Reader's Digest

COMPLETE CAR CARE MANUAL

Reader's Digest

COMPLETE CAR CARE MANUAL

The Reader's Digest Association, Inc.
Pleasantville, New York/Montreal

Complete Car Care Manual

Copyright © 1981 The Reader's Digest Association, Inc.
Copyright © 1981 The Reader's Digest Association (Canada) Ltd.
Copyright © 1981 Reader's Digest Association Far East Ltd.
Philippine Copyright 1981 Reader's Digest Association Far East Ltd.

Library of Congress Catalog Card Number 80-53207
ISBN 0-89577-088-1

Printed in the United States of America

STAFF

Project Editor
Wade A. Hoyt, SAE

Associate Editors
Paul Ahrens
Therese L. Hoehlein
Angus McPherson Laidlaw, SAE
Susan Parker
John Maury Warde

Copy Editor
Diana Marsh

Editorial Assistant
Barbara J. Flinn

Project Art Director
David Lindroth

Art Editors
Donald D. Spitzer
Virginia Wells Blaker

Art Associates
Morris Karol
Edward R. Lipinski
Karen Mastropietro
Joel Musler

Art Assistant
Lisa Grant

Production Associate
Nina Kowaloff

Senior Staff Editor
John Speicher

Group Art Director
David Trooper

CONTRIBUTORS

Chief Technical Consultant
Paul Weissler, SAE

Technical Consultants
Ed Bullman
Rick Clydesdale
N. R. Cooper
Steve DePalma
Carl Haefele
H. J. Hannigan
Bob Lamb
Charles Lewis
Ted Malamus
Paul Pascale
Ronnie Rushneck
John Scott
Jan Zuijdijk

Contributing Writers
Robert Beason
Robert Freudenberger
Lucien Garvin
Cliff Gromer
Mort Schultz
Richard Taylor
Paul Weissler

Contributing Artists
Adolph E. Brotman
Dominic Colacchio
Danmark & Michaels Inc.
Thomas Erik Fornander
Arthur Dale Gustafson
John A. Lind Assoc.
Ken Rice
Gerhard Richter
Danforth R. Robinson & Assoc.
Robert Steimle
Russell J. von Sauers
Whitman Studio Inc.

Contributing Photographers
Morris Karol
Joseph Barnell

Cover: Photo by Ryczard Horowitz.
Auto parts courtesy Fiat Motors of North America Inc.;
Ford Motor Co.; Koni America Inc.; Pirelli Tire Corp.;
Pontiac Motor Div., General Motors Corp.; Volvo of America Corp.

The editors are grateful for the assistance provided by the following organizations

IMPORTERS AND MANUFACTURERS

American Honda Motor Co. Inc.
American Motors Corp.
Chrysler Corp.
   Chrysler-Plymouth Div.
   Dodge Div.
Datsun Nissan Motor Corp.
Fiat Motors of North America Inc.
Ford Motor Co.
   Ford Div.
   Lincoln-Mercury Div.
General Motors Corp.
   Buick Motor Div.
   Cadillac Motor Div.
   Chevrolet Motor Div.
   Oldsmobile Motor Div.
   Pontiac Motor Div.
Jaguar Rover Triumph Inc.
Mazda Motors of America
Renault USA Inc.
Saab-Scania of America
Volkswagen of America Inc.
   Porsche + Audi Div.
   Volkswagen Div.
Volvo of America Corp.

TOOLS AND EQUIPMENT

Brookstone Co.
Burmah-Castrol Inc.
Columbia Motor Corp.
Koni America Inc.
Olympus Camera Corp.
Pioneer Electronics of America
Sears, Roebuck and Co.
3M Co.
J.C. Whitney & Co.

TECHNICAL ASSISTANCE

ACF Industries Inc.
   Carter Carburetor Div.
American Automobile Association
American Petroleum Institute
The Anderson Co.
Automotive Information Council
Belmar Datsun Inc., Belmar, N.J.
Robert Bosch Corp.
Campbell Chain Co., York, Pa.
Ed Carney Ford Inc., East Hanover, N.J.
Champion Cable Chain Inc., Swanton, Vt.
Champion Spark Plug Co.
Colt Industries
   Holley Carburetor Div.
Draf Tool Co. Inc., Bedford Hills, N.Y.
E. I. du Pont de Nemours & Co.
The Echlin Manufacturing Co.
Faette Ford, Clifton, N.J.
Fairchild Camera & Instrument Corp.
Firestone Tire & Rubber Co.
Fletcher Lincoln Mercury Datsun, Summit, N.J.
Garrett Corp.
   Airesearch Industrial Div.
General Motors Corp.
   AC Spark Plug Div.
   Delco Electronics Div.
   Delco Moraine Div.
   Delco-Remy Div.
   Fisher Body Div.
   Harrison Radiator Div.
   Hydra-matic Div.
   Inland Div.
   New Departure Hyatt Bearings Div.
   Rochester Products Div.
   Saginaw Steering Gear Div.
B.F. Goodrich Co.
Goodyear Service Store, Mohegan Lake, N.Y.
Goodyear Tire & Rubber Co.
Gulf Oil Co.
The Hertz Corp.
Intel Corp.
Kayson Chevrolet Inc.
KYB Corp. of America
Loctite Corp.

Fred Mackerodt & Assoc.
Manhattan Ford, New York, N.Y.
Mastermotive Inc.
MEMA Cooling Institute
Michelin Tire Corp.
Mini Motors Inc., Madison, N.J.
Motorola Inc.
National Institute for Automotive
   Service Excellence
National Semiconductor
Ontario Motor League
Phillips Thermo Inc.
Pirelli Tire Corp.
PPG Industries Inc.
   Ditzler Auto Finishes Div.
Purolator Products Inc.
Pyroil Canada Ltd.
Raybestos Friction Material Co.
Rick's: A Body Shop, Kearny, N.J.
Safe Winter Driving League
Sevell's Auto, Westfield, N.J.
Smith Boring and Parts Co., Montclair, N.J.
Society of Automotive Engineers
Standard-Thompson Corp.
Suburban Glass & Mirror, Norwood, N.J.
Temro Automotive Heaters
Tenneco Automotive
   Walker Manufacturing Co.
Texas Instruments Inc.
Tire Buying Service, Elmsford, N.Y
Trico Products Corp.
Union Carbide
Wagner Electric Corp.

About this book

It is the aim of the *Complete Car Care Manual* to make car ownership as trouble-free and as economical as possible. A car that is well cared for will last longer and serve you better than a car that is neglected. Although the typical car lasts 10 years and 100,000 miles, you may get twice that mileage from your car by "overmaintaining" it—that is, by performing regular preventive maintenance jobs at intervals shorter than the carmaker recommends.

The book is divided into four sections. The opening and closing pages deal with general money-saving advice. Chapters 2 and 3 illustrate the mechanical components of cars and explain how they work. Chapters 4 through 6 deal with the maintenance and repair of your car—this is the heart of the book and the section that will help you keep your car running better and longer. The glossary that begins on page 460 explains much of the technical jargon that mechanics use.

Reader's Digest has produced this book with the full cooperation of the major auto manufacturers and importers. The editors, consultants, and contributors have traveled to the automakers' training centers and test tracks in North America and abroad. They learned how to perform many of the jobs shown in the book before they attempted to illustrate or write about them. They have discussed upcoming cars with the engineers who designed them, spoken to technicians from the independent companies that produce major car components or tools for auto service, and learned about "real life," in-the-field problems from experienced mechanics. A large garage was set up in which many repair and maintenance jobs were undertaken and photographed step-by-step. The photos were then transformed into clear, easy-to-understand drawings.

Because there are repairs that are just too complex for a beginner to attempt, each job in the *Complete Car Care Manual* has been rated by degree of difficulty. If you lack the skill, tools, and equipment or a suitable workplace for any procedure described on these pages, we suggest that you leave such repairs to a professional mechanic. We especially urge you to consult your dealer before attempting any work on a car that is still covered by a warranty.

—The Editors

Contents

Warning!

Car care can be dangerous

Working on your car can lead to serious injury unless you observe certain basic precautions. Most of the fluids used in a car are poisonous, corrosive, flammable, or explosive. Many automotive parts become red-hot during normal operation. They can cause severe burns if touched accidentally and can set off a fire or explosion if they come into contact with flammable materials. The potential for injury is great when you work on a car.

Nevertheless, millions of car owners have performed much of their own maintenance and repair work for years without serious injury. The secret is to develop careful work habits, to observe basic safety rules, and to work slowly and deliberately, thinking through each action or step and its possible consequences before you perform it.

Skinned knuckles and minor cuts and burns are a normal part of car repair. Always keep a first-aid kit and a fire extinguisher handy. Never work on a car alone. An adult should always be nearby in case emergency help must be summoned quickly.

Throughout this book, specific safety precautions are given under the heading **Caution**. These special warnings should be strictly observed. So should the following general precautions, which can help to avoid damage to your car and injury to your person.

Personal safety

1. Never work on a car if you are tired, sick, intoxicated, or taking drugs.

2. Never run the engine unless the work area is well ventilated and exhaust gases can escape without building up dangerous levels of poisonous carbon monoxide gas. It is good practice never to run the engine unless the car is outdoors.

3. Do not wear neckties or any loose clothing when working near a car, machine tools, or a running engine. Always tie back long hair and keep it under a cap. If hair or clothing should catch in moving parts, serious injury may result.

4. Beware of hot exhaust manifolds, mufflers, pipes, hoses, radiators, and other car parts that run hot. Do not work near them unless you know that they are cool. If in doubt (or if you must work on a hot car), wear work gloves and heavy clothing with long sleeves to protect yourself from burns.

5. Always stay clear of fan blades. Electric fans may start up even when the engine is off. When working near an electric fan, disconnect the fan's wiring or the battery ground (−) cable.

6. Disconnect the battery ground (−) cable whenever you work on the fuel system or the electrical system. When working with fuel, always work in a well-ventilated area, preferably outdoors, and never smoke, cause sparks, or use a heater. Light switches, fans, and electric motors all create sparks that can ignite explosive gasoline fumes.

7. Before working on a car, remove watches, rings, and other jewelry. They can get caught in moving parts and cause serious injury, or they can cause electrical shorts that will burn or shock the wearer.

8. Never work under a raised car unless it is on level ground and securely supported by jack stands or ramps. Do not support a car on crates, cement blocks, or other makeshift stands. Do not work under a car that is supported only by a jack. If any wheels remain on the ground, chock them securely so that the car cannot roll off its stands.

9. If you work under a car on the ground, make sure that the ground is level. Chock the wheels so that the car cannot roll. Engage the parking brake. Put a manual transmission into *Reverse* and an automatic transmission into *Park*. Disconnect the ignition-coil cable so that no one can start the car.

10. Keep open flame and sparks away from the battery, which can emit explosive hydrogen gas.

11. Catch draining coolant, oil, fuel, or brake fluid in sturdy, tip-proof containers large enough to hold the anticipated amount of fluid without overflowing. Do not use food or beverage containers that might be reused and lead to poisoning. Wipe up spills immediately. Put all soaked rags outside until flammable fumes evaporate, or dispose of the rags in sealed metal containers to prevent spontaneous combustion. Keep all poisonous, flammable, and corrosive fluids away from children, pets, and fire hazards. Follow local environmental and safety regulations when you dispose of drained fluids.

12. If you must heat a garage, never use a heater that has an open flame. Use an electric heater, and keep it far enough from the work area so that you cannot accidentally knock it over as you work.

13. Light your work area well. If you need a portable light, use a safety droplight that has a wire cage around the bulb. If a light bulb breaks, its hot filament can ignite fumes from spilled fuel or lubricants.

Vehicle damage

1. Do not use this manual to work on any car or car component that is not discussed specifically. There are many variations among car parts, and it is impossible to illustrate them all. If the drawings or descriptions in this book do not match the parts on your car exactly, do not use our instructions. You will need a service manual that specifically deals with those components.

2. If you lack the skills, tools, work area, or time listed for any job in this book, do not attempt the job. Take the car to a professional mechanic.

3. Make sure that you have all the tools and materials required before you start any job. Read through the procedures carefully, noting the *Tools* and *Materials* box not only for that job but for any other related job that you might be referred to in the text (for example, the materials needed to bleed the brakes after you replace the shoes). If a part must be removed and inspected before you can determine if a replacement is needed, make sure that the auto parts store will be open, that the part is in stock, and that you have alternate transportation to get to the store.

4. On cars with catalytic converters, you should not run the engine while any spark plug cables are disconnected. Doing so may allow unburned gasoline to reach the catalyst, which can overheat and damage monolith-type converters in a matter of seconds. If it is necessary to disconnect a spark plug cable and run the engine for test purposes, do so for only a few seconds. At the first sign of engine misfiring, check the spark plug cables to be sure that they are all connected tightly.

5. Take care not to spill brake fluid, battery acid, or other corrosive materials onto your car's paint.

6. Use electric or pneumatic tools only to *loosen* threaded fasteners, never to tighten them. Such tools can easily strip threads, especially on lightweight aluminum, titanium, or magnesium parts.

7. Do not improvise with makeshift tools or equipment. Poor tools are dangerous and give poor results.

8. Use only replacement parts recommended by the manufacturer of your car, or substitute parts specifically recommended for your car make and model by a reputable auto parts company. Beware of shoddy off-brand replacements and "pirate" parts that are packaged to resemble the carmaker's original-equipment replacement parts.

The costs of driving

Except for a home, an automobile is the largest single investment that most families will ever make. It is often the biggest drain on the household budget because while most homes increase in value over the years, most cars depreciate in value. Public transportation in many parts of North America is inadequate, so that for many people, owning a car is essential for getting to work, shopping, and leading a normal social life. The following pages will show you how to calculate this major cost of living and should help you to keep your driving costs as low as possible.

Contents

What does it all add up to?

Most car owners are aware that it is becoming increasingly expensive to own and operate an automobile, but many have only a vague notion of exactly how big a bite a car takes out of the family budget.

The traditional North American family car—a four-door sedan with V-8 engine, automatic transmission, air conditioning, and other customary accessories—now costs over $8,000 to buy. During the typical 10 years and 100,000 miles that it will be driven, the car will cost its owner more than $33,000. Assuming that the vehicle is kept by its original owner and sold for scrap at a nominal fee when it is no longer serviceable, the entire $8,000 purchase price will be lost. In addition, it will cost over $5,000 in maintenance and repair costs, over $13,000 for fuel and oil, almost $900 for replacement tires, at least $3,000 for insurance, and more than $2,000 for registration, parking, garage fees, and tolls.

These figures, shown in Tables 1 and 2 at the right, are based on methodology developed by the Highway Statistics Division of the U.S. Department of Transportation (DoT). The figures have been updated to reflect 1980s costs, but they are just estimates. The work sheet found in Table 3 (p.12) is designed to help you calculate your own driving costs.

A typical car passes through two, three, or more owners during its 10-year, 100,000-mile lifetime, but the costs of these changes in ownership, because they are so varied, were not estimated in the DoT study. According to the DoT, it is cheaper to buy a new car and keep it running for 100,000 miles than it is to trade it in for a new model. The need for repairs, or the anticipation of repairs, usually prompts the sale of a car, often through a new- or used-car dealer. As cars become older, they travel fewer miles per year, either because they are used as second or third cars in multi-car families or because they are sold to new owners who do not drive much and therefore don't feel the need for a brand-new car.

Fixed ownership costs

The cost of a car can be broken down into two categories: the fixed cost of ownership, which you pay whether you use the car or not, and the variable cost of operating the car, which is determined by the number of miles you drive each year.

Ownership costs include the purchase price of the car, insurance, garaging, and license and registration

Table 1: Small car ($5,000 purchase price, 30 mpg)

| | YEAR OF OWNERSHIP | | | | | | | | | | |
	1st	2nd	3rd	4th	5th	6th	7th	8th	9th	10th	Totals
Depreciation (%)	12%	11%	11%	11%	10½%	10%	10%	9%	8½%	7%	100%
Depreciation ($)	$600	$550	$550	$550	$525	$500	$500	$450	$425	$350	$5,000
Maintenance and repairs	$190	285	250	650	480	600	600	560	190	80	3,885
Tires	$50	44	38	38	90	100	85	85	85	85	700
Gasoline	$967	867	767	667	660	660	633	567	500	380	6,668
Oil	$30	27	24	21	21	21	20	18	16	12	210
Insurance	$370	350	350	325	325	260	260	260	260	260	3,020
Parking, garage, registration, etc.	$240	230	220	210	210	210	207	200	195	180	2,102
Total cost	$2,447	2,353	2,199	2,461	2,311	2,351	2,305	2,140	1,673	1,347	21,587
Miles driven	14,500	13,000	11,500	10,000	9,900	9,900	9,500	8,500	7,500	5,700	100,000
Cost per mile	16.9¢	18.1¢	19.1¢	24.6¢	23.3¢	23.7¢	24.2¢	25.2¢	22.3¢	23.6¢	21.6¢

Table 2: Large car ($8,000 purchase price, 15 mpg)

| | YEAR OF OWNERSHIP | | | | | | | | | | |
	1st	2nd	3rd	4th	5th	6th	7th	8th	9th	10th	Totals
Depreciation (%)	25%	15%	13%	9½%	7%	6½%	6%	6%	6%	6%	100%
Depreciation ($)	$2,000	$1,200	$1,040	$760	$560	$520	$480	$480	$480	$480	$8,000
Maintenance and repairs	$225	300	620	825	600	700	1,050	420	645	75	5,460
Tires	$60	56	50	50	115	125	110	110	105	110	891
Gasoline	$1,933	1,733	1,533	1,333	1,320	1,320	1,267	1,133	1,000	760	13,332
Oil	$35	31	27	24	24	24	23	20	18	14	240
Insurance	$430	400	400	320	320	280	280	280	280	280	3,270
Parking, garage, registration, etc.	$250	240	230	220	220	220	220	210	205	195	2,210
Total cost	$4,933	3,960	3,900	3,532	3,159	3,189	3,430	2,653	2,733	1,914	33,403
Miles driven	14,500	13,000	11,500	10,000	9,900	9,900	9,500	8,500	7,500	5,700	100,000
Cost per mile	34¢	30.5¢	33.9¢	35.3¢	31.9¢	32.2¢	36.1¢	31.2¢	36.4¢	33.6¢	33.4¢

fees. The purchase price is the most obvious cost, and the least understood. Many people feel that if a car costs $8,000 to buy, that $8,000 is irrevocably lost. But this is not true unless you keep the car until it is a worthless hulk. Most people sell their cars after a few years and recover a portion of the purchase price, although the amount often takes the form of a trade-in allowance on the purchase of their next car, which is not so obvious or gratifying as cash in hand.

If that $8,000 car were sold after several years for $3,000, its real cost would be only the difference between the original purchase price and the selling price, or $5,000. This difference is called *depreciation*, and it is one of the most important concepts to understand regarding car ownership costs.

Any calculation of depreciation is purely theoretical. You will not know exactly how much your car has depreciated until you sell it. If you get less than you might have for your old car, it will have cost you more to own than if you had held out for a higher price. This may seem fairly obvious now, but it is a truth that is often forgotten during the hectic price negotiations for a new car.

As a general rule, you can expect to lose one-third to one-half the value of your new car within the first 3 years, which is why the DoT recommends driving your car for 10 years before selling it. Depreciation is always "front loaded"—that is, your car loses value more rapidly at the beginning of its life. Buyers who trade in frequently lose this money.

Some cars depreciate more quickly than others. The DoT tables show a big car depreciating 25 percent during the first year of ownership, 15 percent the second year, and lesser amounts each subsequent year. Depreciation on the small car in the DoT study was 12 percent the first year, then evened out to between 11 and 10 percent for the next six years. Although these figures are typical for big luxury cars and small economy cars, the rate at which a particular car depreciates depends on how well the car was cared for, how many miles are on the odometer, and how popular the car model is.

Car models that are in high demand or have a good reputation for reliability will depreciate less than the average car. In some recent years, because of international monetary fluctuations, the prices of new German and Japanese cars rose sharply, and this made many used German and Japanese models more valuable than they would otherwise have been. In a few cases, used cars increased in value—a particular two- or three-year-old model sold for more money as a used car than it had cost new.

Such situations are rare and difficult to predict, however. The best way to ensure maximum resale value on a car you presently own is to keep it in good repair and to avoid putting unnecessary mileage on it. If you are buying a new car, pick one that is popular (commonly seen) and has a good reputation for durability (check the frequency-of-repair records in consumer publications). Exotic cars with small, loyal followings *can* have a high resale value, if you can find a member of that small following who wants to buy a used model. Otherwise, these oddball cars may be difficult to sell at all. For more advice on reducing the cost of depreciation, see *How to sell your old car*, p.13.

Insurance costs vary greatly, depending on the amount of coverage you are willing to pay for, the make and model of the car, its age, the area in which you live, and your driving record. A more detailed discussion of insurance costs is found on page 24. In general, the smaller, less expensive, or older the car you drive, and the fewer miles per year it is driven, the less it costs to insure.

Finance charges include the interest you must pay on an auto loan, or the interest lost on money that is withdrawn from savings accounts or other investments in order to pay cash for a car. Because there are so many possibilities—cash purchase, various auto loans, or leasing—no attempt has been made to include finance charges in Tables 1 and 2. There is room for these calculations in Table 3, however, and you should enter your own finance charges there when figuring total costs. For more information on finance charges, see pages 18 to 19.

Local taxes and fees vary widely from area to area but are part of the fixed ownership costs, since they do not depend on the number of miles a car is driven each year. Most states have annual registration fees, plus a fee that is paid each time your driver's license is renewed. In some regions an annual use tax is also levied on each vehicle, or there is a personal property tax that is calculated as a percentage of the car's depreciated value. There may also be state or local sales taxes and title fees, which are usually paid every time a car changes ownership. These last two fees are not included in Tables 1 and 2 but should be entered in Table 3 for the first year a car is owned.

Any sales tax paid on a new car may be deducted from your gross income when computing income taxes. The amount of money you save here depends on the amount of the sales tax and on your personal tax bracket. For example, if you pay $400 in sales tax and are in a 25 percent income tax bracket, deducting $400 from your gross income will save you $400 times .25, or $100. If you are in a 30 percent bracket, it will save you $400 times .3, or $120.

Variable operating costs
The most obvious operating expense is the cost of fuel and oil. Both cars were assumed to run on gasoline that cost $2 per gallon. The large car was assumed to average 15 miles per gallon (mpg); the small car, 30 mpg. They were assumed to use oil at the rate of one gallon of oil for every 167 gallons of gasoline (large car) or every 120 gallons of gas (small car). Oil was figured to cost $1.50 per quart.

You can calculate your own fuel use in one of two ways: One way is to keep a record of every fuel purchase and add up the total for the year. It is a good idea to keep a log of all your operating costs by entering them into a small notebook that you keep in the car. Every time you spend money on the car, note the date, the mileage on the odometer, what was done or added to the car, and the price. This record will help you to calculate your actual operating costs and to keep track of routine maintenance intervals. When you sell the car, its logbook can impress prospective buyers with the care that the car has had.

This logbook will also enable you to calculate your car's gas mileage. If you fill the tank every time you add gas, you can figure out your fuel mileage from the log entries as follows:

DATE	MILEAGE	ITEM	PRICE
6/4	29,562	10.7 gal. gas	$21.40
6/9	29,843	9.5 gal. gas	$19.00
6/14	30,106	11.4 gal. gas	$22.90

Keep a log of car costs in a notebook that you can carry in the glove compartment. This will keep you aware of your car's operating costs and serve as a reminder of when routine service was last performed and, therefore, when it is due again.

What does it all add up to? *(continued)*

To compute the total miles traveled, subtract 29,562 from 30,106 (which equals 544 miles). To find the amount of gas consumed, add all the fill-ups *except the first one* at 29,562. That gives you 9.5 plus 11.4, or 20.9 gallons. Divide the mileage by the gallons (544 by 20.9) to get the miles per gallon (26.02 mpg). If you divide the total cost ($19.00 plus $22.80) of the 20.9 gallons by the mileage (544), you will get the cost-per-mile for fuel (7.7¢ per mile).

If you calculate your fuel mileage for typical driving and know about how many miles you drive each year, you can project your fuel consumption for years to come. For example, if you get 26 mpg and drive 12,000 miles a year, each year you will use 12,000 divided by 26, or 462 gallons of gas. Multiply 462 by the price per gallon in your area, and you will have a rough estimate of your fuel cost per year. (This estimate does not take into account unpredictable changes in the price of fuel.)

The DoT calculations assume that the cars were supplied with radial tires, and that four new radial tires and four new radial snow tires will be purchased during the life of each car. Two extra wheels and two of the snow tires were considered first-year purchases. The cost of tires was spread out over the life

of each tire. Tire costs take a jump from the fifth year onward, when the first group of seven tires wears out at about the same time.

Maintenance and repair calculations include routine maintenance items such as lubrication, tuneups, adjusting headlights, flushing cooling systems, and so on, at the intervals recommended by car manufacturers. Repairs include brake jobs, replacing the water pump and universal joints, carburetor overhaul, and a valve job, all at typical intervals. It was assumed that all work was done by professional mechanics at a labor charge of $20 per hour.

Cutting costs

One obvious way of cutting down on car costs is to do much of the maintenance and repair work yourself, and that is what this book is all about. Tips on being your own mechanic and setting up shop are found on pages 165–180 and 458–459. Hints on getting the best work from professional mechanics are found on pages 454–457.

It is also obvious from Tables 1 and 2 that a small car costs much less to own and operate than a large one. It uses less fuel, and the tires, batteries, and many of the other parts a small car requires also cost

less. Most small engines hold less oil and antifreeze than large ones. Registration, parking, and insurance fees are sometimes lower for small cars, too. However, a small car will usually sustain more damage in an accident than a large car, and therefore cost more to repair. Owning a small car may be impractical for people with large families, car pool commitments, or certain business needs. Because fuel is one of the largest and fastest-growing car costs, it pays to shop for a car with the best fuel economy you can find, whatever the size of the car.

When using Table 3 to calculate your driving costs, make a photostatic copy of p.12 for each car you own, then fill in lines 1 through 12. If you can find out the current resale price of your car, enter it on line 13; otherwise, use Table 1 or 2 to estimate depreciation. If you do not know how many gallons you use each year, fill in line 17 by calculating your car's mpg and dividing it into your annual mileage. Line 20 is an estimate of future repair costs based on the cost of labor in your area. If you have a four-year-old big car, use the repair cost of $825 from Table 2 for this calculation. If you do half the work on your own car and the labor charge for the rest is $25 an hour, divide $25 by 2 and enter that ($12.50) on line 11.

Table 3: How to calculate your ownership costs

Work sheet

1. Purchase price (or down payment) . . . . $ _____

2. Sales tax on purchase . . . . $ _____

3. Monthly installment payments (if any) . . . . $ _____

4. Cost of a tire that fits your car . . . . $ _____

5. Price of fuel (per gallon) . . . . $ _____

6. Price of oil . . . . $ _____

7. Annual insurance premium . . . . $ _____

8. Estimated daily parking cost . . . . $ _____

9. State annual registration fee . . . . $ _____

10. Annual title fee, use tax, or property tax on your car . . . . $ _____

11. Mechanic's hourly labor charge in your area . . . . $ _____

12. Miles driven per year . . . . _____ miles

Ownership costs | YEARLY COST

13. Depreciation (% of original cost from Table 1 or 2) . . . . $ _____

14. Insurance (line 7, above) . . . . $ _____

15. Registration fees (lines 9 and 10, above) . . . . $ _____

16. Finance charges (12 × line 3) . . . . $ _____

Operating costs

17. Fuel cost (annual gallons × line 5) . . . . $ _____

18. Oil (line 12 ÷ your oil change intervals × line 6) . . . . $ _____

19. Tires (line 4 ÷ 2) . . . . $ _____

20. Maintenance and repairs (line 11 ÷ $20 × maintenance and repair cost in Table 1 or 2) . . . . $ _____

21. Parking (250 × line 8, or actual days parked × daily cost) . . . . $ _____

22. Total cost per year (add lines 13–21) . . . . $ _____

23. Cost per mile driven (line 22 ÷ line 12) . . . . _____ ¢

How to sell your old car

Every used car has two price tags: wholesale and retail. The *wholesale* price is the lower of the two; it is the amount a dealer will pay for a car. The *retail* price is the amount the used-car dealer will ask for a reconditioned car. The difference between these two prices pays for any repairs the dealer must make on the car and includes his profit. To get an idea of the wholesale price of your car, ask a few used-car dealers what they would pay for your car. For the retail price, look at the prices of models like yours in used-car lots and classified newspaper ads. Keep in mind that these are only asking prices and that the actual selling prices are usually a few hundred dollars less. There are newsstand publications that list approximate retail and wholesale prices for used cars. The National Automobile Dealers Association (NADA) *Official Used Car Price Guide* also lists wholesale and retail prices. These "official" prices are strictly theoretical, however—a composite of average prices from all around the country. They can only approximate the precise value of your car.

A quick sale to a used-car dealer can have its advantages, but a high price is not one of them. A dealer must offer a lower price because he has expenses to cover: initial car repairs, warranty repairs, and business overhead that includes rent, utilities, insurance, and employee benefits. If you are in a hurry and must sell to a dealer, always show your car to several dealers and take the best offer. A dealer will usually offer more for a trade-in than for a straight sale, but the difference will always be added to the price of the new car you buy from him.

If you are going to sell the car privately, be realistic about your asking price. Being fair about the selling price will save you time. If too much time is wasted trying to sell the car, you could lose some of its real value through additional depreciation. If the car is not in good condition or is minimally equipped, pick a price closer to the wholesale value of a car like yours. If it is in good shape and well equipped, ask for a price closer to its retail value. Have two prices in mind—the highest you think you can reasonably get for your car and the lowest you are willing to take. Keep in mind that you are in competition with the used-car dealer who charges full retail price but who has fixed the car up and offers a warranty. Advertise the higher price, but be prepared to settle for a price between the two. Place ads in local newspapers and on office or supermarket bulletin boards. A For Sale sign in your car window can be effective if it includes both your phone number and asking price. When writing a newspaper ad, be as concise as possible; the fewer words you use, the lower the cost. List only your phone number, not your address or name, in order to prevent thieves from stopping by.

By far the best way to sell a used car in most counties is through local classified advertising publications, such as the *Pennysaver* or *Want Ad Press*. Be sure to include your asking price in any ad; this will save answering unnecessary phone calls to explain your price. Be honest in describing the car to callers. You must also be prepared to spend time showing the car to prospective buyers and doing the necessary paperwork for the title transfer. Make sure you have done all the right paperwork before you even think about selling your car. There is no point in having the car sold, only to find that you have lost the title and cannot complete the deal.

To get the highest price for your car, spend a weekend cleaning it up and doing minor repairs. A coat of wax, a vacuumed interior, and shiny chrome can add hundreds of dollars to the price you get for your car. Don't forget to clean the upholstery, doors, headliner, and windows. Empty the glove compartment and trunk, too. You can clean the engine with an aerosol degreaser. Check all the fluid levels. If the oil is black and dirty, change it. Clean the battery terminals and properly inflate all tires, including the spare. Check to see that all lights are functioning.

When showing your car to prospective buyers, be honest about its condition and defects. By doing this, you will be covering yourself against any future complaints if the car proves to be defective. Collect all your bills for repairs done on the car. That way, a buyer can see proof of regular service and recent repairs. If your car is still under warranty, have your maintenance record available. If a prospective buyer wants to take the car for a test drive, let him do so but go along with him to prevent the car from being stolen or abused. Present your car as honestly as you can. Remember, however, that all used cars are sold "as is," and you have no liabilities to the new owner unless he can prove deliberate fraud.

Never accept a deposit unless you are prepared to sell your car to that person at the agreed price. When accepting any deposit or payment for a car, insist on cash or a certified check. If you are still making loan payments on the car you are selling, you will have to pay off the loan before the car can be transferred to the new buyer. Once the loan is paid in full, the bank will release its lien and sign over the title of ownership to you. You cannot transfer title to the new buyer until this is done.

The certificate of title is only one of the legal papers you must have ready when selling a car; in most states the vehicle registration must be transferred to the new owner as well. Draw up a bill of sale that states the year, make, model, and serial number of the car; the price paid; your name and address; the name and address of the buyer; and that the car is being bought "as is, where is, with no guarantee or warranty of any kind." Federal law requires a statement of mileage, which you can include on the bill of sale. It should say: "The actual mileage on this vehicle, to the best of my knowledge, at the time of sale is _____" and put down the mileage showing on the odometer.

Make two copies of the bill of sale. You and the buyer should sign both copies; give one to the buyer and keep the other for your records. If your car is still under warranty, give the buyer the maintenance schedule. If you have a transferable extended service contract, give him this as well. In some states, license plates are transferable to another car; in others, they must be returned to the motor vehicle bureau. In either case, you will have to get a state form to send to your insurance company with your policy cancellation. You will also need to send back your insurance ID card in order to obtain a premium refund.

Classified ad abbreviations

A/C, or **air** - air conditioning		**pb** - power brakes	
AT - automatic transmission		**ps** - power steering	
bbl - carburetor barrel (2-, 4-)		**pw** - power windows	
CB - citizens band radio		**sacr** - sacrifice	
conv - convertible		**sed** - sedan	
cpe - coupe		**spd** - speed	
cyl - cylinders (4-, 6-, 8-)		**std** - standard	
dlr - dealer		**sun rf** - sunroof	
dr - doors (2-, 4-)		**tape** - tape player	
hdtp - hardtop		**tr** - transmission	
loaded - fully equipped		**trans** - transmission	
lo mi - low mileage		**vnyl** - vinyl top	
man - manual		**wrnty** - warranty	
o.n.o. - or near offer		**wgn** - station wagon	

Deciding on the make and model

For most people, buying a new car is a major event and a relatively large expenditure. The final decision as to what car to buy should be based on intelligent research into the type of car you want or need, and the cars and prices available. This research takes a good deal of time, but it is time well spent. Begin by analyzing the type of driving you generally do (i.e., city driving, short trips, or long trips) and determine how many passengers are usually in the car. Read the car ads and articles in auto magazines to become familiar with the various cars and options available. Narrow your choices down to a few cars of the same type and size that seem to fit your needs best.

Small cars are by far the most economical to buy, own, and operate, and modern small sedans have as much or more interior room than many larger cars. Small cars are excellent for normal commuting, they generally handle better than larger cars, and they are easier to drive and park. Large cars tend to give a better ride because of their longer wheelbase (the distance between the front and rear wheels), but large cars also consume more fuel and money.

Cars are classified into several size groups. The traditional auto industry method is to classify cars by wheelbase, but the U.S. Environmental Protection Agency (EPA) has devised a system based on total interior passenger and cargo volume. The EPA's classes are: *large* (more than 120 cubic feet), such as the Lincoln Continental and Chevrolet Caprice; *mid-size* (110 to 120 cubic feet), such as the Dodge Aspen and Cadillac Eldorado; *compact* (100 to 110 cubic feet), such as the AMC Concord and Ford Granada; *subcompact* (85 to 100 cubic feet), such as the Dodge Omni and Volkswagen Rabbit; and *minicompact* (less than 85 cubic feet), such as the Honda Civic.

Cars are also available in several body styles. There are station wagons, sedans, hatchbacks, coupes, convertibles, and roadsters. *Station wagons* have a large cargo area behind the passenger compartment, and either two or four doors; the rear seats fold down to increase this cargo space. *Sedans* have a closed cargo area separate from the passenger area, and two or four doors. *Hatchbacks* combine the styling of a sedan with the convenience of a station wagon's opening tailgate and folding rear seat. They are sometimes called three-door or five-door sedans (the third or fifth door being the rear cargo hatch). *Coupes* are sporty two-door cars with room for either two

adults or two adults plus two children. The latter models are called *2+2 coupes*. A *convertible* has a folding top and room for four or more people; a *roadster* is a two-passenger convertible.

The number of doors a car has determines how easy it is for passengers to get in and out of the rear seats. Four-door sedans with pillars between the doors are generally sturdier than other body styles. Some four-door sedans now have "childproof" rear door locks that prevent the door from being opened from inside the car. The sedan's separate trunk area allows cargo to be concealed, a fact you should consider if you live in a high-crime area, though most hatchbacks have a removable security panel to conceal the contents of the cargo bin.

Once you have decided which type and size car best suits your needs, visit the showrooms to get some idea of the options and prices available. This is the time to start narrowing down your list to three or four choices. Ask your insurance agent if there are differences in the cost of insuring your choices.

Choosing options

Almost every car make is offered as a *base model* about which price and fuel economy claims are made. The carmaker also offers more expensive *trim levels* plus a long list of *optional equipment* that allows you to outfit your car to your exact needs and taste. On some cars, standard equipment may include a radio, air conditioning, automatic transmission, and power accessories. On "price leader" models, a rear seat and carpets may be extra-cost options.

The purchase price and the cost of owning and operating any car will depend on how you choose to equip it. In general, the larger the car and the more automatic its operation, the more expensive it will be to buy, operate, and maintain. The *Gas Mileage Guide* prepared by the EPA compares the fuel economy and passenger room of all new models. You can obtain a copy from new-car dealers or by writing to Fuel Economy, Consumer Information Center, Pueblo, Colorado 81009.

Engine: In general, the smaller the engine, the more economical it is to operate and maintain. However, the power of the engine must be appropriate for the size and weight of the car. Too small an engine can prove less economical than a larger engine that does not have to work as hard to pull the same load.

The engine offered for the base model almost always has adequate power for safe passing or merging with highway traffic. But if you tow a trailer or load the car with power accessories, you will need a larger engine. When manufacturers offer a choice of three engine sizes, the medium-sized engine is usually the best compromise between power and economy.

Manual transmission: A manual transmission allows more control of the car, especially on slippery roads. When used properly, a manual transmission is also more fuel efficient than an automatic. Manual transmissions are available with three, four, or five forward speeds. Five-speed transmissions usually have overdrive gearing (see p.97), which saves fuel and reduces engine wear. A manual transmission is the most sensible choice for small cars.

Suspension: This supports the weight of the car, cushions passengers from shocks, and provides stable handling (see pp.122–127). The standard suspension on most cars should be adequate for normal driving. If you intend to use your car on rough roads, for fast driving, or to haul heavy loads, you should order a heavy-duty suspension. Special *trailer-towing packages* usually include heavy-duty cooling, electrical, and suspension components; a trailer hitch; and a reinforced frame. Special *police* or *taxi packages* make for an unusually rugged car.

Wheels and tires: Wider wheels and tires can support heavier-than-normal loads safely and provide extra traction and improved handling. Extra-wide tires may rub on the suspension and bodywork, so stick to the options offered by the dealer or factory.

Brakes: There are two basic types of brakes: disc and drum (see pp.105–111). Disc brakes resist fading much better than drums and are standard equipment on most new cars. Power-assisted brakes do not make the brakes work any better, but they do make it easier for you to push the brake pedal and are standard on many new cars.

Steering: Power steering not only makes your car easier to steer, but because the steering ratio (p.129) is quicker with power steering than with manual steering, handling is improved.

Air conditioning: Air conditioning is either factory installed or dealer installed. Dealer-installed "air" may be up to $200 cheaper than a factory-installed unit. If you are paying the extra price for factory air, make certain that you get it. Salesmen tend to be vague on this point, but if they tell you that you are getting factory air and then install an aftermarket unit, that is fraud.

Any air conditioner will reduce the fuel economy of a car when the system is in use. All-season systems, in which you set a thermostat to the desired temperature, operate the compressor winter and summer, thereby increasing fuel consumption the year round. Many cars need a larger-than-standard engine to power the air conditioning. *Tinted glass* will keep the car a little cooler, thereby reducing the amount of work the air conditioner must do; but tinted glass also reduces visibility at night.

Seats: Most cars offer a choice of *seat type* and *seat covering*. A bench seat has a single seat cushion and a single back cushion, both the full width of the car. A variation of the bench seat is the split bench, which is divided into two halves that can be adjusted individually. The bucket seat is a single seat meant for one person; two are placed side by side across the width of the car. On most cars each bucket seat can be individually positioned to fit the person sitting in it. The best bucket seats are shaped to provide side support for your torso when the car is cornering. The seat backs on better bucket seats also adjust to various angles or recline completely.

Vinyl is the most durable and easy to clean upholstery material, and is particularly recommended for families with small children. Fabric seats are more comfortable—cooler in summer, warmer in winter—but can be very difficult to clean. Leather is a luxury that is difficult to maintain and expensive.

Rust-proofing: Although a tar-like *undercoating* is sold as a rust preventive, it may actually trap moisture against the chassis and promote rust. The most effective rust-proofing treatment is a waxy paste sprayed inside the body panels by an aftermarket specialist. He drills holes in hidden areas, sprays in the paste, then plugs the holes. Rust-proofing costs between $150 and $200 but carries a three-year to "lifetime" guarantee against rust-outs.

Silicone-based clear spray can be applied to your car's paint to protect it against chemicals and pollution. Most silicone-based protectants are guaranteed for three years. This *glaze* is applied like old-fashioned wax in only a few minutes. Dealers charge $150 to do this; you can do it yourself for less than $30 by buying the clear spray at an auto supply store.

Getting the best price

The best deal on any new car involves three factors: the purchase price, the dealership, and the warranty. The purchase price is the most immediate cost, and you should try to get the most car for the least money. This will depend on a knowledge of the wholesale price of the car and its options. Retail, or *list,* price is only the manufacturer's suggestion; the dealer can sell his cars for any price he wishes.

The dealer buys his cars at the wholesale price. The difference between the wholesale and list prices is the *dealer markup.* Markup on a small car is about 10 percent; markup on a large car is 20 to 25 percent; markup for options ranges from 25 to 100 percent.

Most cars sell for less than list price, although a few models may command more than list when demand is greater than supply. Most dealers expect to make $300 to $400 profit on each sale, though you can bargain your way down to $150 to $200 over wholesale. You can estimate the wholesale price by using the dealer markups. Subtract 10 percent from the list price—exclusive of options—on mini and subcompact cars, 15 percent on compacts, 20 percent on mid-size and large cars, 25 percent on "luxury" and sports cars. Subtract 50 percent from the list price of all the options added together. The total price of the car plus options will approximate the wholesale price. Add $150 to $200, and that is the price you should pay. You can get the price information you need from the window stickers on the cars in the dealer's lot.

Shop several dealers and get written price quotes from each. The written quote should include a description and separate prices for the car and the options, sales tax, freight and delivery charges, and dealer's preparation fees. Once you have a written deal, ask how much of a trade-in the dealer will give you for your old car. A valid trade-in allowance will be close to the wholesale value of your car (see p.13). Have the trade-in allowance written into the proposed deal after you get a price for the new car. Price quotes and final sales agreements are valid only if they are written and approved by the *sales manager;* the salesman does not have the authority to approve a deal in most dealerships.

Ask your neighbors and the local Better Business Bureau about a particular dealer's reputation for competent and honest service. Also consider the location of the dealership. An out-of-town dealer might have low prices but prove inconvenient for

regular service or emergency repair.

If your choice is between two different car brands, look into the warranty offered by each company. A warranty is a guarantee covering the repair or replacement of specified parts within a limited time and mileage period. One warranty might guarantee that all parts, except tires, that prove to be defective under normal use within 12 months or 12,000 miles (whichever comes first) will be replaced or repaired free of charge. Another might guarantee fewer parts for a longer period of time.

You can also buy an extended service contract from most car manufacturers for around $200. This is a form of insurance that will pay for certain major repairs beyond the limits of the warranty that came with the car. The repairs covered vary with the contract, but many contracts cover only the engine and drive train for three years/36,000 miles to five years/50,000 miles. Most warranties and extended service contracts tie you to the dealer's service department for as long as the warranty is in effect. A dealership service department is usually the most expensive place to have a car serviced.

Test-drive any new car you are considering. Make sure that the car is equipped with the same engine, transmission, and rear-axle ratio you plan to buy. If you test-drive a V-8 loaded with options but order a spartan car with a four-cylinder engine, your test drive will not tell you much. Once you have made the decision to buy a specific car, the salesman will write up a formal sales agreement that should list all the options you ordered, the sales price, and all additional taxes and fees. This agreement should state that your deposit will be returned if the deal fails to go through or if you refuse to accept delivery of a car that is not equipped according to the agreement. Read the agreement carefully and have anything you don't like changed or deleted. Once you and the sales manager sign the agreement, it is final.

The window sticker lists all the options built into each car at the factory and their suggested prices. When your car is delivered, check the sticker against your sales agreement to make sure that the car has all the equipment you ordered, but no extra equipment that you did not order. Refuse to pay for options you did not order. Be sure to test-drive and inspect the car, and have any obvious defects corrected before you accept delivery.

How to find a good used car

The average new car depreciates more than 40 percent in the first 36 months; after that, the rate of depreciation tapers off to less than 10 percent each year. This makes a three-year-old car a particularly good buy; the price is comparatively low, but the car still has tens of thousands of miles of use left in it. The primary disadvantage of buying a used car is the risk of buying a lemon. Even the best used-car warranty lasts only 90 days, and it does not cover all the items covered by a new-car warranty. With a little homework, however, you can make a good used-car buy.

The first and hardest step in selecting any car, new or used, is determining the type and size car that most closely fits your needs (see *Buying a new car,* pp.14-15). The next step is to find out which car has the best reputation for reliability. A car with a good reputation will usually cost more, but your chances of getting a lemon are proportionately less. As a general rule, the most practical used car is a four-door sedan with an uncomplicated medium-sized engine, automatic transmission, few power accessories, and no air conditioning. Read the frequency-of-repair surveys and owner's reports in automobile and consumer magazines to narrow your choices, then ask local mechanics which cars give the least trouble and are easiest to repair.

Once you have settled on a particular model, do some research to determine its value (see p.13). Consult the NADA *Official Used Car Price Guide* or the similar *Kelley Blue Book.* Public libraries or banks that offer automobile loans often have these guides.

Most price guides assume that a car has automatic transmission and a radio. If a late-model used car has no radio, you should deduct $60 from its retail value; if it has a manual transmission, deduct $175. If it has air conditioning, add $200 to $300. If it has power brakes, add $50; power steering, add $65. You should add proportionately less to the price of older cars.

Be sure to use the latest edition of any price guide; prices vary drastically depending on the time of year, availability of gasoline, the state of the economy, and the part of the country you live in. Prices are also dependent on the car's condition. A car in bad condition is worth less than the NADA wholesale price; an excellent car is worth more than the NADA retail price. The best buy in a used car is a low-mileage model in excellent shape. The price "saving" between a poor car and a good car is often less than what it would cost to fix up the car in poor condition.

The best used cars, and the most expensive, are usually found on a new-car dealer's lot. A new-car dealer does not normally have much space for used cars, so he auctions off the dubious trade-ins—cars that are too old, too exotic, or in need of extensive repair. Because the new-car dealer has his own service staff, his used cars have usually been expertly repaired and should be ready for immediate use. You pay for this service, of course. The new-car dealer's prices are invariably higher than those a used-car dealer charges. Any defects should be covered by a 90-day warranty and corrected by the dealer's service department. A new-car dealer often makes a higher profit on a used car than he does on a new car, so the price of a used car is always negotiable.

A used-car dealer sells used cars only. He usually has a number of cars that run the gamut of price and condition. Some of his cars are the unwanted trade-ins from the new-car dealers. Others are bought at auctions or from individuals needing ready cash. Your best bet is to go to a reliable dealer who has been in business for many years. Depending on the dealership, the car may or may not need repairs or be covered by a warranty. The dealership may or may not have a service department.

Rental and leasing companies are another source of used cars. Rental cars get hard use from people who often treat them poorly, and the maintenance may be hit or miss. Because of this, rental cars have a bad reputation and usually sell for bargain prices.

Used cars can also be bought from private sellers. Prices should always be lower than those a dealer charges, but obviously there is no dealer to complain to if the car proves faulty. Unless you can prove deliberate fraud, there is no legal recourse for a lemon purchased from a private party. Experienced buyers spend 25 percent less than they can afford for a used car except when they buy from a new-car dealer. This 25 percent is budgeted for the inevitable repairs the car will need within the first year or so.

Some used cars may still be covered by the manufacturer's original warranty or by a dealer's used-car warranty. Any used-car warranty should cover 100 percent of the cost of parts and labor. Do not settle for a 50-50 warranty, which covers only half the cost; bills can be padded to have you paying for all the work. As with any warranty, you should bring your car back to the dealer as soon as a problem arises. If the car is not repaired satisfactorily, bring it back as often as you have to until the car is fixed.

Extended service contracts, sometimes called extended warranties, are popular options on both new and used cars. These are not true warranties, just a form of insurance on your car. Their terms and prices vary widely, but most contracts cover only the engine and drive train. Some policies require that the work be done by the dealer who sold the car; others allow for repairs nationwide. There are scores of companies selling this service insurance, but not all of them are likely to remain in business. The safest policies are those issued by the car manufacturers.

Before buying any used car, check to see if that model has been recalled and if the particular car has been repaired. If the owner cannot tell you, call the manufacturer's customer service office. If you give them the car's vehicle identification number, they can tell you if that particular car was recalled and fixed. The National Highway Traffic Safety Administration (NHTSA) maintains a toll-free number for recall information: (800) 424-9393. Find out from the manufacturer or NHTSA what the recall was for. A simple fault may not bother you; a serious design defect is a good reason to buy a different model.

A car is assumed to last 10 years or 100,000 miles, whichever comes first, though well-maintained cars can last more than 100,000 miles. A three-year-old car with 60,000 miles is considered to be the equivalent of a six-year-old car and will sell for less than a similar car with 30,000 miles on it.

Every time a car is sold, the seller must give the buyer a statement certifying the actual mileage on the car. Ask the seller to show you the mileage statement he got from the previous owner. This helps to discourage odometer tampering. If you see scratches on the odometer face or holes in the plastic lens over the odometer, be suspicious. While making your road test, check to see that the odometer numbers move smoothly and properly.

On Chrysler cars an ink pad colors each ten-thousandth digit after it comes up on the odometer. If you see a blue ten-thousandth number, the odometer has turned over 100,000 or it has been set back. On GM cars, white lines show up between the numerals if the odometer is tampered with. Ford and AMC odometers simply break if they are turned back.

Road testing a used car

The typical used car is sold because it needs a major repair or because the owner thinks it will soon need repairs. This in itself is no reason to avoid a used car. Anything can be fixed if you spend enough money. There are three things to determine before you buy any used car: Exactly what is wrong with the car? How much will it cost to repair? Is the price of the car, after adding the cost of repairs, still reasonable?

Road test a used car as you would a new one. Are the seats comfortable? Do the ride, handling, and performance meet your standards, and is this the type and size car that best meets your special requirements? When you find a car in which you are seriously interested, take it to your mechanic for a thorough test. He can spot problems and give an estimate of how much it will cost to correct them.

Visual test: Never try to buy a used car at night; you need sunlight to spot defects or poor repairs.

1. Bodywork is expensive, so start by inspecting every corner of the car for rust, dents, signs of repainting, or worn-out old paint. Cars rust from the inside, so surface blisters in the paint are usually an indication that a panel is about to rust through completely. Tap with your fingers along the bottom edge of the body all the way around. Solid metal bodywork will have a metallic ring; quick repairs with plastic body filler will give a dull tap; rusted-out panels will feel spongy or loose. Slide under the car and check the floorboards for rust, too. File marks, paint overspray, or paint shades that don't quite match on adjacent panels mean that the car has been in an accident and was inexpertly repaired.

2. Roll all the windows up and down. Open and close the doors, trunk, and hood. Lock and unlock the doors, using both the outside key lock and inside door lock. If any door or lid does not fit properly, it may indicate that the car has been hit and that the frame or body is permanently bent. Poor window seals and door locks can be expensive to repair.

3. Inspect the tires for uneven wear, which can indicate a bent frame or worn-out suspension. Be suspicious of brand-new tires on a used car; the old tires may have revealed major problems that the owner wants to conceal. Perhaps the shocks are bad, the wheels are out of alignment or bent, or the car was in an accident. If there is excessive tire wear but the odometer shows only low mileage, suspect that the odometer has been tampered with. If the tires

have uneven wear and the car shows signs of accident repairs, the frame is probably bent.

4. While inspecting the front tires, grab the top of each wheel and pull it in and out. If there is excessive movement or noise, check for worn suspension and wheel bearings.

5. Test the shock absorbers. Push down each corner of the car several times, then release it. If the car bounces up and down more than twice, you may need new shock absorbers.

6. Examine the engine for excessive fluid leaks (see p.188). If not the result of an actual crack or faulty seal, a leak could still mean that the car has not been well maintained. Also check the battery and radiator for cracks and proper fluid levels. Oil in the radiator coolant is a sign of a cracked block, blown cylinder head gasket, or leaking transmission cooler. Antifreeze in the automatic transmission fluid means the cooler is leaking. Also check the oil dipstick. Black sludge is a sign of neglect. Water droplets or gray foam in the oil mean that the block has cracked.

7. Check the trunk area for rust, a working jack, and a spare tire. Excessive wear in the trunk or cargo area could mean that the car was used to carry heavy loads, which ages a car quickly.

8. Check out the interior for wear on the seats, floor mats, and pedals. Look for water marks and musty odors, rust, sand under the rugs, and corrosion of electrical connections—all signs that the car was in a flood. Do not buy a car that is flood-damaged.

9. Press down on the brakes. If the pedal goes too low or sinks to the floor, it means that the hydraulic system is defective (see p.210). If the brakes feel spongy, it could mean that there is air in the system.

10. Check the entire exhaust system. Holes or patch jobs indicate a system that needs to be replaced—a job that can cost over $200 on some models.

Road test: If the car has passed its visual inspection, and its estimated repair bill seems reasonable to you, take it for a road test. If the owner will not allow you to road test a car, do not buy it.

1. When you start the engine, listen for unusual noises that can indicate expensive engine repairs (see pp.386–389). Try all the accessories at the same time and make sure that they all work. Check the ammeter to see how well the battery and alternator take the excessive load when everything is working at once. Have a friend stand outside the car to see if the

exterior accessories and lights work properly. If they do not, it may be something as simple as a burnt-out bulb or as complex as an electrical circuit problem.

2. With a friend watching as you drive away, drive slowly in a straight line. If the car travels at a slight angle, it indicates that serious frame damage from an accident has not been repaired properly. Have your friend watch the wheels and tires to see whether they wobble as you drive—a sign of suspension trouble or bent wheels. Have him look for smoke or leaks, too.

3. Accelerate under different road conditions. See if the car picks up speed smoothly. If the engine hesitates, bucks, or makes strange noises after it has warmed up, repairs may be needed (see pp.386–389). While accelerating and after accelerating, look for smoke from the exhaust. Blue smoke indicates worn piston rings or valves. Black smoke means that the carburetor may need overhaul or replacing. White smoke may indicate a blown head gasket.

4. Check the transmission. Put the car into all gears, including *Reverse*. Noise, slippage, or inability to shift means transmission trouble (see p.448).

5. Check the brakes. When pressure is applied, the car should stop smoothly, in a straight line and without grabbing (see p.329). Try the parking brake on a grade to make sure it works.

6. Check to see how well the car steers and responds in sharp turns. The steering should not be loose or sloppy; the car should respond immediately.

7. Test the suspension by driving over a bumpy road. The suspension system may need repairs if the car squeaks or rattles, if you have trouble steering, or if the car bounces excessively (see p.439). If the car wallows long after hitting a bump, the shock absorbers are worn out. Do not confuse *ride* (the comfort of the car on bumpy roads) with *handling* (the way the car responds on turns).

8. At the end of the road test, try to restart the engine while it is hot. Inspect the engine compartment and the underside of the car for leaks.

Mechanic's test: If the car passes your road test and visual test, have your own mechanic check it over. His services will cost you money, but in the long run it will be worth it. Tell your mechanic what you think is wrong with the car. Ask him to inspect the spark plugs and to perform a wet and dry compression test, and a torque converter stall test. If the car has no oil-pressure gauge, have him test the oil pressure.

Driving costs / **Financing**

Shopping for the best car loan

When shopping for any car, new or used, you should also investigate the different methods of financing it. Often, the money saved by shopping for the lowest car price is lost on needlessly expensive financing.

The simplest method of financing, of course, is to pay cash. The chief advantage of this method is that the car is completely yours. Paying cash, however, has its hidden costs—the same amount of money left in a savings account would have earned interest or, if invested elsewhere, could have made a profit.

For most car purchases, money is borrowed from a bank or another lending institution. There are several types of loans, and each carries an additional cost in the form of interest charged on the money borrowed. This interest charge is known as the *annual percentage rate* (APR); it is the total amount of interest charged in a year.

In general, the smaller the amount of money borrowed, the lower the APR charged; and the shorter the duration of the loan, the less the total cost of the loan. The total cost is the amount borrowed plus all finance or interest charges (see tables below). Because interest rates rise with inflation and differ between one lending institution and another, the only way to find the lowest APR available to you is to shop around among several lending institutions.

Other costs

While shopping for a loan, ask about costs or fees other than interest charges. Usually you will be required to make a cash down payment that is equal to a percentage of the car's purchase price. Some institutions will insist that you purchase credit life

insurance to pay off the outstanding balance of the loan in the event of your death. The premiums for this insurance are either separate from, or are automatically added to, the monthly loan payments. You will also be required to carry collision and comprehensive coverage (fire and theft) on your car insurance policy. If the lender can supply this coverage at a lower rate than your insurer's, fine. If not, ask that they accept your insurer's coverage. In no case should you pay for the same coverage from two insurers—they will not pay twice for the same accident. Two other added costs might be a credit investigation fee or a loan application fee. Fees are not tax deductible; interest charges are. Also ask what the penalties are for late or skipped payments and whether or not there is a pre-payment penalty if you pay off the loan before it is due.

Types of loans

The different ways of borrowing money are explained below. Whether or not all types are available to you will depend primarily on your credit rating.

Passbook loans are available from a bank where you have a savings account. Your savings account must contain at least an amount equal to the loan plus the interest and finance charges. While you are paying back the borrowed money, the money in your savings account is gaining its normal rate of interest; so even though you are paying interest charges on the loan, you are accumulating interest on the money in your account. The actual cost to you is the difference between these two rates. A passbook loan is one of the cheapest loans available to many people.

An amount equal to the outstanding loan must remain in your savings account until the loan is repaid. This money acts as collateral; that is, if you default on the loan, the bank will deduct the outstanding amount from your savings.

Borrowing against life insurance: This method applies only to whole life insurance policies that have a built-up cash value. If you have such a policy, you can borrow from the insurance company against the accrued cash value (not face value, the amount paid in case of death). You pay interest charges on the unpaid balance along with your regular premiums. (The APR of the loan was determined the first year the insurance policy was issued, so the interest could be very low by current standards.) You do not have to replace the money borrowed, but if you do not, the balance of the unpaid loan is subtracted from the death benefit paid to your beneficiary.

Loans from credit unions: Credit unions are non-profit organizations, run by some employers or trade unions, that lend money to their members. Interest rates will vary with the organization, but they are usually lower than those of commercial banks. If you belong to a credit union, shop for a better deal elsewhere before you make your decision.

Bank loans: The APR on a loan from a commercial bank can vary greatly from one bank to another. You should go to several in your area and compare their rates. Rates from commercial banks are usually higher than those of savings banks or credit unions. The car serves as collateral for the loan.

Loan companies usually offer loans at higher rates than commercial banks do, often to people with poor credit ratings. Since a predictable number of people will default on these loans, the loan companies must charge a rate high enough to cover their losses.

Loans from car dealers or auto manufacturers: With this type of loan you are paying the cost of a middleman. The middleman is the car dealer; he arranges for a loan from another lending instititution and then charges you those fees plus an additional one for his time and effort. The only advantage to a dealer loan is that it may be offered to people whose credit rating is not good enough for a bank loan.

Personal credit cards: Most cards extend a line of credit from $500 to $5,000. The amount of credit will vary with the card, but the APR is usually close to the maximum allowed in your state.

Table 4: Interest rates

Life insurance policy loan	4%–8%
Bank passbook loan	7%–12%
Credit union loan	9%–12%
Bank loan	10%–15%
Car dealer loan	12%–16%
Finance company loan	18%–23%

Table 5: Typical interest charges on a $1,000 loan

APR	1 YEAR Monthly payment*	1 YEAR Total interest**	2 YEARS Monthly payment*	2 YEARS Total interest**	3 YEARS Monthly payment*	3 YEARS Total interest**	4 YEARS Monthly payment*	4 YEARS Total interest**
10%	$88	$55	$46	$108	$32	$162	$25	$218
12%	89	66	47	130	33	196	26	264
14%	90	77	48	152	34	230	27	312
16%	91	89	49	175	35	266	28	361
18%	92	100	50	198	36	302	29	410

*Includes principal and interest.
**The total interest charge does not represent the APR times the number of months the loan runs (10% of $1,000 × 12, for example). Interest is charged each month only on the amount of the loan outstanding.

Leasing versus buying

There are three types of auto leases: closed-end leases, open-end leases, and maintenance leases.

With a *closed-end lease*—also known as a *net, fixed-cost,* or *walk-away lease*—you (the lessee) contract with a leasing company (the lessor) to rent one of their cars for a certain length of time. At the end of that time, you return the car. The lessor sells the used car and either makes or loses money, depending on the car's resale price. A calculation of the resale price, made at the beginning of the lease, determines the monthly leasing fee. If the actual resale price is more than the amount predicted, the company makes a profit; if the resale is less than predicted, the company loses money. With most closed-end leases there is an additional fee for any excess damage and/or mileage on the car at the end of the lease period.

With an *open-end lease* (also known as a *finance* or *equity lease*) you have an option to buy the car at the end of the lease period. You are not charged for excessive mileage or damage. It is to your benefit, however, to treat the car well, because the monthly payment is affected by a predicted resale price. This is the price at which you can exercise your option to buy the car. If you do not want the car, the leasing company will sell it. If the actual resale price to a third party exceeds the predicted resale figure, you receive the difference; if it is under the predicted price, you must reimburse the lessor.

A *maintenance lease* is an expensive type of closed-end lease in which some or all of the car's maintenance is taken care of by the leasing company.

Be sure you know what all the fees are in any lease agreement. The nominal monthly fee may or may not include sales tax, registration fees, and insurance premiums. Ask the lessor if you are required to carry specific insurance coverages. If the lessor offers insurance, find out the exact coverages and costs to determine if the same coverages are available elsewhere for less. An advance payment or a security deposit may be required. Find out if it is in addition to the monthly payments or whether it will be refunded at the end of the lease.

Look into the penalties. If the lease includes charges for excessive damage or mileage, know what the charges are and exactly what the lessor considers excessive. Know the conditions for terminating the lease and what happens if the car is damaged or destroyed. Have all the details put in writing.

Many times, the decision for or against a lease is based on how its monthly charges compare to those of financing the money for the outright purchase of a car. The table below shows how to compare these costs. Typically, the payments for a three-year lease add up to the full new-car price, in this case 36 payments of $222. If a $500 deposit is required in advance, and this money is taken out of a 7 percent savings account, $113 in interest will be lost over the three-year period (line 3). However, you will not have to pay income tax on that $113, which would save a person in a 30 percent tax bracket $34 in income taxes ($113 times .3), as shown on line 4. The sales tax is also deductible from your gross income in income tax

calculations—in this case saving $400 times .3, or $120.

Line 6 determines exactly how much the lease will cost you. If there are no penalties for damage or mileage, and the car is sold for $500 more than its estimated resale value, that amount is refunded to you. If there are penalties, add them to line 6.

To finance the same car over a three-year period, it was assumed that the buyer put $2,000 down and borrowed $6,000 over three years at an annual interest rate of 13 percent. That would result in a finance charge of $1,278. Over the three-year period, $240 in savings bank interest would be lost on the $2000 down payment (line 11). Income tax savings on this lost interest are $240 times .3 for a person in a 30 percent tax bracket. The finance charges are also tax deductible (line 13).

If the three-year-old car can be sold for $3,760 (see Table 2, p.10), this amount can be deducted from the cost of ownership for three years. All maintenance, insurance, and other costs for the two cars were assumed to be equal.

To fill in the blanks for your case, you must enter the actual costs and charges for leasing or financing the car you want, then estimate its resale value in three years. A leasing company should be glad to give you their estimate.

Leasing is more expensive than buying. It makes sense only for people who use a car for business and can deduct its cost from their taxes. The lease payments become a simple form of record keeping that is seldom questioned in tax audits.

Table 6: Leasing vs. buying costs over three years

Open-end leasing costs for three years	Sample case	Your case
1. 36 monthly payments, plus down payment (if any)	$8,000	$ _____
2. Sales tax on monthly payments	+ 400	_____
3. Interest not earned on any cash used for down payments or deposits	+ 113	_____
4. Tax savings on interest not earned (line 3 × your tax bracket)	− 34	− _____
5. Tax savings on sales tax (line 2 × your tax bracket)	− 120	− _____
6. Surplus (−) or penalty (+) from resale of car	− 500	+/− _____
Total cost:	$7,859	$ _____

Financing costs for three years	Sample case	Your case
7. Purchase price minus down payment	$6,000	$ _____
8. Down payment	+ 2,000	+ _____
9. Sales tax on purchase price and down payment	+ 400	+ _____
10. Finance charge on 36 monthly payments	+ 1,278	+ _____
11. Interest not earned on cash used for down payment	+ 240	+ _____
12. Tax savings on interest not earned (line 11 × your tax bracket)	− 72	− _____
13. Tax savings on finance charges (line 10 × your tax bracket)	− 468	− _____
14. Resale value of three-year-old car	− 3,760	− _____
Total cost:	$5,618	$ _____

You are the best gas-saving device

The best way to save fuel is to drive smoothly and avoid fast starts and sudden stops. Keep an eye on traffic ahead of you. When you see a blockage, coast toward it rather than driving up at high speed, then slamming on the brakes. Avoid unnecessary stops; it takes 20 percent less gas to accelerate to cruising speed from 5 mph than from a full stop.

On the highway, maintain a steady speed. Varying speed by only 5 mph can cost 1.3 miles per gallon (mpg). Stay off the brakes except for emergencies. Steer around slower cars whenever possible, rather than first slowing to their speed, then accelerating past. If you are going too fast, release the gas pedal and coast down to a lower speed, without braking. Keep windows closed at high speeds and use the dash vents for fresh air—vents are quieter and cause less drag. Turn off the engine whenever you will be stopped for more than a few minutes, whether at a store or in a traffic jam. An idling engine can use up to a pint of gas every 5 minutes. Don't let the car idle to warm up the engine. Drive off immediately after starting, but at a low speed. The engine will warm up faster and lubricate better. Keep the engine in tune— a well-tuned engine will not only use less gas, it will start at the first flick of the key.

Never fill the gas tank to the brim. The gas is likely to spill out when the tank is being filled, if you later park facing uphill, or if the sun expands gas that was pumped up from a cold underground storage tank.

Because of differences in rolling resistance, radial tires can save 1 mpg compared to conventional tires, while snow tires can cost you 1 to 3 mpg. Check tire pressures often. A tire that is 8 psi low will cut fuel economy by 2 mpg. Boosting tire pressure 3 to 5 psi above the recommended level will save gas and improve handling, as long as you do not exceed the maximum pressure listed on the tire sidewall.

Always keep a manual transmission in the highest gear possible without straining the engine. Traveling at 50 mph in *Fifth* gear (2,500 rpm) uses less gas than traveling at 30 mph in *Third* (also 2,500 rpm) because the engine turns fewer revolutions per mile.

Do not try to accelerate once you are on a hill and find your speed lagging. Anticipate hills and accelerate to a safe but adequate speed before the incline.

Caution: Never coast downhill in *Neutral* to save gas. You may reach dangerous speeds or overheat the brakes while trying to keep your speed in check.

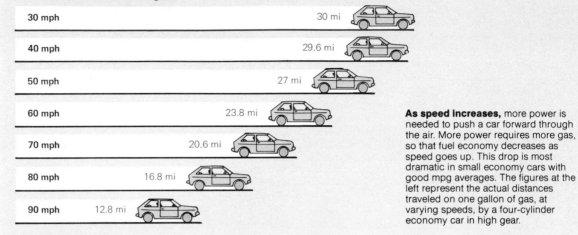

How speed affects mileage

Speed	Distance
30 mph	30 mi
40 mph	29.6 mi
50 mph	27 mi
60 mph	23.8 mi
70 mph	20.6 mi
80 mph	16.8 mi
90 mph	12.8 mi

As speed increases, more power is needed to push a car forward through the air. More power requires more gas, so that fuel economy decreases as speed goes up. This drop is most dramatic in small economy cars with good mpg averages. The figures at the left represent the actual distances traveled on one gallon of gas, at varying speeds, by a four-cylinder economy car in high gear.

Using a manual transmission wisely

In the days when even racing cars had poor brakes, their drivers would shift into lower gears well before a corner to allow the braking action of the engine's compression to slow the car. Some enthusiastic drivers still do this today.

☐ Braking
⬚ Shift point

Start braking — Shift to Third gear — Further braking — Shift to Second gear — Further braking

Gas is saved over this distance by using technique below

The racer's technique shown above wastes gas and puts unnecessary wear on the engine. Modern brakes are adequate to slow a car unaided. Use the brakes alone to slow the car, and shift down when you reach the corner.

Start braking

Shift to Second gear

Shift to Third gear if you can continue

If stop is necessary, use brake; then start again in First

"Straightening out" a one-way highway

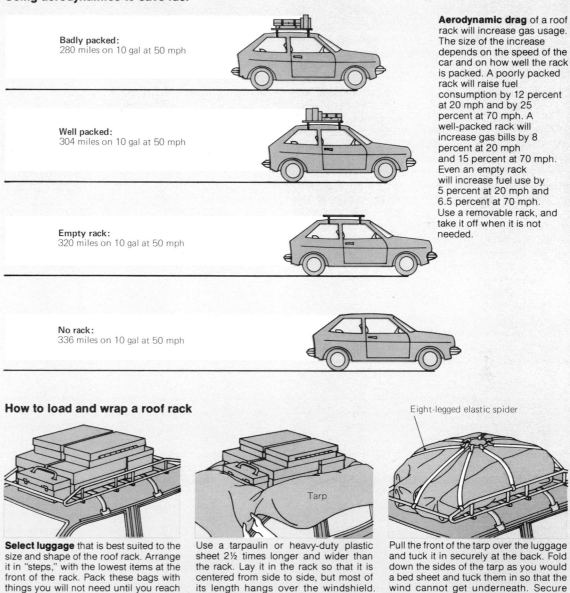

B

6.5%

A   B

A

If a multi-lane highway is uncrowded, you can "straighten it out." Instead of following every zig and zag in the road, follow as straight a path as possible, cutting from curb to curb if necessary. (Be sure always to signal lane changes, keep a careful eye out for other cars coming up behind you, and never cross a yellow line into oncoming lanes.) This will reduce the actual distance you travel from highway entrance to exit and the amount of fuel you consume. On the road pictured above, the difference in length between routes A and B is 6.5 percent.

Using aerodynamics to save fuel

Badly packed:
280 miles on 10 gal at 50 mph

Well packed:
304 miles on 10 gal at 50 mph

Empty rack:
320 miles on 10 gal at 50 mph

No rack:
336 miles on 10 gal at 50 mph

Aerodynamic drag of a roof rack will increase gas usage. The size of the increase depends on the speed of the car and on how well the rack is packed. A poorly packed rack will raise fuel consumption by 12 percent at 20 mph and by 25 percent at 70 mph. A well-packed rack will increase gas bills by 8 percent at 20 mph and 15 percent at 70 mph. Even an empty rack will increase fuel use by 5 percent at 20 mph and 6.5 percent at 70 mph. Use a removable rack, and take it off when it is not needed.

How to load and wrap a roof rack

Eight-legged elastic spider

Tarp

Select luggage that is best suited to the size and shape of the roof rack. Arrange it in "steps," with the lowest items at the front of the rack. Pack these bags with things you will not need until you reach your destination.

Use a tarpaulin or heavy-duty plastic sheet 2½ times longer and wider than the rack. Lay it in the rack so that it is centered from side to side, but most of its length hangs over the windshield. Arrange packed bags as planned.

Pull the front of the tarp over the luggage and tuck it in securely at the back. Fold down the sides of the tarp as you would a bed sheet and tuck them in so that the wind cannot get underneath. Secure with a rope or elastic "spider."

Getting a car off the road

No matter how well you maintain your car, it is not immune to a sudden mechanical failure. No matter how carefully you drive, you are not immune to an accident. The best you can do is to be prepared to handle any road emergency that might arise. Handling road emergencies properly will help to prevent further damage to you and your car, thereby keeping the resulting costs to a minimum. The most important procedure in any emergency is getting your car safely off the road or, if the car is immobile, protecting it and yourself from further harm.

Getting a car safely off the road: Carefully slow down and signal your intention. If you have emergency flashers, use them as you slow down, and indicate turns by hand signals. Ease the car off the road and position it far enough away from traffic so that there is plenty of room to work on the car safely, if necessary. Turn off the engine. If it is dark out, turn on the interior and exterior lights. If you need mechanical assistance, you can do one of three things: If you know the location of a call box, lock the car, walk to the call box, and phone for assistance. If you know the neighborhood and know the location of a gas station, lock the car and walk to the gas station. If you cannot go to a call box or a gas station, open the hood of the car, tie a white cloth to the antenna or to the door handle nearest traffic, and wait for help.

If you cannot get the car off the road: Turn off the ignition and get everyone out of the car. Turn on your emergency flasher lights. If it is dark, keep interior and exterior lights on. Set up flares or reflective warning devices about 20 feet apart in a row extending 100 feet behind the car, as shown below. Do not set flares where they might ignite spilled gas or oil. If any curve or hill within 200 feet of your car will prevent oncoming traffic from seeing your first flare, place another flare over the hill or around the curve. Seek help as described above.

What to do in case of an accident

In the event of an accident, it is very important that you think clearly and remain as calm as possible. Immediately after the accident, stop your car. Get the car safely off the road, if possible, and turn off the ignition. If you cannot get off the road but no one is seriously injured, get everyone out of the car and to safety. If you are trained in first aid, treat injured persons until professional help arrives. As a general rule, do not move an injured person; by doing so you could cause a more severe injury. Only in a dire emergency should you attempt to move an injured person. Such an emergency would be if there is a fire, if gas is leaking from the car, or if a person has been thrown into the path of oncoming traffic. Take care that you are not injured in the rescue attempt. Remember that you can be sued if the rescue aggravates the injuries of an accident victim.

After the injured have been tended to, make a sketch of the accident scene (below); you will need this sketch later to file an accident report. Note the position, direction, and approximate speed of each of the vehicles before and after impact, and what happened at the point of impact. You should also record the length and direction of any skid marks, the road and weather conditions, the physical layout of the road, and the time and place of the accident.

Follow the instructions on the opposite page for getting off the road. Call for the police. Call the fire department if there is a fire or leaking fuel. Call an ambulance if there are injuries. If you cannot go for help, flag down several passing motorists and ask them to go for help; note their license plate numbers, if possible, for your accident report.

Get the names and addresses of all those involved in the accident, including witnesses. Describe each of the cars involved and note the extent of the damages to each car (including your own). Write down the name and address of each person injured, the apparent extent of the injuries, and which car each injured person was in.

The drivers of the cars should exchange driver's licenses and registrations to get the following data: name; address; date of birth; the number and expiration date of the driver's license and car license plate; and the make, model, color, and year of the car. Drivers should also exchange insurance identification cards in order to copy the names of the insurance companies and the policy numbers. The police should be given the same information. You should record the name and badge number of each officer on the scene. Under no circumstances should you admit or deny fault for the accident to anyone, including the police; determining fault is up to the courts.

Most areas require that an accident report be filed with the local authorities. Ask the police or your insurance agent whether or not you must file such a report, and how much time you have for filing. You will also have to file an accident report with your insurance company, whether or not you intend to claim any damages or sue other parties. Both these reports may be introduced in court, so they must agree in every detail. If the accident resulted in only minor damages to your car, it may not be worthwhile to file a claim for damages. If you have $100-deductible coverage and the damages amount to $120, you will be reimbursed $20. But by filing a claim, you risk that your premiums will be increased by an amount higher than the reimbursement.

If you are in doubt about filing a claim, ask your agent to do a cost analysis to see how a particular claim will affect your insurance costs over the next few years. When filing a report, make sure your insurance company knows whether or not you are claiming any damages for your car. It is a good idea to keep a copy of any report you send to the authorities or your insurance company for your records.

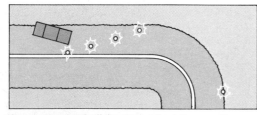

If you cannot get off the road, set out flares as shown.

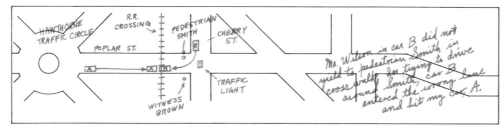

Insurance and police reports usually have an all-purpose map such as this one so that you can make a sketch of the accident scene (shown in color). Make your own sketch at the accident scene, including locations of all the vehicles and witnesses involved, plus other pertinent facts.

Mechanical breakdowns

Flat tire or blowout: If a tire is going flat, you may have difficulty steering the car, the ride may feel sluggish or bumpy, or the car may handle erratically in turns or tilt down toward the flat tire. A blowout happens suddenly. In either case, grip the steering wheel firmly, and gently apply pressure to the brakes; do not slam on the brakes. Pull off the road to change the tire. If necessary, drive slowly until you reach a spot where you can safely pull off the road.

Out of gas: If the engine begins to miss or sputter, you may be running out of gas. Check the fuel gauge. If it reads *Empty,* put the transmission into *Neutral* so that you can coast, and assess your situation. If you are on a road where you are likely to find a service station in a few miles, employ all the fuel-saving tips given on pages 20 and 21. Pull onto the shoulder or slow lane of a multi-lane highway and switch on your emergency flashers. Gently accelerate to 30 mph if you have an automatic transmission, then shift into *Neutral* and let the car coast until it slows to 10 mph, then gently accelerate back to 30 mph. If you have a stick shift, coast downhill whenever possible, but do not let the car slow so much that you are forced to shift out of *High* gear.

If the road is clear of other traffic, wiggle tne steering wheel to slosh extra fuel toward the pickup inside the fuel tank. Do not shut the engine off when coasting; it may be difficult to restart.

If you are not likely to find fuel on the road you are traveling, pull safely off the road before you run out of gas, then call or signal for help. If the car will not restart after it runs out of gas, remove the top of the air cleaner and pour just a few drops of gas into the carburetor, then start the engine. Repeat this procedure until the engine runs without stalling.

Caution: Do not drip fuel onto hot engine parts because a fire may result.

Overheating: The signs of overheating are: steam coming out from under the hood, a temperature gauge registering hotter than normal, or the temperature warning light coming on. Pull the car off the road, let the engine cool down, and find the cause of the problem (see pp.344–345).

Oil-pressure light comes on: The oil-pressure light comes on momentarily when you start the engine. If it stays on, or comes on while you are driving the car, it could mean that the oil pump has failed or that there is not enough oil in the engine. Stop the engine immediately, coast to a safe spot off the road, and check the oil level. Add oil if necessary. If the oil level is satisfactory, suspect a bad oil pump.

Alternator warning light comes on: This light signals a malfunction in the electrical charging system, usually in the alternator or the belt driving it. Do not stop the car; you may not be able to get it started again. Instead, turn off all unnecessary electrical equipment and drive to the nearest gas station for help. You should be able to drive a few miles on the electrical reserve in the battery.

Fire in engine or dashboard: Fires can be caused by a fault in the electrical system or by a leak in the fuel system that allows gas to drip onto a hot engine. Pull off the road, turn off the ignition, and get everyone out of the car. Call for assistance to put out the fire. If you think you can, put the fire out yourself. With your hands covered for protection and your face turned away from the car, carefully open the hood. It will be hot. Use a fire extinguisher, dirt, or a heavy blanket to smother the flames. Do not use water.

A fire in the back of a car is dangerous because most gas tanks are in the back. Get off the road immediately and turn the engine off. Get everyone out of the car and take shelter at least 500 feet away, in case the gas tank explodes. Call for help.

Hood pops open during driving: This is caused by a faulty latch or because the hood was not closed properly. Do not panic and slam on the brakes. Carefully slow down and pull off the road, using your turn signals. Put your head out the window to see ahead, or look through the opening between the cowl and the base of the hood. Once off the road, close the hood. If the latch or hinges are broken, tie the hood closed with rope. Have the hood fixed right away.

Gas pedal stuck: The pedal is stuck because the throttle return spring has broken, because something on top of the pedal is holding it down, or because the throttle linkage is stuck somewhere in the engine compartment. First, try to pull the pedal up with your toe. Shift into *Neutral,* and gently apply the brakes until you are at a safe speed for pulling the car off the road. If the engine is racing, turn the ignition to *Off* (not to the *Lock* position, which may lock the steering). If you have power brakes or steering, the power assist will not work with the engine off; you will still be able to steer and stop, but you will have to work harder to do so. Once off the road, determine what is holding down the pedal or linkage and free it if possible. Test the car before going back into traffic. With the parking brake on and the car in *Neutral,* rev the engine to see if the pedal is working normally. If you cannot fix or find the problem, do not drive.

Brake failure: Try the following three things in rapid succession. Pump the brakes—sometimes this will build up pressure in the system and make the brakes work temporarily. If that does not work, use the parking brake to slow the car. If the parking brake does not work, put the car into a lower gear and ease in the clutch. As engine drag slows the car, keep shifting into lower gears until you are in *First.* Then pull off the road and turn off the ignition.

You can do the same thing on a car with automatic transmission, shifting carefully from *D* to *2* and then to *1* or *L.* If the parking brake will not bring a slowly moving car to a halt, shift momentarily into *R*—not into *P,* which will damage the transmission.

If these three maneuvers fail, then try to sideswipe anything—curbs, guardrails, even parked cars, in an emergency—to help you come to a stop. Once you are off the road, find out what is wrong and have it fixed before moving the car.

If the brakes have faded due to overheating from hard use, let them cool off for 10 or 15 minutes to restore their effectiveness. Drive cautiously in low gear until you are sure they are working properly. Drive slowly in hilly areas if your brakes are prone to fade; shift to a lower gear on downhill runs so that engine drag can help the brakes.

Modern cars have a split braking system. If the rear brakes fail, you may hardly notice their loss. Drive carefully to a repair shop to have them fixed. The front brakes provide up to 80 percent of a car's stopping power, and their loss will increase stopping distances alarmingly. Stop the car well off the road and call for a tow truck.

Steering loss: There is nothing much you can do except try to come to a smooth stop. Apply the brakes gently, but do not jam them on; hard braking might cause the car to swerve. While coming to a stop, honk your horn and put on your emergency flashers to warn other drivers that you are in trouble and that they should get out of your way. When the car finally stops, try to get it off the road. You may need assistance to turn the wheels by hand and push the car off the road. Have the car towed to a repair shop.

How much is enough?

The basic types of auto insurance coverage are: liability, medical payments, collision, comprehensive, and uninsured motorist. The minimum amounts and types of coverage required by law vary from one area to another. Specific information can be supplied by local insurance agents.

Liability insurance will pay the medical and repair bills from an accident caused by you; the amount paid out will depend on the liability limits you contracted for. *Split limits* are represented by three figures separated by slashes, for example, $10,000/$20,000/$5,000 (or $10/20/5). The first number is the maximum amount the insurance company will pay to one person injured (or to his survivors, if he is killed); the second is the most that will be paid to all the people involved; the third is the highest sum the company will pay for damaged property. A *single-liability limit* is stated as one figure—for example, $35,000. It is the total that will be paid for all personal and/or property damage. You and your property are not covered by your liability insurance.

Liability payments are made after a court has determined who caused the accident. The insurance company of the person at fault will pay the damages, but only up to the limits contracted for. Any court settlement above those limits must be paid for by the driver at fault. To protect yourself in the event a high accident award is made against you, you should have adequate liability limits; the more you are worth, the higher your limits should be. If you are penniless and must pay an accident award, you may declare bankruptcy. If you own a home, you might have to sell it to pay a high accident award.

Medical payment insurance will automatically pay medical bills from any accident, no matter who caused it. It covers you, your passengers, or anyone hit by your car. It even covers you if you are injured as a pedestrian. This relatively inexpensive insurance is worthwhile, especially if you habitually have passengers in your car. Medical payment insurance is available with varying limits. If your present health insurance covers the same items, consider taking a higher deductible on it or lowering the limits on your auto medical coverage. Personal health plans usually do not cover passengers. If you have no-fault insurance, medical payments are part of its coverage.

Collision insurance pays for repair or replacement if your car is damaged in an accident caused by you, by an uninsured motorist, or by a hit-and-run driver. The most you will receive is the retail value of the car minus the deductible you contracted for. (If you have a *$100 deductible* policy, you pay the first $100 and the insurance company pays the balance, up to the limits of the policy. The higher the deductible, the lower the premium.) It is usually more economical to take a high deductible, since you are unlikely to be involved in many accidents. Collision insurance is usually not worthwhile if the car is worth less than $1000.

Comprehensive insurance, sometimes called *fire and theft,* will pay for damages done to your car by fire, theft, flood, or most other natural disasters. It will also pay for property in your car that was damaged or stolen. There is usually a deductible amount; the higher the deductible, the lower the premium. As with collision coverage, comprehensive should be dropped once the car's value (or that of the property in it) makes the insurance uneconomical.

Uninsured-motorist coverage will pay medical costs to you or your passengers, within defined limits, for an accident caused by an uninsured motorist or a hit-and-run driver. This coverage should be carried by every car owner.

No-fault insurance means that, no matter who caused the accident, your insurance will pay medical bills (and sometimes damages) to you, your passengers, or pedestrians hit by your car, up to the monetary limits contracted for. Its availability, requirements, and coverages will vary from state to state. In states with no-fault laws, a person involved in an accident loses his right to sue for unmeasurable losses such as "pain and suffering." If an accident results in death or permanent disability, or if the damages exceed your no-fault limits or a minimum threshold amount established by your state, the parties involved can sue the party at fault once the fault has been determined in court. To cover yourself for a possible lawsuit, you should still carry liability and uninsured-motorist coverages. Since no-fault does not usually cover damages to your car, you should also carry collision insurance.

Included in most no-fault policies are payments for wages lost and for services you cannot perform as a result of an accident. For example, child care services may be paid for if a mother is incapacitated. If you already have disability insurance, consider contracting for lower no-fault limits.

Insurance rates

The rates charged for insurance coverages depend on the following factors.

The car: In general, the newer and more expensive the car, the higher the premium. This is because collision and comprehensive insurance will be covering the possible repair or replacement of a vehicle that is more expensive and more likely to be stolen than an older, less expensive car.

Location and use of the car: Rates vary from one area to another but, in general, rates charged for cars used in metropolitan areas are higher than for cars used in suburban or rural areas. The more miles you drive, the higher your rate because your exposure to possible accidents is increased.

Age, sex, marital status: Insurance rates are calculated according to the results of surveys done on the driving records of people in different groups. These studies have shown that, in general, unmarried males under the age of 25 have more accidents and worse driving records than any other group. On the other hand, females and married drivers have proven to be good insurance risks. Depending on the company, young, unmarried, or unemployed drivers of either sex may have to pay higher rates than other drivers pay, or may even be refused insurance.

Your driving record: The worse it is, especially within the last three to five years, the higher your rates. If your record is very bad, you might be considered a high-risk driver and your name put into an *assigned risk pool* with other high-risk drivers. Names are then picked out at random by the companies selling insurance in that state. Drivers in the pool have little or no choice as to which company will sell them insurance. Usually they will be given only the minimum liability limits required by the state.

Discounts on insurance rates are sometimes offered for drivers who have good driving records, have taken driver education courses, do not smoke or drink, own a small car, or have several cars on one policy. There are also special rates for cars used in multiple-car car pools. If your car is the only car pool vehicle, you might need additional liability coverage. If there are teenage drivers in your house, ask if you are eligible for lower rates when the young drivers are away at school. After you have decided what coverages you need, compare the rates of several companies. Premiums for the same coverage can vary a great deal among different companies.

How your car works

Understanding how your car works is the key to diagnosing problems and correcting them. The following 119 pages illustrate all the major parts of a modern car and describe in detail how they work. This chapter makes interesting reading on its own; even if you do not intend to work on your car, it will help you to communicate more confidently and knowledgeably with professional mechanics. If you will be working on your car, you should refer to this chapter before you attempt to service or repair any car component whose operation you do not fully understand.

Contents

Seven steps to understanding how it works

The mass of hoses, wires, pipes, and accessories under the hood of a modern car presents a hopelessly bewildering picture to most people. The average family sedan is assembled from 15,000 parts—1,500 of them synchronized to move together, many of them working within tolerances as small as 0.0001 inch. Nearly 60 different materials—from cardboard, plastic, and rubber to platinum, copper, and steel—are used in a car's construction.

But learning how a car works is not as hopeless as it might seem at first. Many of those 15,000 parts—nuts, bolts, washers, clips, fasteners, insulation, upholstery—are just along for the ride and have little effect on how the car operates. The essential moving parts that make a car start, stop, and turn are relatively few and comparatively similar, whatever the make of the car. Despite enormous differences in styling, performance, and cost, most modern cars work on the same mechanical principles.

Understanding the mechanics of a car can be simplified by dividing the car into the seven subsystems pictured here. Knowing how a car works is the first step toward diagnosing what is wrong when it does not work.

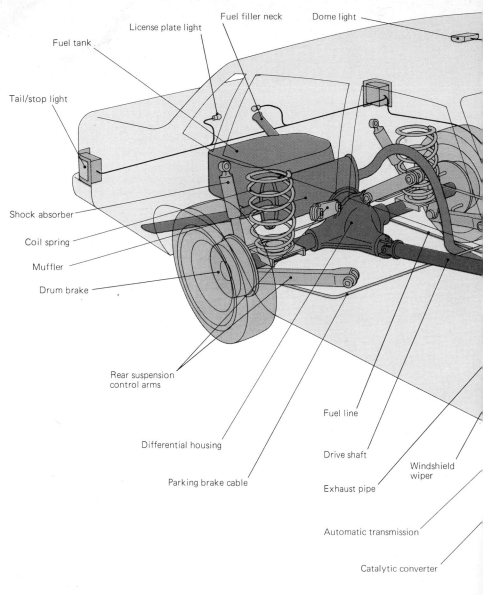

Fuel filler neck — Dome light
License plate light
Fuel tank
Tail/stop light
Shock absorber
Coil spring
Muffler
Drum brake
Rear suspension control arms
Differential housing
Parking brake cable
Fuel line
Drive shaft
Windshield wiper
Exhaust pipe
Automatic transmission
Catalytic converter

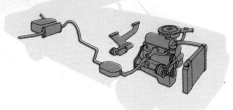

1. Engine: Temperatures of 4500°F or more are produced by fuel burning inside the engine. Less than 20 percent of this heat is converted into useful power. The remainder is dissipated through the cooling and exhaust systems. An engine has 120 to 150 moving parts that must be lubricated with oil to avoid excessive wear. (See pp.28–83.)

2. Drive train: In a conventional car, power is carried from the engine to the rear wheels by the transmission, drive shaft, differential, and rear axle. The transmission contains low gears that provide extra force for starting from rest, climbing hills, or accelerating, as well as high gears for economical highway cruising. (See pp.84–104.)

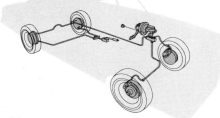

3. Wheels, tires, and brakes: After traveling 60,000 miles—an average five years of normal driving—the typical car wheel has turned 95 million times and worn out nearly two sets of tires. Each time a car comes to a stop from 60 mph, the brakes generate enough heat to boil a half pint of water. (See pp.105-121.)

4. Suspension: Modern suspension systems of torsion bars or springs, anti-sway bars, and shock absorbers move up and down hundreds of times a minute. They help to cushion car occupants against irregularities in the road surface and provide safe and stable handling when the car accelerates, brakes, or turns. (See pp.122–128.)

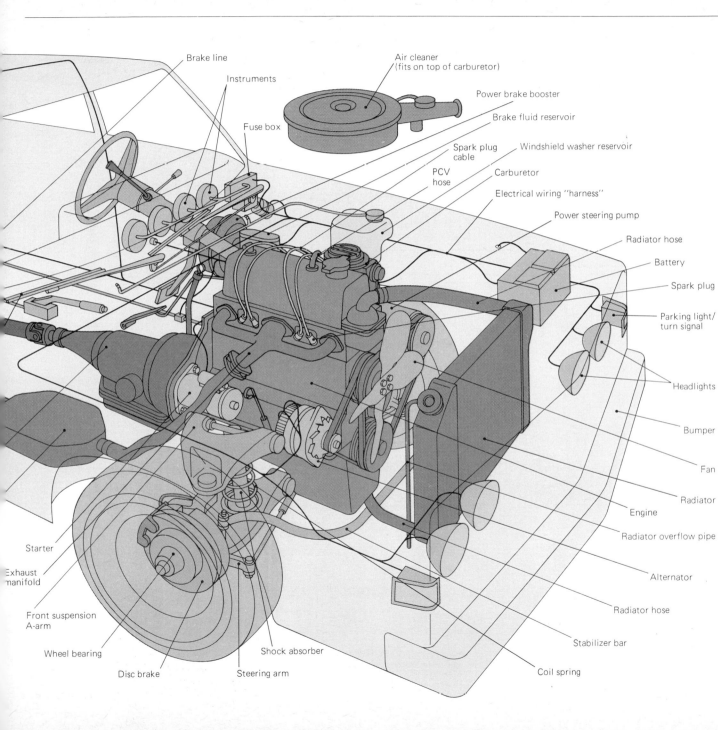

Brake line

Instruments

Fuse box

Air cleaner
(fits on top of carburetor)

Power brake booster

Brake fluid reservoir

Spark plug
cable

Windshield washer reservoir

PCV
hose

Carburetor

Electrical wiring "harness"

Power steering pump

Radiator hose

Battery

Spark plug

Parking light/
turn signal

Headlights

Bumper

Fan

Radiator

Engine

Radiator overflow pipe

Alternator

Radiator hose

Stabilizer bar

Coil spring

Steering arm

Shock absorber

Disc brake

Wheel bearing

Front suspension
A-arm

Starter

Exhaust
manifold

5. Steering: Without the sophistication of modern steering equipment, the 1- to 2-ton weight of the average car would be too difficult to maneuver. A driver must exert up to 30 lb of effort on the steering wheel of a car with manual steering in order to turn it in a tight circle. Power steering cuts this effort to only 5 to 6 lb. (See pp.129–131.)

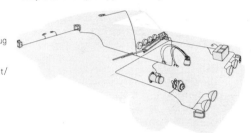

6. Electrical system: A 12-volt battery provides the primary source of power needed to start the engine and operate the lights, radio, horn, windshield wipers, fans, instruments, and other electrical accessories. (See pp.132–139.) These 12 volts are stepped up to as high as 40,000 volts in the engine's ignition system. (See pp.64–72.)

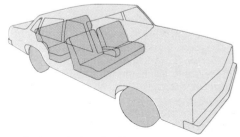

7. Body and chassis: Many new cars have no frame, and it is the bodywork that holds the car together. The average car uses more than 400 sq ft of sheet metal, which varies in thickness from .015 to .035 in. A car's bodywork must be capable of withstanding great stresses imposed when the car is in motion. (See pp.140–144.)

Looking inside the engine

The illustrations at the right show what a simple four-cylinder engine would look like if it were sliced open. The engine is the heart of an automobile. It converts the heat produced by burning gasoline into mechanical energy to turn the wheels. The gasoline is burned in closed *cylinders* inside the engine—hence the term *internal combustion engine.*

The initial impetus to set the engine in motion comes from the *starter*—an electric motor that is powered by the car's battery. The starter is geared to a toothed ring that is fitted to the *flywheel.* When the starter turns the flywheel, the *crankshaft* turns along with it, moving the *pistons* up and down in their individual cylinders. The pistons draw in a mixture of air and gasoline from the *intake manifold* and *carburetor.*

At this point a number of other events are occurring simultaneously. The *camshaft,* which is driven by the crankshaft, begins to open the cylinders' *intake* and *exhaust valves* in the correct sequence. The *distributor,* driven by the camshaft, delivers high-voltage electrical current to the individual *spark plugs* at the proper time, and the engine starts.

Other components, driven by the crankshaft or camshaft, also begin to function. The fuel pump keeps the carburetor supplied with gasoline. The water pump circulates the coolant through the engine and radiator. The fan draws cooling air through the radiator. The oil pump circulates lubricating oil to all the moving parts in the engine. The alternator recharges the battery and supplies electricity to the distributor and other electrical components.

Engine cross section (front view)

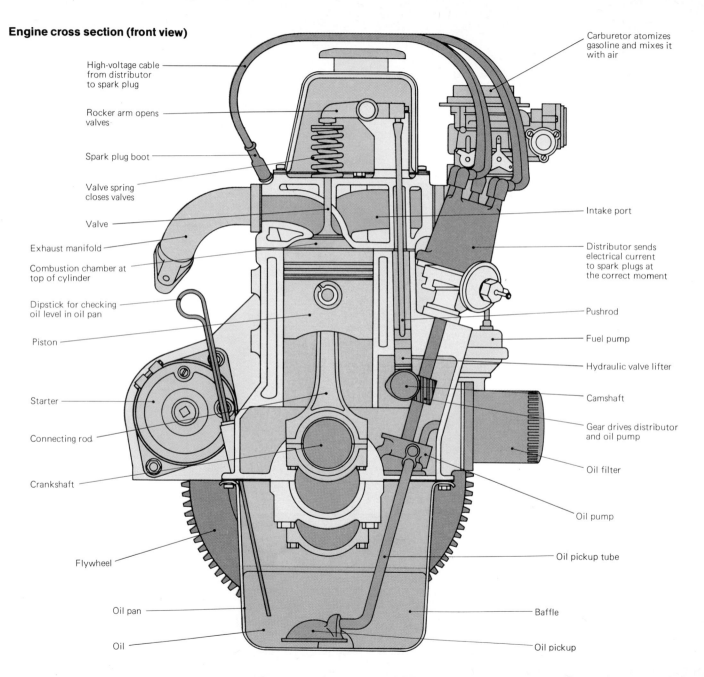

High-voltage cable from distributor to spark plug

Rocker arm opens valves

Spark plug boot

Valve spring closes valves

Valve

Exhaust manifold

Combustion chamber at top of cylinder

Dipstick for checking oil level in oil pan

Piston

Starter

Connecting rod

Crankshaft

Flywheel

Oil pan

Oil

Carburetor atomizes gasoline and mixes it with air

Intake port

Distributor sends electrical current to spark plugs at the correct moment

Pushrod

Fuel pump

Hydraulic valve lifter

Camshaft

Gear drives distributor and oil pump

Oil filter

Oil pump

Oil pickup tube

Baffle

Oil pickup

Engine cross section (side view)

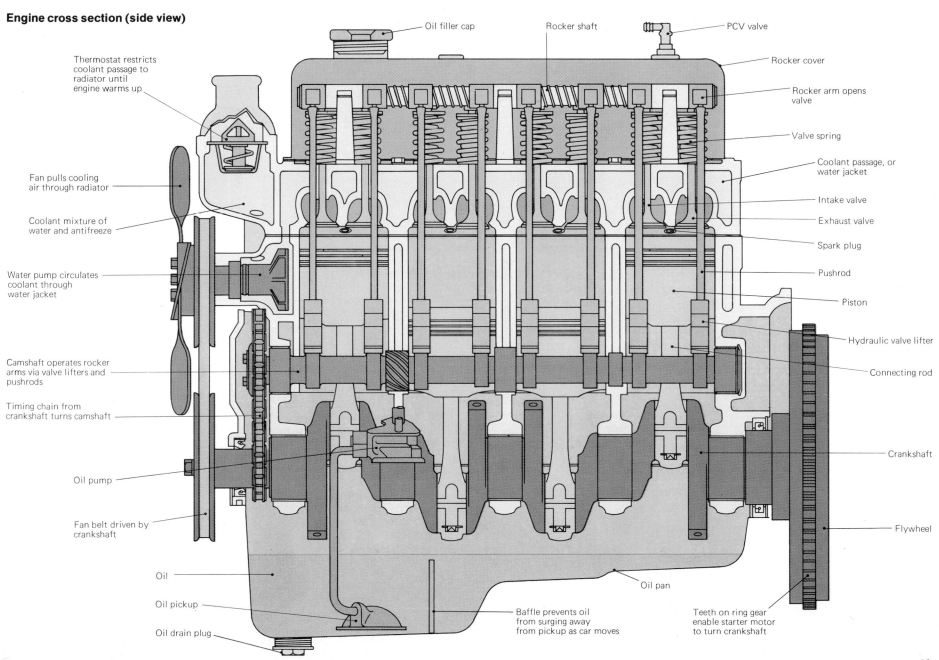

Oil filler cap

Rocker shaft

PCV valve

Thermostat restricts coolant passage to radiator until engine warms up

Rocker cover

Rocker arm opens valve

Valve spring

Fan pulls cooling air through radiator

Coolant passage, or water jacket

Intake valve

Exhaust valve

Coolant mixture of water and antifreeze

Spark plug

Water pump circulates coolant through water jacket

Pushrod

Piston

Hydraulic valve lifter

Camshaft operates rocker arms via valve lifters and pushrods

Connecting rod

Timing chain from crankshaft turns camshaft

Crankshaft

Oil pump

Fan belt driven by crankshaft

Flywheel

Oil

Oil pickup

Oil pan

Oil drain plug

Baffle prevents oil from surging away from pickup as car moves

Teeth on ring gear enable starter motor to turn crankshaft

How your car works / Engine

Four views of a typical engine

Right side

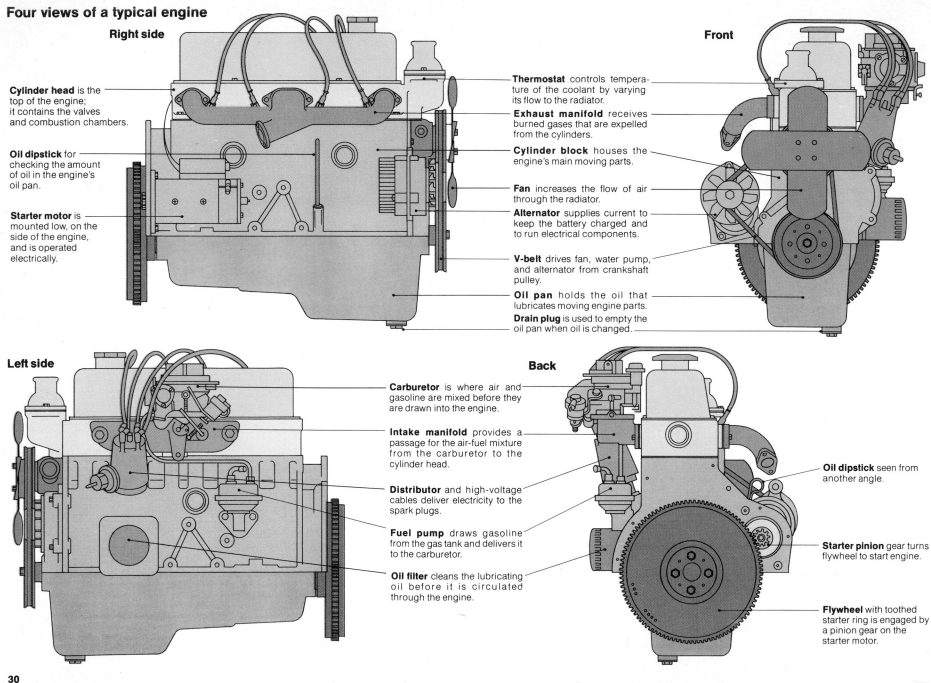

Cylinder head is the top of the engine; it contains the valves and combustion chambers.

Oil dipstick for checking the amount of oil in the engine's oil pan.

Starter motor is mounted low, on the side of the engine, and is operated electrically.

Thermostat controls temperature of the coolant by varying its flow to the radiator.

Exhaust manifold receives burned gases that are expelled from the cylinders.

Cylinder block houses the engine's main moving parts.

Fan increases the flow of air through the radiator.

Alternator supplies current to keep the battery charged and to run electrical components.

V-belt drives fan, water pump, and alternator from crankshaft pulley.

Oil pan holds the oil that lubricates moving engine parts.

Drain plug is used to empty the oil pan when oil is changed.

Front

Left side

Carburetor is where air and gasoline are mixed before they are drawn into the engine.

Intake manifold provides a passage for the air-fuel mixture from the carburetor to the cylinder head.

Distributor and high-voltage cables deliver electricity to the spark plugs.

Fuel pump draws gasoline from the gas tank and delivers it to the carburetor.

Oil filter cleans the lubricating oil before it is circulated through the engine.

Back

Oil dipstick seen from another angle.

Starter pinion gear turns flywheel to start engine.

Flywheel with toothed starter ring is engaged by a pinion gear on the starter motor.

30

Separating the main engine parts

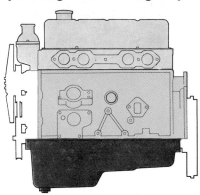

For the sake of clarity, this chapter will deal mainly with a basic four-cylinder engine—the simplest engine found in modern automobiles. The relationship between this engine and other popular designs is shown on page 48.

The engine is a massive structure made up of two basic parts, bolted together. The upper part is the *cylinder head,* which contains the valves and the recesses in which the fuel burns, called *combustion chambers.* Cylinder heads are usually cast iron, although some are made of aluminum to save weight. Passages cast into the cylinder head lead from the intake manifold to the intake valves and from the exhaust valves to the exhaust manifold. Other passages carry cooling fluid from the radiator.

The lower part of the engine is the *cylinder block.* The cylinders are holes bored through the block. The pistons and connecting rods move up and down inside the cylinders, transferring power to the crankshaft to make it rotate. The crankshaft is held against the bottom of the block by a number of brackets that contain the *main bearings.*

A steel pan bolted to the bottom of the block acts as a reservoir for the motor oil. Another sheet-metal stamping covers the valve-operating mechanism at the top of the cylinder head.

Cylinder head contains the valves, the rocker arms that open them, and the springs that close them. The head also contains the intake and exhaust passages and the combustion chambers.

Cylinder block is the largest part of an engine. It has cylinders, or *bores,* for the pistons to move up and down in, passages for fluid that cools the engine, galleries that carry lubricating oil to the various moving parts, and holes for the pushrods (on engines that use pushrods to open the valves).

Crankcase was a separate part on older engines. On modern engines the area enclosed by the oil pan and the bottom of the cylinder block is still referred to as the *crankcase.* The crankshaft is carried in main bearings attached to the base of the cylinder block. The connecting rods cause the crankshaft to rotate as the pistons move up and down. The heavy flywheel at one end of the crankshaft helps to smooth out the power impulses from the individual cylinders. A pulley (not shown) attached to the forward end of the crankshaft drives a V-belt to operate the alternator, water pump, and fan.

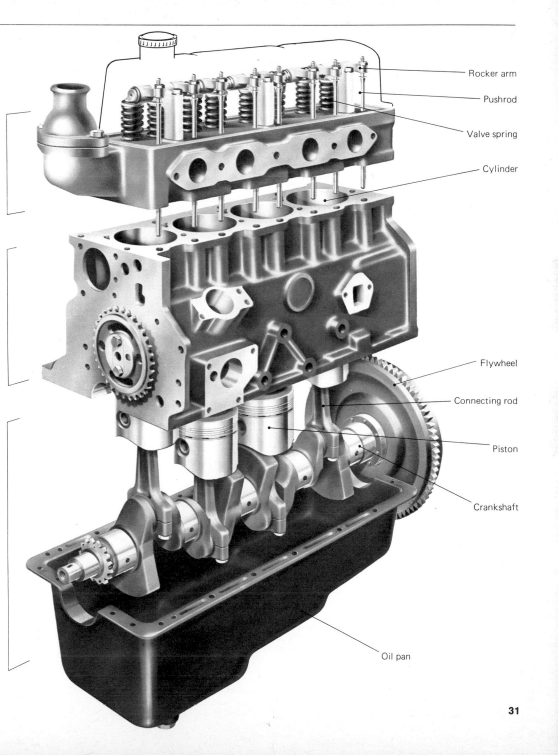

- Rocker arm
- Pushrod
- Valve spring
- Cylinder
- Flywheel
- Connecting rod
- Piston
- Crankshaft
- Oil pan

31

How the engine produces driving power

All the parts of the engine (which are covered in detail on the following pages) exist in order to make possible the process shown here—the internal combustion of gasoline in order to produce useful power at the car's wheels. Heat energy produced by burning gasoline is converted into mechanical power by the pistons, connecting rods, and crankshaft of an engine. This is accomplished by what is known as the four-stroke cycle, illustrated on the opposite page.

Every movement of the piston up or down inside its cylinder is called a stroke. Because of the connecting rod, every two strokes of the piston cause the crankshaft to rotate 360 degrees. Here are the four strokes that make the engine run:

1. Intake stroke: The intake valve opens, the piston descends in its cylinder, and the air-fuel mixture is drawn in.

2. Compression stroke: The intake valve closes, the piston rises, and the air-fuel mixture is compressed at the top of the cylinder, near the spark plug.

3. Power stroke: When the piston is near the top of the cylinder, the spark plug fires the mixture and the piston is forced back down the cylinder by expanding gases.

4. Exhaust stroke: The exhaust valve opens, the piston rises once more, and the burned gases are forced out of the cylinder and into the exhaust port.

Of the four strokes, only the third delivers any power. The other three strokes all absorb power, as the piston and valves essentially act like a pump, moving and compressing gases. For every piston that is delivering power, three more are absorbing some of it for their pumping strokes. More power is absorbed by friction in the engine and transmission, and more still to drive various internal engine parts and external accessories—such as the alternator, air-conditioning compressor, and power steering pump. Whatever power is left, after all these losses, actu-

ally propels the car. Luckily, gasoline is an immensely powerful substance, and one cupful contains the same energy as a dozen sticks of dynamite.

The difference between the volume inside a cylinder when the piston is at the bottom of its stroke and when it is at the top of its stroke is called the compression ratio. The more the air-fuel mixture can be compressed, the higher the horsepower and fuel economy of an engine. However, higher compression ratios can cause excessive combustion temperature peaks that, in turn, produce an air pollutant called nitrogen oxide (NO_x)—a major cause of smog.

The compressed mixture, when ignited by the spark plug, should burn rapidly but smoothly across the top of the piston. It does not explode instantaneously. If the octane rating of the gasoline being used is too low, some of the mixture away from the spark plug may ignite spontaneously when compressed. This causes a condition commonly known as knocking or pinging. Diesel fuel is ignited by compression alone in engines that use no spark plugs but have compression ratios of more than 20:1.

Compression ratio

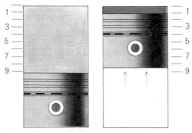

The difference in the volume of gas inside a cylinder at the beginning and end of a piston stroke is the compression ratio. If the gas is reduced to one-ninth of its original volume, the compression ratio is 9:1. Diesels have ratios of about 23:1.

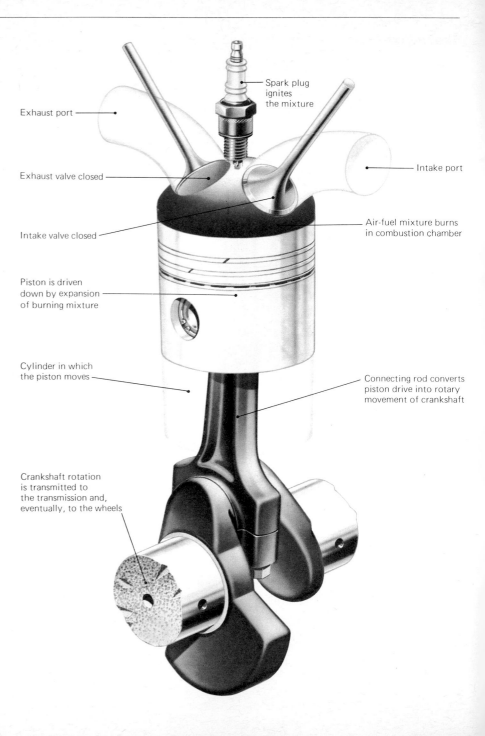

Spark plug ignites the mixture

Exhaust port

Intake port

Exhaust valve closed

Air-fuel mixture burns in combustion chamber

Intake valve closed

Piston is driven down by expansion of burning mixture

Cylinder in which the piston moves

Connecting rod converts piston drive into rotary movement of crankshaft

Crankshaft rotation is transmitted to the transmission and, eventually, to the wheels

The four-stroke cycle

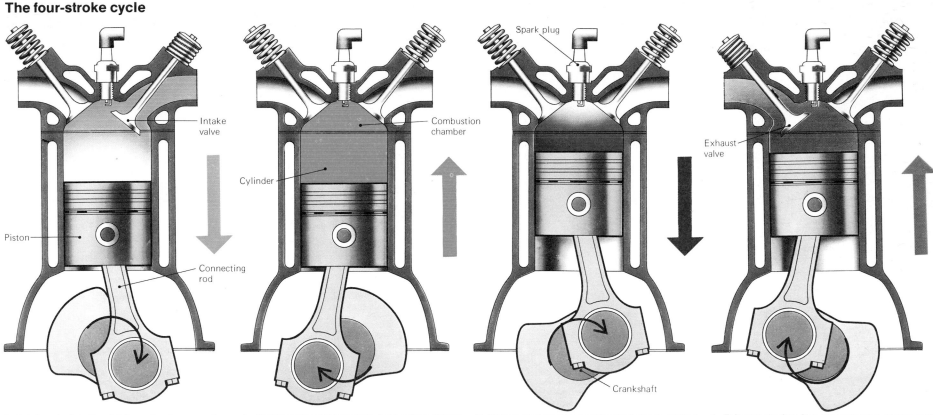

Intake valve

Combustion chamber

Spark plug

Exhaust valve

Cylinder

Piston

Connecting rod

Crankshaft

1. Intake stroke: The intake valve is open, the exhaust valve closed. The piston descends, drawing in air-fuel mixture from the carburetor and intake manifold. Then the intake valve closes.

2. Compression stroke: With both valves closed, the piston rises in the cylinder, squeezing the mixture into an area around the spark plug, called the combustion chamber.

3. Power stroke: The compressed gas is ignited by the spark plug. Expansion of the burning gases drives the piston down. The rotating crankshaft continues to move other pistons in their cylinders.

4. Exhaust stroke: The exhaust valve opens and the piston rises to expel burned gases. Then the intake valve opens, the exhaust valve closes, and the cycle starts again.

Valve overlap

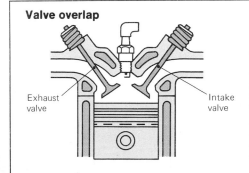

Exhaust valve

Intake valve

In theory, the valves open and close when the piston is at the exact top or bottom of its stroke. In practice, there is a slight *overlap* period during which both valves are open at once. The momentum of the moving gases allows the air-fuel mixture to enter the cylinder and the exhaust gases to exit at the same time, despite the slight up or down motion of the piston at that instant. On some engines, the exhaust valve is allowed to stay open so long that some exhaust gases are drawn back into the cylinder. They lower the combustion temperature peaks and reduce NO_x formation.

Cylinder firing order

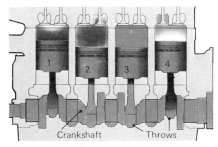

Crankshaft

Throws

The throws on the crankshaft are arranged so that the pistons do not all move up and down at the same time. This allows the power strokes of the pistons to occur at even intervals in most engines, which tends to minimize vibration. In a 4-cylinder engine, the cylinders are numbered from front to back. If the spark plugs fired in numerical order—1,2,3,4—the engine would be out of balance and would vibrate excessively. Vibration is reduced by a firing order of 1,3,4,2 or 1,2,4,3 (shown in the illustration). In-line 6-cylinder engines usually have a firing order of 1,5,3,6,2,4.

Pistons and connecting rods

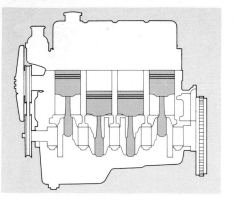

Pistons provide the force that drives the engine. In a small engine running at top speed, each piston may slide up and down inside its cylinder as often as 100 times a second. In a big V-8 engine, 35 times a second is about average at 55 mph (90 km/h). Pistons are made of lightweight aluminum to allow this rapid succession of starts, stops, and reversals. Since heat from the burning fuel expands both the pistons and the cylinder block, there must be some clearance between them so that the pistons can slide freely.

Piston rings of cast iron and spring steel seal this clearance. Two or more *compression rings* keep most of the high-pressure combustion gases from escaping past the piston. If these rings are worn, an excessive amount of gas blows by, reducing engine power. A *scraper*, or *oil control, ring* below the compression rings removes excess oil from the cylinder walls and returns it to the oil pan. A worn oil ring may let oil past the piston, causing a smoky exhaust.

The connecting rods transmit power from the pistons to the crankshaft. These steel forgings or malleable iron castings have parallel holes drilled in each end. A wrist pin in the small hole at the top attaches the piston to the rod. The bottom of the rod is made in two parts so it can be bolted around the crankshaft.

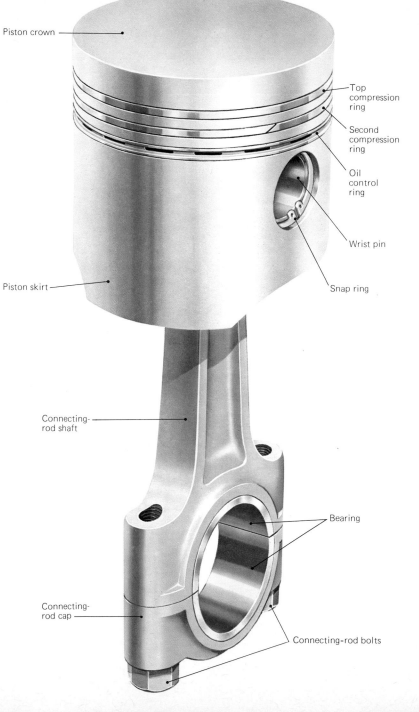

Piston crown

Top compression ring

Second compression ring

Oil control ring

Wrist pin

Snap ring

Piston skirt

Connecting-rod shaft

Bearing

Connecting-rod cap

Connecting-rod bolts

Piston rings

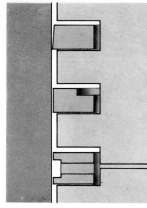

Piston rings fit in grooves around the upper part of the piston. Combustion gas under high pressure passes between the piston and cylinder wall to force the compression ring (top) down in its groove and out against the wall. A small amount of gas will pass the top ring, so a second ring is used. An oil control ring (bottom) scrapes excess oil from the cylinder wall. Gas that gets past all three rings enters the crankcase.

Piston expansion

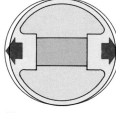 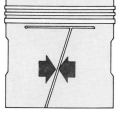

Pistons expand unevenly as the engine warms up. Some are machined to an ellipse (left) so that they become circular and fit the cylinder bore precisely when hot. Other pistons have slots in the skirt (right). As the metal expands, the slot closes and the piston fits the bore closely and runs quietly at all temperatures. Horizontal slots limit heat transfer from the piston crown and keep the skirt relatively cool.

The wrist pin

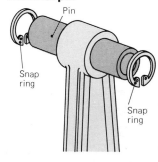

Pin

Snap ring

Snap ring

Wrist pin pivots freely so that the connecting rod can swing to follow the crankshaft's rotation. A free-floating pin (shown) is centered in the piston by snap rings, and the rod pivots around the pin. In another design, the pin is forced into the rod and pivots with it. Friction alone keeps the pin centered in the rod.

The crankshaft

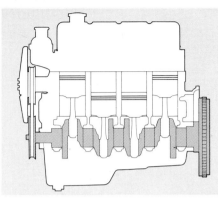

The crankshaft passes power and *torque* (twisting force) to the transmission. It may revolve more than 6,000 times a minute at top engine speeds. Cast or forged in a single piece, it is machined in places to an accuracy within half a thousandth of an inch.

The crankshaft has three major parts: main journals, crankpins, and webs. The crank itself turns on the *main journals,* which ride in the main bearings of the engine block. The connecting-rod bearings run on the *crankpins.* The *webs* join the crankpins and the main journals, and also serve as balance weights for smooth engine running.

The flywheel is an iron or steel disc bolted to one end of the crankshaft. Its momentum smooths out power pulses from the individual pistons. A vibration damper at the other end of the shaft absorbs vibrations from the minute twisting and untwisting of the shaft.

In most engines the crankpins are arranged to deliver the pulses of the pistons at even intervals—every 180 degrees of shaft rotation for a four, every 120 degrees for a six, and every 90 degrees for a V-8. One reason a V-8 tends to run more smoothly than a four or a six is the close spacing of its power pulses.

How the crankshaft works

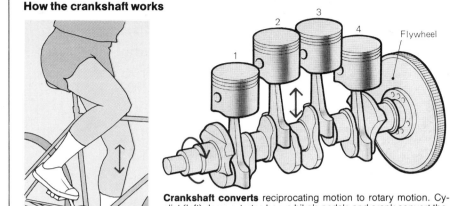

Crankshaft converts reciprocating motion to rotary motion. Cyclist (left) demonstrates how a bike's pedals and crank convert the up-and-down motion of the rider's legs into the rotary motion of the sprocket wheels. Similarly, the connecting rods and crankshaft (above) convert the up-and-down motion of the pistons and connecting rods into rotary motion. On this four-cylinder crankshaft, the two pistons at the top of their strokes (2 and 3) are balanced by two at the bottom of their strokes (1 and 4).

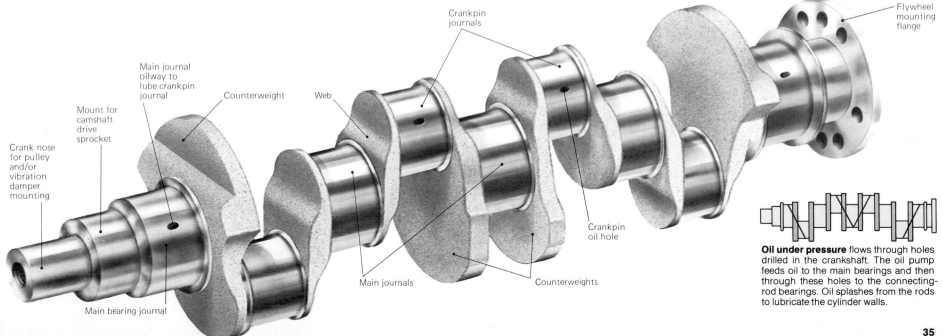

Oil under pressure flows through holes drilled in the crankshaft. The oil pump feeds oil to the main bearings and then through these holes to the connecting-rod bearings. Oil splashes from the rods to lubricate the cylinder walls.

The cylinder block

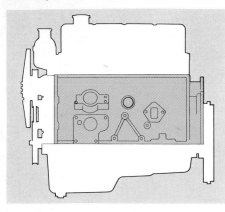

The cylinder block is the main shell of the engine. Most blocks are cast iron, but a few are aluminum, which is lighter and conducts heat better. Because aluminum is too soft to withstand the constant rubbing of the pistons, most aluminum engines have cast-iron sleeves (called *liners*) inserted in the cylinders. An exception was GM's Vega, which had specially treated aluminum cylinders.

Water passages are cast into the block to cool the cylinders. These are connected with the water passages in the cylinder head through openings in the top of the block. The block may crack if water freezes and expands in these passages. Sometimes this expansion will dislodge the core plugs—discs that seal holes required during the casting process—and for this reason the core plugs are sometimes referred to as freeze-out plugs. However, the core plugs are not reliable safety valves, and it is important to maintain at least a 50 percent concentration of antifreeze in the engine's cooling system to prevent the cooling water from freezing. Antifreeze also raises the coolant's boiling point.

The cylinders can be arranged in a row (called an *in-line engine*), in two rows set at an angle (a *V engine*), or in two rows arranged horizontally (a *flat engine*).

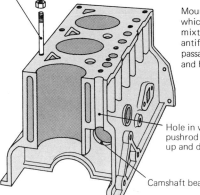

Studs are screwed into the block. Nuts on the top ends of the studs hold the cylinder head in place

Hole in which pushrod moves up and down

Camshaft bearing

Cutaway of cylinder block shows the many passages that must be accurately cast into the block. The big ones are for the pistons; the smaller ones are for the pushrods, studs, oil, and water.

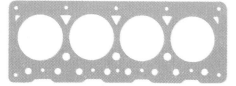

Head gasket forms a seal between the cylinder block and head, to prevent the escape of gases and fluids. It is pierced by many holes, the large ones for the cylinders and the smaller ones for the pushrods, studs, and oil and water passages. The gasket is often made of a compressible material such as asbestos, with a copper or steel cover.

Coolant passage between block and head for water and antifreeze mix

Bores, or cylinders, in which pistons slide

Holes for pushrods

Threaded stud hole

Mounting for water pump, which circulates mixture of water and antifreeze through passages in the block and head to cool engine

Mounting for fuel pump

Distributor mounting. Distributor shaft runs down into block and is driven by camshaft

Mounting for oil filter

Main bearing supports crankshaft

Camshaft bearing

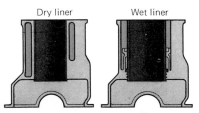

Dry liner   Wet liner

Aluminum blocks use cast-iron or steel cylinder liners. A dry liner (left) is cast into the block during manufacture and is surrounded by aluminum. A wet liner (right) is pressed into the block after it is cast and is exposed to the liquids in the cooling system.

Cylinder head and valves

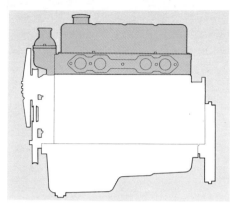

Cast iron is the most popular cylinder head material, but aluminum is not uncommon. In some engines the block may be cast iron and the head aluminum. Aluminum saves weight and conducts heat better than iron, but an aluminum cylinder head needs special inserts to serve as the valve seats and guides. It may also be difficult to maintain an effective seal between an aluminum head and the iron block, as the two metals expand at different rates when heated.

The bottom of the cylinder head is machined to mate perfectly with the top of the cylinder block. Any distortion in the head or block can lead to failure of the head gasket and to leaks. Distortion can be caused by massive overheating, which is often the result of running the engine with insufficient coolant in the cooling system.

The intake valves are usually bigger than the exhaust valves because the gas flow into the cylinder is slower than the exhaust flow out, which occurs under pressure. Because of the high temperatures encountered, the combustion chambers and exhaust ports must be adequately cooled by water passages. The exhaust valves may become red-hot when the car is driven hard, so they are made of a special heat-resistant alloy.

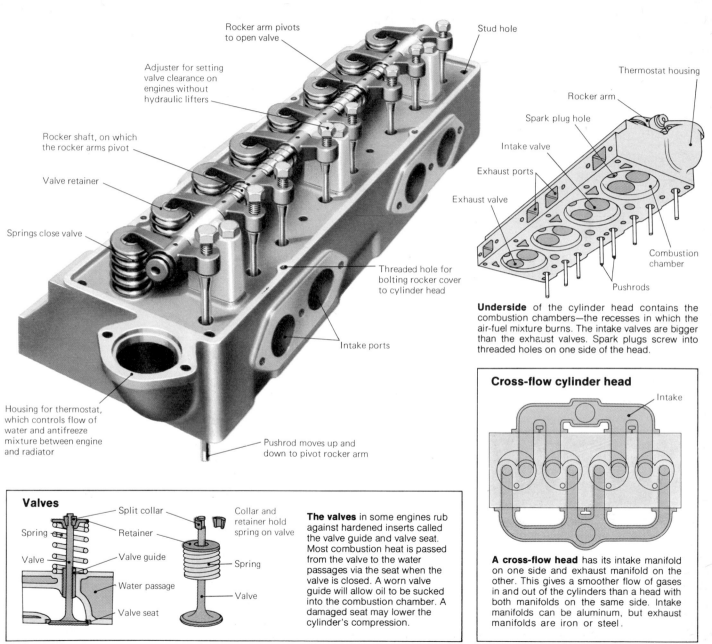

Rocker arm pivots to open valve

Adjuster for setting valve clearance on engines without hydraulic lifters

Rocker shaft, on which the rocker arms pivot

Valve retainer

Springs close valve

Stud hole

Threaded hole for bolting rocker cover to cylinder head

Intake ports

Housing for thermostat, which controls flow of water and antifreeze mixture between engine and radiator

Pushrod moves up and down to pivot rocker arm

Thermostat housing

Rocker arm

Spark plug hole

Intake valve

Exhaust ports

Exhaust valve

Combustion chamber

Pushrods

Underside of the cylinder head contains the combustion chambers—the recesses in which the air-fuel mixture burns. The intake valves are bigger than the exhaust valves. Spark plugs screw into threaded holes on one side of the head.

Valves

Split collar

Spring

Retainer

Valve

Valve guide

Water passage

Valve seat

Collar and retainer hold spring on valve

Spring

Valve

The valves in some engines rub against hardened inserts called the valve guide and valve seat. Most combustion heat is passed from the valve to the water passages via the seat when the valve is closed. A worn valve guide will allow oil to be sucked into the combustion chamber. A damaged seat may lower the cylinder's compression.

Cross-flow cylinder head

Intake

A cross-flow head has its intake manifold on one side and exhaust manifold on the other. This gives a smoother flow of gases in and out of the cylinders than a head with both manifolds on the same side. Intake manifolds can be aluminum, but exhaust manifolds are iron or steel.

How the valves open and close

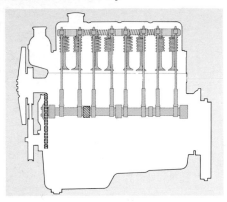

The valves must open and close at the proper moment during each cylinder's four-stroke cycle. This is done by egg-shaped projections called *cams*, which are arranged along a rotating shaft. In most engines, the camshaft is housed low in the cylinder block and operated by a chain that runs to the crankshaft.

As the camshaft rotates, each cam lifts a *tappet,* or *lifter,* and a *pushrod.* The pushrod causes a *rocker arm* to pivot and push the valve down. One or more springs close the valve when further rotation of the cam allows the tappet and pushrod to fall.

There must be some free play in the valve train so that the valve can close completely once the parts have warmed up and expanded. A specific gap called the *valve clearance* is allowed between each closed valve and its rocker arm. On engines with solid tappets, you must be able to adjust the valve clearance periodically in order to compensate for wear in the valve train. If the clearance is too great, the valves will open late and close early, reducing engine power. If the clearance is too small, the valves may not close completely, resulting in compression loss, poor engine performance, and early valve failure. In most engines, oil-filled *hydraulic lifters* automatically adjust for wear.

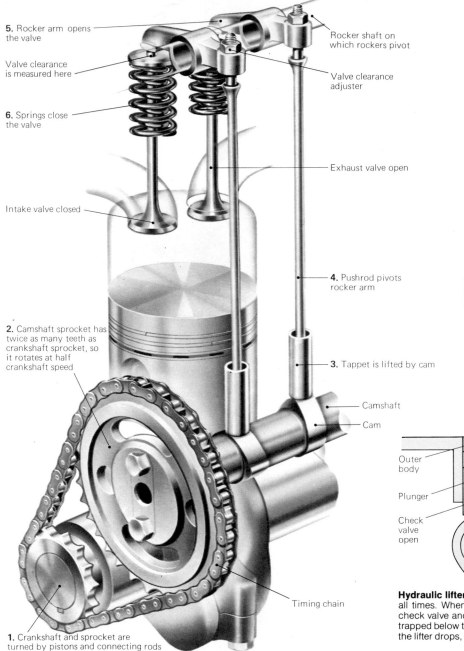

5. Rocker arm opens the valve

Valve clearance is measured here

6. Springs close the valve

Intake valve closed

Rocker shaft on which rockers pivot

Valve clearance adjuster

Exhaust valve open

4. Pushrod pivots rocker arm

2. Camshaft sprocket has twice as many teeth as crankshaft sprocket, so it rotates at half crankshaft speed

3. Tappet is lifted by cam

Camshaft

Cam

Timing chain

1. Crankshaft and sprocket are turned by pistons and connecting rods

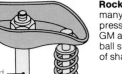

Rocker arms on many cars are made of pressed steel. These GM arms pivot on ball studs instead of shafts.

Stud

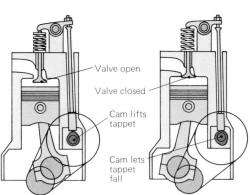

Valve open

Valve closed

Cam lifts tappet

Cam lets tappet fall

Valve operation: As the cam rotates, it lifts the tappet and pushrod, pivots the rocker arm, and opens the valve (left). Further cam rotation allows the tappet and pushrod to fall and the spring to close the valve (right). This design, with the camshaft in the cylinder block, is called an overhead-valve pushrod engine.

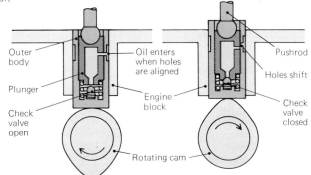

Outer body

Plunger

Check valve open

Oil enters when holes are aligned

Engine block

Rotating cam

Pushrod

Holes shift

Check valve closed

Hydraulic lifters vary their height to maintain zero valve clearance at all times. When the lifter is down (left), pressurized oil flows past a check valve and fills the lifter. As the cam raises the lifter (right), oil is trapped below the check valve and the lifter rises like a solid unit. When the lifter drops, oil leaks out so that the valve can close completely.

Overhead camshafts

Many small or high-performance engines have camshafts in the cylinder head rather than the block. Called *overhead camshafts,* they operate on the valves more directly than the camshaft in a pushrod engine. With fewer parts there is less inertia, so that an overhead cam engine can be run at higher speeds and often produces more power than a comparable pushrod engine.

Older overhead cam designs use long chains to turn the camshafts. Most new designs employ rubber belts that run outside the engine block. These belts need no lubrication and are made of oil-resistant rubber and nonstretch fiberglass or steel cords. To prevent belt slippage—which would cause the valves to open at the wrong time—teeth molded on the inside surface of these belts mesh with matching teeth on the camshaft and crankshaft sprockets.

One or more overhead camshafts may be used on an engine, depending on the desired arrangement of the valves in the combustion chamber. A V-type engine with dual overhead camshafts on each cylinder bank has four camshafts in all. Overhead camshafts can operate directly on the valves, on intermediate rocker arms, or on fingers. When the cam operates the valve directly, a bucket-shaped tappet is often placed between the cam and the valve stem to resist the sideways thrust of the rotating cam.

Newer overhead cam engines often use hydraulic lifters, which are self-adjusting and quieter than solid tappets. Older designs still require periodic valve clearance adjustments.

Valve clearance is adjusted by adding or removing thin metal *shims* to bucket tappets or by turning a tapered screw in the tappet. Finger-operated valves are adjusted by changing the height of the finger's pivot point. Rocker-operated valves have their adjusters at the ends of the rocker arms.

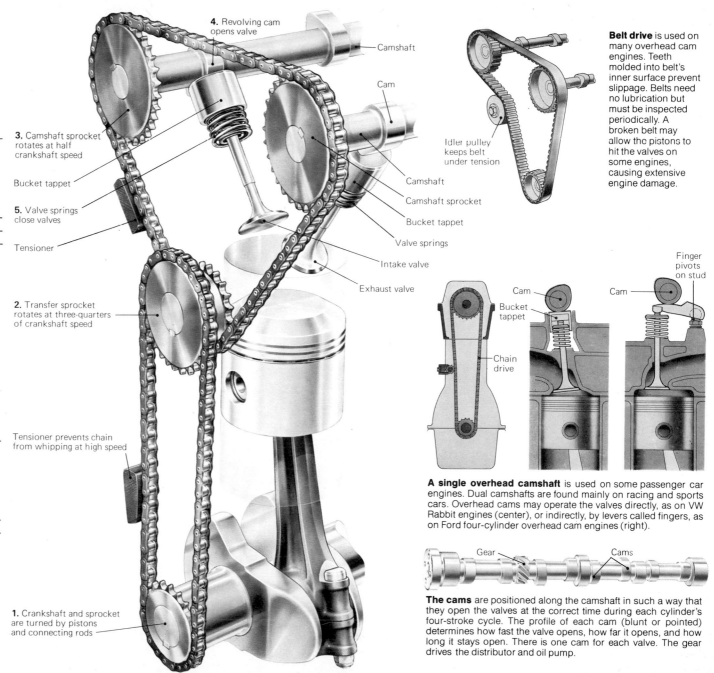

4. Revolving cam opens valve

Camshaft

3. Camshaft sprocket rotates at half crankshaft speed

Bucket tappet

5. Valve springs close valves

Tensioner

2. Transfer sprocket rotates at three-quarters of crankshaft speed

Cam

Camshaft

Camshaft sprocket

Bucket tappet

Valve springs

Intake valve

Exhaust valve

Tensioner prevents chain from whipping at high speed

1. Crankshaft and sprocket are turned by pistons and connecting rods

Belt drive is used on many overhead cam engines. Teeth molded into belt's inner surface prevent slippage. Belts need no lubrication but must be inspected periodically. A broken belt may allow the pistons to hit the valves on some engines, causing extensive engine damage.

Idler pulley keeps belt under tension

Finger pivots on stud

Cam

Cam

Bucket tappet

Chain drive

A single overhead camshaft is used on some passenger car engines. Dual camshafts are found mainly on racing and sports cars. Overhead cams may operate the valves directly, as on VW Rabbit engines (center), or indirectly, by levers called fingers, as on Ford four-cylinder overhead cam engines (right).

Gear

Cams

The cams are positioned along the camshaft in such a way that they open the valves at the correct time during each cylinder's four-stroke cycle. The profile of each cam (blunt or pointed) determines how fast the valve opens, how far it opens, and how long it stays open. There is one cam for each valve. The gear drives the distributor and oil pump.

Combustion chambers

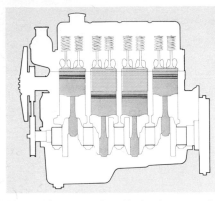

The roof over each cylinder in an engine forms the *combustion chamber*. The chamber's shape determines how well the engine will run, what kind of fuel it needs, how much fuel it burns per horsepower produced, and the volume of pollutants that come out of the tail pipe.

An efficient combustion chamber must meet several requirements: It should be compact to minimize surface area that absorbs heat when the fuel burns. There should be no nooks or crannies, which can cause spontaneous combustion, or *knocking*. It must be possible to move large volumes of air-fuel mixture into, and exhaust gases out of, the combustion chamber conveniently. Room must be available for the spark plug. Because the ignition flame spreads across the chamber at a finite speed, the spark plug should be centrally located to reduce the time needed for all the fuel to ignite. Lastly, the chamber must be capable of reuse up to 50 or more times per second.

A sphere with a spark plug at its center would probably be the ideal shape for the combustion chamber. It would give even burning in all directions with minimal surface area. But it would not be a practical shape for a working engine.

The best compromise for real-life engine efficiency is a half-sphere, but this *hemispherical* chamber is expensive to manufacture because it requires two overhead camshafts or a complex array of rocker arms and pushrods working in several planes to operate its angled valves. *Bathtub, wedge, squish,* and *piston-crown* chambers are therefore more common in passenger car engines.

A bathtub combustion chamber comes by its name for obvious reasons. Both the intake and exhaust valves can be placed side by side in the bottom of the inverted tub so that a single overhead camshaft or a simple row of rocker arms can open them. The spark plug is placed in the side of the tub, making for a compact and efficient chamber.

Wedge chambers chop one side off the tub to make an angled surface for the valves, which are parallel and easy to operate. The closely related squish chamber curves the edge of the wedge and has a flat surface that squirts the gases into the combustion chamber when the piston rises. This squish area swirls the mixture for even distribution but tends to cool it, which may cause excessive hydrocarbon pollution (see p.78).

Placing the chamber in the top of the piston is common practice in diesel truck engines but is rarely done in gasoline engines in this country. The design is more popular in Europe, where it is incorporated in a number of engines.

In the century or more that men have been designing internal combustion engines, almost every conceivable combustion chamber shape has been tried. Lawn mowers still use the once-common *side-valve, L-head,* or *flathead* engine, which has its valves in the block beside the pistons. This makes for a very simple valve-operating mechanism, but the L-shaped combustion chamber normally results in a low compression ratio and is less efficient than those now in common automotive use. Standards for pollution control also help determine the design of combustion chambers.

Hemispherical chamber

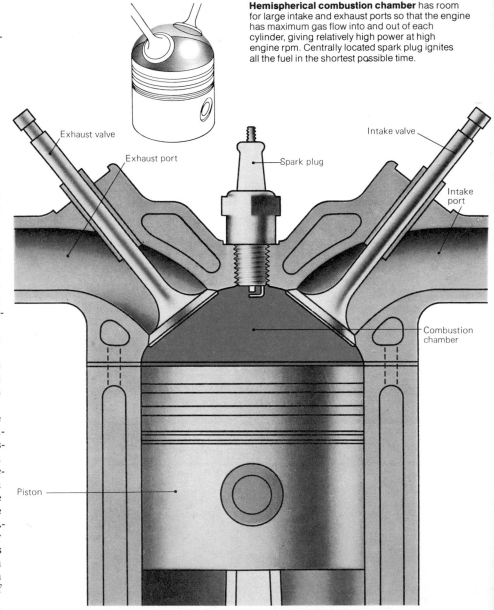

Hemispherical combustion chamber has room for large intake and exhaust ports so that the engine has maximum gas flow into and out of each cylinder, giving relatively high power at high engine rpm. Centrally located spark plug ignites all the fuel in the shortest possible time.

Exhaust valve

Exhaust port

Spark plug

Intake valve

Intake port

Combustion chamber

Piston

Bathtub chamber

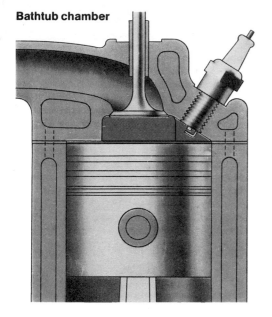 

Bathtub combustion chamber is shaped like an inverted bathtub, with the valves in the bottom of the tub. Since all the valves can be arranged in a single row, the valve-operating camshaft and/or rocker gear are simple to design and operate. The long, oval shape of the bathtub controls excessive turbulence, and the flat areas where the piston comes right up to the head surface supply the squish needed to swirl the mixture. The wide cylinders and short piston strokes in modern engines make it possible to use large valves with bathtub heads for efficient gas flow.

Squish chamber

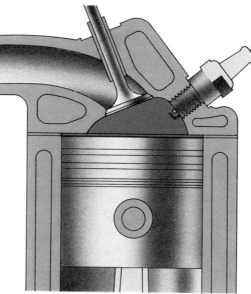 

Squish combustion chamber can be a variation on almost any of the standard forms. The squish area that gives it its name is the flat surface of the cylinder head that almost contacts the piston crown. When the piston rises on the compression stroke, it squishes, or squirts, the gas from this area into the combustion chamber with a swirling motion. This mixes the air-fuel mixture thoroughly for more complete vaporization and combustion. At the same time, the mixture is cooled as it swirls past the chamber walls, which are kept relatively cool by the water passages.

Wedge chamber

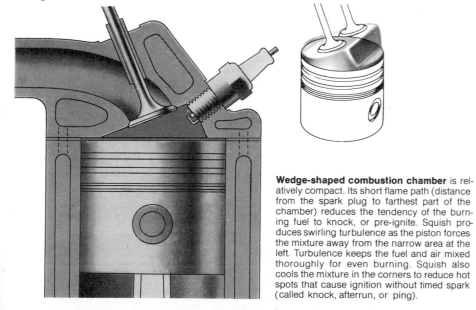

Wedge-shaped combustion chamber is relatively compact. Its short flame path (distance from the spark plug to farthest part of the chamber) reduces the tendency of the burning fuel to knock, or pre-ignite. Squish produces swirling turbulence as the piston forces the mixture away from the narrow area at the left. Turbulence keeps the fuel and air mixed thoroughly for even burning. Squish also cools the mixture in the corners to reduce hot spots that cause ignition without timed spark (called knock, afterrun, or ping).

Piston-crown chamber

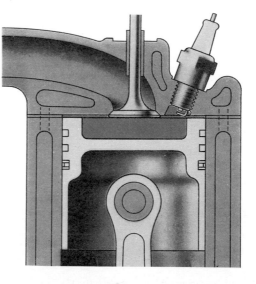 

Piston-crown combustion chamber is used in diesel truck engines and in some European gasoline automobile engines. The advantage in simply machining a flat surface on the cylinder head is offset by the added cost of machining the bowl in each piston and by increased piston weight. Ford uses this design in the Fiesta and for some of its stratified-charge engines (see following page).

Stratified-charge engine

The stratified-charge engine is unique in that the combustion chamber is designed so as not to thoroughly mix the incoming air-fuel mixture but to allow the fuel and air to remain in relatively unmixed layers, or strata.

The theoretically ideal air-fuel mixture for a conventional engine is 14.7 parts air to each part gasoline (by weight), spread uniformly through the combustion chamber. More gas—a *richer* mixture—can produce more power, but it also causes more pollution and gives poorer fuel economy. Less gas—a *leaner* mixture—will not ignite in a conventional engine if the air-fuel ratio is made leaner than 18:1.

Experimental stratified-charge engines allow average ratios as lean as 30:1 to burn smoothly, resulting in less pollution and greater fuel economy than conventional engines do. This is done by allowing a small amount of very rich mixture to accumulate near the spark plug for easy ignition. Once ignited, this rich layer will ignite mixtures as lean as 200:1 elsewhere in the combustion chamber.

One way to stratify the charge is to place the spark plug in a small ante-chamber, called a *pre-chamber*. A rich mixture is introduced into the pre-chamber by a second intake valve or by fuel injection. A lean mixture enters the main chamber by the normal intake valve. This is the system used in Honda's CVCC engine, which has a special multibarrel carburetor that supplies a rich mixture of about 8:1 to the pre-chamber and a lean mixture of 20:1 to the main combustion chamber.

A second method is to isolate rich and lean mixtures aerodynamically, as is done in Ford's Proco engine. Here, fuel is injected at an angle into a conical cavity in the piston crown. As the piston rises, the mixture swirls around and most of the fuel is drawn toward the central spark plug by this whirlpool action.

Honda CVCC (Controlled Vortex Combustion Chamber), introduced in 1973, was the first mass-produced stratified-charge passenger car engine. Complex rocker gear operates three valves per cylinder off a single overhead camshaft.

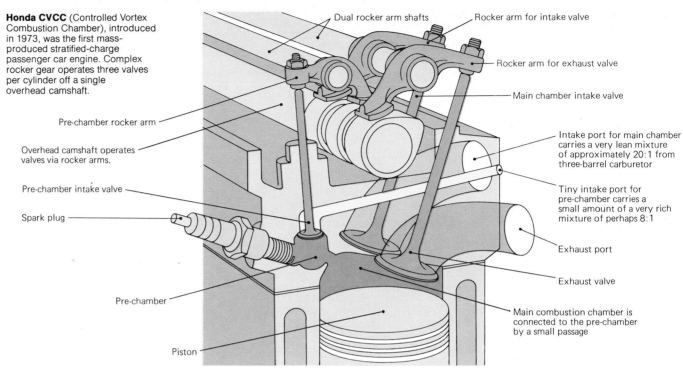

Dual rocker arm shafts

Rocker arm for intake valve

Rocker arm for exhaust valve

Main chamber intake valve

Pre-chamber rocker arm

Overhead camshaft operates valves via rocker arms.

Pre-chamber intake valve

Spark plug

Pre-chamber

Piston

Intake port for main chamber carries a very lean mixture of approximately 20:1 from three-barrel carburetor

Tiny intake port for pre-chamber carries a small amount of a very rich mixture of perhaps 8:1

Exhaust port

Exhaust valve

Main combustion chamber is connected to the pre-chamber by a small passage

Four-stroke cycle in a stratified-charge engine

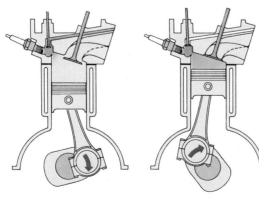 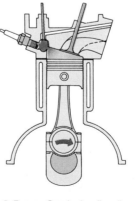 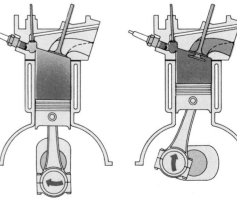

1. Intake: Piston descends, drawing rich mixture into pre-chamber and lean mixture into main chamber.

2. Compression: Piston rises, forming strata and concentrating the rich mixture around spark plug.

3. Power: Spark plug fires the rich mixture, shooting a tongue of flame into the main combustion chamber.

Combustion progresses as lean mixture in main chamber burns and expanding gases move piston.

4. Exhaust: The burned gases are forced past the exhaust valve, and the cycle is ready to begin again.

Diesel engine

A diesel engine has no spark plugs. Ignition is caused by compression, which raises the temperature of the air in the cylinder above the *flash point*, or spontaneous combustion temperature, of the fuel. A typical gasoline engine has a compression ratio of 9:1; diesel engines have compression ratios of more than 20:1.

Diesel fuel, sometimes called *diesel oil*, is similar to kerosene and home heating oil. It does not evaporate as easily as gasoline and is not mixed with the incoming air in a carburetor. Instead, diesel fuel is sprayed under high pressure from an injector into the combustion chamber, where it ignites on contact with the hot compressed air. The timing of this fuel injection must be as precise as the timing of the spark in a gasoline engine if a diesel is to run properly. A pump, driven by the camshaft or crankshaft, delivers fuel in timed pulses to the individual injection nozzles. The accelerator pedal controls the amount and the timing of fuel delivered by the pump, and hence the speed and power of the engine.

Compared to a gasoline engine, diesels generally give greater fuel economy, longer engine life, and produce less pollution. Some diesels produce visible smoke, but the chemical makeup of this smoke is not believed to be as hazardous to health as the invisible pollutants produced by gasoline engines. Because it has no carburetor, distributor, or spark plugs, a diesel engine does not need conventional tuneups. But its lubricating oil and oil filter must usually be changed at relatively short intervals because the products of diesel fuel combustion produce more oil contamination than the products of gasoline combustion do.

Other disadvantages generally include higher cost, greater weight, noisier operation, and less power than in a gasoline engine of the same size. Diesels may also be difficult to start in cold weather and can produce a peculiar odor.

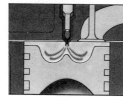

In truck diesels the combustion chamber is often formed by a depression in the piston crown. Unique shape gives a swirling action to the incoming fuel.

Automobile diesels have a pre-chamber design rather than the direct injection used in trucks. The pre-chamber results in quieter operation, at slight cost in fuel economy.

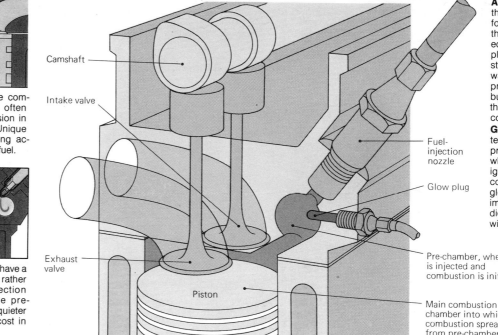

Camshaft

Intake valve

Exhaust valve

Piston

Fuel-injection nozzle

Glow plug

Pre-chamber, where fuel is injected and combustion is initiated

Main combustion chamber into which combustion spreads from pre-chamber

Another advantage of the pre-chamber design for passenger cars is that the pre-chamber can be equipped with a glow plug to facilitate cold starting. A glow plug can warm up the small pre-chamber adequately but could not warm the entire main combustion chamber.

Glow plug raises temperature of pre-chamber to the point where diesel fuel will ignite when it is compressed. Without a glow plug it is difficult or impossible to start a diesel engine on cold winter mornings.

Four-stroke cycle in a diesel engine

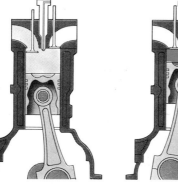
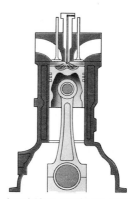
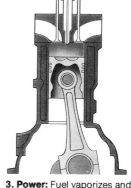
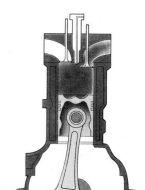

1. Intake: Intake valve is open; exhaust valve is closed. Piston descends and draws air in from manifold.

2. Compression: Both valves close and the piston rises to compress the air. The air's temperature rises.

Just before maximum compression, diesel fuel is injected into the chamber under very high pressure.

3. Power: Fuel vaporizes and ignites almost immediately in the heat of the compressed air. The piston descends.

4. Exhaust: The exhaust valve opens and the rising piston expels exhaust gases in the usual manner.

Why the engine needs oil

The oil in an engine does more than just reduce friction between its moving parts. It also helps to seal the high-pressure combustion gases inside the cylinders, to impede the corrosion of metal parts, to absorb some of the harmful by-products of combustion, and to transfer heat from one part of the engine to another.

Oil is stored in the *oil pan,* at the bottom of the engine. A pump forces the oil through a filter and then through a series of *passages* and *galleries* to lubricate the engine's moving parts. The flow of oil also cools these parts.

Rapidly moving engine parts actually float on a thin film of oil and never make contact with one another. This is called *hydrodynamic* lubrication, and usually begins when an engine reaches idle speed. No shaft can make a perfectly tight fit in its bearing; if it did, it could not turn. There is a tiny clearance between the two surfaces—often as little as .0003 inches (.0076 mm) on a bearing with a diameter of 2 inches (50 mm). Oil is fed into the bearing at a point where the clearance is greatest (usually near the top). The rotation of the shaft pulls the oil around to the point of maximum pressure (near the bottom), where the clearance is smallest. This creates what engineers call an *oil wedge* between the spinning shaft and its bearing, and allows high loads to be borne with little or no wear. Most engine wear occurs when a cold engine is first started, before the oil reaches its normal operating pressure and flow.

An insufficient flow of oil will lead to rapid wear or to seizure of the engine's moving parts by allowing metal to grind against metal. It can also cause engine failure by destroying the sealing surfaces of the piston rings and allowing the combustion gases to escape past the pistons. Sludge or dirt in the oil galleries and passages, a faulty oil pump, a low oil level, or use of the wrong grade of oil can all cause insufficient oil flow.

Separating moving parts

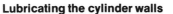

No matter how smooth a metal surface may appear, microscopic examination will reveal jagged irregularities that cause friction (top). Molecules of oil separate the moving parts and reduce the friction between them (bottom).

Wedging action of oil

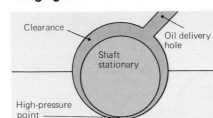

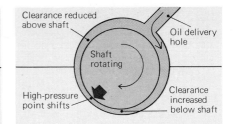

When a shaft is at rest (left), it exerts pressure straight down because of gravity. As it begins to rotate, oil molecules adhering to the shaft are carried around with it, and more oil is drawn into the clearance. As the shaft's rotational speed increases, oil forms a wedge in the high-pressure area, lifting the shaft off the bearing. The greater rotational speed also shifts the high-pressure area to a point directly opposite the oil delivery hole (right).

Lubricating the cylinder walls

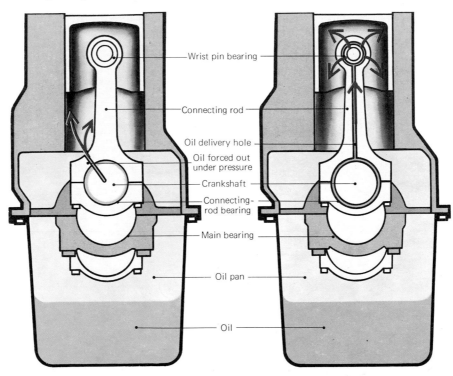

Wrist pin bearing
Connecting rod
Oil delivery hole
Oil forced out under pressure
Crankshaft
Connecting-rod bearing
Main bearing
Oil pan
Oil

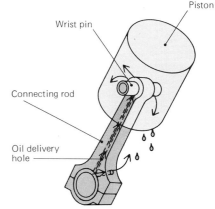

Piston
Wrist pin
Connecting rod
Oil delivery hole

The cylinder walls are lubricated by the oil forced out of the connecting-rod bearings under pressure. In the simplest and least effective system, oil is merely allowed to escape between the connecting rods and crankshaft webs, and some of it inevitably splashes against the cylinder walls. A more certain method is to allow oil to escape through holes drilled in the big end of the connecting rods (far left). The costliest but most effective method is to drill a hole up the center of the connecting rod (left and above). The oil lubricates the wrist pin bearing and escapes in a series of squirts to cool the inside of the piston, then lubricate the cylinder walls. This system is found only in heavy-duty diesel engines.

How oil circulates through the engine

On most engines the oil pump is operated by a shaft driven off a gear on the camshaft. (The distributor is driven off the upper half of this oil pump shaft.) The pump draws oil through a pickup screen from the lowest part of the oil pan, then forces it through the oil filter. From the filter, oil flows into the main oil gallery, which is usually parallel to the camshaft. Smaller passages deliver oil to the camshaft bearings and to the crankshaft main bearings. Holes drilled in the crankshaft force oil under pressure to the connecting rod bearings and from there to the cylinder walls. Oil drips from the cylinder walls back into the oil pan.

A passage branching off the main oil gallery delivers oil through the rocker shaft to the individual rocker arms and valve stems. This oil runs down the pushrod holes to lubricate the tappets and cams. On engines with overhead camshafts, a similar passage delivers oil to the cam lobes and bearings. Passages in the head and block allow this oil to drain back into the oil pan.

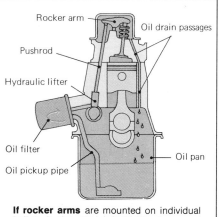

If rocker arms are mounted on individual ball studs, they are lubricated by oil pumped up through hollow pushrods by the hydraulic lifters. This oil drains back into the oil pan through passages in the head and block.

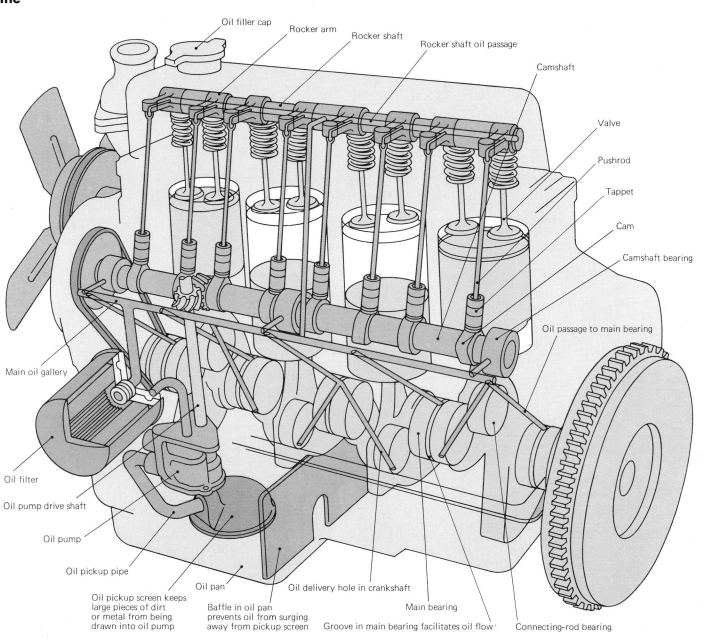

Oil filters and oil pumps

The oil filter removes abrasive particles that enter the lubrication system before they can cause excessive wear. In modern cars, all of the oil passes through the filter before it enters the main oil gallery. The most common filtering medium is a resin-impregnated paper that is folded into accordion pleats in order to accommodate a large filtering area within a small container. A good filter traps more than 95 percent of the particles in the 10- to 40-micron size range each time the oil is passed through it. (A human hair is about 60 microns thick.)

The lubrication system must be fitted with a bypass valve so that the system can continue to function if the filter becomes blocked with dirt or sludge. The spring-loaded bypass valve will usually open if the drop in pressure between the filter intake and outlet exceeds 5 to 12 pounds per square inch (35 to 85 kPa). The valve will also open when the oil is cold and too thick to flow through the filter easily, which is usually the case on a cold morning. On General Motors cars the bypass valve is built into the oil filter mounting, as shown in the illustration below. On most other cars the bypass valve is built into the filter itself. This is one reason why you should always use

the type of filter recommended for your car, not just any filter that physically fits the screw-on filter mount.

The filter should be changed at the intervals recommended by the carmaker; otherwise it will become clogged, the bypass valve will open, and unfiltered oil will circulate through the engine.

Older cars used to employ a bypass filtering system in which only a portion of the oil was filtered before it reached the oil galleries. The filters were commonly made of paper with pores fine enough to trap particles of 5 microns and smaller. However, larger particles in the unfiltered oil might circulate through the engine several times before they were finally trapped by the filter.

Oil pumps: There are two kinds of engine oil pumps in general use: the gear type and the rotor type. Both are usually driven by a shaft with a gear at its end that meshes with a gear on the camshaft.

The oil pump typically keeps pressure in the oil galleries as high as 60 pounds per square inch (410 kPa). A spring-loaded pressure-relief valve near the pump outlet returns oil to the oil pan when the pump is creating excess pressure (at high engine speeds or when the oil is cold and thick).

How the filter works

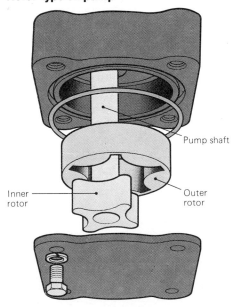

Oil filters are made of pleated paper. They cannot be cleaned but should be periodically replaced. A perforated center tube supports the paper element.

Pleated paper element — Outlet to engine

Bypass valve — Inlet from oil pump

Oil enters the filter through a number of small holes arranged in a circle. The oil flows around the outside of the paper element, through the paper, then back to the engine through the central outlet tube.

Gear-type oil pump

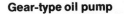
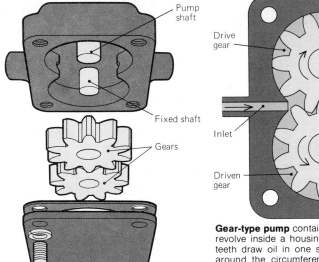

Pump shaft — Fixed shaft — Gears

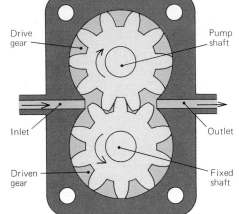

Drive gear — Pump shaft
Inlet — Outlet
Driven gear — Fixed shaft

Gear-type pump contains two meshing gears that revolve inside a housing. The closely fitting gear teeth draw oil in one side of the pump, carry it around the circumference of the housing, then force it out the other side.

Rotor-type oil pump

Pump shaft
Inner rotor — Outer rotor

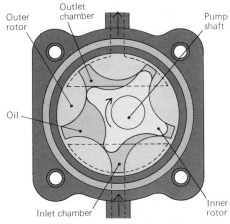

Outer rotor — Outlet chamber — Pump shaft
Oil
Inlet chamber — Inner rotor

Rotor-type pump has a cross-shaped inner rotor that is driven by the pump shaft. The arms of the cross mesh with the cavities in the star-shaped outer rotor. The cross drives the star, but their axes of rotation are different. Thus, the spaces between them vary in size, and the arms of the cross constantly slip from one cavity to the next. This forces oil from one side of the pump to the other.

Engine bearings and motor oil

Bearings are used to minimize friction and to support all the rotating parts of an engine. They fall into two categories: plain bearings and rolling bearings.

Plain bearings consist of outer steel shells with layers of softer metal (mixtures of copper, lead, tin, and antimony) applied to the inner surfaces. Some of the abrasive grit that escapes the oil filter becomes embedded in the soft metal instead of scratching the shaft.

Rolling bearings are used where there is a lot of side force on a shaft (from a tight drive belt, for example). A row of steel balls or cylinders is placed between the shaft and the bearing.

Motor oil: An oil's viscosity (thickness) is identified by its *SAE* (Society of Automotive Engineers) *number*. The thinner an oil, the lower its number. SAE 5W and 10W oils are light enough to flow well at winter temperatures. SAE 30, 40, and 50 oils are heavy enough to provide a protective film at progressively higher operating temperatures. SAE 20 oil is an intermediate weight good for temperate climates. So-called *multi-weight oils* contain additives that give them the characteristics of several viscosity ratings. A 10W-50 oil, for example, is a good all-season oil for climates with large temperature variations. In arctic conditions, a 5W oil will flow more quickly when an engine is first started. Synthetic oils are especially useful in sub-zero weather because they tend to flow at lower temperatures than mineral oils do. An oil's SAE viscosity is often referred to as its *weight* or *grade.*

An oil's *API* (American Petroleum Institute) *Service Classification* is an indication of its service characteristics. It is graded on a scale from SA (the lowest) to SF (the highest) for gasoline engines. Oil for diesel engines must meet different requirements, and it is graded on a scale from CA to CD. Many oils are rated on both the S (spark ignition) and C (compression ignition) scales.

Oil never wears out, but its chemical additives do. Among the other functions they perform, these additives retard corrosion, neutralize acids, and disperse sooty, tarry materials that escape past the piston rings and into the oil pan. Many of these contaminants are vaporized when the engine warms up, and they flow into the positive crankcase ventilation (PCV) system. Those that remain are held in suspension so that they cannot clog oil passages, piston rings, and hydraulic lifters. They are physically removed from the engine when its oil and oil filter are changed. Never postpone an oil change beyond the interval recommended by the carmaker. If a car is used mainly for short trips in which the engine seldom reaches normal operating temperature, you should change oil more often than the carmaker recommends, because the crankcase contaminants do not vaporize at low engine temperatures.

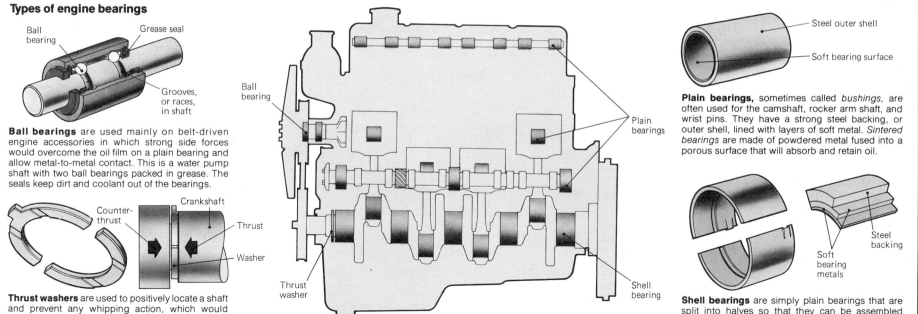

Types of engine bearings

Ball bearings are used mainly on belt-driven engine accessories in which strong side forces would overcome the oil film on a plain bearing and allow metal-to-metal contact. This is a water pump shaft with two ball bearings packed in grease. The seals keep dirt and coolant out of the bearings.

Ball bearing · Grease seal · Grooves, or races, in shaft

Thrust washers are used to positively locate a shaft and prevent any whipping action, which would cause rapid bearing wear. This example is used at the front of the crankshaft to resist the forward thrust applied by the clutch springs. The thrust washer is often built into a main bearing.

Counter-thrust · Crankshaft · Thrust · Washer

Ball bearing · Plain bearings · Shell bearing · Thrust washer

Engine bearings reduce friction and resist wear wherever one metal component rotates within another. There are additional bearings in the distributor, oil pump, alternator, starter, steering system, and drive train.

Steel outer shell · Soft bearing surface

Plain bearings, sometimes called *bushings,* are often used for the camshaft, rocker arm shaft, and wrist pins. They have a strong steel backing, or outer shell, lined with layers of soft metal. *Sintered bearings* are made of powdered metal fused into a porous surface that will absorb and retain oil.

Steel backing · Soft bearing metals

Shell bearings are simply plain bearings that are split into halves so that they can be assembled around the crankshaft. The main bearings and connecting-rod bearings are shell designs. Grooves in the main bearings promote an effective flow of oil, some of which is transferred to the connecting rods.

Common piston engine layouts

The previous pages have described an in-line, four-cylinder engine, the simplest engine mass-produced in North America today. Single-cylinder engines were the rule at the dawn of the automotive age. Two-cylinder engines are still made in Europe and Asia. Saab, the Swedish automobile and aircraft company, produced a three-cylinder engine until 1967.

All modern engines operate in much the same way as the in-line four. For more power or smoothness, five or six cylinders can be arranged in a row. In-line eights were popular before World War II, and General Motors continued to offer them until 1954. Today all eight-cylinder engines, and many sixes, have their cylinders arranged in two rows that form a V. Although V-4 and V-12 engines are produced in Europe, they are imported in small numbers and are not commonly seen in North America. The banks of cylinders in a V-type engine usually form an angle of 90° or, less often, 60°. If the angle between the banks of cylinders is 180°, they form a "flat" engine with horizontally opposed cylinders. Two popular engines of this type were the Volkswagen flat-4 and the Corvair flat-6, both air-cooled designs (see p.75).

Displacement

Engines are classified not only by the number of cylinders they have but also by the size of the cylinders. The volume of air displaced by each piston as it moves from the bottom of its stroke to the top is calculated, then multiplied by the number of cylinders to determine the engine's *displacement,* which is given in cubic inches (cu in.), cubic centimeters (cc), or liters (L). This calculation includes only the *swept volume* of the pistons, not the volume of the combustion chambers. A large-displacement engine will generally use more fuel and produce more power than a typical small-displacement engine does.

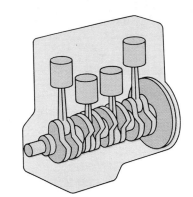

In-line four-cylinder engines are most often found in lightweight economy and sports cars. They are short enough to be placed sideways (called *transverse mounting*) in some front-wheel-drive models. Most fours vibrate noticeably, especially at low engine speeds. One exception is the Silent Shaft Four, used in some Mitsubishi cars sold in the U.S. by Chrysler dealers. It has two balance shafts that rotate in the direction opposite to the crankshaft's, and it is smoother running than some V-8s.

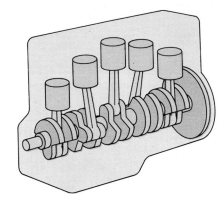

In-line five-cylinder auto engines were unheard of until Mercedes-Benz introduced a five-cylinder diesel passenger car engine in 1974. The Volkswagen-Audi group followed suit a few years later with five-cylinder gasoline and diesel engines. The main advantage of a five is that it produces more power than a four but takes up less space than an in-line six. A V-6, however, is even more compact, and it can be mounted transversely in a front-wheel-drive car, while a five cannot.

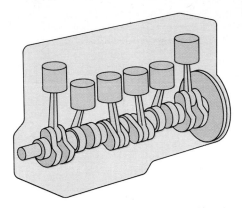

In-line six-cylinder engines are longer and heavier than fours and fives, but are generally smoother and more powerful. Sixes are the traditional "small" engine option in large North American sedans and station wagons. There can be a lot of working room around an in-line six in the engine compartment of a wide modern car. Most sixes stand upright, like the one in the illustration, but Chrysler Corporation slants its six at a 30° angle, which lowers its center of gravity somewhat.

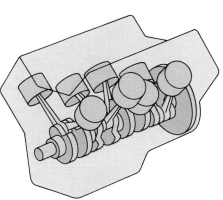

V-8 engines are usually smoother and more powerful than in-line sixes. They are shorter as well. Essentially, they consist of two four-cylinder engines joined to a common crankshaft. Each crankpin is long enough to accommodate two connecting rods. The intake manifold is located inside the V, and an exhaust manifold is found on each side of the engine. Before fuel economy became an important selling point, V-8 engines were found in the majority of cars produced in North America.

Cylinder banks

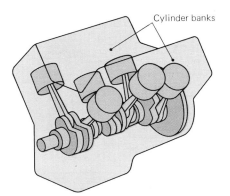

V-6 engines are usually more powerful than fours but short enough to fit into small cars. Those with a 60° angle between the cylinder banks can run as smoothly as V-8s, especially if each connecting rod has its own crankpin. As a manufacturing economy, many V-6s are made on the same machinery as V-8s. They have a 90° angle between the cylinder banks, and two connecting rods per crankpin. They often do not run as smoothly as 60° V-6s because their spark plugs may not fire at even intervals.

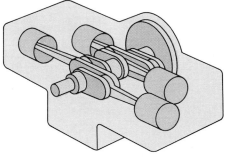

Flat-4 engines have two pairs of cylinders arranged horizontally. Air-cooled flat-4s were made popular throughout the world in Volkswagens. Water-cooled flat-4s are now manufactured by Alfa Romeo, Lancia, and Subaru. Chevrolet once made an air-cooled flat-6 for the controversial Corvair, and Ferrari currently makes a powerful water-cooled flat-12 for the Berlinetta Boxer model. A flat engine's low center of gravity can help to improve a car's handling characteristics.

The Wankel rotary engine

The Wankel engine has no valves, pistons, connecting rods, or crankshaft. Instead, it uses a triangular rotor that revolves in a roughly oval chamber. The four stages of piston engine combustion—intake, compression, power, and exhaust—take place on each of the rotor's three faces as it rotates through the chamber. For clarity, the illustrations below show these events on only one face of the rotor. To grasp the full potential of the rotary engine, you must remember that the same sequence is occurring, in turn, on each of the other rotor faces.

Each rotor has three power "strokes" for every revolution, and during each rotor revolution the output shaft revolves three times. Engineers consider this the equivalent of two four-stroke pistons, so the typical twin-rotor Wankel can be compared to a four-cylinder piston engine. While a twin-rotor Wankel engine has only 7 major moving parts, a comparable four-cylinder engine has more than 50. For the power produced, a

rotary engine is smaller, lighter, and potentially easier to produce than a piston engine. It can also run on low-octane fuel.

Although 20 companies hold licenses to produce Wankel engines, only 2 have built rotary-powered cars in any numbers—Mazda in Japan and Audi-NSU in Germany. One reason is the cost of setting up a production line to build Wankel engines. Another was the high fuel consumption and pollution levels of the early rotary-engine cars, although much progress has been made in these areas recently. Compared to the piston engine, the Wankel is at a much more primitive stage of development; NSU ran the first experimental engine in 1957. With the press of meeting ever-changing fuel economy and antipollution regulations, most carmakers have adopted a wait-and-see attitude toward any completely new engine technology. Other firms have built rotary-powered lawn mowers, motorcycles, outboards, snowmobiles, and model airplane engines.

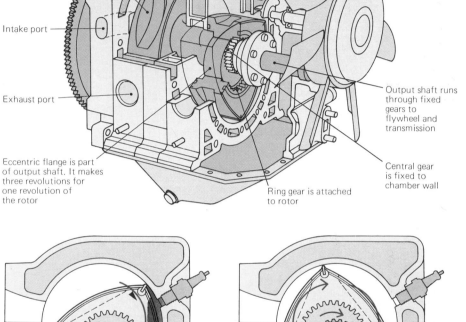

Rotor

Combustion recess in rotor face

Flywheel

Intake port

Exhaust port

Eccentric flange is part of output shaft. It makes three revolutions for one revolution of the rotor

Ring gear is attached to rotor

Output shaft runs through fixed gears to flywheel and transmission

Central gear is fixed to chamber wall

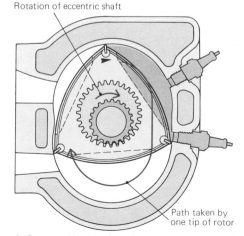

Rotor tip

Intake port

Rotation of eccentric shaft

Fixed gear

Path taken by one tip of rotor

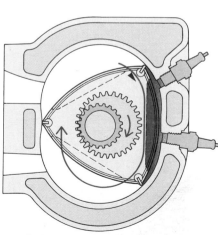

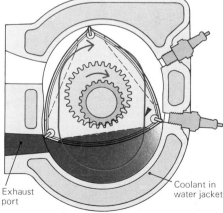

Exhaust port

Coolant in water jacket

1. Intake: The rotor flip-flops around the fixed gear with a motion like that of a hula hoop around a child's waist. As one rotor tip passes the intake port, it creates a chamber of increasing volume and draws in the air-fuel mixture from the carburetor.

2. Compression: As the rotor continues to revolve, the second tip passes the intake port, sealing the fuel mixture in a chamber of decreasing volume. The compression ratio is lower than in piston engines, so very low octane fuel can be used.

3. Power: Ignition causes fuel mixture to burn and expand, imparting energy to the rotor for its power stroke as the size of the chamber again increases. Because of the long, flat shape of the combustion chamber, most Wankels use two spark plugs.

4. Exhaust: The leading tip of the rotor passes the exhaust port and leaves it open for the burned gases to escape as the chamber decreases in size. For every revolution of the rotor, the eccentric flange and output shaft make three revolutions.

From the gas cap to the intake valves

The fuel system begins at the neck of the fuel tank, where liquid fuel is pumped into the car at the corner service station, and ends at the intake valves inside the cylinder head, where the vaporized air-fuel mixture enters the combustion chambers of the engine. Liquid fuel is drawn from the tank by the fuel pump and delivered through several filters into the carburetor, where the fuel is mixed with air and begins to vaporize. (Fuel-injection systems, which have no carburetors, are used on all diesel engines and on some gasoline engines. Fuel injection is covered on pages 60-61.)

Liquid fuel will not burn. When a puddle of gasoline seems to burn, it is actually the vapors rising from the liquid that are aflame. It is therefore important that the fuel be vaporized as much as possible on its way to the combustion chambers, not only to get maximum power and mileage from each drop of gas but also to reduce the pollution caused by incomplete combustion of fuel.

Gasoline is sprayed into the carburetor as a fine mist. When these droplets enter the partial vacuum in the intake manifold, they begin to evaporate. Heat from the exhaust system is routed to the air cleaner and intake manifold on most engines to aid in fuel vaporization.

When any gas—including air—is compressed, its temperature rises. The rising temperature inside the cylinder as the air-fuel mixture is compressed completes the vaporization of the fuel.

Cars sold in the U.S. since 1971 contain an evaporative emission control system to trap fuel vapors that were previously vented into the atmosphere when gasoline in the carburetor and fuel tank evaporated. These vapors are now routed through hoses to a filter or canister impregnated with activated charcoal, which absorbs the vapors. When the car is started, the vapors are drawn into the engine and burned.

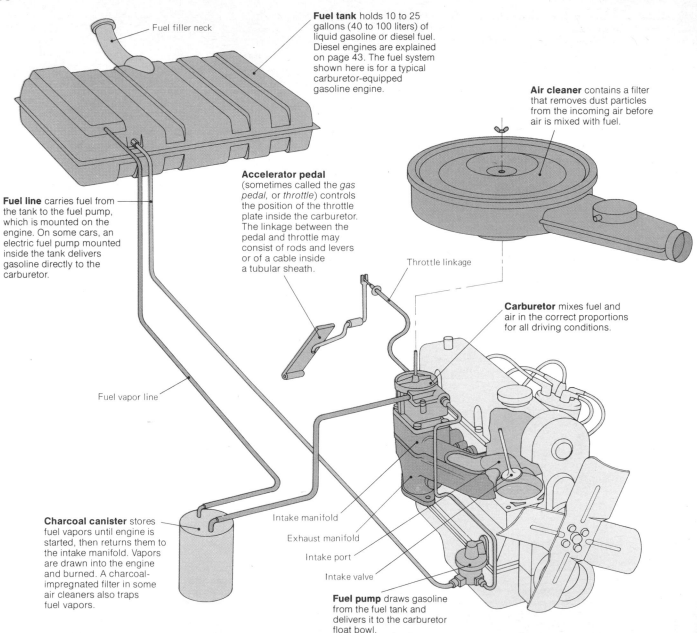

Fuel filler neck

Fuel tank holds 10 to 25 gallons (40 to 100 liters) of liquid gasoline or diesel fuel. Diesel engines are explained on page 43. The fuel system shown here is for a typical carburetor-equipped gasoline engine.

Air cleaner contains a filter that removes dust particles from the incoming air before air is mixed with fuel.

Fuel line carries fuel from the tank to the fuel pump, which is mounted on the engine. On some cars, an electric fuel pump mounted inside the tank delivers gasoline directly to the carburetor.

Accelerator pedal (sometimes called the *gas pedal,* or *throttle*) controls the position of the throttle plate inside the carburetor. The linkage between the pedal and throttle may consist of rods and levers or of a cable inside a tubular sheath.

Throttle linkage

Carburetor mixes fuel and air in the correct proportions for all driving conditions.

Fuel vapor line

Charcoal canister stores fuel vapors until engine is started, then returns them to the intake manifold. Vapors are drawn into the engine and burned. A charcoal-impregnated filter in some air cleaners also traps fuel vapors.

Intake manifold

Exhaust manifold

Intake port

Intake valve

Fuel pump draws gasoline from the fuel tank and delivers it to the carburetor float bowl.

What a carburetor does

As each piston moves downward on its intake stroke, a partial vacuum is created inside the cylinder. The open intake valve allows outside air to rush into the cylinder to fill the vacuum, but first the air must pass through the air cleaner, carburetor, and intake manifold. Due to these restrictions in the air's circuitous path, some vacuum always remains below the throttle plate when the engine is running. Hoses from the intake manifold provide vacuum that operates the power brake booster, heater controls, distributor advance mechanism, and a number of antipollution devices.

As air passes through the carburetor, fuel is drawn out of the float bowl—a small reservoir inside the carburetor—and sprayed into the airstream in carefully measured amounts (pp.52-53). In most engines, a mixture of 14.6 parts air (by weight) to one part gas ensures maximum vaporization and combustion of the fuel. This is called the *stoichiometric* (chemically correct) air-to-fuel ratio. A lower ratio (less air to fuel) is called a *richer* mixture. A higher ratio (more air to fuel) is a *leaner* mixture.

A mixture as rich as seven parts air for each part of fuel (7:1) may be required to start an engine on a cold morning. A mixture as lean as 18:1 may be all that is required for cruising at low speed with a warm engine. Bursts of acceleration and deceleration require constantly changing air-fuel ratios, and it is the function of the carburetor to supply exactly the right mixture at the right time so that the engine can run smoothly.

When gas was cheap and pollution was not a concern, carburetors were tuned to run quite rich. Later, until the advent of today's computer-controlled fuel and ignition systems, auto engineers contrived carburetor settings that would not produce illegal levels of air pollution. As a result, well-tuned smog-controlled engines sometimes stalled and stumbled when cold, or surged in jerky spurts during moderate acceleration and deceleration because they were always running on the leanest possible mixture. These problems have stimulated interest in more expensive but more precise fuel-injection systems (pp.60-61) that would eliminate the carburetor.

A simple carburetor

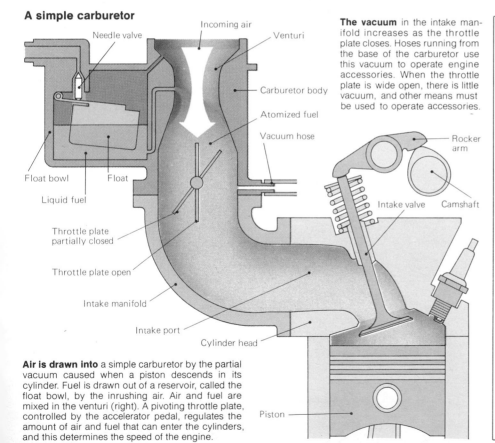

Needle valve · Incoming air · Venturi · Carburetor body · Atomized fuel · Vacuum hose · Rocker arm · Float bowl · Float · Liquid fuel · Intake valve · Camshaft · Throttle plate partially closed · Throttle plate open · Intake manifold · Intake port · Cylinder head · Piston

Air is drawn into a simple carburetor by the partial vacuum caused when a piston descends in its cylinder. Fuel is drawn out of a reservoir, called the float bowl, by the inrushing air. Air and fuel are mixed in the venturi (right). A pivoting throttle plate, controlled by the accelerator pedal, regulates the amount of air and fuel that can enter the cylinders, and this determines the speed of the engine.

The vacuum in the intake manifold increases as the throttle plate closes. Hoses running from the base of the carburetor use this vacuum to operate engine accessories. When the throttle plate is wide open, there is little vacuum, and other means must be used to operate accessories.

The venturi principle

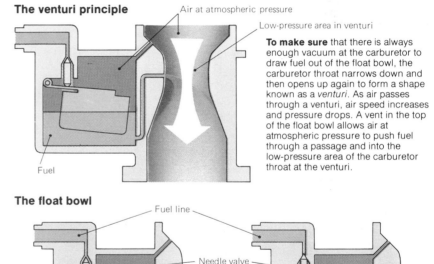

Air at atmospheric pressure · Low-pressure area in venturi · Fuel

To make sure that there is always enough vacuum at the carburetor to draw fuel out of the float bowl, the carburetor throat narrows down and then opens up again to form a shape known as a *venturi*. As air passes through a venturi, air speed increases and pressure drops. A vent in the top of the float bowl allows air at atmospheric pressure to push fuel through a passage and into the low-pressure area of the carburetor throat at the venturi.

The float bowl

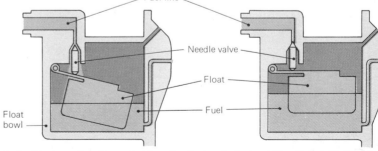

Fuel line · Needle valve · Float · Fuel · Float bowl

As fuel is drawn into the venturi from the float bowl, the float drops and the needle is pushed away from its seat by fuel that is under pressure from the fuel pump.

As the bowl fills with fuel, the float rises, pushing the needle into its seat and blocking the flow of fuel. This system assures a constant supply of fuel at the venturi.

Mixing fuel and air in the correct proportions

The amount of air that can be drawn through the carburetor is controlled by a pivoting flap called the *throttle plate*. If it were not for this plate, an engine would accelerate to its top speed soon after it was started and would run at top speed until something broke. By controlling the position of the throttle plate, the engine can be throttled down to any desired speed. Closing the plate completely will stall the engine. The throttle plate is connected to the accelerator pedal by a cable or a series of levers and rods.

As air passes through the venturi, its pressure drops. Fuel is sucked into this low-pressure area from the float bowl. The more the throttle valve is opened, the faster the air rushes through the venturi; the lower the air pressure drops, the more fuel is sucked in. Thus, more power is

provided in the combustion chambers to drive the engine even faster. It is a sequence that feeds on itself, like a chain reaction, and is controlled only by the throttle plate.

Fuel-metering circuits

The basic carburetor described above might be sufficient for a lawn mower engine, but even the simplest automotive carburetor has at least six separate fuel-metering systems to provide the correct air-fuel ratio needed for different driving conditions. The float bowl system, which assures a proper supply of fuel at all times, is described on page 51. The other major carburetor systems are the idle circuit, the main metering circuit, the accelerator pump circuit, the power enrichment circuit, and the choke system.

These provide, respectively, the proper air-fuel mixture for idling, cruising, accelerating, pulling heavy loads, and starting a cold engine. They are illustrated on the opposite page.

The maximum amount of fuel that can flow through any circuit is controlled by a *jet*—a tube with a hole of precise size drilled in it. Changing the jets will alter an engine's power, fuel economy, and pollution characteristics.

Fuel and air have different flow characteristics. When air flows faster, it becomes less dense, but fuel density remains constant no matter how fast the fuel flows. If this situation were left uncorrected, a carburetor would supply a progressively richer mixture as engine speed (and therefore air speed through the venturi) increased. A number of *air*

bleed jets mix air with the fuel before it is sprayed into the carburetor throat, progressively diluting the fuel mixture as engine speed increases, and thereby adjusts the air-fuel ratio at any engine speed. These air bleed jets are sometimes called *air correction jets,* which is a more descriptive term.

The carburetor illustrated here is a single-barrel carburetor, which means that it has only one venturi and throttle. It is commonly used on four- and six-cylinder engines when maximum economy is desired. Larger engines or those tuned to produce relatively high horsepower have carburetors with as many as four venturis and throttles. Racing engines may use several carburetors, so that each cylinder has its own venturi and throttle, for greater power.

A one-barrel carburetor

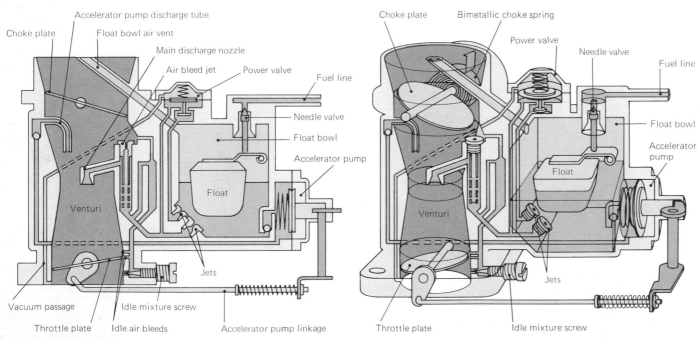

Air bleed jets

As the speed of the air passing through the venturi increases, air density decreases. If the density of the fuel were not adjusted to match that of the air, the mixture would become progressively richer as engine speed increased. The air bleed jet prevents this by mixing varying amounts of air with the gasoline before it enters the venturi. The fuel passes through a well between the float bowl and venturi. Air can enter the well through a perforated tube. As engine speed increases, the level of fuel in the well drops, uncovering more holes in the tube. More air is therefore drawn into the well, automatically giving a leaner air-fuel ratio.

Idle circuit

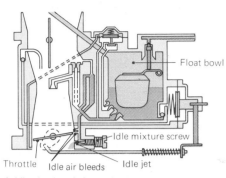

Float bowl

Idle mixture screw

Throttle   Idle air bleeds   Idle jet

At idle, the throttle is nearly closed and fuel must be provided by a jet under the throttle plate. Manifold vacuum, rather than low pressure in the venturi, draws fuel out of the float bowl. The idle jet is a precisely sized hole that limits the rate at which fuel can be drawn from the float bowl. A tapered screw in this hole is used to adjust the air-fuel mixture at idle. As the throttle plate opens, the idle air bleeds are exposed to the vacuum in the intake manifold and fuel is pulled out of them.

Accelerator pump

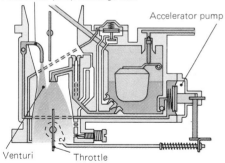

Accelerator pump discharge tube

Accelerator pump

Venturi   Throttle

When the throttle is opened wide for a sudden burst of acceleration, air rushes through the venturi. The fuel, being heavier than air, is slower to speed up to this new rate of flow, and the mixture may momentarily be too lean. This causes the engine to hesitate or stall when the accelerator is first depressed. To avoid this, a small pump squirts a stream of liquid fuel into the venturi whenever the throttle is fully opened, momentarily richening the air-fuel mixture and thereby lessening or preventing hesitation.

Main metering circuit

Main discharge nozzle

Air bleed jet

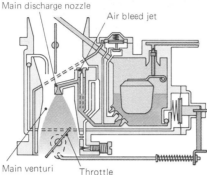

Main venturi   Throttle

This circuit provides the leanest possible mixture for economical cruising at 35 to 70 mph (55 to 110 km/h). The main discharge nozzle is often located inside a miniature venturi of its own. This smaller venturi provides a low-pressure area even at low engine speeds, when the throttle plate is partially closed and airflow through the main venturi is not great enough to provide sufficient vacuum. The air bleed jet maintains the proper air-fuel mixture at all engine operating speeds.

Power enrichment circuit

Diaphragm   Metering valve

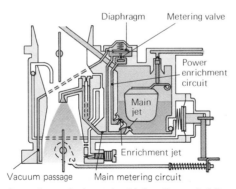

Power enrichment circuit

Main jet

Enrichment jet

Vacuum passage   Main metering circuit

An engine under heavy load (when the car is fully loaded or climbing a hill) may require a richer mixture to produce sufficient torque. The power enrichment circuit provides this richer mixture. As engine load increases, intake manifold vacuum drops. When it drops below a pre-set level, a spring-loaded diaphragm opens a metering valve, which allows more fuel to enter the main metering circuit for improved performance. When manifold vacuum increases, the valve closes again.

The choke

When the engine is cold, fuel does not vaporize properly. The engine is difficult to start and will not run without stalling because the air-fuel mixture is too lean. A choke plate near the top of the carburetor limits the amount of air that can enter the venturi, and this richens the mixture. As the engine warms up, the choke plate opens gradually. Chokes are sometimes operated manually, by a knob on the dashboard, but most North American cars have automatic chokes.

Automatic choke

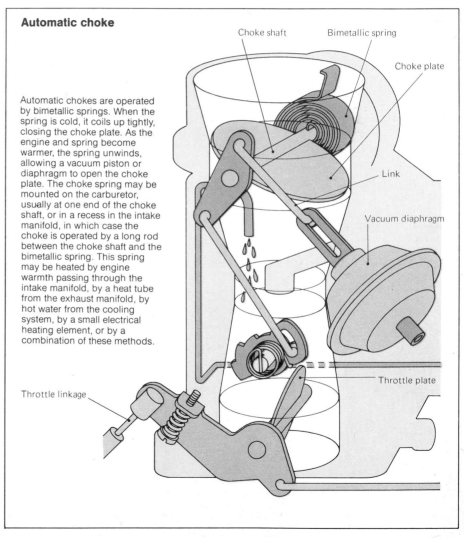

Choke shaft   Bimetallic spring

Choke plate

Link

Vacuum diaphragm

Throttle plate

Throttle linkage

Automatic chokes are operated by bimetallic springs. When the spring is cold, it coils up tightly, closing the choke plate. As the engine and spring become warmer, the spring unwinds, allowing a vacuum piston or diaphragm to open the choke plate. The choke spring may be mounted on the carburetor, usually at one end of the choke shaft, or in a recess in the intake manifold, in which case the choke is operated by a long rod between the choke shaft and the bimetallic spring. This spring may be heated by engine warmth passing through the intake manifold, by a heat tube from the exhaust manifold, by hot water from the cooling system, by a small electrical heating element, or by a combination of these methods.

Two-barrel carburetor

The simple single-barrel carburetor illustrated on pages 52–53 is generally used on four-cylinder engines, and on some six-cylinder engines with relatively low horsepower ratings. Two-barrel carburetors are used on six-cylinder and V-8 engines to provide more power than a single-barrel carburetor would, although at the cost of increased fuel consumption. A two-barrel carburetor is basically a pair of single-barrel carburetors working in tandem: both venturis are covered by a common choke plate; the throttle plates rotate on a single shaft (below); and a common float bowl serves both barrels. ("Barrel" is another term for throat.)

Progressive two-barrel carburetor

A *progressive,* or *compound,* two-barrel carburetor is sometimes fitted to four-cylinder and V-6 engines. It gives the fuel economy of a single-barrel carburetor at low engine speeds and the power of a two-barrel carburetor when the accelerator pedal is floored. At low engine speeds only the smaller *primary* venturi is used (below, left). A slotted throttle link opens the larger *secondary* throttle plate only when the primary throttle is almost fully open (below, right). This provides a surge of extra power when the accelerator is floored for passing, climbing hills, or high-speed cruising. A four-barrel carburetor works the same way.

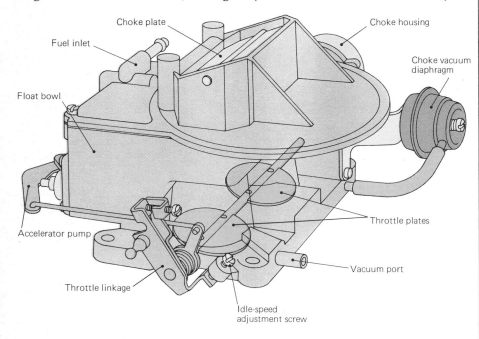

Choke plate
Fuel inlet
Float bowl
Accelerator pump
Throttle linkage
Idle-speed adjustment screw
Choke housing
Choke vacuum diaphragm
Throttle plates
Vacuum port

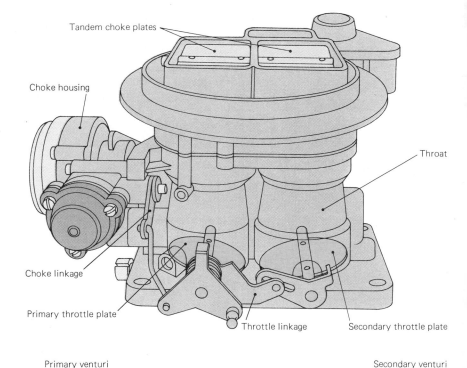

Tandem choke plates
Choke housing
Choke linkage
Primary throttle plate
Throttle linkage
Throat
Secondary throttle plate

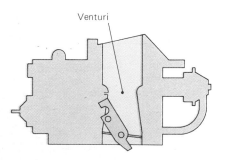

Venturi

Throttle plates closed

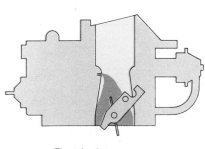

Throttle plates open

Primary venturi

Primary throttle plate open

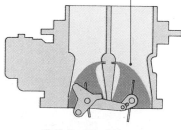

Secondary venturi

Both throttle plates open

Progressive four-barrel carburetor

A progressive four-barrel carburetor is, in effect, two progressive two-barrel carburetors mounted side by side. Some models use a common float bowl to supply fuel to all four barrels; others use separate float bowls for the primary and secondary barrels. At low engine speeds only the primary throttles are open (below, left). When the accelerator pedal is floored, the progressive linkage causes the secondary throttles to spring open (below, right). Some models have a choke plate over the primary barrels only; others have two choke plates that cover all four barrels, with choke linkage that operates them in tandem.

Variable-venturi carburetor

In this unique Ford carburetor, the size of the venturi can be varied to maintain a zone of nearly constant low pressure at the main metering nozzle. Therefore, no accelerator pump or auxiliary metering circuits are required. As the throttle plates open, vacuum from the intake manifold begins to act on the suction chamber, progressively opening the venturi valves (see illustrations below). At the same time, a tapered rod is withdrawn from the metering jet, allowing an increased fuel flow into the square carburetor throat. A thermostatically operated fuel enrichment circuit replaces the conventional choke plate.

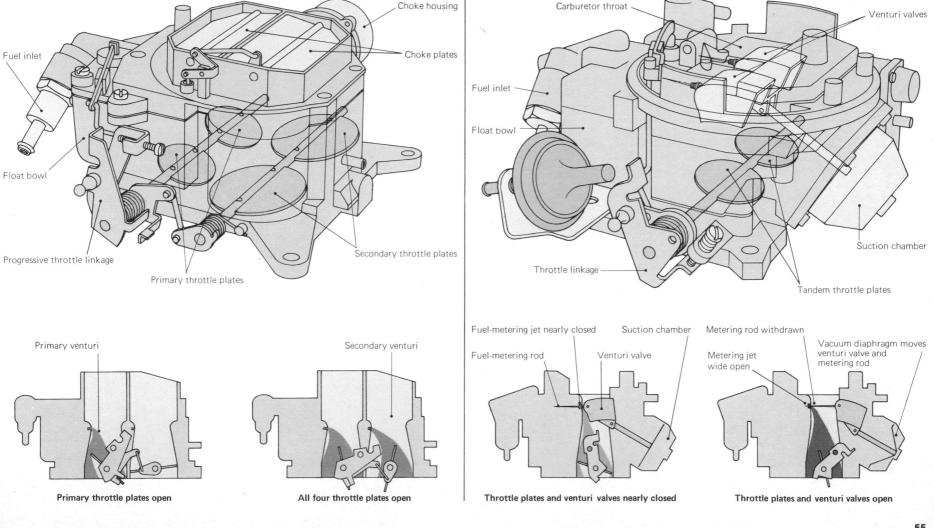

Choke housing

Choke plates

Fuel inlet

Float bowl

Progressive throttle linkage

Primary throttle plates

Secondary throttle plates

Carburetor throat

Venturi valves

Fuel inlet

Float bowl

Throttle linkage

Suction chamber

Tandem throttle plates

Primary venturi

Secondary venturi

Primary throttle plates open

All four throttle plates open

Fuel-metering jet nearly closed

Fuel-metering rod

Suction chamber

Venturi valve

Metering rod withdrawn

Metering jet wide open

Vacuum diaphragm moves venturi valve and metering rod

Throttle plates and venturi valves nearly closed

Throttle plates and venturi valves open

Filtering dust from the air

A typical car uses 14 parts of air to every part of fuel when measured by weight, but there are about 9,000 parts of air for every part of fuel when measured by volume. A car that averages 20 miles per gallon of gasoline (8.5 km/L) will consume 6½ fluid ounces (195 cc) of gas and 450 gallons (1,700 L) of air in one mile. Because such vast amounts of air are pumped through the engine, dust and dirt must be filtered out; otherwise, dirt would soon block the small jets in the carburetor and would rapidly wear down the piston rings and cylinder walls.

The usual *filter* is a pleated sheet of resin-impregnated paper with pores of controlled size. The filter is housed inside a pan-shaped metal or plastic housing called the *air cleaner*. The filter muffles the hissing rush of air through the carburetor, and the shape of the intake snorkel is designed to damp out the noise caused by air pressure fluctuations in the intake manifold.

Modern air cleaners have a number of hoses clamped to them. One small hose supplies filtered air to the *positive crankcase ventilation* (PCV) system. A large hose supplies hot air from the vicinity of the exhaust manifold to the intake snorkel. Two small vacuum hoses and a vacuum diaphragm operate a damper flap inside the snorkel that controls the amount of heated air entering the air cleaner. This supplies the engine with air at a constant temperature. If the damper sticks when open, overheated air will enter the engine, causing a loss of power. If the damper sticks when closed, the car may run unevenly until the engine warms up the air under the hood.

You should inspect the air filter every 12,000 miles or 20,000 km, and replace it when it becomes dirty. A dirty filter can cause overly rich air-fuel mixtures. This may result in a loss of power and, on some cars, a rough idle and an increase in fuel consumption.

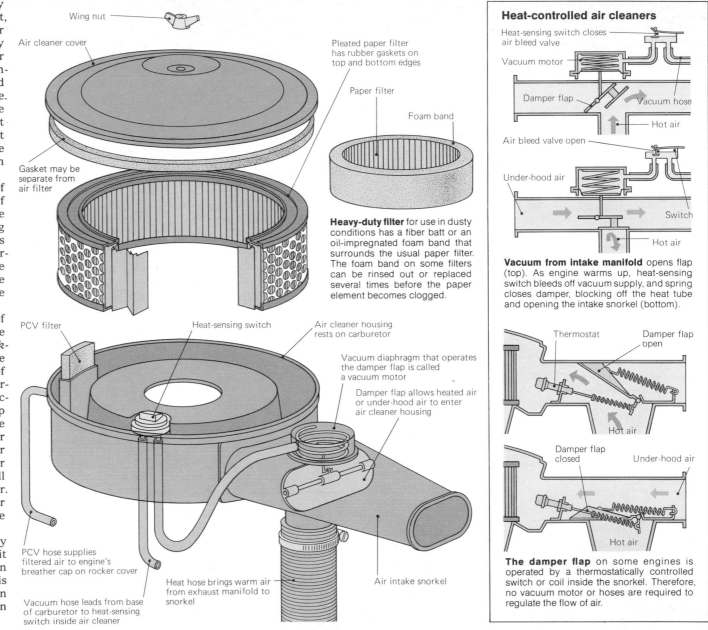

Wing nut

Air cleaner cover

Gasket may be separate from air filter

Pleated paper filter has rubber gaskets on top and bottom edges

Paper filter

Foam band

Heavy-duty filter for use in dusty conditions has a fiber batt or an oil-impregnated foam band that surrounds the usual paper filter. The foam band on some filters can be rinsed out or replaced several times before the paper element becomes clogged.

PCV filter

Heat-sensing switch

Air cleaner housing rests on carburetor

Vacuum diaphragm that operates the damper flap is called a vacuum motor

Damper flap allows heated air or under-hood air to enter air cleaner housing

PCV hose supplies filtered air to engine's breather cap on rocker cover

Vacuum hose leads from base of carburetor to heat-sensing switch inside air cleaner

Heat hose brings warm air from exhaust manifold to snorkel

Air intake snorkel

Heat-controlled air cleaners

Heat-sensing switch closes air bleed valve

Vacuum motor

Damper flap

Vacuum hose

Hot air

Air bleed valve open

Under-hood air

Switch

Hot air

Vacuum from intake manifold opens flap (top). As engine warms up, heat-sensing switch bleeds off vacuum supply, and spring closes damper, blocking off the heat tube and opening the intake snorkel (bottom).

Thermostat

Damper flap open

Hot air

Damper flap closed

Under-hood air

Hot air

The damper flap on some engines is operated by a thermostatically controlled switch or coil inside the snorkel. Therefore, no vacuum motor or hoses are required to regulate the flow of air.

The intake manifold

The intake manifold is a casting of iron or aluminum with chambers that deliver the air-fuel mixture from the carburetor to the intake passages in the cylinder head. The manifold has two jobs: to assist the vaporization of the fuel and to distribute the air-fuel mixture as evenly as possible to each cylinder.

Even distribution would be simpler if the fuel were completely vaporized in the carburetor. Unfortunately, fuel enters the carburetor as a fine mist, and much of the gasoline is still in liquid form when it reaches the engine's intake manifold.

As it passes the throttle valve, the spray of fuel and air enters an area of partial vacuum created by piston suction. Gasoline evaporates more rapidly in a partial vacuum than it would at atmospheric pressure, and the rate of evaporation depends on the degree of vacuum in the intake manifold.

At high engine speeds, when the throttle is fully open, there may be so little vacuum that some of the fuel remains in liquid form and is either carried along in droplets by the inrushing air, or else flows along the walls of the manifold.

If the engine had one carburetor for each cylinder, liquid fuel would still reach each combustion chamber, but in nearly equal amounts. Inside the combustion chambers, this liquid fuel would be vaporized by heat when the mixture was compressed. When one carburetor must supply a number of cylinders, uniform fuel distribution is difficult if the mixture is not completely vaporized.

On many engines, the exhaust manifold is positioned under the carburetor to create a hot spot in the intake manifold in order to improve fuel vaporization. However, too much heat can lower the density of the air in the intake manifold, leading to a loss of power. To prevent this, a thermostatically controlled valve diverts the exhaust gases once a certain engine temperature is reached. In V-type engines the mixture is heated by an exhaust crossover passage in the intake manifold, which is opened or closed by a thermostatic *heat riser valve*.

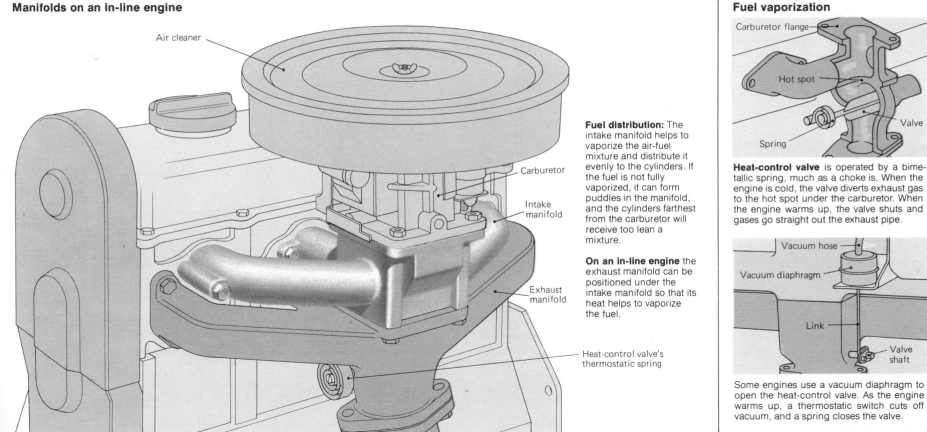

Manifolds on an in-line engine

Air cleaner

Carburetor

Intake manifold

Exhaust manifold

Heat-control valve's thermostatic spring

Fuel distribution: The intake manifold helps to vaporize the air-fuel mixture and distribute it evenly to the cylinders. If the fuel is not fully vaporized, it can form puddles in the manifold, and the cylinders farthest from the carburetor will receive too lean a mixture.

On an in-line engine the exhaust manifold can be positioned under the intake manifold so that its heat helps to vaporize the fuel.

Fuel vaporization

Carburetor flange

Hot spot

Spring

Valve

Heat-control valve is operated by a bimetallic spring, much as a choke is. When the engine is cold, the valve diverts exhaust gas to the hot spot under the carburetor. When the engine warms up, the valve shuts and gases go straight out the exhaust pipe.

Vacuum hose

Vacuum diaphragm

Link

Valve shaft

Some engines use a vacuum diaphragm to open the heat-control valve. As the engine warms up, a thermostatic switch cuts off vacuum, and a spring closes the valve.

Fuel storage

Fuel tanks are positioned well away from the engine in order to reduce the risk of fire—usually in the front of a rear-engine car and in the rear of a front-engine car. A rear-mounted tank is less likely to be ruptured in an accident if it is positioned above or in front of the rear axle, rather than in the more common position immediately ahead of the rear bumper.

Modern fuel tanks often have interior baffles, or perforated walls, to reduce fuel sloshing. Ten gallons (38 L) of gasoline weigh about 62 pounds (28 kg), and this surging mass can have an adverse effect on vehicle handling, especially in a light car. Surging fuel can also disturb the fuel gauge because fuel level is measured by a float. A front-to-rear baffle reduces surging during cornering, and a side-to-side baffle reduces surging during braking or when the car accelerates.

The inside of the tank usually has a coating that prevents moisture in the fuel from forming rust. Molded plastic tanks are completely rustproof, but they are rare, partly because they must be made of materials that will not react with diesel fuel, gasoline, or the many fuel additives used in refining gasoline today.

Older cars had a vent in the gas cap or a vent hose on the tank to prevent the formation of a vacuum as the tank emptied. In new cars, a valve in the gas cap allows air into the tank if necessary. A sealed system transfers fuel vapors to a canister in the engine compartment (see p.50). Cars with catalytic converters must use unleaded fuel. Their gas fillers have a restrictor plate that prevents insertion of the large nozzle used to pump leaded fuel. Unleaded gas is sold from pumps with small nozzles that fit through the hole in the restrictor. All leaded gas is being phased out in the U.S.

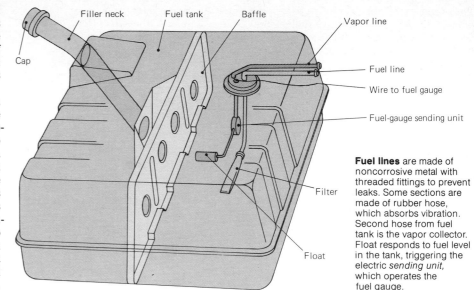

Fuel lines are made of noncorrosive metal with threaded fittings to prevent leaks. Some sections are made of rubber hose, which absorbs vibration. Second hose from fuel tank is the vapor collector. Float responds to fuel level in the tank, triggering the electric *sending unit*, which operates the fuel gauge.

Fuel filters

Two or more filters in the fuel line prevent dirt and moisture from entering the carburetor, blocking tiny fuel passages and affecting engine performance. The first filter is located at the fuel pickup, inside the tank. It is made of fabric and never needs servicing. It traps large particles and most moisture. Older cars may have a screen inside the fuel pump, or a paper filter in a canister that screws onto the pump. New cars have their filters either in the fuel line (between the fuel pump and carburetor) or located at the carburetor's fuel inlet.

Fuel filters should be replaced periodically. A clogged filter exhibits the same symptoms as a faulty fuel pump—hard starting, rough running, stalling, or backfiring. If a small carburetor-mounted filter clogs frequently, discard it and splice a larger-capacity paper filter into the fuel line. (Filter kits are sold in auto parts stores.)

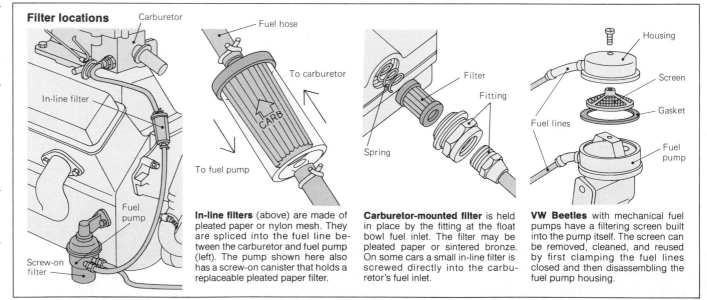

In-line filters (above) are made of pleated paper or nylon mesh. They are spliced into the fuel line between the carburetor and fuel pump (left). The pump shown here also has a screw-on canister that holds a replaceable pleated paper filter.

Carburetor-mounted filter is held in place by the fitting at the float bowl fuel inlet. The filter may be pleated paper or sintered bronze. On some cars a small in-line filter is screwed directly into the carburetor's fuel inlet.

VW Beetles with mechanical fuel pumps have a filtering screen built into the pump itself. The screen can be removed, cleaned, and reused by first clamping the fuel lines closed and then disassembling the fuel pump housing.

Fuel pumps

The fuel pump keeps the carburetor float bowl (p.51) filled with gas. Most cars have a mechanical fuel pump bolted to the side of the engine block and operated by an eccentric lobe on the camshaft. The pump consists of a spring-loaded diaphragm and a pair of one-way valves. When the camshaft rotates, a rocker arm raises the diaphragm and draws fuel past the inlet valve. As the lobe rotates further, the spring pushes the diaphragm downward and forces fuel past the outlet valve and into the fuel line leading to the carburetor. Since the inlet and outlet valves open in only one direction, the up-and-down movement of the diaphragm moves fuel toward the carburetor.

The diaphragm spring does the actual pumping, and it is just strong enough to lift fuel to the level of the carburetor. When the needle valve blocks the float bowl inlet, pressure builds up in the fuel line. The diaphragm spring cannot overcome this pressure, and the diaphragm remains stationary until the needle valve opens to the carburetor again.

Electric fuel pumps work on one of four principles: Some are diaphragm designs, similar to the mechanical pump but run by a solenoid rather than a cam. Some are vane pumps, similar to power steering pumps. The other two types are piston or turbine pumps run by small electric motors, like the GM unit below. The GM pump is submerged in the fuel tank. A small turbine, or impeller, on the end of the motor shaft forces fuel around the motor windings and through the outlet pipe to the carburetor. Gasoline cools and lubricates the pump's moving parts.

An electric pump can be located away from the hot engine compartment, lessening the chance of *vapor lock* in the pump. Vapor lock is caused when engine or exhaust heat vaporizes the fuel in the fuel line or pump. When this vapor pocket reaches the diaphragm chamber, the pump is rendered useless until the fuel recondenses—the diaphragm simply compresses the vapor but does not move the fuel. Most pumps can only move liquid, which is incompressible.

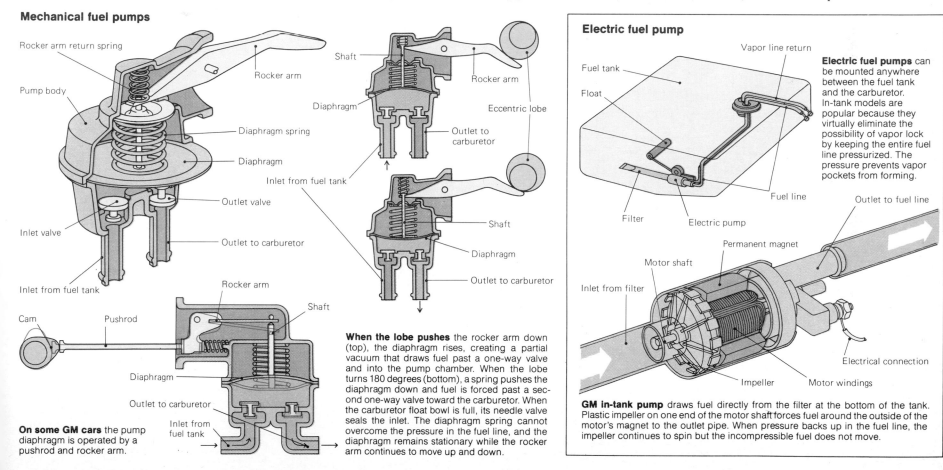

Mechanical fuel pumps

Rocker arm return spring
Rocker arm
Pump body
Diaphragm spring
Diaphragm
Inlet valve
Outlet valve
Outlet to carburetor
Inlet from fuel tank
Shaft
Rocker arm
Eccentric lobe
Outlet to carburetor
Inlet from fuel tank
Shaft
Diaphragm
Outlet to carburetor
Diaphragm

Cam
Pushrod
Rocker arm
Shaft
Diaphragm
Outlet to carburetor
Inlet from fuel tank

On some GM cars the pump diaphragm is operated by a pushrod and rocker arm.

When the lobe pushes the rocker arm down (top), the diaphragm rises, creating a partial vacuum that draws fuel past a one-way valve and into the pump chamber. When the lobe turns 180 degrees (bottom), a spring pushes the diaphragm down and fuel is forced past a second one-way valve toward the carburetor. When the carburetor float bowl is full, its needle valve seals the inlet. The diaphragm spring cannot overcome the pressure in the fuel line, and the diaphragm remains stationary while the rocker arm continues to move up and down.

Electric fuel pump

Vapor line return
Fuel tank
Float
Filter
Electric pump
Fuel line

Electric fuel pumps can be mounted anywhere between the fuel tank and the carburetor. In-tank models are popular because they virtually eliminate the possibility of vapor lock by keeping the entire fuel line pressurized. The pressure prevents vapor pockets from forming.

Outlet to fuel line
Permanent magnet
Motor shaft
Inlet from filter
Electrical connection
Impeller
Motor windings

GM in-tank pump draws fuel directly from the filter at the bottom of the tank. Plastic impeller on one end of the motor shaft forces fuel around the outside of the motor's magnet to the outlet pipe. When pressure backs up in the fuel line, the impeller continues to spin but the incompressible fuel does not move.

Timed fuel injection

Diesel, racing, and a few gasoline engines use fuel injection in place of carburetors. Instead of mixing fuel and air before they enter the intake manifold, a fuel-injection system squirts fuel directly into the combustion chambers (in the case of diesels) or against the intake valve. Because there is one injector nozzle for each cylinder, ideal fuel distribution is possible with fuel injection.

Since no venturi is used, the intake system can be designed for maximum airflow. The precision of the fuel metering permits fuel injection to provide more power than carburetion does while reducing fuel consumption and air pollution.

The disadvantages of fuel injection are its high cost and the fact that it must be serviced by an expert using special equipment and a "clean room" that are not found in service stations.

There are two basic types of fuel injection—timed and continuous; and two modes of operation—mechanical and electronic. In the timed mechanical system shown here, small bursts of fuel are sprayed against the intake valves at intervals, just as each valve is about to open. An electric pump delivers fuel at 100 psi to the metering unit. Pressure is kept constant by a relief valve that returns excess fuel to the fuel tank. An engine-driven rotor inside the metering unit, turning at half the crankshaft speed, distributes fuel to the injectors at the right time. The injector nozzles are held closed by springs until they are opened by fuel pressure. A manual enrichment control provides a rich air-fuel mixture for starting in cold weather, much as the choke does for a carburetor.

In other timed mechanical systems, an electric fuel pump delivers fuel at low pressure to an engine-mounted injection pump—actually a series of small, powerful plungers working in tandem. Each plunger supplies fuel to an individual injector at the correct moment.

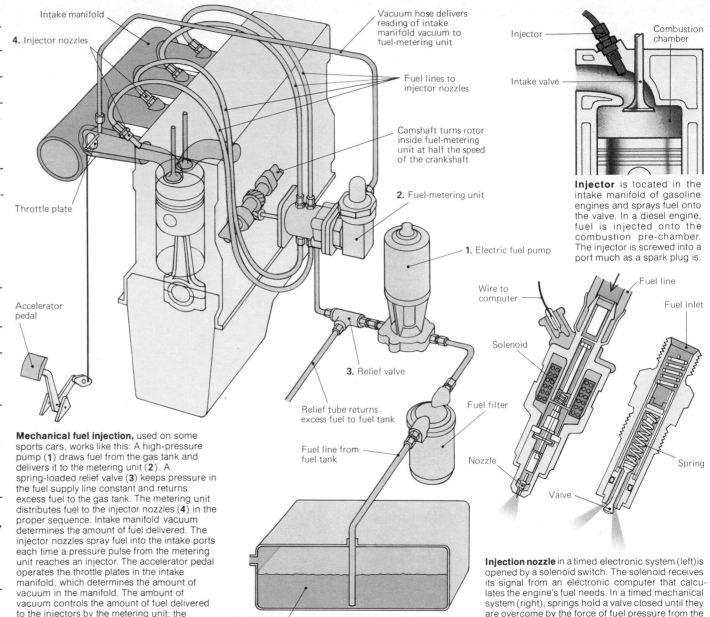

Intake manifold

4. Injector nozzles

Throttle plate

Accelerator pedal

Vacuum hose delivers reading of intake manifold vacuum to fuel-metering unit

Fuel lines to injector nozzles

Camshaft turns rotor inside fuel-metering unit at half the speed of the crankshaft

2. Fuel-metering unit

1. Electric fuel pump

3. Relief valve

Relief tube returns excess fuel to fuel tank

Fuel line from fuel tank

Fuel filter

Fuel tank

Injector

Combustion chamber

Intake valve

Injector is located in the intake manifold of gasoline engines and sprays fuel onto the valve. In a diesel engine, fuel is injected onto the combustion pre-chamber. The injector is screwed into a port much as a spark plug is.

Wire to computer

Solenoid

Nozzle

Valve

Fuel line

Fuel inlet

Spring

Mechanical fuel injection, used on some sports cars, works like this: A high-pressure pump (1) draws fuel from the gas tank and delivers it to the metering unit (2). A spring-loaded relief valve (3) keeps pressure in the fuel supply line constant and returns excess fuel to the gas tank. The metering unit distributes fuel to the injector nozzles (4) in the proper sequence. Intake manifold vacuum determines the amount of fuel delivered. The injector nozzles spray fuel into the intake ports each time a pressure pulse from the metering unit reaches an injector. The accelerator pedal operates the throttle plates in the intake manifold, which determines the amount of vacuum in the manifold. The amount of vacuum controls the amount of fuel delivered to the injectors by the metering unit; the amount of fuel determines engine speed.

Injection nozzle in a timed electronic system (left) is opened by a solenoid switch. The solenoid receives its signal from an electronic computer that calculates the engine's fuel needs. In a timed mechanical system (right), springs hold a valve closed until they are overcome by the force of fuel pressure from the metering pump or fuel distributor.

Continuous fuel injection

Timed fuel injection is necessary on diesel engines because the fuel must be injected directly into the combustion prechamber at the end of each compression stroke (p.43). But timed injection is a needless complication for gasoline engines, since the fuel is sprayed against an intake valve that is opening and closing 4 to 50 times a second, depending on engine speed. Here, a continuous spray of fuel is sufficient, as long as the amount of fuel being sprayed is carefully controlled.

In order to meet today's antipollution laws, the amount of fuel supplied to the cylinders at any moment must be carefully tailored to the constantly changing set of operating conditions that are encountered by an engine from moment to moment. Nothing does this so well as an electronically controlled fuel-injection system. Several versions, both timed and continuous, are used on a number of imported cars as well as on a few domestic models. General Motors offered a hybrid system on some of its V-8 engines. The injection is timed, but the injector nozzles are triggered in pairs, one nozzle squirting against an open valve, the other against a closed valve.

In a timed electronic system, fuel is delivered at relatively low pressure (35 to 40 psi) to the injector nozzles, which are opened at the correct time by solenoids. A small computer determines how long the injector stays open, and this affects the engine's power, economy, and pollution characteristics. The computer is linked to sensors that monitor intake manifold pressure, or airflow; air and coolant temperatures; throttle position; and the rate of acceleration.

The simpler Bosch K Jetronic continuous-injection system shown here is used in Volkswagens and Volvos, among other cars. A counterbalanced metering flap reacts to the mass of air entering the intake manifold, and it adjusts the metering of the low-pressure injection pump accordingly. Since the mass of air is sensed directly, its temperature need not be measured nor its density calculated by a complex computer system.

The throttle plate is connected to the accelerator pedal, and it determines the amount of air that is drawn in by the pistons. A rich mixture is supplied for cold starting by a single enrichment nozzle mounted in the intake manifold. A coolant-temperature sensor in the engine block automatically opens the enrichment nozzle when the engine is cold. An auxiliary air valve is opened at the same time, causing the engine to run faster while it is warming up.

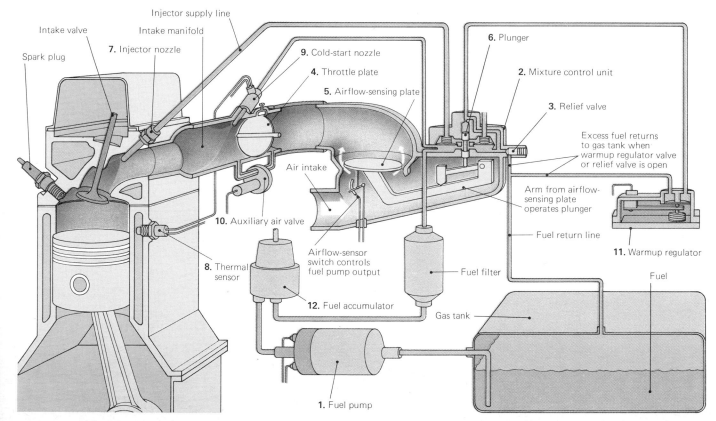

Injector supply line
Intake valve
Intake manifold
7. Injector nozzle
Spark plug
9. Cold-start nozzle
4. Throttle plate
5. Airflow-sensing plate
6. Plunger
2. Mixture control unit
3. Relief valve
Excess fuel returns to gas tank when warmup regulator valve or relief valve is open
Air intake
Arm from airflow-sensing plate operates plunger
10. Auxiliary air valve
Fuel return line
11. Warmup regulator
8. Thermal sensor
Airflow-sensor switch controls fuel pump output
Fuel
Fuel filter
12. Fuel accumulator
Gas tank
1. Fuel pump

Bosch K Jetronic is a comparatively simple mechanical fuel-injection system. Electric fuel pump (**1**) draws fuel from the gas tank and delivers it to the bottom of the mixture control unit (**2**). A spring-loaded relief valve (**3**) keeps pressure in the control unit constant. Accelerator pedal controls the throttle plate (**4**), which admits air to the intake manifold. The airflow-sensing plate (**5**) reacts to the mass of air entering the intake manifold and moves the plunger (**6**) in the mixture control unit up or down. The plunger regulates the amount of fuel that can enter the injector supply lines; throttle position regulates the speed of the engine.
The injection nozzles for each cylinder (**7**) remain open once the engine is started. The rest of the system deals with starting a cold engine. The thermal sensor (**8**) opens the solenoid-controlled cold-start nozzle (**9**) and auxiliary air valve (**10**) whenever the coolant temperature is below a pre-set level. The cold-start nozzle sprays extra fuel into the intake manifold, creating a richer air-fuel mixture; it is the equivalent of the choke on a carburetor. The auxiliary air valve allows more air into the intake manifold, causing the engine to idle faster; it is the equivalent of a carburetor's fast-idle cam. The warmup regulator (**11**) controls fuel pressure acting against the top of the control plunger. When the engine is cold, fuel pressure is reduced, the plunger rises, and a richer mixture is provided by the injector nozzles. An electrically heated bimetallic strip acts as a timer to shut off the cold-start nozzle, the auxiliary air valve, and the warmup regulator after the engine has been running for a pre-set time period. The fuel accumulator (**12**) has a spring-loaded diaphragm that prevents vapor lock by keeping the system pressurized after the engine has been shut off.

Throttle body fuel injection

Throttle body fuel injection has become an increasingly popular replacement for the carburetor. Unlike a conventional fuel-injection system, which has an injector at each cylinder port, the throttle body has a central injection point with one or two injectors or a spray bar. It has no float bowl and no venturi.

A throttle body does not provide the precision cylinder-to-cylinder fuel distribution of conventional fuel injection, but its injectors can be less precise and therefore less costly. Yet the throttle body system mixes air and fuel more completely than a carburetor does.

Throttle body injectors are the solenoid type. When activated, the solenoid pulls on a *pintle valve*, allowing pressurized fuel to spray out. The amount of fuel pressure delivered to the throttle body depends on the injector's design: some injectors need about 40 psi (275 kPa), while others work with only 10 psi (69 kPa). The fuel is pressurized by an electric fuel pump. A pressure regulator on the throttle body allows excess fuel to flow back to the fuel tank to reduce pressure to specifications. A computer determines when and how long the solenoid injectors should be activated.

The spray bar type, designed by Chrysler, uses two fuel pumps: a conventional one that supplies fuel to the throttle body, and a special vane pump, operated by an electric motor, in the throttle body itself. The vane pump, regulated by an *accumulator,* pushes the fuel to the spray bar, which is simply a tube with holes in it. The holes direct a spray of fuel toward the throttle plates.

When the engine is running, there is always some fuel being sprayed from the bar, but the amount is varied by increasing or decreasing the flow of current to the vane pump's motor. This is done by a computer, which bases its decision on information from a number of sensors. One of the sensors measures airflow. The air cleaner snorkel has vanes that cause the incoming air to swirl, forcing some of it up a curved tube, where it pulses against a temperature-sensitive solid-state sensor that is heated by an electric current. The air pulses provide a momentary cooling of the sensor, thus giving a signal that is proportional to the amount of airflow. The signal tells the computer how much air is flowing through the throttle body at any moment.

A second sensor measures the flow of fuel. A light is aimed across the fuel passage to a sensor wired to the computer. A paddle wheel is placed in the passage between the light beam and the sensor. As fuel flows, it spins the paddle wheel, interrupting the beam. This creates a pulsating signal whose rate varies in proportion to the amount of fuel flowing past. The signal enables the computer to measure fuel flow. A motor, also computer controlled, operates the throttle linkage to vary idle speed.

Spray bar type

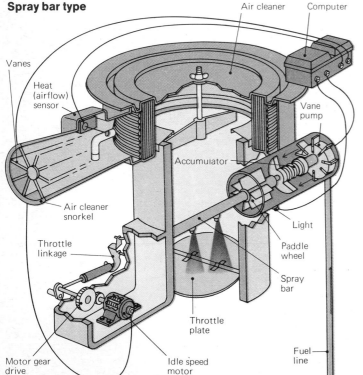

Vanes

Heat (airflow) sensor

Air cleaner snorkel

Throttle linkage

Motor gear drive

Air cleaner

Computer

Vane pump

Accumulator

Light

Paddle wheel

Spray bar

Idle speed motor

Throttle plate

Fuel line

Chrysler's throttle body fuel injector is a relatively simple system, compared to a conventional fuel-injection system. An in-tank electric fuel pump delivers fuel to a small electric vane pump in the throttle body (which looks like a conventional carburetor on the outside). The vane pump forces the fuel past an accumulator —a spring-loaded valve. The accumulator impedes the flow of fuel just enough to ensure that there is always enough pressure for a solid spray of fuel from the spray bar. The computer varies the speed of the vane pump and thus the amount of fuel that is delivered to the spray bar.

Solenoid type

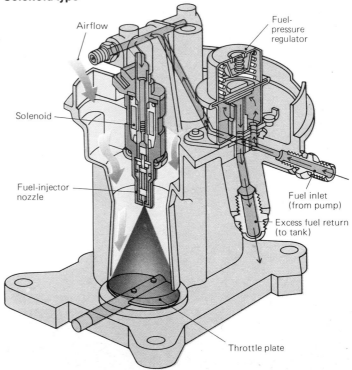

Airflow

Solenoid

Fuel-injector nozzle

Fuel-pressure regulator

Fuel inlet (from pump)

Excess fuel return (to tank)

Throttle plate

Ford's throttle body fuel injector has two solenoid-operated fuel-injection nozzles. They are mounted above the throttle plates in the throttle body. An electric fuel pump supplies fuel at about 80 psi to the spring-loaded fuel-pressure regulator. Exactly 39 psi is needed to open the spring, and when the spring opens, excess fuel is returned to the fuel tank by a separate fuel line. The result is that fuel is delivered from the regulator outlet to the nozzles at exactly 39 psi. A signal from the computer activates the solenoids, which open a pintle valve in each nozzle, allowing fuel to spray into the incoming airstream.

Gasoline and diesel fuel

Gasoline is a mixture of hydrocarbons, the major ones being *octane* and *heptane*. Gasoline must vaporize easily enough to give trouble-free starting on a cold morning, but not so easily as to cause *vapor lock* (p.59) when the engine compartment is hot. Consequently, oil companies decrease the volatility of gasoline in summer. If hot weather arrives suddenly, many gas stations may still have a highly volatile winter blend in their storage tanks. This is why vapor lock is especially common on the first warm days of spring. If your car stalls in hot driving or cannot be restarted a few minutes after being turned off, open the hood and let the engine compartment cool down. Then try to start again.

Fuel line freeze-up will occur if condensation from the fuel tank freezes in the fuel lines. Carburetor icing occurs when moisture in the air condenses and freezes on the carburetor throat and throttle plate. Both will cause a cold engine to buck and stall. The cure is to fill your tank often, especially at night, so that there is no empty space in the tank in which condensation can form. You can also add a chemical deicer to the gas.

The *octane number* is a measure of a gasoline blend's ability to resist knocking. Knocking occurs when gasoline explodes spontaneously upon compression instead of being ignited by the spark plug. A gasoline blend is said to have an octane number of 90 if laboratory tests show that it has the same antiknock properties as a mixture of 90 percent octane and 10 percent heptane.

There are two common systems for measuring gasoline octane—the Motor Method and the Research Method. The same sample of gasoline will have an octane number approximately eight points higher when tested by the Research Method than it will if it is tested by the Motor Method. Many car owner's manuals specify a certain Research Oc-

Normal combustion

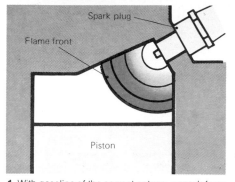

1. With gasoline of the correct octane, a spark from the spark plug ignites the air-fuel mixture.

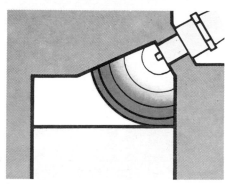

2. The flame front spreads evenly through the mixture as the piston reaches the top of its stroke.

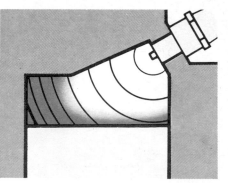

3. Even expansion of the burning gases begins to push the piston back down the cylinder bore.

Knocking

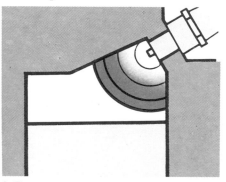

1. The combustion process may begin normally, with the spark plug igniting the air-fuel mixture.

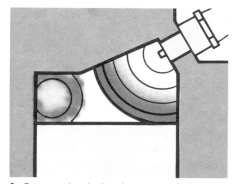

2. Compression ignites low-octane fuel spontaneously in another part of the combustion chamber.

3. Pressure builds violently when the two flame fronts meet. Severe knocking can melt the piston.

tane Number (RON) gasoline for the engine. When octane numbers are posted on gas pumps, they are an average of the Research and Motor ratings. Add four points to the posted octane to get the approximate Research Octane Number.

The gasoline that is distilled from crude oil has very low octane. Its octane number can be raised by further chemical treatments, such as *catalytic reforming,* which are expensive, or by adding lead compounds, which was the normal procedure until the mid-1970s. Lead fouls the

catalytic converters that are used to control pollution on most new cars, and it is being replaced by other octane-raising agents, such as tertiary butyl alcohol.

The octane needs of an engine vary during its lifetime—at first they become greater as deposits build up in the combustion chamber, raising the compression ratio; later the octane requirement drops as the valve seats, and piston rings wear and lower the compression.

Diesel fuel, jet fuel, kerosene, and home heating oil are similar substances.

It is possible to run a diesel engine on kerosene or home heating oil, but this is illegal because no highway taxes are paid on these substances. Diesel fuel often contains lubricants and additives that are not found in heating oil or kerosene.

The *cetane number* of diesel fuel indicates the ease with which it ignites; the higher the cetane, the lower the temperature needed to ignite the fuel. Cetane numbers range from the high 40s to the low 50s. Higher cetane is needed in the winter for easier starting.

How the fuel is ignited

Each cylinder has a spark plug which contains two metal prongs called electrodes. When electricity is fed to the spark plug at sufficient voltage, it jumps the gap between the electrodes in the form of a spark. This spark ignites the air-fuel mixture in the combustion chamber. Very high voltage is required for the spark to penetrate the highly compressed gases inside the combustion chamber. Automobile batteries supply 12 volts. The *coil* boosts available battery voltage to as much as 40,000 volts.

The coil works on the principle that electricity flowing through a wire produces a magnetic field around the wire. Conversely, when a magnetic field breaks down, electricity is generated in any wire within the field's lines of force. This is the same principle used to step voltage up or down in transformers. The coil has two long wires wound tightly around a soft iron core.

One coil of wire, called the *primary winding*, contains a few hundred turns of fairly thick wire. This is the low-voltage winding, and it is connected to the battery. Another coil of wire, called the *secondary winding*, is made up of thousands of turns of fine wire. When the ignition switch is closed, low-voltage current flows through the primary winding into the distributor—if the *breaker points* (p.66) are closed. This generates a magnetic field through and around the iron core. When the breaker points open, the flow of low-voltage current is interrupted and the magnetic field collapses. This generates a current in the secondary winding, which flows through the distributor and to the spark plugs (see opposite page). The voltage of this secondary current is proportional to the ratio of turns between the two windings. If there are 100 turns of wire in the secondary winding for every turn in the primary winding, the voltage in the secondary winding will be 100 times greater.

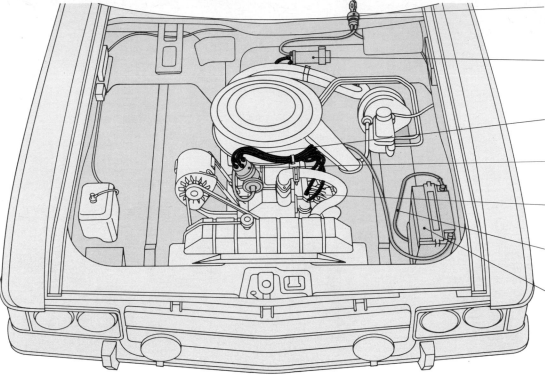

The ignition switch connects the battery to the ignition system and acts as an on-off switch for the engine.

The coil builds up the low-voltage current supplied by the battery to the high voltage needed by the spark plugs.

Heavy ignition cables connect coil, distributor, and spark plugs.

The distributor feeds high-voltage current to each spark plug at the right moment.

Spark plugs, one per cylinder, ignite the air-fuel mixture, producing power to run the car.

One battery cable is grounded to the frame, completing circuit that allows electricity to flow.

The battery supplies electricity to the ignition system and to the other electrical components in the car.

How the coil increases voltage

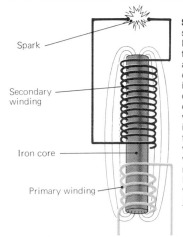

Spark

Secondary winding

Iron core

Primary winding

Schematic diagram of the coil shows how voltage is stepped up. Low-voltage current flowing through the primary winding sets up a magnetic field around the soft iron core. If the flow of current is interrupted, the magnetic field collapses, and this induces a flow of current through the secondary winding. If there are 12 turns of wire in the secondary winding and 4 turns in the primary winding, the voltage in the secondary winding will be three times as great. (The ratio between them is 12:4, or 3:1.) If there is a gap in the high-voltage wire outside the coil, current will jump the gap in the form of a spark.

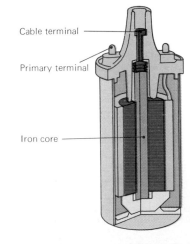

Cable terminal

Primary terminal

Iron core

Cross section of the coil shows the primary winding in yellow and the secondary winding in red. The primary winding has a few hundred turns of heavy wire. The secondary winding has thousands of turns of very fine wire that surround the soft metal core. On a breaker-point ignition system, a resistor in the wire from the ignition switch to the primary winding drops the primary voltage from 12 volts to perhaps 6. When the points first open, a voltage of about 250 is induced from the initial 6 volts in both windings. When the field completes its collapse, the 250 volts is raised to perhaps 40,000 volts in the secondary winding.

Conventional breaker-point ignition

Most cars built in North America since 1975 have electronic ignitions. Most Chrysler cars have used electronic ignition since 1972. These systems are explained on pages 68-69. Older cars, and some new imported cars, use breaker-point ignition systems. The main difference between electronic and breaker-point ignitions is the manner in which the primary current flow to the coil is interrupted. Electronic systems use transistorized electromagnetic or photoelectric devices.

In a conventional ignition system, the breaker points act as an on-off switch to interrupt the flow of low-voltage current through the primary winding of the coil and thereby induce a high-voltage current in the secondary winding.

For electricity to flow, a complete circuit is needed (see *Basic electrical theory*, p.133). In an automobile, all the electrical components are connected, or grounded, to the car's frame. So is the engine block and one battery terminal. The engine and frame therefore complete the circuit and provide a path for electricity to flow back to the battery from the spark plugs, breaker points, and coil.

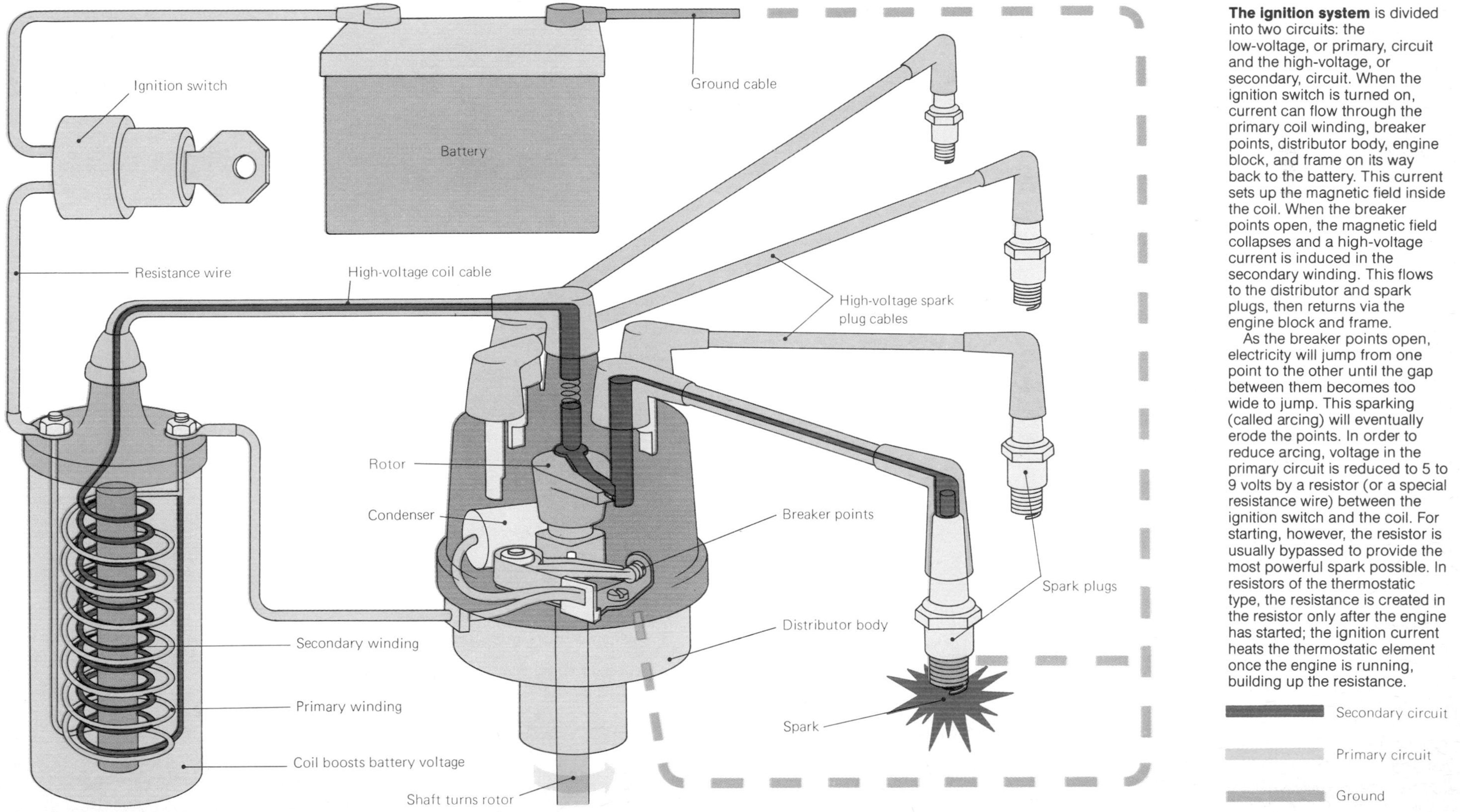

Ignition switch
Battery
Ground cable
Resistance wire
High-voltage coil cable
High-voltage spark plug cables
Rotor
Condenser
Breaker points
Spark plugs
Secondary winding
Distributor body
Primary winding
Spark
Coil boosts battery voltage
Shaft turns rotor

The ignition system is divided into two circuits: the low-voltage, or primary, circuit and the high-voltage, or secondary, circuit. When the ignition switch is turned on, current can flow through the primary coil winding, breaker points, distributor body, engine block, and frame on its way back to the battery. This current sets up the magnetic field inside the coil. When the breaker points open, the magnetic field collapses and a high-voltage current is induced in the secondary winding. This flows to the distributor and spark plugs, then returns via the engine block and frame.

As the breaker points open, electricity will jump from one point to the other until the gap between them becomes too wide to jump. This sparking (called arcing) will eventually erode the points. In order to reduce arcing, voltage in the primary circuit is reduced to 5 to 9 volts by a resistor (or a special resistance wire) between the ignition switch and the coil. For starting, however, the resistor is usually bypassed to provide the most powerful spark possible. In resistors of the thermostatic type, the resistance is created in the resistor only after the engine has started; the ignition current heats the thermostatic element once the engine is running, building up the resistance.

Secondary circuit
Primary circuit
Ground

Breaker-point distributor

The distributor contains the only moving parts in the ignition system. It performs two functions: The breaker points act as an on-off switch to interrupt current flow through the primary winding of the coil (see pp.64–65). The *rotor* and *distributor cap* send the coil's high-voltage current to the spark plugs in the correct *firing order*. Each plug must fire when its piston nears the top of its compression stroke.

High-voltage current travels through a heavy cable from the coil to the center terminal of the distributor cap. A plastic rotor arm with a metal insert rotates beneath the cap. The metal strip is in constant contact with the center terminal of the cap. As the rotor turns, the metal strip makes electrical contact with a number of contacts around the edge of the cap. A heavy cable runs from each of these contacts to one spark plug. In this way the high-voltage current from the coil is passed along to one plug at a time. The spark plug cables are routed in such a way that current is delivered to the plugs in the proper firing order. Any time a spark plug cable is removed, it must be reconnected to both the correct distributor cap terminal and the correct spark plug. If it is misrouted, the spark plugs will fire at the wrong time and serious engine damage may result. It is good practice, therefore, always to remove and replace only one cable at a time. If you must remove several cables, always label each cable and its terminals.

The rotor is driven by the distributor shaft, which is driven by the camshaft on most engines. These parts are geared together so that they both rotate at the same speed, which is half the crankshaft speed. Current is therefore delivered to each spark plug once during every four-stroke cycle of the engine.

As engine speed increases, the spark plug must fire sooner in order to achieve complete combustion. This is done by the distributor's advance mechanism.

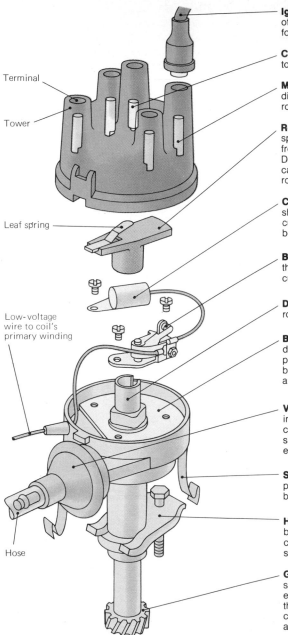

Terminal

Tower

Leaf spring

Low-voltage wire to coil's primary winding

Hose

Ignition cables plug into towers on top of distributor cap. There is one tower for each spark plug, plus one for the coil.

Carbon contact in center of cap touches the leaf spring on the rotor.

Metal contacts around the top of the distributor cap form a link between the rotor and the spark plug cables.

Rotor fits onto distributor shaft and spins with it. Metal insert carries current from carbon contact to metal contacts. Domestic distributors have a fixed carbon contact and a leaf spring on the rotor insert to assure positive contact.

Condenser acts as a sort of electrical shock absorber to store surges of current and reduce arcing (sparking) between points.

Breaker points are the on-off switch that interrupts the flow of low-voltage current through the coil.

Distributor shaft is notched so that the rotor can be installed in only one way.

Baseplate is shifted by the vacuum diaphragm to advance the spark. The points and condenser are bolted to the baseplate and are grounded through it and the distributor body.

Vacuum diaphragm is attached to the intake manifold or the base of the carburetor by a hose. Manifold vacuum shifts the position of the baseplate as engine load changes.

Spring clips hold the distributor cap in place. The cap is notched so that it can be installed in only one way.

Hold-down clamp keeps distributor body from rotating, which would change the timing (the moment the spark plug sparks).

Gears rotate distributor shaft at same speed as the camshaft's. On most engines, the distributor shaft also drives the oil pump; on other engines, the camshaft gear drives both the pump and distributor.

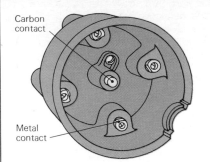

Carbon contact

Metal contact

The distributor cap is made of plastic. High-voltage current from the coil passes from the central carbon contact to the rotor arm. Metal contacts at the edge of the cap are connected to the spark plug cables.

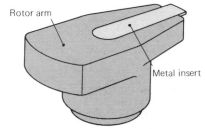

Rotor arm

Metal insert

As the rotor arm turns, current flows through its metal insert from the carbon contact to the spark plug contacts. Imported cars generally have a spring-loaded carbon contact that presses against a flat metal insert.

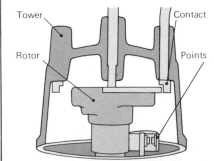

Tower

Contact

Rotor

Points

The rotor arm never touches the spark plug contacts as it rotates, but the high-voltage current easily jumps the gap between them.

How breaker points operate

The breaker points are operated by a cam on the distributor shaft. There is one lobe on the cam for each spark plug in the engine. As the shaft turns, the cam pushes against an arm that forces the breaker points apart. A spring closes the points when the cam rotates further.

Combustion of the air-fuel mixture may take close to the same length of time regardless of engine speed. When the engine is idling, each spark plug fires just before its piston reaches the top of its stroke, which allows time for gas expansion to drive the piston back down. As engine speed increases, there is less time between piston strokes, and the plug must fire sooner to allow time for complete combustion. The *spark advance* mechanisms do this by changing the positions of the points and the cam.

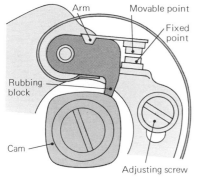

There are two breaker points, one movable and one fixed. The distributor shaft cam has one lobe for each spark plug. As the cam rotates, it pushes the rubbing block, which moves an arm and opens the points.

A leaf spring closes the points as the cam rotates further. The gap between the fully open points is critical and must be adjusted to within a few thousandths of an inch. This is done by changing the position of the plate that holds the fixed point.

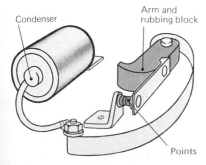

As the points open, electricity will jump between them until the gap is too wide to jump. This sparking (called arcing) can pit and erode the points. The condenser, wired parallel to the points, temporarily stores each surge of electrical power and reduces arcing.

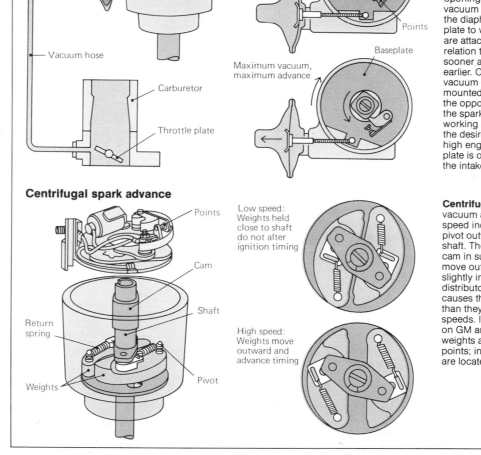

Vacuum spark advance

Centrifugal spark advance

Low speed: Weights held close to shaft do not alter ignition timing

High speed: Weights move outward and advance timing

Vacuum spark advance is provided by a diaphragm attached to the distributor housing. A hose runs from one side of the diaphragm to the carburetor base on most engines. As the throttle opening increases, the partial vacuum in the manifold flexes the diaphragm and rotates the plate to which the breaker points are attached. As the points move in relation to the cam, they open sooner and the spark is delivered earlier. On a few engines a second vacuum diaphragm may be mounted so that it pulls the plate in the opposite direction and retards the spark. The two diaphragms, working against one another, give the desired amount of advance. At high engine speeds, the throttle plate is open wide and vacuum in the intake manifold drops off.

Centrifugal advance takes over as vacuum advance falls off. As engine speed increases, a pair of weights pivot outward from the distributor shaft. The weights are linked to the cam in such a way that, as they move outward, the cam shifts slightly in the direction of the distributor shaft's rotation. This causes the points to open sooner than they would at low engine speeds. In Delco distributors, used on GM and some AMC cars, the weights are located above the points; in most other brands, they are located below the points.

Electronic ignition

An electronic ignition system works in exactly the same way as the breaker-point ignition system shown on pages 64-67 except for the way in which the current to the coil's primary winding is turned on and off. Chrysler made electronic ignition systems standard equipment in 1972, and they have since become standard on most American-built cars.

In a conventional ignition system, the breaker points act as a mechanical switch to turn the current flow through the coil on and off. Electronic ignition systems use nonmechanical devices called *transistors*. A transistor can use a very small flow of current to switch a much larger flow of current (see illustration at lower right). The various makes of electronic ignition differ mainly in the way this small current is generated.

In one of Chrysler's systems, a gear-like *reluctor* turns with the distributor shaft. As each tooth of the reluctor passes a magnetic coil in the distributor, a small electric pulse is generated. This pulse switches the transistor on and off, cutting the flow of low-voltage current through the coil's primary winding.

Other systems use metal detectors, light-emitting diodes, or the Hall effect to generate the small current needed to switch the transistor on and off.

Transistors have several advantages over mechanical breaker points: they have no moving parts that wear or require lubrication; they do not pit or burn; and they can switch higher voltages than points can. The capacity to switch high voltage into the coil enables a transistorized ignition system to produce higher voltage at the spark plug electrodes than a breaker-point system can. This higher voltage can jump a wide spark plug gap, creating the fat spark needed to ignite the lean air-fuel mixtures used in many modern engines without computer-controls. A high-voltage spark will also fire a partially fouled spark plug.

Delco High Energy Ignition (HEI)

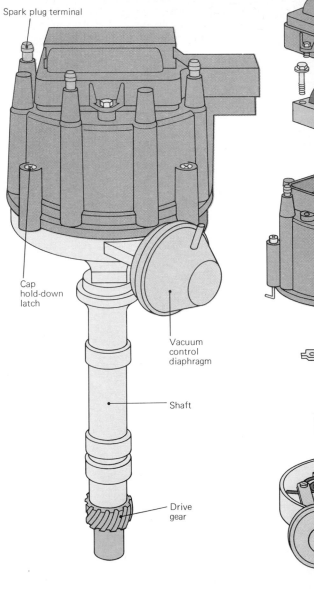

Spark plug terminal

Cap hold-down latch

Vacuum control diaphragm

Shaft

Drive gear

Coil cover in the center of the distributor cap.

Ignition coil is mounted in distributor cap of most HEI distributors. About 100 turns of the primary winding and several thousand of the secondary winding are wrapped around an iron frame, which becomes a magnet when current flows through the primary winding. When the current flow is interrupted, the magnetic field collapses, inducing about 35,000 volts in the secondary winding.

Distributor cap supports high-voltage spark plug cables and determines distributor size. Because of this high voltage, extra distance is required between the cable contacts to prevent arcing from one contact to the next, and the HEI distributor cap is larger than a conventional one.

Rotor inside distributor cap transfers high voltage produced by the coil to each spark plug.

Mechanical advance mechanism fits under the rotor at the top of the distributor shaft. The faster the shaft turns, the farther centrifugal force moves the weights and advances the timing.

Timer core under the advance mechanism turns with the distributor shaft. When the core's external teeth line up with the internal teeth on the stationary pole piece, a voltage pulse is generated. This pulse triggers the transistor.

Magnetic pickup assembly contains a permanent magnet with internal teeth. The pickup coil generates the timing pulse when aligned with a tooth. It is mounted on the baseplate.

Control module contains the transistor that switches current to the coil. It is sealed in epoxy and cannot be repaired; it must be replaced.

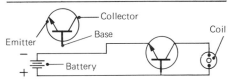

Collector
Base
Coil
Emitter
Battery

Transistor turns *On* when a specified voltage is applied across the base-emitter circuit. This allows a far stronger current to flow across the base-collector circuit. When the base-emitter current stops, so does the flow through the base-collector circuit, and the transistor is *Off*.

Capacitor helps to supress radio interference.

Vacuum control diaphragm moves the pole piece and pickup assembly on the baseplate to advance spark timing, depending on engine load. Many new cars use a computer to adjust timing.

Other methods of switching current without breaker points

Typical transistorized ignition

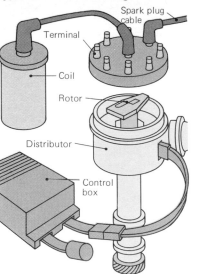
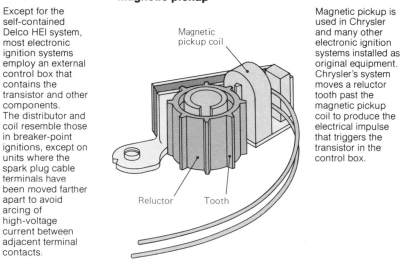

Spark plug cable

Terminal

Coil

Rotor

Distributor

Control box

Except for the self-contained Delco HEI system, most electronic ignition systems employ an external control box that contains the transistor and other components. The distributor and coil resemble those in breaker-point ignitions, except on units where the spark plug cable terminals have been moved farther apart to avoid arcing of high-voltage current between adjacent terminal contacts.

Magnetic pickup

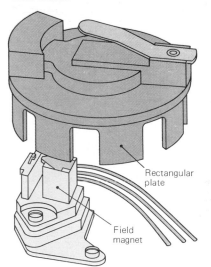

Magnetic pickup coil

Reluctor

Tooth

Magnetic pickup is used in Chrysler and many other electronic ignition systems installed as original equipment. Chrysler's system moves a reluctor tooth past the magnetic pickup coil to produce the electrical impulse that triggers the transistor in the control box.

Hall effect

Rectangular plate

Field magnet

The Hall effect is a voltage shift that is generated when a rectangular plate carrying a current is passed through a magnetic field that is perpendicular to the current flow. This voltage shift triggers the transistor. Since the speed at which the rectangle and the magnet pass each other has no effect on the voltage shift, a Hall effect distributor is equally efficient at any engine speed.

Optical trigger

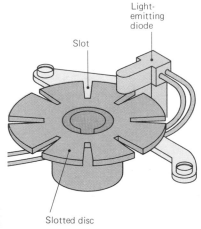

Light-emitting diode

Slot

Slotted disc

Optical triggers for electronic ignition systems aim the light from a light-emitting diode onto a light-sensitive diode. As long as the light-sensitive diode can "see" the light, current passes. The distributor turns a slotted disc between the diodes that intermittently blocks the passage of light and triggers the transistor. This system is often used in electronic ignition kits sold as replacements for breaker points on older cars.

Proximity sensor

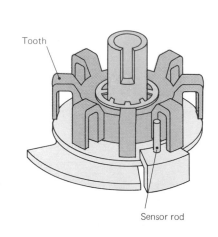

Tooth

Sensor rod

Proximity sensor is used on Prestolite and Motorcraft replacement kits. An external control box sends an oscillating current to the sensor rod, creating an electromagnetic field. When a tooth on the nonconductive trigger wheel shrouds the metal rod, the magnetic field is damped. This changes the current in the sensor rod wiring and triggers the transistor in the control box.

Magnetic coil

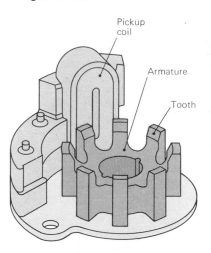

Pickup coil

Armature

Tooth

A magnetic coil is used in Motorcraft systems installed as original equipment on Ford and some AMC cars. When a tooth on the iron *armature* passes the magnetic pickup coil, it induces a small voltage in the coil that triggers the transistor in an external control box.

How the spark plugs work

Spark plugs produce the sparks that ignite the air-fuel mixture in the combustion chambers. Each plug consists of a metal rod, called an *electrode,* surrounded by a ceramic insulator. The lower end of the insulator is encased in a threaded metal shell that is screwed into the cylinder head. Another electrode is welded to the shell. It is separated from the center electrode by a small air gap. High-voltage current from the distributor flows down the center electrode and jumps this gap in the form of a spark.

For good engine performance, this spark must be large enough and last long enough to ignite the fuel mixture efficiently. The wider the gap, the bigger the spark. But wider gaps require higher voltage to produce any spark at all. Every engine has a specified spark plug gap, which may vary from .02 inches (.5 mm) to .08 inches (2 mm). The gap can be adjusted by bending the side electrode. If the gap is too wide, the plug may not fire because the ignition system cannot produce enough voltage to jump the gap. If the gap is too small, the spark may not be big enough to ignite the fuel mixture. The gap must be checked periodically because the electrodes erode with use.

Other causes of weak or erratic sparking are: dirt, oil, or water on the outside of the ceramic insulator; a cracked insulator; or fouled electrodes. All these faults can create an alternate path for the high-voltage current between the ignition cable and the cylinder head. Such current shortcuts are called *short circuits* or just *shorts.* One misfiring spark plug can increase fuel consumption 10 to 15 percent in a V-8 engine and 25 to 35 percent in a four-cylinder engine. Modern spark plugs handle as much as 40,000 volts of electricity and temperatures as high as 4500° F for up to 30,000 miles. Plugs that last 50,000 miles have been made, but they have such expensive features as platinum electrodes.

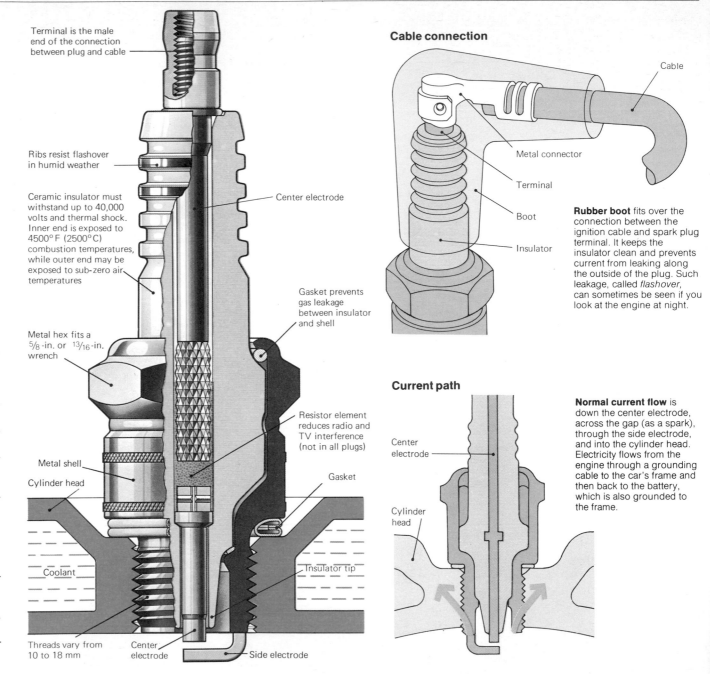

Terminal is the male end of the connection between plug and cable

Ribs resist flashover in humid weather

Ceramic insulator must withstand up to 40,000 volts and thermal shock. Inner end is exposed to 4500° F (2500°C) combustion temperatures, while outer end may be exposed to sub-zero air temperatures

Metal hex fits a ⅝-in. or ¹³/₁₆-in. wrench

Metal shell

Cylinder head

Coolant

Threads vary from 10 to 18 mm

Center electrode

Side electrode

Center electrode

Gasket prevents gas leakage between insulator and shell

Resistor element reduces radio and TV interference (not in all plugs)

Gasket

Insulator tip

Cable connection

Cable

Metal connector

Terminal

Boot

Insulator

Rubber boot fits over the connection between the ignition cable and spark plug terminal. It keeps the insulator clean and prevents current from leaking along the outside of the plug. Such leakage, called *flashover,* can sometimes be seen if you look at the engine at night.

Current path

Center electrode

Cylinder head

Normal current flow is down the center electrode, across the gap (as a spark), through the side electrode, and into the cylinder head. Electricity flows from the engine through a grounding cable to the car's frame and then back to the battery, which is also grounded to the frame.

Choosing the right plugs for your engine

Hundreds of different plugs are manufactured to fit various engines and driving conditions. These plugs vary in physical size and operating characteristics. When replacing plugs, always use the brand and model recommended by the carmaker. Do not use just any plug that fits. Plugs are classified by heat range—their ability to transfer heat from the insulator tip to the engine block. A *hot plug* transfers heat slowly and therefore stays hot. A *cold plug* transfers heat quickly and remains cooler. A plug that is too hot may glow and ignite the fuel mixture before it should, causing pinging. A plug that is too cold may not burn away combustion deposits and will foul—that is, carbon deposits will bridge the gap between the electrodes. A car used mostly for stop-and-go driving may need a hotter-than-normal plug to burn off carbon deposits. A car used mainly for high-speed or long-distance driving may need a colder-than-normal plug to avoid overheating. A car's spark plugs should be inspected periodically and cleaned or replaced when they become worn or fouled (see p.72).

Physical dimensions

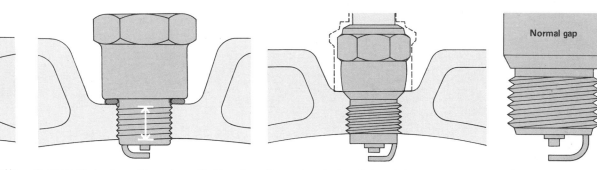

Long-reach plug is used where the cylinder head is very deep. In a thinner head such a plug would project too far into the combustion chamber, possibly striking the piston. Carbon deposits on the exposed plug threads would make it difficult to remove a plug that is too long.

Short-reach plug is used in engines with thin cylinder heads. If used on an engine with a thick cylinder head, this plug's electrodes would be recessed too far for efficient ignition. Carbon deposits in the plug-hole threads would make it difficult to install the proper plug later.

Tapered-seat plug eliminates the need for a gasket. It is tightened into a machined recess in the cylinder head to make a gastight seal. Tapered-seat plugs are usually slimmer than gasket plugs (dotted red line), allowing room in the cylinder head for bigger valves or larger water jackets.

Wide-gap plugs produce a larger spark, which is needed to ignite the lean air-fuel mixtures in some modern smog-controlled engines. A very high voltage ignition system is needed to fire such plugs, which have gaps that range from .05 in. to .08 in. (1.25 mm–2 mm).

Heat range

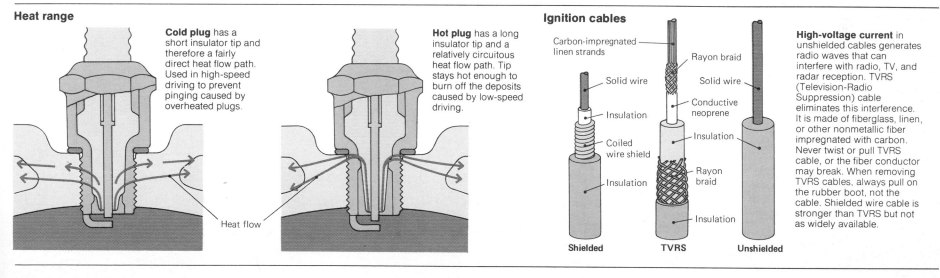

Cold plug has a short insulator tip and therefore a fairly direct heat flow path. Used in high-speed driving to prevent pinging caused by overheated plugs.

Hot plug has a long insulator tip and a relatively circuitous heat flow path. Tip stays hot enough to burn off the deposits caused by low-speed driving.

Heat flow

Ignition cables

Carbon-impregnated linen strands

Rayon braid

Solid wire

Solid wire

Conductive neoprene

Insulation

Coiled wire shield

Insulation

Rayon braid

Insulation

Insulation

Shielded

TVRS

Unshielded

High-voltage current in unshielded cables generates radio waves that can interfere with radio, TV, and radar reception. TVRS (Television-Radio Suppression) cable eliminates this interference. It is made of fiberglass, linen, or other nonmetallic fiber impregnated with carbon. Never twist or pull TVRS cable, or the fiber conductor may break. When removing TVRS cables, always pull on the rubber boot, not the cable. Shielded wire cable is stronger than TVRS but not as widely available.

What plug condition reveals about engine operation

Normal plug has light brown to grayish tan deposits on the insulator tip and electrodes. There is little or no wear on the electrodes. Plug can be gapped and reused. It is the proper heat range for the engine's operating conditions.

Wet black deposits may be caused by oil leaking past worn piston rings or valve guides, brake fluid leaking past the brake booster diaphragm, or transmission fluid leaking past the modulator. Repair car rather than switching to hotter plugs.

Dry black sooty deposits are caused by too rich a fuel mixture, a weak spark, faulty timing, low compression, or wrong heat range. Hotter plugs (within plug maker's approved range for your engine) may burn off deposits, but car should be repaired.

Deposit fouling 1: Red deposits are caused by some brands of lead-free fuel. Manganese antiknock additives leave this harmless deposit. Plugs can be cleaned and reused. Do not confuse these deposits with rust caused by water in the cylinders.

Deposit fouling 2: Additive deposits from leaded fuel range from brown to yellow to white and may be accompanied by a rotten egg smell. This plug should have been cleaned when it looked like normal plug at left. It should be replaced.

Deposit fouling 3: This is the next stage reached if the plug above is further neglected. Powdery, flaky additive deposits fuse into a hard glaze that is difficult to remove even with a professional plug-cleaning machine.

Deposit fouling 4: This occurs when glazed deposits above are neglected for an even longer period. Although deposits seem to be burning off, they have formed an irremovable mass. Replace plugs but do not switch to a different heat range.

Deposit fouling 5: Fused deposit mass bridges gap between electrodes, causing a permanent misfire, which wastes gas and causes pollution. Check plugs used in high-speed driving every 10,000 miles (16,000 km). Check plugs used in city driving twice as often.

Overheating 1: White insulator with spots indicates an overheated plug. This can be caused by pinging, overly advanced timing, too lean a fuel mixture, vacuum leaks, faulty installation, or wrong heat range. If engine is OK, use colder plugs.

Overheating 2: Eroded electrodes and a blistered insulator are the result of extreme or prolonged plug overheating. This is what will happen to the plug above if overheating conditions are not corrected. This plug cannot be reused.

Overheating 3: White insulator and damaged threads may be caused by improper plug installation. Failure to tighten the plug results in poor heat transfer to cylinder head. In some cases, electrodes may melt, fuse together, or be entirely eroded away.

Normal wear ends a spark plug's useful life when erosion increases original gap by more than .01 in. (.25 mm). If such plugs are gapped to the correct setting, they will look like this. There is not enough electrode left on this plug to fire properly.

Handling engine heat

Fuel burns inside the cylinders at temperatures above 4500°F (2500°C). In even the more efficient engines only 20 to 25 percent of this heat energy is used to drive the car. At full throttle, about 35 percent passes out the exhaust system, and 10 percent is lost to internal friction and to heating the lubricating oil. The remaining 30 to 35 percent must be carried away by the cooling system in order to keep the oil from evaporating and engine parts from *seizing* (jamming) or melting. On most cars this is done by circulating a mixture of water and antifreeze through passages in the engine, where heat is absorbed, and then through a radiator, where the heat is given up.

The liquid, called *coolant,* is kept in circulation by the water pump, which is located at the front of the engine and driven by a rubber V-belt from a pulley on the crankshaft. A fan is attached to the water pump pulley, and it keeps air flowing through the radiator when the car is stopped or moving slowly. Cars with front-wheel drive and transverse engines use a small electric motor to run the fan. A thermostatic switch turns the fan motor on and off.

Antifreeze not only lowers the freezing temperature of the coolant but also raises its boiling point. A modern engine needs antifreeze winter and summer. A spring-loaded radiator cap keeps the cooling system under about 14 pounds per square inch (97 kPa) of pressure, which raises the boiling point of a 50-50 mixture of water and antifreeze from 226°F (108°C) to 263°F (128°C). The freezing point of the same mixture would be -34°F (-36°C). Antifreeze concentrations of up to 70 percent can be used, and they produce a boiling point of 274°F (134°C) and a freezing point of -85°F (-65°C) in a 14-psi pressurized system. More than 70 percent antifreeze will raise the freezing point rather than lowering it.

Cylinder wall temperatures of less than 140°F (60°C) can cause condensation and corrosion. A temperature-controlled valve, called a *thermostat,* therefore blocks the flow of coolant to the radiator when the coolant temperature is lower than 185° to 217°F (83° to 102°C), depending on the engine. Normal coolant temperature can reach 250° to 275°F (120° to 130°C), so you must have at least a 50 percent antifreeze concentration and an operating radiator pressure cap to prevent overheating.

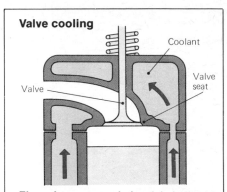

Valve cooling

The valves are cooled mainly by heat transfer from the valve seat to the coolant. Since exhaust valves operate at temperatures as high as 1300°F (700°C), a copious flow of coolant is necessary to prevent the formation of hot spots and steam pockets.

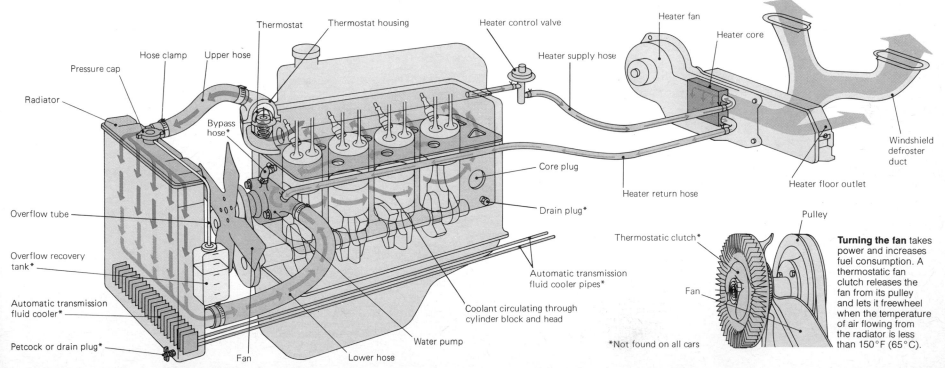

Radiator and thermostat

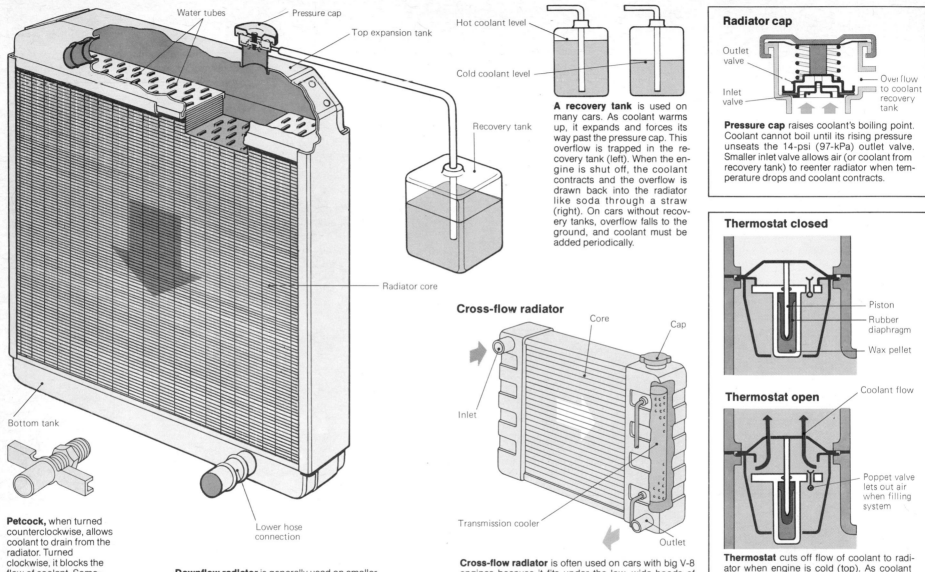

Water tubes

Pressure cap

Top expansion tank

Hot coolant level

Cold coolant level

Recovery tank

Radiator core

Bottom tank

Lower hose connection

Petcock, when turned counterclockwise, allows coolant to drain from the radiator. Turned clockwise, it blocks the flow of coolant. Some radiators have a simple drain plug. A radiator without a petcock or plug is drained by removing the lower hose.

Downflow radiator is generally used on smaller engines. Coolant enters at the top, then flows down through a number of small tubes. Thin metal fins attached to these tubes greatly increase their surface area for maximum heat transfer. Most radiators are brass, but a few are aluminum.

A recovery tank is used on many cars. As coolant warms up, it expands and forces its way past the pressure cap. This overflow is trapped in the recovery tank (left). When the engine is shut off, the coolant contracts and the overflow is drawn back into the radiator like soda through a straw (right). On cars without recovery tanks, overflow falls to the ground, and coolant must be added periodically.

Cross-flow radiator

Core

Cap

Inlet

Transmission cooler

Outlet

Cross-flow radiator is often used on cars with big V-8 engines because it fits under the low, wide hoods of modern cars and is more effective than a downflow design of the same shape. Hot coolant enters tank at left, then travels through long tubes to collector tank at right. Pressure cap and automatic transmission fluid cooler are located at the cool end of the radiator.

Radiator cap

Outlet valve

Inlet valve

Overflow to coolant recovery tank

Pressure cap raises coolant's boiling point. Coolant cannot boil until its rising pressure unseats the 14-psi (97-kPa) outlet valve. Smaller inlet valve allows air (or coolant from recovery tank) to reenter radiator when temperature drops and coolant contracts.

Thermostat closed

Piston

Rubber diaphragm

Wax pellet

Thermostat open

Coolant flow

Poppet valve lets out air when filling system

Thermostat cuts off flow of coolant to radiator when engine is cold (top). As coolant temperature rises, wax pellet melts and expands, forcing piston rod out of its housing. This lowers the housing, allowing coolant to flow to the radiator (bottom).

Water pump

The water pump is driven by a V-belt from the crankshaft pulley and operates whenever the engine is running. Its *impeller* spins inside a cast-iron or aluminum housing. The inlet pipe delivers coolant to the center of the impeller, where centrifugal force flings it outward. The coolant flows through the engine's *water jacket*. When the thermostat is open, the coolant is forced through the radiator and back to the pump inlet. When the thermostat is closed, coolant returns to the pump via a bypass hose or passage. Coolant usually circulates through the heater whether the thermostat is open or closed. A spring-loaded seal prevents coolant from contaminating the water pump's bearing lubricant.

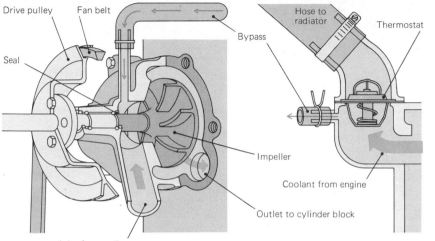

Drive pulley · Fan belt · Seal · Bypass · Hose to radiator · Thermostat · Impeller · Coolant from engine · Outlet to cylinder block · Inlet from radiator

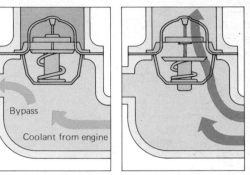

When the thermostat is closed (left), the water pump circulates coolant through the engine's water jacket (or coolant passages) and heater hoses. Coolant returns to the pump via a radiator bypass passage or hose. When thermostat is open (right), coolant flows to the radiator and back via the upper and lower hoses.

Bypass · Coolant from engine

Air-cooled engines

Lawn mowers and most motorcycles use air-cooled engines. Fins cast into the engine block and cylinder head increase the surface area exposed to the air and provide adequate cooling without the need for water pumps, thermostats, hoses, and radiators. Such engines, directly exposed to the flow of air, are easy to air cool.

An air-cooled automobile engine presents several difficulties. First, the engine is enclosed by bodywork. It also has several cylinders, one behind another, and only the forward cylinders can easily be exposed to natural airflow. It is therefore normal practice to enclose an air-cooled car engine in a sheet-metal housing and to force air through this ductwork by a belt-driven fan, in much the same way that the water pump circulates liquid coolant through the water jacket. A large, radiator-like oil cooler is often needed on powerful air-cooled engines, and it becomes debatable whether such engines are air-cooled or oil-cooled. The Corvair and the Volkswagen Beetle were popular air-cooled cars, as are some current Porsche sports models.

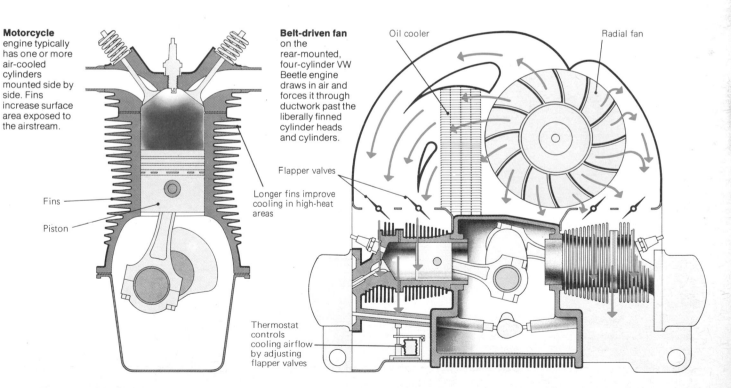

Motorcycle engine typically has one or more air-cooled cylinders mounted side by side. Fins increase surface area exposed to the airstream.

Fins · Piston

Belt-driven fan on the rear-mounted, four-cylinder VW Beetle engine draws in air and forces it through ductwork past the liberally finned cylinder heads and cylinders.

Oil cooler · Radial fan · Flapper valves · Longer fins improve cooling in high-heat areas · Thermostat controls cooling airflow by adjusting flapper valves

Keeping the engine quiet and clean

The exhaust system transports the hot, poisonous exhaust gases from the engine to a point where they can be released into the atmosphere without danger to the car's occupants. The system also reduces the sound of combustion, and usually contains a *catalytic converter*—a chemical reaction chamber in which exhaust pollutants are converted into less harmful substances.

Burned gases are released from the combustion chamber with great force. Several thousand times a minute, high-pressure, supersonic shock waves ricochet through the exhaust manifold.

The *muffler* breaks up or absorbs these pressure waves, reducing them to a legally acceptable noise level. In the case of *glass-pack* mufflers, the noise level may be just barely legal and still objectionable. Baffles and expansion chambers in a conventional muffler allow the exhaust gases to expand and slow down, greatly reducing both pressure and noise. Some cars have two mufflers, mounted one behind the other. The second muffler is called a *resonator* and is designed to absorb the noise frequencies that are not trapped by the first muffler.

Water and road salt eat away at the exhaust system from the outside. Water and acid vapors in the exhaust gases eat away from inside the pipes and mufflers. When the exhaust system is fully warmed up, these vapors pass out the tail pipe with minimal damage. When the system is cold, some vapors condense inside the pipes and mufflers, causing corrosion. Because the exhaust system warms up from the engine rearward, exhaust components toward the back of the car tend to rust away sooner. A car used only for short trips will need more frequent muffler replacements than a car used mostly for long trips. Heavy-gauge exhaust components naturally last longer than those made of thin metal. Stainless steel components last the longest but are expensive. Aluminum-coated parts cost less than stainless steel and last longer than uncoated steel.

Hissing, rumbling, or rattling under the car may indicate a deteriorating exhaust system. Small leaks may not cause much noise, but they still release colorless, odorless carbon monoxide, a gas that can cause headaches, impaired vision, sleepiness, slowed reflexes, nausea, unconsciousness, and death.

Engine faults can often be detected by observing and listening to the exhaust system. An irregular exhaust note may be caused by ignition defects or incorrect carburetor settings. Sooty exhaust smoke may indicate too rich a fuel mixture or failure of the air-injection system. Excessive blue smoke when the car is accelerating shows that oil is leaking past worn valve guides or piston rings and into the combustion chamber. Other causes of a smoky exhaust are brake fluid or automatic transmission fluid that is sucked through vacuum hoses to the intake manifold from a faulty power brake booster or transmission modulator. White smoke indicates a coolant leak.

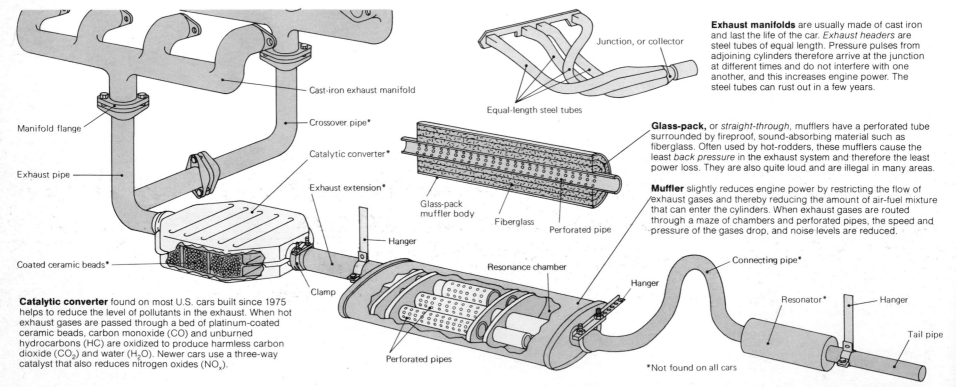

Exhaust manifolds are usually made of cast iron and last the life of the car. *Exhaust headers* are steel tubes of equal length. Pressure pulses from adjoining cylinders therefore arrive at the junction at different times and do not interfere with one another, and this increases engine power. The steel tubes can rust out in a few years.

Glass-pack, or *straight-through,* mufflers have a perforated tube surrounded by fireproof, sound-absorbing material such as fiberglass. Often used by hot-rodders, these mufflers cause the least *back pressure* in the exhaust system and therefore the least power loss. They are also quite loud and are illegal in many areas.

Muffler slightly reduces engine power by restricting the flow of exhaust gases and thereby reducing the amount of air-fuel mixture that can enter the cylinders. When exhaust gases are routed through a maze of chambers and perforated pipes, the speed and pressure of the gases drop, and noise levels are reduced.

Catalytic converter found on most U.S. cars built since 1975 helps to reduce the level of pollutants in the exhaust. When hot exhaust gases are passed through a bed of platinum-coated ceramic beads, carbon monoxide (CO) and unburned hydrocarbons (HC) are oxidized to produce harmless carbon dioxide (CO_2) and water (H_2O). Newer cars use a three-way catalyst that also reduces nitrogen oxides (NO_x).

Labels: Cast-iron exhaust manifold · Crossover pipe* · Catalytic converter* · Exhaust extension* · Manifold flange · Exhaust pipe · Coated ceramic beads* · Junction, or collector · Equal-length steel tubes · Glass-pack muffler body · Fiberglass · Perforated pipe · Hanger · Clamp · Resonance chamber · Perforated pipes · Connecting pipe* · Hanger · Resonator* · Hanger · Tail pipe

*Not found on all cars

Turbocharging for increased power

The pistons and cylinders of an engine act like a pump when they draw in and compress the air-fuel mixture (and also when they force out the burned exhaust gases). The amount of power that an engine can produce is limited by the amount of air and fuel that can be drawn into the cylinders. Air at atmospheric pressure flows through the carburetor and intake manifold to fill the vacuum created when the intake valve opens and a piston descends in a cylinder. Traditional hot-rodding techniques are aimed at making this passage of air easier, thereby allowing more air-fuel mixture into the cylinder before the intake valve closes. Larger carburetors, larger and smoother intake manifolds, larger valves, and exhaust headers are fitted to an en-

gine to increase its horsepower output.

Another way to increase power is to mount a *supercharger* between the carburetor and intake manifold. A supercharger is a chain- or belt-driven pump that forces more air and fuel into the cylinders. Supercharging also raises the effective compression ratio of an engine, which increases its power output.

A *turbocharger* is an exhaust-driven supercharger. A small turbine wheel is mounted in the exhaust system, where the high-speed flow of exhaust gases cause it to spin rapidly. This *exhaust turbine* drives a shaft that is connected to another wheel in the intake manifold called a *compressor*. The compressor forces the air-fuel mixture into the cylinders. The faster the engine runs, the

greater the flow of exhaust gases, and the faster the turbine spins—which in turn causes the engine to run faster still. To prevent this chain reaction from getting out of hand, a safety valve called a *waste gate* diverts exhaust gases around the turbine when pressure in the intake manifold exceeds a pre-set level.

A turbocharger is more efficient than a belt- or chain-driven supercharger because no power is required from the crankshaft to run the pump. The turbine wheel is driven by exhaust heat and pressure, which normally go to waste.

Because the turbocharger raises the engine's effective compression ratio, it can cause pinging (p.63). A system that retards ignition timing as manifold pressure increases can minimize pinging.

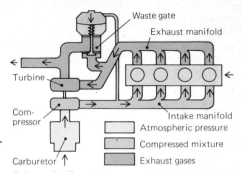

Schematic diagram shows a typical turbocharger installation. The flow of gases in the exhaust manifold spins the turbine, which is connected to the compressor by a shaft. The compressor draws the air-fuel mixture from the carburetor and forces it into the cylinders at higher than normal pressure. If the pressure in the intake manifold becomes too high, the waste gate opens and diverts some of the exhaust gases around the turbine.

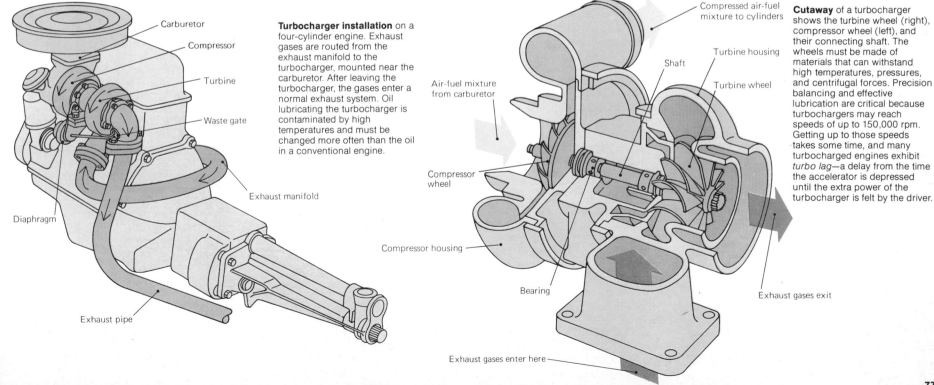

Turbocharger installation on a four-cylinder engine. Exhaust gases are routed from the exhaust manifold to the turbocharger, mounted near the carburetor. After leaving the turbocharger, the gases enter a normal exhaust system. Oil lubricating the turbocharger is contaminated by high temperatures and must be changed more often than the oil in a conventional engine.

Cutaway of a turbocharger shows the turbine wheel (right), compressor wheel (left), and their connecting shaft. The wheels must be made of materials that can withstand high temperatures, pressures, and centrifugal forces. Precision balancing and effective lubrication are critical because turbochargers may reach speeds of up to 150,000 rpm. Getting up to those speeds takes some time, and many turbocharged engines exhibit *turbo lag*—a delay from the time the accelerator is depressed until the extra power of the turbocharger is felt by the driver.

Alternate energy sources

Experts have predicted that petroleum will become so scarce within the next 15 to 25 years that alternate fuels and/or engines will have to be used in the family car. Although many exotic engines have been produced experimentally, the most likely and least expensive solution to a serious petroleum shortage is the development of alternate fuels for existing internal combustion engines. The most promising alternates include: petroleum refined from shale oil; synthetic gasoline and diesel fuel; methyl or ethyl alcohol; liquid petroleum gas (called LPG or propane), synthetic natural gas (SNG), or methane gas; and gaseous hydrogen.

Petroleum can be extracted from oil shale (a rock formation abundant in North America) by heat treatment. Gasoline and diesel fuel can then be refined in the usual way. The drawbacks include the cost of the heat treatment plants and the environmental damage that the strip mining of oil shale produces.

So-called "synthetic" gasoline and diesel fuel can be made from coal, but the process is more complex and expensive than extracting petroleum from oil shale, and strip mining is often involved in obtaining the coal. But if the price of fuel from conventional petroleum sources goes high enough, it will become economically feasible to obtain fuel from oil shale or coal and to pay the cost of repairing the damage done by strip mining.

Alcohol fuels
Alcohol can be added to gasoline to form a mixture called *gasohol*. Widespread use of gasohol could stretch current supplies of gasoline. Mixtures of up to 10 percent alcohol can be used in modern engines without adverse side effects. Alcohol has only one-half to two-thirds the energy content of gasoline, so fuel economy may suffer slightly with a gasohol blend. However, pinging will be reduced, since alcohol has an octane rating of about 140,

compared to about 90 for regular gasoline. Because alcohol burns leaner than gasoline, gasohol mixtures with more than 10 percent alcohol can cause hard starting, hesitation, and bucking in some lean-running smog-controlled engines. Because alcohol is more volatile than gasoline, gasohol mixtures also exhibit an increased tendency toward vapor lock during hot weather.

Engines can be run on 100 percent alcohol, which is often done in racing cars. Brazil has begun a program to convert all of its new cars and many existing cars to burn 100 percent alcohol. Adapting a gasoline engine to 100 percent alcohol fuel involves modifying the carburetor jets and settings to produce a richer air-fuel ratio, changing the ignition timing, and, if maximum use is to be made of the fuel, increasing the compression ratio (p.32) by installing new pistons or machining the cylinder heads. Raising the compression ratio can cost from $200 to more than $400, depending on the engine design and the method used.

When all these modifications are made to a gasoline engine, its power output on alcohol fuel can increase by 20 percent. With an unchanged compression ratio, the performance increase with alcohol is about 8 to 10 percent. It is proportionally lower with gasohol, depending on the percentage of alcohol in the mixture.

There are two kinds of alcohol fuel: methyl alcohol (called *methanol* or *wood alcohol*) and ethyl alcohol (called *ethanol* or *grain alcohol*). Methanol can be produced from coal, natural gas, or garbage, and it is the type of alcohol used in racing engines. However, methanol corrodes the plastic fittings and rubber hoses found in the fuel systems of most cars. It has less than half the energy content of gasoline, so that cars using 100 percent methanol will get half the fuel mileage that they would with gasoline. Engines run on methanol emit two to three times

as many aldehydes (a pollutant that is not now regulated by U.S. law) than the same engines using gasoline.

Ethanol is usually produced from sugar cane, sugar beets, grain, potatoes, yams, or other vegetable matter. It costs about three times as much to produce as methanol, but it has a higher energy content and it does not attack rubber and plastic fittings in existing fuel systems. Fewer pollutants are emitted by engines burning ethanol than by the same engines burning gasoline. Ethanol-powered cars get slightly better fuel economy than methanol-powered cars.

Only a limited quantity of ethanol can be distilled from agricultural by-products and waste. In order to fuel all the vehicles in North America, ethanol would have to be distilled chiefly from crops grown for that purpose. This raises the moral and political question: Should food crops be converted into fuel for automobiles in a world that has not yet solved the problem of widespread hunger?

Propane and natural gas
Industrial vehicles, such as forklift trucks, have been running on propane (LPG) or synthetic natural gas (SNG) for some time. Most commercial vehicles in New Zealand run on LPG. When a car is converted to run on LPG, the original fuel system is left in place, and a switch is installed in the dash so that the driver can switch from LPG to gasoline at will. This is because there are only about 2,000 LPG dealers in the U.S. and Canada who can fuel a car. It costs $800 to $1,200 to convert a car to LPG fuel. Fuel consumption increases 10 to 20 percent on LPG compared to gasoline, but LPG costs 30 percent less. The LPG tank, when full, adds about 300 pounds to the weight of a car, and trunk space is reduced by 20 to 30 percent. In some areas, vehicles carrying LPG are not permitted to travel over bridges or through tunnels.

Methane (sometimes called *marsh gas*) can also be used in an internal combustion engine. It can be fermented from sewage or manure and used to supplement supplies of natural gas and SNG.

Hydrogen
Hydrogen is a nonpolluting fuel that can be produced from water or coal. There are several experimental hydrogen-powered cars in operation, but the use of hydrogen as an everyday fuel is not yet practical. Liquid hydrogen must be stored at a temperature of -423°F (-217°C), which is presently impractical. Metal pellets can be infused with hydrogen and carried in a special tank weighing several hundred pounds. When the pellets are heated by the car's exhaust, they emit gaseous hydrogen, which fuels the engine. The car is started by the gaseous residue that always remains in the tank. Replenishing the hydrogen in the tank takes at least 30 minutes. All the common methods of producing hydrogen require tremendous amounts of heat and electricity, but experimental work is being done to reduce the use of conventional fuels in hydrogen production.

Electricity
Electric vehicles have been available for some time, but their speed and range are limited, and most of their cargo capacity must be utilized to carry heavy lead-acid batteries. New nickel-zinc batteries, expected on the market in a few years, are twice as powerful as lead-acid batteries and will allow a small electric car a range of 100 miles on an overnight charge, which would meet about 90 percent of North America's driving needs. Electricity can be produced by water power, nuclear power, or by burning coal. There is a net loss of energy when petroleum fuels are used to generate electricity to power a vehicle rather than simply being burned in the vehicle's engine.

Internal modifications

Modern engines are modified internally and are equipped with many add-on devices to reduce the formation or prevent the escape of three chemicals believed to be hazardous to human health:

Hydrocarbons (called HC) are unburned or partly burned gasoline. HC may evaporate from the crankcase or fuel system, or may be found in exhaust gases due to incomplete combustion.

Carbon monoxide (CO) is formed when fuel combustion is incomplete because too little oxygen is available (the fuel mixture is too rich).

Oxides of nitrogen (NO_x) are formed in the combustion chamber when peak temperatures are high enough to force the oxygen and nitrogen in the air to combine. HC and NO_x react with sunlight to form *smog*.

Controlling all three of these pollutants at once is difficult. For example, high combustion temperatures that reduce HC can increase NO_x. Carmakers have attacked the problem in many ways.

Where possible, internal modifications have been made to the engine. Compression ratios have been lowered to cut peak temperatures. Combustion chambers have been redesigned to eliminate little nooks, far from the spark plug, that can snuff out the flame and leave gasoline unburned. Camshafts have been designed to close the exhaust valve early, so that some exhaust gases remain in the cylinder to mix with the incoming fuel charge. This dilutes the charge and lowers peak combustion temperatures. The effect is most marked when the engine is at idle or part throttle, for at higher speeds exhaust gases flow out too fast to be caught by the early closing of the valve. At these higher engine speeds, an external exhaust gas recirculation system is used to dilute the fuel charge.

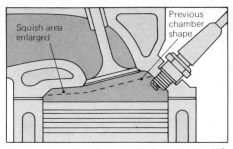

Combustion chamber modified to reduce HC emissions. The height of the squish area in the left-hand part of the chamber has been increased so that the rising piston does not snuff out flame, which would result in unburned hydrocarbons.

Vacuum spark controls

One way to reduce the peak combustion temperatures at which NO_x pollutants form is to retard spark timing, particularly during low-speed acceleration (see *Vacuum spark advance*, p.67). Several systems have been designed to do this:

1. A solenoid vacuum valve is spliced into the vacuum advance hose to the distributor and is wired to a switch on the shift linkage. The solenoid is normally open (allowing normal vacuum spark advance). When the switch closes, it activates the solenoid, closing the vacuum valve and stopping the spark advance. (A vent in the valve bleeds off vacuum from the vacuum advance hose at this time, so that the change is immediate.) The switch is closed in low gears (during acceleration) but opens when the car is cruising in higher gears.

2. In a second design, an electric speed sensor on the speedometer cable transmits a road-speed signal to a combination electronic control unit and solenoid vacuum valve. The vacuum valve closes to stop vacuum spark advance below 23 mph (37 km/h) on acceleration and below 18 mph (24 km/h) on deceleration. In a variation of this system, the speed sensor is wired to an electronic amplifier.

Above 24 to 33 mph (or 38 to 53 km/h, depending on the engine) the amplifier cuts current to the solenoid valve, which springs open and allows vacuum to flow to the vacuum spark advance.

3. A third type of control contains a check valve with a fixed orifice that delays vacuum to the vacuum spark advance by about 17 seconds when the throttle is first opened. When the throttle is released, the valve bleeds all vacuum from the vacuum spark-advance system.

All these systems have some arrangement to provide normal spark advance while the engine is cold and NO_x emission is not a significant problem. In the first two systems, a thermostatic vacuum switch is usually spliced between the vacuum source at the carburetor or manifold and the solenoid vacuum valve or amplifier. With the engine cold, vacuum flows through ports in the switch to bypass the control. When the engine warms up, the switch redirects vacuum to the control. The orifice control contains a bimetallic sensor that responds to temperature in the engine compartment to open a bypass valve, thus allowing full vacuum spark advance when air temperature in the engine compartment is low.

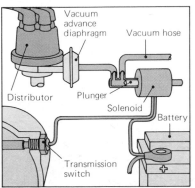

1. Transmission switch is open in *High* gear, as is the solenoid, allowing normal vacuum advance. In other gears the switch is closed, activating the solenoid, which closes the vacuum hose between the intake manifold and vacuum advance diaphragm.

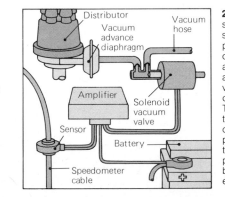

2. Sensor in speedometer cable sends a faint signal proportional to the car's speed through an amplifier and on to a solenoid vacuum valve similar to the one used in System 1. The vacuum supply to the distributor is cut off below certain pre-set speeds. A temperature switch prevents vacuum from being cut off when the engine is cold.

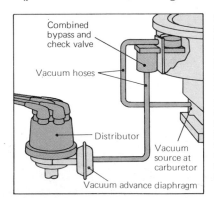

3. A check valve with a tiny orifice impedes the action of the distributor's vacuum advance diaphragm. It takes 10 to 27 sec for enough vacuum to build up to operate the diaphragm during acceleration from idle to part throttle. A thermostatic bypass valve allows normal vacuum spark advance when the engine is cold.

Catalytic converters and air pumps

The catalytic converter is the leading pollution control. An active substance (the catalyst) causes a chemical reaction that turns exhaust emissions into harmless substances. The first catalytic converters contained a platinum-coated ceramic honeycomb or aluminum-oxide pellets coated with platinum. These convert HC and CO into water vapor (H_2O) and carbon dioxide (CO_2). The early catalytic converters, also called *oxidation catalysts*, need extra oxygen to perform properly. Oxygen is often introduced into the exhaust system by an air pump or an air aspirator valve.

New converters are a two-in-one design. The front section is called a *three-way catalyst* because it controls HC, CO, and NO_x by turning them into water, carbon dioxide, and nitrogen. It works only when the exhaust is chemically correct—that is, when the fuel mixture burned in the cylinders has an air-to-fuel ratio of exactly 14.6:1, which is called a *stoichiometric mixture*. Computerized controls maintain this precise ratio.

The rear section is an oxidation catalyst that further reduces HC and CO. It is the only control effective under certain conditions, called *Open Loop*, when the fuel mixture is not stoichiometric.

The air pump supplies air to oxidize some unburned gasoline in the hot exhaust and to provide needed oxygen for the oxidation-type catalytic converter. A belt-driven pump delivers air first to a diverter valve (also called the *air bypass*), then through a check valve into metal tubing called the *injection manifold*. On some engines the air passes through internal passages in the cylinder head.

If the air is pumped into tubing, it flows into the exhaust manifold very close to the cylinder head. On some cars, air may be injected at a single point close to an oxidation converter. On cars with three-way catalysts, it may be injected into the exhaust manifold when the engine is cold, then redirected by a switching valve to an entry between the three-way and the oxidation catalysts. Switching the air also lowers exhaust temperatures on a warm engine, to keep NO_x levels down.

Injecting air into the exhaust is not desirable when a sudden throttle closing momentarily results in a very rich fuel mixture, and much unburned gasoline is released into the exhaust system. If air were injected then, severe backfiring would result. To prevent this, the diverter valve (triggered by high engine vacuum developed during deceleration) pulls on a diaphragm to vent the air into the atmosphere. Some unburned gases then escape into the atmosphere, but not a significant amount.

If an exhaust system does not require much air, a simple *aspirator valve* can be used. Exhaust gases pulsate, producing negative and positive pressures. A negative pulse draws open the aspirator valve and pulls air into the exhaust manifold.

Crankcase and fuel vapors

Combustion gases that blow past an engine's piston rings collect in the crankcase. On old cars these gases were expelled into the atmosphere, but modern positive crankcase ventilation (PCV) systems return combustion gases to the cylinders, where they are burned.

A vacuum hose is attached to the engine rocker cover and to the carburetor base. Engine vacuum draws the vapors from the crankcase, through the rocker chamber, and into the intake manifold, where they are mixed with the fuel.

Fresh air flows through another hose from the air filter to the rocker cover to help purge these vapors and fill the vacuum that is created when they flow out. A flow-control valve (called the PCV valve) regulates vapor flow. When the engine idles and vacuum is high, the plunger on the PCV valve is pulled to a nearly closed position so that vapor flow is light and does not upset the air-fuel ratio. As the throttle is opened, vacuum drops and a spring pushes the valve open, allowing more vapor to flow when the engine can better accept it.

Fuel that would otherwise evaporate from the carburetor and fuel tank when the engine is off is held for later combustion by the *fuel vapor control system*. The fuel tank is sealed with a special cap that contains a pressure-relief valve and a vacuum-relief valve for emergencies. Normally, the fuel tank is vented through a charcoal canister.

When the engine is off, vapor flows through hoses into the canister and is absorbed in the charcoal. When the engine is started and the throttle is opened, engine vacuum flows to a valve in the canister, pulls it open, and draws vapor into the intake manifold.

If the carburetor float bowl has an external vent, it is connected to the canister. On some cars an air filter with a layer of charcoal traps vapors that escape from the carburetor float bowl.

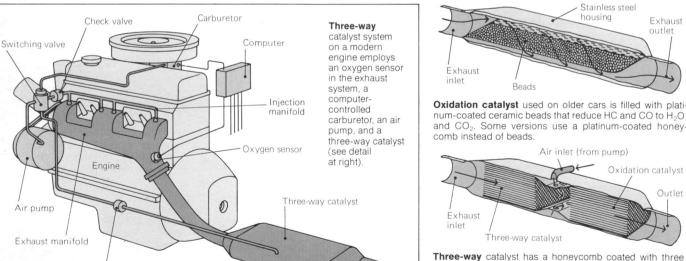

Three-way catalyst system on a modern engine employs an oxygen sensor in the exhaust system, a computer-controlled carburetor, an air pump, and a three-way catalyst (see detail at right).

Labels: Check valve · Carburetor · Switching valve · Computer · Injection manifold · Oxygen sensor · Engine · Three-way catalyst · Air pump · Exhaust manifold · Check valve

Labels: Stainless steel housing · Exhaust outlet · Exhaust inlet · Beads

Oxidation catalyst used on older cars is filled with platinum-coated ceramic beads that reduce HC and CO to H_2O and CO_2. Some versions use a platinum-coated honeycomb instead of beads.

Labels: Air inlet (from pump) · Oxidation catalyst · Outlet · Exhaust inlet · Three-way catalyst

Three-way catalyst has a honeycomb coated with three rare metals: platinum, palladium, and rhodium. The rhodium reduces NO_x when the air-fuel ratio is just right. When the air-fuel ratio is not 14.6:1, the oxidation catalyst continues to reduce emissions of HC and CO.

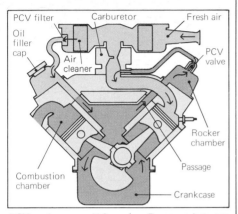

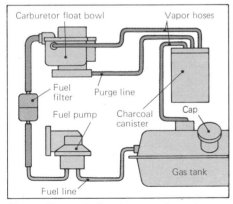

PCV system on a V-8 engine: Passages between the crankcase and rocker chambers provide a path for the flow of air and gases. A hose from the carburetor base to one rocker cover allows intake vacuum to draw blow-by gases from the crankcase and into the cylinders. A second hose from the air cleaner allows filtered air to enter the crankcase. The spring-loaded PCV valve almost closes during idle (when intake vacuum is high) so that excess vapor flow does not cause a rough idle.

Evaporation-control system uses hoses to carry fuel vapors from the gas tank and carburetor float bowl to a canister containing activated charcoal. The charcoal absorbs and stores vapors when the engine is off. When the engine is running, the vapors are drawn through the purge line and into the engine to be burned. Vapor hose also allows air to enter the gas tank as the fuel level drops. Spring-loaded valve in the filler cap acts as a backup in case vapor hose becomes clogged.

Exhaust gas recirculation

Diverting a portion of an engine's exhaust gases back into its combustion chambers lowers peak combustion temperatures and reduces the production of NO_x. A vacuum-operated exhaust gas recirculation (EGR) valve diverts up to 20 percent of the exhaust gases into the intake manifold in modern engines.

Cold engines produce little NO_x, so the EGR device remains off until the engine is warm; it would cause a cold engine to run roughly. EGR is used mainly at part throttle. It is turned off at idle, where it would also cause roughness, and at full throttle, where it would reduce power.

The EGR valve is operated by a diaphragm and mounted on the intake manifold. In V-type engines the exhaust gases are normally routed to the EGR valve through an *exhaust crossover passage* in the intake manifold. On in-line engines the gases are simply diverted from the exhaust manifold to the adjacent intake manifold.

The EGR valve is supplied with vacuum in one of two ways. In some systems, vacuum at the carburetor venturi provides a signal, but it is too weak to

operate the valve and is therefore run into an *amplifier*. Stronger vacuum from the engine also flows into the amplifier. The venturi vacuum operates a weak valve that regulates the flow of engine vacuum to the EGR valve. The vacuum in the venturi is too weak to trigger even the amplifier at idle, and at full throttle, engine vacuum is close to zero.

In other EGR systems the vacuum source is a port just above the throttle plate. When the throttle is closed, vacuum at the port is zero, so that the EGR valve does not operate at idle. Vacuum drops to near zero again at full throttle, and the EGR valve shuts off at these times, too.

To keep the EGR valve off when the engine is cold, a thermostatic vacuum switch is spliced into the vacuum hose leading to the EGR valve or amplifier. The switch, threaded into the intake manifold or water jacket, is closed (blocking vacuum flow) until the engine warms up. On some cars a solenoid vacuum valve triggered by an electronic timer blocks vacuum flow for about half a minute after any startup, even when

the engine is hot, to permit the car to drive away smoothly. After a specified time, the timer switches off current to the solenoid, and a spring opens the valve to permit vacuum flow. Some systems also have a vacuum-relief valve that opens when the engine is at full throttle to release vacuum from the EGR valve.

Diesel engines produce no useful vacuum in their intake manifolds. They must be fitted with special vacuum pumps to operate their pollution-control devices and other accessories. This vacuum is routed to a solenoid vacuum valve and to a valve built into an accelerator-position sensor. At specified accelerator positions, the sensor opens and vacuum flows to a *vacuum-electric switch,* where it pulls on a diaphragm; this completes an electrical circuit from the solenoid valve to the electrical ground. The solenoid then pulls open its valve, and vacuum flows to the EGR valve. There is no modulation in this system; it is either on or off.

Although EGR valves are usually vacuum-operated, some engines with computer controls utilize air from the air pump to operate the EGR valve.

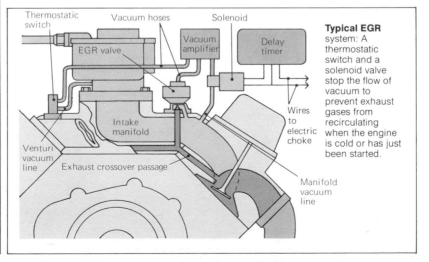

Typical EGR system: A thermostatic switch and a solenoid valve stop the flow of vacuum to prevent exhaust gases from recirculating when the engine is cold or has just been started.

EGR valve: Spring holds valve shut against exhaust pressure until vacuum is strong enough to lift valve. Exhaust gases are then drawn into the intake manifold and cylinders, reducing NO_x emissions.

Some EGR systems are regulated by exhaust pressure. At low engine speeds, control valve is open; vacuum draws air around diaphragm. Exhaust pressure at high speeds closes control valve, and EGR valve works normally.

How computers control engine operation

Minicomputers called *microprocessors* are used to control many systems in modern cars, including spark timing, air-fuel mixture, engine idle speed, automatic choke settings, emission controls, and automatic transmission lockup clutches (see p.97).

The computer box has many circuits and parts, but the computer itself is a tiny chip, programmed to make calculations based on information from various sensing devices. It then issues commands, which do nothing more than supply or deny current to certain electrical terminals to which the chip is connected. These terminals are connected to the operating hardware, which includes electric motors and solenoids.

The computer's sensors may monitor engine coolant and air temperatures, throttle and crankshaft positions, atmospheric pressure, manifold vacuum, pinging, engine speed, the concentration of oxygen in the exhaust, and car speed.

Throttle position: A variable resistor or a cylindrical metal core that slides through a wire coil is connected to the throttle linkage. Movement of the resis-

tor or metal core produces an electric signal to the computer. Throttle position can also be indicated by vacuum-electric switches—diaphragm-operated switches that are opened or closed by the vacuum in the intake manifold to signal when the throttle is closed or wide open.

Crankshaft position: The computer must know the position of each piston in order to trigger the electronic ignition at the proper time.

Manifold vacuum: A vacuum diaphragm or bellows pulls a cylindrical metal core through a wire coil to generate a signal proportional to the vacuum in the intake manifold. In the newest designs, a solid-state pressure sensor, in the same housing as the atmospheric pressure sensor, is used.

Pinging: An electromechanical sensor sends an electric signal to the computer if the engine begins to knock.

Engine speed: This signal is picked up from the electric pulses in the ignition system that fire the spark plugs.

Concentration of exhaust oxygen: An oxygen sensor generates an electric signal based on the percentage of oxygen in

the exhaust gases. This percentage indicates the air-fuel ratio of the mixture just burned in the cylinders, and in that way provides information needed to maintain a precise 14.6:1 air-fuel ratio for most effective operation of the three-way catalyst (see p.80). This is the only sensor that must be replaced at regular intervals, usually every 15,000, 30,000, or 50,000 miles, depending on the car model.

The computer may also draw information from simple wiring connections to the brake switch (to help sense deceleration), to the air-conditioning clutch (to know when the compressor is operating), and to switches that tell which transmission gear is engaged.

The computer issues commands based on the above information. The operating hardware turns these commands into action. To control air-fuel mixture, the computer supplies or cuts current to a *motor* or a *solenoid*.

The motor is located in the carburetor. Depending on which terminals receive current, the motor runs forward or backward, operating a plunger that pushes or pulls on tapered metering rods. These rods may open fuel passages (to enrich the air-fuel mixture) or close them (to lean out the mixture). In other systems the rods open (to lean out) or close (to enrich) air bleed passages. Or, the motor may move a valve that opens or closes a vacuum passage from the intake manifold to the carburetor bowl. When the passage is open, vacuum lowers the air pressure over the fuel, reducing fuel flow into the carburetor's various fuel-metering circuits. When the passage is closed, atmospheric pressure is restored and more fuel flows out of the bowl.

The computer may activate a *solenoid vacuum regulator*. When the solenoid is activated by electric current, it allows vacuum in the manifold to flow to a diaphragm on the carburetor. The vacuum pulls on the diaphragm, which is

attached to a metering valve that controls either a fuel passage (to enrich the air-fuel mixture) or air bleed passage (to lean out the mixture). A spring retracts the solenoid valve when the computer cuts current off. In actual operation, the solenoid continuously pulses on and off.

When used in conjunction with electronic fuel injection, the computer varies the time that the solenoid-type injectors are held open. With mechanical fuel injection, a pulsing solenoid valve bleeds off fuel pressure in the fuel distributor to enrich the mixture.

When the engine is cold, idling, or at wide-open throttle, the computer control is deactivated and the fuel mixture on all systems operates on a built-in setting called *open loop*.

Automatic choke operation is regulated by applying or denying current to electric heaters in the choke housing.

The computer controls spark timing by processing sensor inputs and triggering the electronic ignition at the right time. When the computer gets a signal from the pinging sensor, it retards ignition timing to reduce engine knock.

Idle speed is controlled by a motorized plunger that pushes against the throttle linkage, or by a vacuum-operated plunger that receives vacuum when the computer opens a solenoid-controlled valve in a vacuum line.

Exhaust gas recirculation valves are also controlled by solenoid vacuum valves on many engines.

Computer systems are designed to *failsafe*. If the computer chip fails, arbitrary fixed settings are usually applied to ignition timing, fuel injectors, idle speed motor, and so on, so that the car can still be started and driven. Failures in sensors and operating hardware are more common than computer failures, and the computer chip can act as a troubleshooter by monitoring these components (see pp.388–389).

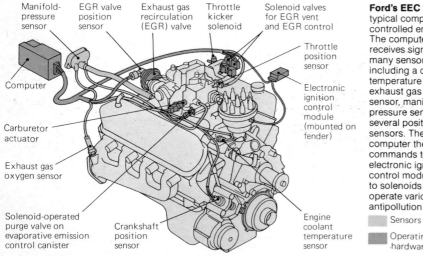

Manifold-pressure sensor
EGR valve position sensor
Exhaust gas recirculation (EGR) valve
Throttle kicker solenoid
Solenoid valves for EGR vent and EGR control
Throttle position sensor
Electronic ignition control module (mounted on fender)
Computer
Carburetor actuator
Exhaust gas oxygen sensor
Solenoid-operated purge valve on evaporative emission control canister
Crankshaft position sensor
Engine coolant temperature sensor

Ford's EEC II is a typical computer-controlled engine. The computer receives signals from many sensors, including a coolant temperature sensor, exhaust gas oxygen sensor, manifold pressure sensor, and several position sensors. The computer then sends commands to the electronic ignition control module and to solenoids that operate various antipollution devices.

☐ Sensors

■ Operating hardware

Sensors

Operating hardware

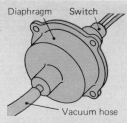

Diaphragm **Switch**

Vacuum hose

Vacuum-electric switch gives gross reading of vacuum in intake manifold by using a diaphragm to operate a simple on-off electrical switch.

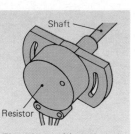

Shaft

Resistor

Throttle position: A variable resistor coupled to the throttle shaft varies amount of current flowing to the computer in proportion to throttle position.

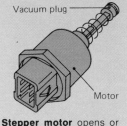

Coil

Throttle link

Throttle position: Iron rod attached to throttle linkage moves in and out of a coil of wire, varying the strength of an electrical signal sent to the computer.

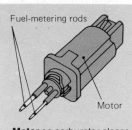

Fuel-metering rods

Motor

Motor on carburetor closes or opens a fuel-metering port to regulate fuel mixture, keeping the air-fuel ratio at exactly 14.6:1 (stoichiometric) at all times.

Vacuum plug

Motor

Stepper motor opens or closes a vacuum passage to the carburetor float bowl. Vacuum reduces flow of fuel into the carburetor's metering circuits.

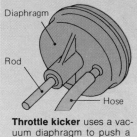

Diaphragm

Rod

Hose

Throttle kicker uses a vacuum diaphragm to push a rod against the throttle linkage to increase idle speed. A solenoid valve controls vacuum supply.

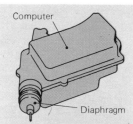

Computer

Diaphragm

Vacuum transducer: Vacuum diaphragm moves an iron rod inside a coil of wire, sending a signal to the computer that is proportional to the amount of vacuum.

Computer chip

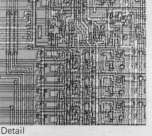

Detail

Microprocessor chip ¼ in. square contains thousands of electrical circuits. It is the "brain" of the computer. The chip's circuits are connected to the car's wiring by strands of 24-carat-gold wire about half the diameter of a human hair. Gold is used because it does not corrode.

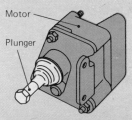

Motor

Plunger

Motor or solenoid operated by the computer can also be used to push a plunger against the throttle linkage in order to increase cold-idle speed.

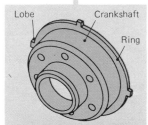

Lobe

Crankshaft

Ring

Crankshaft position: An iron ring is attached to the crankshaft. Whenever a lobe on the ring passes the magnetic sensor, a signal is sent to the computer.

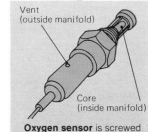

Vent (outside manifold)

Core (inside manifold)

Oxygen sensor is screwed into the exhaust manifold. The difference in the amount of oxygen on either side of the core generates a small voltage signal.

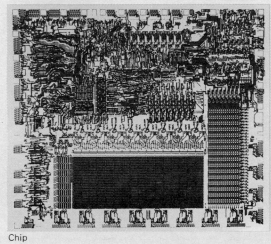

Chip

Fuel lines

Fuel-pressure diaphragm

Solenoid

Solenoid valve bleeds off fuel pressure from the lower half of a continuous fuel injection distributor (p.61) to increase the flow of fuel to the injectors.

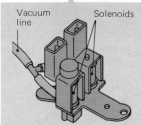

Vacuum line

Solenoids

Solenoid valves on a vacuum line and a vent line can be operated by the computer to modulate the action of an engine's vacuum-controlled EGR valve.

How the engine turns the wheels

The *drive train* transmits power from the engine to the wheels that move the car. In a conventional auto, with its engine in front and drive wheels in the rear, the engine turns shafts in the transmission, which transmits power through a drive shaft to the rear axle. When a car turns, differential gears inside the axle housing permit the outside wheel to make more revolutions than the inside wheel, which has a shorter distance to travel. Universal joints (U-joints) in the drive shaft allow the rear axle to move up and down.

In a front-wheel-drive car or a rear-engine car, there is no drive shaft. The engine drives a combined transmission and differential called a *transaxle,* which turns the two axle shafts that drive the wheels. U-joints in these axle shafts let the suspension move up and down and allow the front wheels to steer a front-wheel-drive car.

A car engine develops useful power at relatively high revolutions per minute (rpm). A typical engine produces its motive power between 1,500 and 3,500 to 5,000 rpm. If the wheels turned once for every crankshaft revolution, the car could travel only between 50 and 270 mph (80 and 435 km/h). Thus, engine speed must be geared down for road use.

Differential gears allow the drive shaft to run two to four times faster than the wheels. Additional gears in the transmission further reduce the speed of the drive wheels while allowing the engine to run in its useful power range. The faster the engine turns in relation to the wheels, the more *torque* (twisting power) it develops; so the transmission acts as a torque multiplier. Maximum torque is developed in the transmission's lowest gears (*First* and *Second*) but they lower the car's speed. Three to five forward gears match engine speeds to driving requirements at any given moment. The gears may be shifted manually or automatically, depending on the type of transmission in the car.

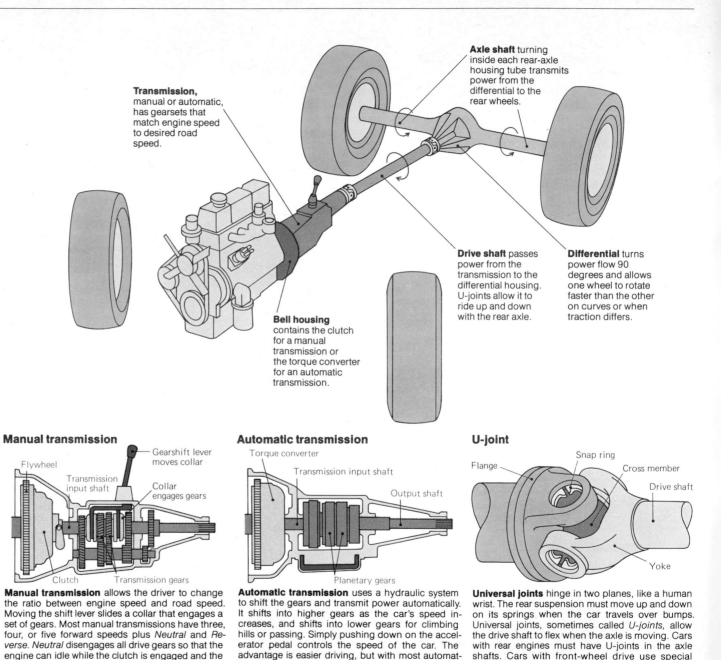

Transmission, manual or automatic, has gearsets that match engine speed to desired road speed.

Axle shaft turning inside each rear-axle housing tube transmits power from the differential to the rear wheels.

Bell housing contains the clutch for a manual transmission or the torque converter for an automatic transmission.

Drive shaft passes power flow from the transmission to the differential housing. U-joints allow it to ride up and down with the rear axle.

Differential turns power flow 90 degrees and allows one wheel to rotate faster than the other on curves or when traction differs.

Manual transmission

Gearshift lever moves collar
Flywheel
Transmission input shaft
Collar engages gears
Clutch
Transmission gears

Manual transmission allows the driver to change the ratio between engine speed and road speed. Moving the shift lever slides a collar that engages a set of gears. Most manual transmissions have three, four, or five forward speeds plus *Neutral* and *Reverse. Neutral* disengages all drive gears so that the engine can idle while the clutch is engaged and the car is stationary.

Automatic transmission

Torque converter
Transmission input shaft
Output shaft
Planetary gears

Automatic transmission uses a hydraulic system to shift the gears and transmit power automatically. It shifts into higher gears as the car's speed increases, and shifts into lower gears for climbing hills or passing. Simply pushing down on the accelerator pedal controls the speed of the car. The advantage is easier driving, but with most automatics there is a loss in fuel economy.

U-joint

Snap ring
Flange
Cross member
Drive shaft
Yoke

Universal joints hinge in two planes, like a human wrist. The rear suspension must move up and down on its springs when the car travels over bumps. Universal joints, sometimes called *U-joints,* allow the drive shaft to flex when the axle is moving. Cars with rear engines must have U-joints in the axle shafts. Cars with front-wheel drive use special U-joints called *constant velocity joints.*

Clutch

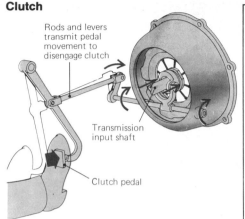

Rods and levers transmit pedal movement to disengage clutch

Transmission input shaft

Clutch pedal

A clutch disengages the engine from the transmission when the pedal is depressed so that the gears in a manual transmission can be shifted smoothly. Part of the clutch is attached to the engine's flywheel and part to the transmission's input shaft. When the clutch pedal is released, the clutch parts are forced together by springs, and the flywheel and input shaft rotate as one piece.

Rear end

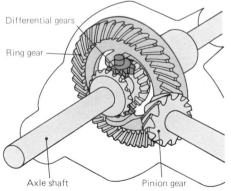

Differential gears

Ring gear

Axle shaft

Pinion gear

The differential reduces drive shaft rpm to useful wheel speed. The pinion gear mates with the ring gear at a right angle, turning the drive to the axle shafts 90 degrees. In the differential *carrier,* differential gears let one axle shaft turn faster than the other so that one wheel can follow the longer path around the outside of a turn. The differential and axle assembly is sometimes called the *rear end.*

Cars without drive shafts

Longitudinal engine

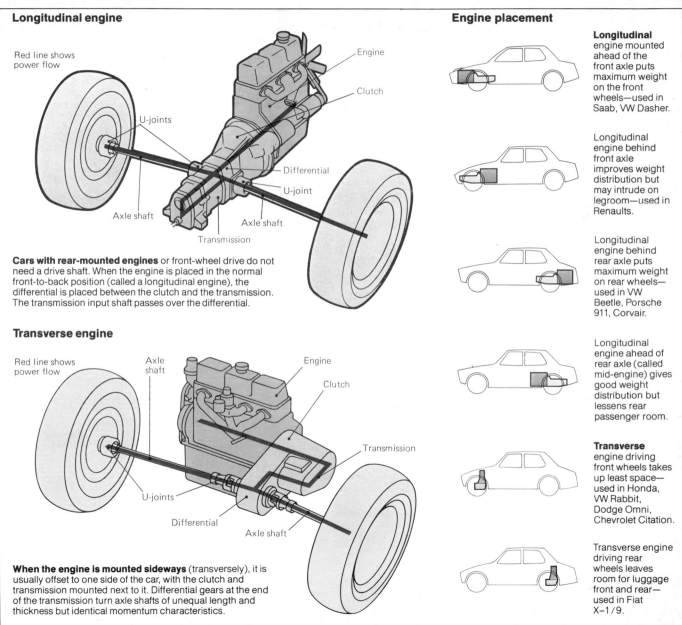

Red line shows power flow

Engine

Clutch

U-joints

Differential

U-joint

Axle shaft

Axle shaft

Transmission

Cars with rear-mounted engines or front-wheel drive do not need a drive shaft. When the engine is placed in the normal front-to-back position (called a longitudinal engine), the differential is placed between the clutch and the transmission. The transmission input shaft passes over the differential.

Transverse engine

Red line shows power flow

Axle shaft

Engine

Clutch

Transmission

U-joints

Differential

Axle shaft

When the engine is mounted sideways (transversely), it is usually offset to one side of the car, with the clutch and transmission mounted next to it. Differential gears at the end of the transmission turn axle shafts of unequal length and thickness but identical momentum characteristics.

Engine placement

Longitudinal engine mounted ahead of the front axle puts maximum weight on the front wheels—used in Saab, VW Dasher.

Longitudinal engine behind front axle improves weight distribution but may intrude on legroom—used in Renaults.

Longitudinal engine behind rear axle puts maximum weight on rear wheels—used in VW Beetle, Porsche 911, Corvair.

Longitudinal engine ahead of rear axle (called mid-engine) gives good weight distribution but lessens rear passenger room.

Transverse engine driving front wheels takes up least space—used in Honda, VW Rabbit, Dodge Omni, Chevrolet Citation.

Transverse engine driving rear wheels leaves room for luggage front and rear—used in Fiat X-1/9.

What the clutch does

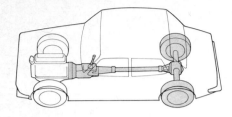

The clutch connects the engine to a manual transmission. Stepping on a foot pedal disengages the clutch so that the engine can run without turning the wheels. This allows the driver to shift the transmission from one gear to another. A friction material on both sides of the clutch disc, similar to that in brake linings, allows the disc to be engaged gradually for smooth starts when the engine is operating at over 1,000 rpm.

The clutch assembly consists of three parts: the engine *flywheel,* the *clutch disc,* and the *pressure plate.* The pressure plate is bolted to the flywheel and turns with it. The clutch disc is a flat steel disc with a splined hub that slides on the transmission input shaft.

Strong springs squeeze the clutch disc between the flywheel and pressure plate. When the clutch disc is locked in place, engine power passes from flywheel to clutch disc to transmission input shaft, thereby driving the car. Depressing the clutch pedal moves the pressure plate back and frees the disc from the flywheel. The disc slides on its *splines* (p.88) so that it touches neither the flywheel nor the pressure plate.

Clutches are named after the kind of pressure springs they employ. *Coil-spring clutches,* once common, are giving way to *diaphragm clutches* because the latter are lighter, cheaper, and reduce pedal pressure. Some coil-spring clutches have centrifugal weights that increase the clamping force of the springs as engine speed increases. They are called *centrifugal clutches.*

Coil-spring clutch

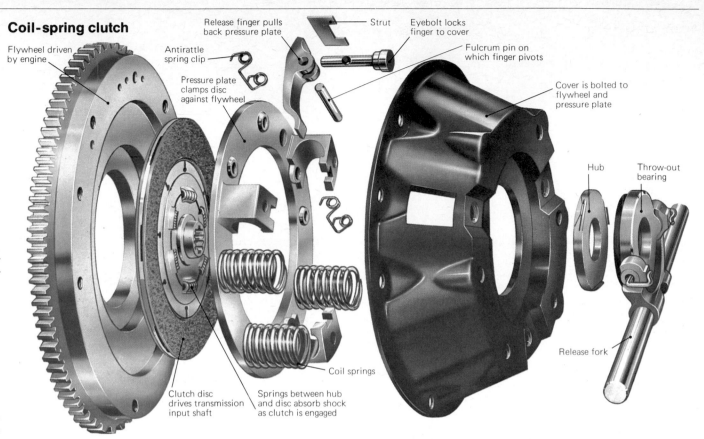

Flywheel driven by engine

Antirattle spring clip

Pressure plate clamps disc against flywheel

Release finger pulls back pressure plate

Strut

Eyebolt locks finger to cover

Fulcrum pin on which finger pivots

Cover is bolted to flywheel and pressure plate

Hub

Throw-out bearing

Release fork

Clutch disc drives transmission input shaft

Coil springs

Springs between hub and disc absorb shock as clutch is engaged

How a clutch works

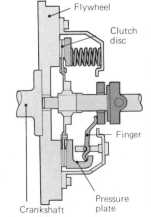

A sanding disc on a drill shows how a clutch works. The disc corresponds to the flywheel, and the drill to the engine. Press a second disc (the clutch) against the first, and friction will turn it too, though more slowly than the disc on the drill. Increase the pressure on the discs, and both will turn together at the same speed.

Coil-spring clutch in operation

Flywheel

Clutch disc

Finger

Crankshaft

Pressure plate

Engaged: Coil springs clamp the clutch disc tightly between the pressure plate and the flywheel. Thus, the flywheel and pressure plate turn the clutch disc at full engine speed. The disc is splined to the input shaft of the transmission; so the engine is firmly linked to the transmission. Only one coil spring and finger are shown, for clarity.

Friction linings on clutch disc

Input shaft

Hub for throw-out bearing

Disengaged: The throw-out bearing presses on the release fingers, which pull the pressure plate away from the flywheel and compress the coil springs. This frees the disc, which slides on its splines so that it touches neither the flywheel nor the pressure plate. Thus the engine turns freely, with no connection to the transmission.

Diaphragm clutch

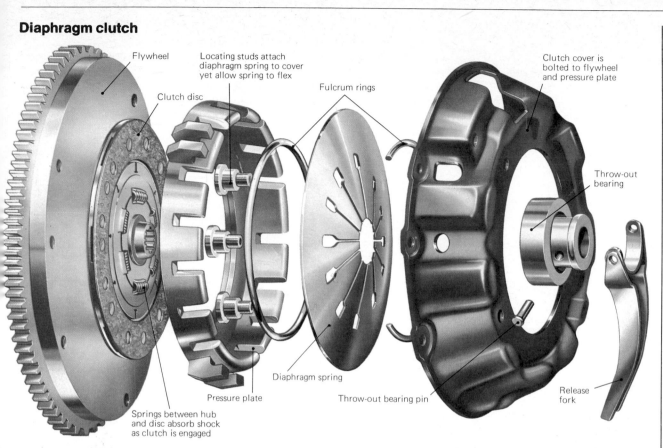

Flywheel

Locating studs attach diaphragm spring to cover yet allow spring to flex

Fulcrum rings

Clutch cover is bolted to flywheel and pressure plate

Clutch disc

Throw-out bearing

Diaphragm spring

Throw-out bearing pin

Pressure plate

Release fork

Springs between hub and disc absorb shock as clutch is engaged

Diaphragm clutch in operation

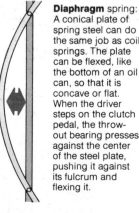

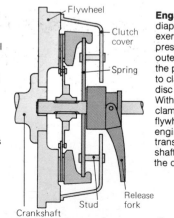

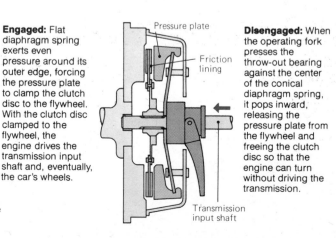

Diaphragm spring: A conical plate of spring steel can do the same job as coil springs. The plate can be flexed, like the bottom of an oil can, so that it is concave or flat. When the driver steps on the clutch pedal, the throw-out bearing presses against the center of the steel plate, pushing it against its fulcrum and flexing it.

Flywheel

Clutch cover

Spring

Crankshaft

Stud

Release fork

Engaged: Flat diaphragm spring exerts even pressure around its outer edge, forcing the pressure plate to clamp the clutch disc to the flywheel. With the clutch disc clamped to the flywheel, the engine drives the transmission input shaft and, eventually, the car's wheels.

Pressure plate

Friction lining

Transmission input shaft

Disengaged: When the operating fork presses the throw-out bearing against the center of the conical diaphragm spring, it pops inward, releasing the pressure plate from the flywheel and freeing the clutch disc so that the engine can turn without driving the transmission.

How the pedal works the clutch

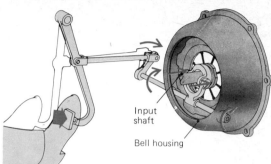

Input shaft

Bell housing

Mechanical linkage: On many large North American cars, the motion of the driver's foot on the clutch pedal is transferred to the throw-out bearing by a system of rods and levers.

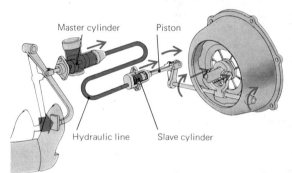

Master cylinder

Piston

Hydraulic line

Slave cylinder

Hydraulic operation: Pushing hydraulic fluid through a pipe from a master cylinder to a slave cylinder provides friction-free thrust to the clutch-operating fork on many imported cars.

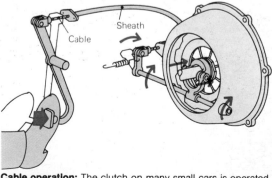

Sheath

Cable

Cable operation: The clutch on many small cars is operated by pulling a cable instead of pushing a rod. The cable slides inside a sheath so that it works smoothly around corners.

What the transmission does

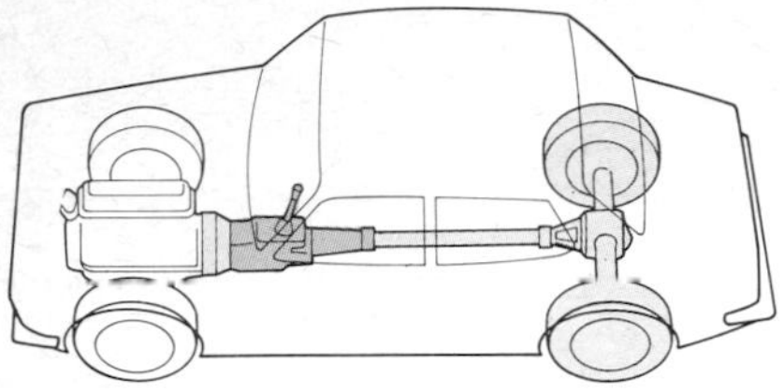

The transmission makes it possible to match the engine's power-producing speeds to the speed of the drive wheels. An engine produces little torque, or twisting power, at low engine rpm. A transmission's lower gears allow the engine to turn very fast in comparison to the drive wheels, thereby providing maximum torque in order to start the car from rest. *High* gear keeps engine rpm low for maximum fuel economy at cruising speeds. When the car encounters a hill, the engine will falter and stall unless an intermediate gear is selected.

The gears between *First* and *High* bridge the gap between the torque required to start a fully loaded car from rest and that required to keep a car rolling along at highway speeds. In the days when engines were big and produced lots of torque, only three forward speeds were needed. Today's smaller engines produce less torque at higher rpm and often require four or five gears.

Manual transmission

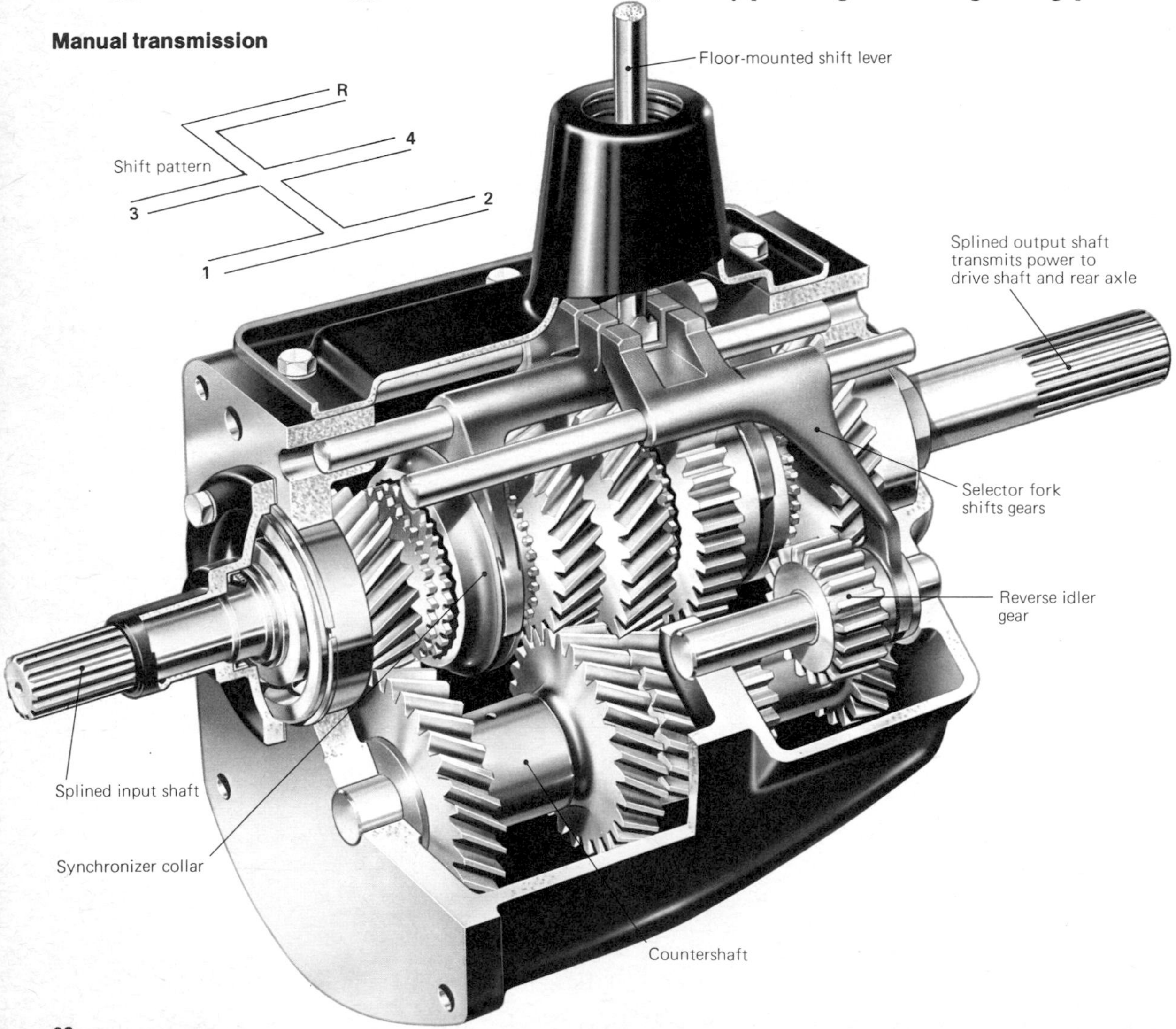

Shift pattern

R
4
3
2
1

Floor-mounted shift lever

Splined output shaft transmits power to drive shaft and rear axle

Selector fork shifts gears

Reverse idler gear

Splined input shaft

Synchronizer collar

Countershaft

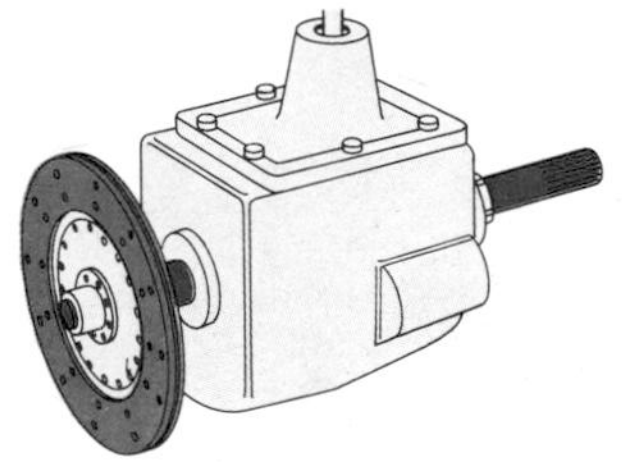

The clutch disc slides on splines cut into the transmission input shaft, turning the shaft whenever the clutch is engaged and the engine is running. Splines are matching parallel grooves in a hub and shaft that allow the hub to slide back and forth on the shaft but force the two parts to turn as one.

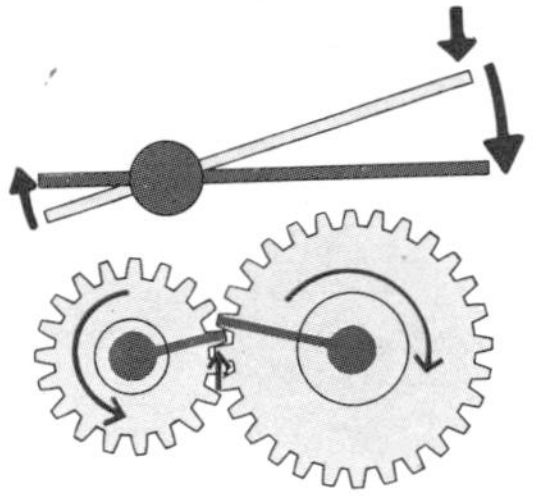

A lever enables a small force moving over a great distance to lift a large weight a lesser distance (top). Gears are toothed wheels that act like a series of levers (bottom). Torque transmitted through a small gear turns a larger gear a lesser amount, multiplying the torque but reducing the original speed.

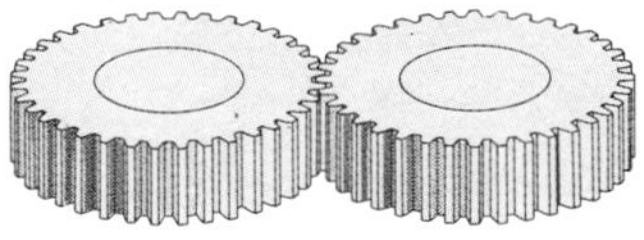

A spur gear has straight teeth cut parallel to its axis of rotation. Spur gears tend to be noisy in operation, but they are cheaper to machine and require slightly less power to turn than helical gears do. Spur gears are used only for *Reverse* on modern transmissions.

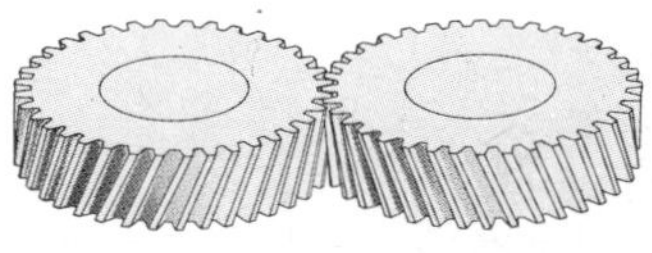

A helical gear has curved teeth cut at an angle to the axis of rotation. The curve forms a spiral (called a *helix*) similar to a screw thread. The overlap between adjoining teeth is greater in helical gears than in spur gears, so that power is transferred more smoothly and quietly.

How a manual transmission works

A manual transmission allows the driver to select the gears he needs to cope with varying road conditions. To shift gears, a driver must depress the clutch pedal to disconnect the engine from the transmission, then move the shift lever. The lever moves collars inside the transmission to engage various sets of gears.

Gear ratios are determined by the number of teeth on the driven gear compared to the driving gear. If the driven gear has 20 teeth and the driving gear has 10, the gear ratio is 2:1. The driven gear will rotate at half the speed of the driving gear, but it will pass on twice the torque.

The lowest gear in the transmission must multiply engine torque enough to start a fully loaded car moving up a steep hill. On a small car with a four-speed transmission, *First* gear might have a ratio of 3.5:1. Other typical ratios would be 2:1 in *Second*, 1.5:1 in *Third*, and 1:1 in *Fourth*. If the rear-axle ratio is 3:1, the overall ratios between crankshaft speed

and wheel speed are found by multiplying the two ratios—10.5:1 in *First*, 6:1 in *Second*, 4.5:1 in *Third*, and 3:1 in *Fourth*.

A car with a bigger engine would not need so much torque multiplication and might use a three-speed transmission with ratios of 2.8:1, 1.5:1, and 1:1, and a rear-axle ratio of 2.75:1.

Neutral

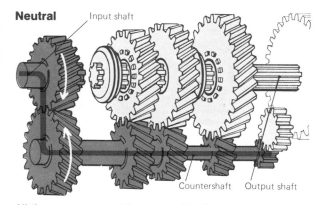

All the gearsets except those needed for *Reverse* are constantly in mesh. The tan gears are fixed to their shafts; those shown in gray revolve on freewheeling hubs. In *Neutral* all the gears on the output shaft are allowed to freewheel, and no power is transmitted.

First gear

When *First* gear is engaged, a collar splined to the output shaft slides into contact with the largest gear and locks it to the shaft so that power is transmitted. The output shaft may rotate once for every three revolutions of the input shaft, providing maximum torque.

Second gear

When the transmission is shifted into *Second*, a selector fork (not shown here) slides the collar forward, out of contact with *First* gear, to engage and drive the second-largest output gear. This gear provides enough torque for brisk acceleration or for climbing steep hills.

Third gear

To shift into *Third*, the rear collar is disengaged from *First* and *Second* gears, and the forward collar slides into engagement with the smallest gear. With its ratio of about 1.5:1, *Third* gear provides enough torque for high-speed passing or for climbing moderately steep hills.

Fourth gear

In *High* gear, called *direct drive* by engineers, the forward collar slides up to bridge the gap between the splined input and output shafts so that they rotate as one. The ratio of this "gear" is obviously 1:1. The other gearsets continue to freewheel and do not transmit power.

Reverse

When *Reverse* is selected, both collars are disengaged and the idler gear is engaged with spur gears on the countershaft and output shaft. This extra gear reverses the output shaft's direction of rotation, causing the car to back up when the clutch is engaged.

How the shift lever changes gears

Linkage from a shift lever, mounted on the floor or steering column, moves the forks inside a manual transmission to engage the gears. The shift forks fit into grooves machined into the circumference of the shift collars. Each two-faced collar locks one gear to the output shaft when moved forward, and locks another gear when it is moved back. That is why *First-Second* and *Third-Fourth* have their own slots in the H-shaped shift pattern.

The only gear that actually shifts is *Reverse*. The others are engaged when the shifting fork forces the collar against an already meshed gear, locking it to the rotating output shaft.

Each shifting fork is attached to a rod in a directly shifted transmission (below),
or to a lever and rod in a transmission with side linkage (right). When the driver moves the shift lever, it pivots on a ball-in-socket joint and moves a control rod in the opposite direction. A collar grips a gear and, when the clutch pedal is released, power is transmitted through the transmission to the wheels.

Synchromesh

Large teeth on the side of each gear engage similar teeth on the shift collars in order to lock a gear to the output shaft. These teeth are called *dogs*. Originally, these dogs were simply forced together by the shift fork until they finally meshed with a great crunch. To do the job more quietly and smoothly, a synchronizing
system has been devised that allows the two sets of dogs to reach the same speed before they are engaged. A typical *synchromesh* system is illustrated on the opposite page.

As the collar is pushed toward a gear, a conical ring on the gear comes into contact with a matching conical hole in the collar. The friction between the two conical surfaces brings the speed of the free-wheeling gear up or down to match the speed of the output shaft and collar. Once their speeds are synchronized, the two sets of dogs can mesh smoothly. A system of blocking rings and spring-loaded sleeves prevents the dogs from being forced into contact until they are rotating at about the same speed.

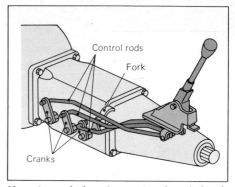

Many transmissions have external control rods that pivot cranks to move the shift forks inside the transmission. These external rods can be operated by a floor-mounted shift lever or, with additional linkage, by a lever on the steering column.

Internal shift linkage

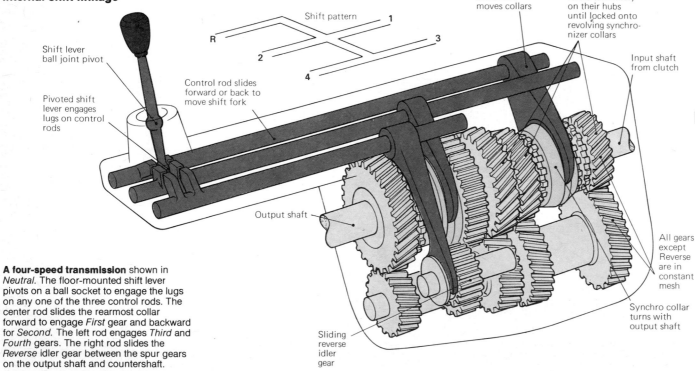

A four-speed transmission shown in *Neutral*. The floor-mounted shift lever pivots on a ball socket to engage the lugs on any one of the three control rods. The center rod slides the rearmost collar forward to engage *First* gear and backward for *Second*. The left rod engages *Third* and *Fourth* gears. The right rod slides the *Reverse* idler gear between the spur gears on the output shaft and countershaft.

Shifting the gears

The shift lever is usually spring-loaded to stay in the center slot unless side force is applied to the shift knob. Pushing the shift lever forward in the center slot (illustration at left) moves the center control rod backward. This moves one shift fork (shown in red) and collar backward to engage *First* gear (tan). Pulling the lever backward engages *Second* gear. Pushing the lever to the right and then forward moves the left rod back to engage *Third* gear (center). When this rod is moved forward, *Fourth* is engaged. Moving the lever left and back engages the *Reverse* idler (right).

How synchromesh works

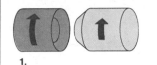

1.

2.

Simplified
illustration shows how synchromesh cones turning at different speeds (1) act like friction clutches to equalize the speed of the two parts as they are forced together (2).

1.

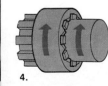

2.

3.

4.

Synchronizer
collar has cones, dogs, and a sliding sleeve. Before shifting (1), conical surfaces on the collar (tan) and freewheeling gear (gray) do not touch. As the shift fork forces the collar and gear together (2), the cones' speeds begin to equalize. When the parts are rotating at the same speed (3), the synchronizer sleeve is forced forward and begins to engage the dogs. In the final stage (4), the dogs lock completely into the splines inside the synchronizer sleeve.

Typical synchromesh system

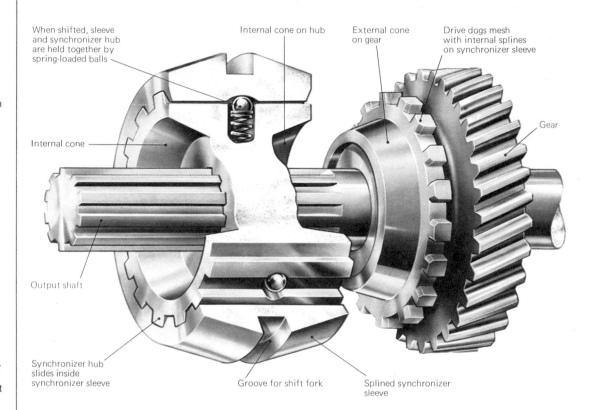

When shifted, sleeve and synchronizer hub are held together by spring-loaded balls

Internal cone on hub

External cone on gear

Drive dogs mesh with internal splines on synchronizer sleeve

Gear

Internal cone

Output shaft

Synchronizer hub slides inside synchronizer sleeve

Groove for shift fork

Splined synchronizer sleeve

The synchronizer collar consists of a hub and a sleeve. The hub has internal splines so that it can slide on the output shaft, and external splines so that the sleeve can slide on it. Internal splines on the sleeve mesh with the dogs on the gear.

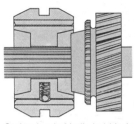

Spring-loaded balls hold hub and sleeve together when they are shifted.

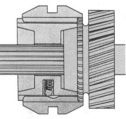

Pressure from shift fork causes splined sleeve to override the spring-loaded balls and slide into engagement with dogs on gear.

The blocker ring system

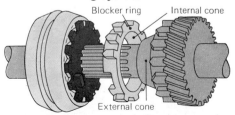

Blocker ring

Internal cone

External cone

Blocker ring turns to hold back synchronizer sleeve

Synchronizer sleeve slides over blocker ring

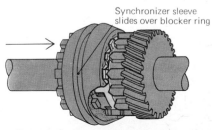

The blocker ring on modern synchromesh systems contains the internal cone. It separates the collar and gear, and prevents the dogs from engaging until all parts are precisely synchronized.

When the shift fork engages the cones, the blocker ring shifts slightly so that its dogs prevent the sleeve from engaging the gear wheel. The shift lever resists any effort to push it into gear.

When the speeds of all three parts are synchronized, the blocker ring shifts again, allowing the sleeve to move forward and engage the aligned dogs on the blocker ring and gear.

Automatic transmission passes power through a fluid

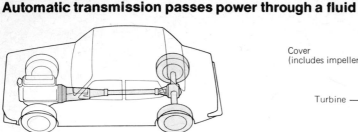

An automatic transmission is made possible by a fluid coupling that is placed between the transmission and the engine. There are two parts in a fluid coupling: the *impeller*, which is driven by the engine, and the *turbine*, which turns the transmission input shaft. Both are bowl shaped and have a number of partitions, called vanes. The two bowls face each other, separated by a small clearance, in a housing filled with oil.

The oil sloshing inside the coupling allows the engine to idle at low speeds. At engine speeds above 1,000 rpm, the impeller imparts so much swirl to the fluid that the turbine also revolves and the car begins to move, if it is in gear and the brakes are released. Above 2,000 rpm the turbine turns at about 98 percent of the speed of the impeller; this 2 percent rpm loss is called *slip*.

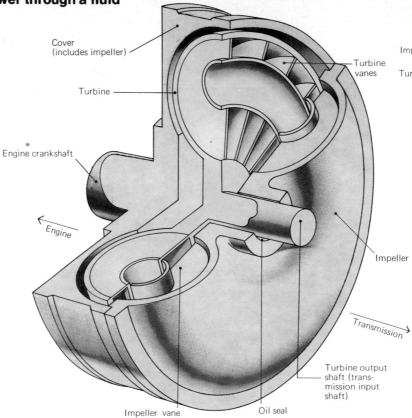

Cover (includes impeller)

Turbine vanes

Turbine

Engine crankshaft

Engine

Impeller

Transmission

Turbine output shaft (transmission input shaft)

Impeller vane

Oil seal

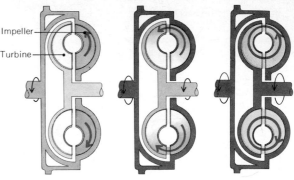

Impeller

Turbine

Progressive engagement of a fluid clutch: The impeller is attached to the engine crankshaft. It faces the turbine in an oil bath. At low rpm (left) the oil transmits too little torque from the impeller to the turbine to move the car, so that the engine idles while the car remains stationary. As engine speed increases, centrifugal force throws more oil from the impeller into the turbine, transmitting some torque (center), but there is still so much slip that the turbine turns the output shaft much more slowly than the engine turns the input shaft. The car begins to move. Once the engine reaches a pre-set speed, usually 1,500 to 2,000 rpm, the circulating oil transmits maximum power (right). Slippage between impeller and turbine rpm drops to as little as 2 percent, and the car accelerates to the speed dictated by the position of the accelerator pedal. Some newer cars are equipped with *lockup converters,* which eliminate all slippage at highway speeds for increased fuel economy. When the car reaches a pre-set speed, a clutch locks the impeller and turbine together, so that they rotate as one.

From the fluid coupling to the modern torque converter

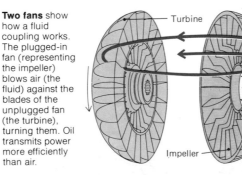

Two fans show how a fluid coupling works. The plugged-in fan (representing the impeller) blows air (the fluid) against the blades of the unplugged fan (the turbine), turning them. Oil transmits power more efficiently than air.

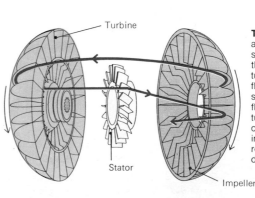

Turbine

Impeller

A fluid coupling engages slowly. Oil flung from the impeller starts the turbine moving. The turbine accelerates as engine speed increases. Above 2,000 rpm, the impeller and turbine turn at nearly the same speed.

Turbine

Stator

Impeller

Torque converter adds a central stator between the impeller and turbine of the fluid clutch. This stator redirects oil flow from the turbine to the center of the impeller while reversing the direction of flow.

The torque converter

The engine torque, or twisting force, applied to the turbine in a fluid coupling can never quite equal the torque delivered by the impeller to the transmission because there is always some slip. This slip accounts for the loss in fuel economy that occurs with automatic transmissions.

At low engine speeds, the oil bounces from the turbine vanes back toward the impeller and circulates in a counterclockwise direction. This is opposite to the clockwise flow that the impeller imparts to the oil, and some engine torque is absorbed in reversing the flow. Modern automatic transmissions use a *torque converter* to overcome this torque loss. A torque converter is a fluid coupling with a third member, called a *stator,* mounted between the turbine and the impeller. A one-way clutch allows the stator to rotate clockwise but locks it in place when it begins to turn counterclockwise.

At low speeds, the counterclockwise flow of oil locks the stator so it cannot turn. The stator vanes divert the oil flowing past them, so that it is again circulating in a clockwise direction when it hits the impeller vanes. This has the effect of doubling the torque that the impeller delivers to the turbine.

As engine speed increases, the oil stops bouncing off the turbine vanes and begins circulating in a clockwise direction. The stator begins to turn on its one-way clutch until it is freewheeling at about the same speed as the turbine and impeller. The stator's multiplication of torque gradually drops from 2.3:1 at startup to zero at cruising speeds.

A modern automatic transmission consists of a torque converter coupled to a two-, three-, or four-speed gearbox. The latest development in automatic transmissions is the *lockup converter.* At cruising speeds, the turbine and impeller are locked together by a clutch to eliminate the slip and lost fuel economy of conventional automatics.

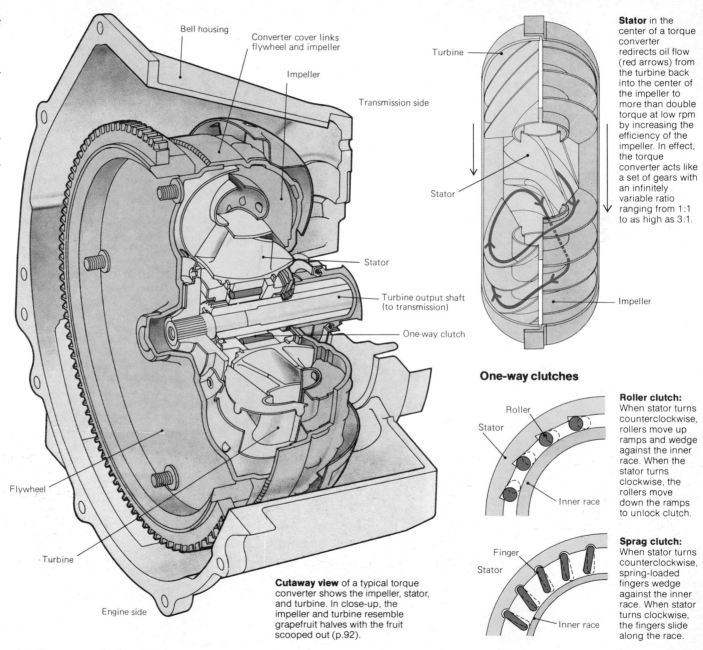

Bell housing

Converter cover links flywheel and impeller

Impeller

Transmission side

Stator

Turbine output shaft (to transmission)

One-way clutch

Flywheel

Turbine

Engine side

Cutaway view of a typical torque converter shows the impeller, stator, and turbine. In close-up, the impeller and turbine resemble grapefruit halves with the fruit scooped out (p.92).

Turbine

Stator

Impeller

Stator in the center of a torque converter redirects oil flow (red arrows) from the turbine back into the center of the impeller to more than double torque at low rpm by increasing the efficiency of the impeller. In effect, the torque converter acts like a set of gears with an infinitely variable ratio ranging from 1:1 to as high as 3:1.

One-way clutches

Roller

Stator

Inner race

Roller clutch: When stator turns counterclockwise, rollers move up ramps and wedge against the inner race. When the stator turns clockwise, the rollers move down the ramps to unlock clutch.

Finger

Stator

Inner race

Sprag clutch: When stator turns counterclockwise, spring-loaded fingers wedge against the inner race. When stator turns clockwise, the fingers slide along the race.

Changing gears without a clutch

The engine needs more torque multiplication than the torque converter alone can supply, in order to start a car up from rest, to climb hills, and to accelerate for passing. This extra torque is provided by *planetary gears* mounted behind the torque converter. Two sets of planetary gears can provide three forward speeds plus reverse, and this is the usual arrangement in an automatic transmission, although some automatics are built with two or four forward speeds.

Planetary gears can be shifted without disconnecting the engine from the transmission. A planetary gearset consists of a *sun gear*, a *ring gear* with internal teeth, and several *planet gears* that rotate between the sun and ring gears, turning a yoke-like *planet carrier*. In a three-speed automatic transmission, the two planetary gearsets have sun gears that are permanently connected. By using hydraulically operated clutches or brake bands to lock or release parts of the two gearsets, varying ratios can be provided. The illustrations (at right and below) show how planetary gears work and (opposite page) how they are arranged in the transmission. The hydraulic shifting system is shown on pages 96-97.

The hydraulic shifting system is shown on pages 96-97.

How a simple planetary gearset works

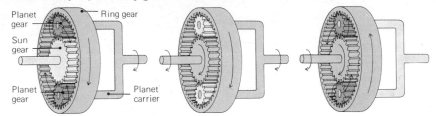

If power is applied to the ring gear and the sun gear is locked (left), the planets will orbit the sun gear, and the planet carrier and ring gear will rotate at different speeds. If the sun gear is locked to the ring gear (center), the planets cannot rotate, and the entire gearset turns as a unit with no change in speed or torque. If the planet carrier is locked and power is applied to the sun gear (right), the planet gears will rotate and drive the ring gear in the opposite direction.

How two planetary gearsets change ratios

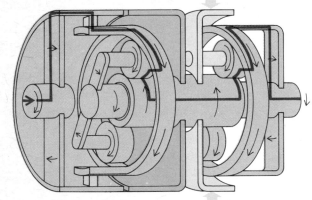

First gear: Foward-drive clutch is engaged so that engine drive (red line) turns the first ring gear. This causes the first planet gears to drive the common sun gear in the opposite direction. The second planet carrier (light gray) is held by its brake band (blue arrows), causing its planets to drive the second ring gear and output shaft in the opposite direction. This produces two reversals of direction and two reductions in engine speed.

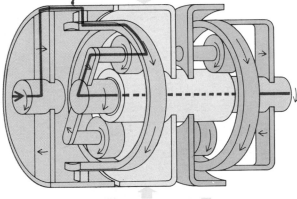

Second gear: When the forward-drive clutch is engaged, the engine drives the first ring gear. The common sun gear (light gray) is braked (blue arrows), so that the first ring gear drives the planet gears around it, and they drive their carrier in the same direction. The carrier shaft is also the output shaft, giving just one speed reduction. The second planet gears and carrier (dark gray) freewheel.

High gear: The forward-drive clutch is engaged, turning the first ring gear. The *Reverse-High* clutch is also engaged, locking the sun gear to the ring gear and causing them both to turn at the same speed. Planet gears (light gray) cannot turn, so their carrier is driven at engine speed. Output shaft turns at engine speed, giving direct drive and no torque multiplication.

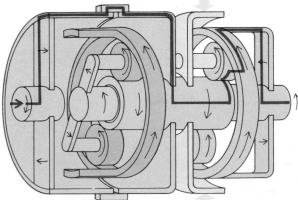

Reverse: Forward-drive clutch is disengaged, allowing the first ring gear to freewheel. *Reverse-High* clutch is engaged, driving the common sun gear. The second planet carrier is braked (blue arrows), so the sun gear causes the second planets to drive the second ring gear in the opposite direction, giving one speed reduction and reverse drive to back up the car.

Inside an automatic transmission

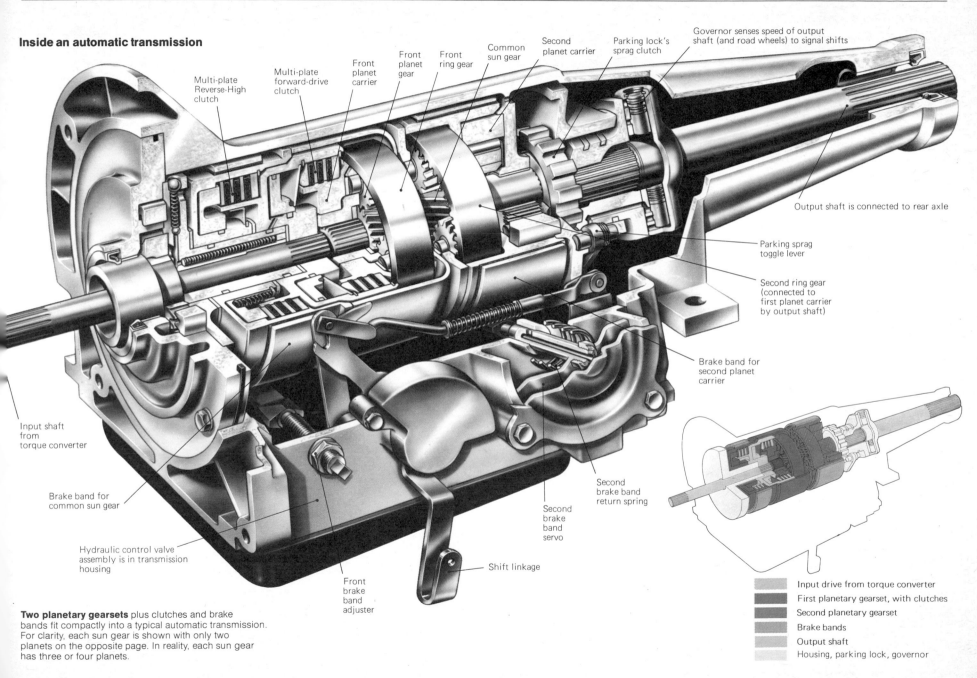

Multi-plate Reverse-High clutch

Multi-plate forward-drive clutch

Front planet carrier

Front planet gear

Front ring gear

Common sun gear

Second planet carrier

Parking lock's sprag clutch

Governor senses speed of output shaft (and road wheels) to signal shifts

Output shaft is connected to rear axle

Parking sprag toggle lever

Second ring gear (connected to first planet carrier by output shaft)

Brake band for second planet carrier

Second brake band return spring

Second brake band servo

Shift linkage

Front brake band adjuster

Hydraulic control valve assembly is in transmission housing

Brake band for common sun gear

Input shaft from torque converter

Two planetary gearsets plus clutches and brake bands fit compactly into a typical automatic transmission. For clarity, each sun gear is shown with only two planets on the opposite page. In reality, each sun gear has three or four planets.

Input drive from torque converter
First planetary gearset, with clutches
Second planetary gearset
Brake bands
Output shaft
Housing, parking lock, governor

How an automatic transmission shifts gears

The *control valve body,* located at the bottom of an automatic transmission, is the "brain" that shifts the gears. It is a complex maze of passages, valves, and springs that shuttles hydraulic pressure to the various pistons and *servo mechanisms* that engage and disengage the brakes and clutches in order to control the planetary gearsets. A pump, driven by the transmission's input shaft, draws transmission fluid from a reservoir, or *oil pan,* at the bottom of the transmission and circulates it through the torque converter, then on to the transmission fluid cooler in the radiator. When it returns from the radiator, the fluid is used to lubricate the moving parts of the transmission. This same fluid, supplied under pressure to the control valve body, is used to shift the planetary gears.

Deciding when to shift

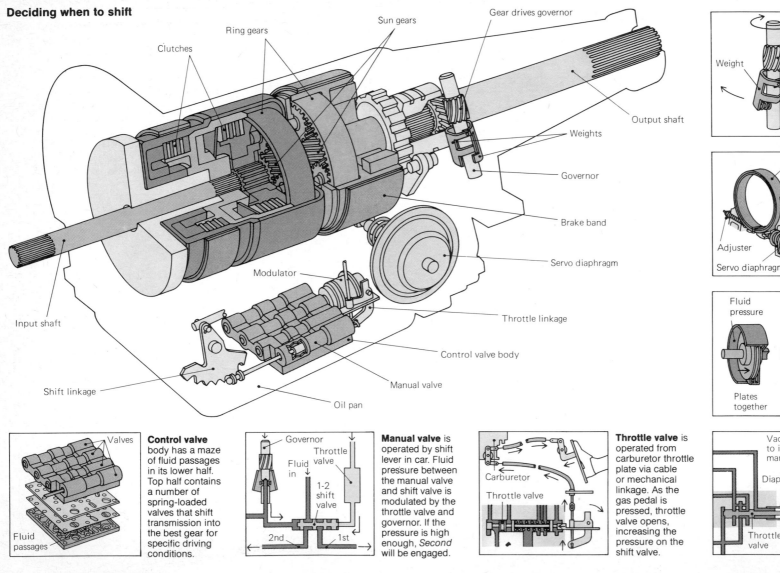

Governor is driven by output shaft. As shaft (and car) speed increase, weights move outward, opening ball valves that increase the fluid pressure on the shift valve.

Brake bands tighten around the sun gear or planet carriers to stop their rotation when fluid pressure is applied to servo diaphragm. Springs release band when pressure drops.

Clutch grips the sun gear or ring gears when fluid pressure on a piston forces the clutch plates together. When fluid pressure is reduced, springs force the clutch plates apart.

Control valve body has a maze of fluid passages in its lower half. Top half contains a number of spring-loaded valves that shift transmission into the best gear for specific driving conditions.

Manual valve is operated by shift lever in car. Fluid pressure between the manual valve and shift valve is modulated by the throttle valve and governor. If the pressure is high enough, *Second* will be engaged.

Throttle valve is operated from carburetor throttle plate via cable or mechanical linkage. As the gas pedal is pressed, throttle valve opens, increasing the pressure on the shift valve.

Modulator can replace mechanical link to throttle plate. Diaphragm responds to changes in the engine's intake manifold vacuum, moving the throttle valve to vary pressure on the shift valve.

The control valve

The control valve body receives signals on vehicle speed, throttle position, engine load, and the gear selected by the driver. It then directs fluid pressure to the appropriate servos to engage the correct gear for the particular driving situation.

When the driver puts the shift lever in *Drive*, he moves a *shift valve* inside the control valve body. The shift valve directs fluid pressure to the servos that engage *First* gear. Two other valves automatically control the shift into *Second*.

The *throttle valve* reacts to the position of the gas pedal. The *governor* senses the speed of the transmission output shaft and generates a fluid pressure signal that is proportional to the car's speed. The two work against each other to shift the gears at various road speeds.

When the car is accelerating gently, throttle valve pressure is low, so that little pressure from the governor (low vehicle speed) is needed to force the shift valve into *Second*. At wider throttle openings, during rapid acceleration, higher pressure from the governor is countered by higher pressure from the throttle valve, blocking the shift until higher engine and vehicle speed are achieved. This is how an automatic transmission can shift gears at low engine speeds to save fuel during gentle driving, or hold the transmission in a lower gear when maximum acceleration is desired. The same system provides the *kickdown* into a lower gear when you floor the accelerator pedal. The shift from *Second* to *High* is made in the same way.

Many transmissions also use a *vacuum modulator,* which responds to intake manifold vacuum in order to modify the action of the throttle valve. During hard acceleration, the modulator causes the throttle valve to increase fluid pressure, which applies the brake bands and clutches more tightly. During gentle driving, it lowers the pressure for smoother shifts.

Overdrive gearing and lockup transmissions

Overdrive gearing improves fuel economy and reduces both engine wear and noise by lowering engine rpm in relation to road speed. An overdrive gearset is one with a ratio of less than 1:1 (such as 0.85:1). That is, for every 0.85 revolutions of the input shaft, the output shaft makes one full revolution.

Overdrive can be achieved by attaching a separate two-speed transmission (one of them overdrive) to the rear of the primary transmission. It is easier and less expensive to design a four- or five-speed manual transmission in which *High* gear has an overdrive ratio.

Cars with rear engines or front-wheel drive usually have a combined transmission and differential unit called a *transaxle* (see pp. 102–103). A manual transaxle has what is known as *all-indirect* gearing. Power enters the transaxle at one end, is transferred by gearsets to an output shaft, and exits from the same end it came in. There is no countershaft, and it is impossible to connect the input and output shafts directly for *High* gear, as is done on a front-engine/rear-drive car (see p.89). Since two gears are required to obtain *High* in an all-indirect transmission, it is as easy to make them overdrive as not, and many front-wheel-drive cars with manual transmissions do use overdrive on *Fourth* and/or *Fifth* speeds.

A benefit similar to overdrive gearing can be achieved on an automatic transmission by a device that mechanically locks the impeller and turbine together, at speeds over 40 mph, to eliminate the usual slippage between them. In the Torque Flite transmissions used in American Motors and Chrysler cars, this is accomplished by a spring-loaded piston that presses the turbine and converter cover together at high speeds. A friction surface on the converter cover causes the two units to lock together like a clutch.

Ford's Automatic Overdrive transmission has a shaft that runs from the converter cover to an extra clutch at the rear of the transmission. At high speeds, this clutch locks the converter cover to the transmission output shaft to eliminate slip and improve fuel economy. *Fourth* gear has an overdrive ratio.

Toyota also offers a four-speed automatic transmission with overdrive gearing, but it has no lockup feature.

A lockup transmission with overdrive

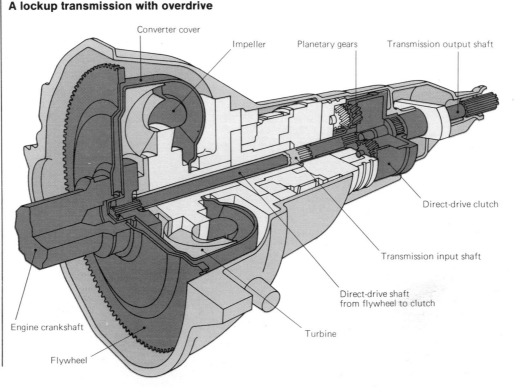

Converter cover · Impeller · Planetary gears · Transmission output shaft · Direct-drive clutch · Transmission input shaft · Direct-drive shaft from flywheel to clutch · Turbine · Engine crankshaft · Flywheel

Ford's Automatic Overdrive transmission has four forward speeds plus a *lockup* feature. When *Fourth* gear is engaged, the fluid coupling of the torque converter is bypassed entirely, and power is delivered from the flywheel to the transmission output shaft by fully mechanical means, eliminating the normal slip in the torque converter and the resultant loss in fuel economy. The transmission input shaft is hollow. A direct-drive shaft runs through it, from a clutch at the rear of the transmission to the torque converter cover (an assembly that includes the flywheel and impeller) at the front of the transmission. When the clutch is engaged, the direct-drive shaft is locked to the transmission's output shaft, and the intervening planetary gearset provides an overdrive ratio of 0.667:1. In *Third* gear, the inner shaft is also locked to the output shaft, but only 60 percent of engine torque is transmitted by this route. The remaining 40 percent is routed through the torque converter and planetary gears with a 1:1 ratio. This dual power flow results in a sharp reduction in converter slippage, but not the complete reduction found in *Fourth*.

The drive shaft

The drive shaft delivers power from the engine-transmission unit in front to the differential gears between the rear wheels of a conventional rear-drive car. This shaft may be 6 feet long or more. It must be able to twist just a bit to absorb torsional shock, but at the same time it must carry heavy torque loads without winding up too much. It must also be able to bend at each end while changing length by about half an inch, to allow for suspension movement.

The drive shaft, sometimes called a *prop shaft,* is a steel tube 3 to 6 inches in diameter. To accommodate angular movement, it has a U-joint at each end. A splined *slip yoke* at the transmission end allows changes in length.

Most drive shafts are long enough to provide the slight cushioning twist required to preserve the gear teeth in the transmission and rear end. Short drive shafts consist of two steel tubes, one inside the other, bonded together with rubber, which absorbs twisting forces. Some cars have two-piece shafts that have three U-joints and are supported in the middle. This arrangement allows each of the three U-joints to flex through a smaller angle than that required for two joints, thereby providing a smoother transfer of power.

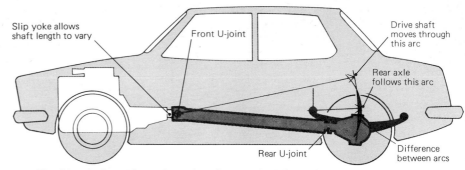

The **drive shaft** must flex and stretch as the rear wheels bounce over rough roads. U-joints at each end of the shaft allow it to change angles. A splined joint at the front of the shaft slides in and out to allow changes in length. A hump, or *tunnel,* in the car floor provides clearance for these movements as well as adding strength to the floor.

Conventional drive shaft components

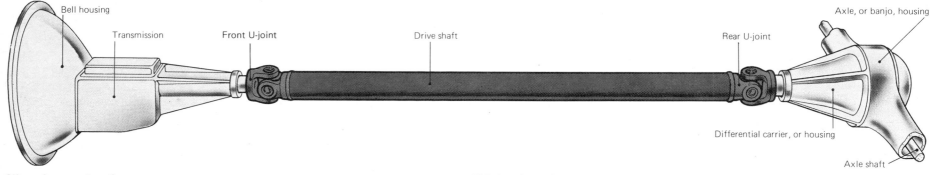

Slip-yoke construction

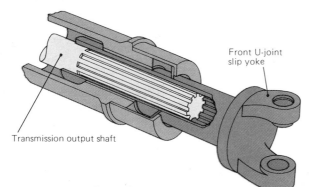

A slip yoke at the front of the first U-joint accommodates changes in drive shaft length as the rear axle assembly moves up and down with the rear suspension. Internal splines on the U-joint yoke slide in and out on the external splines of the transmission output shaft. This splined coupling also allows the drive shaft to be removed from the car when the rear U-joint is disconnected. The drive shaft may fall to the ground and be ruined if either U-joint breaks while the car is in motion.

U-joints in action

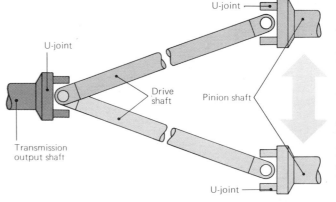

U-joints allow the angle of the drive shaft to change while the transmission output shaft and pinion shaft remain parallel. Some drive shafts are made in two short sections. They require an extra U-joint and must be supported at the center by a bracket and bearing. All the sections must be carefully balanced to avoid vibrations in the drive train. The onset of such vibrations and rattling noises, especially when the car accelerates or climbs hills, is often an early warning of U-joint failure.

Universal joints

The single U-joint is the most common. It consists of two yokes connected by a cross member. Power delivery through a U-joint is not smooth when the joint is operating at an angle. The joint vibrates as the output shaft speeds up and slows down twice during each revolution in order to accommodate the eccentric movements of the cross member, which cannot bend in every direction. The speed variation is proportional to the angle between the shafts. U-joints operate at angles as large as 12°. Combining two U-joints or adding a third joint to the drive shaft minimizes vibrations by halving the angle each must assume.

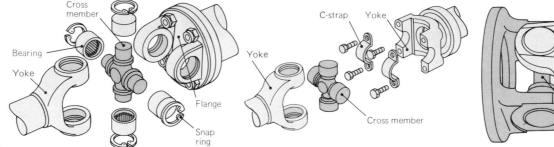

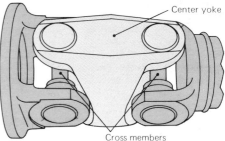

A single U-joint joins the forked ends of two shafts with a swiveling cross member. Roller bearings handle heavy torque loads with minimal friction. In this rear U-joint, the cross member is retained by snap rings, and the drive shaft is removed by first unbolting the flange.

In another design the yoke is bolted to the pinion shaft, and the cross member is held either by U-bolts that pass through the yoke or by steel C-straps that are bolted into holes tapped in the yoke. To remove a drive shaft with such U-joints, the cross member must be unbolted from the yoke.

A double U-joint combines two cross members with a double center yoke to reduce vibration by halving the angle each joint must accommodate. It is used to cope with angles ranging up to 12°. A centering ball equalizes the angles that the two halves of the joint assume.

Rear axles

An axle is a shaft or beam with a wheel at each end. Old cars had a simple beam axle between the front wheels, and modern front-wheel-drive cars often use a flexible-beam axle between the rear wheels.

Axles that transmit power are called *live axles*. A live axle assembly contains two *axle shafts* that transmit power from the differential gears to the wheels. Made of special alloy steel, these axle shafts have splines at their inner ends that fit into matching splines on the differential side gears (p.100). The outer end of each axle shaft is supported by a ball or roller bearing. The axle housing is usually a four-part assembly consisting of a two-piece cast-iron differential housing with a pair of steel axle tubes pressed into it. The two-piece differential housing can be unbolted for access to the gears.

The rear brake drum or disc is attached to the outer end of the axle shaft. Wheel-mounting *lugs* or bolts secure the wheel and the brake drum or disc to the axle flange. Most cars have lugs, because it is easier to change a wheel when there is something to hang it on. However, lugs can break, and on many cars the axle shaft must be removed to replace a lug.

The axle shaft is supported by a tapered roller bearing inside the axle housing. A second bearing supports the differential side gear, which holds the axle. Engineers call this configuration a *semi-floating axle*.

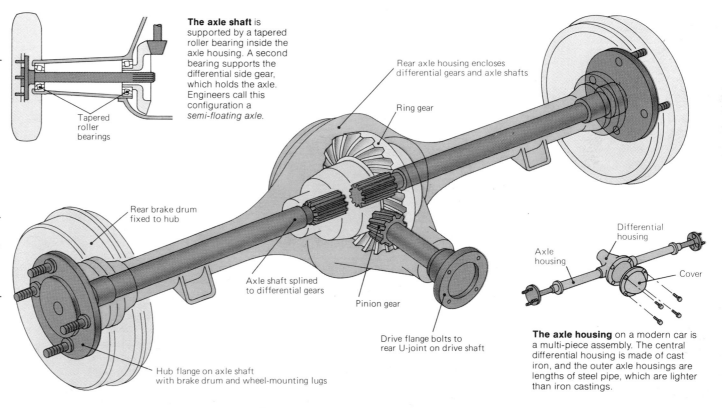

The axle housing on a modern car is a multi-piece assembly. The central differential housing is made of cast iron, and the outer axle housings are lengths of steel pipe, which are lighter than iron castings.

Passing power on to the wheels

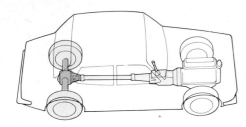

The *rear end* in a front-engine/rear-drive car is the last major link between the engine and wheels. It does three jobs: turning the flow of power 90 degrees, stepping down engine revolutions a final time, and dividing power flow between the rear wheels so that one wheel can turn faster in order to go the long way around the outside of a curve while the other slows down to follow the shorter inside path. The rear end is sometimes called the *final drive* or *differential*.

When a direct-drive transmission is in *High* gear, the drive shaft turns at the same speed as the engine—usually between 2,500 and 4,000 rpm at 55 mph (90 km/h). But at 55 mph the wheels and tires need to turn at only 600 to 950 rpm, depending on their size. The ring gear and pinion gear make this speed reduc-tion, as well as changing the direction of the power flow by 90 degrees.

It takes several revolutions of the pinion to turn the ring gear once. This gives the last gear reduction from engine speed to wheel speed—usually a ratio ranging from 2:1 to 4:1, depending on car size, weight, and use. *High gears* (low numerical ratios like 2:1) give good fuel economy, and *low gears* (high numerical

Main parts of a differential unit

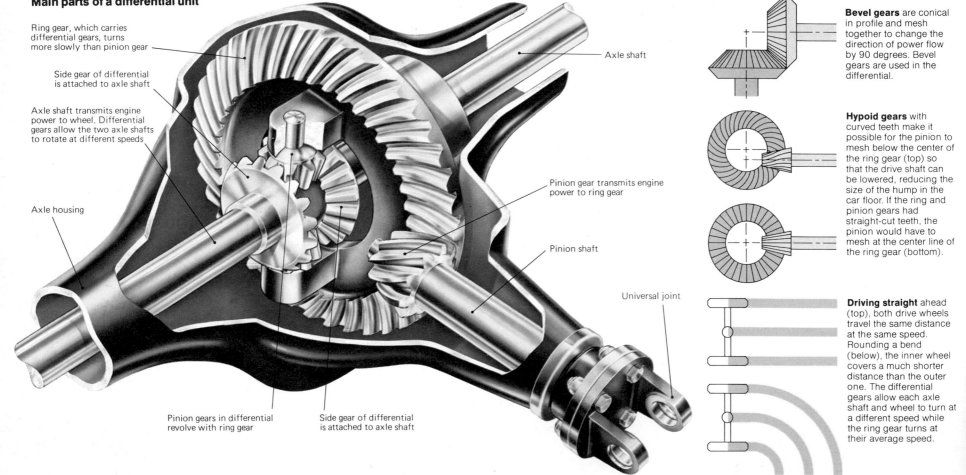

Ring gear, which carries differential gears, turns more slowly than pinion gear

Side gear of differential is attached to axle shaft

Axle shaft transmits engine power to wheel. Differential gears allow the two axle shafts to rotate at different speeds

Axle housing

Pinion gears in differential revolve with ring gear

Side gear of differential is attached to axle shaft

Axle shaft

Pinion gear transmits engine power to ring gear

Pinion shaft

Universal joint

Bevel gears are conical in profile and mesh together to change the direction of power flow by 90 degrees. Bevel gears are used in the differential.

Hypoid gears with curved teeth make it possible for the pinion to mesh below the center of the ring gear (top) so that the drive shaft can be lowered, reducing the size of the hump in the car floor. If the ring and pinion gears had straight-cut teeth, the pinion would have to mesh at the center line of the ring gear (bottom).

Driving straight ahead (top), both drive wheels travel the same distance at the same speed. Rounding a bend (below), the inner wheel covers a much shorter distance than the outer one. The differential gears allow each axle shaft and wheel to turn at a different speed while the ring gear turns at their average speed.

ratios like 4:1) increase acceleration and pulling power.

The ratio selected by car designers is a compromise between power and economy, always deliberately worked out to an odd number—for instance, not 4:1 but 4.11:1. The odd number means that a given tooth on the pinion mates with the same tooth on the ring gear less often than it would if the ratio were an even 4:1.

An imperfection on two matching teeth is therefore much less likely to cause a failure than if the two bad spots hit on every fourth revolution.

Dividing power between a fast-turning outside wheel and a slower-turning inside wheel is the job of the differential—four gears mounted in a cage that is turned by the ring gear. One side gear is splined to the end of each axle shaft. Two pinion gears are meshed with the side gears and attached to the cage. When the car is driven straight ahead, the ring gear turns the cage, which turns the pinions and the axles. When the car rounds a curve, the pinions roll around the side gears so that the inside wheel can turn more slowly and the outside one can speed up. The ring gear and cage turn at the average speed of the two wheels.

Limited-slip differential

Differential gears allow the wheels to turn at different speeds, but divide torque equally. If one wheel is on dry pavement and the other is on a patch of ice, the wheel on the ice will spin at twice the speed of the ring gear, while the wheel with traction does not move at all. Each wheel is getting the same tiny amount of torque needed to spin the wheel on the ice, and the car goes nowhere.

How the differential works

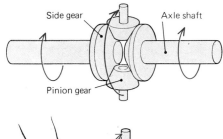

Side gear | Axle shaft

Pinion gear

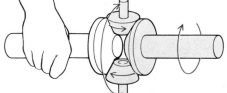

Ring gear

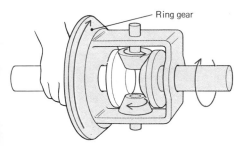

When the axle shafts turn at the same speed, the pinions orbit the side gears but do not revolve on their own axes (top). When one axle shaft is stopped (center), the other can still turn because the pinions roll around the stopped side gear while turning on their own axes. Side gears and pinions are mounted in a cage, which is turned by the ring gear (bottom). The axle shafts pass through this assembly and are splined to the side gears.

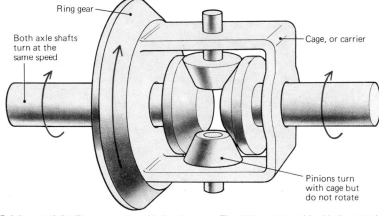

Ring gear

Both axle shafts turn at the same speed

Cage, or carrier

Pinions turn with cage but do not rotate

Driving straight: The cage turns with the ring gear. The pinion gears orbit with the cage but do not rotate, thus driving the side gears and axle shafts.

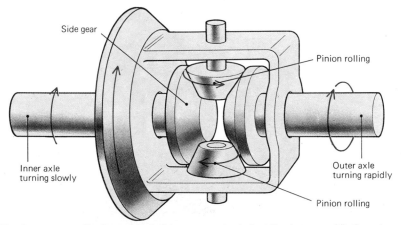

Side gear

Pinion rolling

Inner axle turning slowly

Outer axle turning rapidly

Pinion rolling

Turning a corner: The inner axle shaft turns more slowly than the ring gear while the outer axle shaft, driven by the pinions, revolves correspondingly faster.

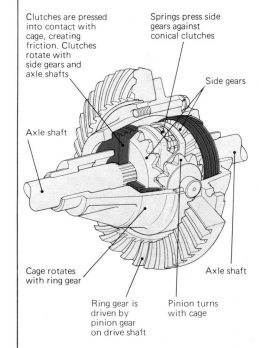

Clutches are pressed into contact with cage, creating friction. Clutches rotate with side gears and axle shafts

Springs press side gears against conical clutches

Side gears

Axle shaft

Cage rotates with ring gear

Axle shaft

Ring gear is driven by pinion gear on drive shaft

Pinion turns with cage

A limited-slip differential contains clutches that limit the movement of the side gears. Springs between the side gears force them outward against the clutches, which in turn are forced against the cage. The friction of the clutches tends to cause the cage and side gears to rotate at the same speed, but the springs are not strong enough to prevent normal differential action on curves. When one wheel is on a slippery spot, however, the clutches will limit the differential action, and some torque will be passed along to the wheel with traction so that the car can move on to firmer ground.

Front-wheel drive

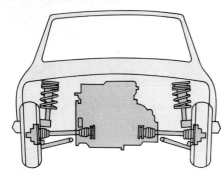

The idea of pulling a car by the front wheels instead of pushing it from behind has intrigued car designers for years. The main advantage of front-wheel drive is that it concentrates all the mechanical parts into a compact package in the nose, leaving up to 80 percent of the car's volume free to accommodate passengers and luggage. Putting the engine weight over the drive wheels also improves stability and traction.

Combining the engine, transmission, and differential in one package eliminates the drive shaft and the hump in the floor that is needed for drive shaft clearance. Axle shafts connect the differential to the front wheels. Both ends of these shafts have constant-velocity (CV) joints which, unlike U-joints, produce smooth, vibration-free rotation even when they are bent at large angles.

Manual transmissions for front-drive cars are usually the all-indirect type (see p.103). Power enters and leaves the transmission at the same end. The output shaft drives the differential's bevel ring gear directly if the engine is mounted longitudinally. It drives a helical differential gear if the engine is mounted transversely. Automatic transmissions in front-drive cars are often driven by heavy chains similar to those used to drive the camshafts on many engines.

Smaller front-drive cars have four-cylinder or V-6 engines placed trans-versely, with the transmission in line with the engine. Axles of different length behind the engine-transmission package drive the front wheels. General Motors automatics have the transmission alongside the engine.

Nearly all front-drive cars use some version of MacPherson strut front suspension, and some have fully independent rear suspensions as well, to increase passenger and luggage space and to improve ride and handling.

Front drive saves weight by eliminating the drive shaft and live axle, but it requires relatively expensive CV joints and complex transmissions. The axle shafts should be of equal length so that the amount of torsional windup is the same on both sides of the car. Otherwise, steering would be affected every time the amount of torque transmitted to the axle shafts was increased or decreased.

It is often convenient to place the engine, clutch, and transmission in a line across the width of the car, which results in axle shafts of different length. There are two ways to resolve this problem: The engineer can make the short shaft solid and the longer one hollow so that both wind up at the same rate. Or he can design two similar axles with a short connecting shaft between them. Volkswagen, Honda, Chrysler, and small GM front-drive cars have transverse engines with axle shafts of unequal length. Ford's Fiesta and GM's longitudinal front-drive V-6s and V-8s use connecting shafts.

The axle shafts turn the CV joints that drive stub axles to turn the wheels. These stub axles fit through hubs in the front suspension, which support the car's weight. Since the bearings in these hubs must also handle steering loads, maintain wheel alignment, and transfer road shocks to the suspension, they must be robust and precise. Special twin-row ball bearings or two single-row bearings pressed into the hub do the job.

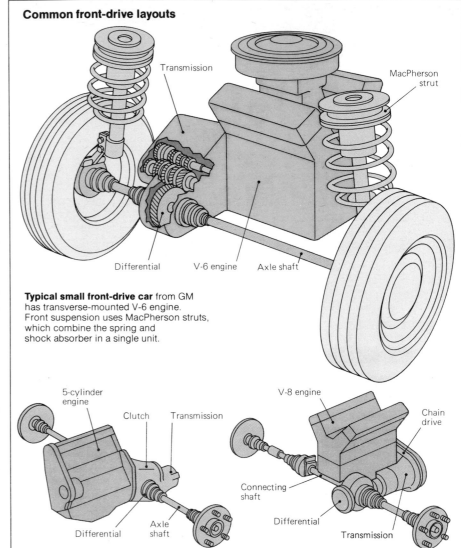

Common front-drive layouts

Typical small front-drive car from GM has transverse-mounted V-6 engine. Front suspension uses MacPherson struts, which combine the spring and shock absorber in a single unit.

Two popular front-drive variations: The larger Audi-Volkswagen sedans have four-, five-, or six-cylinder engines, mounted longitudinally, and front-wheel drive (left). Big GM V-6s and V-8s with front-wheel drive place the engine longitudinally (right). The torque converter is at the rear of the engine; the chain-driven automatic transmission is alongside it. The differential is in front of the transmission, and one axle shaft passes under the engine oil pan.

Transmitting power to the steering wheels

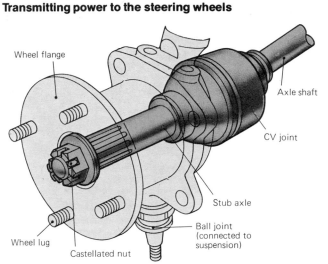

Wheel flange

Axle shaft

CV joint

Stub axle

Ball joint (connected to suspension)

Wheel lug

Castellated nut

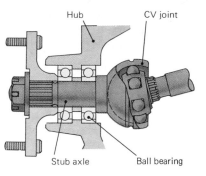

Hub

CV joint

Stub axle

Ball bearing

Short stub axles transmit power from the CV joints to the front wheels. The stub axles are typically supported by ball bearings. The wheels are bolted to flanges that are splined to the stub axles and locked in place with castellated nuts. The inner end of each stub axle is part of the CV joint, which is driven by the final drive via the axle shaft.

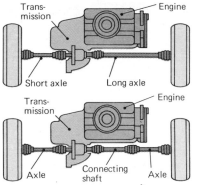

Transmission

Engine

Short axle

Long axle

Transmission

Engine

Axle

Connecting shaft

Axle

Drive axles are of different lengths in most front-drive cars (top). In order for both axles to have equal torque windup, the longer axle can be thicker than the short axle, or it can be hollow. Another solution is to design axles of equal length and to connect them by another shaft placed between the differential and one axle (bottom).

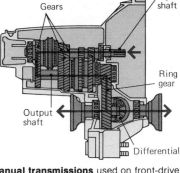

Gears

Input shaft

Ring gear

Output shaft

Differential

Manual transmissions used on front-drive cars are usually all-indirect designs. Power flows from the clutch, along the input shaft, through a pair of engaged gears, and back out the same end of the transmission. The differential ring gear is driven by a gear on the transmission output shaft, rather than by a pinion gear and drive shaft.

Constant-velocity joints

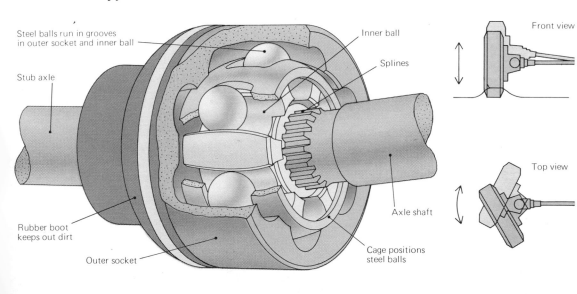

Steel balls run in grooves in outer socket and inner ball

Stub axle

Rubber boot keeps out dirt

Outer socket

Inner ball

Splines

Axle shaft

Cage positions steel balls

Front view

Top view

CV joints transmit torque between angled shafts with less vibration than U-joints do. Steel balls link the major parts of the CV joint. The axle shaft is splined to the inner part of the joint to allow changes in axle length as the suspension moves up and down. A U-joint could handle the small angles involved in suspension movement (upper right), or the large angles involved in steering (lower right), but a CV joint is needed to smoothly transmit power through both angles.

Front suspension

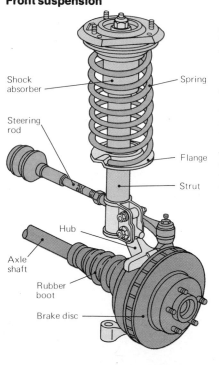

Shock absorber

Spring

Steering rod

Flange

Strut

Hub

Axle shaft

Rubber boot

Brake disc

MacPherson strut suspension is used on most front-drive cars. The main advantage is compactness. A tubular strut serves as the upper suspension link between the wheel and body of the car. The coil spring rests on a flange welded to the strut, and the shock absorber is located in the center of the spring and strut. The axle shaft passes through the hub to the brake disc. The disadvantage of this design is that the spring and brake must often be removed to replace the shock absorber. On this GM design the strut can be unbolted from the steering hub, so the brake need not be removed. On some Ford designs the spring is mounted next to the strut, greatly simplifying replacement of the shock absorber.

Four-wheel drive

The typical four-wheel-drive vehicle is an outgrowth of the World War II jeep. Its front-mounted engine drives the rear wheels through a conventional transmission, drive shaft, and rear axle with leaf-spring suspension. A *transfer case* mounted between the transmission and drive shaft contains a two-speed transmission that provides an extra-low range of gears. These gears supply additional torque for climbing steep hills, for traveling at very low speeds across rugged terrain, or for towing heavy loads.

The transfer case also transfers engine torque to a second drive shaft that runs forward to another differential and axle, mounted on leaf springs. This unit looks like a standard rear axle, but its differential housing is mounted off center, and it has U-joints at the outer ends of the axle shafts, to allow the wheels to steer.

The front and rear wheels cover different distances when a vehicle turns. This makes no difference when driving on dirt or ice, because the wheels that cover the shorter paths are free to spin slightly, eliminating the need for any differential action. On pavement, the front wheels of a part-time four-wheel-drive system must be disengaged to prevent tire wear or damage to the drive train.

Full-time four-wheel-drive systems have a differential in the transfer case, as well as the usual differential in each axle. This allows the use of four-wheel drive on pavement, but it has limitations: If total traction is lost at any one wheel, all the torque will be delivered to that wheel and the vehicle will be immobilized until the driver locks up the transfer case differential by means of a lever inside the vehicle. If a limited-slip differential is used in the transfer case, traction must be lost at both a front wheel and a rear wheel in order to stop the vehicle.

Special *off-road* tires give maximum traction on dirt, sand, mud, snow, or ice for cross-country driving.

Conventional four-wheel drive

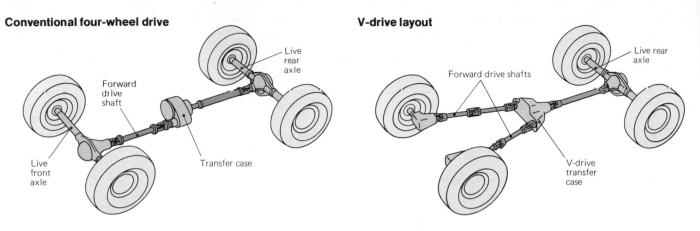

Live rear axle

Forward drive shaft

Live front axle

Transfer case

Typical four-wheel-drive system looks similar to that used on U.S. Army jeeps. Transfer case and forward drive shaft supply torque to the front wheels. Live axles and leaf springs are used front and rear on truck-like vehicles. Some automotive applications have independent front suspensions. There are two basic systems: full-time and part-time four-wheel drive.

V-drive layout

Live rear axle

Forward drive shafts

V-drive transfer case

V-drive system permits the use of independent front suspension for better ride, handling, and traction than the conventional four-wheel-drive system. Because the front drive shafts skirt the engine, vehicle ride height does not have to be raised to install this system. A two-speed transfer case is not available with V-drive. The system is an aftermarket conversion, not a factory-installed option.

Transmitting power to the front wheels

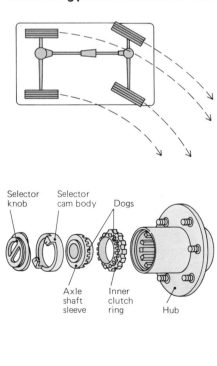

Selector knob

Selector cam body

Dogs

Axle shaft sleeve

Inner clutch ring

Hub

When a vehicle rounds a bend, each wheel covers a different distance. A differential in each axle allows the outer and inner wheels to cover varying distances. If there is no differential in the transfer case, one pair of wheels must be able to spin slightly, or the drive train will be damaged.

Locking hubs allow the front wheels to be disconnected from the drive train to reduce wear and drag after a vehicle has been shifted into two-wheel drive. A dog clutch connects the axle shaft to the wheel hub; ramps on the selector knob force the dogs in and out of engagement.

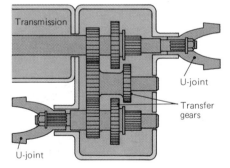

Transmission

U-joint

Transfer gears

U-joint

Transfer case is the heart of a four-wheel-drive system. Gears or a chain transfer torque to the forward drive shaft. Most models also incorporate a two-speed transmission, which can provide high or low overall gearing in four-wheel drive, or rear-wheel drive only, eliminating the need for locking hubs. Full-time four-wheel-drive transfer case has a differential.

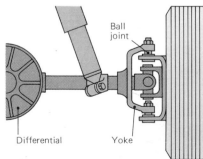

Ball joint

Differential

Yoke

A yoke on the axle housing supports two ball joints that allow the steering knuckle to pivot. Because of the rigid axle, the front wheels pivot only in one plane; they do not change angle with suspension movements, as they would on a car with front-wheel drive. A simple U-joint can therefore be used instead of an expensive constant-velocity joint.

How the brakes stop a car

Brakes stop a car by forcing a high-friction material against spinning iron discs or drums that are bolted to the wheels. This friction causes the car to slow and, eventually, to stop.

Two kinds of brakes are used on modern cars—*disc* brakes and *drum* brakes. Disc brakes work by forcing pads of friction material against the sides of a spinning iron disc. Drum brakes work by forcing curved lengths of friction material against the inside of an iron drum. Of the two, disc brakes are the more effective because the disc is exposed to a cooling flow of air.

When the friction material (called brake *lining*) rubs against the brake disc or drum, it creates heat. If this heat cannot be dissipated fast enough, the brake overheats and ceases to function. This phenomenon is called *brake fade*.

The front brakes supply up to 80 percent of a car's stopping power, making them more susceptible to overheating than the rear brakes. Because disc brakes are less inclined to fade, they are used on the front wheels of most cars. Some high-performance cars and heavy luxury cars have disc brakes on all four wheels.

The friction material is pressed against the brake disc or drum by a hydraulic system. The brake pedal is attached to a master cylinder, and each brake is operated by a wheel cylinder. These cylinders are connected by a system of pipes and hoses filled with hydraulic fluid.

Hydraulic brakes work on the principle that pressure on a liquid in a closed system is equal throughout the system. When the driver pushes the brake pedal, a piston moves against the fluid in the master cylinder, and this applies equal

force at all four wheel cylinders. Pistons inside the wheel cylinders press the linings against the discs or drums.

The hydraulic system can also increase the pressure applied by the wheel cylinders. If the surface area of the piston in the master cylinder is half that of the pistons in the wheel cylinders, the pressure applied to the wheel cylinders doubles. But the distance the wheel cylinder piston travels will be only half that of the master cylinder's piston. Since only a tiny movement is needed to press the linings against the disc or drum, 2 inches of pedal movement can greatly increase the pressure that the driver's leg muscles apply to the brake pedal.

In addition, leverage in the brake pedal can be employed to double or triple the pressure applied to the master cylinder by the driver's leg. Power brakes increase

this even further by using engine vacuum to multiply the force applied to the master cylinder by the brake pedal.

The *parking brake* holds the car in place when it is not being driven. It is a mechanical system of levers and cables that applies the rear brakes. A foot pedal or hand lever applies the brakes, and a ratchet gear holds them on. A knob or button disengages the ratchet and releases the brakes. The system is mechanical because hydraulic systems tend to leak slightly if made to hold high pressure for long periods of time.

A light on the dashboard tells the driver when the parking brake is on. It also serves as a warning light to signal the loss of pressure in the hydraulic system, either because of a leak or because the fluid level is low in the master cylinder's fluid reservoir.

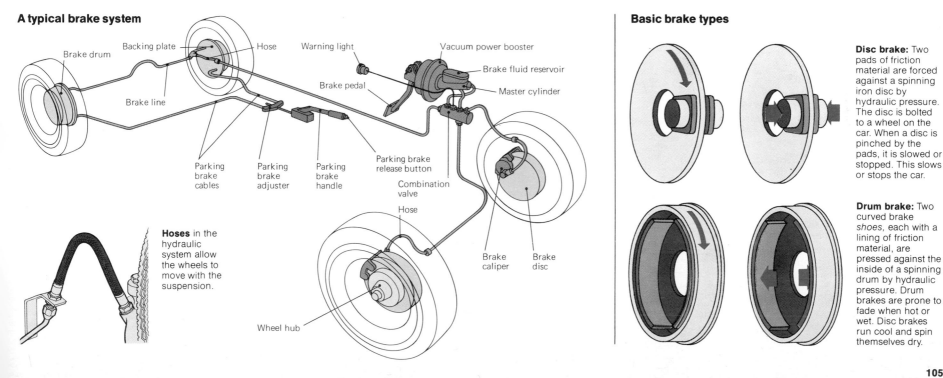

A typical brake system

Brake drum · Backing plate · Hose · Warning light · Vacuum power booster · Brake fluid reservoir · Brake pedal · Master cylinder · Brake line · Parking brake cables · Parking brake adjuster · Parking brake handle · Parking brake release button · Combination valve · Hose · Wheel hub · Brake caliper · Brake disc

Hoses in the hydraulic system allow the wheels to move with the suspension.

Basic brake types

Disc brake: Two pads of friction material are forced against a spinning iron disc by hydraulic pressure. The disc is bolted to a wheel on the car. When a disc is pinched by the pads, it is slowed or stopped. This slows or stops the car.

Drum brake: Two curved brake *shoes*, each with a lining of friction material, are pressed against the inside of a spinning drum by hydraulic pressure. Drum brakes are prone to fade when hot or wet. Disc brakes run cool and spin themselves dry.

Disc brakes

A disc brake consists of a cast-iron disc, or *rotor,* and a *caliper* that clamps friction pads against it. The rotor turns with the wheel. The caliper is mounted on the front suspension.

Most disc brakes have *sliding calipers.* These are mounted so that they can slide from side to side a fraction of an inch. When the driver steps on the brake pedal, hydraulic pressure pushes on a piston inside the caliper and it pushes the brake pad against the rotor. Reaction to this pressure moves the whole caliper on its mounting, pulling the other brake pad against the rotor, too.

Older cars used *fixed-caliper* brakes, which required two or four hydraulic cylinders per wheel. The single cylinder makes the sliding-caliper brake cheaper to manufacture and more reliable because it has fewer hydraulic seals.

The big advantage of disc brakes is their freedom from fade. Brakes fade when they get so hot that the lining material loses its high-friction qualities. Disc brakes transfer heat to the air more rapidly than enclosed drums do. As it heats up and expands, the rotor becomes fatter, thus increasing the pressure against the pads, rather than expanding away from the linings, as a drum can. Water and dirt are thrown off the rotor by centrifugal force, which makes for even braking under adverse conditions.

The disadvantages of disc brakes, compared to drum brakes, include the lack of any built-in *servo,* or power-increasing ability. Disc-brake pads are smaller than drum-brake shoes, so that disc linings wear faster. However, power-brake boosters make disc brakes easy to apply, and easily removed sliding calipers make pad changes simple.

Some disc brakes have pad-wear indicators. The most common type has a spring mounted on the pad. When the pad wears down, the spring rubs on the rotor and squeals.

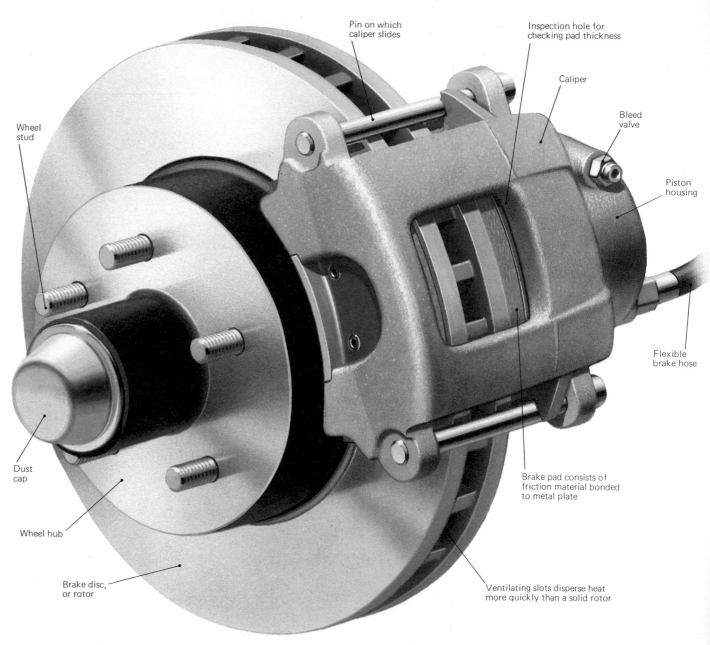

Pin on which caliper slides

Inspection hole for checking pad thickness

Caliper

Wheel stud

Bleed valve

Piston housing

Flexible brake hose

Dust cap

Wheel hub

Brake disc, or rotor

Brake pad consists of friction material bonded to metal plate

Ventilating slots disperse heat more quickly than a solid rotor

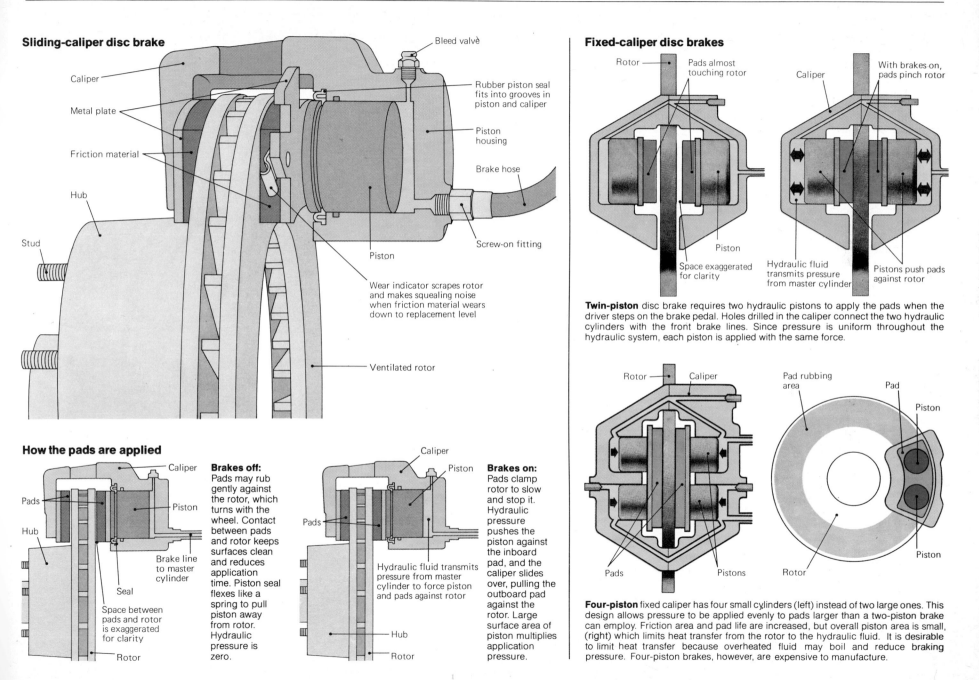

Sliding-caliper disc brake

Bleed valve

Caliper

Metal plate

Rubber piston seal fits into grooves in piston and caliper

Friction material

Piston housing

Hub

Brake hose

Stud

Screw-on fitting

Piston

Wear indicator scrapes rotor and makes squealing noise when friction material wears down to replacement level

Ventilated rotor

How the pads are applied

Caliper

Pads

Piston

Hub

Brake line to master cylinder

Seal

Space between pads and rotor is exaggerated for clarity

Rotor

Brakes off:
Pads may rub gently against the rotor, which turns with the wheel. Contact between pads and rotor keeps surfaces clean and reduces application time. Piston seal flexes like a spring to pull piston away from rotor. Hydraulic pressure is zero.

Caliper

Piston

Pads

Hydraulic fluid transmits pressure from master cylinder to force piston and pads against rotor

Hub

Rotor

Brakes on:
Pads clamp rotor to slow and stop it. Hydraulic pressure pushes the piston against the inboard pad, and the caliper slides over, pulling the outboard pad against the rotor. Large surface area of piston multiplies application pressure.

Fixed-caliper disc brakes

Rotor

Pads almost touching rotor

Caliper

With brakes on, pads pinch rotor

Piston

Space exaggerated for clarity

Hydraulic fluid transmits pressure from master cylinder

Pistons push pads against rotor

Twin-piston disc brake requires two hydraulic pistons to apply the pads when the driver steps on the brake pedal. Holes drilled in the caliper connect the two hydraulic cylinders with the front brake lines. Since pressure is uniform throughout the hydraulic system, each piston is applied with the same force.

Rotor

Caliper

Pad rubbing area

Pad

Piston

Pads

Pistons

Rotor

Piston

Four-piston fixed caliper has four small cylinders (left) instead of two large ones. This design allows pressure to be applied evenly to pads larger than a two-piston brake can employ. Friction area and pad life are increased, but overall piston area is small, (right) which limits heat transfer from the rotor to the hydraulic fluid. It is desirable to limit heat transfer because overheated fluid may boil and reduce braking pressure. Four-piston brakes, however, are expensive to manufacture.

Drum brakes

Drum brakes use a pair of semicircular *shoes* that rub against the inside surface of a metal *drum* to slow and stop the car. The drum turns with the wheel. The shoes are mounted on a *backing plate* that is attached to the axle housing or suspension so that it does not turn. When the driver steps on the brake pedal, hydraulic pressure is developed in the master cylinder and delivered to each wheel cylinder. The *wheel cylinders* push one end of each brake shoe against the drum. The other end of the brake shoe is supported by a pivot point called the *anchor*.

The anchor often incorporates the *brake adjuster*. As the friction material lining the shoes wears down, the shoes must be moved closer to the drum in order to maintain full braking force. This is done by a screw-type adjuster that moves the pivot points closer to the drums. On some cars this adjustment must be made manually at intervals of 3,000 to 6,000 miles (5,000 to 10,000 km).

Most modern cars have disc brakes on the front wheels and drum brakes at the rear. Disc brakes are all self-adjusting, so it makes sense to incorporate self-adjusters in the rear drums that must work with them. Self-adjusters usually operate whenever the brakes are applied while the car is backing up.

WORKING PARTS OF A DRUM BRAKE

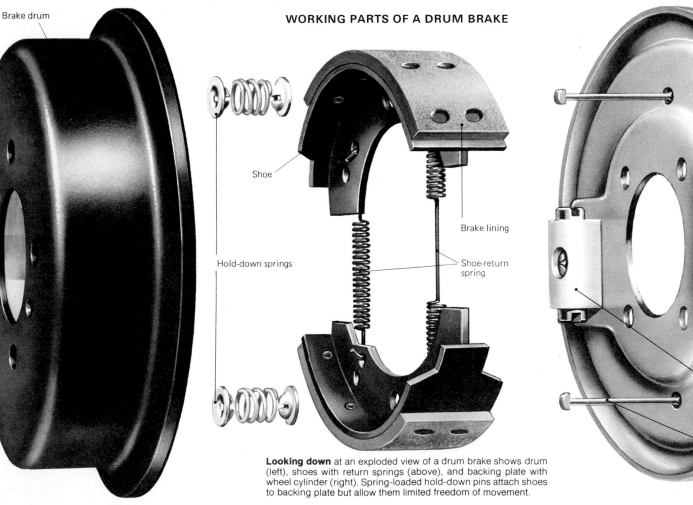

Brake drum

Shoe

Hold-down springs

Brake lining

Shoe-return spring

Backing plate

Brake bleeder

Hydraulic line

Wheel cylinder

Anchor with wedge-type manual adjuster

Brake shoe hold-down pin

Looking down at an exploded view of a drum brake shows drum (left), shoes with return springs (above), and backing plate with wheel cylinder (right). Spring-loaded hold-down pins attach shoes to backing plate but allow them limited freedom of movement.

How servo action increases braking force

Drum brakes can use the rotation of the drum to help apply the shoes. This force-multiplying *servo* action occurs if the friction between the drum and the shoe tends to push the shoe against its pivot point. The drum, in attempting to drag the shoe along with it, pivots the shoe further, increasing the application force between drum and shoe. Such a shoe is called a *primary*, or *leading*, shoe by auto engineers and mechanics.

If the friction between the drum and shoe tends to pull the shoe away from its pivot point, the shoe will swing away from the pivot, and braking force will decrease. Such a shoe is called a *secondary*, or *trailing*, shoe.

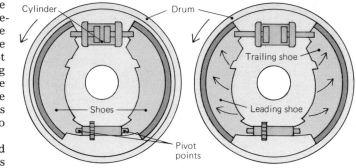

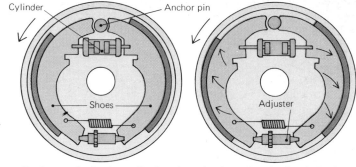

Single-servo brake has shoes that pivot outward from two fixed points (left). Drag from the rotating drum tends to swing the leading shoe around its pivot, increasing pressure between the shoe and the drum (right). The trailing shoe is pushed away from its pivot by drum rotation, decreasing its effectiveness. Backing the car reverses the roles of the leading and trailing shoes.

Dual-servo brake has a fixed anchor pin above the wheel cylinder (left). When the brakes are applied, the shoes shift (right). One shoe pivots on the anchor pin, which increases its braking force. The other shoe pivots on the adjuster, which increases its braking force too. If the driver brakes while backing up, the shoes shift in the opposite direction.

How drum brakes adjust themselves

Disc brakes never need adjustment because the brake pads do not retract very far from the rotors. Each time the brake is applied, the piston is pushed out, and it assumes a new position, which compensates for pad wear.

As the linings on drum brakes wear, the shoes must be adjusted so that they remain close enough to the drums to be applied by the wheel cylinder. The most common adjusting mechanism is a small jackscrew that is turned by a *star wheel*. On a few cars, this wheel must be turned by hand at periodic intervals. Most cars use a rod- or cable-operated *adjuster lever* that turns the star wheel automatically. Each time the brakes are applied when the car is backing up, the rod or cable raises the adjuster lever. When the brakes are released, a spring pulls the lever back down. When the linings wear down to a certain point, the lever is raised enough to engage the next tooth on the star wheel. When the spring pulls the adjuster lever back down, it engages the next tooth on the star wheel and turns the wheel, bringing the brake shoes that much closer to the brake drum.

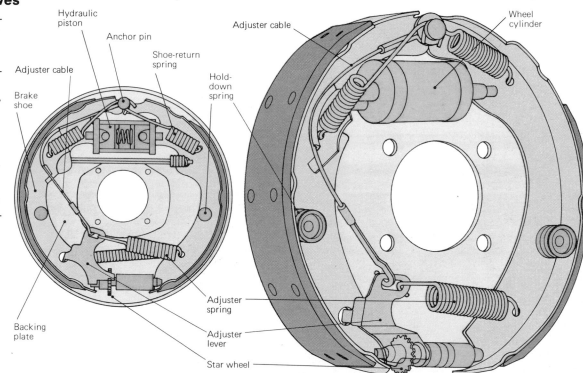

Most brakes are adjusted by turning a star wheel, which advances the adjusting screw to bring the shoes closer to the drums. In self-adjusting brakes an adjuster lever, operated by a rod or cable, rests against a tooth on the star wheel. On this Bendix design, used in Ford cars, a cable raises the adjuster lever whenever the brake shoes shift as the car stops in reverse. As the linings wear down, the shoes shift farther at each stop. When enough wear has occurred, the lever is raised so far that it engages the next tooth on the star wheel. The lever return spring then causes the lever to advance the star wheel by one tooth. Some designs raise the lever whenever the parking brake is set, rather than when the car backs up.

Power brakes

Power brake boosters help the driver push the brake pedal. Most designs utilize vacuum from the engine's intake manifold to develop the power.

The vacuum power booster is a round, stamped-steel canister mounted on the fire wall between the brake pedal linkage and the hydraulic system's master cylinder. Inside the canister are a rubber diaphragm, a return spring, and some valves. The valve-operating rod, which is

moved by the brake pedal, pushes on the end of another rod that moves the master cylinder pistons. If the power booster fails, the brakes will still work. However, it takes greatly increased pressure on the pedal, perhaps all the driver's weight, to operate the brakes if the booster fails. People may mistakenly assume that they have no brakes in these circumstances.

Equal vacuum is supplied to both sides of the diaphragm until the driver steps on

the brake pedal. This moves the operating rod, opening the atmospheric port as it closes the vacuum port. Air at normal atmospheric pressure (14.7 psi, or 101 kPa) enters the chamber on the back side of the diaphragm in proportion to the valve openings. This pushes on the diaphragm to augment the pressure on the operating rod from the driver's foot. When the brake pedal is released, the return spring recenters the diaphragm, opening the

vacuum port and closing the atmospheric port to reestablish equal vacuum on both sides of the diaphragm. Diesel engines and turbocharged gasoline engines produce no vacuum in their intake manifolds. Power brakes and other vacuum-operated accessories on these vehicles can be run by an engine-driven vacuum pump. Some cars have no vacuum booster but use a hydraulic brake booster pressurized by the power steering pump.

Vacuum power booster assembly

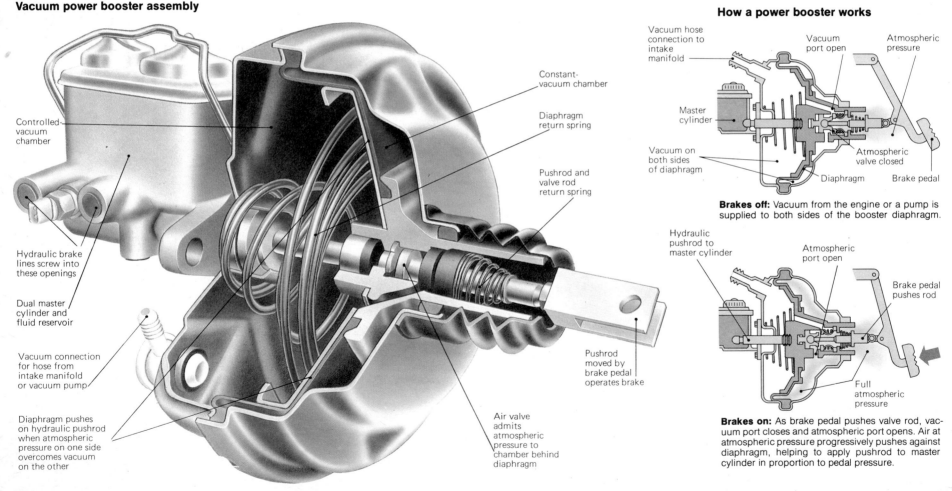

Controlled-vacuum chamber

Hydraulic brake lines screw into these openings

Dual master cylinder and fluid reservoir

Vacuum connection for hose from intake manifold or vacuum pump

Diaphragm pushes on hydraulic pushrod when atmospheric pressure on one side overcomes vacuum on the other

Constant-vacuum chamber

Diaphragm return spring

Pushrod and valve rod return spring

Pushrod moved by brake pedal operates brake

Air valve admits atmospheric pressure to chamber behind diaphragm

How a power booster works

Vacuum hose connection to intake manifold

Vacuum port open

Atmospheric pressure

Master cylinder

Vacuum on both sides of diaphragm

Atmospheric valve closed

Diaphragm

Brake pedal

Brakes off: Vacuum from the engine or a pump is supplied to both sides of the booster diaphragm.

Hydraulic pushrod to master cylinder

Atmospheric port open

Brake pedal pushes rod

Full atmospheric pressure

Brakes on: As brake pedal pushes valve rod, vacuum port closes and atmospheric port opens. Air at atmospheric pressure progressively pushes against diaphragm, helping to apply pushrod to master cylinder in proportion to pedal pressure.

Fail-safe hydraulic brake systems

Simple hydraulic brake systems are quite reliable. However, any leak in the system can result in a complete loss of the car's braking ability. Thus, on the theory that two independent brake systems on the same vehicle are not likely to fail at the same time, major car manufacturers have been installing *dual* brake systems in their vehicles since the mid-1960s.

The master cylinder of a dual brake system has two pistons. These move in tandem when the brake pedal is depressed. Each piston pressurizes its own half of the split hydraulic system and applies braking power to two of the car's wheels. In diagonally split systems, the left front and right rear brakes, and the right front and left rear brakes, are coupled. In front-to-rear split systems, the front and rear brakes are paired with each other.

The efficiency of either system is improved by the inclusion of valves in the brake lines between the master cylinder and the wheels. These are:

A *pressure-differential valve,* shown at

bottom right, is also known as a brake failure warning switch. It is located below the master cylinder. This valve lights a bulb on the dash if either half of the system loses hydraulic pressure. On most cars it is easy to check whether the bulb is working, because it doubles as a parking-brake warning light.

A *metering valve,* used only on disc brake systems, causes the rear brakes to be applied before the front ones. If the front wheels are braked first, the car could be thrown into a skid.

A *proportioning valve,* used only on front-to-rear split brake systems, restricts hydraulic pressure to the rear brakes so that the rear wheels will not lock during a hard stop, thus causing a skid.

A *combination valve* (or control valve) is a pressure-differential valve, metering valve, and proportioning valve combined into a single unit. Combination valves are fitted in most large, late-model North American cars and are found below the master cylinder.

Dual master cylinder with pressure-differential valve

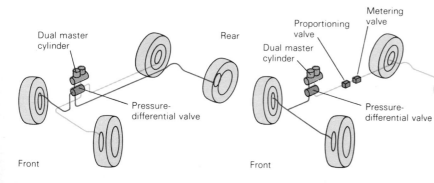

Dual diagonal split is commonly used on front-drive cars. The front suspension is designed to lessen the car's tendency to swerve toward the working front brake, in the event that either half of the brake system springs a leak and fails.

Front-to-rear split is commonly employed on dual brake systems in rear-drive automobiles and in some earlier front-drive models. Front brake loss decreases stopping ability markedly, while rear brake loss tends to affect it considerably less.

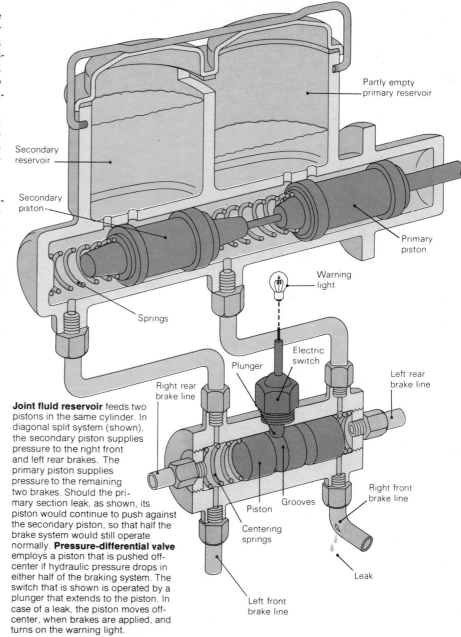

Joint fluid reservoir feeds two pistons in the same cylinder. In diagonal split system (shown), the secondary piston supplies pressure to the right front and left rear brakes. The primary piston supplies pressure to the remaining two brakes. Should the primary section leak, as shown, its piston would continue to push against the secondary piston, so that half the brake system would still operate normally. **Pressure-differential valve** employs a piston that is pushed off-center if hydraulic pressure drops in either half of the braking system. The switch that is shown is operated by a plunger that extends to the piston. In case of a leak, the piston moves off-center, when brakes are applied, and turns on the warning light.

111

How your car rolls on wheels and hubs

Most wheels are made of stamped-steel parts that are welded together. Wire wheels and one-piece cast or forged aluminum wheels (sometimes called *mag wheels*) are available as options on many cars. Magnesium wheels are sometimes used on racing cars to save weight, but they are impractical on the highway because road salt corrodes them in time.

A stamped-steel wheel is made up of two parts called the *rim* and the *center*.

The wheel center is offset to one side to make room for suspension and brake components. It is attached to the hub by bolts with conical heads called *lugs*, or by conical *lug nuts* that fit on *studs*. The mounting holes in the wheel center are also conical so that the lugs or lug nuts can position the wheel accurately. Ventilating holes in the wheel help to keep the brakes cool.

The rim has a *drop center*, or *well*, so that one bead of the tire can fit down into it when the other bead is forced over the *flange*, or *rim wall*, as the tire is installed. Air pressure then seats the tire bead on the rim flanges, which often have *safety ribs*–raised ribs between the flange and the well that help keep the tire in place if it should go flat while the car is moving.

Aluminum wheels are sometimes secured by special lug nuts with separate conical sections. These nuts can be tightened without galling the mounting holes.

Wire wheels are still offered as options on some sports cars and luxury models. Wire spokes in tension support the car's weight; that is, the weight of the car hangs from the spokes at the top of the rim rather than being supported by the spokes below the hub. Wire wheels may be mounted on special splined hubs with a single large nut or on conventional hubs with several small lugs.

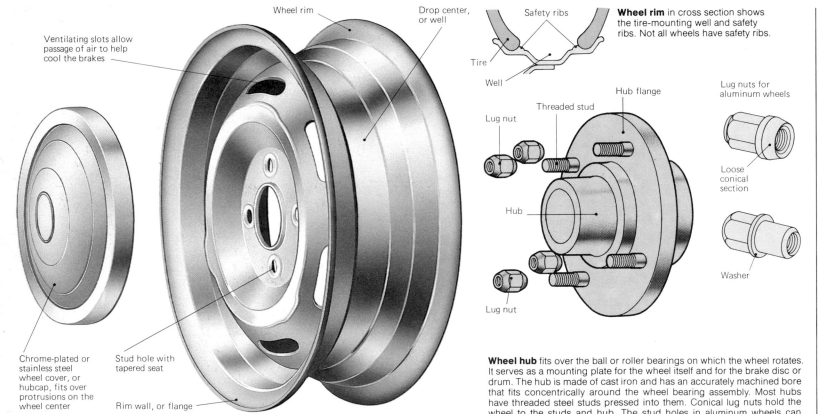

Wheel rim

Drop center, or well

Ventilating slots allow passage of air to help cool the brakes

Safety ribs

Wheel rim in cross section shows the tire-mounting well and safety ribs. Not all wheels have safety ribs.

Tire

Well

Chrome-plated or stainless steel wheel cover, or hubcap, fits over protrusions on the wheel center

Stud hole with tapered seat

Rim wall, or flange

Lug nut

Threaded stud

Hub flange

Lug nuts for aluminum wheels

Hub

Loose conical section

Lug nut

Washer

Stamped-steel wheel for mass-produced automobile has a rolled-steel rim around a stamped center. The center hole fits over the front or rear hub, but the wheel is positioned by the mounting bolts or by lug nuts. Bolts and lug nuts fit into conical holes precisely located to make the wheel run true.

Wheel hub fits over the ball or roller bearings on which the wheel rotates. It serves as a mounting plate for the wheel itself and for the brake disc or drum. The hub is made of cast iron and has an accurately machined bore that fits concentrically around the wheel bearing assembly. Most hubs have threaded steel studs pressed into them. Conical lug nuts hold the wheel to the studs and hub. The stud holes in aluminum wheels can become galled when the lug nuts are tightened and loosened, so special nuts are used with these wheels. Some have conical sections that do not turn with the hexagonal head of the nut (top). Others use a flat washer between the nut and wheel (bottom). Bolts secure the wheel on a few foreign cars. Some hubs and brake drums (or discs) are one-piece units.

Wheel types

Styled steel wheel

Wire wheel

Cast aluminum wheel

How wheel bearings help the wheels revolve

Roller or ball bearings reduce friction so that the wheels on a car can turn freely. *Tapered roller bearings* replaced *ball bearings* in wheel hubs many years ago because rollers can handle heavier loads and higher speeds. Improved ball bearings are now replacing rollers in the newest hubs. They reduce rolling friction (and therefore fuel consumption) and eliminate periodic adjustments to the wheel bearings as a required service.

On free-rolling wheels—the front wheels on a rear-drive car or the rear wheels on a front-drive car—the bearings are mounted on a *spindle*, or *stub axle*, incorporated in the suspension. The spindle does not rotate. Each hub assembly has a large inner ball or roller bearing, and a smaller outer bearing: The hub on which the wheel is mounted turns on these bearings. A *thrust washer*, an *adjusting nut*, and a locking device make it

possible to adjust and maintain a tapered roller bearing's clearance. Special wheel bearing grease is packed into the bearings when they are assembled to lubricate them. A *grease seal* keeps this grease out of the brakes.

Hubs with permanently lubricated, factory-assembled ball bearings are common on front-drive cars. These bearing assemblies require no service and are replaced as a unit if they fail.

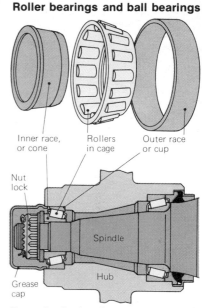

Roller bearings and ball bearings

Inner race, or cone — Rollers in cage — Outer race or cup

Nut lock

Spindle

Grease cap

Hub

Tapered roller bearings on a nonrotating spindle are typical on freewheeling hubs. They require periodic service, but individual parts can be replaced if they fail.

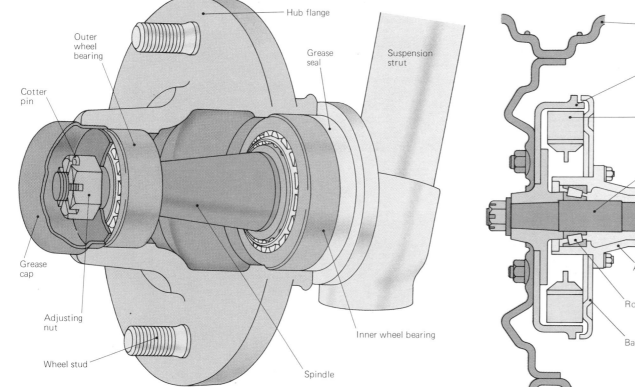

Hub flange

Outer wheel bearing

Cotter pin

Grease cap

Adjusting nut

Wheel stud

Spindle

Inner wheel bearing

Grease seal

Suspension strut

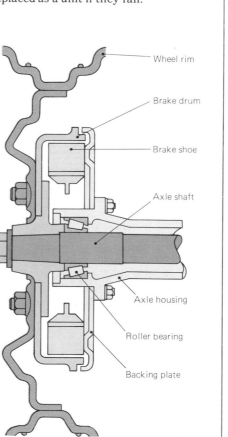

Wheel rim

Brake drum

Brake shoe

Axle shaft

Axle housing

Roller bearing

Backing plate

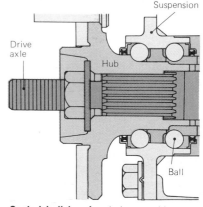

Drive axle

Suspension

Hub

Ball

Sealed ball bearing hub assembly on a drive axle requires no adjustment or lubrication. If the bearing fails, the whole hub assembly is replaced.

Free-turning hub is mounted on tapered roller bearings. It can be disassembled for adjustment, for packing with fresh grease, or for bearing replacement. Tightening or loosening the adjusting nut

changes bearing clearance. When properly adjusted, the nut allows the wheel to turn freely without wobbling. The cotter pin prevents the adjusting nut from unscrewing as the wheel turns.

Rear-wheel hub has ball or roller bearings that are pressed onto the axle shaft inside the rear axle housing. The brake drum and wheel are bolted to a flange on the outer end of each axle shaft.

What the tires do

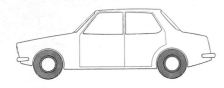

Probably no other parts of a modern automobile are as abused, neglected, and misunderstood as the tires. Yet the tires rival the brakes as the most important safety device on a car.

A tire is an inflatable rubber ring that fits around the wheel. It has four or five parts, depending on the type of tire construction. The *tread* is the part that touches the road and, ideally, provides traction at all speeds and under all weather conditions. Flexible *sidewalls* absorb loads. A strong inner *carcass* resists impacts from potholes and bumps. Metal hoops in the *beads*—the areas where the tire touches the wheel—hold the tire in place. Some tires also have *belts* between the carcass and tread to stabilize the tread and reduce wear.

Besides improving riding comfort by carrying the vehicle on a cushion of air, the tires must cope with the forces that are generated during acceleration, braking, and steering. The problem facing tire engineers is that no one tire is best for all road conditions. A tire must be strong enough to resist damage, yet flexible enough to cushion impacts. It must respond accurately to steering, yet resist deflection by ridges in the road. The rubber must be soft enough to provide good traction on wet pavement, but hard enough to last thousands of miles. Any tire design is a compromise between these conflicting requirements.

Great advances have been made in tire design in recent years. New dimensions, materials, and types of construction have been introduced in an attempt to create the best possible all-around tire. Some cars handle better on a particular type of tire; it is common for car suspensions to be designed for a specific tire type or, occasionally, for a particular tire brand and model.

Tires come in two basic types: tube and tubeless. A tube-type tire has a separate rubber inner tube to contain the air. On tubeless tires the tire beads are shaped in such a way that they form an airtight seal where they are forced against the wheel rim. A soft inner lining prevents air from permeating the sidewalls and tread. A tubeless tire must also use a special grooved valve stem that forms an airtight seal when it is forced through the wheel's valve hole.

Tubeless tires have a number of advantages over the tube types. They are easier to mount on the wheels. When punctured, they deflate more slowly due to the self-sealing effect of the soft lining. Also, flats can be temporarily repaired without removing the tire from the wheel by stopping up the leak with a special rubber plug. As soon as possible, flats should be repaired permanently by removing the tire from the rim, inspecting the carcass for damage, then patching holes up to ¼ inch wide from the inside with a chemical or hot vulcanized patch, or with a head-type plug, which looks like a big rubber nail. The sidewall of a *radial* tire (pp.116–117) usually cannot be repaired if it is punctured; the tire must be replaced. Some tire makers do not recommend patching the sidewall of any tire.

Most cars have tubeless tires. Tubes may be required on some wire wheels to prevent air leaks where the spokes penetrate the rim. Porosity can also cause leaks through some cast-aluminum wheels. One cure is to coat the inside of the wheel with epoxy sealant; another is to use tube-type tires. A tube may be fitted to a tubeless tire to stop a persistent slow leak past the tire bead, but a tube should not be used as a substitute for a proper patch or plug to repair a flat tire.

Tread ribs

Sipes

Tread grooves

Four tire "footprints" like this one, each about the size of the sole on a man's shoe, provide all necessary braking, steering, and accelerating control for a car weighing 1 to 2½ tons.

Tubeless vs. tube-type tires

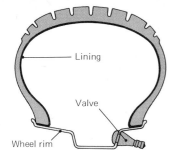

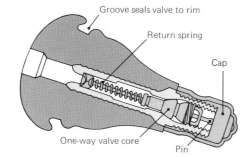

Groove seals valve to rim

Return spring

Cap

One-way valve core

Pin

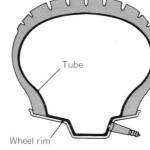

Tube

Wheel rim

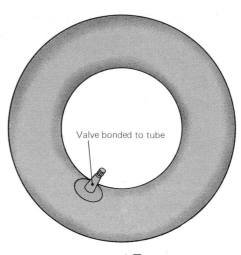

Valve bonded to tube

Inner tube is a dough-nut-shaped rubber bladder. The valve is bonded to it and projects through a hole in the wheel rim, if the tube is properly positioned between the tire and rim. The tire must be removed from the rim in order to patch a punctured inner tube. If a nail penetrates the tire tread, the tube may be punctured repeatedly as it deflates and shifts inside the tire.

Tubeless tire has a soft inner lining that keeps air from leaking between the tire and rim and often forms a seal around a nail or other object that punctures tread. Self-sealing tire holds in air after nail is removed.

Tire valve has a central core that is spring-loaded to allow air to pass inward only, unless the pin is depressed. The core can be un-screwed and replaced if it becomes defective. Airtight cap on the end of the valve is an extra precaution against valve leakage.

Tube-type tire has a rubber inner tube that conforms to the contour of the tire and wheel rim when inflated. When punctured, a tube loses air immediately, sometimes in a sudden rush called a *blowout*.

Tire profile

The ratio between the height of a tire, from wheel rim to tread, and its width, from sidewall to sidewall, is known as the tire's *profile*, or *aspect ratio*. The aspect ratio is expressed as a percentage. A tire that is 145 mm high and 185 mm wide has an aspect ratio of 78 percent (all tires are now built to metric dimensions).

The first tires were circular tubes with 100 percent aspect ratios. It was later discovered that a tire handled better when it was mounted on a wider rim. The next step was to make the tires wider without increasing their height. These

low-profile tires put more tread on the road and gave better handling, better load-carrying capacity, and longer life than the old symmetrical tires. Today's passenger car tires have aspect ratios ranging from 78 to 50 percent. Profiles as low as 35 percent are used on special low-pressure racing car tires. Wider-than-standard wheels and tires can improve both the handling and load capacity of a car, but such tires may also rub against the fenders and suspension, lower the car to a dangerous degree, increase the chance of hydroplaning

(p.118), and give an uncomfortable ride. A new kind of low-profile tire is the *elliptical tire*, which has extremely flex-ible sidewalls that provide a soft ride at high inflation pressures. (High inflation normally improves fuel economy and handling, but increases ride harshness with conventional tires.) Elliptical tires need special wheels to accommodate their bulging sidewalls. Wheels for ellip-tical tires are usually made in odd sizes such as 390 mm (15¼ in.) to prevent mixups with conventional wheels, which have diameters of 13, 14, or 15 inches.

Temporary spares

To save weight and increase trunk space in small, fuel-efficient cars, tire makers have developed a series of temporary spares. They are meant only to get you to the nearest service station and must never be driven faster than 50 mph (80 km/h). The *lightweight spare* is a thin-skinned design about the same size as the tire it replaces. The *high-pressure spare* is the size of a motorcycle tire and is in-flated to 60 psi (413 kPa) to support the same load as a normal tire. The *folding spare* is stored collapsed on its rim and is inflated by a can of compressed gas.

Aspect ratios

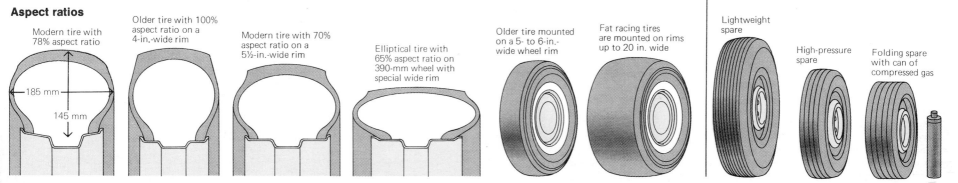

Modern tire with 78% aspect ratio

185 mm

145 mm

Older tire with 100% aspect ratio on a 4-in.-wide rim

Modern tire with 70% aspect ratio on a 5½-in.-wide rim

Elliptical tire with 65% aspect ratio on 390-mm wheel with special wide rim

Older tire mounted on a 5- to 6-in.-wide wheel rim

Fat racing tires are mounted on rims up to 20 in. wide

Lightweight spare

High-pressure spare

Folding spare with can of compressed gas

Tire construction

The *bias-ply* tire reflects the oldest type of tire construction. Its carcass is made up of two or more layers, or *plies*, of rubber-coated fabric. The threads, or *cords*, of these layers cross one another at an angle (on the bias), hence the tire's name. The angle at which the cords intersect has an effect on riding comfort (which is greatest at larger angles) and steering accuracy (best at smaller angles) of the tire; this necessitates yet another compromise in tire design. Most bias-ply tires today are built so that the cords intersect the centerline of the tread at an angle of 35° to 40°.

Two to eight plies of fabric are used in the tire carcass. The more plies, the stronger the carcass but the harsher the ride. Six- to eight-ply tires are used on trucks. When plies were made of cotton, a good passenger car tire required at least four plies. New, stronger ply materials such as nylon, rayon, polyester, and fiberglass have made it possible to build a modern two-ply carcass that is stronger than one of four-ply cotton. The number of plies is not a good indication of tire strength; tires are now rated by "Load Range" (p.119). When new and uninflated, some bias-ply tires have a concave tread. This flattens out when inflated to give a uniform road contact area.

Most new cars are supplied with *radial-ply* tires, but bias-ply tires are popular replacements on older cars because they are cheaper than radials. Radial and bias-ply tires should never be used together on the same car because of their different handling characteristics.

Radial tires are a radical breakthrough in tire construction. Rather than criss-crossing one another, the parallel plies of a radial tire radiate from one bead to the other by the shortest possible route, crossing the tread centerline at a 90° angle. This makes for an extremely flexible sidewall and a soft ride but provides little or no directional stability. Direc-tional stability is supplied by stiff belts of fabric or steel wire that run around the circumference of the tire between the carcass and the tread.

The construction of radial-ply tires reduces cornering wear and increases the overall life of the tire. A problem with bias-ply tires is that the tread tends to distort, or *squirm,* where the tire meets the road. This squirm closes up the tread pattern, reducing its ability to channel away water, and generates considerable heat, which accelerates tread wear. The belts under the tread of a radial or *belted-bias* tire minimize squirm.

One drawback to radial tires is that they tend to produce a harsh ride at low speeds, although the ride smooths out dramatically at highway speeds. If a car is designed with radial tires in mind, the suspension can be tuned to eliminate low-speed ride harshness.

When cornering, the radial tends to roll over onto its sidewall somewhat (see illustration on opposite page, right), so the tread pattern is continued onto the shoulder of most radial-ply tires. Most radials have two-ply fabric sidewalls and either one or two steel belts, or two to six fabric belts. Steel belts add a certain measure of puncture resistance to the tread, but fabric belts can produce a softer ride. Due to their lower rolling resistance, properly inflated radials can give 5 to 7 percent better fuel economy than bias tires.

Concave tread before inflation (left) and after (right), showing its broad, flat road contact area.

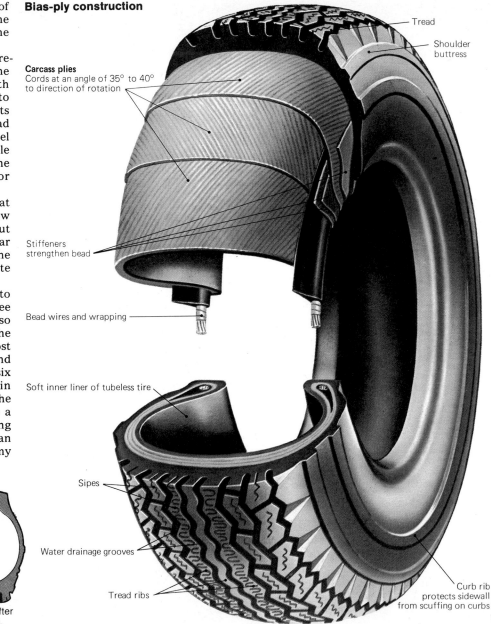

Bias-ply construction

Tread

Shoulder buttress

Carcass plies
Cords at an angle of 35° to 40° to direction of rotation

Stiffeners strengthen bead

Bead wires and wrapping

Soft inner liner of tubeless tire

Sipes

Water drainage grooves

Tread ribs

Curb rib protects sidewall from scuffing on curbs

Radial-ply construction

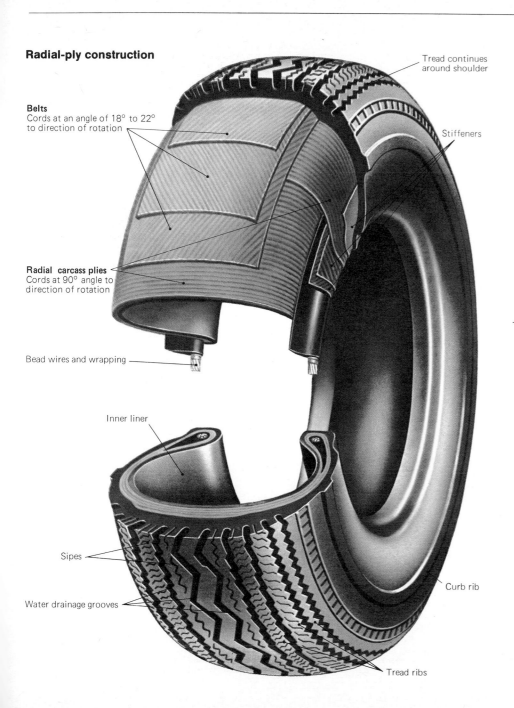

Tread continues around shoulder

Belts
Cords at an angle of 18° to 22° to direction of rotation

Stiffeners

Radial carcass plies
Cords at 90° angle to direction of rotation

Bead wires and wrapping

Inner liner

Sipes

Water drainage grooves

Curb rib

Tread ribs

Radial vs. bias-ply tires

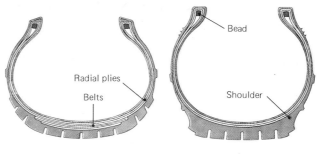

Bead

Radial plies

Belts

Shoulder

Cross sections show the differences between radial and bias-ply tires. Radial tire (left) has reinforcing belts under the tread, and the tread runs partway up the sidewalls. The bias tire (right) has no belts, and there is a sharp delineation between tread and sidewalls.

Radial   **Bias**

A correctly inflated radial-ply tire (left) bulges noticeably just above the contact area between tire and road, due to the radial's flexible sidewall. A properly inflated bias-ply tire (right) has nearly straight sidewalls.

Radial   **Bias**

When a car rounds a curve, centrifugal force tends to pull it toward the outside of the turn. Only the friction between the tire's contact area and the road keeps the car on course in a curve. A radial's flexible sidewall allows the tread to remain flat on the road for maximum traction (left). A bias tire's stiff sidewall pulls a portion of the tread away from the road (right), lessening the contact area and the traction of the tire.

Belted-bias construction

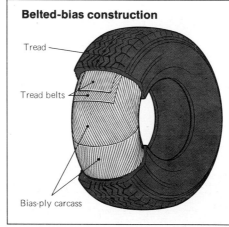

Tread

Tread belts

Bias-ply carcass

The belted-bias tire is unique to North America. Because it can be built on existing bias-ply tire manufacturing equipment, it costs less than a radial tire. The belted-bias design combines the crisscross plies of a bias-ply tire with the tread-reinforcing belts of a radial. The result is a tire with stiff sidewalls and a stiff tread. The tread belts reduce squirm, so the belted-bias tire provides greater fuel economy than a bias-ply tire, but less than a radial does. Tread life and handling qualities approach those of a radial tire. Depending on the suspension design of a particular car, belted-bias tires may provide a harsher ride than bias-ply or radial tires.

What the tread does

Treads are designed to help tires grip the road in any kind of weather. Like the construction of the tire itself, the design of the tread is a compromise between conflicting requirements.

On a dry road, a smooth tire would provide the best grip because the greatest possible area of rubber would be in contact with the road. Most racing tires have smooth treads. But smooth tires have hardly any grip on wet roads.

Water causes skids in two ways: A thin film of water can act as a lubricant. Also, puddles can form a wedge in front of a rolling tire, causing the tire to ride up on the water like a water ski. This causes a type of skid called hydroplaning. The tire is lifted off the road, and all steering and braking control is lost.

Tread ribs do three things in water: First, they either push the water aside or pump it through zigzag grooves from the front of the tire *contact patch* to the back. Second, the film of water left behind is forced into the *sipes*—slits like tiny knife cuts. As the tire revolves beyond the contact area, this water is flung out of the sipes. Third, the ribs grip the remainder of the now-dry contact area.

The high-speed photograph at the left, taken through a thick plate of glass, shows a tire cutting through a puddle of dyed water. Most of the water is pushed around the sides of the tire or pumped through the tread grooves, leaving a small road contact patch.

As speed increases, there is less time for the water to escape via the grooves and sipes. A tire that will not hydroplane at 30 mph may do so at 50 mph on the same wet road. A tire with a badly worn tread cannot pump away as much water as a tire with deep tread. A tire should be replaced when its tread is less than 1/16 inch deep (see p.121).

Different tire manufacturers offer hundreds of different tread patterns designed to cope with varying driving conditions. Some treads are designed to enhance ride comfort or fuel economy, or to minimize road noise.

Snow tires are the best-known example of special-purpose treads. In the tire industry they are known as *mud and snow* tires, and they provide better traction on unpaved roads than conventional treads do. For deep sand, there are *high-flotation* treads designed not to dig down to a firm base the way snow tires do. When they are used on dry roads, snow tires and other designs with rugged treads tend to wear out more rapidly than conventional treads.

The rubber formula, or *tread compound,* represents another compromise. Soft rubber gives the greatest traction, but hard rubber wears longest. A new compound, sometimes called *sticky rubber,* is used on many snow tires. It does not become as hard as conventional compounds when the temperature drops, and thus gives better traction on ice.

Hydroplaning occurs when deep water cannot escape from under the tread, and the tire climbs up a wedge of water, losing contact with the road.

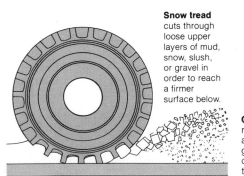

Snow tread cuts through loose upper layers of mud, snow, slush, or gravel in order to reach a firmer surface below.

Conventional tread has narrow water drainage grooves and many sipes. The narrow grooves provide a larger road contact area, improving traction on dry roads.

All-season tire is a radial design with an "aggressive" tread that is a compromise between conventional and snow treads. It is useful on dry roads or light snow.

Mud and snow tire has big ribs that reduce contact area on dry roads but give a good grip on loose surfaces. Most snow treads fling off packed-in snow as the tire revolves.

Studded snow tread is embedded with tiny metal studs for better traction on ice and hard-packed snow. Studs are illegal in many areas because they damage dry roads.

Snow chains provide the best traction on snow and ice, but they cannot be driven at high speed on dry roads without causing noise, vibration, and tire damage.

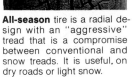

Tire quality grading and other sidewall markings

Information molded into the tire sidewall informs the consumer about a tire's size, construction, and quality. Except for snow tires, all tires sold in the U.S. bear three Uniform Tire Quality Grades, which reflect the outcome of government tests at a Texas track.

Tread wear: A mark of 100 means that the tire would last 30,000 miles at the Texas track. A tire rated 120 would last 20 percent longer, or 36,000 miles. One rated 90 would wear out 10 percent earlier, at 27,000 miles. This grade is no guarantee of the mileage you will get with a set of tires; weather, driving habits, road conditions, and tire maintenance all affect tread life. The tread wear grade merely lets you compare the potential life of various tire brands.

Traction: Hard rubber compounds give long tread life but poor traction. The traction grade lets you weigh tread life against traction on wet roads. The highest grade is A; B is intermediate; C is poor. Since there is no minimum requirement for a C grade, such tires are best avoided in areas with wet climates.

Temperature resistance: This is a measure of a tire's ability to withstand high speeds, overloading, or underinflation. Here again, A is best, B is intermediate, and C is poorest, although there is a minimum requirement for a C rating in temperature resistance.

Other sidewall markings are explained in the illustration at the right.

Buying retreads

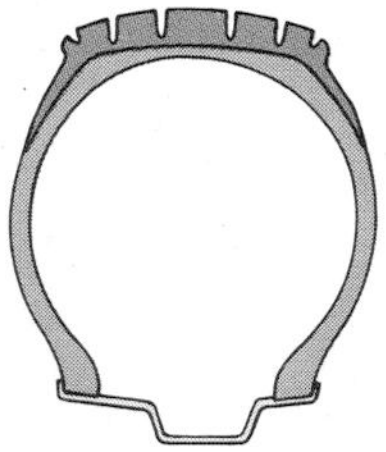

Retreaded tires are cheaper than new tires, but quality can vary widely. New tread is bonded to a bald but otherwise sound tire, usually at a small local factory.

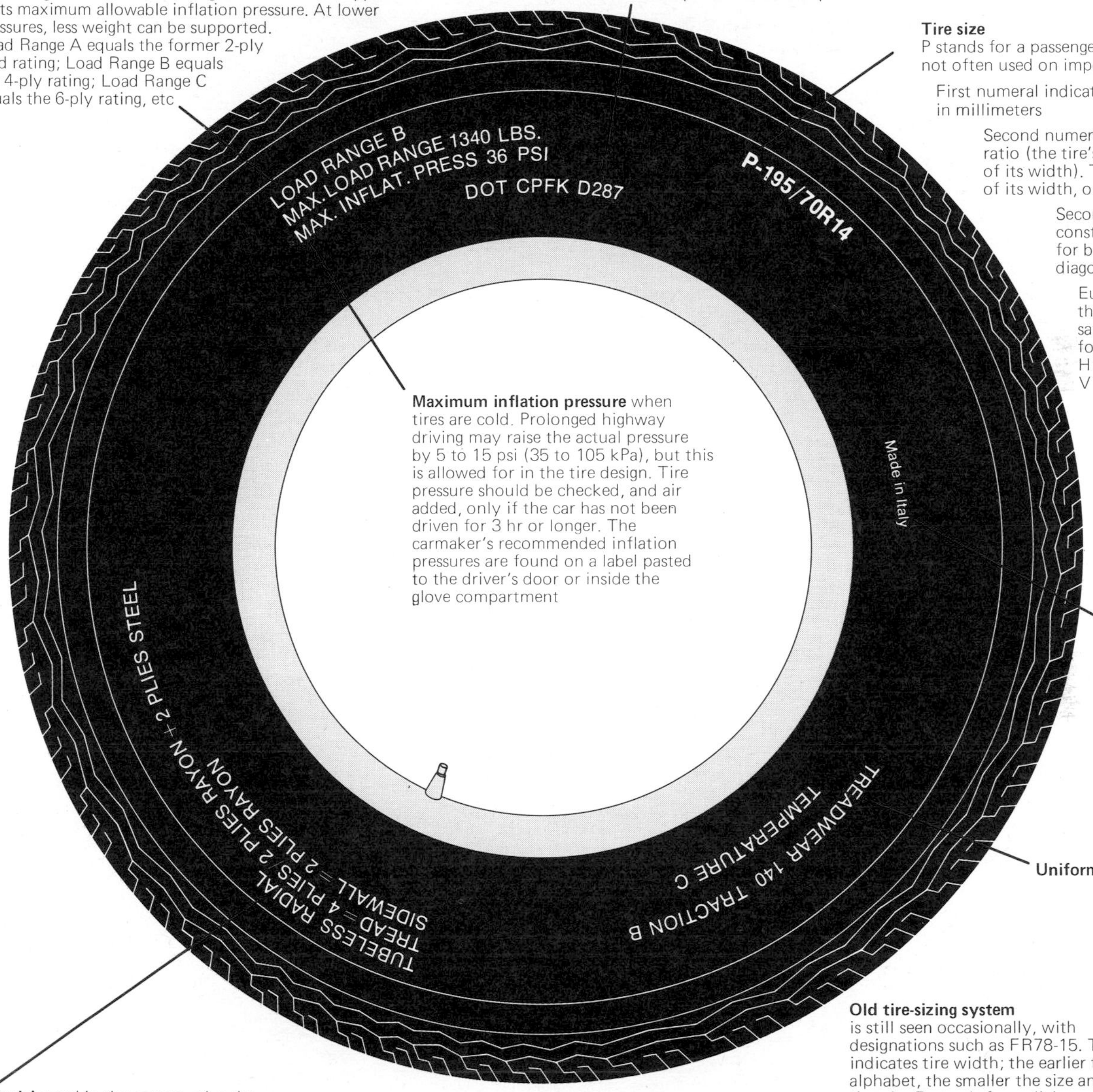

Load range tells how much weight each tire can support at its maximum allowable inflation pressure. At lower pressures, less weight can be supported. Load Range A equals the former 2-ply load rating; Load Range B equals the 4-ply rating; Load Range C equals the 6-ply rating, etc

LOAD RANGE B
MAX. LOAD RANGE 1340 LBS.
MAX. INFLAT. PRESS 36 PSI
DOT CPFK D287

P-195/70R14

Made in Italy

TUBELESS RADIAL 4 PLIES 2 PLIES RAYON
TREAD · 4 PLIES 2 PLIES RAYON
SIDEWALL · 2 PLIES RAYON

TREADWEAR 140 TRACTION B
TEMPERATURE C

Maximum inflation pressure when tires are cold. Prolonged highway driving may raise the actual pressure by 5 to 15 psi (35 to 105 kPa), but this is allowed for in the tire design. Tire pressure should be checked, and air added, only if the car has not been driven for 3 hr or longer. The carmaker's recommended inflation pressures are found on a label pasted to the driver's door or inside the glove compartment

Identification code indicates the tire maker plus the date and place of manufacture

Tire size
P stands for a passenger car tire. (This mark is not often used on imported tires)

First numeral indicates the width of the tire in millimeters

Second numeral indicates the aspect ratio (the tire's height as a percentage of its width). This tire's height is 70% of its width, or 137 mm

Second letter indicates tire construction: R for radial, B for belted bias, or D for diagonal (bias) ply

European tires have a third letter to indicate safe maximum speed: S for 112 mph (180 km/h); H for 130 mph (210 km/h); V for over 130 mph

Third numeral indicates the wheel diameter, either in inches (13, 14, or 15) or millimeters (390)

Country of origin (if other than USA)

Uniform Tire Quality Gradings

Old tire-sizing system is still seen occasionally, with designations such as FR78-15. The first letter indicates tire width; the earlier the letter is in the alphabet, the smaller the size and load rating of the tire. An R stands for radial construction. The numerals indicate aspect ratio and wheel size, respectively

Materials used in the carcass, plus the descriptions "tubeless" or "tube-type"

Proper tire maintenance

The most important factors promoting long tire life are proper balance, wheel alignment, and inflation. No tire or wheel is completely round or uniform. Each has heavy spots that can cause annoying vibrations at high speeds, as well as abnormal tire wear. The wheels and tires should be *dynamically balanced* by a tire dealer or garage. This involves spinning the wheel and tire with a special machine to identify the heavy spots, then crimping lead weights to the rim to compensate for them. If a tire is removed from a wheel (to fix a flat or mount snow tires), it should be rebalanced when it is mounted on the wheel again.

The amount of air pressure in a tire affects not only how fast the tire will wear but how well the car handles and how much fuel it consumes.

Tire balancing

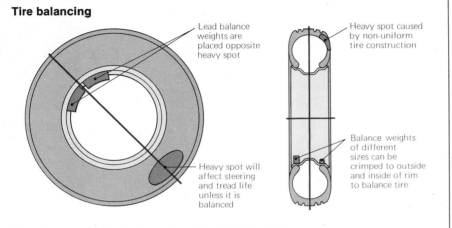

Lead balance weights are placed opposite heavy spot

Heavy spot caused by non-uniform tire construction

Heavy spot will affect steering and tread life unless it is balanced

Balance weights of different sizes can be crimped to outside and inside of rim to balance tire

How tire pressure affects wear, ride, and handling

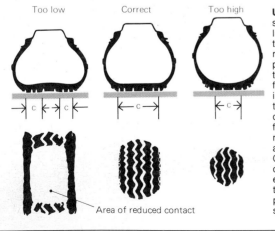

Too low

Correct

Too high

Area of reduced contact

Underinflated tires may give a smooth ride, but handling and tread life suffer. Too little air (left) causes the sidewalls and tread to buckle, reducing the area of the road contact patch (c) and causing a loss of traction, especially on curves. The flexing of an underinflated tire increases fuel consumption and leads to excessive heat buildup, which causes rapid wear and early tire failure. Proper inflation (center) results in maximum road contact area, traction, and fuel economy. Overinflation (right) again reduces the contact area and traction. Fuel economy may increase slightly, but the car's ride will be harsh. Check tire pressure once a month and before starting out on long trips.

Causes of sidewall damage

Flat tire. Running over a curb, pothole, or other obstruction with a flat tire, or driving too far on a flat, can break the sidewall plies.

Carcass failure. Driving too far on a flat can break the sidewall plies radially. Most sidewall damage cannot be seen on the outside of a tire.

Sidewall scuffing. The tire sidewall can wear down to the fabric carcass if the tire is constantly scraped against curbs during parking.

Projection rubbing. The inner sidewall can be damaged if it rubs against steering or suspension parts. Oversized tires may rub only on turns.

Internal fracture. Caused by hitting a pothole or curb at high speed. Tires with major sidewall damage are weakened and must be replaced.

Water damage. Severe bubbling between the plies inside the tire is caused by a barely visible external break or cut. Water can rot rayon plies.

Causes of tread wear

Chronic overinflation causes tire to wear out in the center first, reducing useful tread life. This tire is dangerously worn and must be replaced.

Severe wear will eventually remove tread down to the fabric, exposing the carcass to fracture and water damage and making a tire unsafe for retreading.

Chronic underinflation will cause a tire to wear out at the edges first, reducing useful tread life. This tire's smooth edges may cause skids on wet curves.

Chunking occurs when tread loosens and is torn off the tire by centrifugal force. Chunking is most often caused by defects in a tire's construction.

Incorrect wheel camber (p.128) causes wear at one edge of tire only. Check edges of front tires for irregular wear and have wheels aligned periodically.

Flat spot is caused by skidding on dry pavement when the brakes have locked. Flat spot will throw tire out of balance and may cause future skids.

Feathering of the tread is caused by excessive toe-in or toe-out (p.128) of front wheels, which makes tires slide sideways slightly as they roll.

Bad repair of a flat on a tubeless tire—possibly the use of more than one plug—distorts the tread, resulting in a flat spot and, eventually, in carcass failure.

Cupping, or scalloping, of the tread is uneven wear caused by an unbalanced tire or by faulty suspension parts, steering linkage, or wheel bearings.

When normal wear exposes the wear indicators between two or more adjacent grooves, it is time to replace the tire before the tread wears dangerously low.

Punctured tire should be replaced by the spare at once, even if it has not gone flat. Leave nail in tire so that repairman can easily find the hole.

Nail penetrating tire tread may cause irreparable damage to sidewall plies. Flat tires should always be removed from the wheel and inspected internally.

What the suspension does

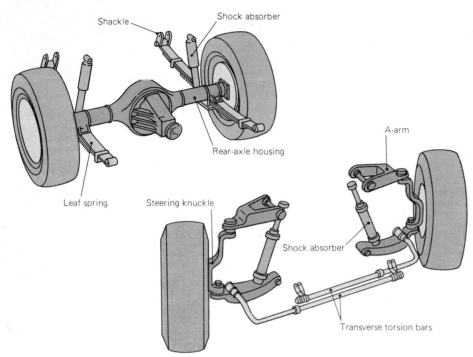

The suspension supports the weight of the car and its cargo, isolates the passengers from the bumps in the road, and keeps the wheels in contact with the ground. This work is accomplished mainly by springs and shock absorbers.

A *spring* is a device that returns to its original shape after being distorted. In a car suspension, springs are placed between the frame and each wheel. When the wheels encounter bumps in the road, the springs absorb the shocks by compressing and extending. A compressed spring, when released, rebounds past its original position, then springs back past the original position again and again. Although each compression and extension is smaller than the previous one, the oscillation can go on long enough to make passengers carsick.

Devices called *shock absorbers* are attached to the springs to dampen these oscillations. Shock absorbers are misnamed—the shock is really absorbed by the springs. The shock absorbers control the excess motion of the springs. This is accomplished by linking the spring to a cylinder partially filled with hydraulic fluid. A piston descends or rises through this fluid in response to spring movement. The piston has calibrated holes or valves that allow the fluid to be forced slowly past the piston. Because fluids cannot be compressed, the size of these valves determines the rate at which the piston can move, which in turn controls the rate at which the spring oscillates.

Three types of springs are used in various combinations in car suspensions.

Leaf springs consist of long, flat leaves. A leaf spring may consist of one leaf that is thicker in the middle than at the ends. More frequently, several leaves of progressively shorter length are bolted together. Both these methods strengthen the spring toward the center, where the greatest force is applied. Leaf springs absorb shock by bending.

Coil springs are rods that have been wound into spirals. They absorb shock by compressing and extending.

Torsion bars absorb shock by twisting. Coil springs are really coiled torsion bars.

Spring steel is specially treated with heat or pressure to make it elastic enough to resume its original shape after being distorted, without becoming brittle from repeated bending.

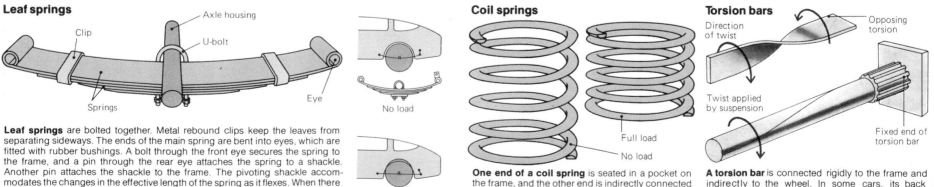

Leaf springs

Leaf springs are bolted together. Metal rebound clips keep the leaves from separating sideways. The ends of the main spring are bent into eyes, which are fitted with rubber bushings. A bolt through the front eye secures the spring to the frame, and a pin through the rear eye attaches the spring to a shackle. Another pin attaches the shackle to the frame. The pivoting shackle accommodates the changes in the effective length of the spring as it flexes. When there is no load on the car, the springs curve down, the distance between the eyes is at its shortest, and the shackles hang straight down (upper right). A full load straightens, and therefore lengthens, the springs; the shackles pivot to accommodate the increase in length (lower right).

No load

Full load

Coil springs

One end of a coil spring is seated in a pocket on the frame, and the other end is indirectly connected to the wheel. (It may be seated in the axle housing or in a suspension control arm.) The spring compresses and extends in response to the up-and-down movements of the wheel.

Torsion bars

A torsion bar is connected rigidly to the frame and indirectly to the wheel. In some cars, its back end is attached to the frame and its front end to a pivoting suspension arm, which acts as a lever. As the wheel moves up and down, the bar twists. In other cars, torsion bars are placed transversely.

Shock absorbers

All modern shock absorbers operate on similar principles, although there are differences in the way the internal valves or orifices are arranged. Special features are added to some shocks to overcome specific problems.

Standard shocks are suitable for ordinary driving without heavy loads.

Heavy-duty shocks have larger fluid capacity and stiffer valving than standard shocks. They give increased control at high speeds or on rough roads.

Adjustable shocks can be made softer or harder by following the manufacturer's instructions. The adjustment changes the orifice calibration so that fluid either passes through the piston faster to give a softer ride or the flow is constricted to give a harder ride. Some brands can be adjusted to harder levels to compensate for wear.

Overload shocks have coil springs wrapped around heavy-duty shocks. These helper springs support excess weight when a car carries heavy loads or tows a trailer.

Air shocks use air chambers to combine the characteristics of adjustable springs and overload shocks. By increasing the air pressure, the chambers become, in effect, helper springs that can support increased loads. When the excess load is removed, air is bled from the chambers, and the assist provided by the air chamber is reduced or eliminated. Air shocks are best suited to cars that carry variable loads or occasionally tow trailers. The air chambers can be filled and bled with a standard tire air valve that is usually mounted in the trunk. Some air shocks are adjusted by a compressor powered by engine vacuum and controlled by a dial on the dashboard.

Some cars level themselves automatically by pumping up their air shocks. These cars have electronic level sensors that operate the pump when the back of the car is riding high or low.

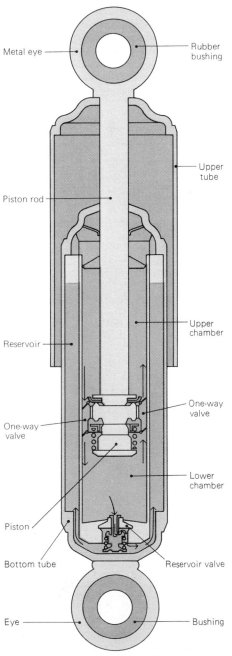

Metal eye
Rubber bushing
Upper tube
Piston rod
Upper chamber
Reservoir
One-way valve
One-way valve
Lower chamber
Piston
Bottom tube
Reservoir valve
Eye
Bushing

The major elements in a shock absorber are two concentric tubes, a piston with precisely calibrated orifices and/or one-way valves, and hydraulic fluid. The top tube with the piston is bolted to the car's frame. The bottom tube, which is sealed and nearly filled with hydraulic fluid, is bolted to a suspension component. The piston fits tightly into the bottom tube, dividing it into an upper and a lower chamber. A reservoir for extra hydraulic fluid is connected to the lower chamber by a two-way valve system.

When the wheel hits a bump, the spring is compressed and the bottom tube telescopes into the top tube, which pushes the piston downward inside the shock. This movement is restricted by the hydraulic fluid, which completely fills the lower chamber. Since fluids cannot be compressed, the only way the tube can move past the piston is by displacing the hydraulic fluid. As the bottom tube moves up, the fluid in the lower chamber is forced past a one-way valve, or through a series of calibrated orifices (depending on the design of the shock). This allows fluid in the lower chamber to be forced into the upper chamber. The bottom tube can move up only as fast as the fluid is displaced.

As the piston rod moves into the upper chamber, its volume displaces additional fluid, which is accommodated by the reservoir. Calibrated valves between the reservoir and the lower chamber offer additional damping control.

On rebound, the spring extends, pulling down the bottom tube. Since the upper chamber is now full, the fluid must pass back through the piston. The fluid is forced into the lower chamber, and some fluid is drawn back from the reservoir. This controls the rate at which the spring can extend.

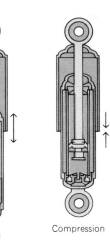

Rebound

Compression

When wheel moves up, so does the bottom tube of the shock absorber. Oil in the lower chamber is displaced through calibrated holes and valves into the upper chamber and reservoir. When the spring rebounds, oil is forced back through the holes and valves from the upper chamber and reservoir into the lower chamber. The action of adjustable shocks can be varied from soft to hard by changing the size of the holes. If shocks are too hard, the springs will not be able to properly absorb road shock, and the car's ride will be very harsh. If they are too soft, the springs will oscillate too much, resulting in excess body movement.

Special-purpose shocks

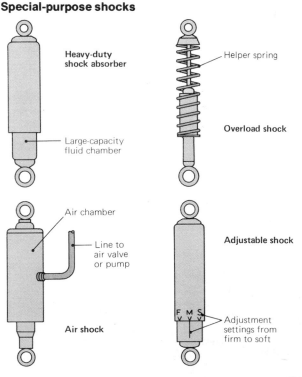

Heavy-duty shock absorber

Large-capacity fluid chamber

Air chamber

Line to air valve or pump

Air shock

Helper spring

Overload shock

Adjustable shock

Adjustment settings from firm to soft

Independent front suspension

Virtually all modern cars have *independent front suspension*, which means that each front wheel is linked to the frame separately. This allows the wheels to react to the road independently so that, for example, the left wheel can go over a bump and move up while the right wheel goes into a depression and moves down without tilting the whole car. Independent suspension offers two advantages over the solid-axle suspension used on old cars and some modern trucks: the ride is more comfortable because the whole car no longer responds to each variation in road surface, and handling is improved because both tires retain better contact with the road.

The front wheels must steer as well as respond to the road surface. *Ball joints,* which can rotate in all directions, allow the wheels to steer left or right and move up or down simultaneously. A *stabilizer bar* is often set between the left and right suspension components to reduce the amount the car's body leans in a turn.

Several engineering solutions to the basic idea of independent suspension are illustrated below.

Double A-arm suspension

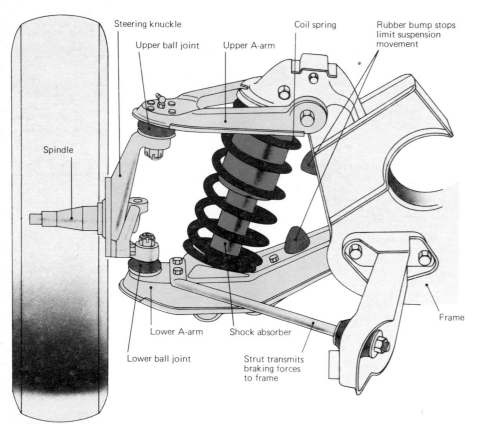

Steering knuckle
Upper ball joint
Upper A-arm
Coil spring
Rubber bump stops limit suspension movement
Spindle
Lower A-arm
Shock absorber
Lower ball joint
Strut transmits braking forces to frame
Frame

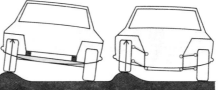

Solid-axle suspension (left) forces both wheels to react when one wheel encounters a bump. This tilts the entire car and disturbs the other tire, reducing its contact with the road. Solid-axle front suspension has not been seen on passenger cars since the days of the Model T Ford, but it is still found on many four-wheel-drive vehicles. Independent front suspension (right) allows both wheels to react separately. If one wheel hits a bump, its suspension absorbs most of the shock, allowing the opposite wheel to stay in contact with the road.

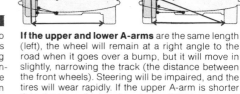

If the upper and lower A-arms are the same length (left), the wheel will remain at a right angle to the road when it goes over a bump, but it will move in slightly, narrowing the track (the distance between the front wheels). Steering will be impaired, and the tires will wear rapidly. If the upper A-arm is shorter than the lower (right), the wheel will tilt inward as it moves up. The track will not vary, steering accuracy will be improved, and tire wear will be reduced. If the car is leaning into a turn, the inward tilt of the wheel will keep the tire perpendicular.

Double A-arm suspension derives its name from the triangular upper and lower control arms that are the main supports of the wheel. The wide ends of both A-shaped arms are hinged to the frame. The narrow ends are attached to the upper and lower ball joints. The steering knuckle (including the *stub axle,* or *spindle,* that carries the wheel bearing and the wheel) is fixed between these ball joints. This configuration allows the wheel to move up and down with variations in the road surface and left and right as it is steered, while keeping the wheel in the correct position with respect to the road and the car. A spring and a shock absorber are set between the frame and the lower A-arm (shown above), or between the frame and the upper A-arm, to absorb road shock and to help control wheel movements.

Grease nipple
Ball stud
Socket

A ball joint consists of a ball stud that fits snugly into a socket. The ball can rotate freely in the socket but cannot slip out of it. Ball joints are placed between the steering knuckle and suspension arms. They allow movement in more than one plane so that the wheels can move up and down with the suspension and can be steered at the same time. Some ball joints have grease nipples (shown) to allow periodic lubrication.

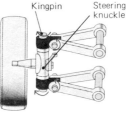

Kingpin
Steering knuckle

Kingpins were used on early solid-axle front suspensions because they were sturdy and allowed the wheels to pivot in one plane for steering. To be adapted to A-arm suspension systems, kingpins had to be fitted with additional pivoting members at the top and bottom. The configuration shown here was typical, with the kingpin running straight through the steering knuckle. Ball joints make for a lighter and less complex arrangement.

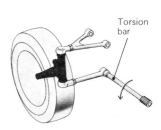

Torsion bar

Torsion bars can be used in place of coil springs to absorb road shocks in A-arm suspensions. Large Chrysler Corporation cars have used torsion-bar front suspensions for decades. The rear end of the torsion bar is attached to a frame member near the fire wall, and the front end is attached to the lower A-arm. Torsion bars can be adjusted to change the ride height of the car and the softness or firmness of the suspension.

MacPherson strut suspension

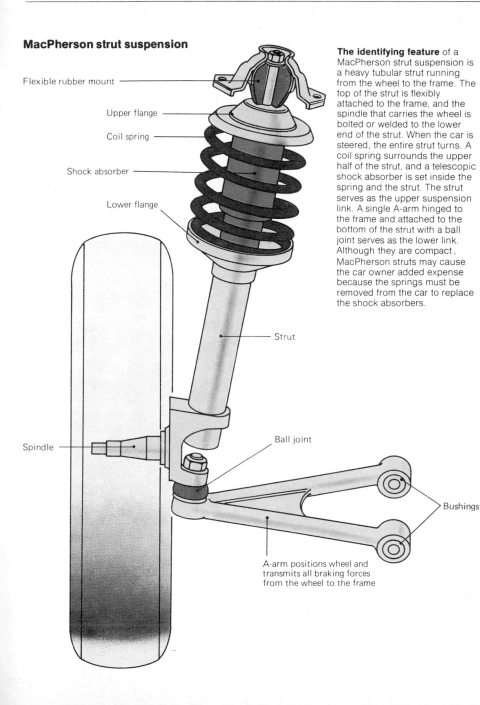

Flexible rubber mount

Upper flange

Coil spring

Shock absorber

Lower flange

Spindle

Strut

Ball joint

Bushings

A-arm positions wheel and transmits all braking forces from the wheel to the frame

The identifying feature of a MacPherson strut suspension is a heavy tubular strut running from the wheel to the frame. The top of the strut is flexibly attached to the frame, and the spindle that carries the wheel is bolted or welded to the lower end of the strut. When the car is steered, the entire strut turns. A coil spring surrounds the upper half of the strut, and a telescopic shock absorber is set inside the spring and the strut. The strut serves as the upper suspension link. A single A-arm hinged to the frame and attached to the bottom of the strut with a ball joint serves as the lower link. Although they are compact, MacPherson struts may cause the car owner added expense because the springs must be removed from the car to replace the shock absorbers.

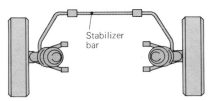

The single A-arms of a MacPherson strut suspension allow very little change in wheel *camber* (tilt from the vertical) as the wheel moves up and down over bumps, thus improving steering accuracy and increasing tire life.

Torsion bars

Trailing arms

Trailing arms, another variation of independent suspension, are used on the VW Beetle. This system permits the distance between the front and back wheels to vary, but camber and track do not change with the up-and-down movement of the wheels.

Stabilizer bars

Stabilizer bar

View from above (left) shows a suspension with a stabilizer bar, MacPherson struts, and lower A-arms. This setup may cost the manufacturer less than the more complicated double A-arm system. The stabilizer bar transfers some of the braking forces from the wheel to the frame and also resists body roll in turns.

In turns, centrifugal force transfers some of the car's weight to the outside wheels. If the wheels are independently suspended, there is nothing to counter this tendency and the car leans toward the outside of the turn, making steering and handling difficult in extreme cases. To minimize this effect, the left and right A-arms are often linked by a stabilizer bar. Essentially a torsion bar that runs across the car, the stabilizer bar twists as the car leans, resisting the motion and keeping the car relatively level. It also restricts the independent action of the wheels somewhat. Stabilizer bars are also called *anti-sway bars, sway bars, anti-roll bars,* or *roll bars.*

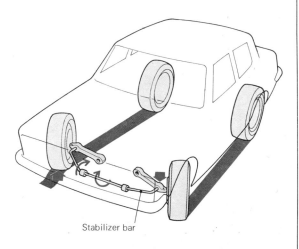

Stabilizer bar

Rear suspension

Rear suspension, like front suspension, is designed to keep the wheels in contact with the road and to give the passengers a comfortable ride, so the two systems have much in common. However, some of the problems that rear suspension must resolve are unique.

The load carried by the front wheels is fairly constant: the weight of the engine and the forward sections of the body and frame. The rear wheels carry a variable load, depending on the number of passengers and the amount of cargo. Rear springs must not sag too much under added load and must not be too stiff without it. If load fluctuations are large, air-adjustable shocks may be needed.

While the front wheels must steer left and right as well as move up and down, the rear wheels should remain straight regardless of their up-and-down movement or the position of the car in turns. Instead of the ball joints used in the front suspension to allow the wheels to swivel freely, the rear wheels are attached to the axles in a way that restricts their movement to the vertical plane.

The most important difference between front and rear suspensions is that in rear-wheel-drive cars, drive-train torque is transferred to the road through the rear wheels. *Torque* is the twisting force that turns the wheels and thereby moves the car. This twisting force also tries to turn parts of the suspension that must be held relatively rigid, so the rear suspension must be designed to resist torque. This is accomplished by precise placement of the suspension components and by adding control arms between the

Live-axle rear suspension

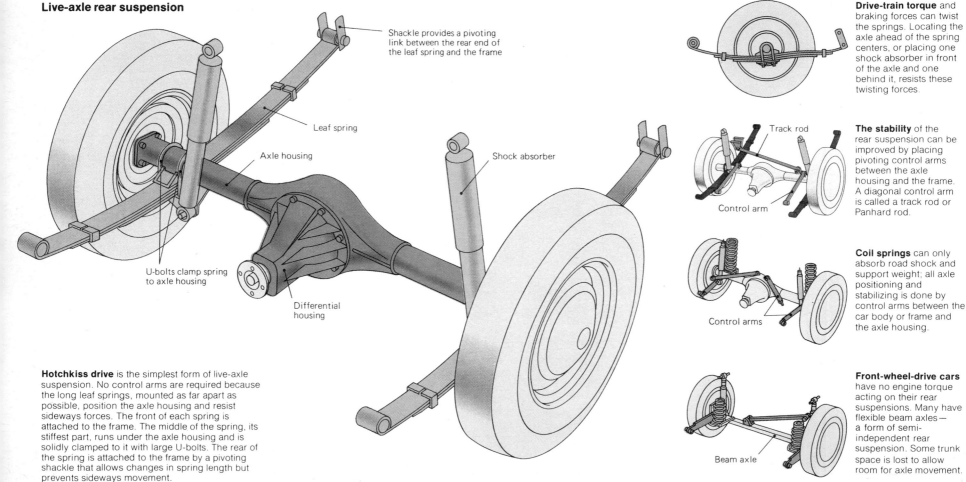

Shackle provides a pivoting link between the rear end of the leaf spring and the frame

Leaf spring

Axle housing

Shock absorber

U-bolts clamp spring to axle housing

Differential housing

Drive-train torque and braking forces can twist the springs. Locating the axle ahead of the spring centers, or placing one shock absorber in front of the axle and one behind it, resists these twisting forces.

The stability of the rear suspension can be improved by placing pivoting control arms between the axle housing and the frame. A diagonal control arm is called a track rod or Panhard rod.

Track rod

Control arm

Coil springs can only absorb road shock and support weight; all axle positioning and stabilizing is done by control arms between the car body or frame and the axle housing.

Control arms

Front-wheel-drive cars have no engine torque acting on their rear suspensions. Many have flexible beam axles — a form of semi-independent rear suspension. Some trunk space is lost to allow room for axle movement.

Beam axle

Hotchkiss drive is the simplest form of live-axle suspension. No control arms are required because the long leaf springs, mounted as far apart as possible, position the axle housing and resist sideways forces. The front of each spring is attached to the frame. The middle of the spring, its stiffest part, runs under the axle housing and is solidly clamped to it with large U-bolts. The rear of the spring is attached to the frame by a pivoting shackle that allows changes in spring length but prevents sideways movement.

frame and the suspension. Two basic types of rear suspension have been developed for rear-wheel-drive cars: *live-axle* and *independent* rear suspension.

Live-axle rear suspension: The predominant feature of a live-axle setup is the axle housing, which runs the width of the car and bounces when either wheel hits a bump. The differential and the axle shafts are contained in the axle housing.

The axle housing itself is positioned by the rear suspension.

If leaf springs are used, they locate the axle and resist sideways thrust in turns, as well as absorbing road shock. A coil-spring suspension requires control arms between the frame and the axle housing to position the axle and resist side thrust, because the coil springs can absorb only vertical forces.

Independent rear suspension: Like independent front suspension, independent rear suspension allows each wheel to respond to the road separately. Because there is no axle housing, the differential is mounted on the car's frame. The suspension does not have to resist drive-train torque, which acts on the frame.

A common problem on older cars with simple swing-axle independent rear suspension was keeping the wheels perpendicular to the road in turns. The rear wheels would develop positive camber (tilt outward at the top), reducing the tire treads' grip on the road and, in extreme cases, causing the car to skid and possibly flip over. Four U-joints and various control-arm modifications are used in modern designs to keep the wheels nearly perpendicular to the road.

Independent rear suspension

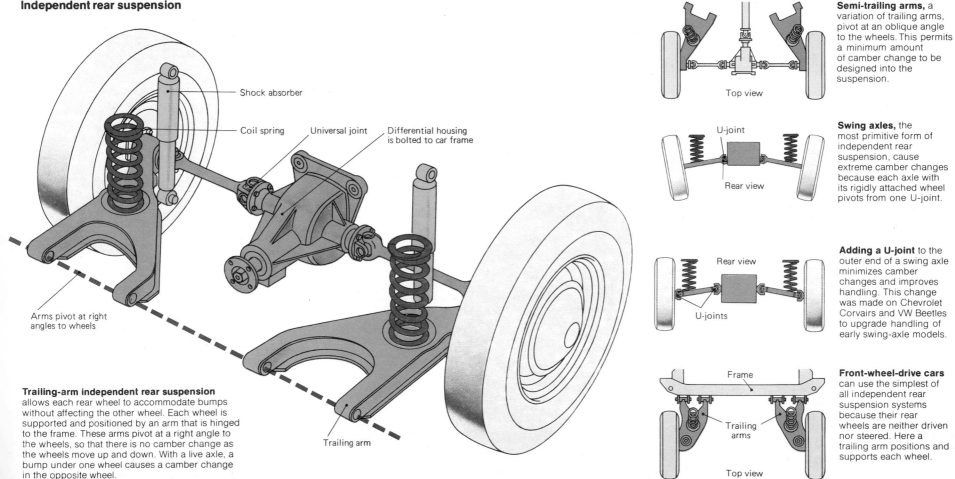

Shock absorber

Coil spring

Universal joint

Differential housing is bolted to car frame

Arms pivot at right angles to wheels

Trailing-arm independent rear suspension allows each rear wheel to accommodate bumps without affecting the other wheel. Each wheel is supported and positioned by an arm that is hinged to the frame. These arms pivot at a right angle to the wheels, so that there is no camber change as the wheels move up and down. With a live axle, a bump under one wheel causes a camber change in the opposite wheel.

Trailing arm

Semi-trailing arms, a variation of trailing arms, pivot at an oblique angle to the wheels. This permits a minimum amount of camber change to be designed into the suspension.

Top view

U-joint

Rear view

Swing axles, the most primitive form of independent rear suspension, cause extreme camber changes because each axle with its rigidly attached wheel pivots from one U-joint.

Rear view

U-joints

Adding a U-joint to the outer end of a swing axle minimizes camber changes and improves handling. This change was made on Chevrolet Corvairs and VW Beetles to upgrade handling of early swing-axle models.

Frame

Trailing arms

Top view

Front-wheel-drive cars can use the simplest of all independent rear suspension systems because their rear wheels are neither driven nor steered. Here a trailing arm positions and supports each wheel.

Wheel alignment

Wheel alignment refers to all of the angular relationships between the front suspension and steering components, wheels, and frame. Five angles are manipulated by the car designer to reach a compromise between optimum tire life, fuel economy, and handling. Maximum fuel economy and tire life are achieved if the tires are perfectly upright and parallel to the direction of travel. But a car steers and handles better if its tires run at a slight angle. This causes them to scuff along the pavement a bit as they roll, which reduces tire life and fuel economy.

Camber is the inward or outward tilt of the wheel, measured in degrees between the tire centerline and the vertical. If the wheel tilts out, camber is said to be *positive;* if it tilts in, the camber is *negative.*

Caster is the angle that the steering axis is offset from the vertical, measured from front to back. If the steering knuckle tilts toward the back, caster is *positive,* and if it tilts toward the front, caster is *negative.*

Steering axis inclination is the angle that the steering axis is offset from the vertical, measured from side to side. If the upper ball joints are farther inward than the lower ones, the wheels will straighten out if the steering wheel is released while the car is moving.

Toe-in means that the front edges of the wheels are closer together than the rear edges. Toe-in counteracts the tendency of the front wheels of rear-drive cars to toe out under power. When the car is moving at highway speeds, toe-in disappears and the wheels roll straight.

Toe-out is sometimes used in front-drive cars to counteract their tendency to toe in under power. Some toe-out on turns is necessary for all cars because the inner wheel must turn at a sharper angle than the outer wheel.

Toe is adjustable on all cars. Caster and camber also are adjustable on most suspension designs.

Zero camber

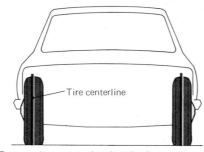

Zero camber means that the wheels are perpendicular to the road, so that the tire treads contact the road evenly. This position minimizes tire wear by distributing the car's weight uniformly across the tread, but steering tends to be heavy.

Negative camber

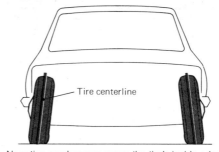

Negative camber can cause the tire's inside edges to wear faster than the outside edges. Independent suspension allows a small amount of negative camber when a wheel moves up going over a bump, so that the track will not vary (see p.124).

Positive camber

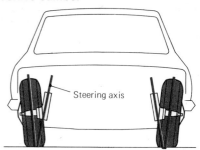

Positive camber can cause the outside edges of the tires to wear faster. Front wheels often have a little positive camber in order to provide stable handling in turns on the typical high-crowned road or when the pavement is bumpy.

Positive caster

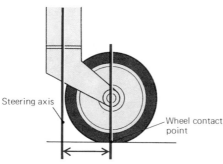

Positive caster is most simply demonstrated by shopping cart wheels. The point where each front wheel touches the ground is behind the steering axis. This puts the load in front of the wheels, and they swing around to follow. The cart then tends to move in a straight line unless it is deliberately steered in a different direction.

Positive caster on a car

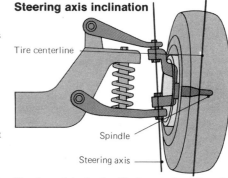

Positive caster is designed into cars for the same reason—to improve directional stability. With the steering knuckle tilted back, the steering axis meets the road ahead of the midpoint of the tire's contact area, and the car, like the shopping cart, tends to travel straight ahead unless the driver steers it in a different direction.

Steering axis inclination

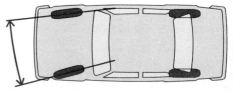

Steering axis inclination tilts the spindles. When the wheels are straight, the spindles are horizontal. When the wheels turn, the outer ends of the spindles try to move down. Since the road prevents this, the inner ends lift up the car. When the steering wheel is released, gravity forces the car down and the wheels straighten out.

Toe-in and toe-out

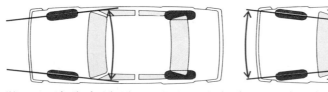

If it were not for the fact that they are firmly attached to the suspension, wheels that toe in would run toward one another (left) and those that toe out would diverge (right). Wheels that toe in or toe out at highway speeds will scuff badly, resulting in uneven tire wear and poor fuel economy.

Toe-out on turns

Toe-out on turns allows the inner wheel to steer through a tighter angle than the outer wheel, so that both wheels can turn around the same point.

How the car is aimed

Steering systems are designed to enable 100-pound people to control 4,000-pound vehicles quickly, accurately, smoothly, and without undue effort. This is done by a set of components that lead from the steering wheel to the front wheels.

Because the steering wheel is a small lever (its radius is only about 7 inches, or 17 cm), the driver needs a *mechanical advantage* to overcome the inertia of the car's weight and the friction between the tires and the road. This advantage is provided by the *steering ratio*—the number of 360° turns of the steering wheel that are required to swivel the front wheels from *lock to lock* (all the way from left to right—usually 60 degrees). For example, a ratio of 15:1 means that 2½ turns of the steering wheel (900 degrees) turn the front wheels 60 degrees. The steering ratio is therefore 900:60, or 15:1. A low ratio responds more quickly to the wheel but requires more power to operate than a high ratio does.

The *steering shaft* runs inside a tubular *steering column*, through the fire wall, and into the steering gearbox in the engine compartment. Modern steering shafts are designed to collapse on impact to protect the driver in a collision.

The *steering gearbox* converts the rotational motion of the steering wheel into the side-to-side motion of the wheels. The gears reduce the large movements of the steering wheel to the small movements of the wheels, giving the driver the necessary mechanical advantage.

The *steering linkage* consists of a series of rods running across the front of the car to connect the front wheels to each other and to the steering gearbox. In the *parallelogram linkage* used on most North American cars, the *Pitman arm* extends from the steering gearbox and transmits gear movement to the left end of a *relay rod*, which runs across the car. An *idler arm,* parallel to the Pitman arm, is attached to the frame to support the right end of the relay rod. *Tie rods* connect the relay rod to the *steering arms,* which transmit movement to the *steering knuckles* to pivot the wheels. Ball joints between the tie rods and steering arms allow steering movement to be transmitted even as the suspension moves up and down over a bumpy road surface.

Parallelogram steering in action

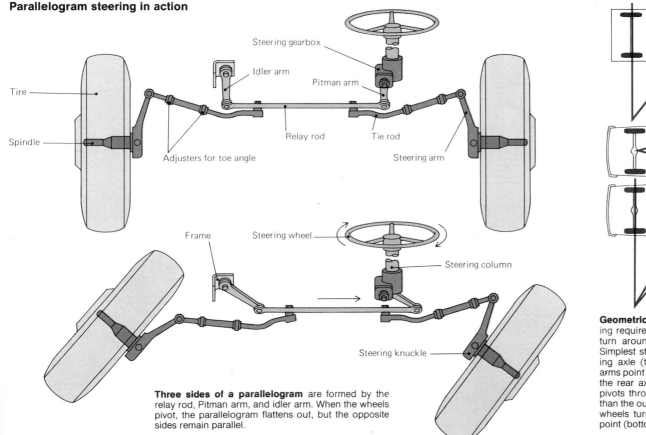

Steering gearbox
Idler arm
Pitman arm
Tire
Spindle
Relay rod
Tie rod
Adjusters for toe angle
Steering arm
Frame
Steering wheel
Steering column
Steering knuckle

Three sides of a parallelogram are formed by the relay rod, Pitman arm, and idler arm. When the wheels pivot, the parallelogram flattens out, but the opposite sides remain parallel.

Geometrically correct steering requires all four wheels to turn around the same center. Simplest steering is by a pivoting axle (top). If the steering arms point toward the center of the rear axle, the inner wheel pivots through a tighter angle than the outer wheel, so that all wheels turn around the same point (bottom).

Collapsible steering columns

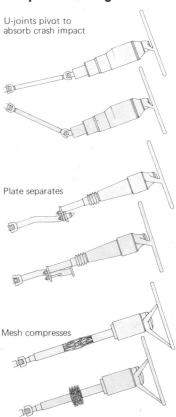

U-joints pivot to absorb crash impact

Plate separates

Mesh compresses

Manual steering

The steering gearbox contains two gears: the *driving gear,* which is mounted on the steering shaft, and the *driven gear,* which moves the steering linkage. The driving gear always turns through the same arc as the steering wheel and shaft, but the larger driven gear moves through only a fraction of its length or circumference for each full revolution of the driving gear. A small force applied through a large angle at the steering wheel is transformed into a large force moving through a small angle at the steering linkage. This provides the mechanical advantage needed to turn the wheels.

Rack and pinion is the simplest form of steering. The small pinion gear on the end of the steering shaft (the driving gear) meshes with the rack (the driven gear), a long bar with teeth cut into one side. The rack runs across the car, and its ends are connected to the tie rods. Turning the steering wheel rotates the pinion, which moves the rack left or right.

The *worm and roller* steering gearbox is named for its component gears. The worm (the driving gear) is a spiral-threaded gear mounted on the end of the steering shaft. It meshes at a right angle with the threads of the roller (the driven gear), a wheel-shaped gear mounted on the Pitman shaft.

The *recirculating-ball* steering gearbox is designed to reduce friction between the gears. This system also uses a worm gear on the end of the steering shaft as the driving gear; but instead of engaging the driven gear directly, the worm gear is threaded into a *ball nut rack,* like a bolt into a nut. About 40 steel ball bearings fit in the thread-like grooves between the worm gear and the ball nut rack. A tube connects the ends of the threads. The balls move into the tube at one end and reemerge at the other end; this gives them a continuous loop to follow and prevents them from piling up at one end of the ball nut rack.

Rack and pinion steering linkage

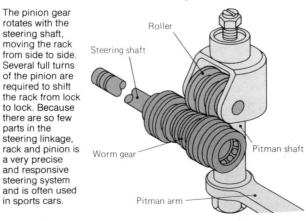

Parallelogram steering linkage

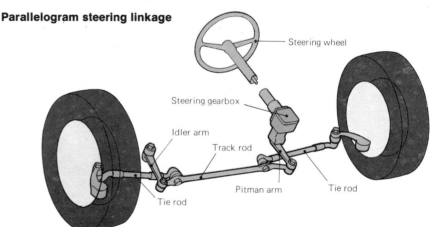

Rack and pinion gearbox

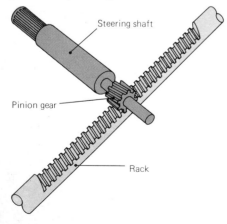

The pinion gear rotates with the steering shaft, moving the rack from side to side. Several full turns of the pinion are required to shift the rack from lock to lock. Because there are so few parts in the steering linkage, rack and pinion is a very precise and responsive steering system and is often used in sports cars.

Worm and roller gearbox

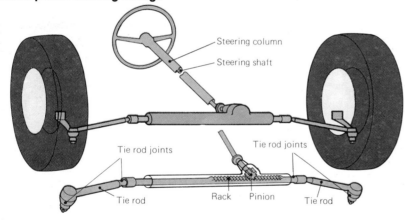

Worm and roller gearbox is used with parallelogram linkage. Threads on the worm gear engage the threads of the roller. Both ends of the worm gear are supported by ball bearings to reduce friction. When the steering wheel is turned, the roller moves along the worm gear, swiveling the Pitman shaft.

Recirculating-ball gearbox

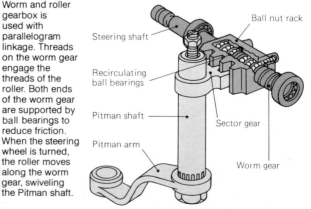

Turning the steering wheel rotates the worm gear, which causes the ball nut rack to move up or down. Teeth on the outer edge of the ball nut rack mesh with the sector gear so that as the rack moves, it swivels the sector gear and Pitman arm. The ball bearings in the grooves reduce friction.

Power steering

Power steering uses hydraulic pressure to reduce the effort needed to steer heavy cars. There are two basic systems. *Integral power steering* applies the pressure inside the steering gearbox. This system, illustrated below, is used in most new cars. *Linkage power steering* employs a separate hydraulic cylinder to apply power assistance directly to the steering linkage. The advantage of the linkage system is that it can be attached to an existing steering system with few modifications. This is usually easier and cheaper for the manufacturer than changing the steering gearbox.

An integral power steering gearbox is similar to a recirculating-ball manual steering gearbox except that the case is filled with hydraulic fluid. The ball nut rack divides this case into two chambers and serves as the piston on which the hydraulic pressure operates.

A control valve in the gearbox, activated by the steering shaft whenever the steering wheel is turned, opens and closes passages that direct fluid into the proper chamber for a left or right turn. The control valve also directs excess fluid back to the reservoir.

Rack and pinion can be designed with power assist, too. A flange on the steering rack acts as a piston, and hydraulic pressure is supplied to either side of it.

The power steering pump is driven by a belt from the engine. A pressure relief valve in the pump protects the system from excess pressure when the engine is turning at high speeds.

Two hoses connect the pump to the steering gearbox. The pressure hose carries fluid under pressures as high as 1,500 psi (10,300 kPa) to the gearbox. The return hose carries fluid back to the pump at a pressure of about 50 psi (350 kPa).

Some power steering systems have variable ratios; the steering ratio changes the further the wheels turn, which speeds up parking maneuvers.

Power steering system

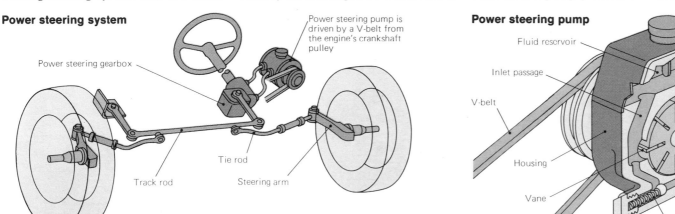

Power steering pump is driven by a V-belt from the engine's crankshaft pulley

Power steering gearbox

Tie rod

Track rod

Steering arm

Power steering pump

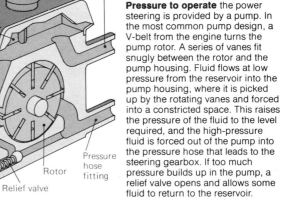

Return hose fitting

Fluid reservoir

Inlet passage

V-belt

Housing

Vane

Relief valve

Rotor

Pressure hose fitting

Pressure to operate the power steering is provided by a pump. In the most common pump design, a V-belt from the engine turns the pump rotor. A series of vanes fit snugly between the rotor and the pump housing. Fluid flows at low pressure from the reservoir into the pump housing, where it is picked up by the rotating vanes and forced into a constricted space. This raises the pressure of the fluid to the level required, and the high-pressure fluid is forced out of the pump into the pressure hose that leads to the steering gearbox. If too much pressure builds up in the pump, a relief valve opens and allows some fluid to return to the reservoir.

Straight ahead

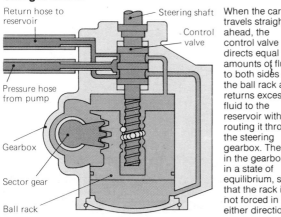

Return hose to reservoir

Steering shaft

Control valve

Pressure hose from pump

Gearbox

Sector gear

Ball rack

When the car travels straight ahead, the control valve directs equal amounts of fluid to both sides of the ball rack and returns excess fluid to the reservoir without routing it through the steering gearbox. The fluid in the gearbox is in a state of equilibrium, so that the rack is not forced in either direction.

Right turn

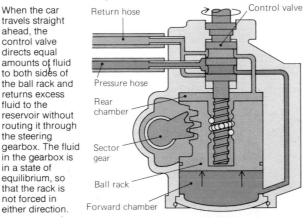

Return hose

Control valve

Pressure hose

Rear chamber

Sector gear

Ball rack

Forward chamber

Turning the wheel clockwise causes the control valve to direct high-pressure fluid to the forward chamber of the gearbox. Fluid helps move the rack and rotate the sector gear and Pitman arm counterclockwise; this pivots the wheels to the right. Fluid from rear chamber enters return hose.

Left turn

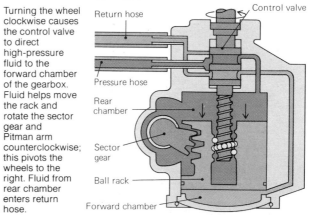

Return hose

Control valve

Pressure hose

Rear chamber

Sector gear

Ball rack

Forward chamber

Turning the wheel counterclockwise moves the control valve into a position that routes high-pressure fluid to the rear chamber of the gearbox. Fluid pressure helps push the rack down and rotate the sector gear and Pitman arm clockwise. Excess fluid is forced from the forward chamber into the return hose.

Car wiring

About 200 feet of wire link the electrical components in a modern car. All the wiring—with the exception of grounding straps, battery leads, and high-voltage ignition wires—is wrapped with insulation of various colors to permit quick recognition when repairs are necessary.

Manufacturer's repair manuals usually include a complete diagram of the car circuits. These diagrams are intended to help you identify the wires by their colors but bear little or no relationship to the actual positions of the wires and components in the car. The diagrams use symbols like those on the facing page to represent components.

Below is a simplified illustration of the wiring and components as they are lo-cated inside a car. The entire system is divided into an ignition circuit, a starter circuit, a charging circuit, lighting circuits, and accessory circuits.

Colors are used in the illustration to distinguish the various circuits; the colors are not meant to represent the color-coding system of a particular car. A few electrical accessories have been omitted below for the sake of clarity.

The battery supports the electrical system by supplying current to the lights and accessories when the engine is not running and by supplying the power that starts the engine. After the engine is running, the *alternator* takes over, recharging the battery and meeting all the other electrical requirements of the car.

Typical wiring harness

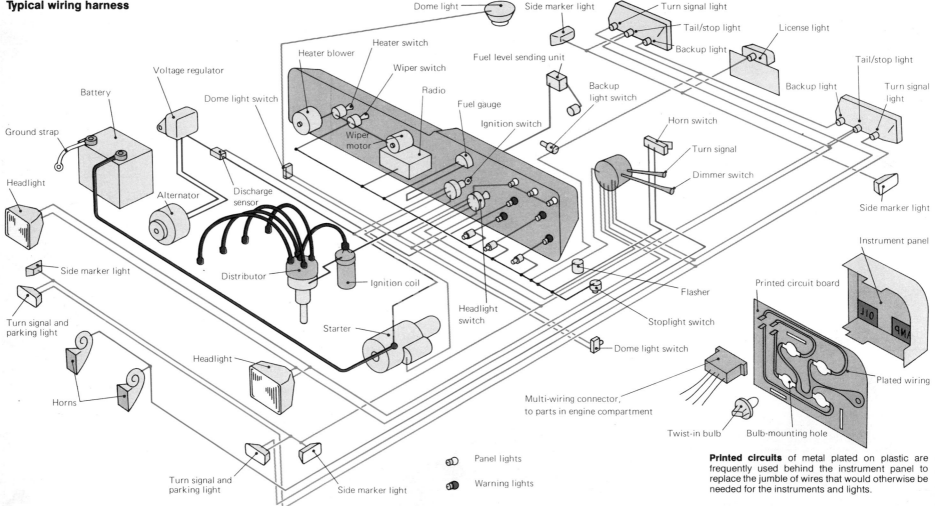

Printed circuits of metal plated on plastic are frequently used behind the instrument panel to replace the jumble of wires that would otherwise be needed for the instruments and lights.

Basic elements of electricity

Electricity is the flow of tiny subatomic particles, called *electrons,* from one place to another. Electrons contain a negative *charge;* they are attracted to particles of opposite (positive) charge and repulsed by particles with the same charge. It is this force that causes electrons to flow, thereby producing electrical power.

The flow of electricity in a wire can be likened to the flow of water through a pipe. An example is water draining a reservoir to run a waterwheel. The reservoir is like a battery, the valve is like a switch, and the pipes are like wires. The wheel is like an *electrical load,* which can

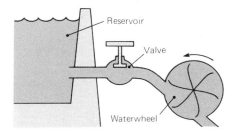
Reservoir
Valve
Waterwheel

be a light bulb, an electric motor, an ignition system, or the like. A diagram of three basic electrical components is shown below. The diagram describes a *circuit.* The circuit includes a return wire

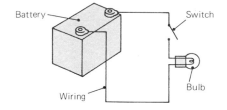
Battery
Switch
Wiring
Bulb

from the load to the battery. All electrical circuits form closed loops; without a return, current could not flow.

The metal body and engine of a car are used as the return wire for all the electrical circuits. This is called *grounding,* and it reduces the actual amount of wire needed by half.

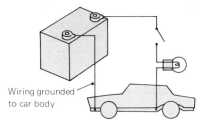
Wiring grounded
to car body

In a waterwheel system it is sometimes desirable to know the pressure of the water when it emerges from the pipe and how much water is flowing out. The same kind of information is often helpful when discussing electrical circuits.

Pressure in a reservoir system can be estimated simply by knowing how high the water is above the waterwheel. The amount of pressure in an electrical circuit, however, is not so easily seen. It is called *voltage,* and an instrument called a voltmeter is needed to measure it. The unit of measurement is a *volt.*

Likewise, the flow of water can be seen, but a flow of electrons is invisible. In a circuit, electron flow is called a *current.* It is measured in *amperes* with an ammeter.

The size of the load in electrical circuits can be measured, too. Load size is called *resistance;* it is measured in *ohms* with an ohmmeter.

These three quantities are connected arithmetically by Ohm's Law:

$$\text{Current} = \frac{\text{Voltage}}{\text{Resistance}}$$

If two of the three quantities are known, the third can be calculated.

For example, if the bulb in the circuit shown above has a resistance of 6 ohms and it is connected to a 12-volt battery, the current flowing through it will be 12 divided by 6, or 2 amperes.

The *power* consumed by a motor or a light is calculated in *watts:* wattage is current times voltage. A 15-ampere headlight operating at 12 volts consumes 180 watts of electrical power.

Coupled to the electric force that sends electrons running through wires is a *magnetic* force that always exerts itself at right angles to the direction of the electron current. In most circuits this force is chaotic and negligible. However, if the electrons are made to flow many times in a spiral—as through many turns of wire wrapped around an iron bar—the forces are lined up and create a magnet:

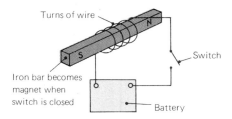
Turns of wire
N
S
Switch
Iron bar becomes
magnet when
switch is closed
Battery

Magnets exert mechanical pull. When oriented in a ring, as in an electric motor, they can be used to pull the motor's shaft continuously around. This is basically the way all electric motors work. It is also the principle behind the operation of *solenoid switches;* the magnetic pull from a coil of wire can move a rod that will close a door lock or engage the starter motor. When the principle operates in reverse, mechanical motion is converted into electricity, as in a car's *alternator.*

Because of the way alternators are built, they produce current that changes direction frequently; this is called alternating current (AC). A *diode* is used to convert this to one-way current, called direct current (DC). Diodes act like one-

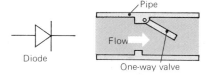
Pipe
Flow
Diode
One-way valve

way valves in water pipes: they allow the current to flow in one direction but block flow in the other direction.

Electrical symbols

Batteries	
Ground connections	
Fuses	
Switches	
Wire coil	
Contact points	
Bulbs	
Diode	
Variable resistors	
Capacitors	
Transistors	
Gauges	
Wires joining	
Wires not joining	
Connectors	

Electrical symbols, many of which are standard throughout the automotive industry, are used in diagrams of car wiring to indicate electrical components and wire connections.

The battery

The battery supplies electricity to the ignition system, starter motor, lights, and a car's other electrical equipment.

The battery is made up of a number of *cells,* each with just over 2 volts, whose terminals are linked by metal bars. Modern car batteries have six cells, giving a total output of 12 volts.

Each cell consists of two sets of plates, or *electrodes,* in a solution of water and sulfuric acid (called the *electrolyte*). One set of plates is made of lead peroxide; the other, of porous lead.

When a cell is functioning, the acid reacts with the plates, converting chemical energy into electrical energy. A positive charge is built up on the lead perox-ide electrode and a negative charge on the lead electrode.

Electric current, measured in *amperes,* flows from one terminal of the battery, through the car's electrical system, to the opposite battery terminal, and then through the electrolyte.

As the chemical reaction goes on, lead sulfate forms on the surface of both electrodes, and the sulfuric acid gradually turns to water. When the surfaces of both plates have become fully coated by lead sulfate, the battery is discharged. Recharging the battery with an electric current restores the electrodes to their original condition and regenerates the sulfuric acid.

A battery eventually goes dead and cannot be recharged for a number of reasons: The plates may become so encrusted with sulfate that a charge cannot get through to them. The plates may disintegrate. Or current leakage between cell plates can cause a short circuit.

Battery capacity is measured in several ways. The most useful is the *zero cold test,* which tells how many amperes a battery can deliver at 0°F over a period of 30 seconds before any cell falls below 1.2 volts. A large engine may need a 400-ampere battery to adequately start it; a small engine, only a 250-ampere battery. Another rating is *reserve capacity*—the number of minutes that a battery can run a car if the alternator is not working.

The heaviest demand made on a battery occurs when the car is being started. During the short period that the starter is turning the engine over, it may be drawing as much as 400 amperes from the battery. (Headlights, in comparison, draw about 15 amperes, and taillights only 1.5 amperes.) Because of this high current drain, the starter should never be operated for more than 30 seconds at a time; it should then be allowed to rest for a minute, to reduce the chance of draining the battery completely.

Once the engine is running, the alternator generates enough current to recharge the battery and keep it charged.

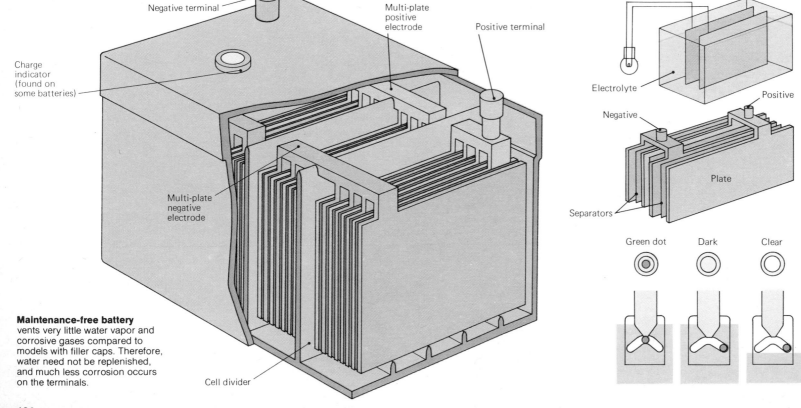

Negative terminal

Multi-plate positive electrode

Positive terminal

Charge indicator (found on some batteries)

Multi-plate negative electrode

Maintenance-free battery vents very little water vapor and corrosive gases compared to models with filler caps. Therefore, water need not be replenished, and much less corrosion occurs on the terminals.

Cell divider

Electrolyte

Negative

Positive

Plate

Separators

Green dot   Dark   Clear

Electrical energy can be stored as well as produced by two metal plates immersed in a chemical solution (top). The larger the surface area of the plates, the more energy can be stored. Large surface areas are achieved by using a stack of plates connected alternately (bottom). Nonconducting, porous plate separators prevent short circuits. Each stack of plates forms a cell with a voltage of slightly more than 2 volts. Cell voltage remains the same no matter how large the cell is made. To achieve higher voltages, cells must be connected in series; for example, six cells will produce 12 volts.

Built-in indicator shows state of charge and level of battery fluid. When battery is more than 65 percent charged, ball floats to tip of plastic rod and is visible in round window as a green dot (left). When battery needs recharging, ball sinks and dot disappears. If window remains dark (center), fluid level still covers plastic rod. When level drops, window becomes clear (right), indicating that water must be added or battery discarded.

The alternator

Without a generator, the electrical demands of a modern car would soon drain a fully charged battery. The generator is mounted at the front of the engine and is connected to the engine crankshaft by the fan belt. Electricity is generated when the engine turns the fan belt.

Car generators used to be the type that produced direct current (DC); now only AC generators—called *alternators*—are used. Alternators generate alternating current (AC), which must be converted to DC. But alternators are lighter and more reliable than the older DC generators.

An alternator can produce more current than a DC generator of the same size. This gives it an advantage in heavy traffic and permits the use of extra electrical accessories.

The amount of current generated depends on how fast a generator turns; the alternator can be geared to run at relatively higher speeds because its interior parts are lighter than those inside a DC generator. As a result, alternators generate some electricity even when the car engine is idling. DC generators could not be adjusted to do this without gearing them to run too fast at highway speeds or setting the idle speed of the engine at an unusually high and wasteful level.

As in a generator, current is produced in an alternator when a wire crosses a magnetic field. In an alternator, however, the wire, in coiled form, is held stationary and the magnetic field is turned.

Because the battery and everything else electrical in the car works on DC, the AC output of the alternator must be converted to DC. This is done with *semiconductor rectifiers* made from silicon. Rectifiers pass current in one direction only. The silicon rectifiers are mounted inside the alternator housing. Before the advent of silicon semiconductors, rectifiers were very large and troublesome to cool, and alternators were used only on large commercial vehicles.

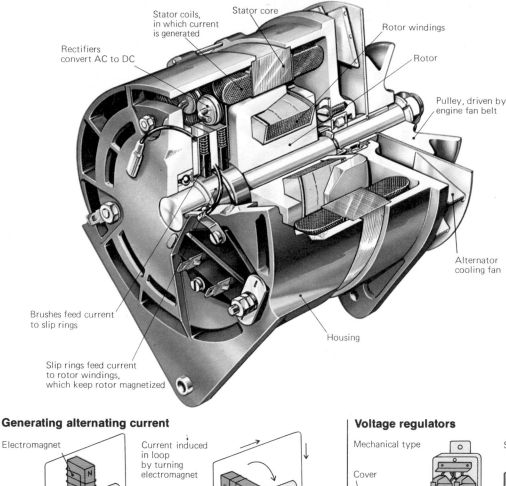

Rectifiers convert AC to DC

Stator coils, in which current is generated

Stator core

Rotor windings

Rotor

Pulley, driven by engine fan belt

Alternator cooling fan

Brushes feed current to slip rings

Slip rings feed current to rotor windings, which keep rotor magnetized

Housing

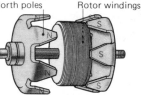

North poles

Rotor windings

Rotating part of alternator (*rotor*) includes an electromagnet that is magnetized by current from the battery. Current flows into rotor windings via slip rings. North and south poles are shaped like interlocking fingers to create an alternating field as the rotor turns.

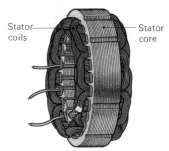

Stator coils

Stator core

Stationary coils in an alternator (called the *stator*) intercept the rotating magnetic field produced by the rotor. Interception of the field is enhanced by a cylindrical core made of laminated soft iron.

Generating alternating current

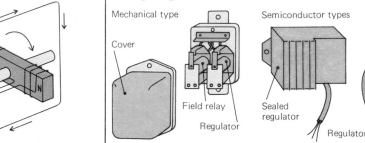

Electromagnet

Current induced in loop by turning electromagnet

Wire loop

Alternator works on the principle that an electric current is generated in a wire whenever the wire passes through a magnetic field. For the field, the alternator has an electromagnet operated by a small amount of current from the battery; the current reaches the electromagnet coils via slip rings on the alternator shaft. As the electromagnet is turned by the car engine, the field is intercepted by the outer loop of wire, and current flows through the wire first in one direction, then in the other, resulting in alternating current.

Voltage regulators

Mechanical type

Cover

Semiconductor types

Alternator

Field relay

Regulator

Sealed regulator

Regulator

Voltage regulator prevents overcharging of the battery by reducing current to the rotating electromagnet as the engine speeds up. This limits the alternator's voltage output. Older type of regulator was an electromechanical vibrator (left); these have mostly been replaced by circuits using semiconductor diodes in a sealed unit mounted inside alternator (right) or sometimes outside it (center). Cars with electromechanical regulators have a field relay in the regulator unit to keep the battery from discharging through the alternator when the engine is off.

The starter

The starter is a conventional electric motor designed to turn the engine until it fires. Most car engines have to be rotated at 50 to 150 rpm before they will start. This requires considerable electric power, particularly in winter, when the engine is cold and the oil is thick.

To manage this high current, a switch called a *solenoid* is frequently used to turn on the starter. The solenoid and/or starter may be triggered by a *relay*.

The starter turns the engine's crankshaft through a pair of gears. One, the *pinion*, is mounted on the starter shaft. It engages with the other, the *flywheel*, which rotates the crankshaft. The gear ratio between pinion and flywheel is generally about 10:1—that is, the torque of the starter is multiplied 10 times.

When the engine fires, the starter pinion must disengage from the flywheel. Otherwise, the engine will run the starter motor at a high speed and damage it.

The starter works in the same way as any electric motor—it depends on the force that magnets exert on each other. The south pole of a magnet is attracted to the north pole of another, and vice versa.

Inside a starter is a set of fixed electromagnets called the *field magnets*, or *field windings*. Between them is the *armature*—another set of electromagnets that change polarity as they turn, becoming south whenever north on a field magnet is approached, and vice versa.

The change of polarity is achieved by a rotating *commutator* that makes contact with a pair of carbon brushes.

Some starters differ from the General Motors unit shown here. Chrysler starters have an extra set of gears between the starter shaft and the pinion to further multiply torque. On Ford starters, the lever that engages the pinion gear is moved by a pole inside the starter rather than by a solenoid switch. The pole is activated whenever current flows through the starter motor coils.

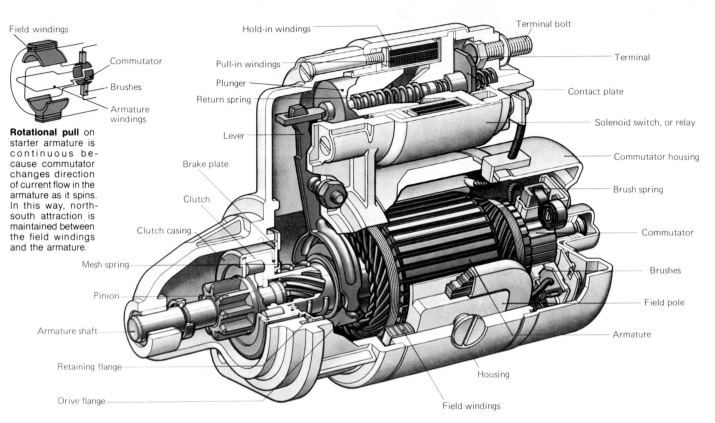

Rotational pull on starter armature is continuous because commutator changes direction of current flow in the armature as it spins. In this way, north-south attraction is maintained between the field windings and the armature.

Labels on main diagram: Field windings · Commutator · Brushes · Armature windings · Hold-in windings · Terminal bolt · Pull-in windings · Terminal · Plunger · Contact plate · Return spring · Solenoid switch, or relay · Lever · Commutator housing · Brake plate · Brush spring · Clutch · Clutch casing · Commutator · Mesh spring · Brushes · Pinion · Field pole · Armature shaft · Armature · Retaining flange · Housing · Drive flange · Field windings

The relay

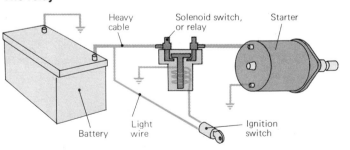

Labels: Heavy cable · Solenoid switch, or relay · Starter · Battery · Light wire · Ignition switch

To start the engine, the driver turns the starter switch, which closes a relay on some cars, allowing current to flow to the starter. A relay is, in effect, a switch turned on by a switch, a complication made necessary because of the high current the starter must handle. Inside the solenoid switch, a small current flows through the electromagnet, which then pulls a contact plate against two heavy-duty, high-current terminals, allowing current to flow.

How the solenoid switch engages the starter

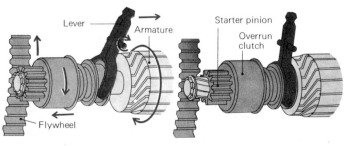

Labels: Lever · Armature · Starter pinion · Overrun clutch · Flywheel

When a solenoid switch is closed, it simultaneously actuates a lever that pushes the starter pinion into engagement with the engine flywheel (left). The starter then cranks the engine until it fires and runs of its own accord. As the engine picks up speed, it is prevented from turning the starter shaft any faster by a one-way overrun clutch, thus protecting the starter from damage. When the driver releases the starter switch, the pinion disengages (right).

Dashboard instruments

Dashboard gauges and lights are electrical devices that are powered by the battery after the ignition switch is turned on. They measure or monitor battery charge, fluid level in the fuel tank, engine oil pressure, and coolant temperature. Mechanically operated gauges indicate car speed and distance traveled. Most dashboard instruments consist of a dial, or a warning light, and a remotely mounted sensing element that is connected to the dial by a wire or cable.

Coolant temperature, for example, is sensed by a *thermistor* element screwed into the engine block so that it makes physical contact with the coolant in the water jacket. Oil pressure is sensed by a device that is screwed into the engine block and penetrates to an oil passage. Battery charge or discharge, on the other hand, is indicated directly by an ammeter inserted in the circuit between the alternator and the battery.

Two kinds of gauge are used to indicate temperature, fuel level, and oil pressure: the bimetallic type (shown for temperature, below) and the multi-coil type (shown for oil pressure). Either gauge can be used for all three measurements.

The ammeter is a third type of gauge. It measures all the current flowing back and forth between the alternator and battery; or, in the variation shown below, the ammeter samples just a small portion of the current—the remainder is bypassed through what is called a *shunt resistance*.

Warning lights are frequently found in place of gauges. These are simpler and less expensive than gauges. They tell less about the condition being monitored but have the advantage of catching the driver's attention as soon as a problem occurs. Warning light sensing units work much as gauges do. For example, an oil-pressure sensing element used with a warning light is like the one shown below, but it has a simple on-off switch, not a variable-resistance element.

Ammeter

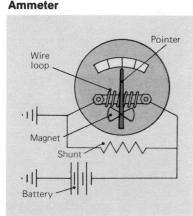

When current flows from alternator into battery (charging condition), it passes through loop of wire in the ammeter, inducing a magnetic field in the loop. The field pulls on the magnet to which the meter's pointer is attached, causing pointer to pivot to the right. When current flows away from battery (discharge condition), pointer swings left.

Temperature gauge

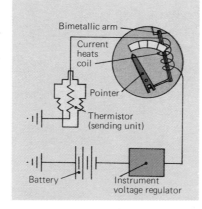

Temperature of engine coolant is sensed by a semiconductor called a thermistor. As coolant temperature rises, the thermistor's electrical resistance decreases, resulting in an increase of electrical current to the temperature gauge. The gauge, in turn, has a *bimetallic arm* that responds to increases in current by bending and pivoting the gauge's pointer toward the high end of the scale.

Fuel gauge

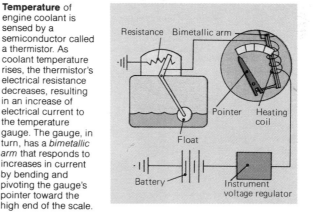

As tank empties, float inside tank drops and resistance to electrical current flow increases. This results in a drop in current through the heating coil in the fuel gauge and a decrease in the coil's temperature. The bimetallic arm around which the coil is wrapped then unbends, pivoting the pointer toward the low end of the scale.

Oil-pressure gauge

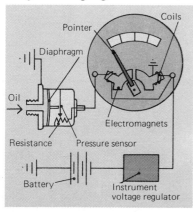

Pressure sensor screwed into engine block has a spring-loaded diaphragm that reacts to increased oil pressure by pushing a slider along a resistance element. The balance of current flow into the pair of coils inside the pressure gauge is then altered. This, in turn, alters the relative strength of the electromagnets, causing the gauge's pointer to read higher on the scale.

Speedometer

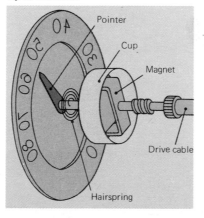

Flexible drive cable connects the speedometer to car's front wheel or to the transmission output shaft. As car speeds up, magnet attached to cable spins faster, which increases its pull on a metal cup that surrounds the magnet. The pull is restrained by a hairspring that lets the cup rotate to a degree directly proportional to the speed of the magnet. The pointer is attached to the cup.

Odometer

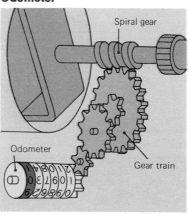

Spiral gear on speedometer shaft is connected via a train of gears to the odometer. The odometer records how much the speedometer cable turns, and is geared so that one rotation of the first odometer wheel is complete after the car has traveled 1 mile. A full rotation of the first wheel turns the second wheel by one digit; a full rotation of the second turns the third one digit.

Lights

Cars are required by U.S. law to have headlights, side marker lights, taillights, a bulb to illuminate the rear license plate, flashing turn signals, four-way hazard warning flashers, backup lights that go on when the transmission is in *Reverse,* and stoplights that turn on when the brakes are applied.

In most states, sealed-beam headlights are required by law. The reflector and lens of a sealed-beam light is manufactured as one piece, hermetically sealed, and evacuated. The entire unit, therefore, functions as one large bulb.

Sealed-beam lights are widely available and inexpensive, but they produce only about 75,000 candlepower of yellowish light. Quartz-halogen headlights can produce over 150,000 candlepower of a bright white light, but they cost much more than conventional lights. Quartz lights are available in two types: sealed-beam units, which are legal in the U.S., and European-style lights with a separate bulb and reflector, which are legal in a few states and in Canada. Headlights are mounted in brackets that can be adjusted by spring-loaded screws so that the headlight beams can be aimed.

Separate bulbs can be used for the taillights and stoplights, but they are often incorporated into a single bulb containing two filaments. Each taillight filament draws about 1.5 amperes of current. The brighter stoplight filaments each draw about 4 amperes.

Taillights are enclosed by red lenses with built-in prisms. The prisms provide a red reflection of the headlights of any car approaching from the rear.

Turn signals on new cars have amber lenses both front and rear. When actuated, the lights are set to blink on and off at a rate of 60 to 120 times per minute. This is accomplished by a *flasher unit* in the turn signal circuit. Another flasher unit activates all four amber lights at once as an emergency hazard warning.

High beam

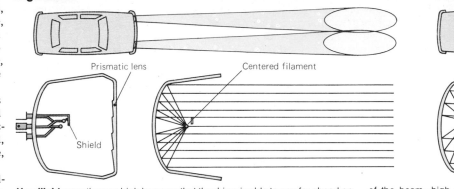

Prismatic lens — Centered filament — Shield

Low beam

Off-center filament

Headlights can throw a high beam so that the driver is able to see far ahead on empty roads at night (left), or a low beam that is directed away from oncoming drivers to protect them from blinding glare. The light source is a tungsten filament, either in a separate bulb or as part of a sealed-beam unit. The direction of the beam—high or low—depends on the placement of the filament; the low-beam filament is placed somewhat off-center, behind a shield (right), which causes the beam to bounce downward off the reflector. The prisms in the glass lens further direct and shape each beam.

Taillight assembly

Housing — Lens — Bulbs

Bulbs

Double filament — Pin — Single filament — Terminal — Single filament in socket

Flasher

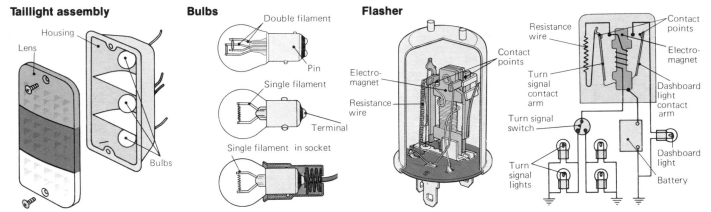

Electromagnet — Resistance wire — Contact points — Turn signal contact arm — Turn signal switch — Turn signal lights — Resistance wire — Contact points — Electromagnet — Dashboard light contact arm — Dashboard light — Battery

Taillights typically consist of two or more tungsten-filament bulbs inside a housing. The housing includes a reflector with bayonet bulb sockets and a plastic lens that is attached to the reflector with screws. This arrangement permits easy access to the bulbs for replacement. On many cars, bulbs are removed from the back of the housing. One bulb with two filaments, covered by a red lens, may be used for both the taillight and the stoplight. A separate bulb with an amber lens is used for the turn signal and hazard warning lights. Another bulb with a white lens serves as a backup light.

Bayonet caps are used on most bulbs. The bulbs are inserted in their sockets by pushing them in and twisting. The sockets have a spring-loaded terminal that maintains electrical contact with the center cap terminal and also locks the bulb in place after it has been twisted into position. Most lights on a car use single-filament bulbs. The bulb in a combination tail/stop light has two filaments and two center terminals on the cap. The locking pins on the sides of single- and double-filament bulbs differ from one another so that they will not be mixed up.

Both sets of contact points are open initially. When the driver activates the turn signal, current begins to flow through the resistance wire and the turn signal contact arm. Since the resistance in the wire is high, the current it lets through is not strong; although this circuit includes the turn signal lights, not enough current passes through the filaments to make them glow. As the current flows, it heats the resistance wire, which expands. This allows the turn signal contact arm, made of spring metal, to straighten. The contact points at the end of the arm then close. As full current flows through the points, the turn signal filaments light up. Almost simultaneously, the electromagnet, activated by the higher current now flowing in its coil, pulls on the other arm. This arm's contact points also close and switch current away from the resistance wire to the turn signal indicator light on the dashboard. The resistance wire cools off and the process reverses. After both contact points have opened, the flashing sequence repeats until the driver, or the self-canceling device in the steering column, terminates it. A similar flasher operates the hazard warning lights.

Headlight assembly

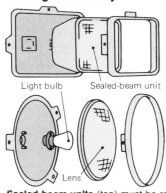

Light bulb   Sealed-beam unit

Lens

Sealed-beam units (top) must be replaced when the filament burns out. Only the bulb has to be replaced on nonsealed lights (bottom).

Halogen lamps

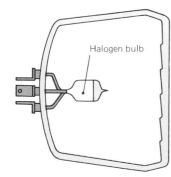

Halogen bulb

Halogen headlights have a separate bulb made of quartz or special high-temperature glass. Small amounts of halogen gas—iodine, bromine, or chlorine—inside the bulb react chemically with the tungsten that evaporates from the filament as it glows white-hot. The reaction causes the tungsten to redeposit on the filament rather than on the inside of the bulb, which happens in an ordinary bulb and reduces light output. This separate bulb can be replaced on European lights; it is permanently molded into the sealed-beam halogen headlights (shown here) used in the U.S.

Horns

Horns sound when an electromagnet causes a diaphragm to vibrate. When the horn button is pushed, current flows in the electromagnet and pulls on the diaphragm plunger—a motion that then disengages the contact points, stops the current, turns off the magnet, and releases the plunger. This cycle repeats several hundred times per second, creating an audible beep. The tone of the beep can be adjusted on some horns by turning an adjusting screw to increase or decrease plunger travel. Some horns have a flared resonating chamber that makes a more musical beep. Various-sized chambers produce various tones. Many cars use a pair of horns with different tones.

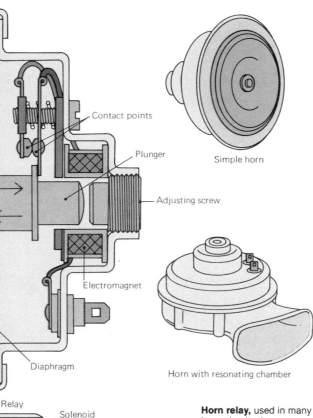

Contact points

Plunger

Simple horn

Adjusting screw

Electromagnet

Diaphragm

Horn with resonating chamber

Relay   Solenoid

Cover

Horn relay, used in many horn circuits, is a heavy-duty solenoid-operated switch. Horns can draw up to 20 amps of current, which requires heavy wiring. A smaller current passing through light-duty wiring to and from the horn button operates the relay switch that sounds the horn.

Wipers

Windshield wipers are operated by a small electric motor. The two-speed motor turns a crank, which converts rotary movement into the push-pull movement needed to operate the wiper blades. In addition to the wiper switch that the driver operates, another switch inside the crank unit is mechanically linked to the gear in the unit. The latter switch remains on when the driver-operated switch is turned off, and keeps the wipers moving until they reach their *Start,* or *Park,* position. Then the gear turns off the switch. Wiper motors are usually protected from damage by a circuit breaker or fuse that will blow if the wipers freeze to the windshield in winter.

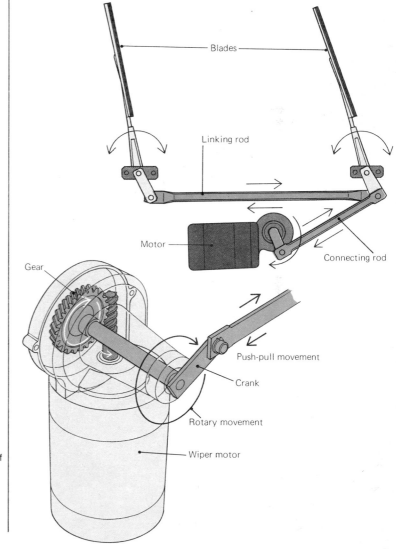

Blades

Linking rod

Motor

Connecting rod

Gear

Push-pull movement

Crank

Rotary movement

Wiper motor

Separate body and frame

Most large North American cars have a separate body and frame, which are bolted together. The frame is made of heavy rectangular, or *box section*, steel tubes that are welded together. The classic frame design, dating back to the 1930s, consists of parallel side members that are combined with an X-shaped bracing across the passenger compartment to provide rigidity. This configuration requires a high floor, to clear the X-member. Today it has been generally abandoned in favor of a series of open rectangles, which are less rigid than the X-frame but allow the floor to be lowered between the rectangles to give increased legroom inside the car.

A fairly recent innovation by some manufacturers is a frame designed with *controlled crushability*. The front and rear sections of the frame are designed to crush into S-shapes in a crash, absorbing much of the energy of a crash and lessening the impact on the passengers.

A separate frame is heavy and not especially rigid. Rust is not a serious safety problem with separate frames because it takes so many years for rust to eat through the thick frame rails.

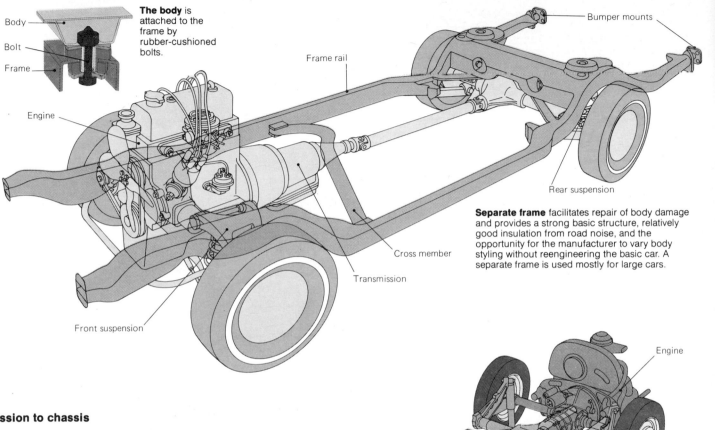

The body is attached to the frame by rubber-cushioned bolts.

Body
Bolt
Frame
Engine
Front suspension
Bumper mounts
Frame rail
Rear suspension
Cross member
Transmission

Separate frame facilitates repair of body damage and provides a strong basic structure, relatively good insulation from road noise, and the opportunity for the manufacturer to vary body styling without reengineering the basic car. A separate frame is used mostly for large cars.

Attachment points of engine and transmission to chassis

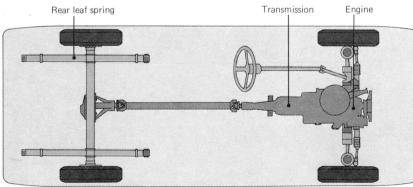

Rear leaf spring
Transmission
Engine

Rubber mountings between the running gear and the frame or unit body are shown in brown.

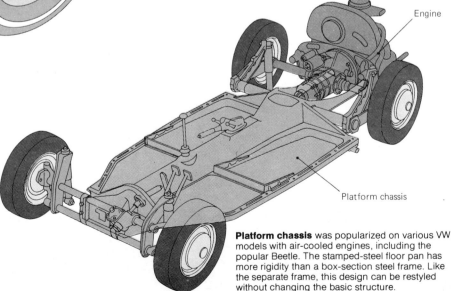

Engine
Platform chassis

Platform chassis was popularized on various VW models with air-cooled engines, including the popular Beetle. The stamped-steel floor pan has more rigidity than a box-section steel frame. Like the separate frame, this design can be restyled without changing the basic structure.

Unit-body construction

A car with *unit-body* construction has no separate frame of steel girders. Instead, comparatively thin pieces of body sheet metal are bent into complex shapes and welded together to provide the strength required for the car's chassis. The result is usually both stiffer and lighter than a separate body and frame, and unit-body construction is therefore common on small, lightweight economy cars.

There are a number of disadvantages to unit-body construction, compared to a separate body and frame: Unit bodies tend to transmit more road noise and vibration. Rust can pose a serious safety problem if it attacks the areas where the engine, transmission, or suspension are attached. Repairing damage after an accident can be expensive; to maintain the structural integrity of a car, a large expanse of bodywork may have to be cut away and replaced. Finally, manufacturing costs are quite high because of the sophisticated metal stamping and welding equipment required.

But mass production can lower these costs, and unit bodies with subframes or platform chassis, plus modern rustproofing, can overcome many of the other disadvantages mentioned above.

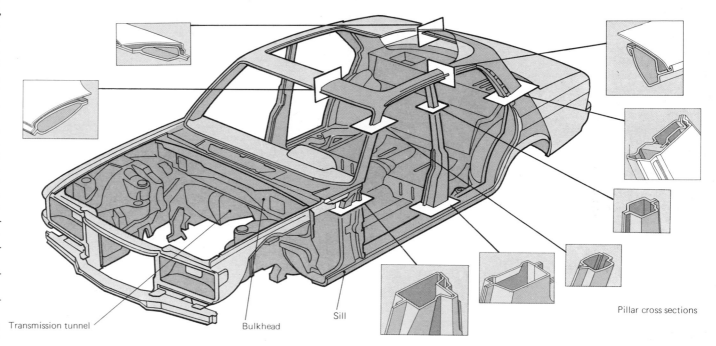

Transmission tunnel

Bulkhead

Sill

Pillar cross sections

Rigidity and strength are obtained in a unit body by welding together boxed-in sections of relatively thin sheet steel. The transmission tunnel and sills under the doors resist front-to-back bending. Bulkheads at the front and rear of the passenger compartment resist side-to-side twisting. Roof, door, and windshield pillars add strength. Complex stampings reinforce areas where the engine and suspension are attached. Many unit bodies incorporate a platform chassis.

Bushings and motor mounts

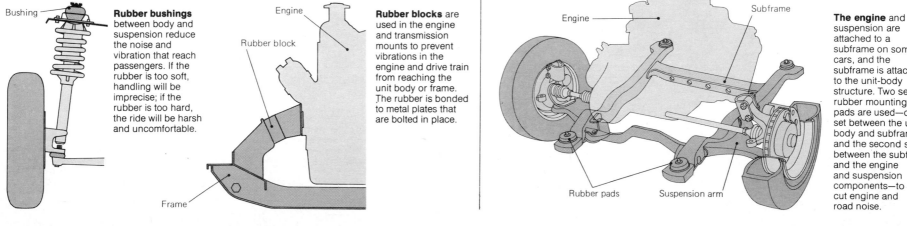

Bushing

Rubber bushings between body and suspension reduce the noise and vibration that reach passengers. If the rubber is too soft, handling will be imprecise; if the rubber is too hard, the ride will be harsh and uncomfortable.

Engine

Rubber block

Frame

Rubber blocks are used in the engine and transmission mounts to prevent vibrations in the engine and drive train from reaching the unit body or frame. The rubber is bonded to metal plates that are bolted in place.

Subframe construction

Engine

Subframe

Rubber pads

Suspension arm

The engine and suspension are attached to a subframe on some cars, and the subframe is attached to the unit-body structure. Two sets of rubber mounting pads are used—one set between the unit body and subframe, and the second set between the subframe and the engine and suspension components—to cut engine and road noise.

Passenger space plus crash protection

Modern car bodies must be designed to protect the driver and passengers in a crash as well as to provide adequate passenger and luggage space. But the need for fuel economy dictates that cars be lighter and smaller than models of the immediate past. These conflicting requirements have brought about basic changes in auto body design.

The separate *chassis frame* once gave a car its structural strength and provided a platform for mounting its mechanical components. The body was bolted to this frame, which made for a high and heavy but quiet and durable automobile.

Many cars now have *unit-body* construction. Stamped sheet-steel parts are welded together to form box structures that work much like the trusses in a bridge to form a light but strong unit.

Some unit-body cars have *subframes* between the basic body box and the engine and suspension. Subframes make the car easier to manufacture, since they can be built on separate assembly lines and then installed. Rubber mounting pads help keep engine and suspension vibrations and noise from traveling through the car.

Unit bodies can be designed to effectively resist collision forces. Thinner sheet metal is used in the nose and tail to make the ends of the automobile relatively soft. Heavier material in the passenger compartment makes it rigid enough to stand up to severe crashes. The strong central box protects the passengers while the crushable nose and tail soften the impact. Passive restraints, either seat belts or air bags, keep car occupants from hitting the inside of the body. This arrangement provides maximum safety, but body damage can be great.

Engine position can increase the interior space available in small cars. Transverse engines driving the front wheels can free up to 80 percent of the body volume for passengers and luggage.

Door locks

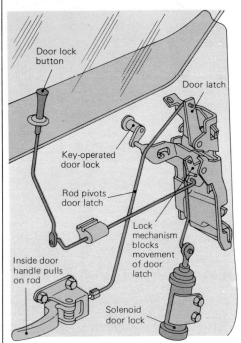

Door lock button

Door latch

Key-operated door lock

Rod pivots door latch

Inside door handle pulls on rod

Lock mechanism blocks movement of door latch

Solenoid door lock

Door latches should keep the door from opening in a crash, resist break-ins, yet not be impossible to open if the key is lost. The door handle is a lever that pulls on a rod to rotate the door latch. The various lock mechanisms interrupt the action of the door latch. In power door locks, the lock mechanism is operated by electric solenoids.

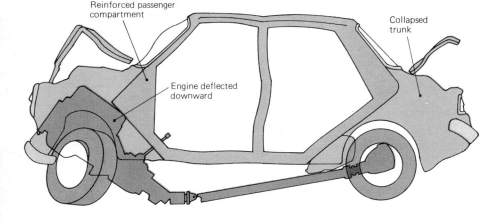

Reinforced passenger compartment

Collapsed trunk

Engine deflected downward

Door

Beam

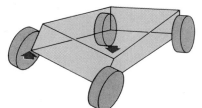

Progressive crumpling at the front and rear of a unit-body car increases the duration of the impact and thus lessens its severity for the occupants. By putting joints in the drive train and designing motor and transmission mounts to shear under crash stresses, these parts can be kept out of the passenger compartment. Passive seat belts or air bag restraint systems protect the passengers.

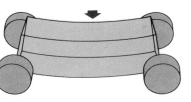

Torsional stiffness resists twisting when one wheel of the car rises over a bump while the opposite wheel falls into a pothole.

Crash beams in the doors help withstand side impacts. Made of tough low-alloy steel, these beams add strength (and weight) to automobiles sold in North America since 1973.

Bending stiffness keeps the body of the car from sagging in the middle. It also allows doors to close smoothly and latch securely. Unit-body designs have exceptionally good bending and torsional stiffness, considering their relatively light weight.

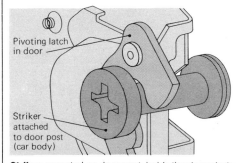

Pivoting latch in door

Striker attached to door post (car body)

Striker, mounted on door post, holds the door shut or allows it to be opened when the latch is rotated by the door handle. The striker must hold the door closed under normal conditions or if the post begins to bend away from the door in a crash.

Window winders

There are two kinds of window-winding mechanisms for automobiles: those that are cranked by hand and those with power. Power windows employ a small electric motor inside the door to turn the crank that raises the window.

Windows may work in one of two ways: The crank may turn a *sector gear* that pivots a pair of arms to raise the *window carrier* and the glass. Or the crank may wind up a ladder-like tape that raises the carrier and the glass.

Metal window winder

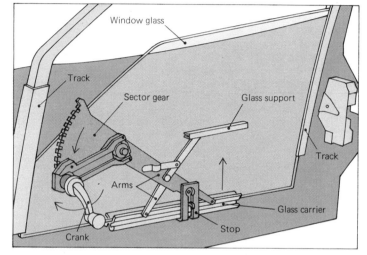

Track
Window glass
Sector gear
Glass support
Track
Arms
Glass carrier
Crank
Stop

Window winder in most car doors has a sector gear that is turned by a hand crank, or by a drive gear on an electric motor. The turning sector gear raises two arms that are attached to the glass carrier that lifts the window glass. In some cars, the glazing in rear doors is fixed and does not go up or down.

Plastic window lift

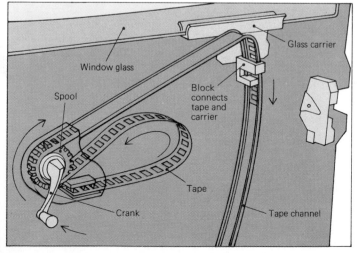

Glass carrier
Window glass
Block connects tape and carrier
Spool
Tape
Crank
Tape channel

Tape mechanism saves weight and space in car doors. Introduced on 1980 GM cars, it uses a tape made of plastic links that look like ladder rungs. These links are wound on or off a spool to raise or lower the glass. The plastic parts will not corrode when rainwater gets into the door. Like many modern plastics, this material needs no lubrication.

Body configurations

The most common body shape for cars is the sedan, with two or four doors and a luggage compartment at the rear. The station wagon, with its rear hatch and large cargo space, is a popular family car. Many carmakers have combined these two designs into a *hatchback* model that incorporates a wagon's rear cargo door with a sloping roofline. A hatchback has more cargo space than a sedan but less than a wagon. Hatchbacks are often called three-door or five-door sedans.

Economy car features two or four doors, a hatchback, and front-drive layout that takes up only 20 percent of the interior space. Car holds four people and may weigh less than a ton.

Mid-engine sports coupe has engine mounted in front of the rear axle. Passenger space is limited to two people. Concentrating the weight in the center of the car improves handling.

Conventional sports coupe has engine in front, driving the rear wheels. Based on sedan components, this layout reduces production costs. Luggage space and rear seat room are sacrificed to sporty styling.

Van may have engine in front or rear. Placing both passenger and luggage space over the driveline provides lots of room inside a relatively short but high vehicle. Some versions seat 15 people. Other variations range from just a driver's seat and cargo space to complete living accommodations.

Contemporary sedan has conventional front-engine/rear-drive configuration. Careful planning allows space for four to six passengers and luggage in a compact package weighing 1½ tons.

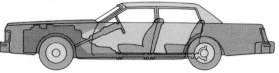

Large sedan of the mid '70s weighed 2 to 2½ tons, but passenger compartment was no bigger than those in the new, smaller sedans. Trunk space was large but often so shallow that shopping bags could not be placed upright.

Flow-through ventilation

Heaters and fresh air ventilation systems are standard equipment on all North American automobiles. The *flow-through ventilation* system takes air in through a duct located at the base of the windshield, passes it through the *heater core*, and distributes it to the inside of the car through vents in the dashboard. Other vents in the rear of the car exhaust the stale air when the car is moving.

The heater core is a small radiator connected to the engine's cooling system in water-cooled cars. Once the engine warms up, the heated coolant warms the air directed through the core. Temperature is regulated by controlling the coolant flow through the heater core and/or by mixing cold outside air with the heated air. Automatic or manual controls allow the driver to adjust the temperature and airflow inside the car. Air flows through ducts and is pushed along by a cylindrical fan called a *squirrel cage*. *Flapper doors* in the ducts direct the air to heating, ventilating, and defrosting vents under, in, and on top of the dashboard. Adjustable louvers on the vents let the car's occupants aim the airflow.

The flapper doors may be operated by cable from levers on the dashboard. On most cars, the flapper doors are operated by vacuum motors powered by vacuum from the engine's intake manifold. On cars with automatic temperature control, these vacuum motors are controlled by thermostatic sensors.

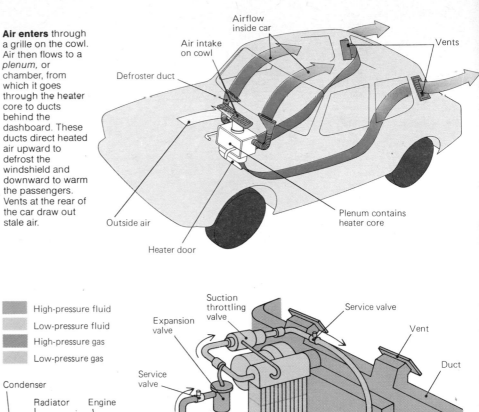

Air enters through a grille on the cowl. Air then flows to a *plenum,* or chamber, from which it goes through the heater core to ducts behind the dashboard. These ducts direct heated air upward to defrost the windshield and downward to warm the passengers. Vents at the rear of the car draw out stale air.

Air conditioning

Air conditioning works on the principle that heat flows from a warmer surface to a colder one. Heat from the air inside the car is transferred to the cold metal fins of the *evaporator*. The *working fluid*—Freon-12 or Refrigerant-12—flows through the evaporator, where it vaporizes and picks up the heat and takes it to a *compressor*. There the gas is pressurized, which concentrates the heat by raising the temperature of the gas.

The gas then goes to the *condenser*, which looks like a thin radiator mounted in front of the car's engine-cooling radiator. Here the Freon gives off its heat to the cooler air flowing through the grille and condenses into a liquid. The liquid goes to a tank called the *receiver-dryer*, where excess fluid is stored and any water is removed. (Water forms hydrochloric acid in an air conditioner, which can produce irreparable corrosion.)

From the *receiver-dryer*, the liquid flows through a hose to the *expansion valve*, which meters it into the evaporator inside the car. Here it expands from a cool, high-pressure liquid into a cold, low-pressure gas. This evaporation, or boiling, absorbs heat and cools the fins that cool the air in the car. The warmed gas then returns to the compressor.

Besides cooling the air, an air conditioner *dehumidifies* it by removing moisture that condenses on the evaporator fins. The condensed water drains through a tube and is released underneath the car. It is normal to find a small puddle of water under an air-conditioned car on a hot, damp day. However, it is a good idea to make sure that any puddle under your car is indeed water from the air conditioner and not coolant, brake fluid, transmission fluid, or oil.

A pressure-sensitive control on the evaporator, called the *suction throttling valve,* keeps condensed moisture from freezing and blocking the cooling fins.

A magnetic clutch in the compressor pulley cycles on and off to regulate temperature in many newer cars. Reduced compressor operation improves fuel economy. A calibrated orifice in the line between the condenser and evaporator replaces the expansion valve.

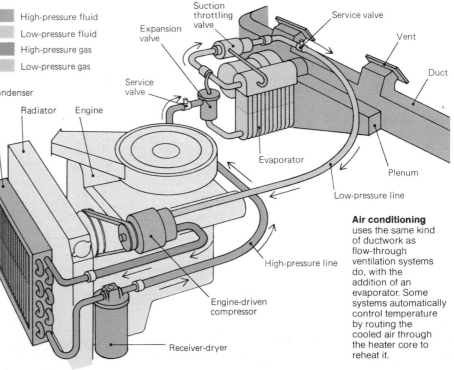

High-pressure fluid
Low-pressure fluid
High-pressure gas
Low-pressure gas

Air conditioning uses the same kind of ductwork as flow-through ventilation systems do, with the addition of an evaporator. Some systems automatically control temperature by routing the cooled air through the heater core to reheat it.

Major components of popular cars

This chapter shows where the various automotive parts discussed in Chapter 2, *How your car works*, are located on popular domestic and imported cars. The models illustrated on the following pages account for more than 90 percent of all the automobiles sold in North America. If your particular car is not shown, you may still be able to locate its major components by referring to a similar model (a front-drive four-cylinder car, for instance, or a rear-drive V-8). Certain models may deviate slightly from those illustrated in this chapter. For example, the alternator may be on the driver's side of some General Motors V-8 engines, not on the passenger side, as illustrated on page 155.

Rear-drive six-cylinder and V-8 cars

AMX, Concord, Gremlin, Hornet, Matador, Pacer, Spirit

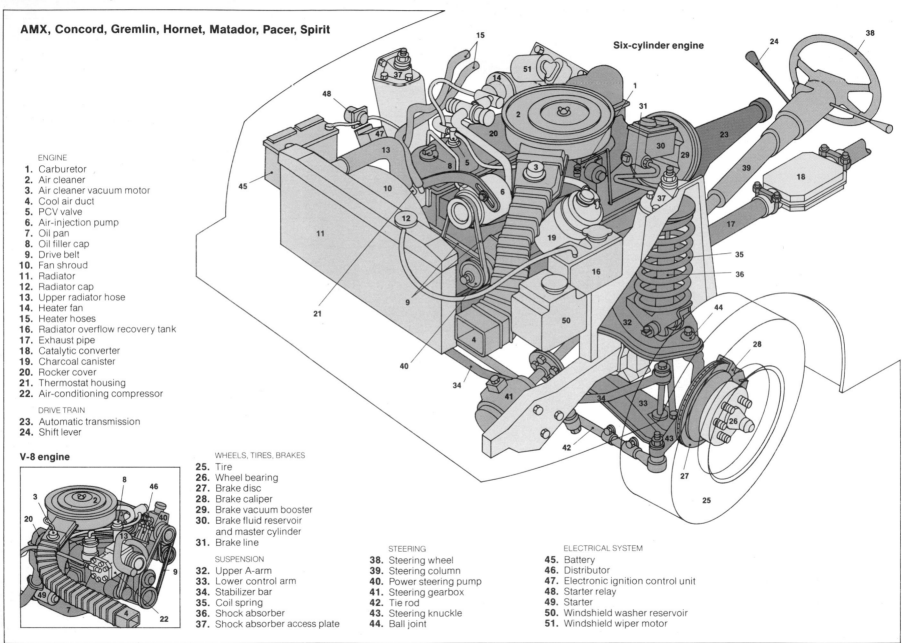

Six-cylinder engine

ENGINE

1. Carburetor
2. Air cleaner
3. Air cleaner vacuum motor
4. Cool air duct
5. PCV valve
6. Air-injection pump
7. Oil pan
8. Oil filler cap
9. Drive belt
10. Fan shroud
11. Radiator
12. Radiator cap
13. Upper radiator hose
14. Heater fan
15. Heater hoses
16. Radiator overflow recovery tank
17. Exhaust pipe
18. Catalytic converter
19. Charcoal canister
20. Rocker cover
21. Thermostat housing
22. Air-conditioning compressor

DRIVE TRAIN

23. Automatic transmission
24. Shift lever

V-8 engine

WHEELS, TIRES, BRAKES

25. Tire
26. Wheel bearing
27. Brake disc
28. Brake caliper
29. Brake vacuum booster
30. Brake fluid reservoir
    and master cylinder
31. Brake line

SUSPENSION

32. Upper A-arm
33. Lower control arm
34. Stabilizer bar
35. Coil spring
36. Shock absorber
37. Shock absorber access plate

STEERING

38. Steering wheel
39. Steering column
40. Power steering pump
41. Steering gearbox
42. Tie rod
43. Steering knuckle
44. Ball joint

ELECTRICAL SYSTEM

45. Battery
46. Distributor
47. Electronic ignition control unit
48. Starter relay
49. Starter
50. Windshield washer reservoir
51. Windshield wiper motor

Rear-drive four-cylinder cars

AMX, Concord, Gremlin, Pacer, Spirit

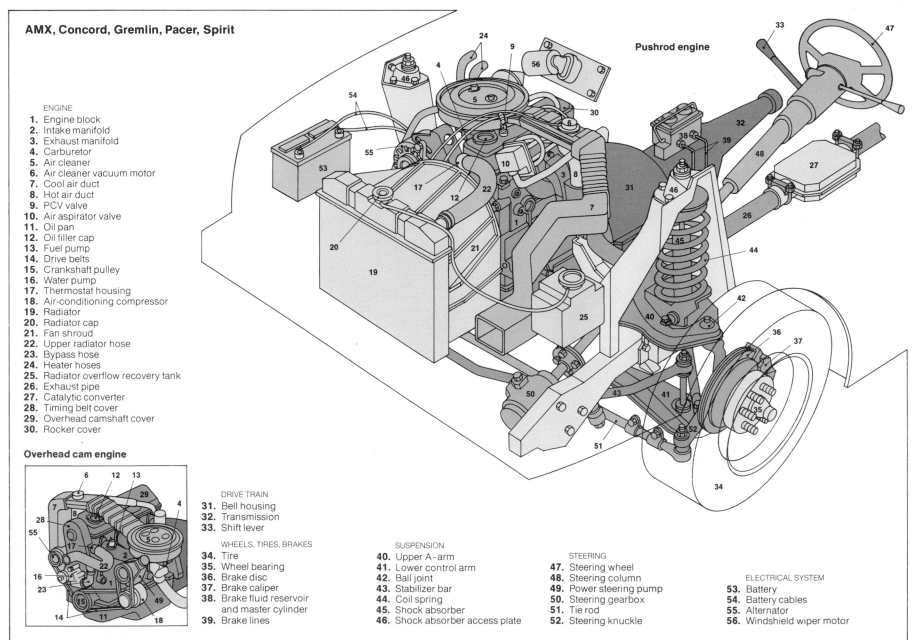

Pushrod engine

ENGINE

1. Engine block
2. Intake manifold
3. Exhaust manifold
4. Carburetor
5. Air cleaner
6. Air cleaner vacuum motor
7. Cool air duct
8. Hot air duct
9. PCV valve
10. Air aspirator valve
11. Oil pan
12. Oil filler cap
13. Fuel pump
14. Drive belts
15. Crankshaft pulley
16. Water pump
17. Thermostat housing
18. Air-conditioning compressor
19. Radiator
20. Radiator cap
21. Fan shroud
22. Upper radiator hose
23. Bypass hose
24. Heater hoses
25. Radiator overflow recovery tank
26. Exhaust pipe
27. Catalytic converter
28. Timing belt cover
29. Overhead camshaft cover
30. Rocker cover

Overhead cam engine

DRIVE TRAIN

31. Bell housing
32. Transmission
33. Shift lever

WHEELS, TIRES, BRAKES

34. Tire
35. Wheel bearing
36. Brake disc
37. Brake caliper
38. Brake fluid reservoir and master cylinder
39. Brake lines

SUSPENSION

40. Upper A-arm
41. Lower control arm
42. Ball joint
43. Stabilizer bar
44. Coil spring
45. Shock absorber
46. Shock absorber access plate

STEERING

47. Steering wheel
48. Steering column
49. Power steering pump
50. Steering gearbox
51. Tie rod
52. Steering knuckle

ELECTRICAL SYSTEM

53. Battery
54. Battery cables
55. Alternator
56. Windshield wiper motor

Rear-drive six-cylinder and V-8 cars

Chrysler, Dodge, and Plymouth

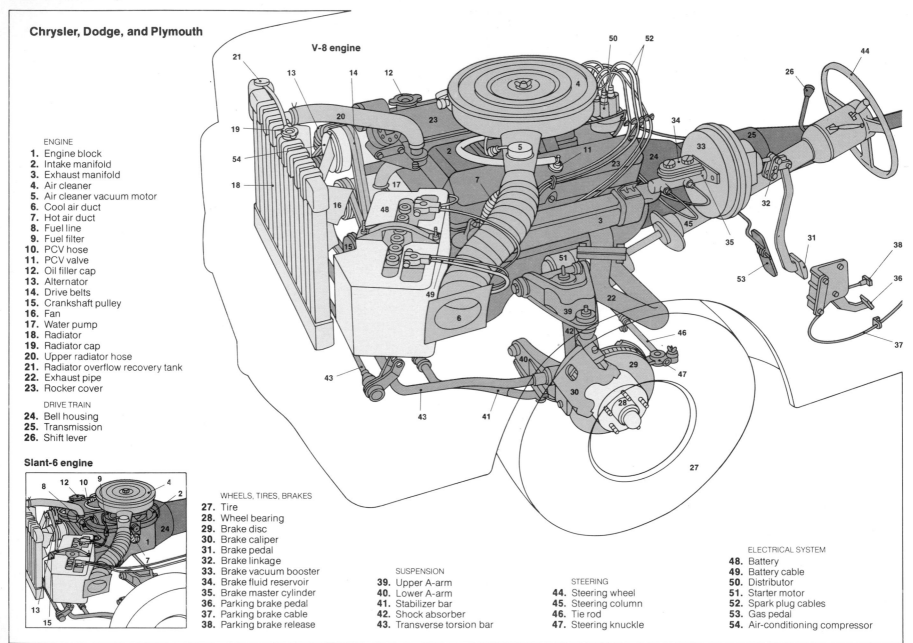

V-8 engine

Slant-6 engine

ENGINE
1. Engine block
2. Intake manifold
3. Exhaust manifold
4. Air cleaner
5. Air cleaner vacuum motor
6. Cool air duct
7. Hot air duct
8. Fuel line
9. Fuel filter
10. PCV hose
11. PCV valve
12. Oil filler cap
13. Alternator
14. Drive belts
15. Crankshaft pulley
16. Fan
17. Water pump
18. Radiator
19. Radiator cap
20. Upper radiator hose
21. Radiator overflow recovery tank
22. Exhaust pipe
23. Rocker cover

DRIVE TRAIN
24. Bell housing
25. Transmission
26. Shift lever

WHEELS, TIRES, BRAKES
27. Tire
28. Wheel bearing
29. Brake disc
30. Brake caliper
31. Brake pedal
32. Brake linkage
33. Brake vacuum booster
34. Brake fluid reservoir
35. Brake master cylinder
36. Parking brake pedal
37. Parking brake cable
38. Parking brake release

SUSPENSION
39. Upper A-arm
40. Lower A-arm
41. Stabilizer bar
42. Shock absorber
43. Transverse torsion bar

STEERING
44. Steering wheel
45. Steering column
46. Tie rod
47. Steering knuckle

ELECTRICAL SYSTEM
48. Battery
49. Battery cable
50. Distributor
51. Starter motor
52. Spark plug cables
53. Gas pedal
54. Air-conditioning compressor

Front-drive four-cylinder cars

Dodge Omni, Plymouth Horizon

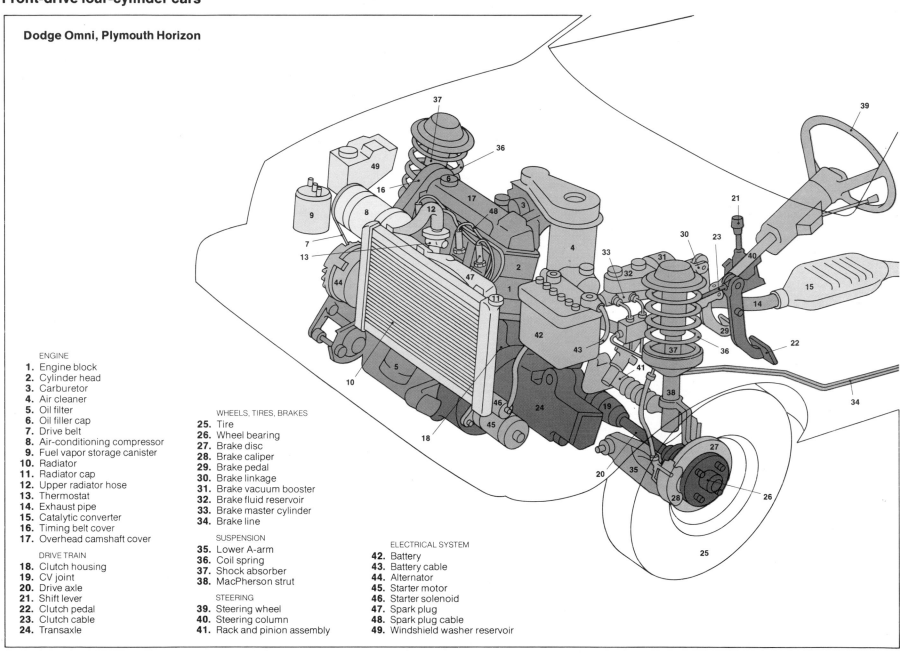

ENGINE

1. Engine block
2. Cylinder head
3. Carburetor
4. Air cleaner
5. Oil filter
6. Oil filler cap
7. Drive belt
8. Air-conditioning compressor
9. Fuel vapor storage canister
10. Radiator
11. Radiator cap
12. Upper radiator hose
13. Thermostat
14. Exhaust pipe
15. Catalytic converter
16. Timing belt cover
17. Overhead camshaft cover

DRIVE TRAIN

18. Clutch housing
19. CV joint
20. Drive axle
21. Shift lever
22. Clutch pedal
23. Clutch cable
24. Transaxle

WHEELS, TIRES, BRAKES

25. Tire
26. Wheel bearing
27. Brake disc
28. Brake caliper
29. Brake pedal
30. Brake linkage
31. Brake vacuum booster
32. Brake fluid reservoir
33. Brake master cylinder
34. Brake line

SUSPENSION

35. Lower A-arm
36. Coil spring
37. Shock absorber
38. MacPherson strut

STEERING

39. Steering wheel
40. Steering column
41. Rack and pinion assembly

ELECTRICAL SYSTEM

42. Battery
43. Battery cable
44. Alternator
45. Starter motor
46. Starter solenoid
47. Spark plug
48. Spark plug cable
49. Windshield washer reservoir

Major car components / **Datsun**

Front-engine rear-drive cars

Four-cylinder pushrod engine (B210)

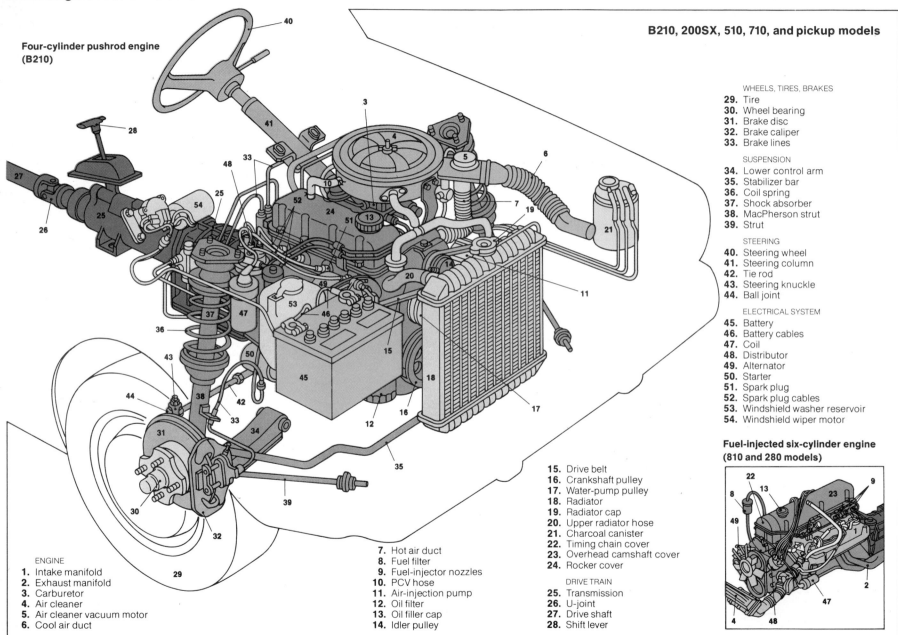

WHEELS, TIRES, BRAKES
29. Tire
30. Wheel bearing
31. Brake disc
32. Brake caliper
33. Brake lines

SUSPENSION
34. Lower control arm
35. Stabilizer bar
36. Coil spring
37. Shock absorber
38. MacPherson strut
39. Strut

STEERING
40. Steering wheel
41. Steering column
42. Tie rod
43. Steering knuckle
44. Ball joint

ELECTRICAL SYSTEM
45. Battery
46. Battery cables
47. Coil
48. Distributor
49. Alternator
50. Starter
51. Spark plug
52. Spark plug cables
53. Windshield washer reservoir
54. Windshield wiper motor

Fuel-injected six-cylinder engine (810 and 280 models)

ENGINE
1. Intake manifold
2. Exhaust manifold
3. Carburetor
4. Air cleaner
5. Air cleaner vacuum motor
6. Cool air duct

7. Hot air duct
8. Fuel filter
9. Fuel-injector nozzles
10. PCV hose
11. Air-injection pump
12. Oil filter
13. Oil filler cap
14. Idler pulley

15. Drive belt
16. Crankshaft pulley
17. Water-pump pulley
18. Radiator
19. Radiator cap
20. Upper radiator hose
21. Charcoal canister
22. Timing chain cover
23. Overhead camshaft cover
24. Rocker cover

DRIVE TRAIN
25. Transmission
26. U-joint
27. Drive shaft
28. Shift lever

Front-drive cars

F10 and 310 models

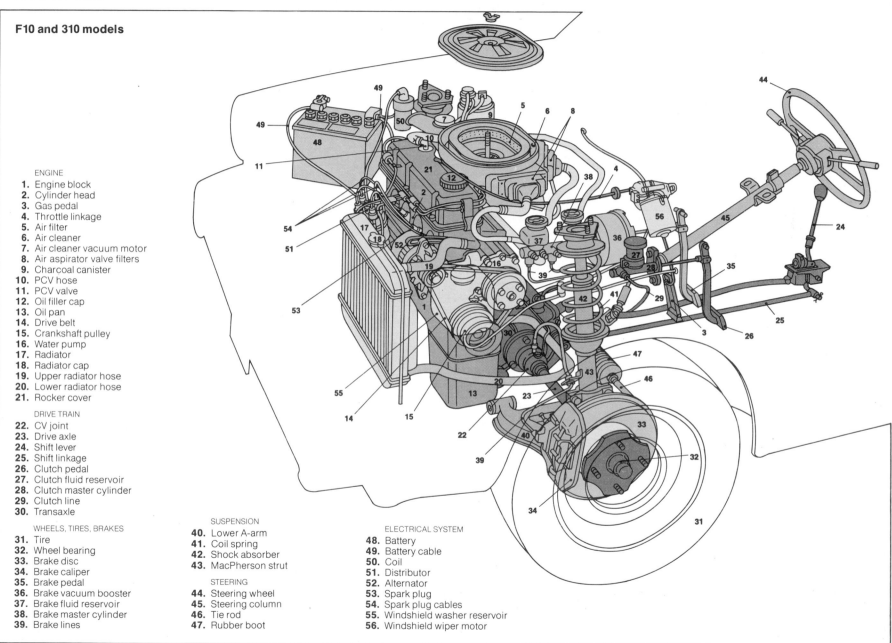

ENGINE
1. Engine block
2. Cylinder head
3. Gas pedal
4. Throttle linkage
5. Air filter
6. Air cleaner
7. Air cleaner vacuum motor
8. Air aspirator valve filters
9. Charcoal canister
10. PCV hose
11. PCV valve
12. Oil filler cap
13. Oil pan
14. Drive belt
15. Crankshaft pulley
16. Water pump
17. Radiator
18. Radiator cap
19. Upper radiator hose
20. Lower radiator hose
21. Rocker cover

DRIVE TRAIN
22. CV joint
23. Drive axle
24. Shift lever
25. Shift linkage
26. Clutch pedal
27. Clutch fluid reservoir
28. Clutch master cylinder
29. Clutch line
30. Transaxle

WHEELS, TIRES, BRAKES
31. Tire
32. Wheel bearing
33. Brake disc
34. Brake caliper
35. Brake pedal
36. Brake vacuum booster
37. Brake fluid reservoir
38. Brake master cylinder
39. Brake lines

SUSPENSION
40. Lower A-arm
41. Coil spring
42. Shock absorber
43. MacPherson strut

STEERING
44. Steering wheel
45. Steering column
46. Tie rod
47. Rubber boot

ELECTRICAL SYSTEM
48. Battery
49. Battery cable
50. Coil
51. Distributor
52. Alternator
53. Spark plug
54. Spark plug cables
55. Windshield washer reservoir
56. Windshield wiper motor

V-8 and six-cylinder rear-drive cars

Ford, Lincoln, and Mercury

ENGINE

1. Engine block
2. Cylinder head
3. Exhaust manifold
4. Carburetor (under air cleaner)
5. Air cleaner
6. Air cleaner vacuum motor
7. Cool air duct
8. Fuel pump
9. PCV hose
10. PCV valve
11. Idler pulley
12. Oil filter
13. Oil filler cap
14. Drive belt
15. Crankshaft pulley
16. Fan
17. Water pump
18. Air-conditioning compressor
19. Radiator
20. Air-conditioning condenser
21. Upper radiator hose
22. Radiator overflow recovery tank
23. Exhaust pipe
24. EGR valve
25. Rocker cover

DRIVE TRAIN

26. Bell housing
27. Automatic transmission
28. U-joint
29. Drive shaft
30. Shift lever

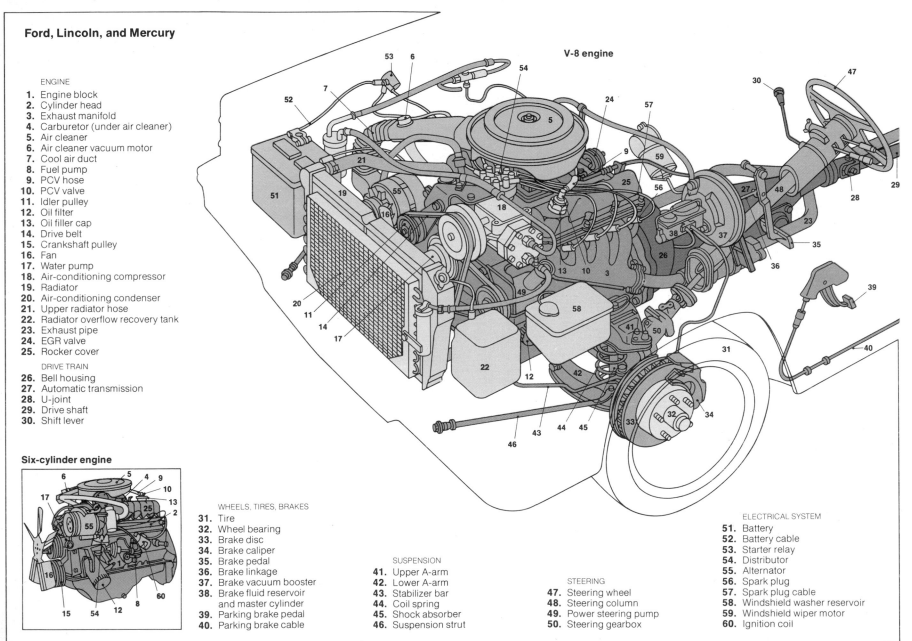

V-8 engine

Six-cylinder engine

WHEELS, TIRES, BRAKES

31. Tire
32. Wheel bearing
33. Brake disc
34. Brake caliper
35. Brake pedal
36. Brake linkage
37. Brake vacuum booster
38. Brake fluid reservoir and master cylinder
39. Parking brake pedal
40. Parking brake cable

SUSPENSION

41. Upper A-arm
42. Lower A-arm
43. Stabilizer bar
44. Coil spring
45. Shock absorber
46. Suspension strut

STEERING

47. Steering wheel
48. Steering column
49. Power steering pump
50. Steering gearbox

ELECTRICAL SYSTEM

51. Battery
52. Battery cable
53. Starter relay
54. Distributor
55. Alternator
56. Spark plug
57. Spark plug cable
58. Windshield washer reservoir
59. Windshield wiper motor
60. Ignition coil

Front-engine rear-drive compact cars

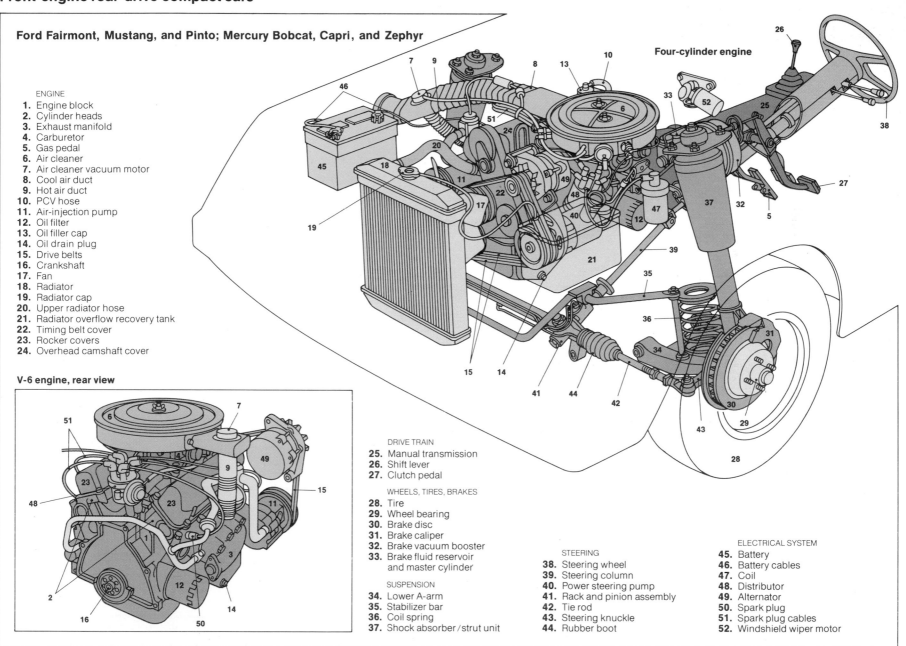

Ford Fairmont, Mustang, and Pinto; Mercury Bobcat, Capri, and Zephyr

Four-cylinder engine

ENGINE
1. Engine block
2. Cylinder heads
3. Exhaust manifold
4. Carburetor
5. Gas pedal
6. Air cleaner
7. Air cleaner vacuum motor
8. Cool air duct
9. Hot air duct
10. PCV hose
11. Air-injection pump
12. Oil filter
13. Oil filler cap
14. Oil drain plug
15. Drive belts
16. Crankshaft
17. Fan
18. Radiator
19. Radiator cap
20. Upper radiator hose
21. Radiator overflow recovery tank
22. Timing belt cover
23. Rocker covers
24. Overhead camshaft cover

V-6 engine, rear view

DRIVE TRAIN
25. Manual transmission
26. Shift lever
27. Clutch pedal

WHEELS, TIRES, BRAKES
28. Tire
29. Wheel bearing
30. Brake disc
31. Brake caliper
32. Brake vacuum booster
33. Brake fluid reservoir
    and master cylinder

SUSPENSION
34. Lower A-arm
35. Stabilizer bar
36. Coil spring
37. Shock absorber/strut unit

STEERING
38. Steering wheel
39. Steering column
40. Power steering pump
41. Rack and pinion assembly
42. Tie rod
43. Steering knuckle
44. Rubber boot

ELECTRICAL SYSTEM
45. Battery
46. Battery cables
47. Coil
48. Distributor
49. Alternator
50. Spark plug
51. Spark plug cables
52. Windshield wiper motor

153

Front-drive four-cylinder cars

Fiesta

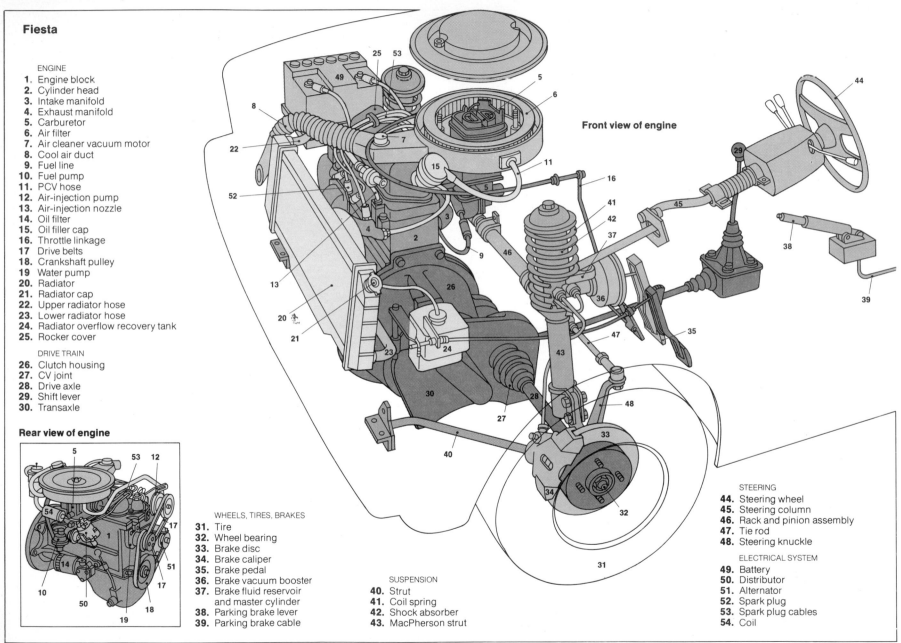

ENGINE
1. Engine block
2. Cylinder head
3. Intake manifold
4. Exhaust manifold
5. Carburetor
6. Air filter
7. Air cleaner vacuum motor
8. Cool air duct
9. Fuel line
10. Fuel pump
11. PCV hose
12. Air-injection pump
13. Air-injection nozzle
14. Oil filter
15. Oil filler cap
16. Throttle linkage
17. Drive belts
18. Crankshaft pulley
19. Water pump
20. Radiator
21. Radiator cap
22. Upper radiator hose
23. Lower radiator hose
24. Radiator overflow recovery tank
25. Rocker cover

DRIVE TRAIN
26. Clutch housing
27. CV joint
28. Drive axle
29. Shift lever
30. Transaxle

Rear view of engine

WHEELS, TIRES, BRAKES
31. Tire
32. Wheel bearing
33. Brake disc
34. Brake caliper
35. Brake pedal
36. Brake vacuum booster
37. Brake fluid reservoir and master cylinder
38. Parking brake lever
39. Parking brake cable

SUSPENSION
40. Strut
41. Coil spring
42. Shock absorber
43. MacPherson strut

Front view of engine

STEERING
44. Steering wheel
45. Steering column
46. Rack and pinion assembly
47. Tie rod
48. Steering knuckle

ELECTRICAL SYSTEM
49. Battery
50. Distributor
51. Alternator
52. Spark plug
53. Spark plug cables
54. Coil

Rear-drive six-cylinder and V-8 cars

Buick, Cadillac, Chevrolet, Oldsmobile, and Pontiac

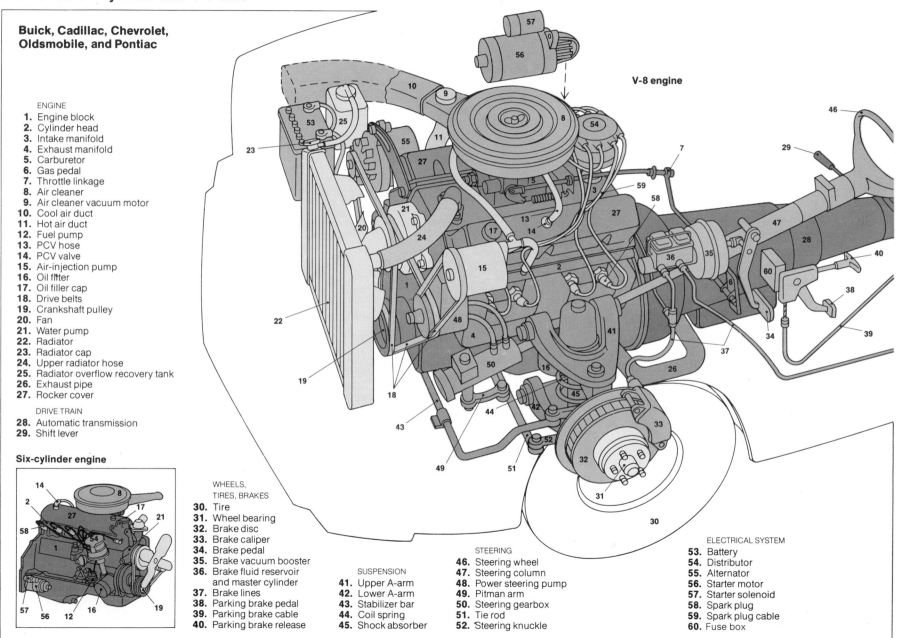

V-8 engine

Six-cylinder engine

ENGINE
1. Engine block
2. Cylinder head
3. Intake manifold
4. Exhaust manifold
5. Carburetor
6. Gas pedal
7. Throttle linkage
8. Air cleaner
9. Air cleaner vacuum motor
10. Cool air duct
11. Hot air duct
12. Fuel pump
13. PCV hose
14. PCV valve
15. Air-injection pump
16. Oil filter
17. Oil filler cap
18. Drive belts
19. Crankshaft pulley
20. Fan
21. Water pump
22. Radiator
23. Radiator cap
24. Upper radiator hose
25. Radiator overflow recovery tank
26. Exhaust pipe
27. Rocker cover

DRIVE TRAIN
28. Automatic transmission
29. Shift lever

WHEELS, TIRES, BRAKES
30. Tire
31. Wheel bearing
32. Brake disc
33. Brake caliper
34. Brake pedal
35. Brake vacuum booster
36. Brake fluid reservoir and master cylinder
37. Brake lines
38. Parking brake pedal
39. Parking brake cable
40. Parking brake release

SUSPENSION
41. Upper A-arm
42. Lower A-arm
43. Stabilizer bar
44. Coil spring
45. Shock absorber

STEERING
46. Steering wheel
47. Steering column
48. Power steering pump
49. Pitman arm
50. Steering gearbox
51. Tie rod
52. Steering knuckle

ELECTRICAL SYSTEM
53. Battery
54. Distributor
55. Alternator
56. Starter motor
57. Starter solenoid
58. Spark plug
59. Spark plug cable
60. Fuse box

Rear-drive four-cylinder and V-6 cars

**Buick Skyhawk, Chevrolet Monza and Vega,
Oldsmobile Starfire, Pontiac Sunbird**

V-6 engine

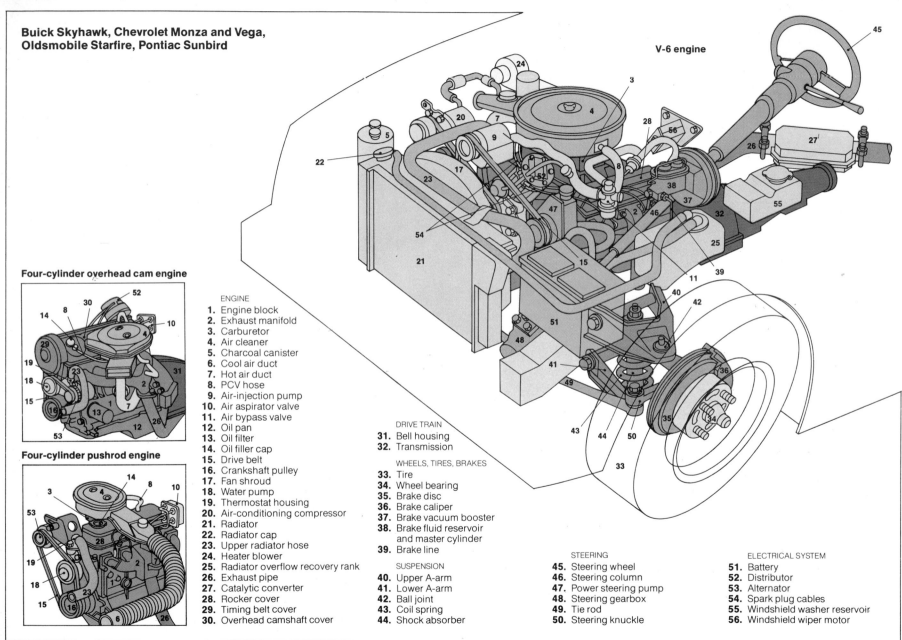

Four-cylinder overhead cam engine

Four-cylinder pushrod engine

ENGINE
1. Engine block
2. Exhaust manifold
3. Carburetor
4. Air cleaner
5. Charcoal canister
6. Cool air duct
7. Hot air duct
8. PCV hose
9. Air-injection pump
10. Air aspirator valve
11. Air bypass valve
12. Oil pan
13. Oil filter
14. Oil filler cap
15. Drive belt
16. Crankshaft pulley
17. Fan shroud
18. Water pump
19. Thermostat housing
20. Air-conditioning compressor
21. Radiator
22. Radiator cap
23. Upper radiator hose
24. Heater blower
25. Radiator overflow recovery rank
26. Exhaust pipe
27. Catalytic converter
28. Rocker cover
29. Timing belt cover
30. Overhead camshaft cover

DRIVE TRAIN
31. Bell housing
32. Transmission

WHEELS, TIRES, BRAKES
33. Tire
34. Wheel bearing
35. Brake disc
36. Brake caliper
37. Brake vacuum booster
38. Brake fluid reservoir
   and master cylinder
39. Brake line

SUSPENSION
40. Upper A-arm
41. Lower A-arm
42. Ball joint
43. Coil spring
44. Shock absorber

STEERING
45. Steering wheel
46. Steering column
47. Power steering pump
48. Steering gearbox
49. Tie rod
50. Steering knuckle

ELECTRICAL SYSTEM
51. Battery
52. Distributor
53. Alternator
54. Spark plug cables
55. Windshield washer reservoir
56. Windshield wiper motor

Front-drive transverse-engine cars

Buick Skylark, Chevrolet Citation, Oldsmobile Omega, Pontiac Phoenix

Four-cylinder engine

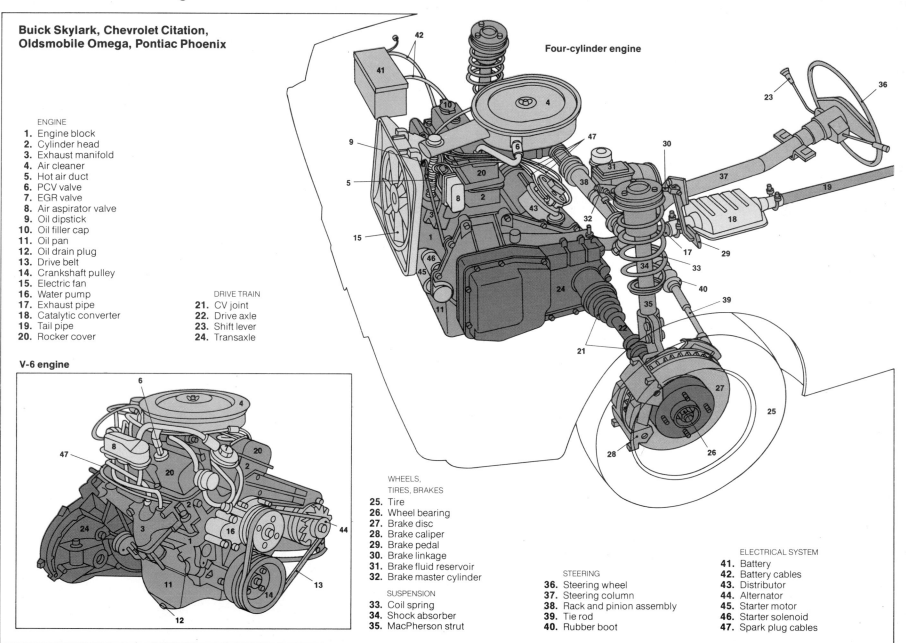

V-6 engine

ENGINE

1. Engine block
2. Cylinder head
3. Exhaust manifold
4. Air cleaner
5. Hot air duct
6. PCV valve
7. EGR valve
8. Air aspirator valve
9. Oil dipstick
10. Oil filler cap
11. Oil pan
12. Oil drain plug
13. Drive belt
14. Crankshaft pulley
15. Electric fan
16. Water pump
17. Exhaust pipe
18. Catalytic converter
19. Tail pipe
20. Rocker cover

DRIVE TRAIN

21. CV joint
22. Drive axle
23. Shift lever
24. Transaxle

WHEELS, TIRES, BRAKES

25. Tire
26. Wheel bearing
27. Brake disc
28. Brake caliper
29. Brake pedal
30. Brake linkage
31. Brake fluid reservoir
32. Brake master cylinder

SUSPENSION

33. Coil spring
34. Shock absorber
35. MacPherson strut

STEERING

36. Steering wheel
37. Steering column
38. Rack and pinion assembly
39. Tie rod
40. Rubber boot

ELECTRICAL SYSTEM

41. Battery
42. Battery cables
43. Distributor
44. Alternator
45. Starter motor
46. Starter solenoid
47. Spark plug cables

Major car components /General Motors

Front-drive longitudinal-engine cars

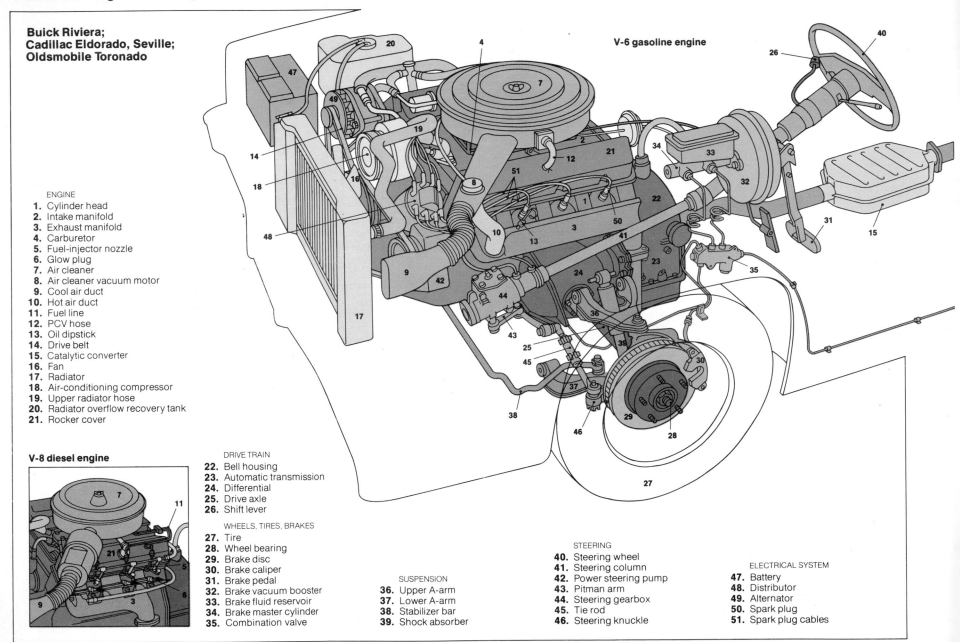

**Buick Riviera;
Cadillac Eldorado, Seville;
Oldsmobile Toronado**

V-6 gasoline engine

ENGINE
1. Cylinder head
2. Intake manifold
3. Exhaust manifold
4. Carburetor
5. Fuel-injector nozzle
6. Glow plug
7. Air cleaner
8. Air cleaner vacuum motor
9. Cool air duct
10. Hot air duct
11. Fuel line
12. PCV hose
13. Oil dipstick
14. Drive belt
15. Catalytic converter
16. Fan
17. Radiator
18. Air-conditioning compressor
19. Upper radiator hose
20. Radiator overflow recovery tank
21. Rocker cover

V-8 diesel engine

DRIVE TRAIN
22. Bell housing
23. Automatic transmission
24. Differential
25. Drive axle
26. Shift lever

WHEELS, TIRES, BRAKES
27. Tire
28. Wheel bearing
29. Brake disc
30. Brake caliper
31. Brake pedal
32. Brake vacuum booster
33. Brake fluid reservoir
34. Brake master cylinder
35. Combination valve

SUSPENSION
36. Upper A-arm
37. Lower A-arm
38. Stabilizer bar
39. Shock absorber

STEERING
40. Steering wheel
41. Steering column
42. Power steering pump
43. Pitman arm
44. Steering gearbox
45. Tie rod
46. Steering knuckle

ELECTRICAL SYSTEM
47. Battery
48. Distributor
49. Alternator
50. Spark plug
51. Spark plug cables

Major car components / Honda

Front-drive transverse-engine cars

Accord and Civic with CVCC engines

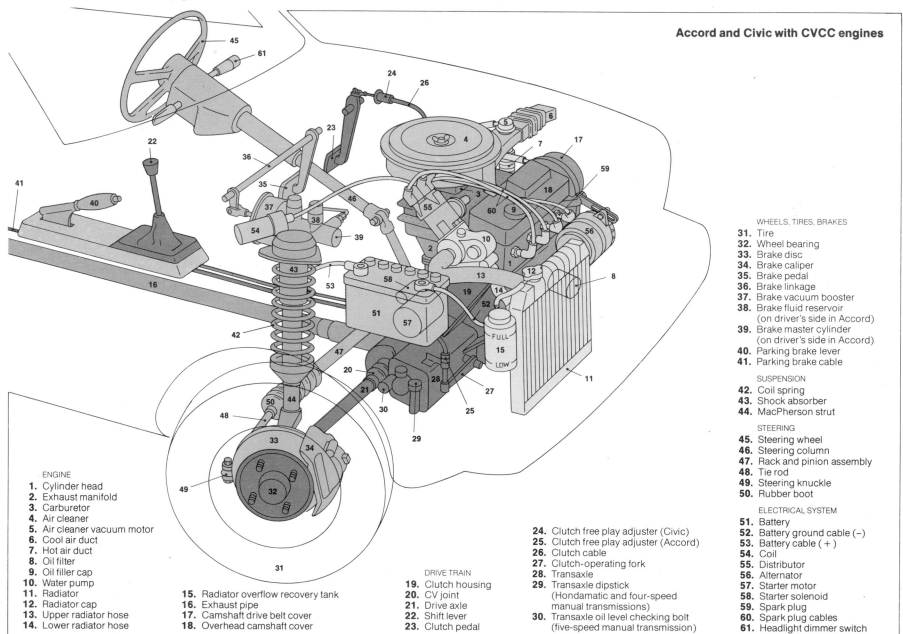

WHEELS, TIRES, BRAKES
31. Tire
32. Wheel bearing
33. Brake disc
34. Brake caliper
35. Brake pedal
36. Brake linkage
37. Brake vacuum booster
38. Brake fluid reservoir
(on driver's side in Accord)
39. Brake master cylinder
(on driver's side in Accord)
40. Parking brake lever
41. Parking brake cable

SUSPENSION
42. Coil spring
43. Shock absorber
44. MacPherson strut

STEERING
45. Steering wheel
46. Steering column
47. Rack and pinion assembly
48. Tie rod
49. Steering knuckle
50. Rubber boot

ELECTRICAL SYSTEM
51. Battery
52. Battery ground cable (−)
53. Battery cable (+)
54. Coil
55. Distributor
56. Alternator
57. Starter motor
58. Starter solenoid
59. Spark plug
60. Spark plug cables
61. Headlight dimmer switch

ENGINE
1. Cylinder head
2. Exhaust manifold
3. Carburetor
4. Air cleaner
5. Air cleaner vacuum motor
6. Cool air duct
7. Hot air duct
8. Oil filter
9. Oil filler cap
10. Water pump
11. Radiator
12. Radiator cap
13. Upper radiator hose
14. Lower radiator hose

15. Radiator overflow recovery tank
16. Exhaust pipe
17. Camshaft drive belt cover
18. Overhead camshaft cover

DRIVE TRAIN
19. Clutch housing
20. CV joint
21. Drive axle
22. Shift lever
23. Clutch pedal

24. Clutch free play adjuster (Civic)
25. Clutch free play adjuster (Accord)
26. Clutch cable
27. Clutch-operating fork
28. Transaxle
29. Transaxle dipstick
(Hondamatic and four-speed
manual transmissions)
30. Transaxle oil level checking bolt
(five-speed manual transmission)

Major car components / **Toyota**

Four-cylinder overhead cam models

Corolla models

Rear-drive Corolla models

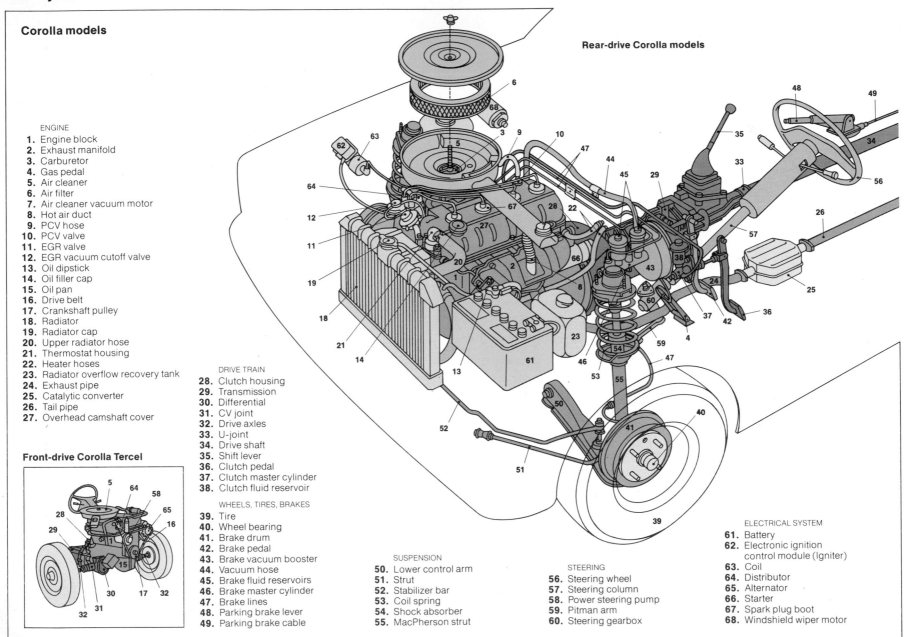

ENGINE

1. Engine block
2. Exhaust manifold
3. Carburetor
4. Gas pedal
5. Air cleaner
6. Air filter
7. Air cleaner vacuum motor
8. Hot air duct
9. PCV hose
10. PCV valve
11. EGR valve
12. EGR vacuum cutoff valve
13. Oil dipstick
14. Oil filler cap
15. Oil pan
16. Drive belt
17. Crankshaft pulley
18. Radiator
19. Radiator cap
20. Upper radiator hose
21. Thermostat housing
22. Heater hoses
23. Radiator overflow recovery tank
24. Exhaust pipe
25. Catalytic converter
26. Tail pipe
27. Overhead camshaft cover

DRIVE TRAIN

28. Clutch housing
29. Transmission
30. Differential
31. CV joint
32. Drive axles
33. U-joint
34. Drive shaft
35. Shift lever
36. Clutch pedal
37. Clutch master cylinder
38. Clutch fluid reservoir

WHEELS, TIRES, BRAKES

39. Tire
40. Wheel bearing
41. Brake drum
42. Brake pedal
43. Brake vacuum booster
44. Vacuum hose
45. Brake fluid reservoirs
46. Brake master cylinder
47. Brake lines
48. Parking brake lever
49. Parking brake cable

SUSPENSION

50. Lower control arm
51. Strut
52. Stabilizer bar
53. Coil spring
54. Shock absorber
55. MacPherson strut

STEERING

56. Steering wheel
57. Steering column
58. Power steering pump
59. Pitman arm
60. Steering gearbox

ELECTRICAL SYSTEM

61. Battery
62. Electronic ignition control module (Igniter)
63. Coil
64. Distributor
65. Alternator
66. Starter
67. Spark plug boot
68. Windshield wiper motor

Front-drive Corolla Tercel

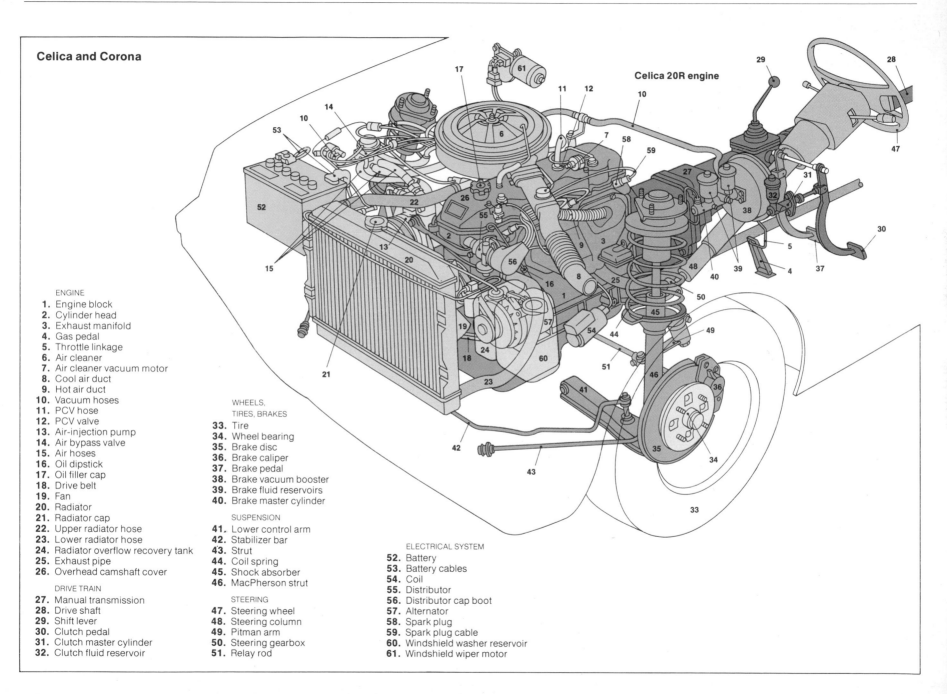

Celica and Corona

Celica 20R engine

ENGINE

1. Engine block
2. Cylinder head
3. Exhaust manifold
4. Gas pedal
5. Throttle linkage
6. Air cleaner
7. Air cleaner vacuum motor
8. Cool air duct
9. Hot air duct
10. Vacuum hoses
11. PCV hose
12. PCV valve
13. Air-injection pump
14. Air bypass valve
15. Air hoses
16. Oil dipstick
17. Oil filler cap
18. Drive belt
19. Fan
20. Radiator
21. Radiator cap
22. Upper radiator hose
23. Lower radiator hose
24. Radiator overflow recovery tank
25. Exhaust pipe
26. Overhead camshaft cover

DRIVE TRAIN

27. Manual transmission
28. Drive shaft
29. Shift lever
30. Clutch pedal
31. Clutch master cylinder
32. Clutch fluid reservoir

WHEELS, TIRES, BRAKES

33. Tire
34. Wheel bearing
35. Brake disc
36. Brake caliper
37. Brake pedal
38. Brake vacuum booster
39. Brake fluid reservoirs
40. Brake master cylinder

SUSPENSION

41. Lower control arm
42. Stabilizer bar
43. Strut
44. Coil spring
45. Shock absorber
46. MacPherson strut

STEERING

47. Steering wheel
48. Steering column
49. Pitman arm
50. Steering gearbox
51. Relay rod

ELECTRICAL SYSTEM

52. Battery
53. Battery cables
54. Coil
55. Distributor
56. Distributor cap boot
57. Alternator
58. Spark plug
59. Spark plug cable
60. Windshield washer reservoir
61. Windshield wiper motor

Front-drive transverse-engine cars

Rabbit, Scirocco, Pickup

ENGINE

1. Engine block
2. Cylinder head
3. Intake manifold
4. Carburetor
5. Fuel-injection distributor
6. Air cleaner
7. Fuel-injector lines
8. Fuel-injector nozzle
9. Gas pedal
10. PCV hose
11. Oil filter
12. Oil filler cap
13. Drive belt
14. Electric fan
15. Water pump
16. Radiator
17. Radiator cap
18. Upper radiator hose
19. Lower radiator hose
20. Exhaust pipe
21. Camshaft drive belt cover
22. Overhead camshaft cover

Carburetor engine

Diesel engine

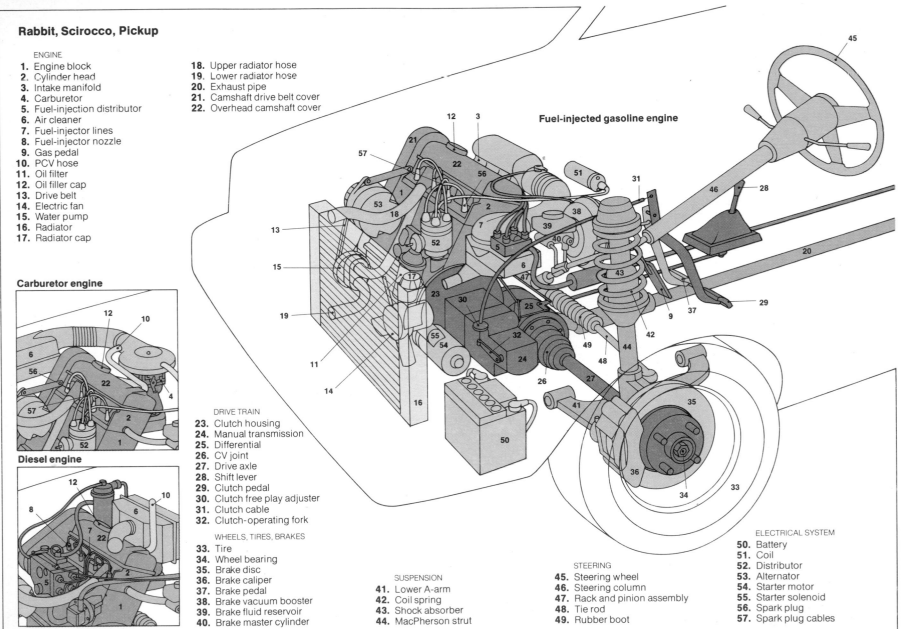

Fuel-injected gasoline engine

DRIVE TRAIN

23. Clutch housing
24. Manual transmission
25. Differential
26. CV joint
27. Drive axle
28. Shift lever
29. Clutch pedal
30. Clutch free play adjuster
31. Clutch cable
32. Clutch-operating fork

WHEELS, TIRES, BRAKES

33. Tire
34. Wheel bearing
35. Brake disc
36. Brake caliper
37. Brake pedal
38. Brake vacuum booster
39. Brake fluid reservoir
40. Brake master cylinder

SUSPENSION

41. Lower A-arm
42. Coil spring
43. Shock absorber
44. MacPherson strut

STEERING

45. Steering wheel
46. Steering column
47. Rack and pinion assembly
48. Tie rod
49. Rubber boot

ELECTRICAL SYSTEM

50. Battery
51. Coil
52. Distributor
53. Alternator
54. Starter motor
55. Starter solenoid
56. Spark plug
57. Spark plug cables

Front-drive longitudinal-engine cars

VW Dasher; Audi Fox, 4000, 5000

Four-cylinder carburetor engine

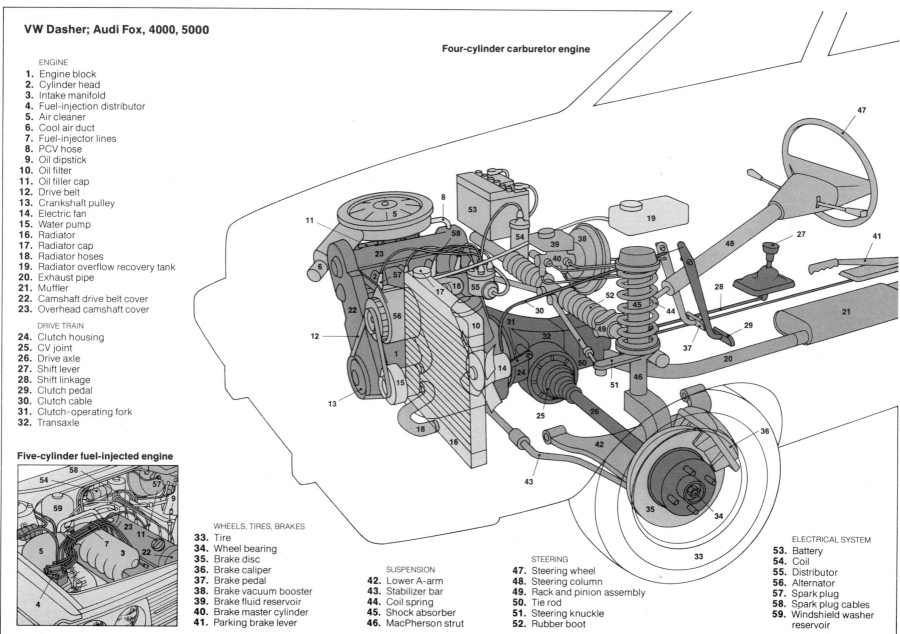

ENGINE
1. Engine block
2. Cylinder head
3. Intake manifold
4. Fuel-injection distributor
5. Air cleaner
6. Cool air duct
7. Fuel-injector lines
8. PCV hose
9. Oil dipstick
10. Oil filter
11. Oil filler cap
12. Drive belt
13. Crankshaft pulley
14. Electric fan
15. Water pump
16. Radiator
17. Radiator cap
18. Radiator hoses
19. Radiator overflow recovery tank
20. Exhaust pipe
21. Muffler
22. Camshaft drive belt cover
23. Overhead camshaft cover

DRIVE TRAIN
24. Clutch housing
25. CV joint
26. Drive axle
27. Shift lever
28. Shift linkage
29. Clutch pedal
30. Clutch cable
31. Clutch-operating fork
32. Transaxle

Five-cylinder fuel-injected engine

WHEELS, TIRES, BRAKES
33. Tire
34. Wheel bearing
35. Brake disc
36. Brake caliper
37. Brake pedal
38. Brake vacuum booster
39. Brake fluid reservoir
40. Brake master cylinder
41. Parking brake lever

SUSPENSION
42. Lower A-arm
43. Stabilizer bar
44. Coil spring
45. Shock absorber
46. MacPherson strut

STEERING
47. Steering wheel
48. Steering column
49. Rack and pinion assembly
50. Tie rod
51. Steering knuckle
52. Rubber boot

ELECTRICAL SYSTEM
53. Battery
54. Coil
55. Distributor
56. Alternator
57. Spark plug
58. Spark plug cables
59. Windshield washer reservoir

Rear-drive rear-engine cars

Beetle, Super Beetle, Karmann Ghia, VW Thing

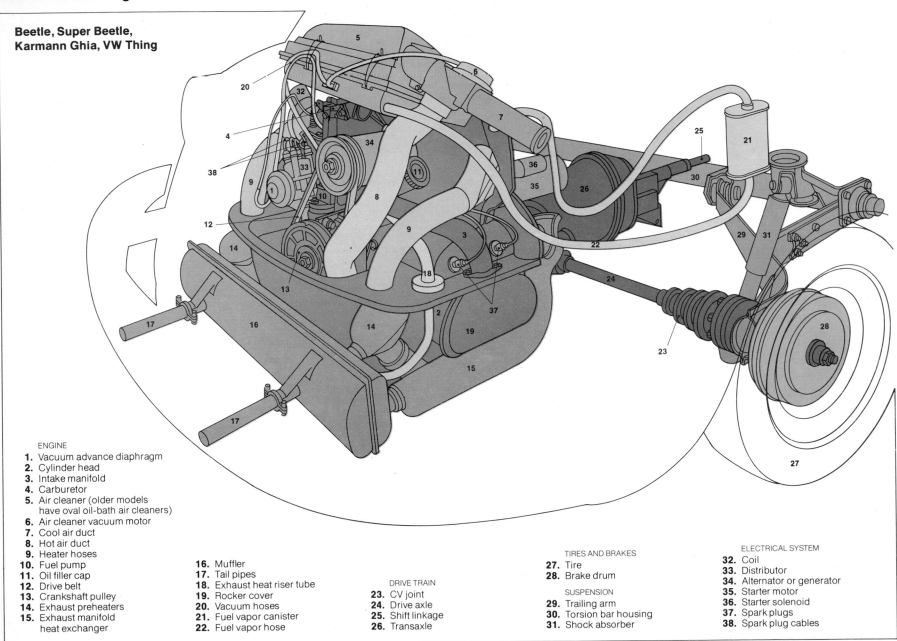

ENGINE
1. Vacuum advance diaphragm
2. Cylinder head
3. Intake manifold
4. Carburetor
5. Air cleaner (older models have oval oil-bath air cleaners)
6. Air cleaner vacuum motor
7. Cool air duct
8. Hot air duct
9. Heater hoses
10. Fuel pump
11. Oil filler cap
12. Drive belt
13. Crankshaft pulley
14. Exhaust preheaters
15. Exhaust manifold heat exchanger

16. Muffler
17. Tail pipes
18. Exhaust heat riser tube
19. Rocker cover
20. Vacuum hoses
21. Fuel vapor canister
22. Fuel vapor hose

DRIVE TRAIN
23. CV joint
24. Drive axle
25. Shift linkage
26. Transaxle

TIRES AND BRAKES
27. Tire
28. Brake drum

SUSPENSION
29. Trailing arm
30. Torsion bar housing
31. Shock absorber

ELECTRICAL SYSTEM
32. Coil
33. Distributor
34. Alternator or generator
35. Starter motor
36. Starter solenoid
37. Spark plugs
38. Spark plug cables

Tools and their uses

You cannot do much work on your car without proper tools. The average homeowner already has a good basic tool kit that includes screwdrivers, hammers, and perhaps some wrenches and an electric drill. But many other specialized tools are required to make car care safe and economical. In most cases, these tools will pay for themselves after only one or two uses because of the money you can save by doing a job yourself rather than taking your car to a mechanic. If a tool is so expensive or so specialized that it will not repay its own cost quickly, it can probably be rented from stores that sell the parts or materials the tool is designed to be used with. This book does not recommend the purchase of expensive, specialized tools that professional mechanics use in order to speed up their work but that the do-it-yourselfer, who can afford to work at a more leisurely pace, does not need.

Contents

The garage workshop

Even a one-car garage can be turned into a surprisingly convenient automotive workshop if you can find another place to store all the bicycles, lawn mowers, and garden tools that clutter up most home garages. Using a garden shed for storage is often the first step to utilizing garage space for a workshop.

Interior: Make your workshop as comfortable and pleasant as possible. Cover the walls with wallboard, and paint them with washable semigloss latex or oil-base paint. White or another light color will reflect as much light as possible. It is pointless to insulate garage walls because so much heat escapes past the typical garage door. Scrub the concrete floor with a special concrete cleaner-etcher to remove grease and grime. Patch any broken spots, then seal the surface with two coats of epoxy concrete floor paint. A bright color will enable you to find lost screws and washers easily.

Lighting: Install a double-tube 8-foot fluorescent fixture with a reflector in the center of the ceiling, and a 4-foot double-tube fluorescent over your workbench. A droplight is essential for working under your car's hood and chassis. A photographer's floodlight on a clamp or tripod is an inexpensive convenience. Used with a 100-watt bulb, it provides good light; if it is used with a heat lamp, it will speed the setting of epoxy or fiberglass patches.

Storage: Plan your work area so that you have easy access to your tools, lots of storage shelves, and plenty of counter space. In a one-car garage, put narrow shelves or cabinets down one side only, and construct your major work area at the end. That way, there will be enough room to move around. Second-hand kitchen cabinets can sometimes be obtained free or very cheaply; they are properly proportioned for standing work and are efficiently planned for storage. Or build your own cabinets for a custom fit. A wall-mounted pegboard is the most efficient way to store the tools you use often. A mechanic's rolling tool chest is an expensive luxury, but very handy if you can afford it. Discipline yourself to clean and put tools away after each job; the most elaborate storage system is pointless if it is unused. Well-ordered tools will speed your work.

Safety: Make sure that your work space is adequately ventilated. Keep a fire extinguisher in an accessible spot, and check it often. Install a smoke alarm. Keep a clearly marked first-aid kit in the shop.

A one-bay workshop

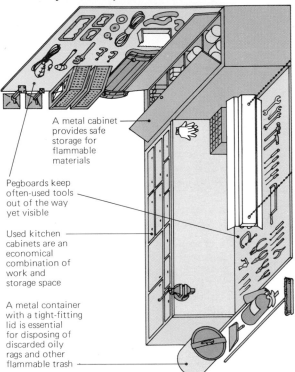

A metal cabinet provides safe storage for flammable materials

Pegboards keep often-used tools out of the way yet visible

Used kitchen cabinets are an economical combination of work and storage space

A metal container with a tight-fitting lid is essential for disposing of discarded oily rags and other flammable trash

Shop supplies

Even the simplest maintenance chores require that certain supplies be on hand continuously, such as oil, hydraulic fluids, cleaners, and paper towels. If you keep the following items on hand, you will probably have what you need when you need it.

Motor oil (buy it by the case to save money), automatic transmission fluid, brake fluid
Radiator antifreeze, fuel line antifreeze
Assorted adhesives: epoxy, clear sealer, "instant" glue
Windshield washer antifreeze solvent, car-wash detergent, engine degreaser
Silicone spray
Touch-up paint (spray can and bottle), polishing compound, chrome polish, car wax
Windshield wiper squeegees
Electrical tape, masking tape, silver duct tape
Air filter, oil filter, fuel filter
Chassis grease, wheel bearing grease, differential gear oil
Carburetor cleaner in an aerosol can
Parts-cleaning solvent
Penetrating oil in an aerosol can
Assorted nuts and bolts, lock washers, flat washers, cotter pins, hose clamps
Electric bulbs, fuses, electrical connectors
Roll of 16-gauge electrical wire
Tuneup kit with spark plugs
Drive belts
Radiator cap
Gasket sealer, bolt-locking compound, tube of RTV silicone
Vacuum hose, radiator hoses, heater hoses, thermostat
Body repair kit, assorted grades of wet and dry sandpaper, vinyl repair kit
Solder
Wiping and polishing towels
Push broom

Shop safety do's and don'ts

Do keep at least one Class B-C fire extinguisher handy.

Do wear safety goggles whenever using a drill or grinder.

Do wear a face mask and have good ventilation when working with chemicals or paint.

Do disconnect the negative battery terminal before starting electrical or engine work.

Don't run the engine without proper ventilation.

Don't wear jewelry, loose clothing, or a necktie while working. Tie back long hair.

Don't smoke in the workshop, particularly around solvents.

Don't crawl under any car that is supported only by a bumper jack.

Shopping for tools

The average professional auto mechanic has $5,000 to $10,000 invested in hand tools, mainly because he must have the proper tool to repair virtually any part on any car, and because having the right tool enables him to work faster and make more money. Although you will need only the tools to fix one or two cars, and speed is not crucial, you will still need a surprisingly large selection of tools, even to do routine maintenance. However, you do not have to buy everything at once. Start with a basic set of tools, then add to it as your interest, needs, and abilities grow.

Never buy cheap tools—they are really no bargain. Most good name-brand hand tools are guaranteed for life; you will still be using them long after inferior tools have broken, possibly injuring you or your car.

If you own few tools, the best buy is often a small or medium-size mechanic's tool set that includes a chest and a selection of tools at a price lower than that of buying the pieces individually. Check catalogs to see which sets contain what you want, and watch for sales. You may also save money by buying a mechanic's test kit that includes a timing light, engine analyzer, compression gauge, pressure gauge, and other test equipment. But be certain that the gauges included will work on your car. Many inexpensive kits contain outdated gauges that will not work properly on new cars with electronic ignitions.

Emergency tools

A compact emergency tool kit kept in the trunk of your car could save money, trouble, and even your life. The items listed below will enable you to cope with most problems.

Unopened can of brake fluid, unopened can of motor oil
Jug of radiator coolant, hose clamps, duct tape
Light bulbs, jumper cables
Distributor cap, rotor, points, condenser
Drive belts
Fire extinguisher, flashlight, highway flares
Aerosol penetrating oil
Wire, solderless connectors, fuses, electrical tape
Wrench set that fits fasteners in your car
Locking pliers, adjustable pliers, wire-cutting pliers
Flat-blade and Phillips screwdrivers
First-aid kit, space blanket
Siphon, empty 1-gal gasoline can
Ice scraper, extra wiper squeegees
Lug wrench, spare tire, scissors jack, a wide board to support a jack on soft ground, tire gauge
Spark plugs, spark plug wrench
Hand cleaner, paper towels

Basic workshop tools

Screwdrivers
Four flat-blade screwdrivers: ⅛ in., ¼ in., ⅜ in., and stubby
Five Phillips screwdrivers: Nos. 1, 2, 3, 4, and stubby
Offset ratcheting screwdriver

Pliers
Slip-joint utility pliers
Lineman's pliers
Wire cutting/stripping pliers
Diagonal wire-cutting pliers
Long-nose pliers
Locking pliers

Wrenches
10-piece combination wrench set, ⅜ in. to 1 in.
10-piece combination wrench set, 6 mm to 19 mm
Ratcheting drive handle, ⅜-in. drive
Four extensions—1 in., 3 in., 6 in., and 10 in.—and U-joint connector
Spark plug socket with rubber insert, ⅝ in. or $^{13}/_{16}$ in.
7-piece socket wrench set, 6 or 12 point, ⅜ in. to ¾ in.
12-piece socket wrench set, 6 or 12 point, 6 mm to 19 mm
Two adjustable wrenches, ½-in. jaws and 1½-in. jaws
15-piece hex-head (Allen) wrench or bit set, .050 in. to .250 in.
10-piece hex-head (Allen) wrench or bit set, 2 mm to 10 mm
Torque wrench, ⅜-in. drive, 0 to 150 lb-ft or 0 to 210 Newton-meters

Hammers and chisels
16- or 24-oz ball peen hammer
Rubber mallet
Flat chisel

Test equipment
Unpowered electrical continuity tester or test light
Compression gauge
Ignition timing light
Dwell/tachometer

Miscellaneous
Flat feeler gauges, .0015 in. to .035 in. and .050 mm to .100 mm
Wire or bar feeler gauge, .020 in. to .100 in., if available
Wire brush
Lug wrench
Tire-pressure gauge, 0 to 60 psi
Battery jumper cables
Oil can spout
Oil filter wrench
Pencil-type soldering gun
Oil drain pan, 1½-gal capacity
Scissors jack
Four jack stands (1½-ton capacity for small cars, 2½-ton for large cars)
Ramps

Optional workshop tools

Water-pump pliers
End-cutting pliers
Compound leverage pliers
Hose-clamp pliers
Pozidriv® screwdrivers (for late-model Ford and GM cars)
Battery-terminal puller
Snap-ring pliers
Brake-spring pliers
Mill file, 8 in.
Taper punches
Pin punches
Center punch
Prick punch
Drift
Impact driver
Plastic-tip hammer
Slide hammer
Hacksaw, 24-tooth-per-inch blades
10-piece ignition wrench set, $^5/_{32}$ in. to $^7/_{16}$ in.
10-piece ignition wrench set, 4 mm to 11 mm
Flex-head ratcheting drive handle, ⅜-in. drive
Open-end wrench sets, ¼ in. to $^{13}/_{16}$ in. and 6 mm to 19 mm
Box-end wrench sets, ¼ in. to $^{15}/_{16}$ in. and 6 mm to 19 mm
Electric drill, ⅜-in. chuck, variable speed, reversible
Drill attachments: sanding disc, polishing wheel, grinding wheel, wire brush, and hole saw
Twist bit set, $^1/_{16}$ in. to ½ in.
Soldering gun
Aluminum rule, 1 yd or 1 m
Dividers
Inside and outside calipers
Tire tread gauge
Thread gauge
Distributor points file
Pocket knife
Long-stem transmission funnel
Grease gun
Radiator coolant hydrometer
Battery hydrometer
Battery charger
Brake-adjusting spoon (to fit your car)
Bench vise
Remote starter switch
Vacuum/pressure gauge
Multi-function engine analyzer (multi-meter)
Mechanic's creeper
Mechanic's tool chest
Mechanic's toolbox
Hydraulic floor jack

The metric system

The metric system, devised during the French Revolution, is a decimal system, which means that it is based on multiples of 10. This greatly simplifies multiplying, dividing, and converting from one metric unit of measure to another. The only arbitrary unit in the metric system is its basic unit of *length*, the meter, from which all other measurements are derived. A meter is divided into 100 centimeters or 1,000 millimeters; 1,000 meters make a kilometer. The metric unit of *volume* is the liter, which is defined as 1,000 cubic centimeters. One cubic centimeter of water at maximum density weighs 1 gram, which is the basic metric unit of *weight*. The Celsius temperature scale (not, of course, based on the meter) defines 0°C as the freezing point of water, and 100°C as the boiling point of water.

Most of the world now uses the metric system. Britain and Canada are presently converting to it, leaving the United States as the only major nation still officially using the English, or inch, system.

Scientists all over the world, including the U.S., have been using the metric system for decades, and now many industries are also changing over. The U.S. auto industry is converting to the metric system on a piecemeal basis—every new engine, transmission, or other major component now designed in Detroit is made to metric measurements, so that the do-it-yourself mechanic will sooner or later be confronted with metric nuts, bolts, and fluid capacities. The biggest problem for mechanics is that while many metric and inch nuts and bolts seem to be about the same size, the thread pitch (the number of threads per inch) and the angle of the threads are quite different. Markings on many fasteners will tell you whether they are metric or English (see p.430). For approximate conversions that you can calculate in your head, use the table below, right. For precise conversions use the tables below and a pocket calculator, or get a slide-type metric-to-English conversion calculator, which can save you time.

Metric prefixes

Prefix	Abbreviation	Number	Decimal
mega	M	million	1,000,000
quinta	q	hundred thousand	100,000
myria	my	ten thousand	10,000
kilo	k	thousand	1,000
hecto	h	hundred	100
deca	da	ten	10
			1
deci	d	one-tenth	.1
centi	c	one-hundredth	.01
milli	m	one-thousandth	.001

By attaching these prefixes to the basic metric units (the meter for length, the liter for volume, and the gram for weight), you can arrive at all other metric units of measure. For example, a kilogram is 1,000 grams, and a milligram is 1/1,000, or .001, gram. Whenever you see an unfamiliar metric term, you can decode it by breaking it into its prefix and base. A decaliter is 10 liters. The English system has no such internal logic: If you were unfamiliar with the word "pint," you could not deduce that it is equal to ½ quart.

Conversion factors and common abbreviations

English system to metric system

To change	Into	Multiply by
inches (in.)	millimeters (mm)	25.40
inches (in.)	centimeters (cm)	2.54
feet (ft)	meters (m)	0.30
yards (yd)	meters (m)	0.91
miles (mi)	kilometers (km)	1.61
square inches (sq in.)	square centimeters (sq cm)	6.45
cubic inches (cu in.)	cubic centimeters (cu cm)	16.39
pints (pt)	liters (L)	0.47
quarts (qt)	liters (L)	0.95
gallons (gal)	liters (L)	3.79
gallons, imperial (gal)	liters (L)	4.54
ounces, mass (oz)	grams (g)	28.35
pounds, mass (lb)	kilograms (kg)	0.45
tons (tn)	metric tons (t)	0.91
ounces, force (oz)	Newtons (N)	0.28
pounds, force (lb)	Newtons (N)	4.44
pound-inches (lb-in.)	Newton-meters (N-m)	0.113
pound-feet (lb-ft)	Newton-meters (N-m)	1.35
horsepower (hp)	kilowatts (kw)	0.75
degrees Farenheit (°F)	degrees Celsius (°C)	(°F−32°) x $\frac{5}{9}$
feet/second² (ft/sec²)	meters/second² (m/sec²)	0.30
inch/second² (in./sec²)	meter/second² (m/sec²)	0.025
pounds per square inch(psi)	kilopascals (kPa)	6.88
*miles per gallon (mpg)	kilometers per liter (km/L)	0.43
*gallons per mile (gal/mi)	liters per kilometer (L/km)	2.35
miles per hour (mph)	kilometers per hour (km/h)	1.61

Metric system to English system

To change	Into	Multiply by
millimeters (mm)	inches (in.)	0.039
centimeters (cm)	inches (in.)	0.39
meters (m)	feet (ft)	3.28
meters (m)	yards (yd)	1.09
kilometers (km)	miles (mi)	0.62
square centimeters (sq cm)	square inches (sq in.)	0.155
cubic centimeters (cu cm)	cubic inches (cu in.)	0.061
liters (L)	pints (pt)	2.11
liters (L)	quarts (qt)	1.06
liters (L)	gallons (gal)	0.264
liters (L)	gallons, imperial (gal)	0.22
grams (g)	ounces, mass (oz)	0.035
kilograms (kg)	tons (tn)	2.21
metric tons (t)	tons (tn)	1.10
Newtons (N)	ounces, force (oz)	3.60
Newtons (N)	pounds, force (lb)	0.225
Newton-meters (N-m)	pound-inches (lb-in.)	8.87
Newton-meters (N-m)	pound-feet (lb-ft)	0.74
kilowatts (kw)	horsepower (hp)	1.34
degrees Celsius (°C)	degrees Farenheit (°F)	$\frac{9}{5}$ x °C + 32°
meters/second² (m/sec²)	feet/second² (ft/sec²)	3.28
meters/second² (m/sec²)	inches/second² (in./sec²)	39.36
kilopascals (kPa)	pounds per square inch (psi)	0.145
*kilometers per liter (km/L)	miles per gallon (mpg)	2.35
*liters per kilometer (L/km)	gallons per mile (gal/mi)	0.43
kilometers per hour (km/h)	miles per hour (mph)	0.62

*Fuel economy ratings for European cars are generally given as a number of liters of fuel consumed per 100 kilometers traveled (L/100 km), while North American cars are rated at the number of miles traveled per gallon of fuel consumed (mpg). To convert L/100 km to mpg, divide the number of L/100 km into 235. To convert mpg into L/100 km, divide the number of mpg into 235.

Useful approximate equivalents

¼-in. wrench may fit 6-mm nut
⁷⁄₁₆-in. wrench may fit 11-mm nut
¹⁵⁄₃₂-in. wrench may fit 12-mm nut
½-in. wrench may fit 13-mm nut
⁹⁄₁₆-in. wrench may fit 14-mm nut
¾-in. wrench may fit 19-mm nut
⅞-in. wrench may fit 22-mm nut
4-mm wrench may fit ⁵⁄₃₂-in. nut
6-mm wrench may fit ¹⁵⁄₆₄-in. nut
8-mm wrench may fit ⁵⁄₁₆-in. nut
10-mm wrench may fit ⅜-in. nut
13-mm wrench may fit ½-in. nut
16-mm wrench may fit ⅝-in. nut
90 km/h = 55 mph
　(1 mph is about .6 km/h)
200 kPa is about 29 psi
　(1 psi is about 7 kPa)
4 L is about 1 gal
1 L is about 1 qt

½ L is about 1 pt
80 km = 50 mi
1,610 m = 1 mi
0°C = 32°F
20°C = 68°F
85°C = 185°F
100°C = 212°F
500 g = 1.1 lb
1 kg = 2.2 lb
1 in. is about 2½ cm
1 mm is about the thickness of a dime
1 cm is about ⅜ in., or roughly the width of your smallest fingernail
4 N-m is about 3 lb-ft
210 N-m is about 155 lb-ft
1 L or 1,000 cc is about 60 cu in.

Caution: Do not use metric wrenches on inch-size nuts and bolts or inch wrenches on metric nuts and bolts except in emergencies. The equivalent sizes given above are theoretically accurate, but wrenches are manufactured to different standards of precision, and not all ½-in. wrenches, for example, are exactly ½ in. To be safe, never use a wrench that does not fit snugly; a wrench that is only slightly too large is likely to round off the corners of the fastener and make it much more difficult to remove.

Screwdrivers

Automotive screwdrivers are precision tools that will last indefinitely when they are used and cared for correctly. Always use the right size and shape screwdriver for the job, or you might damage both the screwdriver and the screw. The tip should always fit snugly in the screw. Wipe the blades with silicone spray periodically to prevent corrosion.

The strongest (and most expensive) screwdrivers are marked "chrome-vanadium steel" and are nickel-chrome plated. They have hardwood or plastic grips riveted to the blade itself; the most comfortable ones have oversized, rounded handles. However, most reasonably priced screwdrivers are made with thin, fluted handles bonded to the shaft. Adding a slip-on rubber grip will make them more comfortable and will give you better leverage.

Your basic tools should include three flat-blade screwdrivers with ⅛-inch, ¼-inch, and ⅜-inch tips; Nos. 1, 2, 3, and 4 Phillips screwdrivers; and two stubby screwdrivers—one flat-blade and one Phillips—for tight spots. An offset screwdriver or a ratcheting screwdriver may fit where nothing else will. A screwdriver with a magnetic tip or a screw-holding tip can help start screws in cramped spots. Buy Reed and Prince, Pozidriv®, and Torx-head® screwdrivers only when you have use for them.

Wrenches

Since cars are primarily held together with nuts and bolts, an auto mechanic's most basic tools are wrenches. The best wrenches are forged from high-carbon steel alloy or chrome-vanadium steel and are heat treated, oil quenched, and nickel-chrome plated. Such wrenches are well worth the extra cost, as cheap wrenches bend or break easily, while the good ones will last a lifetime (some are even guaranteed for life). Use the appropriate wrench for each job, wipe off grease and grit when you are finished, and spray your wrenches with silicone periodically.

Before buying any wrenches, determine whether your car requires metric or inch sizes, or both. Most foreign cars have only metric nuts and bolts; older North American cars use only inch sizes, while newer ones have a combination of metric and inch sizes because retooling at the factory for all-metric sizes is being done gradually. Buying sets of wrenches is more economical than buying them individually, and you will probably have the right size when you need it, even in the smaller sets of 10 or 12 wrenches.

You will need both open-end and box-end wrenches in a variety of sizes. If you don't want to buy separate sets, buying a set of combination wrenches is a good compromise. Combination wrenches have an open-end wrench of a given size at one end and the same-size box-end wrench at the other. Combination wrenches are no help when you need two wrenches of the same size (one to hold a nut and another to turn a bolt, for example). Six-point box-end wrenches contact a hexagonal bolt head on all six sides and can therefore take more torque, but 12-point box ends fit on bolts in more positions.

Obstruction wrenches, sometimes called *starter wrenches,* are open-end or box-end wrenches with curved handles that are designed to clear obstructions. They enable you to do certain jobs faster, although with a little time and ingenuity you can often get at the part with ordinary tools.

Adjustable wrenches are open-end wrenches with one movable jaw. Because they can fit a large number of bolts, they are useful to have for emergencies, but they can slip off tight fasteners and round them off. Moreover, adjustable wrenches are bulky and will not fit into tight spaces. There are two popular sizes: one with jaws that open to ½ inch and one that opens to 1½ inches. Locking adjustable wrenches are stronger than ordinary ones, but there is still some play in their mechanisms, so that they may still slip off nuts and bolts. Make sure that your adjustable wrenches have smooth jaws, since serrated jaws will chew up nuts and bolts.

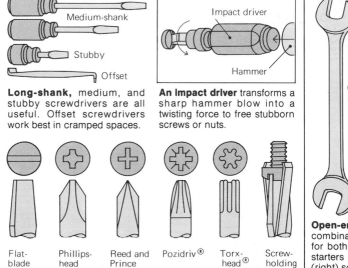

Long-shank, medium, and stubby screwdrivers are all useful. Offset screwdrivers work best in cramped spaces.

An impact driver transforms a sharp hammer blow into a twisting force to free stubborn screws or nuts.

Flat-blade Phillips-head Reed and Prince Pozidriv® Torx-head® Screw-holding

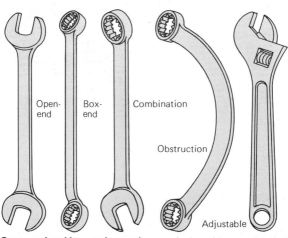

Open-end and box-end wrenches can be bought separately, but combination wrenches are a compact and economical substitute for both. Curved-handle obstruction wrenches make removal of starters and manifolds easier. Always turn an adjustable wrench (right) so that the load is applied to the stronger fixed jaw.

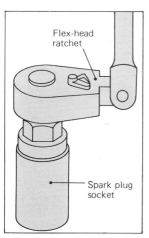

A flex-head ratchet turned 90 degrees and a rubber-lined spark plug socket will simplify the removal of hidden or awkwardly placed spark plugs.

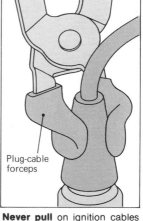

Never pull on ignition cables to remove spark plug boots, or you could damage the cables. Use special puller (p.231) or forceps in tight places.

Socket wrenches

The heart of a socket wrench set is the ratcheting drive handle, which reverses direction to tighten or loosen nuts and bolts. A flex-head ratchet swivels through 90 degrees so that the handle can clear obstructions. Good ratchets are guaranteed for life.

Add 1-inch, 3-inch, 6-inch, and 10-inch extensions, which can be joined together for longer reach. A swiveling U-joint connector will make a ratchet and extensions even more versatile.

Sockets are available with 6 or 12 points; regular length or deep; in inch or metric sizes; and with 1/4-inch, 3/8-inch, 1/2-inch, or 3/4-inch square drive holes. The best socket set for automotive use is one with a 3/8-inch drive and regular-length 6- or 12-point sockets ranging from 3/8 inch to 3/4 inch and 6 mm to 19 mm. You may also need 1/4-inch and 5/16-inch sockets, which may only be available in 1/4-inch drive, in which case you will also need a 1/4- to 3/8-inch drive adapter. Sets containing a ratchet, 3-inch and 6-inch extensions, a U-joint connector, a good range of socket sizes, and a spark plug socket will give you most of what you need at a reasonable price.

There are many specialized sockets that you might find useful. A spark plug socket with a rubber insert that holds the plug by the insulator is invaluable around a hot engine (get one to fit the plugs in your car: 5/8 inch or 13/16 inch). Hex-bit sockets fit Allen-head bolts. Screwdriver-bit sockets allow you to reach awkwardly placed screws with extensions and U-joints. A crowfoot wrench looks like the head of an open-end wrench; a crowfoot head on an extension can reach spots inaccessible to other wrenches.

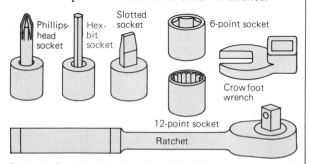

Phillips-head socket
Hex-bit socket
Slotted socket
6-point socket
12-point socket
Crow foot wrench
Ratchet

Stronger 6-point sockets contact the sides of hexagonal nuts; 12-point sockets contact only the corners, but also fit square nuts. Hex-bit sockets on a ratchet make a ratcheting Allen wrench; slotted or Phillips-head sockets make a ratcheting screwdriver. Crowfoot wrenches can reach where other wrenches do not fit.

Special-purpose wrenches

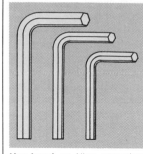

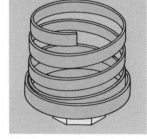

Hex-head, or Allen, wrenches fit into the hexagonal holes in Allen bolts. These L-shaped wrenches are available in inch and metric sizes.

Ignition wrenches come in sets that contain short, thin, open-end or combination wrenches for use on tiny nuts (5/32 to 7/16 in. or 4 to 11 mm).

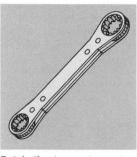

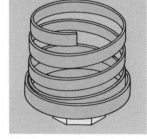

Ratcheting box-end wrenches are long, thin, straight wrenches with fine-tooth ratcheting heads. They can turn nuts and bolts in very tight quarters.

Oil-filter wrench, which looks like a coil spring with a hex nut on the bottom, can spin off tight filters without damage. Other types are available.

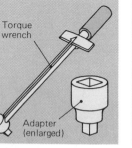

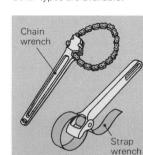

Torque wrench
Adapter (enlarged)
Chain wrench
Strap wrench

Torque wrench that measures up to 150 lb-ft (210 N-m) may be available only with 1/2-in. drive, in which case a 1/2- to 3/8-in. adapter is needed.

Chain wrench can apply tremendous pressure in cramped quarters through lever action on its links. Strap wrench has a nylon strap instead of a chain.

Electric drills

An electric drill functions as a portable power source that can drill, sand, buff, polish, grind, and cut when it is fitted with the proper accessories. For automotive use the most versatile drill has a 3/8-inch chuck, an infinitely variable speed control, a reversible motor, a speed range from 0 to 2,500 rpm, and a motor of at least 3/8 horsepower.

Bits made of high-speed alloy steel (often called *high-speed bits*) are best, for they can cut almost any material. A set of 24 high-quality twist bits ranging from 1/16 inch to 1/2 inch will handle most automotive drilling on mild steel, aluminum, or fiberglass. For heat-treated metals, use a blunt-point bit; for soft plastics and rubber, use a sharp-point bit.

A drill stand converts a hand-held power tool into a bench tool and frees your hands. Other accessories, including a grinding wheel, a polishing wheel, a disc sander, a wire brush, and a hole saw and mandrel set designed to cut metal (not wood) will make your drill even more versatile.

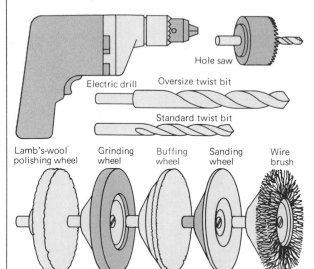

Hole saw
Electric drill
Oversize twist bit
Standard twist bit
Lamb's-wool polishing wheel
Grinding wheel
Buffing wheel
Sanding wheel
Wire brush

A good drill should have a variable-speed, reversible motor and a 3/8-in. chuck. Oversize twist bit is stepped down to fit the chuck; spade bit can be used on plastic and fiberglass. A hole saw with interchangeable blades will cut holes of various sizes; drill bit in center keeps saw from wandering. Sanding disc, muslin buffing wheel, and lamb's-wool polishing wheel make electric drill useful for light bodywork. Wire brush can remove rust and old paint from car body. Grinding wheel can be used to sharpen tools, remove rivet heads, and reshape screwdriver bits.

Hammers, punches, and chisels

Hammers, punches, and chisels must absorb much hard use, so get good ones that will last.

Machinist's hammers: The best hammers have drop-forged, heat-treated steel heads and either fiberglass or hickory wood handles. A ball peen hammer with a 16- or 24-ounce head is the most versatile. Carpenter's claw hammers are not suitable for hammering on hardened steel punches and chisels.

Soft hammers: A rubber mallet will not mar metal, so it can be used for replacing hubcaps and for work on other visible surfaces. A plastic-tip hammer comes with interchangeable tips that range from very hard nylon to very soft rubber. You can also get tips made of brass, copper, and aluminum. Never use soft hammers to strike hard metals or chisels.

Body hammers: Body hammers are made in a variety of shapes and sizes for work on tiny dents as well as large damaged areas. The most common are bumping hammers, for rough contouring; sharply pointed picks, for tapping up small dents; and small finishing hammers. Dollies are shaped blocks of steel that have a variety of curves to fit different body contours. They are used under a dent, either to bump up low spots or to support the hammer while panels are being reshaped. The slide hammer is used to pull out dents that cannot be reached from behind.

Punches: Good punches are drop-forged from tempered chrome-vanadium steel, then nickel-chrome plated. Taper punches are used for aligning the holes in parts before assembly. Pin punches, or *rivet busters*, have straight shafts and flat ends to drive out holding pins without damage to the hole. The center punch has a sharp point to make starting indentations for drills. The prick punch scratches guidelines into metal. Drifts are round punches with flat ends; soft metal drifts can be used to drive out press-fit parts without damaging them.

Chisels: Chisels are heavy-duty cutting tools made from tempered chrome-vanadium steel. Flat chisels have wide cutting edges beveled on two sides.

> **Caution:** To avoid injury, never use a hammer, punch, or chisel that has a chipped or mushroomed head; never use a soft hammer on hard metals; never use the side of a hammer; and never use a hammer with a broken handle. Hammer's face should be at least ½ in. larger than the chisel being hammered. Wear safety goggles.

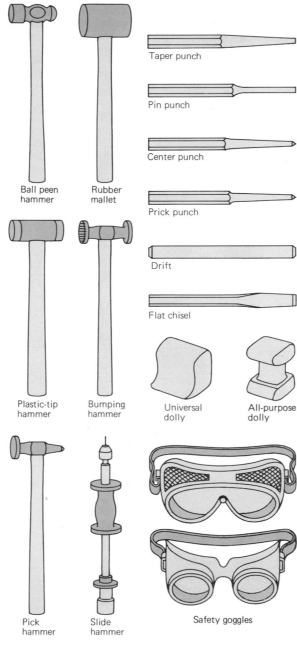

Ball peen hammer · Rubber mallet

Taper punch · Pin punch · Center punch · Prick punch · Drift · Flat chisel

Plastic-tip hammer · Bumping hammer · Universal dolly · All-purpose dolly

Pick hammer · Slide hammer · Safety goggles

Pliers

The best pliers are forged from high-carbon steel and are nickel-chrome plated. Slip-joint pliers have sliding pivots that allow the jaws to open to two or more sizes. The most common slip-joint pliers are utility pliers, which have combination flat and curved jaws, and water-pump pliers, which are larger, stronger, and less likely to slip. Never use slip-joint pliers to turn nuts or bolts—they will round off the corners.

Solid-joint pliers have only one pivot axis. The most common are long-nose pliers, lineman's pliers, and diagonal wire-cutting pliers. Compound-leverage cutting pliers will cut large bolts. End-cutting pliers cut flush to the surface.

Locking pliers apply spring-loaded pressure and lock in position. They are available with a variety of jaw designs. Wire strippers adjust to strip the insulation from wires of various gauges.

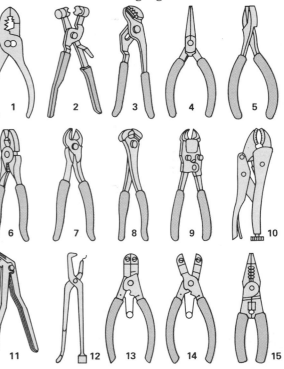

Types of pliers: 1. Utility. 2. Hose clamp. 3. Water pump. 4. Long nose. 5. Duckbill. 6. Lineman's. 7. Diagonal cutting. 8. End cutting. 9. Compound leverage. 10. Locking. 11. Battery terminal. 12. Brake spring. 13. & 14. Snap ring. 15. Wire strippers.

Tools

Files

Files are used to cut metal as well as to smooth it. They vary in shape and in the type and coarseness of their cutting surfaces. Although thousands of different files for different jobs are on the market, only a few are used for general automotive work. These come in combinations of the five shapes (flat, half round, round, square, and triangular); two types of cutting surface (single cut and double cut); and three surface grades (bastard cut, second cut, and smooth cut) that are illustrated at the right.

When deciding which file is best suited for a particular job, you should consider several factors. The shape of the file should match the shape of the surface you will be working on. (For example, use a round file to smooth or enlarge circular holes.) Generally, double-cut files cut through material faster than single-cut files do, but the grade—determined by the number of teeth per inch—also influences the speed and smoothness of the cut.

Many files do not come with handles, which must be purchased separately. Buy a comfortable handle that will grip the tang of the file firmly. A handle that comes off too easily can be annoying to use.

There are several special automotive files that you may use more often than the general-purpose files described above. The ignition-point file is a small, flat file used on distributor points and spark plugs. Some have guides that keep the file from slipping off the points during this tedious filing process. Needle files are very fine cut miniature files that come as a set in a variety of shapes; they are used for precision work or in tight spaces. The thread-restoring file is a square file with eight sets of teeth (four on each end) to fit eight different thread gauges. It will clean rust and dirt out of the threads on bolts and studs, but it cannot repair stripped threads. The perforated file, which looks like a cheese grater, is used in repairing dents, to shape plastic body filler.

Rubbing chalk over a file before using it will help keep the filings from sticking between the teeth, but you will still need to clean the file frequently while you work in order to prevent trapped particles from scratching the surface you are filing. The best way to clean a file is with a file card, which has a wire brush on one side to loosen filings and a bristle brush on the other side to finish the cleaning. Store files so that their teeth do not come in contact with other tools, since a file's cutting surfaces are easily dulled.

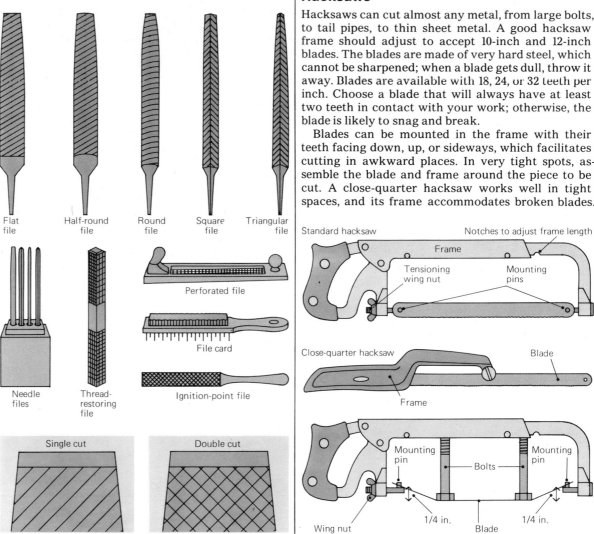

Flat file · Half-round file · Round file · Square file · Triangular file

Needle files · Thread-restoring file

Perforated file

File card

Ignition-point file

Single cut · Double cut

Single-cut files have teeth set in parallel, unbroken diagonal rows. Double-cut files have two diagonal sets of teeth that cross at right angles. Single-cut files produce a smooth surface, while double-cut files remove material rapidly. The coarseness of a file depends on the number of teeth cut into each inch of the file and on the file's length. There are three grades of surface coarseness: bastard, intermediate, and smooth. Bastard is the coarsest grade; smooth is the finest grade. A bastard-cut short file, however, will have smaller teeth than a bastard-cut long file.

Hacksaws

Hacksaws can cut almost any metal, from large bolts, to tail pipes, to thin sheet metal. A good hacksaw frame should adjust to accept 10-inch and 12-inch blades. The blades are made of very hard steel, which cannot be sharpened; when a blade gets dull, throw it away. Blades are available with 18, 24, or 32 teeth per inch. Choose a blade that will always have at least two teeth in contact with your work; otherwise, the blade is likely to snag and break.

Blades can be mounted in the frame with their teeth facing down, up, or sideways, which facilitates cutting in awkward places. In very tight spots, assemble the blade and frame around the piece to be cut. A close-quarter hacksaw works well in tight spaces, and its frame accommodates broken blades.

Standard hacksaw · Notches to adjust frame length · Frame · Tensioning wing nut · Mounting pins

Close-quarter hacksaw · Blade · Frame

Mounting pin · Mounting pin · Bolts · Wing nut · 1/4 in. · 1/4 in. · Blade

Always saw with the blade perpendicular to the surface, not at an angle, or you will not be able to keep at least two teeth in contact with the surface (see text). All cutting is done on the forward stroke, so bear down while pushing forward, then lift saw very slightly on the return stroke. To cut studs or bolts flush with a surface, mount the blade sideways in the frame. Position two bolts between the frame and blade so that the blade is forced down about ¼ in. This will permit the cutting part of the blade to clear the saw's mounting pins and its tensioning wing nut.

Electrical test equipment

One of the most useful devices you can own is a volt-ohm meter (sometimes called a volt-ohm-milliammeter). Unlike most specialized automotive tools, the volt-ohm meter has dozens of uses around the house, from checking appliances to testing fuses. The meter is simple to operate and versatile; it measures voltage and resistance as well as current.

Prices of volt-ohm meters vary widely, depending on the number and range of the scales, their accuracy, and the number of extra convenience features. For general automotive and household use, look for a meter with the following features: The alternating current (AC) and direct current (DC) scales should both measure 0 to 250 volts. The *Low* resistance scale should read 0 to approximately 500 ohms in easily read graduations. Do not buy a meter if the only ohm scale is marked "K-ohms"; this means that the scale is calibrated in 1,000-ohm intervals, which is inadequate for general automotive testing. To measure higher resistances, there should also be higher resistance scales (often labeled R x 10, R x 100, and R x 1,000, for "Resistance times 10" or "times 1,000"). There should also be a control knob to reset the needle to zero each time the ohm scale is changed. A clearly marked switch for selecting function and range is best. Some less expensive meters use jacks for the probes to change the meter's function and range. You will need both alligator-clip and needle test probes. A good selection of volt-ohm meters is available at electronic hobby shops.

If you use and care for your meter properly, it will last indefinitely. Store it in a horizontal position, and remove the batteries whenever the meter will be unused for long periods. Always set the switch for the correct function and range before applying the test probes. When testing unknown voltages, use the highest setting first. Always carefully follow the instructions that come with the meter. By taking these simple precautions, you will avoid unnecessary damage to the meter or the components being tested.

Dwell-tachometer

As the name implies, the dwell-tachometer is a dual-purpose instrument. It measures both dwell angle (the length of time that the distributor points stay closed, measured in degrees of distributor-cam rotation) and engine speed. A dwell-tachometer used to be an optional tool that made tuneups easier and

more precise, but precise tuning has become mandatory for modern engines with complex systems for emission control. For versatility, get a meter that works on four-, six-, and eight-cylinder engines. Beware of cheap instruments from unknown manufacturers—they may not work on cars with electronic ignition systems, even when the package says that they do, or they may give inaccurate readings. Do not buy a meter unless it is returnable; test it immediately to be sure that it works on your car. For instructions on using the meter, see p.223.

Multi-meter

A multi-meter (also called an *engine analyzer*) can perform all the functions of a volt-ohm meter and a dwell-tachometer plus many others. Multi-meters cannot, however, be used to check household current because they have no alternating current (AC) voltage scales. Advances in solid-state electronics have made multi-meters accurate, reliable, and affordable. If you do not own any test instruments, buying a multi-meter can save you money.

When shopping for a multi-meter, there are certain features you should look for. The following description is of an ideal instrument. The ones you see may differ in detail, but they must have essentially the same features to function effectively. Any multi-meter should have separate settings for four-, six-, and eight-cylinder engines; some also have settings for five-cylinder and two-, three-, and four-rotor Wankel engines. A *Low* ohm scale that reads 0 to 500 ohms in easily read graduations is needed to check ignition coils, and a *High* ohm scale from 0 to 500,000 (500 K) ohms is needed to test high-voltage spark plug cables. A voltage scale from 0 to 16 volts or higher can be used to check 12-volt batteries. A *Low* amp scale, from 0 to 100 amps, is used for checking electronic ignition systems, coils, alternators, and generators. A *High* amp scale, from 0 to 400 amps, measures how much current the starter is drawing. Some new computer-controlled multi-meters have digital readouts instead of pointers, which eliminates the problems of accurately reading small, crowded scales or the chance of reading the wrong scale. It is essential to have a complete, comprehensible manual with step-by-step instructions on every test the meter can perform. If your meter sits unused for long periods, remove any batteries to prevent corrosion.

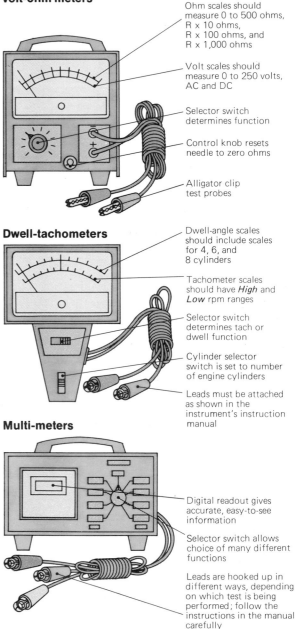

Volt-ohm meters

Ohm scales should measure 0 to 500 ohms, R x 10 ohms, R x 100 ohms, and R x 1,000 ohms

Volt scales should measure 0 to 250 volts, AC and DC

Selector switch determines function

Control knob resets needle to zero ohms

Alligator clip test probes

Dwell-tachometers

Dwell-angle scales should include scales for 4, 6, and 8 cylinders

Tachometer scales should have *High* and *Low* rpm ranges

Selector switch determines tach or dwell function

Cylinder selector switch is set to number of engine cylinders

Leads must be attached as shown in the instrument's instruction manual

Multi-meters

Digital readout gives accurate, easy-to-see information

Selector switch allows choice of many different functions

Leads are hooked up in different ways, depending on which test is being performed; follow the instructions in the manual carefully

Electrical test equipment (continued)

There are also a number of specialized electronic instruments available for automotive work. The most useful of these are described below.

Electronic ignition tester

When the components of an electronic ignition system go bad, they are usually replaced rather than repaired. Replacement units can be very expensive, and they cannot be returned. To be sure that you are replacing parts only when necessary, test the system with an electronic ignition tester—an inexpensive, easy-to-use instrument. There are many electronic ignition testers on the market, but they all perform essentially the same functions. With one hookup, they will tell you if the battery is too weak to perform the tests; then they will test the pickup coil, the control unit, and the ignition coil. If one of these components is malfunctioning, the appropriate light on the tester lights up and you know you must replace that component.

Timing light

Ignition timing (the timed delivery of the spark to the spark plug) seriously affects the way an engine runs. If the timing is too far advanced, the engine will knock and may be damaged. If the timing is retarded, the engine may lose power and overheat. The conventional way to set timing is with a timing light.

Cheap timing lights are usually inadequate. Those with neon lights are so weak that you must work in a darkened garage to see the timing marks. Some inexpensive models draw power from a wall socket instead of the car's battery, which limits where you can work, and they have mechanical pickups that must be inserted between the spark plug and its lead. Good timing lights are considerably more expensive, but worth the price. They have xenon strobe lights, which are clearly visible even in bright sunlight. They are powered by the car's battery, and they have inductive pickups, which can simply be clamped around the spark plug cable without disconnecting anything. Some timing lights even have built-in dwell-tachometers. For complete instructions on adjusting ignition timing, see pp.236–239.

Test light

One of the simplest and most useful devices you can own is a test light, which is nothing more than a

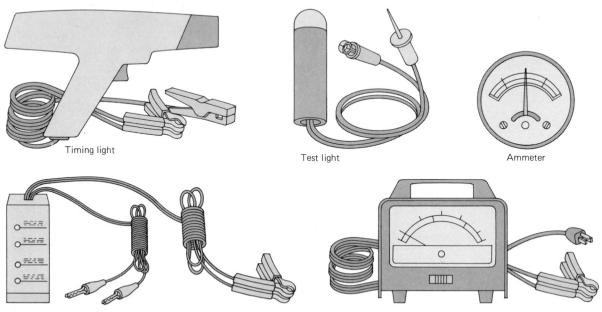

Timing light

Test light

Ammeter

Electronic ignition tester

Battery charger

12-volt bulb with two leads. One lead has a needle probe, and the other has an alligator clip. To locate an open circuit or a short circuit, simply turn on the circuit, attach the alligator clip to a good ground, and probe the wiring and electrical components with the needle. As long as the bulb lights up, the circuit is complete to that point. When the bulb fails to light, you have located an open or short circuit. You can buy a test light, or you can make one as shown on page 361. See *Tracing electrical faults*, pp.361–363, for more complete directions for using a test light.

Battery charger

Whenever possible, a battery should be charged slowly (at low amperage). Professional battery chargers provide 60 to 80 amps to give a quick charge in an emergency, but they also damage the battery and shorten its life. A 6-amp or 10-amp battery charger is perfect for home use, and even a 4-amp unit is adequate, as long as you realize that complete charging may take 24 to 48 hours. (A 10-amp charger will do the job in about 8 hours.) To protect your battery, be sure that any charger you buy has an *automatic cutoff* to prevent overcharging, *reverse polarity protection* in case you hook it up wrong, *solid-state circuitry* to prevent short circuits, and a *meter* so that you can see at what rate the battery is charging. Always hook up the charger before plugging it in (attach its red clamp to the positive battery post, black clamp to the negative post), then plug in the charger and turn it on. Continue charging until the meter reads 1 amp. Turn the charger off and unplug it before removing the cables.

Ammeter

An ammeter measures electric current in amperes, or *amps*. A negative reading indicates that current is being drawn by something (for example, the starter or headlights) faster than the battery is being recharged by the alternator. A positive reading indicates that the generator or alternator is charging the battery. You can test many components of the charging system and starting system with an ammeter. For rough checks, you can get one with an inductive pickup, which clamps to the wires to take a reading; the wires need not be disconnected.

Gauges

In this age of electronics and microchips, some mechanical gauges are still the simplest, the best, or the only way to do a job.

Compression gauge

Before the air-fuel mixture in an engine is ignited, it must be compressed, or the explosion will not produce any useful power. A compression gauge measures this pressure in pounds per square inch (psi). By removing the spark plugs and inserting the gauge in each spark plug hole in turn, then cranking the engine, you will get the compression for each cylinder. All the readings should be at least 90 psi, and all the cylinders should be within 25 percent of each other. Any markedly lower readings indicate that the fuel mixture is leaking out somewhere instead of being compressed, which means that either the piston rings are worn, the head gasket is blown, or the valves are worn or sticking. For complete instructions on using a compression gauge and interpreting the readings, see p.263.

Compression gauges differ in the way they are fitted into the spark plug holes. Cheaper gauges have simple rubber nipples that must be held in place; this type is unsuitable for engines that have little space around their spark plug holes. Better compression gauges have flexible hose connections that screw into the spark plug holes. Some gauges also have "tell-tale" needles that stick at the highest reading until the gauge is reset.

Vacuum gauge

A vacuum gauge measures the difference between air pressure in the manifold and atmospheric pressure. Some new cars have fuel-economy gauges, which are vacuum gauges with color bands instead of numbered scales. These are quite adequate for all vacuum tests, so if your car has one, you will not need to buy another vacuum gauge. Regular vacuum gauges are calibrated in inches of mercury. Vacuum gauge tests can pinpoint problems in carburetor and intake manifold gaskets, ignition timing, air cleaner, valves, valve guides, valve springs, carburetor settings, and the exhaust system. For complete directions on hooking up and using a vacuum gauge, see p.264.

Another useful device is a vacuum pump, a hand pump that produces vacuum and has a vacuum gauge attached. It can be used to test diaphragms, vacuum hoses, and other engine components.

Hydrometers

Two hydrometers are needed for automotive maintenance, one to check the battery acid and one to check the antifreeze. Hydrometers measure the specific gravity of liquids. As the concentration of these mixtures changes, so does their specific gravity.

A hydrometer consists of a syringe with a rubber bulb on top and a floating scale inside. (Inexpensive hydrometers have floating colored balls instead of scales.) Premium hydrometers have built-in thermometers that allow you to correct for temperature, which affects specific-gravity readings. Taking and interpreting battery hydrometer readings is discussed on page 277, and using a hydrometer to check the radiator coolant is covered on page 280.

Tire-pressure gauge

Keep a tire-pressure gauge in your glove compartment and check tire pressures once a month. Check the spare tire when you check the others. For accuracy, always check and adjust tire pressures when the tires are cold. Use your own gauge, since the gauges on air hoses at service stations are often inaccurate. Get a pencil-type gauge, which is cheap and takes up almost no space, or a dial gauge, which is more expensive and bulkier but easier to read.

Feeler gauges

There are three types of feeler gauges: flat blade, wire, and bar. Blade-type gauges are used for setting the breaker-point gap, valve clearances, and other critical adjustments. A typical set has about 15 blades, graduated from .002 to .030 inch or from .1 to .7 millimeter. Wire gauges are best for gapping spark plugs, because they can measure worn electrode tips accurately. However, if your car has an electronic ignition system, you may need a bar-type feeler gauge in order to measure the larger spark plug gaps often specified for these systems; wire feeler gauges are not available in these sizes. Many electronic ignitions require a flat-blade gauge made of brass or plastic so that the magnetic pickup in the distributor will not distort the readings. With any feeler gauge, use the go/no-go method: when the correct-size gauge slides into the gap with slight drag but the next-largest gauge will not fit, the gap is correct.

Compression gauge

Vacuum gauge

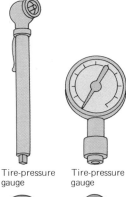

Tire-pressure gauge   Tire-pressure gauge

Floating-ball hydrometer

Floating-scale hydrometer

Vacuum pump

Wire feeler gauge

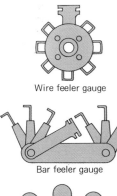

Bar feeler gauge

Flat-blade feeler gauge

Raising a car safely

Raising a car high enough to work under it safely can pose a problem for home mechanics. The bumper jacks and side-lift jacks provided by car manufacturers are flimsy and should never be used for anything but changing a tire. A scissors jack is easier to use and safer. Post-type hydraulic jacks may not fit under your car or, if they do fit, may not raise the car high enough for jack stands to be put in place. A small version of a mechanic's floor jack is expensive but is a good investment if you use it often.

Before jacking up a car, park on level ground. When raising both front wheels or both rear wheels, center the jack under a solid jacking point (below). Once the car is raised sufficiently, put two jack stands under the frame, axle housing, or suspension A-arms, then lower the car onto the stands. For a light car you will need 1½-ton jack stands; for a heavy car, 2½-ton stands. **Caution:** Never get under a car that is supported only by a jack.

If the wheels need not hang free, you can raise the car by driving it up onto ramps. For safety, buy ramps that will support 2½ to 4 tons. They should have stops at their ends and raised edges so that the car cannot roll off the ramps. Ramps must be at least 8 inches wide to accommodate most tires, and they must raise the car at least 8 inches off the ground to give you enough work space. When using either ramps or jack stands, you will need bricks, metal chocks, or 4 by 4s to chock the wheels that remain on the ground. Have a helper direct you when you drive onto the ramps.

Jacking points

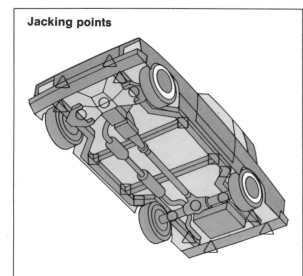

○ You can jack front-engine, rear-drive cars at the rear-axle housing, the lower A-arms of the suspension, any spring attachment points, or the front chassis cross member (if there is one).

△ Cars that come equipped with bumper jacks can also be lifted at the bumpers and the bumper brackets. Do not lift other cars at these points because the bumpers may not be designed to hold the weight of the car.

□ Cars that come with side-lift jacks can be lifted at the special reinforced jacking pads provided for these jacks. On cars with unit-body construction, do not jack at any other points along the body, since only the specified points are properly reinforced to hold the car's weight. Cars with frames can be lifted at almost any point along the frame.

Caution: Always jack up a car on level ground. If the ground is soft, put wood under the jack. Never get under a car that is supported only by a jack; use stands or ramps.

Using a scissors jack and jack stands

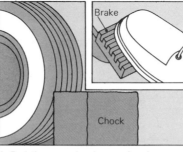

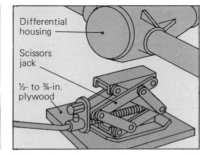

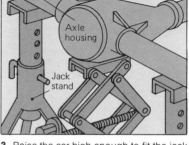

1. Park the car on level ground and engage the parking brake. If you are raising the front wheels of a rear-wheel-drive car or the rear wheels of a front-wheel-drive car, put the transmission in gear (automatics in *Park,* manuals in *Reverse*). Chock the wheels that will stay on the ground with bricks, metal chocks, or 4 by 4s.

2. Place the scissors jack under a central jacking point (here, the differential housing). If the ground is soft, place a piece of plywood under the jack to prevent it from sinking into the ground. Insert the handle, and wind up the jack until it contacts the jacking point. Check that this contact is not wobbly before you raise the car.

3. Raise the car high enough to fit the jack stands under the axle housing (as here) or lower suspension A-arms. If you needed plywood to support the jack, support the stands too. When both stands are in place, slowly lower the car onto them. Do not remove the jack or get under the car until you are sure that the support will hold.

Using drive-on ramps

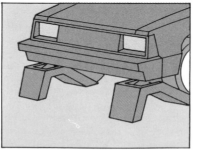

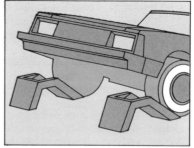

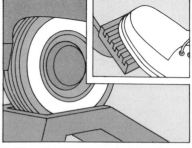

1. Park the car on level ground. Place the ramps so that they are touching the tires and are parallel to each other; be sure that the ramps are on level ground too. If the ground is soft, put sheets of ½- to ¾-in. plywood under the ramps.

2. You must have a helper guide you as you drive onto the ramps so that you will not run off the ends or the edges. Put an automatic transmission in *Low* or a manual in *First.* Slowly, following the signals of your helper, drive up the ramps.

3. When the tires are against the stops at the ends of the ramps, step on the brake pedal and set the parking brake. Put an automatic transmission in *Park* or a manual in *First.* Chock the tires on the ground with bricks, metal chocks, or 4 by 4s.

Lubrication

Wherever moving metal meets metal, lubrication is needed to reduce friction and wear, to prevent the parts from overheating, and to keep them running smoothly. In time, most lubricants break down or get too dirty to work properly and must be replaced. The owner's manual gives the intervals, in months and/or miles, for all oil changes and grease jobs. Complete instructions on how to perform these jobs can be found on pages 191–206.

Only a few tools, none of them expensive, are required for oil changes and chassis lubrication; they are illustrated at the right. Lubricants are not interchangeable, so be sure that you have the right one for the job before you start.

Lubricants

1. Nonstaining, waterproof white grease
2. Household oil
3. Motor oil
4. Chassis grease
5. Graphite
6. Silicone spray
7. Gear oil
8. Automatic transmission fluid
9. Wheel bearing grease
10. Brake fluid
11. Power steering fluid

Lubrication points

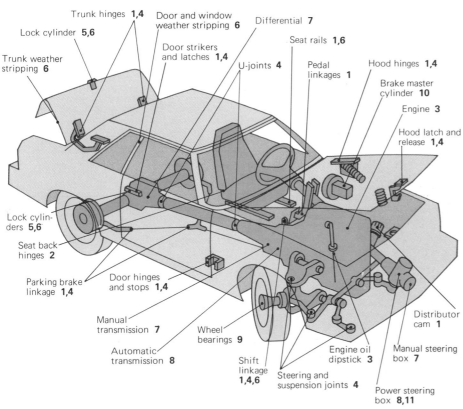

Trunk hinges **1,4**
Door and window weather stripping **6**
Differential **7**
Lock cylinder **5,6**
Seat rails **1,6**
Trunk weather stripping **6**
Door strikers and latches **1,4**
Hood hinges **1,4**
U-joints **4**
Pedal linkages **1**
Brake master cylinder **10**
Engine **3**
Hood latch and release **1,4**
Lock cylinders **5,6**
Seat back hinges **2**
Parking brake linkage **1,4**
Door hinges and stops **1,4**
Manual transmission **7**
Wheel bearings **9**
Automatic transmission **8**
Shift linkage **1,4,6**
Engine oil dipstick **3**
Distributor cam **1**
Manual steering box **7**
Steering and suspension joints **4**
Power steering box **8,11**

Oil-change tools and lubrication tools

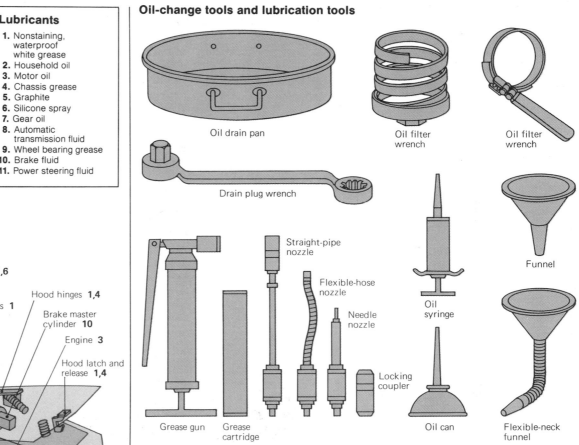

Oil drain pan
Oil filter wrench
Oil filter wrench
Drain plug wrench
Straight-pipe nozzle
Flexible-hose nozzle
Needle nozzle
Oil syringe
Funnel
Grease gun
Grease cartridge
Locking coupler
Oil can
Flexible-neck funnel

To change the oil, you will need a container flat enough to fit under the oil pan and large enough (at least 6-qt capacity) to hold all the oil that drains out. Most oil plugs look like ordinary bolts and can be removed with standard wrenches or sockets. Some axles have rubber plugs that must be pried out. To add oil, you can use a beer can opener plus a funnel, or use an oil spout that punctures the can and directs the flow. A funnel with a flexible neck is good for adding transmission fluid and facilitates access to hard-to-reach oil filler holes. To remove the oil filter, use one of the special oil filter wrenches so as not to crush or puncture the filter.

The basic tool for chassis lubrication is a hand-pumped grease gun. Depending on the type and accessibility of the grease fittings on your car, you will need a variety of nozzles, including a straight pipe (which usually comes with the gun), a flexible hose for getting around obstructions, and a locking grease-fitting coupler. A needle nozzle is needed for the double U-joints used on large GM cars through 1976. Get a gun that holds standard 14½-oz grease cartridges; the cartridges are inexpensive, and the alternative bulk loading of grease is very messy. Use lithium-based *moly* (containing molybdenum disulfide) grease; it lasts longer and lubricates better. To oil some obstructed parts, you will need an oil can with a long nozzle, and in very tight places you might want an oil syringe, available at electronics, crafts, or hobby shops.

Brake tools

The simplest brake job, adjusting the parking brake, can be done with ordinary wrenches and requires no special tools. Bleeding the hydraulic brake system is another simple job easily done at home (see p.217). You can bleed the brakes with a 1-foot length of rubber tubing and an ordinary wrench, but sometimes the bleeder valves are positioned so awkwardly that an offset *brake-bleeder wrench* will make the job easier. Worn master cylinders or wheel cylinders are usually replaced; if you want to rebuild them, you will need a *brake cylinder hone* and an electric drill.

Disc brakes require no adjusting, and most modern drum brakes are self-adjusting. However, for drums that must be adjusted manually, you may need a *brake spoon*. These brake-adjusting tools are made in a variety of shapes to fit through the access holes in the brake backing plates or drums so that adjustments can be made without removing the drums (see p.216). When you do have to remove the drums—for example, to repack the wheel bearings or to replace

the brake shoes—you may find that you need a drum puller in order to exert enough force to get them off. Some auto parts stores or brake jobbers may rent pullers on a daily basis.

You can replace the pads on disc brakes without special tools, although some manufacturers recommend a *sleeve installer* to fit the guide pin sleeves into their holes (see pp.330–333). To replace the brake shoes on most drum brakes, you will need *brake-spring pliers* to remove the return springs and a *retaining-spring tool* to remove and replace springs with retaining-spring caps (see pp.334–337).

Certain major brake work, such as cutting drums that are scored or out-of-round, resurfacing scored disc-brake rotors, and bonding new linings onto brake shoes, requires equipment that no home garage would have. However, if you do need such work done, you can save money by disassembling the brakes yourself, taking the parts to a machine shop, then reinstalling the parts at home.

Exhaust-system tools

Diagnosing and correcting problems in the exhaust system is not difficult, but the work is dirty and uncomfortable. Always wear safety goggles to keep rust out of your eyes and wear heavy gloves to protect your hands from sharp, rusty metal.

Once you have located the defective section of the exhaust system, you must detach it. Penetrating oil may loosen rusted nuts, bolts, and joints enough so that they can be hammered or twisted free, but badly rusted parts or welded joints must be cut. An *exhaust-pipe cutter* fits around the pipe and cuts cleanly in places where movement is restricted. When cutting welded joints, cut next to—not on—the weld. To remove a rusted-on muffler, use a *pipe slitter*, which is basically an offset chisel that allows clearance for your knuckles in tight spots.

Before a new part can be fitted onto an old pipe, you must restore the end of the pipe to a perfectly round, undented contour with a *pipe expander* so that the joint will seal completely.

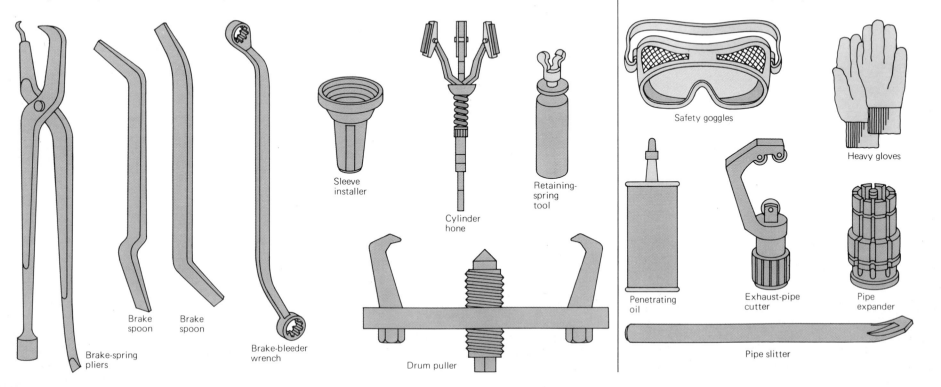

Brake-spring pliers

Brake spoon

Brake spoon

Brake-bleeder wrench

Sleeve installer

Cylinder hone

Retaining-spring tool

Drum puller

Safety goggles

Heavy gloves

Penetrating oil

Exhaust-pipe cutter

Pipe expander

Pipe slitter

Taps and dies

Taps cut internal threads into holes in metal objects. Dies cut external threads onto metal rods. Both taps and dies are available in a range of sizes in three thread standards: National Coarse, National Fine, and Metric. A complete set of taps and dies is very expensive. Begin by purchasing a tap wrench (to turn taps) and a die stock (to turn dies). Buy individual taps and dies only as you need them.

When you are cutting threads to match a specific nut or bolt, use a thread gauge to determine the size and pitch so that you can buy the correct tap or die to cut matching threads. (A thread gauge is a set of templates, one of which matches the profile of virtually any nut or bolt and identifies the standard and size.) When cutting threads, always use a generous amount of cutting fluid to wash away metal chips and to lubricate and cool the area.

Taps come in three basic types, determined by how much of the threaded section is tapered. *Taper taps* are tapered the most—from 6 to 10 threads—for easy starting; they can also be used to finish threading holes that go all the way through the material. *Plug taps,* tapered for three to five threads, are used after taper taps in closed, or *blind,* holes. *Bottoming taps,* with only one tapered thread, are used to finish blind holes that must be threaded to the bottom. To lock a tap into the tap wrench, tighten the chuck as much as possible with your fingers—do not use a wrench.

Dies are made in three configurations. The type you use depends on how precise a fit you need and how tight a spot you must work in. Adjustable dies, the most expensive, have adjusting screws that allow you to cut slightly loose or slightly tight threads to exactly match a certain nut. Solid dies are inexpensive but allow no such adjustment. Six-point and 12-point dies can be turned with wrenches in places with too little clearance for a die stock. All dies have tapered threads at one end for easy starting. To lock a die in the die stock, line up the indentation in the die with the set screw, then tighten the screw.

Using taps

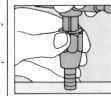
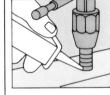

1. Drill a hole with a diameter slightly smaller than that of the tap (taps often have the correct drill size marked on them). Use a square to set the bit perpendicular to the surface before drilling.

2. Secure the taper tap in the tap wrench. Insert the tap in the hole and check that it is perpendicular.

Caution: Only the first thread of the taper tap should fit into the hole; if the hole is too big, the tap might break off in it. Bear down slightly while turning the tap wrench, to start cutting the threads. Once cutting is started, no downward pressure is needed. Reverse the tap a half-turn after every two or three turns to clean out the metal chips, and keep squirting cutting fluid into the hole.

3. If the tap binds, do not force it; broken taps are very difficult to remove. Back the tap out and start again, using plenty of cutting fluid. In a closed hole, repeat this procedure with the plug tap and bottoming tap as necessary.

Using dies

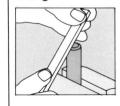
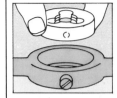

1. Bevel the top of the rod with a file so that the die will go on easily. Secure the rod vertically in a vise, using a square. Lock the die in the die stock, and position it so that it will start to cut with the tapered side of the die facing down.

2. If you are using an adjustable die, start by setting it a little loose, make a trial cut of a few threads, and try the nut. Tighten the adjusting screw a little at a time until the nut fits the threads perfectly. Whatever type of die you use, apply slight downward pressure to start the cutting and use plenty of cutting fluid as you proceed. Keep the die perpendicular to the rod. Reverse the die a half-turn every two or three turns to clean out the metal chips.

3. If the threads must be cut to the end of the rod, first cut all the way down with the tapered side of the die facing down, then reverse the die so that the tapered threads are facing up, and cut full threads to the end.

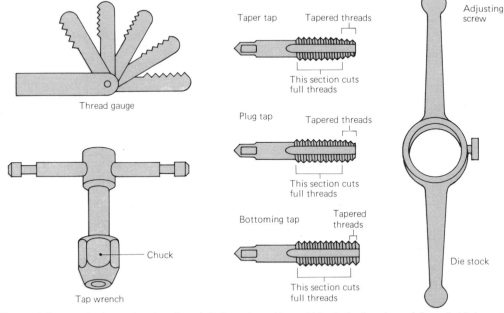

Thread gauge

Tap wrench

Chuck

Taper tap — Tapered threads — This section cuts full threads

Plug tap — Tapered threads — This section cuts full threads

Bottoming tap — Tapered threads — This section cuts full threads

Die stock

Adjusting screw

Adjustable die

Solid die

6-point die

12-point die

Taps and dies can also be used to clean threads that are clogged by corrosion and to repair threads that have been damaged slightly. When you begin to clean or repair existing threads, it is important to start the tool onto the threads carefully, so that it does not begin to cut a set of new threads. Special thread-cleaning taps and dies are sometimes available for this purpose.

Tools / **Setting up shop**

Soldering and solderless connectors

The most permanent way to connect two wires is to solder them together. A 25- or 50-watt, pencil-type soldering iron is most convenient for soldering thin wires in cramped spaces. Use rosin-core solder (hollow wire solder filled with rosin flux) for soldering wires; it requires no additional flux. (Flux prevents oxidation and helps the solder to flow smoothly.) Do not use acid-core solder—the acid will corrode copper wire. The solder itself should be 60 percent tin and 40 percent lead; this type provides the strongest joints and is easiest to work with. Tin the soldering iron as described in Step 2 before soldering the joint. A tinned iron transfers heat better and resists corrosion. Heat-shrink tubing is the best way to insulate a soldered joint. You can also use plastic electrical tape.

Use *solderless connectors* when connecting wires that need to be disconnected occasionally, when connecting a wire to an electrical component, or when you simply do not want to bother with soldering. Solderless connectors are available in a variety of designs for different jobs. Ring and U-shaped connectors are used to attach wires to threaded posts and are themselves held in place by nuts. In-line *butt* connectors are used to splice wires together. Two-piece connectors, both the *bullet* type and the *spade* type, can be disconnected quickly and reconnected after installation. *Wire nuts* are used to hold a number of wires that have been twisted together. *Quick-splice* connectors tap a new wire into a circuit without disconnecting or stripping the wires. Basically, all solderless connectors except the quick-splice type work on the same principle: The connector consists of a metal sleeve in a plastic insulating case. The end of the wire is stripped and inserted into the metal sleeve, then the connector is crimped down firmly to crush the metal sleeve over the wires. This completes the electrical connection and holds the wires in place. Solderless connectors come in various sizes for specific wire gauges. Always use the proper-size connector.

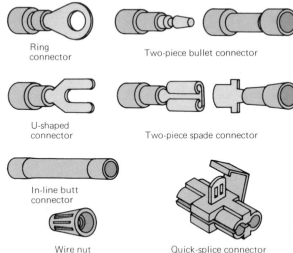

Ring connector

Two-piece bullet connector

U-shaped connector

Two-piece spade connector

In-line butt connector

Wire nut

Quick-splice connector

Soldering wires

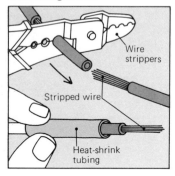

Wire strippers

Stripped wire

Heat-shrink tubing

1. Strip 1 in. of insulation from the end of each wire with wire strippers. Cut a piece of heat-shrink tubing long enough to cover the joint and overlap the insulation by about 1 in. on both sides. Slip the tubing over one wire and push it past the stripped part to keep it out of the way.

Heat-shrink tubing

Twisted wires

Glove

2. Clean the wires and the tip of the soldering iron with sandpaper or steel wool. Twist the wires together; wear gloves, or the oil from your fingers might prevent the solder from adhering. Plug in the soldering iron and let it heat up only enough to melt the solder. To tin the iron, coat its tip with solder, then wipe off the excess with a rag.

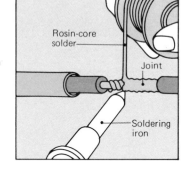

Rosin-core solder

Joint

Soldering iron

3. The correct way to solder a joint is to heat the wires with the soldering iron until they are hot enough to melt the solder. Apply the solder directly to the joint, not to the iron. If you melt the solder with the iron, the solder will not penetrate the splice completely. **Caution:** Always unplug the soldering iron when you are not using it to prevent overheating and burns.

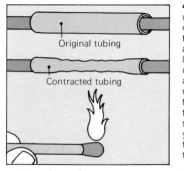

Original tubing

Contracted tubing

4. Allow the solder to cool until it hardens, then center the heat-shrink tubing over the joint. Hold a match or a cigarette lighter under the tubing until it contracts tightly around the wire. If you do not have heat-shrink tubing, wrap the joint tightly with electrical tape, stretching the tape taut as you wind it. Do not stretch tape on the first and last two wraps.

Installing solderless connectors

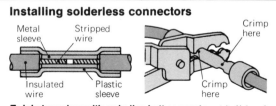

Metal sleeve

Stripped wire

Crimp here

Insulated wire

Plastic sleeve

Crimp here

To join two wires with an in-line butt connector, strip ½ in. of insulation off each wire. Insert the wires into the connector until their insulation butts up against the metal sleeve. No bare wire should extend past the plastic sleeve, or the joint will not be insulated properly. Use pliers to crimp the connector at the two points indicated to crush the metal sleeve over the wires.

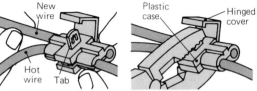

New wire

Plastic case

Hinged cover

Hot wire

Tab

A quick-splice connector can tap a new wire into an existing circuit. Fit existing wire into the open channel, and push the new wire into the unblocked end of the other channel until it touches the stop. Use pliers to push down the metal tab until the top of the tab is flush with the plastic case. The tab cuts through the insulation to contact both wires. Close hinged cover.

How to maintain your car

This chapter is meant to be used with your car's service schedule, which is found in your owner's manual. The service schedule advises you to inspect, adjust, lubricate, or replace certain parts at specified intervals. Maintenance jobs that do-it-yourselfers can perform are shown on the following pages. If parts must be repaired or replaced, refer to Chapter 6. Because certain maintenance jobs are too complex for a beginner, the jobs in this chapter are rated for difficulty, using the system shown below.

🔧	1 wrench means that the job can easily be performed by a NOVICE with no previous car repair experience.
🔧🔧	2 wrenches mean that the job can easily be performed by a BEGINNER with little previous car repair experience.
🔧🔧🔧	3 wrenches mean that the job can be performed by a PRACTICED DO-IT-YOURSELFER with some car repair experience.
🔧🔧🔧🔧	4 wrenches mean that the job should be tackled only by an EXPERIENCED AMATEUR MECHANIC with considerable car repair experience.
🔧🔧🔧🔧🔧	5 wrenches mean that the job should be undertaken only by an ADVANCED AMATEUR MECHANIC with extensive car repair experience.

Contents

An investment in safety and efficiency

Maintenance is defined as keeping something in an existing state of repair or efficiency and preserving it from failure or decline. As applied to automobiles, maintenance refers to the lubrication, adjustment, and parts replacement needed to keep a car running efficiently and to prevent premature wear.

In the 117 pages of this book devoted to *Maintenance,* all the jobs that must be done to maintain your car in an existing state of efficiency and to preserve it from unnecessary deterioration are described in detail. Whether you decide to do all the maintenance jobs your car requires, do some and have some done, or have them all done by professionals, proper maintenance is one of the wisest automotive investments you can make.

This chapter lists all the standard maintenance jobs, then explains exactly how to perform most of them yourself. The wrench symbols (see p.181) tell you at a glance whether a job is easy or difficult. Boxes accompanying most job descriptions contain lists of the parts, tools, supplies, and equipment you will need. If expensive special equipment is required, or the job is simply not worth doing yourself—tire repair, for example—we tell you. However, most maintenance on automobiles is not very complicated.

The engineers who designed your car worked with other engineers, called *service engineers,* who specialize in making it as easy as possible to remove, repair, replace, and maintain a car's components. Although this goal is not always met, most routine maintenance jobs for most car models are fairly simple. After all, the carmaker's employees and his dealers do most of this work while the car is new. Any unnecessary difficulties are a nuisance to the car company. Many of its employees, like you, are not highly trained, experienced, or expert mechanics; they are apprentices. If a maintenance job has been simplified for them, it should be just as easy for you.

Some jobs, like replacing an air filter (p.240), take an experienced mechanic less than five minutes. You can do it just as quickly because you will not have to walk across the shop to the parts department to get the new filter if you keep a spare handy (see *Where to buy auto parts,* p.458).

The time estimates given for most of the jobs in this book were taken from industry *flat-rate manuals* (see p.457). The *low time* is the estimate for a professional mechanic. The *high time* is usually double the low time, our estimate for the time a beginner will need. When the high time is more than twice the low time, it usually reflects a difference in the flat-rate manuals for different makes and models of cars.

If you follow instructions carefully, you may not complete a job as quickly as a professional mechanic, but you will almost certainly do a better job. In the case of the air filter change, most professionals lift out the old filter, drop in a new filter, and put the cover back on the housing. Since you are not trying to beat flat-rate times (p.457), you can take extra time to carefully wipe out the housing with a rag, to make sure that the new filter is properly seated, and to see that the wing nut that secures the cover is properly tightened.

Not only can you often do better work than you can pay for at most shops, you may accomplish the work in less time and at less personal inconvenience. Once you gain a little experience changing the oil in your car (p.196), it will almost certainly take you less time than driving to a service station and waiting around while they do it. Moreover, it can be done at your convenience—after work or on a Sunday, when many stations are closed.

You save money in two ways when you work on your car yourself. You do not have to pay labor charges, which currently average $16 per hour in the U.S. but can go as high as $50 per hour in big-city luxury-car dealerships. Also, you can often get parts and supplies at much lower prices than a garage must charge (see *Where to buy auto parts,* p.458). Oil costs 25 to 50 percent less when bought by the case at discount and auto parts stores than it does when bought by the quart from a service station. Even greater savings are available on popular parts like filters, wiper blade refills, fan belts, and spark plugs.

It is more important that you know what must be done and when than to know how to do it yourself. If proper maintenance is not performed, you can void the warranty on a new car. A poorly maintained car, whether new or old, also burns more fuel; and an inexpensive maintenance job left undone often causes expensive damage that requires major repairs. Neglecting oil changes may save a few dollars initially, but it may lead to expensive engine work and shortened car life later on.

Many maintenance items, such as tires and brakes, affect driving safety. A slightly soft tire can throw your car into a skid when you brake suddenly, turning what should have been a minor emergency into something far more serious. Incorrect air pressure is also the most frequent cause of excessive tire wear and can increase fuel consumption by as much as 2 miles per gallon.

Your owner's manual lists specific time or mileage intervals between major and minor services your car requires. Make sure that all these jobs are done on time. If you do them yourself, you will not void your warranty on a new car (if you can prove that you did the work and that new parts were installed as required). This means that you must keep records and file receipts (which is a good idea for older cars, too).

Many car owners who do their own work record each job in a notebook that they keep in their cars. A garage, if you have one, may be an even more convenient place to keep the notebook because it will not clutter up the car and is less likely to get lost.

Another effective record-keeping system is to keep a note pad and a pen in the garage. Describe each maintenance or repair job on a separate sheet, along with the car's current mileage and the date. The sheets can be stuck on a nail, where they will be handy for reference whenever you are working on the car. Since the sheets are blank, you do not have to conform to other items as you do in a notebook. Because this method is quicker and easier than using a notebook, the record is likelier to be made. Records that are not made because they are too much trouble will be of no help later when you want to know when a tire was replaced, the engine tuned, or when the oil was changed.

You may also find that self-adhesive labels are useful for recording such periodic maintenance jobs as changing the oil or the filters. Labels can be pasted on the inside of the glove compartment door or in the engine compartment. Placing them inside the air cleaner protects them from the weather yet keeps them handy when you are working on the car.

Maintenance and repair jobs overlap when the time comes to replace parts like brake linings, which wear as they work. This chapter covers the jobs that car owners can easily do at home. Troubleshooting charts tell you how to isolate problems. Step-by-step repair procedures tell you what to do about a problem, or, if it is beyond effective home remedy, what to have done about it.

Planning your maintenance schedule

If you operated a fleet of 1,000 cars, your maintenance supervisor would have worked out a schedule for upkeep that would keep costs to a minimum. But if you own one or two cars, probably of different types, your maintenance schedule must be based on faith in what the carmaker tells you each vehicle needs, rather than on personal experience.

Every owner's manual gives you a maintenance schedule. New cars come with a *warranty service booklet* that contains tickets meant to be torn out when certain services have been performed. These services are usually described in detail on the tickets.

What these booklets do not stress is that you can perform the services and sign them off yourself without endangering your new-car warranty, provided that you use reputable parts. Keep receipts and box labels from filters and other parts you replace as proof of service completed. Note all service jobs in your ticket book and in your car maintenance records (opposite page). If a warranty repair comes up, show this material to the car dealer's service manager. If he asks for it, give him only photocopies. You may need the originals if a dispute arises.

Pay special attention to the fine print in owner's manuals, which often defines "normal driving" as highly abnormal, long-distance, high-speed driving, and defines the typical shopping and commuting of most car owners as "severe service." The manuals may require that common maintenance jobs, such as oil and filter changes, be done twice as often under these "severe" conditions.

Making your own periodic maintenance checks is a practical way to get to know the mechanics of your car over a reasonable period of time. This work also prepares you for the more involved semiannual or annual maintenance checks and helps you to progress gradually to doing your own repair work.

Some good habits will make all maintenance jobs easier. Stock the supplies you know you will need. Items like filters and oil do not deteriorate in storage. They can often be picked up at bargain prices when an auto supply store (p.458) runs a special sale. However, never store gasoline in your home.

Start work early in the day. Then, if the job takes longer than you expect (it almost always does, at least the first time), you will have time to get it done. Also, if you find that you need a part or a tool, the store that sells it will still be open.

A typical maintenance schedule

Interval	Service or check
Every week (daily if traveling)	From the driver's seat: check fuel level (on the gauge), brakes (pp.210, 342), warning lights and instuments. Outside the car: check lights and signals (p.360), tires (visual check for obvious softness, see p.184), look for puddles under the car caused by fluid leaks (p.183); clean the lights and glass. Under the hood: check oil level (p.196), coolant (p.187), brake fluid (p.187)
Every month (or every 1,000 miles, 1,600 km)†	Check tire pressure with an accurate gauge (remember to check spare; see p.184). Check battery water (p.277), power steering fluid (p.195), and drive belts (p.286). Top up windshield washer fluid (p.296). Touch up chipped paint (p.314), fluid level in automatic transmission and differential (pp.200, 202)*
Every 3 months (or every 3,000 miles, 4,800 km)†	Change engine oil (p.196).* Check tire tread depth (p.184), vacuum hoses (p.187), and condition of drive belt (p.286). Check exhaust system for leaks (p.434)
Every 6 months (or every 6,000 miles, 9,600 km)†	Change engine oil and filter (pp.196, 198).* Check fuel filter (p.261),* coolant protection (p.281), oil level in manual transmission (p.200),* and free play in clutch pedal (p.207).* Lubricate chassis fittings (p.191),* door locks, and hinges (p.291).* Check headlight aim (p.221). Have wheel alignment checked if tire wear indicates need (p.221). Rotate tires (p.185) *
Every 12 months (or every 12,000 miles, 19,200 km)†	Inspect brakes (p.210) and adjust parking brake (p.218).* Repack wheel bearings (p.219).* Check oil level of steering gearbox (p.194). Check front-drive axle boots (p.187) and air filter (p.240).* Replace antifreeze and spark plugs (if you use leaded fuel, see p.231).* Tune engine with conventional ignition (p.222). Check emission controls (p.254),* air conditioner (p.288), carburetor (p.251)* or fuel injection (p.406),* and distributor cap and rotor (p.408).* Thoroughly wash underbody to remove winter salt (do this each spring). Check for paint failure and body rust
Every 2 years (or every 24,000 miles, 38,400 km)†	Replace spark plugs (if you use unleaded fuel, see p.231).* Replace PCV valve (p.246),* coolant hoses (p.285),* antifreeze (p.284), automatic transmission filter and fluid (p.202),* oil in manual transmission (p.200)* and differential (p.201),* and brake fluid (p.217)*
Every 3 years (or every 36,000 miles, 57,600 km)†	Replace spark plug cables (p.231)* if necessary. Check owner's manual for other specific long-term service requirements for your car, such as inspecting timing belt on overhead cam engines

†Whichever comes first   *Check your owner's manual. Intervals and services vary from car to car

Regular maintenance

procedures, the key to long car life, are covered in your owner's manual and in the table at the left. At first, especially with a new car, you may want a dealer to perform semiannual or major services. But the only way to get weekly, visual inspections done at all is to do them yourself. These are similar to the pre-flight checks that every pilot is required to make before flying his plane, and they take only a few minutes. Record all monthly and more advanced inspections in detail in your service diary or other records.

A pre-vacation check gives you confidence in the condition of your car before you take it on an extended trip. Unless major work or replacements (such as new tires) are needed, you can perform all these checks yourself. Simply make the checks from the *Every week* through *Every 12 months* sections in the schedule at the left. Then consult your owner's manual to make sure that you have included any special checks your car model may require.

Emergency travel kit

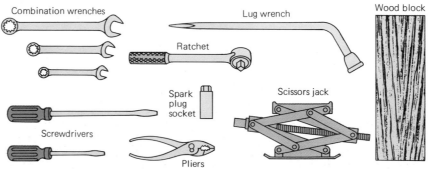

Combination wrenches

Lug wrench

Wood block

Ratchet

Spark plug socket

Scissors jack

Screwdrivers

Pliers

Travel tip: Make up an emergency parts and tools kit to carry in your car. Most of the parts will not cost anything if you save the used parts from maintenance jobs as you perform them. Although used, many parts, such as drive belts or spark plugs, may be good enough to use as spares.

Periodic checks ⏱ 5–10 min

Once a month, check the air pressure in all tires, including the spare. An underinflated tire wears out faster than a properly inflated tire. Moreover, it can affect steering, decrease the load that the tire can safely carry, and increase fuel consumption. The recommended tire pressures for your car are printed in the owner's manual and on a sticker inside the glove compartment or on the driver's door. You can exceed these pressures by about 3 psi as long as the total is still under the maximum pressure given on the sidewall of the tire. The extra pressure will give

you better gas mileage. Check the pressure with an accurate pocket tire gauge when the tires are cold. Gauges on gas station air pumps are often inaccurate. Pressure increases as the tires grow hot from driving; if you adjust the pressure when the tires are hot, they will be incorrectly inflated when they are cold. If the tires need air when cold, and you have to drive to a gas station to fill them, take another reading when you get to the station and add the pressure you know you need to the new reading.

Periodically check the tread depth on the tires.

Also check for unusual tread wear patterns, which could indicate suspension problems (see p.121). If you measure the tread depth across the width of the tire in several places, you can spot uneven wear before the tread is completely worn away. While inspecting the tires, pry out any pebbles or pieces of glass with a screwdriver. If there is a nail in the tire, do not pull it out. Mark the spot, remove the tire, and have it fixed. If the tire has a slow leak and you cannot find any cuts or foreign objects in the tire, suspect a leaking tire valve core or a damaged tire bead.

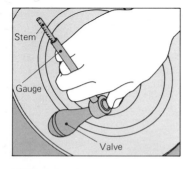

Air pressure in all five tires should be checked at least once a month. As you press this type of gauge down squarely onto the tire valve, the stem of the gauge pops out to indicate how much pressure is in the tire. If there is too much pressure, bleed some air by pushing down on the valve stem.

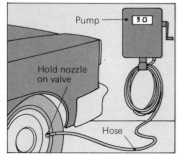

Gas station air pumps are usually set to the desired pressure by turning the handle at the side of the pump. Push the air hose nozzle firmly onto the tire valve; when pump stops ringing; the pressure in the tire equals the setting on the pump. Check the pressure with a pocket tire gauge.

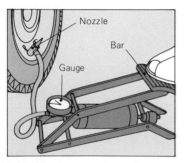
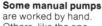

Some manual pumps are worked by hand. Others, like the one shown, are worked by foot. Fasten the air hose nozzle onto the tire valve, and pump air into the tire by pushing down on the bar. Gauge tells you how much air is being pumped into the tire. Check pressure with a pocket gauge.

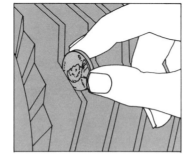

A tread depth of ¹⁄₁₆ in. or less is unsafe, and illegal in most areas. Measure tread depth with a penny, as shown. If the top of Lincoln's head shows, replace the tire. If the tire wear bars show (p.121), replace the tire.

A slow leak in a tire is often caused by a loose or faulty valve core (p.115). To test the core, wet its top with a soapy solution. If bubbles appear, the core is loose or faulty and should be tightened or replaced; use a tire core removal tool.

Tire core removal tool is built into the top of a special tire valve cap. Tool works like a screwdriver either to tighten the core in the stem or to unscrew the core. The tire will go flat when the core is unscrewed, so have a new core and a tire pump at hand before you remove the core.

Tire rotation

To promote even tread wear, rotate tires every 6,000 mi. Rotation patterns differ between bias-ply and radial tires. Tire pressures should be checked after rotation. Rotation may mask the tread wear patterns that identify mechanical defects, so it is not recommended by some manufacturers.

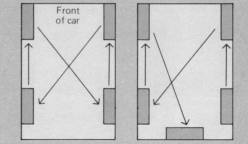

Bias-ply and belted-bias tires can be cross-switched as shown in the illustration above. Include the spare tire in the rotation pattern, if it is usable.

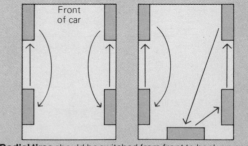

Radial tires should be switched from front to back on each side of the car. If using the spare, include it in the rotation pattern of the tires on only one side of the car.

Types of jacks

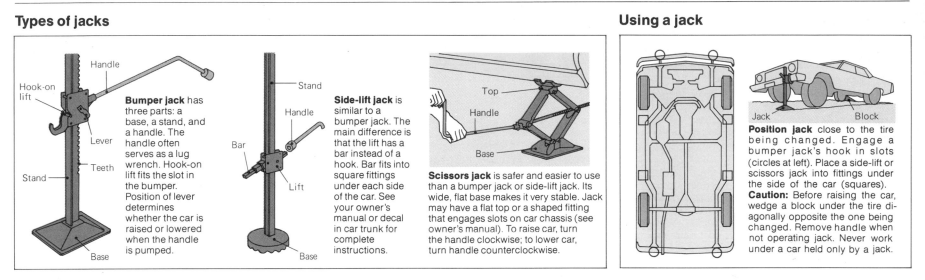

Bumper jack has three parts: a base, a stand, and a handle. The handle often serves as a lug wrench. Hook-on lift fits the slot in the bumper. Position of lever determines whether the car is raised or lowered when the handle is pumped.

Labels: Handle, Hook-on lift, Lever, Teeth, Stand, Base

Side-lift jack is similar to a bumper jack. The main difference is that the lift has a bar instead of a hook. Bar fits into square fittings under each side of the car. See your owner's manual or decal in car trunk for complete instructions.

Labels: Stand, Handle, Bar, Lift, Base

Scissors jack is safer and easier to use than a bumper jack or side-lift jack. Its wide, flat base makes it very stable. Jack may have a flat top or a shaped fitting that engages slots on car chassis (see owner's manual). To raise car, turn the handle clockwise; to lower car, turn handle counterclockwise.

Labels: Top, Handle, Base

Using a jack

Position jack close to the tire being changed. Engage a bumper jack's hook in slots (circles at left). Place a side-lift or scissors jack into fittings under the side of the car (squares). **Caution:** Before raising the car, wedge a block under the tire diagonally opposite the one being changed. Remove handle when not operating jack. Never work under a car held only by a jack.

Labels: Jack, Block

Changing a tire 🕐 10–20 min

Tools: Jack; wheel chock, brick, or block of 4- by 4-in. lumber; jack handle or screwdriver; lug wrench; rubber mallet; tire-pressure gauge.
Material: Penetrating oil.
1. Park well off the road on as level and firm a surface as possible; give yourself enough room to work in safety. Turn off the engine. If car has an automatic transmission, put it into *Park;* put a manual transmission into *Reverse.* Set the parking brake. Get everyone out of the car.
2. Check the pressure in the spare tire; if it is adequate, remove the spare, jack, and tools from the trunk. If spare is flat, have the car towed and have both tires fixed.

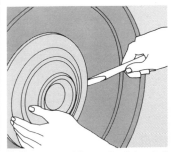

3. Use a screwdriver or the flat end of the jack handle to pry off hubcap.

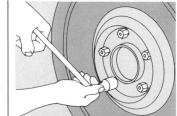

4. Using a lug wrench, loosen the nuts on the wheel. Get a good grip on the wrench and push down on it—never pull up. If the nuts are tight,

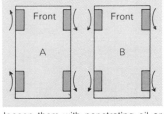

loosen them with penetrating oil or push on the wrench with your foot. Most nuts have right-hand threads and are loosened by turning them counterclockwise (Fig.A, above). Some nuts have left-hand threads and are loosened by turning them

clockwise. If the stud is marked with an L, the nut has left-hand threads. Many Chrysler cars up to the late 1960s have nuts with both left- and right-hand threads. All the nuts on these cars are loosened by turning the wrench toward the back of the car (Fig.B); they are tightened by turning the wrench toward the front of the car (see your owner's manual).
5. Assemble the jack, following the instructions on the decal in the trunk or in your owner's manual.

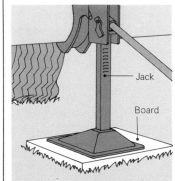

6. Chock the tire diagonally opposite the one being changed so that the car cannot roll off the jack. Then

Labels: Jack, Board

position the jack correctly (see top of page). If the ground is soft, put a wide board or a scrap of plywood under the jack so that it will not sink into the ground.
7. Raise car until tire is just clear of the ground. Remove jack handle.
8. Use wrench to remove lug nuts; put them in hubcap so that they will not be lost. Pull off wheel and tire.
9. Roll the spare into position. Jack up the car a bit more, if necessary, to fit spare. Remove the jack handle. Align the holes in the wheel with the studs and put on the spare.

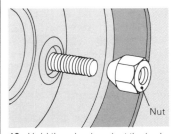

Label: Nut

10. Hold the wheel against the brake with one hand. Using your other hand, screw on each lug nut with its tapered end toward the wheel.
11. Using a wrench, tighten all the nuts in the sequences shown for four- or five-nut wheels. Tightening

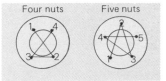

Labels: Four nuts, Five nuts

the nuts in the proper sequence ensures that stress is distributed evenly over the wheel; uneven stress could crack the wheel.

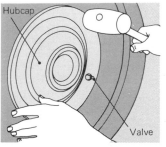

Labels: Hubcap, Valve

12. Lower the car. Remove the jack and block. Tighten all nuts again in the proper sequence. Put the tire valve through the hole in the hubcap, then hammer the hubcap tightly onto the wheel with a rubber mallet or the heel of your hand. Secure all tools in the car. Have the flat tire fixed.

Wheel balancing

In order to compensate for irregularities in their construction, wheels and tires must be *balanced* (see p.120) by a car dealer, front-end shop, tire store, or service station. Unbalanced wheels and tires can cause the steering wheel to shimmy, tires to wear unevenly (see p.121), and in extreme cases will damage the wheel bearings.

A minor imbalance in the rear wheels is not a serious matter, especially on non-independent rear suspensions, so it is not absolutely necessary to balance all four wheels unless you plan to rotate the tires. However, it is a good practice to balance all the wheels. The spare should always be balanced.

The wheels must be balanced every time a tire is removed and reinstalled to repair a flat or to mount snow tires. If you will keep your car for several years, it pays to buy extra wheels for the snow tires from a tire store or wrecking yard. You can then install and remove your own snow tires without paying a mounting and balancing fee each spring and fall.

Severe skids or abnormally high cornering speeds can cause unusual tire-wear patterns that will throw a tire out of balance. Wheels should be *dynamically balanced* on a machine that spins the wheel at high speeds. It may be difficult to balance some wheel and tire combinations. In such cases, you should seek out an experienced shop with special equipment. The better balancing machines allow a wheel to be spun at high speeds and balanced while it is still on the car. The wheel must be removed from the car for balancing on most machines. Special self-adhesive balancing weights should be used on aluminum, or "mag," wheels. Conventional clip-on weights can damage alloy wheels and do not fit onto some types.

Have a problem wheel checked with and without the tire. If the wheel is badly out of balance or bent, it must be replaced. If the tire is badly out-of-round, it may be corrected by shaving the tread slightly. If the tire has a built-in side-to-side wobble, it is defective and must be replaced. Some experts feel that no wheel and tire combination should need more than 4 ounces of weights to balance it.

If a wheel still shimmies after off-car balancing, find a shop that can balance it on the car. This procedure can reveal faulty hubs, brake rotors, brake drums, or wheel bearings. Brake drums and rotors are balanced at the factory, but their balance weights sometimes fall off.

Wide tires

A car's handling can be improved if it is fitted with wider-than-normal tires, which often require wider wheels as well, but the tires must not be so wide that they rub against the car's body, frame, or suspension. Many cars will accommodate tires up to 1 inch (25 mm) wider than the largest size offered by the carmaker. The replacement tires should have the same circumference as the original tires; otherwise, they will throw off the speedometer readings. A radical change in aspect ratio (p.115)—from a 78-series tire to a 50 series, for example—may lower the car enough to affect its ground clearance. Tire dealers have manuals that list tire dimensions. Consult these manuals if you are considering different-size tires. Ask if you can return the tires for a full refund (minus mounting and balancing fees) if the tires rub on your car during a brief road test. If not, shop elsewhere.

Take the car for a short test drive. Make several sharp right and left turns. Drive over sharp dips or humps fast enough to bottom the suspension. You should not hear the tires scraping. Check the tire sidewalls for signs of scuffing or rubbing. If the tires rub, exchange them for a smaller size.

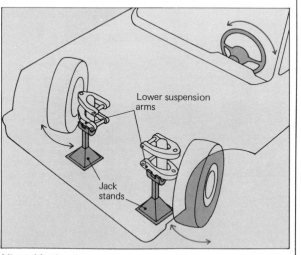

After wide tires are mounted, raise the front of the car (p.176) and support the outer ends of the suspension arms on jack stands. This will compress the springs as much as possible while the car is stationary. Turn the steering wheel as far as it will go in both directions, and make sure that the tires clear the body and chassis by at least ½ in. (12.7 mm). Try to visualize the clearance with the springs fully compressed; it should still be ½ in. (12.7 mm).

Wheel wobble

A wheel that is bent or out-of-round cannot be properly aligned or balanced, and its bearings will be damaged. You can sometimes spot a wheel that is out of shape when you drive behind or alongside a car. Check for a damaged hub or spindle or a loose wheel bearing before you replace a wobbling wheel.

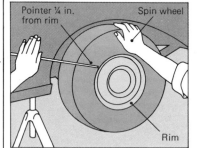

Raise car (p.176). Make sure lug nuts are tight. Hold pointer against fender so that its tip is ¼ in. from wheel rim. Spin wheel. A misshapen wheel will wobble noticeably. If the wheel wobbles, remove it to check for debris on its mounting surfaces. If there is no debris, replace the wheel.

Aftermarket wheels

Aftermarket wheels are popular accessories, but care must be taken to ensure that the replacement wheels have the same *offset* as the original wheels. Offset is the distance between the centerline of the wheel rim and the mounting surface of the wheel. Even wider-than-stock wheels must maintain the original offset, or serious handling and steering problems may result. In addition, excess offset will overload and damage the wheel bearings.

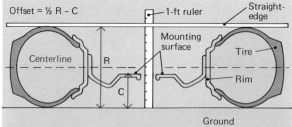

To measure offset, place wheel (with or without tire) on a flat surface with the outside of the wheel facing down. Place a straightedge across the wheel or tire, and measure the distance from the straight edge to the ground (R). Place the ruler through the center hole of the wheel and measure the distance from the wheel's mounting surface to the ground (C). Offset is ½ R − C. If the offset of the replacement wheel does not match the offset of the original wheel, shop around for another wheel that does.

How to identify leaks ⏱ 5–15 min

There are a dozen liquids that can leak out of your car. Only one type of leak is desirable and one other is of minor importance. Leakage of other fluids, if not corrected, can lead to an expensive breakdown.

Some leaks affect driving safety. Gases leaking from the exhaust pipe can let deadly carbon monoxide (CO) enter the passenger compartment. Air leaking out of a tire can create serious handling problems. Of the fluid leaks, brake fluid can be the most serious, and windshield washer solution the least.

A puddle of clear water under your car on a warm day is probably condensation from the air conditioner—the only desirable leak that cars produce. If no condensation is formed, the air conditioner is not dehumidifying the air inside the car.

Not all fluid leaks show up as puddles, but if you notice a stain on the garage floor or in a frequently used parking place, find out what it consists of. It is easier to identify a leaking fluid if you place a small container under the car in the spot where the leak occurs and catch some of the fluid. If the leak is very small, place a piece of white paper under it in order to identify its color. One step in your weekly visual inspection (p.183) should be to look under the car for obvious leaks. Of course, if any fluid level is low, check the appropriate system.

Leaks big enough to make puddles are usually easy to find. Small seepages may lead to expensive safety and mechanical problems too. Although small leaks are harder to find, they may be much easier to repair. If you are lucky, simply tightening a clamp or a few loose bolts may effect a permanent repair.

Fluid leaks do not always show up in obvious places. Sometimes oil or brake fluid can run along the outside of a pipe or body flange to drip at a point several feet away from the source. Some leaks are even less obvious. For example, a leaky master cylinder can let brake fluid enter the vacuum power booster, where it can be sucked into the intake manifold and burned in the engine. The fluid level drops but there are no visible leaks. You can spot this leak by checking inside the power booster's vacuum hose for traces of wetness (p.211, Step 2).

The illustrations at the right and on page 188 show you where to look for leaks on front-engine/rear-drive, front-engine/front-drive, and rear-engine/rear-drive cars. The chart on page 188 tells you how to identify the fluids you may find.

Front-engine/rear-drive cars

Bottom view

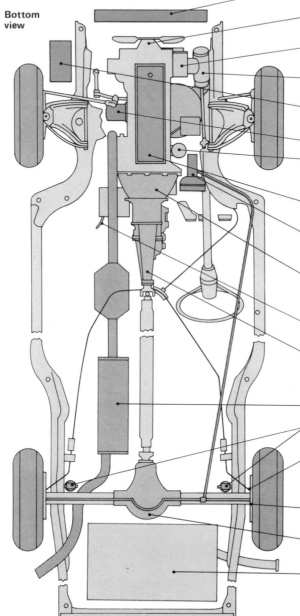

How to find the source of a leak

Radiator: Check seams on bottom or side tanks, drain plug (p.281), and lower hose (p.285). Leak is *antifreeze.*

Water pump: Check vent hole and gasket joint (p.281). Leak is *antifreeze.*

Power steering: Check pump (pp.195,447) and hoses (p.446). Leak is *power steering fluid* or *ATF.*

Steering gear: Check seals at Pitman arm (p.194) or steering rack boots (p.190). Leak is *gear oil.*

Battery: Look for cracked case and loose or missing caps (p.277). Leak is *battery acid.*

Oil filter: Check filter (p.198) and adapter. Leak is *engine oil.*

Fuel pump and lines: Check fittings, hose connections (p.397), filter (p.261), carburetor (p.402). Leak is *gasoline. Engine oil* can leak from pump gasket (p.398).

Oil pan: Check drain plug (p.196), pan gasket (p.245), timing chain cover, and front crankshaft oil seal. Leak is *engine oil.*

Brake master cylinder: Look for wetness around fittings, pushrod, and power brake vacuum hose (p.341). Leak is *brake fluid.*

Bell housing: Check for engine oil at bottom inspection cover (p.202). Check for ATF or gear oil from front seal. Leak may be *engine oil, ATF,* or *gear oil.*

Air conditioner: Clear water under front of passenger compartment is normal if A/C has been in use. Leak is *water.*

Transmission: Check drain plug, if any (p.200), gaskets of cover plate or side plate (tighten bolts evenly), and rear seal. On automatics, check bolts and gasket on oil pan (p.202), and rear oil seal. Leak may be *gear oil* or *ATF.*

Exhaust system: Check for leaks (p.434) of *exhaust gas.*

Shock absorbers: Check for stains or wetness (p.189) and replace leaking front or rear shocks. Leak is *shock absorber oil.*

Brakes: Look for fluid stains on drum backing plates (p.210), disc calipers (p.211), hoses and fittings (p.211). Make sure leak is brake fluid and not grease from wheel bearings (p.213) or front-drive axle boots. Leak is *brake fluid.*

Rear wheel seals: Check drum-brake backing plates, axle ends of differential housing. Leak is *gear oil.*

Differential housing: Check drain plug (if any) and filler plug (p.201), cover-plate gasket (p.425). Leak is *gear oil.*

Fuel tank: Check seams, drain plug, pipe fittings, and any dents. Tighten fittings, replace gasket around sending unit of fuel gauge. Leaks may be *gasoline* or *diesel fuel.*

How to find the source of a leak *(continued)*

Front-engine/front-drive cars

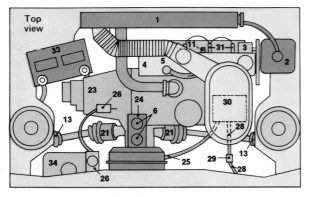

Top view

Front-engine/front-drive cars

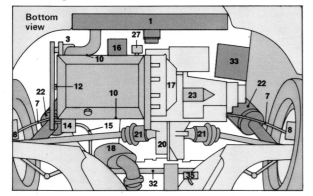

Bottom view

Rear-engine/rear-drive cars

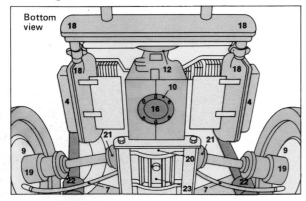

Bottom view

Leaks from cars with designs different from the standard front-engine/rear-drive layout (p.187) come from the same mechanical elements, but these may be arranged differently in the vehicle. Minor seepages, usually repairable by tightening or replacing a clamp or hose, can best be spotted and cured from the engine compartment. Follow each hose and look for signs of wetness where it is attached. Common sources of leaks are keyed to the numbers below.

1. **Radiator and hoses** (p.281): *Antifreeze.*
2. **Coolant reservoir** (p.281): *Antifreeze.*
3. **Water pump** (p.281): *Antifreeze.*
4. **Valve cover** (p.265): *Engine oil.*
5. **PCV valve** (p.246): *Engine oil.*
6. **Brake master cylinder reservoir** (p.210): *Brake fluid.*
7. **Brake hoses** (p.211): *Brake fluid.*
8. **Disc-brake calipers** (p.211): *Brake fluid.*
9. **Drum-brake cylinders** (p.210): *Brake fluid.*
10. **Oil-pan gasket** (p.196): *Engine oil.*
11. **Engine block drain cock or plug** (p.281): *Antifreeze.*
12. **Crankshaft front seal or timing chain cover:** *Engine oil.*
13. **Axle boots** on front-drive outer joints: *Black grease.*
14. **Power steering pump** (p.195): *ATF or power steering fluid.*
15. **Power steering hoses** (p.446): *Power steering fluid or ATF.*
16. **Oil filter** (p.198): *Engine oil.*
17. **Flywheel housing** bottom inspection cover: *Engine oil, ATF, or gear oil.*
18. **Exhaust system** (p.434): *Exhaust gas.*
19. **Rear wheel seals**: *Gear oil or grease.*
20. **Differential housing** (p.201): *Gear oil.*
21. **Inner drive axle boots:** *Gear oil or ATF.*
22. **Shock absorbers** (p.189): *Shock absorber fluid.*
23. **Transmission** (pp.200,202): *ATF or gear oil.*
24. **Brake master cylinder** (p.341): *Brake fluid.*
25. **Brake booster inlet valve** (p.342): *Brake fluid.*
26. **Hydraulic clutch** (p.209): *Brake fluid.*
27. **Fuel pump** (p.397): *Diesel fuel or gasoline.*
28. **Fuel lines and fittings** (p.397): *Diesel fuel or gasoline.*
29. **Fuel filter** (p.261): *Diesel fuel or gasoline.*
30. **Carburetor** (p.402): *Gasoline.*
31. **Fuel injection** (p.406): *Diesel fuel or gasoline.*
32. **Steering gear** (p.190): *Gear oil.*
33. **Battery** (p.277): *Battery acid.*
34. **Windshield washer** (p.302): *Washer solvent.*
35. **Air conditioner** condensation: *Water.*

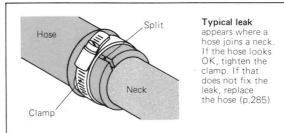

Hose Split

Neck

Clamp

Typical leak appears where a hose joins a neck. If the hose looks OK, tighten the clamp. If that does not fix the leak, replace the hose (p.285)

What can leak out of your car

Liquids

Antifreeze: Clear or tinted (usually green or yellow) liquid slightly thicker than water, with faint, sweet odor. Confirm identification by checking coolant reservoir or top of cold radiator (p.280). *Poisonous.*

ATF (automatic transmission fluid): Light oil, usually red, with a distinctive odor. Confirm identification by matching to fluid on transmission dipstick (p.202). *Poisonous, somewhat flammable.*

Battery acid: Sulfuric acid and water solution with a distinctive odor. If acid touches clothes or your skin, wash immediately and flush with water to prevent burns. *Corrosive, poisonous.*

Brake fluid: Clear, slightly oily liquid, usually with a distinctive odor. Confirm identification by looking into master cylinder reservoir and sniffing. *Somewhat flammable, poisonous, dissolves paint.*

Diesel fuel: Light oil, like home heating oil, that should be dyed red, has distinctive odor. Confirm identification by sniffing fuel filler neck on diesel cars. *Poisonous, flammable.*

Gasoline: Thin, volatile liquid with distinctive odor. Sniff fuel filler neck to confirm identification. *Poisonous, highly flammable, explosive vapors.*

Gear oil: Heavy oil, light tan when new, may turn dark or black with use. Lubricates manual transmissions, axles, differentials, and steering gearboxes. *Poisonous, somewhat flammable.*

Heavy grease: May be black with dirt or additives like lithium or graphite. *Poisonous, somewhat flammable.*

Power steering fluid: Light oil with distinctive odor. Sometimes ATF (automatic transmission fluid) is used, which is usually dyed red. Sniff power steering pump reservoir and check fluid color for identification. *Somewhat flammable, poisonous.*

Shock absorber fluid: Light oil that usually appears as a dark stain in dirt on lower section of tubular shock absorbers. *Poisonous, somewhat flammable.*

Water: Air conditioner condensation is clear, mineral-free water. *Non-poisonous, non-flammable.*

Windshield washer solvent: Water solution containing detergent, as well as wood alcohol to prevent it from freezing. May be tinted various colors. Slightly slippery. *Non-flammable, poisonous.*

Gases

Air: Tires (and windshield washer bottles on older VWs) contain air under pressure up to 65 psi. Slow leaks may hiss audibly. *Harmless* when pressure is released slowly.

Exhaust gas: Hot, pressurized gas with distinctive odor. Makes muttering or louder noises when it leaks out of holes in the exhaust system. Avoid breathing fumes. *Contains odorless, poisonous carbon monoxide (CO).*

Vacuum: Air can leak into the vacuum hoses that operate emission-control equipment, power brake boosters, and valves in the heater system. Leaks make a hissing noise. *Not dangerous.*

Testing springs and shock absorbers ⏱ 15–45 min

It is a simple matter to check the springs in your car. When all four tires are properly inflated and there is one person in the driver's seat, the car should sit level on flat ground. None of the corners should sag, and the front of the car should not be higher or lower than the rear unless the car's suspension has been intentionally modified. If you notice sagging or suspect a spring problem, have a dealer or a shop that specializes in suspension work check the car and perform any necessary service. Spring work requires special tools and equipment that are not found in the typical garage.

If your car handles badly when driven, skitters across rough roads, wallows up and down for a long while after a bump, or if the front end dives sharply in quick stops, the shock absorbers are probably worn. Few original-equipment shocks last more than 25,000 miles. It is often a good investment to buy shocks on sale and save them until they are needed. You can compare their strength with that of your old shocks when deciding whether to replace the shocks. For balanced handling, shocks should always be replaced in pairs (both front shocks or both rears) even if only one is damaged. Buy shocks designed for your car.

Good shocks or bad? Road test your car's suspension

Worn shocks

New shocks

Worn-out shock absorbers cause suspension to bottom out with a loud thunk at rail crossings, bumps, or dips in the road.

With new shocks, ride is firm. Car levels off quickly after passing over railroad tracks or other rough spots on highway.

Checking for worn shocks

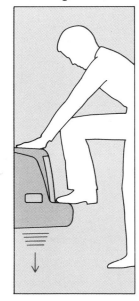

Test your shocks every 5,000 mi by jumping up and down on bumpers at all four corners of vehicle. Car should not bounce freely after you release bumper. Continued rocking indicates poor shocks. This test may not fully determine shock wear, since it simulates slower-than-normal driving speed. Follow up with road test over rough roads.

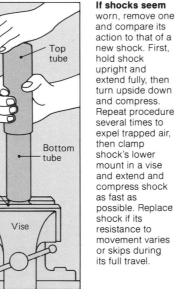

Top tube

Clamp to mount only

Bottom tube

Vise

If shocks seem worn, remove one and compare its action to that of a new shock. First, hold shock upright and extend fully, then turn upside down and compress. Repeat procedure several times to expel trapped air, then clamp shock's lower mount in a vise and extend and compress shock as fast as possible. Replace shock if its resistance to movement varies or skips during its full travel.

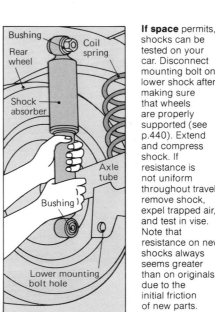

Bushing

Rear wheel

Coil spring

Shock absorber

Axle tube

Bushing

Lower mounting bolt hole

If space permits, shocks can be tested on your car. Disconnect mounting bolt on lower shock after making sure that wheels are properly supported (see p.440). Extend and compress shock. If resistance is not uniform throughout travel, remove shock, expel trapped air, and test in vise. Note that resistance on new shocks always seems greater than on originals due to the initial friction of new parts.

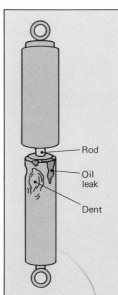

Rod

Oil leak

Dent

Whenever you are under the car to do a grease job or other routine maintenance, inspect the shock absorbers visually. If there is oil leaking from the shock, if the bottom tube has been badly dented by a stone, or if the piston rod is scratched, pitted, or scored, the shock cannot perform properly. Replace damaged shock absorbers (see pp.440–445).

Maintenance / Suspension and steering

Checking the suspension and steering ⚑ 20–40 min

Suspension and steering problems can be difficult to pinpoint. They are often the result of accumulated wear in all of the front-end parts. Making regular checks of the suspension and the steering assemblies enables you to monitor wear as it occurs and greatly simplifies the job of isolating specific problems that may develop later and require repair. To make a complete check of the front end, perform not only the checks shown on this page but also inspect the ball joints (see p.193), wheel bearings (p.213), and the shock absorbers or MacPherson struts (p.189 and p.442). Servicing suspension and steering compo-nents should usually be left to a reputable garage and skilled mechanics. Special tools and precise work-manship are often required. After any service or repair that requires disassembly of front-end parts, the front wheels should be realigned. Regular lubri-cation can extend the life of suspension parts.

Common suspension and steering systems

Double-wishbone suspension

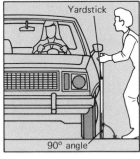

Front — Coil spring — Anti-sway bar — Steering gearbox — Idler arm — Pitman arm — Ball joints — Track rod — Tie rod — Steering knuckle — Control arms (wishbones) — Steering column — Frame

MacPherson strut suspension

Front — Steering knuckle — Anti-sway bar — MacPherson strut — Rubber boot — Rack and pinion steering gear — Tie rod — Ball joint — Steering column — Lower control arm — Frame

Suspension checks

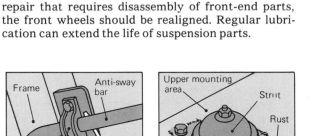

Yardstick — 90° angle

Height of car should be the same at all four corners when driver's seat is occupied. A high or low corner indicates a faulty spring or shock ab-sorber, or a bent frame. First be sure that tires are correct size and properly inflated, and that car is on level ground.

Mounting bolts — Upper arm — Pry bar — Lower arm

Inspect all fasteners for tight-ness. Re-torque loose bolts to carmaker's specifications. Check mounting points on suspension control arms by using a pry bar or tire iron to apply leverage between arms and frame. Movement of con-trol arms should be negligible.

Frame — Anti-sway bar — Bushing

Check condition of rubber bushings, pivot points, grease seals, and bump stops for signs of wear or damage. Poke hard rubber fittings with a screwdriver. Rubber in good condition feels firm. Replace rubber parts that feel spongy or are badly cracked.

Upper mounting area — Strut — Rust — Mounting bolts

Inspect surfaces for deep rust, especially the attachment points on body or chassis. On MacPherson struts, thoroughly check upper mounting areas, usually accessible from above. Have weakened areas rein-forced with welded steel plates if necessary.

Steering checks

Free play

Excess free play in steering wheel indicates wear. To check, measure distance steering wheel rotates in either direction before road wheels begin to move. Worm and roller steering should have no more than 3 in. of play; rack and pinion should have a negligible amount.

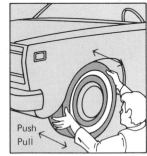

Push Pull

Raise car and have a helper apply brakes. Wiggle each front wheel along its horizontal axis. More than ¼ in. of play indicates wear in ball joint, link-age, or bearing. Watch as helper turns steering wheel. Motion should be smooth, with no clicks or scraping noises.

Seal — Idler arm bracket — Tie rod end — Frame — Bushing — Idler arm

Check each linkage part and shake to check for looseness. Inspect idler arm and Pitman arm for worn bushings, which can cause car to wander on the road, excess play in steering wheel, and wheel shimmy. Idler arm and Pitman arm should have little or no vertical play.

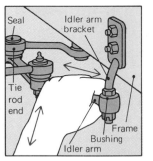

Tie rod end — Seal — Grease fitting

Check spherical joints at ends of tie rods and on other parts of steering linkage. Joints should twist smoothly but should not move up and down. If the tie rod ends are loose, have the rods replaced. If the rubber seals are leaking or cracked, have them replaced.

Performing a grease job 🔧 25 min – 1 hr

Even though many carmakers allow long intervals (up to 36,000 miles, or 57,600 km) between lubrications of the suspension and steering systems, it is a good idea to renew the grease in the suspension and steering components at least once a year, or every 6,000 miles (9,600 km) if driving conditions are severe.

Choose a chassis grease that contains molybdenum disulfide (*moly*) made by a reputable oil company. Most brands are available in cartridge form for use in the ordinary low-pressure, hand-operated grease guns available from auto parts stores. Most cars are equipped with nipple-type grease fittings but some

have plug-type fittings as well. When you purchase a grease gun, make sure to get nozzles that suit the fittings on your car. A flexible hose attachment and some right-angle nipples are also useful, since standard grease fittings are often located in places that may be hard to reach with a hand-powered gun.

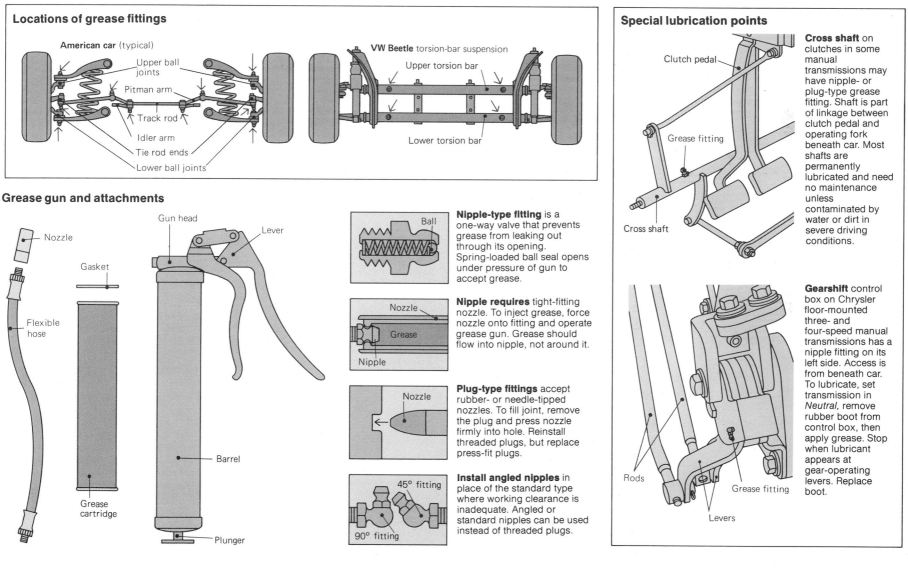

Locations of grease fittings

American car (typical)
- Upper ball joints
- Pitman arm
- Track rod
- Idler arm
- Tie rod ends
- Lower ball joints

VW Beetle torsion-bar suspension
- Upper torsion bar
- Lower torsion bar

Grease gun and attachments
- Nozzle
- Gasket
- Flexible hose
- Grease cartridge
- Gun head
- Lever
- Barrel
- Plunger

Nipple-type fitting is a one-way valve that prevents grease from leaking out through its opening. Spring-loaded ball seal opens under pressure of gun to accept grease.
- Ball

Nipple requires tight-fitting nozzle. To inject grease, force nozzle onto fitting and operate grease gun. Grease should flow into nipple, not around it.
- Nozzle
- Grease
- Nipple

Plug-type fittings accept rubber- or needle-tipped nozzles. To fill joint, remove the plug and press nozzle firmly into hole. Reinstall threaded plugs, but replace press-fit plugs.
- Nozzle

Install angled nipples in place of the standard type where working clearance is inadequate. Angled or standard nipples can be used instead of threaded plugs.
- 45° fitting
- 90° fitting

Special lubrication points

- Clutch pedal
- Grease fitting
- Cross shaft

Cross shaft on clutches in some manual transmissions may have nipple- or plug-type grease fitting. Shaft is part of linkage between clutch pedal and operating fork beneath car. Most shafts are permanently lubricated and need no maintenance unless contaminated by water or dirt in severe driving conditions.

- Rods
- Grease fitting
- Levers

Gearshift control box on Chrysler floor-mounted three- and four-speed manual transmissions has a nipple fitting on its left side. Access is from beneath car. To lubricate, set transmission in *Neutral*, remove rubber boot from control box, then apply grease. Stop when lubricant appears at gear-operating levers. Replace boot.

191

Performing a grease job 🕐 30 min–1 hr

Greasing your car yourself is easy if you prepare for the job before you begin. Have all the tools and materials you will need within easy reach while you are under the car. Wear old clothes and protective eye goggles, and have a good supply of old rags or paper towels on hand. To avoid a messy cleanup later, spread newspapers or a large piece of cardboard beneath the car to catch loose grease and dirt. Work in a well-lit area, or use a droplight. It helps to check the owner's manual before you begin so that you know the locations of all grease fittings. Do not overlook any fittings that are hidden beneath heavy accumulations of road dirt and old grease. If you miss even one fitting, you have not done the job properly.

Caution: Always make sure that you have raised and supported the car safely (see p.176) before you begin to work.

Tools: Jack, jack stands, grease gun, nozzles.
Materials: Moly grease, droplight, rags, old newspaper.

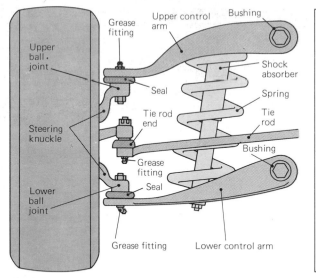

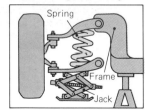
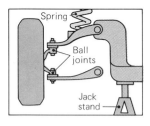

Supporting the ball joints

The weight of the car must be removed from ball joints before they are lubricated if grease is to penetrate the joint properly. On cars with coil springs between upper and lower control arms, support the frame on jack stands and use a jack to raise each lower arm before injecting grease. Where springs are mounted above upper control arms, unload the joint by raising car off the ground and setting jack stands under frame. On all cars, move wheels from side to side when lubricating joints to spread grease.

How to grease joints

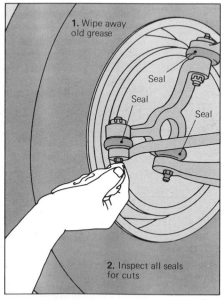

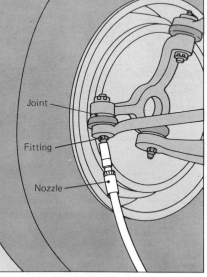

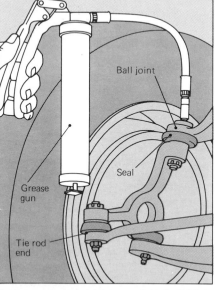

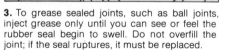

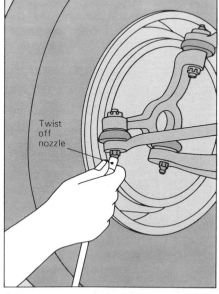

1. First, wipe the fitting and nearby area clean of encrusted old grease and road dirt. Check all rubber seals for cuts. Damaged seals should usually be replaced at a garage.

2. To grease a joint, press nozzle over grease fitting and operate the grease gun. Watch as old grease is forced out at the joint. Stop pumping gun when fresh grease appears at the joint.

3. To grease sealed joints, such as ball joints, inject grease only until you can see or feel the rubber seal begin to swell. Do not overfill the joint; if the seal ruptures, it must be replaced.

4. Remove grease gun by twisting nozzle off the fitting. Do not pull nozzle straight off. On plug-type fittings, reinstall or replace plug. Wipe joint area clean of old grease that was forced out.

Lubricating U-joints ⏱ 5–10 min

Unless they are replacement joints, most U-joints (universal joints) are packed with lubricant and sealed for life. You can identify a U-joint that should be lubricated by noting whether or not there is a grease fitting or plug on the U-joint's cross (the cross-shaped member that joins the pair of U-shaped yokes in the joint).

Lubricate the U-joint when you lubricate the suspension and steering linkage. Clean grease and grime from the fitting first. Inject grease with a grease gun— just one or two pumps on the handle is enough. Also, check for wear in the U-joint. If you find excessive play, replace the U-joint (pp.451–453).

Some drive shafts have double U-joints and some have more than one U-joint, so make sure that you do not miss any lubrication points.

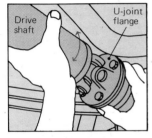

To check U-joint for wear, grip drive shaft with one hand and U-joint flange with the other hand. Try to move the shaft in relation to the flange. If there is any side-to-side movement, the U-joint is worn and should be dismantled and serviced.

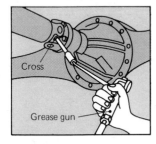

Lubricate U-joint at grease fitting on cross, if there is a fitting. If the cross has a plug instead of a fitting, remove the plug and screw in the fitting to lubricate it. Then reinstall the plug. Do not leave the fitting in place because it will unbalance the drive shaft.

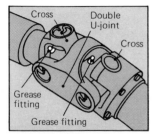

Lubricate double U-joints in the same way as you would single U-joints. There are two crosses in a double joint, and there may be one (GM) to three (Jeep) fittings, depending on the brand. The single, flush fitting on GM U-joints can only be greased with a special needle-tip grease gun adapter.

Checking for play in ball joints ⏱ 10–20 min

Inspect ball joints for wear each time you lubricate them. Worn joints are dangerous. If the joints on your car are worn, have a mechanic replace them.

Ball joints can be checked visually after the tire is jacked up to take the load off the load-carrying joint; it is essentially the same system used when the joints are lubricated (opposite page).

Check the joints for horizontal play and vertical play. If you observe none, the joints are OK. If you observe some play, the joints may still be all right if the play is within manufacturer's tolerances.

To measure the play, you must have an instrument called a dial indicator, and you must know the manufacturer's specification for ball-joint play on your car (which is never more than ¼ in.). Most service stations can make this measurement for you.

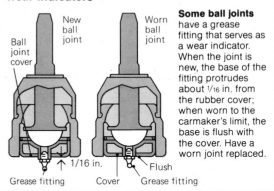

Wear indicators

Some ball joints have a grease fitting that serves as a wear indicator. When the joint is new, the base of the fitting protrudes about 1/16 in. from the rubber cover; when worn to the carmaker's limit, the base is flush with the cover. Have a worn joint replaced.

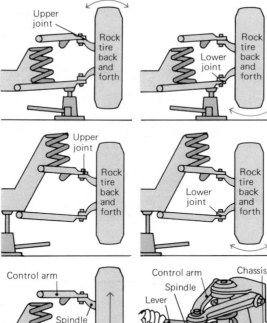

Check horizontal play: If the bottom of the coil spring (torsion bar on some cars) is seated in the lower control arm, the lower ball joint carries the load. To unload the joint, lift the car with a floor jack under the lower control arm. Grasp the top and bottom of the tire and slowly rock it in the manner illustrated. Look at the ball joints as you do this, or have a helper look if you cannot see them. If there is horizontal movement of the steering knuckle with respect to either control arm at either of the joints, the joint has horizontal play and it may be worn. Repeat this test on the other front wheel.

Check horizontal play: If the bottom of the coil spring (torsion bar on some cars) is seated in the upper control arm, the upper ball joint carries the load. To unload the joint, lift the car with a floor jack under the frame or under a cross member. Grasp the top and bottom of the tire and slowly rock it in the manner illustrated. Look at the ball joints as you do this, or have a helper look if you cannot see them. If there is horizontal movement of the steering knuckle with respect to either control arm at either of the joints, the joint has horizontal play and it may be worn. Repeat this test on the other front wheel.

Check vertical play: With the wheel jacked up as shown above, pry the tire upward with a lever or pipe. If you see movement between a control arm and the steering knuckle, the corresponding ball joint has vertical play. For a second check (particularly of the joint that is not load-bearing), apply a lever between the control arm and the spindle as shown, using a part of the chassis as the pivot point. If you can cause vertical movement between the arm and the steering knuckle, the corresponding ball joint has vertical play. You may have to remove the tire to do this properly. Repeat this test on the other front wheel.

Adding oil to a manual steering box ⏱ 5–15 min

On some cars you should check the oil level in the manual steering box once every six months and add oil if necessary. Exceptions are cars made by GM, Honda, Volkswagen, and Chrysler (1975 and later models). In these cars the original lubricant should last the lifetime of the vehicle. As a rule, if the carmaker recommends a periodic oil check and fill, you will see a filler plug on the car's steering box.

Do not confuse the filler plug with a bolt on the steering box cover or with the steering's adjusting screw. The adjusting screw has a locknut as well as a bolt head or a slot for a screwdriver blade. If you turn this screw, you may put the steering off center.

To check the lubricant level on most cars, remove the filler plug and look at the level of the lubricant inside. If lubricant should be added, use the type recommended by the carmaker (see chart below).

On Ford cars, after removing the filler plug and lower cover bolt, turn the steering wheel slowly to the left stop; the level of the lubricant in the cover bolt hole should rise. Turn the steering wheel slowly to the right stop; the level of the lubricant in the filler plug hole should rise. If the lubricant does not rise in one hole or the other, add lubricant.

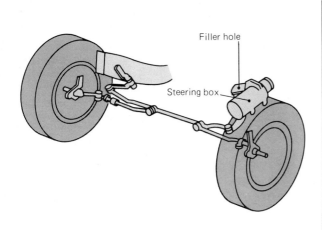

Adding the oil

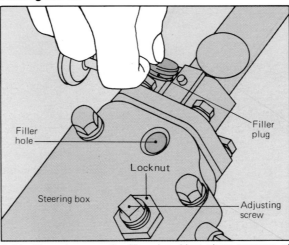

1. Identify and remove the filler plug. Most plugs unscrew, although some can be removed by simply prying them off.

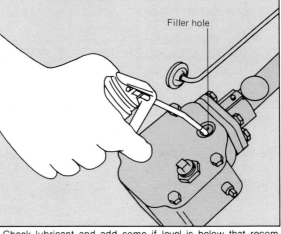

2. Check lubricant and add some if level is below that recommended. See chart for type of lubricant required. Reinstall plug.

Recommended lubricants

Car model	Manual steering lubricant
AMC Ford imports	Lithium grease
Chrysler Chrysler imports	Gear lubricant "For service GL4"
Ford	Power steering fluid
GM (except Cadillacs)	Steering gear lubricant
Datsun Toyota	Gear lubricant "For service GL5"

Filler plug location and fill level

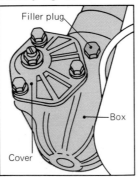

Chrysler cars: Filler plug is offset from steering box cover. Fill box so that lubricant covers the gear inside the box.

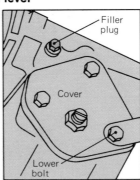

Ford cars: Remove both filler plug and lower bolt on steering box cover. Check oil level as described in text, above.

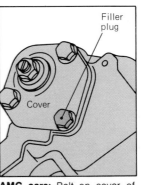

AMC cars: Bolt on cover of steering box serves as the filler plug. Fill so that lubricant covers gear inside box.

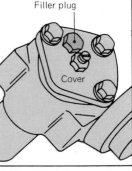

Datsuns and Toyotas: Plug is on steering box cover. Level should be less than 1⅜ in. below upper edge of hole.

Adding power steering fluid ⏱ 5 min

On cars equipped with power steering, the fluid level in the reservoir of the power steering pump should be checked about once every six months. The reservoir is usually housed in the same unit as the pump, near the fan belt, and is readily accessible. Illustrations of common pump reservoirs are found below.

Power steering fluid is specially formulated for hydraulic systems that have rubber hoses. When adding fluid, always use the product that conforms to the carmaker's specifications (see chart below).

The power steering system must have sufficient fluid at all times to maintain precise steering action. To check the level, first turn off the engine. Wipe the outside of the reservoir cap and the reservoir first so that dirt does not fall into the reservoir. Then remove the cap and read the dipstick. If the dipstick has two *Full* marks, the upper one is for a hot engine.

Fluid level will appear abnormally high if the engine is overheated, as may be the case after much stop-and-go driving. Be sure that the engine is cool before you read the dipstick.

If you fill the reservoir above the appropriate *Full* mark, draw off the excess with a mechanic's syringe or a cheap plastic bellows pump.

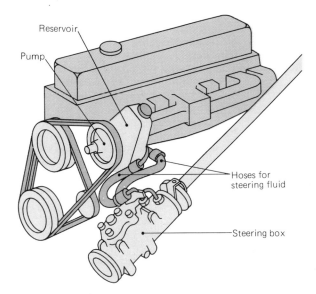

Recommended lubricants

Car model	Power steering lubricant
AMC Chrysler Ford (1973–77) GM	Power steering fluid
Ford (1978 and later)	Automatic transmission fluid, Type F
Chrysler imports Datsun Honda Toyota	DEXRON automatic transmission fluid

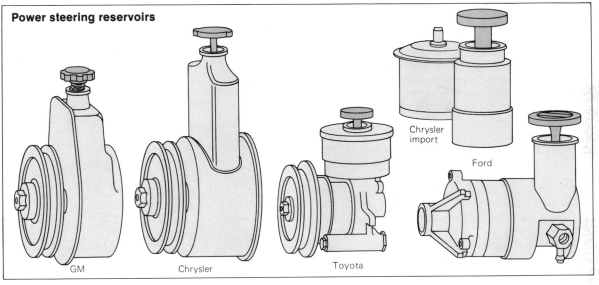

Power steering reservoirs

GM Chrysler Chrysler import Toyota Ford

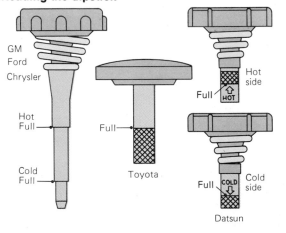

Reading the dipstick

GM Ford Chrysler — Hot Full — Cold Full

Toyota — Full

Hot side — Full HOT

Cold side — Full COLD

Datsun

AMC and GM cars: Run engine up to normal operating temperature and shut it off. Dipstick should read *Hot Full*.

Chrysler cars: Dipstick should read *Cold Full* at engine temperatures around 70°F, *Hot Full* when engine is at normal operating temperature. If pump reservoir does not have a dipstick, fluid level should be 1½ to 2 in. below top of filler neck when the engine is cool, ½ to 1 in. below when engine is at operating temperature.

Ford cars: Run engine up to normal operating temperature. Turn steering wheel all the way to the right and left several times, then shut off engine. Fluid level should be at or near *Hot Full*.

Datsuns: Dipstick has level marks on both sides. Fluid level should read at *Full* mark on hot side of dipstick when engine has been running at normal operating temperature (140° to 175°F), at *Full* mark on cold side when engine is cold.

Toyotas: Add fluid if level is below the bottom of dipstick. Do not add beyond *Full* mark.

Engine oil

The oil in your car's engine must be changed at the intervals specified in your owner's manual. Note that most owner's manuals recommend two oil-change intervals: a longer interval for ideal driving conditions (long trips at relatively steady speeds) and a second, shorter interval for the type of driving that most people do (short trips, stop-and-go driving, or trailer-towing), which is often described by the manual as "severe service." You can buy oil on sale at discount department stores and even in some supermarkets. Just make certain that the oil you buy is of high quality and that it is the type recommended for your car and the conditions under which it is driven.

Motor oil does more than simply lubricate engine parts and prevent destructive metal-to-metal contact. Special additives strengthen the lubricating film so that it can withstand the high pressures found in modern engines. Additives inhibit the formation of sludge, carbon, and varnish deposits; they retard rust, which can result from the action of acids and moisture that form within the engine as by-products of combustion. Moreover, additives keep the oil from becoming either too thick or too thin under extreme operating temperatures, and control foaming of the oil when it is churned up by fast-moving engine parts. Foaming is harmful because the bubbles that form are filled with air, which has no lubricating properties. Other additives keep sludge in suspension until it is removed from the engine during an oil change. These additives dissipate in time, which is why the oil must be changed periodically.

The best type of oil for post-1970 cars with gasoline engines is labeled "For service SE" or "SF." Oil labeled "CC" or "CD" is made for diesel engines. Most diesels require frequent oil changes because their very high compression forces combustion by-products past the piston rings, and this quickly contaminates the oil.

Choose a multi-grade oil that suits your driving conditions. Generally, oil with a viscosity range of 10W-40 is ideal for year-round use. For high-speed, high-altitude, or heavy-duty driving—such as pulling a trailer—heavier 10W-50 oil may be more suitable. At temperatures below 0°F, lightweight 5W-30 or 5W-40 oil is best unless its use is contrary to the carmaker's specifications. When using any 5W oil, avoid speeds above 50 miles per hour.

Synthetic oil is also available, graded and classified in the same way as conventional mineral oils. Though it is expensive and in some cases not recommended for use with diesels, synthetic oil lasts much longer before it must be replaced. Because of its excellent lubricating qualities, synthetic oil is also claimed by its manufacturers to decrease the fuel consumption of engines in which it is used. Before switching to synthetic oil, however, check your car's warranty, if it still applies; make sure that the extra time between changes of synthetic oil will not void the warranty. Also, if you have an older car whose engine leaks oil, switching to a thinner synthetic oil (or to any thin oil) will make it leak even more.

How to check engine oil level

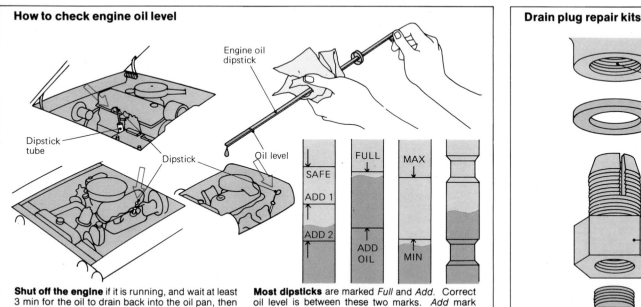

Engine oil dipstick

Dipstick tube

Dipstick

Oil level

SAFE / ADD 1 / ADD 2

FULL / ADD OIL

MAX / MIN

Shut off the engine if it is running, and wait at least 3 min for the oil to drain back into the oil pan, then remove the engine oil dipstick. Wipe the dipstick clean and reinsert it all the way into its tube. Pull the dipstick out again and observe the level of oil clinging to the blade.

Most dipsticks are marked *Full* and *Add*. Correct oil level is between these two marks. *Add* mark means that engine is 1 qt low. Do not add oil before level is down to the *Add* mark, or you may overfill the engine and foaming can result. When checking oil level, be sure car is on level ground.

Drain plug repair kits

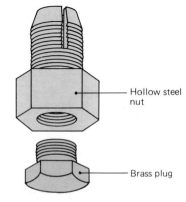

Oil pan

Drain hole

Washer

Hollow steel nut

Brass plug

When reinstalling the oil drain plug (or any threaded fastener), always align the threads carefully and turn the plug by hand as far as you can before gently tightening it with a wrench. If the plug will not turn smoothly, the threads are dirty and should be cleaned (see p.172), or they are misaligned. In either case, do not force the plug with a wrench because you will strip the threads.

If the threads in the oil drain hole are stripped, it is not necessary to replace the oil pan. Instead, you can use one of several drain plug repair kits available from auto parts stores. With the type shown, a self-tapping steel nut is forced into the pan; oil is then drained by removing the small brass plug. Other kits use less durable rubber stoppers.

How to change engine oil ⏱ 15–35 min

Change the engine oil at the intervals specified by the car manufacturer (usually every 3,000 to 10,000 miles, or 5,000 to 16,000 km), more often if you drive only on short stop-and-go trips or over dusty roads. Synthetic oil need not be changed as frequently. If you wish, you can use a beer can opener to open the oil can. A clean funnel will serve to pour the oil, instead of the pour spout shown below. On cars with hard-to-reach filler caps, a funnel with a flexible neck may be needed. Try to drain the oil while the engine is warm; the old oil will drain more quickly and completely, and more of the contaminants that the oil holds in suspension will be removed. Be careful, however, of engine parts that may be too hot to touch. If the engine is cold, let the oil drain for at least 20 to 30 minutes before reinstalling the drain plug.

Tools: Drive-on ramps, jack and jack stands, socket wrench or box-end wrench to fit drain plug, droplight or flashlight, pour spout.
Materials: 6-qt basin or drain pan, rags, fender covers (old blanket, drop cloth, or plastic shower curtain), fresh motor oil, work gloves, safety goggles.

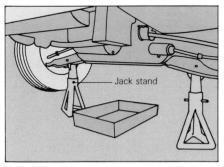

1. Raise front of car and support it on jack stands (unless working clearance under car is adequate). Place basin beneath drain plug. Loosen plug with wrench, then remove plug by hand.

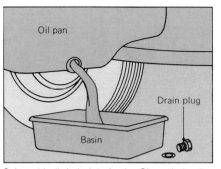

2. Let old oil drain into basin. Clean drain plug and washer with rags. Some plugs are magnetized to trap metal particles. If you are changing the oil filter too, see p.198.

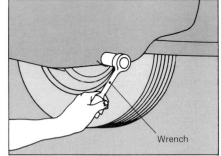

3. Replace plug and washer as soon as old oil has drained. Start plug by hand and tighten it as far as possible. When plug is seated, tighten it another half-turn with a wrench.

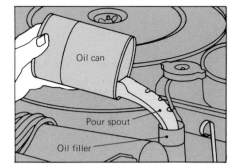

4. Find oil filler. Add amount of oil given in owner's manual, 1 qt less if filter is not changed. Start engine and check for leaks at drain plug. Lower car. Check oil level; adjust if necessary.

Volkswagen oil change

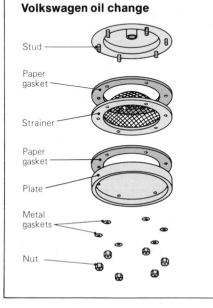

Stud
Paper gasket
Strainer
Paper gasket
Plate
Metal gaskets
Nut

Air-cooled VWs have a wire strainer that must be removed and cleaned in solvent at every oil change. Cars built after 1972 do not have a drain plug; loosen the retaining plate to drain the oil. All gaskets must be replaced; do not reuse them. Gasket kits are sold in auto parts stores.

Drain oil and remove all six nuts that hold retaining plate. Remove and clean strainer. Dry strainer thoroughly, then install paper gaskets, strainer, and retaining plate. Tighten the nuts by hand as far as possible, then tighten them a bit more with a wrench to compress the metal gaskets. The nuts are very easy to strip. Reinstall the drain plug and add about 2½ qt oil. If you strip the threads on a nut, the drain plug, or retaining plate, buy new ones from a dealer. If you strip a stud, replace it (see p.431). If you strip the threaded stud hole, repair it with a thread insert kit (see p.433).

Disposing of old oil

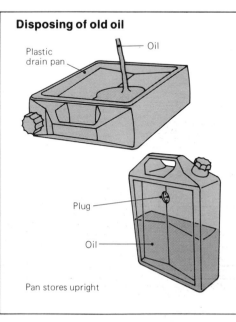

Oil
Plastic drain pan
Plug
Oil
Pan stores upright

Pouring used engine oil down a drain or storm sewer, or even into the ground, not only contributes to pollution but is illegal in many areas. Unless you can find a garage that will accept used oil for forwarding to a recycling plant, you should dispose of old oil by leaving it for the garbage collector in closed, labeled, non-leaking containers, such as polyethylene milk jugs with screw caps. Some oil companies recommend filtering used oil through cheesecloth and adding it to the fuel tank of an oil-burning furnace. Special plastic drain pans that can store several gallons of old oil are available from auto parts stores. These enable you to perform several oil changes before it becomes necessary to dispose of the oil.

Maintenance/**Engine**

Changing the oil filter ⏱ 10–20 min

Changing the oil filter is part of routine engine maintenance. Usually, the oil filter is changed every *other* time you change the engine oil (or at every oil change if driving conditions are extremely dusty), but in any case at least twice a year. Under normal driving conditions, the dirty oil left in the filter will not seriously contaminate the 3 to 5 quarts of fresh oil added at an oil change. The owner's manual for your car should specify the type of filter needed. Filters are available in many types and sizes for different car makes, models, and years and for engines with varying cubic-inch displacements. Your engine's displacement is listed on a decal found on the air cleaner or rocker cover, or on the emission-control decal under the hood. Purchase a reputable brand of filter and one that is designed for the service

you intend it to perform. For instance, if you plan to change the filter at 6,000-mile intervals, you do not need a filter designed to give 15,000-mile service. Virtually all cars today use the *spin-on* type of oil filter shown on these pages, although some trucks and fleet vehicles may be equipped with replaceable-cartridge filters. Volkswagen Beetles do not have oil filters as standard equipment, but kits for adapting spin-on filters to VWs are available from auto parts stores.

> **Tools:** Drive-on ramps or jack and jack stands, oil filter wrench, pour spout or funnel.
> **Materials:** Basin or drain pan, rags, fender cover, replacement oil filter, 1 qt fresh motor oil, work gloves, goggles.

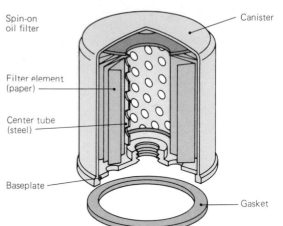

Spin-on oil filter — Canister — Filter element (paper) — Center tube (steel) — Baseplate — Gasket

Locating and reaching the filter

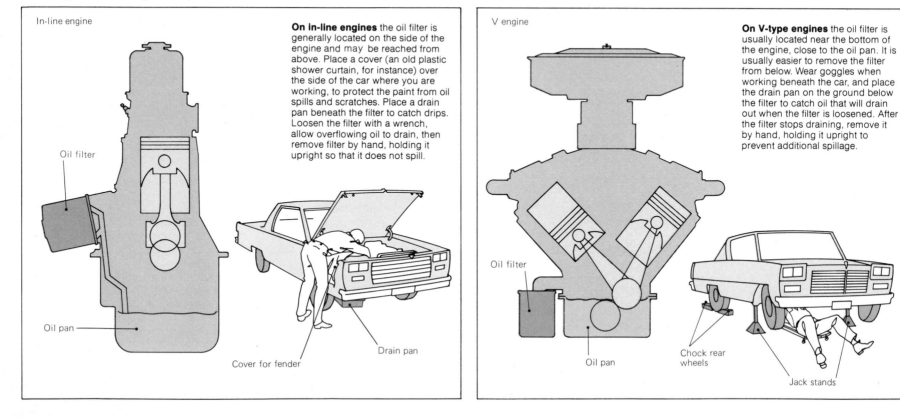

In-line engine

Oil filter

Oil pan

Cover for fender

Drain pan

On in-line engines the oil filter is generally located on the side of the engine and may be reached from above. Place a cover (an old plastic shower curtain, for instance) over the side of the car where you are working, to protect the paint from oil spills and scratches. Place a drain pan beneath the filter to catch drips. Loosen the filter with a wrench, allow overflowing oil to drain, then remove filter by hand, holding it upright so that it does not spill.

V engine

Oil filter

Oil pan

Chock rear wheels

Jack stands

On V-type engines the oil filter is usually located near the bottom of the engine, close to the oil pan. It is usually easier to remove the filter from below. Wear goggles when working beneath the car, and place the drain pan on the ground below the filter to catch oil that will drain out when the filter is loosened. After the filter stops draining, remove it by hand, holding it upright to prevent additional spillage.

Types of oil filter wrenches

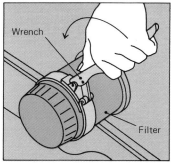

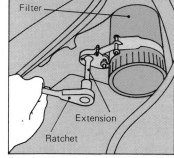

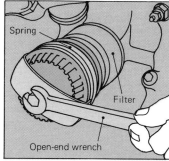

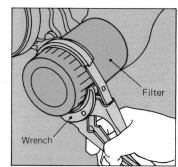

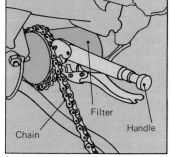

Strap-type wrench with handle. Position wrench so that strap tightens around filter when handle is turned.

Strap-type wrench for use with ratchet and extension fits hard-to-reach areas with little turning room.

Coil-spring wrench fits different-size filters. Spring grips filter when wrench is turned counterclockwise.

Pliers-type wrench works well on filters stuck tight by corrosion, but it requires ample turning room.

Chain-type wrench fits all filters and gives tightest grip. Like pliers type, it requires ample turning room.

Removing stuck filters

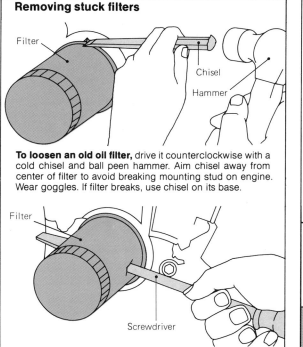

To loosen an old oil filter, drive it counterclockwise with a cold chisel and ball peen hammer. Aim chisel away from center of filter to avoid breaking mounting stud on engine. Wear goggles. If filter breaks, use chisel on its base.

Another technique for removing an old filter is to drive a long screwdriver through the lower half of the filter, near its base. Turn screwdriver, and remove filter by hand. The screwdriver provides plenty of leverage.

Installing a new oil filter

1. Wipe mating surfaces clean on engine and filter; otherwise, leaks may develop. Use soft cloth or fresh paper towel. Then coat rubber gasket on filter with thin film of oil. Failure to oil gasket may hamper removal of filter later.

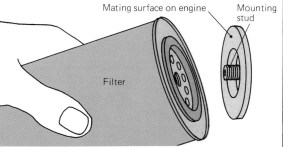

2. Thread filter clockwise onto mounting stud until gasket contacts engine. Tighten filter another three-quarters to one full turn, but no more. Check oil level and add oil. Run engine and check level again. Check for leaks.

Aftermarket oil additives

Many aftermarket engine oil additives contain some of the same chemicals already present in a high-quality engine oil. It should not be necessary to use these additives under normal driving conditions and if you have followed your car manufacturer's recommended schedule for changing the oil and the oil filter. The most common additives found in high-quality engine oils are listed below.

Detergent/dispersants break up varnish, carbon, and sludge deposits and keep them in suspension until they are physically removed when the oil and filter are changed. Detergent/dispersants also help to prevent sludge, varnish, and carbon from forming.

Viscosity-index improvers prevent the oil from thinning out during high-temperature engine operation or from becoming too thick during low-temperature operation.

Pour-point depressants lower the temperature at which the oil will flow readily. They supplement the viscosity-index improvers to provide immediate distribution of oil with each engine start, even in cold weather.

Anti-wear additives enable oil to cling to hard-to-lubricate parts, reducing metal-to-metal contact.

Corrosion inhibitors also enable the oil to coat metal parts to protect them from rust and corrosion.

Oxidation inhibitors retard the formation of acidity in the oil that could cause engine parts to pit, rust, or corrode.

Foam inhibitors reduce the surface tension of the oil in order to prevent the retention of air bubbles that form with the churning of the oil by the engine parts.

If you are using an aftermarket oil additive, follow the package instructions carefully; many are meant to be used only in limited amounts. Kerosene and light-oil additives (sometimes called *upper-cylinder lubricants*) are claimed to loosen or lubricate sticky valves, lifters, and rings. Sealants can stop minor leaks at the engine oil seals by causing dried-out seals to swell.

Adding or changing oil in a manual transmission ⚙️⚙️ 15–30 min

About once every six months, check the oil level in a manual transmission and add oil if necessary. There is a dipstick for checking the oil level in automatic transmissions, but if your car has a manual transmission, you will have to remove a metal or rubber filler plug and check the level with your finger.

Most carmakers do not recommend ever changing the oil in manual transmissions unless the car has had unusually heavy use. Only Honda and Toyota recommend a regular change of oil, about once every two and a half years. This is done in the same way as changing differential oil (opposite page).

Manufacturers are specific about the kind of lubricant that should be used in the transmission. Only Honda recommends engine oil. Consult the chart below for the lubricant recommended for your car.

Lubricants are graded according to viscosity—the higher the viscosity number, the thicker the lubricant. Select a lubricant with a viscosity number appropriate for the climate in which you operate your car. Use the viscosity chart at the right. In areas with temperatures between –40° and 85°F, for example, use a lubricant with a viscosity number of either 80W or 80W–90.

Recommended viscosity numbers

Lubricant viscosity number	Temperature range (FAHRENHEIT)	(CENTIGRADE)
75W	–60° to 50°	–50° to 10°
80W	–40° to 85°	–40° to 30°
80W–90	–40° to 105°	–40° to 40°
85W	10° to 85°	–10° to 30°
90	30° to 105°	0° to 40°
140	50° to 120°	10° to 50°

Adding transmission oil

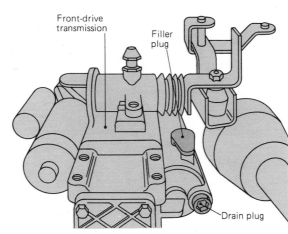

Rear-drive transmission
Filler plug
Drain plug

Front-drive transmission
Filler plug
Drain plug

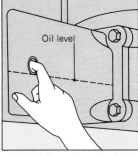

Plug

Oil level

1. Locate filler plug on transmission and remove plug. Do not confuse plug with bolts on the transmission. Accidental removal of a bolt may allow internal parts to spring loose.

2. Insert finger to check oil level. Most transmissions should be filled up to filler hole, but check your owner's manual or the carmaker's service manual for the correct level.

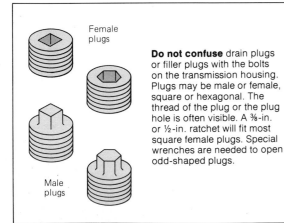

Female plugs

Male plugs

Do not confuse drain plugs or filler plugs with the bolts on the transmission housing. Plugs may be male or female, square or hexagonal. The thread of the plug or the plug hole is often visible. A ⅜-in. or ½-in. ratchet will fit most square female plugs. Special wrenches are needed to open odd-shaped plugs.

Recommended lubricants

Car model	Transmission lubricant
AMC (1977 and earlier models) Chrysler (front-drive cars with VW transaxles) Datsun Toyota VW	Gear lubricant "For service GL4"
AMC (1978 and later models) Chrysler imports Ford GM (3- and 4-speed cars)	Gear lubricant "For service GL5"
Chrysler GM (5-speed cars) GM (small front-drive cars)	DEXRON automatic transmission fluid
Honda	10W–30 motor oil

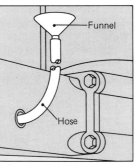

Funnel
Hose

3. If oil is not up to correct level, add more through a length of hose and a funnel. Or use a squeeze bottle such as the one shown on the opposite page for adding lubricant.

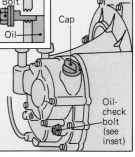

Bolt
Cap
Oil
Oil-check bolt (see inset)

4. Honda five-speed transmissions have a separate filler cap for adding oil. Unscrew oil-check bolt to position shown; remove cap. Add oil until it begins to overflow at bolt.

Checking oil in the differential ⚙⚙ 15–30 min

Check the oil level in the differential every six months and add oil if necessary. The procedure is essentially the same as for manual transmissions.

In front-wheel-drive cars, the differential (sometimes called the *final drive*) is housed with the transmission in a unit called the transaxle. In a manual transmission, the transaxle generally requires only one lubricant and has only one filler hole. When you add oil through the filler hole, you service both the transmission and the differential at the same time.

The transaxle in an automatic transmission is lubricated separately. The transmission lubricant is checked with a dipstick, and oil level in the differential is checked via the filler plug.

Most carmakers do not recommend ever changing the oil in the differential unless the car has been subjected to unusually heavy use. Exceptions are Chrysler cars made in 1972–74, Datsuns, and Toyotas. Change the lubricant in these cars about once every two to three years.

Use the lubricant recommended by the carmaker and indicated by the chart at the right. The lubricant should be of a viscosity appropriate to the temperature range in which the car is being driven, as shown in the chart on the opposite page.

Special lubricants are used in limited-slip differentials, so you must first determine whether or not your car has a differential of that type. Limited-slip units have such trade names as Traction-Lok®, Anti-Spin®, Twin-Grip®, and Positraction®.

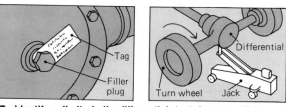

To identify a limited-slip differential, look for a tag. If there is none, raise the rear of the car (p.176) with brake off and transmission in *Neutral.* Turn a rear wheel by hand. If the wheel is easy to turn and the other wheel rotates in the opposite direction, the differential is conventional. If the wheel does not turn easily and the other wheel rotates in the same direction, the differential is the limited-slip type.

Recommended lubricants

Car model	Differential lubricant
AMC (standard models) Chrysler (standard models) GM (standard models except Cadillac) Datsun Toyota VW (front-drive cars, automatic transmission)	Gear lubricant "For service GL5"
Chrysler (front-drive cars)	DEXRON automatic transmission fluid
Ford (standard models)	Hypoid-gear lubricant
AMC (limited-slip) Chrysler (limited-slip) Ford (limited-slip) GM (large front-drive cars) GM (limited-slip and all Cadillacs)	Special lubricant made by each manufacturer for limited-slip differentials

Filler plug near drive shaft — Plug

Plug

Filler plug at rear of differential

Adding or changing oil

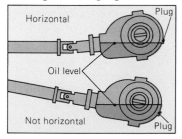

To check oil level, differential must be horizontal. If you want to raise the car, raise and support both ends of the car (p.176) so that it is level.

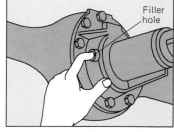

Remove filler plug and insert finger to check oil level. Oil in almost all differentials should reach opening, but check owner's manual to make sure.

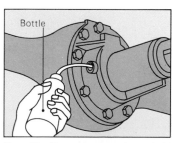

To add oil, use a clean household squeeze bottle (such as a catsup dispenser), or use a hose and funnel as shown on the opposite page.

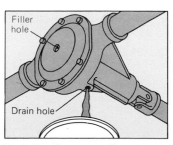

To drain oil, remove filler plug and drain plug. Draining and filling may take several minutes unless lubricant is warm enough to flow quickly.

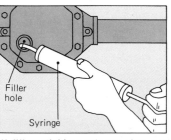

If differential has only one plug, new oil cannot be added until old lubricant is siphoned out. Use a mechanic's syringe or a plastic bellows pump.

Checking automatic transmission fluid ⏱ 5–15 min

Under normal driving conditions, check the level of the automatic transmission fluid every few months. Most car manufacturers recommend checking the fluid level every time you change the engine oil. If you pull a trailer, drive on steep mountain roads at high altitudes, or if you drive consistently in heavy city traffic in temperatures above 90°F, you should check the transmission fluid more often—say, once or twice a month. Never run your car when the transmission fluid is low; doing so could cause serious internal damage. Check the fluid level if you notice the car slipping erratically in and out of gear, a warning sign that is most noticeable when the engine is cold or when the car is being driven up a hill.

The gearbox must be at operating temperature before fluid level is checked. Drive the car 10 to 15 miles or for about 20 minutes. Then stop the car on level ground and apply the brakes. With the engine running, move the gearshift lever through all positions. Finally, put transmission in *Park* on Datsuns, Ford and General Motors cars, and Hondas, or in *Neutral* on American Motors and Chrysler cars, Toyotas, and Volkswagens. Set the parking brake and leave the engine running at idle.

Caution: The parking brake must be in good operating condition; if it will not hold the car stationary on a hill, adjust the parking brake (p.218) before checking the transmission fluid.

Lift the hood, remove the transmission fluid dipstick, and cautiously touch the tip to judge the temperature of the fluid. The end of the dipstick should be too hot to hold comfortably (150° to 200°F).

Note the color of the fluid; it should be red or pink unless your owner's manual specifies otherwise. Compare the color and smell to that of new fluid. Brown or black fluid, especially if it smells burned, often indicates an overheated transmission and the need for maintenance. Wipe the dipstick with a paper towel, being careful not to let any lint cling to the stick. Check the stain for particles or gummy residue. If either are present, the transmission should be inspected by a specialist. Insert the clean dipstick back into the filler tube, making sure that it is seated fully or according to the instructions in the owner's manual. Then withdraw it again and note the level of the fluid clinging to the stick.

On most cars the correct fluid level is at or just below the *Full* mark when the transmission is at operating temperature. If the fluid level seems too high, the transmission may be above normal operating temperature, and you should let it cool for 30 minutes and check the level again. If the fluid seems too low, the transmission may not have been operated long enough to reach the proper temperature. Drive the car again, then recheck the fluid level. Do not rely on a single low reading and add fluid to a cold transmission. You may accidentally overfill it and cause as much damage as you would by operating the car with too little fluid. Compare the fluid level and dipstick temperature to the specifications listed in the owner's manual, and add fluid only if necessary. Use the type and brand of fluid recommended in the manual.

How to add transmission fluid

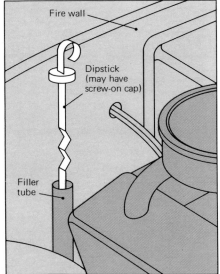

1. Check level of transmission fluid when the car is fully warmed up. Transmission dipstick is located in filler tube behind the engine. Do not confuse it with the engine-oil dipstick. Clean area around tube before removing dipstick.

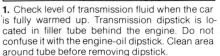
Typical dipstick styles

2. Note dipstick temperature and level of fluid. Transmission oil expands when hot, so consult owner's manual to determine accuracy of reading. Low fluid level may be OK if transmission temperature is below normal.

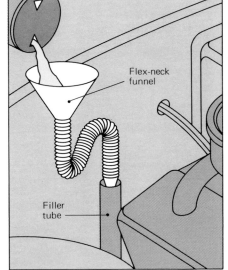

3. Add fluid if necessary. Use clean flex-neck funnel to reach an awkward filler tube opening. Use only fluid that manufacturer recommends for your model. Add fluid in small amounts and check level frequently. Do not overfill.

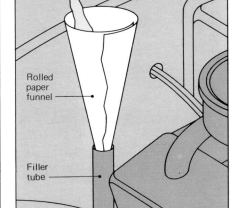

4. You can add fluid in an emergency by using rolled-up paper as a funnel. A magazine cover works well. Make sure that paper is clean and lint-free. Use caution in makeshift situations to avoid contaminating the fluid with dirt or water.

Changing automatic transmission fluid and replacing the filter 🔧🔧🔧🔧 30 min–1½ hr

Many cars with automatic transmissions no longer require regular fluid changes as part of routine transmission maintenance. For other cars, draining and changing the transmission fluid, cleaning the oil pan, and replacing the oil filter is recommended at intervals ranging from every 15,000 miles to every 60,000 miles (25,000 to 100,000 km). Change the fluid more frequently if the car is operated under severe

conditions. Your owner's manual will list the maintenance requirements, if any, for your transmission.

On most cars you will have to remove the transmission's oil pan in order to drain the fluid. Some imported cars, certain Fords, and many pre-1970 cars have transmission fluid drain plugs that can be removed from the oil pan so that transmission fluid can drain before the pan is removed.

Tools: Jack and jack stands, large drain pan, ratchet wrench and sockets, 3-in. extension, screwdriver, putty knife or gasket scraper, torque wrench, funnel, can opener.
Materials: Non-hardening gasket sealer, goggles, work gloves, droplight, rags, fender cover, replacement transmission filter, oil pan gasket, and fresh transmission fluid specifically recommended for your car.

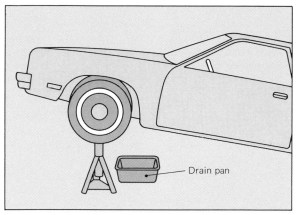

1. Jack up the car and support it on jack stands. Four stands are best, but if only two are available, jack the car as high as possible and place stands under the front of the car. Position a drain pan beneath the transmission to catch the fluid.

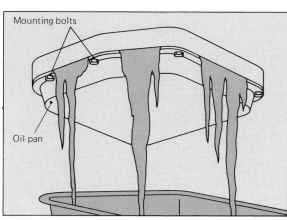

2. With a socket wrench and 3-in. extension, loosen bolts surrounding the transmission's oil pan and remove all except the bolts closest to front of car. Tilt pan down slightly at the rear so that the fluid drains out. Support pan so that it does not bend.

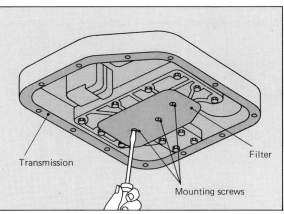

3. When fluid stops draining, remove remaining bolts from oil pan and tilt it to drain more fluid. Lower pan carefully to avoid spilling any remaining fluid. Next, unscrew mounting screws on filter and remove the filter, along with O-ring if one is present.

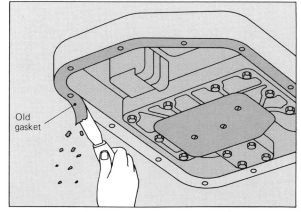

4. Scrape old gasket material off the mating surfaces of the oil pan and the transmission. Clean oil pan with solvent and dry carefully. Inner surface must be lint-free. Apply thin film of gasket sealer to pan to hold gasket in place, then install new gasket on pan.

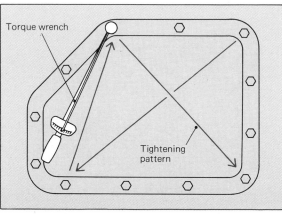

5. Install replacement filter. If filter is O-ring type, make sure that the ring is positioned at the bulge of filter neck. Clean mounting bolts and reinstall the oil pan. Tighten bolts evenly in a crisscross pattern, then torque to manufacturer's specifications.

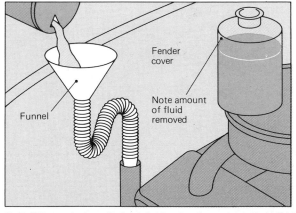

6. Refill transmission with fresh fluid, using the amount of old fluid removed as a guide. Start the engine and run it at idle, shift through all gears, then slowly add more fluid until correct level is reached when the engine is at operating temperature.

Draining the torque converter 🔲🔲🔲 10–20 min

When the transmission's oil pan is removed, only a portion of the transmission fluid drains out. The rest remains in the torque converter and cannot be removed unless the converter has a drain plug or the transmission is disassembled. Torque converters in Chrysler cars through 1977 and in most Fords do have drain plugs. General Motors discontinued them in the mid 1960s. Replacing the amount of fluid that drains out of the transmission when the pan is removed will usually restore the quality of whatever used fluid remains. Draining the converter allows you to change almost all the fluid. Be alert to the condition of the used fluid (p.202). If the fluid is so contaminated that a complete change seems wise, you can drain and refill the transmission several times, driving the car a few miles between changes in order to mix the old and new fluid. Or have the transmission disassembled and inspected by a mechanic.

Reusable filter screens

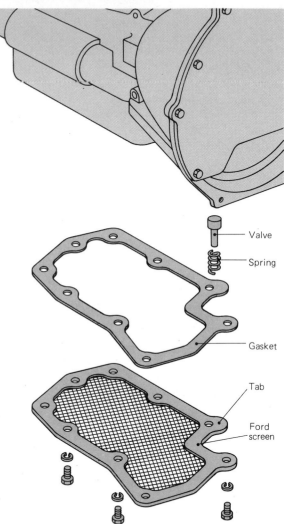

Valve

Spring

Gasket

Tab

Ford screen

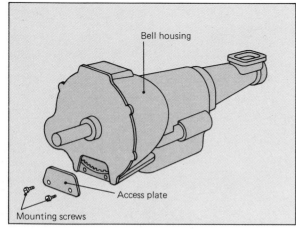

Bell housing

Access plate

Mounting screws

1. Drain converter after removing oil pan. Start by removing drain plug's access plate, located on bottom of bell housing.

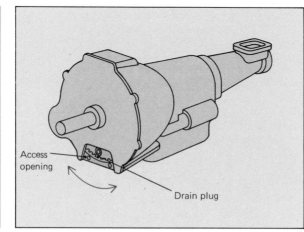

Access opening

Drain plug

2. Move out from under the car. Use short bursts of the starter to rotate the engine until the drain plug is in position to be removed.

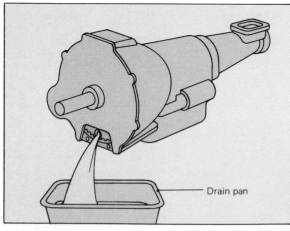

Drain pan

3. Position drain pan beneath the torque converter. Loosen and remove converter's drain plug. Allow fluid to drain into the pan.

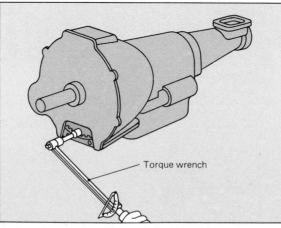

Torque wrench

4. Clean and reinstall drain plug after fluid has drained. Torque plug to manufacturer's specifications. Replace the access plate.

Oil pans of some transmissions have screen mesh filters instead of replaceable paper elements. This type of screen can be cleaned and reused. To remove it, unfasten the screws or clips that hold the screen to the valve body. Gently pull off the gasket or O-rings as well. On Fords, be careful not to lose the throttle's pressure-limit valve and spring, which are held in place by a tab on the screen. Clean the screen in solvent and let it air dry. It must be lint-free. Wipe the gasket with a clean cloth. If either screen or gasket cannot be cleaned thoroughly, buy a new one. To reinstall, place the gasket and screen in position, then replace the screws or clips. Tighten the screws evenly in a crisscross pattern.

Adjusting the gearshift linkage ▱▱▱ 25 min–1½ hr

Adjustments of the gearshift linkage are seldom necessary unless the transmission has been moved in some way or the linkage rods have been bent out of position. Badly damaged linkage rods should be replaced. If the car creeps forward or backward when the gearshift lever is placed in *Park* or *Neutral*, if there is a delay between movement of the shift lever and the engagement of any gear, if the car will not start in *Park* and *Neutral*, or if the transmission does not lock when the shift lever is placed in *Park*, the gearshift linkage is probably out of adjustment. Test the linkage by moving the shift lever slowly until it clicks into *Park*, then try to start the engine. The starter should operate and the car should start. Turn the ignition off and repeat the procedure, this time moving the lever until it clicks into *Neutral*. The

starter should operate with the transmission in this position as well. If the starter does not operate in *Park* and *Neutral*, or if it operates in any gear except these two, the linkage or the *Neutral start* switch may be at fault. First check the *Neutral start* switch (pp.369–370). If the switch is OK, the transmission should be adjusted according to the car manufacturer's instructions for that specific type of transmission and linkage. Confine your adjustments only to the linkage that controls the action of the gearshift lever. Carmaker's service manuals refer to this assembly as the *manual linkage*. Many automatic transmissions have an additional linkage assembly, which operates according to engine vacuum and is attached to the carburetor. Adjustment of this assembly, called the *throttle valve linkage* (or *T.V.*

linkage) is best left to a professional transmission specialist, since the slightest error can cause the transmission to malfunction and result in rapid and extensive internal damage that will require a transmission overhaul.

Even though adjusting the gearshift linkage is not part of routine engine maintenance, regular lubrication of the assembly will help to avoid mechanical failure. The parts of the linkage that need periodic lubrication are those that rub against each other; these are usually obvious upon visual inspection. When lubricating linkage parts, wipe the joint area with a cloth to remove dirt and old grease. Then apply a moderate amount—about a fingerful—of fresh multi-purpose grease, enough to lubricate the pieces and to protect them from rust and abrasive grit.

Common linkage assemblies

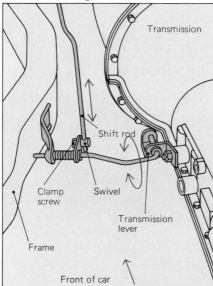

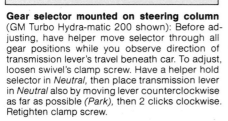

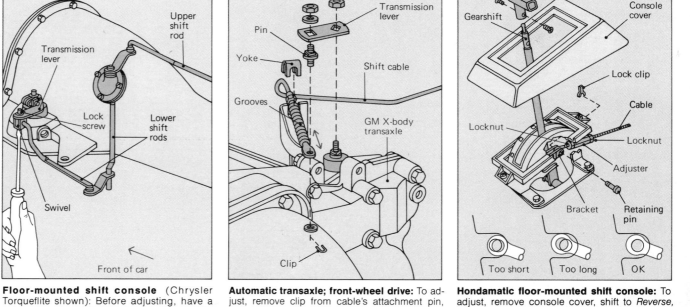

Gear selector mounted on steering column (GM Turbo Hydra-matic 200 shown): Before adjusting, have a helper move selector through all gear positions while you observe direction of transmission lever's travel beneath car. To adjust, loosen swivel's clamp screw. Have a helper hold selector in *Neutral*, then place transmission lever in *Neutral* also by moving lever counterclockwise as far as possible (*Park*), then 2 clicks clockwise. Retighten clamp screw.

Floor-mounted shift console (Chrysler Torqueflite shown): Before adjusting, have a helper move gearshift through all positions while you observe direction of transmission lever's travel beneath the car. To adjust, loosen swivel's lock screw, place gearshift in *Park*, then position transmission lever in *Park* also by moving it all the way to the rear. Tighten swivel's lock screw, making sure that no load is applied to the linkage in either direction as the screw is tightened.

Automatic transaxle; front-wheel drive: To adjust, remove clip from cable's attachment pin, then detach cable. Shift steering column selector into *Neutral*, then position transmission lever in *Neutral* also by moving lever clockwise as far as possible (*Low*), then counterclockwise 4 clicks. Reattach cable to its pin. Eliminate free play in the cable by repositioning yoke in grooves of cable housing. On Omnis, loosen swivel's lock bolt, place selector and lever in *Park*, retighten bolt.

Hondamatic floor-mounted shift console: To adjust, remove console cover, shift to *Reverse*, then remove lock clip and retaining pin from cable end. Loosen locknuts and turn adjuster until hole at end of cable is aligned with holes in bracket of selector arm. Reinstall cable, retaining pin, and lock clip. If resistance is felt as pin is reinstalled, cable is still out of adjustment, and adjuster must be turned farther. Tighten locknuts and reinstall console cover.

Maintaining the gearshift linkage 🖐️🖐️ 20–40 min

The components of the gearshift linkage in manual transmissions should be inspected and lubricated regularly as part of a car's normal maintenance routine. For efficiency, the job may be performed at the same time as the periodic lubrication of the steering and suspension (see pp.191–192). Use fresh multi-purpose grease and apply it to all swivel points in the shift linkage after first wiping away any road dirt and old grease.

Adjust the linkage whenever looseness or free play can be detected. You should not be able to wiggle the shift rods back and forth nor feel any lost motion in the gearshift when you shift from one gear to another. Inspect the shift linkage for worn parts and replace any damaged components, especially threaded fasteners that cannot be tightened. Many American-built manual transmissions have a lockrod to prevent the gearshift from moving out of *Reverse* when the car's ignition switch is in the *Off* or *Lock* position. Adjusting the linkage usually involves a separate adjustment of the lockrod. Some domestic cars and most imported cars (except Hondas and some VWs) have shift linkages mounted inside the transmission. These cannot be serviced.

Column-mounted linkage

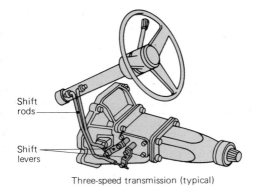

Three-speed transmission (typical)

Floor-shift linkage

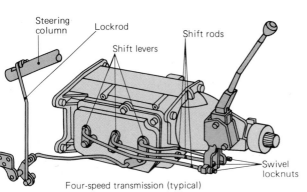

Four-speed transmission (typical)

Small GM front-drive cars

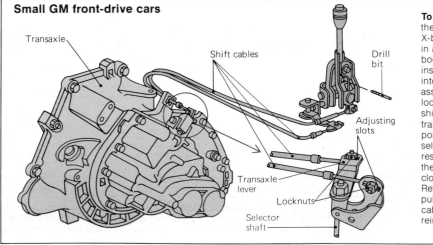

To adjust manual shift linkage on the Citation and other GM J- and X-body cars, first place shift lever in *First* gear, then remove console boot. Lock gearshift in place by inserting a 5/32-in. drill bit into alignment holes in shifter assembly body. Next, loosen the locknuts on each of the two shifter cables. Make sure that transaxle lever is correctly positioned in *First* gear by pushing selector shaft inward until spring resistance is felt, then rotating the transaxle lever counter-clockwise as far as possible. Retighten locknuts while lightly pulling on shift lever to remove cable free play. Remove drill bit, reinstall boot, road-test car.

Adjusting the shift linkage

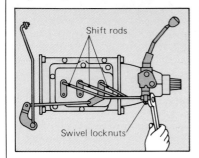

1. Linkage adjustment for three- and four-speed column-mounted or floor shift linkages is basically the same. First place ignition switch in *Off* but unlocked position. Raise car if necessary, then use wrench to loosen swivel locknuts located on shift rods.

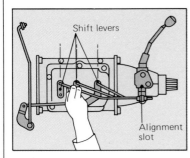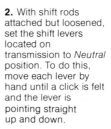

2. With shift rods attached but loosened, set the shift levers located on transmission to *Neutral* position. To do this, move each lever by hand until a click is felt and the lever is pointing straight up and down.

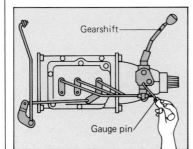

3. Place gearshift in *Neutral,* then lock in position by inserting homemade gauge pin—a punch or drill bit of appropriate diameter—into the alignment slot on the shifter assembly. Eliminate free play from shift rods, then retighten locknuts on swivels.

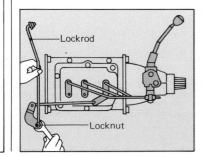

4. Remove gauge pin. Place gearshift in *Reverse,* then loosen locknut on lockrod. Pull rod down to eliminate free play, then retighten locknut. Check that ignition switch moves freely and that all gears shift smoothly.

Maintenance / **Clutches**

Adjusting the clutch linkage 🕐🕐 30–45 min

To avoid early clutch failure, the operating linkage of the clutch should be checked and adjusted periodically. This is often incorrectly called *adjusting the clutch*. Some cars have automatic linkage adjusters. Checks for correct free play in the clutch linkage are required at intervals of 3,000 to 12,000 miles (5,000 to 20,000 km) or every six months, depending on the car. If the clutch slips or the transmission is hard to shift even when the pedal is pressed all the way to the floor, an adjustment is overdue and the clutch may already be damaged. The most common adjustment restores free play in the clutch linkage so that the clutch can engage fully. If this adjustment is not made, the clutch will soon slip and wear itself out.

A slipping clutch can be felt when the engine seems to race but the car does not respond accordingly while accelerating or climbing hills. In severe cases the driver can smell overheated friction material, and the engine may fail to move the car in any gear. If this occurs, it may be possible to restore normal operation by adjusting the clutch linkage, but it is more likely that the clutch will have to be replaced—a job for a professional mechanic.

The clutch pedal should have approximately 1 inch of free play. This is most easily determined by operating the clutch pedal with your hand. For the first inch of pedal movement, you should be able to depress the pedal much more easily than for the final few inches of movement.

If no difference in pressure is required to depress the pedal all the way to the floor, either the linkage needs adjustment or the clutch pedal's return spring is broken or disconnected. To check the return spring (except on Ford vehicles from 1979 onward), lift the pedal. If it flips freely up and down, the return spring has probably broken or come unhooked. The return spring may be connected to the clutch pedal or to the clutch-operating fork. Some cars have a return spring and a linkage tension spring working against one another. On 1979 and later Ford vehicles, check free play by lifting the clutch pedal (see p.208).

There are three types of clutch linkage: rods, cables, and hydraulic systems. Adjustments are usually made between the engine and transmission, where the clutch-operating fork protrudes from the clutch housing. On rear-wheel-drive cars, this is under the car, usually on the driver's side. On front-drive models, adjustments can often be made in the engine compartment without jacking up the car.

The adjusting mechanism varies from one car make to another. Sometimes a tension spring must be removed temporarily to make the adjustment. In some cases you can measure free play at the linkage, using a feeler gauge or ruler, instead of having to go back inside the car to check free play at the pedal.

If in doubt about how to adjust the clutch on your car, unlock the adjuster, turn it a few times in one direction, and check pedal play. If play has increased, you are turning the adjuster the right way; if play has decreased, turn the adjuster in the opposite direction. If there is too much play, the clutch will not disengage fully and the gears will not shift smoothly.

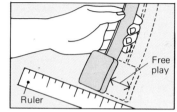

To measure clutch play, hold a ruler beside the pedal and move the pedal by hand. Free play is the first inch or so of movement before resistance increases noticeably. In Ford cars, measure play with the engine running.

Hydraulic clutches

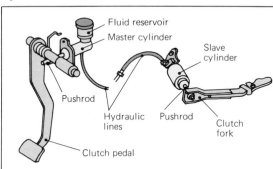

Clutch pedals move a pushrod and piston in a master cylinder to develop hydraulic pressure. Rigid or flexible lines convey this pressure to a slave cylinder mounted on the clutch housing. The piston and pushrod of the slave cylinder move the clutch-release fork to operate the clutch. Separate adjustments on many cars control height of pedal and length of pushrod.
Tools: 1-ft ruler, two open-end wrenches to fit adjusting and locking nuts, locking pliers, bleeder hose and jar.
Materials: Penetrating oil, brake fluid.

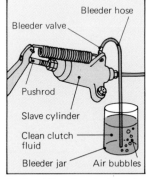

1. Bleed the air out of the hydraulic system first. The procedure is similar to bleeding hydraulic brakes (see p.217). Use a length of tubing in a jar of brake fluid, and have a helper depress the clutch pedal while you open and close the bleeder valve on the slave cylinder until no more bubbles appear.

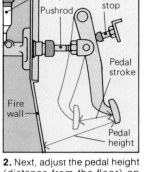

2. Next, adjust the pedal height (distance from the floor) on cars with provisions for this adjustment. Correct pedal height is listed in most owner's manuals. Open the locknut and adjust the rubber stop until the pedal height is within ⅜ in. of specifications. Then tighten the locknut while holding the stop.

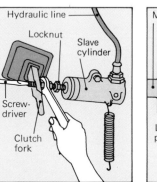

3. Adjust free play by shortening or lengthening the pushrod on the master cylinder or slave cylinder. Pushrod may be a threaded rod with an adjusting nut, or it may consist of two parts that screw together. A locknut holds length adjustment. Clearance may be specified at clutch fork or pedal.

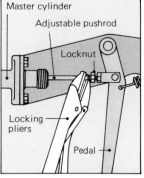

4. Loosen locknut, hold rod with locking pliers, turn adjusting nut until clearance or pedal play is correct. Tighten locknut. Some pushrods are slotted so that they can be held with a screwdriver (see Step 3). **Caution:** Do not use screwdriver to turn the pushrod; the rod may bend.

Adjusting cable-operated clutch linkages 15–30 min

Clutch-operating cables slide inside guide tubes. Adjustments are made by screwing an adjusting nut in or out of a threaded fitting at one end of the cable. Locking devices hold the adjustment. Adjusters may be found at the pedal or at the clutch's operating fork. Rear-drive cars must be raised (p.176) to get at fork adjusters on the clutch housing. Front-drive cars can be adjusted from under the hood, as can rear-drive cars with adjusters on the fire wall.

Approximately 1 inch (2.5 cm) of pedal free play is commonly required, but a smaller clearance can be measured more conveniently with a feeler gauge at the adjuster. On many Ford models from 1979 onward, free play is measured by lifting the pedal. On most earlier Ford cars, free play is measured by depressing the pedal while the engine is running.

Tools: 1-ft ruler, open-end wrenches to fit adjusting and locking nuts, locking pliers, feeler gauge.
Material: Penetrating oil.

Typical cable-operated clutch

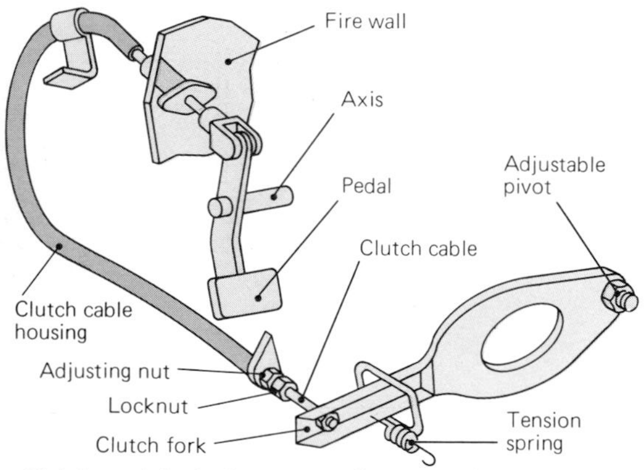

Clutch pedal pivots on an off-center axis to pull on clutch-operating cable. Because it is difficult to reach up under the dash, adjustments are rarely made where the cable is attached to the pedal. Most cable-operated clutches are adjusted at the clutch fork or fire wall. On rear-drive cars the fork is underneath the car, usually on the driver's side of the clutch housing. On most front-drive cars the clutch fork is under the hood, toward the front of the car. Locking mechanisms vary from car to car. See the specific instructions for your car.

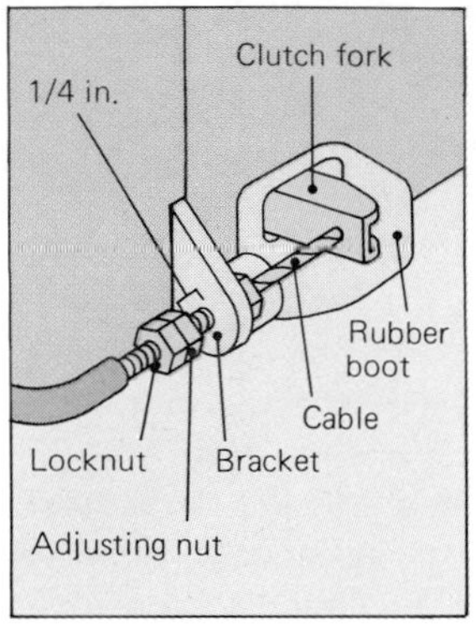

Ford Pinto and Mercury Bobcat: Pull back rubber boot (if any) from clutch fork on lower left side of clutch housing. Loosen locknut. Pull cable forward until you feel resistance. Gap between bracket and adjusting nut should be ¼ in. If it is not, turn adjusting nut until it is ¼ in. from bracket. Release cable and tighten locknut. Reposition rubber boot.

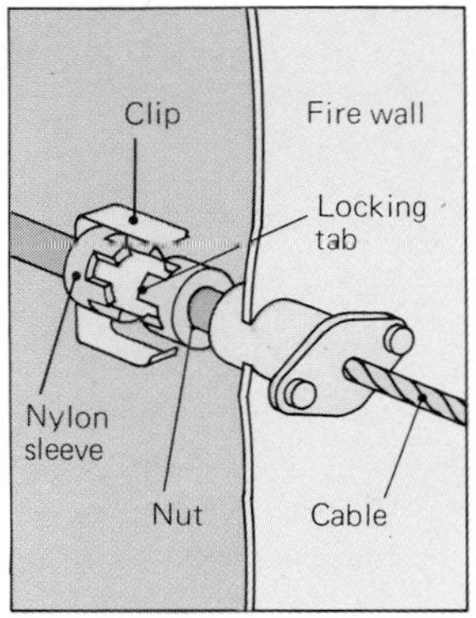

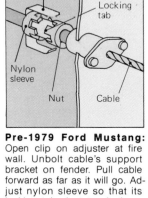

Pre-1979 Ford Mustang: Open clip on adjuster at fire wall. Unbolt cable's support bracket on fender. Pull cable forward as far as it will go. Adjust nylon sleeve so that its locking tabs just touch those on nut. Turn sleeve either way to align tabs and slots, then release cable. Refit clip and bracket. Check for 1 in. pedal clearance with a ruler.

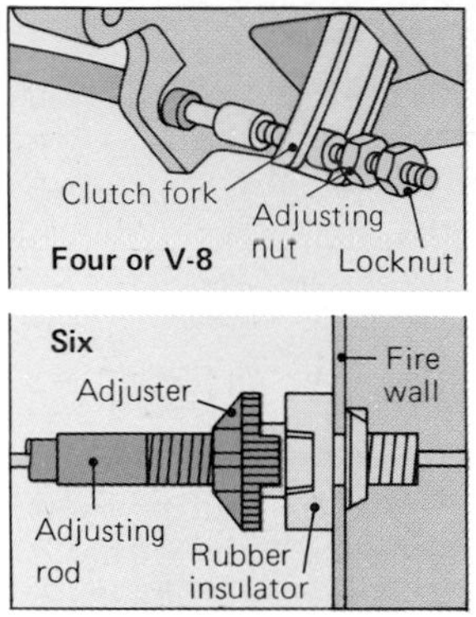

Ford Fairmont and Mustang, Mercury Zephyr and Capri from 1979 onward: Lift pedal to check play—2¾ in. with four- and six-cylinder engines, 1½ in. with V-8s. Six cylinder's adjuster is similar to that on pre-1979 Mustangs. Four-cylinder and V-8 adjusters are similar to Pinto's. Turn adjuster until pedal travel is 6½ in. on V-8s, 5¼ in. on other engines.

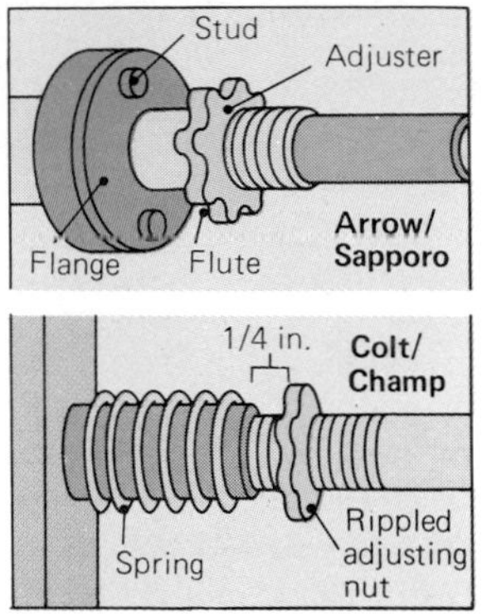

Dodge Colt, Plymouth Champ front-drive car clutches are adjusted at the fire wall. Pull on cable, and turn rippled adjusting nut until clearance is ¼ in. at the nut, 1 in. at the pedal. On rear-drive Colt, Arrow, Challenger, and Sapporo cars, pull on cable and turn fluted adjuster to give ⅛ in. clearance at the adjusting nut and 5½ to 6 in. pedal travel.

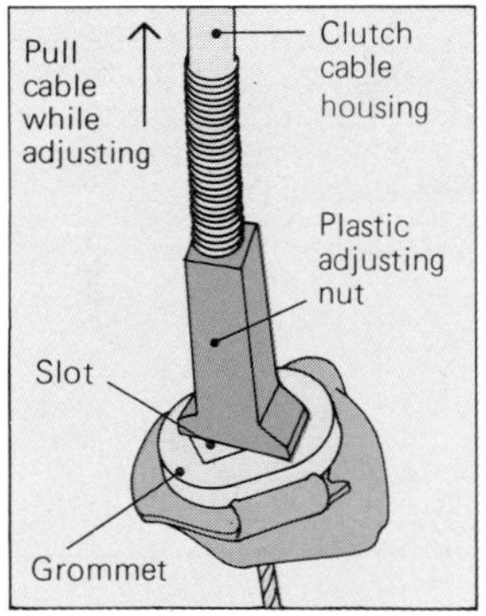

Dodge Omni, Plymouth Horizon front-drive cars have an adjuster that requires no measuring. Pull out cable at transmission until plastic adjusting nut comes out of its recess in the grommet. Turn adjusting nut until it touches the top surface of the grommet. Turn nut the shortest distance to line up with slot in grommet. Release cable to reseat nut in slot.

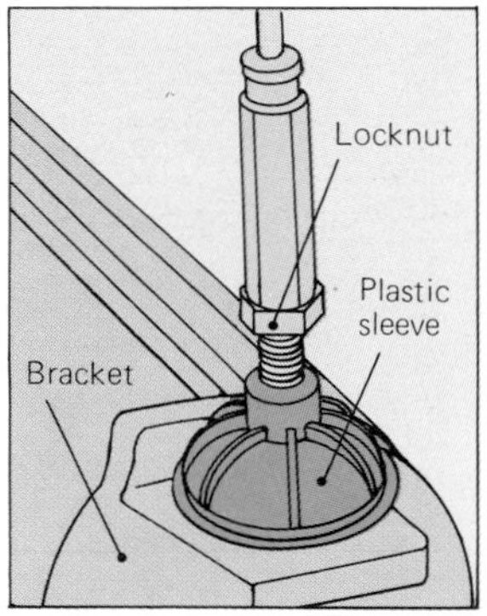

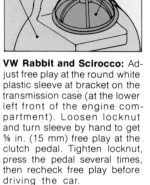

VW Rabbit and Scirocco: Adjust free play at the round white plastic sleeve at bracket on the transmission case (at the lower left front of the engine compartment). Loosen locknut and turn sleeve by hand to get ⅝ in. (15 mm) free play at the clutch pedal. Tighten locknut, press the pedal several times, then recheck free play before driving the car.

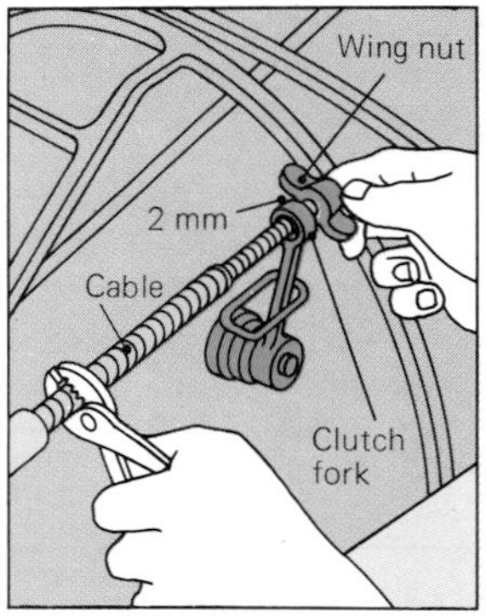

Air-cooled VWs: Raise car (see p.176). Remove left rear wheel and heater hose. Adjust cable at clutch fork on upper left side of transmission. Reach up past axle, and grasp clutch cable with pliers to prevent twisting. Turn wing nut until free play between nut and lever is 2 mm (1/16 in.). Pedal play must be 3/4 to 3/8 in. Turn nut horizontal; seat it in slot in lever.

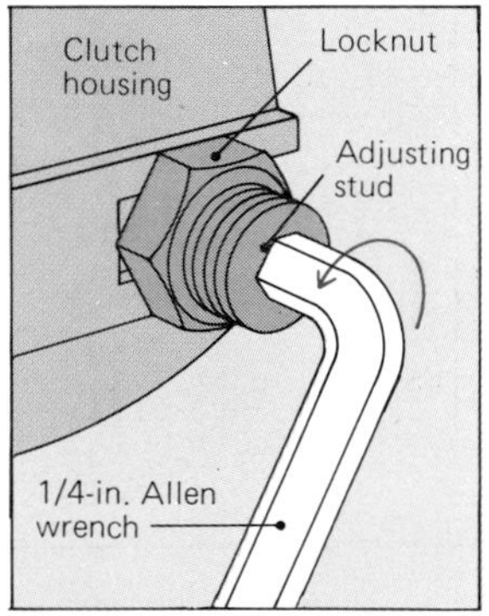

Vega: Raise car (see p.176). Free-play adjustment is made at the clutch fork's pivot point, on passenger's side of clutch housing. Remove dust cap (if any) and loosen locknut. Turn socket-head adjusting stud with a ¼-in. Allen wrench until pedal play measures 1 in. Hold adjusting stud while tightening locknut. Recheck play, then replace dust cap (if any).

Adjusting rod-operated clutches ⚙⚙ 15–30 min

Rod-operated clutches push on levers instead of pulling on a cable to move the clutch fork. These systems are usually found on larger and older cars that require a strong linkage to compress heavy-duty clutch springs. All common rod linkages adjust by a threaded rod that is secured by one or two adjusting or locking nuts. The adjustment is made at the clutch housing, under the car on the driver's side. Free play is measured with a ruler, and should be 1 to 2 inches at the clutch pedal.

First, measure the free play at the pedal and, if it is insufficient, raise the front of the car and support it safely (see p.176). Spray the locking and adjusting nuts with penetrating oil and clean off road dirt before attempting to make the adjustment. When clearance is correct, lock the adjuster.

Tools: 1-ft ruler, two open-end wrenches to fit locking and adjusting nuts, locking pliers.
Materials: Penetrating oil, rags.

Typical rod-operated clutch

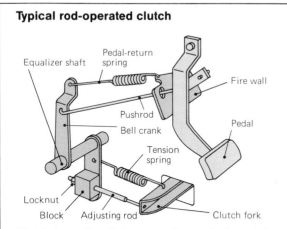

Clutch-operating linkages push on a bell crank to transfer pressure through pushrods to the clutch-operating fork. Adjustments are usually made in the threaded rod that connects the bell crank to the clutch fork in order to maintain from 1 to 2 in. of free play at the clutch pedal. On 1979 and later Ford vehicles, measure clearance by lifting up on the pedal when the engine is idling. On other cars, measure free play (p.207) with the engine off. Sometimes, working clearance is specified at the clutch fork, although pedal's free play is what counts.

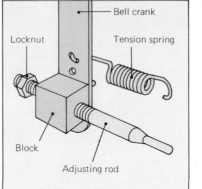

Older GM V-8s with rear drive: Unhook the tension spring and loosen the locknut on the front of the adjusting rod. Screw the adjusting rod into the block on the bell crank to increase clearance or out of the block to decrease clearance. Check pedal's free play, which should be 1 to 2 in. When free play is correct, hold rod with locking pliers to keep it from rotating, and tighten locknut. Recheck pedal play to make sure that it has not changed.

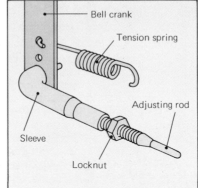

Older GM six-cylinder in-line and V-6 engines in rear-drive cars are adjusted in much the same way as the V-8s, but the adjusting rod screws into a sleeve that pivots on the bell crank instead of screwing into a block. Loosen the locknut on the adjusting rod, and screw the rod into the sleeve to increase pedal play. Check for 1 in. free play at pedal, then hold rod with locking pliers to keep it from rotating, and tighten locknut. Recheck pedal play.

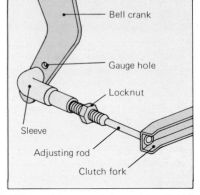

GM rear-drive cars: Late models with V-8, V-6, or in-line six-cylinder engines have a gauge hole in the bell crank just above the adjusting block or sleeve. Loosen locknut. Remove block or sleeve from fork by pulling out retaining clip. Move pivot pin's block or sleeve to gauge hole, and adjust rod so that there is no free play. Grip adjusting rod with locking pliers so that it cannot turn, and tighten locknut. Then reinstall block or sleeve in lower hole.

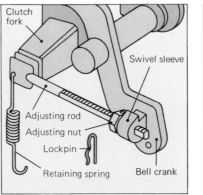

Ford Monarch, Granada: Disconnect clutch's retaining spring from clutch fork, remove lockpin from rod, and loosen adjusting nut. Move fork rearward to take up any free play. Slide rod to seat in fork pocket. Insert .136-in. (9/64-in., or 3.5-mm) spacer or an equivalent stack of feeler gauges between adjusting nut and swivel sleeve. Tighten adjusting nut. Reinstall lockpin and retaining spring. Depress pedal five times. Recheck clearance.

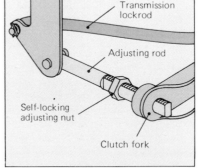

Chrysler cars: Rear-drive cars may have a clutch-transmission lockrod. If so, disconnect it at the transmission end. Adjust linkage by turning the self-locking adjusting nut to get 5/32 in. (4 mm) free movement at the clutch fork, which will produce 1 in. free play at the pedal. Check free play (p.207) with the engine off. When pedal play is correct, reinstall the lockrod on the transmission. Operate the clutch several times and recheck play.

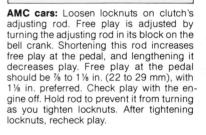

AMC cars: Loosen locknuts on clutch's adjusting rod. Free play is adjusted by turning the adjusting rod in its block on the bell crank. Shortening this rod increases free play at the pedal, and lengthening it decreases play. Free play at the pedal should be 7/8 to 1 1/8 in. (22 to 29 mm), with 1 1/8 in. preferred. Check play with the engine off. Hold rod to prevent it from turning as you tighten locknuts. After tightening locknuts, recheck play.

Inspecting brake systems

Checking and maintaining your car's brakes need not be intimidating, even if you are not an experienced do-it-yourself mechanic. Although they are of vital importance, and some designs do look complicated, brakes are normally maintained by relatively inexperienced personnel. In fact, in many shops, apprentices do a majority of the brake repairs.

The friction material used in brake linings wears away while the brakes slow or stop a car. The kind and rate of wear depends on the lining material, the disc or drum design, and the driving habits of the car's operators. Maintaining passenger car brakes yourself involves three procedures: inspecting them for damage and wear, replacing linings (which are designed to wear and be replaced), and—rarely—the complete overhaul or replacement of parts that fail.

Any car owner can and should inspect his brakes to make sure that the linings are not wearing prematurely and that there are no other signs of incipient failure. Most brake problems develop gradually and can be detected before they become serious by inspecting the system. Brakes can often be inspected by just removing a wheel.

Most lining replacements, especially the first time the job is required, simply involve removing a few mechanical parts, replacing the worn brake shoes or pads, then reassembling the parts.

If more extensive work is required, you can handle the job in exactly the same way most service stations do: you can farm out the portions of the job you do not want to do yourself. For example, if the drums or discs require resurfacing, you can take them to a local machine shop, which has the tools to do the job. The cost can be surprisingly low for such jobs as lathe-cutting brake discs or drums and grinding replacement shoes to match the new drum size exactly.

Replacing a leaking brake hose or hydraulic cylinder is a straight nuts-and-bolts job. Bleeding the brakes afterward to expel air from the system is usually a two-man job but not at all difficult to do.

Generally, brake power-boost systems either work or they fail completely. If the vacuum or hydraulic systems that produce the power are connected and not leaking, repair is a matter of removing the power booster, exchanging it for a new or rebuilt one, and reinstalling it in the car. This is a straightforward job.

Here, in the *Maintenance* section, you will see how to inspect brakes for wear without taking them apart, in systems that allow for this, and how to check out brakes that do require some disassembly. Most disc- and some drum-brake systems can be inspected for lining wear simply by removing the wheel from the brake being checked.

At least once a year it makes sense to remove the drum to check the shoes. Such inspections make it easy to tell how much useful life is left in the brake linings so that you can replace them when the time comes, but not before. Having checked out the brakes yourself, you can have confidence in their safety, efficiency, and condition.

Brake fluid reservoir

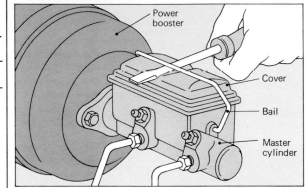

The brake fluid reservoir on many North American autos is an aluminum or iron casting with a stamped-metal cover secured by a spring bail. To check fluid level, pry bail aside.

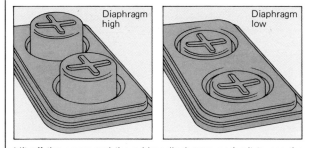

Lift off the cover and the rubber diaphragm under it to see the brake fluid. Diaphragm moves up and down as fluid is pumped into or out of the reservoir so that moisture in the air cannot reach fluid.

Checking for hydraulic leaks ⏱ 5–10 min

As long as they remain sound, hydraulic brake systems rarely, if ever, require the addition of brake fluid. Sometimes, wear in disc-brake pads makes the system appear to be losing fluid. Fluid is transferred from the master cylinder to the brake calipers as the pads wear and move closer to the discs; what is really required in such a case is new pads, not more fluid. Check the fluid level at least once a month.

The first test you should make of the brake system is to apply the brake with the engine off and the transmission in *Neutral*. On cars equipped with power brakes, start the engine; the brake pedal should move down slightly under the pressure of your foot as the power-boost system accumulates vacuum or hydraulic power. The pedal should not move more than halfway to the floor, and it should hold firm under your foot for at least 30 seconds. If the pedal is not firm, there is air in the system. If the pedal sinks slowly to the floor, there is an internal or external fluid leak (see opposite page).

To check the hydraulic fluid level, first find the brakes' master cylinder. In most cars it is under the hood where the pedal linkage comes through the fire wall. On some cars the fluid reservoir is translucent, which allows you to see the level without removing the top. For cars with opaque reservoirs, see illustrations at right. Because brake fluid absorbs moisture, which can corrode parts of the hydraulic system, it is a wise precaution to replace the fluid every two or three years or whenever it becomes discolored.

Caution: Brake fluid softens paint. Wash off spills

Fill reservoir to *Full* mark or to within ½ in. of the top, using only new brake fluid marked DoT 3 or DoT 4. Do not overfill front section if disc-brake pads are worn (low fluid level is normal).

Checking lines and hoses ⏱ 10–20 min

Hydraulic leaks can be internal, where they do not show, or external, where they are usually obvious. There is a leak if the brake fluid level is low but disc-brake pads have not worn excessively, or if the dashboard warning light comes on to indicate a loss of pressure in part of the braking system when the brakes are applied. You must find and repair the leak immediately or have the job done by a mechanic.

External leaks from the master cylinder show up at the pipes around the cylinder, at the seal where the operating rod goes through the power booster, or inside the vacuum hose to the power booster.

With the car supported safely (see p.176), examine the flexible hose at each front wheel and check the brake caliper where the hose screws into it. Do the same at each rear wheel, paying special attention to the bottom of the backing plate. If in doubt, remove the rear drum to look for leaks around the wheel cylinder. A leaky connection may be cured by tightening the affected parts, but leaks in the caliper, cylinder, or hose fitting usually call for replacing these components with new or rebuilt parts.

Internal leaks, in which fluid leaks past one of the pistons, seals, or valves, can be detected by applying continued pressure to the brake pedal for 30 seconds with the engine running. If the pedal sinks slowly to the floor without loss of fluid from the reservoir, the fluid is leaking past the pistons and seals in the master cylinder. The repair is to replace or rebuild the master cylinder (see pp.341–343).

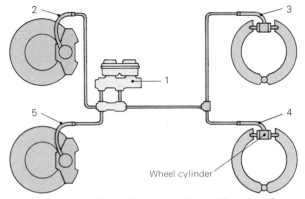

1. Look for leaks starting at the master cylinder (1), and flex hoses at each wheel (2,3,4,5). Raise car and check lines for oily dampness or darkened road dirt that might indicate a leak. Dampness on backing plates or calipers may mean a leaky wheel cylinder or caliper, a defective hose connection, or a loose bleeder valve.

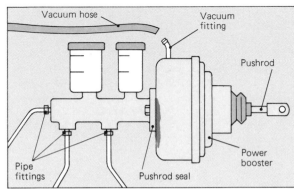

2. Master cylinder leaks are usually internal, but if fluid is being lost, check pipe fittings and pushrod seal. Also examine the inside of the vacuum hose from the intake manifold to the power booster; brake fluid in the hose indicates a leaking power booster. A leaking cylinder or booster should be replaced.

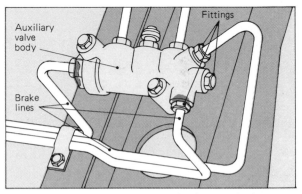

3. Auxiliary valves in the brake system (such as rear brake proportioning valves) may leak or have leaky fittings. Follow the metal brake lines to the valve and then check each fitting carefully for signs of wetness or the smell of brake fluid. If tightening the fitting does not stop the leak, replace the valve.

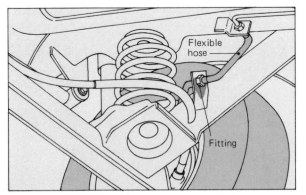

4. Flexible hoses last a long time, but they may crack with age, soften due to rot, or be damaged by stones and debris. Look along the hose and at its fittings for darkened dirt sticking to small leaks, or oily wetness from larger ones. If the hose is mushy or brittle, or if you find any signs of leakage, replace the hose.

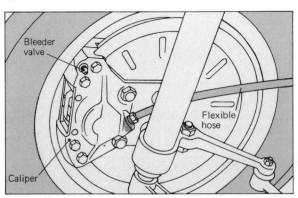

5. Calipers on disc brakes may leak where the flexible hose is screwed in, at the bleeder valve, or around the piston. Tighten leaking bleeder valves or fittings. Replace hoses that are mushy, brittle, or leaking. If a caliper has a leaking piston, replace with a new or rebuilt caliper.

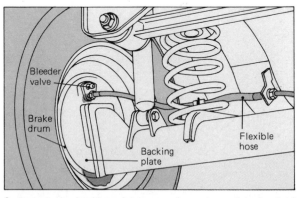

6. Drum-brake backing plates may show signs of brake fluid leakage where the wheel cylinder is mounted, at hose connections, or near bleeder valves. If the leak is serious, you will find fluid at the bottom of the plate or around the edge of the drum. Tighten fittings; if leak does not stop, replace defective parts.

Inspecting brakes without disassembly ⧉⧉ 30–45 min

Once the wheel of a car has been removed, its disc brake is out in the open and can easily be inspected. Drum brakes are enclosed, so that checking their condition on most cars is more difficult. Some drum brakes have inspection holes that enable you to check brake lining wear without removing the drum. In other drum designs, brake inspection is simplified because the drum lifts off relatively easily.

When examining a disc brake visually, make sure that the wear surface on both sides of the disc is smooth, with only light scores. Also check to see that the hydraulic cylinder in the caliper is not leaking, and inspect the pads for thickness and even wear.

Drum brakes may have inspection holes in either the drum or the backing plate. Look for a hole or a rubber plug near the edge of the drum. Sometimes there is a knockout plug, like those seen in an electrical wiring box, in the backing plate. It plugs an adjustment hole, not an inspection opening.

Brake linings wear down with use. New or unworn disc-brake pads are usually between $3/8$ and $1/2$ inch thick. They should be replaced when they wear down to $1/16$ inch. The linings on drum brakes are about $3/16$ inch thick. If the linings are riveted to the shoes, replace the shoes when the lining wears down to $1/32$ inch of the rivet heads. If the linings are bonded to the shoes, they can wear down to $1/16$ inch.

Inspecting drum brakes

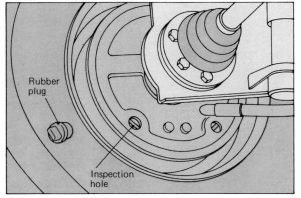

Inspection hole in drum-brake backing plate should have a rubber plug in it. Remove the plug with pliers to check lining thickness visually. Reinstall plug. Replace any missing plugs.

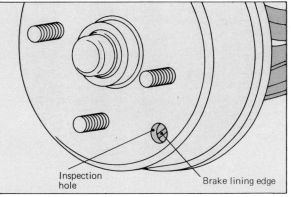

Hole in brake drum near the outer edge lets you see the lining where it meets the rubbing surface of the drum. By turning the drum, you can check the entire lining for thickness and even wear.

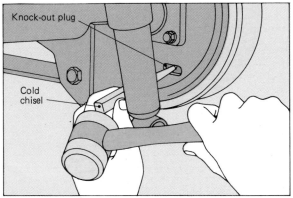

Knock-out plug near center of backing plate makes it possible to back off self-adjusting brakes by hand if necessary to free drums for easier removal. Remove knocked-out plugs that fall into drum.

Inspecting disc brakes

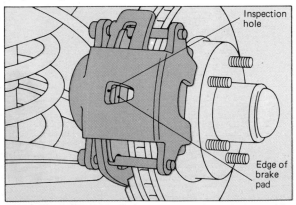

Disc-brake calipers usually have an inspection hole that enables you to see lining thickness of at least one pad without disassembling the brake. Minimum pad thickness should be $1/16$ in.

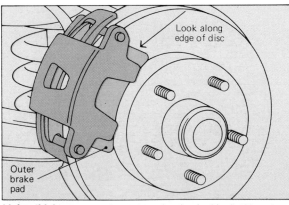

Lining thickness on outer pad can be checked by looking along the side of the disc to see the edge of the pad. The lining thickness should be more than $1/16$ in. at both ends of each pad.

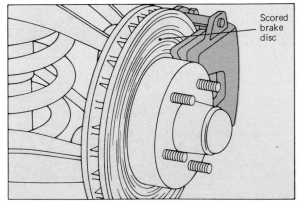

Rubbing surface of disc should be smooth and have no deep scores or ridges. Obvious surface wear that gives the disc an I-shaped cross section calls for a professional check.

Removing the wheel bearings ☑☑☑ 1½–3 hr

Working on the brakes will eventually involve removing a wheel bearing. The drums on many freerolling wheels are cast in one piece with the hub. You must first remove the wheel bearing in order to get such a drum off the spindle. To remove the bearing, first remove the wheel and pry off the dust cap. Next, remove the adjusting nut retainer and the adjusting nut lock, unscrew the adjusting nut, and pull off the drum and bearings. (Instructions for reinstalling and adjusting wheel bearings are on pages 219–220.)

Tools: Water-pump pliers, side cutter pliers, lug wrench, large screwdriver.

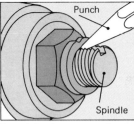

1. A wheel with an integral hub and drum is mounted on a spindle. The most common bearing retainer has a stamped-metal nut lock with a cotter pin to secure the bearing adjusting nut.

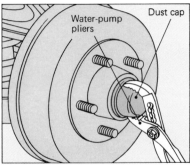

2. Dust cap is driven into the hub. You can often simply pull it off with water-pump pliers, pry it out with a screwdriver, or use a special dust cap puller.

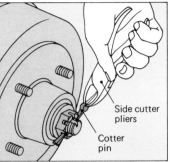

3. A cotter pin usually keeps the wheel bearing adjusting nut from unscrewing. Pull the pin out with side cutter pliers, and unscrew the adjusting nut.

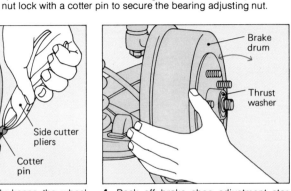

4. Back off brake shoe adjustment star wheel far enough to free the drum (see p.216). Rock drum back and forth to push out thrust washer and outer bearing race.

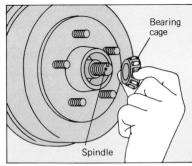

5. Catch thrust washer, inner race, and bearing cage if they pop off spindle when drum is rocked. Otherwise, slide these parts off the spindle.

6. Pull brake drum containing inner bearing and grease seal off spindle (if drum sticks, see p.214). **Caution:** Do not breathe brake dust; it may contain asbestos.

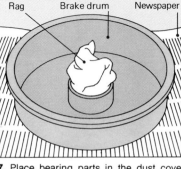

7. Place bearing parts in the dust cover. Stuff a clean rag or paper towel in the hub, and place the drum on clean newspaper to keep abrasive brake dust out of bearings.

Other adjusting nut retainers

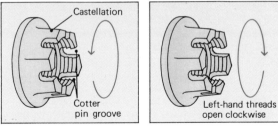

Castellated nut (left) is secured like the more common nut lock, but it allows less precise adjustment. Adjusting nuts on driver's side may have left-hand threads; turn clockwise to remove.

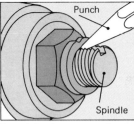

Round dimple secures wheel nut on some French imports. Free it by driving a punch or nail up the groove in the spindle.

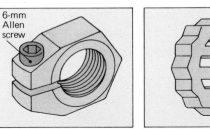

Loosen nut on old VWs and Mercedes with 6-mm Allen wrench, then unscrew nut. Newer models have stamped-metal nut lock.

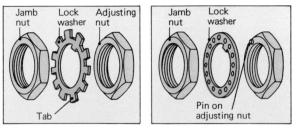

Older VWs have two nuts jammed together over a lock washer. Later version has pin in hole (right). Earlier version has tabs bent against nut flats; unbend tabs to loosen nuts.

Removing drums ▢▢▢ 30 min–1½ hr

Brake drums on drive wheels can be the easiest type to remove or the hardest, depending on their design. If the drum and the hub are separate and have not rusted together, the drum may fall off in your hands when you take off the wheel. Integral drums and hubs, on the other hand, are secured to axle shafts by large nuts, and removing them usually calls for out-size wrenches, brute force, and special pullers.

Some drums, such as those on the rear wheels of most rear-drive North American cars, are so simple to remove that it is practical to make a complete drum-brake inspection every six months. The first time you do this on a new car, you may have to clip off the sheet-metal speednuts that kept the drum from dropping off on the production line.

Integral drums and hubs, or separate ones that are pressed together, are hard to remove. If the drum is a close fit on a shoulder on the end of the axle shaft flange or on a separate hub, it may rust on. Integral drums and hubs often stick over tight-fitting splines or tapered axle ends even after the large retaining nut has been removed. A ¾-inch-drive breaker bar and a special socket are often needed to unscrew the oversized hub nuts on some imported cars. You may have to stand on the wrench or use a long pipe on the bar to work a stubborn hub nut loose.

Once the nut is off, tap the drum with a soft-faced hammer, pry carefully between the drum and the backing plate with screwdrivers, or use a special puller to remove the drum from the axle.

Separate hub and drum

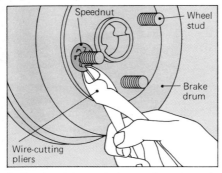

1. Sheet-metal speednuts may have been installed on the production line to keep the drum from falling off before the wheels were mounted. Cut these off with wire-cutting pliers. When rusty, these retainers may be hard to see.

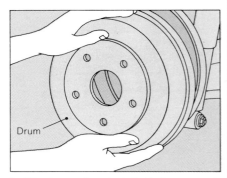

2. Wheel mounting studs hold drum on axle flange or separate hub. Once speednuts have been removed, the drum should lift right off the studs. If it sticks to the brake shoes, adjust the brake by hand to move shoes away from drum.

Integral hub and drum

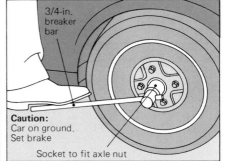

1. Axle nut on an integral drum and hub is usually more than 1 in. wide and torqued to several hundred lb-ft. Loosen it with a ¾-in.-drive socket. Stand on the drive bar if necessary, or use a pipe extender to increase leverage to free the nut.

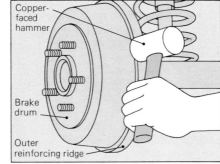

2. Tapping the ridge around the outer lip of the brake drum may slide it off the splines or the shoulder of the axle flange. Use a copper-faced hammer to avoid damaging the drum. If this does not work, use a drum puller (below).

How to remove stuck drums

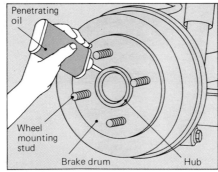

1. Apply penetrating oil around the wheel mounting studs and around the joint where the drum fits against the hub. Tap drum to set up vibrations that may loosen the rust bond. Several applications may be needed to free the drum.

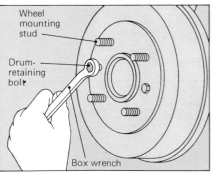

2. Some separate hub and drum assemblies may be held together by Phillips screws or flathead bolts, in addition to the force fit over the flange shoulder. Remove these retainers, which may be hidden under the wheel mounting studs.

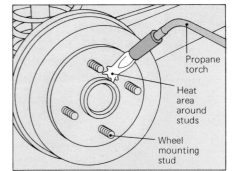

3. Heat from a propane torch applied around the wheel bolts may expand the drum enough to allow easier removal with hammer or puller. **Caution:** Do not heat aluminum drums; they may warp before they come loose.

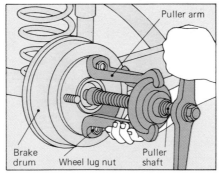

4. Universal drum puller works on all sizes of wheel bolt circles and imparts less shock to bearings than a hammer does. Fasten puller to brake drum with the wheel lug nuts. Tighten center shaft with a wrench to force drum off axle.

Inspecting drum brakes ◨◨◨ 10–20 min

Once the brake drum is off, take a close look at the drum and internal brake parts. To see signs of wear clearly, you must first clean both the drum and the brake mechanism. Mix hot water and liquid dishwashing detergent in a bucket, then dip a brush into this solution and use it to scrub the brake parts. Rinse parts with a garden hose. **Caution:** Avoid inhaling brake dust, which contains asbestos. Do not use a vacuum or compressed air to clean dirty brakes.

Examine the rubbing surface of the drum first. In a car with less than 20,000 miles on the odometer, the rubbing surface should be smoothly polished. Run a fingernail across the surface; it should feel fairly smooth, with no deep ridges or grooves. There should not be a noticeable ridge between the edges of the rubbing surface and the remainder of the drum.

If the drum seems all right, the shoes are wearing evenly from side to side, and there is no glazing of the lining, you can reinstall the drum if a safe amount of lining remains. Replace the shoes (pp.334–337) if they are at or near the wear limit. Riveted linings should not wear beyond 1/32 inch above any rivet. The wear limit for bonded linings is at least 1/16 inch above the brake shoe.

If the linings are uneven from end to end, they may have been ground to compensate for misaligned anchors. Or the springs may be weak, parts bent, or the shoes may be sticking. Uneven side-to-side wear indicates bell-mouthed drums. Have a brake shop check the drums to determine the cause.

1. Drop the drum, open side down, onto hard earth to knock out most of the dust. Wash drum out with a solution of dishwashing detergent and hot water. Rinse with water from a garden hose.

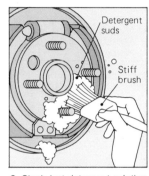

2. Slosh hot detergent solution over drum-brake mechanism, and scrub it with a stiff bristle brush before rinsing with clear water. Do not blow asbestos dust out of brake with a compressed-air hose.

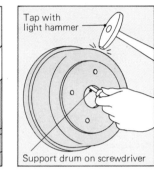

3. Inspect drum's rubbing surface, which should be smooth and unscored. Drag a fingernail across the wear area; nail should not catch on ridges. Surface should not be cracked or discolored.

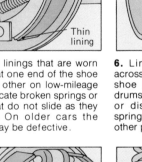

4. Tap drum with a light hammer to make it ring. A dull *thunk* means that drum may be cracked. Special measuring tools reveal bell mouthing, but you can probably spot the condition from lining wear.

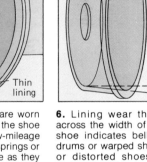

5. Brake linings that are worn thinner at one end of the shoe than the other on low-mileage cars indicate broken springs or parts that do not slide as they should. On older cars the shoes may be defective.

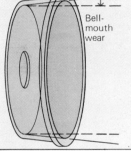

6. Lining wear that tapers across the width of the brake shoe indicates bell-mouthed drums or warped shoes. Worn or distorted shoes, broken springs, and binding parts are other possible causes.

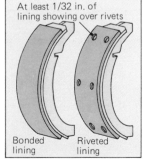

7. Lining thickness indicates brake wear. Bonded linings have no rivets; they should be replaced when they wear down to 1/16 in. thick. Replace riveted linings when they wear to within 1/32 in. of the rivet heads.

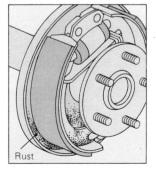

8. Heavily rusted internal brake parts and a buildup like dried mud mean that water is entering the brake. If car has not forded deep water, look for missing plugs in inspection hole or adjustment hole.

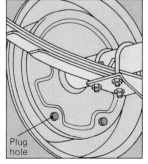

9. Inspection and adjustment access holes in brake backing plate are sealed with plugs. If stamped knockout plugs have been removed, holes should be replugged. Rubber replacement plugs are inexpensive.

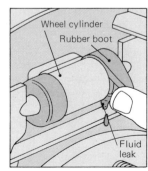

10. Check wheel cylinder for brake fluid leaks. Turn rubber boot back. A little dampness is acceptable, but fluid under the boot indicates a leaky cylinder that should be replaced. See pp.338–339.

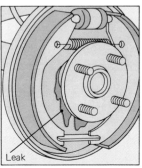

11. Examine the area around the wheel bearing for signs of leaking grease. Any obvious leak requires seal replacement, usually a job for a machine shop equipped to remove and replace axle shafts.

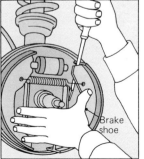

12. Pry against brake shoe with a screwdriver; shoe should move easily against its springs. Adjusters should be free to turn. Frozen, stuck, or binding parts must be freed and lubricated, or replaced.

Manual drum-brake adjustments ⏱ ⏱ 20–45 min

Most drum brakes adjust the position of their shoes automatically to compensate for lining wear. The drum brakes on many North American cars are adjusted when the brakes are applied as the car backs up (pp.108–109). If the brakes do not adjust themselves properly after several hard stops in *Reverse*, the automatic adjusters are stuck, and the drum will have to be removed so that the mechanism can be freed manually, usually with a liberal application of penetrating oil. The automatic adjusters on some cars operate when the parking brake is applied. To be sure that the self-adjusters operate properly, make a point of setting the hand brake firmly.

Manually adjusted drum brakes have an advantage in that you must examine their operation at regular intervals. Most manufacturers recommend adjustment every six months or 6,000 miles (10,000 km), more frequently in salty driving conditions, which can corrode parts and lock them together.

To adjust rear drum brakes, raise the rear of the car and support it on jack stands (p.176) with the front wheels securely chocked. Apply the brakes firmly several times to center the shoes in the drums. Most manually adjusted brakes have star wheel adjusters. You reach the star wheel through an access hole in the brake drum or, more usually, in the backing plate. Turning the star wheel with a screwdriver or a *brake spoon* moves the shoes.

Spin the tire by hand as you adjust the star wheel. When you hear the linings begin to scrape against the drum, continue to turn the adjuster another tooth or two until the wheel becomes difficult to turn.

Then turn the adjuster in the opposite direction until the wheel spins freely with no scraping noise. Apply the brakes two or three times to make sure that the shoes remain centered. If the drum now scrapes when you spin the wheel, back off the adjustment and start again. Repeat the process on the other wheel. If the front drums have manual adjusters, repeat the operation at the front of the car. Reinstall any rubber plugs in the drums or backing plates, lower the car, and take a short test drive.

> **Tools:** Jack and jack stands, wheel chocks, screwdriver or brake spoon that fits through brake adjuster access hole.
> **Material:** Penetrating oil.

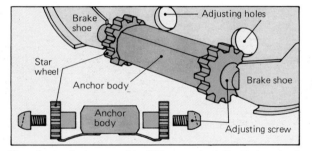

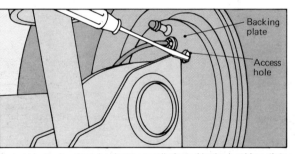

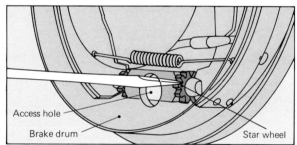

Star wheel adjusters on older VWs are paired. Front star wheel turns clockwise, rear turns counterclockwise, to adjust shoes outward toward drum. If star wheels stick, apply penetrating oil. If this does not free them, replace star wheels.

Access holes for star wheels are usually found in the backing plate. They should be sealed with rubber plugs. The hole acts as a fulcrum for the brake spoon or screwdriver. Lost rubber plugs must be replaced to keep out water and dirt.

Some cars have access holes in the brake drum. A lug bolt hole may double as an access hole. In some cases, the access hole extends through the wheel and is visible when the hubcap is removed. Turn the drum until the hole lines up with the star wheel.

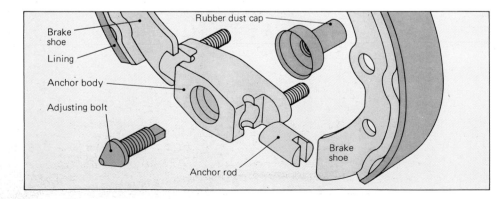

Hondas and VWs retained manual brake adjusters longer than most cars. The bolt on a Honda adjuster has a square head rather than a star wheel. Turning the tapered bolt clockwise forces anchor rods and brake shoes outward.

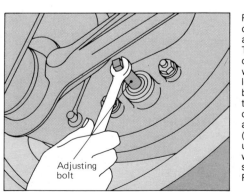

Remove rubber cap from Honda adjusting bolt. Turn bolt clockwise until wheel can no longer be spun by hand. Then turn bolt counterclockwise about two clicks (180°), or just until wheel spins without drag or scraping noise. Replace cap.

Bleeding the hydraulic system ▢▢▢ 30 min–1 hr

Air can be trapped in brake lines due to leaks or when parts are replaced. This will make the brake pedal feel spongy and will reduce the force with which the linings are pressed against the drums or discs. Trapped air must be forced out through bleed valves at the top of each wheel cylinder or caliper.

If your car has power brakes, begin by pumping the brake pedal 10 times, with the engine off, to use up any vacuum in the power booster. Raise the car (see p.176) and attach a length of clean vacuum hose to one of the bleed valves. Insert the other end of the hose into a jar partly filled with fresh brake fluid. Have a helper press firmly on the brake pedal; considerable force may be needed. Use a box wrench to open the valve; the brake pedal will sink. When the pedal reaches the floor, close the valve; then have your helper let the pedal slowly return to its normal position. Repeat this procedure until no more air bubbles or foam come out of the hose. Keep adding fresh fluid to the reservoir so that it will not run dry. To replace, or *flush out,* all the fluid in the system, bleed each wheel until the old fluid runs clear.

When you have finished bleeding the brakes, the brake warning light on the dash will be lit. To turn it off on late-model cars, turn the ignition switch to the *Acc* or *On* position and apply the brakes once.

To shut off the light on older models, you must center the switch inside the metering valve. Open a bleed valve in the circuit opposite the one that was bled last (at a rear wheel, for example, if you bled the front wheels last). Have your helper press the brake pedal slowly with his hand until the light goes out, then close the bleed valve immediately. If the light goes on again, you have overshot the center of the switch and must repeat the procedure at the opposite end of the car. If you have an American Motors model with front drum brakes, unscrew the brake warning light switch from the metering valve before you begin. Replace it when you are through.

Before driving the car, start the engine and pump the brakes to test for a firm pedal. If the pedal feels spongy, there is still air in the system.

Tools: Rubber vacuum hose 1 ft long, clear glass jar, box wrench to fit bleed valves on your car, locking pliers.
Materials: Rags, fresh brake fluid marked DoT 3 or DoT 4.

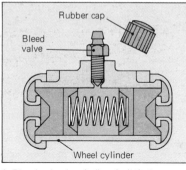

1. Bleed valve is a hollow bolt that screws into a brake caliper or wheel cylinder. Some valves have a rubber cap to keep dirt out. Remove cap and clean off valve.

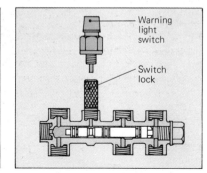

2. To avoid tedious recentering job on some pre-1971 Fords, install a warning light switch lock before bleeding the brakes. Ask dealer if your car requires one.

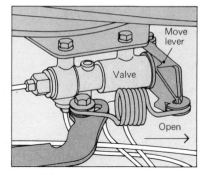

3. Mechanical proportioning valve, used on many small front-wheel-drive cars, senses body angle during braking. Open it by hand before bleeding the brakes.

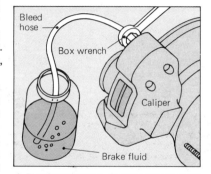

4. Place box wrench over bleed valve, then force hose over valve. Place other end of hose into a jar containing ½ in. of clear brake fluid. Keep hose end submerged.

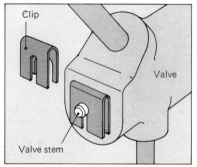

5. Heavy pedal pressure may force fluid past metering or proportioning valve so front brakes can be bled. If not, hold valve open with locking pliers or special clip.

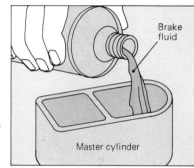

6. Pour new fluid into master cylinder reservoir to keep it full as you bleed brakes. If cylinder empties, air will enter the system, and brake bleeding must be repeated.

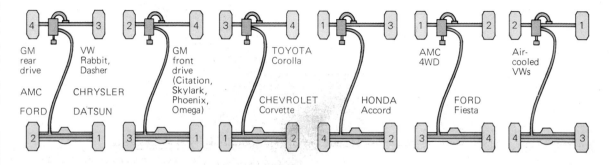

GM rear drive
AMC
FORD

VW Rabbit, Dasher
CHRYSLER
DATSUN

GM front drive (Citation, Skylark, Phoenix, Omega)

TOYOTA Corolla
CHEVROLET Corvette

HONDA Accord

AMC 4WD
FORD Fiesta

Air-cooled VWs

7. Bleed brakes in the sequence recommended by car manufacturer (above), or start at the wheel farthest from the master cylinder and work back to the wheel closest to it. Do not let brake fluid spill on car body (it will ruin the paint). When bleeding is complete, top up fluid reservoir, reset proportioning valve, remove warning light switch lock, and replace any rubber caps.

217

Adjusting parking brakes 🔲🔲 15–30 min

The parking brake is sometimes mistakenly called the emergency brake, but it is designed to keep the car from moving, not to stop it once it is in motion. The parking brake is a system of levers and cables that force the rear brake shoes against the drums.

Constant tension on the parking brake cables stretches them in time, so that the lever or pedal must be applied over greater angles before the brake takes effect. When six or more clicks are required to set the parking brake, it is time to adjust it.

Cable layouts and designs vary, but the adjusters are basically similar. The adjuster shortens the working length of the cable. Most adjusters have a locknut to secure the adjustment. Locking pliers may be required to keep the cable from turning while you make the adjustment.

1. Before making any cable adjustments, make sure that the brakes are correctly adjusted (p.216) and that the whole system is in good order.

2. Raise the car (see p.176) so that the rear wheels can turn freely. Make sure that the parking brake cables are not sticking in their guide conduits and are not kinked, frayed, or corroded. Lubricate the sliding and pivoting friction points with white grease.

3. Locate the adjuster, which is usually at the junction of the cable from the brake pedal or lever and the cable or cables to the rear brakes. If there is no obvious adjuster under the car, it may be inside the car, near the lever or pedal. Your owner's manual may cover parking brake adjustments.

4. The most common procedure is to set the parking brake by one or two clicks of the ratchet (Pontiac specifies seven clicks) and then to turn the adjusting nut until some drag can be felt as each rear wheel is turned by hand. If there is a locknut on the adjuster, it must be loosened before the adjusting nut can be turned, and retightened after the adjustment is made.

5. Release the parking brake. The rear wheels must then spin freely with no brake drag at all.

Some systems used by Chrysler and Oldsmobile are adjusted while the brake is fully released. Back off the adjuster until there is some slack in the parking brake cable. Then adjust the cable until a slight drag can be felt when the rear wheel is turned by hand. Back off the adjuster until the wheel just turns with no trace of drag, then back the adjuster off two or more turns (seven full turns on Oldsmobiles). Lock the adjusting nuts, and lower the car.

With self-adjusting rear drum brakes, it is important that there be no contact between the linings and drums caused by a too-tight parking brake cable. If there is any drag, the self-adjusters will keep the linings rubbing on the drums and will wear out the brake linings within a few thousand miles.

> **Tools:** Locking pliers, screwdriver, jack and jack stands, wrenches to fit adjusting nuts.
> **Materials:** Penetrating oil, white grease.

Foot parking brake

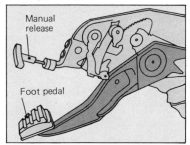

Foot pedal parking brake always has a manual release and may also have an automatic vacuum release. Adjust at threaded rod under car. If vacuum release fails, pull off rubber hoses to check for vacuum. Replace leaky hoses.

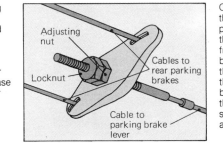

Cable adjusters under the car are most often part of the hardware that joins the cable from the parking brake lever or pedal to the cable or cables that operate the rear brakes. A locknut on the adjusting screw secures the adjustment.

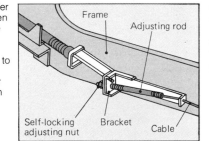

Chrysler Corp. cars (Plymouth, Chrysler, Dodge) built in North America mount cable adjuster on a bracket joining two lengths of cable under the car. A single self-locking adjusting nut sets and retains adjustments to cable length.

Hand parking brake

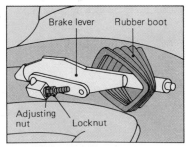

Hand lever parking brake, used in most small cars, may be adjusted under the car or may have adjusters on the lever. Such adjusters may be hidden under a rubber boot. Some boots must be removed, but others have access slots for tools.

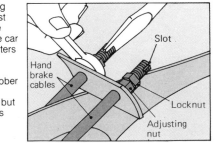

VW and some other parking brake levers have separate cables for each rear brake. Adjust these so that drag is equal on both wheels. Hold screwdriver in slotted rod to prevent rod from turning with adjusting nuts.

Cable shortener

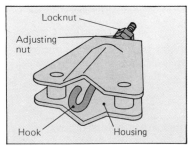

Aftermarket adjusters take up slack after normal adjuster has reached its limit. Hook fits over cable and shortens it by pulling cable into housing. This is easier than installing new cables. Kinked, frayed, stuck, or corroded cables must be replaced.

Reinstalling wheel bearings 🔧🔧🔧 30 min–1 hr

Wheel bearings are precisely machined. When removed from the safety of their grease-packed hub cavities, they must be handled carefully. When you remove the bearings (p.213), leave them in their grease until you are ready to reinstall the hub or drum. Then clean all traces of old lubricant from the hub, spindle, and bearings, inspect the bearings, and repack them with fresh wheel bearing grease before reinstalling them in the hub. Wash the bearings with a brush and parts-cleaning solvent, mineral spirits, or kerosene. Once the cups, cones, and cage are completely clean, you can inspect them. **Caution:** Do not spin the washed bearings at high speed, since this may damage their finely machined surfaces.

Examine the running surface of the races, also called *cups* and *cones,* with a magnifying glass. You can do this without removing the outer cup from the hub. The metal should appear polished, with no tiny pits, cracks, or rough spots and only a trace of grease staining. If the parts are straw-brown or bluish, the metal has been overheated by friction and its hardness lost. If you have any doubt about the condition of a bearing, replace both it and its mate on the same spindle. Whenever you remove a wheel bearing, install new grease seals to keep grease out of the brakes. Old seals should never be reused.

If the bearings are in good shape, you can leave the outer cup in the wheel hub. But if you must replace any part of a bearing, use a brass drift to drive the outer cup from the hub, then install the new cup and bearing. If this proves difficult, you can have a machine shop force the outer cup from the hub and press in a replacement. Make sure that the numbers of the bearing parts match or that the new parts are listed as acceptable replacements in the parts-interchange book at the auto parts store.

Pack the bearing cage with high-temperature wheel bearing grease, working the grease into the cage by hand. You can eliminate mess and keep grit out of the bearing by putting the bearing and a ball of grease about the size of a golf ball into a plastic sandwich bag. Then work the grease into the bearing cage with your fingers from the outside of the bag.

Spread a thin layer of grease inside the hub cavity, between the inner and outer cups, to resist moisture and to retain grease in the cones. Insert the grease-packed inner bearing into its cup and put the cone into the center of the cage, following the steps below.

Some General Motors cars have permanently assembled wheel bearings that require no lubrication or adjustment. The entire hub assembly is unbolted and replaced if it is defective or has too much play.

> **Tools:** Light hammer, hard wood block or hockey puck, brass drift, ball peen hammer, solvent pan, clean brush.
> **Materials:** Parts-cleaning solvent, mineral spirits, or kerosene; high-temperature wheel bearing grease; clean rags; plastic sandwich bags; new grease seals; replacement wheel bearings (if needed); large cotter pins.

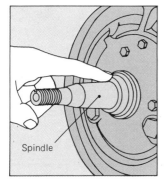

1. Wash old grease and brake grit off spindle with solvent or kerosene, and wipe absolutely clean. Check threads and polished surfaces for signs of galling, heat discoloration, or cracking. Grease spindle lightly with high-temperature wheel bearing grease just before reinstalling bearings, to keep out grit. If threads are damaged, clean them up with a thread-restoring file (p.432) or knife-edge file before greasing the spindle.

Spindle

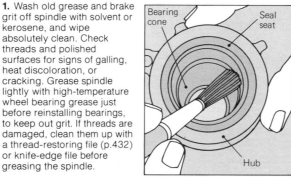

2. Hub and bearing cones must be cleaned of all traces of old grease before they can be inspected and repacked. Do not mix old and new grease; the two may be incompatible and could damage bearing. Smear a thin layer of wheel bearing grease inside the hub, and lightly grease the cones. Wipe grease out of the seal's seating area. Cover hub with rags to keep out any trace of grit or brake dust after hub is lubricated.

Bearing cone   Seal seat   Hub

3. Wash all traces of old grease from bearing cage, using a small pan of clean solvent and a brush. Allow cleaned parts to air dry. If using compressed air to dry the bearing, do not spin the rollers or balls, as this may damage them or the cone. Inspect cones for signs of wear, metal flaking, rust, cracks, or other visible damage, including discoloration. If any part is damaged, replace both bearing assemblies.

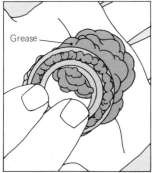

4. Pack the same kind of high-temperature wheel bearing grease into the cages as was used in the hub and on the spindle. Packing can be done inside a plastic bag to keep grit out of the bearing and grease off your hands. Work grease into cage and around rollers or balls until it comes out the other side. Work from the larger side of the bearing to the smaller. Keep bearing in bag until you are ready to install it in hub and put hub back on car.

Grease

5. Install inner bearing assembly in hub. Then insert grease seal in its seat, open side facing bearing. Start seal in its bore by thumb pressure and tap it the rest of the way in with a light hammer and a hockey puck or hard wood block to spread impact load and avoid deforming the seal. Seat seal flush with the outer surface of the hub. Lubricate the lip of the seal by running a greasy finger around it and over the surface of the spindle where it contacts the seal.

Seal   Wood block   Hub   Bearing

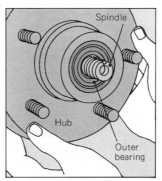

6. Slide the hub, with the inner bearing and seal installed, over the spindle; take care not to cut the lips of the grease seal on the threads. Seat hub by hand pressure and then slip the outer bearing cage into its cup in the hub. Install thrust washer and hub adjusting and retaining nut next. The nut lock and cotter pin are not installed until clearance has been adjusted (see p.220). The grease cap is tapped in place last.

Spindle   Hub   Outer bearing

Maintenance/**Brakes**

Adjusting wheel bearings 🔧🔧🔧 5–15 min

Properly serviced and adjusted, the tapered roller bearings on free-rolling, non-drive wheels will run almost indefinitely without problems. Neglected bearings will eventually seize, causing a wheel to lock, or even to fall off if the spindle breaks. Loose or excessively worn wheel bearings can cause a wheel to wobble. With disc brakes, such eccentricity can knock the pads back into the calipers, which could cause a partial or complete loss of braking power. Scalloping, or cupping, tire wear (see p.121) is often a sign of loose wheel bearings.

Generally, tapered roller bearings support free-rolling wheels. The bearings can be adjusted easily with just a few basic tools. An inexpensive 0- to 100-lb-ft or 0- to 600-lb-in. torque wrench is useful for adjusting tapered roller bearings accurately, but it is not absolutely essential. If you have such a wrench, use it. If not, the other techniques shown here will enable you to approximate the correct torque even if you do not know the specifications.

Volkswagen has devised a method of adjusting bearings that does not even require a torque wrench, but it is intended only for Volkswagens.

No matter which method you use, begin by jacking up the end of the car you will be working on and supporting it on jack stands for safety (see *Raising a car safely,* p.176). Remove the hub cap and pry off the grease cap with a pair of large screwdrivers. Pry gently with the screwdrivers so as not to dent the cap or damage the hub. The cap should come out slowly, moving in small increments. You may also be able to remove a grease cap with water-pump pliers or with a special puller (see p.214). Take off only one cap at a time to prevent dirt from getting into the bearings. After adjusting the first bearing, replace the grease cap before working on the next bearing.

The final check on a wheel bearing's adjustment is made after driving the car. Wheel hubs will run warm to the touch when they are not heated by hard braking, but they should not become uncomfortably hot or untouchable, even after being driven a number of miles at turnpike speeds.

Tools and materials: 12-in. adjustable wrench, water-pump pliers or large socket (usually 1 to 1⅜ in.), 0- to 600-lb-in. torque wrench (optional), cotter pins.

Manual method

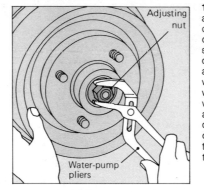

Adjusting nut

Water-pump pliers

1. If you do not have a torque wrench, you can adjust bearing clearance by feel. To seat the rollers in the cones, tighten the adjusting nut with water-pump pliers while turning the wheel by hand. Apply as much force as you comfortably can with one hand. Stop when the plier jaws begin to open.

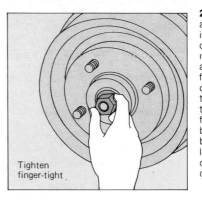

Tighten finger-tight

2. Back off the adjusting nut until it is just free (about one-half turn) and retighten it as tightly as you can with your fingers. This will closely approximate the 10- to 15-lb-in. torque recommended for most cars. It is better to adjust a bearing a little too loosely than to overtighten it. Then do Step 2, below.

Torque wrench method

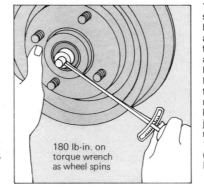

180 lb-in. on torque wrench as wheel spins

1. A torque wrench simplifies wheel bearing adjustment and makes it foolproof. Tighten the adjusting nut to 180 lb-in. (15 lb-ft, or 20 N-m) while spinning the wheel to seat the rollers on their cones. Back off nut until it is just free, then re-torque it to 10 to 15 lb-in. (approximately 1 lb-ft, or 2 N-m).

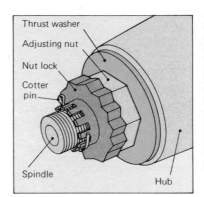

Thrust washer
Adjusting nut
Nut lock
Cotter pin
Spindle
Hub

2. Install nut lock and a new cotter pin. The cotter pin hole in the spindle may be vertical or horizontal. If the slots in the nut lock and the hole in the spindle do not align, loosen the nut, never tighten it. Do not loosen nut more than one-twelfth turn. Spread pin as shown.

Volkswagen method

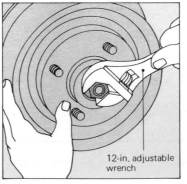

12-in. adjustable wrench

1. No special tools are required for the clearance adjustment devised by Volkswagen. Tighten adjusting nut moderately with 12-in. adjustable wrench, back off until nut is free, and retighten it until you can just slide the thrust washer sideways with gentle pressure of a screwdriver blade.

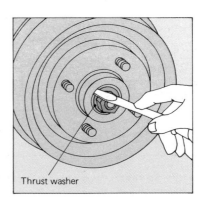

Thrust washer

2. If you have to pry or twist the screwdriver blade to move the thrust washer, the bearing is too tight. When adjustment is correct, position nut lock by trial and error until cotter pin can be inserted with minimal loosening of bearing adjusting nut. Do not turn nut more than one-twelfth turn. (See Step 2, above.)

Servicing ball bearing hubs ⬛⬛⬛⬛ 1–2 hr

Some free-rolling wheels have hubs with ball bearings rather than the more common tapered roller bearings. A few older cars, mostly imports, have ball bearings that come apart in the same way that tapered roller bearings do. These ball bearings are serviced in almost the same way as roller bearings, but they are adjusted more tightly.

Most ball bearings do not come apart like tapered roller bearings. They are manufactured as assemblies and are permanently adjusted. They cannot be readjusted to compensate for wear and must be replaced when they show signs of wear.

Ball bearings are often used in front hubs on front-drive cars. When worn, they must be replaced by a car dealer or machine shop with facilities for pressing the replacement bearings into the hub.

Hubs with ball bearings are found on Honda Civics through 1979 and on some other light cars. The hubs are removed in much the same way as tapered roller bearing hubs are (see p.213). Remove the cotter pin, nut lock (if any), and spindle nut. The hub should then slide off the spindle while the bearings and grease seal stay in the hub. (A little more effort will be required than with tapered roller bearings, which come apart as the hub is removed.)

Generally, you should replace ball bearings rather than repacking them, as the parts are cheap and you will not want to repeat the job when the bearings begin to wear (remember that clearance cannot be adjusted). You can repack ball bearings, if necessary, although most manufacturers (Honda in particular) advise against it. To repack old bearings or pack new ones, which do not come packed in wheel bearing grease, follow the instructions on page 219.

Hubs with ball bearings should spin freely, but you should not be able to feel any play or roughness while turning the wheel by hand. After a high-speed run that does not include heavy braking, the hubs should be warm, but they should not be too hot to touch. Any looseness must be corrected by replacing both the inner and outer ball bearing assemblies.

Tools: Torque wrench, socket to fit spindle nut, hammer, drift, solvent pan, brush.
Materials: Ball bearings, grease seals, parts-cleaning solvent, rags, wheel bearing grease, plastic bag, cotter pins.

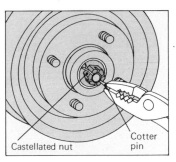

Castellated nut — Cotter pin

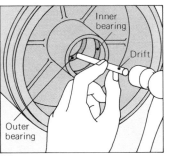

Inner bearing — Drift — Outer bearing

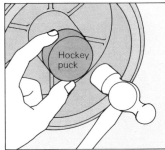

Hockey puck

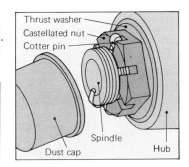

Thrust washer — Castellated nut — Cotter pin — Spindle — Hub — Dust cap

1. Pull out cotter pin and remove nut lock. Use a breaker bar and socket to remove spindle nut on ball bearing hub, which will be tight. Pull hub, bearings, and seal off spindle. In most cases, the hub should not be so tight that a drum puller is needed. Tap hub with a soft hammer to loosen.

2. To remove ball bearings from hub, insert a brass drift through the center of the inner bearing. Push bearing spacer tube to one side so that drift contacts outer bearing race. Use hammer to tap drift while moving it around race to remove bearing without tilting it. Remove grease seal, and tap out inner bearing.

3. To install ball bearings, tap the inner bearing in place with a drift applied to its outer race, replace the bearing spacer, then tap the outer bearing in place. Drive in a new grease seal with a hockey puck or block of wood (see p.219, Step 5) to prevent hammer dents, which can cause a seal to leak.

4. Replace thrust washer, screw the spindle nut onto spindle, and torque nut to specifications (usually about 100 lb-ft). A castellated nut is commonly used with ball bearings. If castellations and hole do not line up, tighten nut to align them. Insert and secure cotter pin. Pack dust cap with grease, and tap it into place.

Wheel alignment

Aligning the wheels is virtually impossible without special equipment, so you should always take alignment problems to a professional with the right equipment. However, you can easily determine whether or not the alignment needs to be checked by a trained mechanic.

The first sign of a problem is usually that the car handles differently or tends to drift to one side or the other when going down a straight, level highway. The most common cause for such abnormal road handling is uneven tire pressure, which can have many of the same effects as incorrect wheel alignment. Inflate the tires to the correct pressure and check them with an accurate gauge. If this does not solve the problem, or if the car suddenly feels strange after a sharp impact with a curb or a pothole, have the alignment checked by a shop that specializes in front-end work as soon as possible. If you continue to drive the car, misalignment will quickly cause the tires to wear badly. You can usually feel this wear pattern before you can see it. Slide your hand in and out across the tread pattern to feel for edges just beginning to feather. Slide your hand around the circumference of the tire for 8 or 10 inches to feel for uneven wear. (See pp.120–121 for illustrations of tire wear patterns and their interpretation.)

If no front-end parts are bent or worn out, simple front-end alignment is relatively inexpensive and can save the cost of a new set of tires.

Unbalanced, bent, or out-of-round wheels or brakes can also cause shimmy and vibrations in the front wheels. You can have wheels balanced at a front-end shop, but bent wheels must be replaced. Raise the front wheels of the car (see p.176). If the disc brakes drag, lever the pads back into the calipers with a screwdriver until the wheel spins freely. Turn the wheel by hand and stop it in four positions. The wheel should rest where you stop it each time. If it turns, it needs to be balanced. Next, clamp a piece of coat hanger wire to the suspension with locking pliers and bend it to within 1/16 inch of the wheel rim. Spin the wheel by hand. If the rim is bent, you will see it wobble in relation to the pointer. Remove the wheel and perform the same test on the brake disc or drum. Replace warped wheels or brakes.

After lowering the car, depress the brake pedal several times to reposition the front disc brake pads before you drive the car.

Maintenance/**Distributor**

Servicing the breaker points and condenser ⚑ 5–15 min

Every six months, check the breaker points on the distributor (see pp.66-67). With normal wear, the points should last for at least 10,000 miles. They may last the entire lifetime of a car, but as a rule you will replace them several times during the car's useful life. Point sets, and the condenser that is usually sold with them, are inexpensive; professional mechanics routinely replace them rather than maintain them.

Maintaining the breaker points generally involves seeing to it that they are aligned, that their surfaces are clean and fairly smooth, and that the spring in the point set has the right tension so that the rubbing block exerts the correct pressure against the cam. When the pressure is too low, the points remain open too long as the engine is revved, causing the engine to misfire at high speed. When the pressure is too high, the rubbing block will wear out quickly.

Whenever you service or replace the breaker points, you must check that they are gapped properly. A quick though inexact way to do this is to measure the gap with a feeler gauge and adjust the gap as described on the next six pages. Do not attempt to measure the gap of points that are very rough or pitted. The measurement will not be true.

To gap the points accurately, check and adjust the dwell angle as described on the opposite page. You will need a dwell meter to do this (p.173). This meter will usually function as a tachometer as well, like the dwell-tachometer illustrated on the opposite page.

Pits in breaker points are usually caused by a defect in the condenser, so replace the condenser when you replace a pitted point set. Pitting is sometimes caused by a poor ground contact between the condenser case and the distributor. Check and clean the condenser mounting bracket or terminal of any dirt or corrosion when you service the distributor.

Too large a dwell angle, an overcharging alternator, or oil on the points will cause the points to burn rapidly. Do not over-lubricate the distributor (p.230). If dwell is correct but burning recurs, check for oil seepage past a worn shaft bushing in the distributor or for a plugged PCV valve.

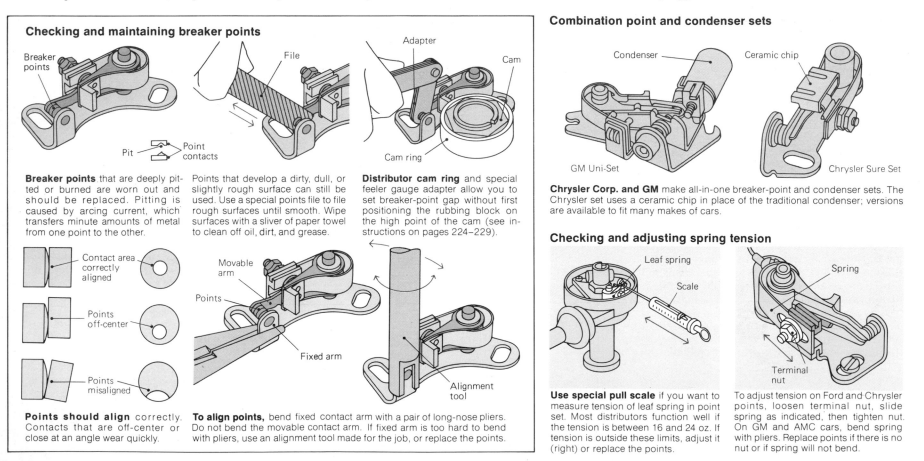

Checking and maintaining breaker points

Breaker points · File · Adapter · Cam · Pit · Point contacts · Cam ring

Breaker points that are deeply pitted or burned are worn out and should be replaced. Pitting is caused by arcing current, which transfers minute amounts of metal from one point to the other.

Points that develop a dirty, dull, or slightly rough surface can still be used. Use a special points file to file rough surfaces until smooth. Wipe surfaces with a sliver of paper towel to clean off oil, dirt, and grease.

Distributor cam ring and special feeler gauge adapter allow you to set breaker-point gap without first positioning the rubbing block on the high point of the cam (see instructions on pages 224–229).

Contact area correctly aligned · Points off-center · Points misaligned

Movable arm · Points · Fixed arm · Alignment tool

Points should align correctly. Contacts that are off-center or close at an angle wear quickly.

To align points, bend fixed contact arm with a pair of long-nose pliers. Do not bend the movable contact arm. If fixed arm is too hard to bend with pliers, use an alignment tool made for the job, or replace the points.

Combination point and condenser sets

Condenser · Ceramic chip · GM Uni-Set · Chrysler Sure Set

Chrysler Corp. and GM make all-in-one breaker-point and condenser sets. The Chrysler set uses a ceramic chip in place of the traditional condenser; versions are available to fit many makes of cars.

Checking and adjusting spring tension

Leaf spring · Scale · Spring · Terminal nut

Use special pull scale if you want to measure tension of leaf spring in point set. Most distributors function well if the tension is between 16 and 24 oz. If tension is outside these limits, adjust it (right) or replace the points.

To adjust tension on Ford and Chrysler points, loosen terminal nut, slide spring as indicated, then tighten nut. On GM and AMC cars, bend spring with pliers. Replace points if there is no nut or if spring will not bend.

Checking and adjusting the dwell angle ⏱ 10–20 min

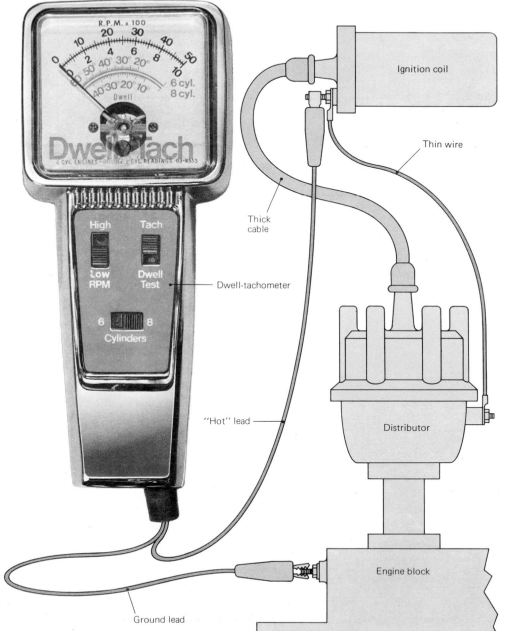

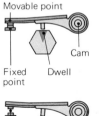

Ignition coil

Thin wire

Thick cable

High

Tach

Low RPM

Dwell Test

Dwell-tachometer

6 | 8
Cylinders

"Hot" lead

Distributor

Engine block

Ground lead

1. Clip the ground lead (usually black) of the dwell-tachometer to any clean metal part of the engine. Clip the other lead (usually red) to the side terminal of the coil that is connected by a thin wire to the distributor. This terminal may be marked –, *CB*, *SW*, or *1*. Check the instructions that come with the dwell-tachometer to make sure that you hook up the leads correctly.

2. Set the meter's function switch to *Tachometer*, turn on the engine, and check the idle speed (see pp.252–253). Adjust idle speed if it does not meet the carmaker's specifications (see *Tuneup Data* supplement).

3. With the engine idling, reset the meter's function switch to *Dwell*. Set the *Cylinders* switch to correspond to the number of cylinders in your engine. (If the engine has four cylinders and *Four* is not on the switch, set the switch to *Eight* and double the reading on the eight-cylinder scale.)

4. Read dwell in degrees from the appropriate scale and compare the reading to the manufacturer's specifications (see *Tuneup Data*). If dwell is correct, proceed to Step 6.

5. Turn off the engine. Adjust breaker-point gap until the dwell falls within the specified range when the engine is idling. The procedure for this depends on your model of car and is given on the next six pages. If the dwell angle is too small, move the points closer together; if the dwell angle is too large, move the points farther apart. The distributors on GM or AMC V-8 engines have a small window through which an Allen wrench can be inserted (p.227). This makes dwell adjustment easier because the dwell can be adjusted without turning off the engine.

6. Check ignition timing and adjust it if necessary (see pp.236–239). This must be done any time the points are adjusted, because point adjustment alters ignition timing.

Caution: When working over a running engine with a dwell-tachometer, be careful to keep loose clothing, long hair, and the meter leads clear of moving fans, pulleys, and belts.

What dwell means

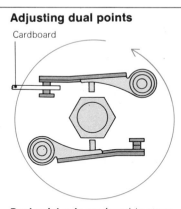

Movable point

Cam

Fixed point

Dwell

Wide gap

Small dwell

Narrow gap

Large dwell

Dwell refers to the time that points remain closed when the engine is running. It is represented by a shaded angle in the illustrations. The angle is varied by changing the position of the fixed breaker point; the larger the angle, the more time points stay closed, and vice versa.

Adjusting dual points

Cardboard

Dual-point sets are found in some Chrysler and Datsun distributors. To adjust dwell on Chrysler cars, block open one of the sets with a sliver of cardboard, plastic, or wood and adjust the other set. Reverse this procedure to adjust the blocked set. Then unblock both sets and take a combined dwell reading. Datsun dual-point sets must be adjusted by an experienced mechanic.

Checking, cleaning, adjusting, and replacing Motorcraft (Ford) points ⏱ 20 – 40 min

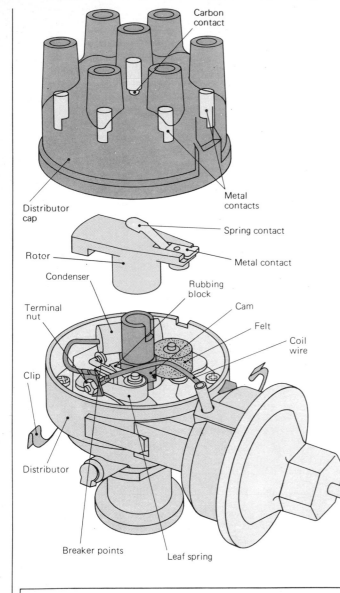

Carbon contact

Distributor cap

Metal contacts

Rotor

Spring contact

Metal contact

Condenser

Rubbing block

Terminal nut

Cam

Felt

Coil wire

Clip

Distributor

Breaker points

Leaf spring

Tools: Screwdriver, screw-holding screwdriver, small file, small ignition wrench, blade-type feeler gauge, offset distributor wrench, dwell meter.
Materials: Chalk or pen, new points and condenser, crocus cloth.

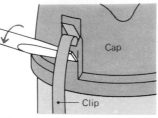

Cap

Clip

1. Pry open clips on the sides of the distributor with a screwdriver, then lift off the cap. Pry carefully to avoid cracking the cap. Lift cap up and out of the way. Do not kink or disconnect the spark plug cables.

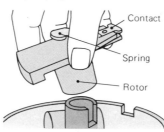

Contact

Spring

Rotor

2. Pull rotor straight up to remove it. Replace it if the spring on the top is weak or if the contact is badly pitted. If the contacts in the cap are badly pitted or discolored, replace the cap (p.231). Clean minor pitting with a crocus cloth.
3. Open the points and inspect their mating surfaces (p.222). If they are pitted or burned, replace the point set. Clean dirty points with a small, clean file until they close evenly.

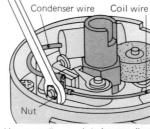

Condenser wire

Coil wire

Nut

4. Use a small wrench to loosen (but not remove) the nut that secures the condenser wire and the coil wire to the terminal on the breaker-point set. Disconnect the wires.

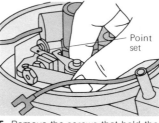

Point set

5. Remove the screws that hold the breaker-point set and ground wire connector in place, then lift out the set. Do not drop the screws; they could lodge inside the distributor.

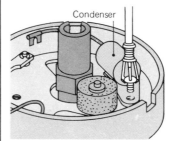

Condenser

6. Take out the screw that holds the condenser in place. Replace the condenser with a new one if the breaker points are pitted. A condenser is difficult to test and is inexpensive; if in doubt about its condition, replace it. Wipe away old grease from parts in the distributor.

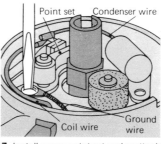

Point set

Condenser wire

Coil wire

Ground wire

7. Install a new point set and reattach the ground wire. Install the replacement set in the same way as the old set was installed. Do not tighten the hold-down screws all the way, but make them snug. Attach the coil wire and condenser wire, and tighten the terminal nut.

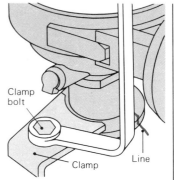

Clamp bolt

Clamp

Line

8. Mark a line with chalk or a felt-tip pen along the distributor and onto the engine. Loosen the clamp bolt, and rotate the distributor until the rubbing block on the point set rests on a high point of the cam.

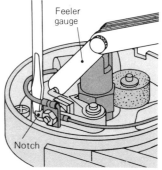

Feeler gauge

Notch

9. Place the blade of a screwdriver in the notch at the base of the point set. With a prying motion, position the fixed breaker point so that the specified feeler gauge (see *Tuneup Data*) can slide between the points with just a slight drag (p.175). Tighten the hold-down screws on the point set.
10. Rotate the distributor so that the chalk or ink marks are realigned, then tighten the clamp bolt. Lubricate the distributor (see p.230).
11. Install the rotor and distributor cap, and measure the dwell angle (p.223). If dwell does not match the specifications for your car (see *Tuneup Data*), remove cap and rotor and readjust gap until dwell is correct. Increase gap to reduce dwell angle; reduce gap to increase dwell.

Checking, cleaning, adjusting, and replacing Chrysler points (Mopar or Prestolite) ⚒ 20 – 40 min

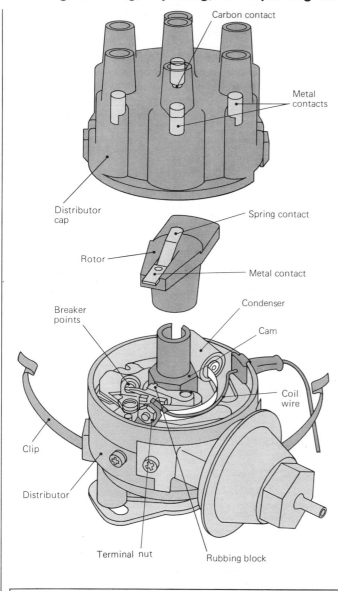

Distributor cap
Carbon contact
Metal contacts
Spring contact
Rotor
Metal contact
Breaker points
Condenser
Cam
Coil wire
Clip
Distributor
Terminal nut
Rubbing block

Tools: Screwdriver, screw-holding screwdriver, small file, small ignition wrench, blade-type feeler gauge, offset distributor wrench, dwell meter.
Materials: Chalk or pen, new points and condenser, crocus cloth.

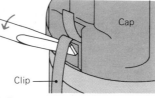

Cap
Clip

1. Pry open clips on the sides of the distributor with a screwdriver, then lift off the cap. Pry carefully against the metal distributor housing to avoid cracking the plastic cap. Lift cap up and out of the way. Do not kink or disconnect the cables.

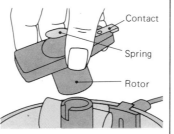

Contact
Spring
Rotor

2. Pull rotor straight up to remove it. Replace it if the spring is weak or the contact is badly pitted. If the contacts in the cap are badly pitted or discolored, replace the cap (p.231). Clean minor pitting with a small piece of crocus cloth.
3. Open the points and inspect their mating surfaces (p.222). If they are pitted or burned, replace the point set. Clean dirty points with a small, clean file until they close evenly.

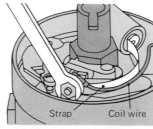

Strap
Coil wire

4. Use a small wrench to loosen (but not remove) the nut that secures the coil wire and the condenser strap to the terminal on the breaker-point set. Disconnect the coil wire and the condenser strap.

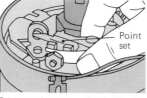

Point set

5. Take out the screw that holds the breaker-point set in place, then lift out the set. Do not drop the screw; if it falls inside the distributor, it may be difficult to recover.

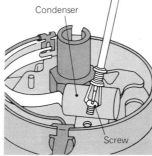

Condenser
Screw

6. Take out the screw that holds the condenser in place. Replace the condenser with a new one if breaker points are pitted. A condenser is difficult to test and is inexpensive; if in doubt about its condition, replace it. Wipe away any grease in distributor.

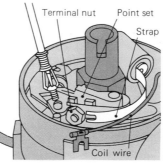

Terminal nut
Point set
Strap
Coil wire

7. Install a new point set in the same way as old set was installed. Do not tighten the hold-down screws all the way, but make them snug. Attach the coil wire and the condenser strap, then tighten the terminal nut.

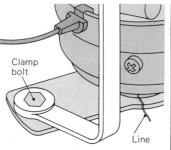

Clamp bolt
Line

8. Turn the starter on and off in short bursts until the rubbing block on the point set rests on or near a high point of the cam. Mark a line with chalk or a felt-tip pen along the distributor and onto the engine. If necessary, loosen the clamp bolt, and rotate the distributor slightly by hand until the rubbing block rests directly on a high point of the cam.

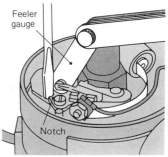

Feeler gauge
Notch

9. Place the blade of a screwdriver in the notch at the base of the point set. With a prying motion, position the fixed breaker point so that the specified feeler gauge (see *Tuneup Data*) can slide between the points with just a slight drag. Tighten the hold-down screw on the point set.
10. Rotate the distributor so that the chalk or ink marks are realigned, then tighten the clamp bolt. Lubricate the distributor (see p.230).
11. Install the rotor and the distributor cap. Measure dwell angle (p.223). If dwell does not match the specifications for your car (see *Tuneup Data*), remove cap and rotor, and readjust gap until dwell is correct. Increase gap to reduce dwell angle; reduce gap to increase dwell.

Checking, cleaning, adjusting, and replacing Delco points (GM and AMC in-line engines) ⟳ 20–40 min

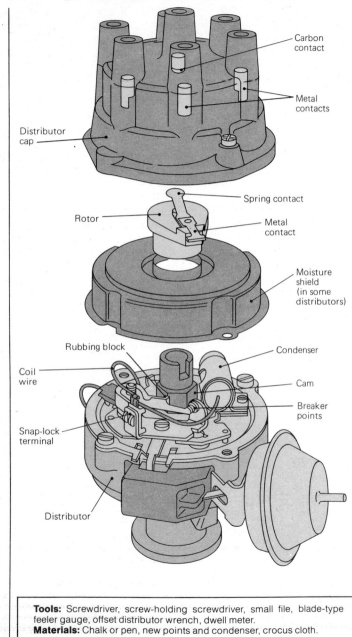

- Distributor cap — Carbon contact
- Metal contacts
- Spring contact
- Rotor — Metal contact
- Moisture shield (in some distributors)
- Rubbing block — Condenser
- Coil wire — Cam
- Breaker points
- Snap-lock terminal
- Distributor

Tools: Screwdriver, screw-holding screwdriver, small file, blade-type feeler gauge, offset distributor wrench, dwell meter.
Materials: Chalk or pen, new points and condenser, crocus cloth.

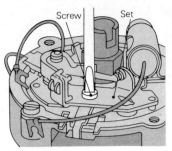

Cap
Hold-down screw

1. Unscrew cap's hold-down screws, then lift off the cap. Lift cap up and out of the way. Do not kink or disconnect the spark plug cables.

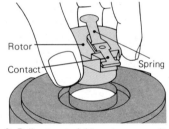

Rotor
Contact
Spring

2. Pull rotor straight up to remove it. Replace it if the spring is weak or the contact is badly pitted. If the contacts in the cap are badly pitted or discolored, replace the cap (p.231). Clean minor pitting with a small piece of crocus cloth.
3. Open the points and inspect their mating surfaces (p.222). If surfaces are pitted or burned, replace the point set. Clean dirty or discolored points with a small, clean file until they close evenly.

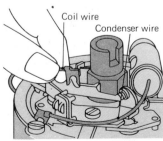

Coil wire
Condenser wire

4. Pry or pull connectors on the coil wire and the condenser wire out of the plastic snap-lock terminal on the breaker-point set.

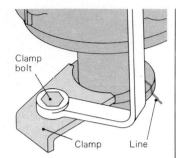

Screw
Set

5. Take out the screw that holds the breaker-point set in place, then lift out the set. Do not drop the screw; if it falls inside the distributor, it may be difficult to recover.

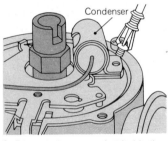

Condenser

6. Remove the screw that holds the condenser in place. Replace the condenser with a new one if the breaker points are pitted. A condenser is difficult to test and is inexpensive; if in doubt about its condition, replace it. Wipe away old grease from parts in the distributor.

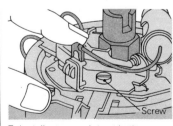

Screw

7. Install a new point set in the same way as the old set was installed. Do not tighten the hold-down screw all the way, but make it snug. Push the connectors on the coil wire and the condenser wire into the plastic snap-lock terminal on the point set.

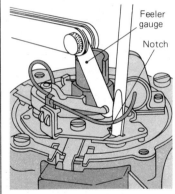

Clamp bolt
Clamp   Line

8. Mark a line with chalk or a felt-tip pen along the distributor and onto the engine. Loosen the clamp bolt, and rotate the distributor until the rubbing block on the point set rests on a high point of the cam.

Feeler gauge
Notch

9. Place the blade of a screwdriver in the notch at the base of the point set. With a prying motion, position the fixed breaker point so that the specified feeler gauge (see *Tuneup Data*) can slide between the points with just a slight drag. Tighten the hold-down screw on the point set.
10. Rotate the distributor so that the chalk or ink marks are realigned, then tighten the clamp bolt. Lubricate the distributor (see p.230).
11. Install the rotor and the distributor cap. Measure dwell angle (p.223). If dwell does not match the specifications for your car (see *Tuneup Data*), remove cap and rotor, and readjust gap until dwell is correct. Increase gap to reduce dwell angle; reduce gap to increase dwell.

Checking, cleaning, adjusting, and replacing Delco points (GM and AMC V-type engines) ▣ 20–40 min

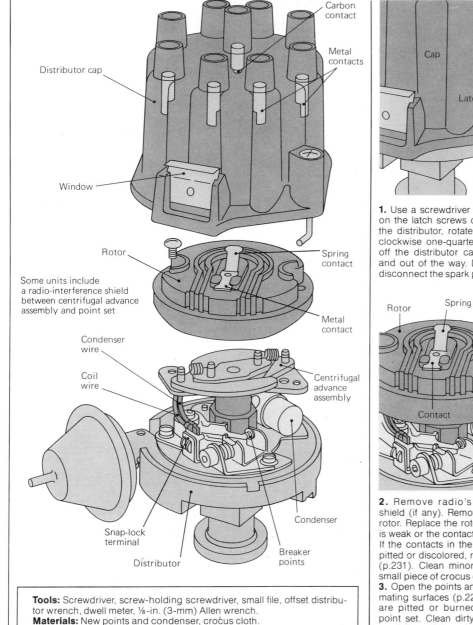

Distributor cap

Window

Carbon contact

Metal contacts

Spring contact

Metal contact

Rotor

Some units include a radio-interference shield between centrifugal advance assembly and point set

Condenser wire

Coil wire

Centrifugal advance assembly

Snap-lock terminal

Condenser

Distributor

Breaker points

Tools: Screwdriver, screw-holding screwdriver, small file, offset distributor wrench, dwell meter, ⅛-in. (3-mm) Allen wrench.
Materials: New points and condenser, crocus cloth.

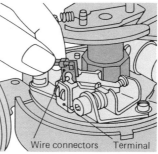

Cap

Latch screw

Latch

1. Use a screwdriver to press down on the latch screws on the sides of the distributor, rotate them counterclockwise one-quarter turn, and lift off the distributor cap. Lift cap up and out of the way. Do not kink or disconnect the spark plug cables.

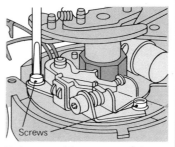

Rotor

Spring

Contact

Screw

2. Remove radio's suppression shield (if any). Remove screws and rotor. Replace the rotor if the spring is weak or the contact is badly pitted. If the contacts in the cap are badly pitted or discolored, replace the cap (p.231). Clean minor pitting with a small piece of crocus cloth.
3. Open the points and inspect their mating surfaces (p.222). If surfaces are pitted or burned, replace the point set. Clean dirty points with a small file until they close evenly.

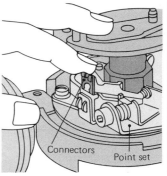

Wire connectors   Terminal

4. Pry or pull the connectors on the coil wire and condenser wire out of the plastic snap-lock terminal on the breaker-point set.

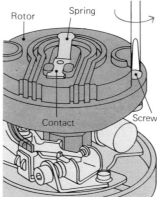

Screws

5. Loosen (do not remove) the screws that hold the breaker-point set in place, and slide the set out from under the screws.

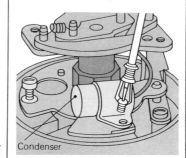

Condenser

6. Remove the screw that holds the condenser in place. Do not drop the screw. Replace the condenser with a new one if breaker points are pitted. A condenser is difficult to test and is inexpensive; if in doubt about its condition, replace it. Wipe away old grease from parts in the distributor.

Connectors   Point set

7. Install a new point set in the same way as the old set was installed. Tighten the hold-down screws. Push connectors on coil wire and condenser wire into plastic snap-lock terminal (or onto stud, if used) as illustrated. If wires are reconnected in any other way, they may interfere with operation of distributor.
8. Reinstall radio shield (if used), rotor, and distributor cap. When installing the rotor, make sure that the square peg on the bottom of the rotor goes into the square hole in the advance mechanism and that the round peg goes into the round hole.

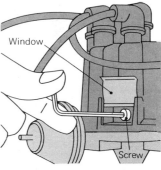

Window

Screw

9. Measure dwell angle (p.223). If dwell does not match specifications for your car (see *Tuneup Data*), adjust breaker-point gap until dwell is correct. To adjust the gap, open the window on the side of the distributor cap, insert a ⅛-in. (3-mm) Allen wrench or special GM tool, and turn adjusting screw with engine running and dwell meter hooked up.

Checking, cleaning, adjusting, and replacing Bosch points (VWs and German Fords) ⏱ 20–40 min

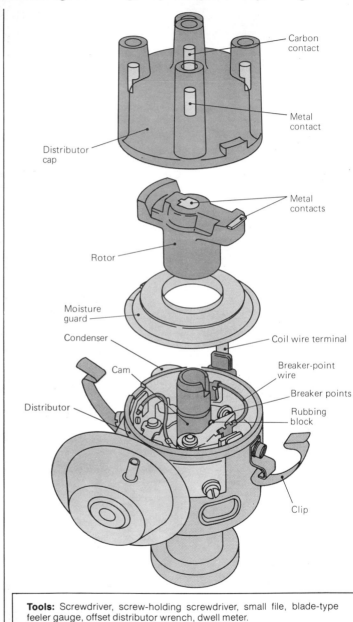

Carbon contact

Metal contact

Distributor cap

Metal contacts

Rotor

Moisture guard

Condenser

Coil wire terminal

Cam

Breaker-point wire

Breaker points

Distributor

Rubbing block

Clip

Tools: Screwdriver, screw-holding screwdriver, small file, blade-type feeler gauge, offset distributor wrench, dwell meter.
Materials: Chalk or pen, new points and condenser, crocus cloth.

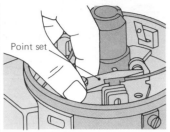

Cap

Clip

1. Pry open clips on the sides of the distributor with a screwdriver, then lift off the cap. Pry carefully to avoid cracking the plastic cap. Lift cap up and out of the way. Do not kink or disconnect the spark plug cables.

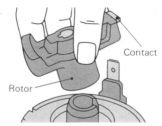

Contact

Rotor

2. Pull rotor straight up to remove it. Replace it if the contact is badly pitted. If the contacts in the cap are badly pitted or discolored, replace the cap (p.231). Clean minor pitting with a crocus cloth.

3. Lift off plastic moisture-guard cap if there is one. Open the breaker points and inspect their mating surfaces (p.222). If surfaces are pitted or burned, replace the point set. Clean dirty points with a small file.

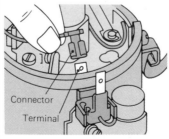

Connector

Terminal

4. Pry or pull breaker-point wire connector off coil wire terminal mounted in the side of the distributor (on bottom of Beetle distributors).

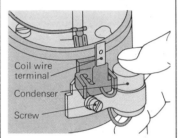

Point set

5. Take out the screw that holds the breaker-point set in place, and lift out the set. Do not drop the screw; if it falls inside the distributor, it may be difficult to recover without removing the distributor from the engine.

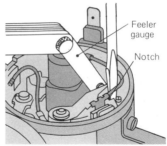

Coil wire terminal

Condenser

Screw

6. Remove the screw that holds the condenser in place. If breaker points are pitted, replace condenser and coil wire terminal to which the condenser is wired with a new condenser-terminal assembly. A condenser is difficult to test and is inexpensive; if in doubt about its condition, replace the condenser. Wipe old grease from distributor.

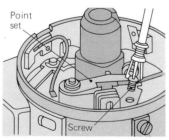

Point set

Screw

7. Install a new point set in the same way as the old set was installed. Do not tighten the hold-down screw all the way, but make it snug. Connect the breaker-point wire to the coil wire

terminal mounted on the side or bottom of the distributor.

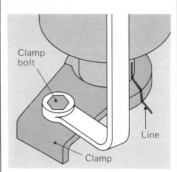

Clamp bolt

Line

Clamp

8. Mark a line with chalk or a felt-tip pen along the distributor and onto the engine. Loosen the clamp bolt and rotate the distributor until the rubbing block on the point set rests on a high point of the cam.

Feeler gauge

Notch

9. Place the blade of a screwdriver in the notch at the base of the point set. With a prying motion, position the fixed breaker point so that the specified feeler gauge (see *Tuneup Data*) can slide between the points with just a slight drag (p.175). Tighten the hold-down screw.

10. Rotate the distributor so that the chalk or ink marks are realigned, then tighten the clamp bolt. Lubricate the distributor (see p.230).

11. Reinstall the moisture guard (if any), the rotor, and the distributor cap. Measure the dwell angle (p.223). If dwell does not match the specifications for your car (see *Tuneup Data*), remove cap and rotor, and readjust gap until dwell is correct. Increase gap to reduce dwell angle; reduce gap to increase dwell.

Checking, cleaning, adjusting, and replacing Nippondenso points (Japanese cars) ⏱ 20–40 min

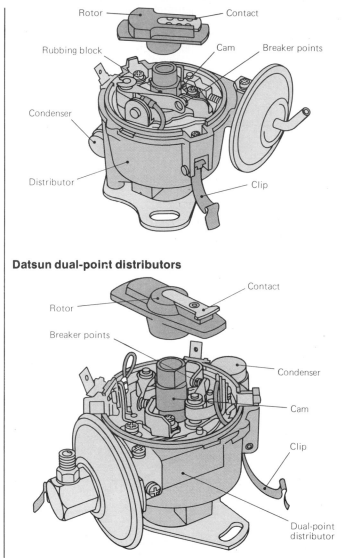

Rotor — Contact
Rubbing block — Cam — Breaker points
Condenser
Distributor — Clip

Datsun dual-point distributors

Rotor — Contact
Breaker points
Condenser
Cam
Clip
Dual-point distributor

Some Datsun distributors have two breaker-point sets instead of one. The procedure for removing either of the sets is the same as that for single-point distributors given on this page. To adjust the point gap in either set, use the prying method described for VW distributors on the opposite page.

Tools: Screwdriver, screw-holding screwdriver, small file, blade-type feeler gauge, offset distributor wrench, dwell meter.

Materials: Chalk or pen, new points and condenser, crocus cloth.

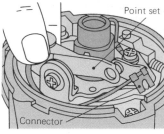

Cap
Clip

1. Pry open clips on sides of the distributor with a screwdriver, then lift off the cap. Pry carefully against the metal distributor housing to avoid cracking the plastic cap. Lift cap up and out of the way. Do not kink or disconnect the cables.

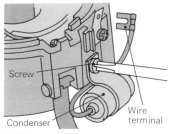

Rotor — Contact

2. Pull rotor straight up to remove it. Replace it if the contact is badly pitted. If the contacts in the cap are badly pitted or discolored, replace the cap (p.231). Clean minor pitting with a piece of crocus cloth.

3. Open the breaker points and inspect their mating surfaces (p.222). If surfaces are pitted or cracked, replace the point set. Clean dirty points with a file until they close evenly.

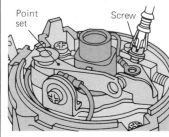

Wire connector
Screw

4. Loosen (do not remove) the screw that secures the coil wire (and condenser wire, in Datsuns) to the terminal on the breaker-point set. Pull wire connector from terminal.

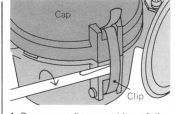

Point set
Connector

5. Loosen the screws (remove them in Toyotas) that hold the breaker-point set and ground wire connector in place, then lift out the set. Do not drop any loose screws.

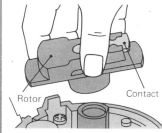

Screw
Condenser — Wire terminal

6. Take out screws that hold condenser and condenser wire connector in place. Replace the condenser with a new one if the breaker points are pitted. A condenser is difficult to test and is inexpensive; if in doubt, replace it. Wipe away old grease from parts in the distributor.

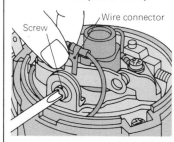

Point set
Screw

7. Install a new point set and reattach the ground wire. Install new set in the same way as the old set was installed. Do not tighten the hold-down screws all the way, but make them snug. Attach coil wire (and condenser wire, in Datsuns) and tighten screw on the terminal.

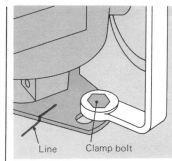

Point set
Line — Clamp bolt

8. Except for Toyotas, turn the starter on and off in short bursts until the rubbing block on the point set rests near a high point of the cam. Mark a line with chalk or a felt-tip pen along the distributor and onto the engine. Loosen the clamp bolt and rotate the distributor by hand so that rubbing block rests directly on a high point of the cam.

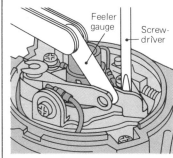

Feeler gauge
Screwdriver

9. Turn the eccentric adjustment screw to position the fixed breaker point so that the specified feeler gauge (see *Tuneup Data*) can slide between the points with just a slight drag. Tighten the hold-down screws. (Toyota point gap adjustment is like that for VW; see opposite page.)

10. Rotate the distributor so that the chalk or ink marks are realigned, then tighten the clamp bolt. Lubricate the distributor (see p.230).

11. Install the rotor and the distributor cap. Measure the dwell angle (p.223). If dwell does not match the specifications for your car (see *Tuneup Data*), remove cap and rotor, and readjust gap until dwell is correct. Increase gap to reduce dwell angle; reduce gap to increase dwell.

Lubricating distributors ⏱ 5–10 min

Motorcraft (Ford)

Remove cap and rotor. Oil the felt in center of shaft with a few drops of SAE 10W engine oil. If distributor has no center felt, it may have a capped oil port at its base. Lift cap and add a few drops of SAE 10W oil to the port.

Smear cam with light film of cam lubricant (cam grease).

Some four-cylinder Ford distributors have a felt ring like that in Delco (right). If felt is dry, add cam grease or replace ring.

Delco distributor with felt ring (GM and AMC)

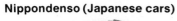

Every 12,000 miles (19,000 km) remove cap, pry off grease-impregnated felt ring, and reinstall it upside down. Every 24,000 miles (38,000 km) replace felt ring with a new one.

Bosch (VWs and German Fords)

Remove cap and rotor. Add a few drops of light engine oil to felt pad, if there is one, in center of shaft.

Smear cam and rubbing block with a small amount of cam lubricant (cam grease).

Add one drop of light engine oil to pivot post of breaker-point set.

Prestolite (Chrysler Corp.)

Remove cap and rotor. Add one drop of light engine oil to felt in center of shaft.

Smear cam with light film of cam lubricant (cam grease).

Delco distributor without felt ring (GM and AMC)

Remove cap and rotor. Smear cam with light film of cam lubricant (cam grease).

Do not let grease get onto points in the breaker-point set.

Nippondenso (Japanese cars)

Remove cap and rotor. Add a few drops of light engine oil to felt pad in center of shaft. In some distributors, grease may be used in the center of the shaft instead of a pad. Pry up plastic cover plug if there is one. Add fresh grease if grease is nearly gone.

Smear cam with light film of cam lubricant (cam grease).

Checking and replacing the distributor cap, rotor, and ignition cables ▶ 15–30 min

A strong spark is needed for proper ignition. The spark is weakened if any current leaks from the ignition cables or distributor. Current can leak if there are cracks or carbon tracks in the distributor cap, or if the insulation or boots of an ignition cable have hardened and cracked.

A quick check for leakage can be made by looking under the hood at night while the engine is running. If you see a spark jump from a cable to the engine block, move the cable away from the engine, then replace the cable as soon as possible.

The spark check illustrated (right) is more effective. Check under dim light. Replace any cable or the distributor cap if you see a spark jump from the part to the screwdriver. **Caution:** Hold screwdriver only by its plastic handle to avoid a shock.

The center contact on the rotor must press against the contact on the inside top of the distributor cap. The necessary pressure is maintained by the springiness of the rotor contact or, in the case of a rotor with a flat center contact, by a spring under the contact in the cap. Replace either part if springiness has been lost, or if either contact is badly worn or burned.

If any cable connection or terminal in the ignition system is corroded, scrub it with a wire brush until it is shiny. If the corrosion cannot be cleaned off, replace the part. Crimp a loose plug terminal with pliers until it fits snugly.

The electrical conductor in modern spark plug cables is made with a high resistance in order to suppress radio interference. Move these cables about gently and do not bend them severely, or you may break their fragile conductors.

A way to check the condition of the ignition spark is to disconnect each spark plug cable, insert a paper clip inside its boot, then check to see how well a spark jumps from the clip to the engine block when the clip is held ½ inch away and the engine is running (see p.414). **Caution:** This test should not be performed on some electronic ignition systems; see pp.414–425.

Spark plug cables can be tested with an ohmmeter. Their resistance should be no more than 15,000 ohms per foot. A 3-foot cable should give a reading of less than 45,000 ohms; the cable should be replaced if the reading is higher. For cables in Fords with electronic ignition, the figure is 60,000 ohms per foot. The correct resistance of replacement cables with shielded metal conductors is 400 to 700 ohms per foot.

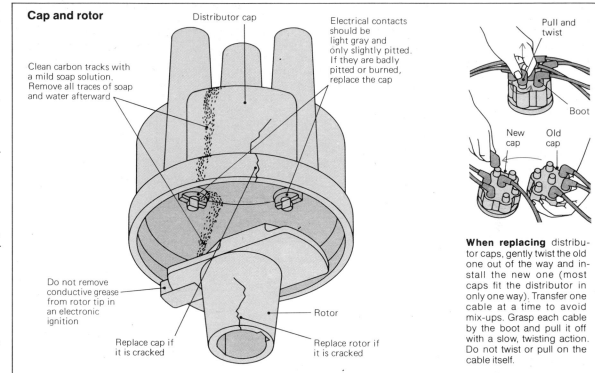

Cap and rotor

Distributor cap

Electrical contacts should be light gray and only slightly pitted. If they are badly pitted or burned, replace the cap

Clean carbon tracks with a mild soap solution. Remove all traces of soap and water afterward

Do not remove conductive grease from rotor tip in an electronic ignition

Replace cap if it is cracked

Rotor

Replace rotor if it is cracked

Pull and twist

Boot

New cap

Old cap

When replacing distributor caps, gently twist the old one out of the way and install the new one (most caps fit the distributor in only one way). Transfer one cable at a time to avoid mix-ups. Grasp each cable by the boot and pull it off with a slow, twisting action. Do not twist or pull on the cable itself.

Ignition cables

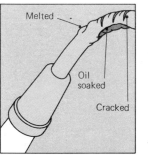

Melted

Oil soaked

Cracked

Inspect cables periodically. Replace any that are cracked, burned, or oil soaked. A full cable set is costly; to save money, buy a spark plug cable kit and cut cables to the appropriate length (see p.408).

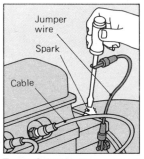

Jumper wire

Spark

Cable

To spark test ignition, connect a jumper wire to a clean electrical ground on engine and to screwdriver shank. Draw the screwdriver along each cable as engine idles. If spark jumps from cable, cable is defective.

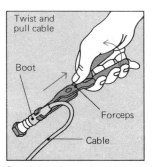

Twist and pull cable

Boot

Forceps

Cable

Special tools can be obtained to disconnect a cable from a spark plug; some tools are small enough to reach the most out-of-the-way plug. With engine off, grasp cable at boot. Do not pull on the cable itself.

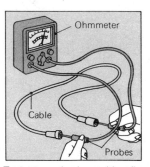

Ohmmeter

Cable

Probes

To test spark plug cable, disconnect it at both ends and touch probes of ohmmeter to each end. With meter set to *High* scale, check and compare resistance with values given in text at left.

Installing spark plug cables 15–30 min

If spark plug cables are not installed correctly, the engine will misfire and may suffer major damage. There are easy ways to reconnect old cables or install new ones. When removing spark plugs, you can disconnect and reconnect one cable at a time, as shown on page 231. When installing new cables, you can tag the old cables before removing them to establish the correct order, as illustrated on page 234.

This page provides a procedure for installing cables if you have removed them all and forgotten the order in which they should go. First, locate the No.1 terminal on the distributor. The terminal is marked on all distributors except those used by AMC and GM. Remove the distributor cap and No.1 spark plug. Hold a finger over the spark plug hole while a helper cranks the starter. When you feel compression,

watch the timing marks. When the marks are aligned, the rotor is pointing at the No.1 terminal.

After locating the No.1 terminal, look up the firing order and cylinder-numbering scheme for your engine (see *Tuneup Data*). Then sketch the correct arrangement of the cables as shown below. This procedure does not apply to Ford EEC engines with bi-level rotors (see p.408).

Finding the No.1 distributor terminal

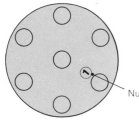

Ford and Chrysler distributors indicate the No.1 terminal with a numeral on the distributor cap.

Numeral

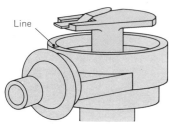

Line

VW distributors have a line incised in the distributor body to indicate the location of the No.1 terminal. To see the line, remove the distributor cap.

Numeral

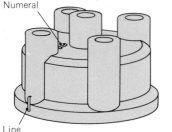

Line

Japanese distributors mark the No.1 terminal with either a numeral or a line molded into the plastic of the distributor cap.

On GM and AMC in-line six-cylinder engines, the No.4 distributor terminal is the one closest to the engine block and the No.1 terminal is to its right. The placement varies on other GM and AMC engines; consult a service manual or see text, above.

Sketching the cable arrangement

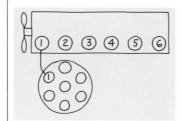

F.O. 1-5-3-6-2-4

1. Draw a diagram of the engine, and number each cylinder (see *Tuneup Data*). Write down the firing order of the cylinders too. Identify in the sketch which direction is toward the front of the car.

2. Sketch the cap of the distributor in about the same location relative to the engine as it appears in your car. Label the No.1 terminal on the cap, and draw a line from the terminal to cylinder 1 on the engine.

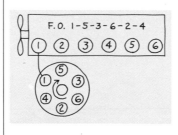

F.O. 1-5-3-6-2-4

3. Turn starter for a second to see which way rotor in the distributor turns. Indicate this direction in sketch with an arrow. From terminal No.1, number terminals in the direction of the arrow, following the sequence of the firing order.

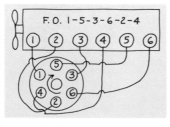

F.O. 1-5-3-6-2-4

4. Draw lines from each numbered distributor terminal to its corresponding cylinder. This sketch shows the correct cable routing. Lay out cables in order of length and install the longest one first, following the routing in the sketch.

Avoiding cross fire

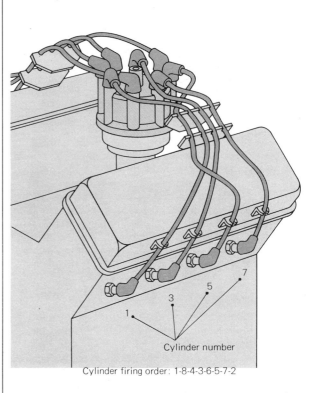

Cylinder number

Cylinder firing order: 1-8-4-3-6-5-7-2

Route cables so that cross fire between them is unlikely. Cross fire can happen between neighboring cables whose spark plugs fire consecutively. The surge of current in one cable creates a magnetic field that induces current in an adjacent parallel cable. This can throw off the timing of the spark through the adjacent cable if it fires immediately afterward, and the engine can misfire. For example, cylinder 7 in the picture fires after cylinder 5; therefore, the cable from the distributor to cylinder 5 has been routed to cross the cable from the distributor to cylinder 7 at a right angle.

Inspecting spark plugs ⏱ 5–10 min

Spark plugs should be inspected every 5,000 to 7,500 miles (8,000 to 12,000 km) and replaced when they are worn or fouled, usually every 10,000 to 15,000 miles (16,000 to 24,000 km). The mileage you get from a plug depends on its construction, on the kind of driving you do, and on the type of gasoline you use. As a rule, plugs that run on lead-free gas last longer than those run on leaded gasoline, which causes lead deposits that can foul the plug electrodes.

Whenever possible, you should buy the brand and model of spark plug recommended by your car's manufacturer. Auto parts stores often stock only two or three popular brands, but they have large manuals that list equivalent spark plug models for most engines. The store can usually supply a plug that will perform satisfactorily in your car. An equivalent plug should have the same physical dimensions as the original plug and a similar heat range (see p.71). An equivalent plug will work well in many engines, but if your inspections show that the equivalent is wearing, overheating, or fouling quickly, you should either switch to an equivalent plug with a more suitable heat range (see below) or, preferably, buy the recommended brand and model plug from another parts store or from your car dealer.

If possible, remove the old spark plugs before buying new ones. Check the condition of the plugs against the color photographs on page 72. The information given there provides clues to possible malfunctions in the engine. Keep the plugs in order, according to their cylinder location, as you remove them; then use the illustrations below to further identify potential engine defects.

Also label removed plugs according to their cylinder location if you expect to take the car to a service station for major repairs; the labeled plugs may help the repairman diagnose the engine's problem.

If a plug has excessive deposits or fouling, you may need a replacement with a higher heat range (sometimes called a *hot plug*), which will burn off these deposits. Note that some deposits are normal, and others are caused by incorrect carburetor adjustments (see p.72). If the plug shows excessive heat erosion or other signs of overheating, you need a replacement with a lower heat range (a *cool plug*).

The way you drive affects the heat range required. The recommended plug for your car is intended for a "normal" mixture of city and highway driving. If your car is used mostly for short trips, stop-and-go driving, or at low speeds, you may need a hotter-than-normal plug to burn off deposits. If your car is used mostly for long-distance, high-speed highway driving, you may need a cooler-than-normal plug to avoid overheating, which can wear plugs rapidly. Overheated plugs should not be confused with an overheating engine (coolant boilover), although either condition can lead to the other.

Although it is possible to clean and reuse fouled plugs, this is a tedious job that is seldom done by professional mechanics.

Diagnosing engine problems

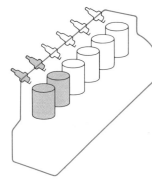

Two adjacent plugs fouled:
This may be due to a blown head gasket between the adjacent cylinders served by the plugs, and can occur in six- or four-cylinder engines or in either bank of an eight-cylinder engine.

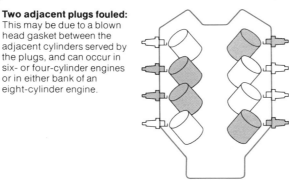

Symmetrical fouling:
Eight-cylinder engines with double-barrel carburetors can exhibit this fouling pattern if the barrels are not balanced. One barrel feeds an overly rich fuel mixture to the four affected spark plugs while the other barrel feeds a normal mixture.

One plug overheated:
There may be a leak in the intake manifold near the affected cylinder. Or, if the overheated plug is the second one to fire in a pair of adjacent plugs that fire consecutively, the overheating may be caused by cross fire between the cables connected to the two plugs. Reroute the cables (see opposite page).

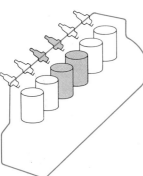

Two center plugs fouled:
Because they are nearest the carburetor, center plugs are the first to be affected by an overly rich fuel mixture, which may allow unburned fuel to enter the cylinders and foul the plugs. Adjustment or overhaul of the carburetor is suggested.

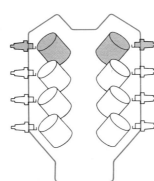

Rear plugs oil-fouled:
Suggests that oil drain holes in the rear of the cylinder head are clogged, forcing oil around the valve stems into the affected cylinders. This is characteristic of eight-cylinder engines that slant toward the rear. There may also be a smoky exhaust and excessive oil consumption.

Rear plugs overheated:
The engine may have a blockage in the cooling system's water jacket. Flush the cooling system to restore coolant circulation (p.283). If the problem is not eliminated, have the engine checked by a professional mechanic.

Checking, cleaning, and replacing spark plugs ⏱ 30 min–2 hr

To remove spark plugs, you will need a spark plug socket. This is a socket deep enough to fit over a plug; it usually has a rubber insert designed to grip the plug's ceramic insulator and lift the plug from the cylinder head. Spark plug sockets are made in two sizes to fit the most common spark plugs: 13/16-inch plugs and 5/8-inch plugs.

To jar a spark plug loose from its seat, hit the wrench with the heel of your hand. If access to the plug is obstructed by engine parts, use extensions and U-joints to improve the reach of the wrench.

Plugs unscrew counterclockwise. Use penetrating oil if a plug sticks. Before completely removing any plug from its hole, use a can of compressed air to clean the surrounding area to prevent dirt particles from falling into the engine. Remove any gaskets that stick to the cylinder head. Whenever you remove plugs that have gaskets, discard the old gaskets and replace them with new ones.

When installing new spark plugs, check their gaps first and make any necessary adjustments. A plug should screw easily into the cylinder head until it seats. Be careful not to cross-thread a plug (screw it into its hole at an angle). If it is difficult to screw a plug into the cylinder head, do not use force. This will strip the threads on the plug or cylinder head. Carbon deposits can make plugs difficult to remove or install. If the plug is hard to remove, clean the threads in the plug hole with a thread chaser (p.432).

Caution: Disconnect the ground cable from the battery before beginning work on any electrical parts. Failure to do so may result in sparks that can damage equipment and burn hands.

> **Tools:** Spark plug socket, ratchet wrench, U-joint, wrench extensions, thread chaser, length of vacuum hose or spark plug cable, bristle brush, plug file, wire or blade feeler gauge, wire brush, pliers.
> **Materials:** Clothespins or tape to label cables, parts-cleaning solvent, anti-seize compound, silicone lubricant, can of compressed air (sold in photo shops).

Removing and installing plugs

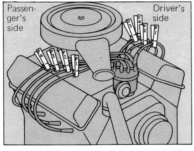

1. To avoid confusion, label plug cables before disconnecting them. Begin numbering the cables from front of engine. On V-type engines, add *D* for the driver's side and *P* for passenger's side.

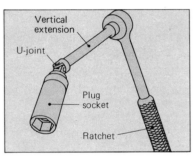

2. Use a ratchet wrench, a U-joint, and a spark plug socket to remove plugs. If a plug is hard to reach, add an extension between the wrench and the socket. Extensions are available in lengths up to 18 in.

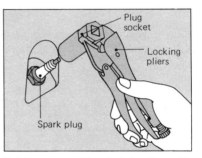

3. If there are overhead obstructions, slip socket over plug first (you can remove the rubber insert for added clearance), then loosen plug by turning the socket with a wrench or with locking pliers.

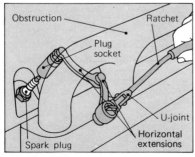

4. Use additional extensions or U-joints to get at plugs that are hard to reach. Extensions and U-joints can be connected in tandem to provide a variety of wrench angles and positions.

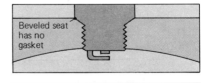

5. To remove loosened hard-to-reach plug, slip length of vacuum hose or spark plug cable over plug terminal, and spin. Reverse procedure to replace plug. Insert a screwdriver into hose to extend reach.

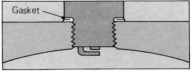

6. Screw plugs in by hand until they seat. If plugs have gaskets, use a wrench to tighten plugs one-quarter or one-half turn more. Tighten plugs without gaskets only 1/16 additional turn.

Removing hard-to-reach GM plugs

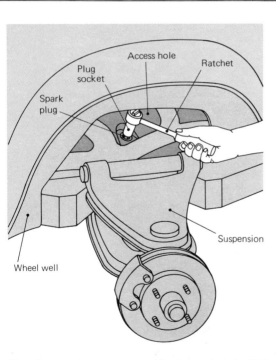

The plugs on the passenger's side of some mid-size GM cars may be blocked by accessories. To reach these plugs, jack up the car and remove the front wheel; the plugs can be reached through an access hole in the wheel well.

Cleaning and adjusting plugs ⏱ 5–10 min

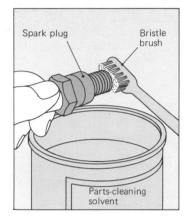

1. If the plugs can be reused (see p.72), wash them with parts-cleaning solvent and a stiff bristle brush; do not use a wire brush. Be careful not to leave bits of bristle on a plug, as these will impair its operation.

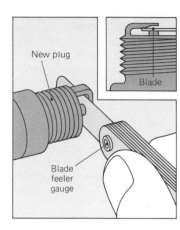

4. A blade feeler gauge can be used to measure the gap of new plugs; their electrodes have not become worn, so that the measurement will not be thrown off. Gap measurement is the number stamped on the feeler blade that will fit between a plug's electrodes without being forced.

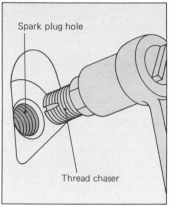

7. If the old plug was difficult to remove, clean the plug hole threads in the cylinder head with a thread chaser (p.432). If the head is made of aluminum, apply anti-seize compound to the threads before installing plugs. The compound comes in tubes and is sold by auto parts stores. You can tell whether or not the head is aluminum by putting a magnet on it; the magnet will stick to iron but not to aluminum.

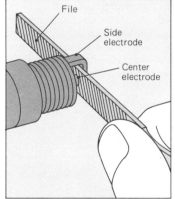

2. After plugs have dried, carefully pry their side electrodes away from the center electrodes. File electrodes until surfaces are flat and horizontal, and edges are sharp. Use a plug file.

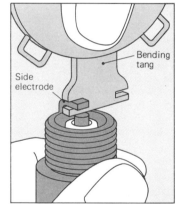

5. Compare the gap you have measured with the correct gap for your engine (see *Tuneup Data*) and adjust if necessary. To increase gap, bend side electrode away from center electrode, using the tang on the gap gauge. To decrease gap, bend the outer electrode toward center electrode. Do not use pliers or a hammer to bend a plug's electrodes.

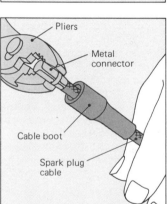

8. If a spark plug cable boot fits loosely on a plug terminal after the plugs are installed, push the rubber boot back and squeeze the metal connector with pliers. If connector is the right-angle type and you cannot push boot back, wrap the plier's jaws with tape and squeeze the boot carefully where it covers the connector.

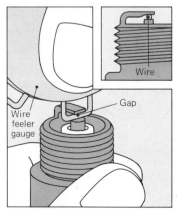

3. Measure the electrode gap on used plugs with a wire feeler gauge. Do not use a blade feeler gauge, since it can give a false reading on worn electrodes (see inset, Step 4). Wire gauges may not be available for the extra-wide plug gaps specified for some modern engines; in that case, use a bar-type gauge designed to measure gaps up to .080 in.

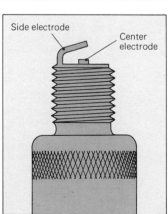

6. Do not bend the side electrode too far. If the outer electrode must be bent away from the center electrode at a sharp angle, as illustrated here, you are trying to adjust a narrow-gap plug for an engine that requires a wide-gap plug (see p.71). Buy only the plug model that is recommended by the carmaker.

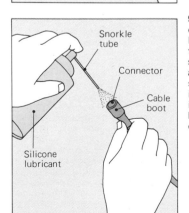

9. To ensure a durable electrical contact between spark plug's terminal and cable, spray silicone lubricant or dab an electrically conductive silicone grease on the inside of the connector in the cable boot. Do this before you attach the cables to the plugs.

Checking and adjusting ignition timing ⚙⚙ 15–30 min

"Timing" refers to the exact moment when the spark plug fires the air-fuel mixture in a cylinder. In most engines this occurs just before the piston reaches the top of its compression stroke (see p.33). The exact moment is specified in terms of crankshaft rotation (the crankshaft rotates 360 degrees to move each piston up and down in its cylinder).

The top of the piston's stroke is called *top dead center* (TDC). A typical timing specification might be 12 degrees before top dead center (12° BTDC). Occasionally, timing may be specified *after top dead center* (ATDC). If the spark timing is moved forward (from 12° BTDC to 15° BTDC, for example) it is said to be *advanced*. If it is moved backward (from 12° BTDC to 6° BTDC), it is said to be *retarded*.

Setting ignition timing is the last electrical step in the tuneup process before the carburetor is checked. On cars with breaker-point ignition systems, the timing changes as the points wear or when the point gap is changed. Whenever new points are installed or old ones are adjusted, the timing should be reset. Cars with electronic ignition may be harder to adjust, but the intervals between adjustments are much longer than those for breaker-point ignitions. Timing on both types should be checked at every tuneup or whenever the point gap has been changed.

Timing is adjusted by turning the distributor until a timing mark on the engine crankshaft lines up with a stationary mark on the engine. A flashing strobe light triggered by the spark to the No.1 cylinder illuminates the timing marks and makes them seem to stand still when the engine is running.

Timing specifications appear on the emission-control information decal in the engine compartment of cars built since 1970 (opposite page), in most owner's manuals, in all workshop manuals, and in the *Tuneup Data* supplement to this book. Follow the instructions for disconnecting and plugging vacuum hoses, turning equipment on or off, and setting engine rpm.

The first step is to locate and clean the timing marks on your engine. Most are on the front crankshaft pulley. Some are on the flywheel and are visible through a small opening in the clutch housing. If the marks are not clear, clean them and chalk or paint the correct timing mark and the pointer so that they will show up clearly in the flash from the timing light. Timing marks are indicated in the same way as the markings on a ruler. If there are five lines and the first one is marked 0 and the last one is marked 5, each line represents 1 degree; if the first line is marked 0 and the last one is marked 10, each line represents 2 degrees. If you cannot see the timing marks because engine accessories or body panels are in the way, you will have to make auxiliary marks; see *How to make your own timing marks*, p.238.

Connect the timing light, following the instructions that came with it. Since engine speed affects timing, connect an accurate tachometer and leave it hooked up while timing the engine. Some timing lights have a built-in tachometer.

Start the engine and aim the timing light at the timing marks, taking care to avoid the *parallax errors* that can occur if your line of sight is not parallel to the beam emitted by the timing light (see Step 5, opposite page). The timing marks should look stationary and clear. If the specified timing marks line up and appear steady, the timing is OK. If the proper marks do not line up, or if they appear to waver unsteadily, double-check the emission-control information decal to make sure that all instructions for setting the timing have been observed. Then loosen the bolt on the distributor clamp, and slowly turn the distributor until the timing marks line up. Shut off the engine, tighten the locking bolt, and recheck timing to make sure that it did not shift as the distributor clamp bolt was tightened.

Timing modules used on 1977 Oldsmobile Misar electronic ignition systems have an adjusting bolt that changes the timing about 1 degree for each turn. Read the timing marks with a timing light as you would on any other car, but shut off the engine before turning the bolt (see p.238).

> **Tools:** Power timing light with electronic or inductive pickup, distributor wrench, nylon strap wrench, tachometer with 0- to 1,200-rpm scale.
> **Materials:** Chalk, paint, or nail polish; rag.

Timing marks on the pulley

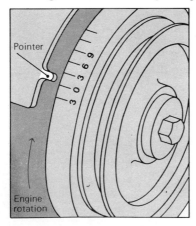

Timing marks are found on the pulley at the front of the crankshaft on many engines. The pointer is on the engine block. The zero indicates TDC and the single 3 refers to 3 degrees after TDC. The marks ahead of the zero indicate degrees before TDC. The direction of engine rotation can be deduced from the timing marks: BTDC numbers must pass the pointer before ATDC numbers can.

Timing marks on the engine

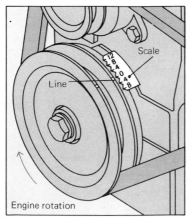

Some engines have a single timing line on the pulley and a degree scale on the engine block. Chalk or paint a narrow white line along the marks for the timing setting for your engine. The extra marks are used by the manufacturer for the variations of your engine. The degree scale may be marked BTDC and ATDC or just A and R (for *Advance* and *Retard*).

Timing marks on the flywheel

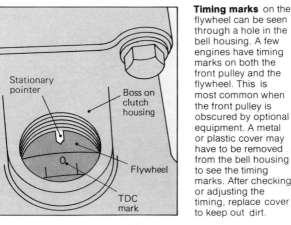

Timing marks on the flywheel can be seen through a hole in the bell housing. A few engines have timing marks on both the front pulley and the flywheel. This is most common when the front pulley is obscured by optional equipment. A metal or plastic cover may have to be removed from the bell housing to see the timing marks. After checking or adjusting the timing, replace cover to keep out dirt.

Types of distributor clamps

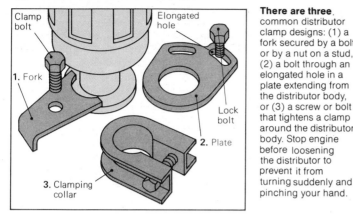

Clamp bolt
Elongated hole
1. Fork
Lock bolt
2. Plate
3. Clamping collar

There are three, common distributor clamp designs: (1) a fork secured by a bolt or by a nut on a stud, (2) a bolt through an elongated hole in a plate extending from the distributor body, or (3) a screw or bolt that tightens a clamp around the distributor body. Stop engine before loosening the distributor to prevent it from turning suddenly and pinching your hand.

Freeing a stuck distributor

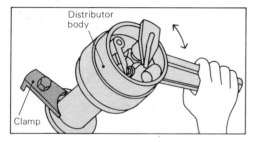

Distributor body
Clamp

If the distributor body will not turn when its clamp is loosened, free it by tapping the housing with a light plastic hammer. Or use a nylon strap wrench to turn the distributor. Do not apply force to vacuum advance diaphragm.

Timing specifications

Ford	FORD MOTOR COMPANY VEHICLE EMISSION CONTROL INFORMATION	SHIFT SCHED	MAINT SCHED	B

ENGINE FAMILY 2.8 "BV" (1X160)EGR/AIR/CATALYST
ENGINE DISPLACEMENT 2.8 (171 CID)   TRANS. AUTO
SPARK PLUG AWSF-42   GAP .032-.036

CATALYST   EVAP. Family is . . .

VALVE LASH	INT. COLD.014 EXH. COLD.016	ALTITUDE	☐ OVER 4000 FT ☒ UNDER 4000 FT	
TRANSMISSION GEAR		NEUTRAL	DRIVE	
IGNITION TIMING ±2°			6°BTDC	IDLE SPEED REDUCTION (LESS THAN 100 MILES)
TIMING RPM			750	
CHOKE SETTING		INDEX		
FAST IDLE ±100 RPM	HIGH CAM			150
	KICK DOWN			
CURB IDLE ±50 RPM	A/C		750	75
	NON A/C		750	

MAKE ALL ADJUSTMENTS WITH ENGINE AT NORMAL OPERATING TEMPERATURE, A/C AND HEADLIGHTS OFF, DISCONNECT SENSOR CONNECTOR AT IGNITION MODULE BEFORE SETTING TIMING OR CURB IDLE (IF SO EQUIPPED). CONSULT SERVICE PUBLICATIONS FOR ADDITIONAL INSTRUCTIONS ON THE FOLLOWING PROCEDURES.

IGNITION TIMING: ADJUST WITH HOSES DISCONNECTED AND PLUGGED AT THE DISTRIBUTOR.

CURB IDLE: ADJUST WITH ALL VACUUM HOSES CONNECTED, AIR CLEANER IN POSITION, AND THROTTLE SOLENOID POSITIONER ENERGIZED (IF SO EQUIPPED).

Specific instructions for setting the timing appear on the emission-control decal located in the engine compartment of cars built since 1970. Manufacturers sometimes change the specifications after a car is built, so check the *Tuneup Data* supplement to this book.

Using a timing light

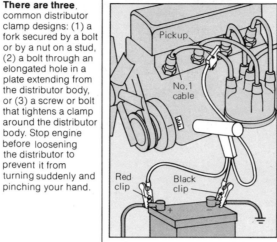

Pickup
No.1 cable
Red clip
Black clip

1. Connect an inductive pickup by clamping the pickup over the spark plug cable to the No.1 cylinder. (See firing order diagrams in *Tuneup Data* to find No.1 cylinder on your engine.) Attach power leads to battery.

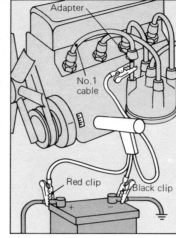

Adapter
No.1 cable
Red clip
Black clip

2. Connect a timing light with direct pickups to the No.1 spark plug cable, using the adapter supplied with the light. Attach the red power lead to the positive battery terminal and the black lead to the negative terminal.

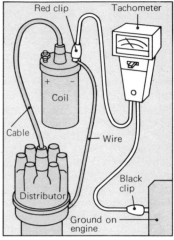

Red clip
Tachometer
Coil
Cable
Wire
Distributor
Black clip
Ground on engine

3. Attach black tachometer lead to a good ground on the engine. Attach red lead to the primary wire contact on the coil. (Attach red lead to terminal marked TACH on GM HEI distributors.) Use adapters when necessary.

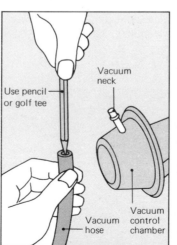

Use pencil or golf tee
Vacuum neck
Vacuum hose
Vacuum control chamber

4. Vacuum hoses to distributor vacuum controls may have to be plugged while timing is adjusted. Follow instructions on emission-control decal in engine compartment. Start engine and set idle speed (p.252).

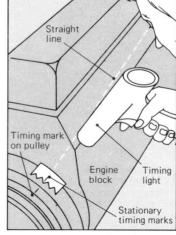

Straight line
Timing mark on pulley
Engine block
Timing light
Stationary timing marks

5. Aim the pistol-like timing light directly at the timing marks on the pulley or engine . Aim in as straight a line as possible. If the line of sight is not parallel to the plane of the pulley or flywheel, parallax errors will result.

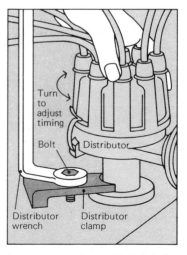

Turn to adjust timing
Bolt
Distributor
Distributor wrench
Distributor clamp

6. Loosen distributor clamp bolt just enough so that you can turn the distributor against light resistance. Turn distributor until nail polish or chalk marks line up in strobe light. Tighten clamp bolt, then recheck timing.

237

Making your own timing marks 🔧🔧🔧 30 min–1 hr

It may be difficult to use a conventional timing light with the timing marks on some new cars. New engines are designed to be timed by special test equipment that is triggered by a magnetic timing probe. Car dealers and modern repair shops may not use the conventional timing marks, which are often obscured by engine accessories. You can use a timing light to check and adjust such engines if you make your own timing marks on a part of the engine that is more accessible.

If your engine has an access hole in the bell housing, you may be able to make your own timing marks on the flywheel. Otherwise, you will have to fabricate a pointer and make timing marks on a visible segment of the crankshaft pulley.

Pick a segment of the pulley that is easy to see and at which a timing light can be aimed easily without its wires becoming tangled in the fan. Next, make a pointer. Then, make the timing marks for ignition advance at idle speed and at the maximum advance engine speed specified on the emission-control decal.

Measure the circumference of the pulley, convert that number to 64ths of an inch, then divide by 360. This gives you the number of inches your crankshaft pulley turns for every degree of crankshaft rotation. Position the No.1 piston at TDC, and mark the pulley as shown in the illustrations below and at the right.

> **Tools:** Tape measure, pocket calculator, file or center punch and hammer, artist's paintbrush.
> **Materials:** Adhesive tape, white paint, rags.

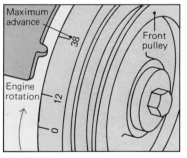

Maker's stationary timing scale

Maker's timing mark on pulley

White tip

Auxiliary stationary timing pointer

Auxiliary timing scale on pulley

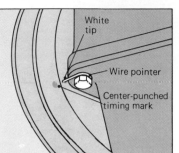

White tip

Wire pointer

Center-punched timing mark

1. Choose a part of the pulley that is clearly visible, then make a pointer from a piece of sheet metal or stiff wire. Attach pointer to engine with an oil-pan bolt or other nearby fastener. Position No.1 piston at TDC (p.237) and punch new TDC mark opposite the pointer.

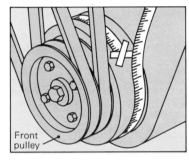

Front pulley

2. Measure pulley circumference. This pulley is 16½ in., or 1,040 64ths. Divide by 360 to get 2.889/64 per degree. To mark 12 degrees of advance, multiply 12 by 2.889, and measure 34.668 64ths (35/64) ahead of TDC mark. Mark this point with a file or center punch.

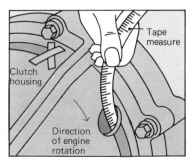

Maximum advance

Front pulley

Engine rotation

3. Paint new pointer and timing marks white. (If the paint becomes cracked, you know the pointer has been bent.) Use new marks to set timing as shown on pages 236–237. The maximum advance mark can be used to check the distributor's advance mechanisms (p.239).

Tape measure

Clutch housing

Direction of engine rotation

4. Measuring and marking the flywheel is more difficult than marking the crankshaft pulley. Mark TDC on flywheel. Attach tape measure to TDC mark with adhesive tape. Turn engine manually (p.275) and feed tape into hole. Calculate and make timing marks.

Auxiliary timing marks

All engines have auxiliary timing marks on internal parts to aid in assembly and rebuilding. Some of these are visible from outside the engine and can be used to position the No.1 piston at TDC. If you can obtain a workshop manual for your car, you can locate these marks on your engine and use them as aids for making new timing marks. Crankshaft pulleys, camshaft pulleys, and flywheels often have these marks, although they may not all be visible when the engine is assembled and installed in the car.

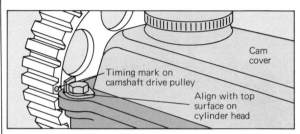

Cam cover

Timing mark on camshaft drive pulley

Align with top surface on cylinder head

Timing marks on the camshaft drive pulley and cam cover of this VW engine are visible when the engine is assembled. When the marks are aligned, the No.1 piston is at TDC.

Oldsmobile timing module

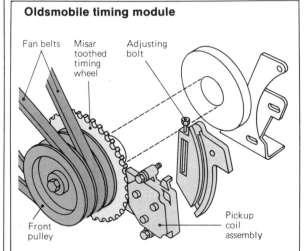

Fan belts

Misar toothed timing wheel

Adjusting bolt

Front pulley

Pickup coil assembly

1977 Oldsmobile Toronados have a Misar computer electronic ignition system. Every revolution of the adjusting bolt on the pickup coil changes the timing by 1 degree. Turn bolt only when engine is off, then start engine and check timing with a timing light (p.237).

Using a timing light to test the distributor ⬛⬛ 10–20 min

Vacuum controls

The vacuum controls on distributors may advance or retard timing. They can be tested with a timing light. Connect light (p.237), run engine at a fast idle, and aim the light at the timing marks. Pull each vacuum hose off the distributor in turn, seal its open end with your finger to prevent vacuum loss, then reconnect hose. Timing should shift noticeably as each hose is connected and disconnected. If it does not, and there is vacuum in the hose, replace the vacuum-control assembly (p.408).

Centrifugal advance

Check centrifugal advance by hand or in operation. To check by hand, remove distributor cap and twist rotor in direction of distributor rotation. Rotor should move about ¼ in., then snap back under spring pressure when released. Timing light check is made with standard hookup (see p.237) and engine at idle. Increase engine speed to about 2,500 rpm. Timing should advance smoothly. If spring action is sluggish or nonexistent, or if advance is jerky, replace springs (p.409) or distributor (p.410).

Distributor condition

Timing marks that jump about or blur in the flash of the timing light may indicate a worn distributor bearing, a weak points spring, or a worn cam. A *dwell-holding test* checks both bearing and cam. Connect dwell-tachometer (p.237) and increase engine speed from idle to about 2,000 rpm. Dwell reading should hold within three degrees. If it shifts more than six degrees, or if shaft can be moved sideways in its bearing with engine off, replace distributor (p.410). Check the points spring (p.222) in older ignition systems.

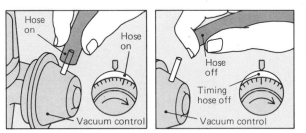

Pull off vacuum-control hose (left) and cover end with a finger. Reinstall hose. Timing marks (insets) should move noticeably.

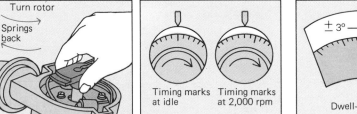

Turn rotor by hand about ¼ in. (left). It should spring back. Timing marks (right) should move smoothly as engine rpm increases.

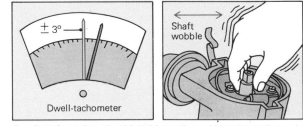

Dwell-tachometer should hold reading within about three degrees as rpm is increased (left). Shaft (right) should not wobble.

Checking timing on cars with electronic ignition ⬛⬛ 10–20 min

In theory, cars with electronic ignition systems should hold spark timing forever. In practice, you should check timing every time you replace spark plugs. A timing check can also indicate the condition of computer components and sensors.

In computerized systems, vacuum, electromechanical, and electronic sensors supply information to the computer (see pp.80–81). The *emission-control decal* tells which controls and sensors should be left alone and which must be disconnected when timing is checked. Follow all instructions exactly.

If the computer fails, a fixed timing setting enables the car to limp home, although with decreased performance and increased fuel consumption. Check the computer with a timing light. Connect the timing light (p.237). If the light performs erratically, split a short piece of rubber tubing and place it around the No.1 spark plug wire under the timing light's inductive pickup. Have a helper start the engine, put the transmission in *Neutral,* hold the throttle briefly at a fast idle, depress the pedal for higher engine speeds, and then back off to idle. You should see definite changes in timing. If the timing marks remain in the same position, have the computer system checked.

On most GM cars with computer-controlled timing

(and on AMC cars with GM engines), you adjust spark timing by turning the distributor. On Cadillacs with throttle-body fuel injection, you must first use a jumper wire to ground the pink wire in the open green test connector near the distributor.

Check timing on Ford EEC I (1978–79 302 V-8s) and EEC II (1979 and some 1980 302 and 351 V-8s with silver emission-control decals) at 28° to 32° with a special timing light or auxiliary timing marks (opposite page). EEC III cars (1980s with gold decals) are checked with the computer system in the self-test mode (pp.388–389). The computer controls timing, which cannot be adjusted except by static rotor alignment (see illustration). If the timing is incorrect, have a Ford shop check and correct the system.

A helper is required to check the timing on Chrysler cars with Lean Burn systems. Ground the carburetor's idle stop switch (see illustration). Connect the timing light (p.237). With the engine fully warmed up, have a helper start the engine, blip the throttle, step on the brakes, then put the transmission in *Drive* and let the engine idle. Watch the timing marks. Timing should show more advance than specified for 1 to 1½ minutes, then settle to specification. If it settles incorrectly, adjust timing (p.237).

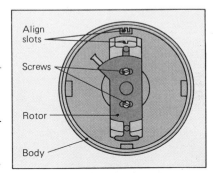

To align rotor on Ford V-8s with EEC III, turn crankshaft pulley until timing marks are at zero (TDC). Slots on distributor body and rotor should be aligned. If not, loosen screws on rotor and align slots (p.409). Retighten screws.

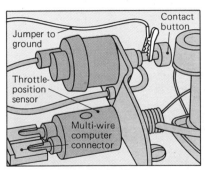

Ground contact button of carburetor's idle switch when timing Chrysler cars with Lean Burn systems. On some models the throttle-position sensor must be disconnected also (check the emission-control decal in the engine compartment).

Periodic checks

From a simple filter mounted on top of the carburetor, the air cleaner has evolved into a complex, thermostatically controlled unit that is part of the car's emission-control system (p.56). Although most air cleaners are mounted on the carburetor, some—especially in fuel-injected or turbocharged engines—are mounted in remote positions (see opposite page). To locate these remotely mounted units, trace the large duct from the carburetor or the fuel-injection system's intake manifold to the air cleaner.

Air cleaners have always required periodic maintenance. The filter inside the housing should be removed and inspected every 12,000 miles (20,000 km). If the filter is wet, damaged, or very dirty, it should be replaced with a new one designed specifically for your engine. Running your car with a clogged filter could result in hard starting, stalling, and poor gas mileage. A damaged filter can cause excess engine wear. When inspecting the air filter, you should also remove and inspect the positive crankcase ventilation (PCV) filter and, if necessary, replace it with a new one. Instructions for servicing the thermostatic controls are on pages 242-243.

In order to perform certain jobs, you will have to remove the entire air cleaner assembly, not just the filter. This usually involves disconnecting several hoses and various clamps that are attached to the snorkel, sides, and underside of the air cleaner (see below). Until you are completely familiar with the air cleaner in your car, label each hose and its attachment point on the air cleaner so that you will be able to reassemble the unit properly.

> **Tools:** Pliers, wrenches, screwdrivers.
> **Materials:** Droplight, compressed air, masking tape, pencil or pen, clean rags.

Removing and inspecting air filters and PCV filters 🕑 10–30 min

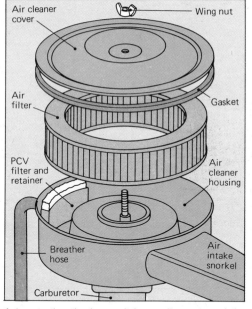

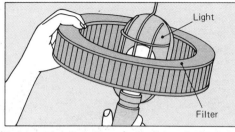

To inspect most air filters, hold a light to the inner side and revolve the filter around the light. If you can see light through the entire filter, it is clean and may be reused. If the filter is slightly dirty, it can be reused after you remove the dirt. To dislodge and remove the dirt, gently tap the filter against a flat surface or blow compressed air through it. If the air filter is so dirty that you cannot see light through it—or if the filter is torn, damaged, or wet—replace it with a new one.

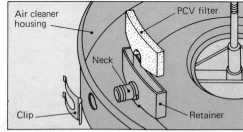

To remove a PCV filter, remove the clip holding the crankcase breather hose to the air cleaner, and pull the hose from the neck of the PCV filter's retainer. Pull filter retainer away from the side of the air cleaner, then slip the filter from the retainer. Inspect the filter; if it is wet, clogged, or very dirty, replace it.

1. Locate the air cleaner. It is usually on top of the carburetor; for variations, see opposite page.
2. Remove the cover from the air cleaner. Cover is usually held in place by a wing nut or by bolts, nuts, or clips. If any hoses attached to the cover interfere with its removal, disconnect them first.
3. Lift out the air filter and inspect it for dirt, tears, or damage. Replace filter if necessary.
4. Remove and inspect the PCV filter; if necessary, replace it with a new one.
5. Reverse removal procedure to reinstall PCV filters and air filters. Secure the cover of the air cleaner.

Removing an air cleaner 🕑 10–30 min

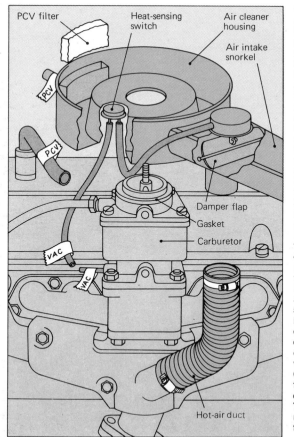

1. Remove the air cleaner cover. Remove and inspect air and PCV filters; replace if necessary.
2. Free any clamps and disconnect any ducts and hoses that interfere with removal of air cleaner. If several hoses must be disconnected, use masking tape to label the hoses and the nipples to which they are attached. This will help you reconnect them properly.
3. Remove any nuts or bolts holding air cleaner to engine. Lift air cleaner off the carburetor.
4. Inspect all ducts, hoses, and lines that were disconnected. Replace any that are damaged.
5. Inspect the gasket between the air cleaner and the carburetor; if it is cracked or soaked with oil, replace it.
6. Wipe the inside of the housing and cover clean.
7. Reverse order of removal to reinstall filters and cleaner.

Removing specific types of air filters ⚡ 10–30 min

Dodge Omni, Plymouth Horizon

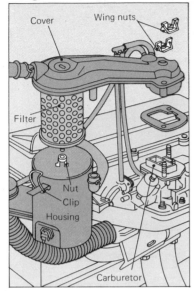

Omnis and Horizons have a canister-like air cleaner next to the carburetor cover. The air cleaner extends to the carburetor. To remove the filter:
1. Remove the two wing nuts holding the cover to the carburetor. Unsnap the two clips that hold the cover to the air cleaner.
2. Lift off the cover; the air filter will come with it.
3. Remove the wing nut at the bottom of the filter, and slip the filter off the rod.
4. Inspect filter and clean or replace it.
5. Reverse order of removal to reinstall the filter.

GM cars with turbocharged V-6 engines

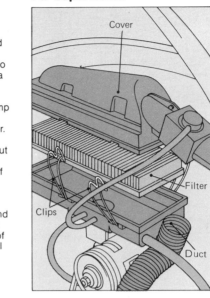

In GM cars with turbocharged V-6 engines, the air cleaner is mounted next to the engine and is connected to the carburetor by a duct. To remove the filter:
1. Loosen the clamp that holds duct to cover of air cleaner. Pull the duct off.
2. Remove wing nut holding cover in place. Lift cover off housing.
3. Lift out and inspect the filter (opposite page) and clean or replace it.
4. Reverse order of removal to reinstall the filter.

VW Super Beetle

VW Super Beetle and several other imported cars have rectangular air cleaners that may be attached to the carburetor (as shown) or remotely mounted and attached to the carburetor by a duct. To remove this type of filter:
1. Open the wire clips by hand.
2. Disconnect hot-air duct and lift cover.
3. Lift out and inspect the filter (opposite page) and replace it if necessary.
4. Reverse order of removal to reinstall the filter and cover.

Datsun Z models

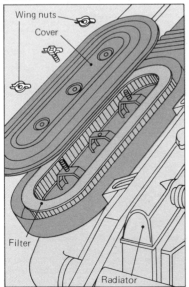

The air cleaner is mounted in front of the radiator on Datsun 240Z, 260Z, 280Z, and 280ZX cars. It is connected to the carburetor or fuel-injection system by a duct. Early models have an oval filter; late models, a rectangular filter. To remove the filter:
1. Remove the wing nuts or wire clips that hold the cover in place.
2. Lift the cover off the housing.
3. Lift out and inspect the filter, and clean or replace it.
4. Reverse order of removal to reinstall the filter.

GM sealed air cleaners

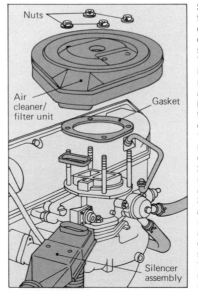

Some GM cars with four-cylinder, overhead cam engines have a sealed air cleaner. The filter cannot be inspected; you must replace the entire unit at 50,000-mile intervals, or sooner if the car exhibits signs of a clogged filter.
1. Remove the bolt or nuts that hold unit to carburetor.
2. Disconnect the silencer assembly and lift the unit out.
3. Inspect gaskets and grommet; replace them if they are wet, cracked, or damaged. Colored side of gasket must face carburetor.
4. Reverse order of steps to install unit.

VW Rabbit with fuel-injected engine

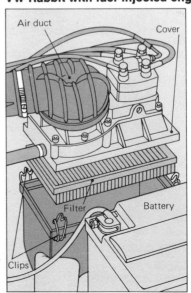

In fuel-injected VW Rabbits the air cleaner is mounted behind the battery. To locate the air cleaner, follow the air duct from the intake manifold. To remove the filter:
1. Unfasten the clips at the back and front of the air cleaner.
2. Lift cover off housing; the fuel distributor and filter will come with it.
3. Pull filter off cover and inspect it (opposite page). Clean or replace the filter.
4. Reverse order of removal to reinstall the filter.

Heat-controlled air cleaners

The heat-controlled air cleaner system (p.56) functions as part of the car's emission-control system; basically, it serves as a preheater for the air in the carburetor. By keeping the temperature of the air that enters the carburetor within a specific range, the carburetor can run much leaner, and pollution emissions are reduced. The heat-controlled air cleaner system also improves the drivability of a cold engine; some systems have an additional control that operates during acceleration, when engine vacuum is low (see *Additional controls*, opposite page).

The heat source for the system is the exhaust manifold. A sheet-metal duct, called a *stove*, around the manifold collects the heat and directs it through a duct connected to the air cleaner's snorkel. The snorkel is also connected to an outside-air intake duct. A damper flap inside the snorkel controls the proportions of heated or outside air that enters the air cleaner and the carburetor. The damper flap may be moved by a mechanical thermostat inside the snorkel, or by a heat-sensing switch inside the air cleaner plus a vacuum diaphragm, called a *vacuum*

motor, on top of the snorkel. Loss of engine power or an engine that runs unevenly until it warms up may indicate a poorly operating damper flap. Check the operation of the damper flap at every tuneup. If you cannot see the flap, reach inside the snorkel with a pencil to feel the flap move.

> **Tools:** Long-nose pliers, screwdrivers, drill and drill bits, small sheet-metal screws.
> **Materials:** Replacement parts as needed.

Checking damper flap operation

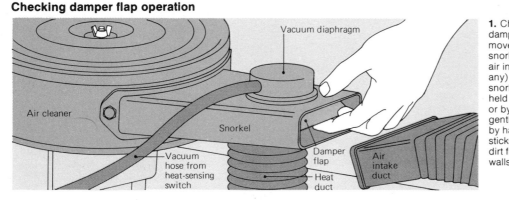

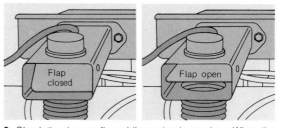

1. Check that the damper flap can move freely inside the snorkel. Remove the air intake duct (if any) from the snorkel; it is usually held in place by clips or by clamps. Then gently work the flap by hand. If the flap sticks, clean off any dirt from the inner walls of the snorkel.

2. Check the damper flap while engine is running. When the engine is cold, the flap should be closed to outside air (left); when the engine is hot, the flap should open (right). If the flap does not move, there is a problem with the controls.
Caution: Do not touch hot or moving engine parts.

Testing a thermostatically operated damper flap 🔧🔧 30 min–1½ hr

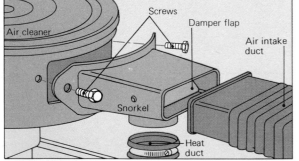

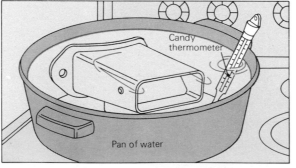

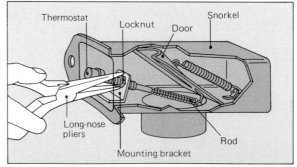

1. With the engine off, remove the snorkel. Disconnect heat duct and air intake duct from the snorkel, then remove the screws holding the snorkel to the air cleaner. If snorkel is part of the air cleaner, remove the air cleaner (p.240). If the spring is disconnected from the damper flap, use long-nose pliers to reconnect it.

2. Immerse snorkel in a pan of water, making sure that the thermostat is covered. Insert a candy thermometer, then heat the water. The flap should be closed when water temperature is below 105° F (40° C), open when temperature exceeds 130° F (54° C). If flap does not move, replace the thermostat or snorkel.

To replace thermostat, use long-nose pliers to loosen locknut. Unhook door rod. Unscrew stat and pull it out. Note position of the locknut, then remove it and screw it onto the new thermostat to exactly the same position. Screw new stat into mounting bracket; reattach door rod. Unscrew stat until door closes. Tighten locknut.

Testing a vacuum-operated damper flap 🔄🔄 30 min–1½ hr

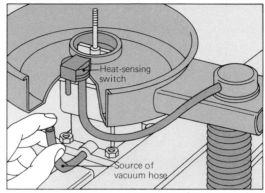

1. Remove air cleaner's cover and filter (p.240). Disconnect the vacuum hose from the heat-sensing switch. Turn on the engine and feel for vacuum. (**Caution:** Do not touch hot or moving engine parts.) If there is no vacuum, turn off the engine. Check that the hose is on tight. If hose is cracked, replace it. Reconnect the hose to the switch.

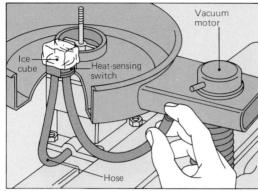

2. Disconnect the hose from the vacuum motor. Make sure that the hose is connected to the heat-sensing switch. If the hose is cracked, replace it. With the engine on, put an ice cube on top of the switch, let the switch cool, then feel for vacuum at the hose end. If there is no vacuum, replace the switch; if there is vacuum, replace the motor.

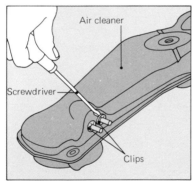

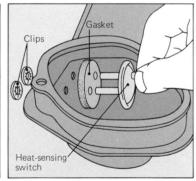

Heat-sensing switch replacement: Disconnect vacuum hoses from the switch and remove the air cleaner. Use a screwdriver to pry off the clips that hold the switch to the air cleaner. Remove switch and gasket. Install a new switch and gasket in the reverse order. Hold new switch by its outer edges; compress gasket to form a tight seal.

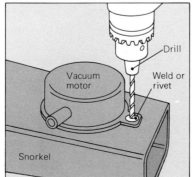

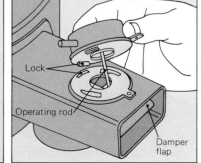

Vacuum motor replacement: Remove the air cleaner and disconnect the hose from the vacuum motor. Drill through the rivets or welds that hold the motor to the snorkel. Tip motor slightly forward to disengage lock, and rotate motor counterclockwise. To disengage the operating rod from the damper flap, slide the motor to one side. Install new vacuum motor in the reverse order. Use small sheet-metal screws to secure motor to snorkel.

Additional controls

Some heat-controlled air cleaner systems have an additional control that affects the temperature and/or the amount of air that enters the system during acceleration, when engine vacuum is low. If your car accelerates poorly, this additional control may be defective and need to be replaced. Have it checked by a professional mechanic.

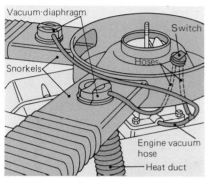

A dual-snorkel air cleaner has a damper flap in each snorkel. One snorkel is attached to the heat duct; the damper flap is controlled by the heat-sensing switch. The flap in the second snorkel is controlled by engine vacuum. During acceleration, both flaps open to admit outside air.

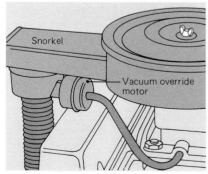

Some Ford cars have a Cold-Weather Modulator on the side of the air cleaner, in the vacuum line between the heat-sensing switch and the vacuum motor. When the outside air is below 55° F (13° C), the modulator traps the vacuum to keep the flap closed to outside air while engine accelerates.

A vacuum override motor is connected to the flap inside the snorkel of some thermostatically controlled damper flap units. When a cold engine is accelerating, the vacuum diaphragm overrides the thermostat control to open the damper flap; this allows outside air as well as heated air to enter the system.

Types of heat-control valves

There are two types of heat-control (*riser*) valves: self-contained and vacuum controlled (p.57). Both types are controlled by a thermostatic device. A self-contained valve is moved by a bimetallic spring that flexes with changes in temperature. A vacuum-controlled valve is moved by a vacuum diaphragm and rod; the vacuum to the diaphragm is controlled by a thermal vacuum switch (TVS) that is in contact with engine coolant or oil. Shown at the right are the typical locations of heat-control valves and their controls on an in-line and a V-type engine. Either kind of engine can have either type of valve.

The most frequent malfunction with a heat-control valve is that it becomes sticky. This can be prevented by applying aerosol penetrating oil to the shaft at every tuneup. Sometimes the control must be replaced. Instructions for replacing a simple spring thermostat, a diaphragm, and a thermal vacuum switch are given on these pages. Removing the valve itself is a more complicated job that involves taking off the exhaust pipes (pp.434-438) and, on many engines, removing the exhaust manifold.

Tools: Hammer, long-nose pliers, wrenches, screwdrivers.
Materials: Heat-control valve lubricant, penetrating oil, sealant, replacement parts as needed.

Self-contained valves on in-line engines

Vacuum-controlled valves in V-engines

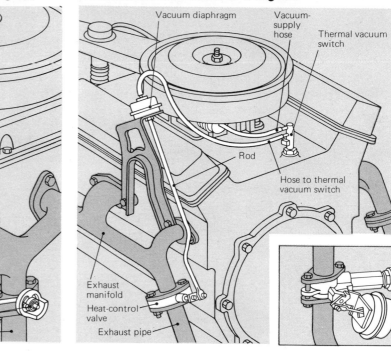

Vacuum diaphragm — Vacuum-supply hose — Thermal vacuum switch — Rod — Hose to thermal vacuum switch — Exhaust manifold — Heat-control valve — Exhaust pipe

Exhaust manifold — Heat-control valve — Exhaust pipe

Checking a self-contained valve ⏱ 5–10 min

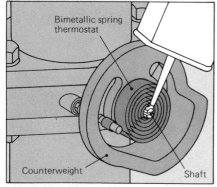

Bimetallic spring thermostat — Counterweight — Shaft

1. With the engine cold, try to turn the shaft by moving the counterweight by hand. If the valve sticks, apply penetrating oil to both ends of the shaft. Let the oil soak in, then work the shaft until it moves freely.

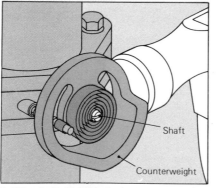

Shaft — Counterweight

2. If the shaft still sticks, apply more penetrating oil to both ends of the shaft, let the oil soak in, then tap the shaft from side to side by hammering on the counterweight. Work the shaft by hand once more until it moves freely.

Replacing a bimetallic-spring thermostat

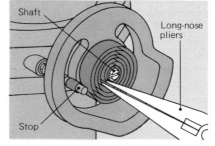

Shaft — Long-nose pliers — Stop

1. Grasp the center of the spring with long-nose pliers and pull it off the shaft. Remove the clip or pin holding the thermostat spring to the shaft, if necessary. The spring will automatically come off the stop.

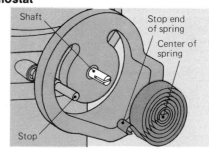

Shaft — Stop end of spring — Center of spring — Stop

2. To install the new spring, align the stop end of the spring with the stop on the manifold, and fit the center of the spring to the shaft. Center usually fits into a slot in the shaft. If necessary, reinstall the retaining clip or pin.

Checking a vacuum-controlled valve ⏱⏱ 10–20 min

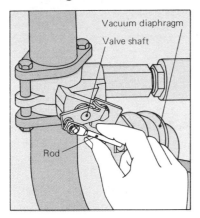

Vacuum diaphragm
Valve shaft
Rod

1. With engine cold, have a helper start the engine while you watch the rod that goes from the vacuum diaphragm to shaft of heat-control valve. Rod and shaft should move. If not, turn off engine and pull on rod to make sure that rod and shaft can move. Then skip to Step 3. **Caution:** Do not touch hot or moving parts; exhaust system heats up quickly.

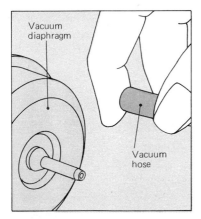

Shaft
Penetrating oil
Rod

2. If rod and shaft will not move, apply penetrating oil to both ends of the shaft. Let the oil soak in, then work the rod and shaft until they move freely. Repeat Step 1. If there is still no movement, proceed to Step 3. If rod and shaft now move freely, skip to Step 5.

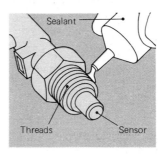

Vacuum diaphragm
Vacuum hose

3. Let the engine cool, then start it up again. Disconnect the vacuum hose from the vacuum diaphragm and feel for vacuum at the hose end. If there is no vacuum, reconnect the hose and proceed to Step 4. If there is vacuum, turn off the engine and replace the diaphragm (right) before proceeding to Step 4.

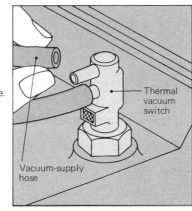

Thermal vacuum switch
Vacuum-supply hose

4. Locate TVS by tracing hose from diaphragm. Start engine. Disconnect vacuum-supply hose from TVS. If there is vacuum at hose, turn off engine and replace TVS (right). If there is no vacuum, turn off engine and clean or replace the vacuum-supply hose. Make sure the other end of the hose is firmly connected. **Caution:** Do not touch hot engine parts.

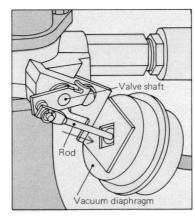

Valve shaft
Rod
Vacuum diaphragm

5. Let engine cool off, then turn it on again. Watch the rod and valve shaft as the engine warms up. When the engine has reached its normal operating temperature, the rod and shaft should move. If rod and shaft do not move, proceed to Step 6.

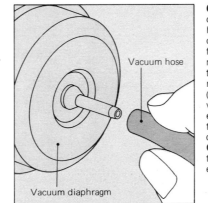

Vacuum hose
Vacuum diaphragm

6. Turn engine on, disconnect vacuum hose from diaphragm, and feel for vacuum. If there is no vacuum, turn off the engine and replace the TVS (right). If there is vacuum, turn off the engine and replace the vacuum diaphragm (right). **Caution:** Do not touch hot or moving engine parts.

Replacing a vacuum diaphragm

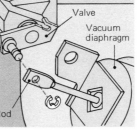

Mounting bracket
Bolt

1. With the engine off and cold, disconnect the vacuum hose from the vacuum diaphragm. Remove the nuts or bolts holding the diaphragm to its mounting bracket.

Valve
Vacuum diaphragm
Rod

2. Disengage the rod from the valve shaft, and remove the diaphragm and rod. Reverse removal procedure to install a new diaphragm. Reconnect the vacuum hose to the diaphragm.

Replacing a thermal vacuum switch

Thermal vacuum switch (TVS)
Hoses

1. With the engine off and cold, locate the TVS by tracing the hose from the vacuum diaphragm. Disconnect both hoses from the TVS. If TVS is in contact with coolant, drain coolant to below the level of the TVS (p.282).

Sealant
Threads
Sensor

2. Unscrew the TVS from the engine; screw in the new TVS. If TVS is in contact with coolant, apply sealant to threads of switch (not to sensor). Reconnect the two hoses; add new coolant if necessary.

Servicing PCV systems ⏱ 15–30 min

Positive crankcase ventilation (PCV) systems help to control automotive pollutants by drawing blow-by gases from the crankcase into the intake manifold, where they are mixed with the air-fuel mixture and burned in the engine (p.80). Yearly inspection and maintenance of the PCV valve, hoses, and filter helps to keep the system working properly. Illustrated below are six engines and the typical locations of PCV parts that need regular maintenance. Use the illustrations as guides to help you locate these parts on your engine. On many V-8s the PCV valve is mounted between the passages of the intake manifold. Specific maintenance procedures are given on the opposite page. If any parts are defective, replace them with new parts designed for your car model.

> **Tools and materials:** Pliers, sheet of paper, solvent.

Typical locations of PCV parts

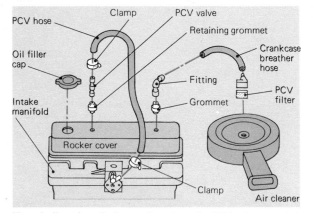

Many in-line six-cylinder engines have the PCV valve mounted in the rocker cover and held by a retaining grommet. The PCV hose runs from the PCV valve into the intake manifold. The crankcase breather hose extends from the rocker cover to the PCV filter inside the air cleaner.

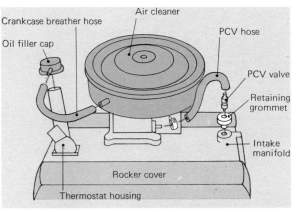

AMC V-8 engines have the PCV valve mounted in a retaining grommet in the intake manifold. The PCV hose goes from the PCV valve to the base of the carburetor. The crankcase breather hose runs from the air cleaner to the oil filler cap; there is a wire mesh filter inside the oil filler cap.

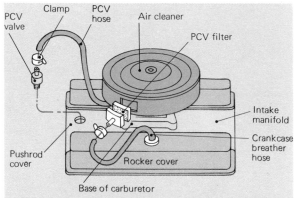

Some Pontiac V-8 engines have the PCV valve mounted in a retaining grommet in the pushrod cover, in front of the thermostat. The PCV hose connects the PCV valve to the intake manifold. The crankcase breather hose runs from the rocker cover to a PCV filter inside the air cleaner.

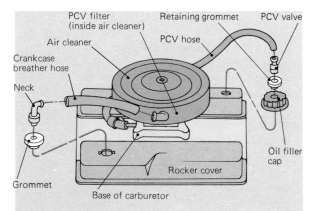

On many Ford V-8 engines the PCV valve is held by a retaining grommet to the oil filler cap, which is mounted on one of the rocker covers. The PCV hose runs from the PCV valve to the base of the carburetor. The crankcase breather hose runs from the other rocker cover to a PCV filter in the air cleaner.

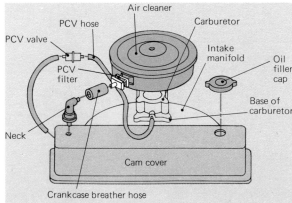

VW four-cylinder overhead camshaft engines used in AMC, Chrysler, and VW cars, have the PCV valve spliced into a hose that runs between the intake manifold and the base of the carburetor. The crankcase breather hose goes from the cam cover to a PCV filter inside the air cleaner.

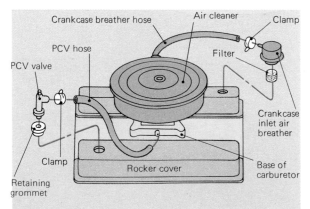

Chrysler V-8 engines have the PCV valve in a grommet in one of the rocker covers. The PCV hose runs from the PCV valve to the carburetor's base. The crankcase breather hose goes from the air cleaner to a crankcase inlet air breather on the other rocker cover. There is a filter inside the breather.

Inspecting and replacing a PCV valve and hose

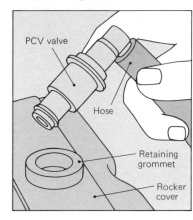

1. With the engine off, locate the PCV valve (see opposite page). Pull the valve out of its retaining grommet (shown). If the valve is spliced into a hose, pull the hose from one end of the valve.

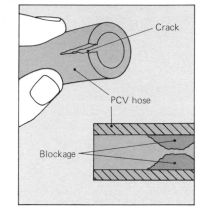

4. Inspect the PCV hose; if the PCV valve is spliced into the hose, be sure to inspect both sections of the hose. If the hose is cracked, blocked, damaged, or collapsed, remove the PCV valve and replace the hose. Then reinstall the PCV valve. Put the PCV valve back into its retaining grommet or other hose section.

2. Shake the PCV valve. If you cannot hear its internal parts rattle, the valve is plugged and should be replaced. Even if the valve rattles, it may be bad. Run the engine with the valve connected to its vacuum source. If you cannot feel strong vacuum at the open end of the valve, replace it.

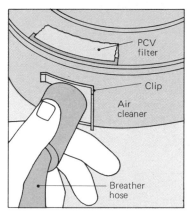

5. With the PCV valve and hose in place, disconnect the crankcase breather hose from the side of the air cleaner.

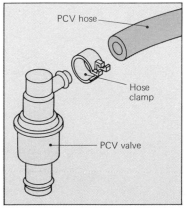

3. To replace a PCV valve, pull the valve out of its hose. It may be necessary to loosen a hose clamp before the valve will come out. Put a new valve into the hose; be sure that the new valve is facing in the same direction as the old one.

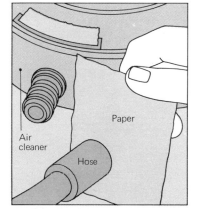

6. With the engine idling, put a piece of paper over the hose end. If vacuum does not hold the paper, the hose will be clogged and should be replaced. If breather hose is connected to a crankcase breather or oil filler cap, the filter in the breather or cap may need replacing or cleaning (right). **Caution:** Do not touch hot or moving engine parts.

Inspecting and replacing PCV filters

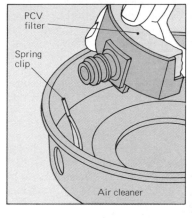

1. The PCV filter is located inside the air cleaner. The filter should be removed and inspected periodically. First, remove the air cleaner cover and filter (p.240). If the filter is dirty, replace it. Some filters are held to the side of the air cleaner by a spring clip. Slip the old filter out of the clip; slip new filter in.

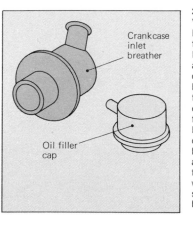

2. Other PCV filters sit in a retainer that is inside the air cleaner. Remove the air cleaner cover and the air filter (p.240). Then remove the clip that holds the crankcase breather hose to the outside of the air cleaner, and pull off the hose. Bring the retainer into the air cleaner; slip the PCV filter out of the retainer. Reverse order of removal to install a new filter.

3. Chrysler and AMC V-8 systems do not have a PCV filter in the air cleaner. Instead, Chrysler has a filter in the crankcase inlet air breather; AMC has a filter in the oil filler cap. To clean these filters, remove the breather or cap and disconnect any hoses that are attached. Then rinse the breather or cap with auto parts solvent. Let part dry before reinstalling it.

Checking automatic choke operation ⏱ 5–10 min

Most cars have an automatic choke that slowly opens as the engine warms up. A sticking choke plate or linkage is a common cause of hard starting. You can often free a sticking choke with an aerosol carburetor and choke solvent (sold in auto parts stores). Check choke operation as part of any tuneup.

The engine must be cold before choke operation can be checked properly. Remove the air cleaner cover. You should now be able to see the choke plate, at the mouth of the carburetor. Floor the accelerator pedal; the choke plate should close completely. Start the engine; the choke plate should open just a crack as the engine starts (see p.250). After 1 to 5 minutes of idling, the choke plate should be completely open (vertical). If the choke does not operate properly, it must be adjusted or repaired.

The choke plate is opened by a vacuum diaphragm or piston and closed by a bimetallic spring that responds to temperature changes by curling up tighter. This spring operates a series of rods and levers (the *choke linkage*) to swivel the choke plate. The spring is mounted in a housing on the carburetor, or in a well in the intake manifold. To locate the spring housing, remove the air cleaner, then jiggle the choke plate and trace the linkage.

The tension of the bimetallic spring can be adjusted, and this determines how quickly the choke plate opens or closes. The adjusting mechanism has a series of marks that may be labeled *Rich* to *Lean* (or *R* to *L*). Adjust the choke to the setting listed in the *Tuneup Data* supplement. "Index" is the center mark. "Two lean" means two marks off center, toward the side marked *L*. The adjusting mechanism may not be labeled. If you turn it in one direction and the choke plate closes, that direction is *Rich*, and the opposite direction is *Lean*. If the spring cannot be adjusted to close the choke plate all the way when the engine is cold, replace the spring unit.

The choke housings on 1981 and later cars are riveted shut and cannot be adjusted. To replace internal parts, you must drill out the rivets, and later attach a new housing with self-tapping screws.

Many newer cars have an electric heating element that speeds the opening of the choke. If this element is disconnected, the choke will open too slowly.

> **Tools:** Screwdrivers and wrenches to fit screws and/or bolts on your car's choke, long-nose pliers, pipe cleaner.
> **Materials:** Carburetor and choke solvent, penetrating oil.

Cleaning the choke linkage

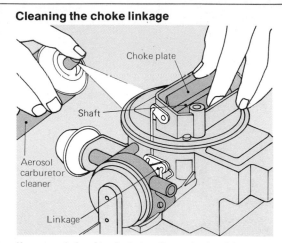

If your car is hard to start when the engine is cold, remove the air cleaner to observe choke operation. When the engine is cold (after standing overnight), floor the gas pedal once. If the choke plate does not close completely, clean the linkage and shaft until they can be moved freely by hand. If the choke plate still will not close tightly, clean the vacuum piston, link, and arm (opposite page).

Carburetor-mounted choke (used on AMC, Ford, most GM cars, and imports)   Manifold-mounted choke (used on Chrysler and some GM cars)

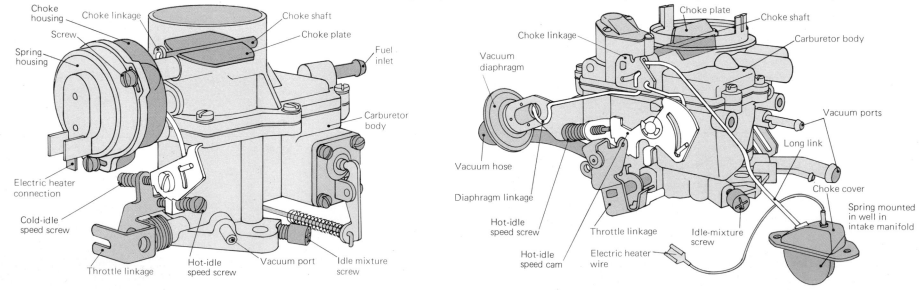

Servicing a carburetor-mounted choke 🔧🔧 30 min–2 hr

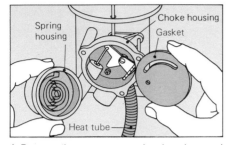

1. Remove three screws, spring housing, and gasket. If there is more than one slot on control arm, note which slot the spring was engaged in. If there are carbon deposits inside choke housing, remove them with solvent. Replace gasket and check heat tube (if any) for leaks.

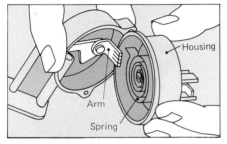

3. Clean spring with solvent and reassemble choke. If control arm has more than one slot, engage spring in original slot or in whichever slot will close choke plate completely when housing is set to the proper index mark (see Step 4). Do not tighten screws.

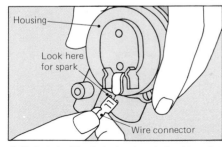

5. To test electric choke heater, start cold engine, pull off heater wire, and rub it along engine. If a spark does not jump gap, trace wiring for an open switch, blown fuse, or shorts (see pp.361–363). If wire sparks but choke does not open after 5 min of idling, replace heating element.

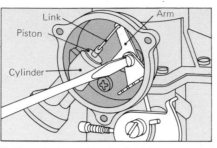

2. If control arm is attached to a vacuum-operated piston, make sure piston can move freely. If it cannot, choke plate will not open when engine is cranked. Spray arm and piston with solvent. If parts still bind, remove arm and piston, clean with solvent, and reassemble.

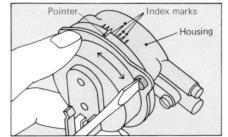

4. Turn housing to align pointer with proper index mark (see *Tuneup Data*). Tighten three screws. With engine cold, floor the gas pedal. If choke does not close completely, loosen screws and turn housing until plate closes. Tighten screws. Replace housing if plate will not close.

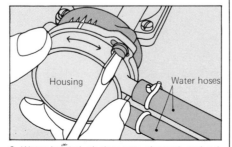

6. Water-heated chokes are cleaned and adjusted like any other carburetor-mounted choke (Steps 1–4). Some may have an electric heater too (Step 5). Feel hoses; if you feel no heat or pressure caused by coolant flow, check them for kinks, blockage, or damage (p.285).

Servicing a manifold-mounted choke 🔧🔧 20 min–1½ hr

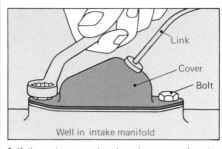

1. If there is no spring housing on carburetor, look for a manifold-mounted spring. Wiggle choke plate to identify its linkage. Follow long link down to its well in the intake manifold. Use a wrench to open bolts on well cover. Use penetrating oil if bolts are rusted tight.

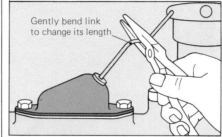

3. With engine cold, floor gas pedal. If choke plate does not close tightly, open manifold well and turn adjusting post (Step 2) until plate will close. On non-adjustable models, bend long link until choke plate closes. If link now rubs against cover, replace spring and link.

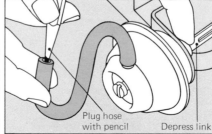

5. If there is vacuum in hose, and diaphragm does not move choke plate slightly, check if diaphragm pulls on the diaphragm link. If diaphragm moves the link but not the choke plate, adjust the vacuum break (p.250). If diaphragm does not move the link at all, it is defective.

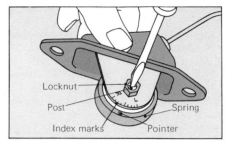

2. Lift spring assembly from well and clean it with solvent. Be sure that pointer is aligned with proper index mark (see *Tuneup Data*). If it is not, loosen locknut, and turn post on adjustable models until index marks are correctly aligned. Tighten locknut and reinstall unit in well.

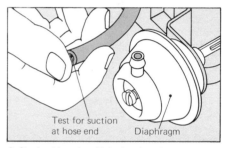

4. Start cold engine. If choke plate does not open slightly, disconnect diaphragm hose and feel for suction. If there is none, shut off engine. Clean out hose and vacuum port with a pipe cleaner. Replace leaking hoses. On cars with two diaphragms, test both.

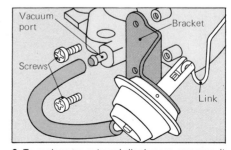

6. To replace an external diaphragm, unscrew it from the carburetor. Disengage link from choke lever. Note carburetor model numbers and take diaphragm to dealer or parts store to buy a replacement. Test an electric choke heater as shown in Step 5 at far left.

Checking and adjusting choke vacuum break ☑☑☑ 10–20 min

A vacuum diaphragm or piston opens the choke plate slightly after the engine starts. This *vacuum-break opening* can be critical—if it opens too much in cold weather or too little in warm weather the engine will stall. Check and correct choke operation first (pp.248–249), then measure the vacuum break on a cold engine.

Check vacuum break under the weather conditions that cause your car to stall. Use a drill bit as a feeler gauge to measure the gap between the choke plate and the carburetor's air horn. Measure the distance between the upper edge of the choke plate and the air horn on Chrysler cars (except those with four-barrel Carter Thermo-Quad carburetors), 1974–78 GM cars (except Chevette), Japanese cars unless otherwise specified, Ford cars with one-barrel Holley carburetors, and AMC cars with two-barrel Carter carburetors or with GM four-cylinder pushrod engines. On Volkswagens, Chevettes, and other Ford and AMC cars, measure the gap between the lower edge of the choke plate and the air horn.

Vacuum-break gaps or angles vary with each engine and carburetor combination. Get the specification from a professional auto parts store where you buy rebuilt parts and have machine work done.

Any of six types of vacuum-break adjusters may be used. **1.** A screw adjuster on a two-piece diaphragm link is used in many GM cars and in some AMC cars with GM engines. **2.** A bendable tang is used on Carter Thermo-Quad carburetors. **3.** A threaded hexagonal sleeve is used on the diaphragm link of some Ford cars. **4.** A screw adjusts the diaphragm of VWs and some AMC, Ford, and GM cars. **5.** A bendable diaphragm link is used in some North American and most Japanese cars. **6.** A choke lever extension is used on chokes that have a vacuum piston.

If there are two choke diaphragms on the carburetor, one may have an air bleed hole to delay its operation. Block any air bleed holes with tape before you check and adjust the vacuum-break opening. Also pull the rubber filter off the vacuum neck, and tape the air bleed under it. When you have finished testing and adjusting vacuum break, remove all tape and replace any filters.

> **Tools:** Choke plate angle gauge or drill bits, slotted bending tool, screwdrivers and wrenches to fit adjusting screws and nuts, pliers, hand-operated vacuum pump.

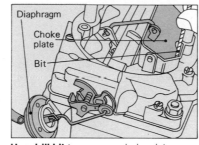

Use drill bit to measure choke plate opening on most cars. Apply vacuum to diaphragm to pull choke plate open while you apply light closing pressure on choke linkage with your finger. Check gap at top or bottom of plate (see text).

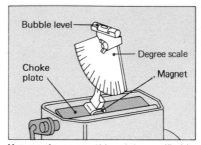

Use angle gauge if break is specified in degrees. Set degree scale to zero and rotate level until bubble is centered. Open choke plate as described at left. Rotate scale to specified angle. Bubble should be centered; if not, adjust vacuum break.

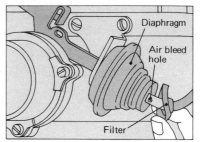

Tape air bleeds (if any) on vacuum diaphragms while adjusting vacuum break. An air bleed is a tiny hole in the vacuum fitting that is sometimes covered by a small doughnut-shaped filter. Remove tape after making the adjustment.

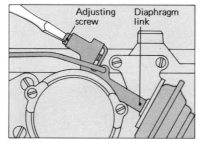

Screw adjuster on diaphragm link from front vacuum break is used to adjust choke plate angle or opening on many GM cars. Turn adjuster until bubble in level is centered when pointer on angle scale is aligned with specified choke plate angle.

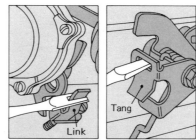

Bend link with a slotted tool to center bubble in level when setting rear vacuum diaphragm on GM carburetor at left. Bend tang on Carter Thermo-Quad with a screwdriver blade. Hold choke plate open with vacuum while you adjust break.

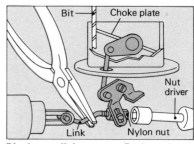

Diaphragm link on some Ford cars has a hexagonal nylon nut. Turn nut to set 1/32-in. clearance at the link when the choke plate is fully closed. Support link with long-nose pliers to keep it from flexing as the adjusting nut is turned.

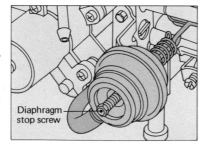

Screw or nut adjusts the diaphragm stop that controls vacuum break on VWs and some AMC, Ford, and GM cars. Hold choke plate open with vacuum and apply light closing pressure to choke linkage while making the adjustment.

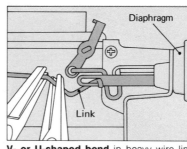

V- or U-shaped bend in heavy wire link can be made carefully to set the vacuum break on most Japanese and many other cars. Close or widen the bend with the pliers until choke plate opening matches the vacuum-break specification.

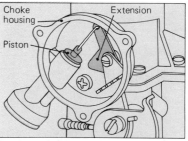

A vacuum piston control on the choke lever extension presents special adjustment problems and should be taken to a mechanic for correction if a vacuum-break check or a stalling problem makes you suspect that adjustment is incorrect.

Setting idle speed and fuel mixture 🔧🔧 10–20 min

As the emission-control standards applied to cars in the 1980s grow more stringent, adjusting the idle speeds and fuel mixtures to a point where they not only conform to these new standards but provide smooth engine performance becomes more complicated. If you cannot tune your engine correctly, have the job done by a professional mechanic. The procedures for adjusting a carburetor are listed on your engine's emission-control decal and in the *Tuneup Data* supplement to this book. These sources will tell you what gear the transmission should be in, the idle-speed specifications, and what hoses or wires must be disconnected.

Although the *cold-idle speed* (sometimes called fast-idle speed) can be set most accurately when the engine is hot and running evenly, this often involves disconnecting certain emission controls in order to simulate cold-engine conditions. If your problem is cold-engine stalling because the cold-idle speed is too low, or racing because the cold-idle speed is too high, set the cold-idle speed when the engine is cold (below). After setting the cold-idle speed, set the *hot-idle speed* (often called curb idle) by adjusting either a screw (below) or a solenoid (p.252). Some cars also specify a third idle-speed setting called *low*, or *slow, idle*; see p.252.

Once the idle speeds are set, set the fuel mixture. One-barrel carburetors have one fuel-mixture adjusting screw. Two- and four-barrel carburetors have two mixture screws. On newer cars these screws are covered with plastic caps that limit how far the screws can be turned. If you cannot get the proper mix within this range, or if the mixture screws are sealed, have the mixture set by a mechanic. (A more precise way of obtaining the correct fuel mixture is with the *propane-enrichment adjustment procedure;* see p.253.) After setting the fuel mixture, recheck the hot-idle speed and readjust it if necessary.

Caution: Always set the parking brake and chock the wheels before you begin to work. Do not touch any hot or moving engine parts.

Tools: Screwdrivers, wrenches, pliers, long-nose pliers, tachometer.

Locating the adjusters

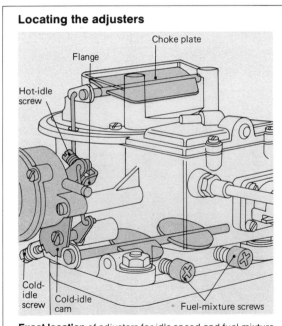

Choke plate · Flange · Hot-idle screw · Cold-idle screw · Cold-idle cam · Fuel-mixture screws

Exact location of adjusters for idle speed and fuel mixture will vary with carburetor design. In general, the cold-idle and hot-idle speed adjusters are near the throttle linkage, and the fuel-mixture screws are at the base of the carburetor. The cold-idle speed adjuster rests against a stepped cam (when the engine is cold) and the hot-idle speed adjuster hits a flange, or stop. Most mixture screws are covered with limiter caps; the mixture screws on cars built since 1981 are sealed and should not be tampered with.

Setting cold-idle speed

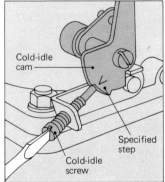

Cold-idle cam · Specified step · Cold-idle screw

Cold-idle speed is usually set by turning a screw. The engine must be cold. Attach a tachometer to the engine (p.223). Remove the air cleaner and start the engine. Pull the throttle linkage back by hand and put the tip of the cold-idle screw on the step of the cold-idle cam that is specified in *Tuneup Data*. Turn the screw until the engine is idling within 100 rpm of the specified speed.

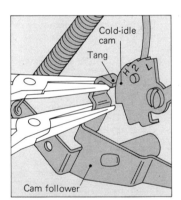

Cold-idle cam · Tang · Cam follower

On some cars, cold-idle speed is set by bending a tang. Connect the tachometer to a cold engine. Position the cam follower's tang on the step of the cold-idle cam that is specified in *Tuneup Data*. While supporting the cam follower with pliers, use long-nose pliers to bend the tang until the engine idles within 100 rpm of the specified speed.

Setting hot-idle speed

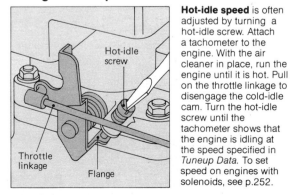

Hot-idle screw · Throttle linkage · Flange

Hot-idle speed is often adjusted by turning a hot-idle screw. Attach a tachometer to the engine. With the air cleaner in place, run the engine until it is hot. Pull on the throttle linkage to disengage the cold-idle cam. Turn the hot-idle screw until the tachometer shows that the engine is idling at the speed specified in *Tuneup Data*. To set speed on engines with solenoids, see p.252.

Adjusting the fuel mixture

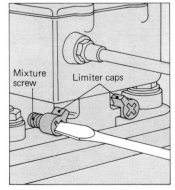

Mixture screw · Limiter caps

Set the fuel mixture after you adjust hot-idle speed. Remove the air cleaner, then open the choke. Turn a mixture screw clockwise, 1/16 turn at a time, until engine speed begins to drop. Back out the screw until idle speed increases and engine runs smoothly. Do the same for the other screw (if any). Check hot-idle speed; readjust it if necessary. If limiter caps prevent proper adjustment, see p.253.

Setting hot-idle speed with a solenoid ⚁⚁ 10–20 min

Hot-idle speed in many cars is set with an idle-stop solenoid located near the throttle linkage. This solenoid is an electromagnet with a plunger that extends when the ignition is turned on and retracts when the ignition is turned off. If the plunger does not behave in this manner, the solenoid or its wiring may be defective, or the solenoid has another purpose. For example, if it is connected to the air conditioning, the solenoid is meant to maintain the hot-idle speed while the air conditioner is on; the plunger will extend only when the A/C is on and will retract when it is off. In a few cars the solenoid is activated by the A/C, but another device or screw is used to set the hot-idle speed. Consult the shop manual for your car if the purpose of a solenoid is not clear.

To set the hot-idle speed with a solenoid, first attach a tachometer to the engine (p.223). Run the engine until it reaches its normal operating temperature. Then, with the air cleaner in place, pull on the throttle to disengage the cold-idle cam. Set the hot-idle speed to specification (see *Tuneup Data*) by adjusting the solenoid. Rev the engine after each adjustment, then wait for the tachometer reading to stabilize. If the solenoid is activated by the air conditioner, make sure that the A/C is off while you set the hot-idle speed (with the solenoid or the separate screw or device). Some engines also have a specification for a low- or slow-idle speed. When setting low-idle speed (below, right), disconnect the wire from the solenoid.

> **Tools:** Screwdriver, open-end wrench, Allen wrench, tachometer.

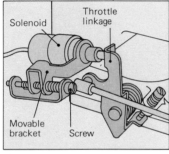

Movable bracket: To adjust hot-idle speed, make sure that the solenoid's plunger is extended. Then turn the screw on the side of the bracket to bring bracket and solenoid closer to, or farther away from, the stop. Adjust the solenoid's position until the proper engine speed is achieved. Rev engine before reading meter.

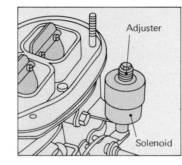

Adjuster on back of the solenoid: To adjust hot-idle speed, turn the adjuster into or out of the solenoid. First make sure that the solenoid's plunger is extended. Then turn the adjuster until the correct engine speed is achieved. Rev engine before reading meter.

Setting low-idle speed

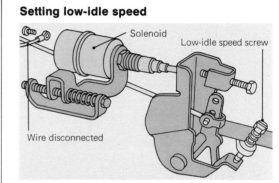

If specs call for a low-idle speed, set the hot-idle speed as shown at left. Then disconnect solenoid's wire, and turn a separate low-idle speed screw (or turn adjuster inside solenoid) to set the low-idle speed.

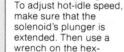
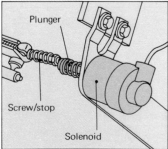

Hex-shaped plunger tip: To adjust hot-idle speed, make sure that the solenoid's plunger is extended. Then use a wrench on the hex-shaped tip of the plunger to screw the plunger out of, or into, the solenoid. Adjust the length of the plunger until the proper engine speed is achieved. Rev engine before reading meter.

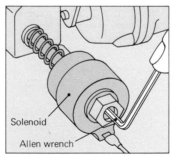

Internal adjuster:
1. Using an Allen wrench, turn the internal adjuster into the solenoid as far as it will go without forcing the adjuster.

Checking a solenoid

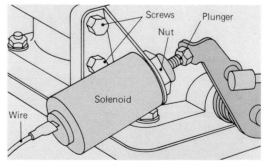

If solenoid plunger never moves, trace its wiring for an electrical fault (pp.361–363). If the wiring checks out but the plunger operates erratically, replace the solenoid; it is usually held in place by a few screws or a nut.

Adjustable screw/stop: With this type of solenoid, the hot-idle speed is adjusted by turning the screw/stop toward or away from the plunger. First make sure that the solenoid's plunger is extended. Then adjust the position of the stop to achieve the proper engine speed. Rev engine before reading meter.

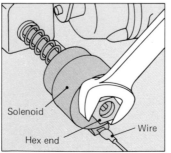

2. Turn the solenoid (on the hex end) until the engine idles at 100 to 150 rpm above the hot-idle specification. (You may need to temporarily disconnect the wiring in order to turn the solenoid.)
3. Reattach the wire and back out the internal adjuster until the engine idles at the specified hot-idle speed.

Propane-enrichment idle mixture adjustment ⏱⏱⏱ 30 min–1 hr

The propane-enrichment adjustment procedure is a more exacting method of adjusting the fuel mixture to make it conform to recent emission-control laws. Chrysler, Ford, and General Motors specify this adjustment procedure; American Motors does not. Since specific details on the procedure may change from time to time, it is recommended that you also refer to the instructions listed in your car's shop manual or on the emission-control decal under the hood of your car. If you cannot achieve the proper mix, have a mechanic do the job. This procedure cannot be done on cars with sealed mixture screws.

Caution: Before you begin, set the parking brake and chock all wheels (p.176). If the car is equipped with a vacuum parking-brake release, disconnect and plug the vacuum hose at the brake. Keep the propane tank vertical, and work in a well-ventilated area that is free from flame and sparks.

Tools: Screwdrivers, wrenches, timing light, tachometer, propane tank, hose, metering valve.

Ford, Lincoln, and Mercury

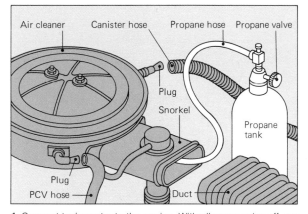

1. Connect tachometer to the engine. With all accessories off, run the engine until it reaches normal operating temperature. Disconnect the vacuum advance hose from the distributor and plug the hose with a golf tee or pencil. Check the engine with a timing light and adjust timing if necessary (pp.236–239). Disconnect the timing light; reconnect the vacuum hose to the distributor.
2. Trace the hoses from the charcoal canister and disconnect them at the engine and at the air cleaner. Plug any open vacuum hose nipples at the engine. Disconnect the hose between the air pump (if any) and the diverter valve.
3. Disconnect the PCV hose at the air cleaner, and plug its nipple. Disconnect the cool-air duct from the snorkel of the air cleaner and insert propane hose three-fourths of the way into the snorkel.
4. Turn fuel-mixture screws counterclockwise to the maximum *Rich* position. Run the engine at 2,500 rpm for about 15 sec.
5. Make sure that hot-idle speed is set to specifications (pp.251–252). Refer to the emission-control decal for the correct gear in which to place the transmission.
6. Slowly open the propane valve and note the maximum gain in engine speed. Check the emission-control decal for the correct specified engine speed gain. If measured gain is higher than specified, the limiter caps on the mixture screws should be removed by a mechanic, who should also readjust the carburetor. If measured speed gain is lower than that specified, turn the mixture screws clockwise, in equal amounts, until you reach the correct specification. If this cannot be achieved within the range of the limiter caps, have a mechanic do the job.
7. Remove the propane hose. Reconnect all hoses and other systems that were disconnected.

General Motors

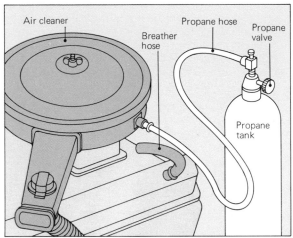

1. Disconnect and plug any vacuum hoses as directed on the emission-control decal. Turn the air conditioner off and run the engine until it reaches normal operating temperature. Choke should be fully open.
2. Disconnect and plug the vacuum advance hose. Connect a tachometer to the engine. Check engine timing with a timing light. Readjust timing if necessary (see pp.236–239). Make sure that the hot-idle speed is set to specifications (pp.251–252). Disconnect the timing light and reconnect the vacuum advance hose.
3. Disconnect the crankcase breather hose from its fitting on the air cleaner, and connect the propane-supply hose to that fitting. Put an automatic transmission in *Drive,* a manual transmission in *Neutral.* Set the parking brake firmly.
4. Open propane valve slowly until the maximum idle speed is reached. If necessary, adjust hot-idle speed screw or solenoid to the enriched rpm setting specified on the emission-control decal.
5. Shut off the propane; shift automatic transmission into *Park.* Run engine at about 2,000 rpm for 30 sec. Return engine to idle, and shift automatic transmission into *Drive.* Check idle speed against that specified on the emission-control decal. If speed is too low, back out mixture screws one-eighth turn at a time until the specified speed is reached. If the speed is too high, turn mixture screws in until the specified speed is reached. If proper speed cannot be achieved within the range of the limiter caps, have a mechanic set the mixture.
6. Remove propane hose. Reconnect all detached hoses.

Chrysler Corp.

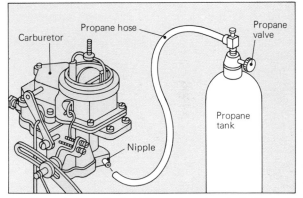

1. Put transmission in *Neutral.* If the car is equipped with Electronic Spark Control (ESC), disconnect and ground the idle-stop carburetor switch with a jumper wire (see p.239). Disconnect and plug the EGR hose at the EGR valve, and the vacuum hose at the spark-control computer. If the car is not equipped with ESC, disconnect and plug the EGR hose at the EGR valve, and plug the vacuum advance hose at the distributor. Refer to the emission-control decal to see if other disconnections are necessary.
2. Connect a tachometer and timing light to the engine. Run the engine until it reaches its normal operating temperature. Adjust the timing if necessary (pp.236–239). Remove the timing light.
3. Disconnect the vacuum hose either for the air cleaner's vacuum motor or for the choke's vacuum diaphragm from the carburetor. Attach propane hose to the nipple on the carburetor.
4. Open propane valve slowly until maximum rpm is reached.
5. Adjust the hot-idle speed screw or solenoid (pp.251–252) until the specified propane-enriched rpm setting is reached (refer to emission-control decal). Then slowly open propane valve to reach highest engine rpm. If maximum rpm is different from that in Step 4, adjust hot-idle speed screw or solenoid to attain the specified propane-enriched rpm.
6. Turn off the propane and adjust the mixture screws for the smoothest idle at the specified hot-idle speed. If this cannot be done within the range of the limiter caps, see a mechanic.
7. Recheck the enriched idle speed by turning the propane back on. If maximum idle speed is 25 rpm more than the enriched rpm specification, readjust the hot-idle speed screw or solenoid to the listed specifications and repeat the procedure.
8. Remove the propane and reconnect all hoses and systems. If this causes any increase in engine rpm, do not readjust.

Servicing air pump systems ☑☑☑ 20 min–3 hr

If the air pump or its associated valves are functioning poorly, you may hear whistling noises or backfire in the exhaust when the car slows down.

The air pump is mounted on a bracket at the front of the engine and is driven by a belt. The tension and condition of this belt should be checked periodically (p.286). At any sign of a problem in the air pump system, inspect all hoses, tubes, and fittings for deterioration or cracks. Check the pressure side of the system for leaks by applying a solution of soap and water to each hose. If there is a leak, bubbles will form when the pump is running. Tighten any leaky fitting. Note how a leaking hose or tube is routed, then replace it.

Most air pump systems have one or two check valves, a *diverter*, or *anti-backfire, valve*, and a *pressure-relief valve*. Each should be checked.

When checking the air pump (below), accelerate the engine to about 1,500 rpm. If the airflow at the hose increases as engine speed increases, the pump is OK. If not, or if there is noise in the relief valve, there may be a leak. Place your finger near the relief valve and feel for any air leakage. There should be none when the engine is running at fast idle. If you are sure there are no other leaks in the system, replace the air pump. If the relief valve is not in the pump, it will be part of the diverter valve. If necessary, substitute a new diverter valve.

In some designs—notably in pre-1981 GM V-6, Chevette, and 1975-78 Ford engines—the diverter valve is replaced by a bypass valve, a vacuum differential valve, and a delay valve. Check the condition of these valves, too (opposite page).

Some air pump systems are made more complex by electronic or computer controls, or by temperature-regulated valves that switch air between the exhaust manifold and a catalytic converter (see p.80). Do not try to repair such systems yourself.

If you cannot find a belt-driven air pump on your car's engine, see *Aspirator valve systems,* opposite.

Tools: Wrenches and screwdrivers as needed, gear puller, hammer, hand-operated vacuum pump.
Materials: Wood block, solvent.

Air pump

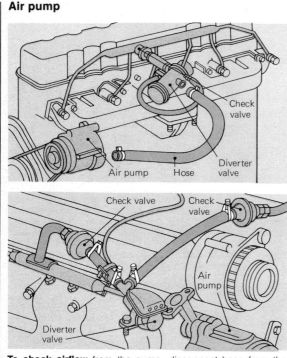

To check airflow from the pump, disconnect hose from the diverter valve and feel whether or not there is flow at the hose's end while the engine is running. If the diverter valve is mounted on the pump, there is no hose; remove the valve to check airflow.
To remove air pump, disconnect any hoses and loosen pump's bracket bolts. Push pump toward engine and remove drive belt from its pulley. Remove bracket bolts and lift out pump.

Relief valve

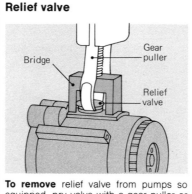

To remove relief valve from pumps so equipped, pry valve with a gear puller or battery terminal puller, using makeshift bridge similar to that shown.

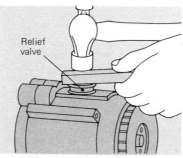

To install relief valve, remove its pressure plug. Tap valve into mounting hole on pump with a hammer and block of wood. Press pressure plug into valve.

Check valve

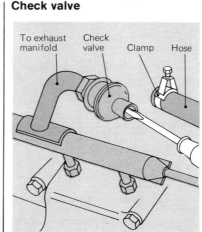

To test the check valve, loosen clamp screw on hose from air pump and disconnect the hose from the check valve. Gently probe spring-loaded metal disc inside valve with a screwdriver. If access to other (exhaust manifold) side of valve is convenient, disconnect valve on that side, too, and probe the disc in the same way. If the disc does not move, soak valve in solvent to free it. If this does not work, replace the valve. If disc moves when it is pressed from exhaust manifold side with a screwdriver, the valve is defective and should be replaced. Another way to inspect the check valve is to operate engine with the air pump hose disconnected from the valve. If you feel exhaust gases coming out of the valve, it is defective.

Diverter valve

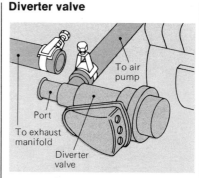

1. Disconnect hose(s) between diverter valve and exhaust manifold. Run engine at idle. If valve is OK, air should come from port where hose was disconnected.

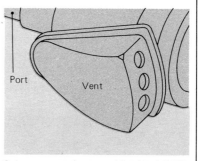

2. Increase engine speed to about 2,500 rpm and quickly release throttle. If valve is OK, air should momentarily stop at valve's port and, instead, exit from the vent.

Bypass, vacuum differential, and delay valves ▯▯▯ 30 min–1½ hr

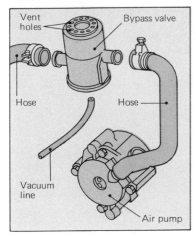

Bypass valve: To check the valve, place your hand over its vent holes while the engine is warm and idling. If air continuously exhausts from the vent holes, replace the bypass valve. Disconnect hoses and vacuum lines, take out mounting bolts, and remove the valve.

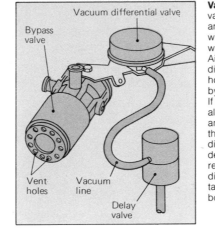

Vacuum differential valve: Quickly open and close throttle while engine is warm and idling. Air should discharge from vent holes on the bypass valve (left). If it does not, and all vacuum lines and fittings are OK, the vacuum differential valve is defective. To replace the valve, disconnect hoses and take out mounting bolts, if any.

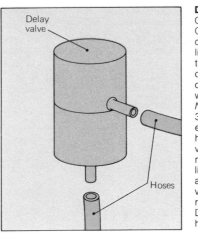

Delay valve: On GM V-6 and Chevette systems, disconnect black line marked VAC that runs to the delay valve, and operate fully warmed engine in *Neutral.* After 15 to 35 sec, air should exhaust from vent holes on bypass valve (left). If it does not, and all vacuum lines and fittings are OK, the delay valve must be replaced. Disconnect its hoses to remove it.

Aspirator valve systems ▯▯ 20 min–1½ hr

Many four- and six-cylinder engines have an aspirator valve instead of an air pump. Some have an assembly of valves, such as GM's Pulsair system. The valves are simple one-way (check) valves that draw fresh air into the exhaust manifold whenever pressure in the manifold is low. If a valve fails, exhaust gas leaks backward into the carburetor via the air cleaner, and the engine performs poorly. Visible signs of this condition may be paint burned off the valve body and deterioration of the rubber hose between the valve and the air cleaner. A hissing valve may also indicate valve failure.

Typical single-valve system

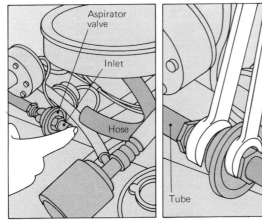

1. Disconnect the hose from the aspirator valve inlet. Feel for vacuum pulses at the inlet while the engine idles. If there are no pulses, replace the valve. Unscrew it from the aspirator tube with two open-end wrenches.
2. Remove the air cleaner and listen for a *putt-putt* noise at inlet of the aspirator valve. If you hear this noise, the valve is OK.

GM multi-valve Pulsair system

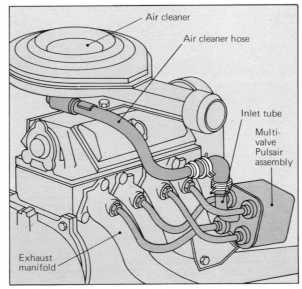

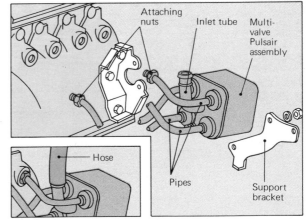

To test Pulsair valves, disconnect air cleaner hose and apply vacuum to valve's inlet tube with a hand-operated vacuum pump. Tube should hold a vacuum. If it does not, replace assembly.
To replace the Pulsair assembly, unscrew attaching nuts on manifold pipes. Remove the bolts that secure assembly to support bracket, if any, and lift assembly off the engine.

Maintenance / **Pollution controls**

Exhaust gas recirculation 🕐🕐 30 min–1 hr

The heart of the exhaust gas recirculation (EGR) system is the vacuum-operated EGR valve. It is mounted on the intake manifold near the carburetor. The EGR valve allows small amounts of exhaust gas into the manifold during moderate acceleration (see p.81). If your engine pings, idles roughly, or the car fails an emissions test because of excess NO_x, there

may be a problem in the EGR valve. The valve will not open if there is a blockage or a leak in one of its vacuum hoses. Make sure that each hose in the system is securely attached to its vacuum port. Replace any leaking or cracked hoses. Check the EGR valve on a warm engine by feeling its diaphragm to make sure that it is moving. Since the valve is hot,

you may have to wear gloves to avoid burning your fingers. Check the other components in the system as illustrated here and on page 257.

Tools: Wrenches and screwdrivers as needed, test light, thermometer, hot plate, hammer, wire brush.
Materials: Bowl of water, piece of vacuum hose.

EGR valve

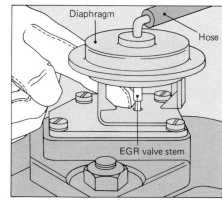

1. Open the throttle while feeling underside of EGR valve's diaphragm. Diaphragm should open (move up) as engine speed increases and close (move down) as throttle is released. A slight vibration of the diaphragm plate is acceptable.

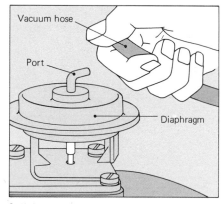

2. If diaphragm does not move, disconnect vacuum hose. With engine running at about 2,000 rpm, feel hose for vacuum. If vacuum is present, skip to Step 5. If not, proceed to Step 3 and check other system components.

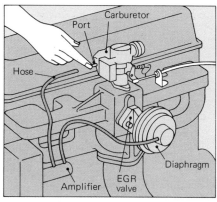

3. Disconnect EGR valve's vacuum hose from its port on carburetor. With engine running at about 2,000 rpm, check for vacuum in port. If there is vacuum, replace hose. If not, clean out port and check engine vacuum (see p.264).

Back-pressure transducer

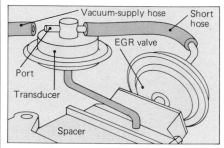

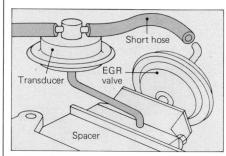

EGR back-pressure transducer, used on some AMC, Ford, and GM vehicles, senses back pressure of engine exhaust and controls the vacuum signal to the EGR valve.
1. With engine idling and at normal operating temperature, disconnect the vacuum supply hose from the transducer. Accelerate engine to about 2,000 rpm and check end of hose with your finger or piece of paper to see if vacuum is present. If there is no vacuum, check other system components (left and opposite page). If there is vacuum, reconnect vacuum hose.
2. At the EGR valve, disconnect the short vacuum hose that runs from the transducer to the valve. Accelerate engine to about 2,000 rpm and check end of hose for vacuum. If there is vacuum, the transducer is OK; if there is none, replace the transducer. Disconnect the other hose from the transducer, take out mounting bolts, and remove the transducer-spacer assembly.

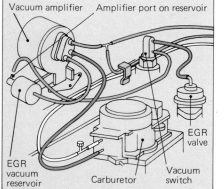

4. If EGR valve's vacuum hose is connected to a vacuum amplifier (see opposite page), check for vacuum at the amplifier port. If there is vacuum, replace EGR valve. If not, check amplifier operation (opposite page).

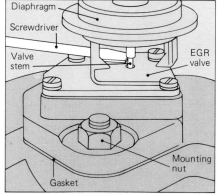

5. Push EGR diaphragm up and release it. If idle speed roughens, then returns to normal, EGR valve is OK. If not, remove the EGR valve. Disconnect the hose, take out the bolts, and remove the valve and gasket from the engine.

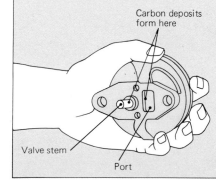

6. Use a wire brush to clean off carbon deposits. Connect a manual vacuum pump to the diaphragm; apply vacuum, then release it. If the valve works smoothly, reinstall it, using a new gasket. If the valve sticks, replace it.

Other EGR system components

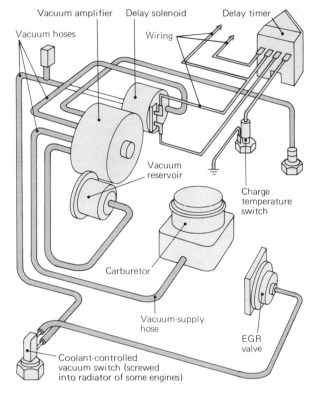

Vacuum amplifier — Delay solenoid — Delay timer

Vacuum hoses — Wiring

Vacuum reservoir

Charge temperature switch

Carburetor

Vacuum-supply hose

Coolant-controlled vacuum switch (screwed into radiator of some engines)

EGR valve

Typical EGR system includes valves and various other components to regulate the EGR valve under diverse operating conditions. An elaborate Chrysler system is shown here. Other systems may include one or more of the above components.

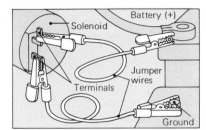

Solenoid — Timer

Test light

Delay timer: With ignition off, remove multi-wire connector from delay solenoid, and connect test light (p.361) across solenoid terminals. Start the engine. Light should go on and stay lit about 30 sec. If light does not go on, or stays on indefinitely, replace timer; unplug connector from timer and take out mounting screws.

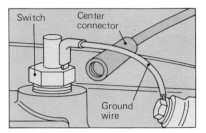

Solenoid — Battery (+)

Jumper wires

Terminals

Ground

Delay solenoid: With ignition off, disconnect solenoid's wiring. Use jumper wires to connect one of the solenoid's terminals to a ground, the other to the positive (+) battery terminal. Solenoid is OK if it clicks when battery connection is made. If there is no click, replace the solenoid. Disconnect wiring and hoses; remove screws.

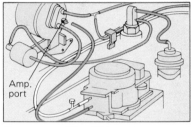

Switch — Center connector

Ground wire

Charge temperature switch: If EGR valve's diaphragm does not move when the engine is warm and speeded up (Step 2, opposite page), remove center connector wire from temperature switch and wait 90 sec. If valve diaphragm now moves, replace temperature switch. Disconnect wiring; unscrew switch from engine.

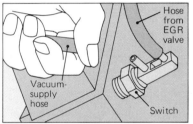

Hose from EGR valve

Vacuum-supply hose

Switch

Coolant-controlled vacuum switch: Disconnect vacuum-supply hose from the vacuum switch. With engine running at about 2,000 rpm, check for vacuum at the hose end. If there is none, look for leaks in the vacuum hose and fittings, and check other components in the system. If there is vacuum, perform the next test (right).

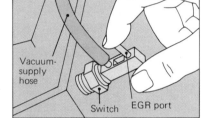

Vacuum-supply hose

Switch — EGR port

Reconnect vacuum-supply hose, then disconnect EGR hose. With engine warm and running at about 2,000 rpm, check for vacuum at the EGR port on the vacuum switch. If there is vacuum, the switch is OK; check hose. If there is no vacuum, replace switch. Test again with engine cold; if there is vacuum, replace switch.

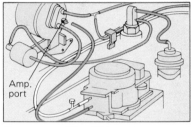

Amp. port

Vacuum amplifier: With engine warm and running just above idle speed, disconnect carburetor hose at amplifier and check hose for vacuum. If there is none, check carburetor port (Step 3, opposite). Reconnect hose and check for vacuum at amplifier port. If there is vacuum in first test but none in the second, replace amplifier.

Volkswagen EGR valve

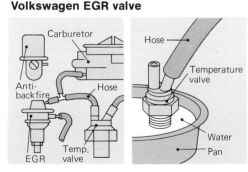

Carburetor

Hose

Temperature valve

Anti-backfire

Hose

EGR — Temp. valve

Water — Pan

1. Let engine idle at normal operating temperature. At the EGR valve, disconnect the hose from the temperature valve. Disconnect hose from anti-backfire valve and attach it to the port on the EGR valve, using a T-connector and extra hose. Engine idle should roughen and slow down. If it does not, check EGR valve for clogging or replace it. If you cannot find the anti-backfire valve (fuel-injection engines have none), use a hand-operated vacuum pump to apply vacuum to the EGR valve.
2. Turn off engine, remove hoses from temperature valve, and unscrew the valve. Place threaded end of valve in a pan of water containing a thermometer. Heat the water. Connect a long piece of hose to the angled port of the valve and suck on the hose. When water reaches 110° to 120°F, valve should open and let air pass through hose as you suck on it. If valve does not open within approximately this temperature range, replace the valve.

Datsun delay valve

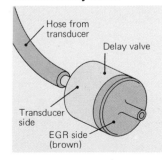

Hose from transducer

Delay valve

Transducer side

EGR side (brown)

Some Datsun EGR systems include a vacuum delay valve in the vacuum line between the EGR valve and back-pressure transducer. To check this delay valve, disconnect its hoses and blow into one side, then into the other. Air should flow freely into the transducer side but encounter some resistance on brown-faced, or EGR-valve, side. If airflow is the same on both sides, replace valve.

Checking vacuum spark emission controls ▢▢▢ 30 min–2 hr

Many types of vacuum-operated spark emission controls help to reduce exhaust emissions in domestic and imported cars built before the early 1980s, when computers took over this function. The operation of the three most common vacuum emission controls is explained on page 79. Many General Motors cars have *Type 1* systems; Ford cars have *Types 1* and *2*; Chrysler cars have *Type 3*; AMC cars have *Type 1* and a variation of it in which the transmission-speed control switch is operated by hydraulic pressure.

If your car has a vacuum spark control, there will be a diaphragm chamber and hose on the distributor. If the hose goes through a plastic fitting (some fittings have wires on them) or into a switch that is screwed into the water jacket on the engine, your engine has vacuum spark emission controls.

Trouble in a vacuum-operated spark-control system may cause the symptoms of incorrect ignition timing—sluggish acceleration in high gear, increased fuel consumption, hot engine temperatures, or pinging during acceleration. If the timing is OK, check out the vacuum spark-control system.

First, test the vacuum control chamber on the distributor. Disconnect the vacuum hose from the chamber and connect a manual vacuum pump in its place. With the engine idling, apply vacuum to the chamber. You should hear the engine speed increase. Shut off the engine and remove the distributor cap. Apply vacuum again and you should see the distributor's baseplate move. If neither of these things occurs, check to see if the vacuum chamber's arm is connected to the baseplate. If not, connect it and perform the tests again. If the arm is connected, the vacuum chamber is faulty and should be replaced. Once the vacuum chamber is working properly, you can proceed with the tests below.

Repair of the more complex systems (pp.259–260) should usually be left to a mechanic, but three simple tests will tell you whether you have a problem in the vacuum spark emission control and—if it is not too complicated—how to make the repair.

To test any vacuum spark-control system, hook up a vacuum gauge with a T-connector at the distributor (below, left). Connect an 8-foot hose to the gauge so that it can be read from the passenger's seat.

Domestic systems supply vacuum to the distributor when the engine is cold and shut off or reduce vacuum to retard the spark when the engine is hot. One Volkswagen system is an exception. Some carbureted Rabbit and Scirocco engines have full vacuum when hot and little or no vacuum when cold.

Test 1: Start the cold engine. You should get a vacuum reading immediately (except on those VWs).

If there is no vacuum reading at cold idle, open the throttle slightly and you should get a reading. If you get no reading either way, check that all vacuum hoses are connected and have no cracks. If the hoses are sound, the control system may be faulty.

Test 2: If there is vacuum in Test 1, warm up the engine. Recheck readings while you drive the car in different gears at varying speeds. Some systems show vacuum only in *High* gear at speeds of 40 mph or more. Others may delay vacuum buildup when the throttle is first opened. The least restrictive designs give vacuum readings at all speeds above idle. If there is no vacuum at any speed, the spark-control system is probably malfunctioning.

Test 3: If Tests 1 or 2 indicate a possible failure in the system, first check for a blown fuse. Then double-check the system by applying vacuum to the distributor control with a hand-held vacuum pump (connected in place of the vacuum gauge) while repeating the driving sequence in Test 2. If applying vacuum to the control cures the car's performance problem, the system is probably faulty. If the procedures on pages 259–260 do not cure the problem, have a repair shop recheck the system.

Tools: Vacuum gauge, T-connector, hand-held vacuum pump, 3-in. and 8-ft lengths of vacuum hose, tachometer.

Hookups for testing vacuum spark controls

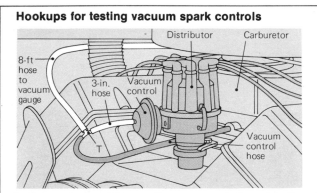

Distributor — Carburetor — 8-ft hose to vacuum gauge — 3-in. hose — Vacuum control — T — Vacuum control hose

Engine compartment: Remove the vacuum control hose from the diaphragm on the distributor. Connect the T-connector and a 3-in. hose to the diaphragm and to the vacuum control hose. Then connect the vacuum gauge to the 8-ft hose on the T. Make certain that the closed hood does not pinch the vacuum hose to the passenger compartment.

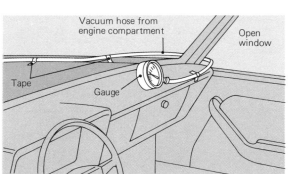

Vacuum hose from engine compartment — Open window — Tape — Gauge

Passenger compartment: Run hose from engine compartment and secure it with tape so that the vacuum gauge can be read by the passenger at a glance. For Test 3, substitute a hand-held vacuum pump for the vacuum gauge. **Caution:** Have a helper drive the car or read the gauge. This is safer and more accurate than trying to do both jobs yourself.

Simple vacuum-hose repairs

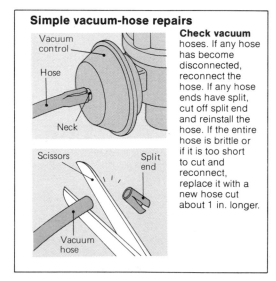

Vacuum control — Hose — Neck — Scissors — Split end — Vacuum hose

Check vacuum hoses. If any hose has become disconnected, reconnect the hose. If any hose ends have split, cut off split end and reinstall the hose. If the entire hose is brittle or if it is too short to cut and reconnect, replace it with a new hose cut about 1 in. longer.

Typical GM system

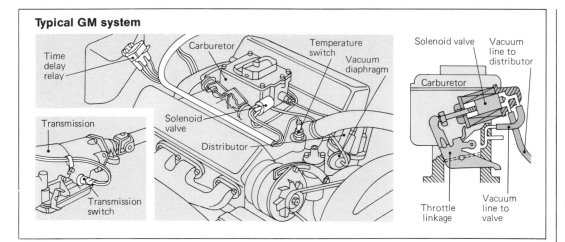

The general tests on page 258 will show you whether your car's vacuum spark control system is working. If simply repairing split or disconnected hoses does not cure the problem, one of the components in the system is probably faulty.

To isolate a malfunctioning solenoid, temperature switch, or other component, you must have a detailed understanding of the system in your car. Only the workshop manual for your specific car make and model lists each step needed to check out every control component. However, most spark-control systems fall into categories. For example, many GM cars have similar components that are checked in the same way on a Chevrolet as they are on some other GM brands. So, too, do AMC, Chrysler, Ford, and imported cars.

GM controls

GM has used many types of vacuum spark controls over the years. Two of the most common are Transmission Controlled Spark (TCS) and, in early 1970 cars, Combined Emission Control (CEC).

TCS, derived from the earlier and more complex CEC system, eliminates vacuum advance until the transmission shifts (or is shifted) into *High* when the engine is warm.

Some cars have a time-delay relay that activates the vacuum solenoid in order to provide normal spark advance for 20 sec after the engine is started, thereby preventing stalling.

There may also be a coolant-temperature switch in the circuit, which is closed below 93°F, opening the vacuum solenoid valve and allowing normal vacuum advance until the engine is warm. At this point the temperature switch opens, and the solenoid opens the vacuum valve when the transmission is in *High.*

1. Check TCS with Test 1 on page 258. The needle on the vacuum gauge should move. If it does not, remove the two wires from the solenoid valve (which is mounted on the intake manifold in TCS systems or on the carburetor in CEC systems). Use a jumper wire to ground one terminal of the solenoid valve, another wire to connect the second terminal to the battery's positive (+) terminal. The solenoid should click as it opens, allowing vacuum to pass through when the engine is running slightly above idle speed. If vacuum does not pass through the solenoid, check its hoses to make sure that vacuum is reaching the solenoid. If there is vacuum at the solenoid valve, the solenoid is faulty; replace it.

2. If the gauge shows that vacuum has been shut off after 20 sec but before the engine temperature rises to more than 92°F (33°C), the time-delay relay is OK but the temperature switch is faulty. Replace the temperature switch in the water jacket.

3. When the engine warms up to normal operating temperature, the vacuum gauge should no longer respond to changes in engine speed. If you still get readings, the temperature switch may be bad. Disconnect wiring from the switch (on cars so equipped) and repeat the test. If the system now performs properly, replace the temperature switch. If the problem remains, the transmission switch is faulty.

4. Perform Test 2 on page 258. The vacuum gauge should produce a reading. If it does not, the transmission switch is defective; replace it.

5. Double-check the system with Test 3 on page 258.

Some late-model GM cars have a control valve that combines full manifold vacuum with carburetor port vacuum. This system is similar to the AMC Non-Linear Vacuum Regulator (NLVR). Follow procedure for AMC on page 260.

Early 1970s GM cars have CEC systems that eliminate vacuum spark advance until the transmission shifts into *High,* and they hold the throttle open during deceleration in *High.* The CEC system has a solenoid vacuum valve combined with a throttle positioner on the carburetor, a coolant temperature switch, and a transmission switch with a *reversing relay.*

When the transmission switch opens in *High* gear, the reversing relay closes and activates the carburetor's solenoid vacuum valve. This allows vacuum to reach the distributor's vacuum control diaphragm and also extends a throttle-positioning plunger at the carburetor, which slows the closing of the throttle in order to lower exhaust emissions. To check out this system, perform the three tests on page 258. Then make the following tests.

1. With the engine cold, turn on the ignition switch and hold the throttle open. The plunger should pop out of the vacuum solenoid switch. If it does not, the solenoid, the temperature switch, or the time-delay relay may be faulty.

2. If the plunger does extend, watch it for 30 sec after turning on the ignition. If plunger retracts in that time, the temperature switch is bad but the time-delay relay is working. Replace the temperature switch, and repeat Tests 1, 2, and 3, p.258.

3. When the engine is revved during Test 1, vacuum gauge's needle should rise until the engine warms up a little. Then, when coolant temperature rises to about 95°F (35°C), the temperature switch should shut off vacuum; the gauge should show no reading as the engine is revved in *Neutral.* Replace the switch if it seems faulty, and retest the system.

4. If the plunger does not extend, test the reversing relay by unplugging its two-wire connector. Its wires are usually tan and brown. The solenoid plunger should extend as the engine is revved. If it does not, the solenoid is OK but the relay is faulty. Replace the relay, then retest it and reconnect the connector.

5. To check the transmission switch on a car with manual transmission, shut off the engine and put transmission in *High.* The plunger on the solenoid vacuum switch should pop out when the ignition switch is turned on. On an automatic transmission, make Test 2 with the car's drive wheels raised clear of the ground (see p.176). (**Caution:** Be sure to raise the front wheels of a front-drive car and the rear wheels of a rear-drive car.) Chock both free-rolling wheels and make certain that

the jack stands hold the car up by its suspension so that the U-joints in the drive train will not be working at excessive angles.

Have a helper start the engine, put transmission in *Drive,* and run engine fast enough to shift transmission into *High* (speedometer should read 45 mph). Stand beside (not in front of) the car, and watch the solenoid vacuum switch. The plunger should pop out and the vacuum gauge should show a reading when the transmission shifts into *High.* If it does not, the transmission switch is faulty and must be replaced.

6. If the throttle-positioning plunger is always extended, the problem is in the solenoid, the reversing relay, or the transmission switch. Pull the purple wire from the relay; if the plunger then retracts, the problem is either in the relay or in the transmission switch. Reconnect the purple wire and disconnect the two-wire connector. If the plunger now retracts, the transmission switch is faulty. If it does not retract, the relay is faulty.

After replacing any part of the system, rerun Tests 1, 2, and 3 to make sure that the original performance problem has been corrected. If it recurs, seek professional help.

Chrysler systems

Chrysler uses an Orifice Spark-Advance Control (OSAC) on many of its North American cars. OSAC delays vacuum advance at the distributor by 10 to 27 sec, depending on the year, engine type, and model of the car. When engine decelerates, there is no spark delay. The OSAC valve is mounted on the air cleaner and has hoses connected to the vacuum port on the carburetor and to the vacuum diaphragm on the distributor. To test the OSAC valve:

1. Hook up the vacuum gauge for Test 1, p.258.

2. Hook up a tachometer (p.237).

3. Start the engine and watch the vacuum gauge while bringing engine speed up to 2,000 rpm. Hold this speed. The needle of the vacuum gauge should rise gradually from zero and stabilize. If the needle jumps up immediately, or if it does not move at all, the OSAC valve is defective and must be replaced.

Checking vacuum spark emission controls *(continued)*

AMC systems

Some AMC cars sold in California have a Transmission Controlled Spark (TCS) system very similar to GM's. It eliminates advance below 33 to 37 mph in *High* gear.

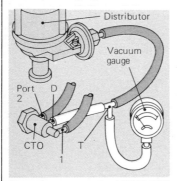

The main components of AMC's TCS system are a solenoid vacuum valve mounted at the right rear of the intake manifold on V-8s or at the rear of the manifold on six-cylinder engines; a pressure-operated speed-sensing switch on the transmission; and a Coolant Temperature Override (CTO) vacuum switch that is screwed into the thermostat housing on V-8s or into the left rear of the cylinder block on sixes.

The transmission switch is closed on automatic transmissions at speeds below 36 mph, and in all gears but *High* on manual transmissions, sending power to the solenoid vacuum valve. This closes off the hose to the distributor's advance diaphragm, preventing vacuum spark advance. The transmission switch opens when cars with automatic transmissions are driven faster than 36 mph or when manual transmissions are shifted into *High*. This deactivates the solenoid vacuum valve, allowing the vacuum advance to operate normally.

The Coolant Temperature Override (CTO) switch may be used alone or combined with a TCS system. To test either arrangement:
1. Pull the hose to the distributor off the center port of the CTO (port is marked *D*) and connect a vacuum gauge with a T-connector and a

short length of vacuum hose.
2. Start the cold engine. At cold idle, the needle on the gauge should show that there is some vacuum.
3. When the engine is warm and idling, the gauge should read zero on a TCS system and nearly zero if TCS is not used. Rev the engine slightly. The gauge reading should remain zero on a TCS engine; it should rise on an engine without TCS. Perform Test 2 (p.258). If there is no vacuum reading in *High* gear above 37 mph, disconnect hose 2 from the CTO and connect the gauge to it. Repeat Test 2. If there is still no vacuum reading, TCS is defective.
4. If there are no vacuum readings at CTO port D in Steps 2 or 3, the CTO is faulty and must be replaced.
5. To check the pressure-operated transmission switch on cars with automatic transmissions, disconnect switch's wire, then connect a test light to it and to the switch with a pair of wires long enough to reach the passenger compartment.
6. Start the engine. The test light should light up.
7. Drive the car and accelerate slowly while a helper watches the speedometer and the light. The light should go out at 33 to 37 mph and stay off at higher speeds.
8. If light does not go out, adjust transmission switch by turning its adjusting screw with a ¹⁄₁₆-in. Allen wrench. Turning the screw clockwise increases the speed at which the light goes out; turning the screw counterclockwise lowers the speed. Alternately turn the screw and road test the car until the light goes out at 33 to 37 mph.
9. If adjusting the switch does not shut test light off at 33 to 37 mph, replace the transmission switch.
10. To check the switch on a manual transmission, hook up the test light between the wire and the switch. Do not start the engine. Turn on the ignition. The light should go on. Put transmission in *High*. Test light should go out. If it does not, replace the switch.

Some AMC TCS systems have a vacuum-delay valve in the hose to the distributor's vacuum control diaphragm in order to maintain some spark advance during acceleration.

To test the delay valve:
1. Disconnect the hose from the distributor when the engine is cold, and connect a vacuum gauge to the end of the hose.
2. Start the engine. The gauge should show engine vacuum.
3. Stop the engine. If the vacuum reading drops off abruptly, replace the vacuum-delay valve.

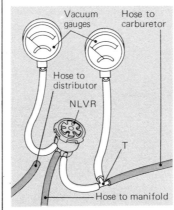

Some late-model AMC cars have a Non-Linear Vacuum Regulator (NLVR) valve to control vacuum spark advance. This valve combines full manifold vacuum with carburetor port vacuum to modulate the vacuum signal to the distributor diaphragm. The NLVR valve is mounted in the vacuum line between the distributor diaphragm and the vacuum sources on the carburetor and intake manifold. It has three ports marked *DIST*, *MAN*, and *CARB*. To check it:
1. Connect one vacuum gauge to the DIST port of the NLVR valve. Trace the hose from the CARB port back to the carburetor and attach a second vacuum gauge there, using a T-connector.
2. With the engine idling, the gauge at the DIST port should read 7 to 9 in.-Hg. If the reading falls outside this range, replace the NLVR valve.
3. Increase the engine speed. The gauge at the DIST port of the NLVR valve should read about the same as the gauge at the carburetor. If it does not, replace the NLVR valve. Remove the vacuum gauges and reconnect the vacuum hoses.

Ford systems

Ford vacuum spark controls on many models use two basic valves to shut off vacuum to the distributor's advance diaphragm—the Spark-Delay Valve (SDV) and Transmission Regulated Spark (TRS) valve. TRS is similar to GM's TCS system covered under *General Motors* (above). Some Ford cars use a variation of TRS—with a speed sensor on the speedometer cable and an amplifier—to control the solenoid valve. A few late-model Ford cars that do not have computer-controlled spark advance have a valve that combines manifold and carburetor vacuum. This valve resembles AMC's NLVR assembly described at the left. Follow the AMC procedure.

The Spark-Delay Valve (SDV) is the simplest and most common Ford spark control. A small plastic disc is spliced into the vacuum hose that leads to the distributor's spark-control diaphragm; it is a one-way delay valve that delays spark advance during acceleration and closes to cut off all advance during deceleration. To check out an SDV:

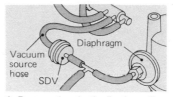

1. Remove the plastic disc by pulling the two hoses (one to the vacuum advance diaphragm and the other to the vacuum source) off SDV nipples. Remember which hose goes on which nipple. One side is usually black, and the other is a different color. The distributor side may be marked. Label the hose ends and nipples with tie-on tags.
2. Blow into the black side of the SDV. You should feel little or no resistance. Blow into the colored side. You should feel strong resistance. If you do not, replace the SDV.
3. If a 1979 5-liter V-8 (except California cars) suffers from poor performance, remove the SDV valve and install a single length of hose directly to the distributor's spark control diaphragm. If performance improves, discard the SDV valve.

Hose-routing decals

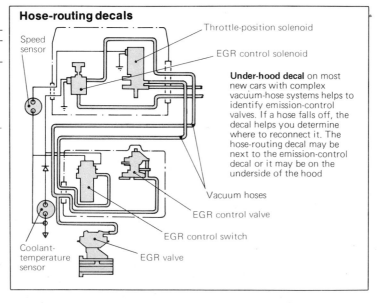

Under-hood decal on most new cars with complex vacuum-hose systems helps to identify emission-control valves. If a hose falls off, the decal helps you determine where to reconnect it. The hose-routing decal may be next to the emission-control decal or it may be on the underside of the hood

Maintenance / Fuel system

Replacing a fuel filter ⚑⚑ 10–30 min

Hard starting, rough running, stalling, and backfiring are all symptoms of a clogged fuel filter. There are basically three types of replaceable fuel filters: an in-line filter, a carburetor-mounted filter, and a fuel pump filter. Some cars have more than one fuel filter. Most have a filter on the fuel pickup inside the tank (see p.58), but this filter seldom clogs.

Caution: Before starting to work, let the engine cool down, then disconnect the battery's ground (−) cable. Work in a well-ventilated area free from smoke and flame. Have rags on hand to wipe up any gasoline that spills out while you work. See additional Cautions on page 397. If you must raise the car to gain access to the filter, see Cautions on page 176.

Tools: Hose-clamp pliers or a screwdriver to remove hose clamps; wrenches; locking pliers or clamps for clamping any flexible fuel lines; strap wrench; rags.
Materials: New filter and any other replacement components needed, such as hoses, clamps, gaskets, or springs.

Carburetor-mounted fuel filters

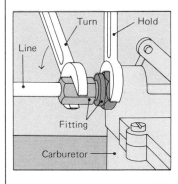

1. To see if there is a filter mounted in or on the carburetor, use two wrenches to disconnect the fuel line fitting at the carburetor. Hold the carburetor steady with one wrench while loosening the fuel line fitting with the second wrench.

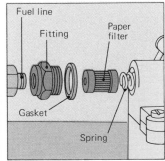

2. Unscrew the fuel filter fitting from the carburetor; be ready to catch the filter, spring, and one or more gaskets. Filter will be made of either sintered bronze or pleated paper. Replace with a pleated paper filter. If necessary, get a new spring and gasket. Install the new filter. Run engine to check for leaks.

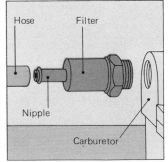

Some cars have an in-line filter that screws into the carburetor. Loosen the hose clamp and carefully pull the hose off the fuel filter. Then unscrew the filter from the carburetor. Replace clamp and hose if they are damaged. Screw new filter into carburetor, then attach hose with clamp. Run engine to check for leaks.

In-line fuel filters

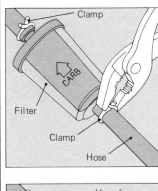

1. To locate an in-line filter, trace the fuel line, starting at the carburetor. (Datsun and Honda filters are near a chassis-mounted fuel pump; see pp.400–401.) Loosen the hose clamps and carefully pull the hoses off the filter. If clamps are the spring type, use special hose-clamp pliers; if they are crimped on, pry them open.

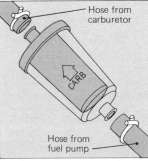

2. Buy a replacement filter and, if necessary, new hoses and clamps. Slip new clamps onto hoses. Attach each hose to each neck of the new fuel filter so that the arrow (if any) on the filter points toward the carburetor. Hold each hose in place with a clamp. Run engine to check for leaks.

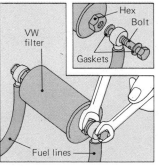

Late-model VWs have an in-line filter that is bolted to the fuel lines. Fuel passes through holes drilled in the bolts. Place a wrench on the hex-shaped end of the filter to hold it steady and use a second wrench to remove the bolts. Install a new filter and gaskets, then run the engine to check for leaks.

Fuel pump filters

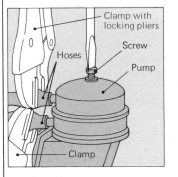

1. Older air-cooled VWs have a filtering screen inside the fuel pump. Before opening the fuel pump, clamp the hose section of each fuel line. Loosen the nut on top of the fuel pump and remove the top of the pump to reach the screen.

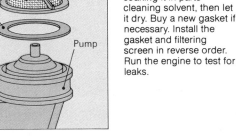

2. Take out the filtering screen and clean it by soaking it in parts-cleaning solvent, then let it dry. Buy a new gasket if necessary. Install the gasket and filtering screen in reverse order. Run the engine to test for leaks.

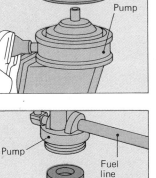

Some older cars have a disposable, pleated paper filter inside the fuel pump. Using a strap wrench, unscrew the housing from the pump. Lift up the housing, and remove the filter and gasket. Install a new filter and gasket in reverse order. Run the engine to test for leaks.

Servicing charcoal canisters ⏱ 20 min –1 hr

Most charcoal canisters have a foam or fiber filter that should be replaced once a year or at 12,000-mile intervals. If the filter becomes clogged, vacuum can build up inside the fuel tank, and the fuel pump must work harder to deliver fuel. A clogged filter can also cause a strong fuel odor.

Canisters that need to be serviced yearly are generally placed in a convenient spot under the hood. In some cars you can feel the filter, pull it out with your fingers, and insert a replacement. The canisters in VWs and Ford cars do not have replaceable filters; the canister must be replaced if it becomes clogged.

Canisters are joined by vapor hoses to the fuel tank and the carburetor, and by a vacuum line to the intake manifold (see p.50). Inspect the hoses and lines yearly. They should be firmly connected. If any hose or line is oil-soaked or cracked, replace it. Use only fuel-resistant hoses made for canister systems.

Canisters themselves are not likely to become defective unless valves are incorporated in the canister body. Some valves, such as those on Datsun canisters, can be disassembled and their parts can be cleaned or replaced individually, although it is usually easier to replace the canister as a unit.

To check the vacuum in a line or hose, place your finger over the end of the disconnected line or hose and feel whether or not there is suction. If a vacuum pump is not available to make the checks at the right, you can suck directly on the line with your mouth, or insert a length of clean tubing or hose onto the line and suck on that.

> **Tools:** Wrench, hand-operated vacuum pump.
> **Materials:** Replacement filter for canister.

Types of canisters

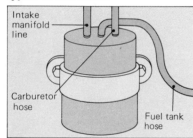

Basic canister has three hoses connected to it. Many units are readily accessible under the hood, although some may be under fender skirt or in air cleaner housing.

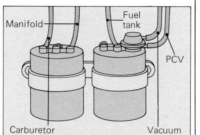

Some canisters are equipped with a vapor vent valve, a purge valve, or both. Purge valve releases fuel vapor to the carburetor when engine speed is above idle.

Dual canisters are found in some Chrysler cars. One canister traps vapors from the fuel tank; the other, from carburetor. Service is the same as for single canisters.

Routine maintenance

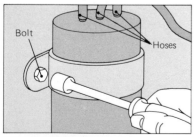

To replace the filter in a canister, first take out its mounting bolts and lift up the unit. Disconnect hoses if the bottom of the canister is still difficult to see or reach.

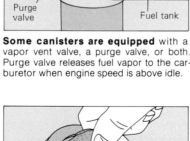

Open spring clip retainer (if any). Work the filter out of its holder in the bottom of the canister, and maneuver a new filter into place. Reinstall the canister.

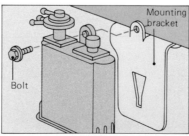

Ford canisters are mounted low in the engine compartment or behind an inner fender skirt. Inspect canister and hoses every two years; replace damaged parts.

Checking vapor vent valves ⏱⏱ 15 min

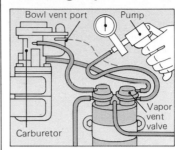

1. With the engine off, disconnect the vapor hose from the bowl vent on the carburetor. Connect hand-operated vacuum pump to hose and apply vacuum. If hose holds a vacuum, see if hose is plugged. If hose is clear, replace the canister.

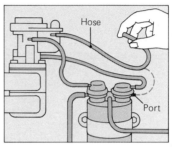

2. Repeat Step 1 with engine idling at normal operating temperature. Suction should now be high. If not, reconnect hose to carburetor and disconnect vacuum line from canister. Check line for vacuum. If there is none, check line for leaks or blockage. If there is vacuum, replace the canister.

Checking canister purge valves ⏱⏱ 15 min

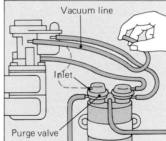

1. Disconnect vacuum line at purge valve. Run engine at 1,500 to 2,000 rpm at normal operating temperature. Check vacuum line. If there is no vacuum, check the EGR system (p.255).

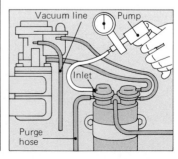

2. If vacuum is present, connect hand-operated vacuum pump to purge valve at vacuum line's inlet. If valve holds a vacuum, it is OK. Otherwise, replace the canister. If valve holds a vacuum, remove vapor purge hose and check it for vacuum as in Step 1. If there is no vacuum, check the PCV system and hoses (p.246).

Testing engine compression 🔧🔧 30 min–1 hr

An engine compression test is a relatively simple way of making sure that the internal components directly affecting compression (the pistons, piston rings, valves, and cylinder head gasket) are sealing properly. If these components are worn or leaking, the engine's performance and fuel economy will be adversely affected, and a tuneup will not restore the engine's performance. Repairs to these internal parts are best left to a professional mechanic.

The tests are done at the spark plug holes. The engine should be hot and the throttle wide open. If you prefer to do the testing on a cold engine, manually open the throttle plate and the choke plate, and hold them open by placing small wedges in their linkages. Do not place wedges in the carburetor throat; they could fall into the engine. Gauges that register pressures of up to 300 pounds per square inch are adequate for gasoline engines. Testing the compression of a diesel engine requires a gauge that registers over 600 psi. The latter tests are done at the glow plug hole or injector hole. Disconnect the fuel pump's solenoid wire (p.343, Step 8) and follow the instructions with the gauge.

Analyzing compression readings

An engine has acceptable compression if the worst cylinder gives a reading of at least 90 psi and the remaining cylinders give readings of at least 75 percent of the highest reading (a range of 90 to 120 psi, for example).

Abnormally high readings in one or more of the cylinders can mean that some exhaust valves are not opening fully or that there is an excessive buildup of carbon inside the engine. Bring the engine up to its normal operating temperature, then disconnect the ignition (Step 2, right) and operate the starter. If the engine tries to start, it means that there is a buildup of hot carbon deposits in some cylinders.

Low readings in one or more cylinders, or readings from two adjacent cylinders that are at least 20 psi below the others, can indicate other problems. To determine the cause, squirt engine oil into the spark plug holes (Step 6, right) and take another set of readings. If the new readings are higher than the first set of readings, the piston rings are worn. If the new readings stay about the same as the first set of readings, the valve seats are worn or the valves are sticking or are burned. If the two adjacent cylinders still read at least 20 psi below the others, the head gasket is damaged between the two cylinders.
Tools: Ratchet wrench and extensions, spark plug socket, jumper wire, compression gauge.
Materials: Masking tape, pencil, paper, engine oil, can of compressed air (sold in photo shops).

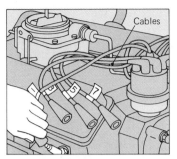

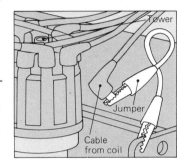

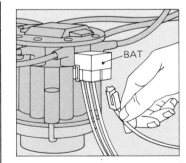

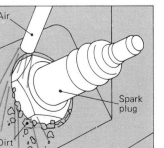

1. Check that the battery is fully charged (p.278). Remove the air cleaner. Run the engine until the choke is fully open. Turn off the engine; check that the oil is at the *Full* mark on the dipstick (p.196). Label each spark plug cable with tape. Disconnect all the cables from the spark plugs.

2. Disconnect the ignition cable from the center tower of the distributor cap. Then use a jumper wire to ground the cable to a metal part of the engine. This will prevent the engine from starting.

Most Delco High Energy Ignition (HEI) systems, have no center tower on the distributor cap. Disconnect the pink battery feed wire (or the main multi-wire harness connector) from the terminal on the side of the distributor cap marked BAT.

3. Using compressed air, clean loose dirt from the area around each spark plug. Remove all the spark plugs (p.234). Inspect the plugs and cables, and replace any that are defective.

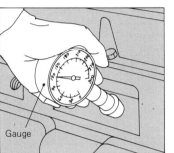

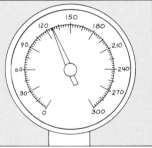

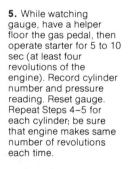

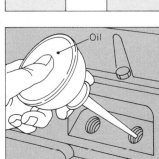

4. To take the pressure reading for each cylinder, install the end of the compression gauge into each spark plug hole. If the gauge has a threaded fitting on the end of a hose, screw the fitting into the spark plug hole.

If the compression gauge has a rubber cone at the end, push the cone into the spark plug hole and hold it firmly in place while taking the pressure readings. If the cone slips, the pressure readings will be inaccurate.

5. While watching gauge, have a helper floor the gas pedal, then operate starter for 5 to 10 sec (at least four revolutions of the engine). Record cylinder number and pressure reading. Reset gauge. Repeat Steps 4–5 for each cylinder; be sure that engine makes same number of revolutions each time.

6. If one or more of the cylinders give low readings, or if two adjacent cylinders give readings at least 20 psi below the others, squirt 1 tablespoon of engine oil into the spark plug holes. Take a new set of readings (repeat Steps 4–5). Then analyze the new readings (see box at left).

Maintenance / Engine

Testing engine vacuum ⏱ 10–20 min

A vacuum gauge (sometimes mounted on the dash and called a fuel economy gauge) can tell you a lot about the internal condition of a gasoline engine. Diesel engines cannot be tested.

Vacuum gauges record the difference in air pressure between the atmosphere and the partial vacuum created in the intake manifold as each piston moves down on its intake stroke. The gauges are calibrated in inches of mercury (in.-Hg), usually from 0 to 30 in.-Hg. Most have color bands indicating engine conditions (or rates of fuel consumption) and a pressure range of up to 10 psi for testing fuel pumps (p.397). You can buy a vacuum gauge for use under the hood as a diagnostic engine tester or in a kit that can be mounted on or under the dashboard.

Measure engine vacuum while the engine is running. Readings indicate general engine condition and pinpoint specific mechanical and adjustment problems (see below). A dash-mounted vacuum gauge should read 10 to 18 in.-Hg (in the yellow or green bands) if you are driving prudently. The higher the reading, the better the fuel economy. At idle, a fully warmed up engine that is properly adjusted and in good mechanical condition will produce a reading between 15 and 22 in.-Hg. Readings will vary with altitude and atmospheric conditions. Every 1,000 feet of altitude lowers the reading by 1 to 2 in.-Hg. A V-8 engine will usually show slightly higher vacuum readings than a six- or four-cylinder engine will.

> **Tools:** Vacuum gauge, rubber vacuum hose, T and adapter fittings, screwdriver, remote starter switch (optional).

Analyzing vacuum readings (engine running)

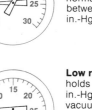

Steady reading between 15 and 22 in.-Hg with the engine warmed up and idling is normal (left, top). Snap the throttle plate open and closed suddenly. The needle should drop to 5 in.-Hg or lower before stabilizing at the normal reading between 15 and 22 in.-Hg (left, bottom).

Low reading that holds steady around 5 in.-Hg indicates a vacuum leak at intake manifold or carburetor gaskets, or a disconnected or leaking vacuum hose.

Low reading that holds steady between 8 and 14 in.-Hg. suggests that ignition timing is off or that piston rings are leaking. Check timing and compression.

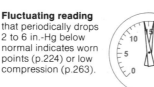

Fluctuating reading that periodically drops 2 to 6 in.-Hg below normal indicates worn points (p.224) or low compression (p.263).

Regular fluctuation between a low reading of about 5 in.-Hg and a slightly lower-than-normal reading means the head gasket is leaking. See a mechanic.

Reading drifts back and forth over a range of 4 to 5 in.-Hg within the normal range to indicate incorrect carburetor adjustment (pp.251, 255).

Rapid needle vibration between 14 and 19 in.-Hg indicates that worn valve guides are letting intake valves chatter as they seat. See a mechanic.

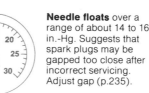

Needle floats over a range of about 14 to 16 in.-Hg. Suggests that spark plugs may be gapped too close after incorrect servicing. Adjust gap (p.235).

Needle that swings erratically between about 10 and 20 in.-Hg when the engine is accelerated smoothly may indicate weak valve springs. See a mechanic.

Steady high reading that holds above 21 in.-Hg indicates restricted air intake. Check for clogged air filter (p.240) or a stuck choke (p.248).

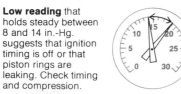

Needle drops to near zero when the engine is accelerated, then climbs back almost to normal level. Exhaust system may be blocked or kinked (p.434).

Testing with a vacuum gauge

Connecting a vacuum gauge for engine testing is easy after you get to know the layout of the vacuum lines on your car.

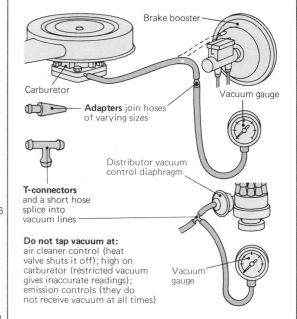

Adapters join hoses of varying sizes

T-connectors and a short hose splice into vacuum lines

Do not tap vacuum at: air cleaner control (heat valve shuts it off); high on carburetor (restricted vacuum gives inaccurate readings); emission controls (they do not receive vacuum at all times)

Testing cranking vacuum

1. Tap into a vacuum line with an adapter or T-fitting, and connect the vacuum gauge. Follow the instructions that come with the gauge. Make sure that the vacuum source gives full manifold vacuum. Some carburetor hoses have restrictors to reduce vacuum to certain controls.
2. Remove and plug the PCV valve at the valve cover, or block its hose with a bolt or your fingertip.
3. Disconnect the high-voltage coil cable from the distributor cap, and ground cable on the engine block (p.263).
4. Close the throttle plate in the carburetor by turning the idle speed screw, or by disconnecting the wire on the idle-stop solenoid if your car has one (p.252).
5. Hook up remote starter switch, following the instructions that come with it, or have a helper crank the engine while you take cranking readings. These will be similar to, but slightly lower than, idling readings (left). If the engine cranks too slowly, check the battery (p.276), starter system (pp.391–396), and compression (p.263).
6. Reconnect the high-voltage coil cable, return idle adjustment to normal, but leave the PCV valve disconnected and plugged while taking vacuum readings.
7. Remove gauge, reconnect vacuum lines and PCV valve.

Maintenance/Valve adjustment

Inspecting valve clearance

Checking and, if necessary, adjusting valve clearances should be a part of the periodic tuneup procedures for your car's engine if it is equipped with solid valve lifters. Engines with hydraulic lifters seldom require valve adjustments.

Normal engine wear generally increases the amount of clearance, or *free play*, between valve train components, causing them to work less efficiently. A common sign of loose valves is poor engine performance even after a tuneup. A steady clicking noise in the valve train that increases with engine speed but lessens when the engine warms up completely is another sign of excessive valve clearance.

Too little valve clearance, known as a *tight valve*, can result from improper adjustment or from excess wear in the valve seat. Valves transfer heat to the coolant only while they are seated. A tight valve is seated for too short a time, which can cause it to *burn*, or overheat. When a valve burns, pieces break off and cylinder compression is lowered. A tight valve may eventually seize or break off, causing extensive engine damage. Tight valves are hard to detect because noise does not develop in the valve train. This is another reason to check valve clearance frequently. Check for tight valves if the engine performs better when it is cold than at normal temperatures. Misfiring in the top or bottom of a gear range or loss of power under load despite other tuneup adjustments may also be signs of tight valves.

Valve clearances are checked with a feeler gauge. Instead of using the tapered go/no-go type, use three separate blades—the correct size plus one size larger and one size smaller. To judge the way the proper blade should feel, slide it through a micrometer set to the specified valve clearance before using the gauge on the valves themselves. For accuracy, always move the gauge parallel to the length of the crankshaft.

Certain pistons must be set at top dead center in order for the valves to be fully closed. To do this, align the engine timing marks according to the manufacturer's instructions. Using a wrench, turn the engine by its crankshaft nut (removing the spark plugs makes turning easier), or put a manual transmission in *High* gear and push the car forward a short distance. You can also "bump" the engine with the starter by flicking the ignition on and off in short bursts until the marks are aligned. A helper or a remote starter switch will simplify the job.

How to identify intake and exhaust valves

Intake valves and exhaust valves usually require different clearance settings. To locate the intake valves on an engine, first remove the valve cover (V-type engines have two valve covers), then observe where each arm of the intake manifold is connected to the engine block. Valves in a direct line with these connections are intake valves. To locate the exhaust valves, note the locations of the exhaust manifold arms. The valves directly in line with these are exhaust valves.

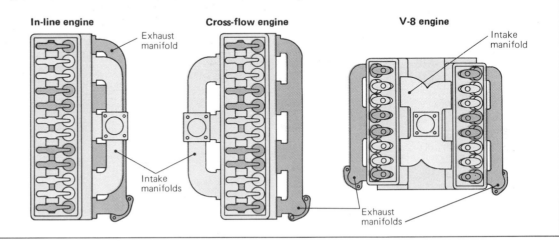

In-line engine — Exhaust manifold, Intake manifolds

Cross-flow engine — Exhaust manifolds

V-8 engine — Intake manifold

How to determine whether a valve is open or closed

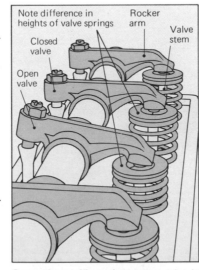

Note difference in heights of valve springs — Rocker arm — Valve stem — Closed valve — Open valve

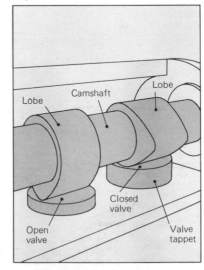

Lobe — Camshaft — Lobe — Closed valve — Open valve — Valve tappet

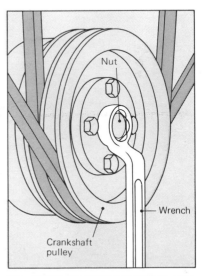

Nut — Wrench — Crankshaft pulley

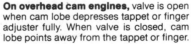

On engines with rocker arms, valve is fully open when rocker arm depresses valve stem fully. When valve is closed, rocker arm exerts no pressure on valve.

On overhead cam engines, valve is open when cam lobe depresses tappet or finger adjuster fully. When valve is closed, cam lobe points away from the tappet or finger.

Use wrench to rotate crankshaft when positioning valves for adjustment. To avoid damaging timing gear, turn engine only in its normal direction of rotation.

Checking for worn parts

Check valve components for wear each time you check or adjust valve clearance. Normally these parts wear very little, because points of contact between them are made of specially hardened material. However, wear has occurred if valves do not hold their settings or require frequent adjustment, or if particular valves must be adjusted substantially tighter or looser than neighboring valves. Limit your inspection to parts that are readily visible; checking internal valve-train components requires engine disassembly.

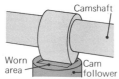

Worn cam followers on overhead cam engines are easy to spot; look for indentations. Replace if excessively worn or if valves will not hold their settings.

Camshaft / Worn area / Cam follower

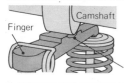

Chipped fingers or rocker arms must usually be replaced. If parts are smoothly worn, careful adjustment of clearance may suffice.

Camshaft / Finger / Chipped area

Check cam lobes on overhead cam engines; crazing indicates softening of surface metal. Have camshaft inspected by a mechanic; a new shaft may be required.

Camshaft / Crazing / Lobe

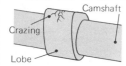

Replace worn adjusters on rocker arms if precise valve settings cannot be maintained. Damaged valve stems require that valves be replaced by a mechanic.

Locknut / Worn screw / Rocker arm

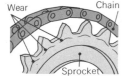

Check timing chain and sprocket for wear. Chain should be taut and should ride smoothly on sprocket. If you can lift chain completely off sprocket teeth, have it replaced.

Wear / Chain / Sprocket

Timing gear drive belt deteriorates with age. Check it often for cracking and for torn or broken teeth. Replace belt at first sign of wear.

Cracking / Drive belt / Torn tooth

Replacing Volkswagen pushrod tubes ▢▢▢▢ 1–2 hr

Leaking or damaged pushrod tubes on air-cooled VW engines can be replaced easily, using expansion tubes available from auto parts stores. Unlike stock tubes, the replacements do not require that the cylinder head be removed, and they can be installed without removing the engine from the car. Because of their high cost, expansion tubes are practical only if you need to replace just a few tubes. If you plan to refit the majority of tubes on either side of the engine, it is usually more economical to have a garage remove the engine, take off the cylinder head, and install stock VW pushrod tubes.

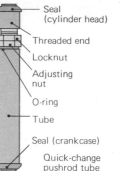

Seal (cylinder head) / Threaded end / Locknut / Adjusting nut / O-ring / Tube / Seal (crankcase) / Quick-change pushrod tube

Tools: Jack, jack stands, large screwdriver, 13-mm socket or box wrench, 1-in. open-end wrench, torque wrench with 13-mm socket, small length of soft wire, metal-cutting shears (optional).
Materials: Replacement pushrod tubes with seals, valve cover gaskets, rocker shaft support seals (pre-1977 cars only).

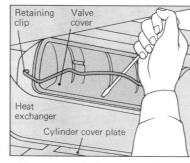

Retaining clip / Valve cover / Heat exchanger / Cylinder cover plate

1. Raise car on jack stands or lift. Clean road dirt from valve cover and area around cylinder head. Using screwdriver, remove lower cylinder cover plate if necessary, then remove valve cover by prying retaining clip outward and down.

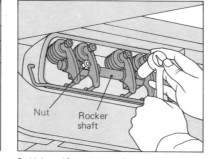

Nut / Rocker shaft

2. Using 13-mm wrench, remove rocker shaft nuts, loosening them alternately, a little at a time. Lift rocker shaft off. Use a piece of soft wire to pry out old support seals from recesses (pre-1977 cars only). Remove rocker shaft's clip, if present.

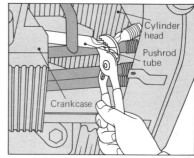

Cylinder head / Pushrod tube / Crankcase

3. Withdraw pushrods from tubes to be replaced. Note order of rods so that you can reinstall them in their original locations. Pry out old pushrod tubes, or cut them in pieces with shears. Remove old tube seals. Wipe mating surfaces clean.

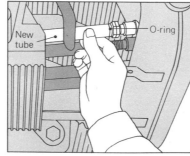

New tube / O-ring

4. Lubricate rubber O-ring on adjusting nut. Install replacement tube with threaded end toward spark plug. Using 1-in. open-end wrench, tighten both nuts to seat tube firmly in cylinder head and crankcase. Do not crush seals by overtightening nuts.

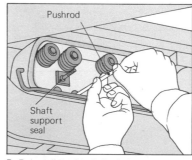

Pushrod / Shaft support seal

5. Reinstall pushrods in their original locations. First roll rods on a flat surface to check for straightness; replace any that wobble. Mount rocker shaft, using new shaft support seals (pre-1977 cars only), and reinstall rocker shaft's clip, if present.

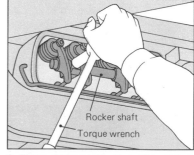

Rocker shaft / Torque wrench

6. Torque rocker shaft nuts to 14 to 18 lb-ft (19 to 24 N·m). Tighten each nut in turn, a little at a time. Reset valves (pp. 267–269), install new valve cover gasket, then install valve cover and cylinder cover plate. Run engine to check for leaks.

Overhead valves

The engines in most large and mid-size North American cars are equipped with overhead valves operated by pushrods (see *How your car works,* p.38). Generally, these engines are also fitted with hydraulic valve lifters and need no adjustment. However, many economy and sports cars, with smaller four- and six-cylinder in-line engines, have overhead valve mechanisms with pushrods and solid tappets that do require periodic maintenance. Pushrod engines have their rocker arms either mounted on a rocker shaft bolted to the top of the cylinder head, or mounted on individual studs. Other variations on some imported cars combine a rocker arm/rocker shaft assembly with an overhead camshaft, thereby eliminating the need for pushrods.

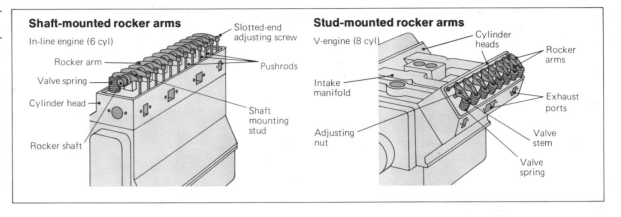

Shaft-mounted rocker arms

In-line engine (6 cyl)
Rocker arm
Valve spring
Cylinder head
Rocker shaft
Slotted-end adjusting screw
Pushrods
Shaft mounting stud

Stud-mounted rocker arms

V-engine (8 cyl)
Cylinder heads
Rocker arms
Intake manifold
Adjusting nut
Exhaust ports
Valve stem
Valve spring

Rocker arm styles on imported cars

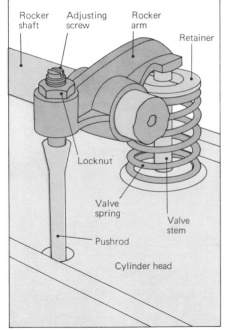

Rocker shaft
Adjusting screw
Rocker arm
Retainer
Locknut
Valve spring
Valve stem
Pushrod
Cylinder head

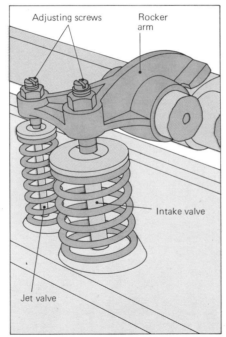

Adjusting screws
Rocker arm
Intake valve
Jet valve

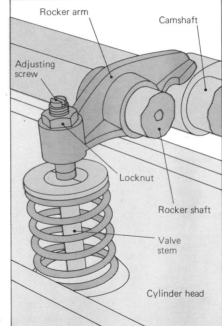

Rocker arm
Camshaft
Adjusting screw
Locknut
Rocker shaft
Valve stem
Cylinder head

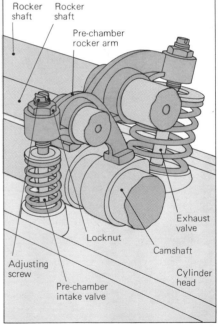

Rocker shaft
Rocker shaft
Pre-chamber rocker arm
Exhaust valve
Locknut
Camshaft
Adjusting screw
Pre-chamber intake valve
Cylinder head

Typical pushrod engine with shaft-mounted rocker arms has clearance-adjusting screws over the pushrods. The screws slotted ends are adjusted with a screwdriver, and the adjustment is held by locknuts that are tightened with a wrench. On air-cooled VW engines, the adjusting screws are located over the valves.

Japanese-built engines used in some Dodge and Plymouth front-drive cars have a *jet valve* that allows extra air into the cylinder. The jet valve is opened by an extension on the rocker arm, and it has a standard adjuster. Loosen intake valve adjusting screw, then adjust jet valve play to .006 in. (.15 mm). Adjust intake valve next.

Toyotas with overhead camshafts operate rocker arms attached to a single rocker shaft located alongside the cam. The clearance-adjusting screws are positioned over the valve stems and are the conventional slotted-end type, adjustable with a screwdriver. Locknuts hold the screws in place after an adjustment is made.

Honda's unique CVCC engine, with three valves per cylinder instead of two, has a conventional overhead camshaft, but its rocker arms are mounted on twin rocker shafts above, rather than beside, the camshaft. Standard slotted-end adjusting screws with locknuts are fitted into each arm, over the valve stems.

Adjusting valve clearance: pushrod engines ☑☑☑ 1–3 hr

The 1,600-cc engines used in Ford Fiestas, and the 2,600-cc and 2,800-cc V-6 engines used in Capris and some other Ford models, have pushrods and overhead valves whose clearance must be adjusted periodically. Other engines with similar designs include Chrysler six-cylinder (slant-6) engines and most European pushrod engines. (Set Chrysler clearance with the engine warmed up and idling.) Japanese pushrod engines include some Datsuns, Mazdas, and Subarus. Dodge Colt, Honda, Plymouth Arrow, and Toyota engines have overhead camshafts that operate shaft-mounted rocker arms similar to those used in pushrod engines, and adjustment procedures are the same. To adjust the valves on a Fiesta, follow the sequence given in the chart below. Check the *Tuneup Data* supplement for adjustment specifications for other engines. Other adjusting mechanisms are shown on page 267.

Fiesta valve-adjustment sequence

Open valves	1 and 6	2 and 4	3 and 8	5 and 7
Adjust valves	3 and 8	5 and 7	1 and 6	2 and 4

Intake valve clearance: .010 in. (.25 mm)	Exhaust valve clearance: .021 in. (.53 mm)

Fiesta valve train

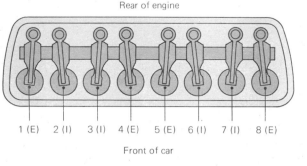

Rear of engine

1 (E) 2 (I) 3 (I) 4 (E) 5 (E) 6 (I) 7 (I) 8 (E)

Front of car

Tools: Flat-blade screwdriver, ratchet wrench, 11-mm or 7/16-in. socket, spark plug socket, 6-in. extension, ratcheting drive handle, blade-type feeler gauge, putty knife, single-edge razor blades and blade holder.
Materials: Clothespins or masking tape, felt-tip pen, new valve-cover gasket, gasket sealant, electrically conductive silicone grease.

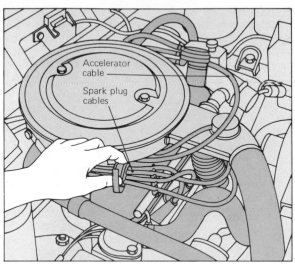

1. Warm up engine to operating temperature, then shut it off. Place transmission in *Neutral* and set parking brake. Working under the hood, disconnect or reposition the vacuum hose and emission-control hose, spark plug cables, and accelerator cable so that air cleaner and valve cover can be removed.

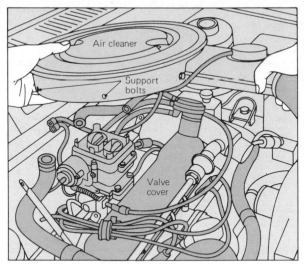

2. Remove air cleaner by loosening the three support bolts at the air cleaner housing, then lifting the entire air cleaner assembly off the carburetor. Do not loosen bolts at EGR valve or intake manifold. Using a flat-blade screwdriver, unscrew the valve cover's hold-down screws, then remove valve cover.

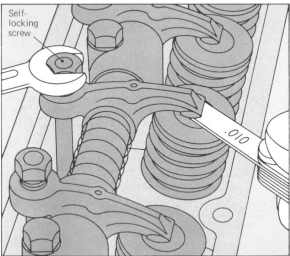

6. To adjust valve clearance, turn self-locking screw clockwise to decrease clearance, or counterclockwise to increase clearance. Use an 11-mm or 7/16-in. socket wrench or box-end wrench. Check final adjustment with a feeler gauge. Measure all valves, rotating engine according to sequence in chart at left, above.

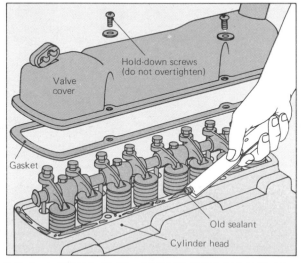

7. Remove all traces of old valve-cover gasket and sealant by scraping surface of cylinder head with a putty knife or razor blade. Be careful not to score gasket surface. Apply a thin bead of gasket sealer to cylinder head, then carefully install new gasket. Clean inside of valve cover and reinstall it, screwing it down evenly.

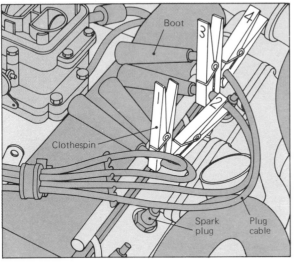

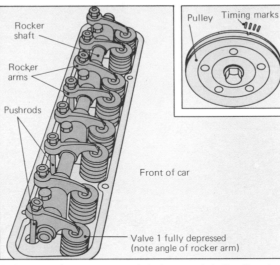

Front of car

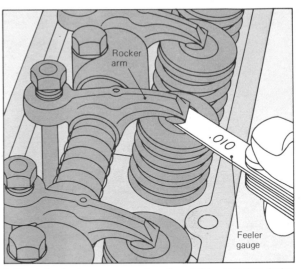

3. Remove spark plugs for inspection and to make engine rotation easier. Label plug cables first, using numbered clothespins or pieces of masking tape. Grasp plug cable by boot only, twist, then pull it off. Wipe plug area clean, then remove plugs with spark plug socket, ratchet wrench, and extension.

4. Rotate engine; use a wrench to turn crankshaft pulley clockwise, or have a helper operate the starter in short bursts until notch in crankshaft pulley is aligned with timing marks. Rotate engine slightly farther until you can see that valves 1 and 6 are fully depressed by the camshaft (fully open).

5. Now check clearance on valves 3 and 8 by inserting feeler gauge between rocker arm and valve stem. Clearance at valve 3 (an intake valve) should be .010 in. (.25 mm). Clearance at valve 8 (an exhaust valve) should be .021 in. (.53 mm). Clearances that are too large or too small must be adjusted.

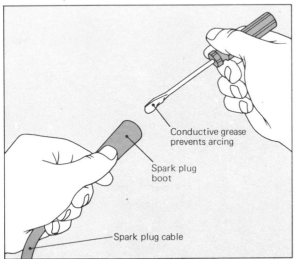

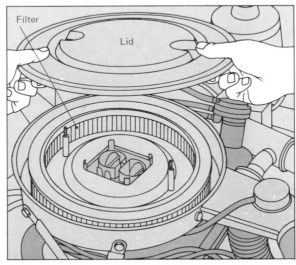

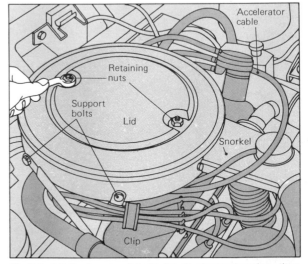

8. Reinstall spark plugs and plug cables. Before attaching cables to plugs, Ford recommends using a small, clean screwdriver to apply a thin film of electrically conductive silicone grease to the interior surfaces of each boot, or spray the inside of each boot with a silicone aerosol spray. Then press the boots over the plugs.

9. Open the air cleaner before reinstalling it (see p.240). Change the filter if necessary. To reinstall cleaner, first install carburetor-to-cleaner gasket on the top of the carburetor, then press the air cleaner housing, with lid removed, onto the carburetor so that it seats firmly without crimping the gasket.

10. Reinstall three support bolts for air cleaner housing, then reinstall air cleaner lid and retaining nuts. Route the accelerator cable over the air cleaner snorkel. Reinstall spark plug cables in plastic clip, making sure that cables in consecutive firing order (1–2–4–3) are not adjacent to each other.

Adjusting valve clearance: shim-type adjusters ▣▣▣ 1½–3 hr

Volkswagens with four-cylinder, water-cooled engines, some Fiats, and many Dodge Omnis and Plymouth Horizons have overhead camshafts and bucket tappet valves (see *Overhead camshafts*, p.39). The tappets have exposed shims recessed into their tops. The shims are metal discs of precise thickness that act as bearing surfaces for the cam lobes during engine operation. The clearance between each shim and cam lobe must be checked periodically according to the manufacturer's specifications, usually at intervals of 10,000 to 15,000 miles. Occasionally, shims must be replaced with thicker ones due to normal valve train wear. Shims of different thicknesses compensate for worn valve train parts and are available from your car dealer's parts department.

Volkswagen valve train

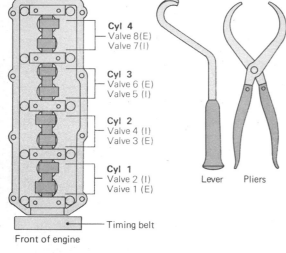

Rear of engine

Cyl 4
— Valve 8 (E)
Valve 7 (I)

Cyl 3
— Valve 6 (E)
Valve 5 (I)

Cyl 2
— Valve 4 (I)
Valve 3 (E)

Cyl 1
— Valve 2 (I)
Valve 1 (E)

— Timing belt

Front of engine

Lever   Pliers

Tools: Ratchet wrench, 10-mm socket, 3-in. extension, spark plug socket, 15-mm box wrench or open-end wrench, 6-mm Allen wrench (not necessary on pre-1980 engines), blade-type feeler gauge, special lever tool and shim pliers, thin knife blade, magnet tool, putty knife, single-edge razor blades and blade holder, four clothespins or masking tape, felt-tip marker.
Special tools for removing shims are available from car dealers and auto parts specialty stores.
Materials: New cam-cover gasket, gasket sealer.

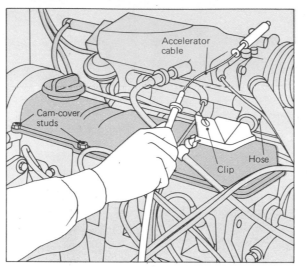

Accelerator cable

Cam-cover studs

Clip

Hose

1. Warm up engine thoroughly, then shut it off. (**Caution:** Run engine only in a well-ventilated area.) Remove hoses and accelerator cable from plastic clips on cam cover. Using 10-mm socket wrench and 3-in. extension, unscrew cam-cover nuts, then remove cam cover and cam-cover flange stiffeners.

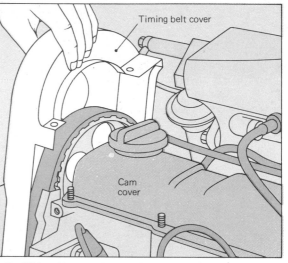

Timing belt cover

Cam cover

2. On 1980 and later models, the timing belt cover fits snugly over the cam cover and must be removed first. To do this, remove the 10-mm nuts and the single bolt holding the cover to the engine. Then, using a 6-mm Allen wrench, remove the retaining screw and washer located at the bottom of the cover.

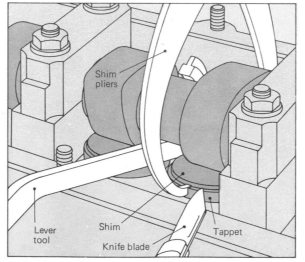

Shim pliers

Lever tool

Shim

Knife blade

Tappet

6. Lift shim out of recess in top of tappet, using shim pliers. Since oil on the tappet often creates a suction seal beneath the shim, making removal difficult, some mechanics slip a thin knife blade or razor blade between the shim and tappet while simultaneously lifting the shim with pliers.

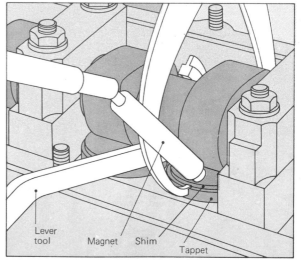

Lever tool

Magnet

Shim

Tappet

7. Shims can also be removed with a magnet tool, used alone or with shim pliers. The number on the underside of the shim indicates its thickness in millimeters. Replacements are available in a wide range of thicknesses, in .002-in. (.05-mm) increments. Calculate the size you need before buying shims.

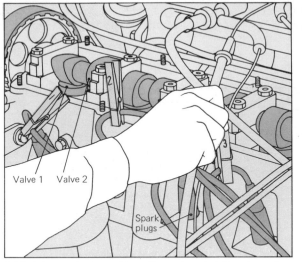

Valve 1 Valve 2

Spark plugs

3. Mark the spark plug cables with numbered clothespins or tape, then remove plugs for inspection and to make engine rotation easier. Using 15-mm open-end or box wrench, turn crankshaft pulley nut clockwise to rotate camshaft until cam lobes over valves 1 and 2 point away from the tappets.

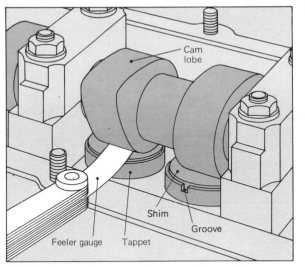

Cam lobe

Shim

Feeler gauge Tappet Groove

4. Use feeler gauge to measure clearances between bottom of cam lobes and tappets. Exhaust valve clearance should be .016 in. to .020 in.; clearance at intake valves should be .008 in. to .012 in. Rotate the camshaft (Step 3) and check each pair of valves, following cylinder firing order: 1–4–3–2.

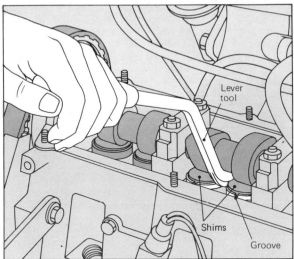

Lever tool

Shims

Groove

5. If clearance is incorrect, remove shims and buy replacements from a VW dealer. To remove shims, rotate tappets so that shim-access grooves are perpendicular to camshaft. Insert lever tool between camshaft and a pair of tappets. Push down on tool to depress tappets. Tool must not contact shims.

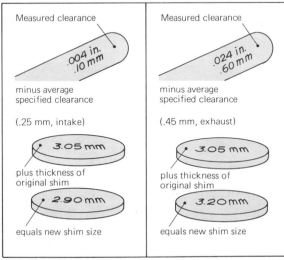

Measured clearance

.004 in. .10 mm

minus average specified clearance

(.25 mm, intake)

3.05 mm

plus thickness of original shim

2.90 mm

equals new shim size

Measured clearance

.024 in. .60 mm

minus average specified clearance

(.45 mm, exhaust)

3.05 mm

plus thickness of original shim

3.20 mm

equals new shim size

8. To compute size of the replacement shim, subtract the average valve clearance allowed by the specifications from the actual clearance measured with a feeler gauge. Add or subtract the difference to the thickness of the original shim to obtain new size needed. Round off answer to the nearest .05 mm.

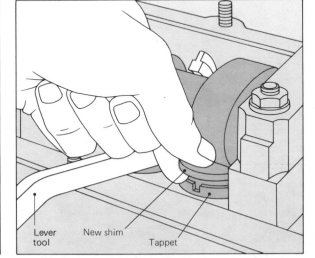

Lever tool New shim Tappet

9. Install replacement shim in tappet recess, with number-etched side facing down. Free tappets by removing lever tool from beneath camshaft. If engine has become cold while shims were being installed, run engine briefly to warm it up to normal operating temperature, then recheck clearances.

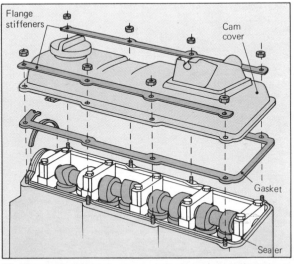

Flange stiffeners

Cam cover

Gasket

Sealer

10. Scrape off old cam-cover gasket, using putty knife or razor blades. Do not damage surface of cylinder head. Apply thin bead of gasket sealer to cylinder head, and carefully install new gasket. Clean and reinstall cam cover, timing belt cover (if necessary), spark plugs, hoses, and accelerator cable.

271

Adjusting valve clearance: screw-type adjusters ▣▣▣ 1– 2 hr

General Motors' four-cylinder engine with aluminum block and overhead camshaft was used in Chevrolet Vegas and Monzas as well as in Pontiac Astres and Sunbirds. The engines in 1971 through 1975 models have adjustable bucket tappets (see *Overhead camshafts,* p.39). The valve clearance on these engines should be checked, and adjusted if necessary, every two years or 30,000 miles, whichever comes first. Engines in 1976 and later models have hydraulic tappets that need no adjustment. Four-cylinder Audis, and AMC cars from 1977 through 1979 (which use Audi engines), have a similar system except for clearance adjustment specifications (see *Tuneup Data* booklet). Adjustments to the Audi as well as to the GM engine should be made with the engine warmed up to its normal operating temperature.

Identifying cams and valves

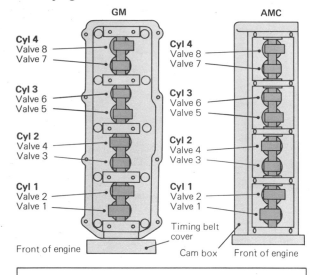

Tools and materials. GM cars: Ratchet wrench, 7/16- and 3/8-in. sockets, 5/8-in. spark plug socket, 3-in. extension, U-joint, 3/4-in. box wrench, blade-type feeler gauge, 1/8-in. Allen wrench, putty knife, single-edge razor blades and blade holder, four clothespins or roll of masking tape, felt-tip marker, cork cam-cover gasket, gasket sealant, rubber bands, heavy-duty plastic wrap, paper towels.
AMC cars: 10-mm socket wrench, 3-mm Allen wrench, cam-cover gasket, gasket sealant, putty knife, razor blades and holder, clothespins or masking tape, felt-tip marker.

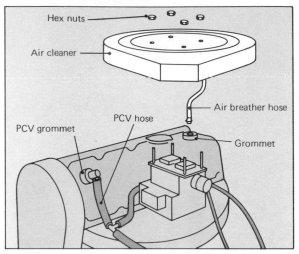

1. Remove the wing nut or hexagonal nuts on top of air cleaner. Pull air breather hose out of rear grommet on cam cover, then lift off air cleaner. Pull PCV hose out of its grommet. Cover carburetor with plastic wrap and a rubber band to keep out dirt. (On AMC cars, air cleaner remains on, but spark plugs, wires, and rear wiring harness must be removed; see Step 3.)

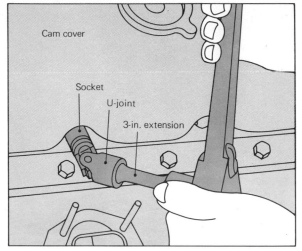

2. Use 3/8-in. socket wrench to remove bolts from cam cover. Use a U-joint and 3-in. extension to reach lower bolts. Loosen cam cover with a blow from a mallet or by prying between cover and gasket with a large screwdriver. Remove cam cover. (AMC cars: Lift cam cover off after removing its stud nuts with a 10-mm socket wrench and extension. U-joint is not needed.)

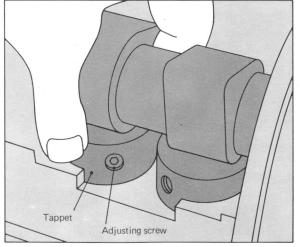

6. The gap size is the number stamped onto the thickest feeler blade that will fit between the cam and the tappet. If the gap between a cam and tappet does not fall into the acceptable range, rotate the tappet until the Allen-head adjusting screw is visible through one of the two holes in the tappet, usually on the right side of the engine (when viewed from the front).

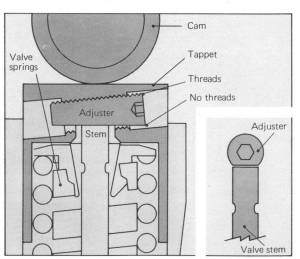

7. The tappet adjuster is a tapered screw with one flat, unthreaded side that must always contact the top of the valve stem. When adjusting the gap between tappet and cam, always turn the adjuster through one or more complete revolutions. Each complete turn changes the valve clearance by .003 in. (.076 mm) on GM cars and by .002 in. (.05 mm) on AMC cars.

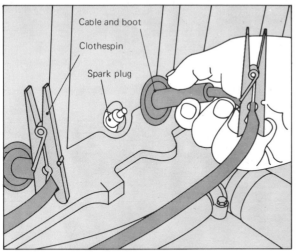

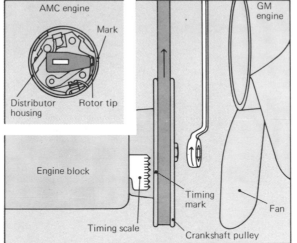

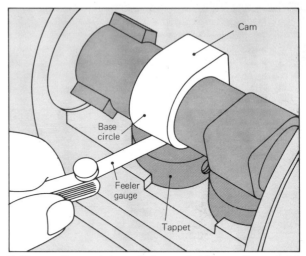

3. Use numbered clothespins or pieces of masking tape to label the spark plug cables, then carefully remove the cables, pulling each by its boot to avoid damage. Remove the spark plugs to check their condition and to make turning the engine (Step 4) easier. Use a ⅝-in. spark plug socket and a 3-in. extension. You may need a U-joint for the rearmost plug.

4. With transmission in *Neutral,* turn engine crankshaft pulley clockwise (when viewed from front of car) until timing mark is about midway along timing scale. This puts camshaft in correct position, with piston No.1 at top dead center (TDC). (On AMC cars, remove distributor cap, then turn crankshaft pulley until rotor tip is aligned with mark stamped on distributor housing.)

5. Measure the gap between bottom end of the cam (base circle) and top surface of the tappet on valves 1, 2, 3, and 6. Gap at valves 1 and 3 should measure between .012 and .018 in. on GM cars, .006 and .009 in. on AMCs. Gap at valves 2 and 6 should measure .027 to .033 in. on GM cars and .016 to .019 in. on AMC models. Normally, the gap increases as the engine wears.

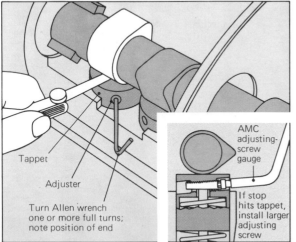

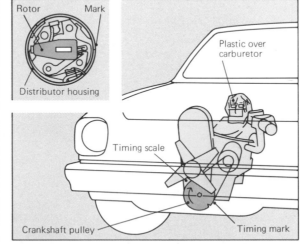

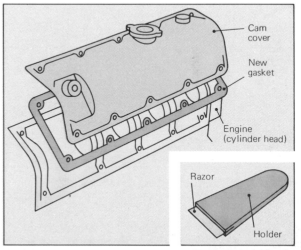

8. Insert Allen wrench (⅛ in. for GM, 7/64 in. or 3 mm for AMC) into the adjuster, and note position of wrench end. Turn adjuster clockwise to increase gap, counterclockwise to reduce gap. Rotate wrench until its end points in original direction. On AMC engines, use special tool to gauge whether adjuster has been screwed in too far. If so, larger-size screw must be installed.

9. Remeasure gap after adjustment. When gaps for valves 1, 2, 3, and 6 are satisfactory, rotate crankshaft pulley one full revolution in its normal direction of travel, so that the camshaft turns 180 degrees. Now measure and adjust gaps on valves 4, 5, 7, and 8. (On AMC engines, rotate crankshaft one full turn until distributor rotor points 180 degrees away from mark on housing.)

10. Scrape all old gasket material from cam cover and cylinder head. Use screwdriver, putty knife, or single-edge razor blade in holder. Apply a thin, continuous bead of gasket sealant to both cover and engine. Position new gasket in groove located on cover or cylinder head so that all holes align. Reinstall cam cover, spark plugs, wiring, and air cleaner (if removed).

Adjusting valve clearance: finger-type adjusters ⚑⚑⚑ 1½–3 hr

Ford Motor Company's overhead camshaft, four-cylinder engine is used in compact and mid-size Ford and Mercury cars as well as in German-built Capris. The 2,300-cc engine, an option since 1974, has hydraulic tappets and. needs no adjustment. The 1,600-cc and 2,000-cc engines have adjustable cam fingers, and their valve clearance should be checked and adjusted every 12 months or 12,000 miles, whichever comes first. After the cam cover is removed (Step 3), rotate the crankshaft (Step 4) and adjust the valves in pairs. Datsun overhead cam engines (both four- and six-cylinder) are similar to Ford's except for the gap specifications (see *Tuneup Data* booklet).

Identifying valves

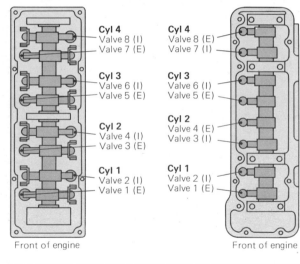

Ford 4-cyl OHC

Cyl 4
Valve 8 (I)
Valve 7 (E)

Cyl 3
Valve 6 (I)
Valve 5 (E)

Cyl 2
Valve 4 (I)
Valve 3 (E)

Cyl 1
Valve 2 (I)
Valve 1 (E)

Front of engine

Datsun 4-cyl OHC

Cyl 4
Valve 8 (E)
Valve 7 (I)

Cyl 3
Valve 6 (I)
Valve 5 (E)

Cyl 2
Valve 4 (E)
Valve 3 (I)

Cyl 1
Valve 2 (I)
Valve 1 (E)

Front of engine

Tools: Ratchet wrench, 10-mm and 12-mm sockets, 13/16-in. spark plug socket, 6-in. extension, 3/4-in. box-end wrench, blade-type feeler gauge, 3/4-in. and 19/32-in. (15-mm) open-end wrenches, putty knife, single-edge razor blades.
Materials: Clothespins or masking tape, felt-tip pen, new cam-cover gasket, gasket sealant, rubber band, heavy-duty plastic wrap, paper towel.
(For Datsuns: 10-mm socket, 14-mm open-end wrench, 17-mm open-end wrench or special Datsun adjusting tool, feeler gauge, masking tape or clothespins, marker, putty knife, razor blades, cam-cover gasket, sealant.)

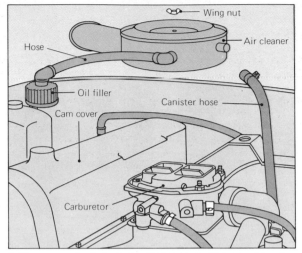

Wing nut

Air cleaner

Hose

Oil filler

Cam cover

Canister hose

Carburetor

1. Warm up engine to operating temperature. Remove wing nut or bolt at top of air cleaner. Disconnect air cleaner hose leading to charcoal evaporative emission control canister. Pull oil filler cap from cam cover, then lift air cleaner off top of carburetor. (Datsuns: Simply remove air cleaner hose from cam cover. It is not necessary to remove the air cleaner.)

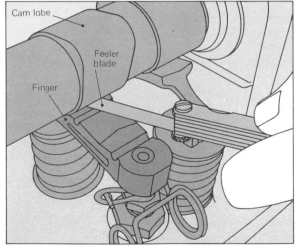

Cam lobe

Feeler blade

Finger

6. Measure the gap between the bottom of the cam lobe and the finger at valves 6 and 7. See *Tuneup Data* supplement for correct clearance at intake and exhaust valves on various engines. Gap size is the number stamped on the thickest feeler blade that will fit between the cam and the finger without undue force. (Datsuns: Check valves 1, 2, 3, and 5 at this time.)

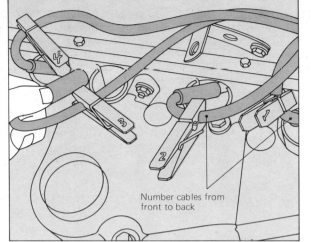

Number cables from front to back

2. Use numbered clothespins or pieces of masking tape to label the spark plug cables. Then remove the cables and plugs, using a 13/16-in. spark plug socket and a 6-in. extension. Removing the plugs will make Step 4 easier. (Datsuns: Spark plugs need not be removed unless they are to be inspected or replaced. However, the plug cables must be removed in order to remove the cam cover.)

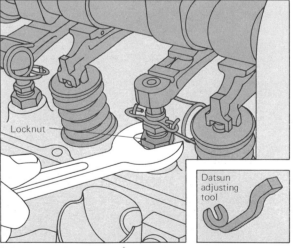

Locknut

Datsun adjusting tool

7. The gap tends to increase as engine parts wear. If the gap is incorrect on any cam, rotate the retaining spring out of the way, then loosen the locknut with a 3/4-in. open-end wrench. (Datsuns: Loosen the locknut with a 17-mm open-end wrench, or use a special Datsun adjusting tool sold by dealers and some auto parts stores. Tool is made to be used with a torque wrench.)

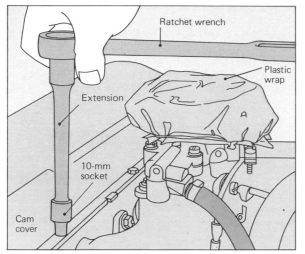

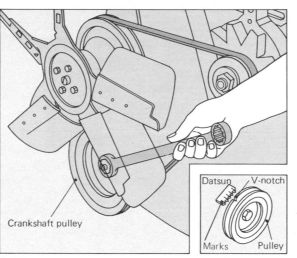

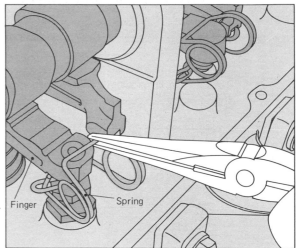

3. Cover the carburetor with plastic wrapping and a rubber band to keep out dirt. Remove the 10 cam-cover bolts, using a ratchet wrench with a 10-mm socket and 6-in. extension. If any dirt drops into the engine, pick it out with paper toweling. (Datsuns: The cam cover has only eight bolts. Cover can be removed without disturbing or covering the carburetor.)

4. With transmission in *Neutral,* turn the crankshaft pulley clockwise (as viewed from the front of the car) until the pointed end of the No.1 cam is pointing straight down, fully compressing the No.1 valve spring. (Datsuns: Position the No.1 *cylinder* at top dead center, using short bursts of the starter to align the timing mark with the V-notch on the crankshaft pulley.)

5. Using long-nose pliers, pull the retaining springs out of their grooves on cam fingers 6 and 7. Pull the springs completely off the fingers so that they hang loosely below. You cannot make an accurate gap measurement with these springs in place. (Datsuns: Removal of retaining springs is not necessary except to provide easy access to adjusting nuts, Step 8.)

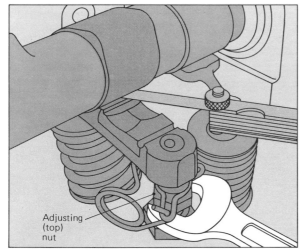

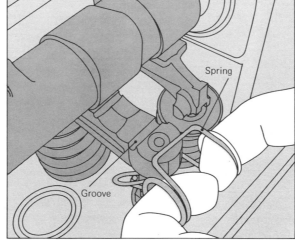

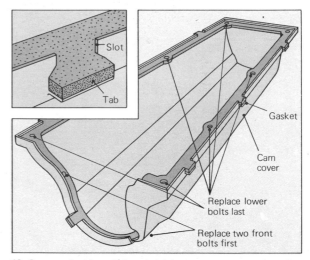

8. Use a thin 15-mm or ¹⁹/₃₂-in. open-end wrench to turn the adjusting nut until the proper feeler blade (*see Tuneup Data supplement*) will just fit into the gap with a slight drag. Turn the adjusting nut clockwise to increase the gap, or counterclockwise to reduce it. (Datsuns: Use a 14-mm wrench. See *Tuneup Data* supplement for proper gap on intake and exhaust valves.)

9. When gap is correct, retighten locknut and reposition spring in groove on finger. Rotate crankshaft to depress valve 2, and check gaps at cams 3 and 8. Then depress valve 3 and check cams 2 and 5. Finally, depress valve 6 and check cams 4 and 1. (Datsuns: Rotate crankshaft until V-notch on pulley is 180° away from timing marks; see Step 4. Adjust clearances at valves 4, 6, 7 and 8.)

10. Scrape all old gasket material from cam cover and engine block. Apply thin, continuous bead of gasket sealant to both cover and engine. (Datsuns have no tabs.) Reinstall cam cover, spark plugs, cables, and air cleaner. Tighten nuts on camshaft cover in stages, working in a spiral pattern to compress gasket evenly. Do not overtighten.

Maintaining hydraulic lifters

Hydraulic valve lifters eliminate the need for valve clearance adjustments because they are designed to compensate for the development of any free play between the lifters and the valve stems caused by normal wear in the valve train (see p.38). If noisiness does develop within the valve train, first check the dipstick to make sure that the engine oil level is neither too low nor too high; either condition can allow air into the lifters and prevent them from working properly. Also check to see that free play has not developed in the valve train due to excess wear or because of earlier faulty adjustments. Pushrod clearance can be eliminated on some engines by tightening the rocker arm studs or adjusting nuts as shown below. If the oil level is correct and there is no free play, the noise may be caused by sticking parts, in which case the engine should be flushed with a commercial valve treatment or special oil, following the manufacturer's instructions. If the condition persists, you must disassemble the valve train and inspect the lifters for wear or damage (see pp.427–429).

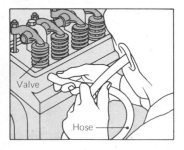

You can hear faulty valve lifters by using a length of hose as an improvised stethoscope. With engine running and valve cover removed, hold one end of the hose against the cylinder head near each valve opening. Listen for a sharp, rapping sound distinct from background noise.

You can feel faulty lifters by holding your finger against valve-spring retainer while engine is running. A malfunctioning lifter transmits a distinct stinging sensation as valve snaps back sharply against its seat. A normal lifter produces smooth valve action.

You can eliminate valve clearance due to worn parts on some engines (see *Tuneup Data*). Loosen adjusting nut on rocker arm or on mounting stud until chatter is audible when engine idles. Retighten nut until noise stops, then tighten amount shown in *Tuneup Data*.

Replacing valve stem seals

The condition of the oil seals located near the tops of the valve stems plays an important part in the amount of oil the engine consumes; oil in the rocker arm chamber can leak past faulty seals and into the combustion chambers. To repair valve guides, you must remove the cylinder head and take it to an automotive machine shop. But it is easy to replace the valve stem seals yourself. Often, this repair is nearly as effective as installing new valve guides. For best results, replace the standard valve stem seals, which are rubber O-rings on many cars, with Teflon or umbrella seals available from auto parts stores. Umbrella-type seals deflect oil that might otherwise be drawn by the suction of the pistons past worn valve guides and into the combustion chambers.

Only one special tool is needed to replace the seals: a valve-spring compressor designed to work with the cylinder head still mounted on the engine.

Caution: Never try to remove springs without a proper tool, since the compressed springs can cause injury if they escape. To prevent the valves from dropping into the engine while the spring is compressed, professional mechanics force compressed air into the cylinders through a special fitting that screws into the spark plug holes. However, packing the combustion chambers with a short length of clothesline, as shown below, also works.

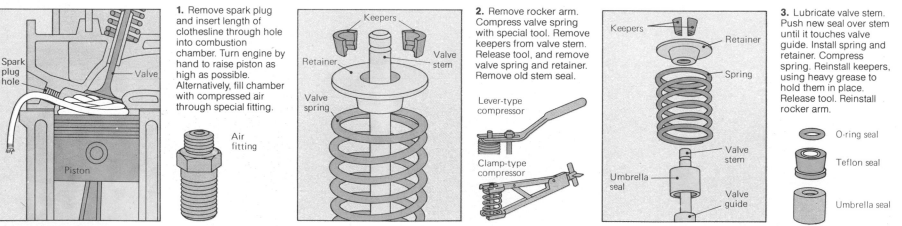

1. Remove spark plug and insert length of clothesline through hole into combustion chamber. Turn engine by hand to raise piston as high as possible. Alternatively, fill chamber with compressed air through special fitting.

2. Remove rocker arm. Compress valve spring with special tool. Remove keepers from valve stem. Release tool, and remove valve spring and retainer. Remove old stem seal.

3. Lubricate valve stem. Push new seal over stem until it touches valve guide. Install spring and retainer. Compress spring. Reinstall keepers, using heavy grease to hold them in place. Release tool. Reinstall rocker arm.

Battery care and replacement

All batteries need care, even the so-called maintenance-free type. This is particularly important in winter, when a well-maintained battery may deliver 40 percent of the power that it delivers in summer.

Batteries lose water through their vents. Check the water level once a month and add water if possible. Low-maintenance batteries should be checked once a year. Maintenance-free batteries can be checked with a built-in indicator (p.134).

Do not add water to a battery in freezing weather unless you intend to drive the car for several miles immediately. If the car is not driven right away, the water will not mix with the battery acid but will freeze and damage the battery.

If a battery has removable vent caps, its charge can easily be checked with a device called a *hydrometer*. It measures the density of the acid-water solution. The denser the solution, the higher the electrical charge in the battery.

In temperate climates a reading of 1.265 or more indicates that the battery is fully charged (far right). But in hot climates, where temperatures do not drop below freezing, your car may have a battery with a milder acid solution, one that reaches full charge at a reading of only 1.225. Similarly, in very cold areas like Alaska your battery will probably be designed to give a full-charge reading of 1.300, to protect the acid solution from freezing.

A hydrometer reads differently when the temperature of the battery fluid changes. If your hydrometer does not have a built-in thermometer, take the measurement when the engine is cold and use the prevailing air temperature to estimate any correction factor (far right). Do not take a hydrometer reading if you have just added water to the battery. Drive the car 15 miles first to allow the water to mix with the acid; otherwise, your reading will be off.

Caution: Batteries contain sulfuric acid, which can seriously injure skin and eyes and damage clothing. If you spill any battery fluid on yourself, wash immediately with water. If acid gets into your eyes, seek prompt medical assistance. Batteries emit explosive hydrogen gas. Never light a match, smoke, or cause a spark near a battery.

Tools: Mirror, funnel or water dispenser, hydrometer.
Material: Distilled water.

Checking fluid level and charge

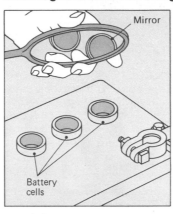

Mirror

Battery cells

Once a month, check the level of fluid in all six battery cells. It should cover the metal plates inside and come to within ¼ in. of the bottom of the filler hole. On some batteries the correct level is specified on the case. Use a pocket mirror to check cells you cannot see into directly.

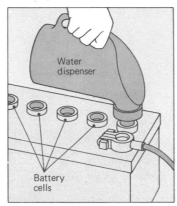

Water dispenser

Battery cells

Add distilled water to battery cells that are low on fluid. Use a small funnel or the special dispenser shown. Do not add water in freezing weather unless car will be driven a few miles afterwards. Wipe top of battery dry after filling. Distilled water, labeled "For steam irons," can be purchased at supermarkets.

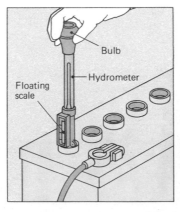

Floating scale

Bulb

Hydrometer

Measure charge of battery with hydrometer. Squeeze the bulb and draw up enough fluid to float the scale inside. Return the fluid to the same cell it was drawn from. Test all six cells and write down the results, then correct the results for temperature (right). If the readings between any two cells differ by more than .050, replace the battery. If readings are closer than .050, the battery can probably be recharged.

Reading a battery hydrometer

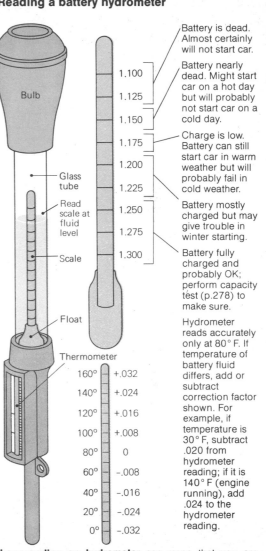

Bulb

Glass tube

Read scale at fluid level

Scale

Float

Thermometer

1.100	
1.125	
1.150	
1.175	
1.200	
1.225	
1.250	
1.275	
1.300	

160°	+.032
140°	+.024
120°	+.016
100°	+.008
80°	0
60°	−.008
40°	−.016
20°	−.024
0°	−.032

Battery is dead. Almost certainly will not start car.

Battery nearly dead. Might start car on a hot day but will probably not start car on a cold day.

Charge is low. Battery can still start car in warm weather but will probably fail in cold weather.

Battery mostly charged but may give trouble in winter starting.

Battery fully charged and probably OK; perform capacity test (p.278) to make sure.

Hydrometer reads accurately only at 80° F. If temperature of battery fluid differs, add or subtract correction factor shown. For example, if temperature is 30° F, subtract .020 from hydrometer reading; if it is 140° F (engine running), add .024 to the hydrometer reading.

Low reading on hydrometer can mean that you are draining the battery with too much stop-and-go driving, that the battery is approaching the end of its useful life, or that there is a defect in the charging system (see pp.374–375). Recharge a battery that reads low by driving car at highway speeds, or use a trickle charger (p.278).

Battery care and replacement *(continued)*

To check a battery's capacity to sustain heavy loads, such as starting in cold weather, you can test it with an expensive battery-starter tester or an inexpensive voltmeter. Note that even a good battery will do poorly in these tests when the weather is very cold. Warm the battery first by running the engine for a few minutes. For greater accuracy, measure the temperature of the battery fluid with a thermometer so that you will know when it is near 80° F.

A battery with a low charge can be recharged either by running the engine (assuming that the alternator and voltage regulator are OK, as discussed on page 374) or by connecting a trickle charger to the battery for several hours or overnight. Leave the charger connected until its meter drops to a reading of less than 1 ampere. If the charger does not have a meter, but the battery has vent caps, check the battery once every hour with a hydrometer (p.277). When the hydrometer indicates no increase in fluid density for three consecutive hours, the battery cannot be charged further. Unplug the charger, then disconnect it from the battery. If the battery cannot be brought to full charge in this way, replace it. Do not try to charge a frozen battery.

A battery in normal operation gives off gases that gradually corrode the terminals. Such corrosion can seriously impair current flow at the terminals. Also, dirt and water can collect on the battery case and provide a medium for current to leak between the terminals and slowly drain the battery. Routinely inspect and clean the battery terminals, the case, and the clamps and support. To do this adequately, you may have to remove the battery. Also tighten the clamps, which can vibrate loose in time.

When removing a battery, disconnect the ground (−) cable first to avoid causing an accidental spark. This is the cable that terminates at the engine block or the car's frame. The positive (+) cable leads to the starter solenoid or relay (see p.136).

Testing battery capacity

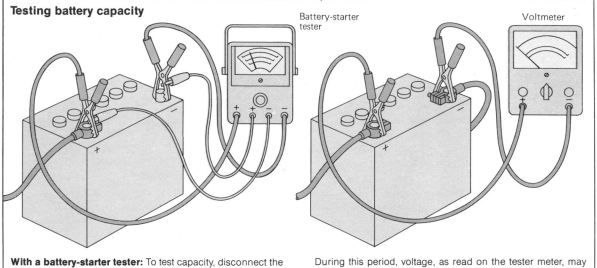

Battery-starter tester

Voltmeter

With a battery-starter tester: To test capacity, disconnect the ground cable from the battery, and connect a battery-starter tester to the battery's terminals. With the tester switch on *Off*, connect its four leads as shown above, at the left. The positive meter lead must go to the positive battery post, the negative lead to the negative post. Consult instructions with tester if you are not certain about the right way to hook up the leads. You may need special terminal adapters to connect the tester to a side-terminal battery. The battery should be at or near full charge. Check it with a hydrometer, if possible, and charge the battery if needed. The temperature of the battery fluid should be about 80° F. Refer to battery specifications to determine the ampere-hour rating of your battery; then turn the tester control knob up so that it points to a current draw equal to three times the ampere-hour figure. If the battery is rated at 100 ampere-hours, for example, current draw on the tester should be adjusted to read 300 amps. Maintain current draw for 15 sec.

During this period, voltage, as read on the tester meter, may drop slowly. Read the voltage after 15 sec, then return the control knob to *Off*. If the voltage does not drop below 9.6 volts on a 12-volt battery (4.8 volts on a 6-volt battery), battery capacity is adequate. If the voltage drops below this figure, the battery has become unreliable and should be replaced.

With a voltmeter: Clip the positive voltmeter lead to the battery's positive post and the negative lead to the negative post. (If you reverse the leads, the meter will read below zero.) The reading you get will be the *battery reference voltage* or *battery non-cranking voltage*. It should be at least 12 volts. Unplug the coil cable from the center terminal on the distributor cap, then ground the cable to the engine block with a jumper cable. (On Delco HEI distributors, just unplug the pink BAT wire from the distributor cap.) Crank the engine for 15 sec and read the meter. This is the *battery cranking voltage*, which should be at least 9.6 volts.

Recharging a battery

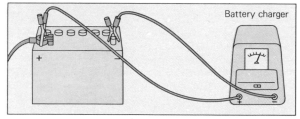

Battery charger

To use a trickle charger, first disconnect ground cable from battery and add water if needed (p.277). Leave vent caps off while you connect charger. Plug charger in and switch it on. When battery is charged, unplug charger, then disconnect battery.

Removing a battery

Bottom clamps

Top clamps

Remove hold-down clamps and any heat shield first. Before you can open clamps, you may have to remove rust with a wire brush and apply penetrating oil. Replace any badly corroded clamps.

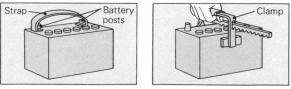

Strap

Battery posts

Clamp

To lift battery from car easily, use a clamp as shown (right). Do not lift it with a strap that grasps the battery's posts; the strap may bend and damage the battery's plates, which are attached to the posts.

Disconnecting battery cables ⏱ 5–10 min

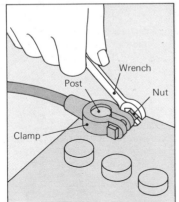

Most battery cables have soft lead bolt-on clamps. Scrape off any built-up corrosion with a wire brush. Loosen the nut on the bolt with a wrench. **Caution:** Batteries emit explosive hydrogen gas. Never light a match or smoke near a battery. Also, remove any rings or jewelry, to avoid causing sparks.

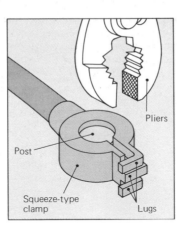

To loosen the clamp from the terminal post, pry it open with a screwdriver as shown. Do not pry up the clamp from underneath, or you could damage the battery case, the post, and the plates inside.

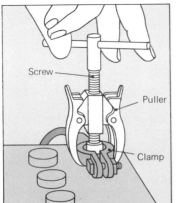

For badly corroded clamps, you may need a special puller. The tool is inexpensive and widely available at auto parts stores. Attach puller so that it grips clamp as shown, then turn center screw. The puller lifts the clamp without applying sideways pressure on the post or case.

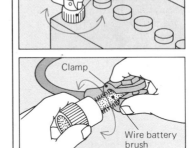

Older GM cars have squeeze-type terminal clamps. To remove the cables, squeeze the lugs with pliers, twist the clamp back and forth, then lift it off the terminal post.

Cables of newer GM cars are bolted to terminals on the side of the battery. Remove bolts with a wrench. Remove cables even if you intend only to inspect them, since even a barely visible amount of corrosion on this type of terminal can impair a car's ability to start.

You need not replace the cable if only its clamp is damaged. Cut off the clamp, strip off ¾ in. of insulation, and bolt on a replacement clamp. (Replace the entire cable if its insulation is cracked or burned, or if its wires are frayed or broken.)

Cleaning a battery ⏱ 5–10 min

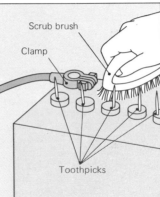

Clean posts and clamps with a wire brush, sandpaper, or steel wool until they are shiny. A special wire brush for cleaning batteries can be purchased at auto parts stores. Clean the hold-down clamps also, and coat them with corrosion-resistant paint if corrosion seems to be weakening them.

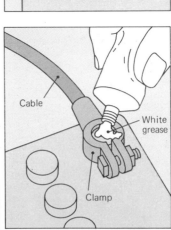

To clean battery (and hold-down clamps), first plug vent holes with tape or with toothpicks, then scrub with a mixture of baking soda and water. Rinse well and wipe dry. Unplug the vent holes. Note that maintenance-free batteries also have vent holes, which may be hidden under a shield. If you remove a battery to clean it, be careful not to spill its fluid (see p.278). Replenish spilled fluid at a service station.

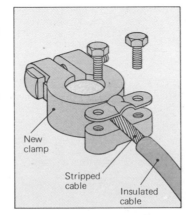

Reattach cable clamps, ground-cable clamp last. Tighten clamps. Coat each post and clamp with white grease or petroleum jelly—or spray them with a rust-preventive lubricant—to inhibit future corrosion. To check that a battery has been reinstalled properly, turn on ignition and lights. If car ammeter reads *Discharge* (or alternator's warning light glows), battery was reinstalled correctly.

Cooling system checks ⏱ 15–30 min

The parts of the cooling system that require periodic maintenance are the hoses and clamps, the drive belt, a few mechanical parts, and the liquid coolant. All work together to get rid of excess engine heat (pp.73–75). To help the cooling system function properly, it is recommended that you do the maintenance checks shown on these two pages and replace the coolant once a year (pp.282–284).

Caution: Do not perform any check for the cooling system (except circulation checks) unless the engine is off and cool. If the car is equipped with an electric fan, be especially wary of a warm engine—it can cause the fan to start unexpectedly, even though the engine is off. Any moving fan can cause injury. Antifreeze is sweet tasting and poisonous; read the warnings on the label and keep antifreeze out of the reach of children and pets.

The most neglected element in the cooling system is the coolant, a mixture of antifreeze and water. The amount and condition of the coolant should be checked periodically. Not enough coolant or a low proportion of antifreeze can lead to overheating (p.345) and can corrode parts of the cooling system.

Coolant loss can be minimized with a *coolant recovery tank* (p.74). Most new cars have a recovery tank that catches and stores coolant overflow. Older cars have an *overflow tube* that allows any boilover to spill out onto the ground. Kits are available for installing recovery tanks on older cars. Coolant loss can also result from a leak in the system. Leaks are usually caused by a faulty seal, broken hose, rust-through, or physical damage to a part, such as the radiator. A leak also reduces the pressure in the cooling system, which lowers the boiling point of the coolant. Check the radiator cap (right) and hoses (p.285) periodically. While the radiator cap is off, check the condition and level of the coolant. If the level is low, you will be able to check for solder bloom (p.348), a formation of deposits in the radiator core that blocks the flow of coolant. Coolant circulation can also be hampered or stopped by a clogged hose or radiator core, a broken water pump, a faulty thermostat, or internal engine deposits.

To ensure that a maximum amount of air passes through the radiator, keep its surface free from debris and make sure that the radiator fan is working. For information on repairing or replacing parts of the cooling system, see pp.344–359.

Checking the radiator cap

Seal

Remove radiator cap and inspect seal on the pressure valve. Seal should be clean, pliable, and free from cracks. If it is dirty, wash it off. If seal is stiff or cracked, replace the entire cap with a new one designed to meet the pressure needs of your car's cooling system (pp.73–74). Clean the neck of the radiator where it mates with the seal in the cap.

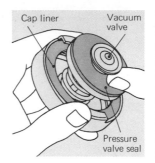

Cap liner   Vacuum valve

Pressure valve seal

Coolant recovery system cap has two seals—one on the pressure valve and another that lines the inside of the cap. Both seals should be clean, pliable, and without cracks. Lift vacuum valve to inspect entire pressure valve seal. If seals are dirty, wash them. If one or both seals are in poor condition, replace the cap with a new one designed for your car.

Checking the condition of the coolant

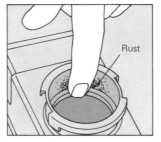

Rust

Rust deposits along neck of radiator mean that the rust inhibitors in the coolant have deteriorated and that the coolant should be replaced (pp.282–284). Bubbles (when the engine is running) or oil in coolant may indicate an internal leak in the engine block. To confirm an internal leak, have system tested by a professional.

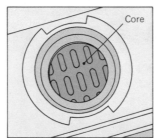

Core

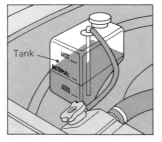

Tank   HOT   NORMAL   ADD

A proper amount of coolant should be in the system at all times. If it is an *overflow system,* there should be enough coolant to cover the core inside the radiator. If the radiator core is exposed (left), add antifreeze/water mix or straight antifreeze until the coolant covers the core or reaches a specific level marked on the radiator. If you have a *coolant recovery system,* the coolant, when cold, should be at the *Normal* or *Cold* mark on the side of the recovery tank (left, below). If necessary, add antifreeze/water mixture or straight antifreeze to the radiator, then to the recovery tank.

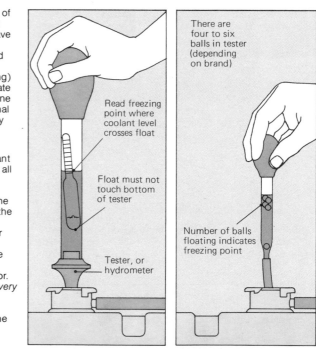

There are four to six balls in tester (depending on brand)

Read freezing point where coolant level crosses float

Float must not touch bottom of tester

Tester, or hydrometer

Number of balls floating indicates freezing point

Test the protection level of the coolant mixture with an antifreeze tester. One type of tester has a floating scale; another has a number of balls. Place tip of tester into coolant and squeeze bulb to draw in some coolant. A scale on the float shows the freezing point of the coolant mixture (left). The number of balls floating indicates the freezing point (right); see package instructions. If protection level is low and coolant has not been replaced for a year, replace old coolant with a new mixture (see pp.282–284).

Cleaning the radiator surface

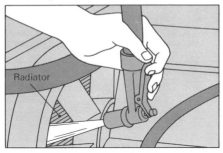

Keep outer surfaces of radiator free from debris. Clean with a soft brush and a detergent/water solution. Flush off with garden hose.

Inspecting and testing radiator fans

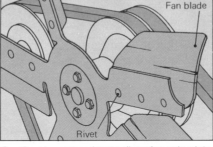

Caution: Inspect and test radiator fan only when engine is off and cold. Replace any fan that has a bent or broken blade or rivet (pp.351–353).

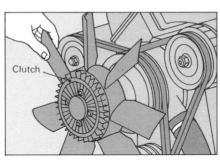

An electric or clutch fan should rotate with some drag when pushed. Silicone in clutch should not leak. Replace bad fan or clutch.

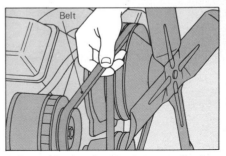

A direct-drive fan should not move easily when pushed. If it does, it may mean that the drive belt needs tightening. Test belt tension (p.287).

Checking for external leaks

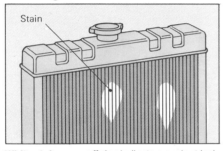

White stains on radiator indicate a coolant leak. Add a sealant to the radiator or remove radiator and take it to a specialist for repair.

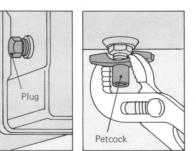

Coolant leak can occur if the radiator drain plug (left) or petcock (right) is loose. To stop the leak, turn the plug or petcock clockwise.

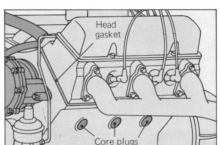

Check for leaks at engine core plugs (freeze-out plugs) and head gasket. If necessary, replace plug (p.347) or have head gasket replaced.

Check hoses and water pump for leaks. Replace leaking hoses or water pump. Minor leaking *(weeping)* at pump is normal.

Checking coolant circulation

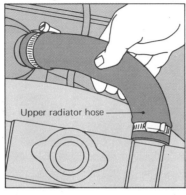

1. Start the engine. Squeeze upper radiator hose to check for coolant flow (hose should become pressurized and hot within a few minutes). If you do not feel the coolant flowing, check for a clogged hose (p.285), a bad thermostat (p.346), or a faulty water pump (p.354). **Caution:** Beware of the fan.

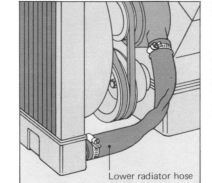

2. With the engine at fast idle, look at the lower radiator hose. If the hose flattens out, it has lost its resilience or the spring inside it has collapsed. Replace it with a new hose (p.285). **Caution:** Beware of the fan.

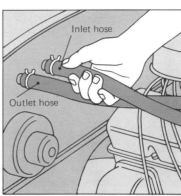

3. Turn heater on. Feel heater inlet and outlet hoses. If they are not close in temperature, suspect a clogged hose (p.285) or a defective heater core or heater control valve (see pp.73, 356–357, 359). Replace any defective part. **Caution:** Beware of the fan.

Removing coolant ⏱ 5–10 min

It is often necessary to remove some coolant in order to maintain or repair the cooling system. This usually involves draining the coolant from the radiator to a level just below that of the part being worked on—a hose or water pump, for example. Coolant can be drained into a large pan and saved for reuse.

All coolant is removed only when you intend to replace the antifreeze (p.284). Antifreeze should be replaced about once a year in most cars.

The best way to remove all the coolant is to *backflush* the system—that is, to force the coolant and water back through the system in a direction opposite to normal coolant flow. Dirt and rust particles are then loosened and swept out of the system. Backflushing is often the only way of removing coolant from the engine block. Some engine blocks have no coolant drain plugs. On engines with drain plugs, the plug is often frozen and impossible to remove, or it is blocked by the frame, engine mounts, or other parts and is inaccessible.

Two methods of backflushing are shown on these pages. The first requires the installation of a *flushing T*. To do this, you need a kit with a flushing T that fits the inside diameter of your heater inlet hose (which is usually ⅜ inch less than its outside diameter). Once

the T has been installed, however, it performs the easier of the two backflushing methods shown here.

The second method, backflushing without a T, has one advantage: it assures the automatic backflushing of the heater core. Often, it is neither necessary nor desirable to backflush the heater core, and when doing so you must be very careful not to use too much water pressure, which can damage the core. A heater core is difficult to repair.

Caution: Do not swallow coolant or let it come in contact with your eyes. Keep coolant away from children. Do not leave puddles of drained coolant where pets can drink it. Do not work with coolant that is hot. Do not open a radiator cap or handle hoses when the engine is hot. Keep hands and face away from the spinning fan when the engine is on. Electric fans can start up without warning even when the engine is off; disconnect the fan before starting work (p.353).

> **Tools:** Large pan, knife, screwdriver or spring-clamp pliers, garden hose, locking pliers.
> **Materials:** T-kit or cork, clean rags.

Draining a radiator

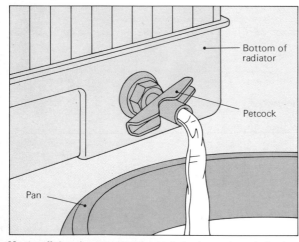

Most radiators have a petcock or a drain plug and are drained as follows: Remove radiator cap, then open petcock or drain plug. When enough coolant has drained, close petcock or plug and reinstall cap. If saving coolant, drain it into a large pan.

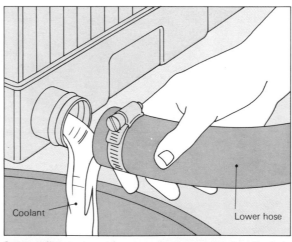

Some radiators do not have a petcock or drain plug. To drain them, remove the cap and disconnect the lower radiator hose (p.285). When enough coolant has drained, reconnect hose and reinstall cap. If saving coolant, drain it into a large pan.

Installing a flushing T ⏱ 5–10 min

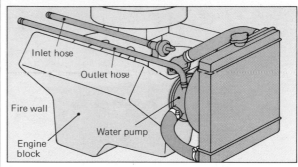

1. Locate the heater inlet hose; it is the one extending from the fire wall to the engine block. (The hose between the water pump and fire wall is the heater outlet hose.) Drain the radiator completely (below, left) or to a level just below that of the inlet hose.

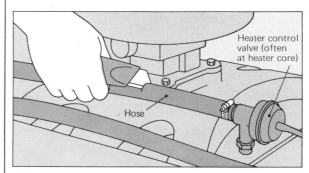

2. Mark a spot on the inlet hose where you want to install the T. It should be in a spot that is easy to reach but not above any electrical component, such as the alternator. Cut through the hose at the spot and slip a hose clamp over each hose end.

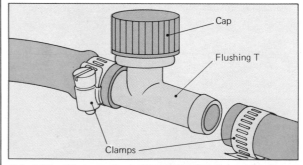

3. Install the T between the cut hose ends. Keeping the cap of the T up, push the ends of the T well into the cut hose ends. Slide both hose clamps back toward cut hose ends, just beyond the ridges in the T, then tighten the clamps. Refill the radiator.

Backflushing with a flushing T ↻ 10–20 min

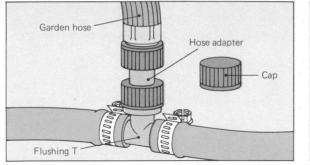

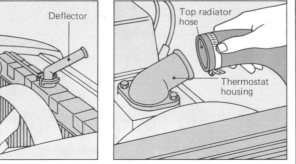

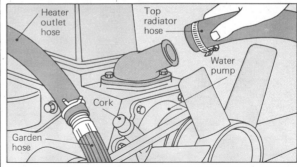

1. Remove the cap from the flushing T. Screw one end of the hose adapter onto the flushing T (the adapter is part of the flushing T kit). Attach a garden hose to the other end of the hose adapter. Make sure that both connections are hand-tight.

2. If the car has a *downflow* radiator (left), insert deflector into the neck of the radiator, pointing it away from the engine. If car has a *crossflow* radiator (right), leave radiator cap on, disconnect top radiator hose (p.285), and point it away from the engine.

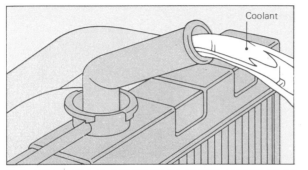

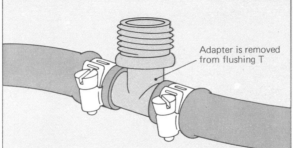

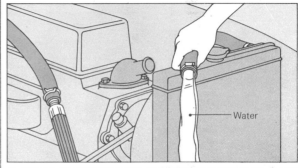

3. Turn the engine on, turn the heater on *High,* and turn on the water tap. Coolant will be forced out through the deflector (or radiator hose). After the escaping water has run clear for 2 min, turn off the heater, the engine, then the water.

4. Remove the deflector (or reconnect the upper radiator hose). Remove the garden hose and adapter from the T; replace the radiator cap. If you wish to backflush the heater core (below), do so before adding a new coolant mix (see p.284).

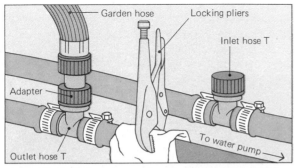

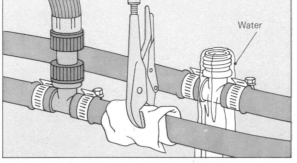

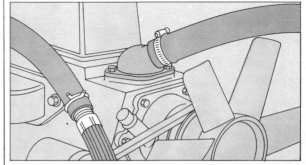

To backflush the heater core, install a T in heater's outlet hose (as was done in inlet hose, facing page). Perform Steps 1–4 above, then attach adapter and hose to outlet T. Pinch outlet hose shut between the T and water pump, using locking pliers.

Remove cap from inlet T. Carefully turn on water (too much water pressure can damage core). When water coming out of T has run clear for 2 min, turn water off. Remove hose and adapter from outlet T; remove locking pliers. Put caps on both T's.

Backflushing without a flushing T ↻

1. Drain radiator (see facing page). Disconnect heater outlet hose (p.285) from water pump. Plug pump opening with a cork; force garden hose into heater hose. When radiator is empty, close all openings. Disconnect top radiator hose; point it away from engine.

2. Turn engine on; turn heater on *High;* turn water tap on. Do not use too much water pressure (over 20 psi), which can damage heater core. When water coming out of radiator hose has run clear for 2 min, turn heater, engine, and water off.

3. Reconnect radiator hose. To add a new coolant mix, see p.284. If system needs more cleaning, use a cooling system cleaner *before* adding new coolant. If system needs a leak sealant, use it *after* adding new coolant. Read package instructions.

Installing new coolant ⏱ 20–30 min

Before a new coolant mixture is installed, the cooling system should be backflushed (pp.282-283). The new coolant mixture is formed by adding antifreeze to the water remaining in the system. The amount of antifreeze is determined by the cooling system's liquid capacity (which is given in the owner's manual) and by the range of temperature protection that you want the coolant to deliver. The temperature protection span varies according to the proportion of antifreeze in the mixture: the more antifreeze, the lower the freezing temperature and the higher the boiling point of the coolant will be (see p.73). For most cars, a 50-50 mix is sufficient. To form a 50-50 mix in a 10-quart cooling system, add 5 quarts of antifreeze to 5 quarts of water. A 70-30 mix (70 percent antifreeze,

30 percent water) is the maximum recommended concentration for any coolant mixture. If there is any antifreeze left, make a supply of coolant mix to use when the system needs to be topped off. If your engine block, cylinder head, or radiator are aluminum, use an antifreeze that is recommended for use with aluminum parts.

Caution: Antifreeze is poisonous. If you siphon a recovery tank, do not use your mouth to start siphoning action. Keep antifreeze away from eyes.

Tools: Funnel, antifreeze tester.
Materials: Antifreeze in the amount needed to form the desired antifreeze / water mix for your car's system.

Systems with recovery tanks

Backflush system (p.283). Close system and let it cool. Drain radiator (p.282) and recovery tank. Add antifreeze to radiator and tank. Top up with water, if necessary. Run engine with heater on *High* for 10 min. Let cool, then test mixture (p.280). If weak, drain some coolant, add antifreeze, run engine. Test again.

Systems equipped with a flushing T

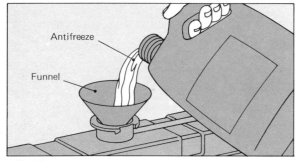

Antifreeze

Funnel

1. Backflush the system and let it cool. Remove the caps on the radiator and on the flushing T in the heater inlet hose. Drain radiator. Pour antifreeze into the radiator through a funnel.

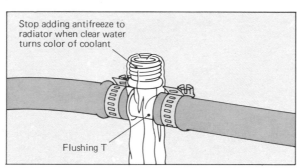

Stop adding antifreeze to radiator when clear water turns color of coolant

Flushing T

2. Water will escape from the flushing T; when antifreeze comes out at T, stop adding antifreeze to radiator. Recap T and radiator. To mix antifreeze, run engine with heater on *High* for 10 to 15 min.

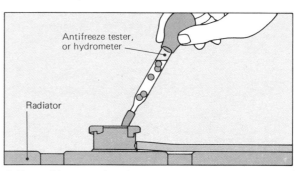

Antifreeze tester, or hydrometer

Radiator

3. Turn off heater and engine, let cool, then test concentration (p.280). If mixture is weak, partially drain radiator, add straight antifreeze, mix it, and test again. Repeat if mixture is still weak.

Systems without a flushing T

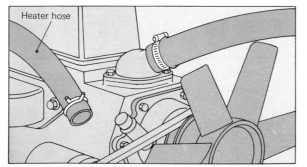

Heater hose

1. Backflush the system and let it cool. Drain radiator, then fill it with straight antifreeze. Remove garden hose from heater hose; direct the heater hose away from the engine.

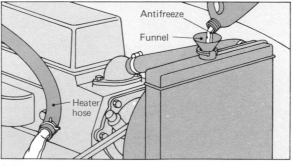

Antifreeze

Funnel

Heater hose

2. To install more antifreeze, turn on engine with heater on *High*. This will force water out of the hose. As the water drains, pour the remaining antifreeze into the radiator.

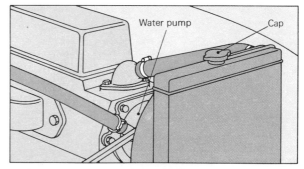

Water pump

Cap

3. When antifreeze is in, quickly turn off heater and engine (you may need a helper) and reconnect heater hose to water pump. Check level of coolant in radiator; top off if low. Recap radiator.

Hoses ⟳ 10–20 min

Most cooling systems are equipped with only four hoses—an upper and lower radiator hose and a heater inlet and outlet hose. Some systems also have a bypass hose near the water pump. On a few engines, one of the heater hoses makes a detour to a water-heated choke, intake manifold, or exhaust gas cooler.

Cooling system hoses should be checked at least every six months. Any hose that is cracked, leaking, oil soaked, or that feels hard or spongy when squeezed should be replaced immediately. Early replacement of a weak hose will prevent the overheating and possible engine damage that a leaking hose can cause. Follow the instructions below when replacing a hose, and be sure that the replacement is

the correct size, length, and shape for your car.

Hoses come in many different diameters, lengths, and shapes to fit particular car models. Lower hoses have an internal spring that helps maintain their shape. Many replacement hoses are pleated. The pleats allow the hose to be bent to conform to different engine and radiator combinations. No matter what hose you use, it is important that it hug the neck tightly. If the hose does not fit snugly, coolant could leak out, even if the hose clamp is tight.

Hoses are held in place by hose clamps. There are several different types, and some are easier to use than others (see bottom of page). Clamps should be inspected periodically. If they are loose, tighten

them. If a spring clamp is loose, it must be replaced, preferably with a worm-drive clamp. As with hoses, clamps come in different sizes to fit the hose and neck to which they will be attached.

Caution: Inspect and replace hoses only when the cooling system is cool. Coolant is sweet tasting and poisonous. Avoid contact with the eyes and keep out of reach of children and pets.

Tools: Large pan, hose-clamp pliers or screwdriver for hose clamps, knife, wire brush.
Materials: Replacement hose and clamps, rag, coolant mixture for topping up the system.

Removing and replacing a hose

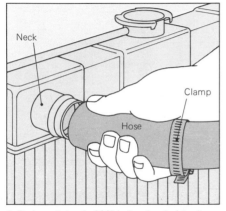

1. Drain radiator (p.282) below level of the hose being replaced; save coolant. Loosen clamp at each hose end and slide clamp back onto hose. Gently twist and pull hose off.

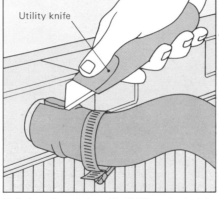

2. If clamp is rusted, cut it off. If hose is stuck to neck, do not force or pry it off. Doing so could damage the neck, radiator, or heater core. Cut hose and peel it off neck.

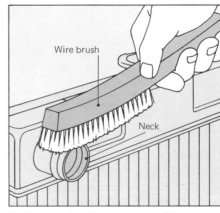

3. Clean neck with a wire brush. Slip two new hose clamps onto replacement hose. Push each hose end onto a neck. (Dipping hose ends in coolant will make them slip on easily.)

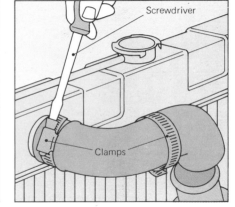

4. Bring clamp toward end of hose, just beyond edge of neck; position clamp so that tightening device is easy to reach. Tighten clamp (below); repeat on other clamp. Pour coolant into radiator.

Loosening or tightening clamps

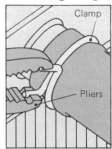

Spring clamp is removed by squeezing ends with pliers. Special hose-clamp pliers have grooves that hold clamp ends and prevent them from slipping. Replace with a worm-drive clamp.

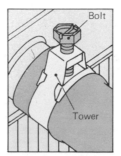

Worm-drive clamp is easiest to use, but vibrations can loosen it. Use a screwdriver to loosen or tighten the bolt; this loosens or tightens the band of the clamp.

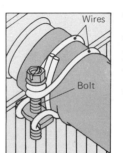

Screw-tower clamp is also loosened or tightened with a screwdriver. You may need to tap the bolt in order to loosen the band. Replace with worm-drive clamp.

Twin-wire screw clamp is loosened or tightened with a screwdriver. If tightened too much, wires can cut into the hose. Replace with worm-drive clamp.

Drive belts

Drive belts operate various engine accessories: the fan, water pump, power steering pump, air-conditioning compressor, alternator, and air-injection pump. One belt can sometimes drive two or more accessories. All these belts are driven by the crankshaft pulley.

Drive belts ride on pulleys. Some pulleys, known as *idler pulleys,* are used as belt-tensioning devices. A pulley will have one track for each belt positioned on it. There are two types of drive belt. The most common has a V-shaped cross section and is called a V-belt. V-belts that must operate at sharp angles may be segmented to make them more flexible. A newer type of belt has longitudinal grooves that fit into the grooved surface of a special pulley. The grooves improve the power transfer between the belt and its pulleys. In a few cars, one long, serpentine, multi-grooved belt is used to drive all the accessories. Both sides of the belt may drive pulleys.

Frequent checks of a belt's condition and tension will help to avoid problems. Defective belts should be replaced immediately. If a fan belt breaks, the water pump will stop circulating coolant and the engine will overheat. If the belt for the power steering pump breaks, you will still be able to steer the car, but with far greater effort than usual.

When buying a new belt, be sure that it is the same size and type as the belt it is replacing. If the accessory is driven by a matched pair of belts and one belt breaks, buy a new matched set. Position any replace-

ment belt on the same pulleys and tracks as the original. You may have to remove all the belts in order to replace the one closest to the engine block. In such a case, it is a good idea to make a sketch of all the belts so that you can reinstall them correctly. Once the belt is in place, tension it properly. The belt must be tight enough so that it will not slip but not so

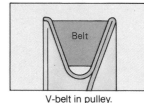
V-belt in pulley.

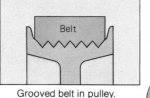
Grooved belt in pulley.

tight that it will exert excess pressure on the accessory's bearings. The tension may need readjustment after the belt has been in place for a few weeks, since new belts stretch with initial use.

Caution: Inspect and replace drive belts only when the engine is off. If the car has an electric fan, disconnect the battery or wait for the engine to cool off; any heat may turn the fan on unexpectedly.

Tools: Belt-tension gauge (optional), wrenches to fit mounting bolts on your car, pry bar, breaker bar (for idler pulley), large screwdriver (for VW pulley).
Material: Replacement belt.

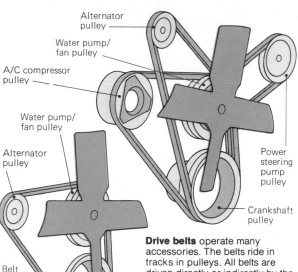

Drive belts operate many accessories. The belts ride in tracks in pulleys. All belts are driven directly or indirectly by the engine's crankshaft. The most basic drive belt is often called the *fan belt* (left). It usually drives the fan, the water pump, and the alternator. On air-cooled VW engines the fan belt drives only the fan and generator. If a car is equipped with optional accessories, such as power steering and air conditioning, there will usually be one or more additional belts to drive them (above).

Inspecting drive belts

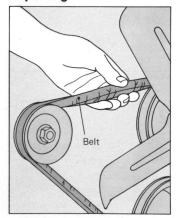

Check the condition of drive belts once a month. Look at each belt in several places; twist the belt to look at its sides and bottom. Replace a belt that is cracked, brittle, oil soaked, badly glazed, or slippery.
Caution: Never touch any belt unless the engine is off. If a car has an electric fan, keep your hands away from the fan until the engine is cold. The fan may start unexpectedly if the engine is warm.

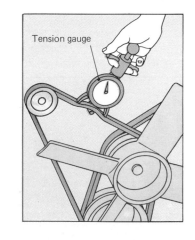

Belt tension should be checked periodically. The most accurate way to check it is with a belt-tension gauge. There are several types; follow instructions that accompany the gauge. To adjust tension, see opposite page. See Caution at left.

A quick test of tension can be performed by pressing down on the belt with your thumb midway along the longest span between pulleys. If belt deflects more than ½ to ¾ in., it is too loose. Although not as accurate as a gauge test, the thumb test is adequate in most circumstances. See Caution, far left.

How to tighten or replace a drive belt ⏱ 5–10 min

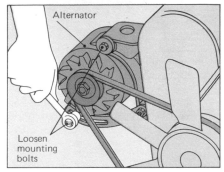

1. Loosen the mounting bolts on all accessories driven by the belt to be replaced. If belt only needs tightening, loosen the mounting bolts on only one accessory and skip to Step 4.

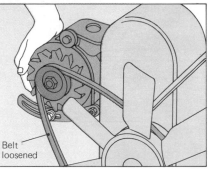

2. Reduce the tension on the drive belt by gently pushing the accessory toward the engine block. If the accessory sticks, loosen its mounting bolts further and push the accessory again.

3. When there is enough slack in the belt, pry it off its pulleys. If there are other belts in the way, they must be removed first. Roll new belt into proper pulley tracks.

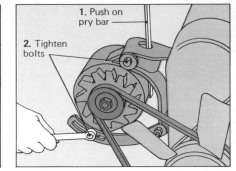

4. To exert tension on belt, pry accessory away from engine and tighten its mounting bolts. Do not pry against fins, power steering pump reservoir, or other fragile parts.

Additional tensioning devices

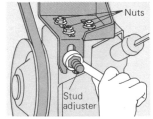

A power steering pump mounted to a large bracket by nuts on its front or top has a stud adjuster on the side. First, loosen mounting nuts. To reduce tension (to move pump toward engine), turn nut on stud counterclockwise. To increase tension, turn nut clockwise. Tighten mounting nuts.

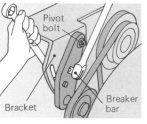

Pivoting idler pulley is maneuvered in much the same way as alternator (top of page). Loosen pivot and sliding bracket bolts. To reduce belt tension, push pulley toward engine. To increase tension, pull it away from engine. Use breaker bar in square hole to hold pulley tight against belt. Tighten bolts.

Eccentric idler pulley has an offset arm between the pulley and engine. First, loosen mounting bolt. Use a wrench on the hex on front of arm to rotate pulley. To reduce tension, move pulley toward engine. To increase tension, move pulley away from engine. Tighten mounting bolt.

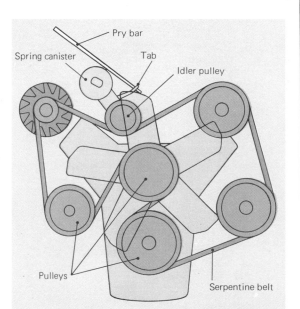

Spring-loaded idler pulley is used on some Ford engines equipped with one long, serpentine drive belt that is wrapped around the pulleys of all the accessories. Idler pulley is pre-set to exert correct tension on the belt. To relieve tension on belt, insert a pry bar into the tab on the spring canister, then push down on bar to lift pulley. To restore tension, let the spring pull the pulley down gently, then remove the pry bar.

Air-cooled Volkswagen drive belt

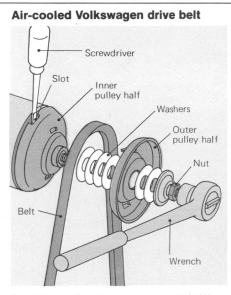

Two-piece pulley is used on air-cooled VW engines. Belt tension is adjusted by adding or removing washers from between the pulley halves. Turn engine over until slot on pulley is at the top. Wedge a screwdriver into the slot to keep the pulley from turning, then remove nut. Remove washers from between pulley halves to increase belt tension; add washers to lessen tension. Replace belt, outer pulley half, and extra washers. Tighten nut. Recheck tension.

Troubleshooting the air conditioner ⏱ 5–10 min

For the average home mechanic, work on a car's air-conditioning system should be limited to the simple maintenance jobs shown on these three pages. Any other job is best left to an air-conditioning (A/C) specialist, not the average mechanic. An important maintenance job is to operate the air conditioning at least once a week whenever the outside temperature is above 50°F (10°C). This circulates the refrigerant and keeps the many seals in the system moist and free from cracks. Cracked seals usually result in leaks. To determine if your system is low on refrigerant, see *Checking the charge* (right). If the refrigerant level is low, recharge the system (p.290). Cooling output can also be helped by using a garden hose to keep the surface of the condenser free of debris, as is done with a radiator (p.281).

If your system is not cooling properly, an inoperative compressor may be the cause. All compressors are belt driven, and all are operated by a magnetic clutch in the center of the compressor pulley. First, with the engine off, check the compressor drive belt; if necessary, adjust its tension or replace it (pp.286–287). If the belt is all right, check the magnetic clutch. With the engine on, have a helper turn on the dashboard A/C switch. When the switch is turned on, the clutch should rotate. (The pulley always rotates as

Pulley

Electrical connection

Magnetic clutch

long as the engine is running. On cycling clutch systems, you may have to wait several minutes for the clutch to engage; the clutch may not engage at temperatures below 50°F.) If the clutch never engages, check that the electrical ground (if any) and the electrical connection at or near the compressor is tight. Then, if necessary, test the fuses and relays in the system (pp.362 and 371); if these are working, have an air-conditioning expert inspect the system and make the necessary repairs.

Although all auto air-conditioning systems work in basically the same way (see p.144), each differs slightly in its components. Use the information given here and the illustrations below to locate those parts necessary for determining the charge (the amount of refrigerant) in your system and, if necessary, for recharging it (p.290).

Every air-conditioning system can be divided into a *high side* and a *low side*. The high side starts at the compressor, continues into the condenser, and ends at a valve or orifice tube at the entrance to the evaporator. (A VIR system means that the valve is in the receiver.) It is referred to as the high side because the refrigerant is highly pressurized.

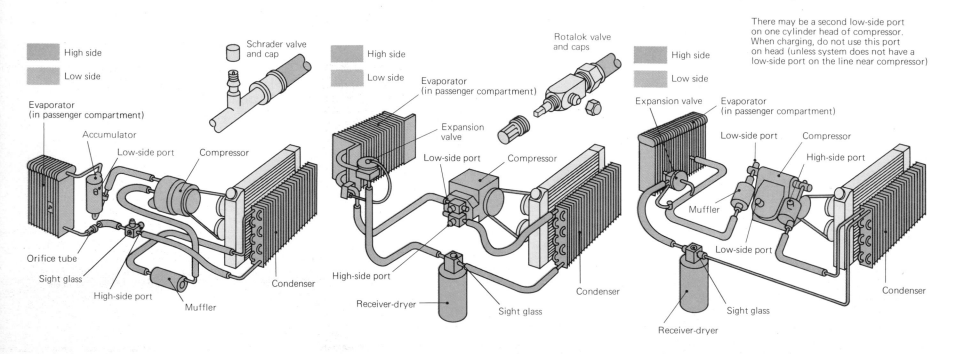

CCOT system (cycling clutch with orifice tube), used on most new Ford and GM cars. Has accumulator instead of receiver-dryer.

CC-TXV system (cycling clutch with thermostatic expansion valve), used on some Ford, AMC cars. Often has Rotalok valves.

EPR (or ETR) system (evaporator pressure regulator or evaporator temperature regulator). Used on older Chrysler cars.

The low side starts at the valve or tube at the evaporator, continues into the evaporator and back to the compressor. It is called the low (or suction) side because the refrigerant has been depressurized and is being sucked back to the compressor.

Every system has a *low-side service port* at which the pressure in the low side can be measured. This measurement helps to determine whether the system needs recharging. The recharging is done through the same low-side service port. There is also a *high-side service port* for taking high-side pressure readings. **Caution:** It is dangerous to charge into the high-side port using the method on page 290.

A service port is actually a valve, either a *Schrader* or a *Rotalok* type. The valve is protected by a removable cap. Schrader valves are easy to use and are the type found on tires. Rotalok valves are more difficult to work than Schrader valves and require a relatively expensive manifold gauge set for taking pressure readings and recharging. Rotalok valves are always at the compressor; Schrader valves can be at the compressor or at other points in the system.

If your system has a *sight glass,* pressure readings are not necessary. You can determine the amount of refrigerant in the system by looking at the refrigerant as it passes under the glass. A sight glass is often on the receiver-dryer, but in some cars it is in a pressure line on the high side of the system.

Caution: When working on an air-conditioning system, wear protective gloves and goggles and work in a well-ventilated area. Refrigerant will freeze anything it contacts. When vapor comes in contact with a flame, a poisonous gas is formed. Handle cans of pressurized refrigerant gently.

Tools and materials: Air-conditioning pressure gauge, work gloves, safety goggles.

Checking the charge

Reading a sight glass
Find sight glass and clean it. Turn on engine and A/C *(Max)*. After 5 min, look at refrigerant under glass:

 If clear, the system is either fully charged or empty. Have a helper turn A/C dash switch off and on. If the system emits cool air or if bubbles appear while switch and clutch are off, the system is charged, not empty.

 A few bubbles mean that the system needs a charge or the clutch is off (some clutches are controlled by a thermostatic switch in addition to the dash switch). Wait for the clutch to go on, then check again.

 If foamy, there is very little refrigerant in the system. Oil streaks (not shown) mean that the system is empty. Have an expert check and recharge the system.

If cloudy, the desiccant in the receiver-dryer or accumulator is breaking up and being circulated through the system. Have the system serviced by an A/C expert.

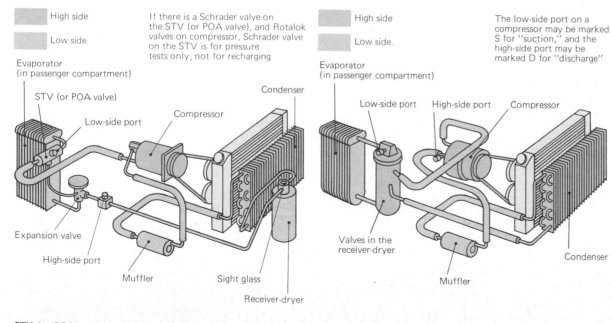

High side

Low side

Evaporator (in passenger compartment)

STV (or POA valve)

Low-side port

Condenser

Compressor

Expansion valve

High-side port

Muffler

Sight glass

Receiver-dryer

If there is a Schrader valve on the STV (or POA valve), and Rotalok valves on compressor, Schrader valve on the STV is for pressure tests only, not for recharging

STV (or POA) system (suction throttling valve or pilot-operated absolute valve). Used on GM and Ford cars.

High side

Low side.

Evaporator (in passenger compartment)

Low-side port

High-side port

Compressor

Valves in the receiver-dryer

Muffler

Condenser

The low-side port on a compressor may be marked S for "suction," and the high-side port may be marked D for "discharge"

VIR system (valves in receiver). Used on some GM cars from 1973 on. Expansion and POA valves are in the receiver-dryer.

Taking pressure readings (Schrader valves)

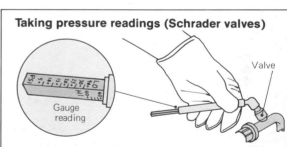

Gauge reading

Valve

Remove caps from high and low service valves; if valve leaks or hisses, replace cap and have an A/C expert service the valve. Take two sets of readings, using an air-conditioning pressure gauge (which is like a tire gauge but has different calibrations). If you get readings different from those given here, have the system checked by an A/C expert. With the engine off, press the gauge onto each valve. If the readings are equal to each other and close to the outside air temperature, the system is charged; if readings are equal but significantly lower than the outside air temperature, the system needs a charge. Turn on the engine and the A/C to *Max;* take a second set of readings. The high side should read about 140 psi; the low side, about 10 to 30 psi. If readings are slightly lower than they should be, the system needs a charge.

Recharging the system 🔲🔲 15–30 min

The need for recharging is determined by pressure readings or sight glass readings (p.288). Use the method shown here only on low-side Schrader valves.

To recharge, you will need a recharging kit and an anti-blowback valve. Additional cans of refrigerant can be bought separately. An anti-blowback valve is a safety device that will prevent the refrigerant in the system from being blown back into the can should you accidentally hook up to the high-side service valve. All dispensing valves have some type of anti-blowback device built into them, but the separate anti-blowback valve is an extra safety measure that is highly recommended. The one can of refrigerant supplied with the recharging kit is usually enough to recharge a system that is slightly undercharged. Do not use more than two cans; if more refrigerant is needed, it could mean that there is a large leak in the system which should be checked out by a mechanic who specializes in air-conditioning work.

Most leaks occur at fittings where lines join each other or where a line connects into another component. Brush a soapy solution on any suspected area; if bubbles form, there is a leak. If the leak is at a joint, tighten the fittings with wrenches. If that does not work or if the leak is at another spot, see an expert.

Caution: When working on air conditioning, wear protective gloves and goggles. Work in a well-ventilated area and away from heat and flame. Handle cans of pressurized refrigerant gently.

Tools: A/C pressure gauge, dispensing valve and collar, charging hose, anti-blowback valve, flare wrenches.
Materials: One or two 13- to 15-oz cans of refrigerant, work gloves, safety goggles.

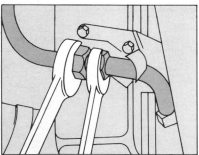

To tighten fittings, use two wrenches and gently push them in opposite directions. Do not overtighten the fittings; you could split the seals inside and cause a bigger leak.

How to set up the recharging kit

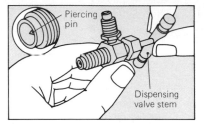

1. Turn the stem of the dispensing valve counterclockwise to bring the piercing pin up into the valve. The point of the pin should not be visible.

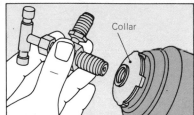

2. Slide the collar onto the can and hold in place while screwing the valve tightly into contact with can. Turn the valve stem clockwise as far as it will go.

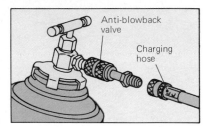

3. Attach the anti-blowback valve tightly to the dispensing valve. Attach the end of the charging hose that has no depressor pin to the anti-blowback valve.

Charging into a low-side Schrader valve

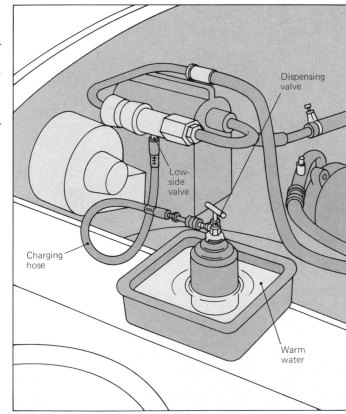

1. Turn on the engine. Turn A/C on *Max*, fan on *High*. Remove the cap from the low-side Schrader valve (see p.289 for typical locations). **Caution:** Wear protective gloves and goggles. If Schrader valve leaks when cap is removed, replace cap and have valve checked out by an A/C expert.

2. Bleed the air from the charging hose. Screw the charging hose to the Schrader valve just enough so that it will not fall off, but not so much that it forms a tight seal. Holding the can upright, turn the dispensing valve stem counterclockwise to open the can and let the refrigerant flow out. Allow gas to hiss out of hose for a few seconds. Then hand-tighten hose connection.

3. Place the can into a pan of warm water (about 125°F, 51°C) and open dispensing valve. **Caution:** Keep the can upright, or liquid refrigerant will enter the system and may damage it.

4. If the system has a sight glass, watch the refrigerant passing under it and stop charging when the glass looks clear. If there is no sight glass, add only one can of refrigerant; then stop charging, and take pressure readings (p.288).

5. To stop charging, first close the dispensing valve. Unscrew the charging hose from the Schrader valve. Put cap back on valve. Turn off the A/C, fan, and engine. If there is any refrigerant left in the can, direct the charging hose toward the ground and open the dispensing valve.

Caution: Wear heavy gloves and safety goggles when handling refrigerant. Keep hands and clothing away from fans, pulleys, belts, and other moving engine parts. Do not keep opened cans of refrigerant.

Lubricating body parts ⏱ 15–30 min

To ensure quiet, smooth, and reliable operation, all moving body parts should be lubricated twice a year. Hoods, trunk lids, and hinges can be damaged if they seize and then are forced. First, clean away any dirt or old lubricant, then apply new lubricant where the parts pivot or where they contact other parts. Work the parts several times to distribute the lubricant, then wipe away any excess. Use engine oil or a waterproof white grease on the hinges and latches on the doors, hood, and trunk. If the parts might touch your clothing, use a non-staining waterproof white grease. Do not apply too much lubricant to the hold-open mechanisms on the door hinges, or the door might not stay open. Nylon or plastic parts are not usually lubricated; consult your owner's manual for the carmaker's recommendations. Lubricate the seat tracks and mechanisms as well as the hinges on the sun visors, glove compartment door, and movable license plate holders.

To lubricate the lock cylinders, use silicone spray or a graphite-based lock lubricant. Do not use oil on a lock cylinder; oil could make the tumblers sticky and hard to operate. Once the lubricant is in the cylinder, work it around by inserting the key into the lock and operating the lock several times. Clean the key before putting it back in your pocket.

Lubricating locks

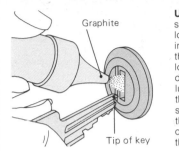

Use graphite or silicone to lubricate locks. Squirt lubricant into the lock; insert the key and work the lock several times to distribute the lubricant. Clean off the key. If lock has a seal, use the tip of the key to hold it open while inserting the lubricant.

Labels: Graphite, Tip of key

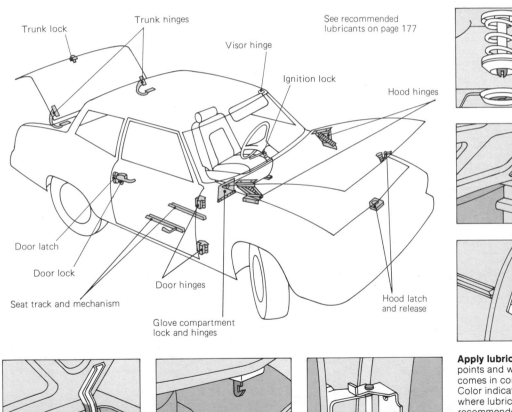

Labels: Trunk lock, Trunk hinges, Visor hinge, Ignition lock, Hood hinges, Door latch, Door lock, Door hinges, Seat track and mechanism, Glove compartment lock and hinges, Hood latch and release

See recommended lubricants on page 177

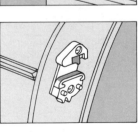

Apply lubricant to the pivot points and where one part comes in contact with another. Color indicates the points where lubricant is recommended.

Drains

To allow for proper drainage, most cars have drains along the bottom of any body part that could possibly collect water. Such body parts include doors, rocker panels, quarter panels, heater housings, cowl/firewall units, the trunk, and the passenger compartment. The drain is often a simple hole or tube through which water can flow, unless the hole or tube becomes clogged with dirt or debris. Sometimes drain holes are fitted with a rubber or plastic plug. When the plug is removed, the water can be swept out through the hole. Such drain plugs should always be reinstalled to prevent fumes from entering the car.

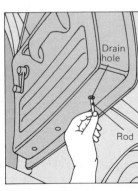

Labels: Drain hole, Rod

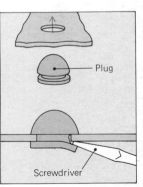

Labels: Plug, Screwdriver

To clear a drain hole or tube, insert a narrow rod into the hole or tube and gently move the rod until all the dirt and debris has fallen out. **Caution:** Wear safety goggles to protect your eyes from falling dirt.

Some drains are fitted with a removable plug. To remove the plug, gently pry on its edges with a screwdriver. Use a whisk broom to sweep accumulated water out. Gently hammer plug back into place.

Preparing a car for winter

Freezing temperatures and snow call for special maintenance procedures and special equipment. Safe driving on roads that are slick with snow or ice requires top efficiency from both the vehicle and its driver. The best policy is to avoid driving in snow, sleet, or freezing rain unless absolutely necessary. If you must drive, do so with extreme caution, and only in a car that has been properly prepared for winter driving. Always drive smoothly and conservatively when roads are slick. Sudden turns, hard braking, or attempts to accelerate rapidly can result in skids. Most winter accidents occur when a car's speed is too great for prevailing conditions.

It is difficult to start a car in cold weather for two reasons. First, cold weather thickens the oil, making it harder to turn the engine over. Second, battery efficiency decreases at lower temperatures. (At 0° F a battery delivers 40 percent of the power that it can deliver at 80° F, and at -30° F the battery may produce as little as 5 percent of its warm-weather power.) Proper maintenance is a key to quick starts and trouble-free operation during the winter months. In fact, a tuneup in the fall makes more sense than the traditional spring tuneup.

Electrical system

For quick, reliable starts in cold weather, be sure that your car's electrical system is in good condition. The battery should be able to deliver all its rated cold-cranking power, spark plug electrodes should be relatively unworn, spark plug gaps should be set to specifications, the alternator belt should be tight, ignition timing should be properly adjusted, and the distributor should be in good working order. Information on service and tuneups can be found on the following pages:

Batteries: pp.277–279
Spark plugs: pp.232–235
Distributors: pp.222–231, 236–239

Since winter is the most demanding time of year for a car, and a breakdown then may not only be inconvenient but potentially hazardous, the safest rule to follow is to replace any electrical part that appears to be damaged or excessively worn. If the battery case is cracked or if it will not accept or hold a charge, replace the battery with a new one. (If you live in a particularly cold area, buy a battery that has at least 20 percent more cold-cranking power than the standard size recommended for your automobile's engine displacement.) Another reason to replace the battery is a variation of more than .05 in specific-gravity reading between any two cells. Spark plugs with damaged shells or badly worn electrodes, battery cables that are frayed or highly corroded, and worn distributor parts also should be replaced. Once the ignition system is tuned up and winterized, finish the job by applying waterproofing solution to all exposed ignition wires. Also consider engine and battery heaters (p.297).

Cooling system

Service the cooling system before cold weather sets in—the job will be easier, your car will be protected against an unexpected cold snap, and you will avoid having to pay premium prices for antifreeze in the event of a shortage.

If the car is more than two years old, the cooling system should be drained and flushed each autumn. Use a chemical flush if the coolant shows signs of extensive rust and scale. Follow the directions that accompany the flushing solution. (See pp.280–287 for detailed information on maintaining the cooling system.)

Examine the system carefully and replace any defective parts. Be sure that the thermostat opens and closes at the temperature marked on it. Inspect hoses and connections on the radiator, heater, heater valve, and heater bypass. Replace any hoses that are rotten, cracked, or brittle; tighten loose clamps and replace damaged ones.

When refilling the system with coolant, add enough ethylene glycol (permanent antifreeze) to protect against freeze-up to the lowest temperature expected. If you do not drain the system, check the coolant with a hydrometer, and add antifreeze if necessary. A mixture of 50 percent antifreeze and 50 percent water is generally satisfactory, not only to prevent freezing but to protect against boilover in the summer (see p.73).

Percent antifreeze	Freezing point	Hydrometer reading at 60°F
50	−34°F	1.080
55	−47°F	1.086
60	−62°F	1.092
65	−80°F	1.097
70	−84°F	1.099

Fuel system

A properly operating fuel system is vital for easy startups in cold weather. Information on maintaining and tuning the fuel system is given on pages 240–262. Pay particular attention to the fuel filter, and replace it at the intervals recommended in your owner's manual. A partially clogged filter can result in an overly lean carburetor mixture—the opposite of what is desired in winter. Check the air filter too. Knock it on the ground to dislodge accumulated debris, then hold a light against its inner surface. If you cannot see the light through the filter, it is time to replace the filter.

A common problem during extremely cold weather is the tendency for ice to form in the fuel line or carburetor, blocking the flow of fuel. To avoid this, add a can of fuel line antifreeze (usually isopropyl alcohol) to the fuel tank every second or third time you buy gasoline. In sub-zero weather add a can with each tankful, especially if the car will be standing outdoors for a day or more. Another way to help prevent icing is to keep the fuel tank at least half full all the time. This will reduce the area in which condensation can form inside the tank.

Automatic chokes on the carburetors of most pre-1981 cars can be adjusted for optimal performance during the different seasons of the year. If your car has an adjustable choke and the engine is hard to start in cold weather, try adjusting the choke for a richer mixture (pp.248–250). Wait until the engine is cold, then turn the adjuster until the choke plate closes fully. If you cannot do this within the range of adjustment marks, replace the choke's thermostatic coil spring.

Exhaust system

Check the exhaust system thoroughly (see pp.434–438) and replace any part that is leaking or shows signs of excessive rust. Most winter driving is done with the windows closed, and as a result the danger of carbon monoxide poisoning is far greater than in warm weather. To avoid this hazard, make sure that all clamps holding the tail pipe and muffler are tight and in good condition. **Caution:** Never start a car or run its engine in a closed garage. Always open the garage door and at least one window for adequate ventilation.

Brakes

Reliable brakes are vital in wintertime. Start by checking the master cylinder; if the fluid is more than ½ in. from the top, check the system for leaks. Next, with the car standing still and the engine idling, press the brake pedal firmly. If the pedal feels spongy, there may be air in the hydraulic line that should be bled off. If the pedal fades, look for leaks in the master cylinder, hydraulic lines, and wheel cylinders and make any necessary repairs. (See pp.210–218 for detailed information on inspecting brake systems.) Try out your brakes on a smooth, dry, straight road. The brakes should not grab, drag, make noise, or cause the car to pull to one side. If any of these symptoms exist, check the brakes (p.329). Finally, examine all brake linings (or brake pads) and replace any that are excessively worn (pp.330–337). If any set of linings or pads must be replaced, always replace the set on the opposite side of the car as well, in order to maintain even braking action and avoid pulling to one side.

Tires

Since the introduction of radial tires, the development of special rubbers, and an increasing variety in tread design, drivers today have a wide range of snow tires to choose from.

Your choice of tread pattern will depend on what part of the country you live in. Open-lugged tires do well in rural areas with heavy snow. A combined lug and drainage-channel design is suitable for areas receiving both snow and rain. A small-lugged pattern is good in sections with moderate snowfall and good snow-removal services.

Steel-belted radial snow tires are the best all-around choice. Most are made of a tread-rubber compound that resists stiffening in near-zero temperatures; they have superior dry-pavement handling characteristics; and some types can be left on all year long. For best traction, mount radial snow tires on all four wheels (that way, your car's cornering performance will benefit, as well as straight-ahead traction and stopping). If you mount radial snow tires on the drive wheels only, be sure that the other two tires are radials: combining radials and other tire types may seriously impair handling.

Studding improves traction on snow and ice, but many states restrict the use of studs (26 states forbid them in warm weather, and 13 ban them altogether). If your car has front-wheel drive and you want to use metal studs, put them in all four tires. Do not put studs in a used tire, and do not try to do the job yourself. Studded tires should not be rotated (neither should any radial winter tires). Mark each tire's position (right rear, etc.) with crayon at the end of winter so that you will know where to remount it the following year.

See and be seen

In addition to slippery roads and freezing temperatures, winter brings a host of severe visibility problems. These range from slush kicked onto the windshield by other vehicles to blinding snowstorms, freezing rain, and wipers caked with ice.

A sturdy plastic scraper for removing ice from windows is essential, but there are other tricks and gadgets that can improve driving visibility. If snow is expected and travel is unavoidable, carry a large, stiff-bristled pushbroom in the trunk of your car. It is much easier to push a foot of snow off your car with such a broom than to flick it away bit by bit with a scraper. Be sure to dress warmly and carry heavy gloves or mittens; scraping a windshield during a blustery, sub-zero winter night with bare hands is an invitation to frostbite. Check all your lights—parking lights, flasher, and turn signal as well as headlights. It can be just as important to *be seen* as it is to see. Not only should all lights be in working order, but they should be clean—dirty, snow-covered brake lights, for example, may be dangerously inadequate.

Your driving habits are important too. When visibility is low because of snow, fog, sleet, or rain, focus your eyes as far up the road as possible. Avert your eyes from oncoming headlights at night to avoid being momentarily blinded; look at the right-hand edge of the road. During snowstorms keep shifting the direction and focus of your sight; falling snow and the movement of your wipers can be hypnotic if you keep staring a fixed distance ahead of your car.

Defogger for rear window is optional equipment on most new cars, but if your car does not have one, it can be added. Easiest to install are paste-on strips with resistance elements that warm the glass electrically.

Fan-type defogger is usually mounted in an opening cut into the rear package shelf. It draws less current than resistance type and can improve the efficiency of the car's main heating and ventilating system by increasing air circulation.

Wiper blades should be resilient and firm; if rubber is brittle or cracked, replace blade. Special winter blade is encased in rubber to prevent wiper from clogging with ice.

Windshield washer fluid is generally a mixture of methyl alcohol, detergent, and water. Like coolant in engine, solution must be more concentrated in winter to keep it from freezing. Chart shows correct proportions.

Side windows can be protected against interior frost with plastic frost shields. Simply peel off protective paper and press self-adhesive shield to inside of car window.

Pump, valves, and hoses of windshield washer should be in working order. Clear blocked valves by flushing system with a syringe filled with warm water. Clear and aim nozzles with a needle or pliers (p.302).

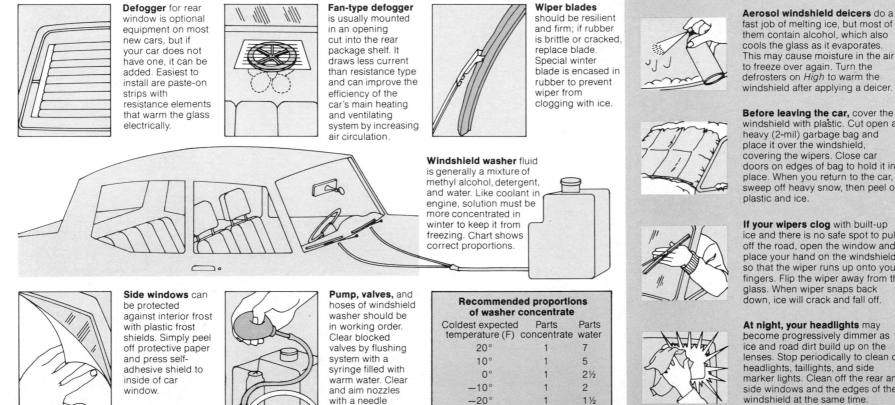

Recommended proportions of washer concentrate		
Coldest expected temperature (F)	Parts concentrate	Parts water
20°	1	7
10°	1	5
0°	1	2½
−10°	1	2
−20°	1	1½
−30°	1	1

Clearing the windshield

Before driving, clear all snow from the windshield, hood, roof, trunk, and all glass areas, including headlights and taillights. Snow left on the car body can swirl up suddenly and block vision, or it can fly off and startle other drivers.

Many types of scrapers are available for removing ice from car windows. If the windshield is covered with ice, let the heater melt it a bit while you scrape. Replace any scraper if its edge has become burred or chipped. You can use the edge of a plastic credit card as an emergency ice scraper.

Aerosol windshield deicers do a fast job of melting ice, but most of them contain alcohol, which also cools the glass as it evaporates. This may cause moisture in the air to freeze over again. Turn the defrosters on *High* to warm the windshield after applying a deicer.

Before leaving the car, cover the windshield with plastic. Cut open a heavy (2-mil) garbage bag and place it over the windshield, covering the wipers. Close car doors on edges of bag to hold it in place. When you return to the car, sweep off heavy snow, then peel off plastic and ice.

If your wipers clog with built-up ice and there is no safe spot to pull off the road, open the window and place your hand on the windshield so that the wiper runs up onto your fingers. Flip the wiper away from the glass. When wiper snaps back down, ice will crack and fall off.

At night, your headlights may become progressively dimmer as ice and road dirt build up on the lenses. Stop periodically to clean off headlights, taillights, and side marker lights. Clean off the rear and side windows and the edges of the windshield at the same time.

Tire chains

Tires with chains outperform even the best snow tires. Weighed against this is the relative inconvenience of chains. Mounting them takes time and energy, particularly if you are forced to do the job during bad weather or in an awkward roadside location. In addition, chains should be removed as soon as conditions improve, and while they are on, speed should be kept below 35 mph to avoid wear and tear on the chains and damage to tires.

Steel-link chains, with or without cleats, are the most common type. Get a set that fits your tire size, and check your owner's manual: in some cases, limited clearance between fender and tire rules out the use of chains or requires the use of special *Class S*

chains. When installing chains, avoid using a jack—it may slip on an icy road, particularly if it is a bumper jack. If you must use a jack, pull well off the road onto a level surface and dig through the snow or ice until the jack's base rests on the ground. If the ground is muddy, place a wide board under the base of the jack to prevent it from sinking.

Types of chains

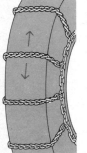 **Steel-link** chains are cheap but wear out quickly and can be difficult to install. They provide good straight-ahead traction (arrows) and shorten braking distances, but give only limited improvement in side traction during turns.

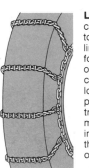 **Lug-reinforced** chains are similar to ordinary steel-link chains except for welded cleats on the links of the chain. They last longer and provide better traction, but cost more. Be sure to install them with the cleats facing outward.

European-style chains have a crisscross pattern that provides traction in many directions (arrows) to improve straight-ahead performance and prevent skids in turns. However, they are expensive and are not widely available.

Strap-on chains provide less grip than other chains but can be useful in emergencies. Install them in pairs (one on each drive wheel). The car need not be moved; simply feed the strap through the wheel slots (if any), and buckle tightly.

Tubular traction aids have cross members made of short lengths of metal tubing threaded onto cables. They are lighter than steel-link chains and can be driven at higher speeds, but they provide less traction and tend to wear out sooner.

Installing steel-link chains

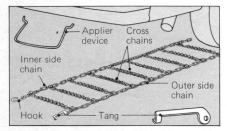

1. Lay chain on ground behind right rear tire. Note that fastener with tang is at outside and to the rear, hook is at inside rear.

2. Slip applier device through front links of chain on either side, then press applier onto tire. Cleats on cross chains must face upward.

3. Drive car slowly forward until chain wraps around tire and applier is back in original position. (Have a helper direct you if possible.)

4. Remove applier, reach behind tire, and slip hook onto link of inner side chain so that chain is snug but does not pull outer side chain.

5. Slip fastener over corresponding link of outer side chain, then push fastener up until its tang engages link of side chain.

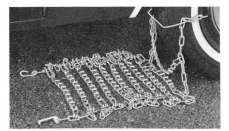

6. To install chain on left rear tire, lay chain *in front* of tire (so that fastener will be on outside and cleats will face up).

7. Move car *backward*, then follow procedure for right tire. Side chains should be centered, cross chains at right angles, when job is done.

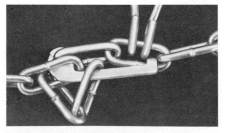

8. Take up slack as chains stretch with use; cut off all but one extra link (or temporarily slip extra links on fastener as shown).

Stopping and starting

Stopping distances increase and traction decreases in winter. The charts below compare tires and chains under two common road conditions: glare ice and loosely packed snow. Although charts are useful, experience is a greater help in winter driving. Veteran drivers learn to "feel" the road by the way their cars handle, and adjust their speeds accordingly.

Braking distance

From 20 mph, after you touch pedal; reaction time averages ¾ sec and adds 22 ft to distances shown below. Percentages show improvement over regular tires.

0 25 50 75 100 125 150	Feet	
Regular tires	145 ft 0%	
Snow tires (rear)	151 ft −1%	
Studded snow tires (used, rear)	129 ft 13%	
Studded tires (used, front and rear)	123 ft 17%	
Studded snow tires (new, rear)	120 ft 19%	
Studded tires (new, front and rear)	103 ft 31%	On glare ice at 25°F
Reinforced tire chains (rear)	75 ft 50%	
Regular tires	60 ft 0%	
Snow tires (rear)	52 ft 13%	On loosely packed snow
Reinforced tire chains (rear)	38 ft 37%	

Traction rating

0 100 200 300 400 500 600 700	Rating	
Regular tires	100 0%	
Snow tires	128 28%	
Studded snow tires (used)	283 183%	
Studded snow tires (new)	318 218%	On glare ice at 25°F
Reinforced tire chains	730 630%	
Regular tires	100 0%	
Snow tires	151 51%	On loosely packed snow
Reinforced tire chains	413 313%	

Source: National Safety Council

The hazards of deep snow

Getting stuck in winter is always an inconvenience and on occasion can be dangerous as well. Tips to help you avoid getting stuck are given below, along with a few ways to extricate your car if it does get stuck. When conditions are particularly severe—during a blizzard, for example—it may happen that nothing will work and that you will find yourself marooned for hours, even days. If you travel long distances in snowy country during the winter months, make a point of taking along emergency equipment. Warm clothing, sleeping bags, extra food, and a small butane or white gas cookstove can keep you warm, well fed, and fairly comfortable while you await the arrival of snow-clearing machinery.

Getting up hills

The key to climbing a steep, slippery hill is to keep your car's wheels from spinning. If no other vehicles are blocking you, pick up as much speed as you safely can before you reach the hill, then use this extra velocity to help carry you over the crest. If the rise is so steep that downshifting is necessary, shift the transmission to a lower gear before you reach the hill; downshifting halfway up the hill will cause the wheels to spin.

Point your wheels ahead

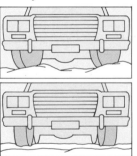

Keep your car's wheels as straight as possible when moving through deep snow, especially when starting from rest. The more your wheels are turned, the more they will act like plows. If a turn is necessary (to pull out of a parking space, for example), accomplish the turn in small, gradual segments, backing up several times, rather than trying to swing out in one forward motion.

Use your jack

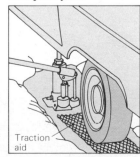

Traction aid

A stuck car can sometimes be freed by jacking up a wheel that is spinning, then sliding a traction aid under the tire. Use a scissors jack or hydraulic jack (a bumper jack is more likely to slip) and dig the snow away until you can set the jack's base on bare earth or pavement. Wire mesh traction mats 32 in. wide and 6 ft long are available. You can also use lengths of roofing paper, twigs, ashes, sand—anything that will increase grip.

Rocking out of snow

Rocking is generally the easiest way to extricate a vehicle that is mired in snow. Keeping the front wheels pointed straight ahead, shift back and forth between *Low* and *Reverse*. Time each shift so that it occurs at the peak of the previous rock. Success in rocking depends on never spinning the tires; as soon as the tires spin, traction is reduced. **Caution:** Excessive rocking can overheat and damage an automatic transmission.

Add weight for traction

Extra weight in the rear improves traction of cars with rear-wheel drive. Be sure to place the weight (75 to 100 lb is enough) in the forward part of the trunk; weight too far in the rear lifts the front wheels, impairs handling, and risks dangerous skids. Use bags of sand or road salt; either material can also be spread on the road to increase the grip of the tires. If you need more traction, have a passenger sit in the rear seat.

Winching a car free

Padding to protect tree

If all else fails, you can extricate a stuck vehicle from deep snow with a length of strong chain and a "come-along" ratchet, a block and tackle, or some other manual hoisting or winching device. Wrap a chain around a sturdy tree and hook one end of the winch to the car frame, the other end to the chain. Standing near the tree, take up the winch gradually, moving the car to firm ground a few inches at a time.

Lubrication

Lubrication is a vital part of winter maintenance. The right kind of engine oil will improve your car's starting performance while at the same time protecting the engine's moving parts at highway speeds. A thorough grease job will do much to shield key parts against the corrosive effects of slush mixed with road salt. A correctly lubricated steering system will help ensure the responsive handling that is so important to safe driving on ice or snow.

The lower the weight, or SAE number, of an oil, the less viscous it is and the more easily the engine will turn over. Multi-viscosity oils that behave like lightweight oils when cold and like heavyweight oils when warm have largely eliminated the need for special pre-winter oil changes. In all but the most frigid sections of the country, 10W-30 or 10W-40 oil is adequate. (The W stands for "winter" and means that the oil has the indicated viscosity at 0°F.) If temperatures in your area consistently fall well below 0°F, you should switch to 5W-20 for winter. In very severe climates, where winter temperatures go below -20°F, a synthetic oil, such as Mobil 1, is useful. This particular oil is rated at 5W-20 but thickens less than conventional oils do when temperatures drop below 0°F. It has good cold-starting qualities at temperatures as low as -40°F. If for some reason you prefer using single-viscosity oil, remember that straight 5W or 10W oil will not provide as much protection as multi-viscosity oil after the engine has warmed up. Consequently, cars using single-viscosity winter-grade oils should not be used for long trips at high speeds. Synthetic oils and lightweight mineral oils also reduce fuel consumption because they reduce internal engine drag. However, you may not notice any difference in fuel economy during cold weather because the choke takes longer to open in winter, and this increases fuel consumption.

A complete pre-winter lubrication of your car's chassis and body points (see pp.191-192) is recommended as an important step in preventing corrosion and protecting the car's performance under severe winter conditions. Check your automatic transmission fluid and adjust the transmission bands if necessary (pp.449-450). Inspect the differential to be sure that the oil is at the proper level—severe strain is placed on the differential when one of the wheels spins, a common occurrence in winter.

Check the power steering fluid level, and top it off to the dipstick mark (p.195). While you are at it, test the steering on a dry road. If the car wanders or if it is difficult to steer, have the front-end alignment checked (p.221). If the tires squeal on turns, check their air pressure (p.184). Also examine the shock absorbers for leaks, damage, and wear (p.189).

Corrosion

One of the most insidious and costly hazards of winter driving is corrosion. The use of road salt not only produces meltwater where none might have existed but also increases the water's corrosiveness. Despite improved rust-proofing at the factory, the severity of any rust is increased by the growing use of thinner sheet metal in auto bodies in order to improve fuel economy by cutting weight. A number of steps can be taken to prevent or reduce corrosion.

Rust-proofing the car can help in many instances, provided that the job is done while the car is still new and is carried out by a reputable firm. The procedure consists of coating all rust-prone surfaces with an oily, waxlike substance. Holes are drilled to reach hard-to-get-at areas, such as the interior of doors, and the rustproofing substance is sprayed inside. The holes are then plugged with plastic. The underside of the car (chassis and suspension) are also sprayed. Because of the special equipment required, rust-proofing is not a task you should attempt yourself. Note that rustproofing should not be confused with *undercoating*, the purpose of which is to decrease road noise by coating the underside of the car with a sound-deadening layer. Undercoating may, in fact, increase rusting either by trapping water against the metal or by forming water-holding crevices as the undercoat cracks with age.

A few other simple pre-winter maintenance chores also help to prevent rust. Inspect painted surfaces on your car; any fractures should be treated immediately. Clear out drain holes and ventilation holes in the trunk, along the bottoms of doors, under the hood, and elsewhere. Spray rubber parts, such as trim, bumper guards, and weather stripping, with silicone as soon as cold weather sets in to keep the rubber from getting brittle. If any of the rubber parts are badly damaged or worn, replace them.

Once winter arrives, wash the car at regular intervals, preferably once a week. Soften up dirt on the underside of the body with a jet of water, wash the dirt off with a sponge and detergent, then rinse thoroughly. Clean and remove caked mud and salt from the car's underside with high-pressure water or steam. Pay particular attention to the wheel housings, bumpers, muffler, tail pipe, and brackets. If you bring your auto to a car wash, avoid stations that use recycled water, which contains a high proportion of salt rinsed off cars that were washed before yours.

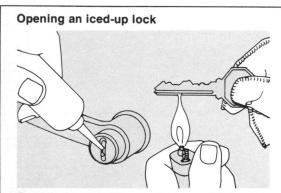

Opening an iced-up lock

Frozen locks can be thawed with an aerosol that squirts a mixture of alcohol and lubricant into the keyhole (left). Another trick is to heat the door key with a match or cigarette lighter (right) before inserting it in a frozen lock. To avoid burning yourself, wear gloves or hold the key with pliers.

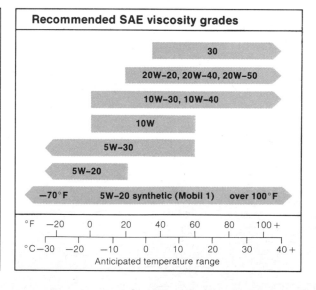

Recommended SAE viscosity grades

	Anticipated temperature range
30	
20W-20, 20W-40, 20W-50	
10W-30, 10W-40	
10W	
5W-30	
5W-20	
−70°F 5W-20 synthetic (Mobil 1) over 100°F	

°F −20 0 20 40 60 80 100 +
°C −30 −20 −10 0 10 20 30 40 +
Anticipated temperature range

Engine heaters and battery heaters

The difficulties of starting a car in winter can be eased by preheating the engine (to make cranking easier) or the battery (to provide more cranking power). The two steps can be used in combination to provide maximum improvement. The diagram below shows the five most common types of engine heaters plus two types of battery heaters. Extension cords to supply power to the heaters should be no more than 25 feet long and should be heavy enough to handle the specified wattage—No.16 wire is adequate for a 1,000-watt heater. All engine heaters require three-wire (grounded) extension cords.

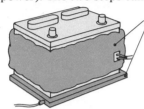

Battery heaters are easy to install and draw only 50 to 100 watts. Plate-type heater (under the battery) operates like a hot plate. Wraparound type resembles a heating pad.

Tank heater is mounted between car heater's outlet hose and the engine block's drain opening; coolant must be drained first. It may be difficult to mount heater near top of block in some cars. Device is very effective in keeping coolant and engine warm.

Radiator hose heater is spliced into lower radiator hose and clamped in place; coolant must be drained first. Device is less effective but easier to install than a tank heater.

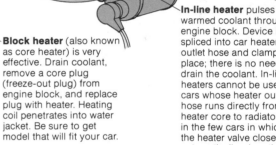

Battery heaters
Car heater supply hose
Car heater
Car heater outlet hose
Car heater outlet hose
T-fitting
Drain opening
Lower radiator hose
Clamps

Block heater (also known as core heater) is very effective. Drain coolant, remove a core plug (freeze-out plug) from engine block, and replace plug with heater. Heating coil penetrates into water jacket. Be sure to get model that will fit your car.

Dipstick heater is a simple, low-cost device that is marginally useful in temperate climates. Insert it in place of dipstick to warm crankcase oil. Replace dipstick before starting car.

In-line heater pulses warmed coolant through engine block. Device is spliced into car heater's outlet hose and clamped in place; there is no need to drain the coolant. In-line heaters cannot be used in cars whose heater outlet hose runs directly from heater core to radiator, nor in the few cars in which the heater valve closes automatically when the engine is turned off.

Caution: This illustration shows the typical placement of several types of heaters on the same engine. Only one heater should be used on any engine.

Tips for safe driving

If you are not accustomed to winter driving, precondition your reflexes by practicing in a safe spot, such as an empty supermarket parking lot, after a snowfall. Once on the road, stay well behind other cars to compensate for longer braking distances. Should you be caught in a snowstorm, keep moving at a moderate, even speed. Avoid unnecessary stops and sudden acceleration, braking, or turning. If you must stop, carefully consider the safety of the place you choose before you pull off the road. (Do not pull to the side of a country road—your tires could sink into a snow-filled drainage ditch.)

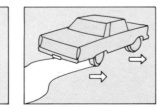

Clothes: Remove heavy outer garments as soon as the heater warms the car. Bulky outer garments restrict movement and increase fatigue. **Caution:** Stop the car in a safe spot before attempting to take off your coat.

Controlling a skid: Let up on the accelerator and steer in the same direction as the rear wheels are skidding. When the skid stops, steer *gently* back on course. Try not to overcorrect, or the car may skid in the opposite direction.

Road sense: Remember that bridges freeze first. Avoid passing if there is snow in the passing lane. Gently tap the brakes occasionally to determine how slippery the road is. Learn to "feel" the road by the way the car handles.

Braking: Gently pump the brake pedal rather than tramping down on it. If the car skids, let up on the brakes briefly—the car will snap out of the skid. In an emergency, steer into a snowbank to avoid an accident.

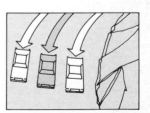

Cornering: Brake before you reach a curve, not in it. Do everything gently. If the curve is sharp, it is generally better to run a bit wide than to risk a skid by cutting the wheel too sharply. If a skid starts, let up on the accelerator.

297

Maintenance

Making your car easier to service

Most of the maintenance jobs you do on your car must be repeated at various intervals. Once you have done a job and become familiar with the procedure, it will seem easier the next time. Also, parts that you have removed before are less apt to be frozen by rust.

When you buy a new car—or a used car that is new to you—you receive two kinds of papers: legal papers and information papers. The legal papers dealing with registrations, insurance, ownership, and licenses must be carried as specified by the laws of your state. If you are not required to keep them in the car, make a folder or envelope for them and keep them at home or in a safe-deposit box where you will always be able to find them.

Information papers include the *owner's manual* and possibly a few instructions that came with the radio, the tire maker's warranty, and instructions for such optional equipment as sun roofs. To this you will want to add a loose-leaf notebook in which to keep track of maintenance or repairs you have done and to store any instructions that come with the parts you buy. You will also want to make your own notes for settings and adjustments, such as the temperature rating of the thermostat (if you should change it from standard) and any other how-to information you collect. You should also include the *Tuneup Data* supplement to this book.

Your car will be much easier to service in the future if you check it out when you first buy it. Some specifications may be hard to find or—like ignition timing on late-model Fords—may not be easily accomplished with the tools you have. By checking timing when the engine is new or properly tuned by a dealer, you can record the settings that work and mark them on the engine pulley (p.238). Then, whenever you want to check the timing, you can do so easily by using your own notes for reference.

Another good maintenance and troubleshooting technique is to label the various relays and electronic black boxes in the engine compartment and under the dash. Nearly all owner's manuals contain a wiring diagram that lists the car's electrical components and shows the wiring that connects them in the form of a map (see p.361). When you are familiarizing yourself with your new car, use the wiring diagram to locate each component that is not obvious. The alternator is easily recognized, but the horn relay, turn signal flasher, and other electrical components are not as easily identified.

You can use nail polish to paint labels on these parts, or you can use stick-on paper labels. Nail polish usually lasts longer and remains more readable because it does not fade or wash off.

You can label parts with their names or simply key them to the numbers in the wiring diagram. If you key the parts to the diagram, have several photocopies made of the wiring diagram and keep one in the car, one on your garage wall where you can refer to it without touching it with dirty hands, and one in your loose-leaf notebook.

If you add any extra equipment to your car, keep a master wiring diagram with your car records and add the new circuits (including the colors of the new wiring) to make future troubleshooting easier.

All cars require some servicing or repair (replacing brake linings, for instance) but usually not until they are several years old. If you plan to keep your car and do these jobs yourself, they will be much easier if you make certain preparations in advance in order to avoid future difficulties.

To get at the brake linings, you must remove the wheel and the brake drum (p.214). If you do this while the car is new, the drum will come right off as it is supposed to do. If you apply anti-seize compound to the fasteners and slip-fit joints, it will be easy to remove the brake drums for inspection and repair later on. If you do not take this precaution, what should be a simple repair may turn into a struggle with parts that are frozen together. Anti-seize compound is available from auto supply stores as a spray or in a brush-lid can.

Some parts worth treating with anti-seize compound are wheel lugs, retaining bolts (if used), brake bleeder valves, and fitted joints on brake drums. Fasteners on shock absorbers and in the exhaust system, removable access panels (if any), headlight-aiming screws, and adjusting nuts on the clutch and the parking brake cable can be treated without removing them or disturbing their adjustment. Spark plugs in aluminum cylinder heads should be treated whenever you remove the plug.

Sooner or later, most drivers will have to change a flat tire. In many instances, the wheel lugs have been tightened by power wrenches at a car dealership or garage. Even if you do not apply anti-seize compound to these fasteners, it is a good idea to change each wheel with the tools you normally carry in the car before you are unexpectedly called upon to do so on the road. You will become familiar with the procedure of jacking up the car. Also, if any of your tools prove to be inadequate, you can purchase better ones and add them to your tool kit.

Carry a short length of heavy board as a jack support. A piece of 2 by 8 wood about 1 foot long will work nicely. Buy or make two chocks to lock a wheel and hold the car in place while you jack it up. A short length of pipe that fits over your lug wrench will allow you to apply extra force to tight lug nuts.

Maintaining a car requires some special tools, or unusual sizes of standard tools. A few wrenches of the right size plus a screwdriver and a pair of locking pliers make a useful tool kit for emergency repairs (see p.167). You should also carry a flashlight and check its batteries once a month.

Buy a small supply of parts that you know you will need to service your car. These may include filters for the air cleaner, fuel system, and crankcase, a complete set of drive belts, cooling system hoses, spark plugs, distributor cap, rotor, and (if your car has conventional ignition) breaker points and a condenser. Seal the electrical parts and belts in a cardboard carton or in a food can with a plastic snap-on lid, then store them in the car trunk so that you will have a replacement for a part that fails while you are driving. Even if you are going to a wedding in your finest clothes and do not want to do the work yourself, you may find a service station that can install a drive belt for you. The station may or may not have the belt you need. If they have it, fine; if they do not have it, supplying your own belt will allow the service station's mechanic to do the job and prevent you from being stranded.

If you do not use these parts for emergency service, you can always employ them for routine maintenance. Then you can save the used parts for emergencies, if they are not too far gone, in much the same way that you would keep the worst tire in your set for the spare and use the best ones on the road.

As you work up to more and more sophisticated maintenance and repair jobs, you will find that your car becomes easier to service and that it runs better and more economically. As your efficiency increases with experience, you will need less time to do the routine maintenance jobs on your car.

How to repair your car

As you follow the maintenance instructions in Chapter 5 (see p.181), you may discover that certain parts of your car need to be repaired or replaced. You can look up these jobs in the list of contents at the right. You can also diagnose car problems with the help of the troubleshooting charts. Because certain repair jobs are too difficult for a beginner to attempt, the jobs are rated for difficulty, using the system shown below. If you feel that a certain job on your car is too complicated (or if it is not illustrated here), have the work done by a professional mechanic.

🔧	1 wrench means that the job can easily be performed by a NOVICE with no previous car repair experience.
🔧🔧	2 wrenches mean that the job can easily be performed by a BEGINNER with little previous car repair experience.
🔧🔧🔧	3 wrenches mean that the job can be performed by a PRACTICED DO-IT-YOURSELFER with some car repair experience.
🔧🔧🔧🔧	4 wrenches mean that the job should be tackled only by an EXPERIENCED AMATEUR MECHANIC with considerable car repair experience.
🔧🔧🔧🔧🔧	5 wrenches mean that the job should be undertaken only by an ADVANCED AMATEUR MECHANIC with extensive car repair experience.

Contents

Windshield wipers

Windshield wipers keep the windshield clear in bad weather and are essential for safe driving. To enable the wipers to work efficiently, keep both windshield and wipers clean by washing them about once a week. Wash the inside of the windshield as well, to maintain good visibility.

The *squeegees*—the parts of the wiper system that actually clean the windshield—are made of natural rubber, which is highly susceptible to deterioration. The squeegees must be flexible enough to follow the contour of the glass, and have edges sharp enough to cut through water and snow cleanly. Air pollution, weather, and time all affect the rubber, making it brittle and inflexible. Road grease can soften the rubber until the squeegees' edges are no longer sharp. Generally, squeegees (often called *refills*) should be replaced every 6 to 12 months. Damage may be visible, as when the rubber is bent, cracked, or eaten away, but often the only evidence of deterioration is an increasingly smeared windshield.

Smearing can also result from a smudged windshield or dirty wipers, so test the squeegees before replacing them. Wash the windshield and squeegees with mild soap and warm water. Rinse them thoroughly to remove all soap residue. Wet the windshield again, and run the wipers through a complete cycle. If they still skip, replace the squeegees.

The *blade assembly* should distribute pressure evenly along the entire length of the squeegee. If the metal is bent or if the swivel joints are corroded, pressure may be uneven, so that the wiper misses some areas of the glass. If so, replace the blade.

Wiper arms contain tension springs that exert the correct pressure on the blades. If the springs break, the arms must be replaced. Whenever you have to replace a part, take the old part with you to make sure you get the correct replacement.

Snow and ice can clog the blade assembly, preventing the wipers from flexing enough to maintain contact with the glass. Special winter wiper blades are made with a rubber boot that covers the entire blade assembly and keeps snow and ice out.

Common windshield wiper problems

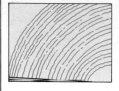

Smearing can be caused by a dirty windshield or wipers, by insufficient solvent or antifreeze in the washing solution, or by worn-out squeegees. Before replacing the squeegees, try cleaning the glass and wipers and adding the correct amount of solvent in summer or antifreeze in winter.

Smearing in only one direction occurs when the squeegee does not flip back and forth. This can be caused by extreme cold. Expose squeegees to warm air or rinse them in warm water. If the squeegees have hardened from age, replace them. The wrong-size squeegee can also cause this problem.

Chattering can be caused by a bent wiper arm that is no longer parallel to the glass or by a frozen squeegee. A bent arm can sometimes be straightened so that it remains parallel to the glass (p.301); if not, replace the arm. Correct a frozen squeegee as described above.

Water beads on the glass result from buildup of grease, oil, wax, or silicone. Thoroughly clean windshield and wipers with clean rags dipped in the solvent normally used to clean grease and silicone from bodywork before painting (p.324). Rinse windshield and wipers until no trace of solvent remains.

Rubber squeegee — Blade assembly — Connector — Wiper arm — Tension spring — Splined shaft

Replacing squeegees ⏱ 5–10 min

There are three basic lock designs for attaching the squeegee to the blade assembly, and the type of refill you need depends on the lock. Anco or Trico-type refill squeegees fit all North American cars and some foreign cars. One or the other of these types is available at most service stations. Many foreign cars use a clip system requiring special squeegee refills that may be available only from the dealer. If you prefer the convenience of the more readily available designs, simply replace the blade assemblies the first time you need squeegees, and thereafter replace only the squeegees. **Caution:** To avoid scratching the windshield, remove the blade assembly from the arm (p.301 before you replace a squeegee. When you have finished installing the new squeegees and have reattached the blade assemblies, tug on them to make sure that they are locked in position.

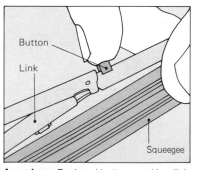

Anco type. Push red button on either link. Pull out squeegee along with the released link. Pull squeegee out of link. Thread refill through the free link, then through link still attached to blade assembly. Snap free link back into place.

Button — Link — Squeegee

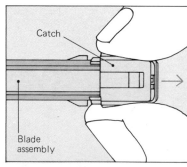

Trico type. Squeeze sides of the spring catch together and pull squeegee out. Thread end of refill without the spring catch onto blade assembly first. Push on the end of the squeegee with the spring catch until catch snaps into place.

Catch — Blade assembly

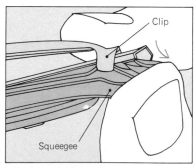

Clip type. Squeeze ends of the squeegee and twist them free of retaining clips. Slide squeegee out. Keep steel reinforcing strips, and fit them into grooves of refill. Slide refill into the blade assembly. Twist refill until clips engage holes in squeegee.

Clip — Squeegee

Replacing wiper blade assemblies ⏱ 5–10 min

Bayonet connector

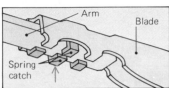

Anco: Press spring catch under blade connector up to release blade from arm, and pull blade off. To install new blade, slide it onto arm until spring catch locks in place.

Trico: Lift connector until post is disengaged from hole, press lever down to release blade from arm, and pull blade off. Slide new blade onto arm until post snaps into hole.

Side pin connector
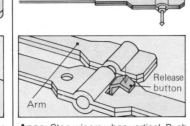
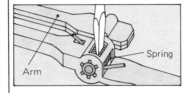

Anco: Stop wipers when vertical. Push in release button, and pull blade off. Push in release button on new blade, and pull pin out. Discard adapter, and push blade onto arm pin.

Trico: Stop wipers when vertical, press spring with screwdriver, and slide blade off. Push new blade onto arm pin, then pinch arm and blade together until spring locks.

Locking connector
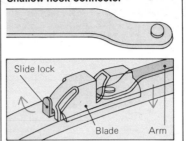
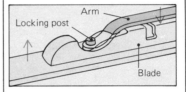

Anco: Pull slide lock out, then lift arm out of connector. Pull out slide lock on new blade, discard adapter, and push bar on arm down into slot in connector until bar locks in position.

Trico: Push blade toward base of arm to unlock connector, and lift arm out of slot in connector. Push bar on arm down into slot in new blade until bar locks securely in place.

Shallow hook connector
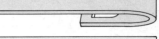
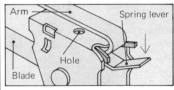

Anco: Pull slide lock out. Rotate blade and pull it off. Pull out slide lock on new blade, fit arm into connector, and rotate blade back to a horizontal position to lock it in place.

Trico: Press arm toward blade, rotate blade until perpendicular to arm, and slide blade out. Fit arm into connector of new blade, and rotate blade back to lock it in place.

Shepherd's crook connector
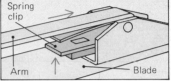

Anco: Squeeze spring clip inside hook upward to release blade, and slide blade off hook. Pull hook through connector on new blade until clip locks securely in position.

Trico: Push spring lever down until post disengages from hole in connector, then slide blade off arm. Pull hook through connector on new blade until post engages hole.

Replacing and adjusting wiper arms ⏱ 5–15 min

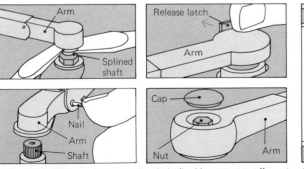

Wiper arms fit snugly onto splined shafts. You can pry off most arms using two screwdrivers (above, left). Do not chip car paint. If arm has a release latch, lift wiper off glass, pull out latch (above, right), then remove arm. If arm has a hole, lift wiper off glass and insert a brad nail into the hole (below, left) to release arm. On some imports, arm is held by a nut. Pry off plastic cap (if any), remove nut, then lift arm off shaft (below, right).

Positioning wiper arms: Wiper arms must be positioned so that they will not hit the sides or the bottom of the windshield frame. With the wipers turned off, fit the arm onto the splines of the shaft so that the blade rests about 1 in. (2.5 cm) from the frame. When positioning recessed windshield wipers, you must open the hood to see where to place the arms. Arms of recessed wipers generally rest on a stop when wipers are in *Park*, or *Off*, position.

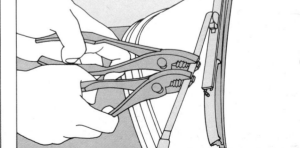

Straightening bent wiper arms: Turn off the engine when wipers are at midstroke. Look carefully at the arms to determine whether they are parallel to the windshield. (A squeegee that is not perpendicular to the glass is also evidence of a bent arm.) If arm is bent, grasp it with two pairs of pliers and twist it until it remains parallel to the glass when released. If tip of arm is bent, remove the blade assembly before twisting arm into shape.

Fixing windshield washers ⏱ 15 min–1 hr

To clean the windshield adequately, not only the wipers but the washer must be in good operating condition. The wipers alone will simply smear road film or light rain, dangerously reducing visibility.

Basically, all windshield washer systems contain the same components: a reservoir to hold the washing solution; a pump, operated either by an electric motor or, rarely, by foot; nozzles to deliver the spray to the windshield; and tubing that connects the pump with the nozzles. If no water, or very little, is being delivered to the windshield, the first and simplest thing to do is to check that the reservoir is full. Even if you filled it recently, bad road conditions can consume a full reservoir of fluid in a short time. Use a solution of windshield washer fluid diluted as instructed on the container. In winter, plain water will freeze and crack the reservoir, but you should use the washer fluid even in summer because it contains special cleaners. Never use engine antifreeze in the washer—it will damage car paint.

Some washer failures are caused by kinks in the tubing or when dirt clogs the system. To find blockages, check the system from end to end. Start at the nozzles, which have small openings that clog easily. Use a sewing needle or straight pin to clear away any dirt. If the nozzles still do not work, disconnect the tubing at the nozzle end and check for water pressure when the pump is working; if water comes out of the tubing but not the nozzles, replace the nozzles. If no

water comes out of the tubing, check it for kinks and straighten it out. Replace any cracked, brittle tubing—it is likely to leak. Next, disconnect the tubing at the pump. If water comes out, you have missed a problem in the tubing or nozzles. If no water comes from the pump, clean the fine wire screen (if any) in the reservoir, which may be clogged.

If none of these procedures work, either there is a problem in the electrical connections (between the pump and the dashboard switch, between the switch and battery, or between the pump and pump ground) or the pump itself is defective. To find a problem in the electrical system, see *Tracing electrical faults*, pp. 361–363. Start by checking for a blown fuse, then for voltage across the pump terminals. The pump is defective if everything else checks out. You can replace the pump with another just like it, but pumps that are mounted in the reservoir (including AMC, Chrysler, Ford, and some GM systems) can be very difficult to remove and replace; doing so may require special tools. An easier and cheaper alternative is to install a *universal windshield washer pump*. These are sold in kits that include a combination pump and motor, plus all the necessary fittings and connectors. The pump is mounted between the reservoir and the tubing to the nozzles, so that the old pump need not be removed—it is simply disconnected and bypassed. A universal kit can also be used to convert a mechanical system to an electrical one.

Cleaning the system

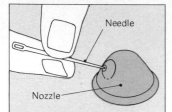

1. Clean the nozzles with a needle or pin, taking care not to enlarge the holes. If the nozzles are still clogged, remove them and blow through them. If this does not work, replace them with new nozzles.

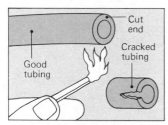

2. Straighten kinked tubing (tubing to wiper arm nozzles is especially prone to twisting). Replace cracked tubing. If only the ends are cracked, cut off ½ in. and soften cut ends by holding them over a match. Flush tubing with warm water.

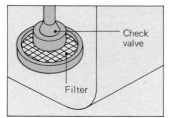

3. A filter screen may be located either at the bottom of the check valve (a one-way valve that prevents fluid from returning to the reservoir) or in the pump inlet tube. Flush the filter with warm water. If the filter is corroded, replace it.

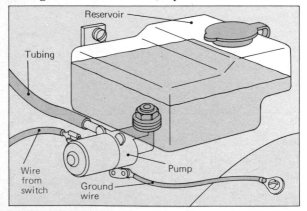

A typical windshield washer system has a combination pump and motor mounted in the bottom of the fluid reservoir. Removing and replacing such pumps may be difficult. You will need a screwdriver and a deep-socket set as well as patience and agility.

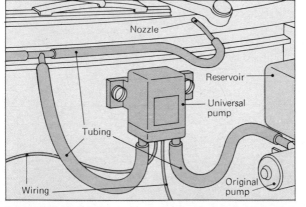

A universal windshield washer pump can be installed to bypass the original pump, which is simply disconnected and left in place. The new pump is mounted outside the reservoir and is spliced into the tubing between the reservoir and the nozzles.

Adjusting the nozzles

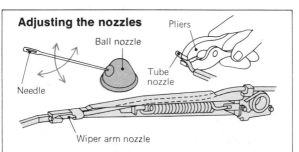

Ball nozzles swivel in their sockets; to redirect the spray, insert a needle into the opening and turn the nozzle. *Tube nozzles* are metal tubes with crimped ends. Sometimes you can move them easily. If not, grasp the tubes gently with pliers and bend the nozzles into position. *Wiper arm nozzles* fit into the wipers and cannot be adjusted. Set adjustable nozzles so that the spray hits the windshield 2 in. below the top of the wiper arc when the car is parked.

Repairing a remote-control mirror 1–2 hr

Remote-control mirrors are operated by three cables, which are attached to a bracket that is an extension of the control knob in the car. The cables are held together by a casing for the length that they are routed through the door, which protects them and keeps them out of the way of the window-winding mechanism. The cables separate again at a bracket behind the mirror glass, and are attached to the mirror in a triangular pattern. When you swivel the control knob, one or more of the cables are pulled; this motion is transmitted through the casing to the mirror, which is swiveled into the desired position.

Because all the connections between the cables and the control knob and between the cables and the mirror are permanent, few repairs can be made. If the cables stick or bind, you can lubricate them at the mirror and the control knob as illustrated at the right. However, if that does not solve the problem, or if one of the cables is broken, you must replace the entire remote-control mirror assembly, since the cables cannot be detached. Before you remove a mirror that sticks, carefully examine the way the cable casing is routed through the door to see if it is kinked or if it is tangled in the window-winding mechanism, as one of these conditions may have caused the problem. (In the latter case, the window will not wind properly either.) If the mirror glass is broken, an auto glass shop can replace it.

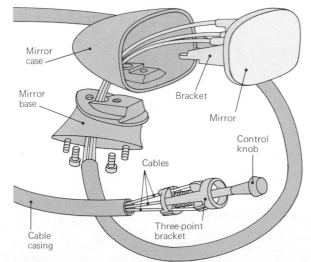

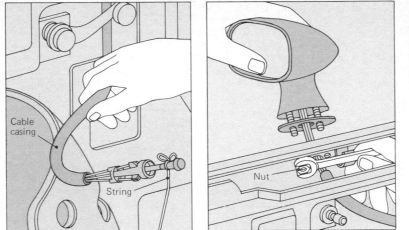

1. Remove the door panel as illustrated on page 308. Note the cable routing very carefully; if it is complex, run a piece of string along the route before removing the cables. If the cable casing is reinstalled in the wrong position, it could interfere with the window-winding mechanism.

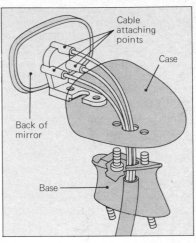

2. Feed the cables through the door panel just far enough to give some slack. Loosen the self-tapping screws or the nuts under the mirror, but do not remove them until you are holding the mirror, or it will fall and break. Lift the mirror and gasket off the door, and carefully pull out the cables.

3. Unscrew the screws inside the mirror base, and remove the base from the mirror. If there are screws or a clip on top of the mirror that hold it in the case, remove them. Pull the mirror, with the attached cables, out of the case so that you have access to the back of the mirror.

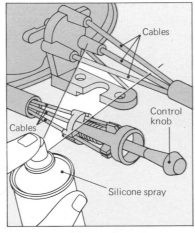

4. Lubricate the cables at the mirror and at the control knob with silicone spray. Do not use oil—it will eventually gum up with dust or dirt and prevent the cables from operating smoothly. Work the cables by hand to free them. If they still stick, replace the entire mirror assembly.

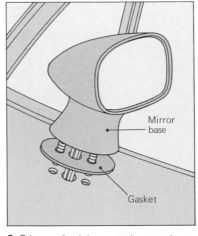

5. Prime and paint a new mirror as shown on pages 322–325. Reassemble a repaired mirror by reversing the order in which you took it apart. Secure the mirror to the door before routing the cable. Remember to install the gasket between the mirror and the door, or the paint will be marred.

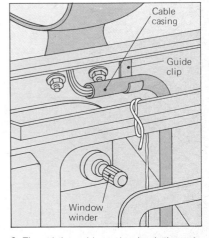

6. Thread the cable casing back through the inside of the door exactly as it came out; follow the string if you used one. Be sure to get the casing in the guide clip at the beginning of the route, and check to be sure that it does not cross any window glass channel.

Finding and fixing body leaks

Water, air, and dust leaks can be annoying and uncomfortable. An unchecked water leak can start a serious rust problem, ruin carpeting, or render the trunk unfit for storing anything except the spare tire. Finding leaks can be tricky, since they do not always originate at the points where water appears inside the car. Before trying to stop a leak, use one or more of the tests illustrated below to locate all problem spots. Because several leaks may be collecting at a single point, or several air leaks may sound like a single noise, always continue testing until all possibilities have been checked.

The *water test* is the only way to find leaks around the windshield, the rear window, or any stationary glass. It can also be used around doors and the trunk lid. Be sure to use a gentle stream of water, since strong water pressure could actually cause a leak. The *chalk test* is best for rubber seals, such as those around the doors and the trunk lid. Always use soft artist's chalk, not hard blackboard chalk. *The paper test* can help determine whether a seal is too tight or too loose. Small air leaks that whistle when the car is moving can be especially hard to pinpoint. Use the *tape test* to locate the source of wind noise that can only be heard when the car is moving. If you cannot tell where a small leak or noise is coming from, or if more than one source seems to be involved, try the *air test*. After you have found a leak, mark the exact spot with masking tape so that, later, you can precisely locate all the points that need repair.

While you are checking, keep in mind some common problems. Damaged weather stripping is the most common cause of leaking doors and trunk lids, but poor alignment might also be at fault (see pp.306–307). Leaks in the trunk might come from the taillight housings or the rear window as well as from the trunk lid. Body leaks can develop at seams or where trim is screwed into holes in the body panels.

Products available at auto parts or hardware stores make sealing most small leaks fairly simple. Clear plastic sealer or silicone caulking compound, available in black or clear, is squeezed directly into the gap between the windshield or other stationary glass and the gasket. Caulking compound is also useful for sealing seams and screw holes in the car body (see p.327). If repositioning the weather stripping does not stop a leak, self-adhesive household weather stripping can be used to shim up uneven auto weather stripping that does not seal properly.

Weather stripping seals the doors and trunk against leaks. If it is badly worn, dried out, cracked, or torn, it cannot seal properly and must be replaced. Weather stripping is not simply glued in place; various combinations of tabs, clips, screws, and integral studs fit into specific holes in the car body. The cross section shapes and the thickness of these seals vary widely from car to car. Since the weather stripping made for one car will not fit most others, buy weather stripping that is identical to the original from a new-car dealer, or have custom replacements made for your car. Weather stripping obtained from wrecking yards is likely to be as old, worn, or dried out as the weather stripping you want to replace.

Testing for leaks ⏱ 15–30 min

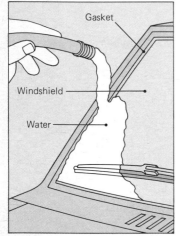

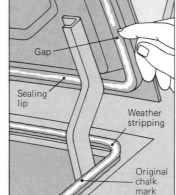

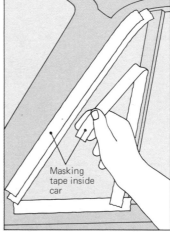

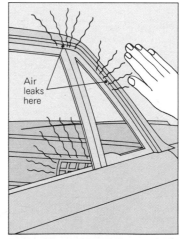

Water test: Slowly run a gentle stream of water over all the gaskets of the area being tested (here, the windshield). Start at the bottom and move up both sides, then across the top. Have a helper inside the car use tape to mark any points that leak.

Chalk test: Open the trunk lid (as here) or the door, and rub soft artist's chalk all along the weather stripping's contact edge. Gently close the lid completely, then reopen it. Spots that have not picked up traces of chalk show where lid is not sealing properly.

Paper test: Close car door on a strip of paper about 2 in. wide and 6 in. long. Pull the paper out; it should drag as you pull on it. If the paper comes out easily or falls out, the weather stripping's seal is too loose. If the paper tears, the seal is too tight.

Tape test: Use masking tape to completely seal the window that seems to be leaking. Drive the car at the speed at which the noise usually occurs. Have a helper slowly peel off the tape until you hear the noise again, then mark the spot that was just uncovered.

Air test: Turn the heater fan on *High*. Roll up all windows and close the doors tightly. Feel along outside all doors and windows for escaping air, and mark each spot. There may be more than one leak, so continue until you have checked all possibilities.

Repairing leaks ⏱ 5–20 min

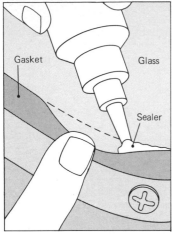

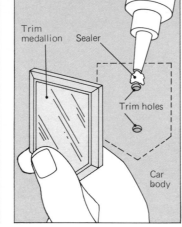

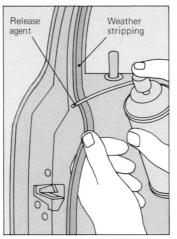

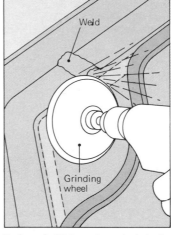

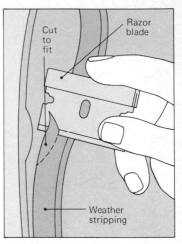

Stationary glass: Gently pry the gasket away from the glass and clean the leaking area thoroughly so that the sealer will adhere properly. Squeeze an even bead of silicone or plastic sealer into the gap. If many spots leak, apply a bead all around the glass.

Body trim holes: Remove the trim as shown on pages 326–327. Repair any small rust spots that have developed as shown on page 324. When the touch-up paint is dry, squeeze a dab of silicone caulking compound into each trim hole, then replace the trim.

Weather stripping: If weather stripping is loose or twisted, spray weather-strip release agent under the rubber before removing it. Clean and dry both exposed surfaces. Apply thin coat of weather-strip adhesive to each surface and press in place.

Bodywork: High spots or dents in the bodywork where it contacts weather stripping can cause leaks. Grind down welds or high spots as shown on page 316. Fill slight depressions with body filler (p.317). Prime and paint the repair (pp.322–325).

Adjustments: Small body irregularities can be corrected. Remove weather stripping. In low spots, add household weather stripping under the original. In high spots, shave down back of weather stripping with a razor. Reglue with weather-strip adhesive.

Installing new weather stripping ⏱⏱ 30 min–1 hr

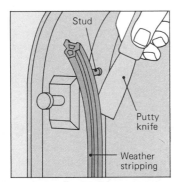

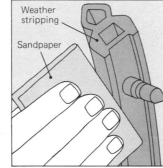

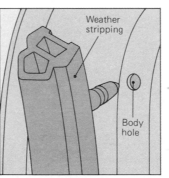

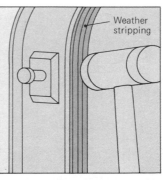

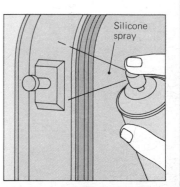

1. Remove all fasteners in the old weather stripping (unscrew screws and pry out any clips or studs). Spray weather-strip release agent under the seal. When adhesive softens, pull stripping off.

2. Remove traces of old adhesive from door with adhesive cleaner or release agent. Clean powder off new weather stripping with adhesive cleaner or lightly sand it off with fine sandpaper.

3. Carefully check correct position for new weather stripping by mounting it in the body holes before applying adhesive. Remove it and apply thin coats of adhesive to door and to weather stripping.

4. Push weather stripping in place on door; work quickly, or adhesive could dry. Push or tap clips or tabs into their holes. Screw in retaining screws. Butt ends together and glue down if necessary.

5. To preserve the new weather stripping and improve the seal, spray it with silicone lubricant. This is also the best treatment for old weather stripping; lubricating it occasionally will keep it in good condition.

305

Adjusting doors, hoods, and trunk lids 🕐 10–20 min

There are several standard means for adjusting the fit of doors, hoods, trunk lids, and other body panels on a car. The most commonly used are slotted holes, caged plates, shims, and adjustable stops. Sometimes two or more of these are used in combination to correctly position or align a body panel.

Slotted holes are simply elongated bolt holes that allow a panel to be shifted either up and down, from side to side, or in and out (but in only one of these directions for each set of holes). The panels are positioned before the bolts are completely tightened; when the bolts are tight, the panel is pinched between the nut and bolt so that it cannot move out of position. Because the bolts do not fit snugly in the holes, flat washers may be placed between the panel and the bolt head to spread the load.

Caged plates are heavy blocks of metal with threaded holes that receive bolts. They are used primarily to adjust the fit of doors. The plates are held in place inside the door or the body by sheet-metal cages that are welded into the door or body. The cages are bigger than the plates so that the plates can be moved around inside them. The difference in size between the cages and the plates determines how much adjustment is possible. The bolt holes in the door and body are larger than the bolts or the threaded holes in the plates. Each caged plate allows horizontal and vertical adjustments to be made simultaneously. Bolts are threaded through the door hinge and into the holes in the plate, the door is shifted to the correct alignment, and the bolts are then tightened. Tightening the bolts squeezes the body metal between the plate and the hinge so that the door cannot be moved out of position.

Shims are metal spacers that are fitted around the shaft of a bolt in order to increase the distance between two parts being bolted together. The shims are placed between the two parts. Shims may be round washers or open on one side so that they can be slipped onto a bolt that has only been loosened, not removed. Often, shims are fitted as part of the original body alignment. Adjustments can be made by removing shims to bring panels closer together, or by adding shims to separate the panels.

Adjustable stops are used on the hood and sometimes on the trunk lid to help the hinges support the panel. Stops also serve to keep corners at the correct height so that the panels will be level with the fenders. An adjustable stop is just a large bolt with a rubber bumper covering the head. The supported panel simply rests on the bumper; the stop does not secure the panel in any way. The bolt is threaded into a nut that is welded to the underside of the body. The bolt is screwed into the welded nut to lower the stop and is unscrewed to raise the stop. A second nut, the *locknut,* is tightened down against the top of the body to lock the bolt in position once it has been adjusted. Some *self-locking* stops have no locknuts; other stops can be adjusted without removing the rubber bumpers. However, all stops function in essentially the same way. When the car's hood is closed, it rests on the stops.

Adjusting doors

The doors of a car should fit flush with the body with a uniform gap of about ¼ inch all around in order to seal properly. The primary support for a door is its hinges, and these should always be adjusted first. The caged plates in the body allow the doors to be moved up and down and forward and back. The caged plates in the door itself allow the door to be moved in and out. Two people are needed to move a heavy door into position; then one person must hold the door steady while the other person tightens the bolts.

When the hinges have been adjusted so that the door hangs properly, close the door gently and note whether it is lifted up, pulled down, forced in, or left too loose by the latch assembly. If so, the striker—the

Door hinges

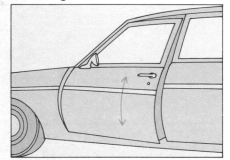

1. Before making any hinge adjustments, open the door and check to see if it is sagging (the most common problem with door alignment). Try to move a sagging door up and down. If it moves, one or more of the hinge bolts is loose and must be tightened. When all the bolts are tight, close the door and examine it to determine what hinge adjustments are necessary. Always make hinge-to-body adjustments first, then hinge-to-door adjustments. Do not try to do both at once.

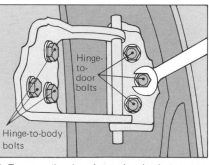

2. To move the door forward or back, or up or down, loosen all the bolts holding the hinges to the body. To move the door in or out, loosen the bolts holding the hinges to the door. Loosen the bolts only enough so that two people can move the door. Push and pull the door into position, then gently close it and check the fit. Readjust as necessary until the alignment is correct, then have an assistant hold the open door steady while you tighten the bolts.

Door latch strikers

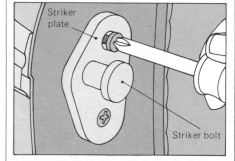

If the door is pulled out of alignment when it is closed and the hinges have already been adjusted, the striker is out of alignment. Loosen a striker bolt with the appropriate tool (p.307). Loosen a striker plate by loosening the screws. Make it just loose enough so that you can move it with light hammer taps. Tap the striker carefully into position. Close the door gently to check the alignment before retightening the striker bolt or striker plate completely.

Hood hinges

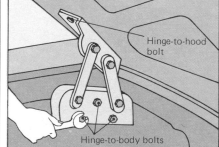

Examine the closed hood carefully to determine what adjustments are necessary. If the hood needs to be lowered or raised, loosen all the bolts holding both hinges to the body just enough so that two people can push and pull the hood into position. If it needs to be moved forward or back, loosen all the bolts holding the hinges to the hood. Partially tighten the bolts. Carefully lower the hood and check the new alignment before tightening the bolts fully.

part of the latch mounted on the body—needs to be adjusted. There are two types of strikers: striker bolts and striker plates. Both are adjusted by shifting their caged plates in or out and up or down until the door closes tightly without being yanked or forced. Striker bolts vary widely; you may need a Pozidriv® screwdriver, Allen wrench, Torx® bit, or locking pliers to make the adjustment. Make sure you have the tool needed to adjust the striker in your car.

Adjusting hoods

A hood should fit flush with the surrounding bodywork with an even gap all around the perimeter. Three support mechanisms keep the hood in place: the hinges position the hood and attach it to the car; adjustable stops keep the opening end of the hood level with the fenders; and the latch keeps the hood closed and supports its opening end.

As the main hood support, the hinges must always be adjusted first. (Welded hinges, of course, are not adjustable.) On bolted hoods, one part of each hinge is bolted to the body through slotted holes that allow the hood to be moved up and down. The other part is bolted to the hood through slotted holes so that the hood can be moved forward and back. Two people should make the adjustment, as hoods are unwieldy.

After the hinges are adjusted properly, set the adjustable stops to keep the hood level with the fenders. Because the corners of the hood rest on the stops, lowering a stop will lower that corner of the hood and raising it will raise the corner. Never use adjustable stops to compensate for misaligned hinges—the hood could be bent out of shape.

Adjust the latch assembly last. Two adjustments are possible on many cars: If the striker is not centered on the latch, shift the striker in its slotted bolt holes until it is centered. If the hood is hard to close or is still loose enough to lift when latched, shift the latch assembly up or down in its slotted holes.

Adjusting lids

Trunk lids, like doors, must fit evenly with about a ¼-inch gap all around if they are to seal properly. The hinges are adjusted first. Generally, only the parts of the hinges bolted to the lid are adjustable. Slotted bolt holes allow the lid to be moved forward and back on the hinges. The height of the lid is often adjusted by adding or subtracting shims between the hinges and the lid. Trunk latches can usually be adjusted from side to side so that the striker is centered in the latch, and up and down so that the lid closes tightly without excessive slamming.

Adjusting devices

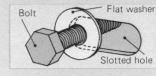

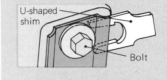

Slotted holes are used for bolts on lids and doors. When bolt is loosened, hinge moves in two directions.

Caged plates have threaded holes for hinge bolts. When its bolts are loosened, a plate can be moved in many directions.

Shims are placed between two parts that are bolted together. Adding or subtracting shims alters the alignment.

Adjustable stops are rubber-tipped bolts that can be adjusted up or down. They use locknuts or are self-locking.

Adjustable stops

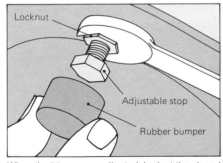

When the hinges are adjusted, look at the closed hood and note whether any corners or edges are higher or lower than the fenders. If so, one or more of the adjustable stops is too high or too low. Pry the rubber bumper off the top of the stop, loosen the locknut with a wrench, and screw the stop up or down as needed. Tighten the locknut and replace the bumper when the stop is at the correct height. Repeat on all the stops until the hood is flush with the body.

Hood and trunk latches

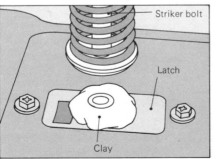

1. To determine whether the striker is centered on the latch, put a lump of clay on the latch and slowly lower the hood or trunk lid until the striker leaves an indentation in the clay. If the mark is off-center, loosen the screws holding the striker, and shift it until it is centered on the latch. On most hoods the latch assembly is mounted on the radiator support, and the striker is mounted on the hood. Trunk lids vary: the latch assembly may be mounted on the lid or on the body.

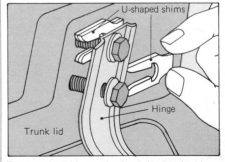

2. Close the hood or lid and note whether it is hard to close or still loose enough to move when it is latched. In either case, loosen the locknut; then screw the striker bolt out to tighten the latch or in to loosen it. Or loosen the bolts holding the latch assembly on the radiator support, then lower or raise the entire latch assembly to tighten or loosen the latch. When properly adjusted, the hood should close tightly without being slammed too hard (all require some slamming).

Trunk hinges

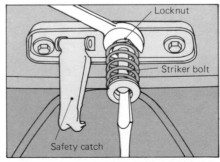

To move the lid forward or back, loosen the hinge bolts just enough to push lid into position. If the lid must be raised, close it and pile shims up on it until they reach the height of the fender. This will be a good approximation of how many shims to add. If the lid should be lowered, pile the shims on the fender until they reach the lid to determine how many shims to remove. Loosen the hinge bolts just enough to slip U-shaped shims on or off. Remove the bolts to add or remove washers.

Repair / **Bodywork**

Removing fixtures and panels from car doors ☑☑☑ 30 min–1 hr

The removal of an inside door panel is the first step in many door-related repairs, such as those to window glass (pp.310–311), remote-control mirrors (p.303), sheet metal on doors (pp.314–317), and lubrication of mechanical parts inside the door. Although it is not difficult to remove the door panel itself (see opposite page), various fixtures must be removed from the panel first. This is because the screws or bolts that hold these fixtures in place go through openings in the panel and are fastened onto the door's inner

metal panels. You will often have to search for the screws or bolts because they are hidden from view by the fixture or by a piece of trim. Sometimes you will also have to search for and remove miscellaneous screws or bolts that do not hold a fixture in place but help to hold the panel to the door. Procedures for removing several different door fixtures are given on these two pages. Since the types of fixtures and the way they are attached vary from one car model to another, use the information given here as a general

guide. To take out the door panel, remove only those fixtures that hold the panel in place. If the panel buckles when you pull on a fixture, that fixture is not holding the panel in place.

> **Tools:** Screwdrivers, awl or punch, metal ruler or spring-clip removal tool, wrenches, special door-panel removal tool, rubber mallet.
> **Materials:** Replacement parts, duct tape.

Window crank handles

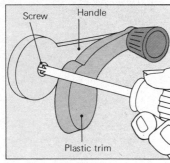

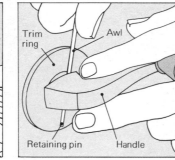

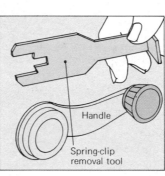

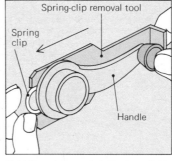

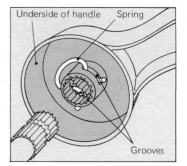

A screw holds some handles in place. To expose the screw, it may be necessary to lift up a strip of plastic trim on the handle (shown). Remove the screw, then pull off the handle.

A retaining pin holds this handle in place. To expose the pin, push the trim ring at the base of the handle against the panel. Force pin out with an awl or punch, then pull handle off.

A spring clip under the base holds this handle in place. To disengage the spring clip, use a metal ruler or a special spring-clip removal tool (shown here).

Hold the ruler or special tool parallel to the arm of the handle, wedge it between the base of the handle and the door panel, then push on the ruler or tool to force the spring out.

If spring is damaged, replace it with a new one. To put handle back on, position spring so that it fits into the grooves of the handle as shown. Then push handle back into place.

Arm rests and door handles

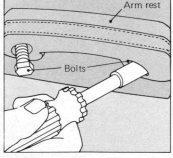

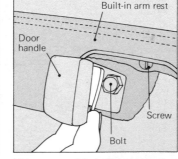

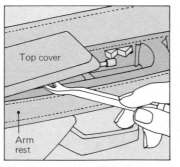

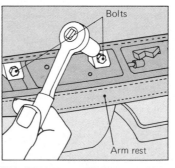

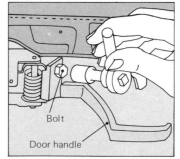

Two bolts, located under the arm rest, hold this arm rest to the door panel. Remove the two bolts. The arm rest will fall away from the panel.

This arm rest is built into the door panel. To remove the panel, the door handle must be removed. Lift handle to remove mounting bolt and screw.

To remove this arm rest, the top cover must be pried off first. Use a screwdriver or another flat-tipped tool. Be careful not to damage arm rest.

With the top cover off, use a wrench to remove the two bolts that hold the arm rest to the inner metal door panel. Then pry panel edges away from door.

If the inside door panel will not clear the door handle, remove the handle from its control mechanism by unscrewing door handle's mounting bolt.

308

Hidden screws

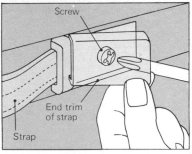

Screw

End trim of strap

Strap

Search for hidden screws and remove them as necessary. To find this screw, pry up the end trim of the door strap.

Removing a door panel

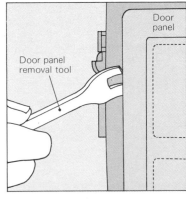

Door panel

Door panel removal tool

1. Remove all screws, bolts, handles, arm rests, and hardware that hinder removal of the door panel. Use a screwdriver, putty knife, or a special door-panel removal tool (shown) to pry the panel off the door.

3. Gently pull the wind-rain barrier off the door. It is usually held in place by tape or by an adhesive bead on the door. The barrier is made of plastic, paper, or felt. If it tears while it is being removed, repair it with silver duct tape, sold in hardware stores.

Power door locks

Screws

Lock panel

Multi-wire connector

Remove arm rest, door handle, and lock panel. Pull out panel; remove screws holding connector to panel.

Removal tool

Door

Clips

Panel

2. Wedge the panel-removal tool between the panel and the door. Working around the edges of the panel, gently pry it off. Metal or plastic clips on the back of the panel hold the panel to the door. If any of the clips are damaged, replace them. Once the panel is free, you can reach any other connections behind it.

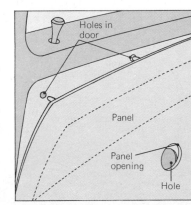

Holes in door

Panel

Panel opening

Hole

4. To reinstall the panel, align the clips on the back of the panel with the holes in the door. Then press panel into place. Gently hammer the panel with a rubber mallet to accurately align the openings in the panel with the screw or bolt holes in the door. Then reinstall all parts that were removed from the door panel.

Door-lock knobs

Knob   Post

Pull off knob

Some lock knobs are removed by unscrewing them from their posts (left). Other knobs are pulled or pried off (right).

Replacing a door-latch mechanism

The door-latch mechanism in many cars is installed from inside the door, and its removal is a complicated job best left to a professional mechanic. In some cars, however, the latch mechanism is installed on the side of the door. It is relatively easy to replace this type of mechanism; all that is needed is an Allen wrench and a replacement mechanism (internal door-latch parts are rarely available separately).

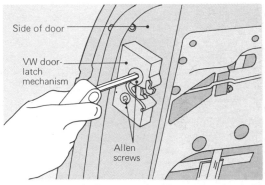

Side of door

VW door-latch mechanism

Allen screws

1. With door panel off, remove the Allen screws that hold the latch mechanism to the side of the door.

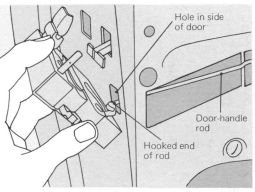

Hole in side of door

Door-handle rod

Hooked end of rod

2. Gently pull the latch mechanism away from the door and disengage the latch from the hooked end of the rod that is operated by the door handle.
3. When installing the new latch mechanism, lift the door handle rod and pull on it so that its hooked end fits into the hole in the side of the door. Then fit the hooked end of the rod into the latch mechanism. Align and position the latch mechanism on the side of the door and reinstall the Allen screws. Reinstall the door panel and all the hardware that was removed from the panel.

Wind-rain barrier

Adjusting window-winding mechanisms ⬛⬛⬛ 1–2 hr

Windows that do not close properly allow annoying leaks and wind noise. Most problems arise when the window binds in its channels, either because the mechanism is corroded or because the window glass is not properly aligned. These faults can be corrected by a home mechanic. Replacing broken glass or installing a new window winder that must be riveted in place are jobs for a professional.

There are two types of movable windows: framed and frameless. Framed windows are surrounded by metal channels that guide the glass. Frameless windows are guided by a mechanism inside the door.

On both types, the same basic components control window movement. The *window winder* is attached directly to the crank inside the door (or to the electric motor on power windows); the winder moves the glass up and down and holds it in position. The *winder arm* is attached to the *lift channel,* which actually holds the glass. The *pivot guide,* also attached to the lift channel, keeps the glass aligned with the top of the door as the window is raised and lowered. *Front and rear channels* (usually on frameless windows), a single *run channel* (usually on framed windows) or a guide tube guide the glass and keep it in position. *Upper stops* and *lower stops* control how far a window can travel. *Glass stabilizers*—padded brackets that press gently against the inside of the window—hold the glass steady.

When a window is binding but you cannot see any obvious misalignment, remove the inner door panels (pp.308–309) and try spraying the mechanism with penetrating solvent to dissolve corrosion. Then spray on silicone lubricant to keep the mechanism operating smoothly. Before making any adjustments, be sure that the door is properly aligned (see pp.306–307) and that the weather stripping is not damaged (see pp.304–305). Whenever the door hinges are adjusted, check the window alignment of frameless windows.

There are four common problems with window alignment. The window may be located too far forward or backward, so that it binds in its channels or frame. The window may be tilted forward or backward, which would cause it to bind and prevent it from opening and closing completely. Or the top edge of the glass may be set too far out or in, so that it does

Framed windows with tape or cable drive
(VW Rabbit and some GM cars, including X-cars)

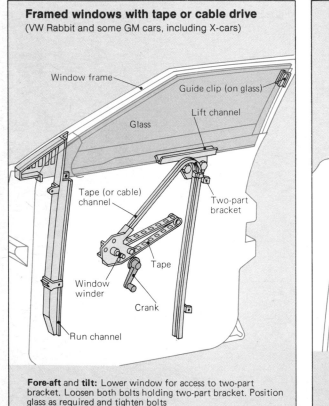

Fore-aft and tilt: Lower window for access to two-part bracket. Loosen both bolts holding two-part bracket. Position glass as required and tighten bolts

Framed windows with a single-run channel
(many AMC, Chrysler, and GM cars)

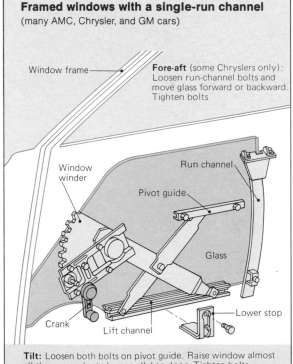

Tilt: Loosen both bolts on pivot guide. Raise window almost all the way and set glass parallel to door. Tighten bolts
Lower stop: Loosen bolt through slotted hole that holds stop in place. Push stop into position and tighten bolt. Adjust all upper and lower stops this way

Frameless windows with run channels
(late-model Chryslers, older Fords, and many GM cars)

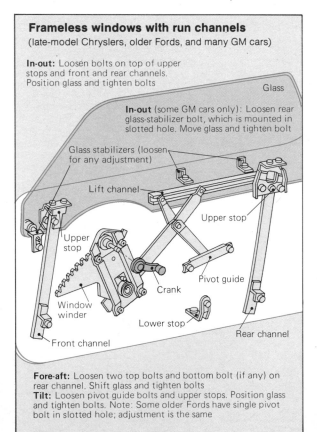

Fore-aft: Loosen two top bolts and bottom bolt (if any) on rear channel. Shift glass and tighten bolts
Tilt: Loosen pivot guide bolts and upper stops. Position glass and tighten bolts. Note: Some older Fords have single pivot bolt in slotted hole; adjustment is the same

not fit against the weather stripping properly. The upper or lower stops may be improperly set, preventing the window from opening or closing completely or allowing it to be raised so high that it breaks.

Because framed windows travel in their channels, adjustments are seldom needed or available. Usually, a single adjustment combines fore-aft position and tilt. Some framed windows have lower stops, but the frame itself sets the upper travel limit for the glass. Aligning frameless windows may require any of the adjustments described above, and sometimes more than one will be needed. To determine exactly what is wrong with a window, examine it carefully in various positions; the type of misalignment is often more obvious at one window height than another. Compare the window that needs adjustment to its counterpart on the other side of the car to see what the correct position should be. If more than one adjustment is necessary, make one at a time. Loosening everything at once is likely to cause problems.

Before you can adjust a window, you must remove the trim panel as shown on pages 308–309. The window-winding mechanism itself is behind the inner sheet metal and is not visible. Some adjusting bolts come through the sheet metal and are tightened against it; other adjustments are made through access holes in the sheet metal. The number, types, and locations of adjusters vary considerably on different car models, but the general procedures are similar. Typical window-winding mechanisms are illustrated on these two pages. Your car may have all or some of them, and their locations may vary slightly. When you think that you have found the proper adjuster, loosen its bolts, nuts, or screws slightly and gently try to move the glass in the desired direction. (You may have to wind the window up or down to reach certain adjusters through the access holes.) Always loosen the glass stabilizers, if any, before making an adjustment. When the glass is aligned, push it out gently against the weather stripping, set the stabilizers so that they just touch the glass, and tighten them. Do not use the stabilizers to force the glass out, or the window will not wind smoothly. Adjust all upper and lower stops as shown in the second illustration on the opposite page.

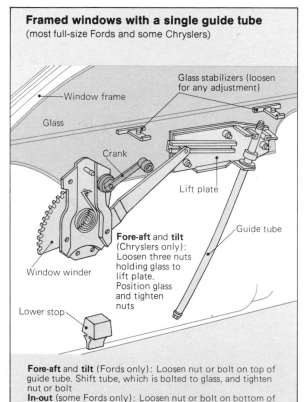

Framed windows with a single guide tube
(most full-size Fords and some Chryslers)

Labels: Window frame; Glass; Glass stabilizers (loosen for any adjustment); Crank; Lift plate; Guide tube; Window winder; **Fore-aft** and **tilt** (Chryslers only): Loosen three nuts holding glass to lift plate. Position glass and tighten nuts; Lower stop

Fore-aft and **tilt** (Fords only): Loosen nut or bolt on top of guide tube. Shift tube, which is bolted to glass, and tighten nut or bolt
In-out (some Fords only): Loosen nut or bolt on bottom of guide tube. Position glass and tighten nut or bolt

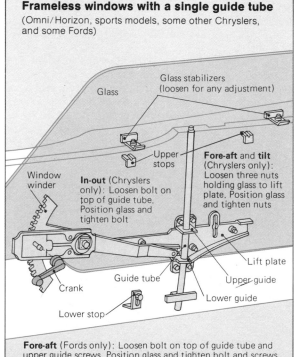

Frameless windows with a single guide tube
(Omni/Horizon, sports models, some other Chryslers, and some Fords)

Labels: Glass; Glass stabilizers (loosen for any adjustment); Upper stops; **Fore-aft** and **tilt** (Chryslers only): Loosen three nuts holding glass to lift plate. Position glass and tighten nuts; Window winder; **In-out** (Chryslers only): Loosen bolt on top of guide tube. Position glass and tighten bolt; Crank; Guide tube; Lift plate; Upper guide; Lower guide; Lower stop

Fore-aft (Fords only): Loosen bolt on top of guide tube and upper guide screws. Position glass and tighten bolt and screws
In-out (Fords only): Loosen lower guide screws. Position glass and tighten screws
Caution: On passenger side, tighten rear lower guide screw first, then front screw

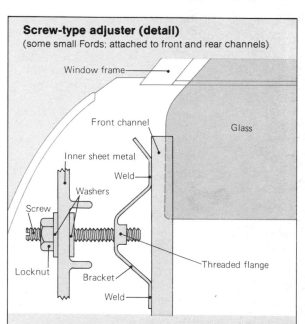

Screw-type adjuster (detail)
(some small Fords; attached to front and rear channels)

Labels: Window frame; Front channel; Glass; Inner sheet metal; Weld; Screw; Washers; Locknut; Bracket; Weld; Threaded flange

Fore-aft, tilt, and **in-out** (depending on location and number of screw adjusters): Loosen all locknuts and screws on front and rear channels. Position glass firmly in upper rear corner and back edge of window frame (Pinto and Bobcat only) or position glass with its top edge 4 in. above bottom of window frame (Maverick and Comet only). While helper holds glass in place, set adjusting screws and tighten locknuts. Turn screw clockwise (tighten it) to pull channel away from glass; turn screw counterclockwise (loosen it) to push channel toward glass

What to do if you lock yourself out of your car ⏲ 5 min–1 hr

It is easy to leave the car keys behind and close an automatically locking car door, but a little common sense can reduce a potentially serious problem to a minor inconvenience. The most important thing is never to lock infants or pets inside a car, even for a moment. If you lock yourself out, children and pets may suffer heat exhaustion, panic, or heart failure if they are confined in a car even for short periods with the windows ajar.

It is a good idea to keep an extra car key on your person for emergencies, but do not carry it in your wallet. If your wallet is stolen, at once the thief will have your address, registration, license, and car key. Do not hide the key anywhere on the car. No matter how cleverly you think you have hidden it, a thief can find it. If you do not have an extra key with you, you probably have one somewhere at home. Before resorting to any of the suggestions below, consider going home or having someone bring you the key.

If your car has button-type locks, you can use a wire coat hanger to unlock the door from the outside. Straighten the hanger, then make a hook on the end large enough to go around the stem of the lock but small enough so that it will not slip over the top. Slide the hanger past the weather stripping as close to the lock as possible. The farther the wire must travel, the

harder it will be to hook and lift the lock.

New-car keys have code numbers, either on knock-out plugs in the key itself or on attached tags. Copy the number and keep it with you. A locksmith can make a key from this number, but you must have the registration to prove that you own the car—a good reason not to leave the registration in the car. In urban areas, locksmiths who make emergency calls 24 hours a day are listed in the Yellow Pages.

If all else fails and you must break a window, choose the window that is smallest and cheapest to replace, provided that you can reach the lock from there. For example, a vent window is ideal if your arm is long and thin enough to reach the lock. On a small two-door car with stationary glass in the back, a side window in the rear might be the best choice. To break glass safely, cover the entire window with masking tape, gently break the glass so that it adheres to the tape, then lift it out carefully. **Caution:** Never break glass with your bare hands. Use a hammer, a rock, or some other makeshift tool.

A key that has broken off in the lock can often be removed with long-nose pliers. If this fails, insert a coping saw blade into the lock and pull out the key as illustrated at the right. Take the broken pieces to a locksmith to have a replacement key made.

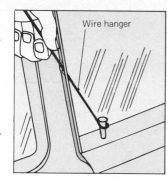

Lifting a button-type lock: Straighten a wire coat hanger and form the end into a hook about ¼ in. across. Slip the hook past the weatherstripping at the point closest to the lock. Fish around until you catch the hook on the lock button, then pull the button up.

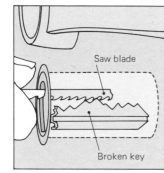

Removing a broken key: Insert a broken coping saw blade into the keyhole. Position the blade so that its teeth are against the cut edge of the key and slanted toward you. Catch the key with the teeth, and draw out the broken piece.

Releasing a stuck seat belt ⏲⏲ 30 min–2 hr

Very few repairs can be made on seat belts; when something breaks, the entire unit is replaced. However, if the belt is stuck in the retractor so that it will neither pull out nor snap back, it is possible that the webbing is twisted or that dirt is jamming the mechanism. Disengaging the release on the cam arm will usually allow you to pull or work the belt free; the most difficult part of the job is gaining access to the retractor. A shoulder belt mounted on the door pillar

might require the removal of seats and trim panels. Rear seat belts are mounted under the seat cushion. Seat cushions are bolted in place or held down by stiff spring catches.

Caution: If possible, leave the retractor mounted while you work on it. In most cases, the seat belts are held in place by special Torx® bolts that can only be removed and replaced with Torx sockets. These bolts must be torqued to exact specifications, and all fit-

tings must be replaced in the correct positions. Any stripped or damaged bolts must be replaced with bolts of identical size and strength. If you must replace seat belts, get the kind designed for your car model from a new-car dealer. Always replace both sections of a two-part belt at the same time. Never get seat belts from a junkyard, since the belts from a car that has been in an accident may be dangerously weakened.

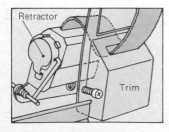

1. Reaching a pillar-mounted retractor may involve many steps. Begin by moving the front seat all the way forward. To remove the trim panels that cover the retractor, first remove anything that overlaps the trim, then remove the caps that hide the trim bolts.

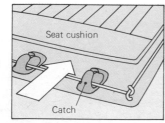

2. Rear retractors are under the seat cushion. Move the front seat forward and kneel on the floor. Locate the spring catches. Put your knee against the cushion just above the catch and push back with all your weight, then lift the cushion up and forward.

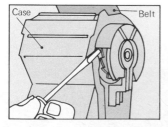

3. Pull belt guard (if any) away from retractor. Do not open retractor case. Poke a long, thin screwdriver into side of case with spring. Push release (either locking bar or cam arm) and pull on belt. When belt comes free, untwist it and clean off any dirt. Work belt a few times to test it.

Repairing a vinyl top 🔲 15–30 min

A vinyl top is more delicate than the painted body of the car and requires more care. Many vinyl tops are damaged through neglect or abuse. To prevent yours from deteriorating, wash it regularly with mild soap and water or with a special foam cleaner made for vinyl. Never use detergent, scouring pads, or abrasive cleaners. After washing, apply one of the waxes made to protect vinyl tops. If your top has already become faded or discolored by weathering or improper cleaning, you can restore it with a vinyl dying kit or a conditioner made for that purpose.

If your vinyl top has begun to peel, you may be able to fix it by melting the old glue with a hair dryer or a heat lamp and pressing the vinyl back in place. If this does not work, reglue the top with automotive trim cement, available at auto supply stores. Be careful to keep the cement on the underside of the vinyl, as it cannot be removed from the surface without damaging the finish. Repair extensive damage, such as cuts and bubbles, by one of the methods shown below.

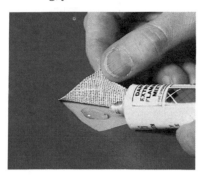

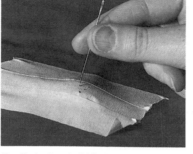

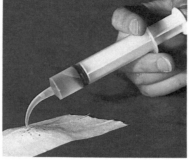

To repair a cut in a vinyl roof, trim off any loose threads. Spread automotive trim cement under the tear right to the edge of the cut; use a thin coat so that no cement oozes onto the surface of the vinyl. Press down until the cement sets, holding the cut edges together as closely as possible.

To eliminate a bubble in a vinyl top, cover the bubble with masking tape before forcing out the excess air; any cement that comes out will get on the tape, not the vinyl. Puncture the bubble with a darning needle at ¼-in. intervals. (An ordinary needle makes too small a hole.)

Heat the area with a hair dryer or a 250-watt heat lamp held 3 to 5 in. from the surface. Press down with a wood block until the cement rehardens. If the old cement will not hold, inject more with a glue injector, available at hobby shops. Press down again with the wood block.

Vinyl repair kits 🔲🔲 30 min–1 hr

Tears, holes, and burns in vinyl or leather can be repaired so that they are virtually invisible with a vinyl repair kit, available from specialty mail-order houses. Each kit contains: patching compound in various colors, which can be mixed to get a perfect match; graining sheets for most grain patterns; and grain mold compound for making graining sheets to match unusual patterns. Some kits include a special heating iron to cure the repair. If kit does not contain a special heater, a household iron is used.

1. Trim off any loose threads around the hole with nail scissors. Clean the repair area with soap and water, remove all soap with a damp cloth or sponge, and let dry. Choose the graining sheet that matches your pattern. If none match, make one according to the instructions in the kit.

2. If none of the patching compounds are the right color, mix a small batch of two or more with a toothpick until you get the right shade, then mix as much as you will need. Fill in the hole with the compound. Make hole level with the original material—do not overfill. Wipe off excess compound.

Repairing carpets and floor mats 🔲 10–15 min

To protect the car's carpeting, always leave the rubber floor mats in place. Use a whisk broom or a vacuum cleaner to clean abrasive dirt from the carpets and mats regularly. Wash the mats occasionally with detergent and water, rinse them well, and let them dry completely before putting them back in the car. If the carpets are very dirty or stained with road salt, remove them from the car and clean them with rug shampoo according to the directions on the can. To remove other stains, follow the directions for *Cleaning cloth upholstery,* p.328. Repair small carpet burns as illustrated below.

1. Cut away any charred carpeting with curved nail scissors. Cut the same number of loops from a hidden area, such as a spot under the seats.

2. Fill in the hole with a clear-drying, waterproof glue. Position the cut loops in the hole with tweezers and hold them upright until the glue sets.

3. Position the graining sheet grain side down over the compound. Apply the heating tool or iron to the graining sheet and hold it in position for 1 min; do not move it around. Be sure to heat every area of the repair this way. Do not allow the heating tool to contact the surrounding vinyl.

4. Allow the repair to cool until the graining sheet is cool to the touch, then peel the sheet off slowly. If the compound has not solidified, replace the sheet and apply heat again as in Step 3. If the finished patch is too shiny, dull it by rubbing it very lightly with emery cloth until patch blends in.

Fixing dents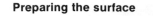

The most important skill to develop for doing bodywork is patience. Mistakes are difficult and sometimes impossible to correct, so always work slowly and carefully. To determine what contours a damaged panel should have, look at its matching part on the other side of the car or on a car like yours.

The most accurate way to judge contours and smoothness is with your hand. The hand is held palm down against the car, with fingers together. Slowly run the entire hand, including the heel of the palm and the fingertips, back and forth over the surface. This technique will enable you to check the contours of a panel, to find high or low spots that are not easily seen, and to feel rough spots or scratches.

The secret to shaping metal is to avoid stretching it any more than the dent already has. Work slowly and carefully, tapping and pulling the panel back to its original contour and no farther. Start at the shallowest part of the damage and work in toward the deepest part. Work cautiously, because if the metal is overstretched, it can be repaired only by an experienced body man working with special tools.

Some dents, such as those made by small stones, are so small that they do not need banging out. In such cases, skip Steps 3 through 9 at the right, and correct the contour with plastic body filler. Do not use filler in deep dents—it should never be applied more than ⅛ inch thick. Filler should be applied on a dry day, even if you are working indoors, since dampness lengthens drying time considerably and can cause rust to form between the metal and filler.

The degree of abrasiveness of sandpaper is noted by its grit number; the higher the number, the finer the paper. Use the recommended grit number or a similar number. Too coarse a sandpaper will scratch the surface, and too fine a paper will not remove enough material. Never use dry sandpaper for wet sanding—the glue used to attach the abrasive is not waterproof. Open-coat sandpaper has less abrasive material per square inch than closed-coat paper and therefore does not clog up as quickly.

After the final sanding of the plastic body filler, the repair area must be as perfect as possible. The edges of the repair must be *feathered*—that is, sanded so smooth that you cannot feel a border between paint, metal, and filler. Paint will emphasize defects, not hide them, so check the contours and surface very carefully before you begin to prime.

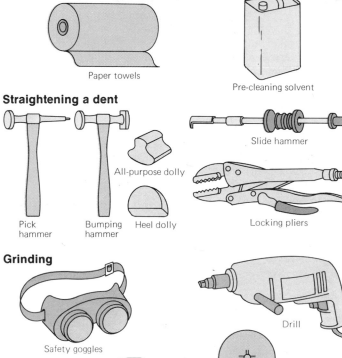

Preparing the surface

Paper towels

Pre-cleaning solvent

Straightening a dent

Pick hammer

Bumping hammer

All-purpose dolly

Heel dolly

Slide hammer

Locking pliers

Grinding

Safety goggles

Wire brush

Drill

Grinding disc

Applying and finishing plastic body filler

Plastic body filler

Hardener

Putty knife

Squeegees

Perforated file

Sanding board

Sanding block

Face mask

Masking tape

Sandpaper

Preparing the surface 5 min

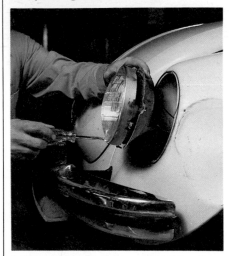

1. Before starting to work on a dent, take off any easily removable chrome trim or lights near the area. Cover any trim you cannot remove with masking tape. Wipe the surface of the repair area and well beyond with water, using clean rags or paper towels. Do not use soap.

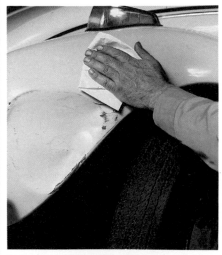

2. Dry the surface with clean rags. Wipe area again with pre-cleaning solvent and clean rags to remove any wax or grease. Wipe off solvent before it dries with clean, dry rags. **Caution:** Do not leave rags soaked in pre-cleaner on the car—it can soften paint and is highly flammable.

Hammering and pulling a dent 1–2 hr

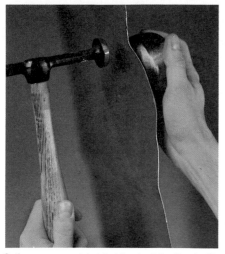

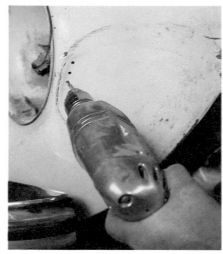
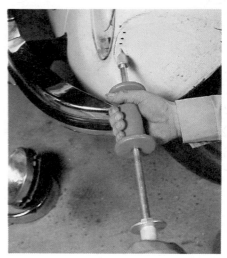

3. If you can reach behind the dent, tap it out with a dolly and hammer. Work from the outside of the dent inward (from the shallowest to the deepest part). If you work outward from the deepest part, the metal will distort too much, and correcting the contour will be much more difficult.

4. Tap from behind with the dolly, then tap down high spots on the front with the hammer. Do not hold the dolly directly behind the spot where you are hammering—sandwiching the metal this way stretches it. Use the dolly to support the metal. Check for smoothness often with your hand.

5. Indented areas that cannot be reached with the dolly must be pulled out. Drill holes with an electric drill and a 1/8-in. bit at 1/2- to 1-in. intervals along the length of the dent. **Caution:** Never run your hand over metal after drilling or pulling—the holes have very sharp burrs.

6. Screw slide hammer into hole at edge of dent. Slide weight back gently while holding outward pressure on handle. If dent does not come out at all, use a little more force. Use a few gentle pulls on each hole. Always work inward from edge of dent, alternating hammering and pulling.

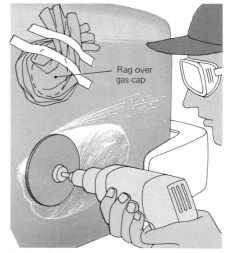

Rag over gas cap

7. Alternate pulling method: If you do not have access to a slide hammer, a No.8 screw, 1½ in. long, and locking pliers make an acceptable substitute. Insert screw into drilled hole two or three turns, grasp it with locking pliers, and pull straight out firmly and smoothly.

8. If the dent does not come out when you first pull on it, tap around the high edge of the dent with a hammer to release pressure, then pull firmly on the screw again with the locking pliers. Never jerk or twist the screw, or you might tear it out of the metal. Use straight, even pressure.

9. Continue tapping out the dent with the dolly and hammer wherever possible—drilling holes and pulling with the slide hammer or pliers when you cannot work from behind—always working in toward the center until contour of panel is as close to the original shape as possible.

10. Caution: Before starting to grind (Step 11), put on safety goggles to keep metal particles and paint chips out of your eyes. Do not rely on ordinary glasses. If you will be grinding near the gas tank, drape a wet rag around the cap to prevent sparks from setting off an explosion.

Repair / **Bodywork**

Grinding a dent ⏱ 15–30 min

11. Grind with a dry No.24 or No.36 closed-coat grinding disc. If it clogs, use an open-coat disc. Grind damage and 1½ in. beyond until finish is down to bare metal and holes have no burrs. Keep disc moving to avoid wearing down one spot or overheating and distorting the metal.

13. If there is any paint left in nicks and cracks after grinding, attach a wire brush to the drill to remove it. (**Caution:** Wear safety goggles.) It is important to remove all traces of the old finish because plastic body filler will not adhere properly to painted surfaces.

12. Allow the metal to cool, then check the surface for smoothness by holding your hand flat and running it back and forth slowly over the entire area, feeling for any remaining paint or burrs. Grinding serves to remove paint, rust, and burrs, not to straighten metal.

14. Check for shape with your hand, and gently tap on high and low spots with the dolly and hammer. Wherever holes have been drilled, tap in the metal to create a slight depression so that body filler will not form a bump there. Straighten and finish the inside lip of the panel.

Applying and finishing plastic body filler ⏱⏱⏱⏱ 2–4 hr

15. Check tape on chrome and retape where necessary to avoid getting filler on trim. Wipe surface with a clean, dry rag. To prepare the filler, carefully follow directions on the can. Mix filler thoroughly with a putty knife or paint-mixing stick until resin on top is completely blended in.

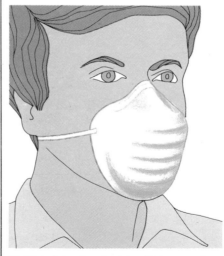

21. When the surface has been filed as smooth as possible, dry-sand it with No.80 sandpaper. Use a sanding board for large areas and a rubber sanding block for small areas. **Caution:** Be sure to wear a face mask to filter out plastic dust while you are sanding.

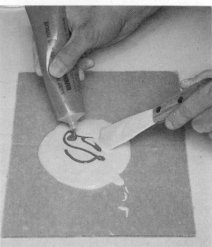

16. Put enough filler onto a piece of cardboard to cover entire repair area with one thin coat. Mix in the specified amount of hardener until no streaks of color show in the filler. Do not add too much hardener, or the filler will harden before you can apply a smooth coat.

22. Sand with the contour, starting from the outer edge of the filler and moving toward the center. Sand the areas around the trim, using a folded sheet of sandpaper wherever the sanding block will not fit. Continue sanding until the filler is smooth, level, and flush with the surface.

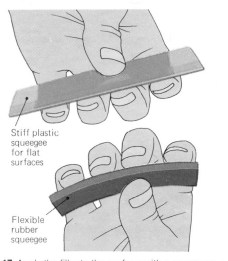

Stiff plastic squeegee for flat surfaces

Flexible rubber squeegee

17. Apply the filler to the surface with a squeegee. For flat surfaces use a fairly stiff plastic squeegee; for contour work use a more flexible rubber squeegee. Both types are sold in a variety of sizes at auto parts stores—choose the size best suited to the size of your repair.

Bare metal

Filler

Paint

Inside Outside

Hole

Filler

Metal

18. For smooth results, work filler in one direction only, applying a thin, even coat over the entire area. Leave a small margin of bare metal around the plastic filler to ensure that no filler gets on the paint. Filler will cover all holes that were drilled for pulling (see inset).

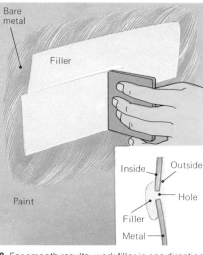

19. Apply filler across repair, working from top to bottom. Use a single swipe across entire width each time. Apply filler quickly—it can dry in minutes on hot, dry days. Let filler dry until it has a rubbery feel. Do not let it dry any longer, or it will be too hard to work with a perforated file.

20. Shave or shred the filler as smooth as possible, using a perforated file and checking often for smoothness with your hand. File in various directions and use moderate pressure so that the file will not dig into any one spot. Filing gives the filler its basic rough contour.

23. With a hammer, gently tap down any high spots where bare metal shows. Check shape with your hand. Feather sanding out onto the metal so that repaired area has no defined edges. Wipe surface thoroughly with a clean, dry rag, then check contour of repair with your hand.

24. You may need several coats of filler to get the contour right. Apply the final coat (a *skim coat*) very thinly with a rubber squeegee. Make it very smooth, working in only one direction. The skim coat is too thin to be filed, and sanding out any unevenness after the filler dries is very hard work.

25. Allow the skim coat of filler to dry 15 to 20 min. The surface must be harder for dry sanding than for filing—the filler cannot be at all tacky. Dry-sand the surface with No.100 sandpaper on a sanding board or block. **Caution:** Always wear a face mask when sanding filler.

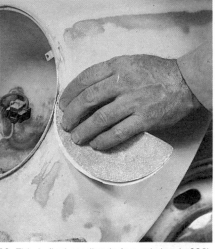

26. This is final sanding before priming (p.322), so filler must be smooth and free of pinholes. Feather edge onto old paint. Use a folded sheet of sandpaper where the block does not fit. Check carefully for smoothness with your hand. Take the time to do the job well.

Fixing small rust-outs ⬜⬜⬜⬜ 3–6 hr

Aluminum tape covered with plastic body filler is a quick, easy way to repair small rust-outs, but such repairs are usually short-lived because it is virtually impossible to remove all the rust. You can, however, maximize the time your repair will last by making certain that you grind away all the visible rust, then treating the remaining metal with metal conditioner. These directions deal with rust that has gone all the way through the metal; to repair small rust spots that do not go through the metal, see *Touching up chipped paint and small rust spots*, p.324.

For a long-lasting repair, a competent body shop will cut away the rusted bodywork back to sound metal, weld in new sheet metal, then undercoat and paint the entire panel. This is a very expensive procedure, but it is the only way to repair serious rust permanently. A cheap repair with plastic body filler is often used to conceal rust damage before a car is sold—look for such repairs before buying a used car.

When all the rust, old paint, and dirt have been removed so that only clean, bare metal remains, treat the metal with metal conditioner, following the directions on the container carefully. Metal conditioner is an acid that etches away rust you cannot see. The conditioner will blacken the metal. Always wipe the conditioner off before it dries, or it could continue etching metal that is sound.

Use aluminum foil tape, sold in hardware stores, to bridge any holes in the bodywork. The tape will adhere only to clean metal, and the taped area cannot be hammered or sanded, so be sure that all shaping and sanding are finished before you apply the tape. Plastic body filler does not adhere well to aluminum tape, so leave a border of bare metal around the tape.

Once the repair is taped, it is completed in exactly the same way as for a dent. *Applying and finishing plastic body filler*, pp.316–317, gives step-by-step instructions for working with filler. *Priming repaired areas*, pp.322–323, and *Painting repaired areas*, pp.324–325, tell you how to achieve a good finish that blends in well with the original paint.

Tools: Electric drill, rubber sanding disc, ball peen hammer, screwdriver, putty knife, squeegee, perforated file, sanding board or block.
Materials: No.40 sandpaper disc, metal conditioner, aluminum foil tape, plastic body filler, No.80 and No.100 sandpaper, masking tape, newspaper, face mask, rags.

Cross section of a temporary repair

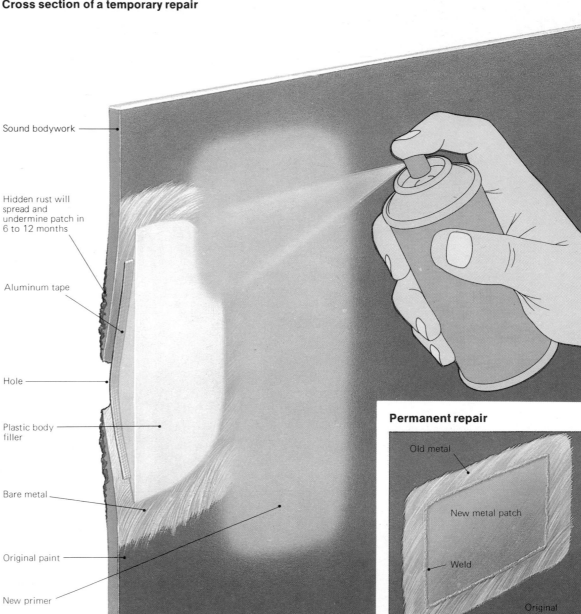

Sound bodywork

Hidden rust will spread and undermine patch in 6 to 12 months

Aluminum tape

Hole

Plastic body filler

Bare metal

Original paint

New primer

Permanent repair

Old metal

New metal patch

Weld

Original paint

1. With an electric drill, grind away all rust and blistered paint, using No.40 (or similar grit) sandpaper on a rubber sanding disc. Grind away the paint at least 1 in. back from rusted or damaged areas, being careful not to cut into adjacent metalwork or tires. This will reveal how far the damage has actually gone.

2. Hammer down any high spots in the good metal with a ball peen hammer. Dislodge as much loose rust and dirt as you can. Restore the original contour of the panel as closely as possible, then indent the metal around the hole slightly so that the plastic body filler will not create a raised spot when it is applied.

3. Use a screwdriver to dig dirt, rust, and any old undercoating or sound-deadening material out of the holes. Grind back the paint at least 1 in. from any holes now visible to allow filler to adhere to sound metal. Treat the metal with metal conditioner, carefully following the directions on the container.

4. Cover holes in the metalwork with aluminum foil tape. Keep your fingers off the tape's gummed surface. If the tape tears, remove it or apply a second layer. With your fingers, press tape down slightly into holes, and press out wrinkles. Leave a border of bare metal exposed between the tape and the original paint.

5. Next, cover the repair with plastic body filler; for complete instructions, see pp.316–317. While working with the filler, be careful not to create peaks and valleys, since these require tedious sanding with fine sandpaper after the filler has dried. Plastic body filler restores the smooth, even contour of the panel.

6. When the repair is sanded as smooth as possible, clean off the sanding dust with a dry rag. Mask off the surrounding areas with paper and masking tape. Leave the inner edge of the tape raised as shown to create a smoother overlap with the original paint. Prime and paint the repair as shown on pages 322–325.

Repairing cracks, breaks, and small holes in fiberglass panels ☑ ☑ ☑ ☑ 2–4 hr

Many cars today are being built with some fiberglass panels to save weight. If you have a crack or small hole in such a panel, repairing it at home is simple and inexpensive, and a good fiberglass patch is as strong as the original panel. If there is major damage, it is easier to replace the whole panel.

Fiberglass repair kits, which include all the materials necessary to make a small repair, are available at auto supply stores. Before buying one, measure the area you plan to cover, since the kits come in different sizes. Follow the manufacturer's directions for mixing hardener with resin and for drying times.

Caution: Although fiberglass is easy to work with, it can be dangerous. Always follow the safety procedures outlined below.

Mix only as much resin as you will use immediately. Resin hardens quickly, and as it cures it generates enough heat to start a fire. The more resin there is in a container, the more heat it will generate. If you do have resin left over after a repair, put it outside until it has hardened completely. Then dispose of it.

Work in a well-ventilated area, preferably with an exhaust fan, to avoid breathing poisonous fumes.

Keep resin away from open flame and sources of high heat, such as a furnace or a space heater. Never smoke when working with fiberglass. Resin fumes are volatile; a spark could set off an explosion.

Fiberglass itself is an irritant. Wear rubber gloves and a long-sleeved shirt to keep fibers from getting into your skin. Wear a mask when grinding or sanding to keep particles and dust out of your lungs.

When your fiberglass patch is finished, treat it as you would any other body repair. Cover the patch with a thin coat of plastic body filler to fill any pinholes or sanding scratches, as illustrated in *Applying and finishing plastic body filler*, pp.316–317. Then follow the instructions for *Priming repaired areas*, pp.322–323 and *Painting*, pp.324–325.

Tools: C-clamps or locking pliers, face mask, safety goggles, electric drill, No.24 grinding disc, grinding bit (rasp), can of compressed air, mixing paddle, rubber dishwashing gloves or disposable surgical gloves, acid brush, heat lamp or hair dryer, scissors, razor blade, No.36 or No.40 dry sandpaper, rubber sanding block.
Materials: Fiberglass repair kit, including fiberglass mat, resin, and hardener (these products can be bought separately or in kits), masking tape, paper.

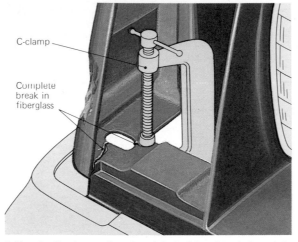

C-clamp

Complete break in fiberglass

1. Examine the damaged area carefully to determine what needs to be done. Remove any trim or adjacent panels in the way. If there is a complete break and the pieces have separated, fit the broken edges together and clamp them with C-clamps or locking pliers. When you have everything clamped in position, reinstall the adjacent panel or trim piece (in this case, the headlight frame) to be sure that the alignment of the clamped edges is accurate.

2. Caution: Always wear a mask and safety goggles when grinding fiberglass. Grind the damaged area and about 2 in. beyond until no paint remains, using a No.24 grinding disc mounted on an electric drill. Use the edge of the disc to make an indentation around the crack or hole; this will hold the new fiberglass patch. Bevel the surrounding area into the indentation so that the surface has a gradual slope, not an abrupt drop.

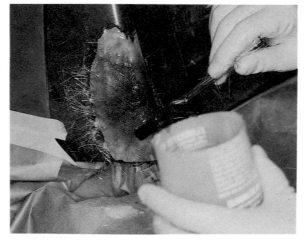

6. Build up the fiberglass patch in thin layers to be sure that each layer of glass is completely saturated with resin before the next layer is applied. Begin by saturating the repair area with resin, using an acid brush (some synthetic brushes dissolve). Make sure that no resin goes beyond the area you have ground down. Apply a thin layer of fiberglass. If the patch must fit into a tight space, trim the glass with scissors. Saturate the glass with resin.

7. Be sure to get out all air bubbles; if there are any left in the patch when it hardens, they will form pinholes when you sand. Look very carefully for bubbles each time you apply resin, and dab at them with the brush until they disappear. Continue applying layers of fiberglass and resin until the patch is slightly higher than the surrounding bodywork. Build up enough material so that you can sand and contour the patch without creating a depression.

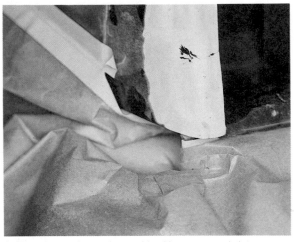

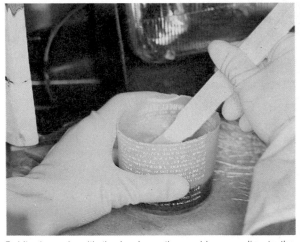

3. Use a grinding bit (rasp) to rout out damaged areas where the grinding disc will not fit. Make the same type of indentation as with the disc (Step 2) to hold the patch. Don't worry if you grind through the fiberglass and make a hole where before there was only a crack—the patch will fill it. After clamping, grinding, and routing, replace the adjacent part again to be certain of the alignment before proceeding with the repair.

4. Clean the repair area thoroughly with compressed air to remove all dust from the surface. (You can buy cans of compressed air at auto supply stores or photography stores.) Fiberglass is porous, so dusting it off with a rag will not get it clean enough. (**Caution:** Wear a face mask and goggles.) Mask off the area around the repair so that the resin will not drip on it; resin is very difficult to remove and will mar the paint.

5. Mix the resin with the hardener thoroughly, according to the directions on the can. **Caution:** Wear a long-sleeved shirt and rubber gloves when working with fiberglass to keep splinters out of your skin. Dishwashing gloves or disposable surgical gloves are the most flexible and easiest to work in. If you do get glass splinters (you will feel very itchy and uncomfortable), do not scratch or rub. Take a shower immediately to rinse the fiberglass off.

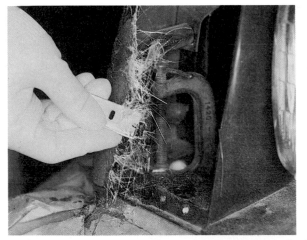

8. A fiberglass patch is very unstable until it is dry, and it can easily be shifted out of position if it is bumped or jostled. Therefore, leave your work in a safe, out-of-the-way place to dry. Resin must cure at 65°F or warmer, or it will not set. If your work area is colder, use a heat lamp or hair dryer. When the fiberglass is completely dry, trim off the excess with a razor blade. Don't worry if the edges are uneven; sanding will smooth them.

9. Sand the edges of the patch until they are flush with the original panel, using No. 36 or No. 40 dry sandpaper on a rubber block. **Caution:** Wear a mask. Use a folded sheet of sandpaper wherever the block does not fit. Feather the edges of the repair into the panel. Test-fit the adjacent part to check the shape of the edge. Sand and contour the remainder of the patch, working from the edges inward. Check for smoothness with your hand frequently.

10. Remove the clamps and blow off dust with compressed air. Grind or rout excess fiberglass from any bolt holes so that the parts will fit back together. If necessary, build up a layered fiberglass patch where the clamps were, as in Steps 5–8. If you see any holes or gaps exposed by sanding, fill them with a little resin, let it dry, and sand it. Then cover the patch with a thin coat of plastic body filler to fill pinholes and sanding scratches.

Priming repaired areas   1–3 hr

Because paint does not adhere well to bare metal, you must apply an intermediate coat of primer before painting. Primer is used to cover plastic body filler and any bare metal as well as a margin of the old paint, so it also provides a uniform surface for new paint. Without primer, paint would not have its characteristic even, smooth, glossy finish.

It is important to match the primer to the paint you will use. A chemical reaction between dissimilar paints can cause the paint to wrinkle and to lift. Use only lacquer primer for lacquer paint and enamel primer for enamel paint. Use a light-colored primer with light paint and a dark primer under dark paint.

By spraying on the primer in the pattern illustrated below, you will be able to cover the area completely with a smooth coat unmarred by runs or blobs.

Glazing putty is applied in a very thin coat to fill sanding scratches and pinholes. Never use a thick coat of putty to contour body panels or to fill anything deeper than scratches. All such repairs must be done by straightening out the dent and finishing it with plastic body filler (see pp.318–321).

Apply glazing putty in one direction only, following the pattern illustrated here. Use strokes that cover the width of the repair, and work from top to bottom, overlapping strokes slightly to be sure there are no gaps. Clean the tools with lacquer thinner.

Putty must be completely dry before it can be sanded. Let it dry for at least half an hour, preferably overnight, but don't leave it out in the cold—putty must cure at a minimum temperature of 60° F.

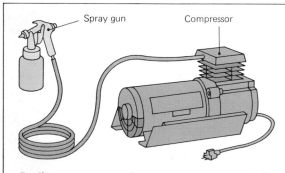

Renting a spray gun and compressor to prime and paint large areas will make the job easier and faster, and you will get more professional results.

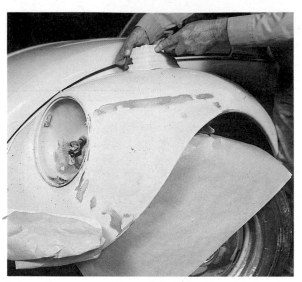

1. Cover large areas near the repair that will not be painted, such as bumper and wheel, with newspaper or brown wrapping paper held in place by masking tape. If work area is drafty, cover the entire wheel. Wipe repaired surface with a clean, dry rag to remove dust.

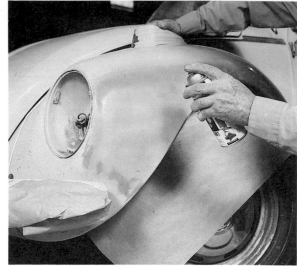

2. Shake spray can vigorously. Spray on several light coats of primer in even strokes, moving can constantly to avoid runs and sags. (**Caution:** Wear a face mask.) Wait 3 to 4 min between coats. Make sure repair area is completely covered. Let primer dry.

6. Let putty dry. Wet-sand with No.220 sandpaper. Use a rubber sanding block for flat areas; for contoured surfaces, hold sandpaper flat in your hand. Keep water flowing on surface by squeezing a sponge over it so that the sandpaper does not clog.

7. Sand lightly across the area in several directions, but avoid any high spots where bare metal appears. Dry the surface and check it with your hand to be sure it is absolutely smooth. Look for pinholes and scratches. If surface is not perfect, wet-sand again.

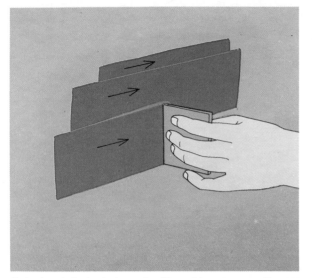

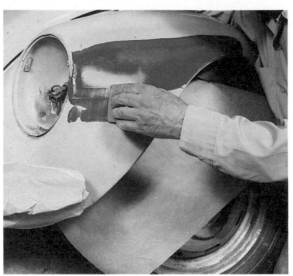

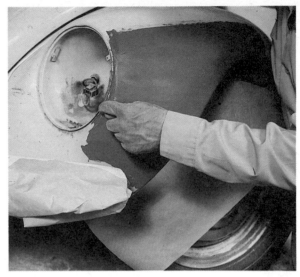

3. Apply auto body glazing putty with a rubber squeegee. Use one stroke to smooth putty across the repaired area in a very thin coat. Move squeegee down a little with each stroke, always applying the putty in the same direction to keep the coat smooth.

4. Continue applying glazing putty until the entire area is covered with a thin, smooth coat of putty. Be sure to glaze the crease around the headlight or other creases. Work quickly, since glazing putty dries fast, and a second coat is difficult to apply.

5. Never go over a spot just puttied, or you will pick up the first coat. If you must go over an area, wait 2 to 3 min, but try to get it right the first time—going over newly applied glazing putty with a squeegee can spoil the smooth finish; a thick coat can crack.

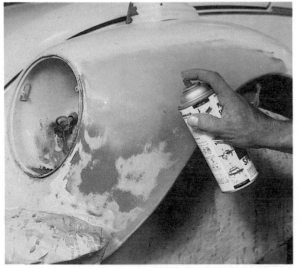

8. Be sure that the surface, including any wells or crevices, is completely dry before priming. Spray primer in repeated light coats as in Step 2, thoroughly covering the area. (**Caution:** Wear a face mask.) Let the primer dry completely.

9. Wet-sand with No.320 sandpaper, using the rubber sanding block for flat areas and holding the paper in your hand for curves. Examine the surface carefully. No bare metal should show through the primer when you finish this sanding.

10. If bare metal does show anywhere, lightly spot-prime those areas; paint will not adhere to bare metal, but primer will. Let the primer dry at least 15 min, then very lightly dry-sand the spot-primed areas with No.400 sandpaper held flat in your hand.

Painting

Two types of paint are used on modern cars: lacquer and enamel. The basic difference between them is that lacquer can be dissolved by thinner no matter how long it has been on the car, while enamel hardens to form a tough, almost impermeable finish after about six months. For this reason, lacquer can be painted over an enamel finish that is at least six months old, but the solvents in some enamels can lift an original lacquer paint job.

For a car owner making his own repairs, *acrylic lacquer* has several advantages. It dries quickly, so dust and dirt will not stick in the paint and ruin the finish; enamel dries slowly and stays tacky for a long time. Acrylic lacquer blends in well with the old finish after the area has been compounded; enamel cannot be compounded until it has cured completely. Runs and mistakes in lacquer can be sanded when dry, and repainted; new enamel cannot be sanded. Therefore, use acrylic lacquer for repairs unless your car has a fresh enamel finish, in which case you should take it to a body shop for repainting.

Before applying any primer or paint, test it on an inconspicuous spot—under the bumper, for example—preferably on the same panel you will be painting. Do not test the inside of the trunk or hood, where a different kind of paint is often used. Give the test area several coats of paint, since solvents may penetrate only after two or more coats.

To control spray paint effectively, you must be able to see how it is going on; place a light so that you can see it reflected by the car's surface.

Metallic paints are applied in several layers, which must be carefully blended to get the right effect. This makes painting at home difficult; to get a good match, take metallic paint repairs to a body shop.

Spray cans of paint are available from dealers and auto supply stores. Aerosol paints seldom match a car's color exactly, as the original paint will have faded. For an exact match, paint must be custom mixed at a body shop and applied with a spray gun. Small bottles of touch-up paint are also available. Use touch-up paint only to fill in small spots of chipped paint. If you take care of tiny knicks and scratches right away, they will not develop into rust spots. However, spots that have been touched up always show—if you want a perfect finish, wet-sand the area with No.320 sandpaper, prime it (see *Priming*, pp.322–323), then spray-paint it. When spraying small areas, cut a nickle-size hole in a piece of cardboard, hold the cardboard about an inch from the surface, then spray. This will limit the area being sprayed without leaving the distinct edge that masking tape would leave.

Touch-up tools and materials: Single-edge razor blade, clean rags, metal conditioner, pre-cleaning solvent, small paintbrushes, primer, bottle of touch-up paint to match your finish.
Spray painting tools and materials: Clean rags, polishing compound, pre-cleaning solvent, masking tape and paper, face mask, acrylic lacquer spray paint to match your finish.

Common problems with spray paint

Runs and sags occur when paint is sprayed in a coat that is too heavy or too wet. Let the paint dry completely, wet-sand the area, then repaint.

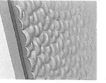

Orange peel (rough, pebbly surface) is caused by spraying too light or too dry a coat. Some orange peel is all right in early coats. Make the final coat wet enough to flow, but not so wet that it runs.

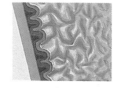

Lifting results when paint is applied over an incompatible base. Sand the area down to bare metal and refinish it with the correct products, after testing them first in an inconspicuous spot.

Fish eyes (small spots where paint does not adhere) form where silicone or wax was not thoroughly cleaned off surface. Wipe off wet paint with lacquer thinner, thoroughly clean surface with pre-cleaning solvent, then repaint.

Touching up chipped paint and small rust spots ▣▣ 30 min–1 hr

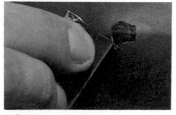

1. Cut away any blistered paint around the damaged spot with the point of a single-edge razor blade, being careful not to cut into the good paint. Blisters are evidence of underlying damage and must be removed. Bevel the edge of the paint around the spot to make the repair less abrupt and obvious.

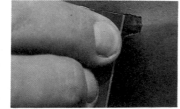

2. With the flat edge of the razor blade, not the point, gently scrape off any loose rust. Use slow, tiny strokes, scraping from the edge of the paint inward so that you will not accidentally scratch the good paint. Keep the repair area as small as possible, while removing all rust.

3. Wipe area with metal conditioner, then wipe it off before it dries. Metal conditioner is a chemical that etches remaining rust from metal and helps primer to adhere better. Conditioner will blacken metal. Next, wipe with pre-cleaning solvent to remove any wax, grease, or tar.

4. Apply the primer only when the pre-cleaning solvent has dried completely. Use a small paintbrush to paint on the primer. Try to fill in just the repair spot without going over onto the paint, but be sure to cover all the metal—paint does not adhere to bare metal. Let the primer dry completely.

5. Shake the touch-up paint vigorously. With the small brush that comes with the paint, paint in the spot as neatly as possible, completely covering the primer. A touch-up will show, no matter how careful you·are; the repair is made chiefly to prevent serious rust damage from developing.

Spray painting techniques 🔲🔲🔲 1–3 hr

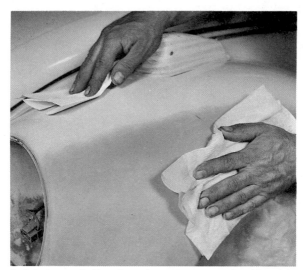

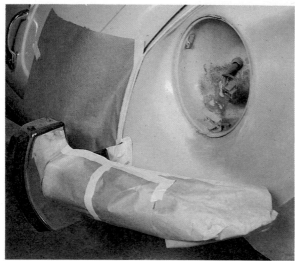

1. Wipe the panel with a clean, damp rag. Dab polishing compound on the old paint surrounding the repair area, covering the entire panel. Rub very hard with a clean rag until the compound disappears. Compounding removes a layer of weathered paint and dirt so that old and new paint will match more closely.

2. Rub the panel with a clean, dry rag to remove all residue of the compound. Next, clean the whole panel, including the repair area, with pre-cleaning solvent. Use two rags simultaneously, one soaked in pre-cleaner and the other dry. Wipe the pre-cleaner on, then wipe it off before it dries.

3. When the entire panel has been thoroughly cleaned, check to be sure that no tape or paper put on before priming overlaps any areas that are to be painted. With more tape and paper, cover all remaining surfaces that abut areas to be painted to protect them from overspray. **Caution:** Always wear a mask when painting.

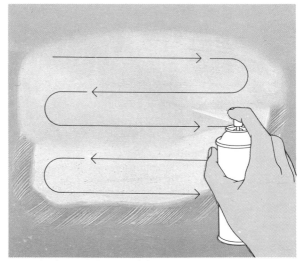

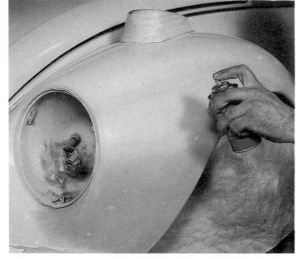

4. Shake the paint thoroughly, following the directions on the can. Keep the can 8 to 12 in. from the surface. Spray the whole area with a sweeping back-and-forth motion, spraying constantly. (Practice on scrap metal until you get good results.) Always keep the can moving—holding it in one place causes runs and sags.

5. Start painting at top of repair area, move downward to bottom, then repeat. (On flat surfaces, start at edge nearest you and move away.) Apply four or five light, even, semi-transparent coats until surface is completely covered. Let each coat dry for 3 to 4 min before applying next coat. Be sure to paint under panel's edge.

6. When the paint is dry to the touch, remove all masking and replace the lights and trim. Allow paint to dry for at least 24 hr, then compound the new paint and the surrounding areas of old paint with polishing compound. This will blend the finishes so that the repair will not show. Do not wax area for 90 days.

Repair/**Bodywork**

Installing vinyl trim ☑☑ 1–2 hr

Many cars develop a line of small dents, chipped paint, and scratches along each side where the doors of other cars, parked alongside, repeatedly bump the bodywork. You can cover such damage, and prevent more from occurring, with protective vinyl trim. This self-adhesive trim is easy to install and is available in a variety of colors and widths. Decorative end caps give the trim a custom-made appearance. If the kit you buy does not have end caps, you can achieve the same effect with the technique shown here. Cut out a long, narrow triangle from the end of the trim.

When the rest of the trim piece has been pressed in place, peel the backing off the cut end, pinch the cut edges together, and press the trim down firmly while holding this position.

To serve as a protective barrier, the trim must protrude farther than the widest part of the bodywork. If your car has a sharp ridge along each side, place the trim just above or just below the ridge (the trim cannot adhere properly to the ridge itself). If there is no ridge, place the trim along the widest part of the car. If in doubt about the widest part, open the door slowly until it contacts a vertical wall; the point of contact will be the widest part. To prevent rust from developing under the trim, fix any chips or scratches as illustrated in *Touching up chipped paint and small rust spots,* p.324. Let the paint dry for 24 hours before applying the trim.

Before you begin to work, carefully determine where you want the trim. Once it has been pressed into place, self-adhesive trim cannot be removed without damaging the paint.

If an existing piece of trim comes loose, you can cement it in place with weatherstrip adhesive. Clean and warm the car body and trim as in Step 1 (right). Apply a thin, even film of adhesive to the back of the trim, and press the trim firmly into position. Use strips of masking tape to hold the trim in place until the adhesive sets, usually about 15 minutes.

Tools and materials: Package of vinyl trim, pre-cleaning solvent or rubbing alcohol, paper towels, hair dryer or heat lamp, ¾-in. masking tape, garden shears.

1. Clean trim area with pre-cleaning solvent or a mixture of half rubbing alcohol, half water, to remove dirt, wax, and silicone from the paint. Wipe dry. Both car and trim must be at least 70°F but less than 125°F for adhesive to hold. Use hair dryer or heat lamp to warm them. (On a hot day they can be left in the sun, but remove the car from direct sunlight before applying trim.)

3. Before applying trim, measure and cut all pieces. Hold trim against the car under guide tape to measure piece for front fender. Remember to leave space for end cap. With garden shears, cut front end of trim straight so that end cap will fit flush against it. Cut other end to match back edge of fender; bevel it at a 45° angle so that the door can open easily.

5. Peel off 6 in. of backing paper, and press first trim piece lightly against panel exactly under tape guide. Do not peel off too much backing at once, or adhesive will get dirty. To get trim on straight, tack down front edge and hold peeled part just far enough from car so that it does not touch. When trim looks straight, press down the whole length at once. Do not stretch or pull the trim.

2. Use ¾-in. masking tape as a guide to get trim on straight. Lay tape along top edge of where trim will go. Attach tape at one end, pull it straight out so that it does not contact car, sight along tape until you can see that it is on correct line, then press other end of tape lightly against car. Step back to see if tape is straight, and adjust as necessary. Press tape down along its entire length.

4. Use the trim piece cut in Step 3 as a template to cut a matching piece for the other side of the car. (This will save you the trouble of measuring half the pieces, and both sides will look the same.) Repeat Steps 3 and 4 for each trim piece needed. Always match the contours of the trim ends to the edges of the fenders and doors except where end caps must fit against the trim.

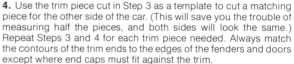

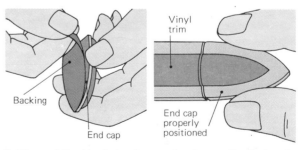

6. When all the trim is in place, make any small adjustments needed to align trim with tape by nudging trim gently. Press trim firmly in place. Put on end caps last. Peel backing off an end cap and carefully align it so that it fits flush against trim, with edges of trim and cap meeting and the point straight. Firmly press cap in place. Repeat this process for each cap.

Removing and replacing exterior trim ⏱ 10–20 min

There are seven basic ways that trim is attached to the car body, with many variations. An example of cemented trim is shown on the opposite page, and the six mechanical methods are illustrated below. Whenever you remove exterior trim, put all the screws, nuts, bolts, and clips in a safe place, since some of these parts can be found only at junkyards.

Trim that is simply screwed to the body is easily removed with a screwdriver. If you do not know how a piece of trim is held in place, feel behind the panel for mounting nuts and unscrew all of them. Once the nuts have been removed—or if there are no nuts—use a putty knife to gently pry the trim away from the panel. (If only the nuts hold the trim in place, it will pull off when they are removed.) Where screws or bolts go through holes in the body, squeeze a dab of silicone caulking compound into each hole before replacing the trim, to prevent leaks, rust, and rattles.

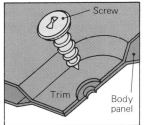

Screws hold the trim to the panel directly. Carmakers use concealed fasteners for most decorative trim.

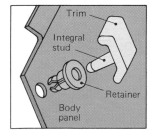

Integral studs on the trim snap into holes in the body; the holes may have retainers. Often used as emblems.

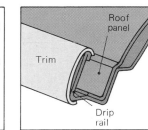

Threaded integral studs snap into holes in the body. Nuts are then screwed on to hold the trim from behind.

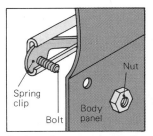

Self-retaining trim—for example, the chrome trim over the drip rail—snaps in position over the body part.

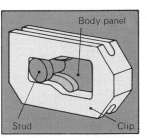

Spring clips snap inside the trim. Bolts or studs protruding from the clips are inserted into holes in the body.

Body panel · Nut · Stud · Clip

Clips attached to the body slip onto studs welded to the panel or are screwed onto the panel. Trim snaps over clips.

Installing or replacing a rear-view mirror ⏱ 30 min–1 hr

Adding a mirror on the right side of your car will increase visibility, particularly in the "blind spot"— the area not reflected by the left and interior mirrors. Mirrors that match those on your car are available from most new-car dealers or from auto parts stores. All necessary hardware and gaskets should be included with the mirror.

If a mirror has been pulled off in an accident or by vandals, the screw holes will be enlarged. You will have to use oversize screws or plastic screw anchors to remount the mirror or to install a new one if the old one is broken. When shopping for oversize screws, take the mirror along to be sure that the screws will fit into the mounting holes. If they do not fit, use the original screws with expanding plastic screw anchors, such as those used to hang pictures. Buy anchors that fit the screws but are not so long that they will interfere with the window glass.

Tools: Ruler or tape measure, felt-tip pen, center punch, hammer, electric drill, drill bits, screwdriver.
Materials: Mirror, self-tapping screws (should come with a new mirror), oversize self-tapping screws or plastic screw anchors, liquid locking compound.

1. Carefully measure the location of the left-hand mirror. Transfer these dimensions to the right side of the car so that the two mirrors will be symmetrical.

4. Hold the drill perpendicular to the surface, with the bit seated in the indentation. First drill pilot holes with a 1/16-in. bit, then drill each hole to the correct size.

2. Hold the mirror in the correct position and mark the screw holes with a felt-tip pen. Remove the mirror. Make an indentation for the drill bit at each mark with a center punch and hammer.

5. Screw on mirror; apply liquid locking compound to each screw before inserting it to prevent rust and keep screws from vibrating loose. Adjust mirror to eliminate blind spot.

3. Use a drill bit the diameter of the screw's shank (not threads) to drill mounting holes. Hold the screw and the bit together to accurately determine which bit has the correct diameter.

To replace a mirror, drill out the enlarged holes for oversize screws or plastic screw anchors. Tap the screw anchors into the holes with a hammer (they should fit snugly).

Cleaning and repairing upholstery

Clean vinyl upholstery as you would a vinyl top, with special products made for the purpose (see p.313). Do not use harsh detergents, abrasives, or cleaning fluid on vinyl, as they will damage the surface. Use a whisk broom or vacuum to remove ordinary dirt from cloth upholstery. If cloth is stained, treat the stain as indicated in the chart at the right. Leather upholstery should be cleaned only with saddle soap and treated with preservatives made especially for leather.

Torn cloth upholstery can sometimes be mended.

However, if it is badly torn or worn out, cover it with a new seat cover. These are made to fit virtually any size and shape seat, in a variety of colors and patterns. To repair torn vinyl upholstery, you must insert a patch between the padding and the cover; if you merely glue the vinyl down, the adhesive will destroy the foam rubber padding. Make the patch for a small tear from the excess material under the seat. For a large tear, buy matching material from an auto upholstery shop or a car dealer.

Repairing vinyl upholstery 30 min–1hr

1. Cut the patch at least ½ in. larger all around than the tear to be sure that no cement will contact the padding. Use nail scissors to trim off all loose threads along the edges of the tear.

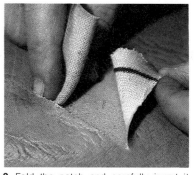

2. Fold the patch and carefully insert it under the tear. Try to avoid ripping the tear any farther. Open the patch so that it lies flat with its finished side facing up, then center it under the tear.

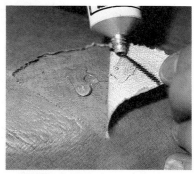

3. Apply auto trim cement evenly to the bottom of the tear and to the top of the patch. Use a thin layer of cement at the edges so that it will not ooze onto the vinyl and mar the finish.

4. Press the torn vinyl gently into place, keeping the edges as close together as possible. If the damage is still visible after the cement has dried, finish it with a vinyl repair kit as described on page 313.

Repairing vinyl piping

A thin wooden matchstick can be used to repair vinyl seat piping that has split. Remove the match head and cut a 1-in. length of wood (too long a piece is impossible to work into the piping).

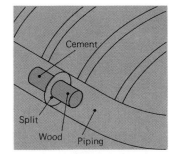

Apply auto trim cement to one end of the stick and insert it halfway into one side of the split. Apply cement to the other end of the stick and work the piping onto it until the edges meet.

Cleaning cloth upholstery 5–10 min

Cloth upholstery in cars is not like that used for home furniture. Car upholstery is chemically treated with a flame retardant, and sometimes with other products to make it stain resistant. Some stains cannot be removed without causing worse damage. For the best results, treat any stain immediately. If this is impossible, blot up or scrape off as much of the stain as you can, and treat it as soon as possible.

STAIN	TREATMENT
Ball-point ink	Use rubbing alcohol. If stain remains after repeated applications, do not try anything else. Ink eradicator will ruin upholstery.
Blood	Wipe with a cloth and cold water. Do not use soap; it may set the stain.
Butter, crayon, oil, grease, margarine	Scrape off excess with a dull knife blade. Use cleaning fluid sparingly.
Candy	Use cloth soaked in lukewarm water for chocolate. Flush other candies with lukewarm water; allow to dry. If necessary, rub lightly with cleaning fluid.
Catsup	Wipe with cloth soaked in cool water. Use mild detergent if more cleaning is needed.
Chewing gum	Harden gum with ice cube, then scrape off with a dull knife blade. Moisten with cleaning fluid and scrape again if necessary.
Coffee, fruit, ice cream, liquor, milk, soda, wine	Wipe with cloth soaked in cold water. If necessary, rub lightly with cleaning fluid. Do not use soap and water, which may set the stain.
Lipstick	Cleaning fluid works on some brands. If stain remains, do not try anything else.
Mustard	Rub with a warm, dampened sponge; then rub mild detergent on dampened stain and work into fabric. Rinse with clean, damp cloth. Repeat several times.
Shoe polish (paste)	Use cleaning fluid sparingly.
Tar	Scrape off excess with a dull knife blade. Moisten with cleaning fluid; scrape again. Rub lightly with more cleaning fluid.
Urine	Sponge with lukewarm soapsuds from a mild soap; rinse with clean cloth soaked in cold water. Soak a cloth in a solution of 1 part ammonia to 5 parts water. Hold it on stain for 1 min. Rinse with a clean, wet cloth.
Vomit	Sponge with a clean cloth dipped in clean, cold water. Wash lightly with lukewarm water and mild soap. If odor persists, treat area with a solution of 1 teaspoon baking soda to 1 cup warm water.

Troubleshooting the brakes

How to use this chart

Find problem at top of chart. Look down column to locate possible causes. First, check out repairs that you can do yourself; then, check repairs you *may* be able to do yourself (possibly with help from a machine shop that specializes in brake work). If problem is still not solved, consult a competent mechanic.

○ You can fix it yourself.
● You *may* be able to make a complete repair.
■ You need a mechanic.
▲ You will need help from a machine shop to make the repair.

Problem column headers (left to right):
1. Brake pedal low (excessive travel)
2. Pedal feels hard
3. Pedal feels spongy
4. Pedal sinks to floor
5. Pedal pulsates
6. Brakes grab
7. One or more brakes drag or lock
8. Brakes pull car to one side
9. Erratic brake performance
10. Brakes are noisy or squeal
11. Brakes do not hold
12. Parking brake does not hold
13. Brake warning light stays lit
14. Brake warning light never lights

1	2	3	4	5	6	7	8	9	10	11	12	13	14	Possible cause	Cure
○		○	○				○			○		○		Low fluid level	Add fluid (p.210). Check for leaks (p.211). Bleed brakes (p.217)
○		○		○			○			○		○		Air in hydraulic system	Bleed brakes (p.217)
●					●	●	●	●	○					Excessive lining clearance	Adjust brakes (p.216), adjust parking brake (p.218), free stuck brake piston (pp.338, 339)
	○							○						Brakes fade due to overheating	Shift into lower gear, coast to a stop, let brakes cool off before driving again
●				●	●	●		●						Grease or fluid on linings or pads	Always replace contaminated pads (pp.330–333) or linings (pp.334–337). Repair leak (pp.338–339)
●					●	●	●	●						Pads or linings are glazed	Replace pads (pp.330–333), linings (pp.334–337), disc (pp.332, 339), or drum (pp.334–337, 339)
○				○		○		○						Brakes are wet	Dry brakes by applying light pedal pressure as you drive until car stops smoothly
●				●		●		●						Faulty vacuum booster	Replace power booster (pp.342–343)
●				●				●						No or low vacuum at booster	Replace vacuum hose (p.342). Troubleshoot engine problems (pp.386–387)
○				○	○	○		○						Linkage binding at pedal or brake	Lubricate pedal linkage or have brakes checked
●	●		●					●						Flexible hoses are weak	Replace all hoses (p.340), bleed brakes (p.217)
				●	●									Loose or worn wheel bearings	Adjust wheel bearings (pp.220–221); replace wheel bearings (p.219)
						■	■							Loose or worn front-end parts	Have steering gearbox adjusted (p.194) or have front-end parts replaced
				■			■							Front wheels are out of alignment	Have wheels aligned
▲			▲	▲		▲	▲							Warped brake disc, out-of-round drum	Remove disc (pp.330–333) or have it removed and refinished or replaced (p.339)
▲	▲	▲	▲		▲	▲	▲		▲			▲		Faulty wheel cylinder or caliper	Replace wheel cylinder (p.338) or caliper (p.339)
●	●	●	●			●		●		●		●		Faulty master cylinder	Replace master cylinder (p.341)
					●	●	●							Weak or broken drum-brake spring	Replace shoe-return springs (pp.334–337)
				▲		▲	▲	▲						Scored brake drums or discs	Remove disc (pp.330–333) or have it removed and refinished or replaced (p.339)
					○		○	○						Dirt in brake mechanism	Inspect and clean brakes (p.210) and free stuck parts (pp.330–337)
●					●	●	●							Kinked brake hose or line	Replace brake hose (p.340) or have brake line replaced
●					●		●		●					Clogged hydraulic system	Bleed brakes (p.217) if possible. Flush hydraulic system (p.217)
											●			Hand brake cable is stuck or broken	Free, lubricate, or replace parking brake (p.218)
●			●		●	●	●	●						Brake linings or pads are worn	Replace disc-brake pads (pp.330–333) or drum-brake linings (pp.334–337)
		○	○	○	○									Incorrect tire pressures. Bald tire	Inflate tires to correct pressures (pp.184–185) or replace tire (pp.184–185)
●					●							●		Loss of pressure in part of dual system	Repair hydraulic system (pp.338–343)
												●		Differential pressure valve not centered	Center differential pressure valve (p.217). Or replace valve and bleed brakes (p.217)
												●	●	Wiring, switch, or bulb is defective	Repair circuit, replace switch or bulb (pp.361–363, 369–371)
●					●		●							Faulty proportioning valve	Replace valve or have it replaced. Bleed brakes (p.217)
●	●	●			●	●	●					●		Contaminated brake fluid	Drain and replace fluid (p.217). Check and replace any damaged hydraulic components (pp.338–347)

Replacing disc-brake pads ⬛⬛⬛ 1–2 hr

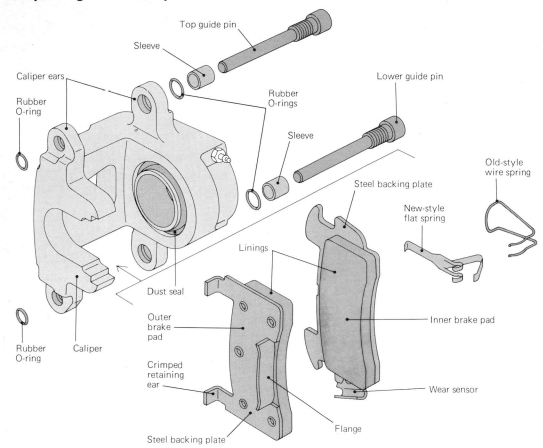

Top guide pin

Sleeve

Caliper ears

Rubber O-ring

Rubber O-rings

Sleeve

Lower guide pin

Old-style wire spring

Steel backing plate

New-style flat spring

Linings

Dust seal

Outer brake pad

Inner brake pad

Crimped retaining ear

Rubber O-ring

Caliper

Wear sensor

Steel backing plate

Flange

The Delco Moraine front disc brake shown here is used on all GM rear-drive cars except the subcompacts. The steps for changing pads on most other disc brakes are basically the same. Front-drive GM cars like the Chevrolet Citation have similar disc brakes but lack the brackets that support the caliper during repairs, so that the caliper must be hung on a wire coat hanger. On some cars you may be able to hang the caliper on a suspension arm or steering knuckle without twisting or stretching the brake hose. Cars with sliding calipers that are held by keys or wedges are serviced in much the same way (see p.332).

Caution: Most brake linings contain asbestos, now considered a health hazard. Wear a respirator or a face mask in order to avoid inhaling dust particles. Keep dust levels down; do not blow or vigorously brush dust from brake parts.

Tools: 7-in. C-clamp, ⅜-in. Allen wrench, wire coat hanger, 12-in. water-pump pliers, small screwdriver, syringe, sleeve installer (optional), wire brush, rubber mallet, jack, jack stands.

Materials: Complete disc-brake pad parts kit, denatured alcohol or disc-brake cleaner, rags, respirator or face mask.

1. Position car on level working area. Put an automatic transmission in *Park,* a manual transmission in *Reverse.* Engage parking brake.
2. Remove hubcaps from both front wheels (see p.185).
3. Loosen lug nuts on both front wheels, but do not remove the nuts.
4. Use 4 by 4 lumber or large stones to chock the rear wheels. Raise and support front end of car (see p.176).
5. Remove lug nuts and both front wheels. From this point onward, work on one brake until it is finished, using the other fully assembled brake as a model to guide you.

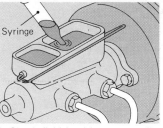

Syringe

6. Check fluid level in master cylinder. If it has been topped up to compensate for pad wear, remove two-thirds of the fluid with a syringe.
Caution: Do not use syringe for anything except brake fluid, which is poisonous. Discard the old fluid; never reuse brake fluid.

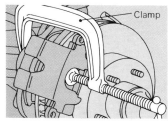

Clamp

7. Place a 7-in. C-clamp over the caliper so that the clamp's screw rests on the outer brake pad and the other end is on the back of the caliper. Tighten the clamp to push the piston back into its bore far enough for the pads to clear the rotor when you lift off the caliper.

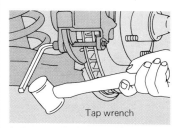

Tap wrench

8. Remove the lower guide pin from the caliper support bracket. This pin usually has a ⅜-in. Allen head, but some cars have been built with hex-head bolts. The pin will be tight; you may have to tap the Allen wrench with a hammer to start it.

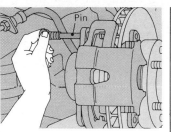

Pin

9. Remove bracket's top guide pin. There is not enough clearance to pull pin all the way out when the car's front wheels are pointed straight ahead. Turn the steering wheel to move the caliper away from the frame and gain working clearance.

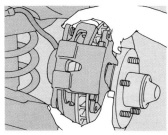

10. Lift caliper off rotor. If pads are pushed back, it should come off. If pads catch on the ridge of rust at the edge of the rotor, repeat Step 7. Sand off severe rust.

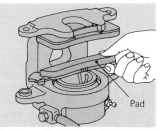

Pad

11. Turn caliper open side up. Lift out inner pad and spring assembly (if any) if it did not fall out as you removed the caliper. Newer support springs are made of flat metal; older springs are wire. Replacement pads work with either kind of spring, but the flat type that clips in place is easier to assemble correctly.

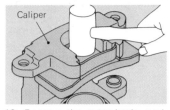

12. Remove the outer brake pad from the caliper. You may need to tap it out with a hammer handle or soft-faced hammer if the pad's ears have been crimped very tightly.

13. Check dust seal on piston for cuts or tears. Gently wipe off brake dust, being careful not to unseat the seal or get dust into the seal's seating edge. If the seal is damaged, have it replaced and the caliper checked or rebuilt by a machine shop. If there is any sign of fluid leakage, replace the caliper or have it rebuilt. To remove caliper, disconnect brake hose (p.340); you will have to bleed the brakes (p.217) when you reinstall the caliper. Inspect rotor surface. If it is scored, worn, or discolored, have machine shop check for warping. Rotor is removed in the same way a drum is (pp.213–214).

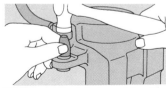

14. Remove the tubular metal guide pin sleeves from the inside upper and lower caliper ears. Sleeves should push out through their rubber O-rings and will move with finger pressure. If a sleeve sticks, drive it out with a light hammer, using a hardwood dowel as a drift.

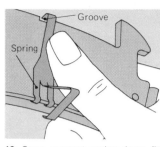

15. Remove the rubber O-rings from the inner and outer caliper ears with a small screwdriver. Take care not to scratch the holes or grooves.
16. Lubricate the new O-rings with any good silicone lubricant. Use your fingers or a dull screwdriver to install O-rings in the grooves in the caliper ears. Be careful not to-cut the rings or mar the grooves.
17. Push the tubular metal guide pin sleeves into their holes in the inner ears of the caliper. The rubber O-rings will hold them in place. A cone-shaped installing tool is recommended to guide the sleeve, but sleeve can often be worked into position with the fingers.

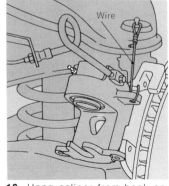

18. Hang caliper from hook on mounting bracket. If there is none, bend a wire coat hanger into a hook, and support caliper from the suspension so that it does not stretch the hydraulic hose. Do not twist or stretch hose as you clean, inspect, or install new pads in the caliper.

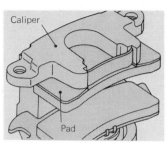

19. Snap support spring (new flat type) onto steel back on inner pad. Upper tab fits in groove, and two lower tabs clip over bottom edge.

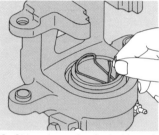

20. Older wire spring for inside pad fits in piston cavity. Holding its top away from piston, install pad with bottom edge of metal backing resting on piston; the two spring ends should bear on center of pad. Push down on top of pad until it lies flat on piston. Spring ends must not stick out.

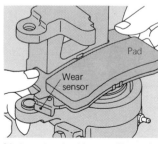

21. Inner pad with new flat spring can be snapped into caliper by thumb pressure on ears. Lining faces rotor, with steel backing against piston and wear sensor down. Spring fits into piston cavity. Spring pressure holds pad.

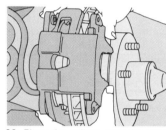

22. Install outer brake pad in the caliper: lining faces the inner pad; steel backing faces the caliper. The two ears on outer pad fit over the two outer ears of caliper. Bottom flange on the pad fits into the cut-out section of the caliper.

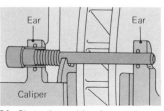

23. Place the caliper over the rotor. Slide caliper down until the holes in the ears line up with the holes in the support bracket. Avoid twisting brake hose. Grooves in the hose should be straight. If they are not, the hose is twisted.

24. Clean the guide pins, and coat their inner ends with silicone lubricant. Push pins through guide sleeves in the inside ears of the caliper and through the holes in support bracket. Pins must go under the ears on the inner brake pad and into the outer ears of the caliper until threads engage support bracket.

25. Tighten the mounting pins to 35 lb-ft (47 N-m) torque if you have an Allen bit and torque wrench. If not, tap the long end of the Allen wrench with a hammer to be sure that the guide pin is tight.
26. Check brake fluid level in the master cylinder. If low, add more.
27. Pump brake pedal to seat new pads on the rotor. The pedal will go to the floor five times or more before the pads seat and you feel the pedal come up to its normal level. Brake fluid level in the master cylinder will drop as the caliper piston pushes the pads against the rotor. Make sure master cylinder does not run dry and allow air into the system. If it does, bleed the brakes (p.217).

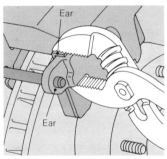

28. Crimp ears on outer brake pad over caliper ears with water-pump pliers until there is no clearance between the pad and the caliper.
29. Go back to Step 7 and replace pads on the other front brake, using assembly you have just finished as a model for how the parts fit.
30. Reinstall the front wheels and tighten the wheel lugs finger-tight.
31. Raise the car off the jack stands, remove the jack stands, and lower the car to the ground.
32. Tighten the wheel lugs in a criss-cross pattern (see p.185).
33. Replace the hubcaps. Tap a rubber mallet around the edges of the hubcaps to seat them so that they will not fall off and get lost.
34. Pump up the brake pedal before moving the car. Recheck fluid level in the master cylinder, and top it up. For maximum service life, use the brakes gently for the first 100 mi to break in the new pads.

Replacing disc-brake pads ☑☑☑ 1–3 hr

Most disc brakes have a single piston and a sliding caliper (see pp.106–107). Some older designs have two or four pistons in fixed calipers. The steps involved in replacing pads on any modern sliding-caliper brake are similar to those on pages 330–331. Other popular designs are shown on these two pages. Work on one brake at a time, keeping the other as a correctly assembled model to guide you.

Do not remove the flexible brake hose from the caliper unless you find that the caliper is leaking or the dust seal is damaged. In that case, take the caliper off the car and exchange it for a new or rebuilt caliper, or have it rebuilt by a machine shop that does brake work. Do not let the caliper hang by the hose; support it with a piece of wire coat hanger. Avoid twisting the hose when you reinstall the caliper.

If you are replacing the pads on one side of the car, always replace the pads for the opposite wheel at the same time. If discs are deeply scored, heavily worn, or discolored, have them checked and resurfaced by a machine shop. Use silicone lubricant on rubber caliper bushings. Always pump the brake pedal until it holds firmly before you drive the car.

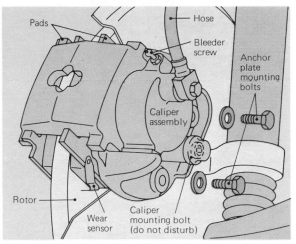

Chevrolet Chevette has Delco Moraine disc brakes with a single piston and two mounting bolts. Push the piston back into the caliper with a 7-in. C-clamp. Remove caliper by taking out two bolts between the anchor plate and steering knuckle. Install new pads so that wear sensor (if any) on inner pad faces rear of car. Bolt caliper to knuckle. Torque bolts to 70 lb-ft (95 N-m).

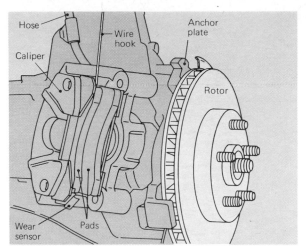

Chevrolet Citation, Pontiac Phoenix, Oldsmobile Omega, and Buick Skylark have a Delco Moraine single-piston caliper closely resembling the one shown on pages 330–331. Pad-changing procedures are similar except that the caliper must be supported on a hook made of coat hanger wire because the anchor has no bracket. Torque mounting bolts to 35 lb-ft (47 N-m).

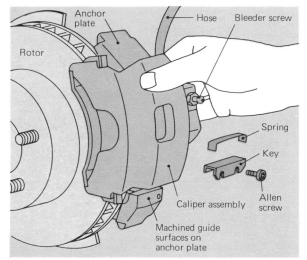

Ford and Chrysler Kelsey-Hayes single-piston sliding calipers are similar. To change pads, remove the Allen screw and take out the caliper-retaining key or keys. Lift the caliper assembly off the anchor plate. Clean machined guide surfaces with a wire brush. During reinstallation, cover the piston with a piece of thin, smooth cardboard to prevent it from cutting the dust boot.

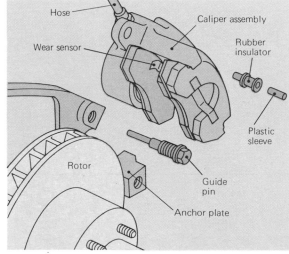

Ford Fairmont, Mustang, Pinto, and Granada; Mercury Capri, Monarch, and Zephyr have Kelsey-Hayes sliding calipers. Unscrew guide pins, then lift off the caliper. Clean sliding surfaces with a wire brush. Inner pads are marked *LH* and *RH* (for left and right wheels). Install outer pads so that wear sensors face forward. Use new rubber insulators and plastic sleeves.

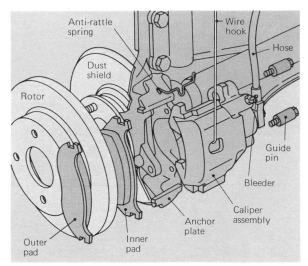

Omni, Horizon: Remove guide pins and anti-rattle spring, then lift caliper off rotor. Remove outer pad from anchor plate, slide rotor off hub studs, and lift out inner pad. Use C-clamp to push piston back. Install inner pad, reinstall rotor, and hold outer pad in position while lowering caliper over disc. **Caution:** Do not cross-thread guide pins; torque them to 35 lb-ft (47 N-m).

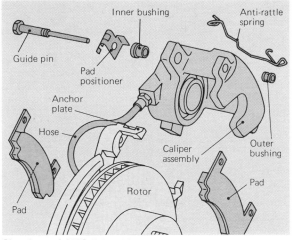

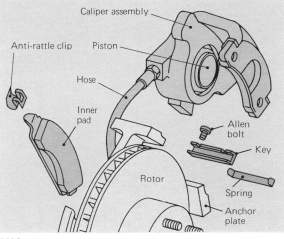

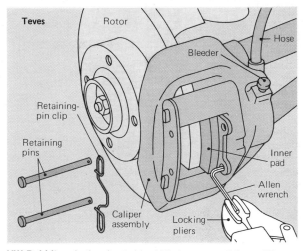

Chrysler and AMC Kelsey-Hayes caliper is secured by two guide pins and, on AMC cars, by anti-rattle clips as well. Remove pins, lift off caliper, slide out pads. Clean sliding surfaces and replace inner and outer bushing in caliper ears. Replace inner pad. Hold outer pad in place while sliding caliper over rotor. Align guide pins; do not cross-thread them. Torque pins to 33 lb-ft (45 N-m).

AMC cars, Ford Pintos, and Mercury Bobcats with Bendix brakes: Push piston into caliper with a C-clamp or by prying on pads with a screwdriver. Remove ¼-in. Allen bolt from anchor plate. Drive out key and spring, then lift off caliper. Clean sliding surfaces and grease them with molydisulfide grease. Outer pad may have to be tapped into position with a hammer.

VW Rabbit and other front-drive VWs have one of three different disc brakes. You can change the Teves and Girling pads on German-made cars without removing the caliper. Drive out retaining pins and pull the pads out with locking pliers. American-built cars have Kelsey-Hayes sliding calipers (far left). Remove anti-rattle springs, guide pins, and caliper to change pads.

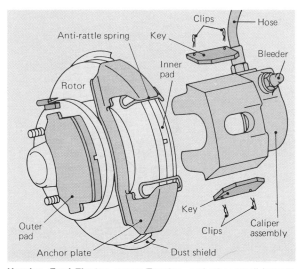

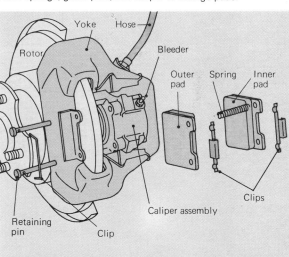

Hondas, Ford Fiestas, many Toyotas, and other small imports have disc-brake calipers with two keys. Remove retaining clips, drive out keys, tip caliper out of anchors, and lift it off the rotor. Push piston into caliper with a C-clamp. Clean keys and machined surfaces, lubricate with silicone grease, fit pads into caliper, place caliper over rotor. Drive keys back in place and reinstall clips.

Datsuns and Toyotas have two-piston, two-cylinder calipers on some models. Remove wire clips and pad-retaining pins from caliper. On cars with electronic wear sensors, remove wiring harness from clamp on knuckle, then unplug wiring from pad. Lift out anti-squeal shims and pads. Replace pads. Arrows on shims must point in direction of disc rotation. Reinstall anti-rattle spring.

Many Datsuns have two pistons in the same caliper cylinder. One pushes on the inner pad, and the other pushes on the yoke that applies the outer pad. Remove clips and pad pins, lift out anti-squeal springs and pads. Push pistons into caliper by prying between piston and disc with a screwdriver; take care not to damage rubber boot. Replace pads; reinstall springs and pins.

Replacing brake linings ▢▢▢ 1½–3 hr

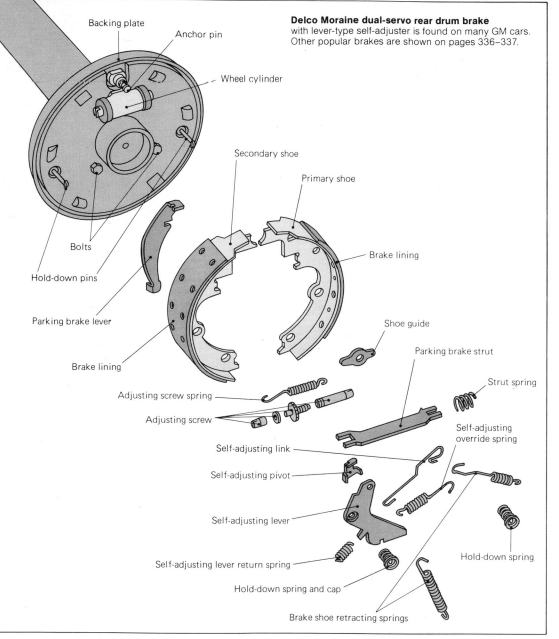

Delco Moraine dual-servo rear drum brake
with lever-type self-adjuster is found on many GM cars. Other popular brakes are shown on pages 336–337.

Backing plate

Anchor pin

Wheel cylinder

Secondary shoe

Primary shoe

Brake lining

Bolts

Hold-down pins

Parking brake lever

Brake lining

Shoe guide

Parking brake strut

Adjusting screw spring

Adjusting screw

Strut spring

Self-adjusting override spring

Self-adjusting link

Self-adjusting pivot

Self-adjusting lever

Self-adjusting lever return spring

Hold-down spring

Hold-down spring and cap

Brake shoe retracting springs

When inspection shows that drum-brake linings have worn too close to the metal surfaces of the brake shoes (see p.215), new linings are required. Linings that are attached to the shoes by rivets should be replaced when worn down to within 1/32 in. of the rivet heads. Bonded linings may wear down to 1/16 in. thick. In order to maintain equal braking action on both sides of the car, the brakes must be serviced in pairs; that is, you must replace the brake shoes and linings on both rear wheels or both front wheels at the same time, even if you find that only one wheel of either set needs new linings. When you purchase new linings, take the brake drums and the old shoes to a dealer or automotive machine shop for inspection. If necessary, have the drums turned on a lathe to correct scoring or distortion. Replace drums that are damaged or warped. Trade in the old shoes for new ones that have been relined and individually machined to fit inside the renewed drums exactly. Label each set of mated drums and shoes and keep them together for correct reinstallation.

Caution: Most brake linings contain asbestos, now considered a health hazard. Wear a respirator or face mask when working on drum brakes in order to avoid inhaling asbestos particles. Keep dust levels down; do not blow or vigorously brush accumulated material from brake parts.

Tools: Brake-spring pliers, locking pliers, long-nose pliers, wire brush, jack, jack stands, wrenches to fit axle nuts and lug nuts.
Materials: Respirator or face mask, paper, pencil, clean rags, detergent/water solution, plastic bags and seals or tape, emery cloth, parts-cleaning solvent, high melting point grease.

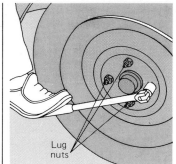

Lug nuts

1. Park car on level ground. Engage *Reverse* (on manual transmissions) or *Park* (on automatic transmissions) and parking brake. Remove hubcaps. Loosen wheel lugs but do not remove them until car is off the ground.
2. Raise car and support it safely on jack stands (p.176). Chock front or rear wheels, depending on which end of car is raised. If you are working on the rear brakes, place transmission in *Neutral* and release parking brake, once car is secure.
3. Remove wheels and brake drums (pp.185, 214). Label axle parts and group them together in plastic bags. Set parts aside for cleaning. Wipe dust from inside of drums, using a cloth soaked in water and detergent. Avoid inhaling dust. Inspect drums for wear, then label and set them aside, open side down.

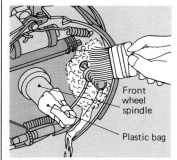

Front wheel spindle

Plastic bag

4. Cover spindles with plastic bags, and tape or seal tightly to keep grit off threads. Slosh detergent/water solution over exposed brake assembly to remove dust.

5. Before removing any parts, sketch or photograph the brake shoe assembly so that you can reinstall the components correctly.

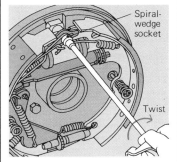

Spiral-wedge socket

Twist

6. Remove brake shoe's retracting springs, using the spiral-wedge socket end of the brake pliers, or ordinary pliers.

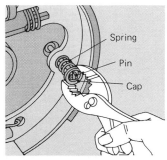

Spring

Pin

Cap

7. Remove brake shoe's hold-down springs by depressing them with brake tool or pliers, then twisting until slotted caps slip off pins.

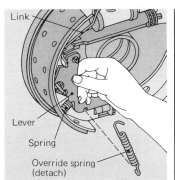

Link

Lever

Spring

Override spring (detach)

8. Lift up on self-adjusting lever and unhook link from anchor pin. Remove link, pin, and lever spring.

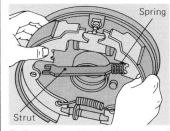

Spring

Strut

9. Remove parking brake strut and spring by spreading brake shoes clear of wheel cylinder. Disconnect parking brake cable from lever. Then remove brake shoes, adjusting screw assembly and spring as a unit.

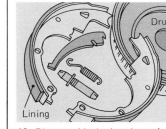

Drum

Lining

10. Disassemble brake shoes from adjusting screw and spring. Remove parking brake lever from secondary brake shoe. Note that primary shoe has shorter lining than secondary shoe. Check both linings for uneven wear patterns. Label shoes, then set them aside with matching drums.

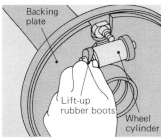

Backing plate

Lift-up rubber boots

Wheel cylinder

11. Clean all brake parts with parts-cleaning solvent or denatured alcohol. Tighten backing plate bolts if necessary. Check wheel cylinders for leaks (p.215). On rear wheels, inspect backing plate for leaks past oil seal of rear wheel bearings.

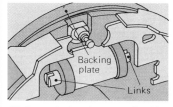

Contact points

12. Using wire brush and emery cloth, remove rust from brake shoe contact points on backing plate. Spread a light film of high melting point grease on contact points.

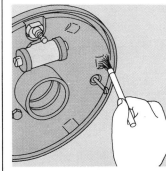

13. Lubricate fulcrum of parking brake lever with high melting point grease. Reattach lever to secondary shoe; make sure lever moves freely.

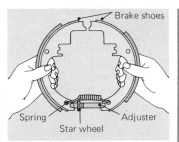

Brake shoes

Spring

Star wheel

Adjuster

14. Open adjuster, clean threads, and lubricate with penetrating oil. If star wheel will not turn freely or has chipped teeth, replace adjuster. Connect relined shoes to adjuster spring, then install adjuster. Spring must not touch star wheel. Right-hand threaded screw goes on left side of car and vice versa. Star wheel must line up with access hole.

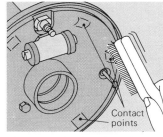

Backing plate

Links

15. Place brake shoes on backing plate by slipping shoes into slotted links in wheel cylinder. Primary shoe faces front. On rear brakes, install parking brake's strut and spring. Reconnect parking brake cable.

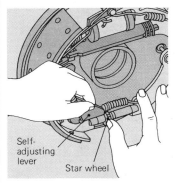

Link

Springs

Lever

16. Reinstall self-adjusting lever, spring, and link.

17. Replace shoe's hold-down springs. If these or any other brake springs are nicked, discolored by heat, or weak, install new ones.

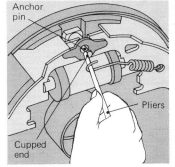

Anchor pin

Pliers

Cupped end

18. Reinstall brake shoe's retracting springs, using brake-spring pliers, long-nose pliers, or locking pliers. Help is sometimes needed to stretch spring and engage its hooked end. Use cupped end of brake pliers to lever springs around anchor pin. Do not damage or distort springs.

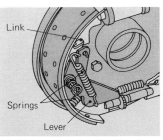

Self-adjusting lever

Star wheel

19. Lift self-adjusting lever, and screw star wheel in or out until diameter of brake shoes is slightly smaller than diameter of brake drum. Then fit drum over brake assembly. Reinstall axle parts and wheels (pp.219–221). Tighten lug nuts finger-tight.

20. Bleed brakes if necessary (p.217). Adjust parking brake (p.218). Check fluid in master cylinder (p.210). Check pedal's firmness and return. Lower car to ground. Tighten wheel lugs. Replace hubcaps. Make several low-speed stops in *Reverse* to set self-adjusters. Brake linings must wear in; try to avoid sudden stops for the next 100 miles.

Popular drum-brake designs

Large and mid-size North American cars generally have dual-servo, self-adjusting drum brakes, similar to the type illustrated on pp.334–335 except for their spring layout and other minor details. "Dual-servo" means that the entire brake shoe assembly shifts in the direction the wheel is turning as the car stops, pivoting against the brake drum to provide extra stopping power (see p.109). The secondary shoes do about 70 percent of the work; their linings must therefore be longer than those on the primary shoes, in order to provide a larger braking surface. Brake linings attached to the secondary shoes are often made of longer-lasting material than that lining the primary shoes. When buying replacement linings for any brakes, always ask for *premium-grade* linings.

Most imported cars, as well as small North American cars with disc brakes on their front wheels, have rear non-servo drum brakes that do not pivot. Instead, the shoes rest against fixed points—usually the wheel cylinder and a stationary anchor plate or block—at both top and bottom. Non-servo brakes have linings of equal length and friction characteristics.

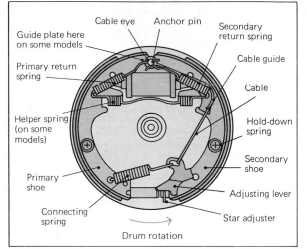

Dual-servo brake with cable-type adjuster is found chiefly on AMC and Ford cars and on a few other makes. Unless it has an anchor-retaining plate, the cable eye should be installed between the primary and secondary shoe-return springs. Replace cable if it is frayed or stretched.

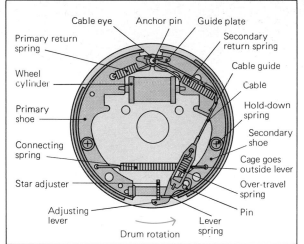

Dual-servo brake with over-travel spring adjuster is found on Chrysler cars. Install shoes and hold-down springs first, then fit lever spring over pin on secondary shoe. Next, install adjusting lever under spring but over anchor pin, as shown. Connect over-travel spring so that its cage is outside adjusting lever.

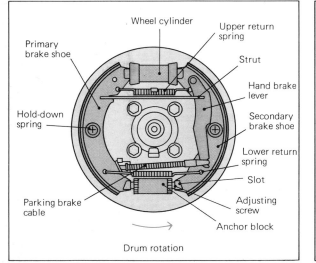

Non-servo rear brake with manual shoe adjusters is found on VW Beetles and other imports. To remove axle nuts, see p.213. Install screw adjusters in anchor block. Position screws so their slots will match angle of brake shoe ends. Then install shoes, strut, return spring, hold-down springs, and parking brake cable.

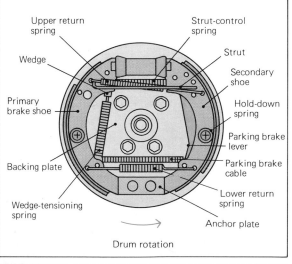

VW Rabbit non-servo rear brake with automatic wedge adjusters is found on 1980 and later models. Wedge fits behind primary brake shoe and passes through slot in hand brake strut. When reassembling brake, attach upper return spring to shoes first, then attach shoes to backing plate.

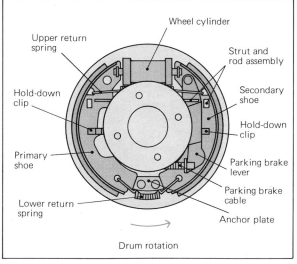

Vega non-servo rear brake used on 1975 and earlier cars has clips instead of hold-down springs. Applying the parking brake adjusts the brake by lengthening a strut and rod assembly. Special tool (available from auto parts stores) is needed to shorten strut to its original length when new brake shoes are installed.

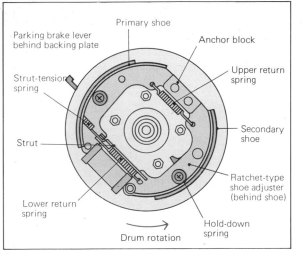

Fiesta non-servo rear brake has automatic ratchet adjuster. Anchor block is near top of backing plate; wheel cylinder is near bottom. Adjuster mechanism connects to parking brake lever protruding through hole in backing plate. Mechanism is complicated; consult service manual for repair procedure.

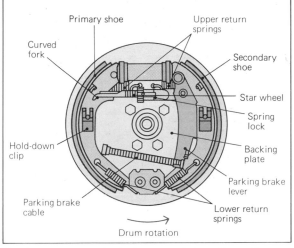

Omni non-servo rear brake has manual shoe adjuster. Fit upper return springs and brake shoes first, then install adjuster between shoes, with curved fork pointing down and spring lock facing away from backing plate. Next, install hold-down clips, the lower return springs, and the parking brake cable.

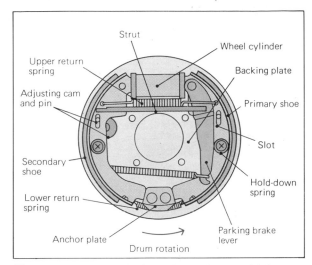

Chevette non-servo rear brake used in 1976–79 models has cam adjusters attached to backing plate. Pin on each adjuster cam fits through slot in each brake shoe. To retract shoes before removing drum, rotate adjusting bolts on outside of backing plate. Turn left-hand bolt clockwise and right-hand bolt counterclockwise.

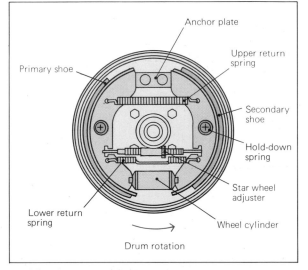

Honda non-servo rear brake has square-drive manual shoe-adjusting mechanism. Parking brake lever is attached to strut and protrudes through hole in backing plate. Sedan brakes have shoe-to-shoe return springs. Upper return springs in station wagons are linked to parking brake strut.

Datsun non-servo rear brake has manual shoe adjuster. Anchor plate is at top of backing plate, wheel cylinder at bottom. Parking brake lever protrudes through hole in plate and attaches to star wheel adjuster, which acts as a strut. Lining on the secondary shoe is mounted higher than lining on the primary shoe.

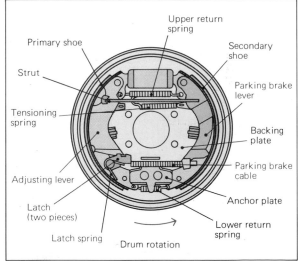

Toyota non-servo rear brake with automatic ratchet adjuster is found in Coronas and Mark IIs. To reassemble, first install secondary shoe and strut on backing plate; then primary shoe, with adjusting lever and latch. Push latch down; move lever toward center of wheel to retract shoes for installation.

337

Replacing a wheel cylinder ⚑⚑⚑⚑ 30 min–2 ½ hr

Wheel cylinders in drum brakes fail when they leak or the pistons stick. If a cylinder is leaking, there will be wetness or excessive fluid inside the rubber dust boot (p.215). Stuck pistons cause erratic braking and uneven lining wear (p.215).

When relining brakes on an older car, many brake shops automatically rebuild wheel cylinders and replace hoses as a precaution. Wear, deposits, and dirty fluid can cause wheel cylinders to leak. If leaking fluid gets on the new linings, they must be discarded. If you are replacing the master cylinder on an old car with high mileage, it is a good idea to replace the wheel cylinders too, as the increased pressure generated by a new master cylinder may dislodge the seals in old wheel cylinders.

It should not be necessary to replace wheel cylinders on newer cars when the brake shoes are replaced unless, of course, the cylinder is leaking. Automatic brake adjusters keep the pistons working in the same portion of the bores, so that problems with them occur far less frequently than with manually adjusted brakes.

Any malfunctioning wheel cylinder must be replaced. Most cast-iron wheel cylinders can be rebuilt from kits of inexpensive parts, but the results, especially in the hands of inexperienced car owners, can be less than satisfactory. Many cylinders cannot be rebuilt because honing can create excessive clearance between the brake piston and cylinder.

Once the brake shoes have been removed (p.334), disconnect the hydraulic hose (p.340) from a front wheel cylinder or from the steel brake line to a rear wheel cylinder. Do not bend a metal line away from the cylinder. Release the retaining clip or remove the bolts that hold the cylinder to the backing plate, then lift the cylinder off.

Install the new wheel cylinder on the backing plate and begin screwing the brake line fitting by hand to avoid cross-threading it. Then install the retaining clip or tighten the mounting bolts, and tighten the hose or brake line fittings completely. Reassemble the other brake parts, and bleed the system (p.217).

Tools: Tubing wrench or flare wrench, socket wrenches, bleeder wrench, 1⅛-in. socket, extension, two ⅛-in. awls.
Materials: Wood block, isopropyl (rubbing) alcohol or brake cleaner, brake fluid, replacement wheel cylinders.

Bolt-on cylinders

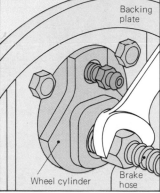

1. Loosen brake lines or hose fitting after removing other parts from backing plate (p.334). Use a tubing wrench or flare wrench. Do not bend tubing away from threaded opening in wheel cylinder; bending the tube will make it difficult to line up with the replacement cylinder. When removing or attaching the brake hose at the wheel cylinder (p.340), do not twist hose.

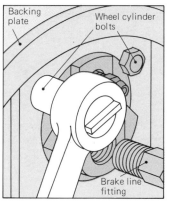

2. Most wheel cylinders fit in holes in the brake backing plate and are held by two small bolts. Cylinders in some GM cars have retainer clips (see details at right). Loosen and remove the bolt or bolts holding the wheel cylinder. Lift cylinder off the backing plate without bending the brake line. Save bolts to mount the replacement.

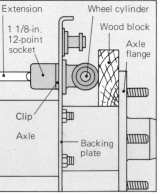

3. Lift wheel cylinder out of its mounting hole in the brake backing plate. Some designs have a lip that hooks over the edge of the opening, in which case cylinder must be tipped out of the backing plate to unhook it. Plug the open end of the brake line with a pencil eraser to keep out dirt. Take the old wheel cylinder to an auto parts store to match it exactly with the replacement, which must have the same bore size.

Clip-on cylinders

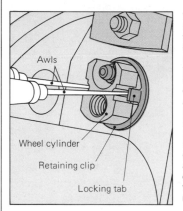

1. Stamped-steel retainers secure the wheel cylinders on the Chevrolet Citation and many other GM cars. If you find no bolts on the backing plate, look for a circular retaining clip. After disconnecting brake pipe (left) or the brake hose (p.340), release the clip by bending its locking tabs outward with two ⅛-in. awls until the tabs spring over the shoulder of the wheel cylinder, releasing it.

2. Lift cylinder off backing plate. Retaining clip must be replaced with a new one, which comes with the new wheel cylinder. Do not reuse the old clip, which will be distorted as you remove it. Plug exposed brake line with a pencil eraser to keep out dirt. When replacing any part of the hydraulic brake system, flush old or discolored fluid out of the system and replace with new DoT 3 or DoT 4 fluid.

3. Insert new wheel cylinder in backing plate hole and screw on pipe fitting by hand. Wedge a wood block between axle flange and wheel cylinder to hold cylinder against backing plate. Position new retaining clip so that its tabs are horizontal and point away from backing plate. Press both tabs under cylinder shoulders, using a 1⅛-in. socket and an extension. Tighten brake line fittings, assemble brake, and bleed system.

Replacing a disc-brake caliper ⏱⏱⏱⏱ 45 min–3 hr

Calipers on disc brakes fail in the same ways as wheel cylinders in drum brakes do. Corrosion causes pistons to stick in their bores, brake fluid leaks out past the seals, or the bleeder valve freezes or breaks off. The cures for these problems are the same: replace the caliper or install a bleeder valve kit (p.340).

If the outer dust shield is undamaged, some sticking caliper pistons can be freed by working them into and out of their bores. Push the piston in all the way with a large C-clamp. When it bottoms, release the C-clamp and have a helper gently tap the brake pedal. The piston will move out of the cylinder about ⅛ inch each time the pedal is tapped. When the piston protrudes about ¼ inch from the caliper, stop tapping the pedal and use the C-clamp to push the piston to the bottom of its bore. Repeat three or four times. If the piston then moves smoothly in its bore, you have solved the problem, at least temporarily.

Any sign of fluid leakage or any damage to the dust seal indicates that dirt has entered the bore and that the caliper must be rebuilt or replaced.

As with wheel cylinders, a caliper can be rebuilt with relatively inexpensive parts, but you are usually better off replacing it. The parts store or machine shop where you get your brake parts can rebuild a caliper if the bore is not corroded or scored. You can also buy a factory-rebuilt caliper from a parts store or a new caliper from a car dealer.

To remove a disc-brake caliper, follow the instructions for changing disc-brake pads (pp.330–333). When the caliper is attached to the car only by its hydraulic hose (as it will be if you discover the need for a new caliper while you are changing brake pads), disconnect the hose, taking care not to twist it. The easy way to hold the caliper while loosening the hose is to temporarily remount it on the car. Plug the exposed end of the brake pipe or hose with a pencil eraser to keep out dirt.

Take the faulty caliper to a parts store to make sure that it is a perfect match with the new or rebuilt replacement. Then turn it in for credit toward the purchase of the replacement. Attach the hose, reassemble the brake, and bleed the system (p.217).

Tools: Flare wrench or open-end wrench.
Materials: Copper washers, brake fluid, pencil eraser.

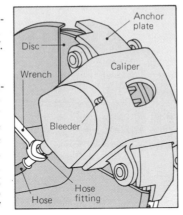

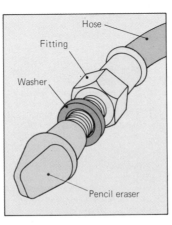

1. Hose fittings on front disc-brake calipers are tight. To hold the caliper firmly while loosening the hose fitting, remount the caliper on the anchor temporarily (p.331). Loosen the fitting with a correctly fitted flare wrench. If you do not have a flare wrench, use a tightly fitting open-end wrench, taking care not to round off the corners on the fitting. When the fitting is loosened, do not unscrew it immediately.

2. Once the fitting is loose, do not twist the brake hose any further. Instead, take caliper out of its mounting on the car and turn the caliper to unscrew it from the hose. Take care not to lose the copper sealing washer on the fitting. This should be replaced with a new one; take the old washer to an auto parts store to be sure you get an exact replacement. Check the hose and replace it if it is cracked, brittle, swollen, or spongy (p.340).

3. Loss of brake fluid through the open end of the hydraulic hose can be prevented by putting one of the rubber caps from a bleeder valve over the tip. If there is no cap or if it will not fit over the threaded fitting on the hose, use a rubber eraser designed to fit over the end of a pencil after the original eraser is worn down. A cap also keeps dirt out of the hydraulic system. Always bleed the system and change all fluid when replacing a caliper.

Brake hose seats

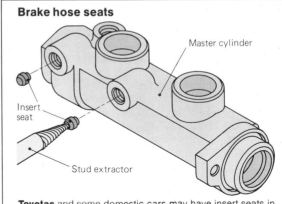

Toyotas and some domestic cars may have insert seats in wheel cylinder or master cylinder hydraulic connections. These must be replaced every time the hose is disconnected. Pull out the old seat with a 0.1-in. stud extractor (p.432) or a self-tapping screw and locking pliers. Drive in the new seat with light hammer taps, using a 5/16-in. rod as a drift. On other hydraulic connections, clean threads and fittings with isopropyl alcohol or brake cleaner, replace copper washers, and use sealing compound on threads.

Wear limit specifications

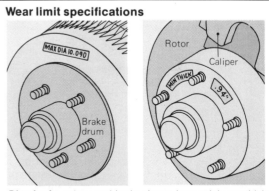

Disc-brake rotors and brake drums have *minimum-thickness* or *maximum-diameter* dimensions cast into the parts. These numbers indicate the minimum thickness or maximum diameter to which a disc or drum can be machined while still leaving it enough material—usually 0.030 in. (0.76 mm)—for wear. A machine shop can measure a disc or drum and refinish it if necessary, or supply a replacement if the part is worn beyond the critical dimension. They can also look up these critical dimensions in brake manuals if the parts on your car are not marked.

Replacing hoses and bleeder valves ☑☑☑ 30 min–2 hr

Replacing a flexible brake hose

Flexible brake hoses may crack, chafe, or weaken so that they swell under pressure. At any sign of leakage or deterioration, replace the hose with another having the same length, strength, and fittings. Some hoses have grooves so that you can tell if they are twisted. Twisting weakens a hose.

A fitting on one end of the hose screws into the wheel cylinder, caliper, or a pipe union. The fitting on the other end is clipped to a bracket on the car body where the hose joins a steel brake line. The clip prevents this connection from turning. Two wrenches, usually of different sizes, must be used to tighten or loosen these fittings to avoid overstressing the hose by twisting it.

> **Tools:** Pliers, flare wrenches, hammer, drift.
> **Materials:** Penetrating oil, brake cleaner, copper sealing washers, bleeder caps or erasers.

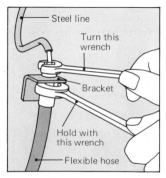

Use pliers to pull out U-shaped clip that secures brake hose to body bracket. If clip sticks, tap it free with a drift and light hammer. It slides toward the side of the clip with the flange. The forked end of the clip fits in a groove around the ferrule on the hose to keep it from twisting. The end of the hose fits through a hole in the bracket, and a flange on the bracket keeps the clip from turning.

Unscrew fitting on steel brake line. Use two wrenches—one to turn the fitting and the other to keep the hose from twisting. Flare wrenches protect soft brass fittings. When hose separates from pipe, plug its end with rubber bleeder cap or eraser. Pull hose through hole in chassis bracket. Unscrew fitting. Reinstall hose, using a new copper sealing washer on the cylinder or caliper joint.

Freeing a stuck bleeder valve

Bleeder valves must always be tight in order to seal properly. Even if they have protective rubber caps, water and salt can corrode the valves tightly in place.

Use penetrating oil and a correctly fitted box wrench or 6-point socket to turn a tight bleeder. If this will not budge it, heat the caliper or wheel cylinder around the valve with a propane torch, taking care not to burn the flexible hose. Then try the wrench again while tapping on the bleeder seat with a light hammer. This usually works. If it does not, get a set of special hammer sockets, which are designed to free stuck bleeders.

If, despite your care, the bleeder valve freezes in place and breaks off, see the procedure at right.

> **Tools:** Box wrench or 6-point socket to fit bleeder, propane torch, light hammer, hammer socket set (if needed).
> **Materials:** Penetrating oil, brake cleaner.

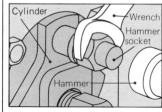

Free stuck bleeder with hammer sockets, available in auto parts stores. Place socket over bleeder, place wrench on socket, and tap with hammer while applying force to wrench. Shock from tapping should free frozen bleeder without breaking it off.

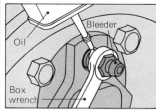

Box wrench, preferably with a 6-point opening, should turn bleeder if hammer socket is not available. Apply penetrating oil around bleeder and down hole. Tap area at base of bleeder with a light hammer while applying force to wrench.

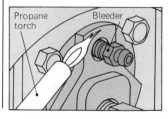

Heat from propane torch applied to area around bleeder may expand threads enough to turn the bleeder. Take care not to overheat caliper or wheel cylinder; avoid burning brake hose. Bleed hydraulic line (p.217) to remove penetrating oil.

Replacing a broken bleeder

Despite the care taken to remove it, a stuck bleeder valve may break off. An inexpensive repair kit can save the cost of replacing an expensive caliper or wheel cylinder. If you cannot do the work yourself, a machine shop that does brake work can install the bleeder screw repair kit for you.

The kit consists of a threaded insert plus a replacement bleeder screw. Specific instructions for drilling out the broken bleeder and retapping the hole come with each kit. See p.433 for procedures. Remove the caliper (p.339) or wheel cylinder (p.338). Clean retapped threads and the entire wheel cylinder or caliper with brake cleaner. Install insert with liquid locking compound. Bleed the brakes (p.217).

> **Tools:** Vise, drill, bits, taps, flare wrenches.
> **Materials:** Bleeder repair kit, brake cleaner, anaerobic liquid locking compound.

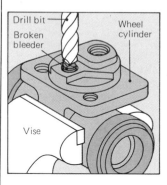

Remove cylinder or caliper from vehicle (pp.338–339) and mount it in a vise. Drill out broken bleeder to the size and depth specified in the instructions that come with repair kit. Enlarging the hole in ⅛-in. increments works better than trying to drill it full size in a single operation. Retap the hole (p.433). Clean out the cylinder and hole with brake cleaner. Remove all metal chips and cutting oil.

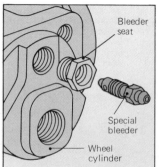

Install bleeder seat insert, using anaerobic liquid locking compound on the threads. Some inserts have hex heads to take a wrench; others are screwed in by turning the bleeder. Torque insert to 35 lb-ft (47 N-m). Remove bleeder. Allow 20 min for locking compound to set. Screw in bleeder and reinstall cylinder (p.338) or caliper (p.339). Reassemble brake and thoroughly flush hydraulic system (p.217) to eliminate contaminants.

Replacing the master cylinder ⏱⏱⏱ 45 min–2 hr

Removing, exchanging, and replacing a master cylinder is easiest on cars with power brakes. Label wires and vacuum lines, unplug any wires, and unscrew the fittings on the lines. Then remove the mounting bolts and lift out the cylinder. Manual brakes on Ford and Chrysler cars may require extra steps (see below). Installing a new or rebuilt cylinder is even easier. To avoid problems with air in the system, pre-bleed the master cylinder before installing it. Then bleed the cylinder at its fittings. If the pedal is firm, you need not bleed the entire system.

Tools: Flare wrenches, sockets, syringe, vise, dowel rod to push in piston, master cylinder bleeder kit.
Materials: New DoT 3 or DoT 4 brake fluid, rags, hot water.

Removing a defective cylinder

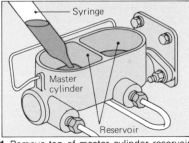

1. Remove top of master cylinder reservoir and draw out all but about ¼ in. of fluid with a syringe. Discard all used brake fluid. **Caution:** Brake fluid is poisonous, and it softens and removes paint. Rinse off spills with water and wipe area dry immediately.

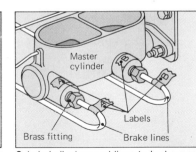

2. Label all wires and lines to brake master cylinder for correct reinstallation. Unplug wires and unscrew brass fittings on steel brake lines. Do not bend lines away from cylinder, but slide fittings back on lines. Plug lines with rubber bleeder caps or erasers.

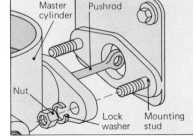

3. Remove nuts and lock washers from studs on booster or fire wall that hold master cylinder in place. Lift out cylinder. On most cars with manual brakes, disconnect pedal linkage as shown at left, below, to free cylinder for removal.

Variations in manual brakes

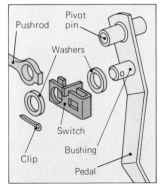

Ford cars with manual brakes have pushrod attached to the brake pedal. To remove cylinder, take spring clip off brake pedal pivot, slide stoplight switch off end of pivot, and lift out switch. Then remove pushrod, washers, and bushings from pivot pin. Lift out master cylinder. When replacing cylinder, carefully insert pushrod and boot through dash, oil washers, and bushings. Then install cylinder on pivot pin with switch and retaining clip.

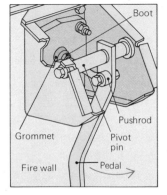

Chrysler cars with manual brakes and aluminum master cylinders have a rubber grommet at fire wall. Pull pushrod through grommet by lifting up hard on brake pedal. Remove and replace master cylinder and grommet. Clean pushrod and attach rod to pedal. Lubricate boot and new grommet with water, and install on pushrod. Seat grommet in fire wall by pressing brake pedal. Grease pedal's pivot pin.

Installing a replacement cylinder

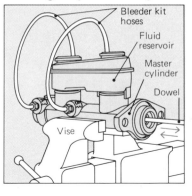

1. Bleed new master cylinder before you install it. Clamp cylinder in a vise and install bleeder kit (if available). Fill cylinder with brake fluid. Use a dowel to depress both pistons slowly. Then pinch hoses closed and allow pistons to return by spring pressure. Repeat until no more bubbles appear in the fluid.

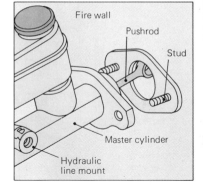

2. Place new or rebuilt master cylinder in position on the fire wall or power booster. Unless you have a Ford or Chrysler car with manual brakes (see procedures at left), pushrod slips into boot on master cylinder as the cylinder goes onto the mounting studs. Avoid bending unattached brake lines.

3. Place lock washers and nuts on mounting studs, but do not tighten. Start brake line fittings by hand to avoid cross-threading. Tighten mounting nuts when fittings are correctly started. Then tighten all fittings, using snug-fitting wrenches or flare wrenches to avoid rounding off corners. Reconnect wires of warning light.

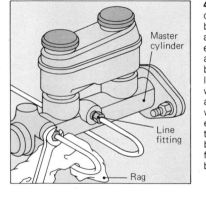

4. Bleed master cylinder by using bleeder valves (if any) or by loosening each fitting while applying pressure to brake pedal. Start at line nearest to fire wall. Catch fluid with a rag. Tighten fittings when no more air is expelled. Wash area to protect paint. If brake pedal is not firm when pressed, bleed brakes (p.217).

341

Checking and replacing a vacuum brake booster ☑☑☑ 45 min–2½ hr

Vacuum power boosters rarely fail on cars less than five years old; make sure that your booster is faulty before buying a replacement. Although some vacuum boosters can be rebuilt, many cannot be repaired without expensive tools. It is more practical to exchange a failed booster for a new or rebuilt one.

If you must exert a great deal of foot pressure to apply the brakes, test the power booster as follows.

1. With the engine off, pump the brake pedal about five times to exhaust the vacuum reserve.
2. Depress the brake pedal and hold it down firmly.
3. Start the engine.
4. The brake pedal should go down a little under foot pressure as the vacuum assist helps you push. On cars with a Hydro-Boost hydraulic power booster (opposite page), the pedal should go down in the same way but then push back up against your foot.

Should your brakes fail this test, check that enough vacuum is going to the brake booster, as shown below, and test or replace the vacuum inlet valve on the power booster. If there is less than 15 inches of vacuum, check the vacuum hose for kinks, blockage, or leaks. Replace the hose if necessary. If the hose is OK, test engine compression (p.263). Have low compression corrected (a major job for a professional mechanic) to raise vacuum to specifications. Do not replace the vacuum booster until you have made sure that the vacuum supply and the vacuum inlet valve are all right. On cars with vacuum pumps (Step 3), make sure that the pump is operating properly. Check for vacuum at the pump outlet when the engine is running. If there is no vacuum, remove the pump and replace it with a new or rebuilt unit; or have the job done at a garage.

On most cars, removing and replacing the booster is a simple nuts-and-bolts job (below). Trade in the defective power booster on a new or rebuilt one.

The operating rod on the new power booster may be preadjusted, or it may require adjustment. A fiberboard or plastic gauge will be supplied with a new booster if the rod must be adjusted. Follow the instructions that come with the booster. A preadjusted rod is simply reattached to the brake pedal linkage, the pin is greased, and the booster is bolted in place. Reattach the vacuum hose, and reinstall the master cylinder on the booster.

The brake fluid level will probably be correct, but check it anyway. Remember, brake fluid is poisonous and a very effective paint remover. Mop up any spills on painted surfaces and rinse with water to remove all traces of spilled fluid.

Test the brakes before you drive the car. The pedal should feel firm, and the power assist should be felt when you test the system. Check to see that the stoplight is operating; adjust the switch if necessary.

Tools: Socket set or open-end wrenches, pliers, screwdriver, vacuum gauge with cone adapter.
Materials: White grease or silicone spray for pedal pivot.

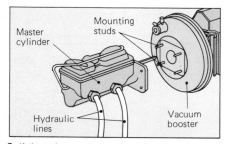

1. If brakes fail test described in text (above) disconnect vacuum hose from inlet valve. Hose may pull off, or it may have a hose clamp similar to those on heater hoses (p.285). Start engine.

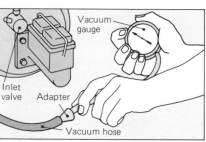

2. Vacuum booster requires at least 15 in. of vacuum in hose at inlet valve. Test by thumb or, preferably, with a vacuum gauge and adapter that fits vacuum hose. Replace a leaky hose.

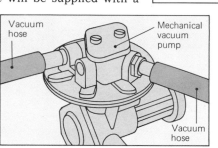

3. Diesels and some gasoline engines use mechanical pumps to supply vacuum for power brakes. If vacuum is below 15 in. and hoses are OK, check and repair, rebuild, or replace pump.

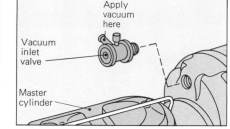

4. Remove vacuum booster's inlet valve, clean it, then test it by sucking on it. It should open in one direction but hold vacuum in the other. Replace a leaking valve. Replace filter, if any.

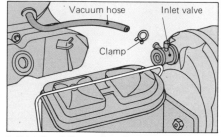

5. If there is vacuum at the inlet valve and the valve is OK, the booster must be faulty. To replace booster, remove mounting nuts on master cylinder. Leave its hydraulic lines connected.

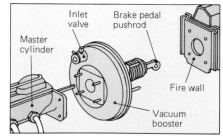

6. Lift out the booster while holding the master cylinder out of the way. If booster catches on brake pedal's pushrod, do not use force. Disconnect linkage to pedal from inside the car.

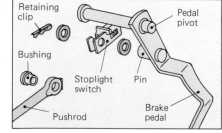

7. Separate pushrod from pedal linkage by removing retaining clip so that pin comes out of eye in pushrod. Then the vacuum booster will lift free while you hold master cylinder to one side.

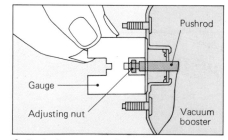

8. Replacing vacuum booster may involve adjusting the pushrod. If pushrod needs adjusting, use fiberboard or plastic gauge and follow instructions supplied with replacement booster.

Replacing a hydraulic power booster ▱▱▱ 45 min–2 hr

Diesels and some gasoline engines do not produce enough engine vacuum to operate the many accessories and pollution controls found on modern engines. Some of these cars employ electric or mechanical vacuum pumps for this purpose. Others, including many North American luxury cars, use hydraulic pressure from the power steering pump and a device called a *Hydro-Boost,* rather than a vacuum-powered brake booster, to provide power-assisted braking.

Test this system in the same way as you would vacuum-powered brakes (p.342). Many problems, including excessive effort to depress the brake pedal for normal stops, can often be cured by topping up the power steering reservoir (p.195), tightening or replacing the drive belt (p.286), or checking the power steering system (p.446).

Check the hoses and Hydro-Boost for leaks. Replace the Hydro-Boost only if there are no symptoms of trouble in the power steering.

Caution: Discharge pressure from the accumulator before working on the Hydro-Boost by applying the brakes four or five times with the engine off. Never put brake fluid in the power steering reservoir nor power steering fluid in the master cylinder reservoir.

Removing and replacing the Hydro-Boost is somewhat similar to changing a vacuum booster. Follow the sequence illustrated below. Wear safety goggles. Loosen line fittings slowly to safely relieve any remaining pressure.

Whenever power steering lines have been disconnected or steering parts have been replaced, bleed air out of the power steering and Hydro-Boost systems by following these steps:

1. Top up the reservoir of the power steering pump to the base of the filler neck.

2. Disconnect the 12-volt wire from the fuel flow solenoid on the injection pump before cranking a diesel engine (below). Ground the coil cable before cranking a gasoline engine (p.263). Crank the engine

for 10 to 15 seconds.

3. Recheck the fluid level; add fluid if needed.

4. Reconnect the diesel's injection-pump wire or a gas engine's coil cable, then start the engine.

5. Turn the steering wheel slowly as far as it will go in each direction, then recenter it.

6. Stop the engine and discharge the accumulator.

7. Check the fluid level and add fluid if needed.

8. Repeat Steps 5–7.

9. If fluid foams, stop the engine and wait 1 hour for foam to dissipate. Start the engine, then repeat Step 5. Recheck the fluid level.

After finishing any brake work, test the system before driving the car. Make trial stops at low speeds to make certain that everything is working correctly.

Tools: Wrenches, pliers, screwdrivers.
Materials: Power steering fluid, safety goggles, drive belt, hoses, new or rebuilt power steering pump and Hydro-Boost (as needed).

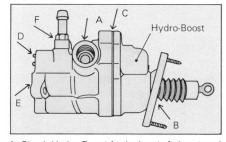

1. Check Hydro-Boost for leaks at: A. Input seal. B. Piston seal. C. Housing. D. Spool valve seal. E. Accumulator cap seal. F. Return port fitting seal. Have leaking seals replaced, or replace booster.

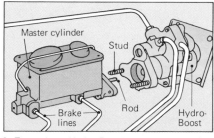

2. To replace Hydro-Boost, remove mounting nuts and pull master cylinder forward until cylinder just clears output rod. Booster can now be pulled forward and out when it is disconnected.

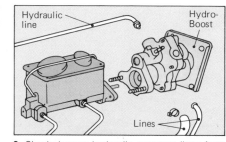

3. Slowly loosen hydraulic pressure lines from Hydro-Boost. Wear safety goggles in case the accumulator is not completely discharged and fluid spurts. Remove lines. Cap openings.

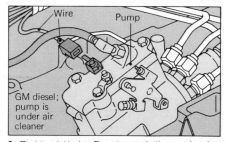

4. Working under dash, disconnect brake pedal linkage from pedal rod. Do not pry rod off pedal arm, as this could damage booster. Disassemble these parts after booster is loose.

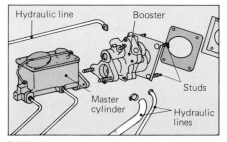

5. Working in the engine compartment, remove nuts from studs that hold Hydro-Boost. Make sure that all hydraulic lines have been removed and that the booster is free.

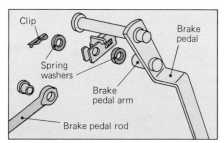

6. Working under the dash, move the brake pedal rod inward until it disconnects from the brake pedal arm. Remove the spring washer from the brake pedal arm.

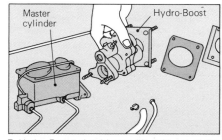

7. Hydro-Boost should now lift right out of the engine compartment. Have it repaired, or trade it in on a rebuilt or new unit. Reverse order of steps used in removal to reinstall the unit.

8. To bleed Hydro-Boost, crank the engine but do not start it. On gasoline engines, ground coil cable (p.263). On diesels, disconnect solenoid wire from fuel-injection pump.

Troubleshooting the cooling system

How to use this chart

Find problem at top of chart. Look down column to locate possible causes.
First, check repairs that you can do yourself; then, check repairs you *may* be able to do yourself.
If problem is still not solved, consult a competent mechanic.

○ You can fix it yourself.
● You *may* be able to make a complete repair.
■ You need a mechanic.

*Applies to air-cooled engines only.

Problem (columns, left to right): Coolant recovery system not working · Unusual noise · Repeated loss of coolant · Engine warms up slowly · Engine overheats

Coolant recovery system not working	Unusual noise	Repeated loss of coolant	Engine warms up slowly	Engine overheats	Possible cause	Cure
○				●	Coolant level too low	Check for leaks (pp.280–281) or have system tested to locate leak; replace defective part (pp.285–287, 345–359)
	○				Coolant level too high	Drain some coolant (p.282)
			○		Incorrect proportion of antifreeze	Check concentration of coolant (p.281) and adjust if necessary
			●		Frozen coolant	Thaw coolant; backflush and refill with correct coolant mixture (pp.282–284)
			○		Deteriorated or contaminated coolant	Backflush system and refill with new coolant mixture (pp.282–284)
				●	Loss of coolant	Check for leaks (pp.280–281) or have system tested to locate leak; replace defective part (pp.285–287, 345–359)
○	○			○	Air trapped in system	Bleed system of air (p.217)
	○			●	Poor circulation; clog in system	Check circulation (p.281), radiator (p.348), heater core (p.359), and water pump (pp.281, 354–355)
○	○			●	Loss of pressure	Check for leaks (pp.280–281) or have system tested to locate leak; replace defective part (pp.285–287, 345–359)
○	○			○	Defective coolant recovery system	Check components and replace any that are defective (p.345)
●	●			●	Leak in system	Check for leaks (pp.280–281) or have system tested to locate leak; replace defective part (pp.285–287, 345–359)
		●		●	Core plug is leaking	Inspect plugs (p.281); replace any that are leaking (p.347)
		■		■	Crack in block or cylinder head	Inspect for leaks (p.281); have mechanic make repair
		■		■	Leaking cylinder-head gasket	Inspect for leaks (p.281); have mechanic replace gasket
○	○			○	Loose or broken fan belt, fan, or shroud	Tighten or replace belt (pp.286–287), fan (pp.351–353), or shroud (pp.348–350)
	○			○	Debris on radiator	Clean off radiator (p.281)
	○	○		○	Thermostat is defective or improperly installed	Check thermostat and replace it if necessary (pp.346–347)
	●				Thermostat missing or stuck open; damper door stuck open*	Check thermostat and replace it if necessary (pp.346–347)
●				●	Thermostat stuck closed; damper door stuck closed*	Check thermostat and replace it if necessary (pp.346–347)
○		○		○	Defective or wrong-type radiator cap	Inspect cap and replace it if necessary (p.280)
●	●			●	Faulty water pump	Replace pump (pp.354–355)
●	●			●	Faulty electric fan switch or motor	Test fan switch and motor; replace one or both as necessary (p.353)
		●		●	Faulty heater control valve	Fix or replace control valve (pp.356–358)
			○	○	Car pulling load too great for cooling system	Reduce load
●				●	Dragging brakes	Check and adjust brakes (pp.210–218)
				●	Exhaust system blocked	Replace bent, dented, or deteriorated parts in exhaust system (pp.434–438)
				○	Late ignition timing	Adjust timing to specifications (pp.236–239)
				●	Idle speed too low	Check and adjust idle speed (pp.251–252)
				●	Air-fuel mixture in carburetor too lean	Adjust carburetor to specifications (pp.248–253)
				○	Clogged fins on engine and/or oil cooler*	Check fins and clean where necessary
		●		●	Misadjusted damper door*	Check position of door and adjust it with the thermostat (p.347)

Overheating 🚗

There are two basic causes of overheating: a mechanical fault that interferes with the operation of the cooling system, or a greater accumulation of heat than the cooling system can handle. The various mechanical faults are listed in the troubleshooting chart on the opposite page, and the information on pages 280–287 and 345–359 tells you how to find and fix most of these faults.

Sometimes an engine overheats simply because more heat builds up than the cooling system can dispose of. This usually happens during stop-and-go driving in hot weather, especially if the air conditioner is on. A temperature gauge can give you advance warning as it creeps up from its normal level toward the danger zone. (A warning light will often not go on until the radiator has already begun to boil over.) If you are stuck in traffic, and other cars are boiling over, you are probably close to the danger point too. Here is what to do to prevent overheating:

1. Shift into *Neutral* and rev the engine at two to three times idle speed so that the fan will pull a greater amount of air through the radiator and the water pump will increase coolant circulation.

2. Stay at least 10 feet behind the car ahead so that its hot exhaust does not flow into your radiator.

3. Turn off the air conditioner. It pumps extra heat into the engine compartment.

4. As a last resort, turn the heater on *High*. Because the heater core acts as a second radiator, the heat it expels will be drawn away from the engine, although this may be a bit hard on you.

5. If possible, get off the crowded highway and onto a freely moving alternate route. If you can keep the car moving at a moderate speed and the air conditioner off, the engine is not likely to overheat.

6. Do not stop and shut off the engine. When you do that, the water pump stops operating but the engine continues to reject built-up heat and will almost certainly boil over. Drive until the engine cools somewhat before shutting it off.

If the engine does boil over, pull off the road and turn off the engine. If you can open the hood without getting burned, do so; otherwise wait at least 15 to 20 minutes for the engine to cool down before opening the hood. Taking care not to burn yourself, check for leaks, burst hoses, a broken drive belt, or other

obvious mechanical faults (see the chart on the opposite page). If you find none, carefully remove the radiator cap, check the coolant level, and top up the radiator as instructed below. **(Caution:** Do not remove cap if steam comes out of the overflow. See instructions below, left.) If you have a coolant recovery system, check it too (below, right).

If your car is equipped with an electric fan, pull off the road at the first sign of overheating. With the engine still running, carefully open the hood and check to see if the fan is operating. If the blades are not moving, the overheating is most probably caused by a defective fan switch or motor. If you cannot start the fan by replacing a fuse or bypassing a faulty fan switch (p.353), have the car towed to a garage.

If your car has an air-cooled engine, the signs of overheating are a loss of power and a hot engine smell. Pull off the road immediately and let the engine cool down. Then inspect the engine for some mechanical fault, such as a broken fan belt or a damper flap that is stuck open. If you can fix the problem, do so. Clean off any debris you find on the fins of the engine or the oil cooler.

Removing the radiator cap from an overheated engine

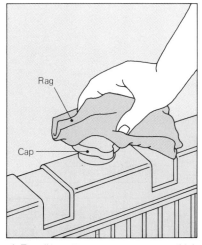

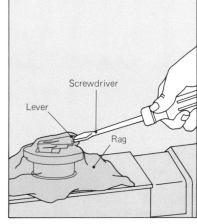

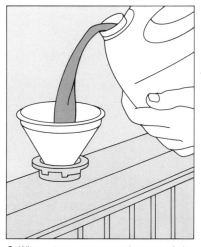

1. To relieve steam pressure, wrap a thick rag around radiator cap and, without pressing down, turn cap counterclockwise to its first stop. Steam will come out of the overflow hose. **Caution:** Do not stand over cap; keep your feet away from overflow.

If the cap has a lever on the top, hold a thick rag around the cap and, using a screwdriver, lift up the lever through the rag. This will release steam through the overflow hose. **Caution:** Do not stand over cap; keep your feet away from overflow.

2. When steam stops coming out of the overflow, press cap down with rag and turn cap to second stop to remove it. Let system cool, then fill radiator with coolant mixture. If only water is available, add antifreeze to adjust mixture as soon as possible.

Checking the coolant recovery system

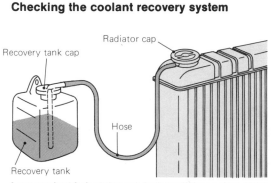

Less coolant is lost through boilover if the coolant recovery system is working properly. (Kits are available for installing a coolant recovery system on cars that have only an overflow hose.) For a coolant recovery system to function properly, all its parts must be in good condition. The tank and hose must be free of cracks and leaks, and the hose must not be clogged. One end of the hose should be fastened securely to the neck of the radiator, the other end to the cap on the recovery tank. The radiator cap and the cap on the tank should be those specified for the system and should be in good condition.

Thermostats 🔧🔧 30 min–2 hr

If your car overheats, takes a long time to warm up, or if the air in the heater system does not warm up, suspect a faulty thermostat. The procedures for replacing a thermostat in any water-cooled engine are basically the same. (Those for thermostats on air-cooled engines are shown on the opposite page.) All thermostats are covered by a housing. Most are located on the top or front of the engine, at the end of the upper radiator hose. If there is a side-mounted water pump (p.355), the thermostat will be either at the base of the water pump or spliced into a hose line above the pump. If you replace a thermostat, make sure that the new thermostat has the correct temperature rating for your car.

Tools: Large pan, wrenches, rubber mallet, putty knife, screwdriver, hose-clamp pliers (if needed), knife, wire brush.
Materials: Liquid sealant, replacement thermostat and gasket (if needed).

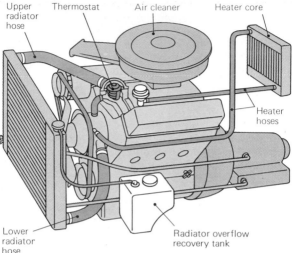

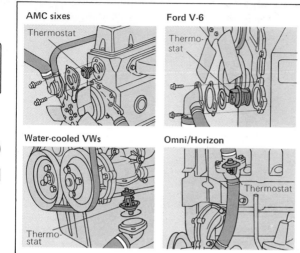

AMC sixes · Ford V-6 · Water-cooled VWs · Omni/Horizon

Replacing a thermostat

1. Disconnect the wiring from an electric fan (p.353). When the cooling system is cold, drain the radiator to a level below the thermostat (p.282); save coolant if it is good. Remove any parts that block access to the housing. Disconnect any electrical lines connected to the housing.

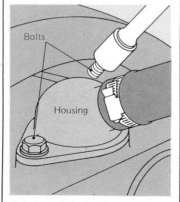

2. Loosen bolts holding thermostat housing in place. Lift housing off (you may need to tap it with a rubber mallet to loosen it). Disconnect any hoses that hamper the removal of the housing (p.285).

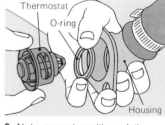

3. Note correct position of thermostat. Remove thermostat and gasket. A retaining ring or an O-ring may have to be removed; some stats must be unscrewed from their housings.

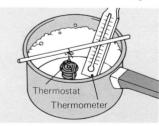

4. Inspect thermostat. Discard it if there is obvious damage. Otherwise, test it. Tie thermostat to a rod and suspend it in a pan of water with a

radiator thermometer or candy thermometer. Neither thermostat nor thermometer should touch bottom of pan. Heat the water. If stat does not open within 5 to 10 degrees of temperature marked on it, replace it.

5. Scrape off any gasket remaining on the housing or engine with a putty knife. Be careful not to gouge the metal. If scraping the engine block, plug the hole in the block with a rag so that no debris falls into the block.
6. Reinstall thermostat. Be sure that it is positioned in the direction indicated by the arrow on the stat. Some stats (not shown) have openings that must align with the bypass openings in the housing. Reinstall any retaining rings or O-rings that were removed during disassembly.

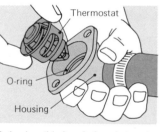

7. Apply a thin bead of gasket sealer around the housing. Do not plug the bolt holes or bypass holes.

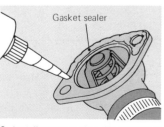

8. Install a new gasket. Align holes in gasket with those on housing; press down on gasket to flatten seal. Then apply a thin bead of sealer on top of the gasket, avoiding any bolt holes or bypass holes.

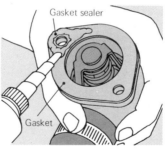

9. Align bolt holes in the housing with those in the engine, then press housing back into place. Reinstall the bolts and tighten them evenly.
10. Reconnect all lines and hoses that were disconnected during disassembly. Put back any parts that were removed to allow access to the housing. Add the coolant. Run the engine with the heater on *High* until the upper radiator hose becomes hot (this means that the thermostat has opened). If a leak occurs or the thermostat does not open, turn off the heater and engine and let the system cool down. When system is cool, drain some coolant and fix the leak, or check that the thermostat was reinstalled correctly.

Thermostat for a VW air-cooled engine

The thermostat in a VW air-cooled engine is located at the lower right-hand side of the engine. It is connected to a door by a rod. When a cold engine starts up, the thermostat contracts and the door is closed; this traps warm air inside a sheet-metal housing around the engine, helping the engine to warm up faster. When the engine is hot, the thermostat expands and the door is opened, allowing outside air in to circulate around the engine and cool it.

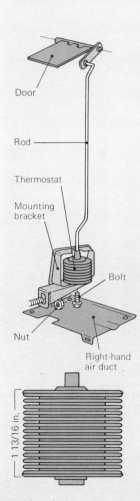

Door

Rod

Thermostat

Mounting bracket

Bolt

Nut

Right-hand air duct

1 13/16 in.

1. Jack up right rear wheel. Remove lower part of right-hand air duct.
2. Remove bolt holding stat to bottom arm of mounting bracket.
3. Push thermostat and rod up as far as they go.
4. Unscrew thermostat from rod. Test stat (below).
5. To replace stat, screw it onto rod. Top of stat should touch top of mounting bracket. If stat is below the top or touches bracket but is not yet fully screwed onto rod, adjust position of bracket. Loosen nut holding bracket in place. If stat is below bracket, slide bracket down to meet it, then tighten nut. If stat is not yet fully screwed onto rod, slide bracket up and screw stat onto rod. Slide bracket down to touch stat, and tighten nut.
6. Pull bottom of stat down so that it rests on bottom arm of mounting bracket. Reinstall bolt and air duct.

To test thermostat:
Suspend thermostat and a candy thermometer in a pan of water. Stat and thermometer should not touch bottom of pan. Heat water. When water is about 149° to 158°F (65° to 70°C), bellows part of stat should measure about 1 13/16 in. (46 mm). If not, replace thermostat.

Core plugs

Core plugs are metal discs that seal the openings left in the engine block during casting (p.281). If they loosen or corrode and allow coolant to escape, they should be replaced. There are three types of replacement plugs: a metal, cuplike disc; a copper expansion plug with an acorn nut; and a rubber expansion plug with a washer and plain nut. Whether or not the opening in the block has straight sides or a lip, both disc plugs and copper expansion plugs must have the same diameter as the top edge of the opening (see below). If you buy a rubber expansion plug to fit a straight-sided opening, the washer must be larger than the opening; the rubber must fit across the opening and be ¼ inch (6.3 mm) deeper than the opening. The extra ¼ inch is what will expand to hold the plug in place. If the opening has a lip, it is preferable that the washer sit on the lip edge. However, if the rubber is so deep that it will create a blockage inside the engine, fit it with a larger washer in order to seat it on the outer edge of the opening. Be sure the rubber is still ¼ inch deeper than the opening.

Caution: If there is an electric fan (p.353), disconnect its wiring and wait until the cooling system is cold before you begin to work.

Tools: Large drain pan, hammer, chisel or screwdriver, drift (flat-head punch), wrenches.
Materials: Non-hardening gasket sealer, antifreeze/water mixture, safety goggles, rags.

Disc plug and copper expansion plug

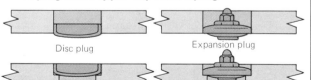

Disc plug

Expansion plug

Rubber expansion plug

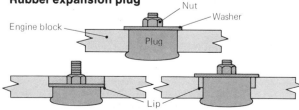

Engine block

Nut

Washer

Plug

Lip

Replacing a core plug 🔧🔧🔧 30 min–5 hr

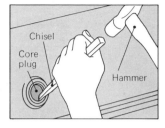

Chisel

Core plug

Hammer

1. Drain the radiator and save the coolant if it is good (p.282). Hammer the tip of a chisel or a screwdriver into the plug; then pry up to remove plug.
Caution: Some coolant will come out as plug is removed; protect your eyes from escaping coolant.

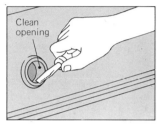

Clean opening

2. Clean off the sides of the core plug opening with clean rags and a wire brush, putty knife, or screwdriver. Insert the new plug. Pour coolant back into the radiator, adding enough to compensate for what was lost. Run the engine to test for leaks.

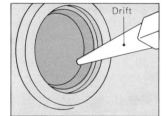

Drift

Cuplike disc plug: Apply gasket sealer to the outer edges of the plug. Insert the plug with its concave side toward the opening. Seat the plug in the opening, tapping along the edges of its base with a drift (flat-head punch) and a hammer.

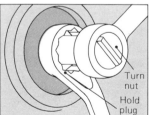

Turn nut

Hold plug

Copper expansion plug: Apply gasket sealer to the edges of the plug. Insert the plug into the opening, nut side out. If necessary, gently hammer plug into place. Then tighten the nut with two wrenches to make the plug expand and tightly fit the opening in the block.

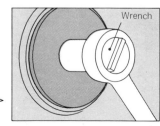

Wrench

Rubber expansion plug: Do not apply gasket sealer to the edges of the plug. Insert the plug into the opening, rubber side first. If necessary, gently hammer plug into place. Then tighten the nut with a wrench to make rubber disc expand and remain firmly in place.

Replacing the radiator 🔧🔧🔧 30 min–3 hr

A clogged or leaking radiator can cause the engine to overheat. Leaks are easily detected by pools of coolant under the car or by stains on the radiator (p.281). Minor leaks may be stopped by adding a cooling system sealer to the radiator. A radiator can be clogged by solder bloom, rust, or old sealer. Remove the cap from a downflow radiator and rev the engine to about 2,500 rpm. If the radiator overflows, it is clogged. Replace the cap and run your hand over the front of the radiator after the engine is warm. If you can feel a sharp difference in temperature, the radiator is probably clogged. Remove it and have it flow-tested by a radiator shop. Slight amounts of solder bloom can be removed by circulating a special cleaner through the cooling system. If leaks or clogging persist, the best remedy is to remove the radiator from the car and take it to a radiator shop. If the shop cannot fix the radiator, replace it with another of at least the same capacity as the old one. There may be several capacities available for your car. Larger capacities are used for cars with air conditioning or those used for towing trailers or for hot stop-and-go driving. Before removing your radiator, read these three pages to see how the radiator is installed in your car. On many cars with air conditioning, the condenser can be tilted out of the way when the radiator is removed and replaced.

Caution: Never open an air-conditioning line in order to remove the radiator. Take the car to a garage or to a radiator specialist.

Tools: Large pan, wrenches, screwdriver, hose-clamp pliers (if necessary), knife, wire brush.
Materials: Antifreeze, water, automatic transmission fluid (for cars with transmission coolers in radiator).

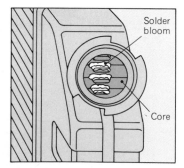

To check for solder bloom, drain some coolant from the radiator (p.282) until the core can be seen by looking down the filler neck. The core cannot be seen through the filler neck on some cross-flow radiators. If this is the case, disconnect upper radiator hose (p.285) and look into the hose neck on the tank.

Preparatory steps

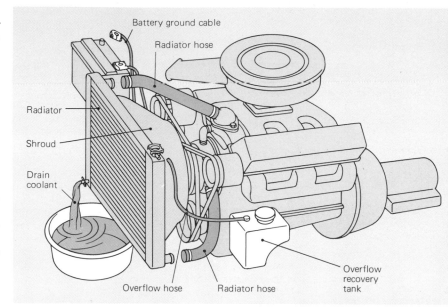

Battery ground cable
Radiator hose
Radiator
Shroud
Drain coolant
Overflow hose
Radiator hose
Overflow recovery tank

1. Disconnect battery ground (–) cable. Drain coolant from radiator into a large, clean pan (p.282). If coolant is good, save it for reuse. Disconnect upper and lower radiator hoses (p.285) and catch any coolant that drains from them. Disconnect any heater hoses connected to the radiator. If there is an overflow recovery tank, disconnect the overflow hose from the radiator's filler neck.

Caution: Do not work on the radiator unless both engine and coolant are cold. Coolant is poisonous; keep it away from children and pets. Do not disconnect any air-conditioning lines. If radiator removal involves opening the air-conditioning system, have the entire job done by a radiator shop or A/C specialist.

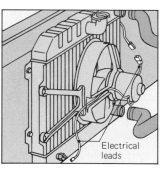

Electrical leads

2. If car has an electric fan, disconnect the electrical lead from the back of the fan (or from the engine). You might have to squeeze the terminal to disconnect the lead. Follow the wires to locate the thermostatic fan switch. If the switch is in a radiator tank, unplug the wiring connector or remove the switch from the tank.

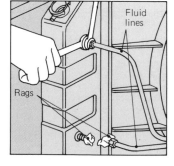

Fluid lines
Rags

3. If the radiator has an automatic transmission cooler, disconnect the two transmission fluid lines from the radiator tank. Use two flare wrenches and turn them in opposite directions to open the fittings. Catch the fluid that drains out. Use clean rags to plug each line and its fitting on the radiator tank.

Hood-release cable
Wiring harness
Hood lock
Shroud

4. Disconnect or remove all other parts that interfere with the removal of the shroud or radiator. In some cars a wiring harness or hood-release cable is clipped to the shroud. Open the clips and push the harness or cable out of the way. It may sometimes be necessary to remove a hood latch; scribe alignment marks for proper reinstallation.

Pivot bolt
Strut

5. Some radiators have a support strut that extends over the radiator and is bolted to the engine and to the body of the car. First, unbolt the strut from the body, then loosen its pivot bolt so that the strut can be swung out of the way.

Removing shrouds

One-piece shrouds

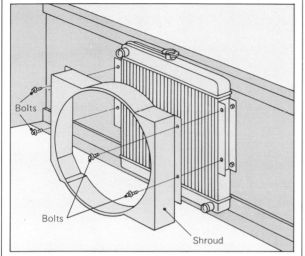

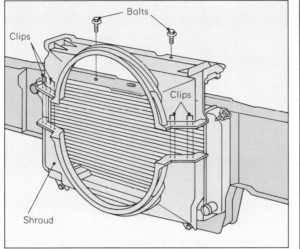

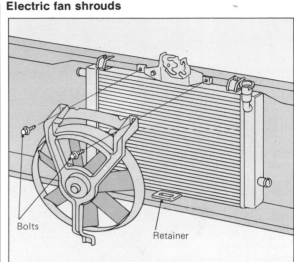

Some one-piece shrouds are bolted to the sides of the radiator. To free this type of shroud, remove the bolts (two on each edge of the shroud and radiator in this case). Lay out any washers and spacers in the order in which they were removed. Remove the shroud from the engine compartment.

Two-piece shrouds

If the top of a two-piece shroud wraps over the top of the radiator, the radiator probably rests in the shroud. Remove only the top half of the shroud. First, remove the clips or screws holding the shroud halves together. Then, unbolt the top half and remove it from the engine compartment.

Electric fan shrouds

If the car has an electric fan, remove the fan and shroud as a unit if possible. First, disconnect the fan (and switch, if necessary; see opposite page). Next, free the fan/shroud unit; for unit above, remove two bolts at the top of the shroud, then lift the unit up to free the base from its retainer.

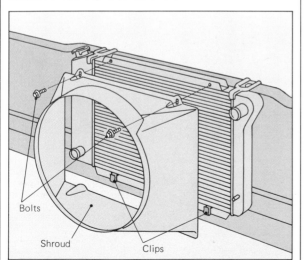

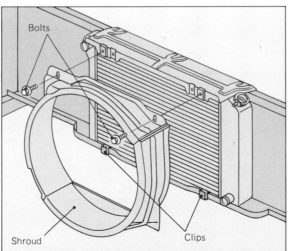

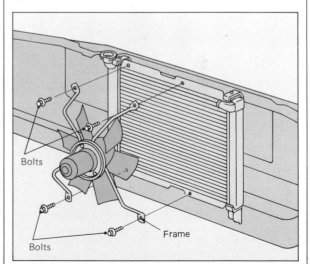

Other one-piece shrouds are held to the top of the radiator housing by bolts and to the bottom of the housing by clips. To free this type of shroud, remove the top bolts, laying out any washers and spacers in the proper order. Then lift the shroud up to free its lower edge from the clips.

Many two-piece shrouds, especially when the top half does not wrap over the radiator, can be removed in the same way as a one-piece shroud. To free the one shown here (which is divided diagonally), remove two bolts holding the top to a mounting panel, then lift the shroud up to free its lower edge from two clips.

Some electric fans are attached to an open frame, like the one shown here, rather than to a shroud. Disconnect the fan (and switch, if necessary; see *Preparatory steps,* opposite page). Remove the bolt at the end of each arm of the frame and lift the fan/frame unit out of the engine compartment.

Removing the radiator

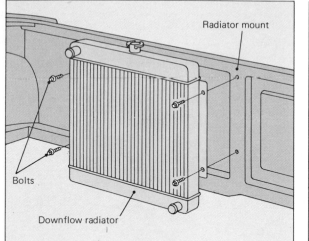

Radiator mount

Bolts

Downflow radiator

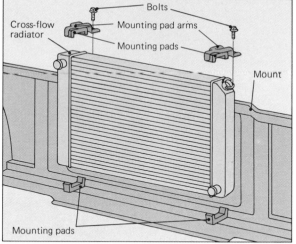

Bolts

Cross-flow radiator

Mounting pad arms

Mounting pads

Mount

Mounting pads

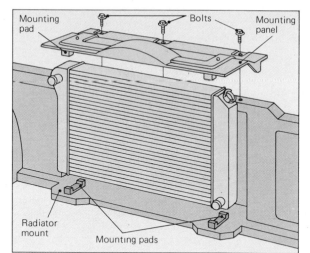

Mounting pad

Bolts

Mounting panel

Radiator mount

Mounting pads

Many radiators are bolted to their mounts. To free the type shown, remove four bolts, two on each side of the mount. Sometimes you must work through the front grille to reach the bolts. Lift the radiator up and out of its mount; be careful not to twist it or hit it against anything that might damage it.

Other radiators are held in place by rubber mounting pads. To free the radiator shown here, unbolt two mounting pad arms from the top of the radiator mount. Then carefully lift the radiator out of its mount. Notice that the radiator was resting on two mounting pads bolted to the bottom of the radiator mount.

With some cars the top rubber mounting pads are attached to the inside of a mounting panel (or the top of a two-piece shroud, as on page 349). Unbolt the mounting panel (or top half of shroud), then carefully lift the radiator out of its housing. Notice that the radiator was resting on two pads at the bottom of the radiator mount.

Reinstalling the radiator

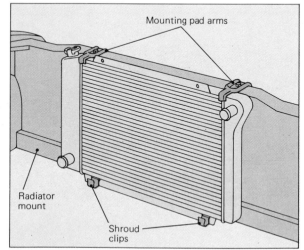

Mounting pad arms

Radiator mount

Shroud clips

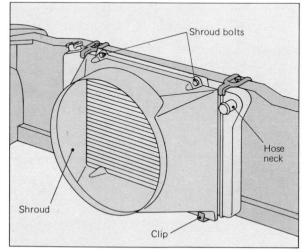

Shroud bolts

Hose neck

Shroud

Clip

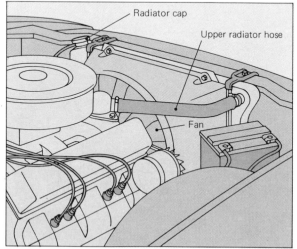

Radiator cap

Upper radiator hose

Fan

Put the radiator back into its mounts, taking care not to twist or damage it. If the radiator is to be bolted in place, align the holes and install the bolts securely. If the radiator is held in place by mounting pads, center the radiator over the bottom mounting pads, then reinstall the top mounting pads.

Reinstall the shroud. If it is a two-piece shroud, fasten the two halves together. If the halves were stapled together, drill holes near the staple locations, and install small nuts and bolts. If the bottom of the shroud is held by clips, center the fan in the shroud, then catch the lower edge in the clips.

Reconnect all hoses and lines that were disconnected in *Preparatory steps,* p.348. Reinstall any hardware that was removed. Put the coolant back into the radiator. Reconnect the battery, and run the engine to test for leaks. Replenish the coolant and automatic transmission fluid, if necessary.

Types of radiator fans

Three types of fans are used in modern cars: direct-drive, clutch, and electric. The type used in your car depends on the cooling needs of its engine as well as on the engine's position in relation to the radiator.

Most longitudinal engines have direct-drive or clutch fans. Both types are located directly behind the radiator and bolted to the water-pump pulley. Both are driven by a V-belt from the crankshaft pulley. If the car is equipped with air conditioning or has a large cooling system, it is probably fitted with a clutch fan (see p.352). The clutch fan can be identified by a finned metal disc bolted to either the front or the back. Both fan types can have either rigid or flexible blades. Flexible blades flatten out at high speeds, when there is more air rushing through the radiator. The blades are less effective when flat, but less power is needed to turn them, which saves gas. The air

forced through the radiator by the forward motion of the car is enough to cool the engine.

Electric fans are used primarily in cars with transverse engines. (Some longitudinal engines have their radiators offset to one side and use an electric fan.)

Electric fans are bolted to the radiator shroud and powered by an electric motor. The motor is turned on and off by a thermostatic switch that is triggered by the coolant temperature. The fan blades, which are always rigid, may be made of plastic or metal.

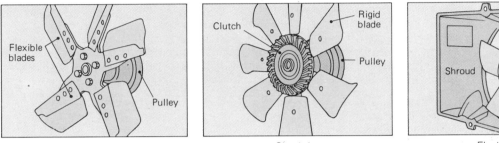

Direct-drive fan   Clutch fan   Electric fan

Replacing a direct-drive fan  30 min–1½ hr

Poor fan operation is usually due to a damaged fan or pulley, or to a loose or defective fan belt. With the engine off, check the tension and condition of the fan belt; if necessary, adjust the tension or replace the belt (pp.286–287). Inspect the blades of the fan; if any are cracked or bent, the fan should be replaced. Also

check the radiator for damage.

Caution: Do not attempt to repair fan blades. They can never be repaired properly, and a damaged blade can fly off, causing injury to you or to the engine. If the fan spacer is cracked, replace it with a spacer that is the same size as the original.

Tools: Large pan, wrenches, screwdrivers, hose-clamp pliers (if needed), knife, wire brush, pry bar or breaker bar for replacing belts.
Materials: Replacement fan, new drive belts (if needed), liquid locking compound.

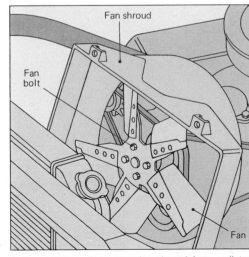

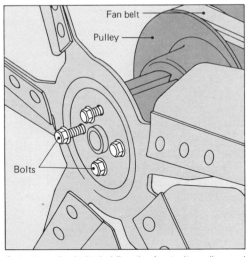

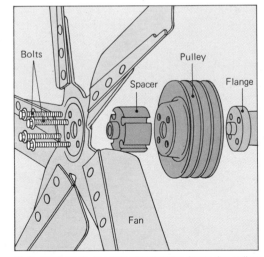

Reassembly: Coat the bolts with a liquid locking compound. Align the bolt holes in the fan, pulley, and spacer with those in the flange. Put a punch through the top set of holes to hold everything in position; then thread bolts into the other holes. Be sure that each part is installed properly, with its front toward the radiator. Tighten the bolts evenly, in a crisscross sequence. Be careful not to damage the fan when reinstalling the shroud (pp.349–350). Check to see that the shroud clears the fan and is securely fastened. Put back and adjust all belts that were removed. Replace damaged belts (pp.286–287).

1. If necessary, disconnect fan shroud from radiator (p.349) to reach bolts on front of fan. Remove the shroud or just push it back toward the engine.

2. Loosen the bolts holding the fan to its pulley and flange. Remove the fan belt from the water-pump pulley and remove any other belt in the way.

3. In most cases, the bolts holding the fan to the pulley also hold the pulley to the water-pump flange. Remove the fan, spacer (if any), and pulley from the flange.

Replacing a clutch fan ⏱⏱ 30 min–2 hr

The speed at which a clutch fan rotates is controlled by fan belt speed and by the silicone oil in the mechanism. As the temperature of the air passing through the radiator rises, the amount of silicone in the coupling increases and so does fan speed. There may be an audible roar when the temperature reads about 150° F (65° C) and the clutch first engages. As the temperature drops, so does the level of silicone in the coupling, causing a decrease in the fan speed. If some or all of the silicone has leaked out of the clutch, the clutch will not perform properly and it should be replaced. Besides checking the tension and condition of the fan belt (pp.286–287), also check the

clutch for leaks (p.281). If there is enough silicone in the clutch, the fan should rotate smoothly but with a slight drag when it is pushed by hand. While checking the clutch and fan belt, inspect the fan blades; if any are bent or cracked, replace the fan. If there is a fan spacer (p.351), check it for cracks as well.

Caution: Perform all fan checks only when the engine is off and cold.

If the mating surfaces of the water-pump pulley and the stem of the clutch do not match exactly, the fan may wobble—a dangerous condition that may also ruin the water-pump bearing. To check for wobble, rub white chalk on the tips of the blades. Turn on

the engine, stand off to one side, and watch the fan revolve. If the chalk marks wobble more than ¼ inch, check to see if the pulley or fan blades are bent or cracked. Replace any defective parts. If the wobble persists, have a radiator shop or dealer add shims to correct the condition.

> **Tools:** Large pan, wrenches, screwdrivers, hose-clamp pliers (if needed), knife, wire brush, pry bar or breaker bar for replacing belts.
> **Materials:** Replacement clutch fan, new drive belts (if needed), liquid locking compound, chalk.

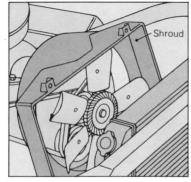

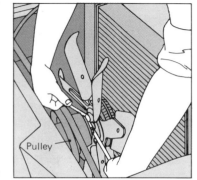

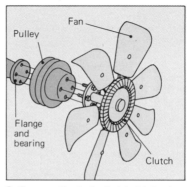

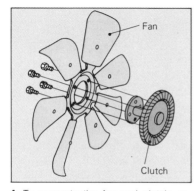

Reassembly: Coat the bolts with a liquid locking compound. Keeping the clutch vertical, align the bolt holes in the fan assembly, pulley, and flange. Put a punch through the top set of holes to hold everything in position; then thread bolts into the other holes. Tighten the bolts evenly in a crisscross sequence. Reinstall the shroud, making sure that it clears the fan and is fastened securely. Reinstall the drive belts, then adjust their tension (pp.286–287).

1. If you cannot reach the front of the fan, disconnect the fan shroud from the radiator (p.349). If necessary, remove the shroud from the engine compartment to make more room. Otherwise, push the shroud back onto the engine.

2. Hold fan. Reach behind fan assembly and loosen bolts that hold it to pulley and flange. Loosen fan belt and any other drive belts in the way, then slip them off pulley. Buy replacements for any belts that are in poor condition.

3. Remove the bolts that hold the fan assembly in place. Be ready to catch the pulley, fan assembly, and shims. Keeping the clutch vertical, remove the fan assembly; if you tip the clutch, silicone may leak out.

4. To separate the fan and clutch, remove the bolts that hold them together. Keeping the clutch vertical, pull the clutch from the fan so that the clutch stem can pass through the center of the fan. Replace defective parts.

Clutch fan variations

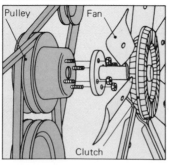

On some cars the clutch and fan are attached to the pulley and flange with nuts and studs. It may be possible to remove the nuts from the pulley and to slide the clutch and fan off without disturbing the pulley, belts, or shroud. Remember to keep the clutch vertical at all times.

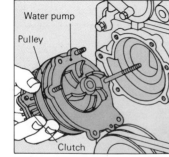

Some Datsuns have a clutch fan in which the clutch is a part of a clutch/pulley/water pump unit. To remove the clutch, you must remove the water pump (p.354). If the clutch is broken, you must replace the entire clutch/pulley/water pump unit.

Clutch shims

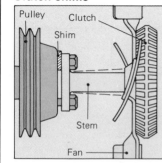

Shims are sometimes placed between the pulley and clutch stem to correct wobble. If you see a shim while you are removing a clutch fan, scribe its outline onto both pulley and clutch stem so that you can reinstall it in the same place. Shims may not be needed with new parts.

Replacing an electric fan ▣▣ 30 min–2 hr

An electric fan is turned on and off by a thermostatic switch that is in contact with the coolant. The switch may be located in the engine block, in one of the radiator tanks, or in a length of pipe spliced into a radiator hose. If an electric fan does not work at all, the cause could be a defective switch or fan motor, a blown fuse in the fan circuit, a defective fan relay (if one is used), or a break in the electrical wiring. First, test the switch; if it is bad, replace it. If the switch is good, test the fan motor. If the motor is defective, remove the fan/shroud unit and replace the motor. If both the switch and the motor are good, then the fault is probably somewhere in the electrical wiring (see *Tracing electrical faults,* pp.361–363). Look through the shroud to inspect the fan; if it is cracked or bent, replace it.

Caution: Wait until the engine is cold before inspecting or working on an electric fan. The thermostatic switch may start the fan unexpectedly if the engine is warm, causing an injury.

Tools: Wrenches, screwdrivers, 14-gauge jumper wire, paper clip, saucepan, candy thermometer, ohmmeter.
Materials: Replacement fan, motor, thermostatic switch (if needed), pipe thread sealer or Teflon plumber's tape.

Testing the fan switch

Locate and disconnect the fan switch (see Step 1, below). Remove the switch by unscrewing it. If the switch is in the radiator tank, first drain the coolant (p.282) to below the level of the switch. Suspend the switch in a pan of water so that only the sensor is immersed. Put a thermometer that reads up to at least 220°F into the pan. Test a two-terminal

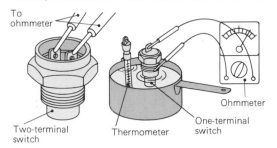

To ohmmeter — Ohmmeter

Two-terminal switch   Thermometer   One-terminal switch

switch by touching ohmmeter probes to each terminal. Test a one-terminal switch by touching one probe to the terminal, the other to the threads of the switch. When the switch is cold, the ohmmeter should read infinity. Heat the pan of water on an oven range; when water is near the boiling point (212°F, 100°C), the switch should close and the ohmmeter should read nearly zero. If the switch does not close, replace it. Before reinstalling the switch, coat its threads with a pipe thread sealer or wrap them with Teflon plumber's tape to ensure a watertight seal.

Testing the fan motor

Disconnect the electrical lead from the motor. If the terminals on the motor are male, clip one end of a jumper wire onto one terminal. If the terminals are female, straighten a paper clip and push one end into the terminal; grasp the other end with the jumper wire. If there are no terminals near the motor, pierce the insulation with a pin.

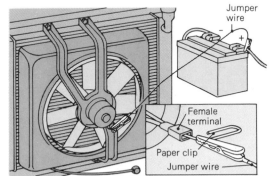

Jumper wire

Female terminal

Paper clip

Jumper wire

(Tape over the hole later.) Stand clear of the fan and touch the other end of the jumper wire to the battery's positive (+) post. Do this on each terminal on the motor until the fan runs. If fan does not move at all, the motor is bad. Locate the fan relay (if any) and place a jumper wire across its terminals. If the fan now runs, replace the relay. If the fan still does not work and switch is OK, replace the motor.

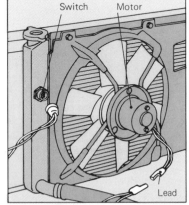

Switch   Motor

Lead

1. Disconnect battery ground (−) cable. Reach behind the fan and disconnect electrical lead from the motor. Follow the line to locate the fan switch; if necessary, disconnect the switch to test it.

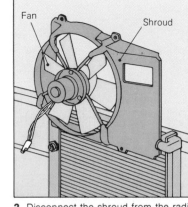

Fan   Shroud

2. Disconnect the shroud from the radiator if necessary. Remove any hoses or wires that are in the way. Remove the fan and shroud as a unit from the engine compartment if necessary.

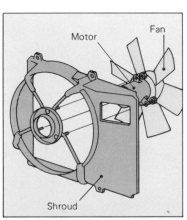

Motor   Fan

Shroud

3. Remove the bolts that hold the motor to the back of the shroud. Then lift the fan and motor from the shroud. Be careful not to damage the fan blades on the shroud as you remove the fan.

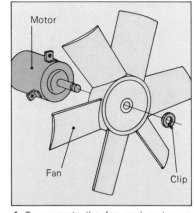

Motor

Fan   Clip

4. To separate the fan and motor, remove the retaining clip or nut that holds them together. Lay out any washers in the order in which they were removed. If fan is bent or cracked, replace it.

Reassembly: Reverse Steps 1–4 at left. Attach the fan to the motor, reinstalling all washers in the correct order. Slip the fan motor into place in the shroud; reinstall the bolts, tightening them snugly. Put the shroud unit back into the engine compartment. Make sure that the fan will clear the radiator, then fasten the shroud securely to the radiator housing. Reconnect the electrical leads to the fan motor and fan switch. Test the fan to see that it runs properly by running the engine long enough to heat the coolant, which causes the fan to operate.

Replacing the water pump 🔧🔧🔧

The water pump circulates the coolant through the cooling system. A failing or an inoperative pump will cause the engine to overheat. Longitudinal engines have their water pumps mounted on the front. The pump shares a pulley with the fan. On transverse engines the pump is mounted on the front, rear, or side of the engine. These pumps do not share a pulley with the fan because transverse engines have electric fans mounted on their radiators (p.353). All pumps are belt driven. If you are having pump problems, first check the tension and condition of the drive belt and, if necessary, adjust its tension or replace it (pp.286–287). If the water pump is noisy, its bearing is usually defective. Try to move the pulley shaft from side to side with the belt off; if there is excessive play, the bearing is faulty and the whole pump must be replaced. If the pump leaks excessively, it means that its inner seal is damaged, and the remedy is to replace the pump. An occasional drop of coolant under the pump (called *weeping*) is normal (p.281).

Caution: Check the pump only when the engine is

Replacing a front-mounted water pump 🔧🔧🔧 1–5 hr

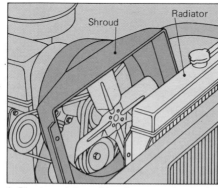

1. Disconnect the wiring from an electric fan. Drain the radiator (p.282). Disconnect the fan shroud. Push it back onto the engine or, if more working room is needed, remove the shroud from the engine compartment. If the radiator is in the way of your work, remove it (pp.348–350).

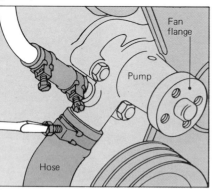

2. Remove the fan if it is attached to the pump (pp.351–352). Remove any drive belts in the way of work (p.287). Disconnect all hoses from the water pump (p.285). Inspect all the parts as you remove them, and buy replacements for any that are defective.

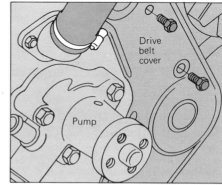

3. Remove (or loosen and swing out of the way) any accessories or parts that impede work, such as the alternator or cover of the camshaft drive belt. Do not remove camshaft drive belt or any parts that require opening the air-conditioning lines. Have such jobs done by a mechanic.

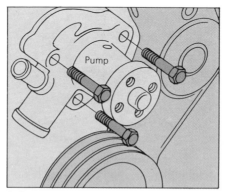

4. Remove bolts holding the pump to the engine. Since bolts can vary in length, draw outline of the pump on a piece of cardboard and make a hole where each bolt goes. When removing bolts, put each one into its respective hole in the cardboard so that bolts will not get mixed up.

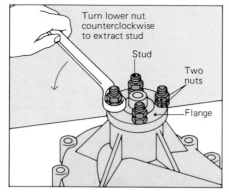

5. Pull off pump and scrape off the old gasket. If necessary, transfer hose nipple, metal baffle, or flange studs to new pump. To remove a stud, thread two nuts onto each stud and lock them together. Then turn lower nut counterclockwise. To install a stud, turn upper nut clockwise.

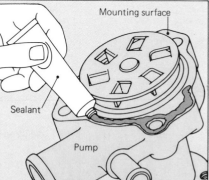

6. Apply a thin bead of liquid gasket sealer along the edges of the replacement pump and around any bolt holes or bypass holes. Install the gasket and apply sealer to the top. Put sealer on the threads of the hose nipple, and screw the nipple into body of the water pump.

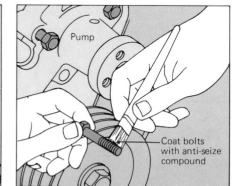

7. Coat bolts with anti-seize compound. Install pump. Then, working in a crisscross sequence, install the bolts, tightening them uniformly. Put back any accessories, parts, and belts that were removed. Replace coolant; reconnect electric fan. Run the engine to test for leaks.

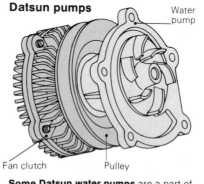

Datsun pumps

Some Datsun water pumps are a part of a combination fan clutch/fan pulley/water pump unit. Remove the fan, then remove the bolts holding the three-part unit to the engine. Install replacement unit.

off and cold, especially if there is an electric fan. Heat can turn the fan on unexpectedly.

Any replacement pump should be the same type and size as the original; if the original pump was aluminum, the replacement should be aluminum. When buying the replacement pump, also get the gasket that fits it. To make sure that dirty coolant will not damage the replacement pump, backflush the cooling system and put in a new coolant mix (pp.282–284) before you remove the old pump, if possible. Rebuilt pumps are much cheaper than new pumps, and they are available from auto parts stores. You should get a trade-in allowance if you turn in your old pump for rebuilding.

Tools: Large pan, wrenches, screwdrivers, knife, wire brush, hose, hose-clamp pliers (if needed), pry bar or breaker bar, rubber mallet, putty knife.
Materials: Replacement water pump and gasket (O-ring for side-mounted pump), liquid or paste-type gasket sealer, anti-seize compound.

Replacing a side-mounted water pump on VW, Dodge, and Plymouth front-drive cars ▨ ▨ ▨ 2–6 hr

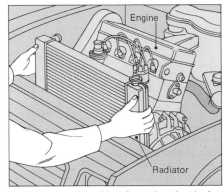

1. Disconnect the wiring from the electric fan. Drain the radiator (p.282); save the coolant if it is good. If more working space is needed, remove the fan/shroud unit and the radiator from the engine compartment (pp.348–350,353). Buy replacements for any defective parts you discover.

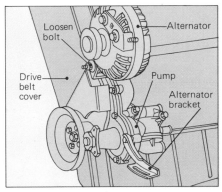

2. Remove the drive belt from the water-pump pulley and remove any other belts impeding work (p.287). Remove bolts holding pump pulley in place, then remove pulley. Disconnect all hoses from water pump. Save coolant that drains from hoses if it is good (p.285).

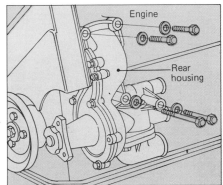

3. Remove (or loosen and swing out of the way) any accessories or parts that impede work, such as the alternator or a camshaft drive belt cover. Do not remove a camshaft drive belt or any parts that require the opening of air-conditioning lines; have such jobs done by a mechanic.

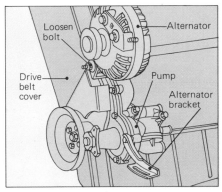

4. Remove the bolts holding the rear housing of the pump to the engine. Make a cardboard pattern (see Step 4, opposite page) for the bolts at the back and front of the pump unit. Pull off the water-pump unit; remove the O-ring between the pump and the engine.

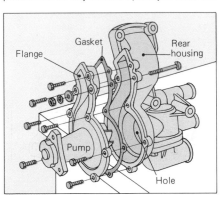

5. Support the pump unit and remove the bolts holding the pump to its rear housing. Hit the flange with a rubber mallet to separate the two parts. Plug up the opening in the rear housing with a clean rag and, using a putty knife, scrape off the old gasket. Do not gouge the metal.

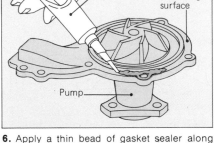

6. Apply a thin bead of gasket sealer along edges of replacement pump and around any bolt holes and bypass holes. Place new gasket on top of sealer; apply a thin bead of sealer over gasket. Coat bolts with anti-seize compound, and bolt pump to its rear housing.

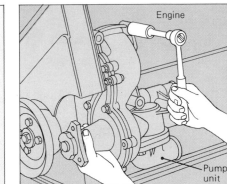

7. Coat remaining bolts with anti-seize compound. Replace the O-ring, and bolt the pump unit to the engine. Tighten the bolts in a crisscross sequence. Reinstall all parts removed in disassembly. Fill the radiator. Connect the fan wiring. Run the engine to test for leaks.

Shared bolts

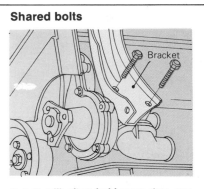

A bolt will often hold more than one part. The two bolts at the bottom of this alternator bracket hold the bracket to the rear housing of the water pump and hold the housing to the engine block.

A typical heating/air-conditioning system

Heating, air conditioning (A/C), defrosting, and ventilation are provided by components that are grouped in ductwork located at the rear of the engine compartment and under the dashboard. The major parts of all heating and air-conditioning systems are the heater core, evaporator, blower fan, and flapper doors. Most systems also have a heater control valve. Although the exact location of each component varies from car to car, all are connected by cables, vacuum hoses and switches, or by electrical wires and switches, to the levers or buttons (controls) on the dashboard control panel.

The *heater core* is a small, radiator-like part whose function is to heat the air in the system. It is connected to the engine's cooling system by two hoses. If there is a *heater control valve,* it will be at the inlet hose or the inlet nipple of the heater core. The heater control valve controls the flow of coolant through the heater core.

The *evaporator* is connected by inlet and outlet lines to the rest of the air-conditioning components in the engine compartment (pp.288–289). The evaporator cools the air in the system.

The small electrical *blower fan* forces air through the system. It is near the heater core and evaporator.

The *flapper doors* direct the air through the ductwork and out the appropriate outlets in the dashboard. Most systems have four doors: a *recirculation* door, a *temperature* door, a *mode* door, and a *defrost* door. Under most operating conditions the recirculation door allows outside air to enter the system through an opening in the cowl, but when additional cooling is desired, the door pivots to close off most of the outside air supply and to draw cool air from the passenger compartment back through the system.

The temperature door is usually placed between the evaporator and the heater core. The position of this door determines how much of the air that has already passed through the evaporator will also pass through the heater core.

The mode door (sometimes called the *heater-A/C* door) is usually at the center of the ductwork. Its position determines whether the air that exits from the center part of the ductwork is directed to the floor, through the outlets in the dash, or both.

The defrost door is also near the center of the ductwork. When the door is fully open, most air passes through outlets at the base of the windshield.

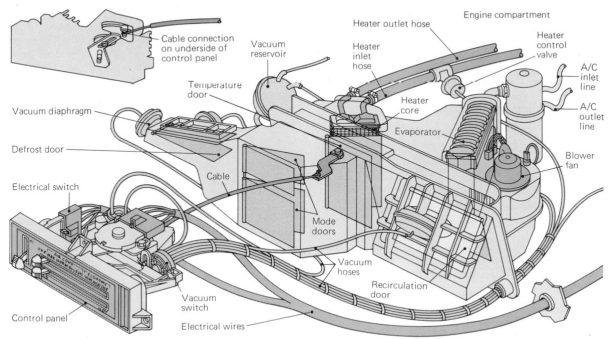

Troubleshooting the heating/air-conditioning system

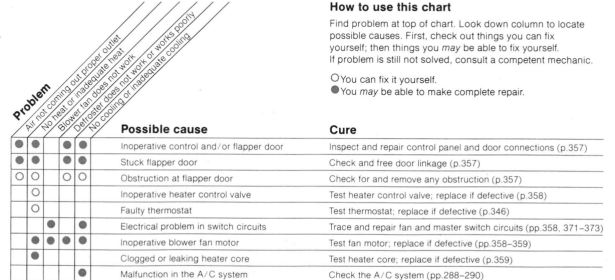

How to use this chart

Find problem at top of chart. Look down column to locate possible causes. First, check out things you can fix yourself; then things you *may* be able to fix yourself. If problem is still not solved, consult a competent mechanic.

○ You can fix it yourself.
● You *may* be able to make complete repair.

Air not coming out proper outlet	No heat or inadequate heat	Blower fan does not work	Defroster does not work or works poorly	No cooling or inadequate cooling	Possible cause	Cure
●	●		●	●	Inoperative control and/or flapper door	Inspect and repair control panel and door connections (p.357)
●	●		●	●	Stuck flapper door	Check and free door linkage (p.357)
○	○		○	○	Obstruction at flapper door	Check for and remove any obstruction (p.357)
	○				Inoperative heater control valve	Test heater control valve; replace if defective (p.358)
	○				Faulty thermostat	Test thermostat; replace if defective (p.346)
		●	●		Electrical problem in switch circuits	Trace and repair fan and master switch circuits (pp.358, 371–373)
●	●	●	●		Inoperative blower fan motor	Test fan motor; replace if defective (pp.358–359)
●					Clogged or leaking heater core	Test heater core; replace if defective (p.359)
				●	Malfunction in the A/C system	Check the A/C system (pp.288–290)

Servicing flapper doors ⚁ ⚁ 15–45 min

If air fails to exit from the proper outlet (see opposite page), suspect trouble with the flapper doors or their controls. Work the controls. With most systems, the temperature control operates the temperature door, and the mode selector works the other three doors. The doors themselves are operated by cable or by vacuum. If they are vacuum operated, they will not work unless the engine is on, and they will make hissing noises as they move. Sometimes the door or outlet is blocked or the door linkage is sticky. Once the obstruction is removed or the linkage is loosened with penetrating oil, air will exit from the proper outlet. At other times the problem is elsewhere in the cable or in vacuum lines between the door and the control panel. To perform the tests below, disengage the control panel and pull it forward. You may have to remove a trim cover and possibly the instrument panel as well (see p.366). In some systems the vacuum hoses are held to the vacuum switch by a connector. Such hoses cannot be pulled off individually for testing; if any are defective, buy a hose-repair kit from an auto parts store.

> **Tools:** Screwdrivers, wrenches, manual vacuum pump.
> **Materials:** Penetrating oil, replacement parts as needed, vacuum hose repair kit (if needed).

Adjusting cable-operated doors

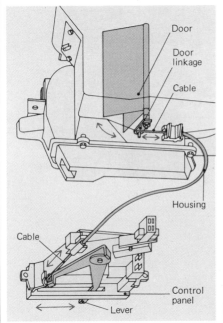

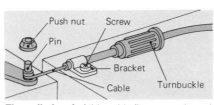

The coiled end of this cable fits over a pin and is held in place by a push nut. A bracket and screw holds the housing in place. To adjust the length of the housing, turn the turnbuckle.

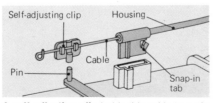

A self-adjusting clip holds this cable to a pin. The coiled end of the cable extends beyond the pin. The housing is held in place by a snap-in tab. To adjust the length of the cable, pull the clip off the pin and slide clip down the cable until 2 in. of cable extends beyond clip. Fit the clip back onto the pin and work the control.

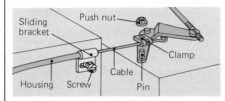

The clamp on this cable fits over a pin and is held in place by a push nut. The coiled end of the cable extends beyond the pin. The housing is held in place by a bracket that is secured by a screw. To adjust its length, loosen the screw, move the housing, then tighten the screw.

A cable-operated door is connected to the back of the control lever by a cable encased in a housing. When the control lever is pivoted, it moves the cable to open or close the door. Typical problems are: the end of the cable is disconnected; the length of the cable or housing is improperly adjusted; or the cable is kinked or broken. There are several ways that cables and their housings are attached and several ways of adjusting their length. Before adjusting length, move the control so that the door is closed, then make the adjustment. If door does not open properly, readjust cable length. If cable is kinked or broken, replace it by snaking a new one through the system (procedure is similar to that of replacing an antenna, p.382).

Troubleshooting vacuum-operated doors

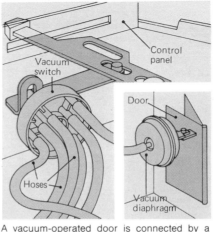

A vacuum-operated door is connected by a hose to a vacuum switch at the back of the control panel. When the control is moved, engine vacuum is routed by hoses through the vacuum switch to a vacuum diaphragm that moves the door. If a vacuum-operated door is not working properly, proceed as follows.

1. Check that all the hoses are attached to the vacuum switch. Then, with the engine on, disconnect one hose at a time (or the connector; see text, above) and feel for vacuum. You should feel vacuum at one hose or at one hole in the connector (the vacuum source). This means vacuum is getting to the switch. Turn off engine.

2. If no vacuum is getting to the switch, check that the other end of the vacuum supply hose is attached at the engine and that the hose is in good condition. If it is kinked, plugged, or leaking, replace it by snaking a new hose through the system (similar to the procedure for replacing an antenna, p.382). If there is a vacuum reservoir, check it for leaks. Also check hoses coming to and from the reservoir. If necessary, replace hoses or reservoir. A reservoir is usually held in place by a few screws.

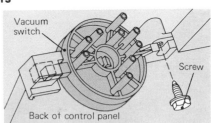

3. If vacuum is getting to the switch but there is no response to any of the controls, the vacuum switch is probably defective and should be replaced. To do this in some cars, you may have to replace the entire control panel. Other switches can be removed simply by removing the screws that hold them to the back of the control panel.

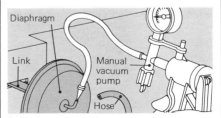

4. If vacuum is getting to the switch but only some of the doors respond to the controls, check the vacuum diaphragm at the affected doors. Disconnect the hose from the diaphragm and, using a manual vacuum pump, apply 7 to 10 in. of vacuum to the diaphragm. If the link on the diaphragm does not move, or if vacuum reading does not hold steady for 1 min, replace the diaphragm. A diaphragm is usually attached with screws.

5. If the vacuum diaphragm is OK, put the hose back onto the diaphragm and apply 7 to 10 in. of vacuum at the other end of the hose (at the vacuum switch). If the door does not respond, the hose is defective. Snake a new hose through the system (see Step 2) and connect it.

Heater control valves 🔧🔧 20 min – 1½ hr

Many heating/air-conditioning systems have a heater control valve to control the flow of engine coolant through the heater core and, therefore, the amount of heat that the air in the system can pick up. If your system has a heater control valve, it is located on the heater inlet hose or on the inlet nipple of the heater core. Some control valves are cable operated, but many are vacuum operated. With either type, the valve is activated by the temperature control (and sometimes the mode selector) to work in unison with the temperature door. When the temperature control

and mode selector are *Off*, the valve and door should be closed and the air should be cool. When the temperature control is *On* and the mode selector is on *Heat*, the valve and door should be open and the air should be hot. If the valve does not produce the desired effect, the fault could be with the valve, the door, or their connections to the control panel.

> **Tools and materials:** Screwdriver, hose-clamp pliers, manual vacuum pump, replacement parts as needed.

Troubleshooting vacuum-operated valves

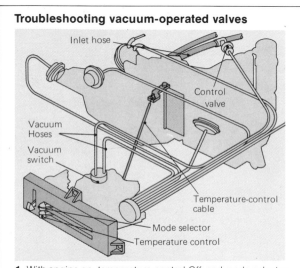

Inlet hose · Control valve · Vacuum Hoses · Vacuum switch · Temperature-control cable · Mode selector · Temperature control

1. With engine on, temperature control *Off,* and mode selector on *Heat,* disconnect the vacuum hose from the heater control valve and feel for vacuum. If there is no vacuum, move temperature control 1 in. and feel again. If there is vacuum in either case, replace the valve.
2. If vacuum is not getting to the valve, turn off the engine and locate a two-hose vacuum switch for the valve (at back of control panel or a temperature door; to remove panel, see p.357). With the engine on and mode selector on *Heat,* disconnect hose from the switch and make sure that vacuum is getting to the switch (Steps 1–2, p.357). Using a manual vacuum pump, apply vacuum to the vacuum source hose neck on the switch and feel for vacuum at the other hose neck while a helper turns the temperature control on and off. If there is no vacuum, the switch is bad and should be replaced (Step 3, p.357) or the temperature-control cable needs adjustment (p.357). If there is vacuum, the hose between the switch and the valve is bad; fix or replace it (Step 2, p.357).

Troubleshooting cable-operated valves

Control valve · Cable · To heater core · Linkage · Inlet hose

1. With the heater off, run engine until it is up to operating temperature. Disconnect cable from the heater control valve (see *Adjusting cable-operated doors,* p.357). Feel the heater inlet hose between the valve and the heater core while you turn the valve linkage. When linkage is turned counterclockwise, the hose should become hot. When linkage is turned clockwise, the hose should cool down. If either condition does not occur, replace the valve (below).
2. If valve is OK, reconnect the cable to the valve and operate the dashboard temperature-control lever. If the cable does not move the linkage, it is disconnected. Remove the control panel and connect the cable (see p.357). If the cable moves the linkage, but not enough to fully open or close the valve, the cable needs adjustment (p.357).

Replacing valves

To replace a heater control valve: Turn off the engine and the heater. When the engine is cool, drain the radiator (p.282) to a level below the valve. Disconnect the cable from a cable-operated valve (see *Adjusting cable-operated doors,* p.357). Disconnect the vacuum hose from a vacuum-operated valve. Disconnect the heater hose; if necessary, replace the hose and clamps (p.285). Remove screws holding valve in place. Install the new valve so that the arrow on the valve points to the heater core. Refill the radiator.

Blower fan controls 🔧🔧 10 – 15 min

The blower fan is a small electrical fan, located near the heater core and evaporator. It is controlled by a switch in the control panel. The switch usually has more than one fan-speed setting. In many systems the fan is also controlled by a master electrical switch. This master switch is activated by the *mode selector,* the same control that operates a vacuum switch for the recirculation door, the defrost door, and the heat/A/C door. Depending on the mode selected, the master switch will turn on the fan and/or the air-conditioning system. Without wiring diagrams of the fan and the master switches, it could be very difficult to trace an electrical problem with

Control panel with fan switch and master switch.

the blower fan. Procedures for tracing electrical faults are on pages 361–363. If you still cannot solve the problem, have an A/C specialist do the job. (If the air conditioner does not work, the problem could also be with the A/C system—see pp.288–290.) However, if there is no activity in the blower, the problem could be the blower motor. Test the motor (below) if you can reach its terminals.

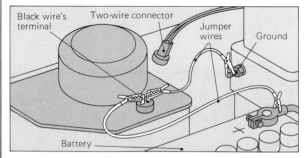

Black wire's terminal · Two-wire connector · Jumper wires · Ground · Battery

To test motor of a GM blower fan: Be sure that engine is off. Unplug the two wires from back of motor. Connect one jumper wire from the black wire's terminal to an electrical ground. Attach another jumper wire to the other terminal. Stand away from motor and touch other end of second jumper wire to battery's positive terminal. If motor does not run, replace it (opposite page).

Replacing a GM blower fan and heater core ▨▨▨ 1–3 hr

If the motor of the blower fan does not work or if the heater core is leaking or clogged (right), replace the faulty component. In many heating/air-conditioning systems, the blower fan and heater core may be difficult to remove because of their awkward location behind the dashboard or under the cowl. In some cases, the air-conditioning refrigerant must be discharged before you can remove the fan or heater core. Such jobs should be done by an air-conditioning specialist at a radiator shop.

The blower fan and heater core on many of the newer General Motors cars are less difficult to locate and to remove, and the GM system has been chosen to illustrate the basic techniques involved in the replacement of a blower fan and heater core. If you work on any other system, use the techniques shown only as general guidelines. If you have a service manual for your car, refer to it for specific instructions. Have the heater core rebuilt (*re-cored*) by a radiator shop, or buy a new one. Handle the new heater core very gently to avoid damaging its fragile fins. While replacing the core, also replace the heater hoses and clamps, and install a fresh coolant mixture.

Caution: Before starting work, turn off the engine and disconnect the battery ground (–) cable.

Tools: Wrenches, hose-clamp pliers, screwdrivers.
Materials: Putty, insulating tape, fresh coolant mixture, replacement parts as needed.

Testing the heater core for clogging

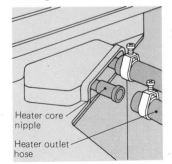

First, check the heater control valve (opposite page). Then, with the engine off, disconnect the heater outlet hose at the heater core nipple. With engine and heater on, turn temperature control to *Hot*. If no coolant or only a trickle flows from heater core, core is clogged.

Heater core nipple

Heater outlet hose

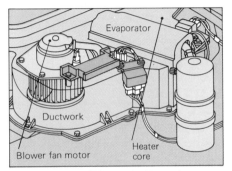

Evaporator

Ductwork

Blower fan motor

Heater core

On many newer GM cars the blower fan motor and its terminals jut out from the top cover of the ductwork. The heater core and evaporator are inside the ductwork to the right of the motor.

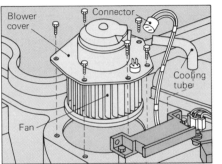

Blower cover

Connector

Cooling tube

Fan

To remove the blower fan, pull off the two-wire connector and the air cooling tube. Remove screws holding blower cover in place. Lift out the fan. Reverse procedure to install a new fan.

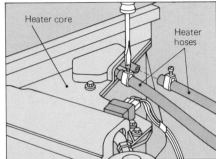

Heater core

Heater hoses

To remove the heater core, proceed as follows:
1. Let engine cool, then drain coolant to a level below that of the heater core (p.282). Disconnect both heater hoses from the core (p.285).

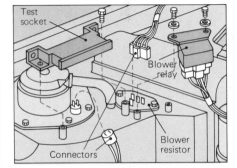

Test socket

Blower relay

Blower resistor

Connectors

2. Unscrew the test socket. Pull off the two-wire connector. Unplug the multi-wire connector from the high-speed blower resistor. Unscrew high-speed blower relay and set it aside.

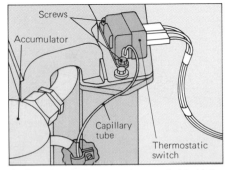

Screws

Accumulator

Capillary tube

Thermostatic switch

3. If car has A/C, remove screws that hold the cycling clutch's thermostatic switch. Unclamp the switch's capillary tube from the A/C tubing. (Do not do this if switch is in the accumulator.)

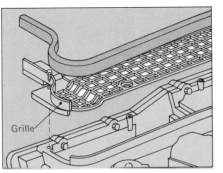

Grille

4. Remove screws holding the grille over the air intake opening; remove the grille. If more working space is needed, also remove the windshield wiper arm (see p.301).

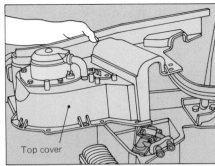

Top cover

5. Remove all screws holding the top cover of the ductwork. Remove the putty sealer from around the evaporator line where it goes into the ductwork. Lift up cover and fan.

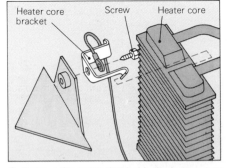

Heater core bracket

Screw

Heater core

6. Remove the screw that holds the heater core bracket. Remove bracket and lift heater core up and out. Reverse these steps to install the new core. Add new coolant mixture (p.284).

Troubleshooting electrical problems

How to use this chart

Find problem at top of chart. Look down column to locate possible causes. First check repairs that you can do yourself. If problem persists, check repairs you *may* be able to do yourself. If none of these procedures work, consult a competent mechanic.

○ You can fix it yourself.
● You *may* be able to make a complete repair.

Possible cause	Oil warning light stays on while engine is running	Oil-pressure gauge reads low	Temperature warning light stays on while engine is running	Temperature gauge indicates overheating	Charge warning light stays on while engine is running	Warning light does not come on when ignition is turned on	Fuel gauge is inaccurate	Headlight or other light on exterior of car does not work	High beams or low beams do not light	Interior light does not work	Instrument panel lamp does not light	Headlights are very dim	Lights dim as car slows or stops	Bulbs blacken or burn out frequently	Brake lights stay on when foot is taken off the brake pedal	Turn signals flash on one side of the car only	Turn signals do not flash at all	Windshield wipers do not work	Horn does not work	Horn will not stop blowing	Electric grid-type defogger does not work	Heater fan does not work at all	Clock or cigarette lighter does not work	Excessive battery wear, causing frequent replacement of battery	Cure
Fuse blown or circuit breaker tripped								○		○	○						○	○	○		○	○	○		Replace fuse or reset circuit breaker (pp.361,367)
Lights dirty												○													Clean lights with water and detergent
Poor electrical contact at bulb socket								○	○	○	○														Clean bulb base and socket with wire brush (opposite page)
Bulb burned out						○		○	○	○	○					○									Replace bulb (pp.364–366); to replace headlights, see p.368
Battery low or defective					○							○	○												Recharge or replace battery (pp.277–279)
Fan belt loose or broken				○	○	○							○											○	Tighten or replace fan belt (pp.286–287)
Alternator overloaded					○								○											○	Reduce usage of accessories, or use heavy-duty alternator (p.374)
Oil problem in engine	●	●																							Check oil level (p.196); investigate oil problem (pp.386–387)
Engine overheating			●	●																					See *Troubleshooting the cooling system,* p.344
Defective switch								●							●	●	●	●	●		●	●			Replace switch (pp.369–371)
Defective relay								●													●	●			Replace relay (p.371)
Faulty dimmer switch									●																Replace dimmer switch (pp.369,371)
Defective flasher																	○								Replace flasher (p.365)
Sticking horn switch																				●					Repair or replace horn switch (p.370)
Sticking horn relay																				●					Replace horn relay (p.371)
Defective horn or horn relay																			●						Replace horn or horn relay (p.371)
Faulty sending unit	●	●	●	●			●																		Replace sending unit (pp.372–373)
Defective gauge		●		●			●																		Replace gauge (p.373)
Faulty instrument voltage regulator		●		●			●																		Replace instrument voltage regulator (pp.373–375)
Defective lighter or clock																							●		Replace defective part (for instrument panel disassembly, see p.366)
Faulty electric motor																		●				●			Replace motor (for wiper motors, see p.383; heater motors, p.358)
Faulty wiring or ground connection	●		●	●	●	●	●	●	●	●	●		●		●	●	●	●	●	●	●	●	●	●	Locate and repair poor ground, short, or open circuit (pp.362–363)
Defective voltage regulator														●										●	Adjust or replace voltage regulator (pp.373–375)
Alternator charging poorly					●																			●	Repair or replace alternator (pp.374–377)
Shorted diode in alternator	●				●																			●	Replace diode assembly (p.377) or replace alternator

Tracing electrical faults ☑☑☑

When a light or an electrical accessory does not work, the fault is either a *short circuit* or an *open circuit* somewhere in the system. Shorts cause fuses to blow, so check your fuse box first. Damaged insulation, broken wires, or open connections can cause short circuits. Open circuits simply prevent a particular component from functioning, and they must be traced. Burned-out bulbs or motors, faulty switches, bad connections, or broken wires cause open circuits. Either type of fault can appear almost anywhere in the electrical system.

Open circuits are commonly caused by an accumulation of oil, dirt, or corrosion at terminals and light bulb sockets, which interferes with the flow of electricity. Vibration, too, can loosen connections in time. When looking for defects, first check and clean all connections. This will sometimes correct the fault, and you may avoid time-consuming circuit tests.

If the battery is dead or its terminals are so badly corroded that current cannot flow out of the battery, none of the car's electrical equipment will work, including the starter. If the starter works but most or all of the remaining electrical equipment does not, a fusible link has probably melted (see pp.362 and 367).

Step-by-step procedures for tracing electrical faults are given on the next two pages. The circuit diagrams in the manufacturer's service manual for your car will help you considerably. The diagrams may seem complicated, but they are readable once you have deciphered the symbols used.

Types of fuses

Glass tube — Good / Blown
Ceramic — Good / Blown
Plug-in — Good / Blown

Removing switches

Rocker switch

Squeeze clips from behind dash. Pull switch from front

Toggle switch

Unscrew ring. Push switch out back

Disconnecting connectors

Squeeze tab to unlock

Lift tab to unlock

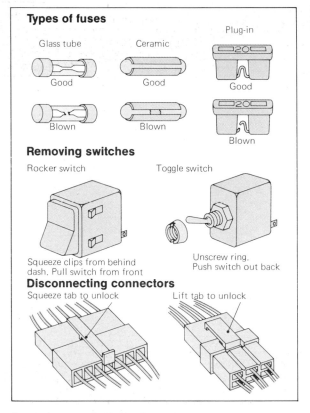

Reading a circuit diagram

Color and size of each circuit wire used is indicated in diagram. 16 LGN, for example, means "16-gauge wire, light green insulation." Check color code chart that accompanies diagram to decipher code. Each terminal at multi-terminal connectors is numbered. Wire 20 BRN, is connected to terminal 11 in the connectors shown. To trace the circuit farther, pick it up from terminal 11 in the matching connector. For meaning of symbols, see p.133.

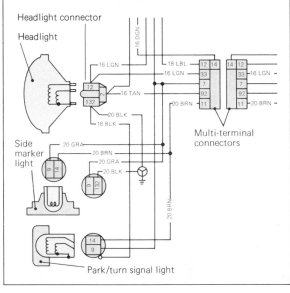

Headlight connector
Headlight
Side marker light
Multi-terminal connectors
Park/turn signal light

How to make a circuit tester

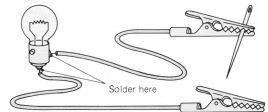

Solder here

To make a test light, you need a 12-volt single-filament auto bulb, two lengths of copper auto wire, two alligator clips, a needle, and a soldering iron. Solder clips to both wires. Solder one wire to bulb sleeve, other wire to center contact of bulb. Use needle to pierce insulation when necessary. A *jumper wire* is a length of auto wire with alligator clips at each end.

Servicing terminals, bulb sockets, and switch contacts

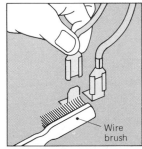

Wire brush

To clean corrosion and other deposits off connectors and terminals, clean metal contact area of each part with a wire brush. When reconnecting parts, join them tightly.

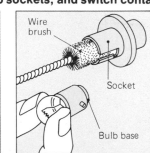

Wire brush
Socket
Bulb base

Brush corrosion from bulb bases and bulb sockets to ensure that full electrical contact is made. When contact is poor, bulbs may burn dimly, erratically, or not at all.

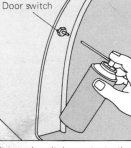

Door switch

Internal switch contacts that are difficult to reach can be cleaned by spraying interior of switch with electrical contact cleaner. Work the switch several times after spraying.

Contact cleaner spray is also useful for cleaning various electrical parts that are difficult to reach with a wire brush, such as fuse terminals in an awkwardly located fuse box.

361

Tracing electrical faults *(continued)* 🔲🔲🔲

First determine whether a fuse has blown, a circuit breaker has tripped, or a fusible link has melted. If so, look for a short in the affected circuit (right). If not, look for an open circuit (see opposite page).

Fuses often blow because of some transient condition that will not recur; replace the blown fuse and see whether the new fuse blows, which would indicate that a true short exists. Circuit breakers reactivate after several seconds, so if a part such as a bulb switches on and off, a breaker is probably cycling on and off. Some shorts may not blow the fuse. To detect such a short, disconnect the battery ground (-) cable, and connect the test light between the cable terminal and battery post. If the bulb lights when all switches are shut off, there is a short somewhere. Disconnect one circuit at a time. When the bulb goes out, you have disconnected the circuit that contains the short. Trace that circuit as shown at right.

Use a test light or an ohmmeter set to the *Low* scale (see p.173) to trace open circuits. The meter is used only to determine whether current passes through a given point (if the needle deflects) or does not pass through (if the needle does not deflect).

If you use an ohmmeter, disconnect the car battery; the meter supplies its own power. Before using a test light, check it by connecting it to the battery terminals. The light will glow if it is working.

Electrical faults can be difficult to find, especially when the fault is intermittent. For example, when vibration momentarily jostles a segment of wire with worn insulation against the car's body, a fuse will blow. Once the fuse is replaced, the problem will recur only if that wire contacts the body again. If finding a fault has you completely stumped, cut out the entire circuit and substitute new wiring.

Sometimes, unexpected things happen. If you step on the brakes and the dome light turns on, this may be caused by a blown fuse. Check the fuses, but also check all other lights to see if any are too dim or too bright, which would indicate that they are on the same circuit. Inspect all ground connections too, since many circuits share a common ground.

Tools: Test light or ohmmeter, jumper wire, wiring circuit diagram for your car model.
Materials: Spare fuses, extra automotive electrical wire.

Checking fuses and fusible links

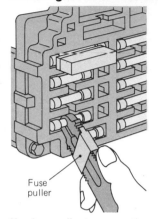

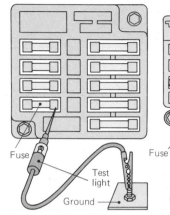

Fusible link

Cable

Fuse puller

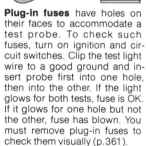

Fuse

Test light

Ground

Fuse

Use fuse puller to remove the glass tube fuses used in many North American cars. Some imported cars have ceramic fuses that can easily be replaced by hand. Plug-in fuses (see pp.361, 367, and illustration at far right) are also replaced by hand. Do not pry out any fuse with a metal tool, such as the blade of a screwdriver; if the blade slipped, it could cause a short.

Fusible link connected to the battery terminal has melted if all of the electrical equipment in the car except the starter has gone dead. Other fusible links located in key positions in the wiring protect large portions of the circuitry. Check them if some but not all of the electrical equipment has gone dead. For information about replacing fusible links, see *Replacing fuses,* p.367.

Use test light to check glass tube or ceramic fuses if uncertain whether or not fuse has blown. Turn on ignition and circuit switches. Clip test light wire to ground. Touch test probe to one side of fuse, then the other side. If light glows for both tests, fuse is OK. If it glows on one side but not the other, fuse has blown. If light does not glow at all, fuse is not receiving power; check wiring for break.

Plug-in fuses have holes on their faces to accommodate a test probe. To check such fuses, turn on ignition and circuit switches. Clip the test light wire to a good ground and insert probe first into one hole, then into the other. If the light glows for both tests, fuse is OK. If it glows for one hole but not the other, fuse has blown. You must remove plug-in fuses to check them visually (p.361).

Tracing a short circuit (fuse blown)

1. Remove the blown fuse and put in a new fuse of the same rating. If it blows, disconnect the circuit part you suspect is shorting out (for example, a bulb or an electric motor) and jump a wire across the gap. The jumper wire must be firmly connected.
2. Insert another fuse. If the fuse does not blow (or the circuit breaker does not trip again), the part that was disconnected caused the short and should be repaired or replaced. If the new fuse blows (or the circuit breaker trips), the short is elsewhere.
3. Replace the disconnected part and repeat Step 2, disconnecting another part, jumping a wire across the gap, and inserting another new fuse. (To disconnect and jump a switch, see opposite page.) Repeat Step 2 as often as necessary, working systematically through the circuit until you find the short.
4. If you cannot find the short in any of the electrical units in the circuit, the fault must be in the wiring. Smoking insulation may lead you to the short. If there is no visible smoke in the engine compartment or under the dash, start at one end of the circuit, disconnect the segment of wire between two connectors, replace it with a jumper wire, and insert a new fuse. If the fuse blows, the short is in another wire segment. Continue testing segments until the fuse does not blow, indicating that the disconnected segment was shorting out. Replace that segment with a new length of wire.

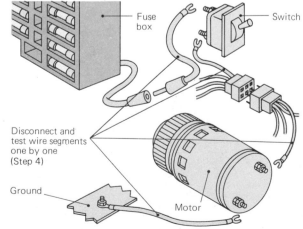

Fuse box

Switch

Disconnect and test wire segments one by one (Step 4)

Ground

Motor

Tracing an open circuit (fuse not blown)

You can find the approximate location of the defect in a complicated circuit with a little detective work. Turn on the circuit and all its switches, including the ignition. Note which units in the circuit work and which do not. The wiring and switches supplying current to units that still work must be all right. Separate wires leading to two or more non-working units are probably all right too, since it is unlikely (but not impossible) that they would go bad simultaneously. By elimination, this means that the circuit segment shared by the non-working units, and no working units, is the most likely site for an open circuit. For example, in the headlight circuit at far right, the low beams work but the high beams do not. If the dimmer switch is OK, there is probably a break in the wire that feeds both high beams but not the low beams.

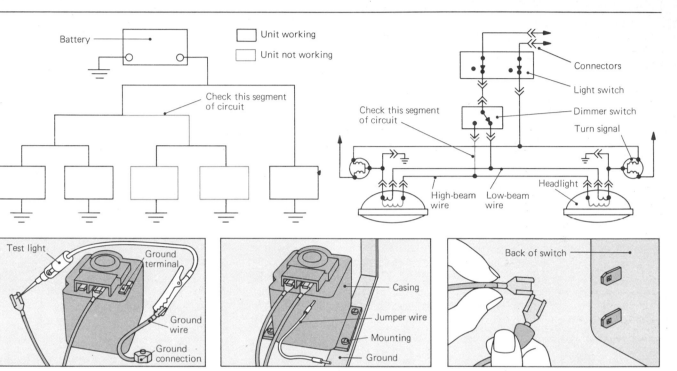

Battery

☐ Unit working

☐ Unit not working

Check this segment of circuit

Connectors
Light switch
Check this segment of circuit
Dimmer switch
Turn signal
High-beam wire
Low-beam wire
Headlight

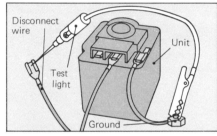

1. To test an inoperative unit with a test light or ohmmeter, turn on ignition and unit. Disconnect wire to unit from switch (see wiring diagram) and attach test light as shown. If light does not glow, circuit is broken elsewhere; go to Step 4. If light glows, proceed to Step 2.

Disconnect wire
Unit
Test light
Ground

2. If unit has a separate ground wire, test as shown. If light glows, unit is faulty and must be repaired. If light does not glow, clean ground connection, tighten, and retest. If light does not glow, ground wire is broken and must be replaced. If light glows, circuit is now OK.

Test light
Ground terminal
Ground wire
Ground connection

3. If unit does not have a separate ground wire, it is grounded through its mounting bolts. Touch jumper wire to unit's metal casing and to ground. If unit then works, clean and tighten its mounting to car body or engine block. If unit still does not work, it is defective. Repair or replace it.

Casing
Jumper wire
Mounting
Ground

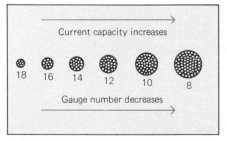

4. Reconnect unit and, with ignition on, test switch that controls it. Remove wires from back of switch and touch them together. If unit works, switch is defective and must be replaced. If unit still does not work, proceed to Step 7. Test plug-in connectors with a jumper wire (see Step 5).

Back of switch

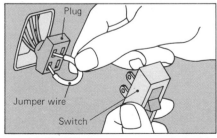

5. Test a switch with a multiple connector by probing each cavity with a grounded test light. Hot cavity will light bulb. Then insert a U-shaped wire between the hot cavity and the others. If unit now works, switch is defective. If unit does not work, proceed to Step 7.

Plug
Jumper wire
Switch

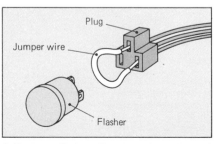

6. To test a flasher, disconnect it and insert a U-shaped wire into the plug from the hot cavity to the other cavities. With the ignition on, try turn signals both ways. If all the turn signal bulbs light (they will stay lit and will not flash), the flasher is defective and must be replaced.

Plug
Jumper wire
Flasher

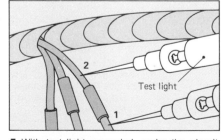

7. With test light grounded, probe the circuit wiring from inoperative unit back toward battery. If test light does not glow when wire is pierced at one point (1) but does glow at next point (2), wire is broken between these points. Cut out break and reconnect wire (see p.180).

Test light

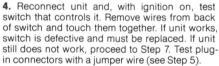

8. If wire is too short to reconnect after removing broken part, insert and connect a new length of wire into the cut-out section. Use wire of the same or heavier gauge than that of the wire it replaces. (The lower the identifying gauge number, the heavier the wire.)

Current capacity increases
18 16 14 12 10 8
Gauge number decreases

Replacing exterior bulbs and flashers ▣▣ 15–30 min

Exterior car lights vary from car to car. It is common to find several bulbs grouped together in one housing. A typical example is a taillight assembly that may include not only the taillight but also the stoplight, backup light, and turn signal light.

Despite the profusion of styles, there are basically three kinds of light housings and three ways to get at a defective bulb. One way is to take off the lens after removing a number of exposed lens-mounting screws. Another way involves detaching the entire light unit from the car and then removing the bulb, with its socket, from the back of the unit. The third method does not require disassembly of the light unit; the bulb is reached from behind—via the trunk, or behind the fender or the bumper. The bulb and socket mount are removed from the rear of the housing. Buy a replacement with the same model number from an auto parts store or your car dealer.

Taillights, stoplights, parking lights, backup lights, and turn signal lights

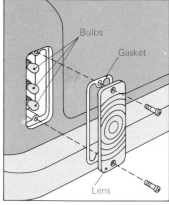

Bulbs in this type of taillight assembly can be reached by removing the screws, then lifting off the lens and lens gasket. Push in bulb, turn it counterclockwise, and lift it out.

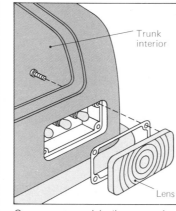

On some car models, the screws (and sometimes nuts) holding the lens to the taillight assembly are hidden. Reach inside the trunk to remove these screws or wing nuts.

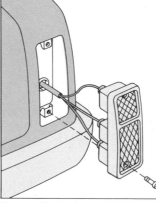

This corner unit consists of front parking and turn signal lights, and also serves as a side marker light. It has a detachable lens. Remove screws and lens, then take out bulb.

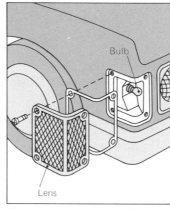

Some taillight assemblies lift off as a unit after the mounting screws have been removed. The bulbs inside these assemblies can be serviced from the back of the unit.

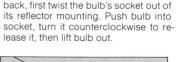

To replace a defective bulb from the back, first twist the bulb's socket out of its reflector mounting. Push bulb into socket, turn it counterclockwise to release it, then lift bulb out.

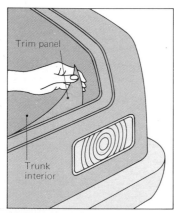

Taillight assembly bulbs on many cars can be reached via the car trunk; no disassembly of light unit is necessary. First remove trim panel, if any, covering back of light unit.

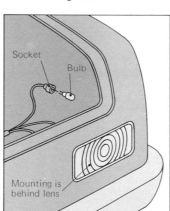

With back of light unit accessible, twist socket of defective bulb, then pull it out of its lens mounting. Next, push bulb into socket, turn bulb counterclockwise, and lift it out.

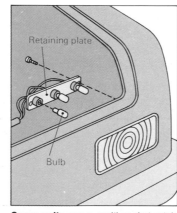

Some units use a multi-socket retaining plate. To replace a bulb, take out screws and remove plate. Then push defective bulb into its socket, rotate, and lift out bulb.

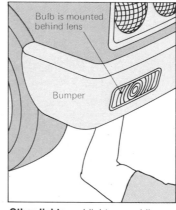

Other lights and light assemblies are housed in the car bumper and also use twist-out bulb sockets. To remove sockets for bulb replacement, reach under and up behind the bumper.

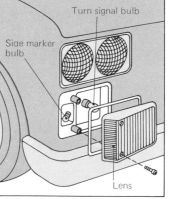

Some front and rear light assemblies, such as this turn signal light, include a separate side marker bulb. To replace either bulb, take out screws, lift off lens, then remove bulb.

Flasher replacement: Flashers are most easily checked by substituting a new flasher unit, which presumably will work. Before going to this trouble, however, check the signal lights to see whether they malfunction as a group or individually.

For example, if the left front turn signal does not blink on when the turn signal lever is actuated, look at the left rear turn signal to see if it lights. Check the right turn signals too. If only one bulb does not light, it is probably burned out. When one bulb is burned out, the remaining bulbs in most systems flash faster. If all four signals do not blink, the flasher is most likely at fault. Flasher units can be mounted anywhere under the dash or, on some imported cars, under the hood. It is a good idea to locate your unit before it fails so that you will know where it is when it does fail. Turn on the signal lights and track down the clicking noise that the flasher unit makes.

Side marker lights

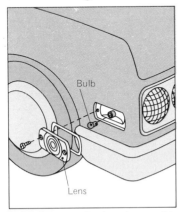

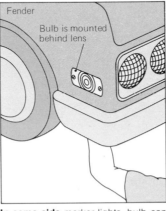

Fender
Bulb is mounted behind lens

Bulbs in many front and rear side marker lights can be reached by first taking out screws and removing lens. To remove bulb, press in, rotate, then lift out bulb.

Some side marker housings lift off the fender when mounting screws are removed. Pry off units held by spring clips. Twist out socket from back of lens, then remove bulb.

In some side marker lights, bulb can be replaced by first reaching under and up behind fender. Twist, then pull out bulb socket. Remove bulb from socket as shown at the left.

License plate lights

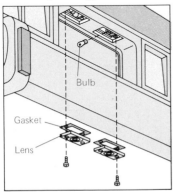

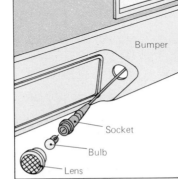

Pair of bulbs in this license plate light can be reached by first taking out screws and lowering lenses and lens gaskets. To remove the bulb, push it in, twist it, then lift it out.

This type of license light assembly can be pried from its bumper mount with a screwdriver. To remove bulb, twist socket out of assembly, then push bulb in, rotate, and lift out.

Disassembly of this light housing is not necessary to remove bulb. Reach under and up behind car bumper to twist socket out of housing; then push bulb into socket, rotate, and lift out.

Turn signal flashers and hazard flashers

To locate a defective flasher, first look in the area under and behind the dashboard, where most car manufacturers put them. You may have to place your head under the dashboard and look around with the help of a flashlight. The cylindrical shape of most flashers is fairly easy to identify. If they cannot be found there, look in the less likely areas illustrated. In some cases, flashers are mounted on the fire wall inside the engine compartment. Turn signals and hazard warning lights have separate flashers.

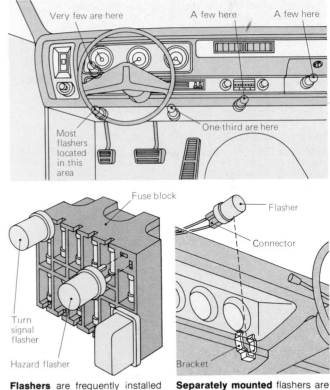

Flashers are frequently installed on the fuse block. To replace, simply unplug flasher from the block and plug in a new one.

Separately mounted flashers are usually supported by a bracket. To replace flasher, pull it off bracket and unplug it from connector.

365

Replacing interior bulbs 🔧🔧

A typical car interior has 15 to 20 light bulbs. Procedures for replacing interior bulbs range from simple to very difficult. The most difficult involve the instrument panel bulbs. Instrument panels vary widely with car decor, and for this reason the arrangements of their lights are not standardized. Variations on the steps shown here should be expected on individual car models.

On some cars the instrument panel bulbs can be removed by simply reaching behind the panel and twisting out the socket that holds the bulb. This step may require some body contortions as well as agile fingers. Since there are a number of sockets behind a panel, it is often difficult to know whether or not the desired socket has been removed. One way to check is to shine a pencil-sized flashlight from behind the dash through the hole vacated by the socket you have removed. If the flashlight illuminates the burnt-out area, you have removed the correct socket.

A defective bulb can often be removed from the front of an instrument panel if you take out the panel-retaining screws and lift off the panel trim and dial lens, and then perhaps one or more instruments. To reach the bulbs in other panels, such as those in some Fords, the instrument panel may have to be removed first. The removal procedure will involve many or all of the steps shown at right, depending on the car model. It is not necessary to disconnect an automatic transmission's PRND21 cable clamp, for example, if the car has a standard shift or if the PRND21 display is not on the dashboard.

Knobs will sometimes have to be removed before the panel will come off. They often pull straight off, but in some cases a screwdriver blade will have to be applied to pinch a locking tab behind the knob. A few knobs screw off, and still others are held by an Allen setscrew. Some Ford knobs require the use of a special tool, made from a bent nail, to release the knob from its shaft.

On some cars a bundle of glass fibers and a single bulb are used to illuminate several areas of the instrument panel. If several "bulbs" seem to burn out at once, suspect this arrangement and look for the single defective bulb responsible.

Caution: Disconnect the ground cable from the battery before beginning work on electrical parts. Failure to do so may result in sparks that can damage equipment and burn hands.

Removing instrument panel bulbs

Some of the more direct ways to gain access to bulbs in the instrument panel are: reaching under and up behind dashboard to instrument panel; reaching through top of dashboard after removing screws and top panel; taking bulbs out from the front after removing panel trim and lens. One type of bulb is simply pulled from its spring-clip socket. Another type must first be pushed in and turned counterclockwise before it can be lifted out.

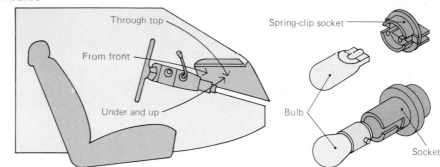

Pulling instrument panel from dashboard

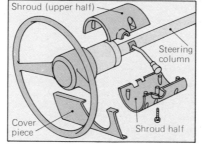

1. Remove upper and lower halves of steering column shroud after taking out screws that secure shroud to column. On some models, additional cover piece (as shown) must also be removed.

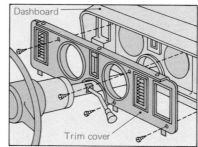

2. Remove instrument cluster trim cover after taking out the screws that secure the cover to the dashboard. Occasionally, the car clock must also be removed before further disassembly can be made.

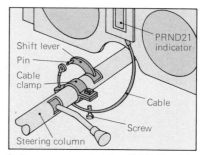

3. Remove screw holding PRND21 cable clamp to steering column. Detach cable from pin on shift lever, then remove clamp from column. On reassembly, set clamp so that PRND21 indicator reads correctly.

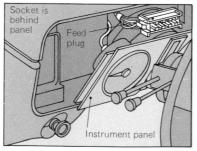

4. Remove screws that hold instrument panel to dash. Unclip speedometer cable housing to provide slack, then pull panel forward. Reach behind panel and pull feed plug out of multi-connector socket.

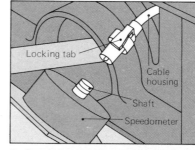

5. Reach behind instrument panel and press locking tab on end of speedometer cable housing. Pull cable off speedometer shaft. On reassembly, tug cable to make sure that catch is properly reengaged.

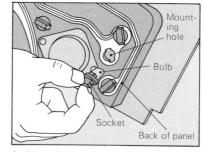

6. Remove instrument panel from dashboard. Twist socket of defective bulb and pull it from instrument panel. Bulb can then be disconnected from socket by pulling or twisting, as illustrated above.

Glove, dome, and trunk lights

Bulb in glove compartment can usually be removed by simply reaching in and taking bulb out of its socket. Some bulbs cannot be reached unless entire lamp and switch assembly is first removed, as shown here. Pry assembly from its mount on the dashboard, then disconnect bulb.

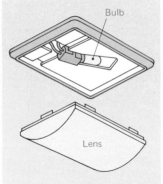

When lens of dome light is removed, bulb can usually be reached. Flexible lenses come off when pressed in on opposite sides. Others are removed by pulling down on one side, by prying, or by twisting. In a few cases, the entire light assembly drops when pulled down, giving easy access to the bulb.

This type of trunk light bulb is directly accessible for removal. In cases where the bulb is covered by a lens, use procedures for dome light (above). If bulb is recessed and difficult to remove with your fingers, use long-nose pliers to slide bulb out of its socket. Do this with care to avoid breaking the bulb.

Replacing fuses 🔧🔧 5–30 min

Fuses, along with *circuit breakers* and *fusible links*, protect a car's electrical system from overheating, which can damage parts or cause fires if a short circuit occurs in the system.

When a fuse blows, replace it. Fuses sometimes blow because of conditions that do not recur. If the replacement fuse also blows, check the circuit the fuse protects for a possible short (pp.361–363).

Fuse ratings are printed on the fuse and by the sockets in the fuse panel. Always replace a fuse with one whose rating matches the fuse panel rating.

Normally, circuit breakers do not have to be replaced, since they switch back on a few seconds after they are tripped by a short circuit. Until the short is fixed, the breakers will continue to trip off and on.

Even when the fuse or circuit breaker has not blown, a circuit may fail if the fuse becomes dirty or corroded, or if it is shaken loose by vibrations of the car. Cleaning or tightening the fuse holder will eliminate these problems (p.361).

Fusible links are special segments of wire that protect portions of the car's wiring system. Because it is made of lighter-than-normal wire, a fusible link will melt first if there is a short. There may be three or four fusible links under the hood of a car.

One fusible link is usually connected to the positive terminal of the car battery. If the link melts through, the battery cable and the connector to which it is joined will have to be replaced as a unit. Other fusible links can be replaced as shown below.

Fuses

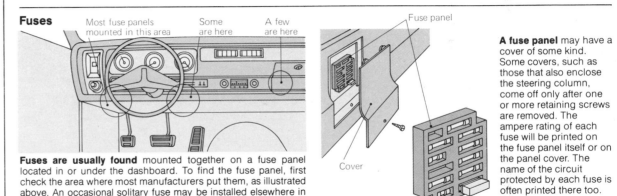

Fuses are usually found mounted together on a fuse panel located in or under the dashboard. To find the fuse panel, first check the area where most manufacturers put them, as illustrated above. An occasional solitary fuse may be installed elsewhere in the car's wiring, most often in the engine compartment wiring.

A fuse panel may have a cover of some kind. Some covers, such as those that also enclose the steering column, come off only after one or more retaining screws are removed. The ampere rating of each fuse will be printed on the fuse panel itself or on the panel cover. The name of the circuit protected by each fuse is often printed there too.

Fusible links

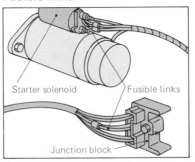

Typical fusible link connections lead to the starter solenoid and to a junction block mounted on the fire wall.

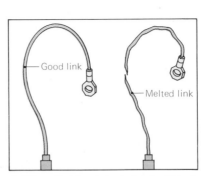

A link melted by a short circuit will look either bloated and discolored or, as shown here, shriveled and broken.

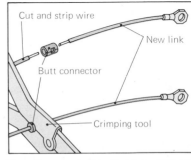

To replace, cut off melted link. Join new link to wire with butt connector. Crimp connector, and wrap it with tape.

Replacing and aiming headlights 🔧🔧 15–30 min

Headlights can burn out. They may also become less effective with age. Their light output decreases as the glass envelope surrounding the filament becomes coated with a thin layer of tungsten. (This problem does not affect halogen headlights.) If a light darkens markedly, it should be replaced.

If the high-beam filament in one of the lights of a four-headlight system burns out, three headlamps remain to illuminate the road ahead, so that it is possible not to notice the loss. Periodic headlight inspections are therefore recommended.

Headlights should be properly aimed. A rough estimate of their aim can be made at night on a long stretch of straight road. High beams should light up not only the road but any adjacent tree or pole for 300 feet ahead. Low beams, on the other hand, should be aimed to cover the road only, or to cover the road and its right-hand margin, where a pedestrian may walk.

Garages use special precision aimers. A less accurate way to aim headlights is to check the light pattern they cast on a smooth, vertical wall. This is best done at night or inside a dark garage. First make sure that the floor is absolutely level, the tires are correctly inflated, the car is carrying its normal cargo load, and the springs are not sagging.

On a four-headlight system, adjust only the inner pair for the high beams. Aim the outer pair by checking the pattern of their low beams only. When checking the inner high beams, first mask the outer headlights with cardboard. If the headlights are arranged one above the other, aim the top pair on low beam only. Then, mask the top pair and aim the bottom pair on the high beam setting.

Headlights can be replaced without disturbing their aim, but it is a good idea to check the aim any time a light is replaced. If the system has recently passed a rigorous state inspection, you need only match the pattern of the replacement lamp to the pattern cast on a wall by its paired opposite lamp.

Headlight mount

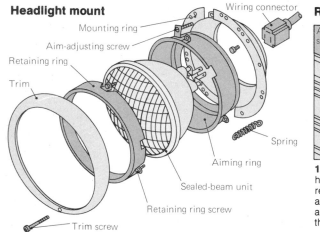

Replacement sequence

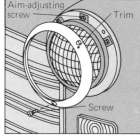 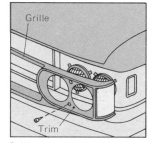 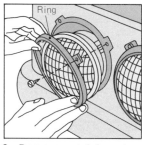 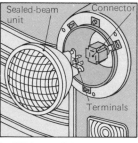

1. Take out screws that secure headlight trim to car body, and remove the trim. Do not disturb aim-adjusting screws that are accessible through a hole in the trim on most models.

2. If headlight trim is an integral part of radiator grille, the entire grille and trim unit will have to be removed. Open the hood, if necessary, and take out all screws that secure grille to car.

3. Remove retaining ring screws, and lift off retaining ring. In some cases, screws need only be loosened; the ring can be rotated counterclockwise slightly, then removed.

4. With retaining ring off, sealed-beam unit is free to fall out or be lifted out. To disconnect wiring, pull the wiring connector off terminals on the back of the lamp.

Aiming sequence

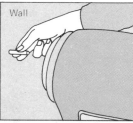 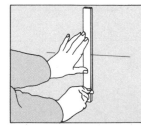 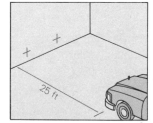 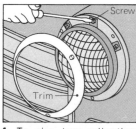 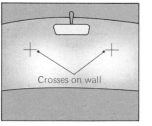 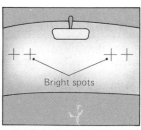

1. Park car on level floor near wall, and mark the point opposite the center of each headlight—two marks for a two-headlight system, four for a four-headlight system.

2. Draw or tape a cross through each mark. In the case of the four-headlight system, note which pair of crosses is for the inner and which pair of crosses is for the outer beams.

3. Back car away from the wall on as straight a line as possible until headlights are 25 ft from the wall. Turn headlights on and adjust their aim as shown in Steps 4-6 at right.

4. To aim, turn adjusting screws on headlight mounting ring. On some models, these screws are directly accessible; on others, trim must be removed first (Steps, 1-2, above).

5. Switch to low beams. Aim headlights (outer pair of four-headlight system) so that beams cast a light pattern as shown, with almost no light appearing above horizontal line.

6. On four-headlight system, switch to high beams. Mask outer lights. Aim inner lights so that beams cast a bright spot on wall that is centered and 2 in. below crosses, as shown.

Replacing switches ⏱⏱⏱ 30 min–1½ hr

There are more than 20 electrical switches inside a modern car. Most of them are mounted on the dashboard or the steering column. A few are in the trunk, the door columns, and on the transmission. Switches for a car's exterior lights are treated on this page; others are covered on the following two pages.

The wide variety of switches used by car manufacturers makes it impractical to describe every type of switch in detail. The lighting switch shown on this page is a relatively standard item on North American cars. It includes not only the headlight and other external light switches but also a built-in rheostat for controlling dashboard lights and, sometimes, an additional switch for turning on the dome light. A circuit breaker is usually built into the switch assembly to protect the taillight, license plate light, parking lights, and side marker lights. Another circuit breaker in the assembly protects the headlights. If any of these components becomes defective, the entire switch assembly should be replaced. On a few cars you may have to remove the instrument panel or a trim panel (see p.366) to replace a switch.

There are two common versions of the switch that actuates the brake light when the brake pedal is depressed. When reinstalling one of the bracket-mounted types, adjust the switch for proper operation. The brake light should turn on when the brake pedal is depressed approximately ½ inch.

The backup light switch may be mounted on the transmission extension, on the steering column, or on the shift linkage under the console. A switch on the transmission extension is actuated by a lever inside the transmission whenever the car is shifted into *Reverse*. This switch often incorporates the *Neutral start switch* (or *Neutral safety switch*), which allows current to flow to the starter only when the transmission is in the *Neutral* or *Park* position.

The dome light switch has a button that is released whenever a door is opened. On some cars the shaft of the switch is threaded so that the distance the button protrudes from the door column can be adjusted. Other common types of automotive switches are illustrated on page 364. Steering column switches are covered on pages 370–371.

Caution: Disconnect the ground cable from the battery before beginning work on electrical parts. Failure to do so may result in sparks that can damage equipment and burn hands.

Light switches and dimmer switches

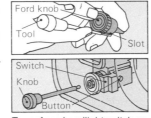

To replace headlight switch on dash, remove knob. Reach behind dash, press release button, and pull out knob. On Fords, pull spring in knob with bent nail or special tool (top).

Unscrew retaining nut that holds the switch to the dashboard. To loosen a recessed unit, remove the retaining nut with a socket wrench or a pair of long-nose pliers.

With retaining nut off, switch assembly can be removed from behind dashboard. Disconnect the multiple-wiring connector from switch to free switch from the wiring harness.

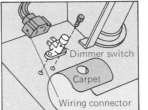

To replace floor-mounted headlight dimmer switch, pull back floor carpet and remove switch mounting screws. Disconnect multiple-wiring connector, then remove the switch.

Brake light switch

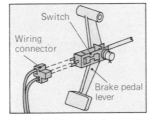

Brake light switch is usually mounted on brake pedal lever, as shown, or on a bracket adjacent to lever (see illustration, far right). To replace switch, first pull off wiring connector.

Pull out the hairpin clip that prevents the brake master cylinder pushrod and the brake light switch assembly from slipping off the end of the brake pedal arm pin.

Slide switch assembly and washers off the brake pedal arm pin. This maneuver can usually be performed without removing the master cylinder pushrod from the arm pin.

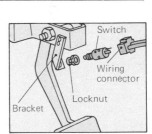

Bracket-mounted brake light switch can be removed by simply unscrewing the switch from the bracket after removing wiring connector. Unscrew locking nut also, if there is one.

Backup light/Neutral start switch

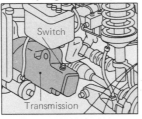

Shift into Neutral to remove backup light/*Neutral start* switch. If switch is mounted on transmission extension, it can be reached under the hood of front-drive cars.

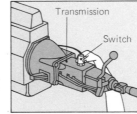

On rear-drive cars, switch may be reached by removing PRND 21 display or center console. If not, switch is on the transmission. Raise car (p.176) and feel for switch with your hand.

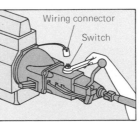

To replace switch, first pull off wiring connector, then unscrew switch from extension. Tighten new switch to a maximum of 5 lb-ft, using a small torque wrench.

Dome light switch

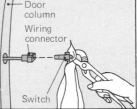

Dome light switch can often be replaced by pulling it out of door column with pliers whose jaws are buffered with cloth to protect shaft threads. Pry off connector with screwdriver.

Repair / Electrical system

Replacing switches and relays ◨◨◨ 30 min–2 hr

Switches are mounted on the steering column in various ways. Some are fairly easy to remove, but others require either that the steering column be lowered or that the steering wheel be removed first.

There are other horn switch configurations in addition to the assembly shown here. Horn switches at the center of the steering wheel can usually be disassembled by first prying off the horn button, then taking the mounting screws out from the top of the wheel rather than from behind it.

The location of a switch on the steering column can differ from the positions shown here. For example, the headlight dimmer switch on some GM and Chrysler cars may be mounted down along the column near the ignition and *Neutral start* switches and operated by a rod from the stalk switch.

If it is necessary to remove the steering wheel, do not attempt to jar the wheel off its shaft with a mallet. This procedure may damage a collapsible steering column. If you must remove the wheel, purchase a special wheel puller tool.

The heater fan and defroster switches shown here are typical of switches mounted on the dashboard. In some cars the fan switch will not turn on the fan until a heater/AC control switch is turned on; so check the control switch before you replace a fan switch.

Mercury-type switches turn on the trunk light by allowing a bubble of liquid mercury to flow over a pair of contacts whenever the switch is tilted. Other trunk light switches function like the dome light switches installed in door columns (see p.369).

Steering column—exploded view

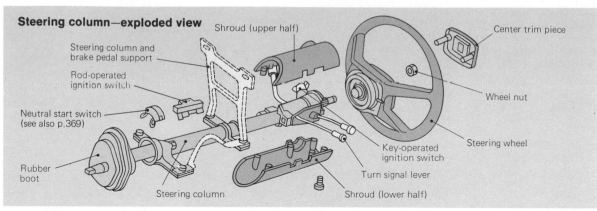

Shroud (upper half)
Center trim piece
Steering column and brake pedal support
Rod-operated ignition switch
Neutral start switch (see also p.369)
Wheel nut
Key-operated ignition switch
Steering wheel
Rubber boot
Turn signal lever
Steering column
Shroud (lower half)

Horn switch

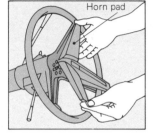
Wheel spoke
Screws

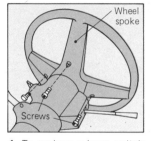
Horn pad

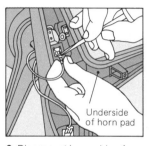
Underside of horn pad

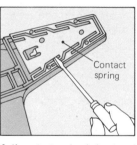
Contact spring

1. To replace a horn switch mounted on the steering wheel, first remove securing screws (or nuts) from behind the wheel spokes.

2. Lift horn pad partway off the steering wheel. Replacing the switch in the horn pad in most automobiles involves replacing the entire pad.

3. Disconnect horn wiring from the pad by pressing in the locking nib on the spade lug, then prying connector off lug with screwdriver. Remove pad.

4. If contact spring is bent and causes horn to blow continuously, a repair is possible. Remove trim pad and bend contact spring back up.

Ignition and Neutral start switches

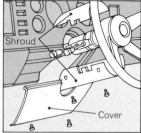
Shroud
Cover

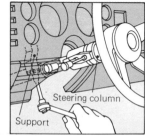
Steering column
Support

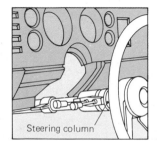
Steering column

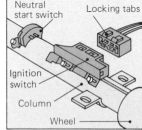
Neutral start switch
Locking tabs
Ignition switch
Column
Wheel

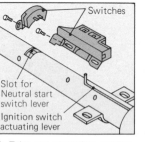
Switches
Slot for Neutral start switch lever
Ignition switch actuating lever

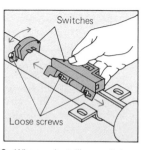
Switches
Loose screws

1. To reach ignition switch and *Neutral start* switch, take out screws and remove steering column cover under dashboard, plus column shroud.

2. Remove the nuts that secure the steering column to the steering-column and brake-pedal support. Two or four nuts will have to be removed.

3. The steering column is now free to tilt downward a few inches. Sometimes it will tilt far enough so that it rests on the driver's seat.

4. Press in on locking tabs of wiring connectors with screwdriver blade, and pull connectors from the switches mounted on the steering column.

5. Take out mounting screws and remove the ignition switch and the *Neutral start* switch. Note how each switch links with actuating levers.

6. When reinstalling switches, adjust by sliding them back and forth in their mounts before tightening screws. Move switch levers to check operation.

Turn signal, dimmer, and hazard warning switches

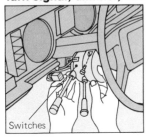

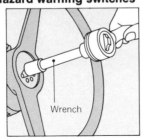

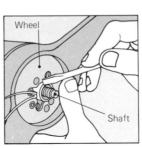

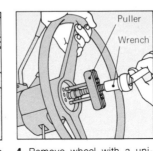

1. Turn signal, dimmer, and hazard switches may unscrew from the steering column after the shroud is removed. If not, remove the steering wheel.

2. Pry off horn pad (see opposite page). Remove nut holding steering wheel to shaft. If a retaining clip holds the nut, pry off the clip first.

3. Use screwdriver to scribe alignment marks on wheel and steering shaft. The marks will help position the wheel correctly for reinstallation.

4. Remove wheel with a universal wheel puller. Grip wheel with one hand to protect steering lock pin. On most imports, switches are now accessible.

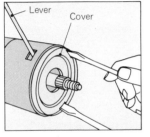

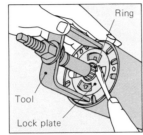

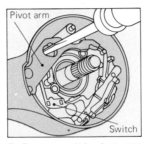

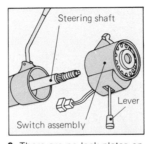

5. Remove trim piece between steering column and dashboard, if necessary. Insert two screwdrivers into slots of plastic cover, and pry cover off.

6. Use pusher tool to push lock plate in just enough to pry retaining ring from groove in shaft. Pull out lever. Push hazard knob in and unscrew it.

7. Remove switch pivot arm. Take out screws holding switch, and lift switch out, taking care not to snag wires. Use new ring for reassembly.

8. There are no lock plates on Fords. Disconnect wiring connectors. Remove switches from shaft. Switches may come off separately or as a unit.

Heater fan, defogger, and trunk light switches

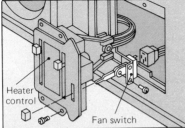

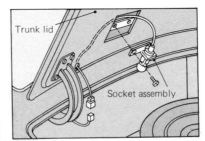

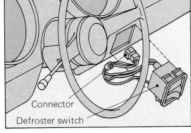

To replace fan switch, first remove instrument panel, if necessary (see p.366). Then take out screws and lift off heater control assembly. Take out retaining screws, disconnect wiring, and remove switch.

Defroster switch and other instrument panel switches like it can sometimes be removed from dashboard by simply prying them off. Pull out wiring until connector appears, then disconnect connector.

Mercury-type trunk light switch is usually part of the bulb socket assembly. Entire assembly should be replaced if switch is defective. To remove it, take out mounting screws and disconnect the wiring.

Replacing relays

A number of switch circuits include relays. A relay is a fairly simple device that is often used in circuits where electric current is strong—for example, in the horn circuit and the ignition circuit. Relays may also be found in the lighting circuit and circuits for the headlight dimmer, the rear window defroster, the hazard warning light, the heater fan, electric radiator fan, and the intermittent windshield wiper.

A working relay clicks whenever it is switched on and off. Check to see that all other parts of the switch-relay circuit are working (see pp.361–363). Then, if you cannot feel the relay clicking with your hand as an assistant operates the switch, the relay is defective and should be replaced.

Relays are easily located and identified on only a few cars. In most cars, you generally do not even know which circuit has a relay until you trace the circuit's wiring or look for the relay on a schematic diagram of the car's wiring. A number of relays may be found clustered on a mounting bracket behind the dashboard. Others are scattered about the engine compartment or in the transmission tunnel.

Before problems arise, it is useful to actuate each car switch sequentially, locate each relay by the sound of its click, then label the relay.

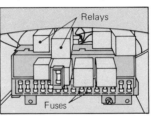

VW relays are mounted with fuses under left side of dashboard to permit easy access and replacement. The relays are labeled and can be unplugged for removal.

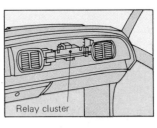

Cluster of relays on some Ford cars is mounted on bracket behind dashboard. Access may require major dashboard disassembly if relays cannot be reached via glove compartment.

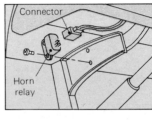

This horn relay is a separate unit mounted on a bracket under the dashboard. To replace relay, pull off its wiring connector and take out the mounting screws.

Checking and replacing sending units, gauges, and warning lights ▢▢▢ 1–3 hr

The warning devices on the instrument panel may be gauges or warning lights. Both types are operated by sending units connected by wires to each gauge or warning light. Many gauges also have an instrument voltage regulator that limits the voltage at each gauge to approximately 5 volts. The regulator may be a tiny replaceable part mounted on the panel's printed circuit board. Some gauges have internal regulators that cannot be serviced separately.

If a warning light does not turn on when the car is started, the bulb is probably defective and should be replaced. This simple solution does not apply to gauges. If a gauge does not work, first check its fuses. Then check the sending unit on the engine block or fuel tank. It may be necessary to remove the air cleaner to gain access to a sending unit on the engine block. After reaching the unit, disconnect its wiring and scrape the terminals clean. Reconnect the wiring so that it is tight, and see if the gauge or warning light now works properly.

Before removing a temperature sending unit, unscrew the radiator cap to lower the pressure in the cooling system. Also, do not confuse the temperature unit with the similar fan thermostat that is found on a number of engines equipped with electric cooling fans. A fan thermostat should have a wire that leads directly to the fan or its relay. **Caution:** Except for tests during which the ignition must be on, disconnect the battery ground cable before beginning work on electrical parts. Failure to do so may cause sparks that can damage equipment and burn hands.

Tools: Wrenches to fit nuts and bolts, water-pump pliers or a hammer and brass drift, voltmeter, ohmmeter.

GM gauges

GM disconnected

Others disconnected

Gauges on GM cars work in the opposite way from other car gauges: they read at the high end of the scale when the gauge is disconnected or when the resistance of the gauge's sending unit is at the high end of its range. When measuring this resistance, therefore, expect the meter readings to be reversed. In addition, GM gauges do not have an instrument voltage regulator.

Fuel-gauge sending unit

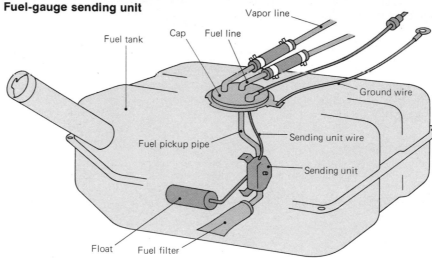

Vapor line · Cap · Fuel line · Fuel tank · Ground wire · Fuel pickup pipe · Sending unit wire · Sending unit · Float · Fuel filter

Sending unit is mounted inside the fuel tank, usually on the fuel pickup pipe. The fuel line and wiring from the sending unit exit the tank through a round plate, or cap, on the top or side of the tank. If this cap is located on the top of the tank and it cannot be reached via the floor of the car or trunk, a mechanic may have to remove the tank from the car.

Caution: When removing the fuel tank's sending unit, take special precautions. Do not smoke or cause sparks. Fuel vapor inside the tank is highly explosive.

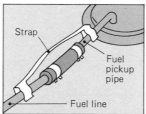

1. The first check in the fuel-gauge system is to examine the ground wire that goes from the sending unit to the car body, or chassis. This wire may corrode, loosen, or break, making the gauge inoperative. To repair the wire, disconnect it, scrape off any corrosion, restore and tighten the connection.

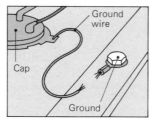

2. On some cars the ground wire for the fuel-gauge sending unit is a strap that is clamped to the fuel pickup pipe at one end and to the fuel line at the other. The strap and its connections should be checked and repaired, if necessary, as shown in Step 1.

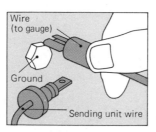

3. Next, check the fuel gauge. Disconnect wire from gauge at sending unit and have assistant turn on car's ignition. Ground the gauge wire briefly (no longer than 5 sec) to body of car. If fuel-gauge needle swings to *Full* (*Empty* on GM units), gauge is OK; otherwise, check gauge and its wiring (see p.373).

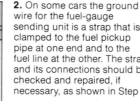

4. Test sending unit if Step 3 shows that gauge is OK. First, disconnect ground strap on battery, then turn tank cap counterclockwise with water-pump pliers. If such pliers are not available, jar cap loose with hammer and a drift or chisel made of brass or other material that will not produce sparks when struck.

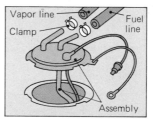

5. Disconnect ground wire, and the wire from the fuel gauge if it is still attached. Loosen clamps, and detach fuel line and fuel vapor line. Then lift fuel-gauge sending unit and fuel pickup assembly out of the tank; be careful not to knock the fragile assembly against the edge of the tank.

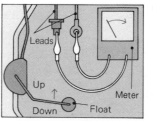

6. Test sending unit resistance with an ohmmeter set to *Low* scale (p.173). Clip meter probes to unit leads. With float down, meter should read from 50 to 300 ohms; with float up, meter should read 2 to 30 ohms. (For GM units, see box at left.) If either test fails, or if meter needle jumps erratically, replace sending unit.

Temperature and oil-pressure sending units

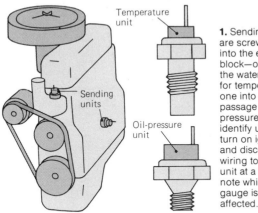

Temperature unit

Sending units

Oil-pressure unit

1. Sending units are screwed into the engine block—one into the water jacket for temperature, one into an oil passage for oil pressure. To identify units, turn on ignition and disconnect wiring to one unit at a time; note which gauge is affected.

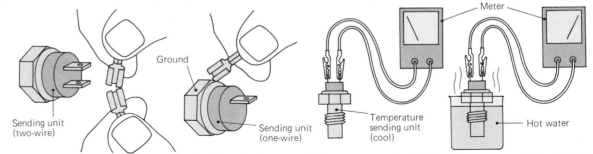

Ground

Sending unit (two-wire)

Sending unit (one-wire)

Meter

Temperature sending unit (cool)

Hot water

2. With ignition on and an assistant at wheel, first check temperature gauge, oil-pressure gauge, or warning light by disconnecting wire(s) at sending unit and shorting it briefly (up to 5 sec). Short the two wires of a gauge system to one another; gauge is OK if needle swings to high end. The reverse is true for GM gauges (see facing page). Ground the single wire of a warning light system on the engine block; light is OK if it turns on.

3. If gauge or warning light is OK, unscrew sending unit from block and test it. Measure temperature unit's resistance with ohmmeter set to *Low* scale (see p.173). If unit is OK, meter will read 50 to 100 ohms when unit is cool, 2 to 30 ohms when unit is immersed in water near the boiling point. (The reverse is true for GM units; see facing page.) The easiest way to check an oil-pressure unit is to substitute one you know is good.

Instrument voltage regulator

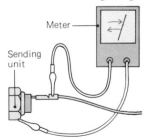

Meter

Sending unit

1. To test instrument voltage regulator, set voltmeter to *Low* scale. Clip meter probes to both terminals of the sending unit (or to one terminal and ground). Turn on the ignition. If voltage regulator is OK, needle of meter will jump to 12 volts, then drop to about 5 volts within a few seconds and fluctuate steadily around that value. The fluctuations indicate that the regulator is turning on and off as it should. If the needle does not move, the regulator is defective and should be replaced. This test can also be performed with a homemade test light like the one shown on page 361. The test light will flicker on and off if the regulator is working properly.

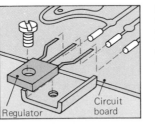

Regulator

Circuit board

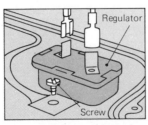

Regulator

Screw

2. If all the gauges on the instrument panel perform erratically or read abnormally high as a group, it means that one voltage regulator serves them all and that the regulator is poorly grounded or defective. Clean and tighten ground connections or replace the faulty regulator.

3. To replace the instrument voltage regulator shown, disassemble instrument panel, if necessary, to gain access to the printed circuit board on which the regulator is mounted (see p.366). Pry regulator from terminals, and install a new one, observing correct polarity (see service manual, if in doubt).

4. Voltage regulator of the type illustrated can be removed from the printed circuit board by taking out its mounting screw and lifting the regulator off. After replacing a regulator, check that it is working before reassembling instrument panel.

Gauges and warning lights

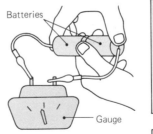

Batteries

Gauge

1. To test an instrument panel gauge, first disassemble the instrument panel, if necessary, to gain access to the back of the gauge (see p.366). Clip a wire to each terminal of the gauge, then hold the other end of each wire against the positive and negative terminals of a pair of fresh flashlight batteries held together in your hands as shown. If the gauge is working, the needle will read about half of full scale (about three-quarters of full scale on GM gauges). If the needle does not move, the gauge is defective and should be replaced. An instrument panel warning bulb can be tested in this manner, too. The bulb will glow dimly if it is working properly.

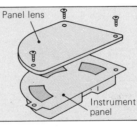

Panel lens

Instrument panel

2. To replace a typical instrument panel gauge, pull the panel from the dashboard, then take out the panel lens mounting screws. Lift the lens off the panel. If there is more than one lens, take off only the one on the gauge in question.

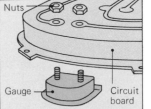

Nuts

Gauge

Circuit board

3. A gauge is usually secured to the printed circuit board by nuts, which also serve to make electrical contact with the board. To remove a gauge, unscrew the nuts and lift the gauge off the board. After replacing a gauge, check its operation before reassembling the instrument panel.

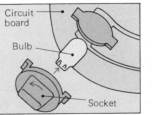

Circuit board

Bulb

Socket

4. To replace a panel warning light mounted on the printed circuit board, twist the socket of the light counterclockwise and remove it. Detach bulb from socket, either by pulling it out as shown or by pushing bulb in, turning it counterclockwise, and lifting it out. Reverse procedure to install a new bulb.

Testing and replacing alternators and voltage regulators ▣▣▣ 30 min–2½ hr

Alternators are part of a car's charging system, which also includes a voltage regulator, the battery, and a dashboard warning light or gauge.

A defect in the charging system will ultimately produce a dead battery, and the car will not start. However, a number of conditions will appear in advance to warn that trouble is brewing.

If a dashboard warning light turns on, it is easily seen. If the car has any meters, they also can signal an abnormality, although you will have to make it a habit to check them periodically. An interpretation of these dashboard warnings is given in the chart on the facing page. Another warning may come from the headlights if they gradually dim during night driving.

The cause of these warnings may be nothing more than an overload on the system, which can occur when such add-on accessories as high-powered audio equipment and high-intensity driving lights are all turned on at once. If so, you must turn off some of the accessories or install a heftier alternator.

At any hint of a problem in the charging system, first look at the fan belt. Turn on all lights and accessories, and have a helper rev up the engine. A loose fan belt will either whine, squeal, or slip; a glazed belt will slip (see pp.286–287).

A belt can also be too tight. Set the tip of a screwdriver against the alternator (if you can reach it) and place your ear against the screwdriver handle. If you hear a rough or grinding noise from the alternator, it means that the bearings are worn, probably by a tight fan belt. Loosening the belt may restore the alternator to service; otherwise, the alternator must be replaced.

A less obvious problem is battery overcharging by a defective voltage regulator. This will cause the battery to need frequent refills or replacements. The on-car tests, opposite, will isolate a faulty regulator.

If you lack the equipment or time for tests, remove the alternator from the car and take it to an auto parts supplier who can test it.

When replacing an alternator, take off the fan, as shown on the next page, and keep it if the replacement alternator does not come with a fan.

Caution: Except for tests during which the engine must be running, disconnect the ground cable from the battery before beginning work on electrical parts. Failure to do so may result in sparks that can damage equipment and burn hands.

Delco (General Motors) alternator

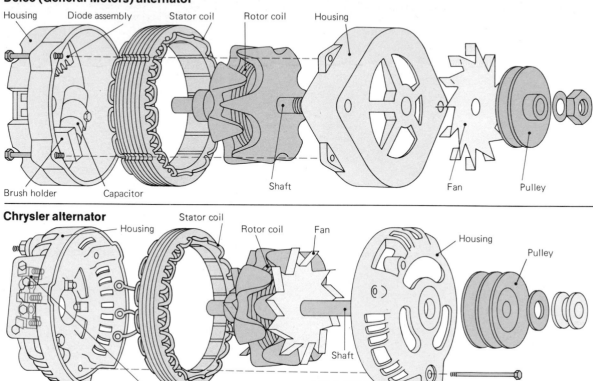

Housing · Diode assembly · Stator coil · Rotor coil · Housing · Brush holder · Capacitor · Shaft · Fan · Pulley

Chrysler alternator

Housing · Stator coil · Rotor coil · Fan · Housing · Pulley · Shaft · Brush assembly is outside housing · Diode assembly is inside housing

Motorcraft (Ford) and Japanese alternators

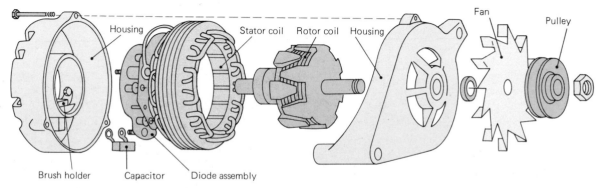

Housing · Stator coil · Rotor coil · Housing · Fan · Pulley · Brush holder · Capacitor · Diode assembly

On-car tests

Some tests can be made on the charging system without disconnecting or removing any part from the car. Tests are for voltage and are made with a voltmeter (p.173) set to a low scale, such as 16 volts.

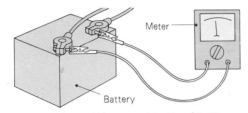

Meter

Battery

1. Begin with a charged battery and ignition off. Clip one meter probe to the positive terminal of the car's battery, the other to the negative terminal. Read the voltage, which will be about 12 volts. This is the *battery reference voltage,* which you must use later.
2. Have an assistant turn on the engine. With lights and all accessories off, run engine at fairly high speed. Read voltage on meter again and compare it to reference voltage.

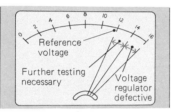

Reference voltage

Further testing necessary

Voltage regulator defective

If voltage has not changed, the alternator is probably defective. To test alternator, see p.376. If voltage is 2 or more volts higher than battery reference voltage, regulator is defective and should be adjusted or replaced (see *Voltage regulators,* p.377). If voltage increase falls between 0 and 2 volts, make the next test.
3. Turn on all lights and accessories, and run engine at high speed. If voltage increases by ½ volt or more above reference voltage, alternator and voltage regulator are OK. If voltage increases by less than ½ volt, proceed with the final test.

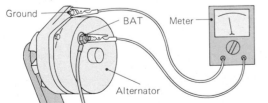

Ground

BAT

Meter

Alternator

4. Turn engine off, then disconnect probes of the voltmeter. Reclip one of the probes to the terminal on the alternator marked BAT, and the other probe to a good ground. Restart engine. With lights and accessories on, run engine at high speed again. If voltage does not increase to more than ½ volt above reference voltage, turn off engine and check alternator for defects. If voltage increases by more than ½ volt, regulator is probably defective.

Dashboard warnings

Cars have either an on-off warning light that shows when the battery is discharging or an ammeter mounted in the dashboard; some cars may have a voltmeter. When the charging system is working well, these instruments will read approximately as indicated in the chart. If they do not, the system is probably faulty. Before reading a meter, let it settle to a steady reading after turning on the engine.

Ignition switch	Car engine	Warning light	Ammeter indication	Voltmeter indication
Off	Stopped	Off	Center	None
On	Running	On	Slight discharge	12 to 13 volts
On	Running	Off	Slight charge	13 to 15 volts

Locating and removing the alternator

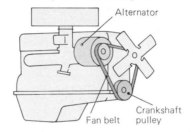

Alternator

Fan belt

Crankshaft pulley

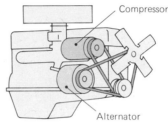

Compressor

Alternator

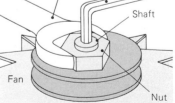

CAUTION HIGH VOLTAGE

Alternators are usually mounted at front of engine and linked by a fan belt to the engine's crankshaft pulley. Those installed high on the engine can be reached and removed from above. Air cleaner may be in the way.

Units mounted low on engine may pose problems, particularly if air conditioner compressor is installed above them. If alternator is too hard to reach, approach it from under the car after removing any splash plate that may be in the way.

Do not confuse regular car alternator with second alternator sometimes installed to defrost the windshield. Such units have special high-voltage warning labels and should be touched only after consulting service manual instructions.

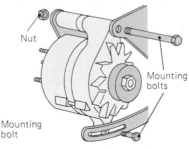

Alternator

Fan belt

Wiring

Mounting bolt

Nut

Mounting bolts

Wrench

Allen wrench

Shaft

Fan

Nut

To remove alternator, first loosen mounting bolt used for adjusting tension of fan belt, and swing alternator toward engine to disengage belt from alternator pulley. Label wires to unit so that they can be reconnected correctly when the alternator is reinstalled.

Disconnect wiring from alternator. The connectors will be either the plug-in type or a simple nut on a stud. Then, remove the nuts from the mounting bolts and, holding the alternator in one hand, pull the bolts out with the other hand. Remove the alternator from the engine.

To remove fan from alternator shaft, use Allen wrench to hold shaft. Remove securing nut with a wrench, then lift fan off shaft. Bolt on most alternator shafts is left-hand threaded and is loosened by turning bolt clockwise; but examine shaft threading to make sure.

Testing and replacing alternators and voltage regulators *(continued)*

There are a number of components inside an alternator that can be tested or checked individually. In some cases, these parts can be purchased separately as well. Not all parts suppliers have all the components in stock, however. Suppliers of domestic car parts are less likely to have everything you need. In some cases, you will have to purchase an entire alternator as a replacement or visit junkyards in the hope of salvaging a needed component.

The voltage regulator is one such component, although in many charging systems it is a unit separate from the alternator. By carrying out the on-car tests on the previous page, you may be able to determine which of the two—regulator or alternator—is faulty.

Certain components, such as the brush assembly, may be mounted in the alternator in such a way that they can be serviced from the outside. To gain access to other components, disassemble the alternator according to the instructions on this page while referring to the exploded views of alternators on page 384.

When an alternator is disassembled, an almost complete set of tests and checks can be made on its components. Most are resistance measurements made with an ohmmeter. Even if a particular component cannot be replaced by a parts supplier, it is still worth determining that an alternator part is causing the difficulty rather than something else, such as the wiring in the charging system.

When measuring coil resistance, it is helpful to know exactly what these resistances should be. You can then determine whether a measured resistance is off just a bit—indicating that a few turns of the coil are shorted to each other, which would cause the alternator to lose some of its efficiency. The required resistances are given in the manufacturer's service manual. The resistance tests given at right are less rigorous by comparison. What they tell is whether or not there is a break in the coil wiring.

Diodes convert the AC that alternators generate into DC. A shorted diode will result in reduced alternator output, which shows up as a whining sound from the alternator or as a dimly glowing dashboard warning light. If one diode becomes defective, the entire set will probably have to be replaced, since the diodes are generally mounted as a unit.

Carbon brushes in a modern alternator usually last the life of the unit. However, checking them for wear may still be worthwhile.

Disassembling alternators

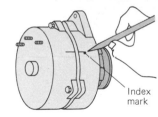

1. Before taking alternator apart, scratch an index mark across the housing halves at a point where they join. Use this mark as a reference to put housing back together correctly when the alternator is reassembled.

Index mark

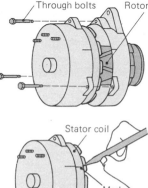

Through bolts   Rotor

2. Unscrew the through bolts that hold the housing together, and pull the housing apart. Shaft with rotor will come out independently. A socket wrench with a slim shank may be needed to get a solid grip on the bolts.

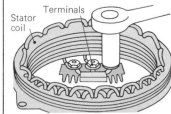

Stator coil

Mark

Housing

3. Scratch another index mark, this time on the housing and core of the stator coil at a point where they join, to ensure that the parts will be reassembled correctly.

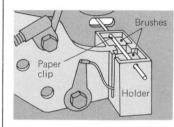

Stator coil   Terminals

4. Remove nuts that secure the stator coil wiring to the terminals inside the alternator housing. Separate the coil from the housing.

Brushes

Paper clip

Holder

5. It is impossible to reassemble some alternators if the brushes are not restrained in their holders. To restrain them, insert a straightened-out paper clip into the hole especially made for this purpose. Pull the clip out after reassembly.

Testing alternator coils

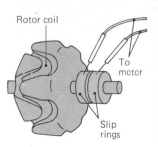

Rotor coil

To meter

Slip rings

1. Test rotor coil for open circuit with an ohmmeter set to the *Low* scale (p.173). Touch one probe to a slip ring on rotor shaft, the other probe to the other slip ring. If meter reads between 2 and 300 ohms, coil is OK. If needle of meter does not move, coil has an open circuit and is defective.

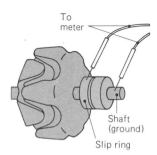

To meter

Shaft (ground)

Slip ring

2. Test rotor coil for short circuit to ground with ohmmeter set to *Low* scale. Touch a probe to one of the slip rings, the other to the rotor shaft. If needle of meter does not move, coil is OK. If needle moves, there is a short circuit and the coil is defective.

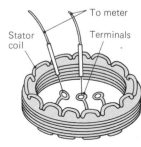

To meter

Stator coil

Terminals

3. Test stator coil for open circuit with meter set as above and coil terminals disconnected from diodes. Touch meter probes to any two pairs of coil terminals. If coil is OK, meter should read almost zero ohms for all pairs selected. If meter needle does not move, coil is open and defective.

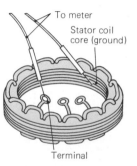

To meter

Stator coil core (ground)

Terminal

4. Test stator coil for short circuit to ground with meter set as above. Touch one probe to any coil terminal, the other to the core of the coil. If meter needle does not move, coil is OK. If needle does move, there is a short and the coil is defective.

Voltage regulators

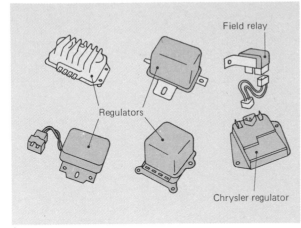

Field relay

Regulators

Chrysler regulator

Regulators that are not part of the alternator are mounted on the fire wall or fender well. They may be hidden behind another part and difficult to spot but will resemble the illustrations at left. To remove such a regulator, disconnect wiring, take out mounting screws, and lift off unit. Note color of each wire attached to each terminal for correct reassembly later. With Chrysler regulators, the field relay, usually found in the regulator circuit, is a separate unit mounted nearby. When replacing this regulator, replace the field relay in the same way.

Alternator diodes

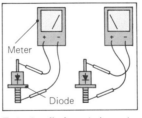

Diodes are found inside the alternator. To gain access to them, disassemble alternator as shown on facing page. Diodes are joined in groups of three or six and look like those in the illustrations at left. An assembled group is usually mounted inside the alternator on the assembly's terminals and can be removed by unscrewing the terminal nuts. In some cases, separate mounting screws will have to be taken out. A radio-suppression capacitor like the one in Delco units may have to be disconnected from the diode assembly first.

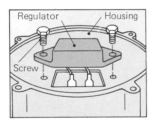

Regulator (cover removed)

Adjusting screw

Ford electronic regulators (installed in 1974–77 Fords, Lincolns, and Mercurys) can be adjusted. Take screws off and remove cover. Turn adjusting screw to raise or lower voltage to meet requirements in On-car test No. 2, p.375.

Regulator   Housing

Screw

Bosch or Motorola charging systems, used in European cars, have their voltage regulators mounted on the alternator housing. To remove regulator, take out mounting screws, disconnect wiring, and lift unit off the alternator.

Resistor

Regulator

Diodes

To replace an internal regulator, first disassemble alternator (opposite page). Take out the screws. Lift out wire resistor and diode assembly (for Delco units). Remove regulator-brush assembly and replace it with a new assembly.

Meter

Diode

To test a diode, set ohmmeter to *Low* scale (p.173). Touch probes to terminals of diode. Reverse probes for second test. If diode is OK, meter needle will not move for one of the tests but will jump to zero for the other test.

Common plate (terminal)

Meter

Diode assembly

Terminals

Three-diode assembly requires that the tests again be made three times. For each diode, touch one probe to the diode terminal, the other to the common mounting plate; then reverse the connections. Repeat test on other two diodes.

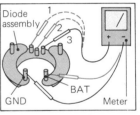

Diode assembly

GND   BAT   Meter

Six-diode assembly requires that the tests (left) be done six times. First three tests are made between three diode terminals and GND terminal. Make second three tests between three diode terminals and BAT terminal.

Removing and checking brushes

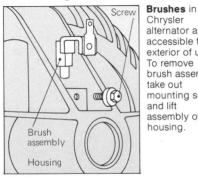

Screw

Brush assembly

Housing

Brushes in Chrysler alternator are accessible from exterior of unit. To remove brush assembly, take out mounting screw and lift assembly off housing.

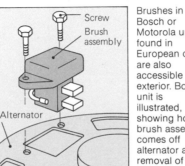

Screw

Brush assembly

Alternator

Brushes in Bosch or Motorola units, found in European cars, are also accessible from exterior. Bosch unit is illustrated, showing how brush assembly comes off alternator after removal of screws.

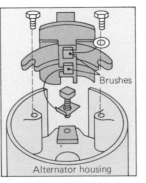

Brushes

Alternator housing

To replace Motorcraft (Ford) brushes, disassemble alternator (facing page). Take out mounting screws and remove brush assembly. Note position of insulating piece under assembly for proper reinstallation.

Brushes

Wear limit

Wear limit is marked on some brushes. Replace brushes if they are worn beyond this limit. If brushes are not marked, consult manufacturer's service manual for wear limit. Most brushes will last the life of the alternator.

Gaining access to and removing car radios ▢ ▢ ▢

The functioning parts of a car radio are the *receiver*, mounted in or beneath the dashboard; the *loudspeaker* or speakers, which may be anywhere inside the passenger compartment but are usually found on the dashboard; and the *antenna*, mounted somewhere on the outside of the car or in the windshield. These parts are connected to each other by cables and wires. The car battery supplies the power that runs the radio. The body and frame of the car serve as a common electrical ground.

The exact arrangement of the radio parts and the cables connecting them varies significantly with different car models. The parts can be quite difficult to reach for inspection or repair and are sometimes even more difficult to remove.

To remove a car radio, first pry off the control knobs, disconnect the speaker wires and cables behind the receiver, and take out the screws and nuts that mount the unit to the dashboard. Next, remove all parts behind the dashboard that could obstruct the radio while it is being removed. These may include the heater and air-conditioner ducts and, in some cases, parts of the instrument panel as well (see *Pulling the instrument panel from the dashboard*, p.366). In some cars you can reach the mounting bolts at the rear of the radio by removing the glove compartment door and bin. When the way is clear, pull the radio from the dashboard. To accomplish all this, you may have to push the front seat as far back as it will go and lie on your back on the seat.

In a few cars the radio can be removed by simply taking out its mounting screws and nuts, then pulling the radio from the front of the dashboard.

Grounding a car radio

A car radio cannot function when it is not properly grounded. The ground runs from the radio chassis, through the radio mounting brackets to the car body, then on through the car frame and engine to the ground terminal of the battery. If the connection is poor at any point, the radio will sound scratchy, play intermittently, or cease to work at all. If this happens, first tighten all the screws and bolts that mount the radio to the dashboard. Then see whether there is a wire that serves as a backup ground (it would be connected from the metal casing on the car radio to the car frame). If you find such a wire, clean and tighten its terminals at both ends. You can check the results of these efforts with an ohmmeter (p.173) set to the *Low* scale. Clip one meter probe to the radio chassis, the other to a bare metal part of the car body—such as a bolt—as far from the radio as the meter probe can reach. If the meter reads close to zero, the ground is OK; if it reads high, the ground is faulty. Attach an additional ground wire if necessary.

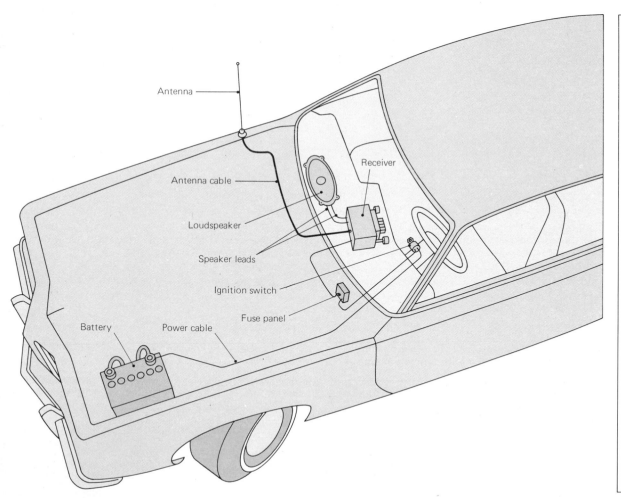

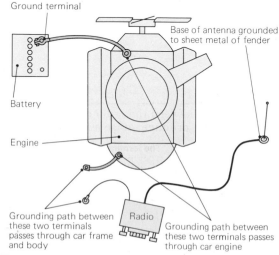

What to do when the radio does not receive any stations or does not come on ◻◻◻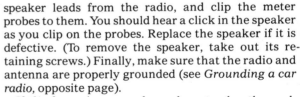

If you cannot receive any stations on the radio, but there is a thumping in the loudspeaker as you turn the set on, or you hear a slight, scratchy noise when you turn the volume control, there is probably a defective connection between the radio and the antenna. To make sure, pull the antenna cable plug from its jack in the back of the receiver and insert a makeshift antenna (such as a length of insulated electrical wire) into the jack. If the radio then picks up stations, albeit poorly, it is likely that the radio is OK and the antenna is at fault. As an added check, you can test the antenna with an ohmmeter (p.173) set to the *Low* scale (see second illustration below). Replace the antenna if it is defective.

If you hear no sound at all when you turn on the radio, check the fuse in the power line from the battery. The power line is on the fuse panel of the car, usually under the dashboard (see p.367). Replace the fuse if it is defective. Next, examine the leads to the loudspeaker to be sure they are making good electrical connections at their terminals. In addition, test the loudspeaker with the ohmmeter. Disconnect the speaker leads from the radio, and clip the meter probes to them. You should hear a click in the speaker as you clip on the probes. Replace the speaker if it is defective. (To remove the speaker, take out its retaining screws.) Finally, make sure that the radio and antenna are properly grounded (see *Grounding a car radio,* opposite page).

If the foregoing procedures do not solve the problem, the receiver itself is probably defective. Remove the receiver (see opposite page) and take it to a repair shop or car dealer for servicing.

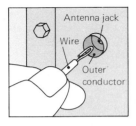

A short piece of wire plugged into the antenna jack in back of the radio serves as a makeshift antenna. Note: Do not let a bare part of the wire touch the outer part of the jack.

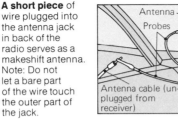

To test the antenna, clip one probe of the ohmmeter to the center conductor of the antenna cable jack, the other probe to the antenna. The meter should read nearly zero.

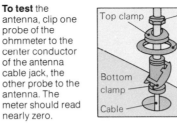

To remove a fender-mounted antenna, loosen the securing nut, then lift the antenna up and out, together with its base trim, clamps, and gaskets and the antenna cable.

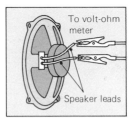

To test the speaker, disconnect its leads. Clip ohmmeter probes to each speaker lead. If you hear a click in the speaker as its leads are touched, it is OK.

Eliminating engine noise in the radio ◻◻◻

A gasoline engine is an inherent source of electrical noise because of the sparks it generates. The hood and fenders of the car shield the car antenna from the interference caused by these sparks. However, this shield will not work effectively unless there is a good electrical connection between the hood and the car body. The connection is made by a braided, flexible strap or by a spring contact on the body that the hood pushes against as you close it. If you hear interference on the radio when the car engine is running, check the condition of this connection and clean or tighten the part where necessary. Replace the strap or spring contact if it is broken.

A poor ground between the radio or antenna and the battery may produce noise too. Check the grounding, and repair it if defective (opposite page).

If the problem persists, listen to determine the type of noise being made. A high-pitched whine that goes up in frequency as the engine accelerates is caused by the alternator. A steady ticking or snapping sound that varies with engine speed is ignition noise.

If you hear ignition noise on the radio, look at the engine at night while it is running. Sparks arcing from the spark plug cables to a grounded part, such as the engine, indicate that the cables are defective and should be replaced. Check the cables with an ohmmeter (p.231) and replace defective cables. In addition, the ignition coil capacitor may be defective. Capacitors are difficult to test. The easiest thing to do is to replace the capacitor with a new one and see if this clears up the interference. Capacitors are cheap.

Even if the car radio was not installed by the manufacturer but at some later time by the owner or car dealer, the car probably has an ignition coil capacitor or spark-suppression cables and suppressor spark plugs as original equipment. (North American cars are equipped with noise-suppression cables and suppressor spark plugs at the factory, whether the car has a radio or not.) Suppressor spark plugs are often called *resistor plugs.*

If the interference is alternator noise, splice a choke into the power line that runs from the fuse box to the radio. The choke, as well as the capacitor and separate spark plug suppressors, can be obtained in most electronic supply stores.

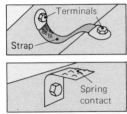

The terminals of a flexible strap connection should be clear of corrosion and tight. If the hood is grounded through a spring contact, the contact should be free of dirt.

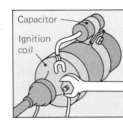

When installing an ignition coil capacitor, follow the instructions that come packaged with the part.

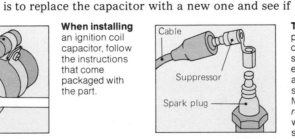

To install spark plug suppressors, connect one suppressor to each plug, then attach cables to suppressors. Most cars have *resistor plugs* with built-in suppressors.

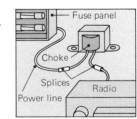

To splice a choke into the power line, cut the line, then solder the leads from the choke to each of the cut ends. Wrap each splice with insulating electrical tape.

Installing a car radio ▢▢▢ 2–3 hr

You can install a radio if your car does not have one, if you want to replace a radio that is broken, or to upgrade your present system with a combination radio and tape player. Replacing the original radio may be difficult (see pp.378–379). If removing an old radio or installing a new one in the dash seems like too much trouble, a new unit can be mounted under the dashboard or on the transmission hump. Brackets and other mounting hardware for under-the-dashboard installation are often supplied with a new unit. Wherever you locate the radio, secure it firmly so that it will withstand jolts and vibration.

Radio manufacturers now make units to fit a wide variety of car dashboards. Check a new radio's specifications to see whether it is designed to fit your car. An in-dashboard installation looks better, is easier to reach, and makes the unit more difficult to steal.

If a dashboard panel is sturdy enough, a radio can be directly supported by the panel, as shown below. If the panel is not securely mounted or if it is shaped too awkwardly for such a purpose, use an additional metal support plate (shown in color outline in the exploded view below, left).

When replacing an old radio, use its mounting plate for the new unit, if possible. Otherwise, a plate may have to be fabricated, and screw holes will have to be drilled and tapped into it and the dashboard.

Before you drill holes and cut openings in the dashboard panel, insert the radio into the allotted space to be sure that it will fit properly. Measure carefully to ensure that the holes and the opening are placed accurately on the dashboard panel.

The easiest way to supply power to the radio is to attach the radio leads to unused accessory terminals on the fuse box, or tap them into the cigarette lighter leads as shown. If the radio includes a tape player, however, its circuit should operate independently of the car ignition; if the ignition switch can turn off the power while the tape player is running, the pinch roller in the player may be damaged. In such a case, find a direct power lead from the battery—near the fuse panel under the dash, for example—and tap the radio power lead directly into that lead.

Before installing the radio in the dash, read the instructions for adjusting the *antenna trim*. Tune in a weak AM station near 1,000 kHz, then turn the antenna trim screw on the back, side, or front of the set to obtain maximum volume.

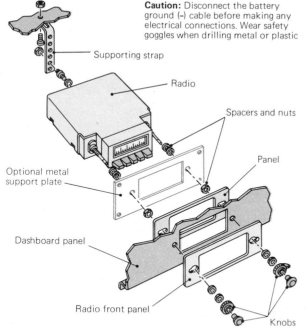

Caution: Disconnect the battery ground (–) cable before making any electrical connections. Wear safety goggles when drilling metal or plastic

Supporting strap
Radio
Spacers and nuts
Optional metal support plate
Panel
Dashboard panel
Radio front panel
Knobs

Tools: Drill, coping saw, file, utility knife, pencil, pliers, wire cutter and stripper, electrician's tape, metal snips (if needed), screwdrivers and wrenches to fit nuts and bolts.
Materials: Extra speaker wire to reach rear speakers (if needed), solderless connectors.

Dashboard installation

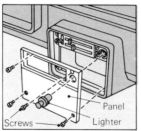

1. Unplug cigarette lighter. Knock out radio-mounting panel (if any), or take out mounting screws and remove dashboard panel that encloses area for radio installation.

Screws — Lighter — Panel

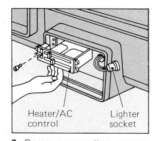

2. Remove mounting screws and pull the heater/AC control forward. Pull out the cigarette lighter socket and any other part that hinders access to space meant for the radio.

Heater/AC control — Lighter socket

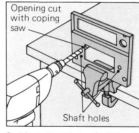

3. Mark location of dial and shafts. Then saw opening for dial, and drill holes for shafts in dash panel. Edges do not have to be perfect, since radio panel will cover them.

Opening cut with coping saw — Shaft holes

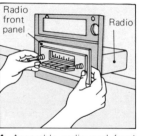

4. Assemble radio and front panels, spacers, washers, nuts, and knobs provided by manufacturer onto dash panel. Insert completed assembly into dashboard to check for fit.

Radio front panel — Radio

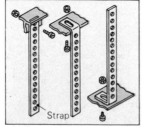

5. Drill hole, then mount supporting strap with screw and nut. Mount strap to any sturdy interior bracket or brace in such a way that radio can easily be secured to strap.

Strap

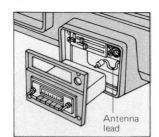

6. Plug antenna lead into antenna jack on back of radio. If car was originally equipped with an antenna, look for its lead in upper part of dash. To install new antenna, see p.382.

Antenna lead

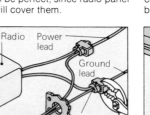

7. Tap radio wires into power lead and ground lead of cigarette lighter (see p.180). Plug speaker wires into radio in the order given in radio manufacturer's instructions.

Radio — Power lead — Ground lead — Taps — Lighter

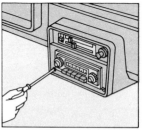

8. Insert radio into dashboard. Secure radio to dashboard with screws. Reach under and behind the dashboard, and bolt the metal supporting strap to the rear of the radio.

Installing speakers ⬚⬚ 1–2 hr

Speakers can be mounted in almost any area of the car. To reproduce stereo sound effectively, however, they should be placed as far apart as possible—for example, in doors or wheel wells on each side of the car. Since car interiors have unusual acoustics, it is advisable to place the speakers in different parts of the car first and to listen to the effect before you cut into panels and install the speakers permanently.

Whether or not your car has a factory-installed radio, manufacturers routinely build speaker-mounting brackets into a car, which makes speaker installation easier. Look for these brackets in the top of the dashboard and under the rear package shelf of a sedan (look from inside the trunk). If you use these brackets, you may still have to cut openings in the fiberboard inner panels for the speaker grilles.

Typical installations

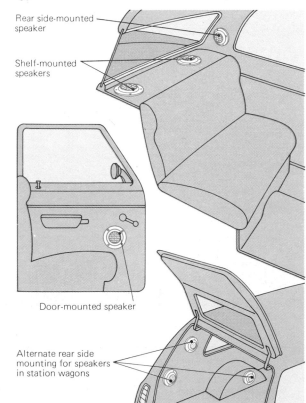

Rear side-mounted speaker

Shelf-mounted speakers

Door-mounted speaker

Alternate rear side mounting for speakers in station wagons

Mounting the speakers

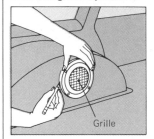

Grille

1. Draw outline of speaker grille on panel to which the speaker is to be mounted. Make sure that when speaker is later mounted in this position, it will fit into space behind panel.

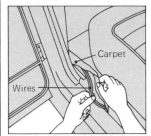

Template

2. Use paper template to draw speaker hole, which must be smaller than the grille. If template is not included in speaker kit, gently trace one onto paper pressed against speaker rim.

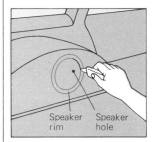

Speaker rim   Speaker hole

3. Cut a speaker hole in the panel with a utility knife or similar cutting tool. Again insert speaker into space behind the hole to be sure that the speaker fits the allotted space properly.

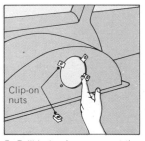

Holes   Speaker with grille

4. Place speaker on car panel so that it mates with outline of grille drawn in Step 1. Use a pencil to mark the location of the screw holes in the speaker rim onto the panel.

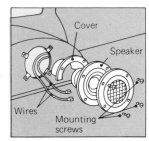

Clip-on nuts

5. Drill holes for screws at the locations marked, and attach clip-on nuts (supplied with speaker) over the holes. Do not drop nuts; they may fall into an inaccessible area of the car.

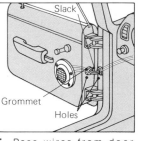

Cover   Speaker   Wires   Mounting screws

6. Connect speaker wires to speaker. Install speaker, grille, and a water-deflecting cover (if one is supplied). Tighten speaker's mounting screws to the clip-on nuts.

Installing the speaker wires

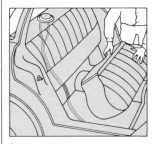

Carpet   Wires

1. Run the wires from a rear speaker under the floor carpet next to the doors, then to the radio. To lift carpet, take out screws and remove chrome trim piece from the door sill.

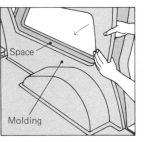

Carpet   Wires

2. Pass speaker wires behind carpet covering the foot well of car, then up to the back of the radio. First pull the carpet forward, then lay the wires and reposition the carpet.

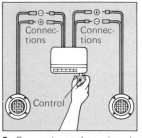

3. If speakers are mounted on a back shelf of a sedan, remove the rear seat cushion. Run the speaker wires through the opening below the back rest, then under the floor carpet.

Space   Molding

4. In places, part of the molding inside the car will have to be loosened to slip speaker wires underneath. First take out mounting screws, then carefully pry the molding loose.

Slack   Grommet   Holes

5. Pass wires from door-mounted speakers through factory-made holes in door and door jamb. Insert rubber grommets in holes. Leave slack in wire so that door can open.

Connections   Connections   Control

6. Connect speaker wires to radio, turn radio on, and operate balance control. If sound comes from right speaker when control is turned left, reverse wire connections.

Installing a radio antenna ☝ 30–45 min

Since antennas break frequently, replacement kits are readily available and often come with installation instructions similar to those given here.

If you want to install a power antenna (one that automatically raises and lowers as you turn the radio on and off), you must find an accessible space large enough to hold the antenna base assembly, which includes a motor and a motor relay. If the antenna cannot be inserted inside the front fender without cutting through inner fender panels, try it on a rear fender where the space underneath can be reached from inside the car's trunk.

If the antenna cable is not long enough to reach the radio from a rear fender, buy a cable extension with a plug and a jack at each end. These are sold in various lengths by radio supply shops.

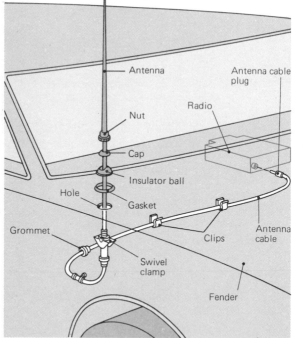

Tools: Electric drill, heavy-duty hole saw attachment for drill, metal file, screwdriver, wrench.
Materials: String, tape, cable extension (if needed).

Replacing an old antenna

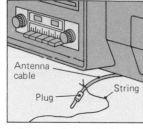

1. Reach under the dashboard and pull antenna cable plug from back of the radio. Tie a string to the plug, one that is long enough to reach the antenna with several feet to spare.

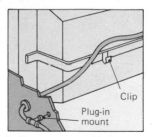

2. Free antenna cable from all clips and other fixtures that moor the cable to inner parts of the dashboard. If necessary, disassemble part of the dash to gain access to the clips.

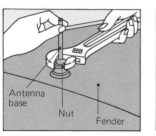

3. Loosen antenna nut and slightly lift nut, cap, and insulator ball. If the base is broken, grasp it with your fingers while loosening nut so that base does not fall inside fender.

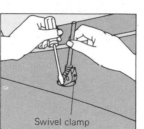

4. Holding on to antenna or to its broken base, reach through fender hole with a screwdriver and push down one side of swivel clamp. Pull the assembly up and out of the hole.

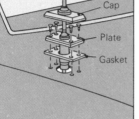

5. Some antennas, such as this type made by Ford, do not have a swivel clamp but are screwed to the fender. To remove this type, pry off snap-on cap, remove screws, and lift out.

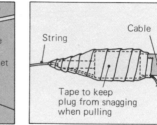

6. Pull antenna cable and string out of fender hole. Undo string; tie and tape it to the new antenna's cable plug. Insert cable, and pull string to guide cable toward dashboard.

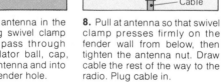

7. Install a new antenna in the fender by tilting swivel clamp so that it can pass through hole. Slip insulator ball, cap, and nut down antenna and into place over the fender hole.

8. Pull at antenna so that swivel clamp presses firmly on the fender wall from below, then tighten the antenna nut. Draw cable the rest of the way to the radio. Plug cable in.

Installing a new antenna

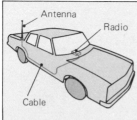

1. If front fender is too narrow, install antenna on rear fender. Route antenna cable under carpeting from inside car trunk to radio (as with rear speaker wires on page 381).

2. Drill pilot hole at the antenna site selected, after having made sure that any part of the antenna assembly to be placed inside the fender will have sufficient clearance.

3. Use a sheet-metal (not carpentry) hole saw to cut a hole in the fender to antenna manufacturer's specifications. Pilot hole in Step 2 serves as a guide for the hole saw.

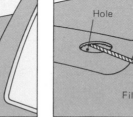

4. File underside of hole edge to provide a good ground for antenna base. Install antenna as in Steps 7–8, above. Route antenna cable to radio, and plug in the cable.

Replacing a windshield wiper motor ▢▢▢ 30 min–2 ½ hr

Before concluding that a wiper motor is defective, check all parts of its electrical system (see *Tracing electrical faults*, pp.361-363). Fuses often blow in winter, when the wiper blades may freeze to the windshield or be used to move heavy accumulations of snow. If the motor operates intermittently, a circuit breaker may be tripping on and off. If the wipers continue to work intermittently or at one speed but not the other, first look for a bad connection in one of the wires in the wiper system, then check the wiper switch for faults (see pp.369-371).

Carmaker's service manuals contain electrical tests for individual wiper motors. The motor may have to be removed to perform these tests. Once the motor crank arm is disconnected from the wiper linkage, try to operate the linkage by hand. If the linkage is binding, the motor may be OK. Free the binding linkage, then reconnect the motor and try it again.

On some Fords, parts of the motor and gearbox can be replaced individually. Otherwise, the entire motor assembly will have to be replaced if any part is defective. When working on a Ford wiper motor, avoid striking it with any hard object. The motor contains some ceramic parts, which shatter easily.

Caution: Disconnect the ground (–) cable from the battery before beginning work on electrical parts. Failure to do so may result in sparks that can damage equipment and burn hands.

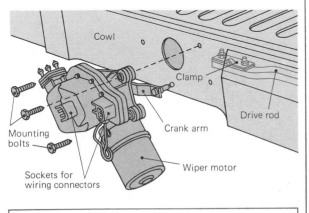

Tools: Wrenches, screwdriver, sockets, extensions and U-joints as needed.
Material: Spray solvent (to free binding linkage).

Engine compartment

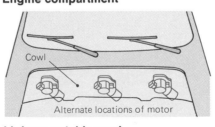

Linkage outside cowl

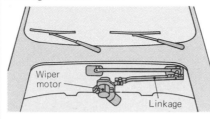

Linkage behind cowl

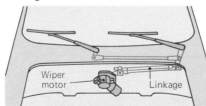

Dashboard mounting (Ford)

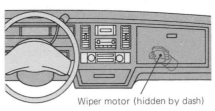

Wiper motor (hidden by dash)

Location of wiper motor on almost all cars is on or near the cowl inside the engine compartment—either centered or in the left or right corner. Wiper linkage may be visible outside the cowl or concealed behind it. On some Fords the wiper motor is behind the dashboard, inside the car. To reach the motor, you must disassemble the dash, panels, heating and air-conditioning ducts, and brackets. Even then, removing and replacing the motor can be difficult; it is a job best left to a professional mechanic.

Removing a wiper motor

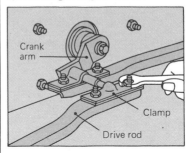

1. To disconnect drive rod of wiper linkage from the motor crank arm in this type of assembly, loosen but do not remove nuts on clamp at the end of the drive rod. Slip rod off end of crank arm.

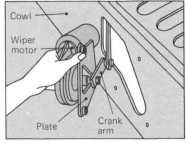

2. In this type of wiper linkage, drive rod can be disengaged from crank arm by simply prying it off with a screwdriver. Whenever disengaging a drive rod, be careful not to bend it.

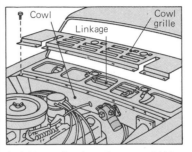

3. If drive rod and crank arm are hidden behind the cowl, you may have to remove cowl grille to reach them (see alternate methods that follow). Remove mounting screws and lift grille out.

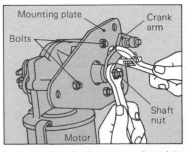

4. In some cases, wiper motor is mounted to a plate bolted to the cowl. To reach and disengage the crank arm, remove bolts and pull motor away from cowl just enough to gain access to arm.

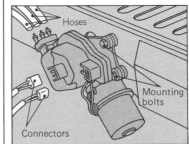

5. With crank arm disengaged, pull multi-wire connectors (and washer hoses, if any) off motor. Remove mounting bolts and motor. When installing new unit, set wipers in *Park* position.

6. If motor is joined to a mounting plate, remove crank arm from motor. Grip crank arm with one wrench; unscrew securing nut with another wrench. Take out bolts, and separate motor from plate.

Repair / Engine

What to do if your car won't start

If your car is to start quickly and run smoothly, three conditions must be met: proper delivery of fuel (mixed with air), correct engine compression, and precise spark timing. If your engine does not start, first determine which of the three conditions are lacking, then follow the systematic procedure at the right to pinpoint the specific cause of the problem.

If there is no spark, for example, trace the electric current from the spark plug back to the battery until you locate the problem. Similarly, fuel delivery is traced from the carburetor or fuel-injection nozzle back to the fuel tank.

Proper compression depends on the mechanical condition of your engine. Trouble in this area can result from a sudden failure of an engine component (such as a timing chain or belt) or from a long and gradual period of engine wear and deterioration. Compression problems are rare and are the most difficult to correct, often requiring extensive repair.

Your car's starting system can malfunction too. For example, when you turn the key there may be no response, or you may hear only a loud click or a series of clicks coming from the starter solenoid. The starter may spin with a whirring sound but fail to crank the engine. If the engine does not crank at all or does so very slowly, the starting system should be checked according to the troubleshooting chart at the right. If the engine is cranking at normal speed but still does not start, determine whether the problem lies in the fuel system or ignition system.

First, check your fuel gauge to verify that there is gas in the tank. Then, remove the air filter and open the choke plate. Pump the accelerator linkage several times and see if gas squirts into the carburetor throat. If it does, the problem is probably not in the fuel system. If you do not see or smell gas, follow the chart for troubleshooting the fuel system. One fast way to determine if a no-start problem is due to lack of fuel is to pour about 2 ounces of gasoline directly into the carburetor throat and then crank the engine. If the engine sputters or attempts to start, the ignition is OK and the problem is in the fuel system.

To check the performance of the ignition system, disconnect a spark plug cable and attach it to a new spark plug. Run a jumper wire from the plug's threaded portion to a metal part of the engine. Then have a helper crank the engine. A strong blue spark at the plug means that the ignition system is OK.

Troubleshooting the starting system

Problem	Troubleshooting procedure		Remedy or test
Engine does not crank with key in *Start* position.	Turn ignition on. Does dash warning light come on? Does ammeter needle show slight discharge? Does voltmeter register close to 12 volts? **YES** ⬇	NO ⮕	*Battery is discharged, disconnected, or missing. If battery is discharged, charge or replace battery (pp.277–279) or jump start car (p.390).*
	Is gear selector in *Park* or *Neutral* position? Is clutch fully depressed? **YES** ⬇	TEST ⮕	*Wiggle gear selector in Park and Neutral positions while attempting to start engine. Release and depress clutch.*
	Turn key to *Start* position. Does warning light stay on? Does ammeter continue to show slight discharge? Does voltmeter continue to show voltage? **YES** ⬇	NO ⮕	*Neutral safety switch is defective. Put transmission in Neutral or Park and connect jumper around switch. Replace switch as soon as possible (pp.369–370).*
	Are seat belts buckled (in 1974 and early 1975 models)? **YES** ⬇	NO ⮕	*Buckle belts even if seat is unoccupied.*
	Is seat belt interlock system defective? **NO** ⬇	TEST ⮕	*Bypass interlock system by standing outside vehicle and reaching in through the window to turn the key. Press emergency override button located under the hood (p.391).*
	Switch on electric wipers or headlights. Do wipers stop or do lights dim when key is in *Start* position? **YES** ⬇	NO ⮕	*There is an open circuit in the starter system if wipers continue to operate or lights stay bright. Test system (pp.391–392).*
	Is ignition switch defective? **NO** ⬇	TEST ⮕	*Connect a jumper wire between ignition switch terminals on the starter solenoid or relay (see p.392). If engine cranks, replace ignition switch (p.370).*
	Is starter system defective?	TEST ⮕	*Check system for loose connections or faulty wiring. Test starter (pp.391–392) or bring car to mechanic.*
Vehicle does not start. Starter cranks engine very slowly.	Switch on electric wipers or headlights. Turn key to *Start*. Do lights dim or wipers slow down? The battery cables may be loose or making poor contact. **YES** ⬇	TEST ⮕	*Remove cables from battery. Clean terminals at both ends of cables. Reinstall and tighten securely (p.279).*
	If lights or wipers are greatly affected by starting attempt or do not work at all, battery may be almost completely discharged.	TEST ⮕	*Check fluid level of battery. Fill to indicated level with water. Check specific gravity of battery if possible (pp.277–279). Trickle charge battery (p.278) or jump start car (p.390). Have charging system checked.*

Repeat the test on other spark plug cables. If you get a spark with some cables but not others, there is a problem in the distributor cap or spark plug cables (see pp.222–231, 408–409, and 414–425).

While the ignition system may be producing a healthy spark in all cylinders, the engine still will not start if the spark is not occurring at the right time. If the distributor is rotated far enough from the correct position, or if the spark plug cables are inserted into the wrong distributor cap terminals, the engine will not start (see pp.231 and 236–239).

Modern engines with extensive pollution-control equipment can be very finicky and difficult to start, even when they are tuned to the carmaker's specifications. It is vital to follow the manufacturer's starting instructions exactly. These instructions are printed in the owner's manual. Most require that you pump the gas pedal once or twice (to set the choke plate), then remove your foot from the pedal and turn the ignition key.

Troubleshooting the ignition system

Problem	Troubleshooting procedure	Remedy or test
Engine cranks normally, has fuel delivery, but will not start.	Remove one spark plug cable and plug. Ground plug by attaching jumper wire to threads and to a good ground or the negative terminal on the battery. Have helper crank engine. Does plug display a healthy, intermittent blue spark? **NO** ⬇	**YES** ⮕ *Check to see if distributor hold-down clamp has loosened. Can distributor be rotated by hand? If so, timing must be reset. Check to make sure that all cables are secure in cap and on plugs. Compare arrangement of cables in cap to specified firing order (p.232).*
	Substitute new plug and repeat test. Does plug show a healthy blue spark? **NO** ⬇	**YES** ⮕ *Original plug is fouled or defective. Replace plug.*
	Remove another plug cable and repeat spark test. Does plug display a healthy, intermittent blue spark? **NO** ⬇	**YES** ⮕ *If one cable sparks but the other does not, check the cap connections and the cables (p.231).*
	Remove distributor cap. Does rotor turn while engine is cranked? **YES** ⬇	**NO** ⮕ *If rotor does not turn, there is a malfunction in timing chain or drive gear.*
	Check condition of rotor. Is it corroded or burned? **NO** ⬇	**YES** ⮕ *Clean rotor by scraping with sharp knife. Do not remove special grease.*
	Check condition of terminals inside cap. Are they corroded or burned? **NO** ⬇	**YES** ⮕ *Clean cap terminals by scraping with sharp knife.*
	Is ignition a Delco HEI unit? **NO** ⬇	**YES** ⮕ *Refer to procedure for troubleshooting HEI distributor, p.414.*
	Remove coil cable from cap. Remove wire from negative terminal on coil. Turn ignition on. Connect jumper to negative terminal of coil. Hold cable close to a ground while intermittently grounding jumper. Does coil cable spark? **YES** ⬇	**NO** ⮕ *If no spark was observed, check for voltage between coil positive terminal and ground with ignition on. If no voltage is present or if it is considerably lower than battery voltage, switch's ballast resistor or wiring is defective, or battery is discharged. If voltage is OK, coil is defective. Replace coil.*
	If a spark can be generated by the above test, examine ignition to determine if it is an electronic design. **NO** ⬇	**YES** ⮕ *If ignition is electronic, refer to specific troubleshooting procedures on pp.414–425.*
	If ignition has breaker points, open points and connect a jumper lead to the movable point arm. Turn ignition on. Touch the lead to ground momentarily. Can you detect a small spark? **YES** ⬇	**NO** ⮕ *If no spark is detected, the primary lead between the negative terminal of the coil and the points is broken or grounded. Replace with wire of the same gauge.*
	Examine condition of the contact points. Are they corroded or pitted? **NO** ⬇	**YES** ⮕ *Replace points and condenser. (pp.222–229).*
	Do points open approximately .015 in. to .025 in. when distributor turns?	**NO** ⮕ *Adjust points to specifications (pp.222–229).*

Troubleshooting the fuel system (carburetors)

Problem	Troubleshooting procedure	Remedy or test
Engine cranks and has good spark, but will not start. Fuel tank contains at least 2 gal of gas.	Remove air cleaner and look straight down into the carburetor while pumping throttle linkage. Can you see a stream of gas shoot into carburetor? **NO** ⬇	**YES** ⮕ *If vehicle is cold, examine the choke plate. It should be almost completely closed. If vehicle is hot, choke plate should be open. If not, adjust choke (p.248). If choke is functioning and fuel is emitted by accelerator pump, engine may be flooded. Hold accelerator pedal to the floor for several minutes, then crank engine with pedal depressed. Do not pump accelerator pedal.*
	Remove fuel line from carburetor and place end in a can, bottle, or glass. Have a helper crank engine. Does engine pump a steady stream of fuel? **NO** ⬇	**YES** ⮕ *Fuel filter is clogged or carburetor is faulty. Do next three tests, then replace or rebuild carburetor. (pp.402–405).*
	Remove in-line fuel filter and repeat test. Does engine pump fuel? **NO** ⬇	**YES** ⮕ *Install new filter (p.261).*
	Disconnect fuel line at inlet side of fuel pump. Remove in-line fuel filter. Blow through fuel line. Can air bubbles be heard at fuel filler opening? **NO** ⬇	**YES** ⮕ *Test fuel pump and replace if defective (pp.397–401).*
	In-tank fuel pickup is clogged. Fuel line is clogged or kinked. There is an air leak in the fuel line. Clean or replace parts.	

Troubleshooting the fuel system (fuel injection)

Problem	Troubleshooting procedure	Remedy or test
Engine cranks and has good spark but will not start. Fuel tank contains at least 2 gal of gas.	Is engine equipped with a coolant-temperature sensor? **NO** ⬇	**YES** ⮕ *Check temperature sensor for open circuit or short circuit. (See p.373).*
	Is engine equipped with a fuel pump relay? **NO** ⬇	**YES** ⮕ *Check to determine that pump relay is delivering voltage to pump (p.397).*
	If there is voltage at fuel pump with engine cranking, does pump pressurize the system? **YES** ⬇	**NO** ⮕ *Replace pump (pp.398–401).*
	Are fuel filters clogged? **NO** ⬇	**YES** ⮕ *Replace filter or filters (p.261).*
	Is system the CFI type? **NO** ⬇	**YES** ⮕ *Check for fuel delivery at the injectors (p.407).*
	Does car have a pressure regulator?	**YES** ⮕ *Perform fuel-pressure check according to directions in shop manual.*

385

How to use this chart

Find problem at top of chart. Look down column to locate possible causes. First, check repairs that you can do yourself. Then, check repairs you *may* be able to do yourself. If problem still is not solved, consult a competent mechanic.

○ You can fix it yourself.
● You *may* be able to make a complete repair.
■ You need a mechanic.

Problem columns (left to right):

1. Starter does not crank; starter is silent
2. Starter clicks, groans, and does not turn
3. Starter cranks normally; engine does not start
4. Hard starting only when engine is cold
5. Hard starting only when engine is hot
6. Engine stalls primarily when hot
7. Engine stalls primarily when cold
8. Engine only runs with key on Start
9. Poor gasoline mileage
10. Excessive oil consumption
11. Strong gasoline odor
12. Engine idles roughly
13. Engine runs roughly at low speeds
14. Engine misfires at high speeds
15. Engine runs roughly at all speeds
16. Engine misfires at all speeds
17. Engine lacks normal power
18. Engine gives poor acceleration
19. Engine runs after it is shut off
20. Engine surges at steady speed
21. Engine rattles or pings

Problem columns 1–21 (see legend)	Possible cause	Cure
1:○	Transmission in gear; seat belts not fastened	Shift to *Park* or *Neutral,* depress clutch; fasten seat belts; bypass *Neutral* start switch (p.383)
1:○ 2:○ 3:○ 4:○	Battery weak or dead, bad connections	Clean corroded connections; check battery (p.277); jump start the car (p.390)
3:○	Out of gas	Add at least 2 gal to tank; check fuel delivery to carburetor (pp.384–385)
3:○ 5:○ 7:○ 11:○	Carburetor flooded	Wait 5 min, then hold gas pedal to floor and operate starter—do not pump gas pedal
2:● 5:● 9:● 10:● 11:● 12:● 13:● 16:●	Faulty ignition circuit	Check out ignition system (pp.384–385); replace parts as required
2:○ 3:○ 4:○ 5:○ 7:○ 9:○ 11:○ 12:○ 13:○ 16:○ 17:○	Choke plate stuck; choke set incorrectly	Close choke manually; clean or adjust linkage (p.248); reset choke (p.249)
2:○ 5:○ 9:○ 11:○ 12:○ 13:○ 15:○ 16:○ 18:○	Vapor lock (warm weather)	Open hood, let engine cool; wrap fuel line and pump with wet rags
3:○ 5:○ 7:○ 9:○ 11:○ 12:○ 15:○ 16:○ 18:○	Air cleaner clogged	Check thermostat operation (p.242); replace air filter (pp.240–241)
2:○ 3:○ 5:○ 9:○ 11:○ 12:○ 15:○ 18:○	Carburetor icing (in cold, damp weather)	Check air cleaner thermostat (p.242); add dry gas (isopropyl alcohol) to fuel tank
6:○ 7:○ 9:○ 11:○ 12:○ 13:○ 15:○ 16:○ 20:○	Heat control valve stuck	Free valve with choke cleaner (pp.244–245); see fuel-system checks pp.384–385
6:○ 7:○ 11:○ 12:○ 13:○ 15:○ 16:○ 20:○	Vacuum hose disconnected	Locate and reconnect or replace disconnected vacuum hose (pp.236, 264)
2:○ 3:○ 6:○ 7:○ 11:○ 13:○ 14:○ 15:○ 18:○	Faulty spark plugs; wrong heat range	Remove spark plugs and inspect, clean, or replace them (pp.233–234)
2:● 6:● 8:● 11:● 12:● 13:● 14:● 15:● 16:● 18:● 21:●	Incorrect ignition timing	Set timing to maker's specifications on emission-control decal (pp.236–238)
2:● 4:● 6:● 8:● 11:● 12:● 13:● 14:● 15:● 16:● 18:● 20:● 21:●	Faulty electronic ignition system	Check function (pp.239, 388, 414), or have system checked by properly equipped shop
8:○ 11:○ 13:○ 15:○ 16:○ 17:○ 21:○	Incorrect grade of gasoline	Switch to a higher-octane fuel (p.63), or have engine adjusted to use available fuel
4:● 5:● 8:● 11:● 12:● 13:● 14:● 15:● 16:● 17:● 18:●	Incorrect carburetor adjustment	Adjust idle speed and mixture to specifications (pp.251–253) or have them adjusted
1:● 2:● 4:●	Faulty starter or starter circuit	Check starting circuit (pp.384, 391)
2:○ 3:○ 5:○ 6:○ 11:○ 12:○ 13:○ 14:○ 15:○ 18:○	Clogged fuel filter, bad pump, ice in line	Inspect fuel filter (p.261); check fuel pump (p.397) and fuel delivery (p.385)
2:● 5:● 8:● 11:● 12:● 13:● 14:● 15:● 16:● 18:●	Dirt or water in gas	Have water drained from fuel tank; replace fuel filter (p.261); have tank and lines cleaned
2:● 4:● 5:● 7:● 8:● 11:● 12:● 13:● 14:● 15:● 16:● 18:●	Worn or dirty carburetor; faulty fuel injection	Clean, rebuild, or replace carburetor (pp.402–405); check fuel-injection system (p.406)
4:○ 6:○ 7:○ 9:○ 13:○	Faulty PCV system	Check PCV hoses for leaks (p.246); clean or replace PCV valve (p.247)
8:●	Engine oil leaking	Tighten oil filter (p.198), drain plug (p.196), and bolts on engine cover gaskets (p.425)
2:■ 6:■ 7:■ 9:■ 11:■ 12:■ 13:■ 16:■ 21:■	Worn or broken internal engine parts	Check engine compression (p.263); have engine inspected and repaired
8:● 11:● 12:● 13:● 14:● 15:● 16:● 18:● 20:●	Vacuum leak at carburetor or manifold	Tighten bolts on carburetor (p.404) or nuts on intake manifold (p.187); replace gaskets
2:○ 6:○ 11:○ 12:○ 13:○ 14:○ 15:○	Ignition system wet	Use paper towels or an aerosol ignition drier to dry ignition cables, rotor, and cap
1:●	Starter gear jammed	Loosen starter bolts and shake starter to free gear (p.393); have starter checked
5:● 6:● 8:● 11:● 12:● 13:● 14:● 15:●	Faulty evaporative emission control system	Test vapor purge valve (p.262); repair or replace parts and hoses as necessary
2:■ 5:■ 6:■ 8:■ 11:■ 12:■ 13:■ 14:■ 15:■ 16:■ 18:■ 20:■	Low compression	Check compression (p.263); have engine inspected and repaired if compression is low
4:● 6:● 8:●	Open circuit in coil wire; defective resistor	Have coil resistance wire or coil resistor replaced
5:● 8:● 12:● 13:● 16:● 18:● 20:● 21:●	Defective EGR system	Test EGR valve (p.255) and replace if necessary

How to use this chart

Find problem at top of chart. Look down column to locate possible causes.
First, check repairs that you can do yourself. Then, check repairs you *may* be able to do yourself.
If problem still is not solved, consult a competent mechanic.

○ You can fix it yourself.
● You *may* be able to make a complete repair.
■ You need a mechanic.

Problem (columns, left to right):
1. Engine vibrates abnormally
2. Engine raps
3. Engine pings
4. Engine ticks rhythmically
5. Screeches in engine compartment
6. Engine boils over
7. Engine runs too hot (gauge)
8. Engine runs too cold (gauge)
9. Oil pressure too low (gauge)
10. Oil pressure too high (gauge or light)
11. Engine leaks oil (gauge or light)
12. Oil visible on outside of engine
13. Oil leaks oil under car
14. Engine backfires through carburetor
15. Engine backfires through exhaust
16. Black smoke from exhaust
17. White smoke from exhaust
18. Blue smoke from exhaust
19. Engine emits oil fumes
20. Engine emits steam

Possible cause	Problem columns (marked)	Cure
Coolant level too low	6○ 7○	Top up coolant with 50-50 antifreeze/water mix (p.280); check for leaks (p.281); see *Overheating* (p.345)
Oil level too low	2○ 4○ 9○ 10○	Top up with engine oil (p.196); if oil consumption is too high, check for leaks (p.187) or oil burning (p.263)
Incorrect grade of gasoline	1○ 3○	Switch to higher-octane gasoline (p.63); have engine adjusted to use available fuel
Incorrect grade of oil	2○ 4○ 9○ 10○ 11○ 12○ 18○ 19○	Change oil and filter (p.196)
Incorrect antifreeze mixture	7○ 8○ 20○	Drain cooling system (p.282); refill with 50-50 antifreeze/water mix (p.284)
Slipping drive belt(s)	5○ 6○ 7○ 20○	Adjust belt tension (p.287); replace worn or glazed belts (p.287)
Faulty spark plugs, or wrong type	1○ 3○	Remove, inspect, and clean spark plugs (p.233); or replace with correct plugs (p.233)
Faulty ignition circuit	1● 4● 5● 15●	Check out ignition system (p.384); replace parts as required (p.231)
Faulty electronic ignition	1● 3● 5● 14● 15● 16●	Check ignition system (pp.239, 388, 414); have system checked by properly equipped shop
Worn distributor	1● 2● 3● 5● 14● 15● 16●	Check distributor wear (p.239); replace distributor (p.410)
Incorrect ignition timing	1● 3● 5● 14● 15● 16●	Set timing to carmaker's specifications on emission-control decal (p.236); have shop check timing
Vacuum control hose disconnected	1○ 3○ 5○ 14○ 15○ 16○	Locate and reconnect or replace disconnected hose (pp.236, 264)
Incorrect carburetor adjustment	1● 3● 14●	Adjust idle speed and idle mixture to specifications (pp.251–253), or have carburetor adjusted
Choke plate is stuck	1○ 16○	Close choke manually; clean or adjust linkage (p.248); reset choke (p.249)
Faulty carburetor or fuel injection	1● 14● 15● 16●	Clean, rebuild, or replace carburetor (pp.402–405); check fuel-injection (p.406)
Clogged air cleaner or stuck valve	16○ 17○	Replace air filter (p.240); check air cleaner's thermostat valve (p.242)
Faulty PCV system	1○ 11○ 12○ 13○ 18○ 19○	Check PCV hoses for leaks or clogs (p.246); clean or replace PCV valve (p.247)
Faulty EGR valve	1● 14●	Check EGR valve operation (p.254); clean or replace valve (p.254)
Faulty sending unit or gauge	8○ 9○ 10○ 11○	Check sending unit (p.372); check wiring to gauge (p.360); check gauge (p.372)
Leaking coolant hose	7○ 8○ 20○	Tighten hose clamp (p.285) or replace hose (p.285)
Faulty engine thermostat	7○ 8○ 9○ 20○	Remove and test thermostat (p.280); replace if necessary
Leaking head gasket	1■ 4■ 5■ 7■ 9■ 10■ 16■ 17■ 20■	Torque cylinder-head bolts or have them torqued to specifications; install sealer (p.283)
Worn or broken engine parts	1■ 2■ 3■ 4■ 7■ 16■ 17■ 18■	Check engine compression (p.263); have engine inspected and repaired
Low compression	1■ 4■ 5■	Check engine compression (p.263); have engine inspected and repaired
Faulty engine valves	1■ 5■	Check compression (p.263); check valve train (p.266); adjust valves (p.267)
Faulty valve train	1● 2● 4● 5● 13● 14●	Check valve clearance (p.265); check valve train (p.266); check hydraulic valve lifters (p.276)
Worn valve guides	1■ 17■ 18■	Replace valve stem seals (p.276), or have valve guides replaced
Worn piston rings	1■ 17■ 18■	Check compression wet (p.263); have engine repaired or rebuilt
Leaking gaskets or joints	1● 4● 7● 9● 10● 18● 19●	Tighten drain plug (p.196), filter (p.198), bolts on engine covers; replace gaskets (p.426)
Faulty air pump diverter valve	16●	Test diverter valve (p.254) and replace if necessary

Troubleshooting computers ⏱ 10–20 min

Many late-model cars have computer systems that control certain engine functions. In four systems the computer is equipped with a self-check circuit so that it may be easily tested for proper operation. For troubleshooting purposes, dashboard lights connected to the computer on some AMC and GM cars display coded information to indicate whether or not the car is working properly, and where any problems are. Check the computer before you begin any engine tuneup or repair work; such work may be impossible to complete or unnecessary if the computer is faulty.

Should the self-check circuit indicate a faulty computer, look only for obvious problems, such as loose connections. If none are found, the car should be taken to a dealer; computer repair is impractical for the home mechanic, and most on-car computers are guaranteed for five years or 50,000 miles.

General Motors systems

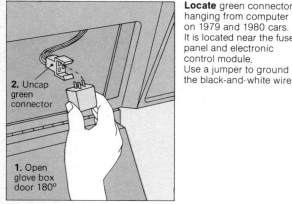

Locate green connector hanging from computer on 1979 and 1980 cars. It is located near the fuse panel and electronic control module. Use a jumper to ground the black-and-white wire.

2. Uncap green connector

1. Open glove box door 180°

Two computer systems have been used on some GM cars since 1979. If the engine malfunctions, a *Check engine* light appears on the dashboard. To find the problem, leave the engine running at idle, shift into *Park*, and set the parking brake. Then, use a jumper wire to ground the trouble code test lead to some metal part of the car. The test lead is a black-and-white wire under the dash. On 1979 and 1980 cars it is in a bright green connector. On 1981 cars it is part of a five-wire connector under the left side of the dash. The *Check engine* light should begin to flash a trouble code (for instance, two flashes, then a pause, then three flashes means code 23). The code is keyed to the

troubleshooting chart below. If more than one part is malfunctioning, the light will flash each trouble code three times. When all the codes have been flashed, the entire series will repeat.

To check the computer's diagnostic system, turn the ignition switch on but do not start the engine. Ground the trouble code test lead as explained above. The *Check engine* light should then flash code 12 to indicate that the system is working properly.

General Motors trouble codes

Code	Problem
12	Computer not receiving rpm signal
13	Defect in oxygen sensor's wiring
14	Short circuit in coolant-temperature sensor's wiring
15	Open circuit to coolant temperature sensor
21, 22	Defect in throttle-position sensor
23	Defect in carburetor solenoid wiring
24	Defect in vehicle-speed sensor
32	Defect in barometric-pressure sensor
35	Short circuit in idle-speed control switch
42	Ground in ignition timing bypass circuit
44	Defect in oxygen sensor
51–53	Defects in computer module
54	Defect in carburetor mixture-control solenoid and/or computer module
55, 56	Defect in throttle-position sensor, oxygen sensor, or computer module (depending on engine model)

Cadillac DEFI system

The Digital Electronic Fuel Injection (DEFI) system has been used on Cadillacs with throttle body fuel injection since 1980. Should the *Check engine* light appear, activate the computer's diagnostic system by simultaneously pressing the *Off* and *Warmer* buttons on the Electronic Climate Control (A/C) panel. This may be done with the engine running, or after the ignition has been switched on for 5 seconds. Hold the buttons down until a dotted line appears on the digital temperature display board. The number 88 should then appear, to indicate that the diagnostic system and all parts of the display board are working correctly, followed by code numbers for each malfunction (see chart below). The entire series will

repeat twice, each time beginning with 88. At the end, the number 70 will appear, signaling the beginning of tests of various switches in the car in which the operator must take part. When the last switch test is completed, the display will show the numbers of any switches that are defective. Then the code number 00 will appear on 1980 cars, signaling that the entire computer diagnosis is finished. Clear trouble codes stored in the computer's long-term memory, if you did not participate in the switch test, by simultaneously pressing the *Off* and *High* buttons on the climate control panel until 00 again appears. Then deactivate the display by turning off the ignition. See a shop manual for additional tests on later cars.

DEFI trouble codes

Code	Problem
00	Diagnostic work is complete
12	Computer not receiving rpm signal
13	Oxygen sensor not ready
14, 15	Fault in coolant-temperature sensor's wiring
16	Battery voltage not within required range
17, 18	Incorrect voltage in starting circuit
19, 20	Incorrect voltage in fuel pump circuit
21, 22	Fault in throttle-position sensor's wiring
23	Ground in ignition timing bypass circuit
24	Vehicle-speed sensor failure
25	Fault in Modular Displacement (V-8-6-4) system
26, 27	Throttle-position switch failure
28–30	Fault in idle-speed control's circuit
31, 32	Fault in pressure sensor's wiring
33	Internal defect in pressure sensor
34	Defect in hose connection to pressure sensor
35, 36	Fault in barometric-pressure sensor's wiring
37, 38	Fault in intake manifold air-temperature sensor's wiring
44, 45	Failure of oxygen sensor
55, 56	Defective computer module
60–64	Defects in Cruise Control system
70	Switch tests to follow
71	Test brake-light switch. (Immediately depress brake pedal when this number appears on display.)
72–79	Additional switch tests (see shop manual)

Ford EEC III system

The Electronic Engine Control (EEC) III system was introduced on some 1980 Ford cars. A gold emission-control decal under the hood distinguishes EEC III-equipped cars from those with the EEC II unit; they have a silver decal. Computer diagnosis is performed with the engine warm and running at idle. You will need a vacuum gauge and a hand-operated vacuum pump to perform the tests.

Working under the hood with the engine off, connect the vacuum gauge in the hose between the air pump diverter valve and the diverter solenoid valve. Next, with the gearshift in *Park* and the parking brake set, start the engine and allow it to reach operating temperature. With the engine idling, connect the vacuum pump to the vent neck on the barometric-pressure sensor. Apply 20 inches of vacuum, hold it for 1 minute, then release it. This activates the diagnostic system. As a self-check, the vacuum-activated throttle kicker (idle speedup device) should come on when vacuum is applied, then retract when vacuum is released. Finally, to signal that the system is working correctly and ready to begin diagnosis, the needle of the vacuum gauge should pulse four times (twice on cars equipped with throttle body fuel injection). If either the diagnostic system or the air pump is defective, the needle will not pulse.

When diagnosis actually begins, the throttle kicker will come on again and stay on for the duration of the tests, which are performed automatically. Near the end, the vacuum gauge will climb briefly to a higher reading, then the needle will pulse two or three times. When the diagnosis is finished, the throttle kicker

will retract and the idle speed will drop. Pulses that convert to the trouble code numbers indicating engine malfunctions (see chart) will then begin to register on the vacuum gauge. For instance, one pulse that is followed by a short pause and two more pulses indicates code 12. If there is more than one malfunction, several code numbers will be delivered, separated by long pauses. When all the results have been delivered, the computer will return to normal operation after a 15-second pause.

EEC III trouble codes

Code	Problem
11	System OK
12	Computer not receiving rpm signal
21	Defect in coolant-temperature sensor's wiring
22	Defect in pressure sensor
23	Defect in throttle-position sensor
31	Position sensor for EGR valve fails to move to *Open* position (may indicate other EGR problem)
32	Position sensor for EGR valve fails to move to *Closed* position (may indicate other EGR problem)
41	Fuel control is keeping mixture too lean
42	Fuel control is keeping mixture too rich
43	Engine coolant temperature staying below 120°F (may indicate defective thermostat)
44	Defect in air pump system

Ford and American Motors MCU system

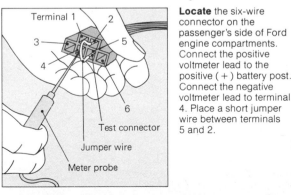

Locate the six-wire connector on the passenger's side of Ford engine compartments. Connect the positive voltmeter lead to the positive (+) battery post. Connect the negative voltmeter lead to terminal 4. Place a short jumper wire between terminals 5 and 2.

The Microprocessor Control Unit (MCU) was introduced in 1980 on Ford 2.3-liter four-cylinder engines

and American Motors six-cylinder engines. Operating hardware on the two makers' systems varies.

In 1981 Ford reprogrammed its MCU to add a self-test capability. Although the 1980 Ford MCU could be checked without special equipment, the procedure (given in the shop manual) is lengthy.

In 1981 Fords a six-wire diagnostic connector can be found over the wheel housing on the passenger's side of the engine compartment. The connector should be connected to an analog (needle-type) voltmeter as shown in the illustration. Warm up the engine, then shut it off. Connect a voltmeter and jumper wire to the connector.

Turn on the ignition; the voltmeter should display a code 11 (one needle pulse to mid-scale, followed by a pause, then a second needle pulse to mid-scale). If you get this signal, the system passes the *Engine off* test. If you get another number, there is a defect.

If you get an 11 code, start the engine. Raise the engine speed of 2.3-liter four-cylinder models to 2,500 rpm or higher; hold this speed until the test is complete. On V-8s let the engine idle for the test.

You should first get two needle pulses (code 20) on the four-cylinder, four pulses on the V-8 (code 40), indicating that the MCU is starting its self-test. If you do not get this code, there is a defect in the system.

If you get the 40 code on a V-8, immediately rap on the intake manifold with a rod and hammer to trigger the knock sensor. If you do not trigger the sensor, or if the sensor is defective, you will get a code 25. After a brief period on either engine, you should get a code 11. Any other number indicates a defect in the system.

On the four-cylinder engine, only the first defect in a programmed order will be indicated. Before you can obtain codes for any other failures that may exist, the first defect must be corrected and the system retested. On the V-8 engine, all failure codes will be given in a row and the sequence will be repeated once. This MCU system is found on all 1981 2.3-liter four-cylinder engines, on 5-liter V-8 Thunderbird and XR-7 California models, and on all other Ford and Mercury large-size V-8 cars outside California.

From 1981 onward the American Motors MCU system provides continuous diagnosis. A light on the dash pulses out a code five times whenever a failure occurs. The codes are given in the shop manual, but because each covers a broad area, lengthy checkouts are specified in the manual for each code.

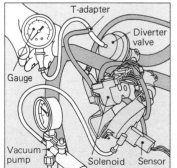

Use T-adapter to connect vacuum gauge between air pump's diverter valve and the diverter solenoid. Connect vacuum pump to vent neck on barometric-pressure sensor (see p.82).

How to jump start a car ☑️☑️ 10–15 min

If your car will not start because the starter does not operate or barely turns over, suspect a dead battery. Remove and clean the battery cables (see pp.277–278), reconnect them, and try again. If your headlights do not work or grow very dim when the starter is operated, you can be fairly certain that the problem is a dead battery. If the lights shine brightly when the starter is in use, the trouble is in the starter or its wiring (see pp.279, 361–363, and 391–394).

A car with a dead battery can be started with a set of jumper cables and a second car that is operating. Be sure that both cars have 12-volt batteries, which have six filler holes, or paired 6-volt batteries.

1. If possible, bring both cars nose to nose and open their hoods. (Some imported cars have their batteries in the trunk or under the rear seat; position these cars so that their batteries are as close to one another as possible.) Do not allow the cars to touch.

2. Set both parking brakes. Put automatic transmissions into *Park,* manual transmissions in *Neutral.* Turn off both ignitions and all electrical accessories.

3. Remove the vent caps (if any) from both batteries and allow any built-up gases to escape. Then cover the vent holes with clean rags.

4. Determine which of the battery posts in each car is the positive terminal. The positive post is generally fatter than the negative post. It may be marked with a plus sign or POS. The positive post is the one that is connected to the starter.

5. Attach the colored booster cable clamps to the positive terminals of both batteries.

6. The other battery post in each car is the negative one. If the posts have different diameters, the negative one will be smaller. It may be marked with a minus sign or NEG. The negative post is the one grounded to the car's chassis or body.

7. Attach one of the black cable clamps to the negative terminal of the good battery. Attach the other black clamp to a good ground (such as an unpainted bolt or flange) on the engine, chassis, or body of the second car. This connection may cause a spark, so pick a ground far from the dead battery.

8. Make sure that everyone's hands and all cables are clear of the fans and other moving parts on both cars. Start the engine of the car with the good battery and have a helper rev it moderately.

9. Start the second engine. If it still will not start, check for additional problems in the ignition and fuel systems (see pp.384–385).

10. Keep the formerly stalled car running, and carefully remove the cables in the opposite order from which they were attached—black cable clamp from the dead car, then from the booster car; colored cable clamp from the dead car, then from the booster car. Be careful not to cause sparks by touching the cables to one another or to a ground.

11. Remove the rags and reinstall the vent caps.

12. Drive the formerly stalled car for at least 30 minutes to recharge its battery.

Push starting

A car with a manual transmission may also be started by pushing if its battery is too weak to turn the starter but not completely dead. This requires a second, operative car with bumpers that match those of the stalled car in size and height. Bring the working car up behind the stalled one until the two cars touch. Check the bumpers to be sure that they are compatible and will not override one another. Turn the ignition key in the stalled car to the *On* position, release the parking brake, and put the transmission into *Neutral.* Have your helper gently push your car with his until your speed reaches 10 to 15 mph. Then your helper should apply his brakes, let you coast ahead, and beep his horn. When you hear the horn, shift into *Second* and ease in the clutch. This should spin the engine over fast enough to start it. Drive the car for at least 30 minutes to recharge its battery.

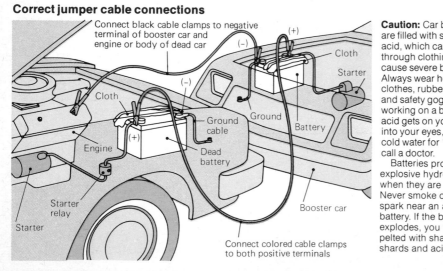

Correct jumper cable connections

Connect black cable clamps to negative terminal of booster car and engine or body of dead car

Cloth · Starter · Cloth · Ground · Ground · Battery · Engine · (+) · Ground cable · Dead battery · Starter relay · Starter · Booster car

Connect colored cable clamps to both positive terminals

Caution: Car batteries are filled with sulfuric acid, which can eat through clothing and cause severe burns. Always wear heavy clothes, rubber gloves, and safety goggles when working on a battery. If acid gets on your skin or into your eyes, rinse with cold water for 15 min and call a doctor.

Batteries produce explosive hydrogen gas when they are recharged. Never smoke or cause a spark near an auto battery. If the battery explodes, you will be pelted with sharp plastic shards and acid.

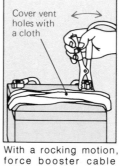

Cables · Clamps

Jumper cables should be made of wire that is 8 gauge or heavier so that they will pass current easily. Cables at least 16 ft long will reach from one battery to another even if the cars cannot be positioned nose to nose. Cable clamps should be color coded, two colored and two black.

Cover vent holes with a cloth

With a rocking motion, force booster cable clamp through any grease or corrosion on the battery terminals and obtain a good, firm contact. Do not allow cable clamps to touch one another or any metal near batteries. This could cause a spark and a battery explosion.

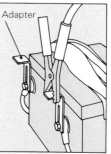

Adapter

It may be difficult to get a firm grip on side terminal batteries with the booster cable jaws. If so, install a set of special adapters, sold in auto parts stores. These will protrude far enough to grip easily. The adapters can be left in place if they do not ground on the hood when it is closed.

Troubleshooting the starter ⚏ ⚏

There are four common symptoms that indicate defects in the starter system. They are described below, together with procedures for correcting them.

Starter spins freely: This happens when the starter pinion does not engage the ring gear on the flywheel properly. The teeth on the pinion or on the ring gear may be worn or broken, the starter overrun clutch assembly may be worn or broken, or the ring gear may be loose on the flywheel. You can often tell that the overrun clutch is malfunctioning by the sound it makes as it momentarily engages and cranks the engine, then slips and lets the starter spin freely.

Remove the starter when the symptom occurs (see pp.393–396) and check the parts involved. If the ring gear teeth are OK but a starter part is faulty, take the starter to an auto parts store to see whether or not the defective part—the pinion or the overrun

clutch—can be purchased separately. If not, you will have to replace the starter. If the ring gear is loose or its teeth are worn, the ring gear must be replaced. This is a job for a professional mechanic.

Engine cranks noisily: This can happen when the starter is improperly bolted to the engine and the pinion teeth do not mesh smoothly with the ring gear teeth. Check the starter's mount for loose bolts, and tighten them. If the noise persists, remove the starter. Check the teeth for wear and check for improper shimming. Replace any worn parts and reinstall the starter. If the starter is still noisy, its bearings are probably worn, or the starter's armature may be misaligned. Replace the starter (pp.393–396).

Engine cranks slowly: This is often caused by poor electrical contact at the battery terminals due to corrosion. This condition can easily be checked by

applying the headlight test (see troubleshooting chart, p.386). If cleaning corroded battery terminals does not correct the problem, check the battery's state of charge (p.278). If the battery is OK, follow the procedure under *Engine cranks slowly,* p.392. When using a voltmeter while cranking the engine, place it where you can read it from the driver's seat, or have someone crank the engine for you. The three most common starter systems are illustrated below. Cars with starters that do not have a relay include GM, Datsun, Omni/Horizon (to 1980), Toyota, and VW.

Engine does not crank: Determine the kind of starter system your car has from the illustrations below and follow the procedure under *Engine does not crank,* p.392. On 1974–75 cars, first check the seat belt interlock system, and repair or disable it if it does not work. If it is OK, proceed to page 392.

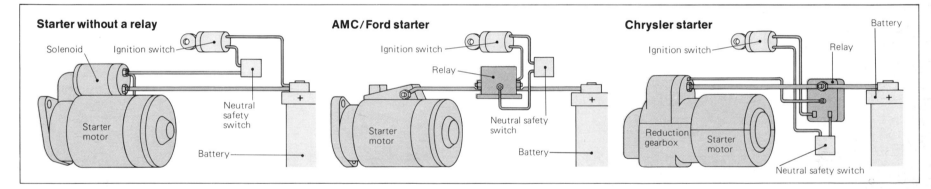

Starter without a relay — Solenoid, Ignition switch, Neutral safety switch, Starter motor, Battery

AMC/Ford starter — Ignition switch, Relay, Neutral safety switch, Starter motor, Battery

Chrysler starter — Battery, Ignition switch, Relay, Reduction gearbox, Starter motor, Neutral safety switch

Checking the seat belt interlock ⚏

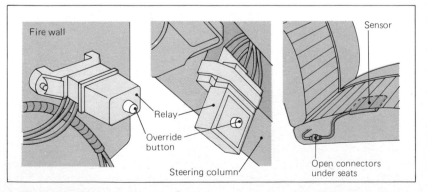

Fire wall, Relay, Override button, Steering column, Sensor, Open connectors under seats

To check seat belt interlock system, press button on the override relay mounted under dash or on the wheel well or fire wall in the engine compartment. This deactivates system temporarily. If starter now works, the interlock system is faulty. Either trace the fault and fix it (see pp.361–363) or disable the system permanently by disconnecting the pressure sensors under the front seats. Bucket seats have one sensor each; bench seats may have three. If the car is Japanese, have a dealer do the job, since disconnecting the sensors will disable the starter too.

Checking the pinion and ring gear ⚏ ⚏ ⚏ ⚏

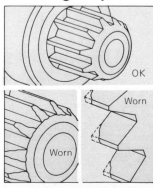

OK, Worn, Worn

To check teeth for wear, remove starter from engine. Worn teeth are often caused by repeated improper meshing of the starter pinion with the ring gear on the flywheel as the starter is engaged. Worn teeth may be found on the starter pinion, the ring gear, or both.

391

Troubleshooting the starter *(continued)*

Engine cranks slowly

1. Disable the engine so that it cannot start when you crank it (see p.263). Crank the engine during each of the following tests, but do not crank longer than 15 sec. Wait 2 min between tests to allow the starter to cool. Set voltmeter to the *Low* DC scale.

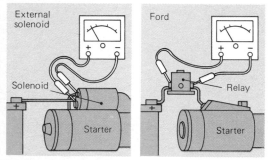

2. If starter has an external solenoid, test solenoid with a voltmeter. Connect meter probes to terminals as shown. If voltage is greater than 0.3 volts while engine is cranked, solenoid is defective and must be replaced. On some cars the solenoid can be removed separately. On other cars the starter must first be removed and disassembled.
3. If the car is a Ford, test starter relay with a voltmeter. Connect meter probes to relay terminals as shown. If voltage is greater than 0.3 volts while engine is cranked, relay is defective and should be replaced. To replace it, disconnect wiring and take out mounting bolts.

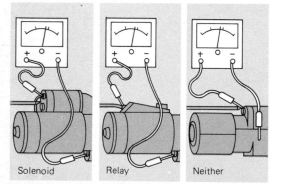

4. Test starter with voltmeter. Depending on starter type, connect meter probes to terminals as shown. If voltage is less than 9.3 volts while engine is cranked at 60°F, disconnect all cables in battery-starter circuit, clean terminals, then reconnect cables. If voltage is still low and you know battery is OK (p.278), replace the starter.

Engine does not crank

Starter without a relay: First, test starter's ignition circuit. If circuit is defective, one of its components—ignition switch, *Neutral* safety switch (if there is one), or the wiring—is faulty (see pp. 361–363, 369). If ignition circuit is OK, test solenoid switch; replace it if defective. Remove solenoid from starter. (To do this on some starters, you have to remove the starter and disassemble it.) If ignition circuit and solenoid switch work, and you know that battery is OK (p.278), starter must be replaced (pp.393–396). **Caution:** Perform all tests with transmission in *Neutral.*

AMC/Ford starter: First, test starter's ignition circuit. If the circuit is defective, one of its components—ignition switch, *Neutral* safety switch (if there is one), or the wiring—is faulty (see pp.361–363, 369). If the ignition circuit is working properly, test starter relay and replace it if defective. To replace the relay, disconnect its wiring and take out its mounting screws. If the ignition circuit and the relay work, and you know that the battery is OK (p.278), the starter is defective and must be replaced (pp.393–396). **Caution:** Perform all tests with the transmission in *Neutral.*

Chrysler starter: First, test starter's ignition and *Neutral* safety circuits. If a circuit is defective, one of its components—the switch or its associated wiring—is faulty and should be repaired (see pp.361–363, 369). If both circuits are OK, test the starter relay and replace it if it is defective. To replace relay, disconnect its wiring and take out its mounting screws. If all the circuits and the relay work, and you know that the battery is OK (p.278), the starter is defective and must be replaced (pp.393–396). **Caution:** Perform all tests with transmission in *Neutral.*

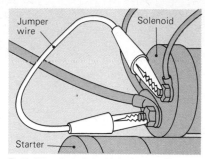

To test the starter's ignition circuit, connect a jumper wire for 1 sec to solenoid terminals as shown. If the starter operates, the ignition key circuit is defective.

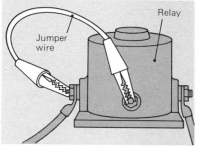

To test starter's ignition circuit, connect jumper wire for 1 sec to relay terminals as shown. If starter operates, ignition key circuit is defective.

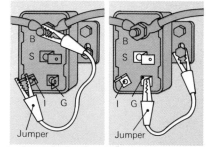

To test ignition key circuit, connect jumper wire to B and I terminals on relay. To test *Neutral* safety circuit, ground terminal G. If starter works on either test, that circuit is bad.

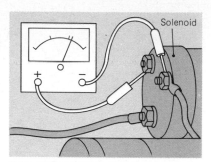

If the solenoid does not click, set voltmeter to *Low* DC scale (p.173) and connect its probes to terminals as shown. If meter reads higher than 10 volts, replace the solenoid.

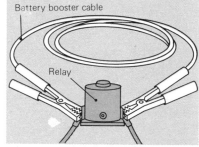

To test the starter relay, touch battery booster cable for a moment to relay terminals as shown. (**Caution:** Beware of sparks.) If starter operates, relay is bad.

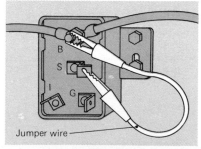

To test the starter relay, connect jumper wire for 1 sec to relay terminals *Batt* and *Sol* as shown. If the starter operates, the relay is defective and must be replaced.

Replacing the starter ☑ ☑ ☑ ☑ 30 min–2 hr

A starter may fail either electrically or because of mechanical damage to its parts. (Troubleshooting procedures for testing a starter are covered on pages 390–391.) But for whatever reason your starter has failed, it is usually best to replace it with a new or rebuilt starter. The individual components of a starter are seldom available, so there is little point in disassembling the starter in the hope of rebuilding it yourself. Most auto parts stores will give credit for an old starter toward the purchase of a new or rebuilt one. Rebuilt starters are cheaper than new ones.

To locate the starter on your car's engine, refer to the illustrations in the chapter *Major components of popular car models* (pp.145–164). Note that the solenoid assembly that actuates the starter on most cars is attached to the starter. The general procedure for removing a starter is illustrated below. First, the wires are disconnected from their terminals on the starter and/or starter solenoid, then the starter's mounting bolts are removed. The new starter is installed by reversing these steps.

The general procedure described here is complicated on many cars by the presence of brackets, nearby lubrication lines, and other engine compo-

nents that may block access to the starter. For this reason you may need more specific information for your car model; exceptions to the general procedure are covered in detail on the following three pages.

Caution: Before beginning to work, disconnect the battery ground (−) cable from its terminal to avoid accidental short-circuiting that can cause sparks. Sparks can ignite hydrogen gas emitted by the battery or touch off fuel vapors, causing an explosion. In most cases, you will have to raise your car and support it on jack stands to remove the starter. See Cautions on page 176 before working under a car.

As you disconnect a wire from the starter or solenoid, mark it with coded tape or some other label to be sure that you reconnect it to the correct terminal when installing the replacement starter. You may want to make a sketch of the starter and solenoid, then key your wires to the sketch. Follow the same procedure with any wire nuts you remove, since different nuts may have different thread sizes. It is a good general practice to thread any wire nuts back onto their studs after the wire or cable has been removed. This will prevent mixups and ensure that the nuts are not lost. Transfer the nuts from the old

starter to the replacement, if necessary.

As you remove the starter, be careful not to damage any surrounding components, such as the seal found on some flywheel housings. Look for shims between the starter and the engine mounting area. Save any you find and scribe their exact position onto the engine so that you can reposition them precisely when installing the replacement starter.

Before installing the new starter, clean the engine and starter mounting surfaces with solvent. If you detect any burrs on the surfaces, use a fine-cut file to remove them. Before attaching wires, use sandpaper or a small wire brush to clean terminals.

Use a torque wrench to tighten the starter mounting bolts to the specifications on page 394. Put a few turns on each bolt successively until all are torqued to specifications. If you cannot reach the starter with a torque wrench, tighten all bolts securely.

Tools: Box wrenches and open-end wrenches to fit the starter and solenoid bolts in your car, torque wrench graduated in lb-ft, wire brush, fine-cut file.
Materials: Automotive parts-cleaning solvent, rags.

General procedure

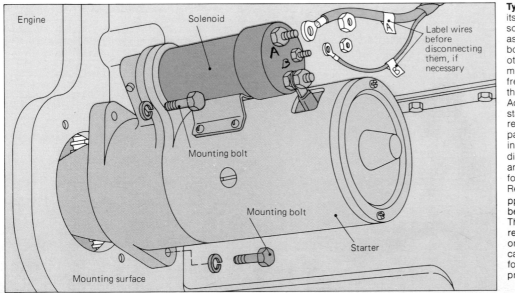

Typical starter with its attached solenoid assembly—plus bolts, brackets, and other parts that must be removed to free it—is shown in this exploded view. Access to the starter may require removing engine parts that are in the way, as discussed above and on the following pages. Refer to pp.394–396 before beginning to work. The steps for replacing the starter on some popular car models do not follow the general procedure.

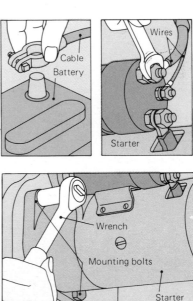

General procedure for removing a starter: First disconnect ground (−) cable from battery terminal, then free wires from starter and solenoid as shown here.

Mounting bolts are removed after all wires have been disconnected and labeled, as described in text. General procedure is reversed to install new starter.

Replacing the starter: exceptions to the general procedure ▢▢▢▢ 30 min– 4 hr

Automobiles for which starter replacement differs significantly from the general procedure (see p.393) are covered here and on the next two pages. If you own a popular car model and do not see it listed on these pages, your starter is replaced by following the general procedure. Among the cars covered by the general procedure are Datsun, Honda, Toyota, and all American Motors models, including Jeep.

As the captions and illustrations on these pages show, most deviations from the general procedure involve gaining access to the starter. In most cases, you will be working under the car, with the vehicle raised and supported on jack stands (see p.176). Access to the starter may be blocked by such parts as chassis cross members, the steering gear and flex coupling at the bottom of the steering column, the steering idler arm, automatic transmission oil cooler tubes, and various other parts of the engine, frame, exhaust, and steering systems. In addition, different sorts of brackets, clips, shields, and shims may be incorporated into the starter mounting assembly. But on all cars the starter is located in generally the same area—at the bottom of the engine toward the rear, on either the left or right side, as shown in the large illustration on page 393. The starter is mounted at the flywheel end of transverse-mounted engines.

Read all the way through the instructions for your car's starter before beginning to work. You may decide that the procedure for your car is too difficult or complicated and that it would be better to leave the job to a professional mechanic.

The chart at the right contains specifications for tightening the mounting bolts on starters in different car models. If you do not have a torque wrench, or if it is difficult to reach the starter bolts with a torque wrench, make sure that all bolts are securely tightened when you install the new starter. Whenever self-locking mounting bolts are removed, they should be replaced with new ones. Remember to disconnect the battery ground (–) cable before doing any work.

Tightening specifications for starter mounting bolts

American Motors	(TORQUE IN LB-FT)
Four-cylinder	33–54
Six- and eight-cylinder	15–20
Chrysler Corporation	
Four-cylinder (except Omni and Horizon)	16–23
Four-cylinder Omni and Horizon	40
Six- and eight-cylinder	50
Datsun	secure
Ford, Lincoln, Mercury	15–20
General Motors	40–50
Honda	32
Toyota	41–55
Volkswagen Beetle	22
Volkswagen Rabbit, Scirocco (automatic transmission or 4-speed manual transmission)	22
Volkswagen Rabbit, Scirocco (5-speed manual transmission)	32

Chrysler Corporation

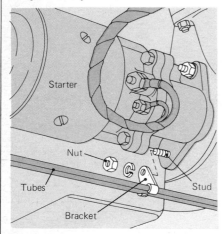

Disconnect battery ground (–) cable and raise vehicle as described on page 176, gaining access to the starter from beneath the car. In some models a bracket that holds tubes for an automatic transmission oil cooler must be pushed back to obtain the clearance required to remove the starter. Free this bracket by removing the stud nut that holds the starter to the flywheel, as illustrated above. The starter is then taken out, following the general procedure outlined on page 393.

Ford, Lincoln, and Mercury

(Pinto, Bobcat, and Fiesta; Granada, Monarch, and Versailles with 5.0- or 4.2-liter V-8s; Mustang and Capri with 5.0-liter V-8s; and Fairmont and Zephyr with 3.3-liter in-line six-cylinder engines are covered elsewhere.)

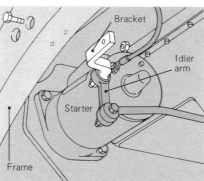

Disconnect battery ground (–) cable. Raise vehicle as described on page 176, gaining access to starter from beneath the car. In some models you may have to remove a brace, disconnect the steering idler arm from the frame, and/or turn the front wheels left or right to reach the starter's mounting bolts or to provide clearance for the starter to come out. Then follow the general procedure outlined on page 393.

Ford Pinto and Mustang; Mercury Bobcat and Capri

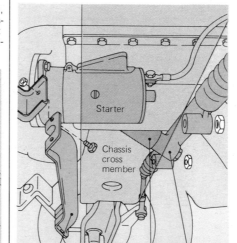

The following procedures apply only to cars with 5.0-liter V-8 engines. (Cars with 4.2-liter V-8 engines are covered under the heading *Ford, Lincoln, and Mercury.*)

1. Disconnect battery ground (–) cable. Raise vehicle as described on page 176 and work from beneath the car.
2. Remove four bolts holding the front cross member of the chassis under the flywheel housing, if vehicle is so equipped. Lower the cross member.
3. Access to the starter is blocked by the steering gearbox. To free the steering gearbox, first remove the clamp screw holding it to the flex coupling at the base of the steering column, as illustrated. Next, remove the three nuts and bolts that anchor the gearbox to the chassis cross member. Finally, disengage the gearbox from the flex coupling and pull the gearbox down to reach the starter.
4. Following the general procedure outlined on page 393, disconnect the starter cable, remove the three starter mounting bolts, and take the starter from the car.

After installing the replacement starter, reconnect the starter cable. Reposition the steering gear's splined shaft in the flex coupling, and attach the gear to the chassis cross member. Then, reinstall the clamp screw that locks the steering gear to the flex coupling. Finally, bolt the chassis cross member back into place if bolts were removed in Step 2.

Ford Fiesta

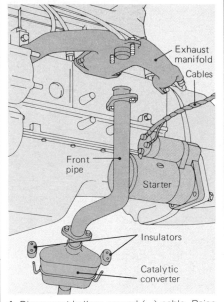

1. Disconnect battery ground (−) cable. Raise vehicle as described on page 176 and work from beneath the car.
2. Disconnect cables and wires, following the general procedure outlined on page 393.
3. Clearance required to remove the starter must be obtained by lowering the exhaust system and emission-control system. A helper should hold these parts as they are lowered, to minimize stress on them. To free the exhaust system, first remove the two rubber insulators supporting the catalytic converter, and the two clamp bolts holding the front pipe to the exhaust manifold, as illustrated. Then, with a helper, carefully lower the exhaust system.

Ford Fairmont and Mercury Zephyr with 3.3-liter in-line six-cylinder engines

1. Working under the hood, disconnect the battery ground (−) cable.
2. Remove the top starter bolt.
3. Remove the exhaust heat shield.
4. Disconnect the starter cable.
5. Raise the front of the car (p.176).
6. Remove the wishbone brace to provide clearance for removing the starter.
7. Remove lower starter bolt(s) and remove the starter from the car.

Ford Granada, Mercury Monarch, and Lincoln Versailles with 5.0- or 4.2-liter V-8 engines

1. Disconnect battery ground (−) cable. Raise front of car (p.176) and work from beneath the car.
2. Disconnect cable from the starter.

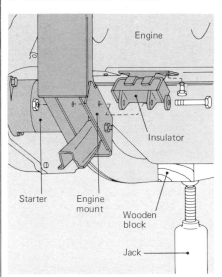

3. The engine must be raised on the passenger's side to provide clearance to remove the starter. Remove the nut and bolt that go through the engine mount on the passenger's side. Remove the other two bolts that hold the insulator to the engine. Pull out the rubber insulator.
4. Place a hydraulic jack under the passenger's side of the engine and raise it slightly. **Caution:** Do not lift the car off the jack stands.
5. Unbolt and remove the starter. After installing the new starter, make sure that all engine mounts are tightened securely.

General Motors

The following procedures apply to all General Motors cars except: Cadillac, Buick Skyhawk, Chevrolet Monza, Oldsmobile Starfire, and Pontiac Sunbird with 231 V-6 engines; Oldsmobiles with 4.3-liter diesel V-8 engines and manual transmissions; and Chevrolet Chevette. These automobiles are covered elsewhere on these pages.
1. Disconnect battery ground (−) cable. Raise vehicle as described on page 176 and work from beneath the car.

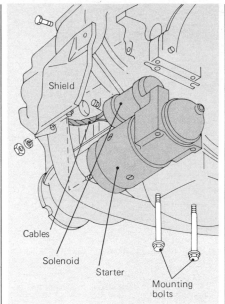

2. Remove any components in the way of the starter mounting bolts, including the starter solenoid switch shield, starter brace, exhaust pipe, and flywheel inspection cover. Some of these parts may be accessible from above the engine.
3. Disconnect cables and wires, following the general procedure outlined on page 393.
4. If the starter is not mounted on a bracket, remove starter's mounting bolts, following the general procedure outlined on page 393.
5. If the starter is mounted on a bracket, loosen the bracket's nut or bolt, then remove starter's mounting bolts. Remove the loosened nut or bolt from the bracket, and rotate the bracket out of the way so that the starter can drop free of the engine. Lower the starter from the car, front end first.
6. When installing the replacement starter, precisely reposition any shims you may have removed along with the starter's mounting bolts. Shims are placed on bolts to ensure proper alignment of the starter's pinion with the flywheel. If the new starter is unduly noisy during cranking, emits a high-pitched whine after the engine fires, or exhibits other unusual symptoms, the shim or shims must be readjusted until the starter performs properly.
   On Chevrolet Corvettes a sealing compound may have been applied where the starter enters the engine splash shield. If so, scrape off old compound and apply fresh compound.

Buick Skyhawk, Chevrolet Monza, Oldsmobile Starfire, and Pontiac Sunbird

1. Disconnect battery ground (−) cable. Raise vehicle as described on page 176 and work from beneath the car.
2. The chassis cross member running under the engine must be loosened to provide clearance for removing the starter. Loosen the six bolts on the cross member and two bolts on stabilizer shaft on the passenger side of the car. Loosen four cross member bolts on the driver's side.
3. Remove two mounting bolts on starter.
4. Pull the starter forward, allowing the front of the parts to drop down, then disconnect cables and wires as described on page 393.
5. While pulling down on the loosened cross member to gain clearance, remove the starter from the car. Remember to tighten bolts on cross member securely after installing the replacement starter.

Skyhawk, Monza, Starfire, and Sunbird with 231 V-6 engines and automatic transmission

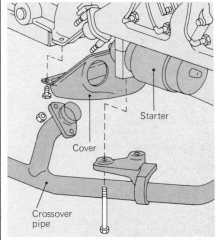

1. Disconnect battery ground (−) cable. Raise vehicle as described in the text on page 176 and work from beneath the car.
2. Remove the exhaust crossover pipe and the flywheel inspection cover as illustrated.
3. Remove two mounting bolts on starter.
4. Pull the starter motor forward and allow the front to drop down. Disconnect the wires and remove the starter from the car.

Replacing the starter *(continued)*

Chevrolet Chevette

Many components must be disconnected from the Chevette engine in order to provide the clearance needed to remove the starter.

1976–79 models without power brakes:
1. Working under the hood, disconnect battery ground (−) cable and remove the air cleaner.
2. Unplug the wiring connector from the oil-pressure sending unit and remove the sending unit from the engine block.
3. Raise the front of the vehicle (p.176).
4. Disconnect wires from the starter solenoid.
5. Remove brace screw from bottom of starter. Remove two screws holding starter to bell housing.
6. Hold starter with both hands and tip it past the engine mounting bracket, then up between the intake manifold and wheel well.

1976–79 models with power brakes, A/C:
1. Working from under the hood, disconnect battery ground (−) cable and remove the air cleaner.
2. Remove starter's upper mounting screw.
3. Remove two screws holding cover of steering column lever.
4. Remove tubular steering column jacket, lower bracket screw, and upper mounting bracket of steering column.
5. Unplug all four multi-wire electrical connectors from the steering column.
6. Remove front of car (p.176) and disconnect the first flexible coupling in the steering column above the steering gearbox.
7. Disconnect wires from the starter solenoid.
8. Remove brace screw and lower mounting screw from the bottom of the starter.
9. Place a hydraulic jack under the left side of the engine and raise it about ½ in. to provide clearance. (**Caution:** Do not lift the car off the jack stands.) Lower starter from engine.

1980 and later models without power brakes:
1. Working under the hood, disconnect the battery ground (−) cable and remove the air cleaner.
2. Disconnect the fuel line at the carburetor (see Cautions on page 397) and push line aside.
3. Disconnect vacuum hoses at the carburetor.
4. Remove the splash shield from the ignition coil and set shield aside.
5. Raise front of the car (p.176).
6. Put together a ratchet handle, extensions totaling 18 in., a U-joint, and a socket to reach the upper starter bolt. Remove the bolt.
7. Remove lower starter bolt, then position starter so that its wiring can be removed. Disconnect the wiring, labeling it for correct reinstallation later.

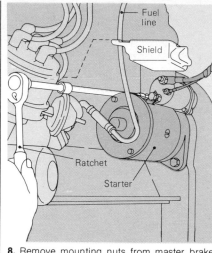

8. Remove mounting nuts from master brake cylinder. Move master cylinder aside to allow removal of starter. Take starter from the car.

1980 and later models with power brakes:
1. Follow Steps 1–2 and 4–6, above.
2. Remove steering column shroud.
3. Remove upper nuts on steering column. Remove screw on floor.
4. Disconnect the first flexible coupling in the steering column above the steering gearbox.
5. Lower the car from jack stands. Move the steering column in order to provide access to the starter.
6. Disconnect wires from the starter solenoid, labeling them for correct reinstallation later.
7. Remove starter's lower mounting bolt and remove the starter from the engine.

Oldsmobile 4.3-liter diesel V-8 engine with manual transmission

1. Working under the hood, disconnect the battery ground (−) cable.
2. Remove screws from radiator fan's shroud and let the shroud hang loose.
3. Raise the front of the car (p.176).
4. Working from beneath the car, remove the clutch's equalizer shaft (see p.209).
5. Disconnect the engine mounts. Place a hydraulic jack under the engine, and jack the engine up 1½ in. to provide working clearance. **Caution:** Do not lift the car off the jack stands.
6. Unbolt and remove the starter. After installing the new starter, make sure that all engine mounts are tightened securely.

Cadillac

Replacing the starter on most 1970–71 and 1979–80 models differs little from the general procedure (p.391). After disconnecting the battery ground (−) cable and the wires from the starter solenoid, remove the spring clip holding the wires to the solenoid housing and push the wires aside. Then remove the two or three mounting bolts and pull the starter forward.

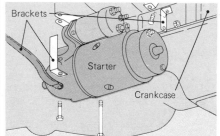

1972–78 models except Sevilles:
1. Disconnect the battery ground (−) cable. On Eldorados, also disconnect starter harness multi-wire connector at right rear of engine.
2. Raise vehicle (p.176). Work beneath the car.
3. Disconnect battery wire from solenoid on all models except Eldorado. On Eldorados, remove spring clip holding wire to solenoid. On all models, disconnect any other wires from solenoid. Label all wires for correct reconnection.
4. Remove bracket (if any) between starter and crankcase. On all models, remove screws that hold starter to the crankcase.
5. Pull starter forward, shifting it toward right front wheel, then up and over the steering linkage toward the rear of the car.

1976–79 Sevilles:
1. Follow Steps 1–3, above.
2. Remove four screws that hold the exhaust crossover pipe. Remove the crossover pipe.
3. Remove support bracket between starter and crankcase.
4. Remove two screws holding the starter to the crankcase. Pull starter out.

1979 and later Eldorados; 1980 and later Sevilles:
1. Disconnect battery ground (−) cables (there are two on diesel engines).
2. Raise vehicle (p.176). Work beneath the car.
3. Remove two screws holding the battery positive (+) cable to the output shaft's support.
4. Disconnect all wires from the starter solenoid, labeling them for correct reconnection.
5. Remove three bolts holding the starter to the crankcase. Remove the starter.

Volkswagen Beetle

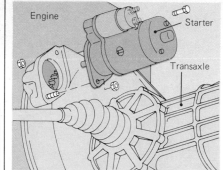

1. Disconnect the battery ground (−) cable. Raise vehicle as described on page 176.
2. Remove the right rear wheel to gain access to the starter.
3. Working through the wheel well, disconnect the wires from the starter, following the general procedure outlined on page 393.
4. Remove the upper and lower mounting bolts. Take the starter from the car.

Volkswagen Rabbit and Scirocco

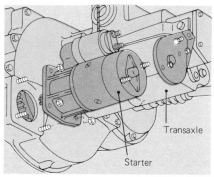

1. Disconnect the battery ground (−) cable. Working inside the engine compartment, remove the wires and upper mounting nuts from the starter, following the general procedure outlined on page 393.
2. Raise the vehicle as described on page 176 and work from beneath the car.
3. If the starter is held by a support bracket, remove the bolt holding the bracket to the transaxle. Then remove the nuts holding the bracket to the starter.
4. With the support bracket released, remove the lower mounting bolts from the starter and take the starter from the car.

Testing mechanical fuel pumps ⬛⬛ 15–30 min

Mechanical fuel pumps are activated by a special cam, called an *eccentric*, that is located on the camshaft. Electric pumps are driven by an electric motor.

Most cars are equipped with mechanical pumps. To determine whether your car is so equipped, trace the fuel line from the carburetor. If the fuel line ends at a pump that is attached to the engine, the car has a mechanical fuel pump; if not, your fuel pump is electric and is located either inside the gas tank or somewhere on the chassis between the gas tank and the carburetor. (Electric pumps, and a list of popular cars that have them, are covered on page 400.)

Caution: Testing and replacing a fuel pump can be a difficult job even for the experienced do-it-yourselfer. The work is potentially hazardous because of the possibility that gasoline will spill from the fuel line or pump; spilled fuel and the resulting vapor present a serious risk of fire or explosion. Read the *Safety precautions* at the right before starting work, and follow them carefully.

A defective fuel pump prevents all or part of the gasoline required by the engine from reaching the carburetor. Thus, the engine may not start; it may start and stall; or it may start and run, only to falter during acceleration. Infrequently, a defective fuel pump may supply too much fuel to the engine, causing similar problems.

There are two methods of testing mechanical fuel pumps: a flow test and a pressure test. The flow test measures the rate of fuel delivery to the carburetor. The pressure test determines by means of a pressure gauge whether fuel pump pressure is above or below the manufacturer's specification. Only the flow test—requiring no special gauge—is used in the procedures described on these pages. If your fuel pump fails the flow test, check the fuel line for a clogged filter and for kinks, obstructions, and leaks. Barring such problems in the fuel line, the fuel pump should be replaced if it fails the flow test.

This section on servicing fuel pumps does not cover cars with diesel engines. Repairing diesel fuel systems requires specialized tools and knowledge.

Tools: Set of open-end wrenches and socket wrenches, fuel line plugs, putty knife, fire extinguisher, vacuum pump.
Materials: Solvent, rags, gasket cement, a watch with a second hand, l-qt jar.

To perform the flow test on the fuel pump, you must disconnect the fuel line at the carburetor.
1. Put a rag under the fuel line's connection to catch dripping fuel.

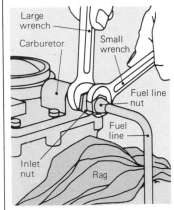

2. Use two wrenches to disconnect a fuel line from the carburetor. Engage the large carburetor inlet nut with a large wrench, as shown, steadying this nut as you loosen the fuel line nut with a smaller wrench. Use pliers to remove the clamp from a fuel hose, then pull the hose off the carburetor's fuel inlet.

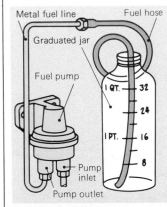

3. Attach a length of fuel hose to a metal fuel line. Extend the hose to a container, a quart or more in volume. A jar graduated in ounces or pints will simplify the test.

4. Have a helper start the engine. (The engine will run on gasoline already in the carburetor long enough to complete the test.)
5. Have your helper shut off the engine when a pint of fuel has collected in the jar. Note the elapsed time. Generally, a V-8 engine should deliver a pint of fuel in 30 sec, a six-cylinder engine in 45 sec, and a four-cylinder engine in 1 min.
6. If the engine does not start, gasoline should still spurt from the fuel line while your helper is operating the starter. If gasoline does not spurt from the line—or if it takes too long to deliver 1 pt—the problem may be either a faulty pump or an obstructed fuel filter or fuel line.

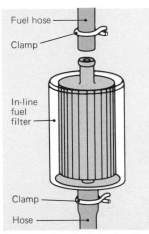

Check the line for kinks, bends, and leaks. Look for an in-line filter between the fuel pump and carburetor, and replace it with a new filter (see p.261). With the line removed, blow through it to see if it is clogged. If the line is free of obstructions and you have replaced the fuel filter but your pump still fails the flow test, remove the fuel pump, following the instructions on pages 398–399. After removing the pump, insert a hand-operated vacuum pump into the fuel line and try to draw fuel from the tank. If you can, replace the fuel pump. If you cannot draw fuel from the tank, have a mechanic check the fuel lines and in-tank filter.

Safety precautions

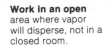

Work in an open area where vapor will disperse, not in a closed room.

Do not work near any source of flame or electrical sparks, including furnaces, fuse boxes, or light switches.

Wipe up any spills immediately and put the soaked rags in a closed metal container.

Keep a fire extinguisher on hand to use in case a fuel spill ignites.

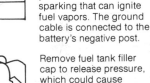

Before beginning work, disconnect the battery ground (−) cable to prevent accidental sparking that can ignite fuel vapors. The ground cable is connected to the battery's negative post.

Remove fuel tank filler cap to release pressure, which could cause gasoline to spurt from fittings as they are disconnected. Have rags ready to wipe up spills immediately. Wash gasoline off skin promptly. Put all fuel-soaked rags in a closed metal container.

Use golf tees or pencil stubs to plug fuel lines as they are disconnected.

Repair / Engine

Replacing mechanical fuel pumps ◨◨◨ 30 min–2 hr

On many cars with mechanical fuel pumps, the pump is accessible from the top of the engine compartment. If it is not, raise and support the front of the car (observing the precautions recommended on page 176) to gain access to the pump from below.

General procedures for replacing a mechanical fuel pump are shown below. Exceptions are detailed on the opposite page. Before beginning work, read the Cautions here and on page 397.

Tools: Open-end or flare wrenches and socket wrenches, fuel line plugs (golf tee, pencil stub), putty knife.
Materials: Solvent, rags, gasket cement, fire extinguisher.

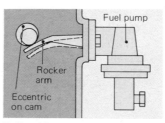

Three common types of mechanical fuel pump are illustrated; two are driven by rocker arms, and the third is driven by a pushrod. Mechanical fuel pumps may be mounted to form a seal with a single gasket or—in many of the pushrod types—with an assembly consisting of a pair of gaskets and a spacer, or mounting plate.

General procedure

Caution: Before beginning work, disconnect the battery ground (−) cable to prevent accidental sparking that can ignite fuel vapors. The ground cable is attached to the battery's negative post and to the car's chassis. Pressure in fuel lines may cause gasoline to spurt through fittings when they are disconnected. Remove the cap from the fuel tank first to relieve pressure. Have rags ready to wipe up any spills immediately, and wash promptly if you get gasoline on your skin.

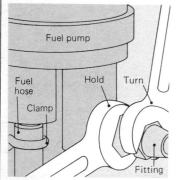

1. Disconnect the fuel inlet and outlet lines from the pump, using two wrenches—one to hold the fitting while the other turns the nut. Using two wrenches minimizes the risk of twisting and deforming the lines and fittings. Flare wrenches work best.

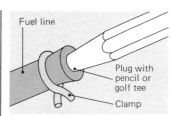

2. Immediately upon disconnecting a line, plug it with a golf tee, pencil stub, or some other suitable object that will prevent spilling.

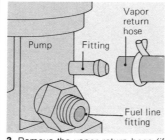

3. Remove the vapor-return hose (if any) from its fitting.
4. Remove the mounting or retaining bolts. There are usually two.
5. Tip the pump to free it as you pull it away from the engine. If you cannot easily remove pump, see Step 9. If the mounting assembly contains separate spacers and gaskets, be careful to retain them as you pull out the pump.

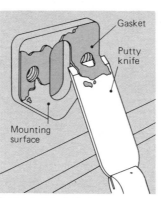

6. Use a putty knife to scrape away old gasket cement from mounting surfaces, spacers, and gaskets. Wipe all surfaces clean, using a cloth dampened with a parts-cleaning solvent. Allow surfaces to dry.
7. Apply fresh sealing cement to gaskets and mounting surfaces, then install the new pump by following the above steps in the reverse order. Remember to attach all the mounting bolts loosely at first, then push the pump firmly against the engine and tighten the bolts alternately until all are secure.
8. After the pump is installed, start the engine and allow it to idle. While the engine idles, check for leaks around the pump. If you see a leak, turn off the engine and tighten the leaky fitting.

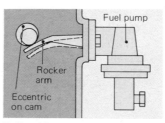

9. Should you have trouble removing the old pump or seating the new one, do not try to force it. The problem probably lies in the position of the eccentric cam on the camshaft inside the engine. The cam's position can interfere with the removal or installation of the pump's rocker arm. You can move the eccentric cam by briefly operating the car's starter to crank the engine.

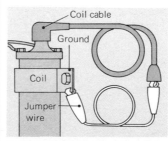

Before cranking the engine, ground the ignition system by disconnecting the cable that runs between the coil

and the distributor cap. Attach one end of a jumper wire to the cable terminal. Attach other end of jumper wire to a metal part of the engine. Finally, reattach the battery ground (−) cable to its battery post.

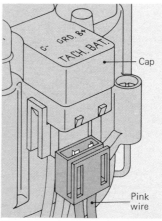

If your car has Delco HEI electronic ignition, with the coil located inside the distributor, disconnect the pink wire from the terminal on the distributor cap marked *BAT* in order to deactivate the ignition.

Crank the engine in short spurts, then try to remove or install the pump after each spurt until you succeed; this will occur when the eccentric cam is at a low point in its revolution.

Buick Skylark, Chevrolet Citation, Oldsmobile Omega, and Pontiac Phoenix

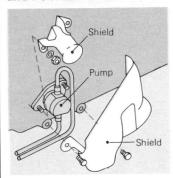

Shield

Pump

Shield

To gain access to the fuel pump in GM X-Body cars with 2.8-liter V-6 engines, remove the oil filter and the two shields over the pump. For clarity, the oil filter is not shown in the illustration.

Chevrolet

Fuel pumps used on some Chevrolet V-8 engines have a pushrod between the eccentric cam and the fuel pump. The pushrod activates a short rocker arm. It is not normally necessary to remove this pushrod. If you

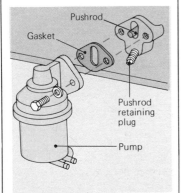

Pushrod

Gasket

Pushrod retaining plug

Pump

have to remove it, the pushrod in 396-, 400-, 427-, and 454-cu-in. engines is kept in place by a plug screwed into the fuel pump mounting. Remove the fuel pump and gasket, then unscrew the plug.

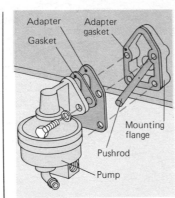

Adapter

Adapter gasket

Gasket

Mounting flange

Pushrod

Pump

In the 262-, 302-, 327-, and 350-cu-in. engines, the pushrod may be pulled from the engine after removing the fuel pump and its gasket, spacer (if any), and adapter. Fuel pump adapter is bolted to engine.

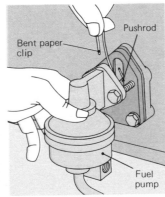

Pushrod

Bent paper clip

Fuel pump

When installing the fuel pump in these V-8 engines, hold the pushrod up so that it engages the pump's rocker arm. This may be done with a heavy paper clip bent to form a hook or by coating the pushrod with heavy grease to hold it in position.
To replace the fuel pump on a Chevette, raise the car (p.176) and remove the distributor cap and ignition coil to gain access to the pump. If the car is equipped with air conditioning, you may also have to loosen or remove the rear bracket on the air-conditioner compressor and raise the compressor.

Dodge Colt and Plymouth Champ

The fuel pump on the Colt and Champ "J" engine (1,400 cc) also has a pushrod between the rocker arm and the eccentric cam. The rod can be taken from the engine after the fuel pump is removed.
Be sure to seat pushrod firmly against eccentric cam when reassembling the unit. Keep rod straight when installing the fuel pump so that it engages rocker arm. If you have trouble keeping pushrod straight, use a paper clip (see *Chevrolet*, left) or coat pushrod with heavy grease to hold it in position.

Ford, Lincoln, and Mercury

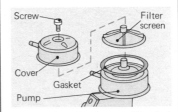

Fuel hose

Wire cutters

Crimped clamp

Pump

If a hose is connected to the fuel pump by a crimped clamp, cut the clamp off with wire cutters. Replace it with a worm-drive clamp.
Models equipped with the 2,800-cc V-6 engine have a fuel pump that uses a pushrod. When installing this pump, insert the pushrod firmly so that it rides on the eccentric cam. Keep the rod straight when installing the new fuel pump so that rod engages rocker arm. If you have trouble keeping pushrod straight, use a paper clip (see *Chevrolet*, left) or coat pushrod with heavy grease to hold it in position.

Volkswagen

To service the fuel pump of the VW Beetle and Karmann Ghia, proceed as follows:

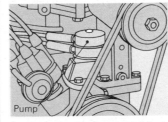

Pump

1. Find the fuel pump, which is located between the distributor and alternator (or generator) support, just below the carburetor.

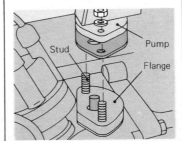

Screw

Filter screen

Cover

Gasket

Pump

2. VW fuel pumps have a filter that will reduce fuel flow if it clogs. Before removing the pump, unscrew its cover and take out the filter. Clean the filter in solvent, let it dry, and reinstall it. Start the car and repeat the fuel flow test (p.397).
3. If a clogged filter is not the problem, pull hoses off the pump. Plug hoses to prevent fuel leakage.

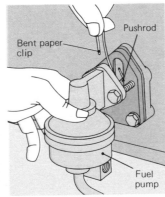

Stud

Pump

Flange

4. Remove the fuel pump's two mounting nuts and washers, and take off the pump and gasket covering the intermediate flange.

---

5. Remove the pushrod from the flange, then remove the flange and the gaskets beneath the flange.
6. Install two new gaskets on the pump's mounting studs on the engine, then install the flange.

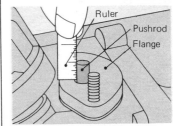

Pushrod

Flange

7. Install the pushrod on the flange, tapered end down.

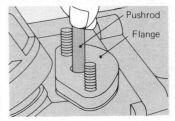

Ruler

Pushrod

Flange

8. Turn the nut on the crankshaft pulley with a wrench until the pushrod rises to its highest point of travel. Measure the distance the pushrod projects above the flange. This distance should be ½ in. (13 mm). If pushrod projects less than ½ in., remove one gasket from under the flange. If pushrod projects more than ½ in., add extra gaskets until measurement is correct.
9. Install a gasket on top of flange.
10. Fill cavity under pump with chassis grease and place pump on mounting studs. Install washers and nuts. Tighten nuts securely.
11. Install fuel hoses, using new hose clamps. Inspect ends of hoses. If hoses are damaged, replace them.

The fuel pumps on VW Rabbit and Scirocco models with carburetors are conventional rocker-arm designs. Follow the general procedures on the opposite page to remove and install these pumps. Fuel-injected Rabbits and Sciroccos have electric fuel pumps (see p.401).

Testing and replacing electric fuel pumps ▨▨▨ 1–3 hr

Electric fuel pumps are found on many late-model cars, including those with fuel-injection systems. Fuel systems with electric pumps are much less prone to vapor lock than mechanical systems and are more uniform in their rate of fuel delivery. In most North American cars so equipped, the electric pump is located inside the fuel tank. Some fuel-injected Cadillacs have two electric pumps—one inside the tank and a second, chassis-mounted pump nearer the engine. Other GM cars with electric fuel pumps include the Chevrolet Vega with four-cylinder engine, Buick Skyhawk, Chevrolet Monza, Oldsmobile Starfire, and Pontiac Sunbird, except those models

with 151-cubic-inch, four-cylinder engines. Cadillacs with throttle body fuel injection also have electric pumps, as do Ford Mustangs and Fairmonts with the turbocharged engine and automatic transmission.

In imported cars the electric pump is often mounted on the chassis somewhere between the tank and the engine. Datsun 280Z and 810 models, Hondas, and Volkswagen Rabbits and Sciroccos with fuel-injection systems all have electric pumps.

In models with the pump inside the fuel tank, the tank must be removed to service the pump—a job for a professional mechanic. Before replacing an electric pump, check for a blown fuse. Also clean and tighten

the connections at both ends of the fuel pump's ground wire (see pp.361–363). To locate the fuel pump in your car, trace the fuel line back from the carburetor or fuel-injection distributor toward the fuel tank. When working on fuel pumps, observe all the Cautions listed on page 397.

> **Tools:** Open-end wrenches and socket wrenches to fit the bolts and fuel line fittings on your car; plugs for fuel hose, such as golf tees or pencil stubs; locking pliers; two jumper wires; putty knife; test light; graduated beaker.
> **Materials:** Rags, solvent, gasket cement.

Datsun 280 and 810 models

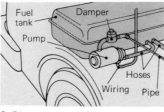

To test the pump, disconnect the fuel line from the top of the fuel filter; the fuel filter is a large canister mounted inside the front fender on the passenger side. Disconnect the wire from the S terminal of the starter motor, and turn the ignition switch to *Start*. If the fuel pump is operative, you will hear a buzzing sound. If not, reconnect the fuel line and starter wire, and turn the ignition on. Check for current at the fuel pump connections. If there is no current, check the circuit for electrical faults (pp.361–363). If there is current at the pump but the pump does not work, replace it.

To replace the electric fuel pump on 1975–76 Datsun 280Z models, proceed as follows:
1. Disconnect the ground(–)cable from the battery.
2. Chock front wheels. Raise and support the rear of the car, observing the Cautions on page 176.

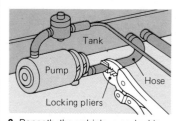

3. Disconnect wires from the fuel pump. The pump is mounted near the fuel tank at the rear wheel on the passenger side.
4. Disconnect the wire from the S terminal of the starter motor.

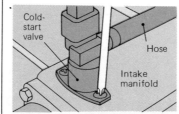

5. Remove the two screws holding the cold-start valve to the engine's intake manifold, and take the valve off the manifold.

6. Reconnect battery ground cable.
7. Place the cold-start valve in a container, such as a large coffee can. Turn the ignition switch to *Start*. This releases fuel line pressure. Fuel will empty itself into the container.

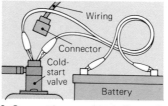

8. Beneath the vehicle, use locking pliers to clamp off the fuel hose between the fuel tank and pump.
9. Disconnect clamps at both sides of the fuel pump. Hold a container under the hoses to catch fuel, then disconnect the fuel hoses.

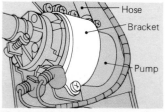

10. Unscrew the two screws holding the fuel pump's bracket and remove the bracket. This uncovers the fuel pump's fasteners. Remove these bolts, then remove the fuel pump.

11. Install the new pump by reversing the above procedures. When installing fuel hoses, clean dirt from the hose fittings, then slide new hose clamps onto the hoses. Push ends of the hoses onto the fittings until hoses contact the pump. Tighten clamps securely.

The procedures for 1977 and later Datsun 280 and 810 models vary as follows:
1. Disconnect both battery cables.
2. Disconnect the multi-wire connector from the cold-start valve on the intake manifold.

3. Connect jumper wires to the positive and negative posts of the battery. Connect the other ends of the jumper wires to the terminals of the cold-start valve for 3 sec. This releases pressure in the fuel system.
Caution: Keep ends of the jumper cables separated. If they touch, they will cause sparks that may result in a fire or explosion.
4. Chock the front wheels, raise and support the rear of the car (see p.176), and remove the cover over the fuel pump. Then follow Steps 8–11 (above) for 1975–76 models.

Early Honda Civic CVCC

To test the fuel pump for proper pressure, proceed as follows:
1. Remove the carburetor air cleaner.
2. Remove clamp and disconnect the fuel hose at the carburetor.

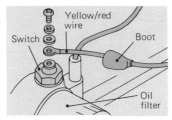

3. Disconnect the striped yellow-and-red wire from the oil-pressure switch, which is on the engine to the right of the oil filter, as illustrated.
4. Hold a calibrated beaker under the fuel hose. With the ignition switch on, hold the hose in the beaker (see flow test, p.397). In 30 sec, turn off the ignition and measure the amount of fuel in the beaker. Normal fuel delivery is 6.75 oz or more in 30 sec. If fuel flow is less than this amount, check the fuel line for obstructions. If there are none, replace the fuel pump. Remember to reconnect the oil-pressure switch and fuel hose, and reinstall the air cleaner.

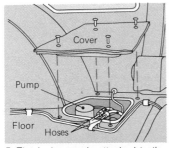

5. The fuel pump is attached to the chassis at the rear of the car, just forward of the rear wheel on the driver's side. To replace the fuel pump, you must raise the rear seat. Remove the bolt in the center at the rear of the seat, then lift the seat up from the rear. Remove the four screws in the fuel pump's cover, and lift off the cover.

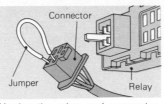

6. Detach both electrical terminals from the pump.
7. Place rags under fuel lines at pump to catch spills. Loosen clamps holding both fuel hoses, and pull the hoses off.
8. Remove the two mounting bolts and take out the pump. Retrieve all fastening hardware, consisting of two bolts, two collars, and the spacer at the left-hand side of the pump support brace.
9. Reverse the above steps to install the new pump. Replace the fuel filter after the first 15,000 miles and every 30,000 miles thereafter.

Honda Accord, Prelude, and late-model Civic

To test the fuel pumps of these models, proceed as follows:

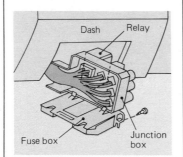

1. With the ignition switch off, remove the fuse box cover under the dash. Locate junction box containing fuel pump's cutoff relay.
2. Trace the two black-and-yellow wires to the cutoff relay connector.

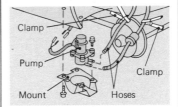

Unplug the relay, and connect a jumper wire between the terminals for the black-and-yellow wires.
3. Disconnect the fuel line at the carburetor, and hold a graduated quart container under the fuel hose.
4. Have a helper turn the ignition switch on for 1 min. Measure the amount of fuel that flows into the container. Replace the fuel pump if less than 23 oz flows into the container from Prelude models, or less than 17 oz flows into the container from Civic and Accord models.
5. To replace Prelude's fuel pump, chock the front wheels. Raise and support the rear of the car, observing the Cautions on page 176.
6. Remove drain bolt from beneath the fuel tank and allow fuel to drain into a clean container.
7. Trace fuel pump wires from the pump to their connector. Disconnect the connector.
8. Trace the fuel hoses from the fuel pump to their clamps. Open the clamps, slide them back, and twist the hoses off their fittings.

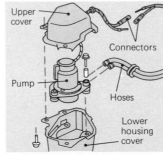

9. Remove bolts from the fuel pump housing, just forward of the rear wheel on the driver's side. Remove the housing.
10. To open the housing, pry up the two tabs on the lower cover to free upper cover. Remove upper cover.

11. Unbolt the fuel pump from the lower cover and lift the pump out of the cover.
12. Slide hose clamps back and twist hoses off fittings to free fuel pump.
13. To install the new fuel pump, reverse order of above procedures.

To replace Civic and Accord pumps, follow the procedures above, but note that the pumps are mounted differently. **Caution:** If there is no drain plug on the fuel tank, clamp the fuel lines closed with locking pliers before removing the hoses from the pump.

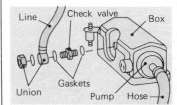

On hatchback models, remove the rear wheel on the driver's side, unbolt the fuel pump mount, and remove the assembly from the car. Then remove bolts that hold the fuel pump to its mount.

The fuel pump in station wagons is mounted to a bracket on the passenger side at the rear of the fuel tank. Remove bolts holding the fuel pump mount to the fuel tank bracket, and lower the pump to the ground. Remove bolts that hold fuel pump to its mount, and remove pump.

Volkswagen Rabbit, Scirocco with fuel injection

To test the fuel pump on 1980 and earlier cars, proceed as follows:
1. Disconnect high-voltage cable from the tower of the ignition coil.

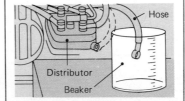

2. Disconnect the fuel-return hose from the fuel distributor. Quickly

place the hose in a container to catch fuel that is expelled.
3. When no more fuel comes from the end of the fuel-return hose, hold an empty calibrated quart beaker under the end of the fuel-return hose. Have a helper operate the starter and crank the engine for 30 sec. At least 14 oz of fuel should be delivered during this time.
4. If fuel pump does not deliver any fuel, check the fuse under the hood. If fuse is OK, remove fuel pump relay (under fuse), connect a jumper wire across terminals 13 and 14, and repeat Steps 1–3. If pump works now, replace relay. If pump does not work, check its wiring (pp.361–363) or have a dealer do it.
5. If fuel delivery in Step 3 is less than 14 oz, check fuel lines and filter for blockage. If lines and filter are OK, replace check valve.
6. Raise car (p.176). Remove right rear wheel to reach fuel pump.
7. Take off the filler cap to relieve any pressure in the fuel system.

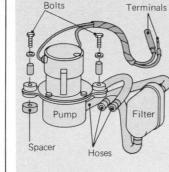

8. Clean dirt off the fuel line union at the side of the pump. Then disconnect the union and remove the line from the fuel-pressure accumulator.
9. Remove the check valve from the fuel pump body with a wrench. Install a new check valve. Use new gaskets. Torque the check valve to 14–18 lb-in. Reconnect the line from the fuel-pressure accumulator.
10. Test fuel delivery again. If fuel output is still not to specification, replace the fuel pump. To replace pump, disconnect the fuel hose from the fuel tank, quickly plugging the end of the hose to prevent excess spillage of fuel. Remove bolts holding the pump's sound-absorbing box to the mounting brackets. Remove the box holding the pump, and take the pump from the box. To install the new pump, reverse the procedure.

When and how to overhaul a carburetor

Only after all other engine systems are operating correctly should you inspect the carburetor. It is the last system to check, adjust, and repair. Carburetors are extremely durable. Parts do not usually wear out before 50,000 miles, nor do they need adjustment as often as most other engine systems.

Carburetor parts do wear eventually: fuel-metering jets become enlarged, sediment may block passages, accelerator pumps develop leaks, and gaskets and diaphragms deteriorate. Then gas mileage falls off and you can no longer adjust the carburetor for smooth performance and a steady idle speed. When this happens, and if all other engine systems check out, it is time to replace or rebuild the carburetor.

You can approach the overhaul of a carburetor in three ways: You can trade in the old carburetor on a new or rebuilt unit, or you can rebuild the old carburetor yourself, using a parts kit. Base your decision on the age and condition of your car as well as on a realistic assessment of your skills as a mechanic.

Replacing a carburetor with a new one is the best and easiest solution, but it is also the most expensive. Pollution controls in 1977- and later-model cars have raised the prices for newer carburetors considerably. Even the simplest one-barrel models, such as the Holley Model 1945 shown on these pages, cost about $125 in 1980. The tamper-proof adjustments legally required for 1981 and later cars limit your choice to a new or rebuilt carburetor for these models.

Rebuilt carburetors cost less than new ones. They come with a guarantee and are what most professional shops install. With the trade-in allowance on the old carburetor, the 1945 Holley cost $80.

The rebuild kit comes with step-by-step instructions and contains most of the small internal parts, seals, and gaskets, but not major items like the float or vacuum break diaphragm. Rebuild kits cost $5 to $25 for simple carburetors.

With care and luck, installing a kit will achieve a complete repair. New or rebuilt carburetors may be the best choice for a home mechanic unless he has considerable skill, knowledge, and experience in diagnosing and repairing carburetor problems.

Tools: Screwdrivers, wrenches, pliers, compressed air.
Materials: Carburetor cleaner, pipe cleaners, brush, replacement carburetor (new or rebuilt) or rebuild kit.

Cleaning a carburetor

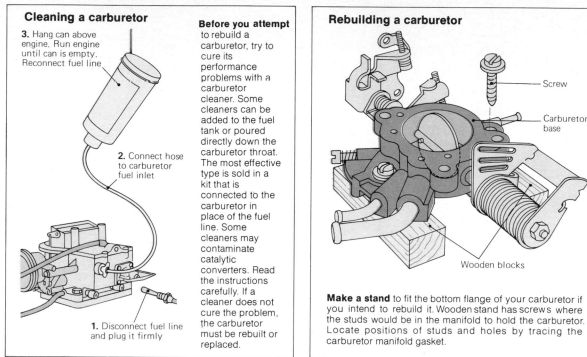

3. Hang can above engine. Run engine until can is empty. Reconnect fuel line

2. Connect hose to carburetor fuel inlet

1. Disconnect fuel line and plug it firmly

Before you attempt to rebuild a carburetor, try to cure its performance problems with a carburetor cleaner. Some cleaners can be added to the fuel tank or poured directly down the carburetor throat. The most effective type is sold in a kit that is connected to the carburetor in place of the fuel line. Some cleaners may contaminate catalytic converters. Read the instructions carefully. If a cleaner does not cure the problem, the carburetor must be rebuilt or replaced.

Rebuilding a carburetor

Screw

Carburetor base

Wooden blocks

Make a stand to fit the bottom flange of your carburetor if you intend to rebuild it. Wooden stand has screws where the studs would be in the manifold to hold the carburetor. Locate positions of studs and holes by tracing the carburetor manifold gasket.

Basic repair procedures

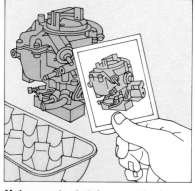

Make rough sketches or take instant photographs to show how parts fit. Instant photos are expensive, but being able to reassemble the parts correctly is worth the price. Sort parts into egg cartons to keep track of them.

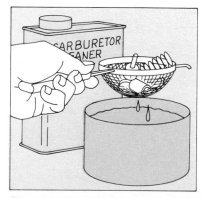

Clean parts in carburetor cleaner as you remove them. Never wash parts in gasoline. Put a few parts at a time into a small kitchen strainer and dip them in cleaner to prevent losing parts or getting them mixed up. Discard strainer.

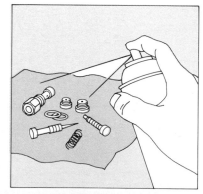

Blow cleaned parts dry with compressed air. If you do not have a compressor, use a hair dryer or a can of compressed air (sold in photo shops). Probe openings with a pipe cleaner. Make certain that all dirt is removed from tiny passageways.

Removing the carburetor from the engine ▯ ▯ ▯ 30 min–1½ hr

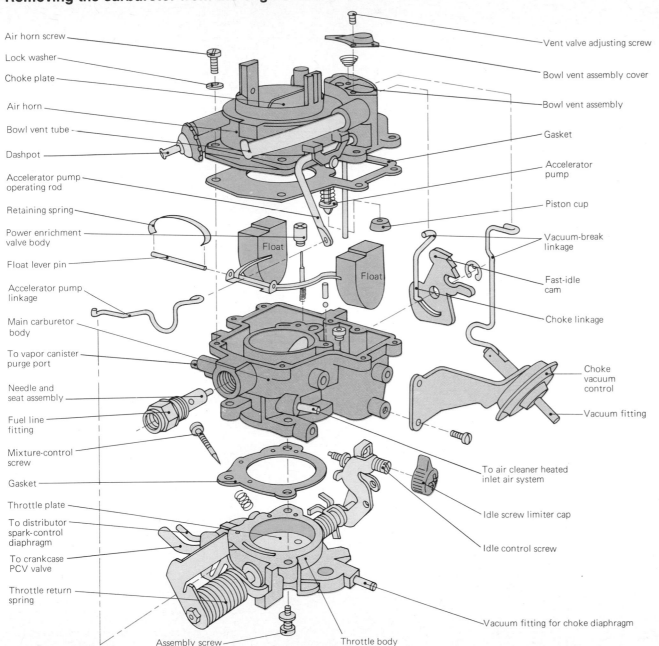

Air horn screw

Lock washer

Choke plate

Air horn

Bowl vent tube

Dashpot

Accelerator pump operating rod

Retaining spring

Power enrichment valve body

Float lever pin

Accelerator pump linkage

Main carburetor body

To vapor canister purge port

Needle and seat assembly

Fuel line fitting

Mixture-control screw

Gasket

Throttle plate

To distributor spark-control diaphragm

To crankcase PCV valve

Throttle return spring

Assembly screw

Float

Float

Throttle body

Vent valve adjusting screw

Bowl vent assembly cover

Bowl vent assembly

Gasket

Accelerator pump

Piston cup

Vacuum-break linkage

Fast-idle cam

Choke linkage

Choke vacuum control

Vacuum fitting

To air cleaner heated inlet air system

Idle screw limiter cap

Idle control screw

Vacuum fitting for choke diaphragm

Removing the carburetor on an older car can be a simple and obvious procedure, but on a newer car with sophisticated emission controls a number of wires, vacuum lines, fuel lines, and control linkages may have to be disconnected first.

If you see a maze of connections when you remove the air cleaner to expose the carburetor (p.240), be sure to disconnect them systematically. Use tape and felt-tip pen to label each hose, wire, or linkage and the point where it attaches to the carburetor. Then, when it is time to reassemble the carburetor, you will know where each part belongs. An instant photograph showing where things fit is also helpful at this stage.

The following instructions are for removing the relatively simple Holley Model 1945 carburetor from a six-cylinder engine. Your car will require steps that are similar and, probably, some that are quite different, depending on the make and model. See Cautions for handling fuel, p.397.

1. Disconnect battery ground (—) cable.

2. Remove air cleaner (p.240).

3. Disconnect and label each hose attached to the carburetor. Label its attachment point on the carburetor. Draw a diagram, or photograph the hookups.

4. Clean the fuel line connection at the carburetor, and put a cup lined with a rag or paper towel under the fuel line fittings. Loosen fittings, using two wrenches (p.261). Separate the line from the carburetor. Insert a plug in the open end of the fuel line to minimize spillage and to keep dirt out of the line. A golf tee or pencil stub works well. Mop up any spilled fuel, and discard rags in a safe fashion (p.8). Label pipes or hoses and their attachment points.

5. Disconnect accelerator linkage. Different kinds of clips are used to attach this linkage, but most are obvious in their operation. A ball-and-socket linkage can usually be released by pulling back on the socket so that the ball slips out. Be careful not to disturb the adjustment of the accelerator or transmission throttle-valve linkage when you disconnect it.

6. Disconnect heat tube (if any) from choke.

7. Disconnect linkage to choke in manifold well, if this type is used (see p.248).

8. Loosen and remove nuts and lock washers that attach the carburetor to the intake manifold. Lift the carburetor off its studs, then mount it on your rebuilding stand (p.402) or take it to a parts store for matching and exchange. If you decide to exchange it for a new or rebuilt carburetor, transfer your connection labels to the new carburetor at the parts counter. This also ensures that the replacement will fit your car correctly.

9. Remove the carburetor-to-manifold gasket.

10. Cover open intake manifold with a rag or press sponge rubber balls into the openings to keep dirt out of the engine while the carburetor is off.

Disassembling a carburetor for rebuilding ▱▱▱▱▱ 1–2 hr

1. Cover workbench with newspapers. Use egg boxes to hold small parts. Make tie-on labels for each part and its mounting. Place carburetor on stand (p.402). Determine how each part works before you remove it. Clean parts with a brush and cleaner. Do not invert carburetor body unless you first cover it with cheesecloth—small parts may fall out and get lost.

2. Remove screws from choke cover and lift cover off after disengaging bimetallic spring (p.249). Place a rubber band over choke lever and remove rubber tube from vacuum break fitting on carb body. Apply vacuum to check diaphragm. If diaphragm does not move or hold vacuum, replace it (p.250).

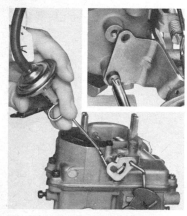

3. Remove vacuum break diaphragm (if any). Remove mounting bolts or screws that hold its bracket to the carburetor body. Disconnect retaining clips of linkage and unhook the linkage to remove it from the carburetor. Put clips back on the linkage so that you can find them later. Reinstall mounting screws on carburetor body for safekeeping also.

4. Disconnect links that run between levers on main carburetor body. Disconnect links from the top half of carburetor (called the *air horn assembly*). You will usually find two linkages: one on the choke plate, the other on the accelerator pump. Screws or clips attach links to levers. Separate links from arms and label them.

5. Remove screws holding air horn assembly to the main body of the carburetor and separate the parts. If air horn sticks to carburetor body, tap with a plastic hammer, then lift off air horn assembly. Do not invert main carburetor body because parts might drop out. Remove moving parts from air horn, but do not attempt to remove choke plate.

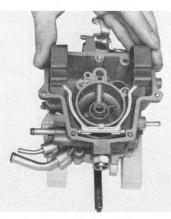

6. Remove float from main carburetor body and check for leaks by shaking float and listening for slosh of fuel inside. Also hold float underwater to check for escaping air bubbles, which indicate leaks. If float has fuel inside or leaks air, replace it. (Most carb rebuild kits do not include floats.) Next, unscrew and lift out needle valve and its seat assembly.

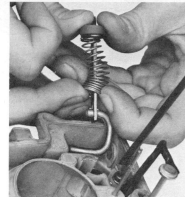

7. Remove accelerator pump. Some rebuild kits have only the rubber plunger; better kits include complete pump assembly (plunger, spring, and pump). Pump piston is held by two tabs squeezed into operating wire. Turn wire so that tabs fit through slot in piston rod, then slide rod off wire. If new piston is not supplied, replace only rubber cup on plunger.

8. Remove all remaining parts that can be removed easily so that you can clean the body of the carburetor effectively. These parts include the main metering jet (a brass fitting with screwdriver slot), power valve (valve body, valve, and return spring), and venturi cluster. Follow the detailed instructions that come with rebuild kit exactly.

9. Remove idle-speed and idle-mixture adjusting screws. Carefully pry off plastic limiter caps if there are new ones in the parts kit, taking care not to bend or turn the screws. (A special puller can be used to remove the caps without breaking them.) Record the number of half-turns needed to remove each screw in order to make roughly correct adjustment when you reinstall screws.

Reassembling and rebuilding a carburetor ☑☑☑☑☑ 2–4 hr

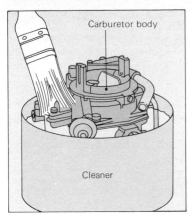

Carburetor body

Cleaner

1. After removing all nonmetallic parts, clean carburetor body by soaking it in carburetor cleaner for about 15 min. If liquid cleaner is not available, use an aerosol cleaner and a brush to remove carbon, gum, and dirt. Rinse carburetor body in hot water to rinse off cleaner. Dry with compressed air. Do not let lint from rags get into the passages.

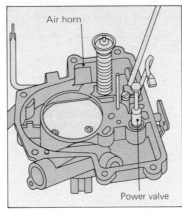

Air horn

Power valve

4. The power valve is not usually replaced when a Holley 1945 carburetor is rebuilt. Valve is held in place in the air horn assembly by metal crimped or staked around valve bore. Valve can only be removed by chiseling the metal away. If valve is faulty, the engine will hesitate when the throttle is opened; replace the carburetor. Replacing the power valve is a job for a carburetor rebuilding shop.

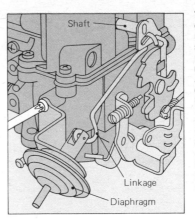

Shaft

Linkage

Diaphragm

7. Reinstall choke diaphragm by hooking up linkage to choke shaft and screwing mounting bracket to main carburetor body. Adjust vacuum break (or pull-down, as it may be called in the instruction sheet) to the specifications given for your carburetor and car (see p.250). Place correct-diameter drill bit between choke plate and air horn to measure gap.

Throttle plate

Shaft

Body

2. To check whether throttle and choke plates are sealing, hold carb body up to a strong light, throttle plate closed. Look through main air passages. Only the tiniest hairline of light should show, and it should be uniform all around the plate. Throttle shaft should not wobble in its holes. If it does, or if plate is off center, replace the carburetor.

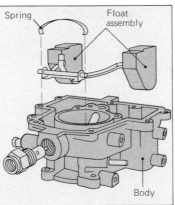

Spring

Float assembly

Body

5. Screw needle valve and seat assembly into main carburetor body. Install float and lever assembly, float pin, and pin's retaining spring. Adjust float level with gauge supplied in rebuild kit. Follow instructions that come with kit exactly. Do not apply force to plastic-tipped needle valve when you bend the float tang to adjust its level.

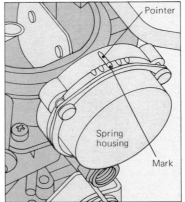

Pointer

Spring housing

Mark

8. Reinstall choke's coil spring in its housing and adjust it (p.249) to the specification for your car. Turn spring housing until the pointer lines up with the correct index mark on the housing. Then tighten the clamping screws firmly to hold the adjustment. If you made your own mark on the housing before disassembly, line it up during reassembly.

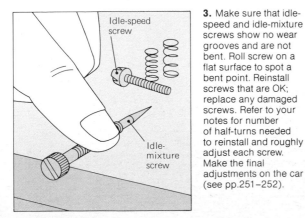

Idle-speed screw

Idle-mixture screw

3. Make sure that idle-speed and idle-mixture screws show no wear grooves and are not bent. Roll screw on a flat surface to spot a bent point. Reinstall screws that are OK; replace any damaged screws. Refer to your notes for number of half-turns needed to reinstall and roughly adjust each screw. Make the final adjustments on the car (see pp.251–252).

Cup

Piston

6. Install new rubber cup on piston of accelerator pump, or replace the entire pump if the parts are supplied in your rebuild kit. Follow the instructions with the repair kit for adjusting the accelerator pump stroke. Note that adjustment specifications vary by car model as well as carburetor model; use the setting given for your car, engine, and transmission.

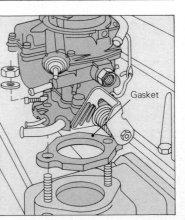

Gasket

9. After you have completed the 73 steps in the instruction sheet, the rebuilt Holley 1945 carburetor can be mounted on the engine. Remove the rag or ball covering opening of intake manifold, and reinstall the carburetor, using a new gasket. Make the carburetor adjustments given on pages 248–253. Better yet, have a shop with a CO tester make the adjustments for you.

Trouble shooting the fuel-injection system ⚡⚡⚡ 30 min–2 hr

Before checking a fuel-injection system, check items that are apt to give trouble, such as the battery, cables, ignition system, compression, and ignition timing. Also, listen to the fuel pump as you crank the engine. It should buzz audibly for one or two seconds; if it does not, check the pump (see pp.397–401).

Common fuel-injection systems are: *electronic fuel injection* (EFI) used by Cadillac, VW, and Datsun; *continuous fuel injection* (CFI) in VW; and *throttle body fuel injection* in Cadillac, Chrysler, and Lincoln.

EFI systems: Follow the procedure given below. If the flap on the airflow sensor is faulty, have a professional mechanic replace it.

Check whether or not fuel reaches the distribution point on the fuel rail while the engine is cranking. This is easy to do if there is a Schrader valve on the rail. See *Safety precautions* on the opposite page. Then remove the cap and push the valve stem in. If fuel squirts forcefully from the valve, fuel delivery is satisfactory. Instead of an airflow sensor, some fuel-injection systems have a manifold-pressure sensor, which is checked by disconnecting the sensor hose. On Cadillacs, this sensor is located inside the electronic control unit. Have a professional mechanic replace the part if it is defective. Test the EFI temperature sensor also, and unscrew and replace it if it is faulty. Check the cold-start injector and the thermal time switch on a cool day (below 50°F) with the engine cold. Replace the injector or switch if either is faulty (see opposite page).

CFI systems: Follow the procedure given on the opposite page. When running a spray test, keep spray time to a minimum to avoid filling the cylinders with fuel; otherwise, engine damage may result.

If fuel delivery and injectors are OK, check the cold-start injector and thermal time switch.

Throttle body injection systems: Check for fuel delivery to the throttle body as described below.

> **Tools:** Pliers, screwdrivers and wrenches as needed, jumper wires, test light.
> **Materials:** Lubricating solvent, jar, cloth.

Checking EFI systems

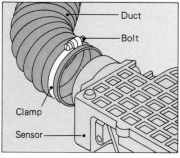

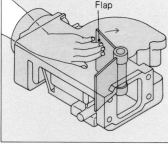

1. In systems that use the airflow sensor, disconnect air duct from the sensor. Loosen bolt on duct clamp, and lift duct away from opening of airflow sensor.

2. Push sensor flap with your hand. Free a stuck flap with solvent. If pump does not work when flap is pushed with ignition on, flap switch is probably faulty.

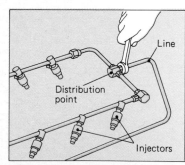

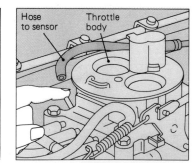

3. To test fuel delivery, look for Schrader valve at distribution point, or loosen line until fuel gushes. Catch fuel with cloth packed around fuel line.

4. To check manifold-pressure sensor, pull sensor hose off intake manifold port, and cover port with a finger. If running engine stalls, sensor is working.

EFI temperature sensor

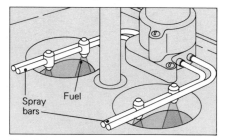

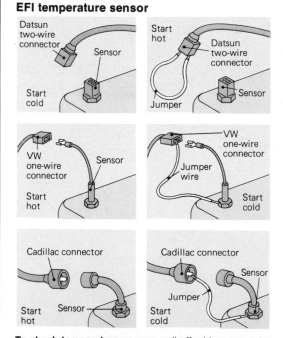

To check temperature sensor, pull off wiring connector, let it dangle, and either connect jumper wire as illustrated or omit the wire. Method chosen depends on whether sensor has one or two terminals, and whether engine is started cold or hot. If engine starts, sensor is bad.

Throttle body injection

Chrysler cars: Remove air cleaner cover and have a helper turn on the ignition as you look into the throttle body. Fuel should squirt from the spray bars. If there is no fuel, check for a plugged fuel filter (p.261). If the filter is OK, check for fuel delivery at the Schrader valve.

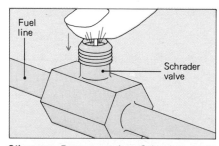

Other cars: Remove cap from Schrader valve in fuel line or on throttle body. Press valve while engine is being cranked to see if there is fuel in the line. If there is none, check the fuel pump, lines (p.397), and filter. If there is fuel, have a mechanic check throttle body.

Checking CFI systems on VWs

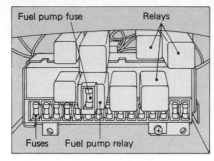

Fuel pump fuse — Relays

Fuses — Fuel pump relay

1. Unplug fuel pump's relay from fuse and relay panel under the dashboard. Plug a jumper wire into terminals 13 and 14 on the panel, as illustrated in the picture at the right. (Terminals are not numbered on 1981 VWs.) This enables the fuel pump to operate when the engine is off.

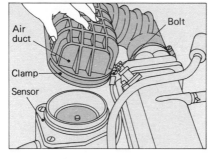

Air duct — Bolt

Clamp

Sensor

2. Remove air duct from top of the airflow sensor to gain access to the sensor plate. Loosen bolt that secures duct clamp, and lift duct up and away from the sensor.

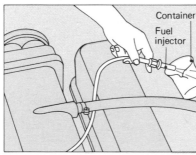

Container

Fuel injector

3. Remove a fuel injector and aim it into a jar. Injector will either be a push-fit type or be held in place by a screw. Take out screw (if any) and pull injector off engine.

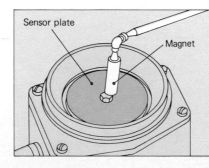

Sensor plate

Magnet

4. Lift airflow sensor plate with a magnet. Fuel delivery is OK if injector sprays when plate is lifted. If there is no spray, check other injectors. If most injectors spray, replace those that do not spray or do not spray properly (right). If no injectors spray, check the fuel filter, lines, and pump.

VW cold-start injector and thermal time switch

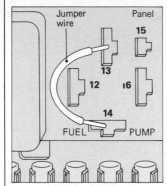

Jumper wire — Panel

15

13

12   16

14

FUEL   PUMP

1. Remove fuel pump's relay from fuse panel under dashboard. Plug jumper wire into terminals 13 and 14 on panel. (Omit this step on EFI systems in VW Beetles.)

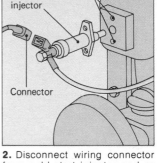

Remove screws

Cold-start injector

Connector

2. Disconnect wiring connector from cold-start injector and remove injector. Connect jumpers between injector terminals and ignition coil and ground (Step 3).

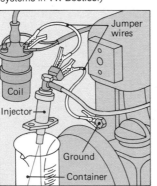

Jumper wires

Coil

Injector

Ground

Container

3. Aim injector into container. Lift airflow plate. On VW Beetles, open air sensor flap (opposite page). Check injector spray (below); replace injector if spray is poor.

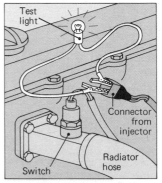

Test light

Connector from injector

Radiator hose

Switch

4. To test thermal time switch, remove and connect test light to connector. Ground ignition (p.263) and operate starter. If test light turns on briefly, time switch is OK.

Fuel-injector spray

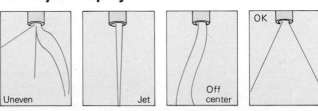

Uneven | Jet | Off center | OK

Injectors should produce a fine, cone-shaped spray as shown at the right. A poor spray pattern will cause engine to stumble, lose power.

Safety precautions

Work in an open area where vapor will disperse, not in a closed room.

Never work near a source of flame or electrical sparks, including furnaces, fuse boxes, or light switches.

Wipe up any spills immediately and put the soaked rags in a closed metal container.

Keep a fire extinguisher on hand to use in case a fuel spill ignites.

Disconnect the battery ground (—) cable to prevent accidental sparking that can ignite fuel vapors (unless you are performing electrical tests).

Remove fuel tank filler cap to release pressure, which could cause gasoline to spurt from fittings as they are disconnected. Have rags ready to wipe up spills immediately. Wash gasoline off skin promptly. Put all fuel-soaked rags in a closed metal container.

Use golf tees or pencil stubs to plug fuel lines as they are disconnected.

Replacing spark plug cables 🔧🔧 20 min–1 hr

Make your selection of replacement spark plug cables after carefully considering the available choices.

Cables are available with three types of rubber insulating jackets: neoprene, hypalon, and silicone. Silicone has the greatest heat resistance and is used as original equipment in late-model cars whose pollution-controlled engines tend to run hot. Hypalon is all right for older cars, particularly if the boots at the spark plug ends of the cables (the areas of greatest heat) are of silicone rubber. Neoprene is the lowest priced, and although it may survive for a while with silicone rubber boots, it may also have a short life and cause engine misfiring. All-silicone cables (jacket and boots) are the most expensive, but their normally long life means that if one cable fails, you need replace only that one; the failure does not indicate that the other cables are nearing the end of their useful lives. Individual silicone cables are available.

Cables are also available with different types of conductors. Conductors made of carbon-impregnated fabric are fragile; you must handle the cable very carefully to avoid internal damage. Some cables have conductors made of aramid (a very strong fiber) or shielded metal wire (see p.71). These cables can take more abuse than fabric-core cables do.

There are three types of replacement cable kits: *full-custom, semi-custom,* and *wire roll.* A full-custom kit is the most expensive, but its terminals are factory-attached at both ends and the cable lengths are very close to the originals, which simplifies installation. On semi-custom kits, the terminals are factory-fitted at the spark plug ends of the cables, which are more critical because they are removed more often and subject to more abuse than the distributor ends. You must trim the distributor end of the cable to the proper length and manually attach a terminal to that end (right).

Wire roll is the least expensive cable, but installing it requires skill and, often, special tools. You cut lengths of cable from the roll and attach terminals to both ends. Unfortunately, the reliability of a manually attached spark plug terminal is limited. This is particularly true of most modern cables, in which the electrically conductive core is not metallic. Never buy a plug cable kit with an unshielded metal-core conductor (non-resistance type), regardless of the kind of insulating jacket or boot.

Types of terminals and boots

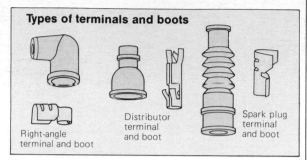

Right-angle terminal and boot

Distributor terminal and boot

Spark plug terminal and boot

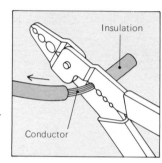

Insulation

Conductor

1. Use a wire stripper or multi-purpose tool to remove insulation. Employ slot that matches the diameter of the conducting core of the cable. (Do not cut the conductor itself; smoothly strip away enough insulation to expose ½ to ¾ in. of conductor.) If you are using a wire roll kit or semi-custom kit, first cut new cables to the lengths of the old cables.

Terminal

Boot

Conductor

Cable

2. Slide the rubber boot onto the cable and push it an inch or two up from the end, to provide room for manipulating the conductor and terminal. Fold back the conductor, then slip the terminal sleeve over the cable so that it makes contact with the conductor. Both boot and terminal may have to be forced.

Crimp tabs on terminal with multi-purpose tool

3. Crimp the metal terminal sleeve firmly to the cable; the conductor should be held tightly in place between the terminal sleeve and the insulating cover of the cable. The reliability of a manually attached terminal at the frequently handled spark plug end is questionable; buy semi-custom kits with factory-attached spark plug terminals.

Replacing distributor parts 🔧🔧🔧

This section covers distributor rotors and vacuum- and centrifugal-timing control units. A screwdriver and pliers are usually the only tools needed to replace distributor components. An alignment tool needed to replace the rotor on Ford electronic ignition systems is described in the captions below.

More information on removing and installing distributor parts is contained on pages 222–231 and 414–425. Instructions for removing and replacing the entire distributor appear on pages 410–413. To diagnose a malfunctioning distributor, refer to *Troubleshooting the engine,* pp.386–387.

Ford electronic ignition rotor

A special rotor alignment tool is needed to remove and install distributors of Ford cars with Electronic Engine Control (EEC) systems. This tool can be purchased from a Ford, Mercury, or Lincoln dealer. For EEC I and EEC II systems (1978–79) the tool part number is T-78P-12200-A. For the EEC III system (1980 and later models) the tool part number is T-79P-12200-A.

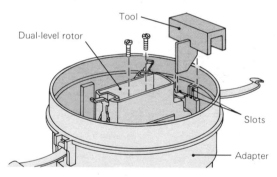

Tool

Dual-level rotor

Slots

Adapter

1. Unlatch and remove distributor cap and put it aside.
2. Rotate crankshaft by hand (p.275) or by cranking the engine until slot of upper distributor rotor blade aligns with slot in distributor adapter.
3. Drop rotor alignment tool in place between two slots.
4. Remove mounting screws, alignment tool, and rotor.
Caution: Do not loosen distributor or turn over engine until rotor is reinstalled.
5. To reinstall rotor, place it on distributor shaft with slot in upper rotor blade opposite slot in distributor housing. Reinstall but do not fully tighten mounting screws.
6. Drop rotor alignment tool in place to make sure of alignment. If the rotor is not aligned, turn it slightly until the alignment tool drops into place.
7. Tighten the rotor's mounting screws.
8. Remove alignment tool and install the distributor cap.

Replacing vacuum control units ☑☑☑ 20–40 min

Except for Toyota, shown at right, the vacuum control unit is replaced in basically the same way in all cars, whether the distributor operates electronically or by means of breaker points. To replace vacuum control unit, proceed as follows.

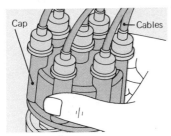

1. Remove distributor cap, with cables attached, and push it aside.

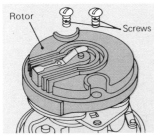

2. Remove distributor rotor by unscrewing its mounting screws (if any) and pulling the rotor straight up.

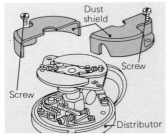

3. In various AMC cars there is a dust shield under the rotor. In some GM models there is an RF (radio frequency) shield to prevent interference with radio reception from the ignition. Remove screws from any such shield or cover and lift it off.

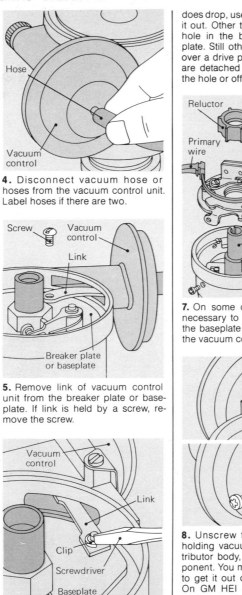

4. Disconnect vacuum hose or hoses from the vacuum control unit. Label hoses if there are two.

5. Remove link of vacuum control unit from the breaker plate or baseplate. If link is held by a screw, remove the screw.

6. If link is held by a retaining clip, pry clip off the drive pin. Be careful not to drop clip into distributor. If clip

does drop, use a small magnet to fish it out. Other types of links fit into a hole in the breaker plate or baseplate. Still others have tangs that fit over a drive pin on the plate. These are detached by lifting them out of the hole or off the drive pin.

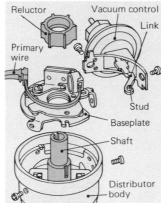

7. On some distributors it may be necessary to disconnect or remove the baseplate in order to disengage the vacuum control link.

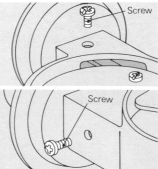

8. Unscrew the screw or screws holding vacuum control unit to distributor body, and remove the component. You may have to tip the unit to get it out of the distributor body. On GM HEI distributors, turn the pickup coil clockwise and push down the vacuum control link to disengage link from pickup coil plate.

To reinstall the vacuum control unit, reverse the above steps.

Toyota vacuum control unit

If your Toyota distributor has breaker points, proceed as follows.

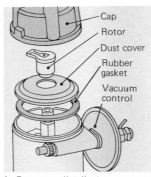

1. Remove distributor cap, with cables attached, and push it aside.
2. Pull off distributor rotor.
3. Remove metal dust cover and rubber gasket.

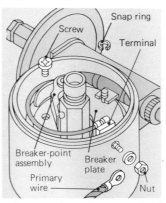

4. Loosen nut on primary wire terminal on outside of distributor body. Detach breaker-point assembly wire from the terminal inside distributor.
5. Remove snap ring from breaker arm pivot and remove contact point screw on the breaker plate. Remove breaker-point assembly.
6. If vacuum control unit has a cap, remove it. Unscrew vacuum control unit's retaining screw. Disengage vacuum control unit from pin on breaker plate, then remove unit.

To reinstall the vacuum control unit, reverse the above steps.

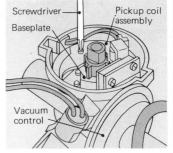

To remove the vacuum control unit from a Toyota electronic ignition distributor, follow the general procedures described for a Toyota distributor with breaker points. However, this distributor is equipped with a pickup coil assembly (signal generator) rather than breaker points. After removing the rotor and dust shield, unscrew pickup coil assembly from the baseplate and remove the coil assembly. Then remove vacuum control unit as explained at left.

Replacing centrifugal advance springs

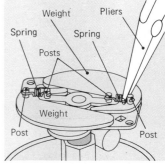

If the centrifugal advance springs are weak or broken, they should be replaced. The springs are simply lifted off the centrifugal advance weights with long-nose pliers. To reach the weights on most Delco breaker-point and HEI distributors, remove cap and rotor (p.228). To reach the weights on other distributors, you must remove the distributor's baseplate. Hook the new springs securely onto the correct posts, then reassemble distributor.

Removing the distributor ⏱ ⏱ 15–30 min

Depending on the position of the distributor in the engine compartment, it may be easier to replace components (see pp.408–409) by removing the distributor and placing it on a workbench. The general procedure illustrated on this page is used to remove both breaker-point and electronic-ignition distributors on most cars, whether the distributor is being repaired or being replaced with a new one. Models that require variations from this procedure are discussed on pages 412–413.

Tools: Set of open-end or box-end wrenches, distributor wrench or socket set with extension (if needed), pliers, screwdriver, awl or file.

1. Disconnect ground (−) cable from its terminal on the battery. If the air cleaner blocks access to the distributor, remove it from the engine (pp.240–241) and set it aside.

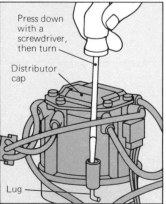

2. Use a screwdriver to pry open the latches on the distributor cap or to open the hold-down lugs. Remove the distributor cap and push it aside; do not disconnect any of the cables from the cap at this time.

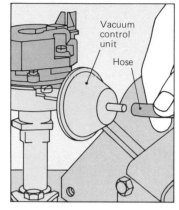

3. Disconnect the vacuum hose (or hoses) from distributor's vacuum control unit(s) by pulling it off. Check the hose for cracks; breaks as small as a pinhole can diminish the effect of the vacuum. Replace any hose that is worn or damaged.

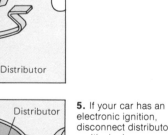

4. If your car has a breaker-point distributor, disconnect the primary ignition wire (for electronic ignitions, see Step 5). You can disconnect the wire either at the ignition coil or at the distributor, whichever location is more convenient.

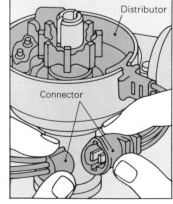

5. If your car has an electronic ignition, disconnect distributor's multi-wire harness connector. It may be attached directly to the distributor or to another harness extending from the side of the distributor (as shown).

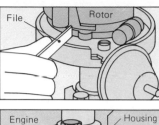

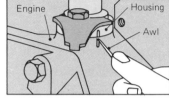

6. Etch a mark on the distributor housing in line with the tip of the rotor. Use an awl or a file. Etch a second mark along the distributor housing and continue it onto the engine block. These marks will ensure that realignment is perfect when you reinstall the distributor. When replacing a distributor, transcribe these marks to the new unit. Also note part of engine compartment at which the rotor is pointing.

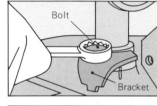

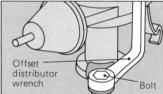

7. Loosen and remove distributor's hold-down bolt. You may be able to use a conventional box-end or open-end wrench, or it may be necessary to employ an offset distributor wrench or a socket and extensions to reach the bolt. If there is a lock washer, remove it and set it aside. Do the same with any bracket that is part of the hold-down assembly.

8. Lift the distributor carefully from the engine. Once the distributor has been removed, check to see if a gasket or an O-ring remains in the distributor's vacant bore in the engine (it may also be clinging to the distributor shaft). Remove and discard the gasket or O-ring. Cover the bore to keep dirt from entering the engine.

Installing the distributor ⏻⏻⏻ 15 min–1 hr

When installing a distributor, you must align it perfectly with the engine. If you are reinstalling a distributor that has been repaired, line up the marks you scribed before removing it from the car (opposite page). Transfer these marks onto a replacement distributor in exactly the same places. It may be hard to mesh the distributor's drive gear and the oil pump drive simultaneously. If you cannot seat the distributor so that its rotor is properly aligned (Steps 3-5), remove it and try again.

Caution: Do not crank the engine (operate the starter) while the distributor is removed from the car or it may be impossible to start the engine.

Car models that require variations from these general procedures are covered on pages 413–414.

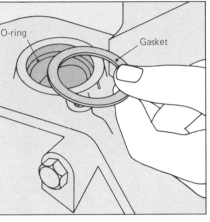

1. If you have a can of compressed air, begin by blowing dirt from the distributor's bore in the engine. Direct the airstream so that dirt is blown away from the engine. A small, dry brush can be used instead of air; brush dirt away from bore.

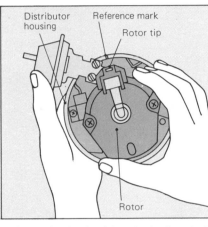

2. If the distributor had a mounting gasket or an O-ring around its shaft (see Step 8, opposite page), place a new gasket or O-ring in the bore of the engine. Use only the replacement parts recommended by distributor's manufacturer.

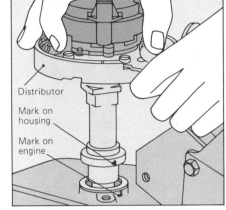

3. Check that the tip of the rotor is aligned with its reference mark on the distributor housing (see Step 6, opposite page). On a new distributor, transcribe this mark in precisely the same spot and align the rotor with it.

4. As you slowly seat distributor, line up marks on housing and engine. Transcribe the marks from your old distributor to a new distributor. Rotor should point in same direction as it did when the old distributor was removed.

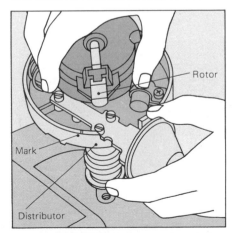

5. To seat new distributor, you may have to turn the rotor slightly to mesh the gear on the shaft with its drive gear inside the engine. The rotor should swing back into alignment with its mark on the housing as the distributor is seated.

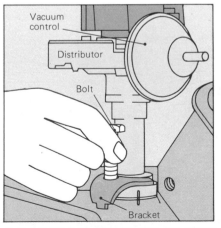

6. Install the hold-down bracket, but do not tighten the bolt fully. Reconnect the primary ignition wire or the multi-wire connector to the distributor. When you attach the distributor cap, be careful not to rotate the distributor.

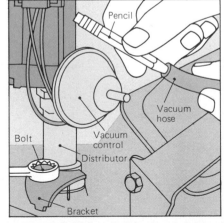

7. With the hold-down bolt in place but not yet tightened and the vacuum hose (or hoses) still unattached, connect a timing light to the engine. Plug the open vacuum hoses. Start the engine and adjust the timing (see pp.236–239).

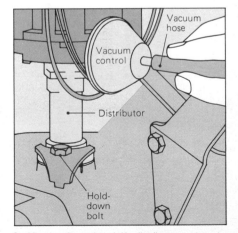

8. After you have timed the distributor and made any necessary adjustments, tighten the hold-down bolt. Reconnect vacuum hose(s) to vacuum control unit(s). Reinstall any components that were removed to reach distributor.

411

Replacing distributors: exceptions to the general procedure ⚡⚡⚡ 15 min–1 hr

Chrysler/Mitsubishi

Cars with distributors that are replaced differently than those shown on pages 410–411 are Arrow, Challenger, Colt, and Sapporo. Their distributors are mounted horizontally on the engine, not vertically, as is usual on most cars. Reference marks have been provided by the manufacturer on most Chrysler/Mitsubishi models.

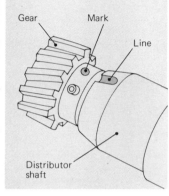

To remove the distributor from an Arrow, Challenger, Colt, or Sapporo, proceed as follows:
1. If there is no mark on the distributor's mounting flange (see Step 3), scribe a mark with an awl or file directly above the mounting stud.
2. Turn the nut on the crankshaft pulley clockwise with a wrench until the timing marks are lined up and the rotor points to the terminal for the No.1 spark plug. (Lift the distributor cap to see the rotor.) Remove the distributor from the engine.

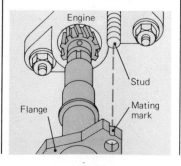

Do not operate the starter or turn the crankshaft pulley while the distributor is out of the engine. To reinstall the distributor:
1. Turn the distributor shaft so that the line on the lower end of the distributor body aligns with the punch mark just above the distributor's drive gear.
2. Slide distributor into the engine.
3. To seat the distributor, align the mark on the distributor's mounting flange with the center of the mounting stud. Install the mounting nut and check the ignition timing (pp.236–239).

Datsun

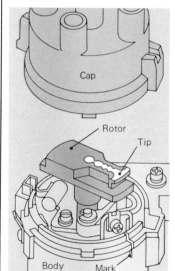

1. To remove the distributor, first disconnect the ground (−) cable from the battery. Then, trace the cable from the spark plug of the No.1 cylinder to the distributor cap. Make a mark on the distributor body in line with the tower for the No.1 cable.
2. Remove the distributor cap.
3. Crank the engine until the tip of the rotor is aligned with your mark on the distributor body.
4. Loosen the distributor's hold-down bolt and remove the distributor as described in the general procedure on page 410.

To install a Datsun distributor, align the tip of the rotor with the mark on the distributor body. Slide the distributor into the engine and proceed as described under the general procedure on page 411.

Ford four- and six-cylinder engines with electronic ignition

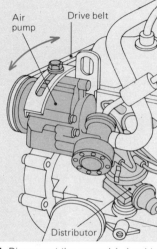

1. Disconnect the ground (−) cable from its terminal on the battery. If the engine is an in-line four- or six-cylinder equipped with an air pump, remove one mounting bolt from the pump, take off the drive belt, and swing the pump to one side to gain access to the distributor.
2. Remove the high-tension cable from the coil and ground it on the engine (p.263). Crank the engine to align its specified timing marks (see *Tuneup Data* supplement). The timing marks must be aligned before you remove the distributor; this can also be done by turning the crankshaft pulley with a wrench (p.275).
3. Remove the distributor as described under the general procedure beginning with Step 2 on page 410. The oil pump's drive shaft fits into a hexagonal recess in the bottom of the distributor shaft and may come out of the engine with the distributor. Retrieve this shaft.

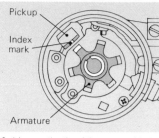

4. Line up the tip of the rotor with the mark you scribed on the body of the distributor (Step 6, p.410); a tooth of the armature should now be in alignment with the manufacturer's index mark on top of the magnetic pickup. To install the distributor, coat one end of the oil pump's drive shaft with heavy grease. Reinsert the shaft, greased end first, into its recess in the distributor shaft (see Step 3, above). Slide the distributor fully into the engine, so that the oil pump's drive shaft seats properly in the oil pump. Complete installation by following the general procedure described on page 411. Reinstall the air pump belt and bolt.

Ford Electronic Engine Control (EEC) systems

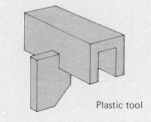

Plastic tool

A special rotor-alignment tool is recommended to remove and install distributors of Ford cars with Electronic Engine Control systems. This tool can be purchased from a Ford, Mercury, or Lincoln dealer. For EEC I and EEC II systems (1978 and 1979) the tool part number is T-78P-12200-A. For the EEC III system (1980 and later models) the tool part number is T-79P-12200-A. You may be able to use a screwdriver if the alignment tool is not available.

Ford EEC I and EEC II systems

1. To remove the distributor, disconnect the ground (−) cable from the battery. Then unlatch the distributor cap and set it aside.

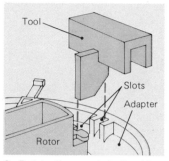

2. Rotate the crankshaft with a wrench (p.275) to bring the slot of the distributor rotor's upper blade into alignment with the slot in the distributor's adapter. Drop the rotor-alignment tool into the two slots.
3. Loosen the distributor's hold-down bolt and clamp as shown on page 410. Remove alignment tool.
4. Slowly withdraw the distributor from the engine. When you feel the distributor's drive gear disengage from the cam in the engine, note the position of one of the rotor blades with respect to distributor base. Mark this position on distributor body for reference during reinstallation.

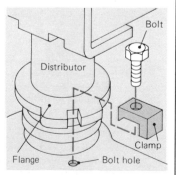

5. To install the distributor, insert it into the engine in such a way that the rotor blade is in the approximate position you marked after withdrawing the distributor (Step 4). Make sure that the slot on the mounting flange of the distributor base lines up with the hold-down clamp's bolt hole in the block. At the same time, the slot in rotor's upper blade must align with slot in distributor's adapter.

6. If rotor and adapter slots are not aligned once the distributor is in the engine, lift the distributor enough to disengage the cam. Rotate the distributor shaft just enough to permit the next tooth on the drive gear to engage the cam. Check the slot alignment. Repeat the procedure until the slots line up.

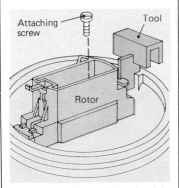

7. Complete the installation by tightening the hold-down bolt (p.411). Drop rotor-alignment tool into place to make sure of alignment. If rotor is not aligned, loosen its attaching screws and turn rotor slightly until alignment tool drops into place. Then install and tighten rotor's attaching screws. Remove alignment tool and install the distributor cap.

Ford EEC III systems

1. To remove the distributor, first disconnect the ground (−) cable from the battery. Then, remove the distributor cap and set it aside.
2. Remove the rotor.
3. Crank the engine or rotate the crankshaft with a wrench (p.275) to bring the specified engine timing marks into alignment (see *Tuneup Data* supplement).
4. Remove distributor's hold-down bolt and clamp (see p.410, Step 7).

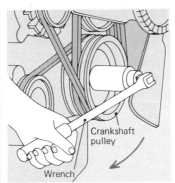

5. Slowly withdraw the distributor from the engine. As the distributor drive gear and cam disengage, note the relative positions of the larger slot in the distributor shaft's sleeve assembly and the alignment slot in the distributor's adapter.

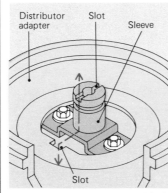

6. To install the distributor, slide it into the engine so that the sleeve assembly and adapter slots are in alignment. The slot on the hold-down flange of the distributor base must align with the clamp's bolt hole in the engine. If these alignment conditions are not met when the distributor is fully seated, lift the distributor out of the engine just enough to disengage the drive gear and cam. Rotate the distributor shaft slightly by hand to allow the next tooth of the drive gear to engage the cam. If all slots are still not aligned, repeat this procedure until correct alignment is achieved.

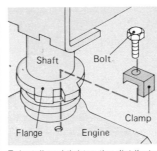

7. Install and tighten the distributor's hold-down clamp and bolt. Drop rotor-alignment tool into the slots of the sleeve assembly and adapter. If the tool does not fit, loosen the two sleeve assembly screws and rotate the sleeve until the tool fits into the alignment slots. Tighten the screws and remove the alignment tool. Install the distributor cap.

Ford Fiesta

It is not necessary to make alignment marks when removing the distributor from a Fiesta; otherwise, removal is performed as described under the general procedure shown on page 410. To install the distributor of a Fiesta, proceed as follows:

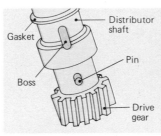

1. Use a wrench to rotate the crankshaft clockwise (p.275) until the notch on the crankshaft pulley lines up with the 12° timing mark on the engine's front cover.
2. After checking that the distributor gasket is in place, align the projecting end of the pin (which holds the drive gear) with the boss in the distributor body. Slide the distributor into the engine and complete installation as described under the general procedure on page 411.

Honda

To remove the distributor, proceed as described under the general procedure on page 410; it is not necessary to scribe alignment marks, since the distributor comes with manufacturer's marks.
To install the distributor:
1. Remove the spark plug from No.1 cylinder and turn the crankshaft with a wrench (p.275) until No.1 piston is at top dead center (TDC).

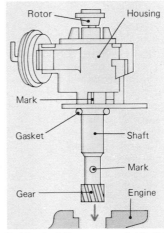

2. After installing a new distributor gasket, line up the mark on the distributor gear's shoulder with the mark on the distributor housing.
3. Slide the distributor straight into the engine.
4. Install the hold-down bolt loosely (see p.410).
5. Install the distributor cap so that the mark on the cap is in line with the rotor (see p.410).
6. Adjust timing and tighten the distributor hold-down bolt.

Toyota

Other than setting the timing mark on the crankshaft pulley to 0° (see p.236), removing and installing the Toyota distributor is the same as described under the general procedure on pages 410–411. To set the timing mark, turn the crankshaft pulley with a wrench (p.275).

VW Beetle

To remove the distributor:
1. Remove the distributor cap and set it aside.
2. Engage the crankshaft pulley nut with a wrench (p.275) and turn the crankshaft until the tip of the distributor rotor points to the notch (the No.1 cylinder mark) cut in the distributor housing.
3. Disconnect ignition coil's primary wire and vacuum hose(s) (p.410).
4. Remove the bolt that holds the distributor bracket, and lift the distributor out of the engine.
5. To install the distributor, reverse this procedure.

VW Rabbit and Scirocco

Remove the distributor the same way as for VW Beetle. To reinstall it:
1. Check to see that the lug on the oil pump's drive shaft is parallel to the engine crankshaft. If it is not, use a screwdriver to get lug into position.
2. Reinstall the washer in the opening of the distributor shaft.
3. Turn the rotor clockwise until the tip of rotor is about 18 degrees past the No.1 cylinder mark cut in the distributor housing.

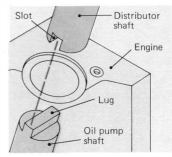

4. Slide the distributor into the engine. As the gears mesh, rotor will turn counterclockwise about 18 degrees, and the lug on the oil pump's drive shaft will engage slot in the lower end of distributor shaft. The rotor should now be aligned with the notch on the distributor housing; if not, withdraw distributor and try again.
5. Complete the installation by attaching wires and hoses, setting timing, and tightening hold-down bolt.

Repair/ Electronic ignition

General troubleshooting ⏱ 5–10 min

When an electronic ignition system (see pp.68–69) is not performing properly, one of the following conditions usually occurs:

1. The engine backfires but fails to start.

2. The engine runs roughly at idle or low speed.

3. The engine misfires at higher speeds.

4. The engine fails to start. Unless the ignition switch circuit is also defective, the starter cranks briskly, ruling out a bad battery or a problem with the starter motor, the battery-to-starter cables, the starter relay, or the starter solenoid.

5. The engine runs well when it is cold but runs roughly or stalls when it warms up.

The causes of conditions 1 and 2 are not usually related to the electronic components in the ignition. If an engine backfires but fails to start, the trouble, if it is ignition related, is most often caused by the distributor cap. Look for moisture inside the distributor cap, or a damaged cap.

If an ignition problem is causing the engine to run roughly at idle or low speeds, or to misfire at higher speeds, the most likely problems are fouled or damaged spark plugs (see p.232), defective spark plug cables (p.231), a malfunctioning vacuum advance diaphram (p.408), or incorrect ignition timing (p.236).

This leaves conditions 4 and 5—failure to start or rough running only at normal operating temperatures. Since malfunctions in the fuel system can produce the same conditions, the trouble must be traced to the ignition system before repairs are attempted. Methods of testing popular electronic ignition systems are outlined on the following pages.

However, there are three ignition parts that can be checked quickly, without any tests: the distributor cap, the rotor, and the various wire and cable connections in the ignition system. The coil and electronic control unit of the most popular GM Delco electronic ignition system are in the distributor (right). Remove the cap to test connections.

Caution: If you must replace the distributor cap or rotor, be sure to get the correct parts for your make and model car. Other parts may fit, but the use of the wrong part will result in poor engine performance, continued problems, and possible damage.

Tools: Screwdriver (to remove distributor cap), timing light, spark plug wrench, volt-ohm meter (to check the non-electronic portions of the system: ignition timing, spark plugs, spark plug cables, and advance mechanism).

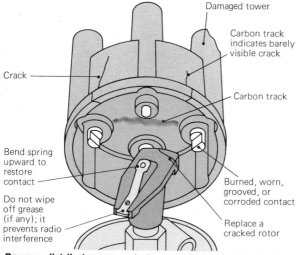

Remove distributor cap and wipe away moisture with a lint-free towel. Replace the cap and rotor if either is cracked, has carbon tracks, or terminals that are worn, burned, or coated with heavy scale. Light scale can be scraped off with a knife.

Labels: Damaged tower; Carbon track indicates barely visible crack; Crack; Carbon track; Bend spring upward to restore contact; Do not wipe off grease (if any); it prevents radio interference; Burned, worn, grooved, or corroded contact; Replace a cracked rotor

Check all connections under the hood to make sure they are tight, including those at the distributor, ignition coil, spark plugs, battery, starter relay, and electronic control unit. If all connections are tight, open one at a time and clean off any corrosion.

Labels: Connectors; Electronic control unit; Coil; Starter relay; Distributor; Spark plug; Battery

GM's Delco HEI system

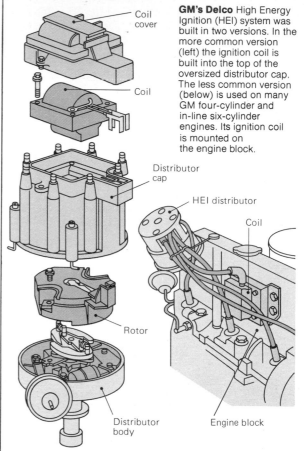

GM's Delco High Energy Ignition (HEI) system was built in two versions. In the more common version (left) the ignition coil is built into the top of the oversized distributor cap. The less common version (below) is used on many GM four-cylinder and in-line six-cylinder engines. Its ignition coil is mounted on the engine block.

Labels: Coil cover; Coil; Distributor cap; HEI distributor; Coil; Rotor; Distributor body; Engine block

GM installed the Delco HEI system on some of its 1974 models and on all of its cars from 1975 onward. The version with the coil built into the distributor cap is found on V-6 and V-8 engines from 1975 onward, on many four-cylinder and in-line six-cylinder engines, and on AMC four-cylinder cars from 1980 onward. If a car with the HEI system does not start, first see the *General troubleshooting* instructions (left). If the HEI system has a built-in coil, follow Steps 1–6 and 10–14 (opposite page). If system has a separate coil, see Steps 1–4 and 7–14. These steps do not apply to cars with electronic fuel injection, Computer-Controlled Catalytic Converter (C-4), or Computer Command Control systems.

Tools: Volt-ohm meter, electronic ignition tester, screwdrivers, ¼-in. socket or nut driver, long-nose pliers, insulated spark plug cable forceps, hand-held vacuum pump, paper clip.

Material: Electrically conductive grease—GE Dielectric Heat Transfer Compound (G642), Dow Corning Heat Sink Compound 341, Dow Corning 5 Compound, or equivalent.

Troubleshooting the Delco HEI system ☑☑☑ 30 min–1 hr

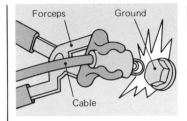

Forceps Ground

Cable

1. Remove any convenient spark plug cable from its plug and force a paper clip into the boot far enough to make contact with the metal terminal inside the boot. Using insulated spark plug cable forceps, hold the paper clip ½ in. away from any clean, dry ground on the engine. (**Caution:** Do not hold the cable or paper clip in your hand, or you may get a shock.) Have a helper crank the engine. If a spark jumps the gap, the HEI system is OK. Check the fuel system for faults (pp.386–387). If there is no spark, proceed to Step 2.

2. Make sure that the multi-wire connector is firmly attached at the distributor cap, that the pink power supply wire is attached to the BAT terminal, and that all spark plug cables are firmly secured. Check the battery cranking voltage (p.278), which should be 9 volts or more. Recharge or replace a weak battery.

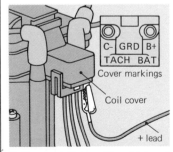

C | GRD | B+
TACH | BAT
Cover markings

Coil cover

+ lead

3. Connect the positive (+) voltmeter lead to the BAT terminal of the distributor. Attach the negative (−) lead to a clean ground on the engine. Turn on the ignition. If the voltmeter reads zero, the circuit between the battery and the BAT terminal is open. Trace the wiring for faults (p.361). If the voltmeter shows any voltage, see Step 4.

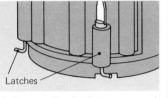

Latches

4. Remove the distributor cap; push down each of the four latches with a screwdriver and rotate it 180 degrees. (**Caution:** To avoid breaking the carbon rotor button in the top of the cap, lift the cap straight up; do not angle it sideways. When reinstalling the cap, lower it straight down onto the distributor body.) Inspect the inside of the cap and the rotor for damage (opposite page). Replace any damaged parts.

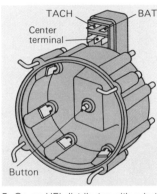

TACH   BAT
Center
terminal

Button

5. On an HEI distributor with a built-in coil, disconnect the battery wire harness from the distributor cap connector. Set the ohmmeter to the *Low* scale (p.173). Connect the meter probes to BAT and TACH terminals. If the meter reads between 0 and 1 ohm, proceed to Step 6. If it reads more than 1 ohm, replace the ignition coil (far right).

6. Set the ohmmeter to the *High* scale (p.173). Connect one probe to the carbon button at the center of the distributor cap and the other probe to the TACH terminal. Note the reading. Switch one probe from TACH terminal to center terminal. Note the reading. If the meter reads infinity for *both* tests, replace the coil (right). Otherwise, proceed to Step 10.

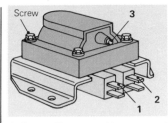

Screw   3

1   2

7. On an HEI system with an external coil, disconnect coil from distributor-to-coil cable and unplug the multi-wire connector from the coil. Set the ohmmeter to the *High* scale. Attach one meter probe to the coil's mounting screw and the other probe to connector terminal 1. If the meter reads infinity, proceed to Step 8. If the meter does not read infinity, replace the ignition coil (right).

8. Set ohmmeter to *Low* scale. Attach probes to connector terminals 1 and 2. If the meter reads 0 to 1 ohm, proceed to Step 9. If the meter reads more than 1 ohm, replace the coil.

9. Set ohmmeter to *High* scale. Connect probes to terminals 2 and 3. If the meter reads infinity, replace the coil. If not, proceed to Step 10.

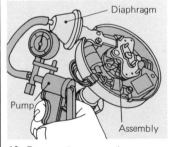

Diaphragm

Pump

Assembly

10. Remove two mounting screws and rotor. Disconnect hose from vacuum diaphragm and connect hand-held vacuum pump. Squeeze pump handles to apply vacuum to diaphragm chamber. If the pole piece and pickup assembly do not rotate as vacuum is applied, unscrew diaphragm unit and replace it. Check wires from pickup to module for tightness. Open connectors and clean any corrosion from their terminals. Repair or replace any wire that has worn insulation.

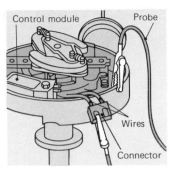

Control module   Probe

Wires

Connector

11. Disconnect the two pickup coil wires from the control module. Set the ohmmeter to the *High* scale. Clip the meter probes to one pickup coil wire and to the distributor body. Apply vacuum until the pole piece and pickup assembly move through their entire range of travel. If meter reads less than infinity at any time, replace the pickup coil (Step 13).

12. Attach ohmmeter probes to both pickup coil wires. Apply vacuum to move pole piece and pickup through their entire range of travel. If meter reads less than 500 ohms or more than 1,500 ohms, replace pickup coil (Step 13).

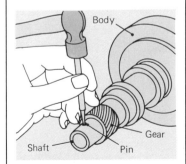

Body

Shaft   Pin   Gear

13. To replace the pickup coil, remove the distributor from the engine (p.410). Drive out the pin that holds the distributor drive gear to the shaft. Remove the rotor, shaft assembly, and pickup coil retainer from the distributor body. Replace the pickup coil and reassemble the distributor. Have a GM dealer or a garage test the distributor on an oscilloscope to make sure that it produces 30,000 volts or more. Reinstall distributor.

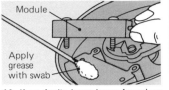

Module

Apply
grease
with swab

14. If no faults have been found so far, check the electronic control module on the car with an electronic ignition tester (which costs less than a new module). Heat module with a hair dryer and test again. If the module is bad, replace it. Do not replace the expensive module, pole piece, or pickup assembly unless you are sure all ignition wiring connections are tight and free of corrosion. Apply electrically conductive grease to underside of module before reinstalling.

Replacing the ignition coil

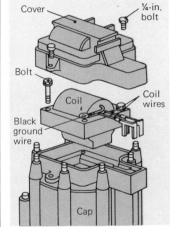

Cover   ¼-in.
                             bolt

Bolt

                        Coil
                        wires

Black
ground
wire

Coil

Cap

Remove ¼-in. bolts between distributor towers. Remove coil cover. Use long-nose pliers to unplug coil wires from distributor cap. Lift out coil. Place new coil into cavity in cap. Push coil wires into terminals in cap without crossing them (left-hand wire into left-hand terminal, etc.). Place the center (black) ground wire under one of the mounting bolts. Install four bolts that hold coil to cap. Install coil cover and its hold-down bolts. Plug in multi-wire connector.

Troubleshooting the AMC BID system 🔧🔧🔧 30 min–1 hr

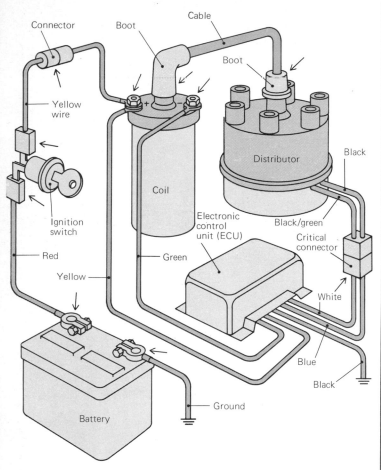

Connector
Boot
Cable
Boot
Yellow wire
Coil
Distributor
Black
Ignition switch
Electronic control unit (ECU)
Black/green
Critical connector
Red
Green
White
Yellow
Blue
Black
Battery
Ground

American Motors' Breakerless Inductive Discharge (BID) system is found on 1975–77 AMC cars and Jeeps with V-8 and six-cylinder engines. A conventional breaker-point distributor is used on 1977–79 four-cylinder cars. The Delco HEI system is used on four-cylinder cars and Jeeps from 1980 onward. AMC cars and Jeeps from 1978 onward use the motorcraft SSI system on V-8 and six-cylinder engines.

Before testing the BID system, make sure that the battery is in good condition and fully charged. Next, see *General troubleshooting,* p.414. Then, check all connections (arrows) for tightness and for corrosion on inner surfaces. The critical connector was the subject of a recall campaign and may have been replaced on your car by a new wiring harness. If the connector is missing from your car, you cannot perform Steps 5–7.

Tools: 12- to 18-in. jumper wire, insulated spark plug cable forceps, paper clip, voltmeter, awl, long-nose pliers, test light (p.361).

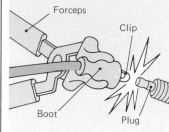

Forceps
Clip
Boot
Plug

1. Disconnect a spark plug cable and force a paper clip into its boot. Grasp the boot with insulated cable forceps and hold the clip about ½ in. from the spark plug terminal. Have a helper crank the engine. If a strong blue spark jumps the gap, the problem is in the distributor sensor, ECU, coil (Steps 7–9) or the fuel system.

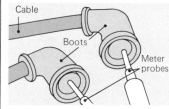

Cable
Boots
Meter probes

2. If no spark occurs in Step 1, reconnect the spark plug cable. Remove the coil-to-distributor cable from the engine. Connect ohmmeter probes to each end of the cable to test its resistance (see p.173). If the resistance is more than 10,000 ohms, replace the cable with a new one and repeat Step 1.

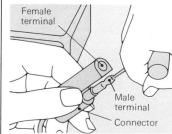

Female terminal
Male terminal
Connector

3. Locate the critical wiring connector between the distributor and the electronic control unit. If the con-

nection is not tight, open the connector. Spread the male terminals open with an awl. Crimp the female terminals closer together with long-nose pliers. Plug the connector halves together, and repeat Step 1.

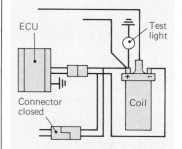

ECU
Test light
Connector closed
Coil

4. If there is still no spark in Step 1, reconnect the cable. Attach a test light between the positive terminal of the coil and a clean ground. Turn the ignition on and then briefly to *Start.* If the test bulb does not light both times, check for a defective ignition switch or a loose wire between the ignition switch and coil.

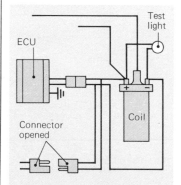

ECU
Test light
Connector opened
Coil

5. If the test bulb lights for both parts of Step 4, turn the ignition off. Connect the test light between the positive and negative coil terminals. Unplug critical connector (see Step 3). Turn on the ignition. If the test bulb does not light, the electronic control unit is probably defective. Replace it with a new unit.

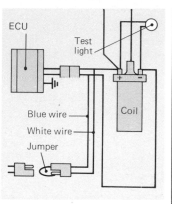

ECU
Test light
Blue wire
White wire
Jumper
Coil

6. If the test bulb lights in Step 5, turn the ignition off but leave the test light in place. Connect the jumper wire across the terminals for the blue and white wires in the critical connector (unplugged during Step 5). Turn on the ignition. If the bulb now lights, the electronic control unit is defective. Replace it.

7. Disconnect one end of the jumper wire placed across the critical connector's terminals in Step 6. Remove the test light. Unplug the coil-to-distributor cable from the distributor. Hold the metal terminal inside the boot ½ in. away from a metal part of the engine, using insulated cable forceps. (**Caution:** If you do not use insulated forceps, you may get a shock. Ordinary pliers can damage the cable.) As a helper cranks the engine, momentarily reconnect the jumper wire across the terminals for the blue and white wires at the unplugged connector. If a spark jumps the gap between the coil cable and the engine, either the ECU or the sensor in the distributor is faulty.

8. Connect an ohmmeter across the terminals for the black and black-and-green wires in the critical connector. (If there is no critical connector, open the connector at the control unit and attach the meter to the terminals for the white and blue wires.) If the meter reads 1 to 4 ohms, replace the ECU. If there is any other reading, replace the sensor inside the distributor (opposite page).

9. If there is no spark in Step 7, replace the ignition coil.

Replacing the BID sensor ☑☑☑ 30 min–1 hr

If Steps 7–8 on the opposite page prove that the sensor in the distributor is defective, it must be replaced with a new unit, available from the parts department of an AMC dealer.

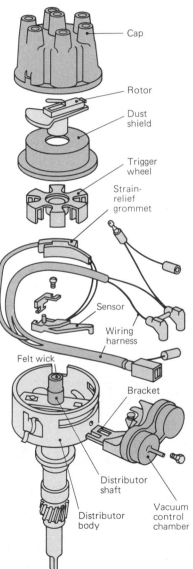

Cap
Rotor
Dust shield
Trigger wheel
Strain-relief grommet
Sensor
Wiring harness
Felt wick
Bracket
Distributor shaft
Distributor body
Vacuum control chamber

Tools: Screwdriver, slip-joint pliers, small gear puller or battery terminal puller, flat washer or coin, chalk or felt-tip pen, deep $^{13}/_{16}$-in. socket, small hammer, timing light.
Materials: SAE 30 motor oil, BID sensor replacement kit.

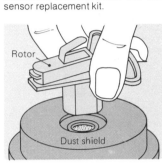

Rotor
Dust shield

1. Remove the air cleaner (p.240) if it blocks access to the distributor. Use a screwdriver to pry open the two clips that lock the distributor cap in place. Remove the distributor cap.
2. Lift off rotor and dust shield. Lay out all parts in the order in which they are removed, to make proper reassembly easier.

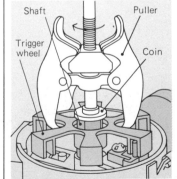

Shaft
Puller
Trigger wheel
Coin

3. Use a gear puller or battery terminal puller to remove trigger wheel. Place a thick washer or a coin on top of distributor shaft. Position puller so that its turn screw rests on the washer or coin and its jaws grip inner shoulders of the trigger wheel. Turn screw clockwise until the jaws pull the trigger wheel free. If the trigger wheel is cracked or damaged, you must buy a new one.

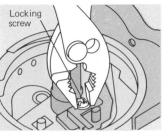

Locking screw

4. Remove the sensor's locking screw. If it is the one originally installed by the manufacturer, the locking screw will have a tamper-proof head; grip this head firmly with pliers and turn it counterclockwise to remove the screw and its washer. Locking screws of replacement sensors have a standard slotted head and are removed with a screwdriver.

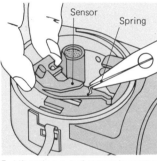

Sensor
Spring

5. Lift spring out of recess in sensor assembly. Slide sensor off bracket on vacuum control chamber. Unplug rubber strain-relief grommet from distributor body, then lift sensor out.

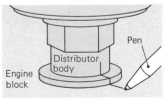

Pen
Distributor body
Engine block

6. Using chalk or a felt-tip pen, draw a line along the lower part of the distributor body and onto the engine block. This line will be used in Step 11 to realign the distributor. Loosen the distributor's hold-down bolt.

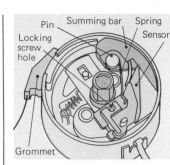

Pin
Locking screw
Summing bar
Spring
Sensor
Locking screw hole
Grommet

7. Position the new sensor on the vacuum control chamber's bracket. Make sure that the sensor's tip fits into the recess in the summing bar. Place the tip of the sensor spring into its recess in the sensor. Route the sensor wire around the sensor spring's pivot pin and press the strain-relief grommet into the notch in the distributor body. The sensor wire must be positioned so that it will not touch the rotating trigger wheel. Install the new washer and the sensor's locking screw, but do not tighten the screw all the way.

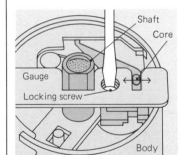

Shaft
Core
Gauge
Locking screw
Body

8. Rotate the distributor body, if necessary, to place the sensor-positioning gauge (supplied with the sensor replacement kit) so that it rests against the flat part of the distributor shaft and surrounds the sensor core. Slide the sensor sideways as necessary to allow the gauge to seat firmly against the upper edge of the distributor. The gauge ensures that the sensor core is the correct distance from the distributor shaft. When the sensor is properly positioned, tighten its locking screw and remove the gauge.

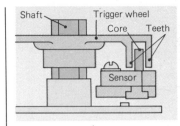

Shaft
Trigger wheel
Core
Teeth
Sensor

9. Put the trigger wheel back in place on the distributor shaft. If the sensor is properly positioned, its core will be centered between the trigger wheel teeth. The rotating trigger wheel must not touch the sensor.

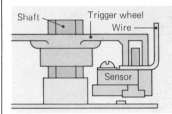

Shaft
Trigger wheel
Wire
Sensor

10. Bend the piece of .050-in. wire in the replacement kit 90 degrees and slide it under a tooth of the trigger wheel so that the wire rests on top of the sensor. Press trigger wheel down until it just rests on the wire. If necessary, place a deep $^{13}/_{16}$-in. socket over the distributor shaft, and tap it lightly with a hammer to seat the trigger wheel. Remove the wire.

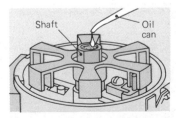

Shaft
Oil can

11. Rotate distributor body until chalk or ink lines from Step 6 are aligned, then tighten distributor hold-down bolt. Apply three drops of SAE 30 oil to felt wick inside the distributor shaft. Reinstall dust shield, rotor, and distributor cap. Set ignition timing to specifications (p.236).

Troubleshooting the Motorcraft SSI system ☑ ☑ ☑ 30 min–1 hr

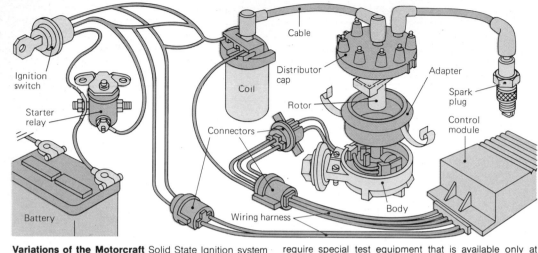

Ignition switch
Starter relay
Battery
Coil
Connectors
Wiring harness
Cable
Distributor cap
Rotor
Adapter
Spark plug
Control module
Body

Repairing the SSI distributor

If the voltmeter needle does not fluctuate in Step 3 at left, the distributor is probably damaged. Inspect the distributor cap and rotor for damage (p.414). To disassemble the distributor and check its magnetic pickup assembly, proceed as follows:

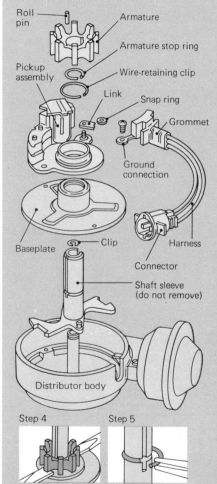

Roll pin
Pickup assembly
Baseplate
Armature
Armature stop ring
Wire-retaining clip
Link
Snap ring
Grommet
Ground connection
Clip
Harness
Connector
Shaft sleeve (do not remove)
Distributor body

Step 4   Step 5

1. Remove air cleaner (if necessary) to gain access to distributor. Remove distributor cap.
2. Remove rotor by pulling it straight up.
3. Push armature. If it moves from side to side, it is worn and must be replaced.
4. Remove armature with a battery terminal puller or by prying it up with two screwdrivers. (**Caution:** Do not lose the tiny roll pin when the armature pops off.) Replace armature if it has any chipped or broken teeth.
5. Using long-nose pliers, remove wire-retaining clip and armature stop ring (if any) from distributor shaft.
6. Remove small snap ring that holds vacuum advance link to magnetic pickup assembly. Remove two Phillips screws, magnetic pickup assembly, and the baseplate.
7. If no obvious faults have been found so far, replace pickup unit.
8. To reassemble distributor, reverse the steps above. Place roll pin in the grooves in the armature and shaft, then push armature back onto shaft, or drive it on with gentle blows from a light hammer. Use a block of wood as a cushion between the armature and hammer. Make sure roll pin does not stick out below armature.
9. Set ignition timing to specifications (p.239).

Variations of the Motorcraft Solid State Ignition system (SSI) have been used on nearly all domestic Ford, Lincoln, and Mercury models since 1974, and on AMC and Jeep V-8 and six-cylinder in-line engines from 1978 onward. The system consists of a distributor, ignition coil, and an electronic control module, all mounted separately in the engine compartment. The procedure outlined here can be used to test all versions of the SSI system except the computerized systems known as Three-Way Catalyst (TWC) and Electronic Engine Control (EEC). The TWC and EEC I and II systems were first introduced on some 1978 engines and

require special test equipment that is available only at new-car dealerships or a very few well-equipped garages. Ford's EEC III system, first introduced in 1980, can be checked with ordinary equipment. Some versions of the SSI system bear the name Duraspark Ignition, but the tests shown here apply to them as well. First check all wires for breaks or burned insulation. Unplug all connectors to check for and correct burned or corroded terminals. Do not remove conductive grease from the terminals.

Tools: Volt-ohm meter, insulated spark plug cable forceps, replacement control module or electronic ignition tester.

---

1. First, see *General troubleshooting*, p.414.
2. Check the battery's cranking voltage (p.278). If it is less than 9.6 volts, recharge or replace the battery. Make sure that the battery cables are clean and tightly connected.

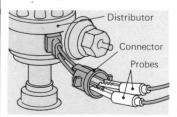

Distributor
Connector
Probes

3. Trace the wiring from the distributor to the first connector. Unplug this connector. The male half will have three blades inside. Connect the voltmeter probes to the two parallel blades for the colored wires (do not

connect a probe to the blade for the black ground wire). Crank the engine. If the meter needle does not fluctuate, there is damage inside the distributor.

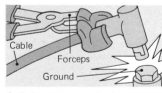

Cable
Forceps
Ground

4. If the meter needle fluctuates in Step 3, reconnect the connector. Remove the coil-to-distributor cable from the center of the distributor. Use insulated cable forceps to hold the metal terminal inside the boot ¼ in. from a clean ground on the engine while a helper cranks the starter. If there is a spark, the SSI system is OK. Check the fuel system.

5. If no spark occurs in Step 4, the electronic control module or coil may be faulty. To test the coil, see Step 3, p.425. Replace the coil if it is defective.
6. The only practical way to test the module is to use an electronic ignition tester (p.174) or to replace the module with one that you know is good. (**Caution:** Modules differ from one year to another; be sure to get the right one for your car. If you cannot borrow a module from a car that is working, you will have to buy one.) Unplug the old module from the distributor, but do not remove it from the car. Plug in the new module and repeat Step 4. If a spark occurs now, the old module is faulty. Replace it. Put electrically conductive grease onto the terminals of the new connectors before plugging them in. Wipe off excess grease after making the connections.

Tools: Screwdrivers, battery terminal puller, long-nose pliers, light hammer, small wooden block, timing light.

Troubleshooting Chrysler ignition systems ▣▣▣ 30 min–1hr

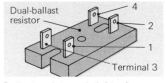

Typical wiring in Chrysler electronic ignition. Check connectors for corrosion and tightness if a failure occurs.

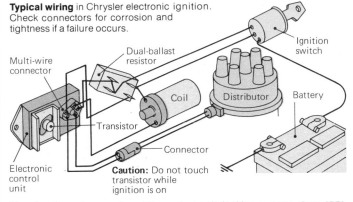

Ignition switch
Dual-ballast resistor
Multi-wire connector
Coil
Distributor
Battery
Transistor
Connector
Electronic control unit

Caution: Do not touch transistor while ignition is on.

Chrysler Corp. has employed three electronic ignition systems since 1971. The basic system (pictured above) consists of an electronic control unit, a dual ballast resistor, ignition coil, and distributor. This system was used on six-cylinder and V-8 engines only. A second system—consisting of a spark-control computer, various sensors, a ballast resistor, ignition coil, and distributor—is used on cars equipped with the Lean Burn engine or the Electronic Feedback Carburetor. Its resistor (Step 5) should show a reading of 1.2 ohms. Other parts of the system can be tested as shown in Steps 7, 9, and 10. The computer can be checked as shown on pages 388–389. The third system—used on Omni and Horizon cars—is shown on page 425.

Tools: Volt-ohm meter with 20,000-ohm capacity, screwdrivers, paper clip, wrench, non-magnetic (plastic or brass) feeler gauge, insulated ignition cable forceps, battery terminal puller (optional).

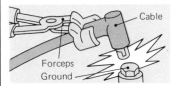

Cable
Forceps
Ground

1. Remove the coil-to-distributor cable from the central distributor tower. Use insulated cable forceps to hold the metal terminal ¼ in. from a clean electrical ground on the engine, and have a helper turn the ignition switch to *Start*. If there is no spark, the trouble may be in the ignition coil. Use an electronic ignition tester (p.174) to test the coil, or follow the procedure in Step 3, p.425. Replace the coil if necessary. If there is a spark, the problem may be in the fuel system or the distributor cap and rotor. Check both (see *General troubleshooting*, p.414).

2. Test the battery voltage (p.278). If it is less than 12 volts, recharge or replace the battery. Make sure that the battery cable's connections are clean and tight.

3. Turn ignition switch and all accessories off. Unplug multi-wire connector from electronic control unit. Turn the ignition on. Connect the negative (−) probe of the voltmeter to clean electrical ground on engine. Connect positive (+) probe to cavity

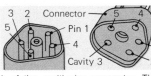

Connector
Pin 1
Cavity 3

1 of the multi-wire connector. The meter reading should be within 1 volt of the battery voltage (Step 2). If it is not, check all connections for tightness and cleanliness.

4. Repeat Step 3 on connector cavities 2 and 3. If all readings are not within 1 volt of the battery voltage, check all connections in ignition.

5. If cleaning and tightening connections does not remedy the voltage discrepancy in Steps 3 and 4, test the dual-ballast resistor. Make a sketch of the wiring connections, then remove the wires from the resistor. Set the ohmmeter to the *Low* scale (p.173) and connect its probes across resistor terminals 1 and 2. The ohmmeter should read 0.5 to 0.6 ohms. Connect the meter across terminals 3 and 4; the reading should be 4.75 to 5.75 ohms at 70°–90°F; if not, replace the resistor. Heat the resistor with a hair dryer and test again. If the readings are off when the resistor is hot, replace unit. Reconnect the wires according to your sketch.

6. If the ballast resistor is OK, switch ignition off. Set ohmmeter to the *High* scale. Connect probes to cavities 4 and 5 in the multi-wire connector. If meter shows 150 to 900 ohms, skip to Step 8.

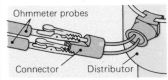

Ohmmeter probes
Connector
Distributor

7. If the meter does not show 150 to 900 ohms in Step 6, open the connector between the control unit and distributor. Connect the ohmmeter between the terminals of the connector that is attached to distributor. If the reading is now 150 to 900 ohms, reconnect the connector tightly. The problem was probably a loose connection. Repeat Step 6. If the meter reading is still not 150 to 900 ohms, replace the magnetic pickup coil (right).

8. Continue testing, if necessary, by connecting the ohmmeter between a good ground and pin 5 on the electronic control unit. The ohmmeter should read close to zero. If there is any reading (over zero), clean and

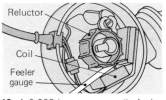

Dual-ballast resistor
Terminal 3

tighten the mounting bolts, which ground the control unit, and test again. If there is still a high reading, replace the control unit and the ballast resistor (a problem with one component is often caused by a problem in the other).

9. Turn ignition off, disconnect ohmmeter, and reconnect all connectors. Remove distributor cap and rotor. Place a large wrench on the crankshaft pulley nut, and turn the pulley clockwise until one tooth of the reluctor is aligned with the pickup coil.

Reluctor
Coil
Feeler gauge

10. A 0.008-in. non-magnetic feeler gauge (0.006 in. on 1978 models) should fit between the reluctor tooth and pickup coil with only slight drag. If it does not, loosen the hold-down screw, insert the correct gauge, and move the coil against it. Then tighten the hold-down screw. If the adjustment is correct, there should be only slight drag when you remove the gauge, and the next-larger gauge should not fit into the gap (do not force it).

11. Remove the distributor's vacuum advance hose from the engine and apply vacuum to the end, either by sucking on it or by using a hand-held vacuum pump. The pickup coil/plate assembly should move. If it does not move, check vacuum hose for leaks and check pickup assembly for binding. Lubricate the distributor and apply vacuum to the hose again. If the pickup does not move, replace the vacuum diaphragm (p.409). When the pickup coil moves, it must not hit any of the reluctor teeth. If it does, the gap is not correct.

12. Turn the crankshaft (Step 9) to rotate the reluctor 180 degrees, then move the pickup coil again. If the teeth on only one side of the reluctor hit the pickup coil, the distributor shaft is bent. Replace the distributor.

13. Reassemble distributor and repeat Step 1.

Replacing the pickup coil

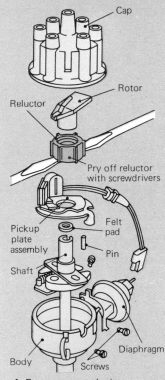

Cap
Rotor
Reluctor
Pry off reluctor with screwdrivers
Pickup plate assembly
Felt pad
Pin
Shaft
Body
Screws
Diaphragm

1. Remove cap and rotor.
2. Remove all screws and lock washers from outside of distributor body.
3. Pry off reluctor with two screwdrivers. Do not damage reluctor teeth or lose the pin.
4. Remove screws and washers from pickup/plate assembly. Disconnect diaphragm arm from pickup/plate assembly and remove diaphragm from body. Replace assembly.
5. Reassemble distributor. Place pin between shaft and reluctor, then press reluctor firmly into place.
6. Set gap (Steps 9 and 10, left). Put one drop of light engine oil onto felt pad inside shaft. Reinstall rotor and cap.

Testing Honda systems for failure to start 🔧🔧🔧 30 min–1 hr

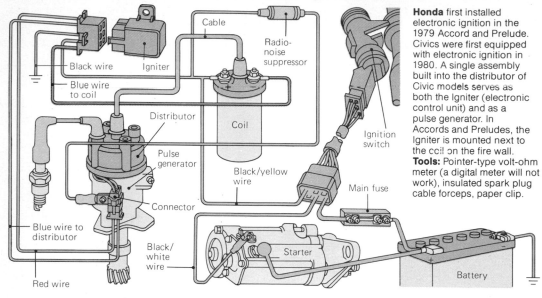

Cable

Radio-noise suppressor

Black wire — Igniter

Blue wire to coil

Distributor

Coil

Pulse generator

Black/yellow wire

Ignition switch

Blue wire to distributor

Connector

Black/white wire

Starter

Main fuse

Battery

Red wire

Honda first installed electronic ignition in the 1979 Accord and Prelude. Civics were first equipped with electronic ignition in 1980. A single assembly built into the distributor of Civic models serves as both the Igniter (electronic control unit) and as a pulse generator. In Accords and Preludes, the Igniter is mounted next to the coil on the fire wall.

Tools: Pointer-type volt-ohm meter (a digital meter will not work), insulated spark plug cable forceps, paper clip.

Accord and Prelude

1. Check battery condition and voltage (p.278). If battery shows less than 12 volts, recharge or replace it.

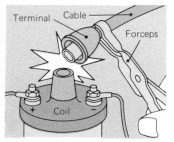

Terminal — Cable

Forceps

Coil

2. Remove the high-voltage cable from the ignition coil tower. Grip the cable with insulated spark plug forceps and hold the metal cable terminal ¼ in. from the ignition coil tower. Have a helper crank the engine. If a strong blue spark shoots from the coil cable, proceed to Steps 3 and 4. If there is no spark, or a weak yellow or orange spark shoots from the coil cable, proceed to Steps 5–10.

3. Reinsert the coil cable and remove a cable from one of the spark plugs. Force a paper clip into the boot until it contacts the metal terminal inside the boot. Use cable forceps to hold the paper clip ¼ in. from a good ground on the engine while a helper cranks the engine.

4. If there is a spark from the clip to the engine, the problem is probably a malfunctioning fuel system, fouled or worn spark plugs, or faulty ignition timing. If there is no spark, the problem may be a damaged spark plug cable, distributor cap, or rotor (see *General troubleshooting*, p.414).

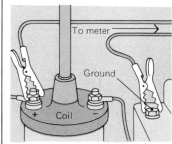

To meter

Ground

Coil

5. If there is no spark from the coil cable (Step 2), suspect a malfunction in the electronic section of the ignition system. Connect the positive voltmeter lead to the positive (+) coil terminal. Connect the negative voltmeter lead to a good electrical ground on the body or engine. Turn on the ignition switch. If the voltmeter does not record battery voltage (see Step 1), the problem lies with the wiring between the ignition switch and coil. Make sure that all connections are tight.

6. If Step 5 shows battery voltage at the positive (+) side of the coil, connect the positive meter lead to the negative (−) side of the coil. Turn on the ignition switch. If the voltmeter does not record battery voltage (see Step 1), the problem lies with the wiring between the ignition coil and Igniter, or with the ignition coil itself. Check the wiring for open circuits (p.363).

7. If Step 6 shows that battery voltage is being delivered to the negative side of the coil, connect the voltmeter between the positive and negative sides of the coil. Have a helper crank the engine. The voltmeter should read between 1 and 3 volts. If it does, the engine's failure to start is probably caused by a weak coil or by

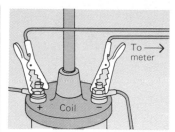

To meter

Coil

defective spark plug cables. Check the cables (p.231) and replace any that are faulty. If the cables are OK, test the coil (see Step 3, p.425), or check the system by substituting a new ignition coil.

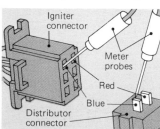

Connector

Black/yellow

Black

Blue wire to coil

8. If Step 7 does not produce 1 to 3 volts, disconnect the multi-wire connector from the Igniter to check the coil side of the connector. Turn the ignition on. Insert a voltmeter probe into the socket for the black wire. Insert the other probe into the socket for the blue wire, then into the socket for the black-and-yellow wire. If the voltmeter does not show battery voltage, the problem lies in the wiring between the ignition coil and Igniter.

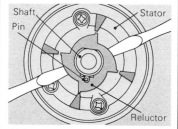

Igniter connector

Meter probes

Red

Blue

Distributor connector

9. If Step 8 reveals no faults, unplug the wiring connector at the distributor. Touch ohmmeter probes to the contacts for the red wire at the distributor connector and at the Igniter

connector. The meter should read almost zero. Repeat this test on the blue wire. (Make sure that you put the meter probe into the socket for the blue wire that runs from the Igniter to the distributor, not into the socket for the blue wire to the coil, which was tested in Step 8.) The reading should be almost zero. If the meter reads close to infinity for either wire, there is a break in the wiring harness; fix or replace it.

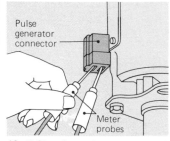

Pulse generator connector

Meter probes

10. If Step 9 produces zero readings, connect the ohmmeter probes to the blue and pink terminals of the pulse generator connector. The ohmmeter should read 600 to 800 ohms (800 to 1,200 for 1980 cars). If it does not, replace the pulse generator. If reading is OK, the starting problem lies with the Igniter.

Shaft — Stator

Pin

Reluctor

11. To replace the pulse generator, remove the distributor cap and rotor. Place a screwdriver on either side of the reluctor and carefully pry off the distributor shaft. Remove the screws that hold the stator and magnetic pickup. Install a new pulse generator and reluctor. Reinstall the magnetic pickup and stator. Drive the reluctor pin back into place with gentle taps from a light hammer. Gap in pin must face away from shaft.

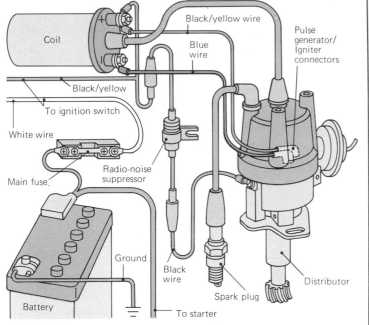

Coil

Black/yellow wire

Blue wire

Black/yellow

To ignition switch

White wire

Main fuse

Radio-noise suppressor

Pulse generator/ Igniter connectors

Black wire

Spark plug

Distributor

Battery

Ground

To starter

Testing the Volkswagen system for failure to start ▣ ▣ ▣ 30 min–1hr

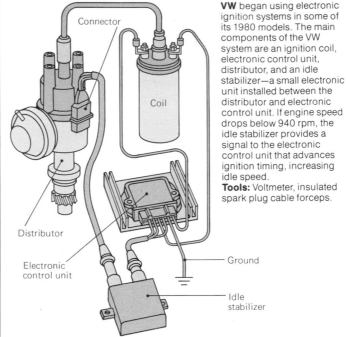

Connector

Coil

Distributor

Electronic control unit

Ground

Idle stabilizer

VW began using electronic ignition systems in some of its 1980 models. The main components of the VW system are an ignition coil, electronic control unit, distributor, and an idle stabilizer—a small electronic unit installed between the distributor and electronic control unit. If engine speed drops below 940 rpm, the idle stabilizer provides a signal to the electronic control unit that advances ignition timing, increasing idle speed.

Tools: Voltmeter, insulated spark plug cable forceps.

Steps 4–6. If the following checks fail to reveal the cause of the problem, replace the wiring harness.

4. Remove the connector from the electronic control unit. Connect a voltmeter between terminals 2 and 4. Turn the ignition on. If the voltmeter reads about 12 volts, the electronic control unit is defective; replace it. If there still is no voltage, reconnect the electronic control unit.

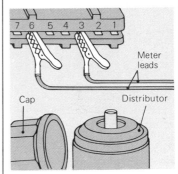

7 6 5 4 3 2 1

Meter leads

Cap

Distributor

5. Pull back the rubber boot of the connector on the electronic control unit. Connect voltmeter leads securely to terminals 3 and 6. Remove the distributor cap and rotor. If necessary, rotate the engine by turning the crankshaft pulley with a wrench until none of the trigger wheel shutters is in the gap between the pickup and magnet. Turn on the ignition. The voltmeter should record no more than 0.4 volt. Now rotate the engine until one of the trigger wheel shutters is in the gap between the pickup and magnet. The voltmeter should record about 9 volts. If you get none or only one of these readings, replace the pickup. If readings are OK, remove the voltmeter and reassemble all components.

6. Connect the positive lead of the voltmeter to terminal 15 of the ignition coil. Connect the negative lead of the voltmeter to terminal 1 of the ignition coil. Remove the connector from the distributor and turn on the ignition. The voltmeter will show about 6 volts. However, it must drop to zero within 2 sec. If this voltage drop does not take place, replace the ignition coil and the electronic control unit.

Civic

Follow Steps 1–7 for the Honda Accord and Prelude (see opposite page). If testing to that point has failed to reveal why the engine will not start, proceed as follows:

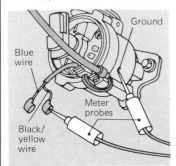

Ground

Blue wire

Meter probes

Black/ yellow wire

8. Disconnect the multi-wire connector from the Igniter in the distributor. Insert a voltmeter probe first in the blue wire's connector and then in the black-and-yellow wire's connector. Hold the other probe against the

body of the distributor to ground it. With the ignition switch turned on, the voltmeter should record battery voltage. If it does not, the fault lies in the wiring from the coil to the Igniter.

9. If Step 8 produces a satisfactory battery voltage reading (see Step 1), check the terminals of the Igniter. With the ohmmeter on the *High* scale, hold one probe to the black-and-yellow wire's terminal, hold the other probe to the blue wire's terminal. The ohmmeter should read close to infinity. Now reverse the probes. The ohmmeter should read close to zero. If the Igniter fails this test, replace it.

10. To replace the Igniter, remove the distributor cap and rotor. Place screwdrivers on opposite sides of reluctor and carefully pry it off distributor shaft. Remove the two screws that hold the Igniter to the breaker plate, and replace the Igniter. Force the reluctor back onto the shaft and gently tap the pin into place with a light hammer; gap in pin must face away from shaft.

To determine what part of the electronic ignition system, if any, is defective when the engine does not start, proceed as follows:

1. Remove the coil-to-distributor cable from the distributor cap. Hold the cable about ¼ in. from a metal part of the engine, using insulated spark plug cable forceps. Crank the engine. If a bright blue spark jumps the gap, the cause of the problem is a damaged distributor cap or rotor (see p.414), defective spark plugs or spark plug cables, or a malfunction in the fuel system. If there is no spark, or if a very weak spark appears, make sure that the battery is fully charged (p.278). If battery voltage is less than 12 volts, recharge or replace the battery.

2. Remove the two connectors from the idle stabilizer and plug them together. Try to start the engine. If the engine now starts but did not start before, the idle stabilizer is defective and should be replaced.

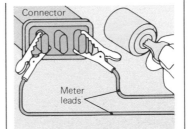

Connector

Meter leads

3. If the engine still does not start, reconnect the idle stabilizer. Remove the connector from the distributor. Connect a voltmeter to the two outside terminals of this connector and turn on the ignition. The voltmeter should show battery voltage (about 12 volts). If there is no voltage, check that the wiring harness connections between the distributor and electronic control unit are securely attached. The problem could also be a defective wire in the wiring harness, but this is unlikely. Continue with

Datsun Trignition systems ⚡⚡⚡ 30 min–1 hr

The Datsun Trignition system consists of a coil, a distributor, and a control unit (called a *Trignition* unit). Prior to 1979 the Trignition unit was mounted high in the passenger's footwell, under the dash. Beginning in 1979 the unit was mounted on the distributor.

The Datsun Trignition system has been used on Datsun 260Z and 280Z models since 1974. It has been used on various California models since 1975. Except for Z models, the first Datsun nationwide to use Trignition was the 1977 B210 High Mileage model. All Datsuns from 1978 onward have the Trignition system.

The Trignition distributor has a reluctor and a pickup coil (or coils) instead of conventional breaker points. The distributor in 1974 to 1976 Z cars with automatic transmissions has two pickup coils, an advance pickup coil and a retard pickup coil. A thermostatic switch screwed into the cylinder head opens a relay when the engine is cold, and the Trig unit is activated by the advance pickup. When the engine warms up, the switch closes the relay and the Trig unit is activated by the retard pickup. If the switch or relay sticks closed, performance will be poor until the engine warms up. Repairs for the four-cylinder, eight-plug engines introduced in 1980 are not covered.

General testing

1. Check battery condition and voltage (p.278). Non-cranking battery voltage should be at least 11.5 volts; cranking voltage should be at least 9.6 volts. If battery voltage falls below these levels, recharge or replace the battery. Write down the non-cranking voltage for use in the tests at the right.

2. Remove the coil-to-distributor cable from the distributor cap. Using plug cable forceps, hold the metal terminal at the end of the cable ½ in. from a clean electrical ground on the engine. Have a helper crank the starter. If there is a spark between the terminal and the engine, the electronic system is OK. Check the distributor cap and rotor for damage (see p.414). Also check the fuel system.

If there is no spark, test the Trignition system by following the procedures listed at the right for your car. Complete each test step before proceeding to the next step. If none of the tests reveals why the engine will not start, test the electronic portion of the system with an electronic ignition tester (p.174), or replace the Trignition unit.

Tools: Insulated spark plug cable forceps, screwdrivers, wrenches, voltmeter and ohmmeter (or a multi-function meter) with the following scales: 0 to 3 volts DC, 0 to 20 volts DC, 0 to 10 volts AC, 0 to 1,000 ohms.

Testing 1979 and later models

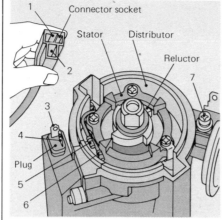

The Trig unit is on the outside of the distributor. Attach meter probes to points 5, 6, and 7 on the distributor to perform tests. Open the connector, and attach meter probes to the connector blades (points 1 and 2) on the Trig unit. Points 3 and 4 are female sockets into which blades 1 and 2 fit.

Testing 1978 models (and the 1977 B210 High Mileage)

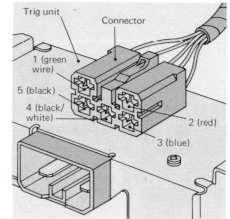

To test the Trignition system in the 1977 B210 High Mileage model and all 1978 models, pull the wiring harness from the Trig unit. You may have to remove the Trig unit from under the dash to reach its connector. Insert meter probes into the appropriate cavities in the multi-wire connector.

Testing the 1977 280Z (and 1975–77 California 280Zs)

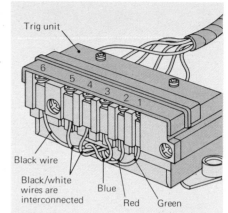

To test the Trignition system in the 1977 280Z model (and in 1975–77 280Z cars made for sale in California), unbolt the Trig unit from its mount to gain easier access to checkpoints. Tests can be made without disconnecting the wiring; attach meter probes to the screws holding the wire terminals to the Trig unit.

ALL MODELS		1979 AND LATER MODELS		1977–78 MODELS		ALL MODELS	
Test step (set meter to *voltage* or *ohms*, as shown)	**Ignition switch position**	**Attach meter's + lead**	**Attach meter's − lead**	**Attach meter's + lead**	**Attach meter's − lead**	**Normal meter reading**	**What to do if reading is not normal**
1. Trig power supply *voltage*	On	2	Ground	4[1]	Ground	Battery non-cranking voltage	Check wires and connectors from ignition switch to Trig unit
2. Trig power supply *voltage*	Start	2	Ground	4[1]	Ground	Not less than 8.6 volts	Check wires and connectors from ignition switch to Trig unit. Also check battery-to-starter circuit
3. Trig ground circuit *voltage*	Start	7	Battery − post	5[2]	Battery − post	0.5 volts or less	Check distributor ground, battery ground wires, and battery cable connections
4. Ignition primary *voltage*	On	1	Ground	3	Ground	Battery non-cranking voltage	Test ignition coil and ignition switch. Check wires from coil to switch
5. Pickup coil resistance *ohms*	Off	5	6	1	2	400[4] ohms ±10%	Check wires and connectors between pickup coil and Trig unit
6. Pickup coil output *voltage*[3]	Start	5	Ground	2[3]	1[3]	Rhythmic needle deflection	Check wires and connectors between pickup coil and Trig unit. Check reluctor for damage; replace a damaged reluctor. Replace pickup coil if reluctor is not damaged

1. Connect lead to screw 5 on 1977 280Z models (and 1975–77 280Zs sold in California)
2. Connect lead to screw 6 on 1977 280Z models (and 1975–77 280Zs sold in California)
3. Set voltmeter on AC range
4. 720 ohms ±10% on 1977–78 models

Testing 1975–76 280Zs (except California cars)

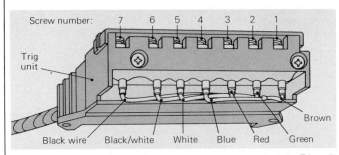

Screw number: 7 6 5 4 3 2 1

Trig unit

Brown

Black wire Black/white White Blue Red Green

To test the Trignition system in 1975–76 280Z models, unbolt the Trig unit from its mount to gain easier access to checkpoints. The tests can be performed without disconnecting the wiring; attach meter probes to the screws that hold the wire terminals to the Trig unit.

Testing the 1974 260Z

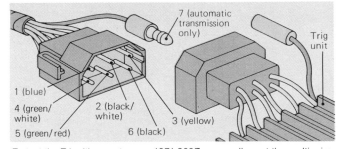

7 (automatic transmission only)

Trig unit

1 (blue)
4 (green/white)
2 (black/white)
5 (green/red)
3 (yellow)
6 (black)

To test the Trignition system on 1974 260Z cars, pull apart the multi-wire connector at the Trig unit. Tests are performed by touching voltmeter or ohmmeter probes to the terminals of the connector half that is attached to the car's wiring harness.

Replacing the reluctor and pickup coil(s)

Replacement procedure for reluctor and pickup coil(s) is the same as for Honda Civic (p.421). Set the pickup coil gap as shown for Chrysler cars (p.419), using a brass or plastic feeler gauge. Correct gap for pre-1979 cars is 0.008 to 0.016 in. (with 0.012 in. preferred). Gap on 1979 and later models should be 0.012 to 0.020 in. (with 0.016 in. preferred).

Testing 1974–76 260Z and 280Z advance-control relay and thermostatic switch

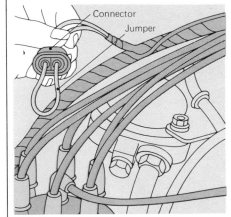

Connector
Jumper

1. Warm up engine, then connect a timing light (p.237). Rev engine slightly to its cold-idle speed. Remove the two-wire connector from the thermostatic switch near the thermostatic housing, at the front of the engine. Ignition timing should advance.
2. If timing does not advance, attach leads of an ohmmeter across the switch terminals. Meter should read near zero. Retest when engine is cold. Meter should read infinity. If thermostatic switch fails either test, replace it.
3. If switch is OK, run warm engine at cold-idle speed. Open connector and attach a jumper wire between a ground and the terminal for the colored wire. Timing should retard as jumper is connected and advance when it is disconnected. If not, replace the advance-control relay.
4. Run warm engine at cold-idle speed. Connect a jumper wire across the terminals of the two-wire connector. Timing should retard. If not, and relay passed test in Step 3, black wire is not making a good ground; clean its ground connection.

ALL MODELS		1975–76 280Z		1974 260Z		ALL MODELS	
Test step (set meter to *voltage* or *ohms*, as shown)	Ignition switch position	Attach meter's + lead	Attach meter's − lead	Attach meter's + lead	Attach meter's − lead	Normal meter reading	What to do if reading is not normal
1. Trig power supply *voltage*	On	6	Ground	2	Ground	Battery non-cranking voltage	Check wires and connectors from ignition switch to Trig unit
2. Trig power supply *voltage*	Start	6	Ground	2	Ground	Not less than 8.6 volts	Check wires and connectors from ignition switch to Trig unit. Also check battery-to-starter circuit
3. Trig ground circuit *voltage*	Start	7	Battery — post	6	Battery — post	0.5 volts or less	Check distributor ground, battery ground wires, and battery cable connections
4. Ignition primary *voltage*	On	4	Ground	1	Ground	Battery non-cranking voltage	Test ignition coil and ignition switch. Check wires from coil to switch
5. Retard pickup coil *ohms*[1]	Off	2	3	4	5	720 ohms[5] ±10%	Check wires and connectors between retard pickup coil and Trig unit
6. Advance pickup coil *ohms*[3]	Off	1	2	3	5	720 ohms[5] ±10%	Check wires and connectors between advance pickup coil and Trig unit
7. Advance control relay *voltage*[3]	On	5	7	7	6	0[4]	Check wires and connectors between advance-control relay and Trig unit. Test water temperature switch and advance-control relay
8. Retard pickup coil *voltage*[1]	Start	2[2]	3[2]	4[2]	5[2]	Rhythmic needle deflection	Check wires and connectors between retard-pickup coil and Trig unit. Check reluctor for damage; replace a damaged reluctor. Replace retard-pickup coil if reluctor is not damaged
9. Advance pickup coil *voltage*[2]	Start	1[2]	2[2]	3[2]	5[2]	Rhythmic needle deflection	Check wires and connectors between advance-pickup coil and Trig unit. Check reluctor for damage; replace a damaged reluctor. Replace advance pickup coil if reluctor is not damaged

1. Cars with manual transmissions have one pickup coil. Cars with automatic transmissions have two pickup coils (advance and retard). This is a test of the retard coil on cars with automatic transmissions, or of the single coil on cars with manual transmissions
2. Set voltmeter on AC range
3. This is a test of the advance pickup coil on cars with automatic transmissions
4. When engine is cold
5. Reading should be between 450 and 750 ohms ±10% on 1974 260Z models

Testing the Toyota Breakerless Ignition system 🔲🔲🔲 30 min–1 hr

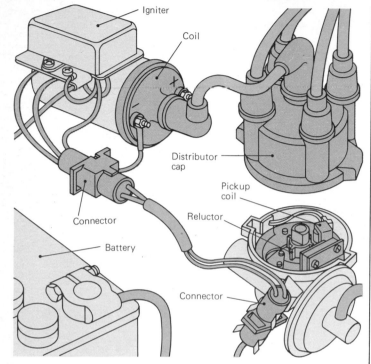

Igniter

Coil

Distributor cap

Pickup coil

Reluctor

Connector

Battery

Connector

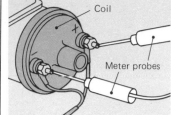

Coil

Meter probes

4. With the engine cold, check the ignition coil's primary resistance by setting the ohmmeter on its *Low* scale. Connect the meter probes to the positive (+) and negative (−) terminals of the coil. The meter should read about 1.3 to 1.7 ohms. If it does not, the coil is bad; replace it.

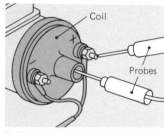

Coil

Probes

5. Set the ohmmeter to its *High* scale. Check the ignition coil's secondary resistance by connecting the probes to the positive (+) coil terminal and to the terminal inside the coil tower. The meter should read 12,000 to 16,000 ohms. If it does not, the coil is defective; replace it.

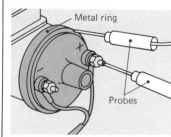

Metal ring

Probes

6. Check ignition coil's insulation by connecting the ohmmeter to the positive (+) coil terminal and to the top ring of the coil. The ohmmeter should read *Infinity*. If it does not, the coil is defective; replace it.

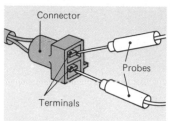

Connector

Probes

Terminals

7. Disconnect the multi-wire connector at the Igniter. Set ohmmeter to the *Low* scale, and touch probes to the brown and the yellow wire terminals of wiring harness. If the ohmmeter reads over 1.2 ohms, the resistance wire in the harness is faulty and the harness should be replaced. This is a job for a Toyota mechanic. Reconnect the multi-wire connector.

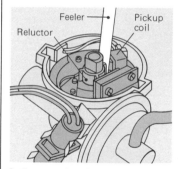

Feeler

Pickup coil

Reluctor

8. Remove the distributor cap. Attach a wrench to the center bolt of the crankshaft pulley and turn clockwise until one tooth of the reluctor is opposite the core of the pickup coil. Use a non-magnetic feeler gauge to check the gap between the reluctor and pickup coil. If the gap is not between 0.008 and 0.016 in., adjust the gap to 0.012 in.

9. To adjust the gap, loosen the adjusting screws on the pickup coil and move the coil until a 0.012-in. non-magnetic feeler gauge can be withdrawn from between the reluctor tooth and pickup coil with only slight drag. Tighten adjusting screws. The next-largest feeler should not fit between the tooth and pickup coil (do not use force on feeler gauge). Replace the reluctor if it has broken teeth. Reassemble the distributor.

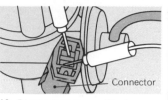

Connector

10. Disconnect the multi-wire connector at the distributor. Connect an ohmmeter across the terminals of this connector. The ohmmeter should read 130 to 190 ohms. If it does not, the pickup coil is defective and must be replaced. This is done in the same way as the pickup coil is replaced in the Datsun Trignition system (p.423).

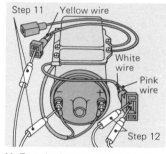

Step 11 Yellow wire

White wire

Pink wire

Step 12

11. Turn the ignition switch on. Connect the positive (+) lead of a voltmeter to the yellow resistor wire terminal of the connector that hooks to the Igniter (see Step 7). Connect the negative (−) lead of the voltmeter to the negative (−) terminal of the coil. If the reading is less than the battery non-cranking voltage (Step 1), the Igniter is faulty and must be replaced. This is done by disconnecting the wires and unbolting the Igniter from its mounting.

12. Turn off the ignition but leave the voltmeter connected as in Step 11. Set the ohmmeter on the *Low* scale. Connect the ohmmeter's positive (+) probe to the pink wire connector of the distributor (Step 10). Connect the ohmmeter's negative (−) probe to the white wire connector of the distributor. Turn on the ignition. This creates resistance in the pickup coil circuit. The voltmeter reading should fall to nearly zero. If it does not, replace the Igniter.

The Toyota Breakerless Ignition system is used in 1978 and later models and in the 1977 Celica GT with 20R engine sold in California. The system has an ignition coil, a distributor with a reluctor and pickup coil rather than breaker points, and an electronic control unit called an Igniter. On some 1976 and 1977 models, Toyota employs a transistorized switching unit (not discussed here) that has breaker points in the distributor.

Tools: Timing light, separate needle-type ohmmeter and voltmeter, non-magnetic (plastic or brass) feeler gauge, wrenches, screwdrivers.

1. Check battery condition and voltage (p.278). Non-cranking voltage must be at least 11.5 volts, and cranking voltage at least 9.5 volts. If battery is weak or dead, recharge or replace it. To be sure that the Igniter is properly grounded, clean and tighten its mounting bolts.

2. Connect a timing light according to instructions on page 237. Crank the engine. If the timing light flashes regularly, the problem is a damaged distributor cap or rotor (p.414) or the fault will be in the fuel system or some other system not related to ignition. If the timing light fails to flash or flashes irregularly, continue the troubleshooting procedure. **Caution:** Do not conduct the above test by disconnecting and grounding a high-voltage ignition cable. This will cause arcing that may damage the Igniter.

3. Check wiring and connections between the distributor, ignition coil, and Igniter. Make sure that connections are clean and tight. Also check the engine's main wiring harness connector, which is located near the right-hand front part of the engine in most models.

Troubleshooting the Omni/Horizon system ▢▢▢ 30 min–1 hr

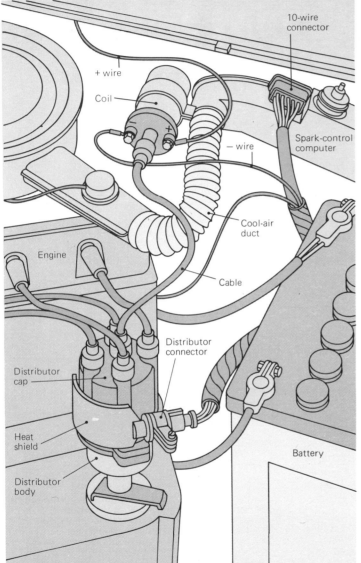

+ wire
Coil
10-wire connector
– wire
Spark-control computer
Cool-air duct
Engine
Cable
Distributor connector
Distributor cap
Heat shield
Distributor body
Distributor connector
Battery

Most of Chrysler Corp.'s front-wheel-drive Dodge Omni and Plymouth Horizon models are equipped with an electronic ignition system that uses a Hall effect pickup unit in the distributor (see p.69) and a spark-control computer. If the car will not start, first follow the *General troubleshooting* tests on page 414. If they do not cure the trouble, make the tests at the right.

Tools: Screwdriver, volt-ohm meter, spark plug cable forceps, jumper wire.

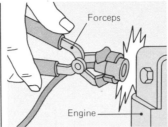

Forceps

Engine

1. Remove the high-voltage coil cable from the center of the distributor. Use insulated spark plug cable forceps to hold it about ¼ in. away from the engine block. Have a helper crank the engine briefly. A spark should jump between cable and engine. **Caution:** Make sure there are no fuel leaks before performing this test. Keep hands, hair, jewelry and loose clothing well away from belts, pulleys, and moving parts.

2. Check battery non-cranking voltage (p.278). If it is less than 12 volts, recharge or replace the battery as necessary. When a voltage above 12 volts is achieved, write down the number. This is the *reference voltage,* needed in the tests to follow.

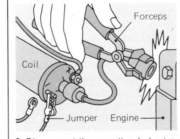

Forceps
Coil
Jumper   Engine

3. Disconnect the negative (–) wire from the coil. Unplug the coil cable from the center tower of the distributor and hold it ¼ in. away from a good ground on the engine block. Turn on ignition. Ground one end of a jumper wire, and momentarily touch the other end to the negative coil terminal. A spark should jump from the coil cable to the engine block when jumper is attached.

4. If a spark does not occur in Step 3, connect a voltmeter between the coil's positive terminal and a good ground. If there are 9 volts or more,

replace the coil. If there are less than 9 volts, check the ballast resistor with an ohmmeter (p.419, Step 5). Check the resistor's wiring and connections for shorts or corrosion.

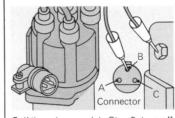

B
Connector   A   C

5. If there is a spark in Step 3, turn off ignition, reconnect the negative coil wire, and disconnect the multi-wire connector from the distributor. Turn ignition back on and connect a voltmeter between hole B on the connector and a good ground. You should get your reference voltage (Step 2). If you do, skip to Step 8.

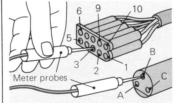

6   9   10
5
3   2   1
Meter probes   B
A   C

6. If you do not get the reference voltage in Step 5, turn off the ignition and disconnect the 10-wire connector from the computer. Connect ohmmeter probes between hole 3 of the computer connector and hole B on the distributor connector (see Step 5). If the meter reads close to infinity, there is a break in the wire between holes 3 and B. Find and repair the break or replace the wire.

7. If the ohmmeter reads close to zero in Step 6, connect voltmeter probes between computer holes 2 and 10. If you do not get the reference voltage from Step 2, check the wiring and connectors for shorts or corrosion. If you do get the reference voltage, the computer is defective.

8. Reconnect all wiring. If the car still will not start, disconnect the coil cable from the center of the distributor cap and have a helper hold it

about ¼ in. from a good ground on the engine (see Step 1). Turn on the ignition. Unplug the distributor connector and momentarily place a jumper wire between holes A and C. If there is a spark now, the problem is in the pickup coil or in the rotor.

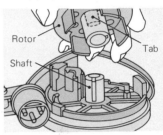

Rotor
Tab
Shaft

9. Remove distributor cap and pull off rotor. Check to see if the metal grounding tab inside the rotor is worn or covered with plastic. Clean the tab or replace the rotor. If the tab is OK, reinstall the rotor, pushing it down firmly so that the tab makes contact with the distributor shaft. If the car still will not start, replace the pickup coil.

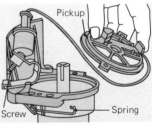

Pickup
Screw   Spring

10. To replace pickup coil, disengage the two lock springs, unscrew the pickup lead's hold-down screw, and lift the pickup unit up and out of the distributor. Reverse these steps to install new pickup coil.

11. If the car still will not start, unplug the computer and distributor connectors again (Steps 5 and 6). Attach ohmmeter leads to holes C and 9, and then to holes A and 5. If the meter reads close to infinity, check for breaks in the wires between the connectors or corrosion on the connectors. If the meter reads close to zero, the computer is probably defective and should be replaced.

Types of gaskets

A gasket is a thin sheet of compressible material placed between two metal parts in order to form a leakproof seal between them. A gasket is usually made of either paper, cork, fiber, neoprene, or composites of neoprene-cork, neoprene-fiber or metal-asbestos. All solid gaskets are shaped to match the surfaces to which they will be applied. Also, there are two products that can be used to make your own gaskets: a silicone rubber paste that cures, or *vulcanizes*, at room temperature (called *RTV sealant*), and an anaerobic compound that dries in the absence of air. The latter product is useful for making a gasket that will not begin to harden, or cure, until the parts are bolted together. Anaerobic compounds are also applied to threaded fasteners to prevent them from vibrating and coming loose. Anaerobic compounds come in two strengths—a permanent formula (usually red) and a non-permanent formula (usually blue). Use the permanent formula on fasteners that you will never want to disassemble again. Metal cylinder-head gaskets are not covered here, since removing the cylinder head is too difficult for most home mechanics.

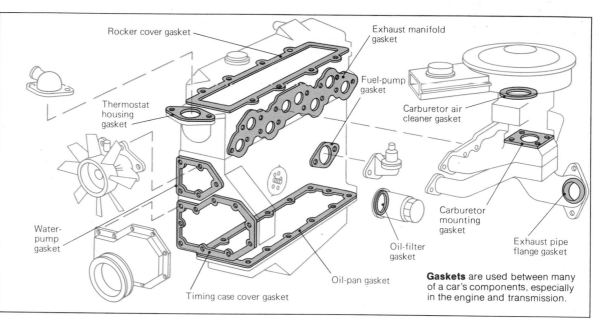

Gaskets are used between many of a car's components, especially in the engine and transmission.

General procedure for installing a gasket ⟳ 5–20 min

Neoprene-rubber gaskets can be reused if they are not damaged or obviously dried up and cracked. Paper, cork, and fiber gaskets should always be replaced. Such used gaskets do not have the compressibility and resilience of new ones, and reusing them could result in leaks. When buying a gasket, be sure that it is the correct size and shape for your car.

Make sure that the mating surfaces to which a new gasket will be applied are clean and are not warped before you install the gasket. Scrape away all remnants of old gasket and sealant (right). Then wipe the mating surfaces clean with a solvent such as alcohol or trichloroethylene, and allow the surfaces to dry before proceeding. To check for warping, lay a straightedge across all areas of the mating surfaces (right). If there is slight warping, a repair may not be necessary; a good seal can often be made with a gasket and pliable gasket sealer. If a surface is severely warped, the part may need to be replaced or machined before any gasket can be installed. Warped sheet-metal parts can often be straightened with a hammer and a block of wood.

When installing a solid gasket, position and align it

correctly on one of the surfaces. Some gaskets must be installed with a particular side up; if so, the gasket will be marked with a warning such as "This side up." If there are bolt holes or screw holes in the gasket, align them with the same holes in the mating surfaces. Some gaskets have a self-adhesive surface that is protected by paper that you must peel off. Other gaskets remain in position either because they fit into a machined groove or because the gasket has tabs that fit into indentations in one of the mating parts. If you need help to hold any solid gasket in place, apply pliable gasket sealer or a thin bead of RTV sealant onto the surface, then press the gasket in place.

Once the gasket is in place, join the two surfaces and tighten the assembly. First, install the bolts finger-tight. Then, using a torque wrench and working in a spiral pattern (p.431), tighten each bolt partially, then go back and tighten each fully. When you are finished, run the engine to test for leaks. (If you used an RTV sealant, wait at least an hour before you test for leaks.) If there is a leak, tighten the bolts a little more. If that fails to stop the leak, take the assembly apart and begin again.

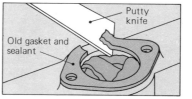

Clean the surfaces by scraping away all old gasket and sealant. Use a putty knife for scraping. Do not gouge the metal.

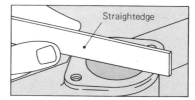

Check for warping. Lay a straightedge in several directions across all areas of both surfaces. If you see light between the straightedge and the surface, the surface is warped.

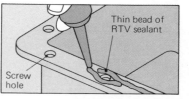

To make a gasket, apply a thin bead of a liquid gasket material along the entire surface and around any bolt holes or screw holes. Check package instructions.

Diagnosing lifter problems ▱▱▱▱▱ 4 – 8 hr

To locate noisy valve lifters, warm up the engine and run it at idle. Use a length of hose to listen to each valve, or place your fingers on top of each valve-spring retainer in order to detect harsher-than-normal valve train action (see p.276). Make sure that the engine oil level is correct, that the valve clearance is properly adjusted, and that any noise or harsh action you detect is not being caused by wear in other components, such as the valve guides. If the noise is coming from the lifters, they should be removed, disassembled, and cleaned. Replace them if they are worn, damaged, or scored. If you find dirt, carbon, or other foreign particles in one lifter, you should service the entire set, since it is probable that all the lifters are contaminated. There should be no clearance in the valve train when the engine is running. When the engine is off, you can compress the lifter by pushing down on the pushrod, but you should feel resistance from the spring inside the lifter. If you feel no resistance, the lifter is defective. Repairing and replacing lifters is not difficult. However, extracting the lifters from the engine often requires extensive disassembly (see p.429). The chart at the right will help you to identify specific lifter problems.

Troubleshooting lifter performance

Noise (when engine is warm)	Probable cause
Hard rapping	Excessive varnish or carbon deposits causing stickiness of lifter parts
	Friction between bore of lifter body and plunger caused by foreign particle wedged between parts
Moderate to light rapping	Excessive oil leakdown rate (lifter malfunction) caused by worn lifter parts
	Lifter check-valve seat is leaking
	Valve clearance needs adjustment
	Excessive valve train wear (have worn parts replaced)
Intermittent clicking	Minute foreign particle occasionally caught between check valve and valve seat
	Valve clearance needs adjustment
General clicking throughout valve train	Engine oil level too low or too high
	Valve clearance needs adjustment

Simple removal techniques

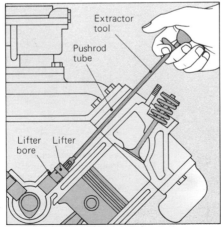

Use special extractor tool, available at auto parts stores, to withdraw hydraulic lifters from the engine. Tool expands inside rim of the lifter body to provide grip for pulling lifter up through the pushrod tube. Long magnetic pickup tool or a length of bent wire may also work.

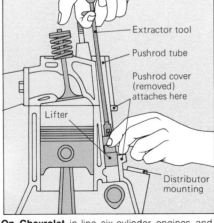

On Chevrolet in-line six-cylinder engines and similar in-line designs, lifters can be removed by using a lifter extractor tool or a long magnetic pickup tool. First remove the pushrods, distributor, and pushrod covers, which are located on the same side of the engine block.

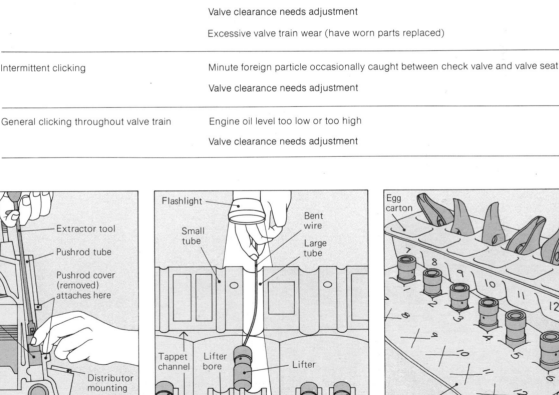

On Ford V-8 engines some of the pushrod tubes are too small for the lifters to pass through. Remove pushrods, and use extractor tool to remove lifters from the large tubes. Then use a bent wire to slide remaining lifters sideways until they are in position under larger tubes.

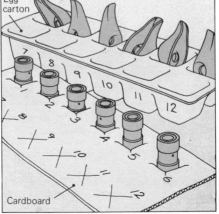

Valve parts to be reused must be reinstalled in their original locations. Number the pushrods and place them in order on a cardboard rack. Label and group other valve parts, including lifters, in numbered egg-carton compartments, plastic bags, or a muffin tin.

Overhauling hydraulic lifters ▣ 30 min–1 hr

Hydraulic lifters should be serviced in an orderly fashion. Work with clean hands in a clean, particle- and grease-free area, preferably at a workbench spread with fresh newspaper. Label each lifter as it is removed from the engine, and keep the lifters in order as you work. Do not take the lifters apart until you are ready to work on them. Disassemble, clean, and reassemble only one lifter at a time to avoid mixing up their internal parts. Lifters can be cleaned in any strong parts-cleaning solvent that will remove varnish, gum, and carbon deposits. Inspect each part carefully, and if any part is rusted, damaged, or worn, replace the lifter. Carefully check the outer wall of the lifter body as well. If the sides are scuffed or scored, there may also be damage inside the lifter bores (where the lifters are installed in the engine block) due to particle wear or poor-quality oil. If the scoring is excessive, or if there is evidence of sticking, the bores must be reamed to a larger size by a machine shop, and oversize lifters installed. Check the *foot* (bottom) of the lifter. If it shows wear, inspect the camshaft lobes. Also check the pushrod seat and, if it is worn, inspect the pushrods. Replace worn pushrods. Have a worn camshaft replaced by a mechanic.

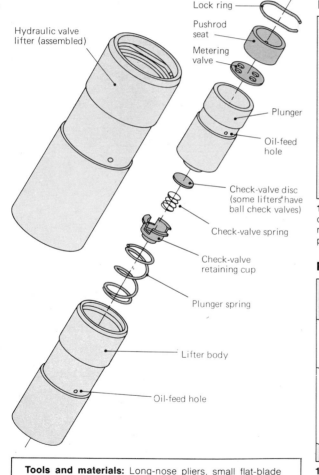

Hydraulic valve lifter (assembled)

Lock ring
Pushrod seat
Metering valve
Plunger
Oil-feed hole
Check-valve disc (some lifters have ball check valves)
Check-valve spring
Check-valve retaining cup
Plunger spring
Lifter body
Oil-feed hole

Tools and materials: Long-nose pliers, small flat-blade screwdriver, pencil with eraser or ¼-in.-diameter dowel rod, paper clip or stiff wire, parts-cleaning solvent, SAE 10 oil, pan and clean rags.

Disassembling a lifter

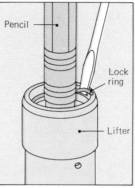

Pencil — Lock ring — Lifter

1. Depress plunger with pencil or dowel. At the same time, remove the wire lock ring with pliers or a screwdriver blade.

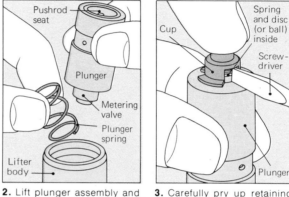

Pushrod seat — Plunger — Metering valve — Plunger spring — Lifter body

2. Lift plunger assembly and spring out of lifter body. Also remove pushrod seat and metering valve from plunger.

Cup — Spring and disc (or ball) inside — Screwdriver — Plunger

3. Carefully pry up retaining cup on check valve, then remove check-valve disc (or check-valve ball) and spring.

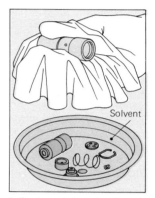

Solvent

4. Soak parts in solvent, such as carburetor cleaner. Check pieces carefully for signs of wear, scoring, or grittiness.

Reassembling a lifter

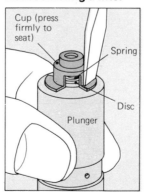

Cup (press firmly to seat) — Spring — Disc — Plunger

1. Place check-valve disc or ball on plunger, then position spring on top. Reinstall cup, seating it firmly by pressing around the edges.

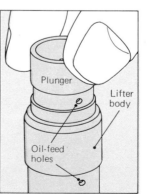

Plunger — Lifter body — Oil-feed holes

2. Place plunger spring in lifter body. Insert plunger, making sure that oil-feed holes in the lifter body and the plunger align when pressed together.

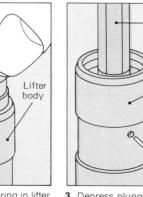

Pencil — Lifter body — Paper clip

3. Depress plunger, using pencil or dowel, until oil-feed holes align. Insert opened paper clip into holes to lock plunger in place. Remove pencil or dowel.

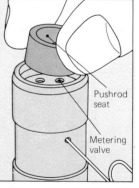

Pushrod seat — Metering valve

4. Fill lifter with SAE 10 oil. Reinstall metering valve, pushrod seat, and wire lock ring. Press against pushrod seat and remove paper clip.

Removing V-engine lifters 🔧🔧🔧🔧🔧

On most V-type engines the valve lifters are inaccessible unless the engine is first partially dismantled and the intake manifold is removed. This is a big job that should not be attempted by a beginner. If you do not have the time to do the job properly, take the car to an experienced mechanic. Before you begin, make sure you understand the removal and reinstallation procedures for each part, and check to see that you have the tools, replacement gaskets, seals, and tune-up equipment necessary to complete the job. You should also have a copy of your car's service manual. Disconnect the battery, and clean the engine before disassembling it. As you work, keep exposed engine ports and passages covered with plastic or blocked with rags to prevent dirt from entering the engine.

Installing new lifters 🔧🔧🔧🔧🔧

To install new or overhauled hydraulic lifters, fill them with oil (p.428), coat them with molybdenum disulfide grease, then place them in their bores. Reinstall the pushrods and rocker assemblies. Tighten the adjusting nut (if any) on each rocker arm (see p.276) while rotating the pushrod with your fingers. When slight resistance is felt as you turn the pushrod, tighten the nut the additional amount specified in *Tuneup Data*. Replace the manifold and other engine parts. Torque the rocker shaft bolts or ball stud nuts to specifications. Refill the crankcase with a premium oil the carmaker recommends. Run the engine at idle until all the lifters fill with oil and become quiet. When the engine is warm, make final adjustments to valve clearance.

Reinstalling the manifold 🔧🔧🔧🔧🔧

Reinstall the intake manifold after the lifters are in place and the valve train has been reassembled. Use new manifold gaskets and seals. First, clean all mating surfaces with solvent, such as lacquer thinner or trichloroethylene, then follow the service manual's instructions to apply silicone rubber sealant at points along the gaskets and engine surfaces. Carefully position the new gaskets and seals on the engine. Then, with help from an assistant, lower the manifold into place without sliding it back and forth. Fasten the manifold bolts and nuts, and torque them according to the manufacturer's tightening pattern and torque specifications. After the engine has been completely reassembled and brought to operating temperature, re-torque the manifold nuts.

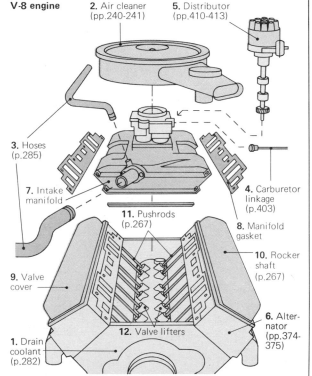

V-8 engine

2. Air cleaner (pp.240-241)
5. Distributor (pp.410-413)
3. Hoses (p.285)
7. Intake manifold
4. Carburetor linkage (p.403)
11. Pushrods (p.267)
8. Manifold gasket
9. Valve cover
10. Rocker shaft (p.267)
12. Valve lifters
6. Alternator (pp.374-375)
1. Drain coolant (p.282)

Typical sequence for removing parts of most V-type engines: Numbers indicate order of removal; page listings refer to specific procedures. Reassemble engine by following this sequence in reverse order. Final step is to give engine a complete tuneup.

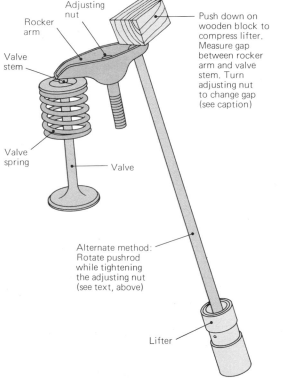

Adjusting nut
Rocker arm
Valve stem
Valve spring
Valve
Push down on wooden block to compress lifter. Measure gap between rocker arm and valve stem. Turn adjusting nut to change gap (see caption)
Alternate method: Rotate pushrod while tightening the adjusting nut (see text, above)
Lifter

To measure valve clearance, rotate the crankshaft until the valve is closed, push down the pushrod to compress the lifter, then measure the gap between the rocker and the valve. Clearance can be adjusted only on Ford V-8s and Chevrolet V-8s and sixes.

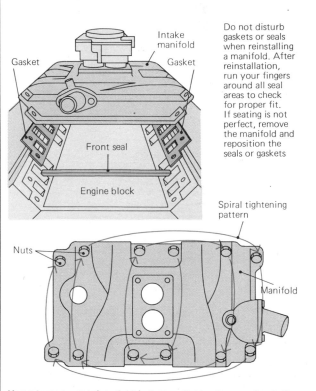

Gasket
Intake manifold
Gasket
Front seal
Engine block
Nuts
Spiral tightening pattern
Manifold

Do not disturb gaskets or seals when reinstalling a manifold. After reinstallation, run your fingers around all seal areas to check for proper fit. If seating is not perfect, remove the manifold and reposition the seals or gaskets

Use a torque wrench to tighten the manifold nuts according to the carmaker's instructions. Torque the nuts gradually, in stages, following a spiral pattern (or carmaker's recommended pattern) to ensure equal distribution of stress throughout the manifold.

Bolts

Bolts, screws, and *studs* are the basic automotive fasteners. Though commonplace items, they are precision made and engineered to meet the specific requirements of particular holding tasks. To be effective, fasteners must be chosen carefully—matched for size, strength, and thread pitch to the jobs they are designed to do. Fasteners must also be installed correctly, neither too loosely nor too tightly. Bolts are the most common type of automobile fastener and the one most often subject to great stress. Their heads have raised markings to indicate tensile strength and thus potential breaking points. Unmarked bolts are designed for no-load use where stress is not a problem.

When replacing a bolt, always substitute another bolt of the same or greater strength. To make sure you obtain a proper replacement, take the old bolt with you to the parts dealer and identify it by its use as well as its size. Also check that the threads of the new bolt fit the threads of the hole into which it is to go; non-metric bolts, studs, and machine screws have either coarse (NC), fine (NF), or special (NS) threads, and a mismatch will result in damage or breakage to both the hole and the fastener.

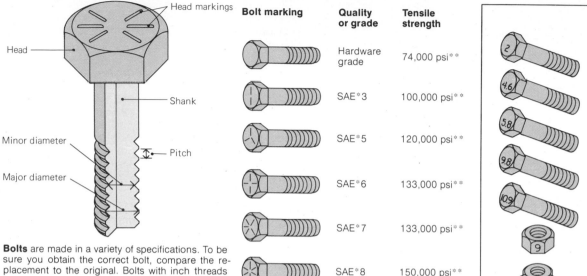

Bolts are made in a variety of specifications. To be sure you obtain the correct bolt, compare the replacement to the original. Bolts with inch threads have symbols to indicate their strength (right). Bolts with metric threads have numerals that indicate their strength (far right). The higher the number, the stronger the fastener.

Bolt marking	Quality or grade	Tensile strength
	Hardware grade	74,000 psi**
	SAE*3	100,000 psi**
	SAE*5	120,000 psi**
	SAE*6	133,000 psi**
	SAE*7	133,000 psi**
	SAE*8	150,000 psi**

*Society of Automotive Engineers
**Pounds per square inch

Screws

Automotive screws are distinguished by their shape, thread character, and type of drive. Slotted and cross-drive (Phillips) screws are the most common. Always be sure that the screwdriver you are using fits correctly, in order to avoid damaging the screw and perhaps making it impossible to turn.

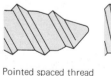

Pointed spaced thread

Blunt-end spaced thread

Self-tapping machine thread

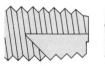

Thread-cutting machine thread

Thread-cutting spaced thread

Multiple-thread drive (for plastic or fiber)

Slotted screw takes flat-blade screwdriver. Blade should be same width as screwhead.

Cross-drive (Phillips) screwdriver is blunt tipped; screw slots curve at junction.

Reed and Prince screwdriver has pointed tip; slots meet at right angles.

Torx® screws with star-shaped drive slots are used in door locks, seat belts, and body parts.

Allen screw requires hexagonal key. Correct-size key will not round off screw corners.

Studs

Studs resemble headless bolts. They may be threaded along their entire length, at each end, or at only one end. One end of a stud is screwed into a threaded hole or pressed into a smooth hole. The other end receives a nut, often tightened to careful torque specifications (see facing page). Studs are often used in engines. Special techniques are needed to install and remove studs without damaging their threads or the holes into which they are driven.

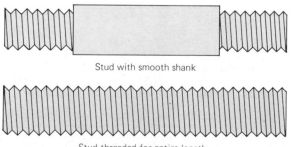

Stud with smooth shank

Stud threaded for entire length

Nuts and washers

Nuts and washers vary as much in shape and size as bolts do. Except in the case of rubber or fiber washers, all three parts should be made of the same metal. This prevents thread damage, seizing, and abrasion damage, called *galling*, which occurs when a hard metal, such as steel, rubs against a softer one, such as aluminum. Washers reduce the chances of seizing and galling, and in addition perform three other functions. Flat washers reduce friction that develops under the head of the fastener and lessen the possibility of breakage. They also distribute load over a greater area than the nut or bolt head. Lock washers, of which there are many varieties, increase friction, usually under the nut, and prevent the fastener from working loose. Nuts and washers are often made as one part, which makes them easier to work with and prevents the washers from getting lost.

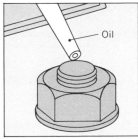

Steel locknut   Nut with integral washer

Flat washer   Lock washers

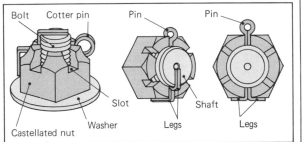

Bolt Cotter pin   Pin   Pin

Slot   Shaft

Castellated nut   Washer   Legs   Legs

A castellated nut is a heavy-duty locknut held in place by a cotter pin that passes through the bolt or stud. To install, tighten nut to proper torque until one pair of slots is aligned with hole in bolt. Loosen slightly, if necessary, to achieve correct alignment. Insert cotter pin so that head seats vertically in slot, cut legs to proper length, then lock by bending one leg of pin over end of shaft, the other down over nut (center). On VW wheel bearing nuts covered by a dust cap with a static collector, insert pin with head sideways, and bend legs around lower portion of nut (right).

Installation tips

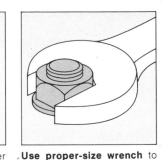

Oil

Check condition of fastener before installing. Clean or replace if necessary. Lubricate threads with light oil or anti-seize compound to prevent rust and to ease removal.

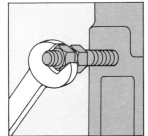

Screw head

Use largest screwdriver that will fit screw in order to benefit from maximum torque. To prevent tip from slipping out of screw, hold blade with other hand as you turn handle.

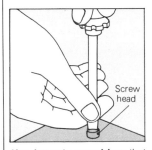

Cam

Stud extractor   Stud

Use stud extractor to install as well as remove studs with smooth shank portions. Tool fits socket wrench handles. Knurled eccentric cam drives stud, fits all common sizes.

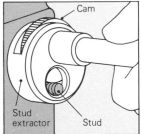

Use proper-size wrench to avoid damaging fastener. Inch-size bolt heads and nuts are 3/16 in. larger than diameter of shank. (Thus, for a 1/4-in. bolt, choose a 7/16-in. wrench.)

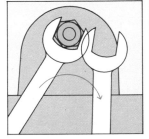

Take advantage of wrench offset in tight places. Turn wrench over after each swing to reverse angle of its opening, thereby increasing the available turning arc.

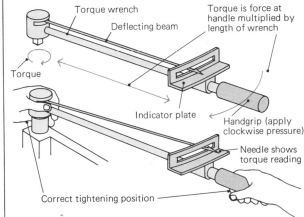

Use two nuts to install or remove fully threaded studs. Tighten nuts firmly against each other, then turn top nut with wrench to install stud, bottom nut to remove it.

Using a torque wrench

Many fasteners must be tightened to precise specifications in order to avoid damaging either the fasteners themselves or the assemblies they hold together. Such exact installing and adjusting requires a torque wrench, which measures the amount of twisting force (torque) being applied to a fastener as it is tightened. Automobile manufacturers list torque specifications in maintenance manuals for individual cars. The standard English units of torque measurement are *pound-feet* (lb-ft); their metric equivalents are *Newton-meters* (N-m).

Torque wrench   Torque is force at handle multiplied by length of wrench

Deflecting beam

Torque

Indicator plate

Handgrip (apply clockwise pressure)

Correct tightening position   Needle shows torque reading

Torque wrench responds to pressure applied by the user and gives readings that also incorporate the length of the wrench handle. To ensure accuracy, hold the wrench at the handgrip portion of the handle only, and apply smooth, steady force.

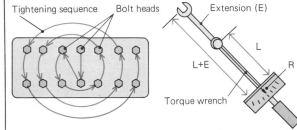

Tightening sequence   Bolt heads   Extension (E)

L

L+E   R

Torque wrench

Tighten groups of fasteners in spiral patterns or according to sequence listed by carmaker. Apply torque in two or three stages, working around gradually until fasteners are all tight.

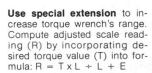

Use special extension to increase torque wrench's range. Compute adjusted scale reading (R) by incorporating desired torque value (T) into formula: $R = T \times L \div L + E$

431

Repair / **Threaded fasteners**

Removing tight fasteners

Threaded fasteners become rusted or corroded easily and are often very difficult to remove. Patience and plenty of penetrating oil are usually effective, even in obstinate cases. Use your imagination and judgment to solve removal problems. For instance, it may be more feasible to break or saw through an expendable fastener than to unscrew it; if it is badly worn, it will have to be replaced anyway. It is better to break a rusted nut purposely than to risk snapping a stud to which it is fastened. A difficult fastener may be part of a larger unit that could be removed first to give you better access for working to free stuck parts.

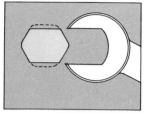

File sides of nut or bolt square if they have become rounded. Use open-end wrench to remove. Replace the part.

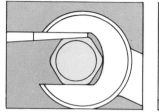

Grip odd-size or rounded-off fasteners by wedging screwdriver between edge of fastener and jaw of open-end wrench.

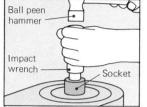

Use impact wrench and sockets to free stuck nuts and bolts. Wrench converts hammer blows into twisting force.

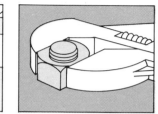

To break off badly rusted nut without damaging bolt or stud, saw off two sides, then twist, using adjustable wrench.

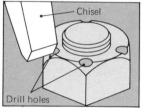

To break large nuts, drill corners, then cut with cold chisel. First make pilot marks with punch to guide drill bit.

Nut splitter is excellent removal tool if space allows. Use one that works from above or the side, as access allows.

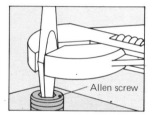

Free a stuck screw by alternate tightening and loosening. To grip damaged screw, use ordinary or locking pliers.

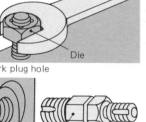

Remove damaged Allen screw by hammering screwdriver into recess; turn screwdriver with adjustable wrench.

Thread care

Preventive maintenance of threaded fasteners keeps them working smoothly and often prevents damage to internal threads on parts that are expensive to replace. Make sure that threads are clean, damage free, and the correct size.

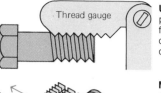

Use a thread gauge to positively identify fasteners, and avoid damage caused by cross-threading parts.

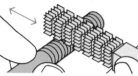

Mildly clogged or rusty threads are cleaned with a thread-restoring file and plenty of penetrating oil.

Clean badly clogged threads with a thread-restoring die. Replace fasteners whose threads are badly corroded.

If spark plugs are hard to remove, clean the spark plug hole with a spark plug *thread chaser* before installing new plugs.

Removing broken studs

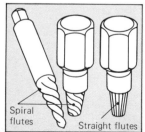

Three types of extractors for broken studs: spiral-fluted types remove right-hand threaded studs only; straight-fluted type removes studs with right- or left-hand threads.

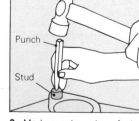

1. To remove stud, first apply generous amount of penetrating oil and allow it to soak in for 15 min or longer. Tap stud with hammer to set up vibrations, which loosen rust.

2. Mark exact center of stud with sharp center punch. Hold punch vertical and strike sharply with ball peen hammer. Indentation provides pilot mark for drilling (next step).

3. Drill hole into center of stud, using drill bit whose diameter is half the diameter of the stud and matches shaft diameter of extractor. Drill hole deep enough to seat extractor.

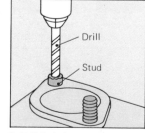

4. Drive splined extractor into hole. Proper size is half the diameter of stud. Avoid glancing blows, which may break brittle extractor. (Spiral extractor is screwed into hole.)

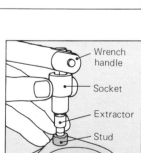

5. Twist out stud, applying force smoothly. Standard-sized wrenches fit extractor ends. Do not use too much force, since a broken extractor is often very difficult to remove.

Repairing stripped threads ◨◨◨ 15–30 min

If the threads on a bolt, screw, or stud become damaged, the best remedy is simply to replace the fastener. However, damaged internal threads in a part such as a cylinder head, engine block, or oil pan, must be repaired, usually by replacing the threads with *threaded inserts*.

Complete insert kits for thread repair are available from several manufacturers. The inserts are of different types intended for different uses. The coil type is best where heat transfer is important, as when replacing stripped threads in spark plug holes (a common problem, especially on cars with aluminum cylinder heads) or when replacing exhaust manifold threads, which must withstand wide ranges of ex-

pansion and contraction. Sleeve-type inserts, less expensive and generally easier to install, work well for such jobs as replacing threads in oil drain plug openings, where stresses are less severe. Special, very thin sleeves are available for spark plug holes.

Most jobs call for drilling out the damaged threads first. You will need an electric drill and a bit of a specific size, which is listed by the kit manufacturer on the package. Make sure that the drill bit fits the chuck of your drill: frequently, large-diameter bits that require a ⅜- or ½-inch drill chuck must be used.

You may not need to use an insert if you can drill out the damaged threads, tap new threads, and use a larger bolt in place of the original.

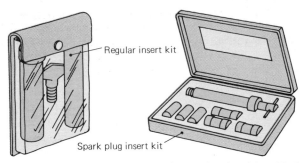

Kits for replacing stripped threads consist of stainless steel thread inserts and matching installation tools. Nearly all sizes are available, including kits for motorcycles and imported cars.

Replacing blind threads

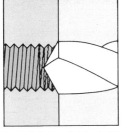 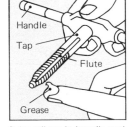 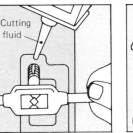 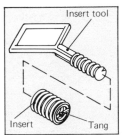 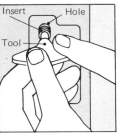 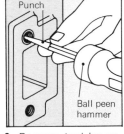 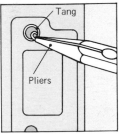

1. Drill hole slightly oversize to remove damaged threads. Use drill size specified in kit instructions. Mark bit with tape to avoid drilling too deep.

2. Install tap in handle and apply grease to flutes to trap metal chips. Handle may not be supplied with some kits. If not, it can be purchased separately.

3. Apply cutting fluid or oil to tap. Then screw tap clockwise into hole. After every two turns forward, back off one-half turn to clear chips from tap.

4. Select proper-size thread insert, and slip it onto insert tool. Tang at end of insert must engage raised portion on end of installation tool.

5. Install insert by screwing tool clockwise into tapped hole until top of insert is one-quarter to one-half turn below top surface of hole.

6. Remove tool by unscrewing it counterclockwise. If insert tang will obstruct fastener, remove tang by striking it sharply with a punch.

7. Tang should break at notch on insert. Extract tang from hole with a bent length of wire, a magnetic pickup tool, or a pair of long-nose pliers.

Replacing threads on spark plug holes

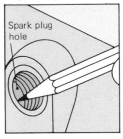 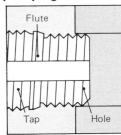 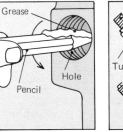 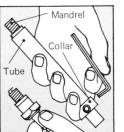 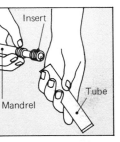 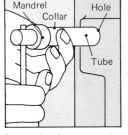 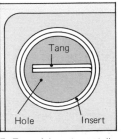

1. Rotate engine so that piston is well clear of plug hole (p.275). Check clearance by inserting long pencil into plug hole until it hits piston.

2. Drill out old threads in cast-iron heads. Use tap alone on aluminum. Grease flutes. Install tap in plug hole; twist clockwise to cut insert threads.

3. Clean metal chips from hole and surrounding area. Use pencil or wire tipped with grease to extract chips that may have fallen inside cylinder.

4. Adjust mandrel so that threaded portion extending beyond tube equals length of plug threads. Lock collar on mandrel with an Allen wrench.

5. Install insert on mandrel, then twist mandrel clockwise into tube until insert engages tube threads. Insert should not protrude beyond mandrel.

6. Hold tube squarely against hole, and rotate mandrel clockwise until collar hits tube. If you feel resistance, remove tool and begin again.

7. Top of insert must lie one-quarter to one-half turn below surface of hole. Use pliers to break and remove tang by bending it at notch.

Inspecting for leaks and wear ⏱ 15–25 min

Excessive or unusual noises—hissing, rumbling, or rattling—coming from beneath the car are almost always signs that the exhaust system needs repair. To inspect your car's exhaust system, place the car on jack stands (p.176) and check each part for damage or misalignment visually and by feel. Start with the tail pipe and work forward toward the engine compartment. Do not overlook the exhaust manifolds; they

can become loose, or their gaskets may wear out. To find leaks where damage is not apparent, make the inspection outdoors with the engine idling. Have a helper partially block the exhaust pipe with a wad of rags. Without touching the parts themselves, carefully place your hands near the exhaust system joints or areas where hissing can be heard. You should be able to feel any jets of escaping gas.

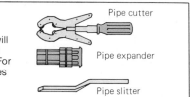

Special tools for exhaust work are shown here. You will also need ordinary mechanic's tools. For safety, wear goggles and work gloves.

Pipe cutter

Pipe expander

Pipe slitter

Troubleshooting the exhaust system

Symptom	Cause	Cure
Excessive noise	Faulty joints	Tighten clamps; reassemble joints with sealer
	Hole in pipe or muffler	Install new parts
	Muffler baffles rusted out	Replace muffler
	Leaking exhaust manifold	Tighten, or install new gasket
Poor engine idle, perform-ance, and eco-nomy after tuneup; pop-ping noise at carburetor	Dented pipe	Repair or replace damaged pipe
	Blockage inside exhaust system	Test muffler and pipes for collapsed inner chambers (p.264); replace if necessary. Check manifolds for casting flash; repair or replace. Check pipes for obstruction
	Manifold heat valve frozen	Free valve with penetrating oil, or replace
Underbody rattles	Loose or mis-aligned parts	Check for broken parts, especially hangers; tighten, realign, or replace

Exhaust manifolds

Hangers

Tail pipe

Manifold heat valve

Resonator

Hanger

Muffler

Clamp

Front pipe

Crossover pipe

Catalytic converter

Exhaust pipe

U-bolt

Clamp

Dented or kinked pipe restricts exhaust flow if dent is deeper than one-quarter of pipe diameter. Check pipe after a rear-end collision, especially over axle.

Check for broken hangers or loose clamps. Vibrating components develop leaks; contact with underbody causes rattles. Severe damage can result if parts droop excessively.

Tap muffler and pipes with wrench to check internal condition. Rust or collapsed inner parts will produce dull thuds or rattles. Clear ringing indicates a part is OK.

Push up on muffler and other fixtures to check condition of end tubes and seams. Check rust damage on all parts by jabbing with a screwdriver. If holes develop, replace parts.

Exhaust manifold heat valves ⏱⏱ 10–20 min

Hard-to-trace performance problems may be caused by a stuck heat valve in the exhaust manifold. Signs that the valve is stuck closed are: difficult warmup, poor idling, and engine stumbling. If the valve sticks open, poor engine performance, lower fuel economy, and vapor lock may result. To check mechanical-type valves, start the engine cold and, as it warms up, watch for movement of the valve shaft end and counterweight. Free a sticking valve by spraying the valve shaft with penetrating oil.

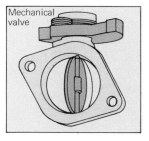

Mechanical valve

To test vacuum-type heat valves, start the engine cold, and watch for movement of the diaphragm link as the engine warms up. If the link does not move, disconnect the vacuum hose to the diaphragm while the engine is running, and check that vacuum is present. If there is none, check all hose connections as well as the switch in the water jacket where the hose begins. If there is vacuum, disassemble the link and diaphragm to check for faults. Starting a warm engine should produce no movement.

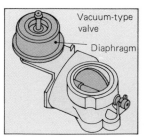

Vacuum-type valve

Diaphragm

Working with pipes and clamps 🔧🔧🔧

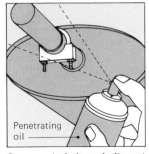

Spray rusted clamp bolts and hangers with penetrating oil to loosen them, unless they are to be replaced. Dry bolts can be broken off with a long wrench.

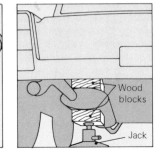

Joints are sometimes packed with sealer. To loosen them, tap around the seams with a hammer, then twist pieces apart with hands or pliers.

When working with flex-mounted parts, steady them by wedging blocks of wood above and below and applying pressure to the pieces with a jack.

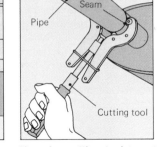

Use pipe-cutting tool to cut away components being replaced. This tool is also needed for work on exhaust systems with welded joints.

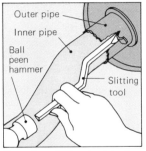

Use pipe-slitting tool to free connections where outer pipe will be replaced. Used carefully, tool peels away outer pipe, leaves inner pipe undamaged.

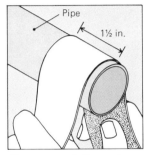

Use pipe expander to restore shape of pipe ends remaining on car. This assures snug fit with new pipes and keeps leaks from developing.

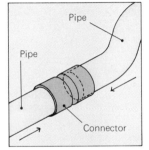

Use emery cloth, sandpaper, or a wire brush to clean a 1½-in. area at the ends of all pipes to be joined. To ensure leak-free fit, sand metal until shiny.

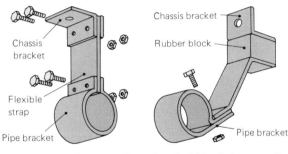

If pipe has a hole or dent limited to a small, straight section, cut out damaged part and replace it with pipe connector, sold at auto parts stores.

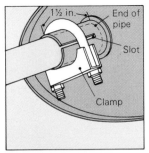

To install U clamps, first join pipes fully. Position clamp over slots in outer pipe, then tighten. Do not overtighten bolts so much that they crush pipes.

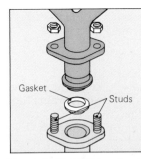

To avoid breaking exhaust pipe flange-joint studs during removal, use plenty of penetrating oil. Install new gaskets or seal rings during reassembly.

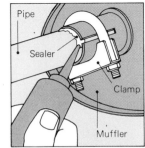

Ball joints are used instead of flange joints for some manifolds and exhaust pipes. Disassemble joint by removing clamp bolts on each side.

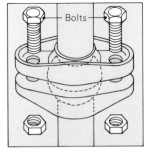

Apply sealer, required on some cars, after joints are clamped and checked for proper alignment. Run engine to harden sealer.

Replacing hangers 🔧🔧 10–20 min

Exhaust pipe hangers are attached to the car underbody. They suspend the exhaust system beneath the car, away from all chassis parts. Many hangers have pipe clamps. There are several different styles of hanger, but each incorporates flexible, nonmetallic portions that accommodate the exhaust system's natural vibrations and prevent them from being transferred to the car itself, where they would produce excessive noise. A stretched or broken exhaust hanger will weaken nearby joints and allow parts to rattle against the underbody. Checking the condition of the hangers and replacing any that are damaged, stretched, or torn should be a part of every exhaust inspection. Try to buy exact duplicates of the original parts; otherwise, improvise with *universal hangers*, available at auto parts stores.

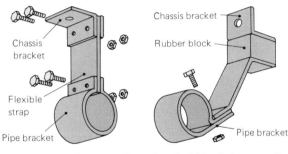

Flexible strap hanger: Remove bolts at chassis and at exhaust pipe. Replace strap. Replace brackets and bolts, if necessary.

Bonded block hanger: Remove top and bottom bolts, and replace entire assembly. Replace pipe bracket and bolt if they are damaged.

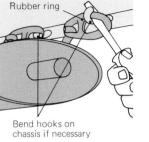

Rubber ring: Cut through old ring to remove, or push up on pipe and slip ring off hook. Stretch new ring to fit, using long screwdriver as lever.

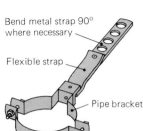

Universal hanger: Bolt metal strap to chassis through hole that will allow exhaust system to hang at proper height. Tighten bracket around pipe.

435

Replacing a muffler ⬚⬚⬚ 1–3 hr

Replacing a damaged or rusted-through muffler or exhaust pipe is not a mechanically difficult task, but it is often complicated by inadequate working space under the car or by corroded or damaged parts that are hard to remove. The car must be raised on sturdy jack stands, and the muffler or damaged pipe cut or chiseled off with special tools. You may prefer to leave muffler replacement to a professional (see

pp.454–455). If you decide to do the work yourself, obtain the necessary tools and equipment, and plan the job carefully before you begin. Some stores that sell mufflers also rent the special tools. Have all the replacement parts you will need at hand, including new hangers, clamps, and sealer. Wear goggles to keep rust particles out of your eyes, and gloves to prevent skinned knuckles.

Exhaust systems usually rust out from the back end forward, so that the tail pipe and muffler will need to be replaced most often. Small holes in other parts of the system can often be repaired with exhaust putty or patches, or by cutting out a short section and replacing it with an exhaust pipe connector. Buy stainless steel or *aluminized* replacement parts if you can afford them; they last longest.

Removing an old muffler

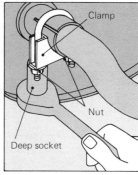

1. Soak muffler clamp fittings and joints with penetrating oil for a few hours before beginning work. Remove clamps from muffler, using a deep socket or a box-end wrench.

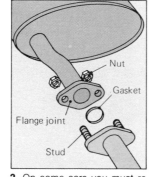

2. On some cars you must remove nuts from flange-joint studs instead of clamps. Be careful not to break the studs. When installing new muffler, use new gaskets.

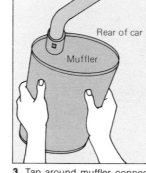

3. Tap around muffler connections with hammer to break any sealer present. Then try to loosen muffler by twisting it up and down by hand, working muffler toward rear of car.

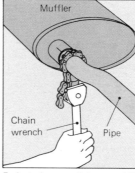

4. Should loosening muffler by hand prove difficult, strike muffler with a wooden or rubber mallet. Direct solid blows against the end seams, forcing muffler off pipes.

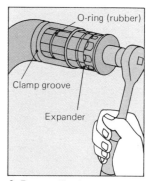

5. A chain wrench is especially useful for twisting pipe connections apart. Use smooth side of chain for best grip on round surfaces. Water-pump pliers can also be used.

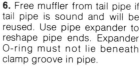

6. Free muffler from tail pipe if tail pipe is sound and will be reused. Use pipe expander to reshape pipe ends. Expander O-ring must not lie beneath clamp groove in pipe.

Installing a new muffler

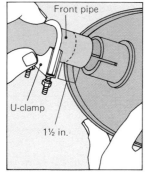

1. Check that ends of front pipe and muffler are round and free of rust. Polish tips with sandpaper or emery cloth until metal shines. Then slip U-clamps over end of each pipe.

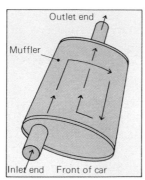

2. Position muffler to fit into or over pipe ends (see maker's instructions). Replacement mufflers are marked to indicate inlet and outlet ends; be sure muffler inlet faces front of car.

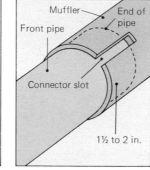

3. Slip front of muffler (inlet end) over end of front pipe. Overlap should not exceed 2 in. Tabs on pipe, if present, should seat firmly in slots of muffler connector section.

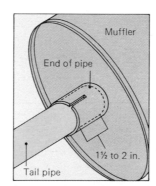

4. Install rear of muffler (outlet end) over tail pipe, following same procedure outlined in Step 3. Check that both pipes protrude into muffler beyond length of connector slots.

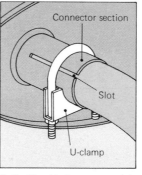

5. Position U-clamps over slots in muffler connectors. Adjust pipes so that they clear all parts of car, then tighten clamps. Use pipe connectors (p.435) if changes in length are needed.

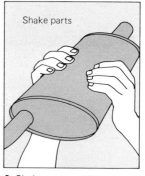

6. Shake reassembled exhaust system to check fit and clearance of parts. Start engine and check exhaust for leaks. Apply sealer to joints if desired or if called for by manufacturer.

Replacing a Volkswagen muffler ▢▢▢▢▢ 2–3 hr

Replacing a Volkswagen muffler differs substantially from working with other makes. The procedures shown here are for the standard, carburetor-equipped "Type I" Beetle, Super Beetle, and Karmann Ghia models. They do not apply to VWs with automatic stick shifts, fuel injection, or catalytic converter exhausts. Owing to emission-control equipment on these cars, their mufflers should be handled

by a Volkswagen dealer or by a professional garage with adequate emission-testing equipment.

Muffler work on a VW can be done with the car on the ground, but the job will be much easier if the car is raised on ramps, jack stands, or a lift, especially if the parts and fasteners to be removed are badly corroded or frozen. Soak fasteners with penetrating oil before trying to loosen them.

Tools: Flat-blade screwdriver, Phillips screwdriver, 13-mm open-end wrench, 10-mm open-end wrench, 10-mm box-end wrench, 10-mm socket wrench (⅜-in. drive), 6-in. socket wrench extension, ¼-in. drift punch.
Materials: Penetrating oil, masking tape, replacement VW muffler, clamps, gasket set, replacement heat exchanger inserts (if necessary).

Preheater pipes
Crankshaft pulley
Cylinder head muffler flange stud
Heat exchanger
Heater hose adapter
Muffler clamp
Rear-engine cover plate
Cylinder head opening gasket
Warm air channel clamp
Muffler
Dual pipes

Removing cover plates

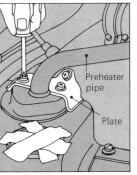

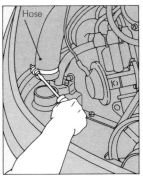

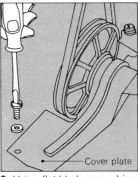

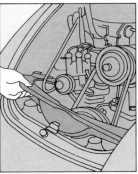

1. Raise and prop engine hood. Pull off preheater hose. Loosen heater clamps, then remove hoses. Remove heater hose adapter and both heater hose grommets.

2. Tape heater hose openings to avoid loosing small parts. Using Phillips screwdriver, remove screws holding right and left preheater pipe protection plates. Remove plates.

3. Using flat-blade screwdriver, remove screws holding crankshaft pulley cover plate in place. Remove plate, exposing crankshaft pulley and large nut on rear end of crankshaft.

4. Using flat-blade screwdriver, remove screws holding rear engine cover plate at right, left, and center. Tilt plate forward and lift up to remove. Clean both plates before reassembly.

Removing an old muffler

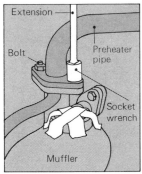

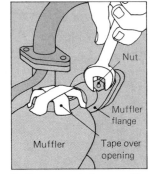

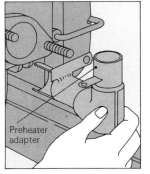

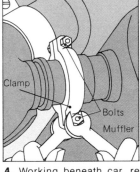

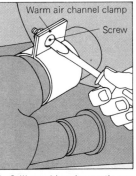

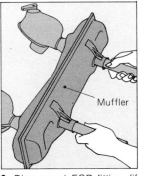

1. Remove bolts attaching right and left preheater pipes to muffler, using 10-mm socket wrench and 6-in. extension. You may need to apply penetrating oil to loosen bolts.

2. Remove nuts from muffler flange studs in right and left cylinder head, using 13-mm open-end wrench. Nuts are hard to reach. Remove lower ones from beneath car.

3. Pull off the carburetor preheater adapter, located on right side beneath engine. Adapter was freed by removing lower nut on right cylinder head's muffler flange stud (Step 2).

4. Working beneath car, remove right and left heat exchanger clamps, using the two 10-mm flat wrenches. Use one wrench to hold bolt heads, the other to turn nuts off shank.

5. Still working beneath car, loosen right and left warm air channel clamps connecting muffler to upper heat exchanger openings. Use flat-blade screwdriver.

6. Disconnect EGR fitting (if any). Grasp tail pipes and pull muffler backward, working it off heat exchanger ends. Clear preheater pipes if they are plugged with rust.

Replacing a Volkswagen muffler *(continued)*

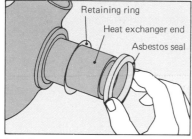

1. Before installing new muffler, polish scale from right and left heat exchanger ends. Install one muffler clamp retaining ring and one asbestos seal on each end, pushing them as far forward as possible.

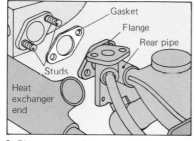

2. Place new gaskets over studs on openings of right and left cylinder heads. Install new muffler by pushing rear pipes over heat exchanger ends until cylinder head flanges seat over studs and gaskets.

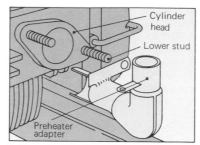

3. Fasten muffler to cylinder head with 13-mm nuts. Before installing lower nut at right cylinder head opening, fit carburetor preheater adapter in place over stud, on top of muffler flange.

Repairing heat exchangers

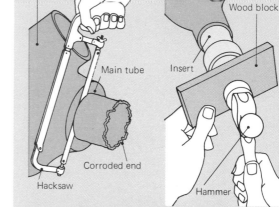

Very often, rust and corrosion destroy the ends of the heat exchangers. Auto supply stores carry inexpensive inserts made of heavy-gauge steel which can be used to restore the heat exchanger ends. To install an insert, use a hacksaw to cut off the corroded exchanger end flush with the main tube. Then, use a heavy ball peen hammer and a block of wood to drive the small-diameter portion of the insert into the opening as far as it will go. Inserts can easily be installed while a muffler is being replaced, but they can also be fitted with the muffler only partially removed.

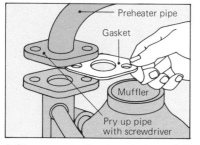

4. Slip new preheater pipe adapter gaskets in place between right and left preheater pipe ends and muffler openings. Fasten pipes with 10-mm bolts. Use drift punch to align holes if necessary.

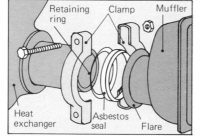

5. Install heat exchanger clamps, using 10-mm bolts, after repositioning asbestos seals and retaining rings to seat against muffler's rear pipes. Clamp surrounds both muffler pipe flare and retaining ring.

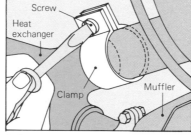

6. Reattach right and left warm air channel clamps, using flat-blade screwdriver. Check all fasteners, reinstall engine cover plates and hoses (see p.437), and remove all tape from covered openings.

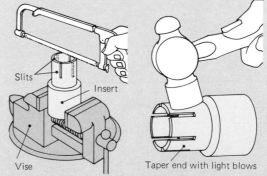

Since a tight fit is best, inserts are often manufactured oversized. Alter them to fit by hacksawing vertical slits along the small-diameter portion, then tap each section lightly with a hammer to taper the end.

Adjusting tail pipes

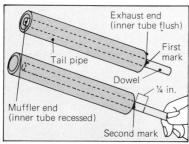
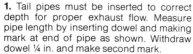

1. Tail pipes must be inserted to correct depth for proper exhaust flow. Measure pipe length by inserting dowel and making mark at end of pipe as shown. Withdraw dowel ¼ in. and make second mark.

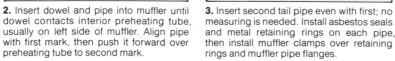

2. Insert dowel and pipe into muffler until dowel contacts interior preheating tube, usually on left side of muffler. Align pipe with first mark, then push it forward over preheating tube to second mark.

3. Insert second tail pipe even with first; no measuring is needed. Install asbestos seals and metal retaining rings on each pipe, then install muffler clamps over retaining rings and muffler pipe flanges.

Troubleshooting steering and suspension problems

Steering and suspension systems are interrelated. If one or more parts in either system are bent, damaged, too loose, or too tight, both steering and handling can be affected. Always be alert to changes in your car's handling characteristics. A malfunction in the steering or suspension can be as serious as faulty brakes. Examine the underbody components periodically, especially the steering linkage, shock absorbers, wheels, and tires, since some of these items require adjustment or replacement at intervals of 25,000 to 50,000 miles. It is a good idea to check all these parts whenever you are working under the car.

How to use this chart

Find problem at top of chart. Look down column to locate possible causes. First, check out things you can fix yourself; then, things you *may* be able to fix yourself. If problem is still not solved, consult a competent mechanic.

- ○ You can fix it yourself.
- ● You *may* be able to make a complete repair.
- ■ You need a mechanic.

Problem column key

1. Car pulls to one side
2. Car wanders from side to side
3. Car vibrates at high speeds
4. Front wheels shimmy
5. Wheel thumps
6. Uneven tire wear
7. Rapid or excessive tire wear
8. Wear on sides of tires (scuffing)
9. Non-parallel wheel tracking ("crabbing")
10. Car hard to steer (manual)
11. Car hard to steer (power)
12. Steering wheel shimmies
13. Poor steering wheel return (manual)
14. Poor steering wheel return (power)
15. Play or looseness in steering
16. Loud squeal in steering
17. Grinding noise in steering
18. Steering noise in steering (power)
19. Steering erratic when brakes are applied
20. Steering wheel kicks back (power)
21. Steering wheel surges or jerks (power)
22. Noise in front end
23. Heavy thumps on rough roads
24. Body leans or sways when car corners
25. Suspension bottoms out on bumps
26. Ride too hard
27. Ride too soft

Possible cause	Applicable problem columns	Cure
Improper tire pressure	1○ 2○ 3○ 4○ 6○ 7○ 9○ 23○ 24○ 26○ 27○	Adjust tire pressure (p.184)
Steering linkage is dry	9○ 13○ 14○	Lubricate linkage (p.191)
Front end is misaligned	1■ 2■ 4■ 6■ 7■ 8■ 9■ 13■ 14■ 19■	Have alignment checked (p.221)
Suspension arms are damaged	1■ 2■ 4■ 6■ 7■ 8■ 22■ 23■	Check and repair suspension (p.190)
Ball joints are binding	9● 13● 14●	Grease or replace ball joints (pp.192–193)
Springs are sagging or broken	1■ 2■ 4■ 8■ 9■ 19■ 22■ 23■ 24■ 25■	Have new or helper springs installed
Power steering belt slips	11○ 14○	Tighten or replace belt (pp.286–287)
Power steering fluid too low	11○ 16○	Add power steering fluid (p.195)
Faulty power steering pump	11■ 18■	Have pump tested and repaired
Loose sway bar, worn bushings	1● 2● 4● 24●	Tighten or replace loose or worn parts
Brakes are dragging or grabbing	1● 19●	Adjust or repair brakes (pp.210–218)
Wheels wobble	3○ 4○ 6○	Have faulty wheel replaced
Dissimilar tires	1○ 4○	Install same-type tires on all wheels
Uneven tire tread	1○ 4○ 6○	Replace tires so tread depth is even on all wheels
MacPherson strut bearing is worn	8● 9● 19●	Replace worn parts (pp.442-445)
Tie rod ends are worn	4■ 6■ 12■ 15■	Have tie rod ends replaced
Bump or blister on tire	3○ 5○ 6○	Replace faulty tire (p.184)
Car is overloaded	24○ 25○	Remove extra weight from car, or install heavier shocks
Rear-axle housing is bent	5■ 8■	Have axle housing checked and repaired
Frame or underbody is misaligned	1■ 5■ 8■ 9■ 19■	Have frame and underbody checked and realigned
Hard driving	6○	Install tires suited to driving habits and road conditions
Excessive speed on turns	5● 6●	Modify driving or install heavy-duty suspension parts
Front wheel bearings are loose	1● 2● 4● 6● 12● 15● 18● 20●	Tighten or replace bearings (pp.213, 219–221)
Ball joints are worn	1■ 2■ 4■ 6■ 12■ 15■ 22■	Have ball joints replaced
Steering linkage is loose	1● 2● 4● 6● 12● 15● 17● 18●	Tighten steering linkage (p.190)
Steering gear misadjusted, or low oil level	1■ 2■ 6■ 10■ 12■ 14■ 16■ 18■	Have steering gear adjusted or lubricated (p.194)
Shock absorbers are worn	2● 3● 4● 5● 6● 7● 22● 23● 24● 25● 26● 27●	Replace shock absorbers (pp.440–445)
Wheels are out of balance	4■ 5■ 8■	Have wheels balanced

Replacing shock absorbers 🔧🔧 1–4 hr

Replacing shock absorbers is seldom difficult. In fact, since shock absorbers are normally replaced several times during the life of an automobile, most types are designed for easy removal and installation. Professional mechanics often use special tools for shock absorber work, which makes the job even simpler. Although these tools are available at auto parts stores and are not overly expensive, most shocks can be removed or installed almost as easily with ordinary socket, box-end, and open-end wrenches.

Not all automobiles have the same arrangements for mounting shock absorbers. In some cars, for instance, the upper mounting bolts on the rear shocks are reached from the trunk or from under the back seat. In other cars, a cover plate in the engine compartment must be removed before you can remove the front shock absorbers.

On cars with coil-spring front suspension, the lower suspension arms must be supported before the shocks are removed; otherwise, the arms may drop under their own weight and damage the brake lines or displace the coil springs. Coil-spring rear axles must be supported for the same reasons. To provide support, place a sturdy piece of lumber, jack stands, a floor jack, or a scissors jack beneath the suspension arm or axle.

Special tools

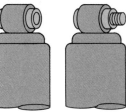

Shock socket

Narrow-jaw open-end wrench

Shock wrench

Types of mountings

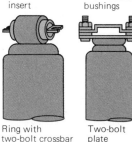

Ring with rubber bushing

Ring with right-angle stud

Ring with metal sleeve insert

Stud mount with rubber bushings

Ring with two-bolt crossbar

Two-bolt plate

Locations of shock mountings

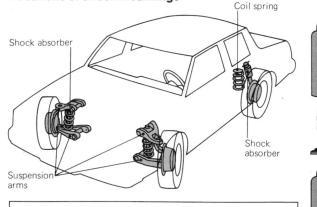

Coil spring

Shock absorber

Shock absorber

Suspension arms

Tools: Ratchet wrench, 8-in. or 10-in. extension, sockets, box-end or open-end wrenches, jack and jack stands.
Materials: Penetrating oil, caulking compound or silicone sealant, replacement shock absorbers.

Replacing front shock absorbers (GM) 🔧🔧 30 min–1 hr

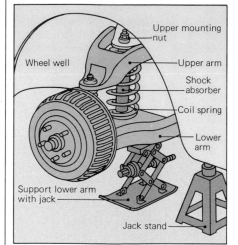

Upper mounting nut

Wheel well

Upper arm

Shock absorber

Coil spring

Lower arm

Support lower arm with jack

Jack stand

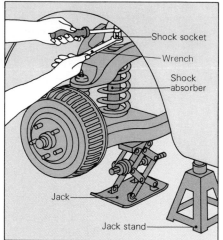

Shock socket

Wrench

Shock absorber

Jack

Jack stand

1. Loosen lug nuts on front wheels. Raise the car and support it on a lift or jack stands. Remove wheel. Support lower suspension arms before removing shocks (see text). Apply a generous amount of penetrating oil to mounting nuts.

2. Remove upper mounting nut, using special tool or two open-end wrenches. Use one wrench to loosen the nut and the other to keep the shaft from turning. Access to upper mounting is through wheel well or engine compartment.

Replacing rear shock absorbers (GM) 🔧🔧 30 min–1 hr

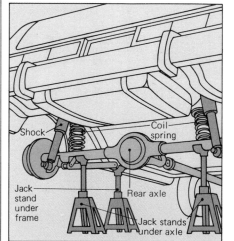

Shock

Coil spring

Jack stand under frame

Rear axle

Jack stands under axle

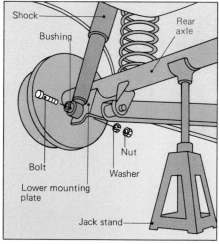

Shock

Rear axle

Bushing

Nut

Bolt

Washer

Lower mounting plate

Jack stand

1. Loosen lug nuts on rear wheels. Raise car, and support it on a lift or jack stands. Remove wheel. If rear suspension has coil springs, support rear axle with jack stands (see text). Leaf-spring suspension requires no support for rear axle.

2. Apply a generous amount of penetrating oil to upper and lower mounting nuts. Allow about 15 min for oil to soak in. Then, using socket wrench or box-end wrench, remove lower mounting bolt, lock washer, and lower mounting nut.

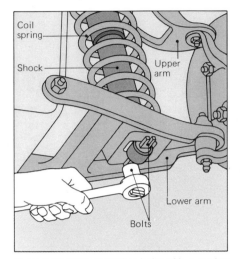

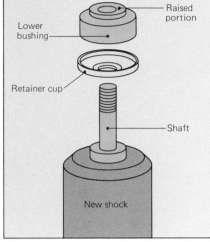

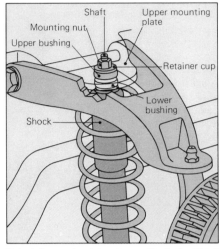

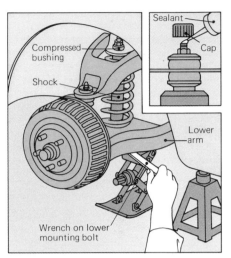

3. Remove lower mounting bolts with a socket wrench or a box-end or open-end wrench. Bolts attach beneath lower suspension arm. Withdraw old shock absorber through hole in suspension arm, pulling shock from within coil spring.

4. Extend new shock absorber. Lengths of old and new shocks should be equal. Using old shock as a guide, install lower bushing's retainer cup on shaft, then rubber bushing. Raised portion of bushing must point toward top of shaft.

5. Install new shock in place, with shaft protruding through hole in upper mounting plate. Install second (upper) bushing and retainer cup. Raised portion of bushing must face down. Reinstall mounting nut, but do not tighten it.

6. Install lower mounting bolts and tighten fully. Then tighten upper mounting nut until bushings compress slightly and are gently rounded. Apply silicone sealant to stud threads to prevent rust. Install protective caps, if any.

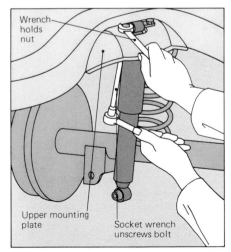

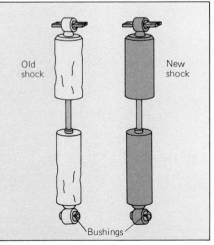

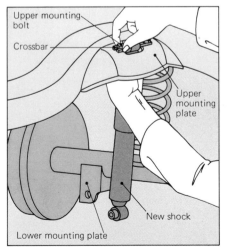

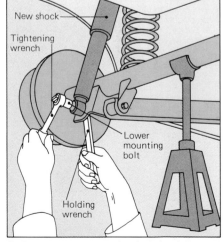

3. Use two wrenches to remove upper mounting bolts. Socket wrench with a long extension is used to unscrew the bolts. Small box-end or open-end wrench prevents the nuts above the mounting plate from turning.

4. Remove old shock absorber. Extend the new shock fully, and check that its length is the same as the original. Using the old shock as a guide, install new rubber bushings, if necessary. Bushings may already be mounted on new shocks.

5. Position new shock absorber and attach upper mounting bolts loosely. Crossbar on shock swivels to allow correct fit. You may need a helper to hold shock and to thread upper bolts through mounting plate and nuts.

6. Fasten lower mounting bolt in place and tighten fully. Then tighten upper mounting bolts. Coat fasteners with caulking compound or silicone sealant to prevent rust. Reinstall wheels, lower car to ground, tighten lug nuts on wheels.

Replacing MacPherson struts 🔧🔧🔧🔧🔧 2–4 hr

MacPherson struts are normally used only in front suspensions. Replace the struts in pairs. Because you must remove the units in order to test them, road test the car first (p.189) to make certain that the shocks are damaged. There are three ways to repair Mac-Pherson struts. You can replace the entire unit. Worn parts can be replaced individually if they are available. Or you can discard the internal parts and substitute a replacement cartridge. A parts store may install the cartridges if you bring them the struts.

Caution: To avoid injury, never stand in front of a compressed spring or point it at anyone.

Tools: Open-end, offset, box-end, and Allen wrenches to fit the suspension parts on your car; awl or file; torque wrench; MacPherson strut; spring compressor; pry bar; anti-seize compound; spanner (for Chrysler cars only).

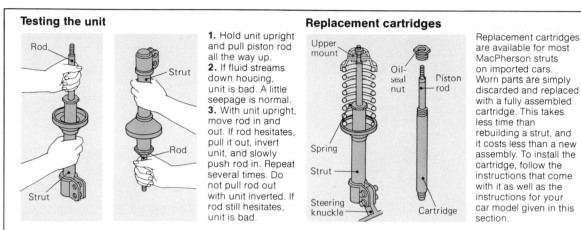

Testing the unit

1. Hold unit upright and pull piston rod all the way up.
2. If fluid streams down housing, unit is bad. A little seepage is normal.
3. With unit upright, move rod in and out. If rod hesitates, pull it out, invert unit, and slowly push rod in. Repeat several times. Do not pull rod out with unit inverted. If rod still hesitates, unit is bad.

Replacement cartridges

Replacement cartridges are available for most MacPherson struts on imported cars. Worn parts are simply discarded and replaced with a fully assembled cartridge. This takes less time than rebuilding a strut, and it costs less than a new assembly. To install the cartridge, follow the instructions that come with it as well as the instructions for your car model given in this section.

GM X-body models and Ford Fiesta

GM X-body models are the Buick Skylark, Chevrolet Citation, Oldsmobile Omega, and Pontiac Phoenix.

Caution: When removing MacPherson struts, take extra care that they do not strike and damage other front suspension components. To remove the struts:

1. Loosen lug nuts. Raise and support front of the car (p.176).
2. Remove the wheel and tire.
3. Remove brake hose clamp, and shift hose out of the way if it interferes with disassembly.

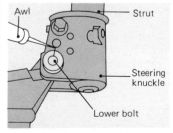

4. The lowest mounting bolt of GM X-body cars also adjusts wheel camber. Before removing this bolt, scribe a mark from bolt onto steering knuckle if strut will be reused; you must line up these marks during re-

assembly. Remove both lower mounting bolts.

6. Open hood and remove the strut's small outer mounting bolts or nuts on top of the wheel wells. Do not loosen the large center bolt.

7. Remove MacPherson assembly and place it on a workbench. You may have to use a pry bar between the frame and the steering control arm to free the MacPherson assembly. Wire the axle to the body so that it cannot fall.

Buy or rent a heavy-duty spring compressor made especially for MacPherson struts.

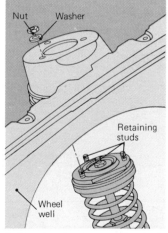

Caution: Do not allow spring to slip

8. Mount spring compressor on spring and coat its threads with anti-seize compound. If your compressor differs from the one shown, follow instructions that come with it.

9. Place MacPherson unit in a vise with protective wooden or rubber spacers between vise jaws and strut.

10. Tighten compressor slowly and evenly on both sides until spring is compressed enough to release tension from top mount of strut. If com-

pressors begin to slip, or "walk" around the spring, loosen them slowly and evenly and start again.

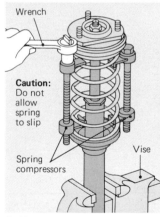

11. Remove the big center retaining nut. Use an Allen wrench to keep the piston rod from rotating as the nut is turned. On many models a box wrench with a sharp offset is needed to reach the recessed retaining nut.

Caution: The spring is under extreme tension; stay out of its line of fire as you remove the upper nut, in case the compressor fails.

12. Remove top mount. Loosen spring compressor slowly. Remove compressor and spring. If the spring is damaged or weak, replace it.

13. Test unit (above). If it fails test, install a replacement cartridge.

14. To reassemble unit, compress spring and seat it in recesses in

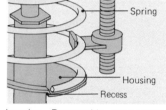

housing. Reassemble components in reverse order of disassembly; tighten retaining nuts securely before releasing compressor.

15. To reinstall assembled unit in the car, slide threaded retaining studs through their holes in the wheel well, working from below. Insert lower mounting bolts. (The Ford Fiesta requires special replacement bolts: buy them from a Ford dealer.)

16. From above, torque top mount's retaining nuts to 18 lb-ft.

17. Torque lower mounting bolts to between 68 and 72 lb-ft for Ford Fiestas, to 140 lb-ft for GM X-Body models. If you are reusing the struts on an X-Body car, align the marks you scribed on the wheel camber adjusting bolt and steering knuckle, even if you must slightly exceed torquing specifications.

18. Reattach the brake hose.

19. Reinstall the wheel and tire.

Caution: After completing this job, have front-end alignment checked.

Servicing MacPherson struts on Chrysler cars ⚑⚑⚑⚑⚑ 2½–5 hr

The Dodge Challenger, Colt, and Sapporo and the Plymouth Arrow and Champ are Mitsubishi cars sold by Chrysler dealers in the U.S. The Dodge Aries and Omni, and the Plymouth Reliant and Horizon are built in the U.S. by Chrysler. All these models have MacPherson struts in front.

Aries/Reliant and Omni/Horizon struts are discussed below, right. Other models are covered in the exploded view at the right, which shows how to remove the units from the cars, and under *Rebuilding Chrysler/Mitsubishi units*, below, where illustrations show how to rebuild the struts. In Colt and Champ hatchbacks, the units are removed in the same way as from GM X-body cars (opposite page).

Removing Chrysler/Mitsubishi units

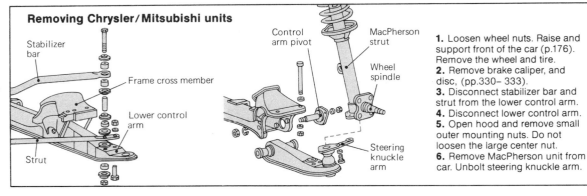

Stabilizer bar · Frame cross member · Lower control arm · Strut · Control arm pivot · MacPherson strut · Wheel spindle · Steering knuckle arm

1. Loosen wheel nuts. Raise and support front of the car (p.176). Remove the wheel and tire.
2. Remove brake caliper, and disc, (pp.330–333).
3. Disconnect stabilizer bar and strut from the lower control arm.
4. Disconnect lower control arm.
5. Open hood and remove small outer mounting nuts. Do not loosen the large center nut.
6. Remove MacPherson unit from car. Unbolt steering knuckle arm.

Rebuilding Chrysler/Mitsubishi units

1. Mount unit securely in a vise.
2. Compress spring (opposite page). Check Cautions first.
3. Pry off the upper dust cover to reveal top mount's securing nut.

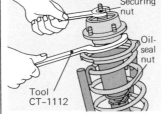

Securing nut · Oil-seal nut · Tool CT-1112

4. Remove securing nut; hold spring seat with a spanner wrench to prevent it from turning as you loosen nut. Chrysler has a special tool (CT-1112) if ordinary spanner wrench does not work.

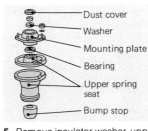

Dust cover · Washer · Mounting plate · Bearing · Upper spring seat · Bump stop

5. Remove insulator washer, upper spring seat, bump stop, and

spring. Use tool CT-1112 to remove nut on oil seal. Discard nut.
6. Drain and discard shock fluid.

Cylinder · Housing · O-ring

7. Use a screwdriver to pry O-ring out of cylinder. Discard O-ring.

Piston rod · Cylinder · Housing

8. Slowly pull piston rod and piston guide out of the cylinder, and pull the cylinder from housing.
9. You can now discard the old components and install a replacement cartridge. If you are rebuilding the unit, examine all parts for damage. Replace all rubber parts and any others that are worn or defective. Clean reusable metal parts in parts solvent and let dry.
To reassemble the strut:
10. Compress piston ring with your fingers and push piston into cylinder. Insert cylinder into strut.

11. Slowly pour 300 cc of shock absorber fluid into cylinder while operating piston to expel air.
12. Slide piston guide over piston.
13. Install a new O-ring, seating it squarely with no deflection.
14. Cover end of piston rod to protect it against accidental damage when you tighten the oil-seal nut.

Spanner · Strut housing · Lower spring seat

Apply fresh shock absorber fluid to the lips of the oil-seal nut, and install the nut. Using a spanner wrench or special tool CT-1112, tighten nut until its edge contacts strut housing.
15. Remove protective cover from end of piston rod. To make sure that air is not trapped in cylinder, move piston rod in and out several times as described under *Testing the unit,* opposite page.
16. Compress spring as illustrated on opposite page. See Caution first. Install spring, making sure that lower coil is seated squarely.
17. Install the bump stop, upper spring seat, insulator, and washer. Look for a D-shaped hole in the

upper spring seat and a reference mark (dent) on the piston rod. Line up the hole and mark.
18. Install securing nut in top mount and tighten it snugly.
19. Loosen spring compressor slowly, allowing spring to extend evenly and seat itself in upper spring seat. See Caution, opposite page.
20. Holding upper spring seat with spanner wrench (Chrysler tool CT-1112), torque securing nut in top mount to 29–36 lb-ft.

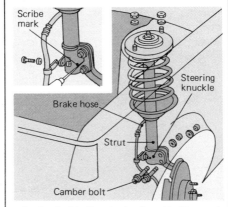

Nut · Torque wrench · Tool CT-1112

To reinstall the strut, reverse the removal procedure, observing the following special procedures:
21. Reattach top of assembly to the mounting bracket on the wheel housing. Torque to 7–11 lb-ft.
22. Reattach lower end of the strut assembly to steering knuckle and torque to 29–36 lb-ft. (On Colt and Champ hatchback models, torque lower mount's retaining bolts to 69–87 lb-ft.)
23. Pack inside of insulator with bearing grease. Install dust cap.
24. Have front-end alignment checked.

Aries/Reliant and Omni/Horizon

If the MacPherson unit is worn out, replace the entire assembly as follows.
1. Loosen wheel nuts. Raise front of the car (p.176) and remove the wheel.
2. If there is a possibility that the unit will be reused (after testing as described on the opposite page), scribe a mark from the camber-

Scribe mark · Steering knuckle · Brake hose · Strut · Camber bolt

adjusting bolt to the steering knuckle. The mark will aid in resetting wheel camber.
3. Detach the brake hose from the strut.
4. Remove bolts from the lower end of strut.
5. Open the hood. Remove small outer retaining nuts that hold upper end of strut to the wheel well. Do not loosen the large center nut.
6. From below, remove the strut from the car.
7. Use spring compressor to transfer spring to new strut. Reverse order of removal to install strut. Tighten upper retaining nuts to 20 lb-ft, lower bolts to 90 lb-ft.
8. Have front-end alignment checked.

Repairing MacPherson struts on Ford cars ⚑⚑⚑⚑ 2–5 hr

German-built Fords—the early Capris (right) and the Fiesta—have conventional MacPherson struts in their front suspensions. The struts in U.S.-built Escorts and Lynxes are similar to those in Fiesta. Many domestic Ford cars use modified struts.

Fairmont/Zephyr from 1978; Mustang/Capri from 1979; T-bird/Cougar from 1980

These cars have modified MacPherson struts. The spring is not part of the strut assembly but is mounted separately. The entire strut must be replaced when it fails:

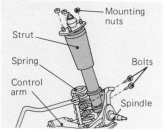

1. Loosen the wheel nuts. Raise and support front of the car (see p.176). Remove the wheel and tire.

2. Place a floor jack under lower control arm on which MacPherson unit is mounted; raise jack to compress unit's coil spring. **Caution:** Be careful not to lift car off jack stands.
3. Working under the hood, remove the 16-mm upper mounting nut(s). Discard the nut(s).
4. Remove the brake caliper, rotor, and dust shield (pp.330–333).
5. From under the car, remove the two lower mounting nuts and bolts that hold the strut to the spindle. Discard the nuts.
6. From under the car, push shock absorber up to compress its piston rod, then remove strut from the car.
To install a new strut:
7. Place the unit against the spindle so that its lower mounting holes align. Install the lower mounting bolts and two new nuts loosely.
8. Extend unit so that its rod passes through hole in upper mounting bracket. Install new upper mounting nut(s), and torque to 60–75 lb-ft. Hold a screwdriver in the slot in the rod to keep rod from turning.
9. Remove floor jack. Torque lower mounting nuts to 150–180 lb-ft.
10. Install brake assembly and wheel, then lower car from jack stands. Have front-end alignment checked.

1971–78 Capris

To remove the MacPherson strut units, proceed as follows.
1. Loosen wheel nuts. Raise and support the front of the car (see p.176). Remove the wheel and tire.

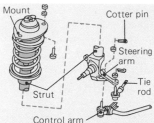

2. Detach brake hose (see pp.338–340). Plug end of hose.
3. Place a hydraulic jack under the control arm. Lift the arm to relieve tension of coil spring.
4. Pull out cotter pin. Remove nut holding tie rod to steering arm. Use Ford tool 3290C to separate rod and arm. Lower jack.
5. Remove cotter pin and nut holding control arm to base of strut. Separate pin and nut.
6. If car has disc brakes, remove brake caliper (see pp.330–333).

7. From top of engine compartment, remove three upper mounting bolts. Do not loosen large center nut.
8. From under car, remove MacPherson strut unit with disc attached, if car is equipped with disc brakes.
To replace the shock absorber:
9. Mount strut in a vise. Install spring compressor, and compress spring. First note Caution on page 442.

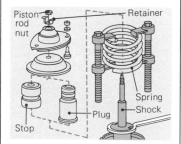

10. Taking care not to dislodge spring compressor, remove large piston rod nut. In some models, nut has collar that fits into a keyway. Using a small punch, force collar out of keyway. Discard such a collared nut. Remove retainer.
11. Lift off the top mount and upper spring seat. Pull rubber bump stop or plug off the housing.

12. Remove spring (see p.442).
13. Using a spanner wrench, unscrew old shock absorber cartridge.
14. Install the new cartridge and tighten it securely.
15. Reinstall parts in reverse order of their removal. If piston rod has a collared nut, install a new one of the same kind. Torque the nut to 5–10 lb-ft. Do not bend collar into keyway yet.
16. Remove spring compressor (see Caution, p.442) and carry assembly to car. Lift assembly into place, and secure top mount to wheel well. Torque the top mounting nuts or bolts to 15–18 lb-ft.
17. Attach control arm to base of strut housing. Torque attaching nut to 30–35 lb-ft. Install new cotter pin.
18. Attach the tie rod end to the steering arm. Torque nut to 18–22 lb-ft. Install a new cotter pin.
19. Reattach brake components and bleed the brakes (p.217). Reinstall the wheel and tire.
20. Lower the car to the ground. Loosen nut on piston rod. Car wheels should face straight ahead when one tab of the top mount retainer faces the engine. With the wheels pointing straight ahead, torque piston rod nut to 28–32 lb-ft. Use a small punch to force its collar (if any) into the piston rod keyway.

Repairing Honda struts ⚑⚑⚑⚑ 3–6 hr

MacPherson struts are used at the front of Honda station wagons and at both the front and rear of other Hondas. The shock absorber is crimped or welded into most Honda struts. You must replace the entire strut or grind the top off the strut housing, following the instructions

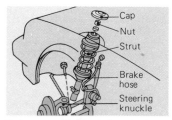

that come with the replacement cartridge. To remove the front struts:

1. Loosen wheel nuts. Raise and support the front of the car (see p.176). Remove the wheel and tire.
2. Remove brake hose clamp from strut housing; releasing brake hose.
3. Remove brake caliper and use a length of heavy wire to hang the caliper from underbody of car.
4. Remove bolt that holds the strut to the steering knuckle.
5. Using a hammer, tap steering knuckle until it separates from strut.
6. Working from the top of the engine compartment, remove rubber cap and upper mounting nut.
7. Remove strut from the wheel well.
The top mount has a roller bearing. Handle it carefully, and lubricate both sides of the bearing with grease before reinstalling it. To reinstall front struts, reverse the removal procedure. Hold piston rod with an Allen

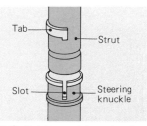

wrench to keep rod from turning when you tighten the spring seat nut. Align tab (if any) on strut housing with slot in steering knuckle. Place a jack under the steering knuckle, and raise car until it just lifts clear of the jack stand. Carefully torque the lower mounting bolt to 36 lb-ft. Torque the top mounting nut to 33 lb-ft. Lower car and have the front-end alignment checked.

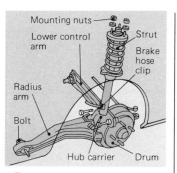

To remove rear Honda struts:
1. Raise and support rear of car, (p.176). Remove rear wheel and tire.
2. Remove brake hose clip from strut housing. Shift hose out of the way.
3. Disconnect parking brake cable from the brake drum.

4. Loosen inner bolt on the lower control arm. Loosen radius arm bolt.
5. Remove lower mounting bolt to free the strut from the hub carrier.
6. From inside luggage area, remove strut's top mounting nuts.
7. From below, maneuver strut from the car. You may have to twist hub carrier to do this.
To install rear strut, reverse the removal procedure. Align tab (if any) on strut housing with slot in hub carrier. Torque the bolt that holds strut to hub carrier to 36 lb-ft. Tighten upper locknut to 24 lb-ft and upper mounting nuts to 17 lb-ft. Place jack under the hub carrier and raise the car just clear of jack stand. Carefully torque the radius arm bolt to 61 lb. ft. Torque the inner bolt on the lower control arm to 40 lb-ft. Attach brake hose to strut housing.

Repairing Toyota struts 🔧🔧🔧🔧🔧 2–5 hr

Several Toyota models use Mac-Pherson struts in front suspensions, including 1971–73 Carinas, 1971 and later Celicas, 1967 and later Corollas, and 1980 and later Tercels. Replacement cartridges (see p.442) are available for all models. To remove Toyota struts:

1. Loosen wheel nuts. Raise and support the front of the car (p.176). Remove the wheel and tire.

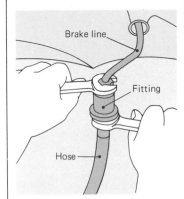

2. Clean area where brake hose is attached to brake line. Disconnect hose and line, and plug end of hose with clean plugs to prevent fluid leakage or the contamination of fluid by foreign matter.

3. If car is equipped with an electronic brake pad wear indicator, disconnect the wires on the brake caliper by pulling them from the multi-wire connector.

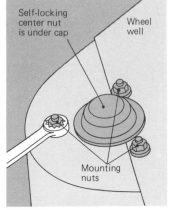

4. From top of the engine compartment, remove strut's top mounting nuts. Do not loosen large center nut.

5. From below, remove the two lower mounting bolts that hold the strut to the steering knuckle. Refer to illustrations on page 442.

6. Pull down the control arm to disengage the strut from the collars on the steering knuckle, and swing strut to one side. Then pull strut and attached brake components down and out of the car.

7. Mount strut in a vise and remove brake components (see pp.329–343). Disassemble the strut, whether you install a replacement cartridge or rebuild the strut (see pp.442–443).

To install a Toyota strut:

8. Reattach the brake components. Check to see that the collars on the

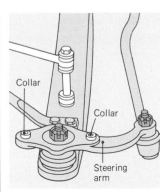

steering arm project 3/16 in. Use a new self-locking nut to hold the piston rod to the upper support plate.

9. Install the strut, guiding the three top studs through the three holes in the wheel well. Position the lower end of the housing over the collars on the steering arm, and loosely attach the two lower mounting bolts to the steering knuckle.

10. Install upper mounting nuts and torque them to 15–22 lb-ft. Torque two lower mounting bolts to 59–66 lb-ft.

11. Reconnect the multi-wire connector for the brake wear indicator (if any). Reattach the brake hose to the brake line. Adjust the front wheel bearings (p.220) on rear-drive models. Pack the area around the piston rod above the support plate with chassis grease. Finally, bleed the brakes (p.217) and have the front-end alignment checked.

Repairing Datsun struts 🔧🔧🔧🔧🔧 2–4 hr

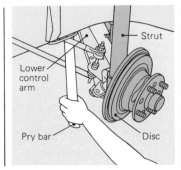

All Datsuns except the pickup truck have front MacPherson struts. Datsun Z models have MacPherson struts in the rear too. Replacement cartridges (p.442) are available for all models. Repair both front and rear MacPherson units by following these general procedures:

1. Loosen wheel nuts. Raise and support the front of the car (see p.176). Remove the wheel and tire.

2. Remove the brake caliper (pp.329–330).

3. Remove lower mounting bolt holding strut to steering knuckle,

and detach knuckle from strut. This can be done by forcing lower control arm down with a pry bar. Allow strut assembly to rest on a jack stand.

4. From above, remove the unit's three top mounting nuts.

5. Remove the strut from the car.

6. Disassemble the strut and install a replacement cartridge or rebuild the unit (see pp.442–443).

7. Install unit by reversing removal procedures. Torque top mounting nuts to 25 lb-ft. Torque lower mounting bolt to 53–72 lb-ft. Have the front-end alignment checked.

Repairing Volkswagen struts 🔧🔧🔧🔧🔧 2–4 hr

The front suspensions of 1971–79 Super Beetles and of all Rabbits and Sciroccos have MacPherson struts. Replacement cartridges are available for all models.

Super Beetle

1. Loosen wheel nuts. Raise and support the front of the car (p.176). Remove the wheel and tire.

2. Pry off speedometer cable's circlip and pull the speedometer cable out of the back of the steering knuckle (on the driver's side only).

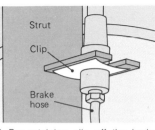

3. Pry retaining clip off the brake hose and shift hose out of the way.

4. On 1970–73 cars, bend lock plates down and remove three bolts that hold the steering knuckle and ball joint to the strut. On 1974–79 models, remove two bolts holding the steering knuckle to the strut.

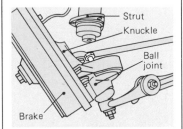

5. Pry the strut and steering knuckle apart. On 1970–73 models, use one of the bolts to temporarily rejoin the ball joint with the steering knuckle.

6. Support strut with a jack stand. From inside luggage compartment, remove upper mounting nuts. Do not loosen the large center nut.

7. Remove strut from car, bring it to workbench, and disassemble unit. Install a replacement cartridge or rebuild strut (see pp.442–443).

8. Install the rebuilt strut, reversing the removal procedure. Torque top mounting nuts to 14 lb-ft. On 1970–73 models, install new lockplates, and torque the mounting bolts to 29 lb-ft. On 1974–79 cars, torque the two mounting bolts to 61 lb-ft, and torque clamp bolt on the steering knuckle's ball joint stud to 25 lb-ft. Finally, have front-end alignment checked.

Rabbit and Scirocco

1. Loosen wheel nuts. Raise and support front of the car (see p.176). Remove the wheel and tire.

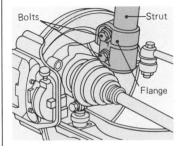

2. The top bolt between the strut and the steering knuckle is used to adjust wheel camber. Scribe a mark across this bolt and onto the flange it passes through. Realign these marks if you reuse the strut.

3. Remove shock absorber's lower mounting bolts.

4. Support the brake and axle assembly with a hook made of coat hanger wire. Attach one end of the hook to the brake, the other end to the chassis.

5. Support strut with a jack stand. From top of engine compartment, remove upper mounting nuts. Do not loosen the large center nut.

6. Take strut from the car, bring it to a workbench, and disassemble the unit. Install a replacement cartridge or rebuilt strut (see pp.442–443). Install rebuilt strut, reversing removal procedure. Torque upper mounting nuts to 14 lb-ft. Torque lower mounting bolts to 58 lb-ft; torque front wheel's camber bolt more, if necessary, to align scribe marks from Step 2. Finally, have front-end alignment checked.

Replacing the power steering pump and hoses 🔧🔧🔧 40 min–3 hr

If a power steering pump or hose becomes defective, one or more of the following symptoms usually occur: a loss of steering assist (the steering wheel becomes extremely difficult to turn), noise from the pump, or fluid leaks from the pump or hoses.

In the case of noise or difficulty in steering, check that the pump reservoir is filled with power steering fluid to the recommended capacity (see p.195) and that the pump drive belt is adjusted correctly (see pp.286–287 and opposite page). Also check the hoses for kinks. In the case of fluid leakage, make sure that the reservoir cap is installed tightly, and check the hoses and their fittings for leaks. If the problem does not lie in any of these areas, have the pump tested at a garage with a power steering pressure gauge to determine whether the pump should be removed from the car for exchange or rebuilding.

Caution: Never work on a power steering pump unless the engine is cold. Contact with hot exhaust system parts near the pump or with hot power steering fluid can cause severe burns.

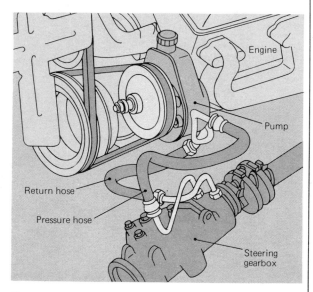

Tools and materials: Set of socket wrenches and set of open-end wrenches (if your car has metric hardware, use metric tools); power steering hose caps; pulley puller, if needed (see Step 11); drain pan.

Removing the pump and hoses

1. Disconnect battery ground (−) cable.

2. Remove or disconnect components that are adjacent to or attached to the power steering system if these parts block access to the pump or prevent its removal. Depending on the vehicle, such components may include drive belts for the air-injection pump or air conditioner compressor, the idler pulley, or the fuel vapor canister and hoses.

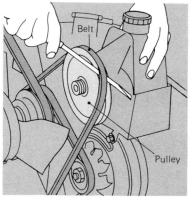

3. Loosen the adjusting bolts on the power steering pump's drive belt, and remove the drive belt from the pump pulley (see *Drive belts*, pp.286–287).
4. Free power steering pump's hoses from any support brackets to which they may be attached. If necessary, raise the car to gain access to the brackets (see safety precautions on page 176).

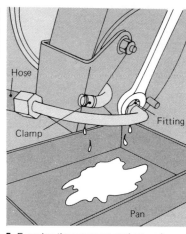

5. Examine the pressure and return hoses for leaks, kinks, dryness, and splits. Replace a suspicious-looking hose by placing a drain pan under it, then detaching the hose from the power steering pump and power steering gear. Be sure to buy a replacement power steering hose specifically recommended by the manufacturer for your car.

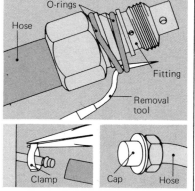

6. If hoses do not have to be replaced, disconnect them from the pump only. Generally, the power steering return hose is held by a clamp, and the power steering pressure hose is held by a fitting, as seen in the illustration for Step 5, above. Discard O-ring seals, and cap the ends of hoses to prevent dirt from entering the lines. Special caps for steering hoses are available from auto parts stores.

7. The car may have a splash shield over the drive belts to protect them from road splashes. If so, remove this shield.

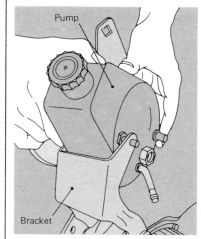

8. Determine if the pump can be released from the bracket or brackets, or whether it is necessary to unbolt the bracket(s) from the engine and to remove pump and bracket(s) as an assembly.

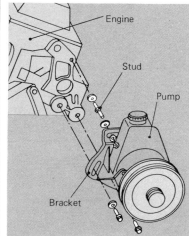

9. If necessary, place the assembly on a workbench after removing it from the car. Then detach the bracket(s) from the pump. The bracket(s) will be transferred to the new pump.

10. In some models the drive belt pulley of the power steering pump is in front of a bracket, while the power steering pump itself is behind the bracket. This makes it necessary to remove the pulley before removing the pump. You may be able to do this by removing the nut that holds the pulley to its shaft.

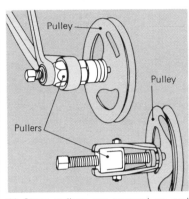

Pulley
Pulley
Pullers

11. Some pulleys are pressed on and must be removed with a special puller. An auto parts store with a machine shop should be able to transfer the pulley to the new pump. To remove the pulley yourself, attach the puller and turn it counterclockwise until the pulley springs loose. (To reinstall the pulley, turn the puller clockwise until the bolt is securely tightened.)

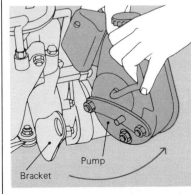

Pump
Bracket

12. If the car has a transverse-mounted engine, detach the pump, then turn it so that it faces the front of the car. Then carefully lift the pump out of the engine compartment.

Installing a new pump and hoses

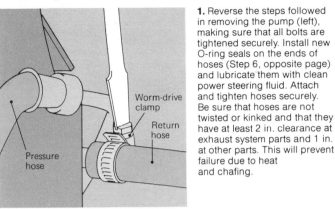

Worm-drive clamp
Return hose
Pressure hose

1. Reverse the steps followed in removing the pump (left), making sure that all bolts are tightened securely. Install new O-ring seals on the ends of hoses (Step 6, opposite page) and lubricate them with clean power steering fluid. Attach and tighten hoses securely. Be sure that hoses are not twisted or kinked and that they have at least 2 in. clearance at exhaust system parts and 1 in. at other parts. This will prevent failure due to heat and chafing.

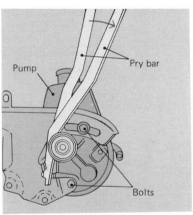

Pump
Pry bar
Bolts

2. Adjust the drive belt (see *Drive belts*, pp.286–287). While tightening bolts, use a bar or length of lumber to lever the power steering pump into position and apply tension on the belt. If the belt deflects more than ½ in., it is too loose.

Fresh fluid
Pump

3. Fill the pump reservoir to the *Cold* or *Add* mark on the cap indicator, or to the bottom of the filler neck if there is no indicator. Use fresh, manufacturer-approved power steering fluid; do not use the fluid you drained from the old pump. Bleed the power steering system as shown at right.

Bleeding the system

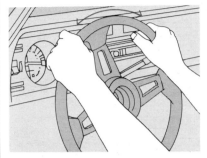

Air in the system hampers normal steering by making it too loose; bleed the steering system of air as follows:
1. Fill the pump reservoir as described in Step 3 at left. Then start the engine, run it at fast-idle, and turn the steering wheel from side to side five times in both directions. Do not allow the wheel to remain at the extreme stop (full-turn) position, as this may damage the power steering system.

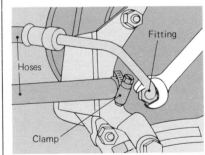

Pump
Remove some fluid with a syringe

2. Return wheels to a straight-ahead position and allow the engine to run at idle for 2 to 3 min longer. Then check the color of the fluid. Fluid that contains air is often a light tan or milky color. If such is the case, bleed the system again by repeating Steps 1 and 2 until fluid clears. If fluid does not clear, it contains water and it should be replaced.

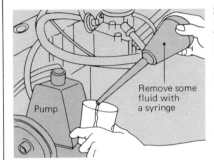

Hoses
Fitting
Clamp

3. Check for fluid leaks at hose fittings. If there is a leak, tighten the fitting securely, using a wrench of the appropriate size. Be careful not to round off the fittings; use a wrench that fits snugly.

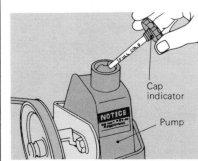

Cap indicator
Pump
NOTICE

4. Fill the pump reservoir with fluid to the *Full* mark on the cap indicator, or to the level suggested in your owner's manual if there is no indicator. Road test the car; steering should be normal and the pump should run quietly.

Repair / Transmission

Troubleshooting transmission problems

How to use this chart

Find problem at top of chart. Look down column to locate possible causes. First, check out repairs that you can do yourself; then, repairs you *may* be able to do yourself. If problem still is not solved, consult a competent mechanic.

○ You can fix it yourself.
● You *may* be able to make a complete repair.
■ You need a mechanic.

Problem — Automatic transmission problems / Manual transmission problems

Column headers (left to right):
1. Delayed shifts
2. Rough (harsh) initial engagement in D or R
3. No drive in one or more gears
4. Slipping or chattering in one or more gears
5. Engine starts with transmission in gear
6. Transmission does not shift at proper speeds
7. No upshifting in D
8. Rough (harsh) 1-2, 2-3 shifting
9. Noisy transmission
10. Transmission overheats
11. Transmission fluid level too low
12. Clutch slips
13. Gears grind (clash) while shifting
14. Gearshift hard to operate
15. Clutch grabs
16. Transmission is noisy
17. Transmission jumps out of gear
18. Transmission cannot be shifted into gear
19. Transmission locked in gear

1	2	3	4	5	6	7	8	9	10	11	12	13	14	15	16	17	18	19	Possible cause	Cure
																			Automatic transmissions	
○	○	○	○		○	○	○	○	○										Incorrect transmission fluid level	Check level; add or drain fluid (p.202)
○	○	○																	Contaminated transmission fluid	Drain and refill transmission; replace filter (pp.202–204)
○		○		■	○	○		○	○										Defective vacuum modulator or governor	Replace modulator (p.450); have mechanic replace governor
●	●	●	●		●	●		●											Improperly adjusted or damaged shift linkage	Adjust linkage (pp.205–206); replace if damaged
■	■	■	■		■	■	■	■		■									Internal transmission damage	Have transmission specialist make repairs
	○				○		○												Engine idling too fast	Adjust engine idling speed (pp.252–253)
●	●																		Loose drive shaft, U-joints, or engine mounts	Inspect; tighten or replace component (pp.451–452)
		●	●		●		●												Transmission band(s) need adjustment	Adjust band(s) (pp.449–450)
				●															Misadjusted or defective *Neutral* start switch	Adjust or replace switch (pp.369–370)
					●		●	●											Defect in EGR system	Repair or replace EGR components (pp.254–260)
○		○			○	○	○												Vacuum hoses misrouted or leaking	Reroute hoses, replace defective hoses
								■	■										Transmission oil cooler lines hitting chassis	Have kinked or leaking lines replaced
									■										Blockage in oil cooler or lines	Have defective parts repaired or replaced
									●										Fluid leaks at gaskets or seals	Add transmission sealant or have gaskets replaced
																			Manual transmissions	
											○	○	○	○					Clutch needs adjusting	Adjust clutch free play (pp.207–209)
											■								Oil or grease on clutch disc	Have clutch disc inspected; replace if necessary
											■	■		■					Worn or warped clutch disc	Have clutch disc inspected; replace if necessary
											■	■							Weak or worn clutch springs	Have clutch springs inspected; replace if necessary
											■	■	■		■	■			Clutch housing misaligned	Have runout at rear face of clutch checked; realign or replace clutch
												■	■		■	■	■	■	Internal transmission damage	Have transmission repaired or replaced
											●	●	●						Clutch linkage or cable binds	Lubricate or adjust clutch linkage (pp.207–209), or have it replaced
												●	●		●	●	●		Shift linkage binds or is bent	Repair or adjust shift linkage (pp.205–206)
												●	●		●	●			Shift linkage incorrectly adjusted	Adjust shift linkage (pp.205–206)
												○	○		○		○		Transmission lubricant level too low	Add lubricant; check for leaks (p.200)
												○	○		○				Incorrect grade of lubricant	Drain and refill transmission (p.200)
												■	■		●	■	■		Shift rail binds, worn, broken	Have defective part of shift rail replaced
															●				Loose clutch-to-engine or transmission-to-clutch bolts	Torque bolts to specifications (see a shop manual)
															●				Foreign matter in transmission	Drain, flush, and refill transmission (pp.202–204)
																■	■	■	Shift lever loose or worn	Tighten shift lever nuts; check for and replace worn parts

Repair / Automatic transmissions

Adjusting automatic transmission bands ▣▣▣▣ 30 min–1½ hr

The transmission bands on contemporary passenger cars seldom need adjusting. If you do need to adjust them, you must first know the model of the transmission in your car. Check the vehicle identification or certification label for a code letter or get the part number of the transmission from its housing beneath the car, then consult the parts department of a dealer for that make of car. Usually, the only tools you will need for making band adjustments are standard socket wrenches and a torque wrench. Sometimes, specialized torque-wrench adapters may be required to reach the adjusters on some cars or to fit the adjusting mechanism. Adapters may be obtained at auto parts stores. All band adjustments are made with the transmission in *Neutral*.

Ford vehicles

Automatic transmissions on Ford vehicles should receive band adjustments after the first 12,000 or 15,000 miles, depending on the type of vehicle; the specific interval is listed in the owner's manual. No additional band adjustment is regularly required for any Ford product unless the vehicle is driven under extreme service conditions. To identify the transmission model installed in your car, compare the listings in the chart below with the code letter stamped on the vehicle certification label. The label should be on the door lock post on the driver's side and should be visible when the door is open.

Code letter	Transmission model
V	C3
U	C6
Z	C6 (Police)
W	C4
X	FMX
S	JATCO
B or D	Needs no adjustment

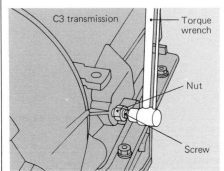

Transmission models C3 and C6 require only one band adjustment. To adjust C3 transmissions, you must first remove the downshift rod from the downshift lever in order to gain access to the adjusting screw, which is located on the left side of the transmission case, close to the rear of the torque converter. On both types, carefully clean and oil the threads on the band's adjusting screw, then remove and discard the locknut on the screw. Use a torque wrench to

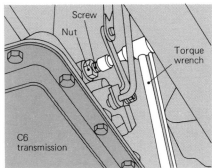

C6 transmission

tighten the adjusting screw to 10 lb-ft, then back the screw off 1½ turns. Loosely install a new locknut. To complete the adjustment, use a wrench to hold the adjusting screw steady so that it does not turn, then tighten the locknut securely. Reinstall shift rod on C3 transmissions.

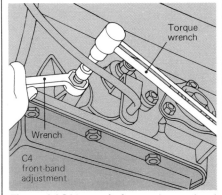

C4 front-band adjustment

The model C4 transmission requires two band adjustments. The front adjusting screw is located on the left side of the transmission case, near the rear of the torque converter. The rear adjusting screw is on the right side of the case, also to the rear of the converter. To adjust the front band, clean and oil the threads of the adjusting screw, then remove and discard its locknut. Using a torque wrench, tighten the adjusting screw to 10 lb-ft, then back the screw off 1¾ turns. Install a new locknut, hold the adjusting screw firmly with a wrench so that it

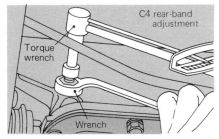

C4 rear-band adjustment

does not turn, and tighten the locknut securely. To adjust the rear band, follow the same procedure, but back the adjusting screw off three turns. Replace the old locknut with a new one as described above, and tighten it securely.

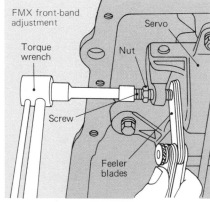

FMX front-band adjustment

The FMX transmission requires front and rear band adjustments. To adjust the front band, you must first drain the transmission and remove the oil pan and screen (pp.202–204). The front adjusting screw is located on the right side of the valve body near the front of the transmission case. Loosen the locknut two full turns. Pull back the adjusting rod and insert a 0.25-in. stack of feeler blades between the servo piston stem and the adjusting screw. Using a torque wrench, tighten the adjusting screw to 10 lb-ft, then remove the feelers and tighten the adjusting screw three-quarters of a turn more. Use a wrench to hold the adjusting screw firmly so that it does not turn, then tighten the locknut se-

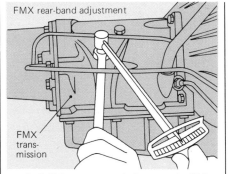

FMX rear-band adjustment

curely. Refit the screen and oil pan, and refill the transmission with fresh fluid.

The rear band's adjusting screw is on the outside of the transmission, on the right side, near the midpoint of the case. To adjust, follow the procedures outlined under *Transmission models C3 and C6* on this page.

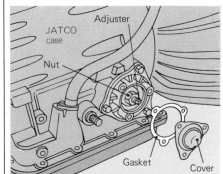

The JATCO transmission requires only one band adjustment. Before you begin, obtain a new servo-cover gasket from an auto parts store or a Ford parts dealer. First, remove the servo cover from the right side of the transmission case. Loosen the locknut on the adjusting screw, then use a torque wrench to tighten the adjusting screw to 10 lb-ft. Back the adjusting screw off two turns. Use a wrench to hold the adjusting screw so that it does not turn, and retighten the locknut securely. Reinstall the servo cover, using the new gasket.

Adjusting automatic transmission bands (continued)

AMC and Chrysler cars

Most AMC and Chrysler cars use the same transmissions: the Chrysler Torqueflite 904 or 727. (AMC calls the transmission *Torque-Command*.) AMC also uses a Chrysler model 998 and, on the AMC Eagle, a model 999. The transmission part number for all models is stamped on the left side of the transmission case above the mating surface of the oil pan or on the right side of the torque converter housing. Except for the AMC Eagle, neither AMC nor Chrysler recommends band adjustment as part of routine maintenance unless your car is driven in city traffic at temperatures above 90°F more than half the time, or if you use it to tow a trailer. AMC recommends that the bands be adjusted every 15,000 mi on the Eagle.

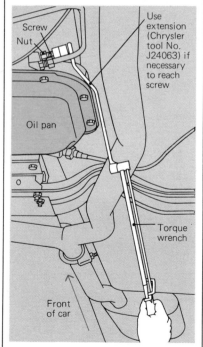

To adjust the front (kickdown) band on the Torqueflite (or Torque-Command) transmission, first find band's adjusting screw, which is on the left side of the transmission case. On Omnis and Horizons, the screw is on the left side, top front, of the transaxle case. On Eagles

only, mark (for realignment) and disconnect the front drive shaft from the axle yoke and move the shaft aside to gain working clearance (see pp.451–452). Next, on all models, loosen the adjusting screw's locknut until the screw turns freely, then use a torque wrench to tighten the adjusting screw to 72 lb-in. After tightening, back the adjusting screw off two turns if the transmission is a model 904, 998, or 999. Back the screw off 2½ turns if it is a model 727, or three turns if it is an Omni or Horizon. To complete adjustment on all models, hold loosened adjusting screw steady, then retighten locknut securely. If adjusting screw accidentally turns as you tighten the locknut, make adjustment again.

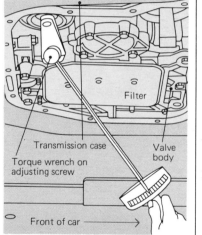

No rear (*Low/Reverse*) band adjustment is possible on Omnis or Horizons. To adjust the rear band on other models, first remove the transmission's oil pan (see pp.203–204). Then, find the rear band's adjusting screw and locknut, which protrude from a spot alongside the transmission's valve body. On model 727 transmissions, loosen the locknut until the screw turns freely. On all other models, remove the locknut altogether. Use a torque wrench to make the band adjustments. On all AMC models, tighten the adjusting screw to 41 lb-in., then back the screw off 7½ turns (four turns on the model 998 and Eagle). Holding the screw steady, tighten the locknut securely. On Chrysler model 727 transmissions,

tighten the adjusting screw to 72 lb-in. Back the screw off two turns, then retighten the locknut securely. On the Chrysler model 904 (except when used with the 225-cu-in. engine), tighten the adjusting screw to 72 lb-in., back the screw off four turns, then retighten the locknut securely. On the Chrysler model 904 with the 225-cu-in. engine, tighten the adjusting screw to 41 lb-in., back the screw off seven turns, then tighten the locknut securely.

General Motors cars

The Turbo Hydra-matic 250 and the Chevrolet Powerglide/Pontiac M-35 of the mid-1970s are the only GM automatic transmissions that require band adjustments. The identifying number for the 250 is on the right side of the transmission case. On the Powerglide and M-35, it is on the rear of the transmission's oil pan.

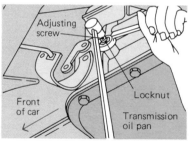

The 250 should be adjusted every 24,000 mi, or sooner if the transmission is slipping. To make the adjustment, first loosen the locknut on the adjusting screw (located on the right side of the transmission case) a quarter-turn. Using a torque wrench, tighten the adjusting screw to 30 lb-in., then back the screw off three turns. Hold the adjusting screw so that it does not move, then retighten locknut securely in order to hold the adjustment.

The Powerglide and M-35 should be adjusted every 12,000 mi. The adjusting screw and locknut are located under a protective cap on the left side of the transmission case. To make the adjustment, first remove the cap and loosen the adjusting screw's locknut three-quarters of a turn. Then hold the locknut steady, and with a torque wrench tighten the adjusting screw to 70 lb-in. Back the screw off four turns, retighten the locknut securely, and replace the protective cap.

Replacing the vacuum modulator ⏱ 30 min

Most Ford and General Motors automatic transmissions use a vacuum modulator to ensure smooth shifting at all throttle openings. Symptoms of a defective modulator are harsh shifting, delayed upshifting, a slipping transmission, overheating in the transmission, and loss of transmission fluid.

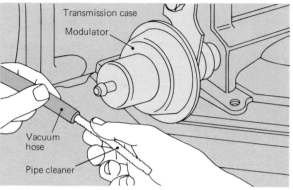

To check the modulator, first inspect all hoses leading to and from the unit for cracks and holes. Replace damaged hoses. Next, disconnect the vacuum hose at the modulator end, and insert a pipe cleaner as far as possible into the hose. Withdraw the pipe cleaner. If there is transmission fluid on the pipe cleaner, the modulator is leaking and must be replaced.

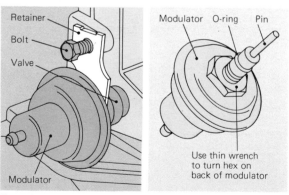

To replace the modulator, disconnect its vacuum hose. Unscrew bolt that holds retainer, and remove modulator and its valve. If there is no retainer, slip a thin wrench or special tool between modulator and transmission case, and unscrew the modulator from the case. Have a pan on hand to catch any fluid that drains from transmission when modulator is removed. Transfer pin (if any) and O-ring to new modulator, unless replacements are supplied. Install new modulator and valve. Replace transmission fluid and check its level (p.202), then road test the vehicle.

Repair / Drive train

Replacing universal joints ▱▱▱ 45 min−3 hr

Hard-to-trace vibrations, or noise at low driving speeds, may mean that the universal joints are worn or damaged. To inspect them, raise the car so that the wheels hang free (see p.176). Grasp the drive shaft near each U-joint and twist the two sections of the shaft in opposite directions. If you can feel movement at the rear joint, tighten the flange bolts and twist the shaft again. If there is movement at either U-joint, the joint is probably defective. In order to replace a U-joint, the drive shaft must be removed first. You will need ample work space and a work bench equipped with a sturdy vise that opens at least 5 inches. Repair kits or replacements for single U-joints are available from a car dealer or auto parts store. Double U-joints cannot be repaired.

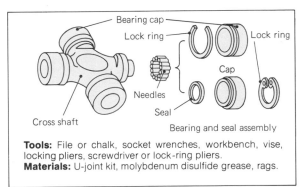

Bearing cap
Lock ring
Lock ring
Cap
Needles
Seal
Cross shaft
Bearing and seal assembly

Tools: File or chalk, socket wrenches, workbench, vise, locking pliers, screwdriver or lock-ring pliers.
Materials: U-joint kit, molybdenum disulfide grease, rags.

Removing the drive shaft

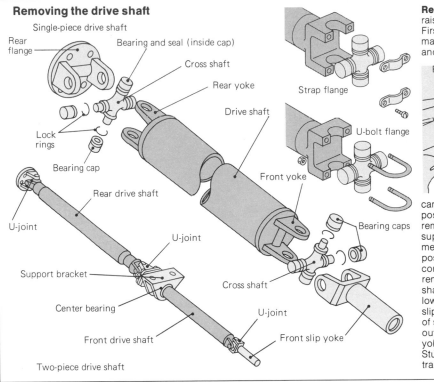

Single-piece drive shaft
Rear flange
Bearing and seal (inside cap)
Cross shaft
Rear yoke
Drive shaft
Strap flange
Lock rings
Bearing cap
Front yoke
U-bolt flange
Bearing caps
Rear drive shaft
U-joint
U-joint
Cross shaft
Support bracket
Center bearing
U-joint
Front drive shaft
Front slip yoke
Two-piece drive shaft

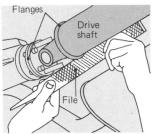

Remove drive shaft with car raised (transmission in *Neutral*). First, use a file or chalk to make marks across the shaft's yokes and axle flanges so that the shaft

Flanges
Drive shaft
File

can be reinstalled in its original position. If shaft is two-piece type, remove the bolts that hold the support bracket to the frame cross member, and record the order and position of shims (if any) for correct reinstallation later. Next, remove bolts or clamps that attach shaft to rear axle flange. Then, lower shaft clear of flange, and slide slip-joint yoke at front of shaft off the splined transmission output shaft. Do not allow slip yoke to fall to the ground. Stuff clean rags into open end of transmission to stop fluid loss.

Disassembling an old U-joint

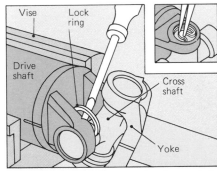

Vise
Lock ring
Drive shaft
Cross shaft
Yoke

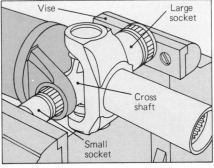

Vise
Large socket
Cross shaft
Small socket

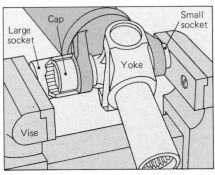

Cap
Large socket
Small socket
Yoke
Vise

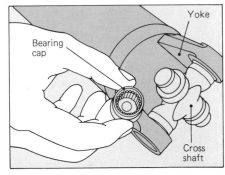

Yoke
Bearing cap
Cross shaft

1. Clamp drive shaft in vise, and scribe or chalk reference marks across yokes. Then, using a screwdriver or lock-ring pliers, remove the lock rings from the bearing caps. If caps have plastic retainers instead of lock rings, proceed to Step 2.

2. Place U-joint between jaws of vise. Position the open end of an ordinary large wrench socket (about 1 ⅛-in. diameter) against one bearing cap, and the closed end of a smaller socket (about 9/16-in. diameter) against the opposite cap.

3. Tighten the vise jaws carefully against both sockets until the smaller socket presses into the U-joint and forces the opposite bearing cap out of the joint and into the large socket. Plastic retainers will break. Do not to bend the yokes.

4. Loosen the vise and remove the bearing cap. If cap sticks in yoke, pull it free with locking pliers, or lock cap in vise and tap on shaft with a hammer until cap comes free. Repeat Steps 1–4 on the other caps.

451

Replacing universal joints (continued)

Installing a new U-joint

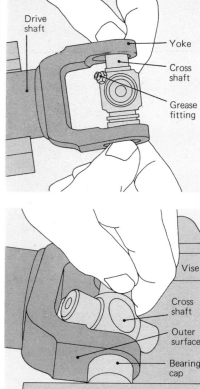

Drive shaft
Yoke
Cross shaft
Grease fitting

1. If replacement bearing caps are not pre-lubricated, smear the needle bearings inside the caps with grease. Use the vise to press one cap into the yoke. Install cross shaft into the yoke, slipping its stem into the cap. If the cross shaft has a grease fitting, it should face the drive shaft.

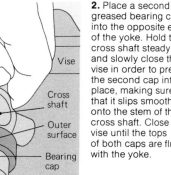

Vise
Cross shaft
Outer surface
Bearing cap

2. Place a second greased bearing cap into the opposite ear of the yoke. Hold the cross shaft steady and slowly close the vise in order to press the second cap into place, making sure that it slips smoothly onto the stem of the cross shaft. Close the vise until the tops of both caps are flush with the yoke.

Socket
Cross shaft
Yoke
Yoke
Vise

3. If necessary, use the vise and a small socket to press the bearing caps even farther into the yokes in order to expose the grooves for the lock rings. This is always necessary with the type of ring that fits into a recess in the yoke (see inset here and in Step 1, p.451).

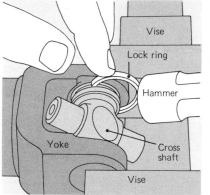

Vise
Lock ring
Hammer
Yoke
Cross shaft
Vise

4. Install the two lock rings with light blows of a hammer or work into place using a screwdriver and pliers.

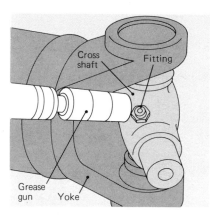

Cross shaft
Fitting
Grease gun
Yoke

5. Release the vise jaws and lubricate the cross shaft's grease fitting with a grease gun if necessary (see p.191). Not all cross shafts are equipped with grease fittings.

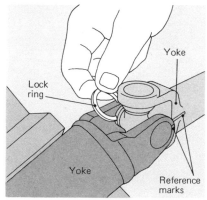

Lock ring
Yoke
Yoke
Reference marks

6. Turn the drive shaft 90° and install the other yoke that makes up the U-joint. Before you begin, be sure to align the reference marks made earlier across each of the two yokes. Repeat Steps 1–6 to press-fit all remaining bearings and caps into the yoke arm and to attach the lock rings.

Reinstalling the drive shaft

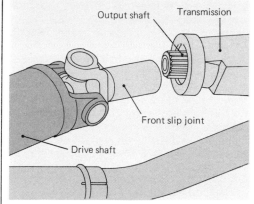

Output shaft
Transmission
Front slip joint
Drive shaft

1. To reinstall the drive shaft after the U-joints have been replaced, first clean and lightly grease the end of the front slip joint, then slide it carefully back onto the splined transmission output shaft so that the reference marks will align when you raise the rear of the drive shaft to meet the rear axle flange. Do not turn the drive shaft to align the marks; remove and reinstall it. Then reinstall the bolts or clamps that hold the shaft to the flange. If the drive shaft is a two-piece type, reinstall the center bracket and shims.

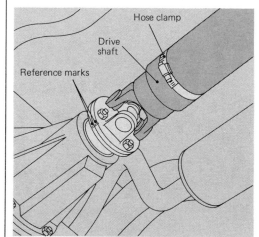

Hose clamp
Drive shaft
Reference marks

2. Road test the car. Minor vibration caused by imbalanced shaft parts can be eliminated or minimized by attaching an ordinary worm-drive hose clamp to the drive shaft and experimenting with the position of its tightening screw until vibration is reduced.

Tracking down strange noises ⏱ 10–30 min

Before you can analyze strange sounds, you must be aware of how your car normally sounds. Walk around the car as it idles and listen to the noises it makes. Listen to it as you drive. Open the window as you pass by a wall or through a tunnel and listen to the sounds that are reflected back at you.

To determine where a new noise is coming from, drive the car at different speeds on different road surfaces and analyze the results. If a noise occurs all the time, even when the car is standing still and in *Neutral*, the source is probably the engine or one of its belt-driven accessories. If the noise occurs only while the car is moving, it is probably coming from the transmission, chassis, or suspension. If the noise occurs only when you apply the brakes, the cause is probably in the braking system.

Sometimes, the source of the noise is not so obvious. A sound can travel through a car's body and chassis. Some sounds are intermittent or may clear up when the engine warms up. A noise that you would describe as a harsh, rapping sound might be regarded as a mild clicking sound by a mechanic.

The chart at the right defines some common automotive noises and their likely sources. Use the cross references and the index to check out the malfunctions. Engine sounds can often be checked with a mechanic's stethoscope or with a length of hose. Place one end of the stethoscope or hose to your ear, and move the other end from one car component to another as the engine idles. The volume of the noise will intensify when you place your listening device on a malfunctioning component.

Caution: Do not touch hot or moving engine parts. Never work under a car that is not properly supported (see *Raising a car safely*, p.176).

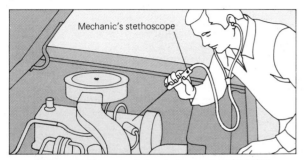

Using a stethoscope to locate the source of a noise.

SOUND/LOCATION	POSSIBLE CAUSES
Bang: A sharp, heavy, loud explosion *from the exhaust* or intake manifold	Incorrect ignition timing (p.236) or fuel mixture (p.251); cracked distributor cap (p.408); defective valve, valve spring (p.266), or air pump
Buzz: A low-pitched, beelike hum *from around the dashboard area*	Loose dashboard component or part of heating system (p.356)
Chatter: A steady, rapid, tapping sound *From the rear* in cars with limited-slip differentials *From the engine*, the sound increases or decreases with engine speed	Limited-slip differential may be filled with wrong lubricant (p.201) Defect or wear in valve train (p.266)
Chirp: A shrill, pulsating, whistling sound *from front wheels* of cars with power steering when wheels are turned. (When steering wheel is turned as far as it will go, a chirping noise is normal)	Loose drive belt on power steering pump (p.286)
Click: A sharp, tapping, metallic sound *From wheels*, the sound intensifies as the speed increases *From engine compartment*, sound changes with engine speed *From the inside of a cold engine* only when it is first started *From inside the engine*, the sound continues as long as engine is on *From inside the engine*, the noise decreases as the engine warms up	Loose hubcap; stone in hubcap; defective wheel bearing (pp.220–221) Bent or loose fan blade is hitting the radiator (pp.351–353) Engine low on oil (p.196); loose manifold heat-control valve (p.244) Hydraulic valve lifter that fails to fill with oil (p.276) Excessive valve lash (p.265); piston slapping against cylinder (p.265)
Clunk: A dull, thumping sound *from beneath a car* with rear differential; may occur more frequently as the speed increases	Defective U-joint
Grind: A grating, scraping sound *from clutch* as it is depressed	Defective clutch throw-out bearing (p.207)
Groan: A low-pitched, creaking, moaning sound *from the front wheels* of cars with power steering when wheels are turned	Insufficient power steering fluid (p.195)
Growl: A low-pitched, muffled sound *From the front wheels*, the sound lessens when brakes are applied *From the rear end* of cars with rear differentials, the sound occurs during turns and is more intense on left turns than right turns *From the rear end* of cars with rear differentials, the sound occurs during acceleration and deceleration *From the rear end* of cars with rear differentials, the sound is steady while car is coasting and becomes more intense as time passes *From the dash area*, the sound intensifies with car speed	Worn front-wheel bearings (p.213) Worn differential Differential end play (may be normal); snow tire hum (normal) Worn axle shaft bearings (pp.220–221) Defective speedometer cable or gears
Hiss: A sharp, high-pitched, buzzing hum *from any component* that is under pressure (e.g., tires, valves) or vacuum (hoses)	Leak in the component; component poorly installed; defective gasket (p.426)
Knock (Ping): A heavy pounding or clanking sound *from the engine* during acceleration. Some light pinging is normal on new cars tuned for maximum economy	Detonation because of low-octane fuel (p.63), improper ignition timing (p.236), defective spark plug (p.232), or overheating (p.344); pre-ignition due to a carbon buildup in engine or to overheated spark plugs (p.232); failure of electronic knock controls
Put-put: Flat, short, regular explosions *from the tail pipe*	Leaking exhaust valves; over-rich fuel mixture; faulty air pump system
Rap: Metallic, tapping noises *from the engine* while car is coasting	Worn connecting rods
Scrape: A sharp, rubbing, scratchy, grating sound *from the wheels* as the brakes are applied	Worn brake pads or linings (p.329). Some disc brake pad warning devices scrape or squeak when pads need replacement
Screech: A high-pitched, shrieking sound *from the engine compartment* as the engine, while in Neutral or Park, is accelerated	Loose drive belt (p.286); defective bearing in a belt-driven acccessory
Squeak: A high-pitched, shrill squeal *From the wheels* as the brakes are applied *From the chassis or body* as the car goes over a bump or dip in road	Defective drum-brake linings (p.329); defective disc-brake pads (may be normal on some brakes; see p.329) Chassis points require lubrication; worn suspension bushings (p.190)
Thud: A heavy, dull, low thump *From the engine*, the sound occurs regularly *From the engine* when it is under a heavy load *From under car* when driven on rough roads	Loose flywheel Loose or worn main bearings (p.386) Loose or misaligned exhaust system (pp.434–438)
Whine: A high-pitched cry from the engine	Defective timing gear, oil pump drive, or distributor drive (p.408)
Whir: Continuous quick, fluttering, vibrating sounds *from under the car*	Unbalanced drive shaft

How to complain effectively

Complaints about cars fall into two categories: the vehicle's construction and its repair. Complaints about the vehicle's construction are sometimes resolved by its warranty. Most new cars are sold with a 12,000-mile or 12-month warranty (whichever occurs first) that entitles the new-car owner to replacement or repair of specified parts that break down within the span of the warranty. New-car dealers may hesitate to do warranty work because the factory often pays less for such repairs than consumers are normally charged. If a dealer balks at warranty work, contact the car company's zone office or headquarters. If you do not get satisfaction there, get in touch with the local Better Business Bureau or a consumer group (see p.459).

U.S. law requires carmakers to guarantee the emission-control performance of their engines for 50,000 miles. If an expensive part of the carburetion, fuel injection, ignition, or computer system malfunctions, it will affect the engine's emissions. These parts are not normally covered by the 50,000-mile emission warranty, but some car owners have been successful in getting carmakers to replace them.

"Secret" warranties come about when a manufacturer decides to replace defective parts beyond the limits of the original warranty at little or no cost to the car owner. Since these special warranty extensions are not announced publicly, dealers may make them available only to persistent complainers.

If you have a complaint about auto service, go back to the shop that repaired the car. Be calm but firm with the garage owner or customer-service representative. If you are not satisfied with the treatment you receive, contact one of the consumer complaint agencies listed on page 459. Give them your name and address; the name and address of the shop; the make, model, and year of your car; then explain your problem fully.

Your last recourse is to sue the mechanic or garage. If you have paid a disputed garage bill of more than $50 in your home state by credit card, the Fair Credit Billing Act of 1975 may allow you to get your money back. If you notify the credit card company or bank in writing that negotiations with the mechanic have failed, you can withold the disputed amount from your credit card payments, and the amount will be charged to the mechanic's bank. If the mechanic wants to pursue the matter further, he must sue you.

How to choose a mechanic

Consumer protection groups receive far more complaints about auto service and repair than about any other business. The Federal Trade Commission has estimated that one-third of the money spent for automobile repairs each year is unnecessary. A Department of Transportation survey indicates that 53 cents of every auto-repair dollar is wasted.

There are many reasons for this poor showing on the part of the auto-repair industry, including the increasing complexity of modern automobiles and a nationwide shortage of qualified mechanics. When even an incompetent mechanic can earn a comfortable living, a good mechanic is likely to be overworked. Haste and incompetence are at the root of most auto-service complaints. Intentional fraud plays a much smaller role than many people imagine, although it does exist.

Common practices

Many mechanics work on a commission basis and do not receive a fixed hourly wage (see p.457). They may receive up to half the hourly rate that the shop charges the customer for labor. This flat-rate system encourages haste and sloppy work and often results in a "shotgun" approach to repair. Instead of carefully diagnosing a problem and replacing only defective parts, a mechanic may simply replace one part after another until the problem is solved. The flat-rate system also discourages repairing an old part; it is easier to replace it. In some cases, installing a $30 part is cheaper than two hours of diagnosis and repair, but in other cases it would be cheaper to repair the part. However, few mechanics have the time to do this. Some shops even give their mechanics a commission on parts sold, thereby further reducing incentive to do honest, professional work.

Shopping for a mechanic

The task of weeding out the good mechanics from the bad is difficult but not impossible. Listed below are some things to look for.

1. A neat and orderly shop. An efficient mechanic is usually neat and well organized. If a shop looks orderly, the work is probably done systematically.

2. A certification of competence. The National Institute for Automotive Service Excellence (NIASE) administers voluntary tests and certifies competent mechanics on a national basis. A certified mechanic wears a patch indicating the tests he has passed—engine tuneup or repair, automatic or manual transmission, front end, brakes, electrical system, and heating and air conditioning. A *certified general mechanic* has passed all these tests. You can purchase a directory of shops that employ certified mechanics from NIASE, Suite 515, 1825 K Street NW, Washington, DC 20006. Keep in mind that not every mechanic in the shop is necessarily certified, and that a mechanic certified on brake systems may be useless in diagnosing air-conditioning problems.

The AAA certifies shops on a state-by-state basis. The program is not yet nationwide. For more information, contact The American Automobile Association, 8111 Gatehouse Road, Falls Church, VA 22042.

3. A group of satisfied customers. Ask your friends and relatives if they can recommend a mechanic whose work has been reliable.

4. A written guarantee on all parts and labor.

5. A cooperative attitude. A good mechanic will solicit information about you and your car in a businesslike fashion. Badgering and pushiness will be kept to a minimum.

Take in a minor repair to evaluate a mechanic you are unfamiliar with. If he does the job efficiently and at reasonable cost, go back to him with bigger jobs. Keep a record of your repairs. If you do this, you will avoid having duplicate jobs done within a short span of time. The record will also help the mechanic to diagnose problems and eliminate possible causes.

When you have found a mechanic who seems competent and trustworthy, patronize him regularly. A mechanic who sees you only once or twice a year is not as likely to go out of his way for you as he might for a regular customer.

The mechanic's lien

Dishonesty in auto repairs is a two-way street, and there are customers who give mechanics bad checks or refuse to pay for honest but expensive work. In many states the repair shop has a legal recourse called the *mechanic's lien*. In these states a mechanic may seize a car and sell it to satisfy an unpaid bill.

If there is a mechanic's lien in your state, it would be better to pay a disputed bill and then take the shop to court to recover your costs, rather than suffer the inconvenience of being without a car for a long time or run the risk that the shop might sell your car.

Picking a repair facility

Picking a repair facility is difficult, but the auto repair business is highly competitive and there are many choices. Before you take your car to any shop, consider these factors about the shop:

1. The shop's reputation. Ask friends or relatives who may have dealt with the shop. Check with local consumer groups or the Better Business Bureau. It is usually best to deal with a facility that has existed for a while and has built up a good reputation.

2. How does the shop look? A good shop is usually clean and well organized. An efficient facility will probably be busy, but not overburdened with work.

3. Are the mechanics certified by an independent agency, such as NAISE? If the mechanics are certified, the shop will display a notice to this effect. If you do not see one, don't be afraid to ask.

4. Does the shop engage in ethical business practices? The facility should be willing to give you a written estimate and an itemized bill of service. All work should be guaranteed in writing for 100 percent of parts and labor for a specified mileage or time period. Minor repairs should be guaranteed for 30 days or 1,000 miles; major overhauls, for up to six months or 6,000 miles.

Listed below are the kinds of shops that exist, their services, and how these compare in cost.

An auto dealer's service department is the best place to go if your car is under warranty or needs work on such complex items as power seats, fuel injection, or electronic gadgetry. The dealer has the specialized tools and the latest information needed for work on new cars. And you might void your warranty if unauthorized parts are used in your car.

A dealer's facility has certain drawbacks. You often have no direct contact with a mechanic but deal through a service manager, or "writer," whose job is to sell service. Because the mechanics work on a commission basis, they will often choose the fastest way to make a repair, which is not necessarily the cheapest way. This can lead to sloppy work or to the replacement of parts that could have been repaired.

An independent garage is often your best bet for receiving adequate and reasonably priced car care. The owner of such a shop depends on establishing and maintaining a good reputation. The work is not as expensive as a dealer's, and you can often talk directly to the mechanic who will work on your auto. The mechanics are more likely to repair than to replace parts, and the cost of the parts is often less than at a dealer's service department.

There are certain disadvantages to using an independent garage. Some parts may not be on hand and will have to be ordered. Labor charges are relatively high because many of the mechanics are highly trained. However, if your car needs a routine tuneup, brake work, or work on the transmission, air conditioning, cooling, electrical, or suspension systems, get a written estimate from an independent garage and compare it to those from shops listed below.

The local gas station is still used most often because of its accessibility. Gas stations continue to provide routine lubrication, tuneups, and parts replacement. Labor charges are low because the mechanics do relatively simple work that does not command high pay.

A gas station that does a high volume of work is often able to buy its parts at a larger discount than an independent garage can. A gas station cannot afford to tie up its service bays with complex jobs, so it will farm them out to a specialized shop and add its own markup to the shop's fee.

If at all possible, avoid dealing with gas stations that are located on main highways. Prices for parts and labor are usually inflated because of high rents. Such shops may take advantage of the motorist who experiences problems far from home.

Department store chains tend to offer limited service "packages" at reasonable cost, if you need all the items in the package. Parts are cheaper than at the local gas station because department stores order in high volume. The mechanics are not highly trained, so that the cost of labor is low. The stores usually specialize in the sale of batteries, tires, brake service, lights, mufflers, and shock absorbers.

Specialty shops are often the best equipped to deal with more complex problems. There are two types of specialty shops: the franchised operator and the independent. The franchised operator advertises heavily and must pay franchise fees. The result is often an added cost to the consumer. Check out the prices and guarantees at an independent shop before you visit the franchise, where the hard sell is a way of life. Below is a list of some different specialty shops.

Muffler shops: Always check your exhaust pipe, muffler, and tail pipe before you go to a muffler shop. Muffler shops prefer replacing large sections of the exhaust system to repairing small sections, which could save you money.

Radiator shops: These concentate on cooling-system and air-conditioning work, and on repairing and rebuilding radiators. Some shops repair only radiators that are brought to them, and you can save up to 50 percent of the service station's charge by taking a radiator out yourself and bringing it to the shop.

Automatic transmission shops: Because of its complexity, the transmission is probably the most misdiagnosed part in your car. Be wary of shops that push for a complete overhaul or use hard-sell tactics to sell a rebuilt transmission when less extensive repairs or adjustments might suffice. Ask a few local gas stations where they have transmission work done. They are not likely to farm work out to incompetent or dishonest shops. Do not go to a shop that specializes only in expensive overhauls or replacements and is unwilling to undertake minor band adjustments, fluid changes, or filter replacements.

Body shops concentrate on repairing and repainting vehicles. If the body of your car must be repaired, this type of shop is the only place to go.

Auto glass shops specalize in replacing cracked and broken glass. They do cheaper work than auto dealers, who farm the work out anyway. You can locate glass shops in the Yellow Pages. Some car dealers and glass shops can repair minor chips with a clear epoxy (called the *Novus method*), which is cheaper than replacing a windshield.

Mechanics on wheels are a relatively new phenomenon in auto service. In effect, they make house calls. The mechanic usually works out of a van, thereby eliminating a large part of his overhead, which allows him to charge low prices. Because he relies on word-of-mouth advertising and satisfied customers, he usually does adequate work on routine jobs that do not require lifts or heavy equipment.

Diagnostic centers were once regarded as the answer to consumers' needs. However, motorists were often reluctant to pay for just a checkup. Today, diagnostic centers are usually combined with repair shops. The impressive diagnostic computer printout may be used to sell repairs that are not absolutely necessary. In many cases, the car owner would do better to consult a reliable mechanic who combines less expensive test equipment with commonsense judgment about when to replace parts.

Explaining your problem so that it is fixed the first time

Like most machines, a car is apt to malfunction occasionally; the wear and tear of daily use creates a strain on all its parts. Unfortunately, getting the car fixed properly without having to make repeated trips to the garage is seldom a simple matter.

If you cannot fix your own car or do not have the time to do so, your only recourse is to bring it in to a repair facility. Misdiagnosis and faulty repair often require the car owner to bring his vehicle back to the facility so that it can be repaired properly. There are few things more frustrating than spending a lot of money to have a job done, only to have to make a return trip to the garage because the problem resurfaced after only a few hours or days. The waste in time and money is enough to drive any car owner into a malfunctioning state.

Mechanics, or their employers, do not like a job to "come back." The shop loses money whenever faulty work must be corrected at no charge to the customer. "Comebacks" cannot be attributed solely to dishonest or incompetent mechanics. Part of the problem lies in the motorist's inability to describe the car's problem. A recent U.S. government-financed study showed that the key to service satisfaction is effective communication between motorist and mechanic. The solution to an automotive problem depends, more often than not, on an accurate description of the symtoms plaguing your automobile. Often, a car is not repaired properly because the mechanic has been furnished with a sketchy and unclear description of the trouble. The survey showed that when a motorist and mechanic understood one another, the customer was more likely to be satisfied with the work done.

Because communication is a complicated process, there are no hard and fast rules to follow in dealing with a repair facility, but the following guidelines should facilitate any exchange of information:

1. Keep in mind that you are the only one who can describe your car's symptoms. Since the car cannot speak for itself, proper repair depends on your ability to describe the problem clearly and accurately. Being attuned to the normal sounds of your automobile will enable you to detect the warning signals that sometimes precede a breakdown. Moreover, you will be better able to describe the problem if you can pinpoint the abnormalities in the car's performance.

2. Always keep written records of previous work done on your car. A logbook (p.182) will do. All records should be kept in the glove compartment for inspection by the mechanic. Unnecessary work can be avoided simply by checking to see what work was recently done on the vehicle.

3. Before you approach a repair facility, write down the things you want checked or repaired. Take the time to note any symptoms you have noticed. For instance, how long has the problem existed? Does it happen constantly or only under certain conditions? Is an odor associated with the problem?

4. Before you bring the car in for service, call ahead and make an appointment. Most reliable shops are busy and will have to schedule a date in advance. Shops that are not busy may not be the best ones to do business with. A busy shop may be able to squeeze you into their schedule for a genuine emergency, but like the boy who cried "wolf," you should not cry emergency for a mere annoyance.

5. When you do bring the car in, do not just leave it without explaining what is wrong. Describe the problem accurately and give the person you're dealing with a written copy of the symptoms. Very often, the first person you deal with is not going to work on the car, so make sure that you have the vehicle's problem in written form, and keep a copy.

If you are sure what the problem is, have the shop draw up a service order. Before you authorize the work, make certain that the order includes only necessary repairs. If you are not sure what is wrong with your automobile, have the service order made out for a diagnosis only. Ask the shop to call you before any repair work is begun. Never give a shop blanket approval to do repairs unless you know them well and trust them completely. Otherwise you may wind up getting the costliest job possible.

6. If at all possible, try to have your car serviced by the same mechanic. If you can establish a rapport with him, you'll have a much better chance of having your car worked on correctly. Not only will he be familiar with your car and its particular quirks, but he will also be more likely to service your car professionally if he knows you personally. If you are lucky enough to have a good mechanic, let him know you are pleased with his work. Tipping is not a bad idea, since it is an investment for any future work.

7. Be polite but firm in your dealings with the mechanic. Stick to the facts. Don't offer opinions unless they are from an expert. Try to explain the symptoms in plain and simple language. Unless you are really knowledgeable about automobiles, do not tell the mechanic what to do. Nothing aggravates a mechanic more than to have an "expert" tell him what to do. Unless you're absolutely certain about it, do not tell the shop to replace a particular part. The mechanic might find that the source of your trouble lies with another part, but he will replace both parts just to satisfy your demand. The result is added expense to you.

8. Do not be intimidated by a shop or mechanic. You are entitled to know what the problem is and what you are paying for. If you learn something about your car, you can ask intelligent questions and understand the mechanic's explanation. He is less likely to be condescending if he thinks you know what you are talking about. Also, he will listen more closely to your description of the car's symptoms.

9. Before you sign any service order, ask for an estimate of the job. Make sure that the estimate is written in the work order. Also be sure to write down your phone number in case any extra work has to be commissioned. If the shop is uncooperative about writing out the estimate, take your car elsewhere. You are not bound by law to have any shop work on your car until you authorize it in writing.

10. Make sure that all work is guaranteed before you authorize it. The guarantee is only valid if it is written out. It should be validated on the day the work is completed. Always save the bill and guarantee in case the repairs prove to be faulty.

11. After the work is completed, take the car out for a road test. If it doesn't run the way it should, or if the problem persists, bring the car right back to the shop. If the problem reappears after a few days, call the shop and explain the situation. If the shop balks at fixing a recurring problem, or if they try to charge you again to fix the same problem, let them know you will not be bullied. Your recourse would be to contact the Better Business Bureau or local consumer groups. Most shops do not want to deal with governmental agencies and give in when threatened. You should not have to go this far; if you have dealt with the shop fairly and to the best of your ability, an honest shop will respond to you in similar fashion. Some new-car dealers subscribe to binding third-party arbitration in order to settle disputes over repairs.

Repair costs and how they are computed

More than half the complaints received by consumer groups are directed against the automobile repair industry. Consumers have complaints against all types of facilities, from car dealers to chain stores. The charges range from faulty repair to overpricing. The relationship between the two becomes clear when you realize how repair costs are computed.

Repair facilities, like all capitalistic ventures, remain solvent by making adequate profit on their transactions. The overhead costs of such establishments, typically high, must be passed on to the consumer. New equipment must be purchased to keep pace with the changes in automotive engineering, and because of inflationary pressure, the cost of parts and labor is high. Competent mechanics are in short supply and therefore demand high salaries. Add these expenses to the increased cost of rent, heat, and electricity, and the result is a high overhead.

One way to offset this overhead is to mark up prices of the auto parts that are installed. However, the markup on parts is not nearly enough to offset the cost of running a shop. The bulk of the facility's profit must come from the service charge. That elusive charge, called "labor," so noticeable on every bill, provides the proprietor with his profit. It is also the chief cause of much of the billing abuse that exists within the industry.

Labor charges

The charge for labor in most facilities is determined by multiplying two factors, labor *rate* and the *time* it takes to complete a job. Labor rates vary throughout the country but are usually higher in cities because of higher expenses, such as rent and insurance. Rates range from $15 to $40 per hour. The problems in computing the labor charge arise in calculating the time it takes to complete a job. This time may not be measured by actual clock time. Most automobile repair businesses use *flat-rate manuals* to estimate the time of completion. Originally, flat-rate manuals were intended to average out the time differences between fast and slow workers and to protect consumers from paying excessive fees to unqualified or incompetent mechanics.

The two most commonly used manuals are *Chilton's Labor Guide and Parts Manual* and *Motor's Parts & Time Guide*. Carmakers issue their own manuals to avoid overcharges for warranty repairs performed by their dealers. These manuals consistently show lower time estimates for jobs than the independent manuals do. When performing work that the customer pays for, most dealerships refer to the more liberal *Chilton* or *Motor* manuals.

Critics of flat-rate manuals say that the books greatly exaggerate the time an average mechanic would take to do a job. *Consumer Reports* did a comparative study in 1979 and found that the estimated times in the manuals were 25 percent longer than actual times observed in shops. Other studies have repeatedly shown that an average mechanic can easily beat the estimated time, sometimes by 50 percent. The flat-rate manual provides a convenient way for a garage to give a written estimate for a job. If the job actually takes longer than the estimate, not all shops will absorb this extra cost. But if a mechanic "beats the book" and does the job in less time than is given in the manual, the customer will usually be charged for the full manual estimate.

The relationship of cost computation to faulty repair becomes apparent when you examine how a mechanic earns his salary. A mechanic usually makes one-half the labor rate that a garage charges. If the rate is $20 an hour, the mechanic makes $10 an hour. If a shop uses a flat-rate manual to compute labor rates, mechanics are not paid for actual time worked but rather for the flat-rate time. Hence, a mechanic who does repairs in a 10-hour day for which customers are charged 14 hours of flat-rate time is paid for 14 hours. Thus, built into the system is an incentive for the mechanic to work as quickly as possible. The result is that mechanics are constantly trying to beat the clock in order to increase their income. Not only do they sometimes do sloppy work, but they often wind up using a "shotgun approach" to repair, replacing parts that are likely to be faulty until the problem is corrected rather than performing tests that might isolate the problem to one or two parts. This merely increases the final cost to consumers. The car owner winds up paying for new parts that are not needed.

By shopping around, you may be able to find a shop that pays mechanics by actual time worked. The labor rates might be a bit higher than at a similar shop that charges "manual time," but at least you would be more likely to encounter a systematic approach to diagnosis and repair.

Job charges

Many shops have certain fixed prices for routine jobs, such as brake work or oil changes, in which there is no separate fee for parts and labor. Naturally, the most experienced and highest-paid mechanic in the shop does not perform these routine jobs. His skills are employed elsewhere. However, even when low-paid apprentices and off-brand parts are used, the price may still seem alarmingly high to a cost-conscious consumer. The economics of the marketplace often conspire to drive the price of even a simple job like an oil change to unreasonable levels.

Before you can bring your car into a shop for an oil change, someone must book the appointment. This takes time. The person must be fairly literate and well organized, or the shop would be a shambles. In a small garage, the owner may perform this function, but in a larger facility it is likely to be a full-time or part-time secretary. Because some people make appointments and never show up, a shop may overbook to protect itself. If everyone does show up, there will be delays, which further annoy the customer.

When the car arrives for its oil change, it may be left all day, so the shop owner must rent space to store many cars that are sitting idle. When the work is finally done, the car must be put on a lift, which for 15 or 20 minutes ties up a service bay that could be doing more profitable work. The apprentice is working fast on a cold engine, so not all the old oil is likely to drain out. Unless you ask for it specifically, the shop may not use the highest-quality oil.

In addition to the worker's salary, the shop owner must pay a certain percentage to government medical plans and social security. He must also hire an accountant to deduct the proper federal, state, and local taxes from employee's wages. In larger shops, he may contribute to private medical insurance and pension plans. What the shop owner sees is a job he must charge $15 to $20 for in order to make a profit. (If he charges less to be competitive, he must make it up on other jobs or sell the customer additional, more profitable work.) What the customer sees is a job, hastily done, that requires little skill, $5 worth of oil, and a $3 filter. When he is charged $18 for such work, the customer feels cheated. This is the reason so many people perform their own car service and repair. When a job is relatively simple, it makes more sense to do it yourself.

Being your own mechanic

Because professional mechanics are expensive and in short supply, and labor rates have risen steadily over the past decade, you can save substantial charges by paying only for parts and doing the routine maintenance and minor repair work on your car yourself.

Many otherwise handy people are afraid to work on their cars. This is a natural reaction to the confusing maze of hoses and wires to be found under the hood of a modern automobile. The average car today has more than 15,000 parts. Fortunately, only a few of these parts regularly wear out or need adjustment. Some can be fixed only by a professional mechanic who has special tools and expensive instruments. Others can easily be adjusted or repaired by anyone with the necessary time and knowledge. It is the intention of this book to provide that knowledge and to give tips on when to take a car to a repair shop. Common maintenance and repair procedures are illustrated, and there are troubleshooting charts for all the major systems of the car: brakes, cooling, electrical, engine, exhaust, suspension, steering, and transmission. Use the index when the troubleshooting charts do not pinpoint a particular problem.

Working on your own car is mainly a matter of self-confidence. When attempting a particular job for the first time, many novice mechanics prefer to have some coaching from a neighbor or friend who regularly works on his own car. Once you have performed a few jobs successfully, you will gain confidence in your abilities and will want to do more.

How much can you save?

The bill reproduced here is a facsimile of an actual bill for routine 24,000-mile service on a four-cylinder economy car, performed by the service department of a new-car dealership. No repairs were made. The dealer's labor rate was $16 an hour (which is less than half the rate charged in some big-city dealerships). Parts cost full list price. The circled items show how much the owner of this car could have saved by purchasing the parts at a discount auto parts store and doing the work himself.

This car owner could have saved $47.70 in parts and $6.40 in labor by telling the dealer not to add a pint of expensive oil additive to his engine and not to replace the charcoal canister (scheduled for 24,000-mi replacement) until it malfunctions. Even a beginning do-it-yourself mechanic could have saved more than $20 on parts and the entire $62.40 labor charge by getting the following parts from a discount store and installing them himself: spark plugs, oil and oil filter, breaker points and condenser, air filter, and drive belt.

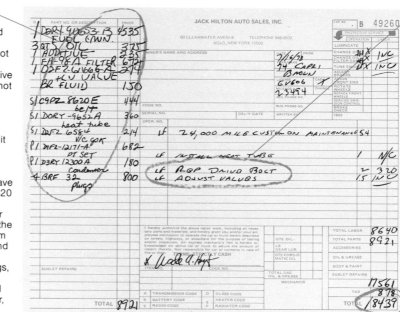

An experienced home mechanic could have saved another $24 in labor charges by doing his own valve adjustment.

By investing less than $30 in discount auto parts, the owner of this car could have performed the entire 24,000-mi service job himself, for a net saving of more than $155.

Where to buy auto parts

Today you can buy auto parts at many drugstores and supermarkets, as well as at more traditional outlets. Where you buy the parts will determine their price and, to some extent, their quality. Here are the most popular sources for parts:

The parts department of a new-car dealership that handles your make of car should have (or should be able to order) most mechanical parts for cars up to 10 years old. The parts will be duplicates or improved versions of those that were on the car when it was new. They will also be relatively expensive.

Professional auto parts stores carry an extensive selection of parts made by aftermarket manufacturers. These are the parts you would get if you took the car to a gas station or garage for repair rather than to the service department of a new-car dealership. They are duplicates of the original parts.

The auto parts store also sells many rebuilt parts, such as alternators, carburetors, and starters, which have been refurbished by firms specializing in such work. Rebuilt parts are less expensive than new parts and are sometimes of even higher quality, because they are inspected more thoroughly during and after manufacture than original parts are.

Auto parts stores are open to the public and offer discounts of 25 to 40 percent off list price to anyone who comes in. The staff is usually highly knowledgeable and used to helping do-it-yourselfers. Some stores incorporate machine shops.

Discount chains, department stores, supermarkets, and even some drugstores carry a limited stock of the most popular auto parts and supplies (usually filters, spark plugs, breaker points, and oil). Their prices can be very low, but the quality of the merchandise can also be low if the store does not carry familiar brand names. The sales staff may be unable to answer technical questions.

Wrecking yards are a good source of parts that are hard to find elsewhere (including body panels, trim, instruments, and seats). Modern auto dismantlers subscribe to a teletype service that can track down parts within reasonable shipping distance. Reputable yards offer a guarantee that all parts sold are in good working condition, although you may have to install the part first to determine its fitness.

Where to buy it guide

Most of the tools and materials pictured in this book were supplied by the firms listed on page 5 or were purchased at professional auto parts stores (see *Where to buy parts,* opposite page) and are readily available across the nation. In a few cases, it was necessary to use unusual tools and materials that may be difficult to find. As a service to readers, the list below contains the names and addresses of firms that supplied these hard-to-find tools and materials. This list in no way constitutes a testimonial or recommendation by Reader's Digest of the companies listed. You may be able to find similar items of higher quality or lower cost elsewhere. Your best bet is first to attempt to locate such items locally. Remember that most professional auto parts stores can order items that they do not have in stock from a local distributor and deliver them in a few days. If you cannot obtain an item locally, you can contact one of the sources listed below. Reader's Digest cannot guarantee the quality or availability of any item.

PAGE	DESCRIPTION/SOURCE
169	**Patented screwdrivers for screws shown:** The Stanley Works Stanley Tools Div. 600 Myrtle Ave. New Britain, Conn. 06050 or The Cooper Group Xcelite Div. Orchard Park, N.Y. 14127
175	**Hand-operated vacuum pump:** Neward Enterprises, Inc. P.O. Box 725 Cucamonga, Calif. 91730
197	**Plastic oil drain pan/ storage container:** The Brookstone Co. 127 Vose Farm Rd. Peterborough, N.H. 03458
241	**GM distributor repair kit:** Thexton Manufacturing Co., Inc. 7685 Parklawn Ave. Minneapolis, Minn. 55435
250	**Carburetor choke-plate angle gauge:** Borroughs Tool & Equipment Corp. 2429 North Burdick St. Kalamazoo, Mich. 49007
270	**VW lever tool and shim pliers:** Columbia Motor Corp. 136 West 21st St. New York, N.Y. 10011
289	**Air-conditioning pressure gauge:** Draf Tool Co., Inc. 333 Adams St. Bedford Hills, N.Y. 10507

PAGE	DESCRIPTION/SOURCE
293	**Winter wiper blades:** Champion Spark Plug Co. P.O. Box 910 Toledo, Ohio 43661
294	**European-style chains:** Jersey Chain and Metal Co., Inc. 198 Rte. 206 S. Sommerville, N.J. 08876
294	**Lug-reinforced chains:** Campbell Chain Co. 3990 East Market St. York, Pa. 17402
294	**Tubular traction aids:** Burns Bros. Inc. Security Chain Div. Fourth St. Swanton, Vt. 05488
297	**Wraparound battery heater; radiator hose heater:** Budd Canada Inc. Temro Automotive Div. P.O. Box 962 Winnipeg, Man. Canada R3C 2V3
297	**Plate-type battery heater:** Phillips Termo, Inc. 9700 West 74th St. Eden Prairie, Minn. 55344
297	**Dipstick heater:** Pyroil Canada Ltd. 1330 Crestlawn Dr. Mississauga, Ont. Canada L4W IP8

PAGE	DESCRIPTION/SOURCE
297	**Block heater; in-line heater:** Mastermotive Inc. 5440 West 125th St. Savage, Minn. 55378
313	**Glue injector for vinyl roof repair:** The Brookstone Co. 127 Vose Farm Rd. Peterborough, N.H. 03458
340	**Brake bleeder screw repair kit:** Thexton Manufacturing Co., Inc. 7685 Parklawn Ave. Minneapolis, Minn. 55435
371	**Steering wheel lock plate remover:** Lisle Corp. 807 East Main St. Clarinda, Iowa 51632
430	**Patented screwdrivers:** For source, see entry for p.169.
432	**Thread-restoring files and dies:** Jaw Manufacturing Co. P.O. Box 213 Reading, Pa. 19603 or J.C. Whitney & Co. 1917–19 Archer Ave. Chicago, Ill. 60680
433	**Kits for repairing stripped threads:** Heli-Coil Products Div. of Mite Corp. Shelter Rock Lane Danbury, Conn. 06810
443	**O-ring removal tool:** Owatonna Tool Co. Owatonna, Minn. 55060

Where to address complaints

Complaints about car construction or repairs should be addressed to one or more of the following:

The president of the car's manufacturing or importing company (see owner's manual for address).

Automobile Owner's Action Council, 1025 Vermont Ave. N.W., Suite 750, Washington, D.C. 20005; or phone (202) 638-5550

Automotive Service Councils, Inc., 188 Industrial Dr., Elmhurst, Ill. 60126; or phone (312) 530-2330

Center for Auto Safety, 1223 DuPont Circle Bldg., Washington, D.C. 20030; or phone (202) 659-1126

Consumer Product Safety Commission, 1111 18th St. N.W., Washington, D.C. 20207; or phone (202) 634-7700

Council of Better Business Bureaus, Inc., 1150 17th St. N.W., Washington, D.C. 20036 (attention: Automotive Programs); or phone (202) 862-1200

Department of Energy, 1000 Independence Ave. S.W., Washington, D.C. 20505; or phone (202) 252-5000

Environmental Protection Agency, 401 M St. S.W., Washington, D.C. 20460; or phone (202) 755-2673

Federal Energy Regulatory Administration, 12th St. and Pennsylvania Ave. N.W., Washington, D.C. 20037; or phone (202) 252-5000

Federal Highway Administration, 400 7th St. S.W., Room 4208, Washington, D.C. 20590; or phone (202) 426-0677

Federal Trade Commission, Bureau of Consumer Protection, Pennsylvania Ave. at 6th St. N.W., Washington, D.C. 20580 (or its regional offices); or phone (202) 724-1524 (about defects in new cars only)

Insurance Institute for Highway Safety, Suite 300, 600 New Hampshire Ave. N.W., Washington, D.C. 20037; or phone (202) 333-0770

National Automobile Dealers Association, 8400 Westpark Dr., McLean, Va. 22101 (attention: AUTOCAP); or phone (202) 821-7000. A list of local offices is available from the national headquarters

National Highway Traffic Safety Administration, 400 7th St. S.W., Washington, D.C. 20590; or phone (202) 426-1828

The state attorney general in your state capital

White House Office of Consumer Affairs, New Executive Office Bldg., Washington, D.C. 20506; or phone (202) 456-1414. (People registering complaints are sent the *Consumers Resources Handbook,* which gives tips on how to seek help locally)

Glossary

A

AC Abbreviation for alternating current.

A/C or **a/c** Abbreviation for air conditioner or air conditioning.

acceleration An increase in speed.

accelerator Sometimes called *gas pedal* or *throttle*. (1) A foot-operated pedal or hand-operated lever connected by linkage or a cable to the throttle plate in the carburetor. (2) There is no throttle plate in a diesel engine; its accelerator is connected to a fuel flow control valve on the fuel-injection pump. In either case, the position of the accelerator determines engine speed.

accelerator pump A small pump mounted inside most carburetors and linked to the accelerator. If the accelerator is depressed rapidly when the engine is cold or running at low speed, the accelerator pump squirts additional fuel into the carburetor throat, enriching the air-fuel mixture to improve engine operation.

accessories (1) Items of comfort or convenience added to a basic vehicle, such as power windows, air conditioning, radio, or tape player. (2) *Engine accessories* include such vital appendages to an engine as the alternator, fuel pump, air pump, water pump, as well as optional devices such as the air-conditioning compressor and power steering pump.

accumulator (1) A trap for liquid refrigerant built into some air-conditioning systems. (2) A pressure regulator used in the pumps of many fuel-injection systems. (3) A valve in the automatic transmission that regulates the flow of transmission fluid to the brake bands' servo diaphragms.

additive Any product added to another substance to improve its performance. Best known are additives for lubricating oils and gasoline.

advance Any automatic or manual adjustment of the distributor to produce ignition spark earlier in relation to piston position.

afterboil The boiling of engine coolant after the engine is stopped. (Fuel in close proximity to a hot engine sometimes boils also.) Condition is due to the inability of a stopped engine to rid itself of excess heat.

aftermarket Industry term for auto parts and accessories that are not supplied by the carmaker but are added to a car after it has been purchased.

afterrunning Condition in which the engine continues to operate after the ignition switch is turned off. Can be destructive to an engine. Also called *run-on* and *dieseling*.

after top dead center The position of the piston after it has reached the top of its stroke. Piston position is measured in degrees of crankshaft rotation. Abbreviation is ATDC. Spark timing may be specified in terms of degrees ATDC.

aiming screws Spring-loaded screws that hold the headlights to a support frame. The screws permit the headlights to be aimed in horizontal and vertical planes.

A.I.R. Abbreviation for air-injection reactor, a type of air pump system.

air aspirator valve A one-way valve mounted on the exhaust manifold of some engines. It allows air to enter the exhaust system to provide extra oxygen, which helps to complete the combustion of unburned hydrocarbons and convert carbon monoxide to carbon dioxide. Used instead of an air pump. Also called a *gulp valve*.

air bag A passive restraint device consisting of bags in front of the driver and passengers. The bags automatically inflate with gas to provide cushioning against the impact of a collision.

air bleed A nozzle or opening that admits air into a flow of fuel.

air bypass valve A valve in the air pump system. At high engine vacuum, it vents pressurized air from the air pump to the atmosphere in order to prevent backfiring. At other times it sends air to the exhaust manifold; on cars with a three-way catalyst, it sends air only to the oxidation catalyst when the engine warms up. Also known as the *anti-backfire valve* or *diverter valve*.

air cleaner A filter assembly ordinarily mounted in a housing on top of the engine to catch and hold dust and other damaging particles found in the air that is drawn into the carburetor or fuel-injection system.

air-cooled engine An engine that radiates excess heat directly into the atmosphere by means of cooling fins rather than through a liquid.

air filter Usually refers to the air cleaner's filter that captures and holds harmful particles so that they cannot be drawn into the cylinders. There are other air filters in the PCV system, air-injection system, and elsewhere.

air-fuel mixture The combustible product of air and fuel that is produced in the carburetor of engines that have carburetors, in the throttle body of engines with throttle-body fuel injection, or in the intake ports or cylinders of engines equipped with individual cylinder fuel injection.

air-fuel ratio The amount of air as compared to the amount of fuel in an air-fuel mixture. The measurement is by weight. Given as two numbers separated by a colon, such as 14:1.

air gap The space between the spark plug electrodes, the distributor points, the armature and pickup coil of an electronic distributor, or the rotor and stator of electric motors and generators. Also known as *gap*, this distance can often be adjusted to obtain optimum performance.

air horn The top part of a carburetor barrel through which incoming air passes in amounts controlled by the choke plate and throttle plate.

air-injection reactor A system in which fresh air is mixed with hot exhaust gases in the exhaust manifold to cause combustion that will consume particles of gasoline that have escaped unburned from the cylinders. Abbreviation is A.I.R.

air-injection system An emission-control design in which fresh air is mixed with hot exhaust gases to cause the combustion of unburned particles. See also *air-injection reactor.*

air nozzle The device that supplies air to an air-injection system.

air pollution Substances introduced into the atmosphere that are harmful to humans, animals, or vegetation.

air pressure (1) See atmospheric pressure. (2) Air that is compressed to produce pressures higher than normal atmospheric pressure. (3) Air that is evacuated to produce pressures lower than normal atmospheric pressure.

air pump A device employing a piston, a rotor with sliding vanes, or a turbine blade to produce a flow of air at higher than atmospheric pressure.

aligning drift A rod or shaft used to align parts during assembly.

alignment Adjustment of the relationship between two or more objects to form a single line or parallel lines.

Allen wrench A six-sided (hexagonal) tool used to turn screws that have matching recessed hexagonal heads.

alloy (1) A mixture of two or more metals. For example, brass is an alloy of copper and zinc. (2) British term for lightweight metals, such as aluminum and magnesium.

alternating current A flow of electricity that periodically reverses direction; two flows of current, one in each direction, are called a *cycle*. Household current in the U.S. flows at 60 cycles per second. Abbreviation is AC.

alternator Belt-driven generator on the engine that produces a flow of alternating current and converts it to direct current. The current is stored in the battery and used to supply all electrical needs of a car. During the 1960s the alternator replaced the DC generator. Alternators are lighter and can provide more current at lower engine speeds.

ambient temperature (1) The temperature of air in the natural state in a given location. (2) The temperature of the air surrounding a car or an engine.

ammeter A device that measures the flow of electricity in a circuit; readings are given in *amperes*.

amperage The amount of electricity flowing in a circuit as read in amperes.

ampere A unit of measurement for electric current; 1 ampere flowing at 1 volt equals 1 watt of power.

anti-backfire valve See *air bypass valve.*

antifreeze An additive that lowers the freezing point of a liquid, as ethylene glycol lowers the freezing point of water in a radiator. Alcohol-based antifreeze solutions are used in fuel systems and windshield-washer systems.

anti-friction bearing A bearing employing balls or rollers. Differs from a plain, or shell, bearing, which is sometimes called a *friction bearing.*

antiknock compound Any fuel additive that prevents the air-fuel mixture in the cylinders from burning too quickly or spontaneously (which produces an audible knock). Tetraethyl lead is the best-known antiknock compound.

anti-percolator A carburetor valve that opens to vent vapor when the throttle plate is closed. Otherwise, unvented pressure would cause fuel to dribble (percolate) into the carburetor throat from the fuel nozzle.

anti-rattle spring A spring that holds parts in clutches and disc brakes together and keeps them from rattling.

anti-roll bar See *stabilizer bar.*

anti-sway bar See *stabilizer bar.*

anti-theft device Any of several devices (some required by U.S. law) designed to slow down or discourage a car thief. These include mechanical locks on the steering wheel and ignition switch plus electric or mechanical aftermarket devices that shut off the ignition system, block the flow of fuel, or sound an alarm.

arcing (1) The jumping of an electrical spark from one electrode to another, as in the spark plug. (2) The undesired sparking between electrical conductors or between a conductor and ground when insulation is insufficient or damaged.

armature The moving part of a generator or electric motor, consisting of coils of wire around a metal core. When the armature moves through a magnetic field, an electric current is created, as in the generator. The application of an electric current through the armature causes it to turn, as in a motor. Thus, a motor can sometimes act as a generator, and vice versa.

aspect ratio A percentage figure used to express the ratio of a tire's height to its width. A figure of 80 would mean that a tire is 80 percent as high as it is wide. Also called the *tire profile.*

assembly A group of parts that are joined together and function as a unit, such as a brake caliper assembly, a wheel bearing assembly, or an oil pump assembly.

ATDC Abbreviation for after top dead center.

atmospheric pressure The weight or pressure of the earth's atmosphere, amounting to 14.7 pounds per square inch (psi) at sea level but less at higher altitudes. Pressure is due to the earth's gravitational pull on the air mass. (The pressure of compressed air is sometimes expressed in *atmospheres* rather than psi; 5 atmospheres would equal about 73.5 psi.)

automatic choke A choke system that enriches the air-fuel mixture in a cold engine when the accelerator is first depressed. As the engine reaches normal operating temperatures, the choke plate is opened automatically.

automatic level control A system composed of two air-chamber shock absorbers in the rear of the car. These are fed compressed air by an electric compressor. The pressure in the air chambers is determined automatically by a sensing system to keep the car's body at a predetermined height no matter what load it is carrying.

axle ratio A figure expressing the speed in revolutions per minute (rpm) of the drive shaft in relation to the speed of the drive wheels. A figure of 3.5 means that the shaft turns three and a half times while the wheels turn once.

B

babbitt A low-friction metal alloy. It is up to 90 percent tin, to which copper, antimony, lead, zinc, and sometimes other metals are added in small amounts. A soft material with a low (600°F) melting point, babbitt is widely used to coat friction bearings of harder metals. Babbitt was once used for casting journal or sleeve bearings.

backfire Ignition of the air-fuel mixture in the intake or the exhaust manifold. Backfire occurs if the intake or exhaust valves are open when there is a mistimed ignition spark, or if there is a malfunction in the air pump system.

backflush A method of cleaning a car's cooling system in which a fluid (such as water) is pumped through the system in a direction opposite to the normal flow of coolant. Also known as *reverse flush.*

backlash The clearance between gear teeth — how far one gear can be moved without moving another.

back pressure A limitation to the free flow of gases or liquid. For example, the gases in an exhaust system compress and exert a force back to the engine. Excess back pressure makes an engine work too hard to purge itself, reducing engine power.

ballast resistor A resistor in the supply circuit to the ignition coil that limits voltage. It is necessary because the charging voltage from the alternator to a 12-volt battery must be more than 12 volts, but after passing beyond the battery, 12 volts can damage the ignition system. The ballast resistor reduces 12 volts to as little as 5 volts.

ball bearing (1) A spherical bearing. (2) One or more rows of steel balls held between two races to form a bearing assembly. See also *bearing.*

ball check valve A valve in which the closing device is spherical. Flow is permitted in one direction but is checked in the opposite direction when the ball is carried against a ring-shaped seat, closing the valve's passage.

ball joint A design that joins two members by means of a sphere on one side and a matching socket on the other, permitting rotation in all planes. Widely used in suspension and steering systems.

ball peen The half-spherical back of the head of a machinist's hammer, used to shape or flatten metal. There is usually a flat face at the opposite end of the head. Sometimes spelled *ball pein.*

ball stud A stud with a ball-shaped end that is widely used in steering linkages and engine valve trains.

barrel (1) A unit of liquid measure that varies from one industry to another but usually equals 31.5 gal. When referring to oil, one bbl is equivalent to 42 gal. (2) A throat or bore in a carburetor. (3) The removable individual cylinders of an air-cooled engine.

base circle On a camshaft, the side opposite a lobe (or cam) that ordinarily has a greater radius than the shaft.

battery acid A solution of sulfuric acid used as the electrolyte in automotive storage batteries.

battery charge (1) The amount of energy stored in a battery. (2) The application of an electric current that is converted to chemical energy for storage in a battery.

BDC Abbreviation for bottom dead center.

bead The inner lips of a tire, designed to fit into the metal rim.

bearing A device fitted between two moving parts to reduce friction.

bearing clearance The space between the bearing and the shaft into which lubricant can be pumped.

bearing cups See *race.*

before top dead center The position of the piston before it has reached the top of its stroke. Piston position is measured in degrees of crankshaft rotation. Abbreviation is BTDC. Spark timing may be specified in degrees BTDC.

bell crank A rigid L-shaped arm that pivots on a fixed point at its elbow. Often used to change linear motion to rotational motion around its pivot. In some steering systems, the crank is fitted at one front wheel and its motion is transferred to the other wheel by a connecting-rod assembly.

bell mouthing The uneven wear of a brake drum or similar mechanism toward the open end. Flared wear pattern usually resembles the mouth of a bell. Also called *bell wear.*

bellows A device that achieves expansion and contraction by means of folds, as in some cameras. Design is used in some thermostats and in the control devices in many air-conditioning systems.

belt (1) A flat band of material that lies beneath the tread of a tire. Often made of nylon, rayon, fiberglass, or steel. (2) A drive belt.

belted-bias tire Tire with basic body plies arranged at an angle, or bias, to the tire's centerline and to each other. Unlike bias-ply tires, belted-bias tires incorporate reinforced belts between the plies and tread.

Bendix drive Drive system design used to engage the starter motor shaft with the gear teeth on the flywheel. Disengages automatically when the engine starts. Rare on modern cars.

bevel gear A gear whose teeth are set at an angle to its shaft. Used in pairs to transmit power at angles.

bias-ply tire Tire in which the body plies are set on an angle, or bias, to the centerline of the tire.

big end The end of the connecting rod that fits onto the crankshaft.

bimetal A strip made up of two metals that have different expansion characteristics. When heat is applied, the strip bends toward the metal that expands less. These strips are used in thermostatically controlled devices.

bleeding Exhausting the air from hydraulic brake lines.

block See *cylinder block.*

blow-by The passage of gases from the combustion chamber past piston rings into the crankcase, due to worn rings or excess pressure. Some blow-by is normal, even in sound engines.

blower (1) Electric fan in the heater/evaporator housing that blows air into the passenger compartment. The air may be heated or cooled, depending on the driver's selection. (2) Slang term for a supercharger.

bore Automotive specification for the diameter of a cylinder. Also refers to any cylinder —in the engine block, hydraulic system, or elsewhere.

bore out To increase the size of a cylinder by boring. Sometimes called *reboring.*

boring bar The tool used to bore out a cylinder.

bottom dead center The piston's position at its lowest point of travel. Abbreviation is BDC.

brake drag The continuous contact between pad or lining with the brake disc or drum. Usually caused by misadjustment, although in many disc-brake systems, a small amount of brake drag is normal.

brake drum A metal housing, shaped like an oversize jar lid and bolted to a car wheel. Brake shoes covered with a friction material are forced against the cylindrical inner surface of the drum to stop it, and therefore the wheel to which it is bolted.

brake fade Loss of braking effectiveness when excessive heat reduces the friction between the pad and disc or the shoe and drum.

brake fluid A liquid used to transmit force through brake lines. A high boiling point is an essential characteristic.

brake grab Sudden and undesirable increase in braking force, often on only one wheel.

brake lines Pipes and hoses filled with fluid that transmits force from the brakes' master cylinder to the wheel cylinders or pistons.

brake lining Heat-resistant friction material that is pressed against the metal drum or disc to achieve braking force in a brake system.

brake pads The parts of a disc brake that are periodically replaced; pads of friction material are bonded to rectangular metal plates. Sometimes called *disc-brake shoes,* but not to be confused with drum-brake shoes.

brake shoe Metal assembly on which a friction lining is mounted in the drum-brake system. Fitted in pairs at each wheel, shoes bring the linings into contact with the drum.

breakerless ignition system See *electronic ignition.*

breaker points A switch in the distributor. When it closes, it completes a circuit through the ignition coil. When it opens, the ignition coil discharges a high voltage to a spark plug. Also called *contact points.*

breather pipe An open pipe that vents fumes, or serves as an air inlet when venting takes place elsewhere. Commonly used in PCV systems to allow fresh air to enter the engine crankcase, to replace fumes drawn into the engine for burning. Also called *crankcase breather.*

British thermal unit A measurement of the heat content of a fluid, or the amount of heat removed. Each British thermal unit equals the amount of heat required to raise the temperature of 1 lb. water by 1° F. Abbreviation is Btu.

brush A pad of electrically conductive material that bears on the commutator to form an electrical circuit between rotating and stationary components. See also *commutator.*

BTDC Abbreviation for before top dead center.

Btu Abbreviation for British thermal unit.

bump stop Rubber blocks fitted to some suspension systems to limit the amount of spring compression that results when the car hits a bump or dip in the road.

burned valve A valve that has been so deformed or otherwise damaged by excessive heat that it is defective.

bushing A removable metal, rubber, or plastic sleeve placed between two parts, either or both of which may move. The bushing may absorb shock, perform bearing-like functions, or help to position parts.

butterfly valve A circular plate mounted on a shaft so that it can pivot to open or close a cylindrical passage. The chokes and the throttles in carburetors and in some fuel-injection systems are butterfly valves.

bypass A secondary passage for the flow of liquid or gas.

bypass filter Oil-filtering system in which contaminants are removed from a secondary flow of oil rather than from the main flow.

bypass valve Valve that opens under certain conditions to permit a flow of liquid or gas by some alternate to its normal route. There are bypass valves in oil filters, AIR systems, and power steering pumps.

Glossary

C

caliper (1) A two-legged instrument that measures distances between points, such as the diameter of a rod or the size of a cylinder bore. (2) The assembly in a disc brake that brings the pads to bear on the disc.

cam (1) A lobe or lump on a rotating shaft that is used to open the intake and exhaust valves. (2) A shaft in a breaker point distributor; the lobes (one for each cylinder) push the breaker points open. (3) Slang for camshaft.

camber The angle at which a vertical plane passing through the circumference of a wheel-tire assembly meets the ground. *Positive camber* is created when a wheel leans out at the top; *negative camber* when it leans inward.

camshaft A rotating shaft with lobes that open intake and exhaust valves.

capacitive discharge Ignition system in which primary power is stored in a capacitor; ignition spark is created by discharge of the capacitor. Also called *capacitor discharge*.

capacitor Electrical storage component also known as a *condenser*. Wired across the distributor's breaker points, a capacitor absorbs electricity when points open, discharges it when they close. Capacitors are also used to suppress radio interference.

capacity (1) The volume of liquid that can be held in a container or auto system. Examples are fuel tank capacity, crankcase capacity, radiator capacity, and cooling system capacity. (2) See *displacement*.

carbon Black residue of the combustion process.

carbon dioxide A harmless gas that is one component of auto emissions. Abbreviation is CO_2.

carbon-fouled The buildup of carbon deposits on internal engine parts or on spark plug electrodes. Fouled spark plugs may misfire, causing a loss of power and wasting fuel.

carbon monoxide A deadly gas, composed or carbon and oxygen, that is a component of auto exhaust emissions. Abbreviation is CO.

carburetion The combining of air and fuel outside the cylinder, using a carburetor or carburetors.

carburetor A device that combines air and fuel for burning in cylinders.

carcass The basic body of a tire on which the plies and the tread are laid.

caster The angle described by drawing one line through the steering axis of a wheel and a second line through the hub to the spot where the wheel contacts the ground. Caster is expressed in degrees.

catalyst Any agent that encourages a chemical reaction but is not consumed in the reaction.

catalytic converter A component of the exhaust system that causes a chemical reaction that converts certain air pollutants in the exhaust gases into harmless substances.

cc Abbreviation for cubic centimeters.

Celsius The metric temperature scale in which water at sea level freezes at 0° and boils at 100° (as compared to the 32° freezing point and 212° boiling point of water on the Fahrenheit scale). Also known as *centigrade*.

centimeter Metric unit of measure that is equal to 1/100 meter and 0.390 in. Abbreviation is cm.

centrifugal advance Weight-controlled system in the distributor that changes spark timing in relation to engine speed.

centrifugal clutch Clutch design that has weights attached to pivots around the circumference of the rotating part of the clutch. As the clutch rotates, the weights are spun outward by centrifugal force and increase the locking pressure on the clutch. In some designs, the weights have friction surfaces and, when spun outward, the weights lock against the inside of a drum on a second shaft, thereby transmitting power to it.

centrifugal force The force that is exerted outward from a center of rotation.

cetane number A measure of the combustibility of diesel fuel. The higher the number, the more readily the fuel will ignite in the hot air of the diesel's combustion chamber.

charcoal canister A filter, with charcoal as the active element, used to trap gasoline fumes.

charging Filling or refilling a container or system, such as a battery or air-conditioning system.

charging rate The size or quantity of flow at which a charge is delivered. See *charge*.

chassis The frame, running gear, steering, and suspension of a car.

check valve A valve that permits flow in only one direction.

choke (1) A device in most carburetors that enriches the air-fuel mixture by choking off, or restricting, the airflow. (2) The knob or handle that operates the choke.

choke plate A flat plate in the carburetor that pivots to the degree desired to choke off the airflow. See *choke*.

Chrysler cars Cars produced by the divisions of the Chrysler Corporation, with Plymouth, Dodge, and Chrysler nameplates.

Chrysler vehicles Cars and trucks produced by the divisions of the Chrysler Corporation.

CID Abbreviation for cubic-inch displacement.

circlip A circular clip used to hold parts together. See *snap ring*.

circuit (1) A conductor through which electricity flows before it returns to its source (thus having completed a circuit). (2) Passages or piping through which liquid or gas flows before returning to its source.

circuit breaker A mechanical device that opens contacts when an electric flow is excessive; used in place of a fuse. When current flow returns to normal, the circuit breaker in a car closes.

clearance A defined space between two parts, as between a shaft and a bearing, one or both of which are usually moving.

clutch Mechanical device capable of coupling and uncoupling a drive shaft from its power source. In a car, the clutch is placed between the engine and the transmission.

clutch disc A plate faced with friction material and mounted on the transmission input shaft between the engine flywheel and a movable pressure plate. When pressed between the flywheel and pressure plate, the disc transmits power from the engine to the transmission. Also called *friction disc*.

clutch fork A metal component, resembling a tuning fork, that positions the throw-out bearing behind the pressure plate.

clutch housing A large metal case, resembling a bell, that surrounds the clutch and flywheel. Also called the *bell housing* or *flywheel housing*.

cm or **Cm** Abbreviation for centimeter.

CO Chemical symbol for carbon monoxide.

CO_2 Chemical symbol for carbon dioxide.

coil An assembly of two wire coils in a transformer that steps up low-voltage current to the high levels needed to produce an ignition spark.

coil spring A steel wire or rod bent into a series of loops that make a cylindrical shape. Coil springs resist compression or extension and are widely used in car suspensions.

cold cranking rate A rating for automotive batteries in a 30-sec discharge test; measured in amperes at either 0°F. or −20°F.

cold idle An engine idle speed, higher than hot idle, that helps to prevent the engine from stalling when it is cold. Also called *fast idle*. See *idle*.

cold patch Piece of rubber applied to an inner tube or tire to mend a hole, using an air-drying adhesive only.

cold plug A spark plug with a low heat range.

cold-start test A test administered by the U.S. Environmental Protection Agency to gauge auto emissions when a cold engine is started.

combined octane number Average of the octane numbers generated by the Research and Motor methods, posted on gasoline pumps in the U.S.

combustion chamber That portion of the cylinder between the piston and cylinder head in which combustion takes place.

commutator A slotted metal ring on the end of the rotor of a generator or electric motor. When in contact with stationary brushes, segments of the commutator conduct electricity to or from the turning rotor.

compensating port Tiny opening between a brake master cylinder and brake-fluid reservoir that permits passage of fluid between the two.

compression Increasing the pressure of a gas by reducing its volume.

compression ignition Spontaneous combustion of air-fuel mixture caused by heat due to high compression, as in a diesel engine.

compression ratio Volume of the cylinder at the piston's lowest point of travel compared to the volume at the piston's highest point of travel. Expressed as two numerals: 10-to-1 or 10:1.

compression ring Type of piston ring fitted to the uppermost grooves of a piston to prevent combustion gases from passing into the crankcase. Most pistons have two compression rings.

compression stroke Upward stroke of a piston that squeezes the air-fuel mixture into a tiny space, raising its pressure and causing it to explode with greater force when ignited.

compression tester Instrument that can be fitted into a spark-plug hole to give readings of compression pressure in pounds per square inch (psi) or in kilopascals (kPa).

compressor A mechanical device, usually employing a piston or a rotor with sliding vanes, that compresses gases, such as air for tire inflation or refrigerant in an air conditioner.

condenser (1) The heat-radiator in an air conditioner that extracts heat from the refrigerant and converts it from a gas to a liquid. (2) The capacitor in a breaker-point distributor.

conduction The physical passage of heat or electrical energy in a designed pathway from one point to another.

conductor A material, normally metallic, that permits easy passage of heat or electricity.

connecting rod Steel part connecting the piston to the crankshaft.

constant-velocity joint A type of universal joint that maintains exact speeds between driving and driven shafts even when the two shafts are operating at sharp angles to each other.

contact points See *breaker points*.

control arm A part of the suspension that supports a wheel.

convection The transfer of heat by the natural circulation of a fluid. When heated, the fluid at the bottom of a vessel expands, becomes lighter than the surrounding fluid, and rises to the top of the vessel. Colder fluid settles to the bottom of the vessel where it, too, is heated and rises. If the fluid at the bottom of the vessel is always hotter than the fluid at the top, a constant circulation will take place.

coolant In a car, the liquid that carries excess heat from the engine to the radiator. Water alone was once used, but modern coolant is usually a mixture of water and antifreeze.

coolant recovery tank An auxiliary tank designed to receive the overflow when coolant in the radiator expands. When coolant in the radiator contracts, the overflow is drawn back from the recovery tank.

cooling system A set of components that rid an engine of excess heat.

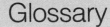

core (1) The central metal part inside a coil, as in a transformer. (2) The section of a heat exchanger (radiator, heater, or air-conditioning condenser or evaporator) that is composed of tubing and fins. (3) A faulty but rebuildable automotive component traded in on a new or rebuilt one.

core plug A small metal disc that is force-fit into openings in the water jacket of an engine block. If the coolant freezes, one or more core plugs may pop out to relieve pressure so that the block does not fracture. Also called a *freeze-out plug.*

cotter pin A split metal pin whose ends are bent to secure it in a hole as a fastener. A loop of metal forms a head at the other end of the pin.

countershaft The secondary shaft in a conventional manual transmission. The cluster of gears that rotate on the countershaft are in constant mesh with the freewheeling gears on the transmission's input and output shafts. When the transmission is put into gear, one of the freewheeling gears is locked to its shaft, and power is transmitted from the engine to the rear wheels when the clutch is engaged.

counterweight Any weight used to offset another weight of similar size. On a crankshaft, metal lobes on the side opposite the cranks act as counterweights to prevent vibration.

courtesy light A small light inside the car that switches on automatically when the door is opened.

cowl The top forward portion of a car body on which the windshield and instrument panel are mounted.

crabbing (1) Attitude of a car when the back wheels are not in line with the front wheels — causing the car, when driven straight ahead, to appear to be moving slightly sideways, in the manner of a crab. (2) Turning the front wheel into a crosswind to keep the car moving as straight down a road as possible. Also called *dog tracking.*

crank (1) A rod bent into an offset handle and used to start an engine. (2) The U-shaped bends in a crankshaft. (3) Slang for crankshaft.

crankcase Metal housing of the crankshaft and related components, a section of which is the oil pan.

crankcase breather A port or tube that vents fumes from the crankcase. An inlet breather allows fresh air into the crankcase. See *breather pipe.*

crankpin The outermost part of a crankshaft to which a connecting rod is attached. Also called a *connecting-rod journal.*

crankshaft The part of an engine that converts the reciprocating power produced by the pistons into rotary power, which is transmitted to the drive wheels. Named for the offsets, called *cranks* or *crank throws*, to which connecting rods are attached.

crank throw The offset part of a crankshaft with webs on either side and the crankpin as the outermost part. Sometimes called a *crank.*

crank web The side members of a crank throw.

crashworthiness Engineering term for the relative protection offered to car occupants in the event of a crash. A car with good crashworthiness will protect occupants from death or serious injury during a crash at higher speeds than a car with poor crashworthiness will.

crazing A series of minute cracks on the surface of an object.

cross fire An undesirable jumping of electrical current from one spark plug cable to another. Aggravated by poor insulation and poor routing of plug cables. Causes the engine to misfire.

cross-flow radiator A radiator in which the coolant flows through horizontal tubing.

cross-thread The mismating of threads — as a nut on a bolt, or a stud in a hole — that causes threads to cross and thereby damages them.

cubic centimeter A unit of volume in the metric system. There are 16.38 cc in 1 cu in.

cubic-inch displacement A measurement of cylinder volume. Abbreviation is CID.

curb idle See *idle.*

curb weight The weight of a vehicle ready for operation — that is, carrying fuel, coolant, and lubricants but no passengers or payload.

current A flow of electricity. Under the Current Theory, flow is from negative to positive poles.

cycling clutch system Design for air conditioners in which cooling is controlled by a sensing thermostat that opens or closes a solenoid. The solenoid, in turn, engages or disengages a magnetic clutch to produce on-off cycles in the compressor.

cylinder block The basic engine casting in which power components operate. Usually made of iron, sometimes of aluminum. Also called the *block* or *engine block.*

cylinder head An iron or aluminum casting that is bolted to the top of the cylinder block. Normally contains the combustion chambers, valves, spark plugs, and coolant passages. Also called the *head.*

cylinder head gasket A gasket of compressible metal and asbestos placed between the cylinder head and block to prevent combustion gases from escaping and coolant from entering the cylinders.

cylinder-leakage tester An instrument for locating leaks from the combustion chamber. Tester fits into the spark plug hole and applies air at high pressure while piston is at top dead center and the valves are closed.

cylinder liner A metal sleeve that fits into a cylinder to form a facing between the cylinder walls and piston.

D

dashpot A damper device in the carburetor that prevents the throttle from closing as soon as the driver's foot is taken off the gas pedal. This prevents the engine from stalling or prevents an overly rich fuel mixture that would increase exhaust emissions.

DC Abbreviation for direct current.

deceleration A decrease in speed.

defroster A device that uses electrical resistance wires or heated air to warm the windshield or other car windows in order to melt ice or evaporate condensation. Also called a *defogger.*

degree (1) A measurement of the angle between two intersecting lines; a quarter circle contains 90°; a full circle, 360°. (2) A measurement of temperature. See *Celsius* and *Fahrenheit.*

Department of Transportation A U.S. government agency in overall charge of federal laws and policies that affect vehicles and transportation. Abbreviation is DoT.

deposit ignition Untimed ignition of the air-fuel mixture by glowing bits of material, usually carbon, deposited on surfaces of the combustion chamber.

detent A design for restraining a mechanical device; often a spring-loaded ball or pawl that fits into a hole or de-

pression. A detent holds a transmission lever in the position chosen (*Drive, Neutral, Reverse*, etc.).

detonation In a gasoline engine, a sound created by ignition that occurs without a spark. (Also see *deposit ignition.*) The ignition commonly occurs in a recess in the combustion chamber and upsets the normal combustion pattern. Also known as *knock, ping, dieseling, afterrun, run-on.*

diaphragm See *vacuum diaphragm.*

die A metal tool used to cut outside threads on a rod or pipe, or to help clean or restore damaged threads on a bolt or stud.

diesel engine An engine that achieves ignition from the heat generated by extreme compression of the air-fuel mixture and without an electrical spark.

dieseling See *afterrunning.*

differential Gear assembly design that permits the drive wheel on one side of a car to turn faster than its mate, as on a curve. Term is derived from *speed differential.*

dimmer switch Hand- or foot-operated switch that turns the high-beam filaments of headlights on or off.

diode Electrical device that permits current to flow in only one direction. Most often used as a component in electronic controls and accessories. Also converts an alternator's AC output to DC.

dipstick Metal rod, round or flat, that indicates the level of oil in a container. Used in the engine's crankcase, automatic transmission's oil pan, and power steering pump's reservoir.

direct current Electric current flowing in one direction. Abbreviation is DC.

disc (1) A round, flat component. (2) The part attached to the wheel in a disc-brake system; also called a *rotor.*

disc brake Brake design in which the member attached to the wheel is a steel disc, and braking force is applied by two friction pads that are squeezed against the disc by a caliper.

disc runout A measurement of how much a brake disc wobbles from side to side as it rotates. Also called *runout.*

discharge side The high-pressure part of an air-conditioner circuit.

dispersant An additive that keeps sludge, such as particles in a lubricant, suspended. Suspended particles can then be removed when the lubricant and filter are changed. Also called a *detergent-dispersant.*

displacement The total volume (expressed in cu in., cc, or L) of the space inside the cylinders occupied and then evacuated (swept) by all the pistons of an engine.

distributor Electromechanical device that distributes high-voltage electricity to the individual spark plug cables.

diverter valve See *air bypass valve.*

dog tracking See *crabbing.*

DOHC Abbreviation for double overhead camshaft.

dolly A formed piece of metal used to back metal sheets, such as body panels, while they are being hammered.

DoT Abbreviation for the U.S. Department of Transportation.

double overhead camshaft An engine design in which one camshaft operates the intake valves and a second operates the exhaust valves. Both cams are located atop the cylinder head. Abbreviation is DOHC.

dowel pin A metal pin or rod that keeps two parts in alignment.

downdraft Carburetor design with a vertical intake throat.

downflow Radiator design in which the coolant pipes are vertical and the coolant flows from top to bottom.

downshift To shift to a lower gear. In an automatic transmission, downshifting to the next lower, or *passing*, gear may be achieved by flooring the accelerator. This is called *kickdown.*

drift A specialized type of punch with a cylindrical tip that ends with a flat facing rather than in a point.

driveability Engineering term for an engine's response to the accelerator pedal. An engine that accelerates smoothly, with no bucking or hesitation, runs at constant speed when the accelerator is held steady (and does this when cold as well as warm) is said to have good driveability. An engine that hesitates, or *stumbles*, on acceleration, or one that fluctuates in speed, or *hunts*, when the accelerator is held steady has poor driveability.

drive belt A reinforced rubber belt, usually with a V-shaped cross section, used to drive various engine accessories such as the alternator, air-conditioning compressor, and water pump. Also called *fan belt.* Belts with molded teeth are often used to drive overhead camshafts.

driveline The shaft or shafts that carry power from the transmission to the differential.

Glossary

driven disc A disc attached to a clutch shaft that transmits power when pressed between pressure plate and flywheel. Also called *clutch disc, driven plate,* and *friction disc.*

driven wheels See *free-rolling wheels.*

drive shaft Metal tube that transmits power from the transmission to the differential; includes universal joints. Also known as *propeller shaft* or *prop shaft.*

drive train Term covers all power-transmitting components between the engine and wheels, including the clutch, transmission, drive shaft, differential, and axles.

drive wheels The wheels that receive power from the engine and drive train to drive the car.

drop-center wheel Wheel rim design in which the center is lower than the flanges in which the tire beads fit.

droplight A shaded electric bulb with a protective cage and a long cord used to illuminate a work area. Also called a *work light.*

drum brake Brake design in which the component attached to the wheel is shaped like an open-ended drum or a jar cap. Shoes press the friction linings against the inside of the drum to provide braking action.

dry sump Engine lubricating design in which lubricant is stored in a remotely mounted reservoir rather than in an oil pan below the crankcase. Oil is circulated through tubing between the engine and reservoir by a pump.

dry weight Weight of a car without any of its required operating fluids, such as fuel, coolant, or lubricants.

dwell The angle, in degrees, described by the distributor cam while the breaker points are closed. In an electronic ignition system, dwell is the amount of time that the primary circuit is completed by transistorized circuitry. Dwell is always expressed in degrees of distributor shaft rotation.

dwell meter Electronic instrument used to read dwell.

dwell-tachometer An instrument that combines the functions of a dwell meter and a tachometer.

dynamic balancing Balancing a wheel while it is turning in order to eliminate uneven tire wear and annoying wheel shimmy on the road.

dynamometer A machine used to measure power output. An *engine dynamometer* measures power at the crankshaft; a *chassis dynamometer* measures power at the drive wheels.

eccentric (1) A projection or a lobe on a shaft. The eccentric transmits power to a rod to convert rotary motion into reciprocating motion. (2) The undesirable off-center operation of a wheel, disc, or drum.

E-clip A circular clip with tabs that vaguely resembles the letter E. Used to hold parts together. See *snap ring.*

efficiency (1) Net, or usable, horsepower produced by an engine as compared to its total horsepower. (2) The percentage of power transmitted through the drive train compared to the power input from the engine.

EGR Abbreviation for exhaust gas recirculation.

electric choke An automatic choke design in which a tiny ceramic resistance wire is used to heat the choke coil.

electrode Posts or plates having an electrical potential with respect to each other, as in a spark plug or battery. Electrodes are positive or negative.

electrolyte Chemical filler in a battery; acts on electrodes to cause the flow of electricity. Sulfuric acid is the electrolyte in a car battery.

electromagnet A magnet that derives its power from the flow of electric current in a coil around a pole piece, usually made of soft iron.

electron In an atom, a minute particle that rotates around the nucleus. A flow of free electrons becomes an electric current.

electronic ignition An ignition system in which the distributor's breaker or contact points are replaced by electro-magnetic sensors and transistorized circuitry to trigger the ignition coil. Also called *breakerless ignition.*

emergency brake See *parking brake.*

emergency flasher See *hazard warning system.*

emission control A device or engine modification that alters the byproducts of combustion to make them less hazardous to man and the environment.

emission standards Legal standards for the maximum amounts of pollutants that may be discharged into the atmosphere. Federal standards are best known but they may be superseded by stricter local standards, such as those in California and certain high-altitude U.S. counties.

end play The amount that a shaft, such as the crankshaft, moves longitudinally in its bearings.

energy The capacity to exert force or perform work. Measured in British thermal units (Btu's).

engine block See *cylinder block.*

Environmental Protection Agency U.S. government department charged with preserving and improving the quality of our air and water, among other tasks. Abbreviation is EPA.

epoxy A family of thermosetting resin adhesives composed of oxygen and carbon. An epoxy is normally marketed as two compounds that, when mixed and set, form a bond of great strength.

ethyl A term for premium gasoline that contains tetraethyl lead, which raises the fuel's octane rating.

ethylene glycol Chemical solution used as an antifreeze. It lowers the freezing point and raises the boiling point of water.

evaporation control An emission-control design in which fuel vapors are trapped in charcoal when the engine is stopped, then fed to the intake system when the car starts.

evaporator The part of an air-conditioning system in which the liquid refrigerant expands rapidly and absorbs heat.

exhaust gas analyzer An instrument used to measure some of the ingredients of exhaust gases.

exhaust gas recirculation system An emission-control system in which a portion of the exhaust gases are routed through the intake manifold to mix with the air-fuel mixture in order to reduce peak combustion temperatures and thereby reduce the formation of oxides of nitrogen. Abbreviation is EGR.

exhaust manifold That part of the exhaust system closest to the engine. It collects gases from the engine's exhaust ports and passes them on to the rest of the exhaust system.

exhaust pipe The pipe in the exhaust system that leads from the exhaust manifold to a catalytic converter, resonator, or muffler.

exhaust stroke The final stroke of a piston in a combustion engine. The exhaust stroke pushes exhaust gases out of the cylinder.

exhaust system All components involved in controlling, converting, and finally carrying away an engine's exhaust gases.

expansion tank See *coolant recovery tank.*

expansion valve Air-conditioner component that controls the flow of liquid refrigerant into the evaporator.

fast charging The restoration of energy in a battery at a rapid rate. Fast charges may take only 20 to 30 min., but they shorten the life of the battery.

fast flushing A method of cleaning a car's cooling system with a chemical solution and a pressure machine whose action is faster than the flow rate of an engine's water pump — which is the alternate method of circulating the chemical solution.

fast idle See *cold idle.*

fast-idle cam Cam used in the carburetor linkage to hold the throttle valve open for a faster-than-normal idle speed when the engine is cold.

feeler gauge A tool made of strips of metal of identified thicknesses. It is used to check clearances between automotive parts.

female A hollow component designed to receive a mating male part.

field coil A coil of wire, usually with an iron core, that produces a magnetic field. Term often describes the stationary components of a motor or generator that produces the magnetic field in which the rotor turns, although it is not restricted to this meaning. Also called *field winding.*

field winding See *field coil.*

filler cap A cap that seals the filler neck, filler tube, or filler hold on a gas tank, rocker cover, cam cover, transmission, or other part.

fins Thin metal projections designed to conduct excess heat from an engine or radiator to the atmosphere, or to help a heat exchanger to pick up heat from the surrounding air.

firing order The sequence in which the spark plugs ignite the air-fuel mixture in a car's cylinders.

fit To install. See also *force-fit.*

flasher Device in the turn-signal system that opens and closes the circuit to produce flashes of light.

flat rate A book method of determining the labor charge in a repair bill in terms of listed times that may be more or less than the actual time a mechanic spends on a particular job.

flat spot (1) A momentary hesitation of an engine in the midst of acceleration. (2) The wearing away of the tire tread in one place.

float (1) A hollow metal or plastic part in the carburetor that operates the valve through which fuel flows from the fuel pump into the float bowl. (2) A hollow or buoyant part of the fuel-level sensor in the fuel tank.

float bowl Carburetor chamber containing a fuel reserve from which fuel is drawn during the fuel-intake process. Fuel level in bowl is controlled by the float. Also called a *fuel bowl.*

float level Fuel level in a float bowl as maintained and regulated by a float.

flooding Condition in which the air-fuel mixture is too rich to permit easy combustion. Often leads to a coating of raw fuel on spark plug electrodes and makes starting difficult.

fluid coupling An assembly in which power is transmitted from one turbine wheel to another through a liquid medium. Such a device is used in the torque converter to couple the engine crankshaft to the automatic transmission's input shaft.

flywheel A heavy wheel that, by its inertia, smooths out a flow of power produced in uneven cycles. In a car the flywheel is attached to the engine crankshaft and ordinarily has a toothed ring pressed onto its outer circumference. The teeth mesh with a gear on the starter motor.

force (1) The exertion of strength or power upon a body or surface, as combustion exerts force on a piston. (2) The joining of two components that fit together closely.

force fit A method of joining two parts that are nearly identical in size by forcing them together so that they are held in place by friction alone.

Ford cars Cars produced by the divisions of the Ford Motor Company, with Ford, Lincoln, or Mercury nameplates.

Ford vehicles Cars and trucks produced by the divisions of the Ford Motor Company.

four-stroke cycle An engine's use of four piston strokes to convert an air-fuel mixture into mechanical power. The cycles are intake, compression, power, and exhaust; together, they are known as an Otto cycle.

four-way-flashers See *hazard warning system.*

four-wheel drive Design in which all four wheels of a vehicle are driven by the engine. Abbreviation is 4WD.

frame An assembly of steel components, usually including two long rails, that supports a car's body and engine and is in turn supported by the suspension system.

free play Clearance. (1) The free movement possible in the valve train without opening of the valve. (2) The free movement at the clutch pedal before the clutch begins to disengage.

free-rolling wheels The wheels that roll along while the car is propelled by the drive wheels. They are the front wheels in a rear-drive car and the rear wheels in a front-drive car. Sometimes called *driven wheels*.

freewheeling (1) Any part that rotates freely and does not transmit power. (2) A non-powered wheel, as the front wheels in a rear-drive car. (3) A method of power transmission used in the 1930s in which cars coasted on downhill grades to save fuel.

freeze-out plug See *core plug*.

Freon Trademark for a refrigerant used in most automotive air conditioners. Also called *Refrigerant-12*.

friction The resistance to movement of two bodies in contact. Friction creates heat and absorbs power, a characteristic that is generally undesirable except in brakes.

friction disc See *clutch disc*.

front drive See *front-wheel drive*.

front-end alignment (1) The measuring, with special equipment, of the angular relationships of the wheels and suspension parts to each other and to the road. (2) The correcting of these relationships with adjustments or the installation of shims. *Caster, camber,* and *toe* are the adjustable angles (although caster and camber are not adjustable on all vehicles).

front-wheel drive A car in which engine power is transmitted to the front wheels. Also called *front drive*. Abbreviation is FWD.

frozen Condition in which a mechanism, such as an engine, is unable to operate or sometimes to move at all because its parts are corroded or heat-warped. Also called *seized*.

fuel bowl See *float bowl*.

fuel injection Fuel system in which the carburetor is replaced by jets that inject fuel directly into the cylinders, at intake ports, or into a throttle body that is mounted on the intake manifold (replacing the carburetor).

fuel lines Tubes and hoses carrying fuel from the tank to the carburetor.

fuel nozzle (1) The tip of the tube that delivers fuel from the float bowl to the carburetor throat. The nozzle protrudes slightly into the flow of incoming air. (2) A fuel injector.

fuel pump A mechanical or electrical device that moves fuel from the fuel tank to the carburetor.

fuel system All the components, from the fuel tank to the intake manifold, that handle the storage and delivery of fuel in a car.

full-floating axle An axle whose sole job is the transmission of power. It does not support any of a vehicle's weight.

full-flow filter An oil-filtering system in which all the oil flows through a filter as it leaves the oil pump, as contrasted to a bypass system, in which only a portion of the oil is filtered.

fuse A metal link in a circuit that melts when the current flow is excessive, thereby breaking the circuit.

fuse block An assembly concentrating most or all of a car's fuses at one point.

fusible link A wire or bar designed to melt if more than a certain amount of electrical current is transmitted through it. Often used as a main fuse or backup fuse for large sectional portions of a car's electrical system.

FWD Abbreviation for front-wheel drive.

G

gall The wearing-away of a softer metal by a harder one at their point of contact.

gallery A passageway through which lubricating oil flows.

gap See *air gap*.

gas (1) A state of matter in which the molecules are far apart. Air is a mixture of gases, as are the exhaust emissions of an engine. Gases have no shape or volume but tend to expand to fill any container they are put in. Otherwise, gases share many of the physical properties of liquids. (2) Slang for gasoline.

gas cap See *filler cap*.

gasket A compressible material (often cork or metal) that makes a leak-free seal by filling in minor irregularities between rigid mating surfaces.

gasket cement An adhesive used for the installation of gaskets. It holds the gasket in position while filling in any irregularities in the gasket's mating surfaces.

gasoline A derivative of crude oil that is more volatile than many other liquid hydrocarbons. With additives, it becomes automotive fuel.

gas pedal See *accelerator*.

gassing The venting of hydrogen bubbles from battery acid as the battery is recharged.

gauge pressure A reading in pounds per square inch or kilopascals on a gauge set to read zero in the open air, thereby ignoring normal atmospheric pressure.

gear oil A lubricant for gears; it is thicker than engine oil.

gear ratio The number of turns made by a driving gear compared to those of a driven gear. For example, two turns by the driving gear to one by the driven gear would be a ratio of 2 to 1 (2:1).

gearshift A lever by which gears are engaged or disengaged. Also refers to the intermediate parts between the shift lever and the transmission.

gear-type pump Pump design in which the pump's force is produced by two gears in mesh.

General Motors cars Cars produced by the divisions of General Motors Corporation with Chevrolet, Oldsmobile, Buick, Cadillac, and Pontiac nameplates. Abbreviation is GM cars.

General Motors vehicles Cars and trucks produced by the divisions of the General Motors Corporation.

generator An electromechanical device that converts mechanical power into electricity.

glow plug An assembly that resembles a spark plug but with a heating element instead of electrodes. Used at the beginning of the starting cycle in a diesel engine to aid compression ignition. Sometimes spelled *glo plug*.

GM Abbreviation for General Motors.

go/no-go feeler gauge A gauge used to measure clearances (gaps) accurately. The gauge contains several blades of graduated thickness. Each blade is thinner at its outer end than at its inner end. The transition from the thin to thick ends is in the form of a sharp step. The gap between two objects is the thickness etched onto the blade whose thin end will just slip between the objects, but whose thick end will not fit between them without being forced.

governor Mechanism controlling the speed of an engine or machine.

gpm Abbreviation for gallons per minute (a rate of flow) or grams per mile (a measure of exhaust emissions).

grade (1) General term for the quality of an item, such as oil or tires, which is often described as *premium grade* — a rating with no specific legal definition. (2) The steepness of a hill, measured either in degrees of slope or as a ratio of a hill's height to its length.

grams per mile A measure of weight, that describes the quantity of any measured element contained in a car's exhaust gases during operation over 1 mile. Abbreviation is gpm.

grease fitting A spring-loaded ball-valve assembly, threaded into a part that requires periodic injections of grease. The tip of the fitting is shaped to accept the nozzle of a grease-injection gun. Grease fittings are found on the joints in steering and suspension systems, drive shafts, and clutch linkage. See also *zerk fitting*.

grease rack See *lift*.

grommet A circular device, usually of rubber, used to hold a wire, cable, or tube without damaging it. Grommets often fit into holes drilled through metal panels and are then used as bumpers between the metal and the parts that pass through the holes.

gross horsepower A calculation of the total power developed by an engine without subtracting the power used by such accessories as the water pump or alternator.

grounding Connecting one side of a car's electric circuit to the chassis, body, or engine. These parts then provide a metal path that conducts electrical current back to the car's battery to complete a circuit. Grounding may be done with a jumper wire.

gulp valve See *air aspirator valve*.

H

H The chemical symbol for hydrogen.

hand brake See *parking brake*.

handling Evaluation of a car's stability in turns and on rough roads. Not to be confused with *ride*.

hazard warning system Electrical switching device and associated lights (usually the front and rear turn-signal lights) producing flashes of light to indicate that a car is in a distress situation. Also called *emergency flasher* or *four-way flashers*.

head See *cylinder head*.

header Usually, an exhaust manifold of special design. Sometimes used to describe a stock exhaust manifold.

heat-control valve Device in the exhaust system that feeds heat to the intake system when the engine is cold. Also called the *manifold heat-control valve* or *heat riser*.

heated-air system Design in which exhaust heat is supplied to the carburetor or throttle body fuel-injection module to help vaporize fuel when the engine is cold.

heater core An assembly of tubes and fins in a car's heater system; it resembles a small radiator. Hot coolant passing through the tubes in the heater core warms the air that is forced over the fins by a blower fan.

heat exchanger Tubular part with fins that pick up or reject heat. Radiators, heater cores, and air-conditioning condensers give up heat to the surrounding air. Air-conditioning evaporators pick up heat from the surrounding air.

heat range A classification for spark plugs. The higher the number, the "hotter" the plug runs, which means that the plug does not dissipate heat as quickly as a "cooler" plug does.

heat riser See *heat-control valve*.

heat soak (1) A large buildup of heat in a body or mechanism, sometimes used to temper a metal part during production. (2) In a car engine, heat soak occurs after operation is stopped and can be damaging if excessive.

helical gear A gear whose teeth are set in a spiral (helix).

hesitation Momentary pause during acceleration.

hood The hinged panel that covers the engine.

Glossary

horn relay Electromagnetic circuit-closing device that switches electricity to the horn when the horn button is depressed.

horsepower A measurement of power or work; one unit equals 33,000 foot-pounds of work per minute. Abbreviation is hp or HP.

Hotchkiss drive Suspension design in which the motive force of the drive wheels is transmitted forward through the rear springs.

hot-idle compensator A valve in the carburetor which smooths out engine idle during hot weather by opening to admit hot and expanded air.

hot patch A piece of rubber that is applied with heat and cement to an inner tube or tire to mend a hole.

hot plug A spark plug with a high heat range.

hp or **HP** Abbreviation for horsepower.

hub The center part of a wheel.

hydraulic brakes Brake design in which fluid in tubes transmits force to operate the brakes.

hydraulic clutch Clutch design in which fluid transmits force to operate the clutch. Often used in imported cars.

hydraulic lifter A valve-lifter design using oil pressure to keep the lifter itself in contact with the camshaft on one end and the valve stem on the other. This eliminates all clearance in the valve train when the engine is running.

hydraulic pressure Measurement, in pounds per square inch or kilopascals, of the force exerted by a fluid under pressure.

hydrocarbon A chemical composition made up of hydrogen and carbon, such as petroleum.

hydrogen Highly flammable elemental gas. Chemical symbol is H.

hydrometer An instrument used to measure the specific gravity of liquids. Hydrometers can be calibrated to indicate the charge level of a battery or the percentage of antifreeze in a coolant mixture.

hypoid gear Design in which a gear is mounted lower than center, or lower than normal. A common example is in the typical rear axle of rear-drive cars, in which the pinion gear, at the input to the rear axle, is below the center of the ring gear it drives.

I

idle A low engine speed, sufficient to keep the engine running smoothly when a car is at rest. Also called *hot idle, curb idle,* or *idle speed.*

idle limiter A fitting on the idle-mixture screw that limits the adjustment of the idle mixture to prevent it from being set so rich that the exhaust would contain excessive air pollutants. Limiters were used until the idle mixture adjusting screws were capped, beginning in 1979 on some cars.

idle mixture The specific mixture of air and fuel supplied to an engine at idle.

idle-mixture screw An adjusting screw that leans or enriches the idle mixture. See also *idle limiter.*

idler arm Component of the steering linkage that supports the tie rod and transmits steering force. One end attaches to the car frame.

idle speed See *idle.*

idle-speed solenoid See *throttle solenoid positioner.*

idle-stop solenoid Electromechanical device with a plunger that bears against the throttle linkage to hold the idle speed. When the ignition is turned off, the plunger is retracted by a spring and the throttle closes completely so that the engine will not stall.

idle system The special components of the carburetor or fuel-injection system that are used only when the engine is idling.

ignition (1) The start of the burning of the air-fuel mixture in a cylinder. (2) Slang for the electromechanical system that produces the spark at the spark plugs.

ignition coil Term applied to what is actually a transformer with two coils, or windings; pulsed low-voltage direct current in the primary winding produces high-voltage spark impulses in the secondary winding.

ignition switch Key-operated main power switch in a car. Its chief function is to close the primary ignition circuit, but modern designs include several other circuits and even a steering column lock.

ignition system All the components that together produce the ignition spark at the spark plugs: battery, distributor, ignition coil, spark plugs, and associated switches and wiring.

J

jack stand A safety device that is placed under a car to guard against jack failure. It is usually made of steel and its height is adjustable.

jet A tube or opening of calibrated size through which air or fuel flows.

journal The smoothly finished part of a shaft that turns on a bearing.

juice A slang term for electricity.

K

key (1) A small piece of metal that fits into slots (keyways) of mating parts to hold them in a fixed position. A key can be used to ensure that a gear turns with a shaft, rather than rotating around it. (2) A small metal device capable of operating a lock.

kg or **KG** Abbreviation for kilogram.

impact wrench (1) A professional garage tool operated by compressed air, used to turn bolts or nuts by means of a series of strokes (impacts). (2) A manual tool that converts hammer blows into twisting force.

impeller A wheel equipped with blades to move a gas or liquid.

induction The spontaneous creation of an electric current in a coil as it passes through a magnetic field.

infrared analyzer An expensive professional instrument used to measure exhaust emissions.

injector The nozzle that supplies fuel in a fuel-injection system.

in-line engine Engine with all its cylinders in a single line.

inner tube Thin rubber bag used as an air container inside a tire. Once a standard component, now largely eliminated by tubeless tires.

insulator A nonconductor or poor conductor of heat or electricity.

intake manifold An engine component that conducts the air-fuel mixture from the carburetor or throttle body fuel-injection module to the cylinders. Often made of cast iron.

intake stroke The downward movement of the piston during which the air-fuel mixture is drawn in through the open intake valve.

intake valve The valve through which the air-fuel mixture enters the cylinder.

kickdown Switch, activated by flooring the accelerator, that causes an automatic transmission to shift down into a lower gear.

kilogram A unit of weight in the metric system; equals 1,000 grams or 2.2 pounds. Abbreviation is kg or KG.

kilometer A unit of linear measurement in the metric system; 1,000 meters (1 kilometer) equals .62 miles. Abbreviation is km or KM.

kilopascal Unit of pressure in the metric system, equal to .145 pounds per square inch. Abbreviation is kPa.

kilowatt A measurement of power equal to 1,000 watts. 100 volts flowing at the rate of 10 amperes equals 1 kilowatt. Abbreviation is kw or KW.

kingpin The metal rod or pin on which the steering knuckle turns. Still used in many heavy-duty vehicles, but has been replaced by ball joints in modern passenger cars.

km or **KM** Abbreviation for kilometer.

knock Sound produced when a car's air-fuel mixture is ignited by something other than the spark plug, such as a hot spot in the combustion chamber. Light knock is normal in modern engines during heavy acceleration or under other high-load conditions, such as climbing steep grades. Severe knock may be caused by fuel with too low an octane rating or by improper adjustment of the ignition system, and it will harm the engine. Also called *detonation* or *ping.*

knuckle Steering gear component that is also part of the suspension. It has a spindle that supports the wheel, and it pivots (typically on ball joints) to allow the wheels to be steered.

knurl A machined metal surface with a pattern of ridges and grooves.

kPa Abbreviation for kilopascal.

kw or **KW** Abbreviation for kilowatt.

L

L or **l** Abbreviation for liter.

lash The amount of play or free movement between parts, such as sets of gear teeth or valve train components.

lead (1) An elemental metal that is heavy, pliable, and easily melted. (2) Abbreviated term for tetraethyl lead. (3) A wire in an electric circuit.

leaded gasoline Gasoline to which tetraethyl lead has been added.

lead sulfate A product of the electrochemical action in a lead-acid battery. The sulfate forms on the plates and slowly fouls the battery.

lean mixture A mixture in a gasoline engine with an air-to-fuel ratio greater than 14.6:1, usually above 16:1.

lift Garage machine capable of lifting an entire car. It normally utilizes compressed air to provide power for a hydraulic system. Sometimes called a *grease rack.*

lifter Cylindrical metal component in contact with the camshaft on one end and the pushrod, rocker arm, or valve stem on the other. Oil inside the lifter transfers the cam's up-and-down action to the pushrod, rocker arm, or valve stem by hydraulic action.

limited-slip differential Differential design in which the amount of power that goes to a slipping wheel is limited by spring-loaded clutches so that some power can be transferred to a wheel with better traction. This prevents a car from becoming hopelessly stuck in sand, snow, or on ice.

linkage An assembly of rods, levers, and links designed to transmit motion.

liquefied petroleum gas A hydrocarbon gas reduced to liquid form by pressure. The gas can be manufactured or natural, although the latter is usually called *liquefied natural gas* (LNG). Abbreviation is LPG.

liter A metric unit of volume. Equal to 1,000 cubic centimeters or 2.2 pints. In engine displacement, 1 liter equals approximately 61 cubic inches. Abbreviation is L or l.

live axle A drive axle to which a wheel is rigidly attached.

load test (1) A test for starter motors in which the current draw is measured while the engine is cranking. (2) A battery test.

lobe A rounded projection on a shaft. See also *cam.*

locknut A nut designed to resist loosening once it has been tightened.

lock washer A washer, usually with a split or projections, designed to be placed under a nut to secure it.

low-lead gasoline Gasoline with a small amount (½ g per gal) of tetraethyl lead additive.

LPG Abbreviation for liquefied petroleum gas.

lug (1) Sputtering action of an overloaded engine, cured by shifting to a lower gear. (2) The stud, nut, or bolt that holds a car wheel to its hub.

M

m or **M** Abbreviation for meter.

machine screw Threaded rod of uniform diameter with a head on one end and often a nut on the other.

machining Shaping a metal part by mechanically turning or grinding it.

MacPherson strut Suspension design that combines the shock absorber and a spring in a single assembly that links the lower control arm and chassis.

mag Slang for magnesium wheel and for wheels of like design.

magnetic field The space that is subject to the force produced by a magnet.

magnetic pole The ends of a magnet, called *north* and *south*, where the magnetic lines of force converge and enter the magnet.

magnetic switch A switch operated by a small electromagnet. Solenoids and relays are magnetic switches.

magneto A type of generator whose high-voltage output is strong enough to fire a spark plug. The name is derived from permanent magnets used in the generator. Once used in place of distributors in some cars, magnetos are still used in many small gasoline engines for lawn mowers, chain saws, and the like.

main bearings The bearings in which the crankshaft turns.

main jet A calibrated tube whose outlet nozzle is in the carburetor venturi. It supplies fuel when the engine runs faster than idle speed.

main metering system A group of components that supply fuel to the carburetor between very low speeds and maximum engine speed.

male A protruding part or member designed to fit into a hollow (female) part.

manifold A housing with chambers. An *exhaust manifold* has chambers that connect the exhaust port of each cylinder to an exhaust pipe that leads to the muffler. An *intake manifold* has chambers that connect the cylinder's intake ports to a carburetor or fuel-injection throttle body.

manifold heat-control valve See *heat-control valve.*

manifold vacuum Low pressure in the intake manifold caused by evacuating action of pistons and cylinders.

master cylinder Piston and cylinder assembly that receives mechanical force from the brake pedal and transmits hydraulic force to individual wheel cylinders and/or calipers.

mesh The fitting together of the teeth of two or more gears.

meter (1) Unit of linear measurement in the metric system equal to 39.37 in. Abbreviation is m or M. (2) The readout device on measuring instruments. (3) A mechanism that measures or controls flow, as the jet in a carburetor.

metering rod A pointed rod, fitting inside a jet, that controls fuel flow through the jet; a carburetor component.

metering valve Hydraulic brake component that momentarily delays the application of front disc brakes until the rear drum brakes begin to move. Helps provide balanced braking.

millimeter Unit of linear measurement in the metric system; equals .039 in. Abbreviation is mm or MM.

misfiring Condition of an engine when one or more cylinders are not producing power.

mm or **MM** Abbreviation for millimeter.

modulator A vacuum-diaphragm device in automatic transmissions. Connected to a source of vacuum on the engine, the modulator provides an engine-load signal to the transmission.

MON Abbreviation for Motor Octane Number.

motor Electromechanical device that converts electricity into mechanical movement.

Motor Octane Number Index of the antiknock properties of gasoline arrived at through a laboratory test of this name, using a single-cylinder engine. Abbreviation is MON. See also Research Octane Number.

muffler Component of the exhaust system, most commonly containing tubes and baffle plates, or a fiberglass packing. It reduces (muffles) exhaust noise and extracts some heat from exhaust gases.

multi-grade See *multi-viscosity oils.*

multi-viscosity oils Lubricants that, with additives, meet the viscosity requirements for more than one grade of oil. For example, a 10W–50 oil meets the requirements of grade 10W through grade 50. The letter W means that the oil meets the viscosity requirement at 0°F. If there is no W, the viscosity is measured at 210°F. Also called *multi-grade oils* and *multiple - viscosity oils.*

N

N Chemical symbol for nitrogen.

needle bearing A roller bearing with rollers of small diameter.

needle valve Carburetor-valve design in which the valve and matching seat taper almost to a point. The carburetor float controls such a valve.

neoprene A synthetic rubber. In cars it is used as a gasket material and as a light-duty insulation for cables.

net horsepower The power developed by an engine after the power used by such accessories as the water pump, alternator, and the like has been subtracted.

Neutral Condition in a transmission when there is no connection between input and output shafts.

Neutral safety switch See *Neutral start switch.*

Neutral start switch Switch, operated by the transmission linkage, that permits starting in *Park* or *Neutral* but prevents starting in *Reverse* or in any forward gears. Also called the *Neutral safety switch.*

nitrogen An elemental gas which is inert. Seventy-eight percent of the air is nitrogen. Chemical symbol is N.

nitrogen oxides Products of an engine's combustion process, formed by the combination of nitrogen with oxygen at high temperatures. Also called oxides of nitrogen.

no-load test A test for starter motors in which current draw is measured when the starter's pinion gear is not engaged.

NO$_x$ Abbreviation for nitrogen oxides or oxides of nitrogen.

nozzle (1) The orifice at the end of a tube or like components, such as the tip of the fuel injector. (2) Slang for the delivery valve of a service-station gasoline pump.

nut (1) A shaped piece of metal containing a threaded hole designed to fit on a bolt. (2) A component in recirculating-ball steering systems that rides on the worm gear and transmits steering movements to the Pitman arm. Steel balls travel through the nut's channels.

O

O Chemical symbol for oxygen.

octane rating Index of antiknock properties in gasoline; the higher its octane rating, the less likely that the gasoline will cause knock.

octane requirement The minimum octane rating that a car requires to operate without knocking.

odometer Component of the speedometer that registers miles traveled. The *trip odometer* can be reset to measure individual trips.

OEM Abbreviation for original-equipment manufacturer.

OHC Abbreviation for overhead camshaft.

ohm The unit of measurement for resistance to a flow of electricity.

ohmmeter An instrument that measures electrical resistance of a conductor in units called ohms.

OHV Abbreviation for overhead valve.

oil (1) Petroleum derivative used for lubrication. (2) Sometimes refers to diesel fuel, as in *diesel oil.*

oil cooler A small radiator that is used to cool oil.

oil dilution An undesirable thinning of lubricating oil by raw gasoline that slips past the piston rings.

oil filter Device that often uses resin-impregnated, heat-cured paper to trap dirt particles and much of the sludge in the oil. The paper element of the filter unit is usually not replaceable; instead, the entire filter canister is replaced.

oil pan The metal housing at the bottom of the engine. Serves as an oil reservoir.

oil pump Device that forces lubricating oil through an engine.

oil ring Bottom piston ring that prevents an excessive amount of oil from going up past the piston. Also called an *oil scraper* because it scrapes excess oil from the cylinder walls and lets it drain back into the oil pan.

oil scraper See *oil ring.*

oil seal Component that prevents oil from leaking along a shaft or other moving part.

oil strainer A screen mounted at or near the oil pump to prevent the passage of large-scale solid impurities.

one-way clutch (1) A clutch that transmits power between shafts in only one direction. (2) A clutch that permits a rotating part to turn in only one direction. Often used in automatic transmissions and torque converters. Also used in starters. Sometimes called an *overrunning clutch.*

open circuit An electrical circuit that — because of a break or because a switch has failed to close — is not complete. See also *short circuit.*

orifice tube Tube with a plastic filter and calibrated opening. It has replaced the expansion valve in many air-conditioning systems.

original-equipment manufacturer Automotive term describing replacement parts supplied by the carmaker, as opposed to *aftermarket* parts supplied by firms other than the original manufacturer. Abbreviation is OEM.

O-ring Circular soft plastic or rubber ring used to seal a joint.

oscilloscope Instrument that converts voltage and frequency readings into traces on a cathode-ray tube.

overcenter spring Component of some clutch systems that, by its action, lessens the effort required to depress the pedal without reducing the pressure of the clutch plate.

overcharging Continuing to charge a battery after it has a full charge; can damage the battery.

overdrive (1) A gear ratio that causes the drive shaft to turn faster than the crankshaft. (2) A mechanism outside the transmission that produces overdrive. A transmission gear can achieve the same results.

overflow tank See *coolant recovery tank.*

overhaul A major disassembly of an engine or other mechanism; replacing worn parts or reconditioning them to close to their original specifications. In a minor overhaul, only parts that have failed are replaced, and the engine is not expected to operate as well as it did when new.

overhead camshaft Engine design in which the camshaft is mounted on the cylinder head. Abbreviation is OHC.

overhead valve Engine design in which the valves are mounted in the cylinder head rather than in the block. Abbreviation is OHV.

overrunning clutch See *one-way clutch.*

Glossary

oversquare Engine design in which the bore (diameter) of the cylinders is greater than the stroke (travel) of the pistons.

oversteer A handling characteristic in which a car's rear wheels will begin to skid in a turn at a lower speed than the front wheels do. Often found in rear-engine cars or other tail-heavy vehicles unless the suspension has been especially designed to overcome this trait.

owner's manual A book of operating and maintenance instructions that is supplied with a new car. Not to be confused with a *service manual*.

oxidation The combination of any material with oxygen in a chemical reaction. Oxidation of iron is called *rust*.

P

pad The friction material in a disc brake. The pad is pressed against the spinning disc by a hydraulically operated piston.

parallax error An error in reading an instrument (or timing marks) when the pointer and dial are viewed at an angle rather than head-on.

parallel Electrical design in which two or more circuits, batteries, or components share common negative and positive connections.

parallelogram linkage Steering design in which the steering linkage elements form a parallelogram.

parking brake Brake system that prevents the car from rolling when it is parked. The brake usually locks the rear wheels, rarely the front wheels. In some designs, it locks the drive shaft. Also called the *emergency brake* and *hand brake*.

particulate A tiny bit of solid matter found in exhaust gases.

parts per million A measure used in emission analyses. Abbreviation is PPM or ppm.

passage An opening in a solid body that permits a gas or liquid to flow through. This opening is usually of some length, not merely a hole.

pawl A metal rod or arm that can be moved into a hole or slot to lock something in place.

PCV Abbreviation for positive crankcase ventilation.

peen To spread, bend, or flatten the end of a rivet or pin with a hammer.

percolation Undesirable condition in a stopped engine in which heat causes the air or fuel in the float bowl to expand so that fuel is forced into the intake manifold. A properly working float bowl vent should prevent percolation.

permanent magnet A piece of metal that retains its power to attract metal.

photochemical Adjective describing the action of light (photo) on air pollutants (chemicals), which creates smog.

pickup coil An electromagnetic device in the distributor of electronic ignition systems that creates an electromagnetic field. When the magnetic field is crossed by a wheel spinning past it, the pickup coil transmits an electric signal to an electronic control unit that causes the ignition coil to discharge its high-voltage spark.

ping See *knock*.

pinion (1) The bevel gear at the end of the drive shaft (or pinion shaft) that engages the ring gear in the differential. (2) The smallest gear or gears in any assembly of gears. A typical differential contains two pinion gears in its carrier housing.

piston Sliding metal part fitted to operate within a cylinder under hydraulic, mechanical, or combustion pressures. In an engine, the piston is attached to a rod and, through that rod, transfers power to the crankshaft. In a brake system, mechanical pressure from the brake pedal on the master cylinder's piston develops hydraulic pressure that pushes against pistons in the wheel cylinders and calipers.

piston crown The top of a piston. Sometimes called the *piston head*.

piston rings Steel rings that operate in grooves in a piston and bear against the cylinder walls. The rings are designed to prevent compression forces from leaking past the pistons and into the crankcase, and excess oil from leaking past the pistons and into the combustion chambers.

pitch (1) A measurement from the center of one gear tooth to the center of the next. (2) The variation in degrees from a flat plane of a fan or like blade. (3) The number of threads per inch on a bolt or screw.

Pitman arm A short arm in the steering system linking the track rod to the rest of the steering linkage.

pivot A rod, pin, or projection upon which another component swings or turns.

planet gear A gear in a planetary gearset. Its outside meshes with the teeth inside of a ring gear; its inside meshes with the sun gear.

planetary gearset A gearset comprised of a sun gear, a ring gear, and several planet gears.

plate (1) Component of a storage battery, one of a series of flat lead sheets with which acid reacts to produce electricity. (2) A pivoting flap in the choke or throttle valve of a carburetor. (3) To apply a coating or layer of one material over another.

plenum Chamber containing an air supply in a heating system or intake manifold.

pliers Metal pincers used to hold, turn, or bend.

ply The fabric layer in a tire.

pneumatic tool A tool that is powered by compressed air.

points See *breaker points*.

polarity The difference in properties or powers between two bodies or the ends of one body, as in a magnet. According to the Current Theory, polarities in an electric circuit are established by an excess of electrons on one side (negative) and a deficiency on the other (positive).

poppet valve Valve design with a flat head attached to a stem, as are the engine exhaust and intake valves.

port An opening. In an engine, openings through which the air-fuel mixture and exhaust gases flow.

ported vacuum Vacuum tapped from a passage just above the throttle plate in a carburetor.

ported vacuum switch See *vacuum control valve*.

positive crankcase ventilation An emission-control system that routes engine crankcase fumes into the intake manifold, where they are drawn into the cylinders and burned along with the air-fuel mixture. Abbreviation is PCV.

pounds per square inch A measurement of pressure equivalent to a certain weight distributed over a given area. Abbreviation is psi.

pour point Lowest temperature at which a lubricating oil can be poured.

power The ability to exert force; common automotive measurements of power are *horsepower* and *kilowatt*.

power brakes (1) A brake system that employs vacuum to help the driver to produce braking force. (2) A hydraulic system, operated by the power steering pump, that assists the hydraulic system operated by the driver's foot on the brake pedal. Also called *power-assist brakes*.

power stroke Downward movement of the piston after the ignition of the air-fuel mixture in an engine cylinder.

power team Automotive term for the combination of engine, transmission, and differential.

PPM or **ppm** Abbreviation for parts per million.

precombustion chamber A small side chamber on some diesel engines into which fuel is injected to start the combustion cycle. Similar chambers are used in some stratified-charge gasoline engines.

pre-ignition Undesirable ignition of the air-fuel mixture before the spark occurs at the spark plug. Often caused by glowing carbon deposits. Can harm the engine. Also called *knocking* or *pinging*.

preload To place light pressure on a mechanism, such as a bearing or joint, before the actual working load is added; makes for more stable operation. Preloading is also used during wheel bearing adjustments.

premium (1) Term distinguishing high-octane from low-octane fuels. (2) Synonym for "better quality" in tires, brake linings, and other automotive parts. The term is applied loosely by manufacturers, and is not an official quality grading.

press-fit parts Parts so similar in size that, when forced together, they will hold together by friction alone, without fasteners.

pressure bleeder Garage device that injects fluid under pressure into a hydraulic brake system and forces air out.

pressure cap Radiator cap designed to permit a limited buildup of pressure but to vent excess pressure.

pressure plate A spring-loaded metal plate that pushes the clutch disc against the flywheel to complete the coupling of the engine with the transmission.

pressure-relief valve A valve designed to open at a pre-set pressure.

pressure tester Instrument used at garages to test a pressure-type cooling system for leaks and to test a pressure cap to see if it holds to its pre-set value.

primary (1) A low-voltage circuit or part of a circuit. (2) The input coil of a transformer.

printed circuit Electrically conductive metal paths that are produced by printing a pattern on a board, then etching away all areas that are not printed.

progressive linkage Carburetor linkage design in which one barrel after another is brought into operation as the throttle opening increases in the primary barrel.

propeller shaft See *drive shaft*.

proportioning valve A valve in a hydraulic braking system that regulates the proportion of braking force of the front and rear brakes.

prop shaft See *drive shaft*.

psi or **PSI** Abbreviation for pounds per square inch.

pull Condition in which a car drifts to one side.

puller Tool used to separate parts, such as a wheel puller. Usual components are jaws for holding and a forcing screw for pressure.

pulsation (1) Energy that is brought to bear in surges. (2) Undesirable surges in braking action or brake pedal resistance found in a faulty braking system.

pumping oil Slang term for the action of an engine in which oil is getting past the piston rings and burning in the combustion chambers.

purge To clean a system, such as a radiator, by flushing with water so as to rid the system of contaminants.

purge valve A valve that controls the flow of fuel vapors in an evaporation-control emission system.

pushrod A rod in overhead valve engines that is fitted between the rocker arm and the valve lifter or tappet.

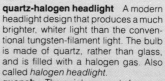

Q

quartz-halogen headlight A modern headlight design that produces a much brighter, whiter light than the conventional tungsten-filament light. The bulb is made of quartz, rather than glass, and is filled with a halogen gas. Also called *halogen headlight*.

quench The quick removal of excess heat from the combustion chamber; the heat is carried away (quenched) by the engine block and by coolant.

R

race Hard, smoothly finished steel sleeves against which ball or roller bearings turn. Also called *bearing cup*.

rack and pinion Steering gear design that uses a pinion gear at the end of the steering column to move a toothed bar (rack) left or right to transmit steering movements.

radial tire Tire design in which the cords of the body plies run at right angles (radially) to the tire's centerline.

radiator In a car, the component of the cooling system that dissipates excess engine heat into the atmosphere.

ratio The size or number of one thing or group as compared to the size or number of another thing or group.

reboring See *bore out*.

recapping Tire-renewal process in which a new tread (cap) is vulcanized to a used-tire carcass. Also known as *retreading*.

receiver-dryer Device in an air conditioner that removes contaminating moisture from the refrigerant. It also filters out some impurities from the refrigerant and stores extra refrigerant to compensate for any minor leakage or heavier-than-normal demand upon the A/C system.

recharge (1) To restore energy to a battery by means of an electric current. (2) To restore the level of a substance in a system, as recharging an air conditioner with refrigerant.

reciprocating movement A back-and-forth motion.

recirculating ball Steering gear design in which steering movements are transmitted by steel balls placed between a worm gear and a nut. Widely used on North American cars.

rectifier Electrical device that permits alternating current to flow in only one direction thereby transforming it into direct current.

reed valve A valve design that incorporates a thin strip of metal shaped like the reed of a musical instrument. Fluid or gas can push past the reed in one direction but not in the other.

refit See *reinstall*.

refrigerant A material that transports heat from one part of an air-conditioning system to another. It absorbs heat while turning into a gas, gives off heat when becoming a liquid.

reinstall To put back a part that was previously removed. Sometimes called *refit*. See also *replace*.

relay An electromechanical switch that is operated by a mechanical switch. A small current passing through the mechanical switch activates a solenoid in the electromechanical switch, closing a set of heavy contacts and allowing a large current to flow. Used in starters, horns, and other systems where is it undesirable for a large current to flow through the mechanical switches on the dashboard.

release bearing See *throw-out bearing*.

release levers Clutch components that relieve spring pressure whenever the clutch pedal is depressed in order to disengage the clutch.

relief valve The component of the hydraulic system that protects against excessive hydraulic pressure.

repair manual See *service manual*.

replace To install a new part in place of a defective one. See also *reinstall*.

Research Octane Number A measurement of the antiknock properties of gasoline. The number is calculated by means of a laboratory test called the Research Method.

reserve capacity The length of time that a fully charged battery, at 80°F, will remain functional when it is discharging at a rate of 25 amps. This rating is intended to tell the driver how long the car can be operated, with headlights and certain other accessories on, after an alternator failure.

residual magnetism Slight magnetic properties retained by metal, such as a wiring coil in a generator, after it has passed through a magnetic field.

resistance The opposition offered by a conductor to a flow of electricity; measured in ohms.

resonator A second, muffler-like, sound-reduction device located behind the muffler in an exhaust system.

retainer A part whose primary function is to hold other parts together. Nuts, bolts, clips, and rings are commonly used as retainers.

retard Any automatic or manual action that delays an ignition spark in relation to piston position.

retreading See *recapping*.

return spring A spring designed to return a component to its original position after it is no longer subject to another force.

revolutions per minute A measure of the rotational speed of a shaft or an engine. Abbreviation is rpm.

rich mixture An air-fuel mixture with a high proportion of fuel. A mixture in which the proportion of air to fuel is lower than 14 to 1 (by weight) is considered to be rich.

ride Evaluation of a car suspension's ability to cushion bumps in a road without transmitting shocks to the passengers. Not to be confused with *handling*.

ring (1) A ring-shaped metal part that is fitted around a piston and is used to seal the combustion chamber of the engine; see *piston ring*. (2) Similar rings may also be used on shafts in automatic transmissions. (3) Rings are also used as retainers, to keep parts in place on shafts.

ring gear Usually, a large gear that resembles a ring, such as the large differential gear engaging the pinion, the large gear in an automatic transmission's planetary gearset, or the gear on a flywheel that engages the starter drive.

rocker arm A metal member that pivots (rocks) on a shaft or on a ball-shaped stud. Rocker arms are used to change upward force on one end into downward force on the other in some valve trains.

rolling radius A measurement from the center of an axle to the ground.

roll-over bar Safety device, usually a pipe, mounted over the driver's head to protect him if the car turns over. Also called a *roll bar*.

RON Abbreviation for Research Octane Number.

room temperature Temperature (usually 70°F ± 2°) required for efficient operation or adjustment of certain automotive components.

rotary engine An engine, such as the Wankel rotary engine, whose power is developed by a rotor moving in a circular pattern within a chamber.

rotor (1) The part of a rotary engine, motor, or generator that revolves. (2) The disc in a disc brake. See *disc*. (3) The rotating part of a distributor that transfers current from the coil cable to the spark plug cables.

rotor pump Pump design in which eccentric rotors move a fluid.

rpm or **RPM** Abbreviation for revolutions per minute.

R&R Abbreviation for remove and reinstall, often found on bills. Means that a part has been removed, serviced, and reinstalled.

run-on See *afterrunning*.

runout See *disc runout*.

S

SAE Abbreviation for Society of Automotive Engineers.

safety rim A tire rim with an extra ridge on the inside that helps to hold the bead of a flat tire in place.

schematic diagram Symbolic representation of an electric circuit or vacuum-hose circuit.

Schrader valve A type of spring-operated valve.

scraper ring See *oil ring*.

screwdriver A tool designed to insert or remove screws by turning them.

scuffing Roughness developed on the surface of a material that has been rubbing against another material.

seal Material or design used to prevent the passage of gas or fluid at a joint.

sealed-beam Headlight design incorporating filaments, a reflector, and a lens in a unit with no separate bulb.

sealer A liquid or paste compound designed to seal or help to seal a joint.

seat (1) The surface on which a part, such as a valve, rests. (2) The final mating of parts after a period of wear.

secondary (1) A high-voltage circuit or part of a circuit. (2) The output coil of a transformer.

sector gear A gear whose shape comprises a segment of a circle.

seized See *frozen*.

self-locking screw A screw that once tightened, resists loosening.

self-tapping screw A screw that cuts its own threads as it is turned.

semiconductor General term for transistors, integrated circuits, and other electronic devices made of materials, such as silicone, that conduct electricity poorly.

series An electrical connection in which two or more circuits, batteries, or components are connected negative-to-positive. The opposite of *parallel*.

service manual A large, detailed maintenance and repair handbook designed mainly for use by professional mechanics. Also called *repair manual* or *shop manual*.

service rating A grading system that identifies the kind of service for which automotive lubricants are intended. Engine oils are rated from SA through SF for gasoline engines, and from CA to CD for diesel engines. SE, SF, CC, and CD oils are the only ones recommended for modern engines.

servo An apparatus that transmits a force, often after multiplying it. Examples of servo mechanisms are the brake master cylinder and the piston device that applies the brake bands in an automatic transmission.

setscrew A screw that passes through one part and presses against a second part in order to hold it in a fixed position.

shackle A flexible connecting link between two components, such as the link between one end of a leaf spring and the chassis.

shift valve Valve that controls the shifting of the gears in an automatic transmission.

shim A thin metal strip used to separate one component or surface from another or to change the angle of a part.

shimmy (1) The wobble of a front wheel upon its steering axis; can sometimes be violent. (2) A shaking in the car body that occurs on rough roads or is due to misalignment or imbalance of the wheels.

shock absorber A hydromechanical device that limits the travel of a spring and prevents its continued oscillation.

shoe The metal component in a drum-brake system that holds the lining and brings it into contact with the drum.

shop manual See *service manual*.

short circuit Defect in an electric circuit in which electricity flows directly from one conductor to another rather than through the intended circuit.

shrink fit (1) Heating a component so that it expands and passes over or around another component or member and then, after cooling, contracts (shrinks) to make a tight fit. (2) Electrical insulation that shrinks when heated.

shroud (1) A partial housing around a fan that directs and improves the efficiency of the airflow. (2) Any partial cover, such as the one under the steering column inside the car.

shunt circuit A minor side circuit that parallels and feeds off a main circuit.

sight glass Small window that opens into a fluid line to allow a visual check of level or flow. Used in some air-conditioning systems.

Glossary

single overhead camshaft An engine design with a single camshaft placed above the cylinder head. Abbreviation is sohc or SOHC.

skirt The hollow, lower part of a piston.

slap Sound made by a loose-fitting piston as it hits a cylinder wall.

sleeve A replaceable liner that fits into a hole or cylinder and bears against a shaft or piston.

sliding vane pump A pump with a slotted rotor in which blades (vanes) slide. Either the rotor motion or the housing into which the rotor fits is eccentric. The turning of the rotor and the sliding of the vanes create chambers of varying sizes, through which a fluid is drawn in, compressed, and forced out. Design is used for power steering pumps, fuel pumps, and air-conditioning compressors.

slip ring A circular conductor on a rotor or armature that contacts brushes. Electricity flows from the brushes to the slip ring, thus allowing current to pass from a stationary part to a rotating part.

slow charge Administering a charge to a battery over a long period of time and at a low rate, as happens with a trickle charger.

small end The end of a connecting rod that fits into the piston.

smog Air pollution created by the action of sunlight on nitrogen oxides.

snap ring Circular spring-steel clip that can be snapped into retaining grooves on a shaft or in a hole to hold parts together. Various-shaped snap rings are called *circlips* or *E-rings*.

Society of Automotive Engineers A professional organization that sets standards for many automotive products, including fasteners, lenses, and lubricants. Abbreviation is SAE.

socket wrench Wrench with a hood (socket) designed to grasp a nut or a bolt head. A ratchet or handle provides a grip for turning the socket.

sodium-cooled valve An engine valve with a hollow area inside the stem filled with sodium crystals that conduct heat away from the valve head.

SOHC or **sohc** Abbreviation for single overhead camshaft.

solder A lead/tin compound with a low melting point; used to join metal components by adhesion.

solenoid An electromagnet employed to move a metal rod or metal strip. Sometimes synonomous with *relay*.

solenoid relay A switching component in the starter motor circuit. Light current operates the solenoid, which closes the contacts carrying the heavy current to the starter motor.

solenoid switch A switch operated by a solenoid.

solenoid vacuum switch Any one of a variety of engine control devices that combine a solenoid switch and a vacuum valve. The solenoid opens or closes a valve in a vacuum line, usually as part of a pollution-control system.

solid state General term for transistors and related electronic components that are replacing vacuum tubes.

solvent (1) A liquid capable of dissolving a solid or thinning another liquid. (2) A chemical that dissolves rust, hardened road film, and grease.

spark deceleration valve A valve that operates on engine vacuum to advance the spark, or ignition timing during engine deceleration. Also called *spark decel valve*.

spark plug Electrical component that produces a spark to ignite the air-fuel mixture in the cylinders.

specific gravity The weight of a given volume of a liquid as compared to the weight of the same volume of water.

speed The velocity or rate of motion of an object.

speedometer An instrument for measuring the speed of cars. Car speed is measured in miles per hour (mph) or kilometers per hour (kph).

spindle A short, tapered axle that supports a free-rolling wheel. Also called a *stub axle*.

splines Grooves cut into shafts so that two parts can mesh together. When the parts are splined together, they can slide along each other but must rotate together. An example is a clutch friction disc splined onto the input shaft of a transmission.

spongy pedal Brake pedal that does not give firm resistance to foot pressure.

spring rate A measure of the firmness of a spring.

sprockets See *timing gears*.

sprung weight The total weight of a car that bears on the suspension.

spur gear A gear with teeth that are cut parallel to the shaft.

squish The action in the combustion chamber in which some of the air-fuel mixture is pushed around (squished) during the compression stroke.

stabilizer bar A bar linking the two front suspension systems in order to help them resist sway. Also called an *anti-roll bar, roll bar, anti-sway bar* and *sway bar*.

stall test (1) A test for starter motors in which current draw is measured while the motor is stalled by a load. (2) A test of the one-way clutch in an automatic transmission's torque converter.

starter The electric motor and drive mechanism used to start an engine.

stator (1) The stationary coils or poles of an electric motor or generator. (2) A vaned wheel in an automatic transmission that directs fluid flow.

steering arm The component in the steering system that links the steering knuckle and the tie rod.

steering column The shaft between the steering wheel and steering gear.

steering gearbox The housing that holds the gears at the end of the steering wheel's shaft.

steering knuckle A suspension/steering-system component that supports a front wheel and, pivoting on ball joints, permits the wheels to be steered.

steering lock (1) Mechanism that locks the steering shaft in one position when the ignition key is turned to *Off*. (2) The limits (to the left and right) to which the steering wheel can be turned.

stoichiometric Chemically correct. An air-fuel mixture is considered stoichiometric when it is neither too rich nor too lean; stoichiometric ratio is 14.6 parts of air for every part of fuel.

stratified charge Method of drawing the air-fuel mixture into the combustion chamber so that there is a layer of fuel at the spark plug rich enough to be ignited by a spark, and so that layers are progressively leaner as the distance from the spark plug increases.

stroke The distance a piston travels from top dead center (TDC) to bottom dead center (BDC).

strut A bar or rod that keeps two components in a fixed relationship.

stub axle See *spindle*.

stumble A pause in the acceleration of an engine that sometimes occurs in cold weather.

suction line The refrigerant line in an air-conditioning system that connects the evaporator and compressor and in which the compressor's suction may be measured.

sun gear The center gear in a planetary gearset.

supercharger An engine-driven air compressor that delivers a large supply of air-fuel mixture to the intake manifold in order to increase engine power.

surface grinder Machine used at professional garages to grind down flat metal surfaces.

surge Undesirable sudden acceleration of an engine while the accelerator is held steady.

suspension The system of springs, arms, shock absorbers, and related components that connect a car's body and frame to its wheels and axles.

sway bar See *stabilizer bar*.

synchro Short term for synchromesh or synchronizer.

synchromesh Transmission design that synchronizes the speed of the gears before they are meshed.

T

tachometer Instrument that measures engine speed in revolutions per minute.

taillight (1) A light on the rear of a vehicle covered by a red lens. (2) General term applied to the entire rear light cluster, including the taillight, brake light, turn signal, and backup light.

tap A metal male tool used to cut or restore the inside (female) threads in a hole or nut.

tappet A solid valve lifter with no hydraulic fluid. See *lifter*.

TDC Abbreviation for top dead center.

tetraethyl lead Chemical compound used as an antiknock agent in gasoline.

thermal reactor Exhaust manifold design using heat and air to burn unburned hydrocarbons in the exhaust gases in order to reduce air pollution.

thermostatic vacuum switch (1) Device in the cooling system that senses high coolant temperature in an idling engine and opens a vacuum line. This advances ignition timing to speed up the engine and cool it. (2) Any vacuum switch or valve that is controlled by the temperature of coolant or air.

thread chaser A tap-like metal tool used to clean and straighten threads in spark plug holes.

threaded insert A metal sleeve with outside and inside threads. When the sleeve is inserted into a rebored and retapped hole, the inside threads match those of the original hole.

three-way catalyst A catalyst designed to convert hydrocarbons, carbon monoxide, and oxides of nitrogen into harmless substances. Only effective when the exhaust gases are chemically correct, that is, when the air-fuel ratio of the mixture burned in the cylinders is 14.6:1. See also *stoichiometric*.

throat The bore, barrel, or venturi of a carburetor.

throttle (1) A flat-plate valve or butterfly valve at the bottom of the carburetor throat that is linked to the accelerator pedal. It controls the flow of the air-fuel mixture and, therefore, engine speed. (2) The accelerator pedal or lever.

throttle body (1) The carburetor body. (2) The section of a simple fuel-injection system that contains the throttle valve.

throttle body fuel injection A simplified fuel-injection system built into a housing that resembles a carburetor.

throttle solenoid positioner A solenoid that holds the throttle valve slightly open when the engine is idling and closes it when the engine is stopped. Also called the *idle speed solenoid*. (2) A device that slows the throttle's closing in order to reduce emissions.

thrown rod A broken connecting rod that pierces the engine.

throw-out bearing A bearing that the clutch-pedal linkage moves into the release arms to disengage the clutch. It is at the back of the clutch assembly. Also called a *release bearing*.

thrust bearing A bearing that resists side or end movement, as can happen, for example, on the crankshaft.

tie rod Steering system component that moves the steering arms.

tie-rod end The ball-and-socket joint at the end of a steering rod.

timing (1) Regulation of the spark impulse so that the spark occurs at the proper time for ignition. (2) Regulation of a valve's opening and closing.

timing belt A belt with cogs (squared teeth) that drives an overhead camshaft. On some diesels, the belt also drives a fuel-injection pump.

timing chain A crankshaft-driven chain that turns the camshaft to open and close valves at the proper time.

timing gears The gears on the crankshaft and camshaft on which the timing chain runs. Also called *sprockets*.

timing light An instrument with a strobe that pulses in unison with the No. 1 spark plug to permit checking and adjustment of ignition timing.

tire rotation Systematically changing the location of tires to different wheel positions in order to equalize wear.

toe-in The amount that a front wheel points inward.

toe-out The amount that a front wheel points outward.

top dead center The piston's position at the highest point of travel. Abbreviation is TDC.

torque A twisting or turning force measured in pound-feet or Newton-meters.

torque converter A mechanism that couples an engine to an automatic transmission. It employs a fluid medium, a pump (called an impeller) at the flywheel, and a turbine (attached to the transmission's input shaft). A finned wheel (a stator) between the impeller and the turbine directs the oil flow.

torque wrench A wrench fitted with a gauge that indicates the amount of torque being applied.

torsional vibration The back-and-forth twisting of a shaft along its length.

torsion bar A suspension component making use of a special steel rod's resistance to twisting in order to achieve spring action.

tramp Excessive up-and-down motion of a car's axle and/or wheels.

transfer case A gearbox that divides power between the front and rear wheels of a four-wheel-drive vehicle.

transistor Solid-state electronic component widely used to replace vacuum tubes and switches.

transmission A mechanical device that uses gears, shafts, and other components to multiply the torque produced by the engine and to allow the engine to run at efficient speeds while the drive wheels turn at lower speeds.

tread The outside part of a tire that contacts the road.

trickle charger Device designed to charge a battery at a slow rate.

tube See *inner tube*.

tuned intake Intake system designed to deliver a greater-than-normal supply of air or air-fuel mixture for combustion.

tuneup A package of services, such as those performed on the engine, fuel, and ignition systems, intended to restore engine performance.

turbocharger A supercharger powered by exhaust gases.

turbulence A violent disturbance of a fluid or gas.

twist drill A drill bit with flutes that form a spiral.

U

U-bolt A rod bent to the shape of the letter U and having threads on both ends. Used to secure parts of suspension and exhaust systems.

understeer A handling characteristic in which a car's front wheels, in a turn, will begin to skid at a lower speed than the rear wheels. This causes the car to continue in a straighter line than the angle of the steering wheel would indicate. Understeer is common in front-drive cars and is considered easier to cope with than *oversteer*.

unit body Car design incorporating the frame and body into one unit. Also called *unitized body* or *unibody*.

universal joint Flexible joint that couples two shafts to permit either shaft to swivel with respect to the other.

unloader Device, fitted to the throttle valve, that opens the choke valve when the accelerator is fully depressed.

upshift To shift to a higher gear.

unsprung weight Combined weight of all components of a car that are not supported by the springs.

V

vacuum (1) The absence, or relative absence, of air. (2) All conditions of less-than-atmospheric pressure.

vacuum control valve A valve controlled by a thermostatic sensor. In response to a pre-set air or coolant temperature, the valve opens (to allow vacuum flow) or closes (to block vacuum flow). Commonly used to regulate the vacuum control for spark advance in the distributor. See also *thermostatic vacuum switch*.

vacuum diaphragm Mechanism using engine vacuum to distort a flexible diaphragm that, in turn, pulls or pushes a rod to close or open a switch, advance ignition timing, move heater doors, etc. See also *vacuum motor*.

vacuum-electric switch An electrical switch that is operated by vacuum and a spring.

vacuum modulator The component of an automatic transmission that regulates hydraulic pressure in response to engine vacuum.

vacuum motor A vacuum diaphragm.

vacuum pump A device used to produce vacuum.

valve A mechanical device designed to open, close, or restrict the flow of liquid or gas within a passage.

valve clearance The free play, or clearance, in a valve train; it is measured with the valve closed.

valve float An undesirable condition in an engine when the valves cannot close before combustion begins.

valve grinding Resurfacing a valve and valve seat mechanically or manually with grinding compounds.

valve guide Passage in which the valve stem slides.

valve-in-head Engine design in which the valves are located in the cylinder head. See *overhead valve*.

valve lash See *valve clearance*.

valve lifter See *lifter*.

valve overlap Momentary interval in many four-stroke engine cycles when both the exhaust and intake valves are open.

valve rotator A component in some engines that turns a valve slightly each time it is opened in order to distribute wear and prolong valve life.

valve seat The surface on which a valve rests when it is closed.

valve-seat insert A replaceable valve seat.

valve stem The rod-like part of a valve that moves within the valve guide.

valve-stem seal The seal around a valve stem that limits the passage of oil down the valve guide.

valve train All the valve's operating components, including the valve, camshaft, spring, and any tappets, push-rods, or rocker arms.

vane A flat, extended section of a wheel-shaped part; it affects or is affected by a flow of liquid or gas. An example is a turbine vane.

vaporization (1) A change of state in a liquid or a solid in which its particles form a vapor in gas. (2) Evaporation.

vapor lock Vaporization of gasoline within a fuel line, a condition that prevents the fuel pumps from working.

vapor-recovery system See *evaporation control*.

vehicle identification number The serial number of a vehicle. Abbreviation is VIN.

V engine Engine design with two banks of cylinders set at an angle to each other and operating a common crankshaft. Common varieties are the V-4, V-6, and V-8.

venturi The narrowing of a passage that increases the speed of a flow of gas or air while decreasing its pressure. Such a design occurs in a carburetor, and the resulting vacuum is used to draw in fuel.

vibration damper A weighted device, attached to a crankshaft, to smooth out power flow and prevent torsional vibration. See *torsional vibration*.

VIN Abbreviation for vehicle identification number.

viscosity The resistance of a liquid, such as oil, to flow.

viscosity index A measure of an oil's ability to resist viscosity changes during temperature fluctuations.

viscosity rating Numerical rating of oil viscosity based on tests devised by the Society of Automotive Engineers. Common readings run from 5W to 60 for engine oil and to 140 for gear oil. The higher the number, the thicker the oil and the slower its rate of flow.

volatility The ability of a substance to vaporize quickly, which affects its flammability.

volt The unit of measurement for the force or pressure of a flow of electricity.

voltage drop A lowering of the voltage in a circuit when resistance, such as a load, is added.

voltage regulator A device that prevents excessive voltage on, or overcharge of, the battery by the generator or alternator.

voltmeter An instrument that measures the voltage in an electric circuit.

vulcanization (1) Heat treatment that improves the elasticity and strength of rubber. (2) The fusing together of two or more pieces of rubber.

W

water jacket The passages around an engine's cylinders through which coolant flows and collects excess combustion heat.

water pump An engine-operated pump that circulates engine coolant.

watt A measurement of power. One volt multiplied by 1 amp equals 1 watt, and 746 watts equal 1 horsepower. A *kilowatt* is 1,000 watts.

wear indicator (1) A strip of material that is placed in a tire tread, brake lining, and the like to give a visual or audible signal when a pre-determined amount of wear has occurred. (2) A projection from a ball joint that recedes into the joint as the joint wears.

wheel alignment The adjustment of automotive suspension and steering parts, particularly at the front wheels, that brings the wheels into a specified relationship with the road and each other. Alignment of rear wheels is done on some cars with independent rear suspension.

wheelbase The distance between the centers of the front and rear wheels.

wheel cylinder Mechanism located at each wheel in a hydraulic drum-brake system. The cylinder converts hydraulic pressure into braking force by moving curved brake shoes against the drum to stop the wheel from turning.

window winder The mechanism, including the hand crank, used to raise and lower a window. Also called a *window regulator*.

windshield wiper Motor-driven mechanism that moves a rubber blade back and forth on a windshield to wipe away rain or snow.

wire feeler gauge (1) Wire loop of specified diameter that is used to check the gap between a spark plug's electrodes. (2) A set of different-size wire loops mounted on a holder.

wiring harness A bundle of insulated electrical wires covered by an additional insulating jacket. The individual wires emerge from the harness at different points to go to various terminals.

work light See *droplight*.

worm gear A gear composed of a long, thin cylinder that has spiraling (helical) threads.

wrist pin A short rod that fits into two holes in the piston. It passes through the small end of the connecting rod and holds the piston to the rod.

XYZ

yoke A split, fork-like component that is used to hold, support, or apply pressure to another part in two places.

Zerk fitting Brand name for one type of grease fitting.

Index

Index

Index

Index

Index

Illustration Credits

p.70 Spark plug cutaway:
      Robert Bosch GmbH
p.72 Deposit fouling 1 photo:
      Champion Spark Plug Co.
p.83 Computer chip photos, black
      and white: INTEL Corp.
      Color: Texas Instruments Inc.
p.120 Carcass failure photo:
      Michelin Tire Corp.
p.135 Alternator drawing:
      Robert Bosch GmbH
p.136 Starter drawing:
      Robert Bosch GmbH
p.141 Unit-body drawing:
      Daimler-Benz AG
p.223 Dwell-tachometer photo:
      Joseph Barnell
p.294 Tire chain photos:
      Campbell Chain Co.
p.319 Rust repair photos:
      Joseph Barnell
Color photos and drawings on pages
28, 29, 31–41, 43, 44, 46, 47, 52, 60,
63, 64, 66, 67, 70–75, 84–95, 98–101,
103, 105, 107, 108, 110, 112–121,
124–130, 135, 136, 138–142, and 144
copyright © 1970 Drive Publications
Ltd., London
All other photos by Morris Karol